Organizational Behavior

Stephen P. Robbins   Timothy A. Judge

Liberty University Edition

with Self-Assessment Library

Required for BUSI 500

Taken from:
Organizational Behavior, Thirteenth Edition
by Stephen P. Robbins, Timothy A. Judge

Custom Publishing

New York   Boston   San Francisco
London   Toronto   Sydney   Tokyo   Singapore   Madrid
Mexico City   Munich   Paris   Cape Town   Hong Kong   Montreal

Cover Art: *Glass Tower*, by Barry Cronin

Taken from:

Organizational Behavior, Thirteenth Edition
by Stephen P. Robbins, Timothy A. Judge
Copyright © 2009, 2007, 2005, 2003, 2001 by Pearson Education, Inc.
Published by Prentice Hall
Upper Saddle River, New Jersey 07458

This special edition published in cooperation with Pearson Custom Publishing.

Printed in the United States of America

15 16 17 18 19 20 V3NL 16 15 14 13

2008160501

DM

**Pearson
Custom Publishing**
is a division of

www.pearsonhighered.com

ISBN 10: 0-555-01227-1
ISBN 13: 978-0-555-01227-7

Preface xxiii

1 Introduction

1 What Is Organizational Behavior? 2

2 The Individual

2 Foundations of Individual Behavior 42
3 Attitudes and Job Satisfaction 72
4 Personality and Values 102
5 Perception and Individual Decision Making 136
6 Motivation Concepts 172
7 Motivation: From Concepts to Applications 212
8 Emotions and Moods 248

3 The Group

9 Foundations of Group Behavior 282
10 Understanding Work Teams 320
11 Communication 348
12 Basic Approaches to Leadership 382
13 Contemporary Issues in Leadership 410
14 Power and Politics 448
15 Conflict and Negotiation 482

4 The Organization System

16 Foundations of Organization Structure 516
17 Organizational Culture 548
18 Human Resource Policies and Practices 582

5 Organizational Dynamics

19 Organizational Change and Stress Management 616

Appendix 658
Comprehensive Cases 665

Preface xxiii

1 Introduction

Chapter 1
What Is Organizational
Behavior? 2

The Importance of Interpersonal Skills 4

What Managers Do 5

Management Functions 6 • Management Roles 6 • Management Skills 8 • Effective Versus Successful Managerial Activities 8 • A Review of the Manager's Job 10

Enter Organizational Behavior 10

Complementing Intuition with Systematic Study 11

Disciplines That Contribute to the OB Field 13

Psychology 13 • Social Psychology 14 • Sociology 15 • Anthropology 15

There Are Few Absolutes in OB 16

Challenges and Opportunities for OB 16

Responding to Globalization 16 • Managing Workforce Diversity 18 • Improving Quality and Productivity 21 • Improving Customer Service 21 • Improving People Skills 22 • Stimulating Innovation and Change 22 • Coping with "Temporariness" 23 • Working in Networked Organizations 23 • Helping Employees Balance Work–Life Conflicts 24 • Creating a Positive Work Environment 25 • Improving Ethical Behavior 26

Coming Attractions: Developing an OB Model 26

An Overview 26 • The Dependent Variables 27 • The Independent Variables 31 • Toward a Contingency OB Model 32

Global Implications 34

Summary and Implications for Managers 34

Self-Assessment Library How Much Do I Know about Organizational Behavior? 4

Myth or Science? "Preconceived Notions Versus Substantive Evidence" 12

OB in the News Other Disciplines Make Use of OB Concepts 15

International OB Transfer Pricing and International Corporate Deviance 30

Point/Counterpoint In Search of the Quick Fix 35

Questions for Review 36
Experiential Exercise 36
Ethical Dilemma 37
Case Incident 1 "Data Will Set You Free" 37
Case Incident 2 Workplace Violence 38

The Individual

Chapter 2
Foundations of Individual Behavior 42

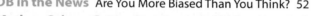

Ability 44

Intellectual Abilities 45 • Physical Abilities 47

Biographical Characteristics 48

Age 48 • Gender 50 • Race 51 • Other Biographical Characteristics: Tenure, Religion, Sexual Orientation, and Gender Identity 51

Learning 54

A Definition of *Learning* 54 • Theories of Learning 55 • Shaping: A Managerial Tool 58

Global Implications 64

Intellectual Abilities 64 • Biographical Characteristics 64 • Learning 65

Summary and Implications for Managers 65

Self-Assessment Library What's My Attitude Toward Older People? 44
International OB The Benefits of Cultural Intelligence 46
OB in the News Are You More Biased Than You Think? 52
Myth or Science? "You Can't Teach an Old Dog New Tricks!" 58
Self-Assessment Library How Good Am I at Disciplining Others? 59
Point/Counterpoint All Human Behavior Is Learned 66

Questions for Review 67
Experiential Exercise 67
Ethical Dilemma 67
Case Incident 1 The Flynn Effect **68**
Case Incident 2 Professional Sports: Rewarding and Punishing the Same Behavior? **69**

Chapter 3
Attitudes and Job Satisfaction 72

Attitudes 75

What Are the Main Components of Attitudes? 75 • Does Behavior Always Follow from Attitudes? 76 • What Are the Major Job Attitudes? 79

Job Satisfaction 83

Measuring Job Satisfaction 83 • How Satisfied Are People in Their Jobs? 84 • What Causes Job Satisfaction? 84 • The Impact of Satisfied and Dissatisfied Employees on the Workplace 87

Global Implications 91

Is Job Satisfaction a U.S. Concept? 91 • Are Employees in Western Cultures More Satisfied with Their Jobs? 91

Summary and Implications for Managers 92

Self-Assessment Library How Satisfied Am I with My Job? 74
International OB Chinese Employees and Organizational Commitment 80

Self-Assessment Library Am I Engaged? 82

OB in the News Why Is Job Satisfaction Falling? 83

Myth or Science? "Happy Workers Are Productive Workers" 86

Point/Counterpoint Managers Can Create Satisfied Employees 93

Questions for Review 94
Experiential Exercise 94
Ethical Dilemma 95
Case Incident 1 Albertsons Works on Employee Attitudes **95**
Case Incident 2 Long Hours, Hundreds of E-Mails, and No Sleep: Does This Sound Like a Satisfying Job? **96**

Chapter 4
Personality and Values 102

Personality 104

What Is Personality? 105 • The Myers-Briggs Type Indicator 107 • The Big Five Personality Model 108 • Other Personality Traits Relevant to OB 111

Values 117

The Importance of Values 117 • Terminal Versus Instrumental Values 117 • Generational Values 119

Linking an Individual's Personality and Values to the Workplace 121

Person–Job Fit 121 • Person–Organization Fit 123

Global Implications 123

Personality 123 • Values 124

Summary and Implications for Managers 127

Self-Assessment Library Am I a Narcissist? 104

Myth or Science? "Entrepreneurs Are a Breed Apart" 115

International OB A Global Personality 116

OB in the News Are U.S. Values Different? 121

Point/Counterpoint Traits Are Powerful Predictors of Behavior 128

Questions for Review 129
Experiential Exercise 129
Ethical Dilemma 129
Case Incident 1 The Rise of the Nice CEO? **130**
Case Incident 2 A Diamond Personality **131**

Chapter 5
Perception and Individual Decision Making 136

What Is Perception? 139

Factors That Influence Perception 139

Person Perception: Making Judgments About Others 140

Attribution Theory 141 • Frequently Used Shortcuts in Judging Others 142 • Specific Applications of Shortcuts in Organizations 145

The Link Between Perception and Individual Decision Making 146

Decision Making in Organizations 147

The Rational Model, Bounded Rationality, and Intuition 147 • Common Biases and Errors in Decision Making 150

Influences on Decision Making: Individual Differences and Organizational Constraints 153

Individual Differences 154 • Organizational Constraints 155

What About Ethics in Decision Making? 156

Three Ethical Decision Criteria 157 • Improving Creativity in Decision Making 158

Global Implications 160

Summary and Implications for Managers 162

Self-Assessment Library What Are My Gender Role Perceptions? 139

International OB Can Negative Perceptions Dampen International Business Relationships? 144

Myth or Science? "No One Thinks They're Biased" 152

Self-Assessment Library Am I a Deliberate Decision Maker? 153

OB in the News Google and the Winner's Curse 154

Self-Assessment Library How Creative Am I? 160

Point/Counterpoint When in Doubt, Do! 164

Questions for Review 165
Experiential Exercise 165
Ethical Dilemma 166
Case Incident 1 Natural Disasters and the Decisions That Follow 166
Case Incident 2 Whistle-Blowers: Saints or Sinners? 167

Chapter 6
Motivation Concepts 172

Defining Motivation 175

Early Theories of Motivation 175

Hierarchy of Needs Theory 176 • Theory X and Theory Y 177 • Two-Factor Theory 178 • McClelland's Theory of Needs 180

Contemporary Theories of Motivation 181

Cognitive Evaluation Theory 182 • Goal-Setting Theory 185 • Self-Efficacy Theory 188 • Reinforcement Theory 191 • Equity Theory 192 • Expectancy Theory 197

Integrating Contemporary Theories of Motivation 199

Global Implications 201

Summary and Implications for Managers 202

Self-Assessment Library How Confident Am I in My Abilities to Succeed? 174

Myth or Science? "Women Are More Motivated to Get Along, and Men Are More Motivated to Get Ahead" 178

OB in the News Paying Employees Not to Work 182

International OB How Managers Evaluate Their Employees Depends on Culture 184

Self-Assessment Library What Are My Course Performance Goals? 187
Point/Counterpoint Failure Motivates! 204

Questions for Review 205
Experiential Exercise 205
Ethical Dilemma 205
Case Incident 1 Do U.S. Workers "Live to Work"? **206**
Case Incident 2 Bullying Bosses **206**

Chapter 7
Motivation: From Concepts to Applications 212

Motivating by Job Design: The Job Characteristics Model 215

The Job Characteristics Model 215 • How Can Jobs Be Redesigned? 217
• Alternative Work Arrangements 221 • Ability and Opportunity 224

Employee Involvement 225

Examples of Employee Involvement Programs 225 • Linking Employee
Involvement Programs and Motivation Theories 227

Using Rewards to Motivate Employees 227

What to Pay: Establishing a Pay Structure 228 • How to Pay: Rewarding
Individual Employees Through Variable-Pay Programs 228 • Flexible
Benefits: Developing a Benefits Package 233 • Intrinsic Rewards: Employee
Recognition Programs 234

Global Implications 236

Summary and Implications for Managers 238

Self-Assessment Library What's My Job's Motivating Potential? 214

Myth or Science? "Everyone Wants a Challenging Job" 219

OB in the News Motivating with Performance Reviews 233

International OB Cultural Differences in Job Characteristics and Job Satisfaction 237

Point/Counterpoint Praise Motivates 240

Questions for Review 241
Experiential Exercise 241
Ethical Dilemma 242
Case Incident 1 Reducing Travel Costs at Applebee's **242**
Case Incident 2 Thanks for Nothing **243**

Chapter 8
Emotions and Moods 248

What Are Emotions and Moods? 251

The Basic Emotions 252 • The Basic Moods: Positive and Negative Affect 253
• The Function of Emotions 254 • Sources of Emotions and Moods 256

Emotional Labor 260

Affective Events Theory 262

Emotional Intelligence 264

The Case for EI 264 • The Case Against EI 266

OB Applications of Emotions and Moods 267

Selection 267 • Decision Making 267 • Creativity 268 • Motivation 268 • Leadership 268 • Negotiation 269 • Customer Service 269 • Job Attitudes 270 • Deviant Workplace Behaviors 270 • How Managers Can Influence Moods 270

Global Issues 271

Summary and Implications for Managers 272

Self-Assessment Library How Are You Feeling Right Now? 250
Self-Assessment Library What's My Affect Intensity? 256
Myth or Science? "People Can't Accurately Forecast Their Own Emotions" 258
International OB Emotional Recognition: Universal of Culture Specific? 260
Self-Assessment Library What's My Emotional Intelligence Score? 266
OB in the News Crying at Work Gains Acceptance 271
Point/Counterpoint The Costs and Benefits of Organizational Display Rules 273

Questions for Review 274
Experiential Exercise 274
Ethical Dilemma 274
Case Incident 1 The Upside of Anger? 275
Case Incident 2 Abusive Customers Cause Emotions to Run High 276

Chapter 9
Foundations of Group
Behavior 282

3 The Group

Defining and Classifying Groups 284

Stages of Group Development 286

The Five-Stage Model 286 • An Alternative Model for Temporary Groups with Deadlines 287

Group Properties: Roles, Norms, Status, Size and Cohesiveness 288

Group Property 1: Roles 289 • Group Properties 2 and 3: Norms and Status 292 • Status 297 • Group Property 4: Size 299 • Group Property 5: Cohesiveness 301

Group Decision Making 302

Groups Versus the Individual 302 • Groupthink and Groupshift 304 • Group Decision-Making Techniques 306

Global Implications 309

Summary and Implications for Managers 310

Self-Assessment Library Do I Have a Negative Attitude Toward Working in Groups? 284
Self-Assessment Library Do I Trust Others? 292

International OB Group Cohesiveness Across Cultures 302

Myth or Science? "Are Two Heads Better Than One?" 303

OB in the News Groupthink for an Enron Jury? 305

Point/Counterpoint All Job Should Be Designed Around Groups 312

Questions for Review 313
Experiential Exercise 313
Ethical Dilemma 314
Case Incident 1 "If Two Heads Are Better Than One, Are Four Even Better?" **315**
Case Incident 2 The Dangers of Groupthink **315**

Chapter 10
Understanding Work Teams 320

Why Have Teams Become So Popular? 322

Differences Between Groups and Teams 323

Types of Teams 324

Problem-Solving Teams 324 • Self-Managed Work Teams 324 • Cross-Functional Teams 325 • Virtual Teams 326 • Creating Effective Teams 326 • Context: What Factors Determine Whether Teams Are Successful 328 • Team Composition 330 • Work Design 334 • Team Processes 335

Turning Individuals into Team Players 337

Beware! Teams Aren't Always the Answer 339

Global Implications 339

Summary and Implications for Managers 340

Self-Assessment Library How Good Am I at Building and Leading a Team? 322

International OB Global Virtual Teams 327

OB in the News Surgical Teams Lack Teamwork 329

Myth or Science? "Old Teams Can't Learn New Tricks" 334

Self-Assessment Library What Is My Team Efficacy? 336

Point/Counterpoint Sports Teams Are Good Models for Workplace Teams 341

Questions for Review 342
Experiential Exercise 342
Ethical Dilemma 342
Case Incident 1 Teamwork: One Company's Approach to High Performance **343**
Case Incident 2 Team-Building Retreats **344**

Chapter 11
Communication 348

Functions of Communication 351

The Communication Process 352

Direction of Communication 353

Downward Communication 353 • Upward Communication 354 • Lateral Communication 355

Interpersonal Communication 355

Oral Communication 355 • Written Communication 356 • Nonverbal Communication 357

Organizational Communication 358

Formal Small-Group Networks 358 • The Grapevine 359 • Electronic Communications 360 • Knowledge Management 364

Choice of Communication Channel 366

Barriers to Effective Communication 368

Filtering 368 • Selective Perception 368 • Information Overload 368 • Emotions 369 • Language 369 • Communication Apprehension 370 • Gender Differences 370 • "Politically Correct" Communication 370

Global Implications 372

Summary and Implications for Managers 375

Self-Assessment Library Am I a Gossip? 351
Myth or Science? "People Are Good at Catching Liars at Work" 356
OB in the News Starbucks' Great Communicator 365
International OB Lost in Translation? 373
Self-Assessment Library How Good Are My Listening Skills? 375
Point/Counterpoint Keep It a Secret 376

Questions for Review 377
Experiential Exercise 377
Ethical Dilemma 378
Case Incident 1 Dianna Abdala 378
Case Incident 2 Do You Need a Speech Coach? 379

Chapter 12
Basic Approaches to Leadership 382

What Is Leadership? 385

Trait Theories 386

Behavioral Theories 388

Ohio State Studies 389 • University of Michigan Studies 390 • Summary of Trait Theories and Behavioral Theories 390

Contingency Theories: Fiedler Model and Situational Leadership Theory 391

Fiedler Model 392 • Hersey and Blanchard's Situational Theory 395 • Path-Goal Theory 396 • Path-Goal Variables and Predictions 397 • Summary of Contingency Theories 398

Leader–Member Exchange (LMX) Theory 398

Decision Theory: Vroom and Yetton's Leader-Participation Model 400

Global Implications 401

Summary and Implications for Managers 402

Self-Assessment Library What's My Leadership Style? 384

OB in the News Bad Bosses Abound 387

Myth or Science? "Narcissists Make Better Leaders" 388

Self-Assessment Library What's My LPC Score? 392

International OB Cultivating an International Perspective: A Necessity for Leaders 401

Point/Counterpoint Leaders Are Born, Not Made 404

Questions for Review 405
Experiential Exercise 405
Ethical Dilemma 405
Case Incident 1 Moving from Colleague to Supervisor **406**
Case Incident 2 The Kinder, Gentler Leader? **406**

Chapter 13
Contemporary Issues
in Leadership 410

Inspirational Approaches to Leadership 412

Charismatic Leadership 413 • Transformational Leadership 418

Authentic Leadership: Ethics and Trust Are the Foundation of Leadership 422

What Is Authentic Leadership? 422 • Ethics and Leadership 423 • What Is Trust? 423 • Trust and Leadership 424 • Three Types of Trust 425 • Basic Principles of Trust 427

Contemporary Leadership Roles 428

Mentoring 428 • Self-Leadership 430 • Online Leadership 431

Challenges to the Leadership Construct 432

Leadership as an Attribution 432 • Substitutes for and Neutralizers of Leadership 434

Finding and Creating Effective Leaders 435

Selecting Leaders 435 • Training Leaders 436

Global Implications 437

Summary and Implications for Managers 438

Self-Assessment Library How Charismatic Am I? 412

Self-Assessment Library Am I an Ethical Leader? 423

Myth or Science? "Men Make Better Leaders Than Women" 430

International OB Cultural Variation in Charismatic Attributions 433

OB in the News Before and After 434

Point/Counterpoint Keep Leaders on a Short Leash 439

Questions for Review 440
Experiential Exercise 440
Ethical Dilemma 441
Case Incident 1 The Making of a Great President **441**
Case Incident 2 Generation Gap: Mentors and Protégés **442**

Chapter 14
Power and Politics 448

A Definition of *Power* 451

Contrasting Leadership and Power 451

Bases of Power 452

Formal Power 452 • Personal Power 452 • Which Bases of Power Are Most Effective? 453

Dependency: The Key to Power 454

The General Dependency Postulate 454 • What Creates Dependency? 455

Power Tactics 456

Sexual Harassment: Unequal Power in the Workplace 459

Politics: Power in Action 461

Definition of *Organizational Politics* 461 • The Reality of Politics 462

Causes and Consequences of Political Behavior 463

Factors Contributing to Political Behavior 463 • How Do People Respond to Organizational Politics? 466 • Impression Management 469

The Ethics of Behaving Politically 471

Global Implications 472

Politics Perceptions 472 • Preference for Power Tactics 472 • Effectiveness of Power Tactics 473

Summary and Implications for Managers 473

Self-Assessment Library Is My Workplace Political? 450
International OB Influence Tactics in China 458
Myth or Science? "Power Breeds Contempt" 463
Self-Assessment Library How Good Am I at Playing Politics? 469
OB in the News Excuses Are Everywhere 471
Point/Counterpoint Managing Impressions is Unethical 474

Questions for Review 475
Experiential Exercise 475
Ethical Dilemma 476
Case Incident 1 Dressing for Success 476
Case Incident 2 The Politics of Backstabbing 477

Chapter 15
Conflict and Negotiation 482

A Definition of *Conflict* 484

Transitions in Conflict Thought 485

The Traditional View of Conflict 485 • The Human Relations View of Conflict 486 • The Interactionist View of Conflict 486

The Conflict Process 486

Stage I: Potential Opposition or Incompatibility 486 • Stage II: Cognition and Personalization 489 • Stage III: Intentions 489 • Stage IV: Behavior 491 • Stage V: Outcomes 492

Negotiation 495

Bargaining Strategies 496 • The Negotiation Process 499 • Individual Differences in Negotiation Effectiveness 501 • Third-Party Negotiations 503

Global Implications 504

Conflict and Culture 504 • Cultural Differences in Negotiations 505

Summary and Implications for Managers 505

Self-Assessment Library How Do I Handle Conflict? 484

Myth or Science? "High Starting Bids Lead to High Auction Sales" 498

Self-Assessment Library What's My Negotiating Style? 502

International OB Negotiating Across Cultures 503

OB in the News "Marriage Counseling" for the Top Bosses 504

Point/Counterpoint Conflict Benefits Organizations 508

Questions for Review 509
Experiential Exercise 509
Ethical Dilemma 510
Case Incident 1 David Out-Negotiating Goliath: Apotex and Bristol-Meyers Squibb **510**
Case Incident 2 Negotiation Puts Hockey in the Penalty Box **511**

4 The Organization System

Chapter 16 Foundations of Organization Structure 516

What Is Organizational Structure? 519

Work Specialization 519 • Departmentalization 521 • Chain of Command 522 • Span of Control 523 • Centralization and Decentralization 524 • Formalization 524

Common Organizational Designs 526

The Simple Structure 526 • The Bureaucracy 527 • The Matrix Structure 529

New Design Options 530

The Virtual Organization 530 • The Boundaryless Organization 532

Why Do Structures Differ? 534

Strategy 534 • Organization Size 535 • Technology 536 • Environment 537

Organizational Designs and Employee Behavior 539

Global Implications 540

Summary and Implications for Managers 541

Self-Assessment Library Do I Like Bureaucracy? 518

Self-Assessment Library How Willing Am I to Delegate? 524

OB in the News Siemens's Simple Structure—Not 525

International OB Structural Considerations in Multinationals 528

Myth or Science? "People Are Our Most Important Asset" 538

Point/Counterpoint Downsizing Improves Organizational Performance 543

Questions for Review 544
Experiential Exercise 544
Ethical Dilemma 544
Case Incident 1 Can a Structure Be *Too* Flat? **545**
Case Incident 2 No Bosses at W. L. Gore & Associates **545**

Chapter 17
Organizational Culture 548

Institutionalization: A Forerunner of Culture 550

What Is Organizational Culture? 551

A Definition of *Organizational Culture* 551 • *Culture* Is a Descriptive Term 552 • Do Organizations Have Uniform Cultures? 553 • Strong Versus Weak Cultures 554 • Culture Versus Formalization 554

What Do Cultures Do? 555

Culture's Functions 555 • Culture as a Liability 556

Creating and Sustaining Culture 558

How a Culture Begins 558 • Keeping a Culture Alive 559 • Summary: How Cultures Form 563

How Employees Learn Culture 564

Stories 564 • Rituals 564 • Material Symbols 564 • Language 565

Creating an Ethical Organizational Culture 566

Creating a Positive Organizational Culture 567

Spirituality and Organizational Culture 570

What Is Spirituality? 570 • Why Spirituality Now? 570 • Characteristics of a Spiritual Organization 570 • Criticisms of Spirituality 572

Global Implications 573

Summary and Implications for Managers 573

Self-Assessment Library What's the Right Organizational Culture for Me? 550
International OB A Good Organizational Culture Knows No Boundaries 555
Myth or Science? "People Socialize Themselves" 558
OB in the News Change Jobs, and You May Be in for a Culture Shock 566

Self-Assessment Library How Spiritual Am I? 572
Point/Counterpoint Organizational Cultures Can't Be Changed 575

Questions for Review 576
Experiential Exercise 576
Ethical Dilemma 577
Case Incident 1 Mergers Don't Always Lead to Culture Clashes **577**
Case Incident 2 Wegmans **578**

Chapter 18
Human Resource Policies and Practices 582

Selection Practices 585

How the Selection Process Works 585 • Initial Selection 585 • Substantive Selection 587 • Contingent Selection 589

Training and Development Programs 590

Types of Training 591 • Training Methods 593 • Individualizing Formal Training to Fit the Employee's Learning Style 594 • Evaluating Effectiveness 594

Performance Evaluation 595

Purposes of Performance Evaluation 595 • What Do We Evaluate? 595 • Who Should Do the Evaluating? 596 • Methods of Performance Evaluation 598 • Suggestions for Improving Performance Evaluations 600 • Providing Performance Feedback 601

Managing Diversity in Organizations 602

Work–Life Conflicts 603 • Diversity Training 605

Global Implications 605

Selection 605 • Performance Evaluation 606

Summary and Implications for Managers 607

Self-Assessment Library How Much Do I Know about Human Resource Management (HRM)? 585

Myth or Science? "It's First Impressions That Count" 589

International OB Cultural Training 592

OB in the News The Rise and Fall of Forced Ranking 600

Self-Assessment Library How Good Am I at Giving Performance Feedback? 602

Point/Counterpoint Telecommuting Makes Good Business Sense 609

Questions for Review 610
Experiential Exercise 610
Ethical Dilemma 610
Case Incident 1 Job Candidates Without Strong SAT Scores Need Not Apply **611**
Case Incident 2 Job Candidates Without Strong SAT Scores Need Not Apply **611**

5 Organizational Dynamics

Chapter 19
Organizational Change and Stress Management 616

Forces for Change 619

Planned Change 620

Resistance to Change 622

Overcoming Resistance to Change 623 • The Politics of Change 625

Approaches to Managing Organizational Change 625

Lewin's Three-Step Model 625 • Kotter's Eight-Step Plan for Implementing Change 627 • Action Research 628 • Organizational Development 628

Creating a Culture for Change 633

Stimulating a Culture of Innovation 633 • Creating a Learning Organization 635

Work Stress and Its Management 637

What Is Stress? 637 • Potential Sources of Stress 638 • Individual Differences 641 • Consequences of Stress 642 • Managing Stress 644

Global Implications 647

Summary and Implications for Managers 648

Self-Assessment Library How Well Do I Respond to Turbulent Change? 619

Myth or Science? "Meetings Stress People Out" 639

Self-Assessment Library How Stressful Is My Life? 642

OB in the News The Ten Most Stressful Jobs—And One More That Didn't Make the List 643

International OB Coping with Stress: Cultural Differences 644

Point/Counterpoint Managing Change Is an Episodic Activity 650

Questions for Review 651
Experiential Exercise 651
Ethical Dilemma 652
Case Incident 1 Innovating Innovation 652
Case Incident 2 The Rise of Extreme Jobs 653

Appendix 658

Comprehensive Cases 665

Credits 682

Indexes 685

Glindex 700

Stephen P. Robbins

Education

Ph.D. University of Arizona

Professional Experience

Academic Positions: Professor, San Diego State University, Southern Illinois University at Edwardsville, University of Baltimore, Concordia University in Montreal, and University of Nebraska at Omaha.

Research: Research interests have focused on conflict, power, and politics in organizations, behavioral decision making, and the development of effective interpersonal skills.

Books Published: World's best-selling author of textbooks in both management and organizational behavior. His books are used at more than a thousand U.S. colleges and universities, have been translated into 16 languages, and have adapted editions for Canada, Australia, South Africa, and India. These include

- *Essentials of Organizational Behavior*, 8th ed. (Prentice Hall, 2005)
- *Management*, 8th ed. with Mary Coulter (Prentice Hall, 2005)
- *Human Resource Management*, 8th ed., with David DeCenzo (Wiley, 2005)
- *Prentice Hall's Self-Assessment Library 3.0* (Prentice Hall, 2005)
- *Fundamentals of Management*, 5th ed., with David DeCenzo (Prentice Hall, 2006)
- *Supervision Today!*, 4th ed., with David DeCenzo (Prentice Hall, 2004)
- *Training in Interpersonal Skills*, 3rd ed., with Phillip Hunsaker (Prentice Hall, 2003)
- *Managing Today!*, 2nd ed. (Prentice Hall, 2000)
- *Organization Theory*, 3rd ed. (Prentice Hall, 1990)
- *The Truth About Managing People . . . And Nothing But the Truth* (Financial Times/Prentice Hall, 2002)
- *Decide and Conquer: Make Winning Decisions and Take Control of Your Life* (Financial Times/Prentice Hall, 2004).

Other Interests

In his "other life," Dr. Robbins actively participates in masters' track competition. Since turning 50 in 1993, he's won 14 national championships, 11 world titles, and set numerous U.S. and world age-group records at 60, 100, 200, and 400 meters. In 2005, Dr. Robbins was elected into the USA Masters' Track & Field Hall of Fame.

Timothy A. Judge

Education

Ph.D. University of Illinois at Urbana-Champaign

Professional Experience

Academic Positions: Matherly-McKethan Eminent Scholar in Management, Warrington College of Business Administration, University of Florida; Stanley M. Howe Professor in Leadership, Henry B. Tippie College of Business, University of Iowa; Associate Professor (with tenure), Department of Human Resource Studies, School of Industrial and Labor Relations, Cornell University; Lecturer, Charles University, Czech Republic, and Comenius University, Slovakia; Instructor, Industrial/Organizational Psychology, Department of Psychology, University of Illinois at Urbana-Champaign.

Research: Dr. Judge's primary research interests are in (1) personality, moods, and emotions, (2) job attitudes, (3) leadership and influence behaviors, and (4) careers (person-organization fit, career success). Dr. Judge published more than 100 articles in these and other major topics in journals such as *Journal of Organizational Behavior, Personnel Psychology, Academy of Management Journal, Journal of Applied Psychology, European Journal of Personality, and European Journal of Work and Organizational Psychology.*

Fellowship: Dr. Judge is a fellow of the American Psychological Association, the Academy of Management, the Society for Industrial and Organizational Psychology, and the American Psychological Society.

Awards: In 1995, Dr. Judge received the Ernest J. McCormick Award for Distinguished Early Career Contributions from the Society for Industrial and Organizational Psychology, and in 2001, he received the Larry L. Cummings Award for mid-career contributions from the Organizational Behavior Division of the Academy of Management. In 2007, he received the Professional Practice Award from the Institute of Industrial and Labor Relations, University of Illinois.

Books Published: H. G. Heneman III, and T. A. Judge, *Staffing Organizations*, 5th ed. (Madison, WI: Mendota House/Irwin, 2006).

Other Interests

Although he cannot keep up (literally!) with Steve's accomplishments on the track, Dr. Judge enjoys golf, cooking and baking, literature (he's a particular fan of Thomas Hardy, and is a member of the Thomas Hardy Society), and keeping up with his three children, who range in age from 19 to 5.

Welcome to the thirteenth edition of *Organizational Behavior!* Long considered the standard for all organizational behavior textbooks, this edition continues its tradition of making current, relevant research come alive for students. While maintaining its hallmark features—clear writing style, cutting-edge content, and compelling pedagogy—the thirteenth edition has been updated to reflect the most recent research within the field of organizational behavior.

Key Changes to the Thirteenth Edition

New Global Emphasis. In addition to the International OB highlights, a Global Implications section—which discusses the global implications of each chapter's material—has been added to each chapter.

Updated and Expanded S.A.L. S.A.L. (Self-Assessment Library), the top-selling self-assessment product on the market, has been improved and updated. An additional 25 tests have been added to S.A.L. Moreover, the S.A.L. assessments have been integrated into each chapter, including a S.A.L. assessment at the beginning of each chapter, which allows a seamless self-assessment of a key concept in each chapter.

New Learning Objectives. Each chapter has new learning objectives to allow students to quickly grasp the core concepts in each chapter. In addition to being highlighted at the beginning of each chapter, these learning objectives are keyed to the presentation of the material in the text, and then are highlighted again in the chapter *Questions for Review.*

Experiential Exercises. An experiential, hands-on, in-class exercise is included in each chapter, along with material in the Instructor's Manual that will make for unique and entertaining exercises to highlight a key chapter concept.

Streamlined Length. The text has been streamlined—it is shorter than the last edition of Robbins/Judge, done so by eliminating older material that is less on the cutting edge.

Updated Material. In nearly every chapter, the *Opening Vignette, OB in the News,* and *Myth or Science?* sections are new. In addition, many of the *Case Incident, Ethical Dilemma,* and *Point/Counterpoint* sections are new to this edition.

Chapter-by-Chapter Changes

- New material on evidence-based management (Chapter 1).
- New section on creating a positive work environment and discussion of positive organizational scholarship (Chapter 1).
- New material on general mental ability (Chapter 2).
- New material on sexual orientation and gender identity in the workplace (Chapter 2).
- Revised treatment of cognitive dissonance (Chapter 3).

- Updated sections on personality determinants and how the Big Five predict behavior at work (Chapter 4).
- Updated and revised material on stereotyping and profiling (Chapter 5).
- Enhanced integration of material on the rational model of decision making, bounded rationality, and intuition (Chapter 5).
- Revised treatment of McClelland's Theory of Needs (Chapter 6).
- Streamlined treatment of implementing goal-setting theory and Management by Objectives (Chapter 6).
- Updated treatment of variable-pay programs (Chapter 7).
- New section on gender and emotions (Chapter 8).
- Revised treatment of group norms (Chapter 9).
- New material on virtual teams (Chapter 10).
- New material on personality and team performance (Chapter 10).
- Updated material on diversity effects on team performance (Chapter 10).
- New material on team reflexivity and team mental models (Chapter 10).
- Revised treatment of downward communication (Chapter 11).
- Revised and updated coverage of electronic communication, including new sections on networking software and Internet logs (blogs) (Chapter 11).
- New material on gender differences in communication (Chapter 11).
- Updated material on authentic and ethical leadership (Chapter 13).
- New section on how trust can be regained (Chapter 13).
- New section on political skill (Chapter 14).
- Updated treatment of sexual harassment (Chapter 14).
- Revised recommendations for effective use of distributive bargaining tactics (Chapter 15).
- Revised treatment of individual differences in negotiation, including new coverage of gender differences in negotiation (Chapter 15).
- Revised and updated treatment of the virtual organization (Chapter 16).
- New section on creating a positive organizational culture (Chapter 17).
- Updated material on forces for change in OB (Chapter 19).
- New section on implementing organizational changes fairly (Chapter 19).
- Additional material on challenge and hindrance stressors (Chapter 19).

Instructor's Resource Center

At www.prenhall.com/irc, instructors can access a variety of print, digital, and presentation resources available with this text in downloadable format. Registration is simple and gives you immediate access to new titles and new editions. As a registered faculty member, you can download resource files and receive immediate access and instructions for installing course management content on your campus server.

If you need assistance, our dedicated technical support team is ready to help with the media supplements that accompany this text. Visit www.247.prenhall.com for answers to frequently asked questions and toll-free user support phone numbers.

The following supplements are available to adopting instructors (for detailed descriptions, please visit www.prenhall.com/irc):

- **Instructor's Resource Center (IRC) on CD-ROM**—ISBN: 0-13-602669-9
- **Printed Instructor's Manual**—ISBN: 0-13-602670-2
- **Printed Test Item File**—ISBN: 0-13-602683-4
- **TestGen Test Generating Software**—Available at the IRC online
- **PowerPoint Slides**— Available at the IRC online and on CD-ROM
- **Custom Videos on DVD**—ISBN: 0-13-602675-3

AACSB Learning Standards Tags in Test Item File

What Is the AACSB?

AACSB is a not-for-profit corporation of educational institutions, corporations, and other organizations devoted to the promotion and improvement of higher education in business administration and accounting. A collegiate institution offering degrees in business administration or accounting may volunteer for AACSB accreditation review. The AACSB makes initial accreditation decisions and conducts periodic reviews to promote continuous quality improvement in management education. Pearson Education is a proud member of the AACSB and is pleased to provide advice to help you apply AACSB Learning Standards.

What Are AACSB Learning Standards?

One of the criteria for AACSB accreditation is the quality of the curricula. Although no specific courses are required, the AACSB expects a curriculum to include learning experiences in such areas as:

- Communication
- Ethical Reasoning
- Analytic Skills
- Use of Information Technology
- Multicultural and Diversity
- Reflective Thinking

These six categories are AACSB Learning Standards. Questions that test skills relevant to these standards are tagged with the appropriate standard. For example, a question testing the moral questions associated with externalities would receive the Ethical Reasoning tag.

How Can I Use These Tags?

Tagged questions help you measure whether students are grasping the course content that aligns with AACSB guidelines noted above. In addition, the tagged questions may help to identify potential applications of these skills. This in turn may suggest enrichment activities or other educational experiences to help students achieve these goals.

OneKey Online Courses: Convenience, Simplicity, and Success

OneKey offers complete teaching and learning online resources all in one place. OneKey is all that instructors need to plan and administer courses, and OneKey is all that students need for anytime, anywhere access to online course material. Conveniently organized by textbook chapter, these resources save time and help students reinforce and apply what they have learned. OneKey is available in three course management platforms: Blackboard, CourseCompass, and WebCT.

Vango Notes

Study on the go with VangoNotes (www.VangoNotes.com), detailed chapter reviews in downloadable MP3 format. Now wherever you are and whatever you're doing, you can study on the go by listening to the following for each chapter of your textbook:

- Big Ideas: Your "need to know" for each chapter
- Practice Test: Gut check for the Big Ideas—tells you if you need to keep studying

- Key Terms: Audio "flashcards"—help you review key concepts and terms
- Rapid Review: Quick-drill session—use it right before your test

VangoNotes are **flexible**: Download all the material (or only the chapters you need) directly to your player. And *VangoNotes* are **efficient**: Use them in your car, at the gym, walking to class, wherever you go. So get yours today, and get studying.

CourseSmart eTextbooks Online

Developed for students looking to save money on required or recommended textbooks, CourseSmart eTextbooks online save students money compared with the suggested list price of the print text. Students simply select their eText by title or author and purchase immediate access to the content for the duration of the course using any major credit card. With CourseSmart eText, students can search for specific keywords or page numbers, make notes online, print-out reading assignments that incorporate lecture notes, and bookmark important passages for later review. For more information, or to purchase a CourseSmart eTextbook, visit www.coursesmart.com.

OneKey Online Course Management Materials

OneKey offers complete teaching and learning online resources all in one place. OneKey is all that instructors need to plan and administer courses, and OneKey is all that students need for anytime, anywhere access to online course material. Conveniently organized by textbook chapter, these resources save time and help students reinforce and apply what they have learned. OneKey is available in three course management platforms: Blackboard, CourseCompass, and WebCT.

What's Key for Students?

- **Learning Modules** — Every section of all 19 chapters is supported by section-level pretest, content summary for review, learning application exercise, and post-test. Learning modules are a great way to study for exams and are not connected to the instructor grade book, offering unlimited practice.
- **Prentice Hall's Self-Assessment Library (S.A.L.)**
- **Research Navigator™** is the easiest way for students to start a research assignment or research paper. Complete with extensive help on the research process and four exclusive databases of credible and reliable source material—including the EBSCO Academic Journal and Abstract Database, *New York Times* Search by Subject Archive, "Best of the Web" Link Library, and *Financial Times* Article Archive and Company Financials—Research Navigator helps students quickly and efficiently make the most of their research time.

What's Key for Instructors?

Instructor Resource Center — Faculty can access all instructor resources in one place.

Companion Website

This Web site serves as a student study and review site. Accessible at www.prenhall.com/robbins, this site includes chapter quizzes and student PowerPoints.

Updated and Expanded Self-Assessments

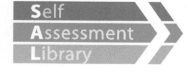

Prentice Hall's Self-Assessment Library (S.A.L.)

A hallmark of the Robbins series, S.A.L. is a unique learning tool that allows you to assess your knowledge, beliefs, feelings, and actions in regard to a wide range of personal skills, abilities, and interests. Self-Assessments have been integrated into each chapter, including a self-assessment at the beginning of each chapter. S.A.L. helps students better understand their interpersonal and behavioral skills as they relate to the theoretical concepts presented in each chapter.

Highlights

- **68 research-based self-assessments** — Our entire collection of 68 instruments are from sources such as *Journal of Social Behavior and Personality, Harvard Business Review, Organizational Behavior: Experiences and Cases, Journal of Experimental Education, Journal of Applied Measurement,* and more.
- **Work–life and career focused** — All self-assessments are focused to help individuals better manage their work lives or careers. Organized in four parts, these instruments offer you one source from which to learn more about yourself.
- **Choice of Formats** — The Prentice Hall Self-Assessment Library is available in either CD-ROM or online format. It is integrated into the Robbins authored OneKey materials for use within the course-management context for his textbooks.
- **Save Feature** — Students can take the self-assessments an unlimited number of times, and save and print their scores for class discussion.
- **Scoring Key** — The key to the self-assessments has been edited by Steve Robbins to allow students to quickly make sense of the results of their score.
- **Instructor's Manual** — An *Instructor's Manual* guides instructors in interpreting self-assessments and helps facilitate better classroom discussion.

For the *Thirteenth Edition*, S.A.L. is included on CD-ROM with every new copy of the text. Additionally, faculty can select to ValuePack S.A.L. in an online format. (stand-alone Web site or within your OneKey course management course offered in WebCT, Blackboard, and CourseCompass). S.A.L. is also available for stand-alone purchase.

Prentice Hall's Self-Assessment Library (S.A.L.) Table of Contents

I. WHAT ABOUT ME?

A. **Personality Insights**
   1. What's My Basic Personality?
   2. What's My Jungian 16-Type Personality?
   3. Am I a Type-A?
   4. How Well Do I Handle Ambiguity?
   5. How Creative Am I?

B. **Values and Attitude Insights**
   1. What Do I Value?
   2. How Involved Am I In My Job?
   3. How Satisfied Am I with My Job?
   4. What Are My Attitudes Toward Workplace Diversity?

C. **Motivation Insights**
   1. What Motivates Me?
   2. What Are My Dominant Needs?
   3. What Rewards Do I Value Most?
   4. What's My View on the Nature of People?
   5. What Are My Course Performance Goals?
   6. How Confident Am I in My Abilities to Succeed?
   7. What's My Attitude Toward Achievement?
   8. How Sensitive Am I to Equity Differences?
   9. What's My Job's Motivating Potential?
   10. Do I Want an Enriched Job?

D. **Decision-Making Insights**
1. What's My Decision-Making Style?
2. Am I a Procrastinator?
3. How Do My Ethics Rate?

E. **Other**
1. What's My Emotional Intelligence Score?
2. What Time of Day Am I Most Productive?
3. How Good Am I at Personal Planning?
4. Am I Likely to Become an Entrepreneur?

II. WORKING WITH OTHERS

A. **Communication Skills**
1. What's My Face-to-Face Communication Style?
2. How Good Are My Listening Skills?

B. **Leadership and Team Skills**
1. What's My Leadership Style?
2. How Charismatic Am I?
3. Do I Trust Others?
4. Do Others See Me as Trusting?
5. How Good Am I at Disciplining Others?
6. How Good Am I at Building and Leading a Team?

C. **Power and Conflict Skills**
1. How Power-Oriented Am I?
2. What's My Preferred Type of Power?
3. How Good Am I at Playing Politics?
4. How Well Do I Manage Impressions?
5. What's My Preferred Conflict-Handling Style?
6. What's My Negotiating Style?

III. LIFE IN ORGANIZATIONS

A. **Organization Structure**
1. What Type of Organization Structure Do I Prefer?
2. How Willing Am I to Delegate?
3. How Good Am I at Giving Performance Feedback?

B. *Careers*
1. What's the Right Organizational Culture for Me?
2. How Committed Am I to My Organization?
3. Am I Experiencing Work/Family Conflict?
4. How Motivated Am I to Manage?
5. Am I Well-Suited for a Career as a Global Manager?

C. **Change and Stress**
1. How Well Do I Respond to Turbulent Change?
2. How Stressful Is My Life?
3. Am I Burned Out?

IV. NEW ASSESSMENTS

A. **Personality Insights**
1. Am I a Narcissist?
2. Am I a Deliberate Decision Maker?
3. How Confident Am I in My Abilities to Succeed?
4. How Spiritual Am I?

B. **Motivation Insights**
1. Am I Engaged?

C. **Values and Attitude Insights**
1. What's My Attitude Toward Older People?
2. What Are My Gender Role Perceptions?

D. **Mood and Emotion Insights**
   1. How Are You Feeling Right Now?
   2. What's My Affect Intensity?

E. **Leadership and Team Skills**
   1. Do I Have a Negative Attitude Toward Working in Groups?
   2. What Is My Team Efficacy?
   3. Am I a Gossip?
   4. Am I an Ethical Leader?
   5. What Is My LPC Score?

F. **Organization Structure**
   1. Is My Workplace Political?
   2. Do I Like Bureaucracy?

G. **Other**
   1. How Much Do I Know about Organizational Behavior?
   2. How Much Do I Know about HRM?

Getting this book into your hands was a team effort. It took faculty reviewers and a talented group of designers and production specialists, editorial personnel, and marketing and sales staff. Sincere appreciation goes to Bob Stretch, Southwestern College, for his skillful and dedicated work on the Instructor's Manual; Cara Cantarella, Acumen Enterprises, Inc., for her tireless work on perfecting the Test Item File; Kate Demarest, Carroll Community College, for her work on the imaginative Online Content; Nick Kaufman Productions for its professional work on the Videos; Brent Scott, Michigan State University, for his dedicated work on the updating of the Self-Assessment Library; and finally Donald Truxillo, Portland State University for his work on the VangoNotes.

More than 100 instructors reviewed parts or all of *Organizational Behavior, Thirteenth Edition*. Their comments, compliments, and suggestions have significantly improved the final product. The authors would like to extend their sincerest thank you to the following instructors:

David Abramis, California State University

Chris Adalikwu, Concordia College

Basil Adams, Notre Dame de Namur University

Vicky Aitken, St Louis Community College

Lois Antonen, CSUS

Lucy Arendt, University of Wisconsin, Green Bay

Mihran Aroian, University of Texas Austin

Christopher Barlow, DePaul University

Jacqui Bergman, Appalachian State University

Anne Berthelot, University of Texas at El Paso

David Bess, Shidler College of Business

Bruce Bikle, California State University Sacramento

Michael Bochenek, Elmhurst College

Alicia Boisnier, State University of New York

William H. Bommer, Cleveland State University

Bryan Bonner, University of Utah

Jessica Bradley, Clemson University

Dr. Jerry Bream, Empire State College/Niagara Frontier Center

Jeff Bruns, Bacone College

Pamela Buckle, Adelphi University

Patricia Buhler, Goldey-Beacom College

Edith Busija, University of Richmond

Michael Cafferky, Southern Adventist University

Scott Campbell, Francis Marion University

Elena Capella, University of San Francisco

Don Capener, Monmouth University

Dan Caprar, University of Iowa

Carol Carnevale, SUNY Empire State College

Donald W. Caudill, Bluefield College

Anthony Chelte, Midwestern State University

David Connelly, Western Illinois State University

Jeffrey Conte, San Diego State University

Jane Crabtree, Benedictine University

Suzanne Crampton, Grand Valley State University

Douglas Crawford, Wilson College

Michael Cruz, San Jose State University

Robert Cyr, Northwestern University

Nancy Da Silva, San Jose State University

Joseph Daly, Appalachian State University

Denise Daniels, Seattle Pacific University

Marie Dasborough, Oklahoma State University

Christine Day, Eastern Michigan University

Emmeline de Pillis, University of Hawaii Hilo

Roger Dean, Washington & Lee University

Robert DelCampo, University of New Mexico

Kristen Detienne, Brigham Young University

Cynthia Doil, Southern Illinois University

Jennifer Dose, Messiah College

David Duby, Liberty University

Ken Dunegan, Cleveland State University

Michael Dutch, Greensboro College

Lenny Favara, Central Christian College

Claudia Ferrante, U.S. Air Force Academy

Andy Fitorre, Nyack College

Kathleen Fleming, Averett University

Erin Fluegge University of Florida

Lucy Franks, Bellevue University

Diane Galbraith, Slippery Rock University

Janice Gates, Western Illinois University

James Gelatt, University of Maryland University College

Matthew Giblin, Southern Illinois University

Cindi Gilliland, The University of Arizona

David Glew, University of North Carolina at Wilmington

Leonard Glick, Northeastern University

Reginald Goodfellow, California State University

Richard Grover, University of Southern Maine

John Guarino, Averett University

Linda Hackleman, Concordia University Austin

Deniz Hackner, Tidewater Community College

Jonathon Halbesleben, University of Missouri-Columbia

Dan Hallock, University of North Alabama

Nell Hartley, Robert Morris University

Erin Hayes, George Washington University

Douglas Heeter, Ferris State University

David Henderson, University of Illinois at Chicago

Scott Henley, Oklahoma City University

Susan Herman, University of Alaska Fairbanks

James Hess, Ivy Tech Community College

Kim Hinrichs, Minnesota State University Mankato

Kathie Holland, University of Central Florida

Brooks Holtom, Georgetown University

Lisa Houts, California State University Fullerton

Paul Hudec, Milwaukee School of Engineering

Charlice Hurst, University of Florida

Warren Imada, Leeward Community College

Christine Jackson, Purdue University

Marsha Jackson, Bowie State University

Alan Jackson, Peru State College

Kathryn Jacobson, Arizona State University

Paul Jacques, Western Carolina University

Elizabeth Jamison, Radford University

Michael Johnson, University of Washington

David Jones, South University

Rusty Juban, Southeastern Illinois University

Carole L. Jurkiewicz, Louisiana State University

John Kammeyer-Mueller, University of Florida

Edward Kass, Saint Joseph's University

James Katzenstein, California State University

John Keiser, SUNY College at Brockport

Mark Kendrick, Methodist University

Mary Kern, Baruch College

Hal Kingsley, Erie Community College

Jeffrey Kobles, California State University San Marcos

Frederick Lane, Baruch College

Rebecca Lau, Virginia Polytechnic Institute and State University

Julia Levashina, Indiana State University Kokomo

Don Lifton, Ithaca College

Ginamarie Ligon, Villanova University

Beth Livingston, University of Florida

Barbara Low, Dominican University

Doyle Lucas, Anderson University

Alexandra Luong, University of Minnesota

Rick Maclin, Missouri Baptist University

Peter Madsen, Brigham Young University

J. David Martin, Midwestern State University

John Mattoon, State University of New York

Brenda McAleer, University of Maine at Augusta

Christina McCale, Regis Colllege

Don McCormick, California State University Northridge

Bonnie McNeely, Murray State University

Steven Meisel, La Salle University

Catherine Michael, St. Edwards University

Sandy Miles, Murray State University

Leann Mischel, Susquehanna University

Atul Mitra, University of Northern Iowa

Paula Morrow, Iowa State University

Mark Mortensen, Massachusetts Institute of Technology

Judy Nixon, University of Tennessee at Chattanooga

Jeffrey Nystrom, University of Colorado at Denver

Heather Odle-Dusseau, Clemson University

Miguel Olivas-Lujan, Lujan Clarion University

Laura Finnerty Paul, Skidmore College

Anette Pendergrass, Arkansas State University at Mountain Home

Jeff Peterson, University of Washington

Nanette Philibert, Missouri Southern State University

Larry Phillips, Indiana University Southbend

Eric Popkoff, Brooklyn College

Aarti Ramaswami, Indiana University Bloomington

Amy Randel, San Diego State University

Anne Reilly, Loyola University Chicago

Chris Roberts, University of Massachusetts Amherst

Sherry Robinson, Pennsylvania State University Hazleton

Andrea Roofe, Florida International University

Manjula Salimath, University of North Texas

Mary Saunders, Georgia Gwinnett College

Elizabeth Scott, Elizabeth City University

Mark Seabright, Western Oregon University

Joseph Seltzer, LaSalle University

John Shaw, Mississippi State University

John Sherlock, Western Carolina University

Heather Shields, Texas Tech University

Stuart Sidle, University of New Haven

Bret Simmons, University of Nevada Reno

Lynda St. Clair, Bryant University

John B. Stark, California State University, Bakersfield

Merwyn Strate, Purdue University

Karen Thompson, Sonoma State University

Linda Tibbetts, Antioch University McGregor

Ed Tomlinson, John Carroll University

Bob Trodella, Webster University

Albert Turner, Webster University

William Walker, University of Houston

Ian Walsh, Boston College

Charles F. Warren, Salem State College

Christa Washington, Saint Augustine

Jim Westerman, Appalachian State University

William J. White, Northwestern University

David Whitlock, Southwest Baptist University

Dan Wiljanen, Grand Valley State University

Dean Williamson, Brewton-Parker College

Hilda Williamson, Hampton University

Alice Wilson, Cedar Crest College

Craig Wishart, Fayetteville State University

Laura Wolfe, Louisiana State University

Melody Wollan, Eastern Illinois University

Evan Wood, Taylor University Fort Wayne

Chun-Sheng Yu, University of Houston-Victoria

Over the last editions this text has grown stronger with the contribution and feedback of the following instructors:

Janet Adams, Kennesaw State University

Cheryl Adkins, Longwood College

David Albritton, Northern Arizona University

Bradley Alge, Purdue University

Anke Arnaud, University of Central Florida

Gary Ballinger, Purdue University

Deborah Balser, University of Missouri at St. Louis

Joy Benson, University of Wisconsin at Green Bay

Lehman Benson III, University of Arizona

Richard Blackburn, University of North Carolina–Chapel Hill

Weldon Blake, Bethune-Cookman College

Bryan Bonner, University of Utah

Peggy Brewer, Eastern Kentucky University

Jim Breaugh, University of Missouri

Deborah Brown, North Carolina State University

Reginald Bruce, University of Louisville

Allen Bures, Radford University

Holly Buttner, University of North Carolina at Greensboro

David Carmichael, Oklahoma City University

Suzanne Chan, Tulane University

Bongsoon Cho, State University of New York–Buffalo

Savannah Clay, Central Piedmont Community College

Evelyn Dadzie, Clark Atlanta University

Emmeline de Pillis, University of Hawaii

Doug Dierking, University of Texas at Austin

Ceasar Douglas, Florida State University

Ken Dunegan, Cleveland State University

Kathleen Edwards, University of Texas at Austin

Berrin Erdogan, Portland State University

Ellen Fagenson Eland, George Mason University

Jann Freed, Central College

Carolyn Gardner, Radford University

Edward Fox, Wilkes University

Alison Fragale, University of North Carolina at Chapel Hill

Dean Frear, Wilkes University

Crissie Frye, Eastern Michigan University

Janice Gates, Western Illinois University

David Glew, University of North Carolina at Wilmington

Ellen Kaye Gehrke, Alliant International University

Joe Gerard, University of Wisconsin at Milwaukee

Donald Gibson, Fairfield University

Mary Giovannini, Truman State University

Jeffrey Goldstein, Adelphi University

Jodi Goodman, University of Connecticut

Claude Graeff, Illinois State University

W. Lee Grubb III, East Carolina University

Rebecca Guidice, University of Nevada at Las Vegas

Andra Gumbus, Sacred Heart University

Dan Hallock, University of North Alabama

Edward Hampton, University of Central Florida

Vernard Harrington, Radford University

Nell Hartley, Robert Morris University

Barbara Hassell, Indiana University, Kelley School of Business

Tom Head, Roosevelt University

Ted Herbert, Rollins College

Ronald Hester, Marymount University

Patricia Hewlin, Georgetown University

Chad Higgins, University of Washington

Kathie Holland, University of Central Florida

Elaine Hollensbe, University of Cincinnati

Kristin Holmberg-Wright, University of Wisconsin at Parkside

Abigail Hubbard, University of Houston

Stephen Humphrey, Florida State University

Gazi Islam, Tulane University

Elizabeth Jamison, Radford University

Stephen Jenner, California State University, Dominguez Hills

John Jermier, University of South Florida

Jack Johnson, Consumnes River College

Ray Jones, University of Pittsburgh

Anthony Jost, University of Delaware

Louis Jourdan, Clayton College

Marsha Katz, Governors State College

Robert Key, University of Phoenix

Sigrid Khorram, University of Texas at El Paso

Jack Kondrasuk, University of Portland

Leslie A. Korb, University of Nebraska at Kearney

Glen Kreiner, University of Cincinnati

James Kroeger, Cleveland State University

David Leuser, Plymouth State College

Benyamin Lichtenstein, University of Massachusetts at Boston

Robert Liden, University of Illinois at Chicago

Kathy Lund Dean, Idaho State University

Timothy A. Matherly, Florida State University

Lou Marino, University of Alabama

Paul Maxwell, Saint Thomas University

James McElroy, Iowa State University

Melony Mead, University of Phoenix

Nancy Meyer-Emerick, Cleveland State University

Janice Miller, University of Wisconsin at Milwaukee

Linda Morable, Richland College

Lori Muse, Western Michigan University

Padmakumar Nair, University of Texas at Dallas

Alison O'Brien, George Mason University

Kelly Ottman, University of Wisconsin at Milwaukee

Peg Padgett, Butler University

Jennifer Palthe, Western Michigan University

Dennis Passovoy, University of Texas at Austin

Karen Paul, Florida International University

Bryan Pesta, Cleveland State University

William Pinchuk, Rutgers University at Camden

Paul Preston, University of Montevallo

Scott Quatro, Grand Canyon University

Jere Ramsey, Cal Poly at San Luis Obispo

Clint Relyea, Arkansas State University

David Ritchey, University of Texas at Dallas

Christopher Ann Robinson-Easley, Governors State University

Tracey Rockett Hanft, University of Texas at Dallas

Joe Rode, Miami University

Bob Roller, LeTourneau University

Philip Roth, Clemson University

Craig Russell, University of Oklahoma at Norman

Andy Schaffer, North Georgia College and State University

Holly Schroth, University of California at Berkeley

Ted Shore, California State University at Long Beach

Daniel Sherman, University of Alabama, Huntsville

Stuart Sidle, DePaul University

Randy Sleeth, Virginia Commonwealth University

William Smith, Emporia State University

Kenneth Solano, Northeastern University

Shane Spiller, Morehead State University

John Stark, California State University at Bakersfield

Joo-Seng Tan, Cornell University

Tom Tudor, University of Arkansas at Little Rock

William D. Tudor, Ohio State University

Daniel Turban, University of Missouri

Jim Turner, Morehead State University

Leslie Tworoger, Nova Southeastern University

M.A. Viets, University of Vermont

Roger Volkema, American University

Barry Wisdom, Southeast Missouri State University

Jun Zhao, Governors State University

Lori Ziegler, University of Texas at Dallas

Gail Zwart, Riverside Community College

We owe a debt of gratitude to all those at Prentice Hall who have supported this text over the last 30 years and who have worked so hard on the development of this latest edition. On the development and editorial side, we want to thank Development Editor, Elisa Adams; Director of Development, Steve Deitmer; Editorial Assistant, Elizabeth Davis; Editor, Jennifer Collins; Editor in Chief, David Parker; and Editorial Director, Sally Yagan. On the design and production side, Senior Managing Editor Judy Leale did an outstanding job. Last but not least, we would like to thank Marketing Manager, Nikki Jones, and Director of Marketing, Patrice Jones and their sales staff who have been selling this book over its many editions. Thank you for the attention you've given this book.

What Is Organizational Behavior?

The stellar universe is not
so difficult of comprehension
as the real actions of other
people.

—Marcel Proust

1

LEARNING OBJECTIVES

After studying this chapter, you should be able to:

1 Demonstrate the importance of interpersonal skills in the workplace.

2 Describe the manager's functions, roles, and skills.

3 Define *organizational behavior (OB)*.

4 Show the value to OB of systematic study.

5 Identify the major behavioral science disciplines that contribute to OB.

6 Demonstrate why there are few absolutes in OB.

7 Identify the challenges and opportunities managers have in applying OB concepts.

8 Compare the three levels of analysis in this book's OB model.

anagers make a lot of mistakes. Some come from inexperience. Others reflect lack of knowledge. And some are just dumb.

But few mistakes could be considered as stupid as what managers of home security company Alarm One, Inc., did.

As part of a "team building" exercise, employees were paddled with rival companies' yard signs as part of a contest that pitted sales teams against one another. The win-

Is That Any Way to Treat an Employee?

ners threw pies at the losers, fed them baby food, made them wear diapers, and, yes, spanked them. Sometimes coworkers made comments such as, "bend over baby," and "you've been a bad girl."

Outside the "team building" contests, Alarm One also routinely spanked employees who were late for work.

One of the employees who was spanked—Janet Orlando (see photo above)—was so humiliated that she quit shortly after the episode and later decided to sue Alarm One.

During the trial against Alarm One, in his closing arguments, Orlando's attorney said, "No reasonable middle-aged woman would want to be put up there before a group of young men, turned around to show her buttocks, get spanked and called abusive names, and told it was to increase sales and motivate employees."

It's not surprising that a jury of six men and six women ruled in favor of Orlando, awarding her more than she'd asked for: $500,000 in compensatory damages and $1.2 million in punitive damages.

Why did Alarm One do this in the first place? The Anaheim, California, company defended the spankings by saying they were part of a voluntary program to build camaraderie and were not discriminatory because they were given to both male and female workers.

After the trial, Orlando and Alarm One agreed to a payment of $1.4 million, in lieu of Alarm One's appealing. As of now, though, the company has not paid Orlando a dime, forcing her to sue all over again. "These guys have lied since day one," says Orlando.[1] ∎

*Y*ou might think incidents like the one at Alarm One illustrate that managing people is all about common sense. After all, you don't need a textbook to tell you not to spank employees. However, as we'll see, not all aspects of management are common sense. Mistakes like spanking employees are visible and obvious mistakes, but managers commonly make other mistakes due to their lack of knowledge. This is where organizational behavior comes into play.

To see how far common sense gets you, try the following from the Self-Assessment Library.

HOW MUCH DO I KNOW ABOUT ORGANIZATIONAL BEHAVIOR?

In the Self-Assessment Library (available on CD and online), take assessment IV.G.1 (How Much Do I Know About OB?) and answer the following questions:

1. *How did you score? Are you surprised by your score?*
2. *How much of effective management do you think is common sense? Did your score on the test change your answer to this question?*

The Importance of Interpersonal Skills

Although practicing managers have long understood the importance of interpersonal skills to managerial effectiveness, business schools have been slower to get the message. Until the late 1980s, business school curricula emphasized the technical aspects of management, specifically focusing on economics, accounting, finance, and quantitative techniques. Course work in human behavior and people skills received minimal attention relative to the technical aspects of management. Over the past 2 decades, however, business faculty have come to realize the importance that an understanding of human behavior plays in determining a manager's effectiveness, and required courses on people skills have been added to many curricula. As the director of leadership at MIT's Sloan School of Management recently put

1 Demonstrate the importance of interpersonal skills in the workplace.

Succeeding in management today requires good people skills. Communication and leadership skills distinguish managers such as Jeffrey Immelt who rise to the top of their profession. Immelt, CEO of General Electric, joined the company in corporate marketing in 1982 and spent 20 years in sales, marketing, and product development leadership positions before moving into GE's top management job. Outgoing and adept at building relationships, Immelt travels the world, meeting with customers, employees, suppliers, and stockholders. In this photo, Immelt interacts with schoolchildren in a reading program funded by GE.

it, "M.B.A. students may get by on their technical and quantitative skills the first couple of years out of school. But soon, leadership and communication skills come to the fore in distinguishing the managers whose careers really take off."[2]

Recognition of the importance of developing managers' interpersonal skills is closely tied to the need for organizations to get and keep high-performing employees. Regardless of labor market conditions, outstanding employees are always in short supply.[3] Companies with reputations as good places to work—such as Starbucks, Adobe Systems, Cisco, Whole Foods, American Express, Amgen, Goldman Sachs, Pfizer, and Marriott—have a big advantage. A national study of the U.S. workforce found that wages and fringe benefits are not the main reasons people like their jobs or stay with an employer. Far more important is the quality of the employee's job and the supportiveness of the work environment.[4] So having managers with good interpersonal skills is likely to make the workplace more pleasant, which, in turn, makes it easier to hire and keep qualified people. In addition, creating a pleasant workplace appears to make good economic sense. For instance, companies with reputations as good places to work (such as the companies that are included among the "100 Best Companies to Work for in America") have been found to generate superior financial performance.[5]

We have come to understand that technical skills are necessary, but they are not enough to succeed in management. In today's increasingly competitive and demanding workplace, managers can't succeed on their technical skills alone. They also have to have good people skills. This book has been written to help both managers and potential managers develop those people skills.

What Managers Do

2 *Describe the manager's functions, roles, and skills.*

Let's begin by briefly defining the terms *manager* and *organization*—the place where managers work. Then let's look at the manager's job; specifically, what do managers do?

Managers get things done through other people. They make decisions, allocate resources, and direct the activities of others to attain goals. Managers do their work in an **organization**, which is a consciously coordinated social unit, composed of two or more people, that functions on a relatively continuous basis to achieve a common goal or set of goals. On the basis of this definition, manufacturing and service firms are organizations, and so are schools, hospitals, churches, military units, retail stores, police departments, and local, state, and federal government agencies. The people who oversee the activities of others and who are responsible for attaining goals in these organizations are managers (although they're sometimes called *administrators*, especially in not-for-profit organizations).

Management Functions

In the early part of the twentieth century, a French industrialist by the name of Henri Fayol wrote that all managers perform five management functions: planning, organizing, commanding, coordinating, and controlling.[6] Today, we have condensed these to four: planning, organizing, leading, and controlling.

Because organizations exist to achieve goals, someone has to define those goals and the means for achieving them; management is that someone. The **planning** function encompasses defining an organization's goals, establishing an overall strategy for achieving those goals, and developing a comprehensive set of plans to integrate and coordinate activities. Evidence indicates that this function is the one that increases the most as managers move from lower-level to midlevel management.[7]

Managers are also responsible for designing an organization's structure. We call this function **organizing**. It includes determining what tasks are to be done, who is to do them, how the tasks are to be grouped, who reports to whom, and where decisions are to be made.

Every organization contains people, and it is management's job to direct and coordinate those people. This is the **leading** function. When managers motivate employees, direct the activities of others, select the most effective communication channels, or resolve conflicts among members, they're engaging in leading.

The final function managers perform is **controlling**. To ensure that things are going as they should, management must monitor the organization's performance. Actual performance is then compared with the previously set goals. If there are any significant deviations, it is management's job to get the organization back on track. This monitoring, comparing, and potential correcting is what is meant by the controlling function.

So, using the functional approach, the answer to the question "What do managers do?" is that they plan, organize, lead, and control.

Management Roles

In the late 1960s, Henry Mintzberg, a graduate student at MIT, undertook a careful study of five executives to determine what those managers did on their jobs. On the basis of his observations, Mintzberg concluded that managers perform 10 different, highly interrelated roles—or sets of behaviors—attributable to their jobs.[8] As shown in Exhibit 1-1, these 10 roles can be grouped as being primarily (1) interpersonal, (2) informational, and (3) decisional.

Interpersonal Roles   All managers are required to perform duties that are ceremonial and symbolic in nature. For instance, when the president of a college hands out diplomas at commencement or a factory supervisor gives a group of high school students a tour of the plant, he or she is acting in a

Exhibit **1-1**	Mintzberg's Managerial Roles

Role	Description
Interpersonal	
Figurehead	Symbolic head; required to perform a number of routine duties of a legal or social nature
Leader	Responsible for the motivation and direction of employees
Liaison	Maintains a network of outside contacts who provide favors and information
Informational	
Monitor	Receives a wide variety of information; serves as nerve center of internal and external information of the organization
Disseminator	Transmits information received from outsiders or from other employees to members of the organization
Spokesperson	Transmits information to outsiders on organization's plans, policies, actions, and results; serves as expert on organization's industry
Decisional	
Entrepreneur	Searches organization and its environment for opportunities and initiates projects to bring about change
Disturbance handler	Responsible for corrective action when organization faces important, unexpected disturbances
Resource allocator	Makes or approves significant organizational decisions
Negotiator	Responsible for representing the organization at major negotiations

Source: Adapted from *The Nature of Managerial Work* by H. Mintzberg. Copyright © 1973 by H. Mintzberg. Reprinted by permission of Pearson Education.

figurehead role. All managers also have a *leadership* role. This role includes hiring, training, motivating, and disciplining employees. The third role within the interpersonal grouping is the *liaison* role. Mintzberg described this activity as contacting outsiders who provide the manager with information. These may be individuals or groups inside or outside the organization. The sales manager who obtains information from the quality-control manager in his or her own company has an internal liaison relationship. When that sales manager has contacts with other sales executives through a marketing trade association, he or she has an outside liaison relationship.

Informational Roles   All managers, to some degree, collect information from outside organizations and institutions. Typically, they obtain it by reading magazines and talking with other people to learn of changes in the public's tastes, what competitors may be planning, and the like. Mintzberg called this the

managers *Individuals who achieve goals through other people.*

organization *A consciously coordinated social unit, composed of two or more people, that functions on a relatively continuous basis to achieve a common goal or set of goals.*

planning *A process that includes defining goals, establishing strategy, and developing plans to coordinate activities.*

organizing *Determining what tasks are to be done, who is to do them, how the tasks are to be grouped, who reports to whom, and where decisions are to be made.*

leading *A function that includes motivating employees, directing others, selecting the most effective communication channels, and resolving conflicts.*

controlling *Monitoring activities to ensure that they are being accomplished as planned and correcting any significant deviations.*

monitor role. Managers also act as a conduit to transmit information to organizational members. This is the *disseminator* role. In addition, managers perform a *spokesperson* role when they represent the organization to outsiders.

Decisional Roles   Mintzberg identified four roles that revolve around making choices. In the *entrepreneur* role, managers initiate and oversee new projects that will improve their organization's performance. As *disturbance handlers*, managers take corrective action in response to unforeseen problems. As *resource allocators*, managers are responsible for allocating human, physical, and monetary resources. Finally, managers perform a *negotiator* role, in which they discuss issues and bargain with other units to gain advantages for their own unit.

Management Skills

Still another way of considering what managers do is to look at the skills or competencies they need to achieve their goals. Robert Katz has identified three essential management skills: technical, human, and conceptual.[9]

Technical Skills   **Technical skills** encompass the ability to apply specialized knowledge or expertise. When you think of the skills of professionals such as civil engineers or oral surgeons, you typically focus on their technical skills. Through extensive formal education, they have learned the special knowledge and practices of their field. Of course, professionals don't have a monopoly on technical skills, and not all technical skills have to be learned in schools or other formal training programs. All jobs require some specialized expertise, and many people develop their technical skills on the job.

Human Skills   The ability to work with, understand, and motivate other people, both individually and in groups, defines **human skills**. Many people are technically proficient but interpersonally incompetent. They might be poor listeners, unable to understand the needs of others, or have difficulty managing conflicts. Because managers get things done through other people, they must have good human skills to communicate, motivate, and delegate.

Conceptual Skills   Managers must have the mental ability to analyze and diagnose complex situations. These tasks require **conceptual skills**. Decision making, for instance, requires managers to identify problems, develop alternative solutions to correct those problems, evaluate those alternative solutions, and select the best one. Managers can be technically and interpersonally competent yet still fail because of an inability to rationally process and interpret information.

Effective Versus Successful Managerial Activities

Fred Luthans and his associates looked at the issue of what managers do from a somewhat different perspective.[10] They asked the question "Do managers who move up the quickest in an organization do the same activities and with the same emphasis as managers who do the best job?" You would tend to think that the managers who are the most effective in their jobs would also be the ones who are promoted the fastest. But that's not what appears to happen.

Luthans and his associates studied more than 450 managers. What they found was that these managers all engaged in four managerial activities:

1. **Traditional management.**   Decision making, planning, and controlling
2. **Communication.**   Exchanging routine information and processing paperwork

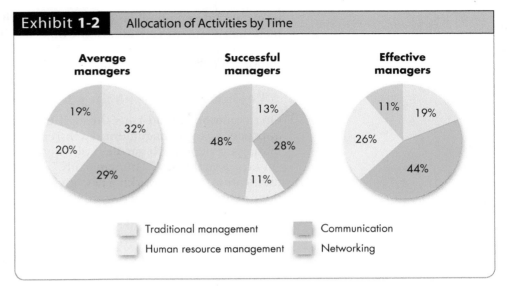

| Exhibit **1-2** | Allocation of Activities by Time |

Source: Based on F. Luthans, R. M. Hodgetts, and S. A. Rosenkrantz, *Real Managers* (Cambridge, MA: Ballinger, 1988).

3. Human resource management. Motivating, disciplining, managing conflict, staffing, and training

4. Networking. Socializing, politicking, and interacting with outsiders

The "average" manager in the study spent 32 percent of his or her time in traditional management activities, 29 percent communicating, 20 percent in human resource management activities, and 19 percent networking. However, the amount of time and effort that different managers spent on those four activities varied a great deal. Specifically, as shown in Exhibit 1-2, managers who were *successful* (defined in terms of the speed of promotion within their organization) had a very different emphasis than managers who were *effective* (defined in terms of the quantity and quality of their performance and the satisfaction and commitment of their employees). Among successful managers, networking made the largest relative contribution to success, and human resource management activities made the least relative contribution. Among effective managers, communication made the largest relative contribution and networking the least. More recent studies, conducted in a variety of countries (Australia, Israel, Italy, Japan, and the United States), further confirm the link between networking and success within an organization.[11] For example, one study found that Australian managers who actively networked received more promotions and enjoyed other rewards associated with career success. And the connection between communication and effective managers is also clear. A study of 410 U.S. managers indicates that managers who seek information from colleagues and employees—even if it's negative—and who explain their decisions are the most effective.[12]

This research adds important insights to our knowledge of what managers do. On average, managers spend approximately 20 to 30 percent of their time on each of the four activities: traditional management, communication, human resource management, and networking. However, successful managers don't

technical skills *The ability to apply specialized knowledge or expertise.*

human skills *The ability to work with, understand, and motivate other people, both individually and in groups.*

conceptual skills *The mental ability to analyze and diagnose complex situations.*

give the same emphasis to each of those activities as do effective managers. In fact, their emphases are almost the opposite. This finding challenges the historical assumption that promotions are based on performance, and it illustrates the importance of networking and political skills in getting ahead in organizations.

A Review of the Manager's Job

One common thread runs through the functions, roles, skills, activities, and approaches to management: Each recognizes the paramount importance of managing people. Regardless of whether it is called "the leading function," "interpersonal roles," "human skills," or "human resource management, communication, and networking activities," it's clear that managers need to develop their people skills if they're going to be effective and successful.

Enter Organizational Behavior

We've made the case for the importance of people skills. But neither this book nor the discipline on which it is based is called "people skills." The term that is widely used to describe the discipline is *organizational behavior.*

Define organizational behavior (OB).

Organizational behavior (often abbreviated OB) is a field of study that investigates the impact that individuals, groups, and structure have on behavior within organizations, for the purpose of applying such knowledge toward improving an organization's effectiveness. That's a mouthful, so let's break it down.

Organizational behavior is a field of study, meaning that it is a distinct area of expertise with a common body of knowledge. What does it study? It studies three determinants of behavior in organizations: individuals, groups, and structure. In addition, OB applies the knowledge gained about individuals, groups, and the effect of structure on behavior in order to make organizations work more effectively.

Microsoft understands how organizational behavior affects an organization's performance. The company maintains good employee relationships by providing a great work environment, generous benefits, and challenging jobs. The two-story wall painting shown here is one of 4,500 pieces of contemporary art displayed at Microsoft's corporate campus for employees' enjoyment. Other benefits, such as valet parking, dry-cleaning and laundry service, free grocery delivery, and take-home meals, help employees focus on their work. At Microsoft, employee loyalty and productivity are high, contributing to the company's growth to $44 billion in revenues since its founding in 1975.

To sum up our definition, OB is concerned with the study of what people do in an organization and how their behavior affects the organization's performance. And because OB is concerned specifically with employment-related situations, you should not be surprised to find that it emphasizes behavior as related to concerns such as jobs, work, absenteeism, employment turnover, productivity, human performance, and management.

There is increasing agreement as to the components or topics that constitute the subject area of OB. Although there is still considerable debate as to the relative importance of each, there appears to be general agreement that OB includes the core topics of motivation, leader behavior and power, interpersonal communication, group structure and processes, learning, attitude development and perception, change processes, conflict, work design, and work stress.[13]

Complementing Intuition with Systematic Study

Each of us is a student of behavior. Since our earliest years, we've watched the actions of others and have attempted to interpret what we see. Whether or not you've explicitly thought about it before, you've been "reading" people almost all your life. You watch what others do and try to explain to yourself why they have engaged in their behavior. In addition, you've attempted to predict what they might do under different sets of conditions. Unfortunately, your casual or commonsense approach to reading others can often lead to erroneous predictions. However, you can improve your predictive ability by supplementing your intuitive opinions with a more systematic approach.

4   Show the value to OB of systematic study.

The systematic approach used in this book will uncover important facts and relationships and will provide a base from which more accurate predictions of behavior can be made. Underlying this systematic approach is the belief that behavior is not random. Rather, there are certain fundamental consistencies underlying the behavior of all individuals that can be identified and then modified to reflect individual differences.

These fundamental consistencies are very important. Why? Because they allow predictability. Behavior is generally predictable, and the *systematic study* of behavior is a means to making reasonably accurate predictions. When we use the phrase **systematic study**, we mean looking at relationships, attempting to attribute causes and effects, and basing our conclusions on scientific evidence—that is, on data gathered under controlled conditions and measured and interpreted in a reasonably rigorous manner. (See Appendix A for a basic review of research methods used in studies of organizational behavior.)

An approach that complements systematic study is evidence-based management. **Evidence-based management (EBM)** involves basing managerial decisions

organizational behavior (OB) *A field of study that investigates the impact that individuals, groups, and structure have on behavior within organizations, for the purpose of applying such knowledge toward improving an organization's effectiveness.*

systematic study *Looking at relationships, attempting to attribute causes and effects, and drawing conclusions based on scientific evidence.*

evidence-based management (EBM) *Basing managerial decisions on the best available scientific evidence.*

MYTH OR SCIENCE?   *"Preconceived Notions Versus Substantive Evidence"*

*a*ssume that you signed up to take an introductory college course in finance. On the first day of class, your instructor asks you to take out a piece of paper and answer the following question: "What is the net present value at a discount rate of 12 percent per year of an investment made by spending $1,000,000 this year on a portfolio of stocks, with an initial dividend next year of $100,000 and an expected rate of dividend growth thereafter of 4 percent per year?" It's unlikely you'd be able to answer that question without some instruction in finance.

Now, change the scenario. You're in an introductory course in organizational behavior. On the first day of class, your instructor asks you to write the answer to the following question: "What's the most effective way to motivate employees at work?" At first you might feel a bit of reluctance, but once you began writing, you'd likely have no problem coming up with suggestions on motivation.

That's one of the main challenges of teaching, or taking, a course in OB. You enter an OB course with a lot of *preconceived notions* that you accept as *facts*. You think you already know a lot about human behavior.[14] That's not typically true in finance, accounting, or even marketing. So, in contrast to many other disciplines, OB not only introduces you to a comprehensive set of concepts and theories; it has to deal with a lot of commonly accepted "facts" about human behavior and organizations that you've acquired over the years. Some examples might include: "You can't teach an old dog new tricks," "leaders are born, not made," and "two heads are better than one." But these "facts" aren't necessarily true. So one of the objectives of a course in organizational behavior is to *replace* popularly held notions, often accepted without question, with science-based conclusions.

As you'll see in this book, the field of OB is built on decades of research. This research provides a body of substantive evidence that is able to replace preconceived notions. Throughout this book, we've included boxes titled "Myth or Science?" They call your attention to some of the most popular of these notions or myths about organizational behavior. We use the boxes to show how OB research has disproved them or, in some cases, shown them to be true. Hopefully, you'll find these boxes interesting. But more importantly, they'll help remind you that the study of human behavior at work is a science and that you need to be vigilant about "seat-of-the-pants" explanations of work-related behaviors. ■

on the best available scientific evidence. We'd want doctors to make decisions about patient care based on the latest available evidence, and EBM argues that we want managers to do the same. That means managers must become more scientific in how they think about management problems. For example, a manager might pose a managerial question, search for the best available evidence, and apply the relevant information to the question or case at hand. You might think it's difficult to argue against this (what manager would argue that decisions shouldn't be based on evidence?), but the vast majority of management decisions are still made "on the fly," with little or systematic study of available evidence.[15]

Systematic study and EBM add to **intuition,** or those "gut feelings" about "why I do what I do" and "what makes others tick." Of course, a systematic approach does not mean that the things you have come to believe in an unsystematic way are necessarily incorrect. As Jack Welch noted, "The trick, of course, is to know when to go with your gut." If we make all decisions with intuition or gut instinct, we're likely making decisions with incomplete information—sort of like making an investment decision with only half the data.

The limits of relying on intuition are made worse by the fact that we tend to overestimate the accuracy of what we think we know. A recent survey revealed that 86 percent of managers thought their organization was treating their employees well. However, only 55 percent of the employees thought they were well treated.

We find a similar problem in chasing the business and popular media for management wisdom. The business press tends to be dominated by fads. As a writer for *The New Yorker* put it, "Every few years, new companies succeed, and they are scrutinized for the underlying truths they might reveal. But often there is no underlying truth; the companies just happened to be in the right place at the right time."[16] Although we try to avoid it, we might also fall into this trap. It's not that the business press stories are all wrong; it's that without a systematic approach, it's hard to separate the wheat from the chaff.

Some of the conclusions we make in this text, based on reasonably substantive research findings, will only support what you always knew was true. But you'll also be exposed to research evidence that runs counter to what you may have thought was common sense. One of the objectives of this text is to encourage you to enhance your intuitive views of behavior with a systematic analysis, in the belief that such analysis will improve your accuracy in explaining and predicting behavior.

We're not advising that you throw your intuition, or all the business press, out the window. Nor are we arguing that research is always right. Researchers make mistakes, too. What we are advising is to use evidence as much as possible to inform your intuition and experience. That is the promise of OB.

Disciplines That Contribute to the OB Field

5 *Identify the major behavioral science disciplines that contribute to OB.*

Organizational behavior is an applied behavioral science that is built on contributions from a number of behavioral disciplines. The predominant areas are psychology and social psychology, sociology, and anthropology. As you shall learn, psychology's contributions have been mainly at the individual or micro level of analysis, while the other disciplines have contributed to our understanding of macro concepts such as group processes and organization. Exhibit 1-3 is an overview of the major contributions to the study of organizational behavior.

Psychology

Psychology is the science that seeks to measure, explain, and sometimes change the behavior of humans and other animals. Psychologists concern themselves with studying and attempting to understand individual behavior. Those who have contributed and continue to add to the knowledge of OB are learning theorists, personality theorists, counseling psychologists, and, most important, industrial and organizational psychologists.

Early industrial/organizational psychologists concerned themselves with the problems of fatigue, boredom, and other factors relevant to working

intuition   *A gut feeling not necessarily supported by research.*

psychology   *The science that seeks to measure, explain, and sometimes change the behavior of humans and other animals.*

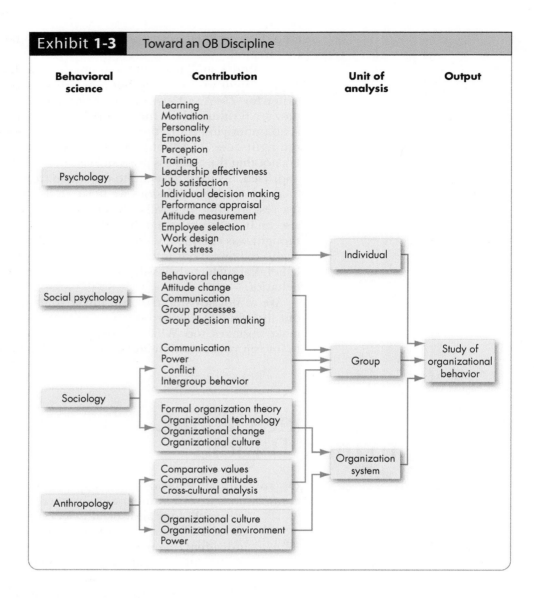

Exhibit **1-3**   Toward an OB Discipline

Behavioral science	Contribution	Unit of analysis	Output

(Figure contents:)

Psychology → Learning, Motivation, Personality, Emotions, Perception, Training, Leadership effectiveness, Job satisfaction, Individual decision making, Performance appraisal, Attitude measurement, Employee selection, Work design, Work stress → **Individual**

Social psychology → Behavioral change, Attitude change, Communication, Group processes, Group decision making

Communication, Power, Conflict, Intergroup behavior → **Group**

Sociology → Formal organization theory, Organizational technology, Organizational change, Organizational culture → **Organization system**

Comparative values, Comparative attitudes, Cross-cultural analysis

Anthropology → Organizational culture, Organizational environment, Power

Individual, **Group**, **Organization system** → **Study of organizational behavior**

conditions that could impede efficient work performance. More recently, their contributions have been expanded to include learning, perception, personality, emotions, training, leadership effectiveness, needs and motivational forces, job satisfaction, decision-making processes, performance appraisals, attitude measurement, employee-selection techniques, work design, and job stress.

Social Psychology

Social psychology blends concepts from both psychology and sociology, though it is generally considered a branch of psychology. It focuses on peoples' influence on one another. One major area receiving considerable investigation from social psychologists has been *change*—how to implement it and how to reduce barriers to its acceptance. In addition, we find social psychologists making significant contributions in the areas of measuring, understanding, and changing attitudes; communication patterns; and building trust. Finally, social psychologists have made important contributions to our study of group behavior, power, and conflict.

OB In the News

Other Disciplines Make Use of OB Concepts

It may surprise you to learn that, increasingly, other business disciplines are employing OB concepts.

Of the business disciplines, marketing has the closest overlap with OB. One of the primary areas of marketing is consumer research, and trying to predict consumer behavior is not that different from trying to predict employee behavior. Both require an understanding of the dynamics and underlying causes of human behavior, and there's a lot of correspondence between the disciplines.

What's perhaps more surprising is the degree to which the so-called hard disciplines are making use of soft OB concepts. Behavioral finance, behavioral accounting, and behavioral economics (also called *economic psychology*) all have grown in importance and interest in the past several years.

On reflection, this shouldn't be so surprising. Your common sense will tell you that humans are not perfectly rational creatures, and in many cases, our actions don't conform to a rational model of behavior. Although some elements of irrationality are incorporated into economic thought, increasingly, finance, accounting, and economics researchers find it useful to draw from OB concepts.

For example, investors have a tendency to place more weight on private information (information that only they, or a limited group of people, know) than on public information, even when there is reason to believe that the public information is more accurate. To understand this phenomenon, finance researchers use OB concepts. In addition, behavioral accounting research might study how feedback influences auditors' behavior, or the functional and dysfunctional implications of earnings warnings on investor behavior.

The point is that while you take separate courses in various business disciplines, the lines between them are increasingly being blurred as researchers draw from common disciplines to explain behavior. We think that's a good thing because it more accurately matches the way managers actually work, think, and behave.

Source: Based on W. Chuang and B. Lee, "An Empirical Evaluation of the Overconfidence Hypothesis," *Journal of Banking and Finance*, September 2006, pp. 2489–2515; and A. R. Drake, J. Wong, and S. B. Salter, "Empowerment, Motivation, and Performance: Examining the Impact of Feedback and Incentives on Nonmanagement Employees," *Behavioral Research in Accounting* 19 (2007), pp. 71–89.

Sociology

While psychology focuses on the individual, **sociology** studies people in relation to their social environment or culture. Sociologists have contributed to OB through their study of group behavior in organizations, particularly formal and complex organizations. Perhaps most importantly, sociology has contributed to research on organizational culture, formal organization theory and structure, organizational technology, communications, power, and conflict.

Anthropology

Anthropology is the study of societies to learn about human beings and their activities. For instance, anthropologists' work on cultures and environments has helped us understand differences in fundamental values, attitudes, and behavior between people in different countries and within different organizations. Much of our current understanding of organizational culture, organizational environments, and differences between national cultures is a result of the work of anthropologists or those using their methods.

---

social psychology *An area of psychology that blends concepts from psychology and sociology and that focuses on the influence of people on one another.*

sociology *The study of people in relation to their social environment or culture.*

anthropology *The study of societies to learn about human beings and their activities.*

There Are Few Absolutes in OB

6 *Demonstrate why there are few absolutes in OB.*

There are few, if any, simple and universal principles that explain organizational behavior. There are laws in the physical sciences—chemistry, astronomy, physics—that are consistent and apply in a wide range of situations. They allow scientists to generalize about the pull of gravity or to be confident about sending astronauts into space to repair satellites. But as a noted behavioral researcher aptly concluded, "God gave all the easy problems to the physicists." Human beings are complex. Because we are not alike, our ability to make simple, accurate, and sweeping generalizations is limited. Two people often act very differently in the same situation, and the same person's behavior changes in different situations. For instance, not everyone is motivated by money, and you may behave differently at church on Sunday than you did at a party the night before.

That doesn't mean, of course, that we can't offer reasonably accurate explanations of human behavior or make valid predictions. However, it does mean that OB concepts must reflect situational, or contingency, conditions. We can say that *x* leads to *y*, but only under conditions specified in *z*—the **contingency variables**. The science of OB was developed by applying general concepts to a particular situation, person, or group. For example, OB scholars would avoid stating that everyone likes complex and challenging work (the general concept). Why? Because not everyone wants a challenging job. Some people prefer the routine over the varied or the simple over the complex. In other words, a job that is appealing to one person may not be to another, so the appeal of the job is contingent on the person who holds it.

As you proceed through this book, you'll encounter a wealth of research-based theories about how people behave in organizations. But don't expect to find a lot of straightforward cause-and-effect relationships. There aren't many! Organizational behavior theories mirror the subject matter with which they deal. People are complex and complicated, and so too must be the theories developed to explain their actions.

Challenges and Opportunities for OB

7 *Identify the challenges and opportunities managers have in applying OB concepts.*

Understanding organizational behavior has never been more important for managers than it is today. A quick look at a few of the dramatic changes now taking place in organizations supports this claim. For instance, the typical employee is getting older; more and more women and people of color are in the workplace; corporate downsizing and the heavy use of temporary workers are severing the bonds of loyalty that historically tied many employees to their employers; and global competition is requiring employees to become more flexible and to learn to cope with rapid change. The war on terror has brought to the forefront the challenges of working with and managing people during uncertain times.

In short, there are a lot of challenges and opportunities today for managers to use OB concepts. In this section, we review some of the most critical issues confronting managers for which OB offers solutions—or at least some meaningful insights toward solutions.

Responding to Globalization

Organizations are no longer constrained by national borders. Burger King is owned by a British firm, and McDonald's sells hamburgers in Moscow. ExxonMobil, a so-called American company, receives almost 75 percent of its

Dallas, Texas–based Pizza Hut is responding to globalization by expanding its restaurants and delivery services worldwide. Pizza Hut introduced pizza to Chinese consumers in 1990. Today, Pizza Hut management targets mainland China as the number-one market for new restaurant development because of the country's enormous growth potential. In this photo, Pizza Hut passes out free samples in Nanjing to promote its delivery service. Managers expect delivery to become increasingly important as economic activity continues to expand, placing increased time demands on Chinese families.

revenues from sales outside the United States. New employees at Finland-based phone maker Nokia are increasingly being recruited from India, China, and other developing countries—with non-Finns now outnumbering Finns at Nokia's renowned research center in Helsinki. And all major automobile manufacturers now build cars outside their borders; for instance, Honda builds cars in Ohio, Ford in Brazil, Volkswagen in Mexico, and both Mercedes and BMW in South Africa.

These examples illustrate that the world has become a global village. In the process, the manager's job is changing.

Increased Foreign Assignments If you're a manager, you are increasingly likely to find yourself in a foreign assignment—transferred to your employer's operating division or subsidiary in another country. Once there, you'll have to manage a workforce that is likely to be very different in needs, aspirations, and attitudes from those you are used to back home.

Working with People from Different Cultures Even in your own country, you're going to find yourself working with bosses, peers, and other employees who were born and raised in different cultures. What motivates you may not motivate them. Or your style of communication may be straightforward and open, but they may find this approach uncomfortable and threatening. To work effectively with people from different cultures, you need to understand how their culture, geography, and religion have shaped them and how to adapt your management style to their differences.

Coping with Anticapitalism Backlash Capitalism's focus on efficiency, growth, and profits may be generally accepted in the United States, Australia, and Hong Kong, but these capitalistic values aren't nearly as popular in places

contingency variables *Situational factors: variables that moderate the relationship between two or more other variables.*

like France, the Middle East, and the Scandinavian countries. For instance, because Finland's egalitarian values have created a "soak the rich" mentality among politicians, traffic fines are based on the offender's income rather than the severity of the offense.[17] So when one of Finland's richest men (he is heir to a sausage fortune), who was making close to $9 million a year, was ticketed for doing 80 kilometers per hour through a 40-kilometer zone in central Helsinki, the Finnish court hit him with a fine of $217,000!

Managers at global companies such as McDonald's, Disney, and Coca-Cola have come to realize that economic values are not universally transferable. Management practices need to be modified to reflect the values of the different countries in which an organization operates.

Overseeing Movement of Jobs to Countries with Low-Cost Labor   It's increasingly difficult for managers in advanced nations, where minimum wages are typically $6 or more an hour, to compete against firms who rely on workers from China and other developing nations where labor is available for 30 cents an hour. It's not by chance that a good portion of Americans wear clothes made in China, work on computers whose microchips came from Taiwan, and watch movies that were filmed in Canada. In a global economy, jobs tend to flow to places where lower costs provide business firms with a comparative advantage. Such practices, however, are often strongly criticized by labor groups, politicians, local community leaders, and others who see this exporting of jobs as undermining the job markets in developed countries. Managers must deal with the difficult task of balancing the interests of their organization with their responsibilities to the communities in which they operate.

Managing People During the War on Terror   If you read the paper or watch the evening news, chances are you will find that the war on terror is one of the top stories. But when you think about the war, do you think about the workplace? Probably not. So you might be surprised to learn that the war on terror has had a profound effect on the business world. In fact, surveys suggest that fear of terrorism is the number-one reason business travelers have cut back on their trips. But travel isn't the only concern. Increasingly, organizations need to find ways to deal with employee fears about security precautions (in most cities, you can't get into an office building without passing through several layers of airport-like security) and assignments abroad (how would you feel about an assignment in a country with substantial sentiments against people from your country?).[18] An understanding of OB topics such as emotions, motivation, communication, and leadership can help managers to deal more effectively with their employees' fears about terrorism.

Managing Workforce Diversity

One of the most important and broad-based challenges currently facing organizations is adapting to people who are different. The term we use for describing this challenge is *workforce diversity*. Whereas globalization focuses on differences between people *from* different countries, workforce diversity addresses differences among people *within* given countries.

Workforce diversity means that organizations are becoming a more heterogeneous mix of people in terms of gender, age, race, ethnicity, and sexual orientation. A diverse workforce, for instance, includes women, people of color, the physically disabled, senior citizens, and gays and lesbians (see Exhibit 1-4). Managing this diversity has become a global concern. It's not just an issue in the United States but also in Canada, Australia, South Africa, Japan, and Europe. For instance, managers in Canada and Australia are finding it necessary to adjust to large influxes of Asian workers. The "new" South Africa is increasingly

Exhibit **1-4**	Major Workforce Diversity Categories

Gender

Nearly half of the U.S. workforce is now women, and women are a growing percentage of the workforce in most other countries throughout the world. Organizations need to ensure that hiring and employment policies create equal access and opportunities to individuals, regardless of gender.

Race

The percentage of Hispanics, blacks, and Asians in the U.S. workforce continues to increase. Organizations need to ensure that policies provide equal access and opportunities, regardless of race.

National Origin

A growing percentage of U.S. workers are immigrants or come from homes where English is not the primary language spoken. Because employers in the United States have the right to demand that English be spoken at the workplace on job-related activities, communication problems can occur when employees' English-language skills are weak.

Age

The U.S. workforce is aging, and recent polls indicate that an increasing percentage of employees expect to work past the traditional retirement age of 65. Organizations cannot discriminate on the basis of age and need to make accommodations to the needs of older workers.

Disability

Organizations need to ensure that jobs and workplaces are accessible to the mentally and physically challenged, as well as to the health challenged.

Domestic Partners

An increasing number of gay and lesbian employees, as well as employees with live-in partners of the opposite sex, are demanding the same rights and benefits for their partners that organizations have provided for traditional married couples.

Religion

Organizations need to be sensitive to the customs, rituals, and holidays, as well as the appearance and attire, of individuals of non-Christian faiths such as Judaism, Islam, Hinduism, Buddhism, and Sikhism, and ensure that these individuals suffer no adverse impact as a result of their appearance or practices.

characterized by blacks holding important technical and managerial jobs. Women, long confined to low-paying temporary jobs in Japan, are moving into managerial positions. And the European Union cooperative trade arrangement, which opened up borders throughout much of Western Europe, has increased workforce diversity in organizations that operate in countries such as Germany, Portugal, Italy, and France.

Embracing Diversity   We used to take a melting-pot approach to differences in organizations, assuming that people who were different would somehow automatically want to assimilate. But we now recognize that employees don't set aside their cultural values, lifestyle preferences, and differences when they come to work. The challenge for organizations, therefore, is to make themselves more accommodating to diverse groups of people by addressing their different lifestyles, family needs, and work styles. The melting-pot assumption is being replaced by one that recognizes and values differences.[19]

workforce diversity   *The concept that organizations are becoming more heterogeneous in terms of gender, age, race, ethnicity, sexual orientation, and inclusion of other diverse groups.*

Haven't organizations always included members of diverse groups? Yes, but they were a small percentage of the workforce and were, for the most part, ignored by large organizations. Moreover, it was assumed that these minorities would seek to blend in and assimilate. For instance, the bulk of the pre-1980s U.S. workforce were male Caucasians working full time to support their nonemployed wives and school-aged children. Now such employees are the true minority![20]

Changing U.S. Demographics   The most significant change in the U.S. labor force during the last half of the twentieth century was the rapid increase in the number of female workers.[21] In 1950, for instance, only 29.6 percent of the workforce was women. By 2003, it was 46.7 percent. So today's workforce is rapidly approaching gender balance. In addition, with women now significantly outnumbering men on U.S. college campuses, we can expect an increasing number of technical, professional, and managerial jobs to be filled by the expanding pool of qualified female applicants.

In the same way that women dramatically changed the workplace in the latter part of the twentieth century, the first half of the twenty-first century will be notable for changes in racial and ethnic composition and an aging baby boom generation. By 2050, Hispanics will grow from today's 11 percent of the workforce to 24 percent, blacks will increase from 12 percent to 14 percent, and Asians will increase from 5 percent to 11 percent. Meanwhile, the labor force will be aging in the near term. The 55-and-older age group, which currently makes up 13 percent of the labor force, will increase to 20 percent by 2014.

Implications   Workforce diversity has important implications for management practice. Managers have to shift their philosophy from treating everyone alike to recognizing differences and responding to those differences in ways that ensure employee retention and greater productivity while, at the same time, not discriminating. This shift includes, for instance, providing diversity training and revamping benefits programs to accommodate the different needs of different employees. Diversity, if positively managed, can increase creativity and innovation in organizations as well as improve decision making by providing different perspectives on

With more than 370,000 employees in 200 countries, United Parcel Service embraces the value of diversity. Since 1968, UPS senior managers participate in a 4-week community internship program that deepens their responsiveness to the needs of a diverse workforce and customer base while helping with charitable causes in the community. In this photo, UPS managers from Germany and California help a bicycle shop owner reorganize his business.

problems.[22] When diversity is not managed properly, there is a potential for higher turnover, more difficult communication, and more interpersonal conflicts.

Improving Quality and Productivity

In the 1990s, organizations around the world added capacity in response to increased demand. Companies built new facilities, expanded services, and added staff. The result? Today, almost every industry suffers from excess supply. The retail world suffers from too many malls and shopping centers. Automobile factories can build more cars than consumers can afford. The telecom industry is drowning in debt from building capacity that might take 50 years to absorb, and most cities and towns now have far more restaurants than their communities can support.

Excess capacity translates into increased competition. And increased competition is forcing managers to reduce costs and, at the same time, improve their organizations' productivity and the quality of the products and services they offer. Management guru Tom Peters says, "Almost all quality improvement comes via simplification of design, manufacturing, layout, processes, and procedures." To achieve these ends, managers are implementing programs such asquality management and process reengineering—programs that require extensive employee involvement.

Today's managers understand that the success of any effort at improving quality and productivity must include their employees. These employees will not only be a major force in carrying out changes but increasingly will actively participate in planning those changes. OB offers important insights into helping managers work through these changes.

Improving Customer Service

American Express recently turned Joan Weinbel's worst nightmare into a non-event. It was 10:00 P.M. Joan was home in New Jersey, packing for a week-long trip, when she suddenly realized she had left her AmEx Gold Card at a restaurant in New York City earlier in the evening. The restaurant was 30 miles away. She had a flight to catch at 7:30 the next morning, and she wanted her card for the trip. She called American Express. The phone was quickly answered by a courteous and helpful AmEx customer service representative. He told Ms. Weinbel not to worry. He asked her a few questions and told her "help was on the way." To say Joan was flabbergasted would be an understatement when her doorbell rang at 11:45 P.M.—less than 2 hours after she had called AmEx. At her door was a courier with a new card. How the company was able to produce the card and get it to her so quickly still puzzles Joan. But she said the experience made her a customer for life.

Today, the majority of employees in developed countries work in service jobs. For instance, 80 percent of the U.S. labor force is employed in service industries. In Australia, 73 percent work in service industries. In the United Kingdom, Germany, and Japan, the percentages are 69, 68, and 65, respectively. Examples of these service jobs include technical support representatives, fast-food counter workers, sales clerks, waiters or waitresses, nurses, automobile repair technicians, consultants, credit representatives, financial planners, and flight attendants. The common characteristic of these jobs is that they require substantial interaction with an organization's customers. And because an organization can't exist without customers—whether that organization is DaimlerChrysler, Merrill Lynch, L.L.Bean, a law firm, a museum, a school, or a government agency—management needs to ensure that employees do what it takes to please customers.[23] For example, at Patagonia—a retail outfitter for climbers, mountain bikers, skiers and boarders, and other outdoor fanatics—managers are held

It's an annual tradition for Michael Dell to work the phone lines, helping customers in Dell, Inc.'s consumer department. Dell models the customer-responsive culture he created in founding Dell Computer Corporation in 1984 with the idea of building relationships directly with customers. He attributes his company's climb to market leadership as the world's top computer systems company to a persistent focus on the customer. Dell employees deliver superior customer service by communicating directly with customers via the Internet or by phone.

directly responsible for customer service. In fact, customer service is the store manager's most important general responsibility: "Instill in your employees the meaning and importance of customer service as outlined in the retail philosophy, 'our store is a place where the word "no" does not exist'; Empower staff to "use their best judgment" in all customer service matters."[24] OB can help managers at Patagonia achieve this goal and, more generally, can contribute to improving an organization's performance by showing managers how employee attitudes and behavior are associated with customer satisfaction.

Many an organization has failed because its employees failed to please customers. Management needs to create a customer-responsive culture. OB can provide considerable guidance in helping managers create such cultures—cultures in which employees are friendly and courteous, accessible, knowledgeable, prompt in responding to customer needs, and willing to do what's necessary to please the customer.[25]

Improving People Skills

We opened this chapter by demonstrating how important people skills are to managerial effectiveness. We said that "this book has been written to help both managers and potential managers develop those people skills."

As you proceed through the chapters, we'll present relevant concepts and theories that can help you explain and predict the behavior of people at work. In addition, you'll gain insights into specific people skills that you can use on the job. For instance, you'll learn ways to design motivating jobs, techniques for improving your listening skills, and how to create more effective teams.

Stimulating Innovation and Change

Whatever happened to Montgomery Ward, Woolworth, Smith Corona, TWA, Bethlehem Steel, and Worldcom? All these giants went bust. Why have other giants, such as Sears, Boeing, and Lucent Technologies implemented huge cost-cutting programs and eliminated thousands of jobs? To avoid going broke.

Today's successful organizations must foster innovation and master the art of change, or they'll become candidates for extinction. Victory will go to the organizations that maintain their flexibility, continually improve their quality, and beat their competition to the marketplace with a constant stream of innovative products and services. Domino's single-handedly brought on the demise of thousands of small pizza parlors whose managers thought they could continue doing what they had been doing for years. Amazon.com is putting a lot of independent bookstores out of business as it proves you can successfully sell books from an Internet Web site. After years of lackluster performance, Boeing realized it needed to change its business model. The result was its 787 "Dreamliner" and becoming again the world's largest airplane manufacturer.

An organization's employees can be the impetus for innovation and change, or they can be a major stumbling block. The challenge for managers is to stimulate their employees' creativity and tolerance for change. The field of OB provides a wealth of ideas and techniques to aid in realizing these goals.

Coping with "Temporariness"

With change comes temporariness. Globalization, expanded capacity, and advances in technology have combined in recent years to make it imperative that organizations be fast and flexible if they are to survive. The result is that most managers and employees today work in a climate best characterized as "temporary."

Evidence of temporariness is everywhere in organizations. Jobs are continually being redesigned; tasks are increasingly being done by flexible teams rather than individuals; companies are relying more on temporary workers; jobs are being subcontracted out to other firms; and pensions are being redesigned to move with people as they change jobs.

Workers need to continually update their knowledge and skills to perform new job requirements. For example, production employees at companies such as Caterpillar, Ford, and Alcoa now need to know how to operate computerized production equipment. That was not part of their job descriptions 20 years ago. Work groups are also increasingly in a state of flux. In the past, employees were assigned to a specific work group, and that assignment was relatively permanent. There was a considerable amount of security in working with the same people day in and day out. That predictability has been replaced by temporary work groups, teams that include members from different departments and whose members change all the time, and the increased use of employee rotation to fill constantly changing work assignments. Finally, organizations themselves are in a state of flux. They continually reorganize their various divisions, sell off poor-performing businesses, downsize operations, subcontract noncritical services and operations to other organizations, and replace permanent employees with temporary workers.

Today's managers and employees must learn to cope with temporariness. They have to learn to live with flexibility, spontaneity, and unpredictability. The study of OB can provide important insights into helping you better understand a work world of continual change, how to overcome resistance to change, and how best to create an organizational culture that thrives on change.

Working in Networked Organizations

Computerization, the Internet, and the ability to link computers within organizations and between organizations have created a different workplace for many employees—a networked organization. These technology changes allow people to communicate and work together even though they may be thousands of miles apart. They also allow people to become independent contractors, who can telecommute via computer to workplaces around the globe and change employers as the demand for their services changes. Software programmers, graphic designers, systems analysts, technical writers, photo researchers, book editors, and medical transcribers are just a few examples of people who can work from home or other non-office locations.

The manager's job is different in a networked organization, especially when it comes to managing people. For instance, motivating and leading people and making collaborative decisions "online" requires different techniques than are needed in dealing with individuals who are physically present in a single location.

As more and more employees do their jobs linked to others through networks, managers need to develop new skills. OB can provide valuable insights to help with honing those skills.

Helping Employees Balance Work–Life Conflicts

The typical employee in the 1960s or 1970s showed up at the workplace Monday through Friday and did his or her job in 8- or 9-hour chunks of time. The workplace and hours were clearly specified. That's no longer true for a large segment of today's workforce. Employees are increasingly complaining that the line between work and nonwork time has become blurred, creating personal conflicts and stress.[26] At the same time, however, today's workplace presents opportunities for workers to create and structure their work roles.

A number of forces have contributed to blurring the lines between employees' work life and personal life. First, the creation of global organizations means their world never sleeps. At any time and on any day, for instance, thousands of General Electric employees are working somewhere. The need to consult with colleagues or customers 8 or 10 time zones away means that many employees of global firms are "on call" 24 hours a day. Second, communication technology allows employees to do their work at home, in their cars, or on the beach in Tahiti. This lets many people in technical and professional jobs do their work any time and from any place. Third, organizations are asking employees to put in longer hours. For instance, over a recent 10-year period, the average American workweek increased from 43 to 47 hours; and the number of people working 50 or more hours a week jumped from 24 percent to 37 percent.

Merrill Lynch is committed to helping its employees achieve a work–life balance. The company provides adoption assistance to employees such as Keli Tuschman, shown here with her adopted daughter from China. Other employee-support systems include day-care facilities, paid time-off child-care leave for birth and adoption, a "school's out" program that provides child care during school holidays, and working-parent networks. Creating a family-friendly workplace helps Merrill Lynch attract and retain a motivated workforce.

Source: Jessica Kourkounis/ The New York Times

Finally, fewer families have only a single breadwinner. Today's married employee is typically part of a dual-career couple. This makes it increasingly difficult for married employees to find the time to fulfill commitments to home, spouse, children, parents, and friends.

Employees are increasingly recognizing that work is infringing on their personal lives, and they're not happy about it. For example, recent studies suggest that employees want jobs that give them flexibility in their work schedules so they can better manage work–life conflicts.[27] In fact, evidence indicates that balancing work and life demands now surpasses job security as an employee priority.[28] In addition, the next generation of employees is likely to show similar concerns.[29] A majority of college and university students say that attaining a balance between personal life and work is a primary career goal. They want "a life" as well as a job. Organizations that don't help their people achieve work–life balance will find it increasingly difficult to attract and retain the most capable and motivated employees.

As you'll see in later chapters, the field of OB offers a number of suggestions to guide managers in designing workplaces and jobs that can help employees deal with work–life conflicts.

Creating a Positive Work Environment

Although competitive pressures on most organizations are stronger than ever, we've noticed an interesting turn in both OB research and management practice, at least in some organizations. Instead of responding to competitive pressures by "turning up the heat," some organizations are trying to realize a competitive advantage by fostering a positive work environment. For example, Jeff Immelt and Jim McNerney, both disciplines of Jack Welch (former CEO of GE), have tried to maintain high performance expectations (a characteristic of GE's culture) while also fostering a positive work environment in their organizations (GE and Boeing). "In this time of turmoil and cynicism about business, you need to be passionate, positive leaders," Mr. Immelt recently told his top managers.

At the same time, a real growth area in OB research has been **positive organizational scholarship** (also called *positive organizational behavior*), which concerns how organizations develop human strengths, foster vitality and resilience, and unlock potential. Researchers in this area argue that too much of OB research and management practice has been targeted toward identifying what's wrong with organizations and their employees. In response, these researchers try to study what's *good* about organizations.[30]

For example, positive organizational scholars have studied a concept called "reflected best-self"—asking employees to think about situations in which they were at their "personal best" in order to understand how to exploit their strengths. These researchers argue that we all have things at which we are unusually good, yet too often we focus on addressing our limitations and too rarely think about how to exploit our strengths.[31]

Although positive organizational scholarship does not deny the presence (or even the value) of the negative (such as critical feedback), it does challenge researchers to look at OB through a new lens. It also challenges organizations to think about how to exploit their employees' strengths rather than dwell on their limitations.

positive organizational scholarship *An area of OB research that concerns how organizations develop human strength, foster vitality and resilience, and unlock potential.*

Improving Ethical Behavior

In an organizational world characterized by cutbacks, expectations of increasing worker productivity, and tough competition in the marketplace, it's not altogether surprising that many employees feel pressured to cut corners, break rules, and engage in other forms of questionable practices.

Members of organizations are increasingly finding themselves facing **ethical dilemmas**, situations in which they are required to define right and wrong conduct. For example, should they "blow the whistle" if they uncover illegal activities taking place in their company? Should they follow orders with which they don't personally agree? Do they give an inflated performance evaluation to an employee whom they like, knowing that such an evaluation could save that employee's job? Do they allow themselves to "play politics" in the organization if it will help their career advancement?

What constitutes good ethical behavior has never been clearly defined, and, in recent years, the line differentiating right from wrong has become even more blurred. Employees see people all around them engaging in unethical practices—elected officials are indicted for padding their expense accounts or taking bribes; corporate executives inflate company profits so they can cash in lucrative stock options; and university administrators "look the other way" when winning coaches encourage scholarship athletes to take easy courses in place of those needed for graduation in order to stay eligible. When caught, these people give excuses such as "everyone does it" or "you have to seize every advantage nowadays." Is it any wonder that employees are expressing decreased confidence and trust in management and that they're increasingly uncertain about what constitutes appropriate ethical behavior in their organizations?[32]

Managers and their organizations are responding to this problem from a number of directions.[33] They're writing and distributing codes of ethics to guide employees through ethical dilemmas. They're offering seminars, workshops, and other training programs to try to improve ethical behaviors. They're providing in-house advisors who can be contacted, in many cases anonymously, for assistance in dealing with ethical issues, and they're creating protection mechanisms for employees who reveal internal unethical practices.

Today's manager needs to create an ethically healthy climate for his or her employees, where they can do their work productively and confront a minimal degree of ambiguity regarding what constitutes right and wrong behaviors. In upcoming chapters, we'll discuss the kinds of actions managers can take to create an ethically healthy climate and help employees sort through ethically ambiguous situations. We'll also present ethical-dilemma exercises at the end of each chapter that will allow you to think through ethical issues and assess how you would handle them.

Coming Attractions: Developing an OB Model

We conclude this chapter by presenting a general model that defines the field of OB, stakes out its parameters, and identifies its primary dependent and independent variables. The end result will be a "coming attraction" of the topics in the remainder of this book.

> *8 Compare the three levels of analysis in this book's OB model.*

An Overview

A **model** is an abstraction of reality, a simplified representation of some real-world phenomenon. A mannequin in a retail store is a model. So, too, is the

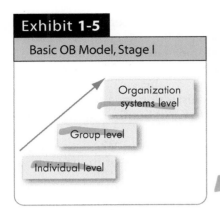

Exhibit 1-5

Basic OB Model, Stage I

Organization systems level

Group level

Individual level

accountant's formula Assets + Liabilities = Owners' Equity. Exhibit 1-5 presents the skeleton on which we will construct our OB model. It proposes that there are three levels of analysis in OB and that, as we move from the individual level to the organization systems level, we add systematically to our understanding of behavior in organizations. The three basic levels are analogous to building blocks; each level is constructed on the previous level. Group concepts grow out of the foundation laid in the individual section; we overlay structural constraints on the individual and group in order to arrive at organizational behavior.

The Dependent Variables

A **dependent variable** is the key factor that you want to explain or predict and that is affected by some other factor. What are the primary dependent variables in OB? Scholars have historically tended to emphasize productivity, absenteeism, turnover, and job satisfaction. More recently, two more variables—deviant workplace behavior and organizational citizenship behavior—have been added to this list. We'll briefly discuss each of these variables to ensure that you understand what they mean and why they have achieved their level of distinction.

Productivity   An organization is productive if it achieves its goals and does so by transferring inputs to outputs at the lowest cost. As such, **productivity** implies a concern for both **effectiveness** and **efficiency**.

A hospital, for example, is *effective* when it successfully meets the needs of its clientele. It is *efficient* when it can do so at a low cost. If a hospital manages to achieve higher output from its present staff by reducing the average number of days a patient is confined to a bed or by increasing the number of staff–patient contacts per day, we say that the hospital has gained productive efficiency. A business firm is effective when it attains its sales or market share goals, but its productivity also depends on achieving those goals efficiently. Popular measures of organizational efficiency include return on investment, profit per dollar of sales, and output per hour of labor.

We can also look at productivity from the perspective of the individual employee. Take the cases of Mike and Al, who are both long-distance truckers. If Mike is supposed to haul his fully loaded rig from New York to Los Angeles in 75 hours or less, he is effective if he makes the 3,000-mile trip within that time period. But measures of productivity must take into account the costs incurred in reaching the goal. That's where efficiency comes in. Let's assume that, with identical rigs and loads, Mike made the New York to Los Angeles run in 68 hours and averaged 7 miles per gallon. Al, however, made the trip in 68 hours also but averaged 9 miles per gallon. Both Mike and Al were effective—they accomplished their goal—but Al was more efficient than Mike because his rig consumed less gas and, therefore, he achieved his goal at a lower cost.

Organizations in service industries need to include attention to customer needs and requirements in assessing their effectiveness. Why? Because in these types of businesses, there is a clear chain of cause and effect running from employee attitudes and behavior to customer attitudes and behavior to an

ethical dilemmas   *Situations in which individuals are required to define right and wrong conduct.*

model   *An abstraction of reality. A simplified representation of some real-world phenomenon.*

dependent variable   *A response that is affected by an independent variable.*

productivity   *A performance measure that includes effectiveness and efficiency.*

effectiveness   *Achievement of goals.*

efficiency   *The ratio of effective output to the input required to achieve it.*

organization's productivity. Sears, in fact, has carefully documented this chain.[34] The company's management found that a 5 percent improvement in employee attitudes leads to a 1.3 percent increase in customer satisfaction, which in turn translates into a 0.5 percent improvement in revenue growth. More specifically, Sears found that by training employees to improve the employee–customer interaction, it was able to improve customer satisfaction by 4 percent over a 12-month period, which generated an estimated $200 million in additional revenues.

In summary, one of OB's major concerns is productivity. We want to know what factors will influence the effectiveness and efficiency of individuals, of groups, and of the overall organization.

Absenteeism   **Absenteeism** is defined as the failure to report to work. Absenteeism is a huge cost and disruption to employers. For instance, a recent survey found that the average direct cost to U.S. employers of unscheduled absences is $789 per year per employee—and this doesn't include lost productivity or the additional costs for overtime pay or hiring temporary employees to cover for absent workers.[35] Comparable costs in the United Kingdom are also high—approximately $694 per year per employee.[36] In Sweden, an average of 10 percent of the country's workforce is on sick leave at any given time.[37]

It's obviously difficult for an organization to operate smoothly and to attain its objectives if employees fail to report to their jobs. The work flow is disrupted, and often important decisions must be delayed. In organizations that rely heavily on assembly-line production, absenteeism can be considerably more than a disruption; it can result in a drastic reduction in the quality of output, and, in some cases, it can bring about a complete shutdown of the production facility. Levels of absenteeism beyond the normal range in any organization have a direct impact on that organization's effectiveness and efficiency.

Are *all* absences bad? Probably not. Although most absences have a negative impact on the organization, we can conceive of situations in which the organization may benefit by an employee's voluntarily choosing not to come to

Employees of Worthington Industries take part in a lunchtime kickboxing class at the company's fitness center. The class is part of Worthington's employee health and wellness initiative that helps reduce absenteeism and increase productivity. Worthington also operates an on-site medical center staffed with doctors and nurses. The center helps reduce the time employees spend on doctors' visits and minimizes absenteeism through preventive screenings and wellness programs.

work. For instance, in jobs in which an employee needs to be alert—consider surgeons and airline pilots, for example—it may be better for the organization if an ill or fatigued employee does *not* report to work. The cost of an accident in such jobs could be disastrous. But these examples are clearly atypical. For the most part, we can assume that organizations benefit when employee absenteeism is low.

Turnover   **Turnover** is the voluntary and involuntary permanent withdrawal from an organization. A high turnover rate results in increased recruiting, selection, and training costs. What are those costs? They're higher than you might think. For instance, the cost for a typical information technology company in the United States to replace a programmer or systems analyst has been estimated at $34,100; and the cost for a retail store to replace a lost sales clerk has been calculated as $10,445.[38] In addition, a high rate of turnover can disrupt the efficient running of an organization when knowledgeable and experienced personnel leave and replacements must be found and prepared to assume positions of responsibility.

All organizations, of course, have some turnover. The U.S. national turnover rate averages about 3 percent per month, which is about a 36 percent turnover per year. This average, of course, varies a lot by occupation (for example, the monthly turnover rate for government jobs is less than 1 percent versus 5 to 7 percent in the construction industry).[39] If the "right" people are leaving the organization—the marginal and submarginal employees—turnover can actually be positive. It can create an opportunity to replace an underperforming individual with someone who has higher skills or motivation, open up increased opportunities for promotions, and add new and fresh ideas to the organization.[40] In today's changing world of work, reasonable levels of employee-initiated turnover facilitate organizational flexibility and employee independence, and they can lessen the need for management-initiated layoffs.

But turnover often involves the loss of people the organization doesn't want to lose. For instance, one study covering 900 employees who had resigned from their jobs found that 92 percent earned performance ratings of "satisfactory" or better from their superiors.[41] So when turnover is excessive, or when it involves valuable performers, it can be a disruptive factor that hinders the organization's effectiveness.

Deviant Workplace Behavior   Given the cost of absenteeism and turnover to employers, more and more OB researchers are studying these behaviors as indicators or markers of deviant behavior. Deviance can range from someone playing his music too loudly to violence. Managers need to understand this wide range of behaviors to address any form of employee dissatisfaction. If managers don't understand *why* an employee is acting up, the problem will never be solved.

We can define **deviant workplace behavior** (also called *antisocial behavior* or *workplace incivility*) as voluntary behavior that violates significant organizational norms and, in doing so, threatens the well-being of the organization or its members. What are organizational norms in this context? They can be company policies that prohibit certain behaviors such as stealing. They also can be

---

absenteeism   *The failure to report to work.*

turnover   *Voluntary and involuntary permanent withdrawal from an organization.*

deviant workplace behavior   *Voluntary behavior that violates significant organizational norms and, in so doing, threatens the well-being of the organization or its members.*

International OB

Transfer Pricing and International Corporate Deviance

Workplace deviance isn't limited to the harmful behaviors of employees within one location. There are cases of corporate deviance that extend across country borders. Consider transfer pricing, which is the price that one part of a company charges another part of the same company for a product or service. What happens with transfer pricing if various parts of a company are located in different countries, which is becoming increasingly common as more and more companies extend their operations across the globe to become multinational businesses?

Tax rates on company profits differ—sometimes greatly—from country to country. Transfer pricing, when used to shift income from high-tax countries to low-tax countries, can be a deviant corporate policy if it is abused. One way to increase overall profit—that is, the combined profit of the multinational's headquarters and its subsidiaries—is to take profits in the country with the lower taxes.

Take the case of a multinational firm whose headquarters sold toothbrushes to a subsidiary for $5,000— each. The subsidiary, with the higher tax of the two, claimed a loss (after all, it paid $5,000 per toothbrush). The multinational firm, with the lower tax of the two, took the profit and paid the tax on it. Because the two firms were part of the same organization, they combined the results of the transaction, and the company made a staggering profit.

Transfer pricing, according to a survey by the international auditing firm Ernst & Young, has become a heated issue among multinational companies. Why? The U.S. Multistate Tax Commission estimated that states were losing almost one-third of their corporate tax income because of tax-sheltering practices by multinational companies—transfer pricing among them. The U.S. Internal Revenue Service is keeping a watchful eye on international transactions.

Source: Based on "Case of the U.S. $5000 Toothbrush," *Finance Week,* April 27, 2005, pp. 45–46.

---

unspoken rules that are widely shared, such as not playing loud music in one's workspace. Consider, for example, an employee who plays Metallica's "St. Anger" at work with the speakers amped up. Yes, he may be showing up at work, but he may not be getting his work done, and he could also be irritating coworkers or customers (unless they are Talli fans themselves). But deviant workplace behaviors can be much more serious than an employee playing loud music. For example, an employee may insult a colleague, steal, gossip excessively, or engage in sabotage, all of which can wreak havoc on an organization.

Managers want to understand the source of workplace deviance in order to avoid a chaotic work environment, and workplace deviance can also have a considerable financial impact. Although the annual costs are hard to quantify, estimates are that deviant behavior costs employers dearly, from $4.2 billion for violence to $7.1 billion for corporate security against cyberattacks to $200 billion for theft.[42]

Deviant workplace behavior is an important concept because it's a response to dissatisfaction, and employees express this dissatisfaction in many ways. Controlling one behavior may be ineffective unless one gets to the root cause. The sophisticated manager will deal with root causes of problems that may result in deviance rather than solve one surface problem (excessive absence) only to see another one crop up (increased theft or sabotage).

Organizational Citizenship Behavior   **Organizational citizenship behavior (OCB)** is discretionary behavior that is not part of an employee's formal job requirements but that nevertheless promotes the effective functioning of the organization.[43]

Successful organizations need employees who will do more than their usual job duties—who will provide performance that is *beyond* expectations. In today's dynamic workplace, where tasks are increasingly done in teams and where flexibility is critical, organizations need employees who will engage in "good citizenship" behaviors such as helping others on their team, volunteering for extra work, avoiding unnecessary conflicts, respecting the spirit as well as the letter of rules and regulations, and gracefully tolerating occasional work-related impositions and nuisances.

Organizations want and need employees who will do those things that aren't in any job description. And the evidence indicates that organizations that have such employees outperform those that don't.[44] As a result, OB is concerned with OCB as a dependent variable.

Job Satisfaction   The final dependent variable we will look at is **job satisfaction**, which we define as a positive feeling about one's job resulting from an evaluation of its characteristics. Unlike the previous five variables, job satisfaction represents an attitude rather than a behavior. Why, then, has it become a primary dependent variable? For two reasons: its demonstrated relationship to performance factors and the value preferences held by many OB researchers.

The belief that satisfied employees are more productive than dissatisfied employees has been a basic tenet among managers for years, though only now has research begun to support this theory after decades of questions about the satisfaction–performance relationship.[45] Recently, a study of more than 2,500 business units found that units scoring in the top 25 percent on the employee opinion survey were, on average, 4.6 percent *above* their sales budget for the year, while those scoring in the bottom 25 percent were 0.8 percent *below* budget. In real numbers, this was a difference of $104 million in sales per year between the two groups.[46]

Moreover, it can be argued that advanced societies should be concerned not only with the quantity of life—that is, concerns such as higher productivity and material acquisitions—but also with its quality. Researchers with strong humanistic values argue that satisfaction is a legitimate objective of an organization. Not only is satisfaction negatively related to absenteeism and turnover, but, they argue, organizations have a responsibility to provide employees with jobs that are challenging and intrinsically rewarding. Therefore, although job satisfaction represents an attitude rather than a behavior, OB researchers typically consider it an important dependent variable.

The Independent Variables

What are the major determinants of productivity, absenteeism, turnover, deviant workplace behavior, OCB, and job satisfaction? Our answer to that question brings us to the independent variables. An **independent variable** is the presumed cause of some change in a dependent variable.

Consistent with our belief that organizational behavior can best be understood when viewed essentially as a set of increasingly complex building blocks, the base, or first level, of our model lies in understanding individual behavior.

Individual-Level Variables   It has been said that "managers, unlike parents, must work with used, not new, human beings—human beings whom others

---

organizational citizenship behavior (OCB)   *Discretionary behavior that is not part of an employee's formal job requirements but that nevertheless promotes the effective functioning of the organization.*

job satisfaction   *A positive feeling about one's job resulting from an evaluation of its characteristics.*

independent variable   *The presumed cause of some change in a dependent variable.*

have gotten to first."[47] When individuals enter an organization, they are a bit like used cars. Each is different. Some are "low mileage"—they have been treated carefully and have had only limited exposure to the realities of the elements. Others are "well worn," having been driven over some rough roads. This metaphor indicates that people enter organizations with certain intact characteristics that will influence their behavior at work. The most obvious of these are personal or biographical characteristics such as age, gender, and marital status; personality characteristics; an inherent emotional framework; values and attitudes; and basic ability levels. These characteristics are essentially in place when an individual enters the workforce, and, for the most part, there is little management can do to alter them. Yet they have a very real impact on employee behavior. Therefore, each of these factors—biographical characteristics, ability, values, attitudes, personality, and emotions—will be discussed as independent variables in Chapters 2 through 4 and 8.

There are four other individual-level variables that have been shown to affect employee behavior: perception, individual decision making, learning, and motivation. Those topics will be introduced and discussed in Chapters 2, 5, 6, and 7.

Group-Level Variables   The behavior of people in groups is more than the sum total of all the individuals acting in their own way. The complexity of our model is increased when we acknowledge that people's behavior when they are in groups is different from their behavior when they are alone. Therefore, the next step in the development of an understanding of OB is the study of group behavior.

Chapter 9 lays the foundation for an understanding of the dynamics of group behavior. That chapter discusses how individuals in groups are influenced by the patterns of behavior they are expected to exhibit, what the group considers to be acceptable standards of behavior, and the degree to which group members are attracted to each other. Chapter 10 translates our understanding of groups to the design of effective work teams. Chapters 11 through 15 demonstrate how communication patterns, leadership, power and politics, and levels of conflict affect group behavior.

Organization System-Level Variables   Organizational behavior reaches its highest level of sophistication when we add formal structure to our previous knowledge of individual and group behavior. Just as groups are more than the sum of their individual members, so are organizations more than the sum of their member groups. The design of the formal organization; the organization's internal culture; and the organization's human resource policies and practices (that is, selection processes, training and development programs, performance evaluation methods) all have an impact on the dependent variables. These are discussed in detail in Chapters 16 through 18.

Toward a Contingency OB Model

Our final model is shown in Exhibit 1-6. It shows the six key dependent variables and a large number of independent variables, organized by level of analysis, that research indicates have varying effects on the former. As complicated as this model is, it still doesn't do justice to the complexity of the OB subject matter. However, it should help explain why the chapters in this book are arranged as they are and help you to explain and predict the behavior of people at work.

For the most part, our model does not explicitly identify the vast number of contingency variables because of the tremendous complexity that would be

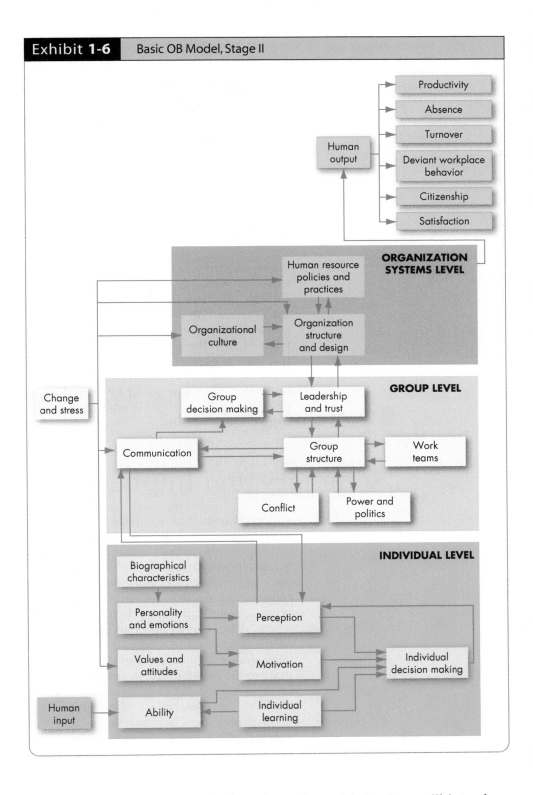

Exhibit 1-6 Basic OB Model, Stage II

involved in such a diagram. Rather, throughout this book we will introduce important contingency variables that will improve the explanatory linkage between the independent and dependent variables in our OB model.

Note that we have included the concepts of change and stress in Exhibit 1-6, acknowledging the dynamics of behavior and the fact that work stress is an individual, group, and organizational issue. Specifically, in Chapter 19, we will discuss the change process, ways to manage organizational change, key change issues currently facing managers, consequences of work stress, and techniques for managing stress.

Also note that Exhibit 1-6 includes linkages between the three levels of analysis. For instance, organizational structure is linked to leadership. This link is meant to convey that authority and leadership are related; management exerts its influence on group behavior through leadership. Similarly, communication is the means by which individuals transmit information; thus, it is the link between individual and group behavior.

Global Implications

We've already discussed how globalization presents challenges and opportunities for OB. We want to draw your attention to this spot in the chapter, though, because in every subsequent chapter, we will have a section at this spot—titled "Global Implications"—that discusses how some of the things we know about OB are affected by cultural differences within and between countries. Most OB research has been conducted in Western cultures (especially the United States). That's changing, however, and compared to even a few years ago, we're now in a much better position to answer the question "How does what we know about OB vary based on culture?" You'll find that some OB principles don't vary much across cultures, but others vary a great deal from culture to culture.

Summary and Implications for Managers

Managers need to develop their interpersonal, or people, skills if they are going to be effective in their jobs. Organizational behavior (OB) is a field of study that investigates the impact that individuals, groups, and structure have on behavior within an organization, and it applies that knowledge to make organizations work more effectively. Specifically, OB focuses on how to improve productivity; reduce absenteeism, turnover, and deviant workplace behavior; and increase organizational citizenship behavior and job satisfaction.

We all hold generalizations about the behavior of people. Some of our generalizations may provide valid insights into human behavior, but many are erroneous. Organizational behavior uses systematic study to improve predictions of behavior that would be made from intuition alone. But because people are different, we need to look at OB in a contingency framework, using situational variables to moderate cause-and-effect relationships.

Organizational behavior offers both challenges and opportunities for managers. It offers specific insights to improve a manager's people skills. It recognizes differences and helps managers to see the value of workforce diversity and practices that may need to be changed when managing in different countries. It can improve quality and employee productivity by showing managers how to empower their people, design and implement change programs, improve customer service, and help employees balance work–life conflicts. It provides suggestions for helping managers meet chronic labor shortages. It can help managers to cope in a world of temporariness and to learn ways to stimulate innovation. Finally, OB can offer managers guidance in creating an ethically healthy work climate.

- Day-care services (after company contribution) = $2,000 for all of an employee's children, regardless of number
- Company-provided transportation to and from work = $750
- College tuition reimbursement = $1,000
- Language class tuition reimbursement = $500

The Task

1. Each group has 15 minutes to develop a flexible benefits package that consumes 25 percent (and no more!) of their character's pay.

2. After completing step 1, each group appoints a spokesperson who describes to the entire class the benefits package the group has arrived at for their character.

3. The entire class then discusses the results. How did the needs, concerns, and problems of each participant influence the group's decision? What do the results suggest for trying to motivate a diverse workforce?

Source: Special thanks to Professor Penny Wright (San Diego State University) for her suggestions during the development of this exercise.

Ethical Dilemma

LYING IN BUSINESS

Do you think it's ever okay to lie? If you were negotiating for the release of hostages, most people would probably agree that if lying would lead to the hostages' safety, it's okay. What about in business, where the stakes are rarely life or death? Business executives such as Martha Stewart have gone to jail for lying (submitting a false statement to federal investigators). Is misrepresentation or omitting factors okay as long as there is no outright lie?

Consider the negotiation process. A good negotiator never shows all his cards, right? And so omitting certain information is just part of the process. Well, it may surprise you to learn that the law will hold you liable for omitting information if partial disclosure is misleading or if one side has superior information not accessible to the other.

In one case (*Jordan v. Duff and Phelps*), a company (Duff and Phelps) withheld information from an employee—Jordan—about the impending sale of the company. The problem: Jordan was leaving the organization and therefore sold his shares in the company. Ten days later, when the sale of the company became public, those shares became worth much more. Jordan sued his former

employer on the grounds that it should have disclosed this information to him. Duff and Phelps countered that it had never lied to Jordan. The Court of Appeals argued that in such situations, one party cannot take "opportunistic advantage" of the other. In the eyes of the law, sometimes omitting relevant facts can be as bad as lying.

Questions

1. In a business context, is it ever okay to lie? If yes, what are those situations? Why is it okay to lie in these situations?

2. A recent survey revealed that 24 percent of managers said they have fired someone for lying. Do you think it's fair to fire an employee who lies, no matter what the nature of the lie? Explain.

3. In business, is withholding information for your own advantage the same as lying? Why or why not?

4. In a business context, if someone has something to gain by lying, what percentage of people, do you think, would lie?

Source: Based on "Lying at Work Could Get You Fired," *UPI*, March 5, 2006; "Brain Scans Detect More Activity in Those Who Lie," Reuters, November 29, 2004; www.msnbc.msn.com/id/6609019; and P. Ekman and E. L. Rosenberg, *What the Fact Reveals: Basic and Applied Studies of Spontaneous Expression Using the Facial Action Coding System (CAPS)*, 2nd ed. (New York: Oxford University Press, 2004).

Case Incident 1

"DATA WILL SET YOU FREE"

Ford CEO Alan Mulally is known for starting meetings by saying "Data will set you free" and for trying to change Ford's culture to one that is based on increased accountability,

more information sharing, and hard metrics. "You can't manage a secret," he is also fond of saying. Although it's not clear whether Mulally's approach will work at Ford, which is known for its self-contained fiefdoms where little information is shared, some companies have found that managing people according to hard metrics has paid off. Consider Freescale Semiconductor, a computer chip manufacturer based in Austin, Texas.

Freescale has discovered that in order to have the right people at the right time to do the right job, it needs an extensive and elaborate set of metrics to manage its 24,000 employees in 30 countries. Of particular concern to Freescale is retention. "There's no greater cost than human capital, especially in the technology industry," says Jignasha Patel, Freescale's director of global talent sourcing and inclusion. "When you've got a tenured employee that decides to walk out the door, it's not just one person leaving, it's that person's knowledge and network and skills."

To manage talent and prevent turnover, Freescale holds line managers accountable for recruiting, hiring, and retaining employees. To do that, managers need to project their talent needs into the future and reconcile those with projected availabilities. Patel provides line managers with census data that help them make their projections, but at the end of the day, the responsibility is theirs. "What we have done is taken all of our inclusion data, all our

metrics, and we've moved the accountability over to the business unit," Patel says.

Patel also provides Freescale managers with benchmark data so they can compare their effectiveness with that of other units. The benchmark data include the number of people hired, turnovers, and promotions—and breakdowns by demographic categories. "There's [a return on investment] for everything we do," says Patel.

Questions

1. Why do you think Freescale focuses on metrics? Why don't more organizations follow its approach?

2. As a manager, would you want to be accountable for the acquisition and retention of employees you supervise? Why or why not?

3. In general, what do you think are the advantages and limitations of such metrics?

4. Freescale focused on metrics for the acquisition and retention of employees. Do you think metrics can be applied to other areas of management, such as employee attitudes, employee performance, or skill development? How might those metrics be measured and managed?

Source: Based on R. R. Hastings, "Metrics Drive Winning Culture," *SHRM Online*, April 9, 2007, www.shrm.org.

Case Incident 2

WORKPLACE VIOLENCE

On Wednesday, January 26, 2005, 54-year-old Myles Meyers walked into DaimlerChrysler's Toledo, Ohio, assembly plant holding a double-barrel shotgun under his coat. Myers, a Jeep repairman, approached Yiesha Martin, a 27-year-old stock supervisor, and stated his intentions. He was there to murder three supervisors: Mike Toney, 45, Roy Thacker, 50, and Carrie Woggerman, 24. Afterward, he said, he would turn the gun on himself. "I was shaking and I started to cry," said Martin. Meyers told her not to cry and to page Toney. Although he was usually eating lunch at his desk around this time, Toney was busy dealing with a problem on the production line. On Martin's second attempt, Toney responded.

Thacker, however, was the first of Meyer's intended victims to approach the former employee. When Thacker asked Meyers why he was at the office, "[Meyers] turned from the partition and just shot him," Martin recalled. "I just saw the shells go. He reloaded in front of me." Martin ran, grabbing a radio in the process. As she ran away, calling into her radio for help, she heard another gunshot. Mike Toney had just arrived and was now the second victim. Carrie Woggerman was able to flee after the

first shot, but Paul Medlen, 41, while attempting to come to the aid of Toney, was shot in the chest by Meyers just before Meyers turned the gun on himself, taking his own life. Of the three employees shot by Meyers, two survived. Unfortunately, Thacker died from his wounds.

Regrettably, the shooting at the Toledo assembly plant was not an isolated incident. Just 2 years earlier, Doug Williams, an employee at Lockheed Martin, left in the middle of an ethics meeting, went to his car, and came back with several guns. He then shot six coworkers to death and wounded eight others before committing suicide. Every year, nearly half of U.S. workers report having faced aggression from coworkers, customers, or supervisors. And according to the Occupational Safety and Health Administration (OSHA), roughly 20,000 assaults and 792 homicides occurred at workplaces throughout the United States in 2005. Such violence prompted the Centers for Disease Control and Prevention to label workplace violence a "national epidemic."

In addition to the obvious devastation workplace violence causes victims and their families, businesses often experience serious repercussions, including legal action.

Lockheed Martin is still embroiled in a legal battle over whether the company should assume part of the responsibility for the shooting that took place at its plant. And Paul Medlen has filed suit against DaimlerChrysler and the plant's security firm, Wackenhut Corp., alleging that both failed to provide adequate security. Given the tremendous damage that companies and employees face following violent episodes, why aren't businesses doing more to curtail workplace violence? According to a recent study by the American Society of Safety Engineers, only 1 percent of U.S. businesses have formal antiviolence policies.

Advice on how to reduce workplace violence abounds. According to former FBI agent Doug Kane, people who behave violently often announce or hint at their intentions before the violence occurs. Managers, then, need to be aware of at-risk employees who may commit violent acts and should encourage employees to report any threatening or suspicious behavior. Some employees of the DaimlerChrysler plant are even suggesting that metal detectors be installed to prevent future violence. Whatever measures are taken, it is clear that workplace violence is an issue that needs to be addressed for employees to feel safe at work.

Questions

1. How liable should companies be for violent acts committed during work by their own employees?

2. Can companies completely prevent workplace violence? If not, what steps can they take to reduce it?

3. Why do you think only 1 percent of companies have formal antiviolence policies?

4. Some companies are considering installing metal detectors to prevent workplace violence. Do you think these measures infringe too much on individual privacy? In other words, can a company take prevention too far?

5. What factors might lead to violent acts in the workplace? Are these acts committed by only a few "sick" individuals, or are many individuals capable of committing acts given certain circumstances?

Source: Based on "Half of U.S. Workers Face On-the-Job Violence," *Forbes*, January 26, 2006, www.Forbes.com; A. K. Fisher, "How to Prevent Violence at Work," *Fortune*, February 21, 2005, pp. 42; and C. Hall, "Witness Recounts Moments of Horror and Heartbreak," *The Toledo Blade*, January 29, 2005, http://toledoblade.com/apps/pbcs.dll/article?AID=/20050129/NEWS03/501290378.

Endnotes

1. "Spanked Employee Seeks $1.2 Million," *CNN.com Law Center*, April 27, 2006, p. 1; and "Clovis Woman Who Sued Successfully over Spanking Is Suing Again," *Fresno Bee*, December 14, 2006, www.SFGate.com.

2. Cited in R. Alsop, "Playing Well with Others," *Wall Street Journal*, September 9, 2002.

3. See, for instance, C. Penttila, "Hiring Hardships," *Entrepreneur*, October 2002, pp. 34–35.

4. *The 2002 National Study of the Changing Workforce* (New York: Families and Work Institute, 2002).

5. I. S. Fulmer, B. Gerhart, and K. S. Scott, "Are the 100 Best Better? An Empirical Investigation of the Relationship Between Being a 'Great Place to Work' and Firm Performance," *Personnel Psychology*, Winter 2003, pp. 965–993.

6. H. Fayol, *Industrial and General Administration* (Paris: Dunod, 1916).

7. A. I. Kraut, P. R. Pedigo, D. D. McKenna, and M. D. Dunnette, "The Role of the Manager: What's Really Important in Different Management Jobs," *Academy of Management Executive* 19, no. 4 (2005), pp. 122–129.

8. H. Mintzberg, *The Nature of Managerial Work* (Upper Saddle River, NJ: Prentice Hall, 1973).

9. R. L. Katz, "Skills of an Effective Administrator," *Harvard Business Review*, September–October 1974, pp. 90–102.

10. F. Luthans, "Successful vs. Effective Real Managers," *Academy of Management Executive*, May 1988, pp. 127–132; and F. Luthans, R. M. Hodgetts, and S. A. Rosenkrantz, *Real Managers* (Cambridge, MA: Ballinger, 1988). See also F. Shipper and J. Davy, "A Model and Investigation of Managerial Skills, Employees' Attitudes, and Managerial Performance," *Leadership Quarterly* 13 (2002), pp. 95–120.

11. P. H. Langford, "Importance of Relationship Management for the Career Success of Australian Managers," *Australian Journal of Psychology*, December 2000, pp. 163–169; and A. M. Konrad, R. Kashlak, I. Yoshioka, R. Waryszak, and N. Toren, "What Do Managers Like to Do? A Five-Country Study," *Group & Organization Management*, December 2001, pp. 401–433.

12. A. S. Tsui, S. J. Ashford, L. St. Clair, and K. R. Xin, "Dealing with Discrepant Expectations: Response Strategies and Managerial Effectiveness," *Academy of Management Journal*, December 1995, pp. 1515–1543.

13. See, for instance, C. Heath and S. B. Sitkin, "Big-B Versus Big-O: What Is *Organizational* about Organizational Behavior?" *Journal of Organizational Behavior*, February 2001, pp. 43–58. For a review of what one eminent researcher believes *should* be included in organizational behavior, based on survey data, see J. B. Miner, "The Rated Importance, Scientific Validity, and Practical Usefulness of Organizational Behavior Theories: A Quantitative Review," *Academy of Management Learning & Education*, September 2003, pp. 250–268.

14. See L. A. Burke and J. E. Moore, "A Perennial Dilemma in OB Education: Engaging the Traditional Student," *Academy of Management Learning & Education*, March 2003, pp. 37–52.

15. D. M. Rousseau and S. McCarthy, "Educating Managers from an Evidence-Based Perspective," *Academy of Management Learning & Education* 6, no. 1 (2007), pp. 84–101.

16. J. Surowiecki, "The Fatal-Flaw Myth," *The New Yorker*, July 31, 2006, p. 25.

17. "In Finland, Fine for Speeding Sets Record," *International Herald Tribune*, February 11, 2004, p. 2.

18. Chris Woodyard, "War, Terrorism Scare Off Business Travelers," *USA Today*, March 25, 2003.

19. O. C. Richard, "Racial Diversity, Business Strategy, and Firm Performance: A Resource-Based View," *Academy of Management Journal*, April 2000, pp. 164–177.

20. "Bye-Bye, Ozzie and Harriet," *American Demographics*, December 2000, p. 59.

21. This section is based on M. Toosi, "A Century of Change: The U.S. Labor Force, 1950–2050," *Monthly Labor Review*, May 2002, pp. 15–27; and *CBO's Projections of the Labor Force* (Washington, DC: Congressional Budget Office, September 2004).

22. See M. E. A. Jayne and R. L. Dipboye, "Leveraging Diversity to Improve Business Performance: Research Findings and Recommendations for Organizations," *Human Resource Management*, Winter 2004, pp. 409–424; S. E. Jackson and A. Joshi, "Research on Domestic and International Diversity in Organizations: A Merger That Works?" in N. Anderson et al (eds.), *Handbook of Industrial, Work & Organizational Psychology*, vol. 2 (Thousand Oaks, CA: Sage, 2001), pp. 206–231; and L. Smith, "The Business Case for Diversity," *Fortune*, October 13, 2003, pp. S8–S12.

23. See, for instance, S. D. Pugh, J. Dietz, J. W. Wiley, and S. M. Brooks, "Driving Service Effectiveness Through Employee-Customer Linkages," *Academy of Management Executive*, November 2002, pp. 73–84; and H. Liao and A. Chuang, "A Multilevel Investigation of Factors Influencing Employee Service Performance and Customer Outcomes," *Academy of Management Journal*, February 2004, pp. 41–58.

24. See www.patagonia.com/jobs/retail_asst_mgr.shtml; and "Patagonia Sets the Pace for Green Business," *Grist Magazine*, October 22, 2004, www.grist.org.

25. See, for instance, M. Workman and W. Bommer, "Redesigning Computer Call Center Work: A Longitudinal Field Experiment," *Journal of Organizational Behavior*, May 2004, pp. 317–337.

26. See, for instance, V. S. Major, K. J. Klein, and M. G. Ehrhart, "Work Time, Work Interference with Family, and Psychological Distress," *Journal of Applied Psychology*, June 2002, pp. 427–436; D. Brady, "Rethinking the Rat Race," *BusinessWeek*, August 26, 2002, pp. 142–143; J. M. Brett and L. K. Stroh, "Working 61 Plus Hours a Week: Why Do Managers Do It?" *Journal of Applied Psychology*, February 2003, pp. 67–78.

27. See, for instance, *The 2002 National Study of the Changing Workforce* (New York: Families and Work Institute, 2002).

28. Cited in S. Armour, "Workers Put Family First Despite Slow Economy, Jobless Fears."

29. S. Shellenbarger, "What Job Candidates Really Want to Know: Will I Have a Life?" *Wall Street Journal*, November 17, 1999,

p. B1; and "U.S. Employers Polish Image to Woo a Demanding New Generation," *Manpower Argus*, February 2000, p. 2.

30. F. Luthans and C. M. Youssef, "Emerging Positive Organizational Behavior," *Journal of Management*, June 2007, pp. 321–349; and J. E. Dutton and S. Sonenshein, "Positive Organizational Scholarship," in C. Cooper and J. Barling (eds.), *Encyclopedia of Positive Psychology* (Thousand Oaks, CA: Sage, 2007).

31. L. M. Roberts, G. Spreitzer, J. Dutton, R. Quinn, E. Heaphy, and B. Barker, "How to Play to Your Strengths," *Harvard Business Review*, January 2005, pp. 1–6; and L. M. Roberts, J. E. Dutton, G. M. Spreitzer, E. D. Heaphy, and R. E. Quinn, "Composing the Reflected Best-Self Portrait: Becoming Extraordinary in Work Organizations," *Academy of Management Review* 30, no. 4 (2005), pp. 712–736.

32. J. Merritt, "For MBAs, Soul-Searching 101," *BusinessWeek*, September 16, 2002, pp. 64–66; and S. Greenhouse, "The Mood at Work: Anger and Anxiety," *New York Times*, October 29, 2002, p. E1.

33. See, for instance, G. R. Weaver, L. K. Trevino, and P. L. Cochran, "Corporate Ethics Practices in the Mid-1990's: An Empirical Study of the Fortune 1000," *Journal of Business Ethics*, February 1999, pp. 283–294; and C. De Mesa Graziano, "Promoting Ethical Conduct: A Review of Corporate Practices," *Strategic Investor Relations*, Fall 2002, pp. 29–35.

34. A. J. Rucci, S. P. Kirn, and R. T. Quinn, "The Employee-Customer-Profit Chain at Sears," *Harvard Business Review*, January–February 1998, pp. 83–97.

35. J. Britt, "Workplace No-Shows' Cost to Employers Rise Again," *HRMagazine*, December 2002, pp. 26–29.

36. "Absence-Minded Workers Cost Business Dearly," *Works Management*, June 2001, pp. 10–14.

37. W. Hoge, "Sweden's Cradle-to-Grave Welfare Starts to Get Ill," *International Herald Tribune*, September 25, 2002, p. 8.

38. "Employee Turnover Costs in the U.S.," *Manpower Argus*, January 2001, p. 5.

39. See http://data.bls.gov (May 11, 2005).

40. See, for example, M. C. Sturman and C. O. Trevor, "The Implications of Linking the Dynamic Performance and Turnover Literatures," *Journal of Applied Psychology*, August 2001, pp. 684–696.

41. Cited in "You Often Lose the Ones You Love," *IndustryWeek*, November 21, 1988, p. 5.

42. R. J. Bennett and S. L. Robinson, "Development of a Measure of Workplace Deviance," *Journal of Applied Psychology* 85, no. 3 (2000), pp. 349–360; A. M. O'Leary-Kelly, M. K. Duffy, and R. W. Griffin, "Construct Confusion in the Study of Antisocial Work Behavior," *Research in Personnel and Human Resources Management* 18 (2000), pp. 275–303; and C. Porath, C. Pearson, and D. L. Shapiro, "Turning the Other Cheek or an Eye for an Eye: Targets' Responses to Incivility," paper interactively presented at the annual meeting of the National Academy of Management, August 1999.

43. D. W. Organ, *Organizational Citizenship Behavior: The Good Soldier Syndrome* (Lexington, MA: Lexington Books, 1988), p. 4; and J. A. LePine, A. Erez, and D. E. Johnson, "The Nature and Dimensionality of Organizational Citizenship Behavior: A Critical Review and Meta-Analysis," *Journal of Applied Psychology*, February 2002, pp. 52–65.

44. P. M. Podsakoff, S. B. MacKenzie, J. B. Paine, and D. G. Bachrach, "Organizational Citizenship Behaviors: A Critical Review of the Theoretical and Empirical Literature and Suggestions for Future Research," *Journal of Management* 26, no. 3 (2000), pp. 543–548; and M. C. Bolino and W. H. Turnley, "Going the Extra Mile: Cultivating and Managing Employee Citizenship Behavior," *Academy of Management Executive*, August 2003, pp. 60–73.

45. T. A. Judge, C. J. Thoresen, J. E. Bono, and G. R. Patton, "The Job Satisfaction–Job Performance Relationship: A Qualitative and Quantitative Review," *Psychological Bulletin* 127 (2001), pp. 376–407.

46. M. Buckingham and C. Coffman, *First, Break All the Rules: What the World's Greatest Managers Do Differently* (New York: Simon & Schuster, 1999).

47. H. J. Leavitt, *Managerial Psychology*, rev. ed. (Chicago: University of Chicago Press, 1964), p. 3.

Foundations of Individual Behavior

I think that God in creating Man somewhat overestimated his ability.

—Oscar Wilde

LEARNING OBJECTIVES

After studying this chapter, you should be able to:

1 Contrast the two types of ability.

2 Define *intellectual ability* and demonstrate its relevance to OB.

3 Identify the key biographical characteristics and describe how they are relevant to OB.

4 Define *learning* and outline the principles of the three major theories of learning.

5 Define *shaping* and show how it can be used in OB.

6 Show how culture affects our understanding of intellectual abilities, biographical characteristics, and learning.

eet Alexandra Hai, the first woman to operate a gondola in Venice.

For more than a millennium, gondolas have been navigating the canals of Italy's most fabled city. And for more than a millennium, they've been operated by men. Until 2007, when Hai won her right to operate one. But it didn't come without a fight. Hai, a 40-year-old of German and Algerian descent, had to go to court. The court ruled in her favor but restricted her operations to transporting the guests of a local hotel.

Paddling Against the Tide

Source: Dave Yoder/The New York Times

Whenever Hai is out, people stop, gawk, take pictures, and shout ("Brava, Gondoliera! Brava!" shouted one resident from his balcony). Not all the reactions are so positive, though.

Roberto Luppi, president of the Venice gondoliers' association, said that Hai has been proven incapable of operating a gondola, having failed four tests. He says the court's decision to allow her to operate is a publicity stunt. He defends the threats she's received from some male gondoliers, arguing, "After a person accuses gondoliers of being racists and sexists, what does she expect?" he said. "That they are supposed to give her kisses?"

Compared to the United States and especially the Scandinavian countries, Italy differentiates markedly between gender roles (though, of course, there is a lot of individual variation within Italy, as within most countries). In Venice, the first women was allowed to wait on tables in St. Mark's Square only 8 years ago. That waitress, Ljubica Gunj, still waits on tables at the Aurora Café. However, next door, the Firoian Café allows women to wait on tables only indoors.

Even though Hai continues to operate her gondola, locals still dispute her right to be on the water. Hai maintains that she failed the tests because they were rigged against her. Luppi and many other Venetians see it differently. "She needs to look in the mirror and accept that she cannot drive," he said. To most of the gondoliers, the job is fit only for a man since it requires strength and the ability to navigate currents and paddle in reverse, and even for aesthetic reasons (relating to the traditional garb of the gondoliers). Says one gondolier, "Let's leave just one tradition intact. Being a gondolier is a tradition, and it is very difficult work."

For her part, Hai argues that her job has been doubly difficult because she's had to fight for her job. "There is nothing worse than to do something like this," she said. "I would have preferred to do something more useful in life, like helping save the rain forests."[1] ■

*g*ender is but one characteristic that people bring with them when they join an organization. In this chapter, we look at how individual differences in the form of ability (which includes intelligence) and biographical characteristics (such as age) affect employee performance and satisfaction. Then we show how people learn behaviors and what management can do to shape those behaviors.

But before we move on to the next section, check out the following Self-Assessment Library, where you can assess your views on one of the characteristics we'll discuss in this chapter—age.

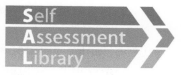

WHAT'S MY ATTITUDE TOWARD OLDER PEOPLE?

In the Self-Assessment Library (available on CD or online), take assessment IV.C.1 (What's My Attitude Toward Older People?) and answer the following questions:

1. *Are you surprised by your results?*
2. *How do your results compare to those of others?*

Ability

1 *Contrast the two types of ability.*

Contrary to what we were taught in grade school, we weren't all created equal. Most people are to the left or to the right of the median on some normally distributed ability curve. For example, regardless of how motivated you are, it's unlikely that you can act as well as Scarlett Johansson, play basketball as well as LeBron James, write as well as J. K. Rowling, or play the guitar as well as Pat Matheny. Of course, just because we aren't all equal in abilities does not imply that some individuals are inherently inferior to others. Everyone has strengths and weaknesses in terms of ability that make him or her relatively superior or inferior to others in performing certain tasks or activities. From management's standpoint, the issue is not whether people differ in terms of their abilities. They clearly do. The issue is knowing *how* people differ in abilities and using that knowledge to increase the likelihood that an employee will perform his or her job well.

What does *ability* mean? As we will use the term, **ability** refers to an individual's capacity to perform the various tasks in a job. It is a current assessment of what one can do. An individual's overall abilities are essentially made up of two sets of factors: intellectual and physical.

Intellectual Abilities

Intellectual abilities are abilities needed to perform mental activities—for thinking, reasoning, and problem solving. People in most societies place a high value on intelligence, and for good reason. Compared to others, smart people generally earn more money and attain higher levels of education. Smart people are also more likely to emerge as leaders of groups. Intelligence quotient (IQ) tests, for example, are designed to ascertain a person's general intellectual abilities. So, too, are popular college admission tests, such as the SAT and ACT and graduate admission tests in business (GMAT), law (LSAT), and medicine (MCAT). Testing firms don't make the argument that their tests assess intelligence, but experts know that they do.[2] The seven most frequently cited dimensions making up intellectual abilities are number aptitude, verbal comprehension, perceptual speed, inductive reasoning, deductive reasoning, spatial visualization, and memory.[3] Exhibit 2-1 describes these dimensions.

2 Define intellectual ability and demonstrate its relevance to OB.

Exhibit **2-1**	Dimensions of Intellectual Ability	
Dimension	**Description**	**Job Example**
Number aptitude	Ability to do speedy and accurate arithmetic	Accountant: Computing the sales tax on a set of items
Verbal comprehension	Ability to understand what is read or heard and the relationship of words to each other	Plant manager: Following corporate policies on hiring
Perceptual speed	Ability to identify visual similarities and differences quickly and accurately	Fire investigator: Identifying clues to support a charge of arson
Inductive reasoning	Ability to identify a logical sequence in a problem and then solve the problem	Market researcher: Forecasting demand for a product in the next time period
Deductive reasoning	Ability to use logic and assess the implications of an argument	Supervisor: Choosing between two different suggestions offered by employees
Spatial visualization	Ability to imagine how an object would look if its position in space were changed	Interior decorator: Redecorating an office
Memory	Ability to retain and recall past experiences	Salesperson: Remembering the names of customers

ability *An individual's capacity to perform the various tasks in a job.*

intellectual abilities *The capacity to do mental activities—thinking, reasoning, and problem solving.*

Intelligence dimensions are positively related, so that high scores on one dimension tend to be positively correlated with high scores on another. If you score high on verbal comprehension, for example, you're more likely to score high on spatial visualization. The correlations aren't perfect, meaning that people do have specific abilities. However, the correlations are high enough that for some time, researchers have recognized a general factor of intelligence, called **general mental ability (GMA)**. GMA doesn't deny that there are specific abilities, but it suggests that it makes sense to talk about overall, or general, intelligence.

Jobs differ in the demands they place on incumbents to use their intellectual abilities. The more complex a job is in terms of information-processing demands, the more general intelligence and verbal abilities will be necessary to perform the job successfully.[4] Of course, a high IQ is not a requirement for all jobs. For jobs in which employee behavior is highly routine and there are few or no opportunities to exercise discretion, a high IQ is not as important to performing well. However, that does not mean that people with high IQs cannot have an impact on jobs that are traditionally less complex.

It might surprise you that the most widely used intelligence test in hiring decisions takes only 12 minutes. It's called the Wonderlic Personnel Test. There are different forms of the test, and each form has 50 questions. Here are a few examples of questions from the Wonderlic:

- When rope is selling at $.10 a foot, how many feet can you buy for $.60?
- Assume the first two statements are true. Is the final one:
  1. true, 2. false, 3. not certain?
     a. The boy plays baseball.
     b. All baseball players wear hats.
     c. The boy wears a hat.

The Wonderlic tests both speed (almost nobody has time to answer every question) and power (questions get harder as you go along), so the average

International **OB**

The Benefits of Cultural Intelligence

Have you ever noticed that some individuals seem to have a knack for relating well to people from different cultures? Some researchers have labeled this skill *cultural intelligence*, which is an outsider's natural ability to interpret an individual's unfamiliar gestures and behaviors in the same way that others from the individual's culture would. Cultural intelligence is important because when conducting business with people from different cultures,

misunderstandings can often occur, and, as a result, cooperation and productivity may suffer.

Consider the following example. An American manager was meeting with his fellow design team engineers, two of whom were German. As ideas floated around the table, his German colleagues quickly rejected them. The American thought the feedback was harsh and concluded that his German colleagues were rude. However, they were merely critiquing the ideas, not the individual—a distinction that the American was unable to make, perhaps due to a lack of cultural intelligence. As a result, the American became wary of contributing potentially good ideas. Had the American been more culturally

intelligent, he likely would have recognized the true motives behind his colleagues' remarks and thus may have been able to use those remarks to improve his ideas.

It is unclear whether the notion of cultural intelligence is separate from other forms of intelligence, such as emotional intelligence, and even whether cultural intelligence is different from cognitive ability. However, it is clear that the ability to interact well with individuals from different cultures is a key asset in today's global business environment.

Source: Based on C. Earley and E. Mosakowski, "Cultural Intelligence," *Harvard Business Review*, October 2004, pp. 139–146.

score is pretty low—about 21/50. And because the Wonderlic is able to provide valid information at a cheap price ($2–$6/applicant), more and more companies are using the test in hiring decisions. For example, the Factory Card & Party Outlet, which has 182 stores nationwide, uses the Wonderlic. So do Subway, Peoples Flowers, Security Alarm, Workforce Employment Solutions, and many others, including the NFL, as you'll see in Chapter 18 Most companies that use the Wonderlic don't use it in place of other hiring tools such as application forms or interviews. Rather, they add the Wonderlic as another source of information—in this case, because of the test's ability to provide valid data on applicants' intelligence levels.

Interestingly, while intelligence is a big help in performing a job well, it doesn't make people happier or more satisfied with their jobs. The correlation between intelligence and job satisfaction is about zero. Why? Research suggests that although intelligent people perform better and tend to have more interesting jobs, they are also more critical in evaluating their job conditions. Thus, smart people have it better, but they also expect more.[5]

Physical Abilities

Though the changing nature of work suggests that intellectual abilities are becoming increasingly important for many jobs, **physical abilities** have been and will remain important for successfully doing certain jobs. Research on the requirements needed in hundreds of jobs has identified nine basic abilities involved in the performance of physical tasks.[6] These are described in Exhibit 2-2. Individuals differ in the extent to which they have each of these abilities. Not surprisingly, there is also little

3 Identify the key biographical characteristics and describe how they are relevant to OB.

Exhibit **2-2**	Nine Basic Physical Abilities
Strength Factors	
1. Dynamic strength	Ability to exert muscular force repeatedly or continuously over time
2. Trunk strength	Ability to exert muscular strength using the trunk (particularly abdominal) muscles
3. Static strength	Ability to exert force against external objects
4. Explosive strength	Ability to expend a maximum of energy in one or a series of explosive acts
Flexibility Factors	
5. Extent flexibility	Ability to move the trunk and back muscles as far as possible
6. Dynamic flexibility	Ability to make rapid, repeated flexing movements
Other Factors	
7. Body coordination	Ability to coordinate the simultaneous actions of different parts of the body
8. Balance	Ability to maintain equilibrium despite forces pulling off balance
9. Stamina	Ability to continue maximum effort requiring prolonged effort over time

general mental ability (GMA) *An overall factor of intelligence, as suggested by the positive correlations among specific intellectual ability dimensions.*

physical abilities *The capacity to do tasks that demand stamina, dexterity, strength, and similar characteristics.*

relationship among them: A high score on one is no assurance of a high score on others. High employee performance is likely to be achieved when management has ascertained the extent to which a job requires each of the nine abilities and then ensures that employees in that job have those abilities.

Biographical Characteristics

As discussed in Chapter 1, this textbook is essentially concerned with finding and analyzing the variables that have an impact on employee productivity, absence, turnover, deviance, citizenship, and satisfaction. The list of those variables—as shown in Exhibit 1-6—is long and contains some complicated concepts. Many of the concepts—motivation, say, or power and politics or organizational culture—are hard to assess. It might be valuable, then, to begin by looking at factors that are easily definable and readily available—data that can be obtained, for the most part, simply from information available in an employee's personnel file. What factors would these be? Obvious characteristics would be an employee's age, gender, race, and length of service with an organization. Fortunately, a sizable amount of research has specifically analyzed many of these **biographical characteristics**.

Age

The relationship between age and job performance is likely to be an issue of increasing importance during the next decade for at least three reasons. First, there is a widespread belief that job performance declines with increasing age. Regardless of whether this is true, a lot of people believe it and act on it. Second, as noted in Chapter 1, the workforce is aging. The third reason is U.S. legislation that, for all intents and purposes, outlaws mandatory retirement. Most U.S. workers today no longer have to retire at age 70.

What is the perception of older workers? Evidence indicates that employers hold mixed feelings.[7] They see a number of positive qualities that older workers

Home Depot values the work ethic of older employees such as assistant manager Ellen Van Valen shown here, who is in her late 60s. Home Depot is one of a growing number of firms that are recruiting older workers because, compared with younger workers, they have lower turnover rates and training costs and, in many cases, better work performance. Van Valen believes that age has little to do with the desire to work but says that "older folks seem to catch on a lot quicker."

Source: Douglas Healey/ The New York Times

bring to their jobs, such as experience, judgment, a strong work ethic, and commitment to quality. But older workers are also perceived as lacking flexibility and as being resistant to new technology. And in a time when organizations are actively seeking individuals who are adaptable and open to change, the negatives associated with age clearly hinder the initial hiring of older workers and increase the likelihood that they will be let go during cutbacks. Now let's take a look at the evidence. What effect does age actually have on turnover, absenteeism, productivity, and satisfaction?

The older you get, the less likely you are to quit your job. That conclusion is based on studies of the age–turnover relationship.[8] Of course, this shouldn't be too surprising. As workers get older, they have fewer alternative job opportunities. In addition, older workers are less likely to resign than are younger workers because their long tenure tends to provide them with higher wage rates, longer paid vacations, and more attractive pension benefits.

It's tempting to assume that age is also inversely related to absenteeism. After all, if older workers are less likely to quit, won't they also demonstrate higher stability by coming to work more regularly? Not necessarily. Most studies do show an inverse relationship, but close examination finds that the age–absence relationship is partially a function of whether the absence is avoidable or unavoidable.[9] In general, older employees have lower rates of avoidable absence than do younger employees. However, they have higher rates of unavoidable absence, probably due to the poorer health associated with aging and the longer recovery period that older workers need when injured.

How does age affect productivity? There is a widespread belief that productivity declines with age. It is often assumed that an individual's skills—particularly speed, agility, strength, and coordination—decay over time and that prolonged job boredom and lack of intellectual stimulation contribute to reduced productivity. The evidence, however, contradicts that belief and those assumptions. For instance, during a 3-year period, a large hardware chain staffed one of its stores solely with employees over 50 and compared its results with those of five stores with younger employees. The store staffed by the over-50 employees was significantly more productive (measured in terms of sales generated against labor costs) than two of the other stores and held its own with the other three.[10] Other reviews of the research find that age and job performance are unrelated.[11] Moreover, this finding seems to be true for almost all types of jobs, professional and nonprofessional. The natural conclusion is that the demands of most jobs, even those with heavy manual labor requirements, are not extreme enough for any declines in physical skills attributable to age to have an impact on productivity; or, if there is some decay due to age, it is offset by gains due to experience.[12]

Our final concern is the relationship between age and job satisfaction. On this issue, the evidence is mixed. Most studies indicate a positive association between age and satisfaction, at least up to age 60.[13] Other studies, however, have found a U-shaped relationship.[14] Several explanations could clear up these results, the most plausible being that these studies are intermixing professional and nonprofessional employees. When the two types are separated, satisfaction tends to continually increase among professionals as they age, whereas it falls among nonprofessionals during middle age and then rises again in the later years.

biographical characteristics   *Personal characteristics—such as age, gender, race, and length of tenure—that are objective and easily obtained from personnel records.*

Gender

Few issues initiate more debates, misconceptions, and unsupported opinions than whether women perform as well on jobs as men do. In this section, we review the research on that issue.

The evidence suggests that the best place to begin is with the recognition that there are few, if any, important differences between men and women that will affect their job performance. There are, for instance, no consistent male–female differences in problem-solving ability, analytical skills, competitive drive, motivation, sociability, or learning ability.[15] Psychological studies have found that women are more willing to conform to authority and that men are more aggressive and more likely than women to have expectations of success, but those differences are minor. Given the significant changes that have taken place in the past 40 years in terms of increasing female participation rates in the workforce and rethinking what constitutes male and female roles, you should operate on the assumption that there is no significant difference in job productivity between men and women.[16]

One issue that does seem to differ between genders, especially when the employee has preschool-age children, is preference for work schedules.[17] Working mothers are more likely to prefer part-time work, flexible work schedules, and telecommuting in order to accommodate their family responsibilities.

But what about absence and turnover rates? Are women less stable employees than men? First, on the question of turnover, the evidence indicates no significant differences.[18] Women's quit rates are similar to those for men. The research on absence, however, consistently indicates that women have higher rates of absenteeism than men do.[19] The most logical explanation for this finding is that the research was conducted in North America, and North American culture has historically placed home and family responsibilities on the woman. When a child is ill or someone needs to stay home to wait for a plumber, it has been the woman who has traditionally taken time off from work. However, this research is undoubtedly time bound.[20] The historical role of the woman in caring for children and as secondary breadwinner has definitely changed in the past generation, and a large proportion of men nowadays are as interested in day care and the problems associated with child care in general as are women.

JPMorgan Chase, a global banking and financial services firm, believes that women perform as well on jobs as men do. Almost 60 percent of the firm's employees are women, and 50 percent of its managers and professionals are women. The many working moms at JPMorgan appreciate flexible work schedules such as job sharing, compressed workweeks, flextime, and telecommuting. JPMorgan also provides on-site, back-up child-care centers for employees whose usual child-care arrangements fall through. Shown here are stockbrokers and traders at company headquarters in New York City.

Race

Race is a controversial issue. It can be so contentious that it's tempting to avoid the topic. A complete picture of individual differences in OB, however, would be incomplete without a discussion of race.

What is race? Before we can discuss how race matters in OB, first we have to reach some consensus about what race is, and that's not easily done. Some scholars argue that it's not productive to discuss race for policy reasons (it's a divisive issue), for biological reasons (a large percentage of us are a mixture of races), or for genetic and anthropological reasons (many anthropologists and evolutionary scientists reject the concept of distinct racial categories).

Most people in the United States identify themselves according to a racial group. (In contrast, in some countries, such as Brazil, people are less likely to define themselves according to distinct racial categories.) The Department of Education classifies individuals according to five racial categories: African American, Native American (American Indian/Alaskan Native), Asian/Pacific Islander, Hispanic, and white. We'll define race as the biological heritage people use to identify themselves. This definition allows each individual to define his or her race. Tiger Woods, for example, refuses to place himself into a single racial category, emphasizing his multiethnic roots.

Race has been studied quite a bit in OB, particularly as it relates to employment outcomes such as personnel selection decisions, performance evaluations, pay, and workplace discrimination. Doing justice to all of this research isn't possible here, so let's summarize a few points.

First, in employment settings, there is a tendency for individuals to favor colleagues of their own race in performance evaluations, promotion decisions, and pay raises.[21] Second, there are substantial racial differences in attitudes toward affirmative action, with African Americans approving of such programs to a greater degree than whites.[22] Third, African Americans generally fare worse than whites in employment decisions. For example, African Americans receive lower ratings in employment interviews, are paid less, and are promoted less frequently.[23]

The major dilemma faced by employers who use mental ability tests for selection, promotion, training, and similar personnel decisions is concern that they may have a negative impact on racial and ethnic groups.[24] For instance, some minority groups score, on average, as much as 1 standard deviation lower than whites on verbal, numeric, and spatial ability tests, meaning that only 10 percent of minority group members score above the average for whites. However, after reviewing the evidence, researchers have concluded that "despite group differences in mean test performance, there is little convincing evidence that well-constructed tests are more predictive of educational, training, or occupational performance for members of the majority group than for members of minority groups."[25] The issue of racial differences in cognitive ability tests continues to be hotly debated.[26]

Other Biographical Characteristics: Tenure, Religion, Sexual Orientation, and Gender Identity

The last set of biographical characteristic we'll look are tenure, religion, and sexual orientation.

Tenure   With the exception of gender and racial differences, few issues are more subject to misconceptions and speculations than the impact of seniority on job performance.

Extensive reviews have been conducted of the seniority–productivity relationship.[27] If we define *seniority* as time on a particular job, we can say that the

Are You More Biased Than You Think?

One late Wednesday afternoon, a 34-year-old white woman sat down in her Washington, DC, office to take a test. She prided herself on being a civil rights advocate, and her office décor gave ample testament to her liberal causes.

The woman accessed a test on a Web site run by a research team at Harvard. The test was relatively simple; it asked her to distinguish between a series of black and white faces. When she saw a black face, she was to press a key on the left, and when she saw a white face, she was to press a key on the right. Next, she was asked to distinguish between a series of positive and negative words. Words such as "wonderful" required pressing the "i" key, words such as "terrible" required pressing the "e" key. The test remained simple when two categories were combined: The person pressed "e" if she saw either a white face or a positive word, and she pressed "i" if she saw either a black face or a negative word.

Then the groupings were reversed. The woman's index fingers hovered over her keyboard. The test now required her to group black faces with positive words and white faces with negative words. She leaned forward intently. She made no mistakes, but it took her longer to correctly sort the words and images.

Her result appeared on the screen, and the activist became very silent. The test found she had a bias for whites over blacks.

"It surprises me I have any preferences at all," she said. "By the work I do, by my education, my background. I'm progressive, and I think I have no bias. Being a minority myself, I don't feel I should or would have biases."

As it turns out, evidence is starting to accumulate—there are more than 60 studies so far—showing that most people have these sorts of implicit biases. They're implicit because we don't consciously realize they're there. But there they are. We may have implicit biases against minorities or women, or people of a certain religion or sexual orientation. Some people do not have an implicit bias in one area (say, toward race), but do in another area (say, toward Republicans).

Are these biases set in stone? Are they changed by experience? That's not yet clear. Some of the researchers argue that such biases are so primitive that simple training exercises or experiences are unlikely to change them. Like race or gender, they may be part of who we are. "Mind bugs operate without us being conscious of them," says one of the Harvard researchers. "They are not special things that happen in our heart because we are evil."

Source: Based on S. Vedantam, "See No Bias," *Washington Post*, January 23, 2005, p. W12; and A. S. Baron and M. R. Banaji, "The Development of Implicit Attitudes: Evidence of Race Evaluations from Ages 6 and 10 and Adulthood," *Psychological Science*, January 2006, pp. 53–58.

most recent evidence demonstrates a positive relationship between seniority and job productivity. So tenure, expressed as work experience, appears to be a good predictor of employee productivity.

The research relating tenure to absence is quite straightforward. Studies consistently demonstrate seniority to be negatively related to absenteeism.[28] In fact, in terms of both frequency of absence and total days lost at work, tenure is the single most important explanatory variable.[29]

Tenure is also a potent variable in explaining turnover. The longer a person is in a job, the less likely he or she is to quit.[30] Moreover, consistent with research which suggests that past behavior is the best predictor of future behavior,[31] evidence indicates that tenure on an employee's previous job is a powerful predictor of that employee's future turnover.[32]

The evidence indicates that tenure and job satisfaction are positively related.[33] In fact, when age and tenure are treated separately, tenure appears to be a more consistent and stable predictor of job satisfaction than is chronological age.

Religion   Religion is a touchy subject. Not only do religious and nonreligious people question each other's belief systems, often people of different religious faiths conflict. As demonstrated by the war in Iraq and the past conflict in Northern Ireland, there are often violent differences among sects of the same religion. U.S. federal law prohibits employers from discriminating against employees based on their religion, with very few exceptions. However, that doesn't mean religion is a non-issue in OB.

Perhaps the greatest religious issue in the United States today revolves around Islam. There are nearly 2 million Muslims in the United States, and across the world, Islam is one of the most popular religions. For the most part, U.S. Muslims have attitudes similar to those of other U.S. citizens (though the differences tend to be greater for younger U.S. Muslims). Still, there are both perceived and real differences. Nearly 4 of 10 U.S. adults admit that they harbor negative feelings or prejudices toward U.S. Muslims. Fifty-two percent believe that U.S. Muslims are not respectful of women.

Some in the United States take these general biases a step further. Motaz Elshafi, a 28-year-old software engineer for Cisco Systems who was born and raised in New Jersey, received an e-mail from a coworker addressed, "Dear Terrorist." Although such acts are relatively isolated, they do occur.

There are limits to which workplaces can be adapted to fit the views of some Muslims. For example, it may be difficult for certain employers to accommodate some Muslims' practice of praying five times a day or wearing a beard or head scarf.

But we need to be careful of laying down blanket judgments of all Muslims; they're no more accurate than judgments of all Christians or all the people in any other group. As one Islamic scholar has noted, "There is no such thing as a single American Muslim community, much as there is no single Christian community. Muslims vary hugely by ethnicity, faith, tradition, education, income, and degree of religious observance."[34]

Sexual Orientation and Gender Identity   Employers differ a lot in how they treat sexual orientation. Federal law does not prohibit discrimination against employees based on sexual orientation, though many states and municipalities do have anti-discrimination policies. Many employers ignore it (practicing some version of the "don't ask, don't tell" military policy), some do not hire gays, but an increasing number of employers are implementing policies and practices protecting the rights of gays in the workplace. Take defense contractor Raytheon, builder of Tomahawk cruise missiles and other defense systems. Raytheon offers domestic partner benefits, supports a wide array of gay rights groups, and wants to be an employer of choice for gays. Why has Raytheon done this? Because it believes these policies give it an advantage in the ever-competitive market of hiring engineers and scientists.

Raytheon is not alone. More than half of the Fortune 500 companies offer domestic partner benefits for gay couples. This includes companies such as American Express, IBM, Intel, Morgan Stanley, Motorola, and Wal-Mart. That doesn't mean, though, that all employers are on board. Some companies are against domestic partner benefits or nondiscrimination clauses for gay employees. Among those companies are Alltel, ADM, ExxonMobil, H. J. Heinz, Nissan, Nestle, and Rubbermaid.[35]

As for gender identity, companies are increasingly putting in place policies to govern how their organization treats employees who change genders (often called *transgender employees*). In 2001, only eight companies in the Fortune 500 had policies on gender identity. By 2006, that number had swelled to 124. IBM is one of them. Brad Salavich, a diversity manager for IBM, says, "We believe that having strong transgender and gender identification policies is a natural extension of IBM's corporate culture." Dealing with transgender employees requires some special considerations, such as bathrooms, names, and so on.[36]

Learning

4 *Define* learning *and outline the principles of the three major theories of learning.*

All complex behavior is learned. If we want to explain and predict behavior, we need to understand how people learn. In this section, we define *learning*, present three popular learning theories, and describe how managers can facilitate employee learning.

A Definition of Learning

What is **learning**? A psychologist's definition is considerably broader than the layperson's view that "it's what we did when we went to school." In actuality, each of us is continuously "going to school." Learning occurs all the time. Therefore, a generally accepted definition of *learning* is "any relatively permanent change in behavior that occurs as a result of experience."[37] Ironically, we can say that changes in behavior indicate that learning has taken place and that learning is a change in behavior.

The previous definition suggests that we can see changes taking place, but we can't see the learning itself. The concept is theoretical and, hence, not directly observable:

> You have seen people in the process of learning, you have seen people who behave in a particular way as a result of learning and some of you (in fact, I guess the majority of you) have "learned" at some time in your life. In other words, we infer that learning has taken place if an individual behaves, reacts, responds as a result of experience in a manner different from the way he formerly behaved.[38]

Our definition has several components that deserve clarification. First, learning involves change. Change may be good or bad from an organizational point of view. People can learn unfavorable behaviors—to hold prejudices or to shirk their responsibilities, for example—as well as favorable behaviors. Second,

The U.S. military uses cultural sensitivity training to provide soldiers with an experience that will lead to positive and permanent changes in their behavior. Soldiers learn how to communicate with village leaders in Afghanistan by practicing with role players who are Afghan citizens living in the United States. They learn in a realistic setting by sitting on the floor in a room decorated to resemble the home of an Afghan village leader. Instructors evaluate the training sessions to determine whether changes in behavior take place as a result of the learning process.

the change must become ingrained. Immediate changes may be only reflexive or a result of fatigue (or a sudden burst of energy) and thus may not represent learning. Third, some form of experience is necessary for learning. Experience may be acquired directly through observation or practice, or it may be acquired indirectly, as through reading. The crucial test still remains: Does this experience result in a relatively permanent change in behavior? If the answer is "yes," we can say that learning has taken place.

Theories of Learning

How do we learn? Three theories have been offered to explain the process by which we acquire patterns of behavior. These are classical conditioning, operant conditioning, and social learning.

Classical Conditioning   Classical conditioning grew out of experiments to teach dogs to salivate in response to the ringing of a bell, conducted in the early 1900s by Russian physiologist Ivan Pavlov.[39] A simple surgical procedure allowed Pavlov to measure accurately the amount of saliva secreted by a dog. When Pavlov presented the dog with a piece of meat, the dog exhibited a noticeable increase in salivation. When Pavlov withheld the presentation of meat and merely rang a bell, the dog did not salivate. Then Pavlov proceeded to link the meat and the ringing of the bell. After repeatedly hearing the bell before getting the food, the dog began to salivate as soon as the bell rang. After a while, the dog would salivate merely at the sound of the bell, even if no food was offered. In effect, the dog had learned to respond—that is, to salivate—to the bell. Let's review this experiment to introduce the key concepts in classical conditioning.

In Pavlov's experiment, the meat was an *unconditioned stimulus*; it invariably caused the dog to react in a specific way. The reaction that took place whenever the unconditioned stimulus occurred was called the *unconditioned response* (or the noticeable increase in salivation, in this case). The bell was an artificial stimulus, or what we call the *conditioned stimulus*. Although it was originally neutral, after the bell was paired with the meat (an unconditioned stimulus), it eventually produced a response when presented alone. The last key concept is the *conditioned response*. This describes the behavior of the dog; it salivated in reaction to the bell alone.

Using these concepts, we can summarize classical conditioning. Essentially, learning a conditioned response involves building up an association between a conditioned stimulus and an unconditioned stimulus. When the stimuli, one compelling and the other one neutral, are paired, the neutral one becomes a conditioned stimulus and, hence, takes on the properties of the unconditioned stimulus.

Classical conditioning can be used to explain why Christmas carols often bring back pleasant memories of childhood; the songs are associated with the festive holiday spirit and evoke fond memories and feelings of euphoria. In an organizational setting, we can also see classical conditioning operating. For example, at one manufacturing plant, every time the top executives from the head office were scheduled to make a visit, the plant management would clean up the administrative offices and wash the windows. This went on for years.

---

learning   *A relatively permanent change in behavior that occurs as a result of experience.*

classical conditioning   *A type of conditioning in which an individual responds to some stimulus that would not ordinarily produce such a response.*

Eventually, employees would turn on their best behavior and look prim and proper whenever the windows were cleaned—even in those occasional instances when the cleaning was not paired with a visit from the top brass. People had learned to associate the cleaning of the windows with a visit from the head office.

Classical conditioning is passive. Something happens, and we react in a specific way. It is elicited in response to a specific, identifiable event. As such, it can explain simple reflexive behaviors. But most behavior—particularly the complex behavior of individuals in organizations—is emitted rather than elicited. That is, it's voluntary rather than reflexive. For example, employees *choose* to arrive at work on time, ask their boss for help with problems, or "goof off" when no one is watching. The learning of those behaviors is better understood by looking at operant conditioning.

Operant Conditioning Operant conditioning argues that behavior is a function of its consequences. People learn to behave to get something they want or to avoid something they don't want. Operant behavior means voluntary or learned behavior in contrast to reflexive or unlearned behavior. The tendency to repeat such behavior is influenced by the reinforcement or lack of reinforcement brought about by the consequences of the behavior. Therefore, reinforcement strengthens a behavior and increases the likelihood that it will be repeated.

What Pavlov did for classical conditioning, the Harvard psychologist B. F. Skinner did for operant conditioning.[40] Skinner argued that creating pleasing consequences to follow specific forms of behavior would increase the frequency of that behavior. He demonstrated that people will most likely engage in desired behaviors if they are positively reinforced for doing so; that rewards are most effective if they immediately follow the desired response; and that behavior that is not rewarded, or is punished, is less likely to be repeated. For example, we know a professor who places a mark by a student's name each time the student makes a contribution to class discussions. Operant conditioning would argue that this practice is motivating because it conditions a student to expect a reward (earning class credit) each time she demonstrates a specific behavior (speaking up in class). The concept of operant conditioning was part of Skinner's broader concept of **behaviorism**, which argues that behavior follows stimuli in a relatively unthinking manner. In Skinner's form of radical behaviorism, concepts such as feelings, thoughts, and other states of mind are rejected as causes of behavior. In short, people learn to associate stimulus and response, but their conscious awareness of this association is irrelevant.[41]

You see apparent illustrations of operant conditioning everywhere. For example, any situation in which it is either explicitly stated or implicitly suggested that reinforcements are contingent on some action on your part involves the use of operant learning. Your instructor says that if you want a high grade in the course, you must supply correct answers on the test. A commissioned salesperson wanting to earn a sizable income finds that doing so is contingent on generating high sales in her territory. Of course, the linkage can also work to teach the individual to engage in behaviors that work against the best interests of the organization. Assume that your boss tells you that if you will work overtime during the next 3-week busy season you'll be compensated for it at your next performance appraisal. However, when performance-appraisal time comes, you find that you are given no positive reinforcement for your overtime work. The next time your boss asks you to work overtime, what will you do? You'll probably decline! Your behavior can be explained by operant conditioning: If a behavior fails to be positively reinforced, the probability that the behavior will be repeated declines.

Toyota Motor Corporation applies social learning theory in teaching employees skills they need to meet the company's high standards of quality and efficiency. At its new Global Production Center training facility in Toyota City, Japan, employees from factories around the world learn production techniques through observation and direct experience. Trainees first watch computerized "visual manuals" to learn basic skills. Then, under the tutelage of an experienced production master, they practice the skills. In this photo, a trainer (left) models a spray-painting technique while a trainee practices the skill.

Social Learning   Individuals can learn by observing what happens to other people and just by being told about something as well as through direct experiences. For example, much of what we have learned comes from watching models—parents, teachers, peers, motion picture and television performers, bosses, and so forth. This view that we can learn through both observation and direct experience is called **social-learning theory**.[42]

Although social-learning theory is an extension of operant conditioning—that is, it assumes that behavior is a function of consequences—it also acknowledges the existence of observational learning and the importance of perception in learning. People respond to how they perceive and define consequences, not to the objective consequences themselves.

The influence of models is central to the social-learning viewpoint. Four processes have been found to determine the influence that a model will have on an individual:

1. **Attentional processes.**   People learn from a model only when they recognize and pay attention to its critical features. We tend to be most influenced by models that are attractive, repeatedly available, important to us, or similar to us in our estimation.
2. **Retention processes.**   A model's influence depends on how well the individual remembers the model's action after the model is no longer readily available.
3. **Motor reproduction processes.**   After a person has seen a new behavior by observing the model, the watching must be converted to doing. This process then demonstrates that the individual can perform the modeled activities.

operant conditioning   *A type of conditioning in which desired voluntary behavior leads to a reward or prevents a punishment.*

behaviorism   *A theory that argues that behavior follows stimuli in a relatively unthinking manner.*

social-learning theory   *The view that people can learn through observation and direct experience.*

4. **Reinforcement processes.** Individuals are motivated to exhibit the modeled behavior if positive incentives or rewards are provided. Behaviors that are positively reinforced are given more attention, learned better, and performed more often.

Shaping: A Managerial Tool

Because learning takes place on the job as well as prior to it, managers are concerned with how they can teach employees to behave in ways that most benefit the organization. When we attempt to mold individuals by guiding their learning in graduated steps, we are **shaping behavior**.

Consider a situation in which an employee's behavior is significantly different from that sought by management. If management rewarded the individual only when he showed desirable responses, there might be very little reinforcement taking place. In such a case, shaping offers a logical approach toward achieving the desired behavior.

We *shape* behavior by systematically reinforcing each successive step that moves the individual closer to the desired response. If an employee who has chronically been a half-hour late for work comes in only 20 minutes late, we can reinforce that improvement. Reinforcement would increase as responses more closely approximated the desired behavior.

Methods of Shaping Behavior   There are four ways to shape behavior: through positive reinforcement, negative reinforcement, punishment, and extinction.

Following a response with something pleasant is called *positive reinforcement*. This would describe, for instance, a boss who praises an employee for a job well done. Following a response by the termination or withdrawal of something unpleasant is called *negative reinforcement*. If your college instructor asks a question and you don't know the answer, looking through your lecture notes is likely

Define shaping *and show how it can be used in OB.*

MYTH OR SCIENCE?

"You Can't Teach an Old Dog New Tricks!"

*t*his statement is false. It reflects the widely held stereotype that older workers have difficulty adapting to new methods and techniques. Studies consistently demonstrate that older employees are perceived as being relatively inflexible, resistant to change, and less willing and able to be trained than their younger counterparts.[43] But these perceptions are mostly wrong.

Evidence does indicate that older workers (typically defined as people aged 50 and over) are less confident of their learning abilities (perhaps due to acceptance of societal stereotypes). Moreover, older workers do seem to be somewhat less efficient in acquiring complex or demanding skills, and, on average, they are not as fast in terms of reaction time or in solving problems. That is, they may take longer to train. However, once trained, research indicates that older workers actually learn more than their younger counterparts, and they are better at transferring what they have learned to the job.[44] And age actually improves some intellectual abilities, such as verbal ability, and older brains are packed with more so-called expert knowledge—meaning they tend to have better outlines for how to solve problems.[45]

The ability to acquire the skills, knowledge, or behavior necessary to perform a job at a given level—that is, trainability—has been the subject of much research. And the evidence indicates that there are differences between people in their trainability. A number of individual-difference factors (such as low ability and reduced motivation) have been found to impede learning and training outcomes. However, age has not been found to influence these outcomes. In fact, older employees actually benefit more from training. Still, the stereotypes persist.[46] ■

to preclude your being called on. This is a negative reinforcement because you have learned that looking busily through your notes prevents the instructor from calling on you. *Punishment* is causing an unpleasant condition in an attempt to eliminate an undesirable behavior. Giving an employee a 2-day suspension from work without pay for showing up drunk is an example of punishment. Eliminating any reinforcement that is maintaining a behavior is called *extinction*. When the behavior is not reinforced, it tends to be gradually extinguished. College instructors who wish to discourage students from asking questions in class can eliminate this behavior in their students by ignoring those who raise their hands to ask questions. Hand raising will become extinct when it is invariably met with an absence of reinforcement.

Both positive and negative reinforcement result in learning. They strengthen a response and increase the probability of repetition. In the preceding illustrations, praise strengthens and increases the behavior of doing a good job because praise is desired. The behavior of "looking busy" is similarly strengthened and increased by its terminating the undesirable consequence of being called on by the teacher. However, both punishment and extinction weaken behavior and tend to decrease its subsequent frequency. In shaping behavior, a critical issue is the timing of reinforcements. This is an issue we'll consider now.

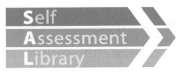

HOW GOOD AM I AT DISCIPLINING OTHERS?

In the Self-Assessment Library (available on CD or online), take assessment II.B.5 (How Good Am I at Disciplining Others?).

Schedules of Reinforcement   The two major types of reinforcement schedules are *continuous* and *intermittent*. A **continuous reinforcement** schedule reinforces the desired behavior each and every time it is demonstrated. Take, for example, the case of someone who historically has had trouble arriving at work on time. Every time he is not tardy, his manager might compliment him on his desirable behavior. With **intermittent reinforcement**, on the other hand, not every instance of the desirable behavior is reinforced, but reinforcement is given often enough to make the behavior worth repeating. This latter schedule can be compared to the workings of a slot machine, which people will continue to play even when they know it is adjusted to give a considerable return to the casino. The intermittent payoffs occur just often enough to reinforce the behavior of slipping in coins and pulling the handle. Evidence indicates that the intermittent, or varied, form of reinforcement tends to promote more resistance to extinction than does the continuous form.[47]

An intermittent reinforcement can be of a ratio or interval type. *Ratio schedules* depend on how many responses the subject makes. The individual is reinforced after giving a certain number of specific types of behavior. *Interval schedules* depend on how much time has passed since the previous reinforcement. With interval schedules, the individual is reinforced on the first appropriate

---

shaping behavior   *Systematically reinforcing each successive step that moves an individual closer to the desired response.*

continuous reinforcement   *Reinforcing a desired behavior each time it is demonstrated.*

intermittent reinforcement   *Reinforcing a desired behavior often enough to make the behavior worth repeating but not every time it is demonstrated.*

behavior after a particular time has elapsed. A reinforcement can also be classified as fixed or variable.

When rewards are spaced at uniform time intervals, the reinforcement schedule is a **fixed-interval schedule**. The critical variable is time, which is held constant. This is the predominant schedule for most salaried workers in North America. When you get your paycheck on a weekly, semimonthly, monthly, or other predetermined time basis, you're rewarded on a fixed-interval reinforcement schedule.

If rewards are distributed in time so that reinforcements are unpredictable, the schedule is a **variable-interval schedule**. When an instructor advises her class that pop quizzes will be given during the term (the exact number of which is unknown to the students) and the quizzes will account for 20 percent of the term grade, she is using a variable-interval schedule. Similarly, a series of randomly timed unannounced visits to a company office by the corporate audit staff is an example of a variable-interval schedule.

In a **fixed-ratio schedule**, after a fixed or constant number of responses are given, a reward is initiated. For example, a piece-rate incentive plan is a fixed-ratio schedule; the employee receives a reward based on the number of work pieces generated. If the piece rate for a zipper installer in a dressmaking factory is $5 per dozen, the reinforcement (money in this case) is fixed to the number of zippers sewn into garments. After every dozen is sewn in, the installer has earned another $5.

When the reward varies relative to the behavior of the individual, he or she is said to be reinforced on a **variable-ratio schedule**. Salespeople on commission are examples of individuals on such a reinforcement schedule. On some occasions, they may make a sale after only 2 calls on a potential customer. On other occasions, they might need to make 20 or more calls to secure a sale. The reward, then, is variable in relation to the number of successful calls the salesperson makes. Exhibit 2-3 summarizes the schedules of reinforcement.

Reinforcement Schedules and Behavior Continuous reinforcement schedules can lead to early satiation, and under this schedule, behavior tends to weaken rapidly when reinforcers are withheld. However, continuous reinforcers are appropriate for newly emitted, unstable, or low-frequency responses. In contrast, intermittent reinforcers preclude early satiation because they don't follow every response. They are appropriate for stable or high-frequency responses.

In general, variable schedules tend to lead to higher performance than fixed schedules (see Exhibit 2-4). For example, as noted previously, most

Exhibit **2-3**	Schedules of Reinforcement		
Reinforcement Schedule	**Nature of Reinforcement**	**Effect on Behavior**	**Example**
Continuous	Reward given after each desired behavior	Fast learning of new behavior but rapid extinction	Compliments
Fixed-interval	Reward given at fixed time intervals	Average and irregular performance with rapid extinction	Weekly paychecks
Variable-interval	Reward given at variable time intervals	Moderately high and stable performance with slow extinction	Pop quizzes
Fixed ratio	Reward given at fixed amounts of output	High and stable performance attained quickly but also with rapid extinction	Piece-rate pay
Variable-ratio	Reward given at variable amounts of output	Very high performance with slow extinction	Commissioned sales

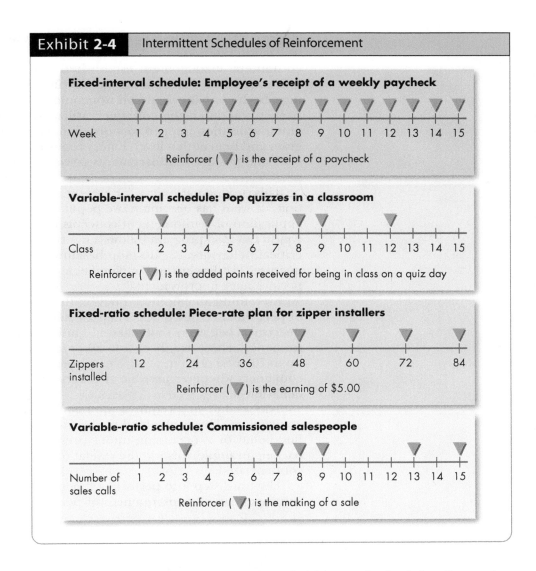

Exhibit 2-4 | Intermittent Schedules of Reinforcement

Fixed-interval schedule: Employee's receipt of a weekly paycheck

| Week | 1 | 2 | 3 | 4 | 5 | 6 | 7 | 8 | 9 | 10 | 11 | 12 | 13 | 14 | 15 |

Reinforcer (▼) is the receipt of a paycheck

Variable-interval schedule: Pop quizzes in a classroom

| Class | 1 | 2 | 3 | 4 | 5 | 6 | 7 | 8 | 9 | 10 | 11 | 12 | 13 | 14 | 15 |

Reinforcer (▼) is the added points received for being in class on a quiz day

Fixed-ratio schedule: Piece-rate plan for zipper installers

| Zippers installed | 12 | 24 | 36 | 48 | 60 | 72 | 84 |

Reinforcer (▼) is the earning of $5.00

Variable-ratio schedule: Commissioned salespeople

| Number of sales calls | 1 | 2 | 3 | 4 | 5 | 6 | 7 | 8 | 9 | 10 | 11 | 12 | 13 | 14 | 15 |

Reinforcer (▼) is the making of a sale

employees in organizations are paid on fixed-interval schedules. But such a schedule does not clearly link performance and rewards. The reward is given for time spent on the job rather than for a specific response (performance). In contrast, variable-interval schedules generate high rates of response and more stable and consistent behavior because of the high correlation between performance and reward and because of the uncertainty involved—the employee tends to be more alert because there is a surprise factor.

Behavior Modification   A now-classic study took place a number of years ago with freight packers at Emery Air Freight (now part of FedEx).[48] Emery's management wanted packers to use freight containers for shipments whenever possible because of specific economic savings. When packers were asked about the percentage of shipments contained, the standard reply was

fixed-interval schedule   *Spacing rewards at uniform time intervals.*

variable-interval schedule   *Distributing rewards in time so that reinforcements are unpredictable.*

fixed-ratio schedule   *Initiating rewards after a fixed or constant number of responses.*

variable-ratio schedule   *Varying the reward relative to the behavior of the individual.*

90 percent. An analysis by Emery found, however, that the actual container utilization rate was only 45 percent. In order to encourage employees to use containers, management established a program of feedback and positive reinforcements. Each packer was instructed to keep a checklist of daily packings, both containerized and noncontainerized. At the end of each day, the packer computed the container utilization rate. Almost unbelievably, container utilization jumped to more than 90 percent on the first day of the program and held at that level. Emery reported that this simple program of feedback and positive reinforcements saved the company $2 million over a 3-year period.

This program at Emery Air Freight illustrates the use of behavior modification, or what has become more popularly called **OB Mod**.[49] It represents the application of reinforcement concepts to individuals in the work setting. The typical OB Mod program follows a five-step problem-solving model: (1) identify critical behaviors; (2) develop baseline data; (3) identify behavioral consequences; (4) develop and implement an intervention strategy; and (5) evaluate performance improvement.[50]

Everything an employee does on the job is not equally important in terms of performance outcomes. The first step in OB Mod, therefore, is to identify the critical behaviors that make a significant impact on the employee's job performance. These are those 5 to 10 percent of behaviors that may account for up to 70 or 80 percent of each employee's performance. Freight packers using containers whenever possible at Emery Air Freight is an example of a critical behavior.

The second step requires the manager to develop some baseline performance data. This is obtained by determining the number of times the identified behavior is occurring under present conditions. In the Emery freight-packing example, this was the revelation that 45 percent of all shipments were containerized.

The third step is to perform a functional analysis to identify the behavioral contingencies or consequences of performance. This tells the manager the

Convenience-store retailer 7-Eleven, Inc., uses OB Mod to strengthen desirable performance behaviors. Using employee performance software, 7-Eleven measures the efforts of 2,400 store managers and 30,000 employees at company-owned stores in Canada and the United States. The company ties employee compensation to performance outcomes based on 7-Eleven's five fundamental strategic initiatives—product assortment, value, quality, service, and cleanliness—as well as for meeting goals set for new products. The system identifies top performers and rewards them with incentive bonuses.

antecedent cues that emit the behavior and the consequences that are currently maintaining it. At Emery Air Freight, social norms and the greater difficulty in packing containers were the antecedent cues. This encouraged the practice of packing items separately. Moreover, the consequences for continuing the behavior, prior to the OB Mod intervention, were social acceptance and escaping more demanding work.

Once the functional analysis is complete, the manager is ready to develop and implement an intervention strategy to strengthen desirable performance behaviors and weaken undesirable behaviors. The appropriate strategy will entail changing some elements of the performance–reward linkage—structure, processes, technology, groups, or the task—with the goal of making high-level performance more rewarding. In the Emery example, the work technology was altered to require the keeping of a checklist. The checklist plus the computation, at the end of the day, of a container-utilization rate acted to reinforce the desirable behavior of using containers.

The final step in OB Mod is to evaluate performance improvement. In the Emery intervention, the immediate improvement in the container-utilization rate demonstrated that behavioral change took place. That it rose to 90 percent and held at that level further indicates that learning took place. That is, the employees underwent a relatively permanent change in behavior.

A number of organizations have used OB Mod to improve employee productivity; to reduce errors, absenteeism, tardiness, and accident rates; and to improve friendliness toward customers.[51] For instance, a clothing manufacturer saved $60,000 in 1 year due to fewer absences. A packing firm improved productivity 16 percent, cut errors by 40 percent, and reduced accidents by more than 43 percent—resulting in savings of over $1 million. A bank successfully used OB Mod to increase the friendliness of its tellers, which led to a demonstrable improvement in customer satisfaction.

Problems with OB Mod and Reinforcement Theory   Although the effectiveness of reinforcements in the form of rewards and punishments has a lot of support in the literature, that doesn't necessarily mean that Skinner was right or that OB Mod is the best way to reward people. What if the power of reinforcements isn't due to operant conditioning or behaviorism? One problem with behaviorism is, as research shows, that thoughts and feelings immediately follow environmental stimuli, even those explicitly meant to shape behavior. This is contrary to the assumptions of behaviorism and OB Mod, which assume that people's innermost thoughts and feelings in response to the environment are irrelevant.

Think about praise from a supervisor. For example, assume your course instructor compliments you for asking a good question. A behaviorist would argue that this shapes your behavior because you find the stimulus (the compliment) pleasant and therefore respond by attempting to ask other questions that will generate the same reward. However, imagine, for example, that you had to weigh the pleasant feelings produced by your professor's praise against the snickers of jealous classmates who whispered "brown noser." Your choice of what to do would likely be dictated by weighing the value of these stimuli, which may be a rather complex mental process involving thinking and feeling.

OB Mod   *The application of reinforcement concepts to individuals in the work setting.*

Also, is it really shaping if the compliment was given without an intention of molding behavior? Isn't it perhaps overly restrictive to view all stimuli as motivated to obtain a particular response? Is the only reason we tell someone we love them because we wish to obtain a reward or to mold their behavior?

Because of these problems, among others, operant conditioning and behaviorism have been superseded by other approaches that emphasize cognitive processes.[52] There is no denying, though, the contribution of these theories to our understanding of human behavior.

Global Implications

As you will see, there may be no global or cross-cultural research on some of the topics we discuss in a chapter, and this chapter is no exception. We therefore confine our comments here to areas where there has been the most cross-cultural research: (1) How does research on intellectual abilities generalize across cultures? (2) Do biographical characteristics such as gender and age operate similarly across cultures? and (3) Do the principles of learning work in different cultures?

6 Show how culture affects our understanding of intellectual abilities, biographical characteristics, and learning.

Intellectual Abilities

Evidence strongly supports the ideas that the structures and measures of intellectual abilities generalize across cultures. Thus, someone in Venezuela or Sudan does not have a different set of mental abilities than a U.S. or Czech worker. Moreover, data from across many cultures support the finding that specific mental abilities indicate a higher-order factor we call general mental ability (GMA). There is some evidence that IQ scores vary to some degree across cultures, but those differences are much smaller when we consider educational and economic differences.[53]

Biographical Characteristics

Obviously, some biographical characteristics vary across cultures. Some cultures are more racially homogenous than others, and the average age of citizens varies across countries (for example, in Italy and Japan, a far greater percentage of the population is over 65 than in India or China). That doesn't mean, however, that the relationships we've described between age and performance, or between gender and turnover, are different across cultures. Frankly, we don't have much good scientific evidence on whether, for example, gender or age affects absenteeism similarly across cultures. One Accenture survey of U.S. managers in eight countries revealed some surprising differences. Compared with British managers, female managers in the Philippines believed that their country was more supportive of women's advancement into leadership positions.[54] While such survey results are interesting, they don't substitute for systematic study. Thus, we really don't know the degree to which gender (or other biographical factors) varies in importance in predicting OB outcomes in different countries.

OB researchers don't always answer the questions we want them to answer. AACSB International, the largest accreditation association for business schools, frequently faults business schools for not producing research that's relevant to managers. Though we think OB research has a lot to offer, it's not perfect either, and this is a case in point.

Learning

There is little research on how theories of learning generalize to organizations and employees in different cultures. This is due in part to the fact that much of the research on learning theories is fairly old, conducted before there was a lot of cross-cultural research. For example, two major recent reviews of cross-cultural research in OB did not mention learning theories, reinforcement theory, or behavioral modification. That doesn't mean these theories are necessarily culturally bound; it means we really don't yet know one way or the other.

Summary and Implications for Managers

This chapter looked at three individual variables—ability, biographical characteristics, and learning. Let's now try to summarize what we found and consider their importance for a manager who is trying to understand organizational behavior.

Ability Ability directly influences an employee's level of performance. Given management's desire to get high-performing employees, what can be done?

First, an effective selection process will improve the fit. A job analysis will provide information about jobs currently being done and the abilities that individuals need to perform the jobs adequately. Applicants can then be tested, interviewed, and evaluated on the degree to which they possess the necessary abilities.

Second, promotion and transfer decisions affecting individuals already in the organization's employ should reflect the abilities of candidates. As with new employees, care should be taken to assess critical abilities that incumbents will need in the job and to match those requirements with the organization's human resources.

Third, the fit can be improved by fine-tuning the job to better match an incumbent's abilities. Often, modifications can be made in the job that, while not having a significant impact on the job's basic activities, better adapt it to the specific talents of a given employee. Examples would be changing some of the equipment used or reorganizing tasks within a group of employees.

Biographical Characteristics Biographical characteristics are readily observable to managers. However, just because they're observable doesn't mean they should be explicitly used in management decisions. We also need to be aware of implicit biases we or other managers may have.

Learning Any observable change in behavior is *prima facie* evidence that learning has taken place. Positive reinforcement is a powerful tool for modifying behavior. By identifying and rewarding performance-enhancing behaviors, management increases the likelihood that those behaviors will be repeated. Our knowledge about learning further suggests that reinforcement is a more effective tool than punishment. Although punishment eliminates undesired behavior more quickly than negative reinforcement does, punished behavior tends to be only temporarily suppressed rather than permanently changed. And punishment may produce unpleasant side effects, such as lower morale and higher absenteeism or turnover. In addition, the recipients of punishment tend to become resentful of the punisher. Managers, therefore, are advised to use reinforcement rather than punishment.

Point ⟫⟪ Counterpoint

ALL HUMAN BEHAVIOR IS LEARNED[55]

*h*uman beings are essentially blank slates that are shaped by their environment. B. F. Skinner, in fact, summarized his belief in the power of the environment to shape behavior when he said, "Give me a child at birth and I can make him into anything you want."

Following are some of the societal mechanisms that exist because of this belief in the power of learned behavior:

Role of parenting.   We place a great deal of importance on the role of mothers and fathers in the raising of children. We believe, for instance, that children raised without fathers will be hindered by their lack of a male role model. And parents who have continual run-ins with the law risk having government authorities take their children from them. The latter action is typically taken because society believes that irresponsible parents don't provide the proper learning environment for their children.

Importance of education.   Most advanced societies invest heavily in the education of their young. They typically provide 10 or more years of free education. And in countries such as the United States, going on to college after finishing high school has become the norm rather than the exception. This investment in education is undertaken because it is seen as a way for young people to learn knowledge and skills.

Job training.   For individuals who don't go on to college, most will pursue job-training programs to develop specific work-related skills. They'll take courses to become proficient as auto mechanics, medical assistants, and the like. Similarly, people who seek to become skilled trades workers will pursue apprenticeships as carpenters, electricians, or pipe fitters. In addition, business firms invest billions of dollars each year in training and education to keep current employees' skills up-to-date.

Manipulation of rewards.   Organizations design complex compensation programs to reward employees fairly for their work performance. But these programs are also designed with the intention to motivate employees. They are designed to encourage employees to engage in behaviors that management desires and to extinguish behaviors that management wants to discourage. Salary levels, for instance, typically reward employee loyalty, encourage the learning of new skills, and motivate individuals to assume greater responsibilities in the organization.

These mechanisms all exist and flourish because organizations and society believe that people can learn and change their behavior.

*a*lthough people can learn and can be influenced by their environment, far too little attention has been paid to the role that evolution has played in shaping human behavior. Evolutionary psychology tells us that human beings are basically hardwired at birth. We arrive on Earth with ingrained traits, honed and adapted over millions of years, that shape and limit our behavior.

All living creatures are "designed" by specific combinations of genes. As a result of natural selection, genes that produce faulty design features are eliminated. Characteristics that help a species survive tend to endure and get passed on to future generations. Many of the characteristics that helped early *Homo sapiens* survive live on today and influence the way we behave. Here are a few examples:

Emotions.   Stone Age people, at the mercy of wild predators and natural disasters, learned to trust their instincts. Those with the best instincts survived. Today, emotions remain the first screen to all information we receive. We know we are supposed to act rationally, but our emotions can never be fully suppressed.

Risk avoidance.   Ancient hunter-gatherers who survived were not big risk takers. They were cautious. Today, when we're comfortable with the status quo, we typically see any change as risky and, thus, tend to resist it.

Stereotyping.   To prosper in a clan society, Early humans had to quickly "size up" whom they could trust or not trust. Those who could do this quickly were more likely to survive. Today, like our ancestors, we naturally stereotype people based on very small pieces of evidence, mainly their looks and a few readily apparent behaviors.

Male competitiveness.   Males in early human societies frequently had to engage in games or battles in which there were clear winners and losers. Winners attained high status, were viewed as more attractive mates, and were more likely to reproduce. The ingrained male desire to do public battle and display virility and competence persists today.

Evolutionary psychology challenges the notion that people are free to change their behavior if trained or motivated. It doesn't say that we can't engage in learning or exercise free will. What it does say is that nature predisposes us to act and interact in particular ways in particular circumstances. As a result, we find that people in organizational settings often behave in ways that don't appear to be beneficial to themselves or their employers.

Case Incident 2

PROFESSIONAL SPORTS: REWARDING AND PUNISHING THE SAME BEHAVIOR?

Baseball Commissioner Bud Selig has felt the heat for some time, and it's not the kind a 90-mile-per-hour fastball brings. When allegations of steroid use among some of Major League Baseball's biggest stars first surfaced, Selig argued that the league's policy on steroids was "as good as any in professional sports." The policy? Random drug testing, with a 10-day suspension for first-time offenders. Congress and the general public were not satisfied. So, Selig announced a tougher "three strikes and you're out" policy: A 50-game suspension for a first offense, a 100-game suspension for a second, and a permanent ban from baseball for a third. Players may incur fines as well. Other professional leagues have followed suit. The PGA Tour even announced its own drug-testing policy, which began in the 2008 season.

But here's the problem: The same system that punishes those who take performance-enhancing drugs may also reinforce such behavior. And the current repercussions for players may not serve as a strong deterrent. A fine of $10,000 or a 10-day suspension may be a relatively minor setback compared to the millions that can be earned for becoming an all-star power hitter.

Take Rafael Palmeiro as an example. He tested positive for steroids. Though Palmeiro insists he took them inadvertently, the type found in his system (stanozolol) is not the kind found in dietary supplements. His punishment? Palmeiro received a 10-day suspension and forfeited $167,000 of his $3 million salary, and a banner celebrating his 3,000th hit was removed from Camden Yards.

Now consider all-time home-run king Barry Bonds. Bonds has set records, and made millions, by hitting lots of home runs. Although there are widespread and detailed reports that he has taken performance-enhancing drugs (particularly between 1998 and 2003, when federal agents raided the company that was allegedly supplying him), the allegations have never been enough to get him banned from baseball. His fame and fortune continue. And the rewards of hitting home runs are not limited to the players. Revenues from increased game attendance and sports merchandise, as well as a team's rising popularity and success, are incentives for players to perform at high levels and for owners to reward them.

In the NFL, the situation is not much different. For example, Oakland Raiders safety Jarrod Cooper tested positive for steroids before the 2007–2008 season. His penalty? Suspension from the preseason games and the first four regular-season games. Although a four-game suspension can mean a large loss of income (the average NFL salary tops $1 million), such punishment still may not prevent steroid use because the money that can be made from endorsements and winning games can far exceed players' salaries.

It appears that professional sports may be trying to have their cake and eat it, too. As we have seen, behavior that may lead individuals and teams to fame and fortune may also be behavior that demands punishment.

Questions

1. What type of reinforcement schedule does random drug testing represent? Is this type of schedule typically effective or ineffective?

2. What are some examples of behaviors in typical organizations that supervisors reward but that may actually be detrimental to others or to the organization as a whole? As a manager, what might you do to try to avoid this quandary?

3. If you were the commissioner of baseball, what steps would you take to try to reduce the use of steroids in baseball? Is punishment likely to be the most effective deterrent? Why or why not?

4. Is it ever okay to allow potentially unethical behaviors, which on the surface may benefit organizations, to persist? Why or why not?

Source: "Bonds Exposed," *Sports Illustrated,* March 7, 2006; M. Lewis, "Absolutely, Power Corrupts," *New York Times Magazine,* April 24, 2005, p. 46; and "Former K-State Wildcat Jarrod Cooper Violates NFL Steroids Policy," *Kansas City Star,* July 20, 2007.

Endnotes

1. Based on P. Kiefer, "On the Canals, a Woman Paddles Against the Tide," *New York Times,* May 14, 2007, pp. A1, A4.

2. L. S. Gottfredson, "The Challenge and Promise of Cognitive Career Assessment," *Journal of Career Assessment* 11, no. 2 (2003), pp. 115–135.

3. M. D. Dunnette, "Aptitudes, Abilities, and Skills," in M. D. Dunnette (ed.), *Handbook of Industrial and Organizational Psychology* (Chicago: Rand McNally, 1976), pp. 478–483.

4. J. F. Salgado, N. Anderson, S. Moscoso, C. Bertua, F. de Fruyt, and J. P. Rolland, "A Meta-analytic Study of General Mental Ability Validity for Different Occupations in the European Community," *Journal of Applied Psychology,* December 2003, pp. 1068–1081; and F. L. Schmidt and

J. E. Hunter, "Select on Intelligence," in E. A. Locke (ed.), *Handbook of Principles of Organizational Behavior* (Malden, MA: Blackwell, 2004).

5. Y. Ganzach, "Intelligence and Job Satisfaction," *Academy of Management Journal* 41, no. 5 (1998), pp. 526–539; and Y. Ganzach, "Intelligence, Education, and Facets of Job Satisfaction," *Work and Occupations* 30, no. 1 (2003), pp. 97–122.

6. E. A. Fleishman, "Evaluating Physical Abilities Required by Jobs," *Personnel Administrator*, June 1979, pp. 82–92.

7. K. Greene, "Older Workers Can Get a Raw Deal—Some Employers Admit to Promoting, Challenging Their Workers Less," *Wall Street Journal*, April 10, 2003, p. D2; and K. A. Wrenn and T. J. Maurer, "Beliefs About Older Workers' Learning and Development Behavior in Relation to Beliefs About Malleability of Skills, Age-Related Decline, and Control," *Journal of Applied Social Psychology* 34, no. 2 (2004), pp. 223–242.

8. D. R. Davies, G. Matthews, and C. S. K. Wong, "Ageing and Work," in C. L. Cooper and I. T. Robertson (eds.), *International Review of Industrial and Organizational Psychology*, vol. 6 (Chichester, UK: Wiley, 1991), pp. 183–187.

9. R. D. Hackett, "Age, Tenure, and Employee Absenteeism," *Human Relations*, July 1990, pp. 601–619.

10. Cited in K. Labich, "The New Unemployed," *Fortune*, March 8, 1993, p. 43.

11. See G. M. McEvoy and W. F. Cascio, "Cumulative Evidence of the Relationship Between Employee Age and Job Performance," *Journal of Applied Psychology*, February 1989, pp. 11–17; and F. L. Schmidt and J. E. Hunter, "The Validity and Utility of Selection Methods in Personnel Psychology: Practical and Theoretical Implications of 85 Years of Research Findings," *Psychological Bulletin* 124 (1998), pp. 262–274.

12. See, for instance, F. J. Landy, et al., *Alternatives to Chronological Age in Determining Standards of Suitability for Public Safety Jobs* (University Park, PA: Center for Applied Behavioral Sciences, Pennsylvania State University, 1992).

13. R. Lee and E. R. Wilbur, "Age, Education, Job Tenure, Salary, Job Characteristics, and Job Satisfaction: A Multivariate Analysis," *Human Relations*, August 1985, pp. 781–791.

14. K. M. Kacmar and G. R. Ferris, "Theoretical and Methodological Considerations in the Age–Job Satisfaction Relationship," *Journal of Applied Psychology*, April 1989, pp. 201–207; and W. A. Hochwarter, G. R. Ferris, P. L. Perrewe, L. A. Witt, and C. Kiewitz, "A Note on the Nonlinearity of the Age–Job Satisfaction Relationship," *Journal of Applied Social Psychology*, June 2001, pp. 1223–1237.

15. See E. M. Weiss, G. Kemmler, E. A. Deisenhammer, W. W. Fleischhacker, and M. Delazer, "Sex Differences in Cognitive Functions," *Personality and Individual Differences*, September 2003, pp. 863–875; and A. F. Jorm, K. J. Anstey, H. Christensen, and B. Rodgers, "Gender Differences in Cognitive Abilities: The Mediating Role of Health State and Health Habits," *Intelligence*, January 2004, pp. 7–23.

16. See M. M. Black and E. W. Holden, "The Impact of Gender on Productivity and Satisfaction Among Medical School Psychologists," *Journal of Clinical Psychology in Medical Settings*, March 1998, pp. 117–131.

17. S. Shellenbarger, "More Job Seekers Put Family Needs First," *Wall Street Journal*, November 15, 1991, p. B1.

18. R. W. Griffeth, P. W. Hom, and S. Gaertner, "A Meta-analysis of Antecedents and Correlates of Employee Turnover: Update, Moderator Tests, and Research Implications for the Next Millennium," *Journal of Management* 26, no. 3 (2000), pp. 463–488.

19. See, for instance, K. D. Scott and E. L. McClellan, "Gender Differences in Absenteeism," *Public Personnel Management*, Summer 1990, pp. 229–253; and A. VandenHeuvel and M. Wooden, "Do Explanations of Absenteeism Differ for Men and Women?" *Human Relations*, November 1995, pp. 1309–1329.

20. See, for instance, M. Tait, M. Y. Padgett, and T. T. Baldwin, "Job and Life Satisfaction: A Reevaluation of the Strength of the Relationship and Gender Effects as a Function of the Date of the Study," *Journal of Applied Psychology*, June 1989, pp. 502–507; and M. B. Grover, "Daddy Stress," *Forbes*, September 6, 1999, pp. 202–208.

21. J. M. Sacco, C. R. Scheu, A. M. Ryan, and N. Schmitt, "An Investigation of Race and Sex Similarity Effects in Interviews: A Multilevel Approach to Relational Demography," *Journal of Applied Psychology* 88, no. 5 (2003), pp. 852–865; and G. N. Powell and D. A. Butterfield, "Exploring the Influence of Decision Makers' Race and Gender on Actual Promotions to Top Management," *Personnel Psychology* 55, no. 2 (2002), pp. 397–428.

22. D. A. Kravitz and S. L. Klineberg, "Reactions to Two Versions of Affirmative Action Among Whites, Blacks, and Hispanics," *Journal of Applied Psychology* 85, no. 4 (2000), pp. 597–611.

23. J. M. Sacco, C. R. Scheu, A. M. Ryan, and N. Schmitt, "An Investigation of Race and Sex Similarity Effects in Interviews: A Multilevel Approach to Relational Demography," *Journal of Applied Psychology* 88, no. 5 (2003), pp. 852–865.

24. P. Bobko, P. L. Roth, and D. Potosky, "Derivation and Implications of a Meta-Analytic Matrix Incorporating Cognitive Ability, Alternative Predictors, and Job Performance," *Personnel Psychology*, Autumn 1999, pp. 561–589.

25. M. J. Ree, T. R. Carretta, and J. R. Steindl, "Cognitive Ability," in N. Anderson, D. S. Ones, H. K. Sinangil, and C. Viswesvaran (eds.). *Handbook of Industrial, Work, and Organizational Psychology*, vol. 1 (London: Sage Publications, 2001), pp. 219–232.

26. See J. P. Rushton and A. R. Jenson, "Thirty Years of Research on Race Differences in Cognitive Ability," *Psychology, Public Policy, and the Law* 11, no. 2 (2005), pp. 235–295; and R. E. Nisbett, "Heredity, Environment, and Race Differences in IQ: A Commentary on Rushton and Jensen (2005)," *Psychology, Public Policy, and the Law* 11, no. 2 (2005), pp. 302–310.

27. M. A. Quinones, J. K. Ford, and M. S. Teachout, "The Relationship Between Work Experience and Job Performance: A Conceptual and Meta-analytic Review," *Personnel Psychology*, Winter 1995, pp. 887–910.

28. I. R. Gellatly, "Individual and Group Determinants of Employee Absenteeism: Test of a Causal Model," *Journal of Organizational Behavior*, September 1995, pp. 469–485.

29. P. O. Popp and J. A. Belohlav, "Absenteeism in a Low Status Work Environment," *Academy of Management Journal*, September 1982, p. 681.

30. Griffeth, Hom, and Gaertner, "A Meta-analysis of Antecedents," pp. 463–488.

31. R. D. Gatewood and H. S. Field, *Human Resource Selection* (Chicago: Dryden Press, 1987).

32. J. A. Breaugh and D. L. Dossett, "The Effectiveness of Biodata for Predicting Turnover," paper presented at the National Academy of Management Conference, New Orleans, August 1987.

33. W. van Breukelen, R. van der Vlist, and H. Steensma, "Voluntary Employee Turnover: Combining Variables from the 'Traditional' Turnover Literature with the Theory of Planned Behavior," *Journal of Organizational Behavior* 25, no. 7 (2004), pp. 893–914.

34. M. Elias, "USA's Muslims Under a Cloud," *USA Today*, August 10, 2006, pp. 1D, 2D; and R. R. Hastings, "Muslims Seek Acknowledgement of Mainstream Americans," *HRWeek*, May 11, 2007, p. 1.

35. *HRC Corporate Equality Index*, 2006, www.hrc.org/cei; and R. R. Hastings, "Necessity Breeds Inclusion: Reconsidering 'Don't Ask, Don't Tell'," *HRWeek*, January 2007, pp. 1–2.

36. B. Leonard, "Transgender Issues Test Diversity Limits," *HRMagazine*, June 2007, pp. 32–34.

37. See H. M. Weiss, "Learning Theory and Industrial and Organizational Psychology," in M. D. Dunnette and L. M. Hough (eds.), *Handbook of Industrial & Organizational Psychology*, 2nd ed., vol. 1 (Palo Alto, CA: Consulting Psychologists Press, 1990), pp. 172–173.

38. W. McGehee, "Are We Using What We Know About Training? Learning Theory and Training," *Personnel Psychology*, Spring 1958, p. 2.

39. I. P. Pavlov, *The Work of the Digestive Glands*, trans. W. H. Thompson (London: Charles Griffin, 1902). See also the special issue of *American Psychologist*, September 1997, pp. 933–972, commemorating Pavlov's work.

40. B. F. Skinner, *Contingencies of Reinforcement* (East Norwalk, CT: Appleton-Century-Crofts, 1971).

41. J. A. Mills, *Control: A History of Behavioral Psychology* (New York: New York University Press, 2000).

42. A. Bandura, *Social Learning Theory* (Upper Saddle River, NJ: Prentice Hall, 1977).

43. T. Maurer, K. Wrenn, and E. Weiss, "Toward Understanding and Managing Stereotypical Beliefs About Older Workers' Ability and Desire for Learning and Development," *Research in Personnel and Human Resources Management* 22 (2003), pp. 253–285.

44. J. A. Colquitt, J. A. LePine, and R. A. Noe, "Toward an Integrative Theory of Training Motivation: A Meta-Analytic Path Analysis of 20 Years of Research," *Journal of Applied Psychology* 85, no. 5 (2000), pp. 678–707.

45. S. Begley, "The Upside of Aging," *New York Times*, February 16, 2007, pp. W1, W4.

46. Wrenn and Maurer, "Beliefs About Older Workers' Learning and Development Behavior," pp. 223–242.

47. A. D. Stajkovic and F. Luthans, "A Meta-analysis of the Effects of Organizational Behavior Modification on Task Performance, 1975–95," *Academy of Management Journal*, October 1997, pp. 1122–1149.

48. "At Emery Air Freight: Positive Reinforcement Boosts Performance," *Organizational Dynamics*, Winter 1973, pp. 41–50.

49. F. Luthans and R. Kreitner, *Organizational Behavior Modification and Beyond: An Operant and Social Learning Approach* (Glenview, IL: Scott, Foresman, 1985); Stajkovic and Luthans, "A Meta-Analysis of the Effects of Organizational Behavior Modification on Task Performance, 1975–95," pp. 1122–1149; and A. D. Stajkovic and F. Luthans, "Behavioral Management and Task Performance in Organizations: Conceptual Background, Meta-Analysis, and Test of Alternative Models," *Personnel Psychology*, Spring 2003, pp. 155–192.

50. Stajkovic and Luthans, "A Meta-analysis of the Effects of Organizational Behavior Modification on Task Performance, 1975–95," p. 1123.

51. See F. Luthans and A. D. Stajkovic, "Reinforce for Performance: The Need to Go Beyond Pay and Even Rewards," *Academy of Management Executive*, May 1999, pp. 49–57; and A. D. Stajkovic and F. Luthans, "Differential Effects of Incentive Motivators on Work Performance," *Academy of Management Journal* 44, no. 3 (2001), pp. 580–590.

52. E. A. Locke, "Beyond Determinism and Materialism, or Isn't It Time We Took Consciousness Seriously?" *Journal of Behavior Therapy & Experimental Psychiatry* 26, no. 3 (1995), pp. 265–273.

53. N. Barber, "Educational and Ecological Correlates of IQ: A Cross-National Investigation," *Intelligence* (May–Jun 2005), pp. 273–284.

54. S. Falk, "The Anatomy of the Glass Ceiling," *Accenture*, 2006, www.accenture.com.

55. Points in this argument are based on N. Nicholson, "How Hardwired Is Human Behavior?" *Harvard Business Review*, July–August 1998, pp. 135–147; and B. D. Pierce and R. White, "The Evolution of Social Structure: Why Biology Matters," *Academy of Management Review*, October 1999, pp. 843–853.

56. J. Stripling, "UF Requirement for Partner Benefits: You Must Have Sex," *Gainesville (Florida) Sun*, January 20, 2006, pp. 1A, 7A.

Attitudes and Job Satisfaction

Attitude isn't everything, but it's close.

—*New York Times* headline, August 6, 2006

After studying this chapter, you should be able to:

1 Contrast the three components of an attitude.

2 Summarize the relationship between attitudes and behavior.

3 Compare and contrast the major job attitudes.

4 Define *job satisfaction* and show how it can be measured.

5 Summarize the main causes of job satisfaction.

6 Identify four employee responses to dissatisfaction.

7 Show whether job satisfaction is a relevant concept in countries other than the United States.

*i*t seems that Google will spare no expense to keep its workers happy. Unlimited amounts of chef-prepared food all day. A huge gym with state-of-the-art equipment, including a climbing wall, a volleyball court, and two lap pools. A masseuse is there, too. On-site car washes, oil changes, haircuts, and dry cleaning. And free doctor checkups and free dental work, again on site. Child care next door and a backup child-care service in case the employee is running late.

Google: Is This a Great Place to Work or What?

Free transportation is the latest benefit. Silicon Valley, the location of Google's main operations, is home to some of the worst traffic in the United States. A recent survey of Silicon Valley residents indicated that traffic is their number-one concern—for the 10th straight year! So Google now provides its employees with free high-tech shuttle buses equipped with comfortable leather seats, bicycle racks, and wireless Internet access, powered by biodiesel engines. About one-quarter of Google's employees take advantage of the service. Riders can even sign up to receive alerts on their PCs and cellphones about changes in schedules or delays. The morning service starts at 5:05 A.M., and the evening run goes until 10:05 P.M.. During peak hours, pickups are as frequent as every 15 minutes. "We are basically running a small municipal transit agency," says Marty Lev, the Google director who oversees the program. Bent Hagemark, a software engineer, loves Google's shuttle so much he said, "If they cut the shuttle, it would be a disaster."

Although its free shuttle and other benefits programs have attracted the most attention, Google offers a host of other benefits, less flashy but no less valued, including:

- Automatic life insurance at two times annual salary
- For employees with 6 or more years of seniority, 25 vacation days per year
- For new parents, parental leave at 75 percent pay for 6 weeks and reimbursement for up to $500 for take-out meals during the first 4 weeks at home with the new baby
- Tuition reimbursement of $8,000 per calendar year
- A $2,000 bonus for referral of employees who are hired and stay at least 60 days
- A gift-matching program for employee contributions up to $3,000 per year to nonprofit organizations
- Reimbursement up to $5,000 to use toward adoption expenses

A recent survey suggested that of all the factors that might increase job satisfaction, employees believe benefits are the most important. Google seems to get that.[1] ■

*l*ike Google, many organizations are very concerned with the attitudes of their employees. In this chapter, we look at attitudes, their link to behavior, and how employees' satisfaction or dissatisfaction with their jobs affects the workplace.

What are your attitudes toward your job? Use the following Self-Assessment Library to determine your level of satisfaction with your current or past jobs.

HOW SATISFIED AM I WITH MY JOB?

In the Self-Assessment Library (available on CD or online), take assessment I.B.3 (How Satisfied Am I with My Job?) and then answer the following questions. If you currently do not have a job, answer the questions for your most recent job.

1. *How does your job satisfaction compare to that of others in your class who have taken the assessment?*
2. *Why do you think your satisfaction is higher or lower than average?*

Attitudes

Attitudes are evaluative statements—either favorable or unfavorable—about objects, people, or events. They reflect how we feel about something. When I say "I like my job," I am expressing my attitude about work.

Attitudes are complex. If you ask people about their attitude toward religion, Paris Hilton, or the organization they work for, you may get a simple response, but the reasons underlying the response are probably complex. In order to fully understand attitudes, we need to consider their fundamental properties or components.

> **1** Contrast the three components of an attitude.

What Are the Main Components of Attitudes?

Typically, researchers have assumed that attitudes have three components: cognition, affect, and behavior.[2] Let's look at each.

The statement "my pay is low" is a description. It is the **cognitive component** of an attitude—the aspect of an attitude that is a description of or belief in the way things are. It sets the stage for the more critical part of an attitude—its **affective component**. Affect is the emotional or feeling segment of an attitude and is reflected in the statement "I am angry over how little I'm paid." Finally, and we'll discuss this issue at considerable length later in this section, affect can lead to behavioral outcomes. The **behavioral component** of an attitude refers to an intention to behave in a certain way toward someone or something (to continue the example, "I'm going to look for another job that pays better").

Viewing attitudes as being made up of three components—cognition, affect, and behavior—is helpful in understanding their complexity and the potential relationship between attitudes and behavior. Keep in mind that these components are closely related, and cognition and affect in particular are inseparable in many ways. For example, imagine you concluded that someone had just treated you unfairly. Aren't you likely to have feelings about that, occurring virtually instantaneously with the thought? Thus, cognition and affect are intertwined.

Exhibit 3-1 illustrates how the three components of an attitude are related. In this example, an employee didn't get a promotion he thought he deserved; a coworker got it instead. The employee's attitude toward his supervisor is illustrated as follows: the employee thought he deserved the promotion (cognition), the employee strongly dislikes his supervisor (affect), and the employee is looking for another job (behavior). As we previously noted, although we often think that cognition causes affect, which then causes behavior, in reality these components are often difficult to separate.

In organizations, attitudes are important for their behavioral component. If workers believe, for example, that supervisors, auditors, bosses, and time-and-motion engineers are all in conspiracy to make employees work harder for the same or less money, it makes sense to try to understand how these attitudes formed, their relationship to actual job behavior, and how they might be changed.

> **2** Summarize the relationship between attitudes and behavior.

---

attitudes *Evaluative statements or judgments concerning objects, people, or events.*

cognitive component *The opinion or belief segment of an attitude.*

affective component *The emotional or feeling segment of an attitude.*

behavioral component *An intention to behave in a certain way toward someone or something.*

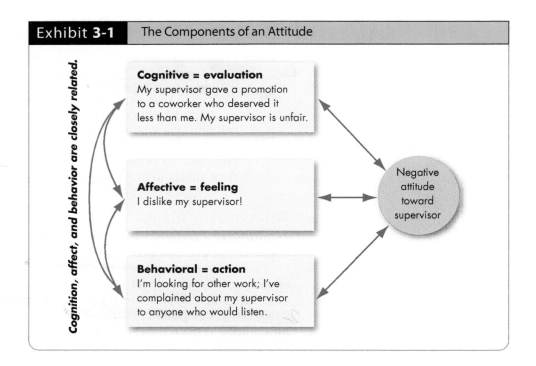

| Exhibit **3-1** | The Components of an Attitude |

Cognition, affect, and behavior are closely related.

Cognitive = evaluation
My supervisor gave a promotion to a coworker who deserved it less than me. My supervisor is unfair.

Affective = feeling
I dislike my supervisor!

Behavioral = action
I'm looking for other work; I've complained about my supervisor to anyone who would listen.

Negative attitude toward supervisor

Does Behavior Always Follow from Attitudes?

Early research on attitudes assumed that they were causally related to behavior; that is, the attitudes people hold determine what they do. Common sense, too, suggests a relationship. Isn't it logical that people watch television programs they like, or that employees try to avoid assignments they find distasteful?

However, in the late 1960s, this assumed effect of attitudes on behavior was challenged by a review of the research.[3] One researcher—Leon Festinger—argued that attitudes *follow* behavior. Did you ever notice how people change what they say so it doesn't contradict what they do? Perhaps a friend of yours has consistently argued that the quality of U.S. cars isn't up to that of imports and that he'd never own anything but a Japanese or German car. But his dad gives him a late-model Ford Mustang, and suddenly U.S. cars aren't so bad. Festinger argued that these cases of attitude following behavior illustrate the effects of **cognitive dissonance**.[4] *Cognitive dissonance* refers to any incompatibility an individual might perceive between two or more attitudes or between behavior and attitudes. Festinger argued that any form of inconsistency is uncomfortable and that individuals will attempt to reduce the dissonance and, hence, the discomfort. They will seek a stable state, in which there is a minimum of dissonance.

Research has generally concluded that people seek consistency among their attitudes and between their attitudes and their behavior.[5] They do this by altering either the attitudes or the behavior or by developing a rationalization for the discrepancy. Tobacco executives provide an example.[6] How, you might wonder, do these people cope with the ongoing barrage of data linking cigarette smoking and negative health outcomes? They can deny that any clear causation between smoking and cancer, for instance, has been established. They can brainwash themselves by continually articulating the benefits of tobacco. They can acknowledge the negative consequences of smoking but rationalize that people are going to smoke and that tobacco companies merely promote freedom of choice. They can accept the research evidence and begin actively working to make less dangerous cigarettes or at least reduce their

Marriott Corporation strives for consistency between attitudes and behavior through its motto "Spirit to Serve." CEO Bill Marriott (left in photo) models the behavior of service by visiting hotel employees throughout the year. "I want our associates to know that there really is a guy named Marriott who cares about them," he says. Marriott honors employees with job excellence awards for behavior that exemplifies the attitude of service.

availability to more vulnerable groups, such as teenagers. Or they can quit their job because the dissonance is too great.

No individual, of course, can completely avoid dissonance. You know that cheating on your income tax is wrong, but you "fudge" the numbers a bit every year and hope you're not audited. Or you tell your children to floss their teeth every day, but *you* don't. So how do people cope? Festinger would propose that the desire to reduce dissonance depends on the *importance* of the elements creating it and the degree of *influence* the individual believes he has over the elements; individuals will be more motivated to reduce dissonance when the attitudes or behavior are important or when they believe that the dissonance is due to something they can control. A third factor is the *rewards* of dissonance; high rewards accompanying high dissonance tend to reduce the tension inherent in the dissonance.

These moderating factors suggest that just individuals who experience dissonance will not necessarily move directly toward reducing it. If the issues underlying the dissonance are of minimal importance, if individuals perceive the dissonance is externally imposed and substantially uncontrollable, or if rewards are significant enough to offset it, an individual will not be under great tension to reduce the dissonance.

While Festinger questioned the attitudes–behavior relationship by arguing that, in many cases, attitudes follow behavior, other researchers asked whether there was any relationship at all. More recent research shows that attitudes predict future behavior and confirmed Festinger's original belief that certain "moderating variables" can strengthen the link.[7]

Moderating Variables   The most powerful moderators of the attitudes–behavior relationship are the *importance* of the attitude, its *correspondence to behavior*,

cognitive dissonance   *Any incompatibility between two or more attitudes or between behavior and attitudes.*

"Giving back to the communities in which we live and work" is an important value of Deloitte & Touche USA. The company gives its employees a direct experience with this attitude through its annual Impact Day, a one-day example of the company's year-round commitment to volunteer service. On this day, employees are allowed to leave their regular work to participate in a community service project. In this photo, the firm's CEO, Barry Salzberg (center), talks with an employee volunteer at a send-off party for a Make-A-Wish recipient.

its *accessibility*, whether there exist *social pressures*, and whether a person has *direct experience* with the attitude.[8]

Important attitudes reflect fundamental values, self-interest, or identification with individuals or groups that a person values. Attitudes that individuals consider important tend to show a strong relationship to behavior.

The more closely the attitude and the behavior are matched or correspond, the stronger the relationship. Specific attitudes tend to predict specific behaviors, whereas general attitudes tend to best predict general behaviors. For instance, asking someone specifically about her intention to stay with an organization for the next 6 months is likely to better predict turnover for that person than if you asked her how satisfied she was with her job overall. On the other hand, overall job satisfaction would better predict a general behavior such as whether the individual was engaged in her work or motivated to contribute to her organization.[9]

Attitudes we remember easily are more likely to predict our behavior. Interestingly, you're more likely to remember attitudes you frequently express. So the more you talk about your attitude on a subject, the more you're likely to remember it, and the more likely it is to shape your behavior.

Discrepancies between attitudes and behavior are more likely to occur when social pressures to behave in certain ways hold exceptional power. This situation tends to characterize behavior in organizations. It may explain why an employee who holds strong anti-union attitudes attends pro-union organizing meetings or why tobacco executives, who are not smokers themselves and who tend to believe the research linking smoking and cancer, don't actively discourage others from smoking in their offices.

Finally, the attitude–behavior relationship is likely to be much stronger if an attitude refers to something with which the individual has direct personal experience. Asking college students with no significant work experience how they would respond to working for an authoritarian supervisor is far less likely to predict actual behavior than asking that same question of employees who have actually worked for such an individual.

What Are the Major Job Attitudes?

3 *Compare and contrast the major job attitudes.*

A person can have thousands of attitudes, but OB focuses our attention on a very limited number of work-related attitudes. These tap positive or negative evaluations that employees hold about aspects of their work environment. Most of the research in OB has looked at three attitudes: job satisfaction, job involvement, and organizational commitment.[10] A few other attitudes attracting attention from researchers include perceived organizational support and employee engagement; we'll also briefly discuss these.

Job Satisfaction   The term **job satisfaction** describes a positive feeling about a job, resulting from an evaluation of its characteristics. A person with a high level of job satisfaction holds positive feelings about his or her job, while a dissatisfied person holds negative feelings. When people speak of employee attitudes, they usually mean job satisfaction. In fact, the two are frequently used interchangeably. Because of the high importance OB researchers have given to job satisfaction, we'll review this attitude in detail later in this chapter.

Job Involvement   Related to job satisfaction is **job involvement**.[11] Job involvement measures the degree to which people identify psychologically with their job and consider their perceived performance level important to self-worth.[12] Employees with a high level of job involvement strongly identify with and really care about the kind of work they do. Another closely related concept is **psychological empowerment**, which is employees' beliefs in the degree to which they influence their work environment, their competence, the meaningfulness of their job, and the perceived autonomy in their work.[13] For example, one study of nursing managers in Singapore found that good leaders empower their employees by involving them in decisions, making them feel their work is important, and giving them discretion to "do their own thing."[14]

High levels of both job involvement and psychological empowerment are positively related to organizational citizenship and job performance.[15] In addition, high job involvement has been found to be related to a reduced number of absences and lower resignation rates.[16]

Organizational Commitment   The third job attitude we'll discuss is **organizational commitment**, a state in which an employee identifies with a particular organization and its goals and wishes to maintain membership in the organization.[17] So, high job involvement means identifying with your specific job, while high organizational commitment means identifying with your employing organization.

There are three separate dimensions to organizational commitment:[18]

1. **Affective commitment.**   An **affective commitment** is an emotional attachment to the organization and a belief in its values. For example, a Petco

---

job satisfaction   *A positive feeling about one's job resulting from an evaluation of its characteristics.*

job involvement   *The degree to which a person identifies with a job, actively participates in it, and considers performance important to self-worth.*

psychological empowerment   *Employees' belief in the degree to which they affect their work environment, their competence, the meaningfulness of their job, and their perceived autonomy in their work.*

organizational commitment   *The degree to which an employee identifies with a particular organization and its goals and wishes to maintain membership in the organization.*

affective commitment   *An emotional attachment to an organization and a belief in its values.*

employee may be affectively committed to the company because of its involvement with animals.

2. **Continuance commitment.**   A **continuance commitment** is the perceived economic value of remaining with an organization compared to leaving it. An employee may be committed to an employer because she is paid well and feels it would hurt her family to quit.

3. **Normative commitment.**   A **normative commitment** is an obligation to remain with the organization for moral or ethical reasons. For example, an employee who is spearheading a new initiative may remain with an employer because he feels he would "leave the employer in the lurch" if he left.

A positive relationship appears to exist between organizational commitment and job productivity, but it is a modest one.[19] A review of 27 studies suggested that the relationship between commitment and performance is strongest for new employees, and it is considerably weaker for more experienced employees.[20] And, as with job involvement, the research evidence demonstrates negative relationships between organizational commitment and both absenteeism and turnover.[21] In general, affective commitment seems more strongly related to organizational outcomes such as performance and turnover than the other two commitment dimensions. One study found that affective commitment was a significant predictor of various outcomes (perception of task characteristics, career satisfaction, intent to leave) in 72 percent of the cases, compared with only 36 percent for normative commitment and 7 percent for continuance commitment.[22] The weak results for continuance commitment make sense in that it really isn't a strong commitment at all. Rather than an allegiance (affective commitment) or an obligation (normative commitment) to an employer, a continuance commitment describes an employee who is "tethered" to an employer simply because there isn't anything better available.

Chinese Employees and Organizational Commitment

Are employees from different cultures committed to their organizations in similar ways? A 2003 study explored this question and compared the organizational commitment of Chinese employees to that of Canadian and South Korean workers. Although results revealed that the three types of commitment—normative, continuance, and affective—are present in all three cultures, they differ in importance.

Normative commitment, an obligation to remain with an organization for moral or ethical reasons, was higher in the Chinese sample of employees than in the Canadian and South Korean samples. Affective commitment, an emotional attachment to the organization and a belief in its values, was also stronger in China than in Canada and South Korea. Chinese culture may explain why. The Chinese emphasize loyalty to one's group, and in this case, one's "group" may be the employer, so employees may feel a certain loyalty from the start and become more emotionally attached as their time with the organization grows. To the extent that the Chinese view their organization as part of their group and become emotionally attached to that group, they will be more committed to their organization. Perhaps as a result of this emphasis on loyalty, the normative commitment of Chinese employees strongly predicted intentions to maintain employment with an organization.

Continuance commitment, the perceived economic value of remaining with an organization compared with leaving it, was lower in the Chinese sample than in the Canadian and South Korean samples. One reason is that Chinese workers value loyalty toward the group more than individual concerns.

So, although all three countries experience normative, continuance, and affective commitment, the degree to which each is important differs across countries.

Source: Based on Y. Cheng and M. S. Stockdale, "The Validity of the Three-Component Model of Organizational Commitment in a Chinese Context," *Journal of Vocational Behavior,* June 2003, pp. 465–489.

There is reason to believe that the concept of commitment may be less important to employers and employees today than it once was. The unwritten loyalty contract that existed 30 years ago between employees and employers has been seriously damaged, and the notion of employees staying with a single organization for most of their career has become increasingly irrelevant. Given that, "measures of employee–firm attachment, such as commitment, are problematic for new employment relations."[23] This suggests that *organizational commitment* is probably less important as a work-related attitude than it once was. In its place, we might expect something akin to *occupational commitment* to become a more relevant variable because it better reflects today's fluid workforce.[24]

Perceived Organizational Support   Perceived organizational support (POS) is the degree to which employees believe the organization values their contribution and cares about their well-being (for example, an employee believes his organization would accommodate him if he had a child-care problem or would forgive an honest mistake on his part). Research shows that people perceive their organization as supportive when rewards are deemed fair, when employees have a voice in decisions, and when their supervisors are seen as supportive.[25] Although less research has linked POS to OB outcomes than is the case with other job attitudes, some findings suggest that employees with strong POS perceptions are more likely to have higher levels of organizational citizenship behaviors and job performance.[26]

Employee Engagement   A new concept is **employee engagement**, an individual's involvement with, satisfaction with, and enthusiasm for, the work she does. For example, we might ask employees about the availability of resources and the opportunities to learn new skills, whether they feel their work is important and meaningful, and whether their interactions with coworkers and supervisors are rewarding.[27] Highly engaged employees have a passion for their work and feel a deep connection to their company; disengaged employees have essentially "checked out"—putting time but not energy or attention into their work. A recent study of nearly 8,000 business units in 36 companies found that, compared with other companies, those whose employees had high-average levels of engagement had higher levels of customer satisfaction, were more productive, had higher profits, and had lower levels of turnover and accidents.[28] Molson Coors found that engaged employees were five times less likely to have safety incidents, and when one did occur, it was much less serious, and less costly, for the engaged employee than for a disengaged one ($63 per incident versus $392). Engagement becomes a real concern for most organizations because surveys indicate that few employees—between 17 percent and 29 percent—are highly engaged by their work. Caterpillar set out to increase employee engagement and concluded that its initiative resulted in an 80 percent drop in grievances and a 34 percent increase in highly satisfied customers.[29]

Because of some of these promising findings, employee engagement has attracted quite a following in many business organizations and management consulting firms. However, the concept is relatively new, so we have a lot to learn about how engagement relates to other concepts, such as job satisfaction, organizational

---

continuance commitment   *The perceived economic value of remaining with an organization compared with leaving it.*

normative commitment   *An obligation to remain with an organization for moral or ethical reasons.*

perceived organizational support (POS)   *The degree to which employees believe an organization values their contribution and cares about their well-being.*

employee engagement   *An individual's involvement with, satisfaction with, and enthusiasm for the work he or she does.*

Employee engagement at Good People Company, Ltd., in Seoul, South Korea, includes a monthly "Pyjamas Day" during which all employees work in the clothing the company designs. Good People managers then hold meetings with employees to solicit their feedback and inspirations about company products, making employees feel that their contributions are important and meaningful.

commitment, job involvement, or intrinsic motivation to do one's job well. Engagement may be broad enough that it captures the intersection of these variables. In other words, it may be what these attitudes have in common.

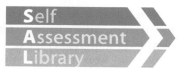

AM I ENGAGED?

In the Self-Assessment Library (available on CD or online), take assessment IV.B.1 (Am I Engaged?). (Note: If you do not currently have a job, answer the questions for your most recent job.)

Are These Job Attitudes Really All That Distinct?   You might wonder whether these job attitudes are really distinct. After all, if people feel deeply involved in their job (high job involvement), isn't it probable that they like it (high job satisfaction)? Similarly, won't people who think their organization is supportive (high perceived organizational support) also feel committed to it (strong organizational commitment)? Evidence suggests that these attitudes are highly related, perhaps to a troubling degree. For example, the correlation between perceived organizational support and affective commitment is very strong.[30] The problem is that a strong correlation means the variables may be redundant (so, for example, if you know someone's affective commitment, you basically know her perceived organizational support).

But why is this redundancy so troubling? Why have two steering wheels on a car when you need only one? Why have two concepts—going by different labels—when you need only one? Redundancy is inefficient and confusing. Although we OB researchers like proposing new attitudes, often we haven't been good at showing how they compare and contrast with each other. There is some measure of distinctiveness among these attitudes, but they overlap greatly. The overlap may exist for various reasons, including the employee's personality. Some people are

OB In the News

Why Is Job Satisfaction Falling?

There is increasing evidence that job satisfaction levels in the United States are dropping. The Conference Board, which surveys large numbers of workers every year, reports the following percentages of individuals reporting that they are at least moderately satisfied with their jobs:

1987	61%
1995	59%
2000	51%
2005	52%
2006	47%

What are the strongest areas of dissatisfaction? Only one in five employees is satisfied with his company's promotions and bonus plans. Surprisingly, satisfaction has dropped the most among those making the highest incomes (although they still have somewhat higher satisfaction than those with relatively low earnings).

Even though U.S. workers remain relatively satisfied with their jobs, especially compared to employees in other countries, this doesn't explain why job satisfaction levels are dropping. One reason may be that in their drive to increase productivity, many companies continue to downsize, leaving the remaining workers overburdened. Downsizing also lowers the morale of layoff survivors. Why? Not only are the survivors saddled with the duties of their coworkers, but they often miss their coworkers and also wonder whether they'll be next. A recent survey suggested that only one in four employees believes her organization is loyal to her. It shouldn't be a surprise that job attitudes fall as a result.

Source: Based on K. Gurchiek, "Show Workers Their Value, Study Says," *HR Magazine*, October 2006, p. 40; "U.S. Job Satisfaction Declines," *USA Today*, April 9, 2007, p. 1B; S. Moore, L. Grunberg, and E. Greenberg, "The Effects of Similar and Dissimilar Layoff Experiences on Work and Well-Being Outcomes," *Journal of Occupational Health Psychology*, July 2004, pp. 247–257.

predisposed to be positive or negative about almost everything. If someone tells you she loves her company, it may not mean a lot if she is positive about everything else in her life. Or the overlap may mean that some organizations are just all-around better places to work than others. This may mean that if you as a manager know someone's level of job satisfaction you know most of what you need to know about how the person sees the organization.

Additional activities designed to change attitudes include arranging for people to do volunteer work in community or social service centers to meet individuals and groups from diverse backgrounds and using exercises that let participants feel what it's like to be different. For example, when people participate in the exercise *Blue Eyes–Brown Eyes*, in which people are segregated and stereotyped according to their eye color, participants see what it's like to be judged by something over which they have no control. Evidence suggests that this exercise reduces participants' negative attitudes toward individuals who are different from them.[31]

Job Satisfaction

4 *Define* job satisfaction *and show how it can be measured.*

We have already discussed job satisfaction briefly. Now let's dissect the concept more carefully. How do we measure job satisfaction? How satisfied are employees in their jobs? What causes an employee to have a high level of job satisfaction? How do dissatisfied and satisfied employees affect an organization?

Measuring Job Satisfaction

We've defined job satisfaction as a positive feeling about a job resulting from an evaluation of its characteristics. This definition is clearly a very broad one.[32] Yet breadth is inherent in the concept. Remember, a person's job is more than just the obvious activities of shuffling papers, writing programming code, waiting on customers, or driving a truck. Jobs require interacting with coworkers and bosses, following organizational rules and policies, meeting performance standards, living with working conditions that are often less than ideal, and the like.[33] This means that an employee's assessment of how satisfied he is with the job is a complex summation of a number of discrete job elements. How, then, do we measure the concept?

The two most widely used approaches are a single global rating and a summation score made up of a number of job facets. The single global rating method is nothing more than a response to one question, such as "All things considered, how satisfied are you with your job?" Respondents circle a number between 1 and 5 that corresponds to answers from "highly satisfied" to "highly dissatisfied." The other approach—a summation of job facets—is more sophisticated. It identifies key elements in a job and asks for the employee's feelings about each. Typical elements here are the nature of the work, supervision, present pay, promotion opportunities, and relations with coworkers.[34] Respondents rate them on a standardized scale, and researchers add the ratings to create an overall job satisfaction score.

Is one of these approaches superior to the other? Intuitively, summing up responses to a number of job factors seems likely to achieve a more accurate evaluation of job satisfaction. The research, however, doesn't support the intuition.[35] This is one of those rare instances in which simplicity seems to work as well as complexity, and comparisons of the two methods indicate that one is essentially as valid as the other. The best explanation for this outcome is that the concept of job satisfaction is inherently so broad that the single question captures its essence. Another explanation may be that some important facets are left out of the summation of job facets. Both methods are helpful. For example, the single global rating method isn't very time-consuming, which frees managers to address other workplace issues and problems. And the summation of job facets helps managers zero in on where problems exist, making it easier to deal with unhappy employees and solve problems faster and more accurately.

How Satisfied Are People in Their Jobs?

Are most people satisfied with their jobs? The answer seems to be a qualified "yes" in the United States and in most other developed countries. Independent studies conducted among U.S. workers over the past 30 years generally indicate that more workers are satisfied with their jobs than are dissatisfied.[36] However, two caveats need to be mentioned. First, as we noted earlier, job satisfaction levels in the United States appear to be dropping.

Second, research shows that satisfaction levels vary a lot, depending on which facet of job satisfaction you're talking about. As shown in Exhibit 3-2, people are, on average, satisfied with their jobs overall, with the work itself, and with their supervisors and coworkers. However, they tend to be less satisfied with their pay and with promotion opportunities. It's not really clear why people dislike their pay and promotion possibilities more than other aspects of their jobs.[37]

What Causes Job Satisfaction?

5 *Summarize the main causes of job satisfaction.*

Think about the best job you've ever had. What made it so? Chances are you probably liked the work you did. In fact, of the major job-satisfaction facets (work itself, pay, advancement opportunities, supervision, coworkers), enjoying the work is almost always the one most strongly correlated with high levels of overall job satisfaction. Interesting jobs that provide training, variety, independence, and control satisfy most employees.[38] In other words, most people prefer work that is challenging and stimulating over work that is predictable and routine.

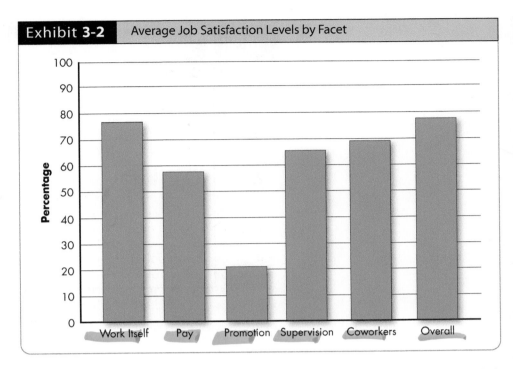

Exhibit 3-2   Average Job Satisfaction Levels by Facet

You've probably noticed that pay comes up often when people discuss job satisfaction. There is an interesting relationship between salary and job satisfaction. For people who are poor (for example, living below the poverty line) or who live in poor countries, pay does correlate with job satisfaction and with overall happiness. But, once an individual reaches a level of comfortable living (in the United States, that occurs at about $40,000 a year, depending on the region and family size), the relationship virtually disappears. In other words, people who earn $80,000 are, on average, no happier with their jobs than those who earn close to $40,000. Take a look at Exhibit 3-3. It shows the relationship between the average pay for a job and the average level of job satisfaction. As you can see, there isn't much of a relationship there. Jobs that are compensated handsomely have average job satisfaction levels no higher than those that are paid much less. To further illustrate this point, one researcher even found no significant difference when he compared the overall well-being of the richest people on the Forbes 400 list with that of Maasai herdsmen in East Africa.[39] As we saw in the Google example at the beginning of the chapter, good benefits do appear to satisfy employees, but high pay levels much less so.

Money does motivate people, as we will discover in Chapter 6. But what motivates us is not necessarily the same as what makes us happy. A recent poll by UCLA and the American Council on Education found that entering college freshmen rated becoming "very well off financially" first on a list of 19 goals, ahead of choices such as helping others, raising a family, or becoming proficient in an academic pursuit. Maybe your goal isn't to be happy. But if it is, money's probably not going to do much to get you there.[40]

Job satisfaction is not just about job conditions. Personality also plays a role. People who are less positive about themselves are less likely to like their jobs. Research has shown that people who have positive **core self-evaluations**—who

core self-evaluations Bottom-line conclusions individuals have about their capabilities, competence, and worth as a person.

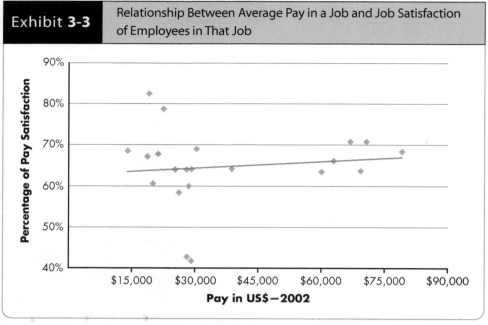

| Exhibit **3-3** | Relationship Between Average Pay in a Job and Job Satisfaction of Employees in That Job |

Source: T. A. Judge, R. F. Piccolo, N. P. Podsakoff, J. C. Shaw, and B. L. Rich, "Can Happiness Be "Earned"?: The Relationship Between Pay and Job Satisfaction," working paper, University of Florida, 2005.

believe in their inner worth and basic competence—are more satisfied with their jobs than those with negative core self-evaluations. Not only do they see their work as more fulfilling and challenging, they are more likely to gravitate toward challenging jobs in the first place. Those with negative core self-evaluations set less ambitious goals and are more likely to give up when confronting difficulties. Thus, they're more likely to be stuck in boring, repetitive jobs than those with positive core self-evaluations.[41]

MYTH OR SCIENCE?

"Happy Workers Are Productive Workers"

*t*his statement is generally true. The idea that "happy workers are productive workers" developed in the 1930s and 1940s, largely as a result of findings drawn by researchers conducting the Hawthorne studies at Western Electric. Based on those conclusions, managers worked to make their employees happier by focusing on working conditions and the work environment. Then, in the 1980s, an influential review of the research suggested that the relationship between job satisfaction and job performance was not particularly high. The authors of that review even went so far as to label the relationship as "illusory."[42]

More recently, a review of more than 300 studies corrected some errors in that earlier review. It estimated that the correlation between job satisfaction and job performance

is moderately strong. This conclusion also appears to be generalizable across international contexts. The correlation is higher for complex jobs that provide employees with more discretion to act on their attitudes.[43]

The reverse causality might be true: Productive workers are likely to be happy workers, or productivity might lead to satisfaction.[44] In other words, if you do a good job, you intrinsically feel good about it. In addition, your higher productivity should increase your recognition, your pay level, and your likelihood of promotion. Cumulatively, these rewards, in turn, increase your level of satisfaction with the job.

Both arguments are probably right: Satisfaction can lead to high levels of performance for some people, while for others, high performance is satisfying. ■

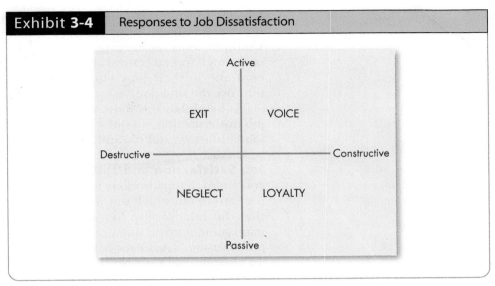

Exhibit **3-4**	Responses to Job Dissatisfaction

The Impact of Satisfied and Dissatisfied Employees on the Workplace

6 *Identify four employee responses to dissatisfaction.*

There are consequences when employees like their jobs and when they dislike their jobs. One theoretical model—the exit–voice–loyalty–neglect framework—is helpful in understanding the consequences of dissatisfaction. Exhibit 3-4 illustrates the framework's four responses, which differ from one another along two dimensions: constructive/destructive and active/passive. The responses are defined as follows:[45]

- *Exit.* The **exit** response involves directing behavior toward leaving the organization, including looking for a new position as well as resigning.
- *Voice.* The **voice** response involves actively and constructively attempting to improve conditions, including suggesting improvements, discussing problems with superiors, and undertaking some forms of union activity.
- *Loyalty.* The **loyalty** response involves passively but optimistically waiting for conditions to improve, including speaking up for the organization in the face of external criticism and trusting the organization and its management to "do the right thing."
- *Neglect.* The **neglect** response involves passively allowing conditions to worsen, including chronic absenteeism or lateness, reduced effort, and increased error rate.

Exit and neglect behaviors encompass our performance variables—productivity, absenteeism, and turnover. But this model expands employee response to include voice and loyalty—constructive behaviors that allow individuals to tolerate unpleasant situations or to revive satisfactory working conditions.

---

exit *Dissatisfaction expressed through behavior directed toward leaving the organization.*

voice *Dissatisfaction expressed through active and constructive attempts to improve conditions.*

loyalty *Dissatisfaction expressed by passively waiting for conditions to improve.*

neglect *Dissatisfaction expressed through allowing conditions to worsen.*

It helps us to understand situations, such as those sometimes found among unionized workers, for whom low job satisfaction is coupled with low turnover.[46] Union members often express dissatisfaction through the grievance procedure or through formal contract negotiations. These voice mechanisms allow them to continue in their jobs while convincing themselves that they are acting to improve the situation.

As helpful as this framework is in presenting the possible consequences of job dissatisfaction, it's quite general. We now discuss more specific outcomes of job satisfaction and dissatisfaction in the workplace.

Job Satisfaction and Job Performance   As the "Myth or Science?" box concludes, happy workers are more likely to be productive workers, although it's hard to tell which way the causality runs. Some researchers used to believe that the relationship between job satisfaction and job performance was a management myth. But a review of 300 studies suggested that the correlation is pretty strong.[47] As we move from the individual level to that of the organization, we also find support for the satisfaction–performance relationship.[48] When satisfaction and productivity data are gathered for the organization as a whole, we find that organizations with more satisfied employees tend to be more effective than organizations with fewer satisfied employees.

Job Satisfaction and OCB   It seems logical to assume that job satisfaction should be a major determinant of an employee's organizational citizenship behavior (OCB).[49] Satisfied employees would seem more likely to talk positively about the organization, help others, and go beyond the normal expectations in their job. Moreover, satisfied employees might be more prone to go beyond the call of duty because they want to reciprocate their positive experiences. Consistent with this thinking, evidence suggests that job satisfaction is moderately correlated with OCBs, such that people who are more satisfied with their jobs are more likely to engage in OCBs.[50] More recent evidence suggests that satisfaction influences OCB through perceptions of fairness.

A major focus of Nissan Motor Company's Diversity Development Office in Japan is helping female employees develop their careers. Nissan provides women such as the assembly-line workers shown here with one-on-one counseling services of career advisors and training programs to develop applicable skills. Women can also visit Nissan's corporate intranet to read interviews with "role models," women who have made substantial contributions to the company. Nissan believes that hiring more women and supporting their careers will contribute to the company's competitive edge.

Why do those satisfied with their jobs contribute more OCBs? Research indicates that fairness perceptions explain the relationship, at least in part.[51] What does this mean? Basically, job satisfaction comes down to conceptions of fair outcomes, treatment, and procedures.[52] If you don't feel that your supervisor, the organization's procedures, or pay policies are fair, your job satisfaction is likely to suffer significantly. However, when you perceive organizational processes and outcomes to be fair, trust develops. And when you trust your employer, you're more willing to voluntarily engage in behaviors that go beyond your formal job requirements.

Job Satisfaction and Customer Satisfaction   As we noted in Chapter 1, employees in service jobs often interact with customers. Since the management of service organizations should be concerned with pleasing those customers, it is reasonable to ask: Is employee satisfaction related to positive customer outcomes? For frontline employees who have regular contact with customers, the answer is "yes."

The evidence indicates that satisfied employees increase customer satisfaction and loyalty.[53] Why? In service organizations, customer retention and defection are highly dependent on how frontline employees deal with customers. Satisfied employees are more likely to be friendly, upbeat, and responsive—which customers appreciate. And because satisfied employees are less prone to turnover, customers are more likely to encounter familiar faces and receive experienced service. These qualities build customer satisfaction and loyalty. The relationship also seems to apply in reverse: Dissatisfied customers can increase an employee's job dissatisfaction. Employees who have regular contact with customers report that rude, thoughtless, or unreasonably demanding customers adversely affect the employees' job satisfaction.[54]

A number of companies are acting on this evidence. Service-oriented businesses such as FedEx, Southwest Airlines, Four Seasons Hotels, American Express, and Office Depot obsess about pleasing their customers. Toward that end, they also focus on building employee satisfaction—recognizing that

Service organizations know that whether customers are satisfied and loyal depends on how frontline employees deal with customers. Singapore Airlines has earned a reputation among world travelers for outstanding customer service. The airline's "putting people first" philosophy applies to both its employees and customers. In recruiting flight attendants, the airline selects people who are warm, hospitable, and happy to serve others. Through extensive training, Singapore molds recruits into attendants focused on complete customer satisfaction.

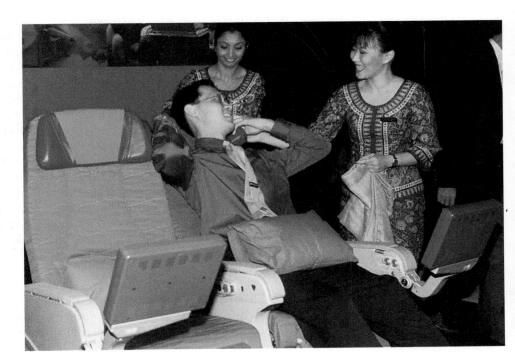

employee satisfaction will go a long way toward contributing to their goal of having happy customers. These firms seek to hire upbeat and friendly employees, they train employees in the importance of customer service, they reward customer service, they provide positive employee work climates, and they regularly track employee satisfaction through attitude surveys.

Job Satisfaction and Absenteeism   We find a consistent negative relationship between satisfaction and absenteeism, but the correlation is moderate to weak.[55] While it certainly makes sense that dissatisfied employees are more likely to miss work, other factors have an impact on the relationship and reduce the correlation coefficient. For example, organizations that provide liberal sick leave benefits are encouraging all their employees—including those who are highly satisfied—to take days off. Assuming that you have a reasonable number of varied interests, you can find work satisfying and yet still want to take off to enjoy a 3-day weekend or tan yourself on a warm summer day if those days come free with no penalties.

An excellent illustration of how satisfaction directly leads to attendance, when there is minimal impact from other factors, is a study done at Sears, Roebuck.[56] Sears had a policy of not permitting employees to be absent from work for avoidable reasons without penalty. The occurrence of a freak April 2 snowstorm in Chicago created the opportunity to compare employee attendance at the Chicago office with attendance in New York, where the weather was quite nice. (Satisfaction data were available on employees at both locations.) The storm crippled Chicago's transportation system, and individuals knew they could miss work this day with no penalty. If satisfaction leads to attendance when there are no outside factors, the more satisfied employees should have come to work in Chicago, while dissatisfied employees should have stayed home. The study found that on this particular April 2, absenteeism rates in New York were just as high for satisfied groups of workers as for dissatisfied groups. But in Chicago, the workers with high satisfaction scores did indeed have much higher attendance than did those with lower satisfaction levels, exactly what we would have expected if satisfaction is negatively correlated with absenteeism.

Job Satisfaction and Turnover   Satisfaction is also negatively related to turnover, but the correlation is stronger than what we found for absenteeism.[57] Yet, again, other factors, such as labor-market conditions, expectations about alternative job opportunities, and length of tenure with the organization, are important constraints on an employee's decision to leave her current job.[58]

Evidence indicates that an important moderator of the satisfaction–turnover relationship is the employee's level of performance.[59] Specifically, level of satisfaction is less important in predicting turnover for superior performers. Why? The organization typically makes considerable efforts to keep these people. They get pay raises, praise, recognition, increased promotional opportunities, and so forth. Just the opposite tends to apply to poor performers. The organization makes few attempts to retain them. There may even be subtle pressures to encourage them to quit. We would expect, therefore, that job satisfaction is more important in influencing poor performers to stay than in influencing superior performers to stay. Regardless of level of satisfaction, the latter are more likely to remain with the organization because the receipt of recognition, praise, and other rewards gives them more reasons to do so.

Job Satisfaction and Workplace Deviance   Job dissatisfaction predicts a lot of specific behaviors, including unionization attempts, substance abuse, stealing at work, undue socializing, and tardiness. Researchers argue that these behaviors are indicators of a broader syndrome that we would term *deviant* *behavior in the workplace* (or *employee withdrawal*).[60] The key is that if employees don't like their work environment, they'll respond somehow. It is not always easy to forecast exactly *how* they'll respond. One worker's response might be to quit. Another might take work time to surf the Internet, take work supplies home for personal use, and so on. In short, evidence indicates that workers who don't like their jobs "get even" in various ways—and because employees can be quite creative in the ways they do that, controlling one behavior, such as having an absence control policy, leaves the root cause untouched. If employers want to control the undesirable consequences of job dissatisfaction, they should attack the source of the problem—the dissatisfaction—rather than try to control the different responses.

Managers Often "Don't Get It"   Given the evidence we've just reviewed, it should come as no surprise that job satisfaction can affect the bottom line. One study by a management consulting firm separated large organizations into high morale (where more than 70 percent of employees expressed overall job satisfaction) and medium or low morale (lower than 70 percent). The stock prices of companies in the high morale group grew 19.4 percent, compared with 10 percent for the medium or low morale group. Despite these results, many managers are unconcerned about job satisfaction of their employees. Still others overestimate the degree to which their employees are satisfied with their jobs, so they don't think there's a problem when there is. One study of 262 large employers found that 86 percent of senior managers believed their organization treated its employees well, but only 55 percent of the employees agreed. Another study found 55 percent of managers thought morale was good in their organization, compared to only 38 percent of employees.[61] Managers first need to care about job satisfaction, and then they need to measure it rather than just assume that everything is going well.

Global Implications

Is Job Satisfaction a U.S. Concept?

> 7   *Show whether job satisfaction is a relevant concept in countries other than the United States.*

Most of the research on job satisfaction has been conducted in the United States. So, we might ask: Is job satisfaction a U.S. concept? The evidence strongly suggests that this is *not* the case; people in other cultures can and do form judgments of job satisfaction. Moreover, it appears that similar factors cause, and result from, job satisfaction across cultures. For example, we noted earlier that pay is positively, but relatively weakly, related to job satisfaction. This relationship appears to hold in other industrialized nations as well as in the United States.

Are Employees in Western Cultures More Satisfied with Their Jobs?

Although job satisfaction appears to be a relevant concept across cultures, that doesn't mean there are no cultural differences in job satisfaction. Evidence suggests that employees in Western cultures have higher levels of job satisfaction than those in Eastern cultures.[62] Exhibit 3-5 provides the results of a global study of the job satisfaction levels of workers in 15 countries. (This study included 23 countries, but for presentation purposes, we report the results for only the largest.) As the exhibit shows, the highest levels of job satisfaction appear to be in the United States and western Europe.

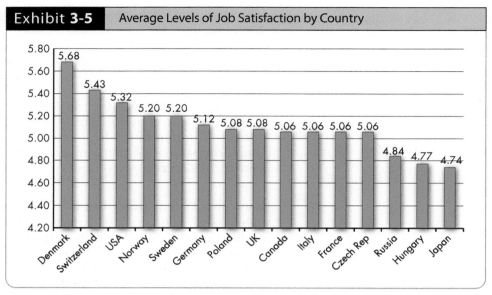

| Exhibit **3-5** | Average Levels of Job Satisfaction by Country |

Source: M. Benz and B. S. Frey, "The Value of Autonomy: Evidence from the Self-Employed in 23 Countries," working paper 173, Institute for Empirical Research in Economics, University of Zurich, November 2003 (http://ssrn.com/abstract=475140).

Note: Scores represent average job-satisfaction levels in each country as rated on a 1 = very dissatisfied to 10 = very satisfied scale.

Is the reason that employees in Western cultures have better jobs? Or are individuals in Western cultures simply more positive (and less self-critical)? Although both factors are probably at play, evidence suggests that individuals in Eastern cultures value negative emotions more than do individuals in Western cultures, whereas those in Western cultures tend to emphasize positive emotions and individual happiness.[63] That may be why employees in Western cultures such as the United States and Scandinavia are more likely to have higher levels of satisfaction.

Summary and Implications for Managers

Managers should be interested in their employees' attitudes because attitudes give warnings of potential problems and because they influence behavior. Satisfied and committed employees, for instance, have lower rates of turnover, absenteeism, and withdrawal behaviors. They also perform better on the job. Given that managers want to keep resignations and absences down—especially among their most productive employees—they'll want to do things that generate positive job attitudes. As one review put it, "A sound measurement of overall job attitude is one of the most useful pieces of information an organization can have about its employees."[64]

The most important thing managers can do to raise employee satisfaction is focus on the intrinsic parts of the job, such as making the work challenging and interesting. Although paying employees poorly will likely not attract high-quality employees to the organization, or keep high performers, managers should realize that high pay alone is unlikely to create a satisfying work environment. Creating a satisfied workforce is hardly a guarantee of successful organizational performance, but evidence strongly suggests that whatever managers can do to improve employee attitudes will likely result in heightened organizational effectiveness.

Point   Counterpoint

MANAGERS CAN CREATE SATISFIED EMPLOYEES

a review of the evidence has identified four factors conducive to high levels of employee job satisfaction: mentally challenging work, equitable rewards, supportive working conditions, and supportive colleagues.[65] Management is able to control each of these factors:

Mentally challenging work.   Generally, people prefer jobs that give them opportunities to use their skills and abilities and offer a variety of tasks, freedom, and feedback on how well they're doing. These characteristics make work mentally challenging.

Equitable rewards.   Employees want pay systems that they perceive as just, unambiguous, and in line with their expectations. When pay is seen as fair—based on job demands, individual skill level, and community pay standards—satisfaction is likely to result.

Supportive working conditions.   Employees want their work environment both to be safe and personally comfortable and to facilitate their doing a good job. In addition, most prefer working relatively close to home, in clean and relatively modern facilities, with adequate tools and equipment.

Supportive colleagues.   People get more out of work than merely money and other tangible achievements. For most employees, work also fulfills the need for social interaction. Not surprisingly, therefore, having friendly and supportive coworkers leads to increased job satisfaction. The boss's behavior is also a major determinant of satisfaction. Studies find that employee satisfaction is increased when the immediate supervisor is understanding and friendly, offers praise for good performance, listens to employees' opinions, and shows a personal interest in employees.

t he notion that managers and organizations can control the level of employee job satisfaction is inherently attractive. It fits nicely with the view that managers directly influence organizational processes and outcomes. Unfortunately, a growing body of evidence challenges the notion that managers control the factors that influence employee job satisfaction. The most recent findings indicate that it is largely genetically determined.[66]

Whether a person is happy or not is essentially determined by gene structure. Approximately 50 to 80 percent of people's differences in happiness, or subjective well-being, has been found to be attributable to their genes. Identical twins, for example, tend to have very similar careers, report similar levels of job satisfaction, and change jobs at similar rates.

Analysis of satisfaction data for a selected sample of individuals over a 50-year period found that individual results were stable over time, even when the subjects changed employers and occupations. This and other research suggests that an individual's disposition toward life—positive or negative—is established by genetic makeup, holds over time, and carries over into a disposition toward work.

Given these findings, there is probably little most managers can do to influence employee satisfaction. Despite the fact that managers and organizations go to extensive lengths to try to improve employee job satisfaction by manipulating job characteristics, working conditions, and rewards, people will inevitably return to their own "set point." A bonus may temporarily increase the satisfaction level of a negatively disposed worker, but it is unlikely to sustain it. Sooner or later, a dissatisfied worker will find new areas of fault with the job.

The only place managers will have any significant influence is in the selection process. If managers want satisfied workers, they need to screen out negative people who derive little satisfaction from their jobs, irrespective of work conditions.

Questions for Review

1   What are the main components of attitudes? Are these components related or unrelated?

2   Does behavior always follow from attitudes? Why or why not? Discuss the factors that affect whether behavior follows from attitudes.

3   What are the major job attitudes? In what ways are these attitudes alike? What is unique about each?

4   How do we measure job satisfaction?

5   What causes job satisfaction? For most people, is pay or the work itself more important?

6   What outcomes does job satisfaction influence? What implications does this have for management?

7   Is job satisfaction a uniquely U.S. concept? Does job satisfaction appear to vary by country?

Experiential Exercise

WHAT FACTORS ARE MOST IMPORTANT TO YOUR JOB SATISFACTION?

Most of us probably want a job we think will satisfy us. But because no job is perfect, we often have to trade off job attributes. One job may pay well but provide limited opportunities for advancement or skill development. Another may offer work we enjoy but have poor benefits. The following is a list of 21 job factors or attributes:

- Autonomy and independence
- Benefits
- Career advancement opportunities
- Career development opportunities
- Compensation/pay
- Communication between employees and management
- Contribution of work to organization's business goals
- Feeling safe in the work environment
- Flexibility to balance life and work issues
- Job security
- Job-specific training
- Management recognition of employee job performance
- Meaningfulness of job
- Networking
- Opportunities to use skills/abilities
- Organization's commitment to professional development
- Overall corporate culture
- Relationship with coworkers
- Relationship with immediate supervisor

- The work itself
- The variety of work

On a sheet of paper, rank-order these job factors from top to bottom so that number 1 is the job factor you think is most important to your job satisfaction, number 2 is the second most important factor to your job satisfaction, and so on.

Now gather in teams of three or four people and try the following:

1. Appoint a spokesperson who will take notes and report the answers to the following questions, on behalf of your group, back to the class.

2. Averaging across all members in your group, generate a list of the top five job factors.

3. Did most people in your group seem to value the same job factors? Why or why not?

4. Your instructor will provide you with the results of a study of a random sample of 600 employees conducted by the Society for Human Resource Management (SHRM). How do your group's rankings compare with the SHRM results?

5. The chapter says that pay doesn't correlate all that well with job satisfaction, but in the SHRM survey, people say it is relatively important. Can your group suggest a reason for the apparent discrepancy?

6. Now examine your own list again. Does your list agree with the group list? Does your list agree with the SHRM study?

Ethical Dilemma

ARE U.S. WORKERS OVERWORKED?

Europeans pride themselves on their quality of life, and rightly so. In a recent worldwide analysis of quality of life, the United States ranked 13th. The 12 nations that finished ahead of the United States were all from Europe. Factors considered in the analysis included material well-being, health, political stability, divorce rates, job security, political freedom, and gender equality.

Many Europeans would credit their high quality of life to their nations' free health care, generous unemployment benefits, and greater emphasis on leisure as opposed to work. Consider that most European nations mandate restricted workweek hours and a month or more of vacation time, but U.S. workers have among the fewest vacation days and longest average workweek in the world. Juliet Schor, a Harvard economist who has written on the subject, argues that the United States "is the world's standout workaholic nation" and that U.S. workers are trapped in a "squirrel cage" of overwork. Some argue that mandated leisure time would force companies to compete within their industry by raising productivity and product quality rather than by requiring workers to put in more hours.

Many European nations also place limits on the hours employers can require employees to work. France, Germany, and other nations limit the workweek to 35 hours. Recently, after much debate, the French parliament voted to do away with the rule that set 35 hours as the maximum workweek. The justification was that more flexible rules would allow French companies to compete more effectively

so that, if business required it, they could pay employees for longer hours. Opponents of the new rule argue that it puts the decision about how much to work in the individual's hands and that it will inevitably detract from quality of life and give employers power to exploit workers. A French union leader said, "They say it's the worker who will choose how much to work, but they're lying because it's always the employer who decides."

Questions

1. Why do you think quality of life is lower in the United States than in many European nations? Do you think it would improve if the U.S. government required a minimum number of vacation days or limited workweek hours?

2. Do you think the French parliament was right to eliminate the 35-hour workweek limit? Do you think the quality of French life will suffer? Why or why not?

3. Do you think employers have an obligation to consider the quality of life of their employees? Could such an obligation mean protecting employees from being overworked?

4. Do you think it makes a difference in the research results that the unemployment rate in Europe is roughly double that of the United States and that Europe's gross domestic product (GDP) is about half that of the United States?

Sources: Juliet Schor, *The Overworked American: The Unexpected Decline of Leisure* (New York: Basic Books, 1992); C. S. Smith, "Effort to Extend Workweek Advances in France," *New York Times*, February 10, 2005, p. A9; "The Economist Intelligence Unit's Quality-of-Life Index," *The Economist*, 2005, www.economist.com/media/pdf/QUALITY_OF_LIFE.pdf; E. Olsen, "The Vacation Deficit," *Budget Travel*, October 29, 2004, www.msnbc.msn.com/id/6345416/.

Case Incident 1

ALBERTSONS WORKS ON EMPLOYEE ATTITUDES

Albertsons is a huge grocery and drug company. It has more than 2,400 supermarkets, and its Osco and Savon brands make it the fifth-largest drugstore company in the United States. In a typical year, shoppers make 1.4 billion trips through its stores.

Albertsons competes in tough businesses. Wal-Mart, in particular, has been eating away at its market share. With revenues flat and profits falling, the company hired Larry Johnston to turn the business around.

Johnston came to Albertsons from General Electric. And it was while he was at GE that Johnston met a training specialist named Ed Foreman. Foreman endeared himself to Johnston when the latter hired Foreman to help him with a serious problem. At the time, Johnston had been sent to Paris to fix the European division of GE Medical Systems, which made CT scanners. Over the previous decade, four executives had been brought in to turn the division around and try to make it profitable. All had failed. Johnston responded to the challenge by initiating some important changes: He made a number of acquisitions, he closed down inefficient plants, and he moved factories to eastern European countries to take advantage of lower labor costs. Then he brought in Ed Foreman to charge up the troops. "After we got Ed in," says Johnston, "people began to live their lives differently. They came to work with a spring in their step." In 3 years, the division was bringing in annual profits of $100 million. Johnston gives a large part of the credit for this turnaround to Foreman.

What is Foreman's secret? He provides motivation and attitude training. Here's an example of Foreman's primary program, called the Successful Life Course. It lasts 3 days and begins each morning at 6 A.M. The first day begins with a chapter from an inspirational handout, followed by 12 minutes of yoga-like stretching. Then participants march up a hill, chanting, "I know I can, I know I can." This is followed by breakfast and then a variety of lectures on attitude, diet, and exercise. But the primary focus of the program is on attitude. Says Foreman, "It's your attitude, not your aptitude, that determines your altitude." Other parts of the program include group hugs, team activities, and mind-control relaxation exercises.

Johnston believes strongly in Foreman's program. "Positive attitude is the single biggest thing that can change a business," says Johnston. He sees Foreman's program as being a critical bridge linking employees with customers: "We're in the business of the maintenance and acquisition of customers." And with so many shoppers going through his stores, Johnston says this "provides a lot of opportunities for customer service. We've got to energize the associates." To prove he's willing to put his money where his mouth is, Johnston has committed $10 million to this training. By year-end 2004, 10,000 managers had taken the course. They, in turn, are training all 190,000 Albertsons associates, with the help of tapes and books.

Foreman says his program works. He cites success at companies such as Allstate, Milliken & Co., and Abbott Labs. "The goal is to improve mental, physical, and emotional well-being," he says. "We as individuals determine the success of our own lives. Positive thoughts create positive actions."

Questions

1. Explain how Foreman's 3-day course could positively influence the profitability of Albertsons.

2. Johnston says, "Positive attitude is the single biggest thing that can change a business." How valid and generalizable do you think this statement is?

3. If you were Johnston, what would you do to evaluate the effectiveness of your $10 million investment in Foreman's training program?

4. If you were an Albertsons employee, how would you feel about going through Foreman's course? Explain your position.

Source: Based on M. Burke, "The Guru in the Vegetable Bin," *Forbes*, March 3, 2003, pp. 56–58.

Case Incident 2

LONG HOURS, HUNDREDS OF E-MAILS, AND NO SLEEP: DOES THIS SOUND LIKE A SATISFYING JOB?

Although the 40-hour workweek is now the exception rather than the norm, some individuals are taking things to the extreme:

- John Bishop, 31, is an investment banker who works for Citigroup's global energy team in New York. A recent workday for Bishop consisted of heading to the office for a conference call at 6:00 P.M. He left the office at 1:30 A.M. and had to be on a plane that same morning for a 9:00 A.M. presentation in Houston. Following the presentation, Bishop returned to New York the same day, and by 7:00 P.M., he was back in his office to work an additional 3 hours. Says Bishop, "I might be a little skewed to the workaholic, but realistically, expecting 90 to 100 hours a week is not at all unusual."

- Irene Tse, 34, heads the government bond-trading division at Goldman Sachs. For 10 years, she has seen the stock market go from all-time highs to recession levels. Such fluctuations can mean millions of dollars in either profits or losses. "There are days when you can make a lot, and other days where you lose so much you're just stunned by what you've done," says Tse. She also states that she hasn't slept completely through the night in years and frequently wakes up several times during the night to check the global market status. Her average workweek? Eighty hours. "I've done this for 10 years, and I can count on the fingers of one hand the number of days in my career when I didn't want to come to work. Every day I wake up and I can't wait to get here."

- Tony Kurtz, 33, is a managing director at Capital Alliance Partners, and he raises funds for real estate investments. However, these are not your average properties. He often travels to exotic locations such as Costa Rica and Hawaii to woo prospective clients. He travels more than 300,000 miles per year, often sleeping on planes and dealing with jet lag. Kurz is not the only one he knows with such a hectic work schedule. His girlfriend, Avery Baker, logs around 400,000 miles a year, working as the senior vice president of marketing for Tommy Hilfiger. "It's not easy to maintain a relationship like this," says Kurz. But do Kurz and Baker like their jobs? You bet.

- David Clark, 35, is the vice president of global marketing for MTV. His job often consists of traveling around the globe to promote the channel as well as to keep up with the global music scene. If he is not traveling (Clark typically logs 200,000 miles a year), a typical day consists of waking at 6:30 A.M. and immediately responding to numerous messages that have accumulated over the course of the night. He then goes to his office, where throughout the day he responds to another 500 or so messages from clients around the world. If he's lucky, he gets to spend an hour a day with his son, but then it's back to work until he finally goes to bed around midnight. Says Clark, "there are plenty of people who would love to have this job. They're knocking on the door all the time. So that's motivating."

Many individuals would balk at the prospect of a 60-hour or more workweek with constant traveling and little time for anything else. However, some individuals are exhilarated by such professions. According to the Bureau of Labor Statistics, in 2004, about 17 percent of managers worked more than 60 hours per week. But the demands of such jobs are clearly not for everyone. Many quit, with turnover levels at 55 percent for consultants and 30 percent for investment bankers, according to Vault.com. However, it is clear that such jobs, which are time-consuming and often stressful, can be satisfying to some individuals.

Questions

1. Do you think only certain individuals are attracted to these types of jobs, or is it the characteristics of the jobs themselves that are satisfying?

2. What characteristics of these jobs might contribute to increased levels of job satisfaction?

3. Given that the four individuals we just read about tend to be satisfied with their jobs, how might this satisfaction relate to their job performance, citizenship behavior, and turnover?

4. Recall David Clark's statement that "there are plenty of people who would love to have this job. They're knocking on the door all the time." How might Clark's perceptions that he has a job many others desire contribute to his job satisfaction?

Source: Based on L. Tischler, "Extreme Jobs (And the People Who Love Them)," *Fast Company,* April 2005, pp. 55–60, www.glo-jobs.com/article.php?article_no=87.

Endnotes

1. M. Helft, "Google's Buses Help Its Workers Beat the Rush," *New York Times,* March 10, 2007, pp. A1, B9; E. Esen, *SHRM Job Satisfaction Series: 2005 Job Satisfaction* (Alexandria, VA: Society for Human Resource Management, 2005); and "Benefits," *Google.com,* www.google.com/support/jobs/bin/static.py?page=benefits.html&benefits=us.

2. S. J. Breckler, "Empirical Validation of Affect, Behavior, and Cognition as Distinct Components of Attitude," *Journal of Personality and Social Psychology,* May 1984, pp. 1191–1205; and S. L. Crites, Jr., L. R. Fabrigar, and R. E. Petty, "Measuring the Affective and Cognitive Properties of Attitudes: Conceptual and Methodological Issues," *Personality and Social Psychology Bulletin,* December 1994, pp. 619–634.

3. A. W. Wicker, "Attitude Versus Action: The Relationship of Verbal and Overt Behavioral Responses to Attitude Objects," *Journal of Social Issues,* Autumn 1969, pp. 41–78.

4. L. Festinger, *A Theory of Cognitive Dissonance* (Stanford, CA: Stanford University Press, 1957).

5. See, for instance, I. R. Newby-Clark, I. McGregor, and M. P. Zanna, "Thinking and Caring About Cognitive Consistency: When and for Whom Does Attitudinal Ambivalence Feel Uncomfortable?" *Journal of Personality & Social Psychology,* February 2002, pp. 157–166; and D. J. Schleicher, J. D. Watt, and G. J. Greguras, "Reexamining the Job Satisfaction-Performance Relationship: The Complexity of Attitudes," *Journal of Applied Psychology* 89, no. 1 (2004), pp. 165–177.

6. See, for instance, J. Nocera, "If It's Good for Philip Morris, Can It also Be Good for Public Health?" *New York Times,* June 18, 2006.

7. See L. R. Glasman and D. Albarracín, "Forming Attitudes That Predict Future Behavior: A Meta-analysis of the Attitude–Behavior Relation," *Psychological Bulletin,* September 2006, pp. 778–822; I. Ajzen, "The Directive Influence of Attitudes on Behavior," in M. Gollwitzer and J. A. Bargh (eds.), *The Psychology of Action: Linking Cognition and Motivation to Behavior* (New York: Guilford, 1996), pp. 385–403; and I. Ajzen, "Nature and Operation of Attitudes," in S. T. Fiske, D. L. Schacter, and C. Zahn-Waxler (eds.), *Annual Review of Psychology,* vol. 52 (Palo Alto, CA: Annual Reviews, Inc., 2001), pp. 27–58.

8. Ibid.

9. D. A. Harrison, D. A. Newman, and P. L. Roth, "How Important Are Job Attitudes? Meta-analytic Comparisons of Integrative Behavioral Outcomes and Time Sequences," *Academy of Management Journal* 49, no. 2 (2006), pp. 305–325.

10. P. P. Brooke, Jr., D. W. Russell, and J. L. Price, "Discriminant Validation of Measures of Job Satisfaction, Job Involvement, and Organizational Commitment," *Journal of Applied Psychology*, May 1988, pp. 139–145; and R. T. Keller, "Job Involvement and Organizational Commitment as Longitudinal Predictors of Job Performance: A Study of Scientists and Engineers," *Journal of Applied Psychology*, August 1997, pp. 539–545.

11. See, for example, S. Rabinowitz and D. T. Hall, "Organizational Research in Job Involvement," *Psychological Bulletin*, March 1977, pp. 265–288; G. J. Blau, "A Multiple Study Investigation of the Dimensionality of Job Involvement," *Journal of Vocational Behavior*, August 1985, pp. 19–36; C. L. Reeve and C. S. Smith, "Refining Lodahl and Kejner's Job Involvement Scale with a Convergent Evidence Approach: Applying Multiple Methods to Multiple Samples," *Organizational Research Methods*, April 2000, pp. 91–111; and J. M. Diefendorff, D. J. Brown, and A. M. Kamin, "Examining the Roles of Job Involvement and Work Centrality in Predicting Organizational Citizenship Behaviors and Job Performance," *Journal of Organizational Behavior*, February 2002, pp. 93–108.

12. Based on G. J. Blau and K. R. Boal, "Conceptualizing How Job Involvement and Organizational Commitment Affect Turnover and Absenteeism," *Academy of Management Review*, April 1987, p. 290.

13. K. W. Thomas and B. A. Velthouse, "Cognitive Elements of Empowerment: An 'Interpretive' Model of Intrinsic Task Motivation," *Academy of Management Review* 15, no. 4 (1990), pp. 666–681; G. M. Spreitzer, "Psychological Empowerment in the Workplace: Dimensions, Measurement, and Validation," *Academy of Management Journal* 38, no. 5 (1995), pp. 1442–1465; G. Chen and R. J. Klimoski, "The Impact of Expectations on Newcomer Performance in Teams as Mediated by Work Characteristics, Social Exchanges, and Empowerment," *Academy of Management Journal* 46, no. 5 (2003), pp. 591–607; A. Ergeneli, G. Saglam, and S. Metin, "Psychological Empowerment and Its Relationship to Trust in Immediate Managers," *Journal of Business Research*, January 2007, pp. 41–49; and S. E. Seibert, S. R. Silver, and W. A. Randolph, "Taking Empowerment to the Next Level: A Multiple-Level Model of Empowerment, Performance, and Satisfaction," *Academy of Management Journal* 47, no. 3 (2004), pp. 332–349.

14. B. J. Avolio, W. Zhu, W. Koh, and P. Bhatia, "Transformational Leadership and Organizational Commitment: Mediating Role of Psychological Empowerment and Moderating Role of Structural Distance," *Journal of Organizational Behavior* 25, no. 8, 2004, pp. 951–968.

15. J. M. Diefendorff, D. J. Brown, A. M. Kamin, and R. G. Lord, "Examining the Roles of Job Involvement and Work Centrality in Predicting Organizational Citizenship Behaviors and Job Performance," *Journal of Organizational Behavior*, February 2002, pp. 93–108.

16. G. J. Blau, "Job Involvement and Organizational Commitment as Interactive Predictors of Tardiness and Absenteeism," *Journal of Management*, Winter 1986, pp. 577–584; K. Boal and R. Cidambi, "Attitudinal Correlates of Turnover and Absenteeism: A Meta Analysis," paper presented at the meeting of the American Psychological Association, Toronto, Canada, 1984; and M. R. Barrick, M. K. Mount, and J. P. Strauss, "Antecedents of Involuntary Turnover Due to a Reduction in Force," *Personnel Psychology* 47, no. 3 (1994), pp. 515–535.

17. Blau and Boal, "Conceptualizing," p. 290.

18. J. P. Meyer, N. J. Allen, and C. A. Smith, "Commitment to Organizations and Occupations: Extension and Test of a Three-Component Conceptualization," *Journal of Applied Psychology* 78, no. 4 (1993), pp. 538–551.

19. M. Riketta, "Attitudinal Organizational Commitment and Job Performance: A Meta-analysis," *Journal of Organizational Behavior*, March 2002, pp. 257–266.

20. T. A. Wright and D. G. Bonett, "The Moderating Effects of Employee Tenure on the Relation Between Organizational Commitment and Job Performance: A Meta-analysis," *Journal of Applied Psychology*, December 2002, pp. 1183–1190.

21. See, for instance, W. Hom, R. Katerberg, and C. L. Hulin, "Comparative Examination of Three Approaches to the Prediction of Turnover," *Journal of Applied Psychology*, June 1979, pp. 280–290; H. Angle and J. Perry, "Organizational Commitment: Individual and Organizational Influence," *Work and Occupations*, May 1983, pp. 123–146; J. L. Pierce and R. B. Dunham, "Organizational Commitment: Pre-Employment Propensity and Initial Work Experiences," *Journal of Management*, Spring 1987, pp. 163–178; and T. Simons and Q. Roberson, "Why Managers Should Care About Fairness: The Effects of Aggregate Justice Perceptions on Organizational Outcomes," *Journal of Applied Psychology* 88, no. 3 (2003), pp. 432–443.

22. R. B. Dunham, J. A. Grube, and M. B. Castañeda, "Organizational Commitment: The Utility of an Integrative Definition," *Journal of Applied Psychology* 79, no. 3 (1994), pp. 370–380.

23. D. M. Rousseau, "Organizational Behavior in the New Organizational Era," in J. T. Spence, J. M. Darley, and D. J. Foss (eds.), *Annual Review of Psychology*, vol. 48 (Palo Alto, CA: Annual Reviews, 1997), p. 523.

24. Ibid.; K. Lee, J. J. Carswell, and N. J. Allen, "A Meta-analytic Review of Occupational Commitment: Relations with Person- and Work-Related Variables," *Journal of Applied Psychology*, October 2000, pp. 799–811; G. Blau, "On Assessing the Construct Validity of Two Multidimensional Constructs: Occupational Commitment and Occupational Entrenchment," *Human Resource Management Review*, Fall 2001, pp. 279–298; and E. Snape and T. Redman, "An Evaluation of a Three-Component Model of Occupational Commitment: Dimensionality and Consequences Among United Kingdom Human Resource Management Specialists," *Journal of Applied Psychology* 88, no. 1 (2003), pp. 152–159.

25. L. Rhoades, R. Eisenberger, and S. Armeli, "Affective Commitment to the Organization: The Contribution of Perceived Organizational Support," *Journal of Applied Psychology* 86, no. 5 (2001), pp. 825–836.

26. Z. X. Chen, S. Aryee, and C. Lee, "Test of a Mediation Model of Perceived Organizational Support," *Journal of Vocational Behavior*, June 2005, pp. 457–470; and J. A. M. Coyle-Shapiro

and N. Conway, "Exchange Relationships: Examining Psychological Contracts and Perceived Organizational Support," *Journal of Applied Psychology*, July 2005, pp. 774–781.

27. D. R. May, R. L. Gilson, and L. M. Harter, "The Psychological Conditions of Meaningfulness, Safety and Availability and the Engagement of the Human Spirit at Work," *Journal of Occupational and Organizational Psychology* 77, no. 1 (2004), pp. 11–37.

28. J. K. Harter, F. L. Schmidt, and T. L. Hayes, "Business-Unit-Level Relationship Between Employee Satisfaction, Employee Engagement, and Business Outcomes: A Meta-analysis," *Journal of Applied Psychology* 87, no. 2 (2002), pp. 268–279.

29. N. R. Lockwood, *Leveraging Employee Engagement for Competitive Advantage* (Alexandria, VA: Society for Human Resource Management, 2007); and R. J. Vance, *Employee Engagement and Commitment* (Alexandria, VA: Society for Human Resource Management, 2006).

30. L. Rhoades and R. Eisenberger, "Perceived Organizational Support: A Review of the Literature," *Journal of Applied Psychology* 87, no. 4 (2002), pp. 698–714; and R. L. Payne and D. Morrison, "The Differential Effects of Negative Affectivity on Measures of Well-Being Versus Job Satisfaction and Organizational Commitment," *Anxiety, Stress & Coping: An International Journal* 15, no. 3 (2002), pp. 231–244.

31. T. L. Stewart, J. R. LaDuke, C. Bracht, B. A. M. Sweet, and K. E. Gamarel, "Do the 'Eyes' Have It? A Program Evaluation of Jane Elliott's 'Blue-Eyes/Brown-Eyes' Diversity Training Exercise," *Journal of Applied Social Psychology* 33, no. 9 (2003), pp. 1898–1921.

32. For problems with the concept of job satisfaction, see R. Hodson, "Workplace Behaviors," *Work and Occupations*, August 1991, pp. 271–290; and H. M. Weiss and R. Cropanzano, "Affective Events Theory: A Theoretical Discussion of the Structure, Causes and Consequences of Affective Experiences at Work," in B. M. Staw and L. L. Cummings (eds.), *Research in Organizational Behavior*, vol. 18 (Greenwich, CT: JAI Press, 1996), pp. 1–3.

33. The Wyatt Company's 1989 national WorkAmerica study identified 12 dimensions of satisfaction: work organization, working conditions, communications, job performance and performance review, coworkers, supervision, company management, pay, benefits, career development and training, job content and satisfaction, and company image and change.

34. See E. Spector, *Job Satisfaction: Application, Assessment, Causes, and Consequences* (Thousand Oaks, CA: Sage, 1997), p. 3.

35. J. Wanous, A. E. Reichers, and M. J. Hudy, "Overall Job Satisfaction: How Good Are Single-Item Measures?" *Journal of Applied Psychology*, April 1997, pp. 247–252.

36. A. F. Chelte, J. Wright, and C. Tausky, "Did Job Satisfaction Really Drop During the 1970s?" *Monthly Labor Review*, November 1982, pp. 33–36; "Job Satisfaction High in America, Says Conference Board Study," *Monthly Labor Review*, February 1985, p. 52; E. Graham, "Work May Be a Rat Race, but It's Not a Daily Grind," *Wall Street Journal*, September 19, 1997, p. R1; and K. Bowman, "Attitudes About Work, Chores, and Leisure in America," *AEI Opinion Studies*, August 25, 2003.

37. W. K. Balzer, J. A. Kihm, P. C. Smith, J. L. Irwin, P. D. Bachiochi, C. Robie, E. F. Sinar, and L. F. Parra, *Users' Manual for the Job Descriptive Index (JDI; 1997 Revision) and the Job In General Scales* (Bowling Green, OH: Bowling Green State University, 1997).

38. J. Barling, E. K. Kelloway, and R. D. Iverson, "High-Quality Work, Job Satisfaction, and Occupational Injuries," *Journal of Applied Psychology* 88, no. 2 (2003), pp. 276–283; F. W. Bond and D. Bunce, "The Role of Acceptance and Job Control in Mental Health, Job Satisfaction, and Work Performance," *Journal of Applied Psychology* 88, no. 6 (2003), pp. 1057–1067.

39. E. Diener, E. Sandvik, L. Seidlitz, and M. Diener, "The Relationship Between Income and Subjective Well-Being: Relative or Absolute?" *Social Indicators Research* 28 (1993), pp. 195–223.

40. E. Diener and M. E. P. Seligman, "Beyond Money: Toward an Economy of Well-Being," *Psychological Science in the Public Interest* 5, no. 1 (2004), pp. 1–31; and A. Grant, "Money= Happiness? That's Rich: Here's the Science Behind the Axiom," *The (South Mississippi) Sun Herald*, January 8, 2005.

41. T. A. Judge and C. Hurst, "The Benefits and Possible Costs of Positive Core Self-Evaluations: A Review and Agenda for Future Research," in D. Nelson & C. L. Cooper (eds.), *Positive Organizational Behavior* (London, UK: Sage Publications, 2007), pp. 159–174.

42. M. T. Iaffaldano and M. Muchinsky, "Job Satisfaction and Job Performance: A Meta-analysis," *Psychological Bulletin*, March 1985, pp. 251–273.

43. T. A. Judge, C. J. Thoresen, J. E. Bono, and G. K. Patton, "The Job Satisfaction–Job Performance Relationship: A Qualitative and Quantitative Review," *Psychological Bulletin*, May 2001, pp. 376–407; T. Judge, S. Parker, A. E. Colbert, D. Heller, and R. Ilies, "Job Satisfaction: A Cross-Cultural Review," in N. Anderson, D. S. Ones, H. K. Sinangil, and C. Viswesvaran (eds.), *Handbook of Industrial, Work, & Organizational Psychology*, vol. 2 (Thousand Oaks, CA: Sage, 2001), p. 41.

44. C. N. Greene, "The Satisfaction–Performance Controversy," *Business Horizons*, February 1972, pp. 31–41; E. E. Lawler III, *Motivation in Organizations* (Monterey, CA: Brooks/Cole, 1973); and M. M. Petty, G. W. McGee, and J. W. Cavender, "A Meta-analysis of the Relationship Between Individual Job Satisfaction and Individual Performance," *Academy of Management Review*, October 1984, pp. 712–721.

45. See D. Farrell, "Exit, Voice, Loyalty, and Neglect as Responses to Job Dissatisfaction: A Multidimensional Scaling Study," *Academy of Management Journal*, December 1983, pp. 596–606; C. E. Rusbult, D. Farrell, G. Rogers, and A. G. Mainous III, "Impact of Exchange Variables on Exit, Voice, Loyalty, and Neglect: An Integrative Model of Responses to Declining Job Satisfaction," *Academy of Management Journal*, September 1988, pp. 599–627; M. J. Withey and W. H. Cooper, "Predicting Exit, Voice, Loyalty, and Neglect," *Administrative Science Quarterly*, December 1989, pp. 521–539; J. Zhou and J. M. George, "When Job Dissatisfaction Leads to Creativity: Encouraging the Expression of Voice," *Academy of Management Journal*, August 2001, pp. 682–696; J. B. Olson-Buchanan and W. R. Boswell, "The Role of Employee Loyalty and Formality in Voicing Discontent," *Journal of Applied Psychology*, December 2002, pp. 1167–1174; and A. Davis-Blake, J. P. Broschak, and E. George, "Happy Together? How Using Nonstandard Workers Affects Exit, Voice, and Loyalty Among Standard

Employees," *Academy of Management Journal* 46, no. 4 (2003), pp. 475–485.

46. R. B. Freeman, "Job Satisfaction as an Economic Variable," *American Economic Review,* January 1978, pp. 135–141.

47. T. A. Judge, C. J. Thoresen, J. E. Bono, and G. K. Patton, "The Job Satisfaction–Job Performance Relationship: A Qualitative and Quantitative Review," *Psychological Bulletin,* May 2001, pp. 376–407.

48. C. Ostroff, "The Relationship Between Satisfaction, Attitudes, and Performance: An Organizational Level Analysis," *Journal of Applied Psychology,* December 1992, pp. 963–974; A. M. Ryan, M. J. Schmit, and R. Johnson, "Attitudes and Effectiveness: Examining Relations at an Organizational Level," *Personnel Psychology,* Winter 1996, pp. 853–882; and J. K. Harter, F. L. Schmidt, and T. L. Hayes, "Business-Unit Level Relationship Between Employee Satisfaction, Employee Engagement, and Business Outcomes: A Meta-analysis," *Journal of Applied Psychology,* April 2002, pp. 268–279.

49. See T. S. Bateman and D. W. Organ, "Job Satisfaction and the Good Soldier: The Relationship Between Affect and Employee 'Citizenship'," *Academy of Management Journal,* December 1983, pp. 587–595; P. Podsakoff, S. B. MacKenzie, J. B. Paine, and D. G. Bachrach, "Organizational Citizenship Behaviors: A Critical Review of the Theoretical and Empirical Literature and Suggestions for Future Research," *Journal of Management* 26, no. 3 (2000), pp. 513–563.

50. B. J. Hoffman, C. A. Blair, J. P. Maeriac, and D. J. Woehr, "Expanding the Criterion Domain? A Quantitative Review of the OCB Literature," *Journal of Applied Psychology* 92, no. 2 (2007), pp. 555–566; D. W. Organ and K. Ryan, "A Meta-analytic Review of Attitudinal and Dispositional Predictors of Organizational Citizenship Behavior," *Personnel Psychology,* Winter 1995, pp. 775–802; and J. A. LePine, A. Erez, and D. E. Johnson, "The Nature and Dimensionality of Organizational Citizenship Behavior: A Critical Review and Meta-analysis," *Journal of Applied Psychology,* February 2002, pp. 52–65.

51. J. Fahr, P. M. Podsakoff, and D. W. Organ, "Accounting for Organizational Citizenship Behavior: Leader Fairness and Task Scope Versus Satisfaction," *Journal of Management,* December 1990, pp. 705–722; R. H. Moorman, "Relationship Between Organization Justice and Organizational Citizenship Behaviors: Do Fairness Perceptions Influence Employee Citizenship?" *Journal of Applied Psychology,* December 1991, pp. 845–855; and M. A. Konovsky and D. W. Organ, "Dispositional and Contextual Determinants of Organizational Citizenship Behavior," *Journal of Organizational Behavior,* May 1996, pp. 253–266.

52. D. W. Organ, "Personality and Organizational Citizenship Behavior," *Journal of Management,* Summer 1994, p. 466.

53. See, for instance, B. Schneider and D. E. Bowen, "Employee and Customer Perceptions of Service in Banks: Replication and Extension," *Journal of Applied Psychology,* August 1985, pp. 423–433; D. J. Koys, "The Effects of Employee Satisfaction, Organizational Citizenship Behavior, and Turnover on Organizational Effectiveness: A Unit-Level, Longitudinal Study," *Personnel Psychology,* Spring 2001, pp. 101–114; and J. Griffith, "Do Satisfied Employees Satisfy Customers? Support-Services Staff Morale and Satisfaction Among Public School Administrators, Students, and Parents," *Journal of Applied Social Psychology,* August 2001, pp. 1627–1658.

54. M. J. Bitner, B. H. Booms, and L. A. Mohr, "Critical Service Encounters: The Employee's Viewpoint," *Journal of Marketing,* October 1994, pp. 95–106.

55. E. A. Locke, "The Nature and Causes of Job Satisfaction," in M. D. Dunnette (ed.), *Handbook of Industrial and Organizational Psychology* (Chicago: Rand McNally, 1976), p. 1331; R. D. Hackett and R. M. Guion, "A Reevaluation of the Absenteeism–Job Satisfaction Relationship," *Organizational Behavior and Human Decision Processes,* June 1985, pp. 340–381; K. D. Scott and G. S. Taylor, "An Examination of Conflicting Findings on the Relationship between Job Satisfaction and Absenteeism: A Meta-analysis," *Academy of Management Journal,* September 1985, pp. 599–612; R. Steel and J. R. Rentsch, "Influence of Cumulation Strategies on the Long-Range Prediction of Absenteeism," *Academy of Management Journal,* December 1995, pp. 1616–1634; and G. Johns, "The Psychology of Lateness, Absenteeism, and Turnover," p. 237.

56. F. J. Smith, "Work Attitudes as Predictors of Attendance on a Specific Day," *Journal of Applied Psychology,* February 1977, pp. 16–19.

57. W. Hom and R. W. Griffeth, *Employee Turnover* (Cincinnati, OH: South-Western Publishing, 1995); R. W. Griffeth, P. W. Hom, and S. Gaertner, "A Meta-analysis of Antecedents and Correlates of Employee Turnover: Update, Moderator Tests, and Research Implications for the Next Millennium," *Journal of Management* 26, no. 3 (2000), p. 479; G. Johns, "The Psychology of Lateness, Absenteeism, and Turnover," p. 237.

58. See, for example, C. L. Hulin, M. Roznowski, and D. Hachiya, "Alternative Opportunities and Withdrawal Decisions: Empirical and Theoretical Discrepancies and an Integration," *Psychological Bulletin,* July 1985, pp. 233–250; and J. M. Carsten and P. E. Spector, "Unemployment, Job Satisfaction, and Employee Turnover: A Meta-analytic Test of the Muchinsky Model," *Journal of Applied Psychology,* August 1987, pp. 374–381.

59. D. G. Spencer and R. M. Steers, "Performance as a Moderator of the Job Satisfaction–Turnover Relationship," *Journal of Applied Psychology,* August 1981, pp. 511–514.

60. K. A. Hanisch, C. L. Hulin, and M. Roznowski, "The Importance of Individuals' Repertoires of Behaviors: The Scientific Appropriateness of Studying Multiple Behaviors and General Attitudes," *Journal of Organizational Behavior* 19, no. 5 (1998), pp. 463–480.

61. K. Holland, "Inside the Minds of Your Employees," *New York Times* (January 28, 2007), p. B1; "Study Sees Link Between Morale and Stock Price," *Workforce Management* (February 27, 2006), p. 15; and "The Workplace as a Solar System," *New York Times* (October 28, 2006), p. B5.

62. M. J. Gelfand, M. Erez, and Z. Aycan, "Cross-Cultural Organizational Behavior," *Annual Review of Psychology* 58 (2007), pp. 479–514; A. S. Tsui, S. S. Nifadkar, and A. Y. Ou, "Cross-National, Cross-Cultural Organizational Behavior Research: Advances, Gaps, and Recommendations," *Journal of Management,* June 2007, pp. 426–478.

63. M. Benz and B. S. Frey, "The Value of Autonomy: Evidence from the Self-Employed in 23 Countries," working paper 173, Institute for Empirical Research in Economics, University of Zurich, November 2003 (http://ssrn.com/

abstract=475140); and P. Warr, *Work, Happiness, and Unhappiness* (Mahwah, NJ: Laurence Erlbaum, 2007).

64. Harrison, Newman, and Roth, "How Important Are Job Attitudes?" pp. 320–321.

65. Judge, et al., "Job Satisfaction: A Cross-Cultural Review"; T. A. Judge and A. H. Church, "Job Satisfaction: Research and Practice," in C. L. Cooper and E. A. Locke (eds.), *Industrial and Organizational Psychology: Linking Theory with Practice* (Oxford, UK: Blackwell, 2000), pp. 166–198; L. Saari and T. A. Judge, "Employee Attitudes and Job Satisfaction," *Human Resource Management* 43, no. 4 (2004), pp. 395–407.

66. See, for instance, R. D. Arvey, B. McCall, T. J. Bouchard, Jr., and P. Taubman, "Genetic Influences on Job Satisfaction and Work Values," *Personality and Individual Differences*, July 1994, pp. 21–33; D. Lykken and A. Tellegen, "Happiness Is a Stochastic Phenomenon," *Psychological Science*, May 1996, pp. 186–189; and D. Lykken and M. Csikszentmihalyi, "Happiness—Stuck with What You've Got?" *Psychologist*, September 2001, pp. 470–472; and "Double Take," *UNH Magazine*, Spring 2000, www.unhmagazine.unh.edu/sp00/twinssp00.html.

Personality and Values

I am driven by fear of failure.
It is a strong motivator for me.

—Dennis Manning, CEO of
Guardian Life Insurance Co.

LEARNING OBJECTIVES

After studying this chapter, you should be able to:

1 Define *personality*, describe how it is measured, and explain the factors that determine an individual's personality.

2 Describe the Myers-Briggs Type Indicator personality framework and assess its strengths and weaknesses.

3 Identify the key traits in the Big Five personality model.

4 Demonstrate how the Big Five traits predict behavior at work.

5 Identify other personality traits relevant to OB.

6 Define *values*, demonstrate the importance of values, and contrast terminal and instrumental values.

7 Compare generational differences in values and identify the dominant values in today's workforce.

8 Identify Hofstede's five value dimensions of national culture.

*J*ohn Ruskin wrote that the first test of a truly great man is his humility. Don't tell that to Stephen Schwarzman, chief executive of the Blackstone Group. Schwarzman says his mission in life is to "inflict pain" and "kill off" his rivals. "I want war," he told the *Wall Street Journal*," not a series of skirmishes." And win in business he has. In 20 years, he has made Blackstone one of the most profitable—and most feared—investment groups on Wall Street, with assets approaching $100 billion.

The Seven-Billion-Dollar Man

Source: Fred R. Conrad/The New York Times

Recently, Blackstone went public, and Schwarzman profited to the tune of $7.75 billion. His successes as an investment banker are so legendary that, in 2007, *Fortune* dubbed him the "King of Wall Street." David Rubenstein, co-founder of rival buyout firm Carlyle Group, told Schwarzman, "I wish you would retire so you wouldn't compete with us on deals."

Not only is the 5'6" Schwarzman combative, he likes the attention his success has produced. When he turned 60, his birthday party was anything but modest. The affair was emceed by comedian Martin Short. Rod Stewart performed. Marvin Hamlisch put on a number from *A Chorus Line*. Singer Patti LaBelle led the Abyssinian Baptist Church choir in a song about

Schwarzman. Who staged this event? Why, Schwarzman himself. When Blackstone executives prepared a video tribute to him to be played at the event, Schwarzman intervened to squelch any roasting or other jokes played at his expense.

As you might imagine, Schwarzman is not the easiest guy to work for. When he was sunning himself at his 11,000-square-foot estate in Palm Beach, Florida, he complained that an employee wasn't wearing the proper black shoes with his uniform. On another occasion, he reportedly fired a Blackstone executive for the sound his nose made when he breathed.

The image of an enormously successful, demanding, and, yes, glamorous business leader does not daunt Schwarzman. "You wouldn't have a party for 500 people or buy trophy properties in Palm Beach or on Park Avenue if you didn't relish the notoriety," says one longtime Wall Street executive.

No matter what you think of what a Harvard roommate of Schwarzman calls his desire "to be above the crowd," there is no denying that Schwarzman has been a huge success. You may even be interested in working for him. If you do, just be careful how you breathe.[1] ■

Our personalities shape our behaviors. So if we want to better understand the behavior of someone in an organization, it helps if we know something about his or her personality. In the first half of this chapter, we review the research on personality and its relationship to behavior. In the latter half, we look at how values shape many of our work-related behaviors.

One of the personality traits we'll discuss is narcissism. Like many other CEOs and celebrities, Stephen Schwarzman might be described as relatively narcissistic. Check out the Self-Assessment Library to see how you score on narcissism (remember: be honest!).

AM I A NARCISSIST?

In the Self-Assessment Library (available on CD or online), take assessment IV.A.1 (Am I a Narcissist?) and answer the following questions.

1. *How did you score? Did your scores surprise you? Why or why not?*
2. *On which facet of narcissism was your highest score? your lowest?*
3. *Do you think this measure is accurate? Why or why not?*

Personality

1 *Define personality, describe how it is measured, and explain the factors that determine an individual's personality.*

Why are some people quiet and passive, while others are loud and aggressive? Are certain personality types better adapted than others for certain job types? Before we can answer these questions, we need to address a more basic one: What is personality?

What Is Personality?

When we talk of personality, we don't mean that a person has charm, a positive attitude toward life, a smiling face, or a place as a finalist for "Happiest and Friendliest" in this year's Miss America contest. When psychologists talk of personality, they mean a dynamic concept describing the growth and development of a person's whole psychological system. Rather than looking at parts of the person, personality looks at some aggregate whole that is greater than the sum of the parts.

Defining *Personality*   The definition of *personality* we most frequently use was produced by Gordon Allport nearly 70 years ago. He said personality is "the dynamic organization within the individual of those psychophysical systems that determine his unique adjustments to his environment."[2] For our purposes, you should think of **personality** as the sum total of ways in which an individual reacts to and interacts with others. We most often describe it in terms of the measurable traits a person exhibits.

Measuring Personality   The most important reason managers need to know how to measure personality is that research has shown that personality tests are useful in hiring decisions. Scores on personality tests help managers forecast who is the best bet for a job.[3] And some managers want to know how people score on personality tests to better understand and more effectively manage the people who work for them. Far and away the most common means of measuring personality is through self-report surveys, with which individuals evaluate themselves by rating themselves on a series of factors such as "I worry a lot about the future." Though self-report measures work well when well constructed, one weakness of these measures is that the respondent might lie or practice impression management—that is, the person could "fake good" on the test to create a good impression. This is especially a concern when the survey is the basis for employment. Another problem is accuracy. In other words, a perfectly good candidate could have just been in a bad mood when the survey was taken.

Observer-ratings surveys provide an independent assessment of personality. Instead of self-reporting, a coworker or another observer does the rating (sometimes with the subject's knowledge and sometimes not). Even though the results of self-report surveys and observer-ratings surveys are strongly correlated, research suggests that observer-ratings surveys are a better predictor of success on the job.[4] However, each can tell us something unique about an individual's behavior in the workplace.

Personality Determinants   An early debate in personality research centered on whether an individual's personality was the result of heredity or of environment. Was the personality predetermined at birth, or was it the result of the individual's interaction with his or her surroundings? Clearly, there's no simple black-and-white answer. Personality appears to be a result of both hereditary and environmental factors. However, it might surprise you that research in personality development has tended to better support the importance of heredity over the environment.

Heredity refers to factors determined at conception. Physical stature, facial attractiveness, gender, temperament, muscle composition and reflexes, energy

personality   The sum total of ways in which an individual reacts to and interacts with others.

heredity   Factors determined at conception, one's biological, physiological, and inherent psychological makeup.

A study of identical twins reared apart concluded that heredity plays an important role in determining personality. Dr. Nancy Segal, co-director of the University of Minnesota research project, is shown here with twins separated at birth, reared in different family environments, and reunited after 31 years. Segal and her team of researchers discovered that the sets of twins studied shared more personality characteristics than siblings raised in the same family.

level, and biological rhythms are generally considered to be either completely or substantially influenced by who your parents are—that is, by their biological, physiological, and inherent psychological makeup. The heredity approach argues that the ultimate explanation of an individual's personality is the molecular structure of the genes, located in the chromosomes.

Studies of young children lend strong support to the power of heredity.[5] Evidence demonstrates that traits such as shyness, fear, and aggression can be traced to inherited genetic characteristics. This finding suggests that some personality traits may be built into the same genetic code that affects factors such as height and hair color.

Researchers in many different countries have studied thousands of sets of identical twins who were separated at birth and raised separately.[6] If heredity played little or no part in determining personality, you would expect to find few similarities between the separated twins. But the researchers found a lot in common. For almost every behavioral trait, a significant part of the variation between the twins turned out to be associated with genetic factors. For instance, one set of twins who had been separated for 39 years and raised 45 miles apart were found to drive the same model and color car. They chain-smoked the same brand of cigarette, owned dogs with the same name, and regularly vacationed within three blocks of each other in a beach community 1,500 miles away. Researchers have found that genetics accounts for about 50 percent of the personality differences and more than 30 percent of the variation in occupational and leisure interests.

Interestingly, the twin studies have suggested the parental environment doesn't add much to our personality development. In other words, the personalities of identical twins raised in different households are more similar to each other than to the personalities of the siblings they were actually raised with. Ironically, the most important contribution our parents may have made to our personalities is giving us their genes!

This is not to suggest that personality never changes. Over periods of time, people's personalities do change. Most research in this area suggests that while

Exhibit **4-1**

Source: PEANUTS. Reprinted with permission of United Features Syndicate, Inc.

some aspects of our personalities do change over time, the rank orderings do not change very much. For example, people's scores on measures of dependability tend to increase over time. However, there are still strong individual differences in dependability, and despite the fact that most of us become more responsible over time, people tend to change by about the same amount so that the rank order stays roughly the same.[7] An analogy to intelligence may make this clearer. Children become smarter as they age so that nearly everyone is smarter at age 20 than they were at age 10. Still, if Madison is smarter than Blake at age 10, she is likely to be so at age 20, too. The same holds true with personality: If you are more dependable than your sibling now, that is likely to be true in 20 years, even though you both should become more dependable over time.

Early work on the structure of personality tried to identify and label enduring characteristics that describe an individual's behavior. Popular characteristics include shy, aggressive, submissive, lazy, ambitious, loyal, and timid. When someone exhibits these characteristics in a large number of situations, we call them **personality traits**.[8] The more consistent the characteristic and the more frequently a trait occurs in diverse situations, the more important that trait is in describing the individual.

A number of early efforts tried to identify the primary traits that govern behavior.[9] However, for the most part, they resulted in long lists of traits that were difficult to generalize from and provided little practical guidance to organizational decision makers. Two exceptions are the Myers-Briggs Type Indicator and the Big Five Model. Over the past 20 years, these two approaches have become the dominant frameworks for identifying and classifying traits.

The Myers-Briggs Type Indicator

> *2 Describe the Myers-Briggs Type Indicator personality framework and assess its strengths and weaknesses.*

The **Myers-Briggs Type Indicator (MBTI)** is the most widely used personality-assessment instrument in the world.[10] It's a 100-question personality test that asks people how they usually feel or act in particular situations. On the basis of their answers, individuals are classified as extraverted or introverted (E or I), sensing or intuitive (S or N),

---

personality traits *Enduring characteristics that describe an individual's behavior.*

Myers-Briggs Type Indicator (MBTI) *A personality test that taps four characteristics and classifies people into 1 of 16 personality types.*

Indra Nooyi, CEO and chair of PepsiCo, scores high on all personality dimensions of the Big Five model. She is described as sociable, agreeable, conscientious, emotionally stable, and open to experiences. These personality traits have contributed to Nooyi's high job performance and career success at PepsiCo; she joined the company in 1994 as senior vice president of strategy and development, and she was promoted to president and chief financial officer before moving into the firm's top position.

thinking or feeling (T or F), and judging or perceiving (J or P). These terms are defined as follows:

- *Extraverted versus introverted.*   Extraverted individuals are outgoing, sociable, and assertive. Introverts are quiet and shy.
- *Sensing versus intuitive.*   Sensing types are practical and prefer routine and order. They focus on details. Intuitives rely on unconscious processes and look at the "big picture."
- *Thinking versus feeling.*   Thinking types use reason and logic to handle problems. Feeling types rely on their personal values and emotions.
- *Judging versus perceiving.*   Judging types want control and prefer their world to be ordered and structured. Perceiving types are flexible and spontaneous.

These classifications together describe 16 personality types. To illustrate, let's take several examples. INTJs are visionaries. They usually have original minds and great drive for their own ideas and purposes. They are skeptical, critical, independent, determined, and often stubborn. ESTJs are organizers. They are realistic, logical, analytical, and decisive and have a natural head for business or mechanics. They like to organize and run activities. The ENTP type is a conceptualizer. He or she is innovative, individualistic, versatile, and attracted to entrepreneurial ideas. This person tends to be resourceful in solving challenging problems but may neglect routine assignments. A book profiling 13 contemporary businesspeople who created super-successful firms including Apple Computer, FedEx, Honda Motors, Microsoft, and Sony found that all were intuitive thinkers (NTs).[11] This result is particularly interesting because intuitive thinkers represent only about 5 percent of the population.

The MBTI is widely used in practice by organizations including Apple Computer, AT&T, Citigroup, GE, 3M Co., many hospitals and educational institutions, and even the U.S. Armed Forces. In spite of its popularity, the evidence is mixed as to whether the MBTI is a valid measure of personality—with most of the evidence suggesting that it isn't.[12] One problem is that it forces a person into either one type or another (that is, you're either introverted or extraverted). There is no in-between, though people can be both extraverted and introverted to some degree. The best we can say is that the MBTI can be a valuable tool for increasing self-awareness and providing career guidance. But because results tend to be unrelated to job performance, managers probably shouldn't use it as a selection test for job candidates.

The Big Five Personality Model

3 *Identify the key traits in the Big Five personality model.*

The MBTI may lack for strong supporting evidence, but the same can't be said for the five-factor model of personality typically called the **Big Five Model**, or the "Big Five." An impressive body of research supports its thesis that five basic dimensions underlie all others and encompass most of the significant variation in human personality.[13] The Big Five factors are:

- *Extraversion.*   The **extraversion** dimension captures one's comfort level with relationships. Extraverts tend to be gregarious, assertive, and sociable. Introverts tend to be reserved, timid, and quiet.
- *Agreeableness.*   The **agreeableness** dimension refers to an individual's propensity to defer to others. Highly agreeable people are cooperative, warm, and trusting. People who score low on agreeableness are cold, disagreeable, and antagonistic.
- *Conscientiousness.*   The **conscientiousness** dimension is a measure of reliability. A highly conscientious person is responsible, organized, dependable,

and persistent. Those who score low on this dimension are easily distracted, disorganized, and unreliable.

- *Emotional stability.*   The **emotional stability** dimension—often labeled by its converse, neuroticism—taps a person's ability to withstand stress. People with positive emotional stability tend to be calm, self-confident, and secure. Those with high negative scores tend to be nervous, anxious, depressed, and insecure.

- *Openness to experience.*   The **openness to experience** dimension addresses one's range of interests and fascination with novelty. Extremely open people are creative, curious, and artistically sensitive. Those at the other end of the openness category are conventional and find comfort in the familiar.

How Do the Big Five Traits Predict Behavior at Work? Research on the Big Five has found relationships between these personality dimensions and job performance.[14] As the authors of the most-cited review put it: "The preponderance of evidence shows that individuals who are dependable, reliable, careful, thorough, able to plan, organized, hardworking, persistent, and achievement-oriented tend to have higher job performance in most if not all occupations."[15] In addition, employees who score higher in conscientiousness develop higher levels of job knowledge, probably because highly conscientious people exert greater levels of effort on their jobs. The higher levels of job knowledge then contribute to higher levels of job performance.[16]

Although conscientiousness is the Big Five trait most consistently related to job performance, the other traits are related to aspects of performance in some situations. All five traits also have other implications for work and for life. Let's look at the implications of these traits one at a time. Exhibit 4-2 summarizes the discussion.

People who score high on emotional stability are happier than those who score low. Of the Big Five traits, emotional stability is most strongly related to life satisfaction, job satisfaction, and low stress levels. This is probably true because high scorers are more likely to be positive and optimistic in their thinking and experience fewer negative emotions. People low on emotional stability are hyper-vigilant (looking for problems or impending signs of danger), and high scores are associated with fewer health complaints. One upside of low emotional stability, however, is that when in a bad mood, such people make faster and better decisions than emotionally stable people in bad moods.[17]

Compared to introverts, extraverts tend to be happier in their jobs and in their lives as a whole. They experience more positive emotions than do introverts, and they more freely express these feelings. They also tend to perform better in jobs that require significant interpersonal interaction, perhaps because they have more social skills—they usually have more friends and spend more time in social situations than introverts. Finally, extraversion is a relatively

4 *Demonstrate how the Big Five traits predict behavior at work.*

Big Five Model   *A personality assessment model that taps five basic dimensions.*

extraversion   *A personality dimension describing someone who is sociable, gregarious, and assertive.*

agreeableness   *A personality dimension that describes someone who is good natured, cooperative, and trusting.*

conscientiousness   *A personality dimension that describes someone who is responsible, dependable, persistent, and organized.*

emotional stability   *A personality dimension that characterizes someone as calm, self-confident, secure (positive) versus nervous, depressed, and insecure (negative).*

openness to experience   *A personality dimension that characterizes someone in terms of imagination, sensitivity, and curiosity.*

Exhibit 4-2	Model of How Big Five Traits Influence OB Criteria

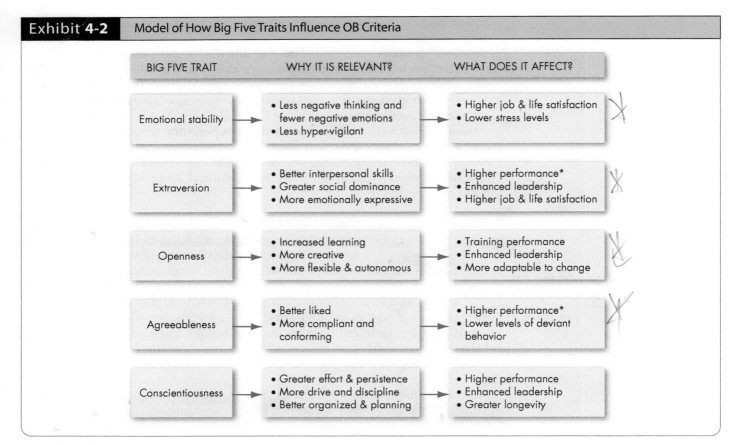

BIG FIVE TRAIT	WHY IT IS RELEVANT?	WHAT DOES IT AFFECT?
Emotional stability	• Less negative thinking and fewer negative emotions • Less hyper-vigilant	• Higher job & life satisfaction • Lower stress levels
Extraversion	• Better interpersonal skills • Greater social dominance • More emotionally expressive	• Higher performance* • Enhanced leadership • Higher job & life satisfaction
Openness	• Increased learning • More creative • More flexible & autonomous	• Training performance • Enhanced leadership • More adaptable to change
Agreeableness	• Better liked • More compliant and conforming	• Higher performance* • Lower levels of deviant behavior
Conscientiousness	• Greater effort & persistence • More drive and discipline • Better organized & planning	• Higher performance • Enhanced leadership • Greater longevity

*In jobs requiring significant teamwork or frequent interpersonal interactions.

strong predictor of leadership emergence in groups; extraverts are more socially dominant, "take charge" sorts of people, and they are generally are more assertive than introverts.[18] One downside of extraversion is that extraverts are more impulsive than introverts; they are more likely to be absent from work and engage in risky behavior such as unprotected sex, drinking, and other impulsive or sensation-seeking acts.[19]

Individuals who score high on openness to experience are more creative in science and in art than those who score low. Because creativity is important to leadership, open people are more likely to be effective leaders. Also, open individuals are more comfortable with ambiguity and change than are those who score lower on this trait. As a result, open people cope better with organizational change and are more adaptable in changing contexts.[20]

You might expect agreeable people to be happier than disagreeable people, and they are, but only slightly. When people choose romantic partners, friends, or organizational team members, agreeable individuals are usually their first choice. Thus, agreeable individuals are better liked than disagreeable people, which explains why they tend to do better in interpersonally oriented jobs such as customer service. Agreeable people also are more compliant and rule abiding. Agreeable children do better in school and as adults are less likely to get involved in drugs or excessive drinking.[21] Thus, agreeable individuals are less likely to engage in organizational deviance. One downside of agreeableness is that it is associated with lower levels of career success (especially earnings). This may occur because agreeable individuals are poorer negotiators; they are so concerned with pleasing others that they often don't negotiate as much for themselves as do others.[22]

Interestingly, conscientious people live longer than less conscientious people because they tend to take better care of themselves (eat better, exercise more) and engage in fewer risky behaviors (smoking, drinking/drugs, risky sexual or driving behavior).[23] Still, there are downsides to conscientiousness. It appears that conscientious people, probably because they're so organized and structured, don't adapt as well to changing contexts. Conscientious people are generally performance oriented. They have more trouble than less conscientious people learning complex skills early in the training process because their focus is on performing well rather than on learning. Finally, conscientious people are often less creative than less conscientious people, especially artistically.[24]

Other Personality Traits Relevant to OB

5 *Identify other personality traits relevant to OB.*

Although the Big Five traits have proven to be highly relevant to OB, they don't exhaust the range of traits we can use to describe someone's personality. Now we'll look at other, more specific, personality attributes that have been found to be powerful predictors of behavior in organizations. The first relates to one's core self-evaluation. The others are Machiavellianism, narcissism, self-monitoring, propensity for risk taking, and the Type A and proactive personalities.

Core Self-Evaluation People differ in the degree to which they like or dislike themselves and whether they see themselves as capable and effective. This self-perspective is the concept of **core self-evaluation**. People who have positive core self-evaluations like themselves and see themselves as effective, capable, and in control of their environment. Those with negative core self-evaluations tend to dislike themselves, question their capabilities, and view themselves as powerless over their environment.[25] We discussed in Chapter 3 that core self-evaluations relate to job satisfaction because people with positive core self-evaluations see more challenge in their job and actually attain more complex jobs.

But what about job performance? People with positive core self-evaluations perform better than others because they set more ambitious goals, are more committed to their goals, and persist longer at attempting to reach these goals. For example, one study of life insurance agents found that core self-evaluations were critical predictors of performance. In life insurance sales, 90 percent of sales calls end in rejection, so an agent has to believe in him- or herself to persist. In fact, this study showed that the majority of successful salespersons had positive core self-evaluations.[26]

You might wonder whether someone can be *too* positive. In other words, what happens when someone thinks he is capable, but he is actually incompetent? One study of Fortune 500 CEOs, for example, showed that many are overconfident, and their perceived infallibility often causes them to make bad decisions.[27] Teddy Forstmann, chairman of the sports marketing giant IMG, said of himself, "I know God gave me an unusual brain. I can't deny that. I have a God-given talent for seeing potential."[28] One might say that people like Forstmann are over-confident, but very often we humans sell ourselves short and are less happy and effective than we could be because of it. If we decide we can't do something, for example, we won't try, and not doing it only reinforces our self-doubts.

core self-evaluation *The degree to which an individual likes or dislikes himself or herself, whether the person sees himself or herself as capable and effective, and whether the person feels in control of his or her environment or powerless over the environment.*

A positive core self-evaluation helps U.S. Secretary of State Condoleezza Rice meet the daunting challenges and complexity of her job. Confident, skilled in diplomacy, and possessing a relentless work ethic, Rice views her job as an opportunity to shape U.S. foreign policy and to take a global leadership role in spreading democracy and constructing a peaceful international climate. Rice works toward these goals by managing relationships with foreign leaders and diplomats, such as with Alexander Downer, Australia's Minister of Foreign Affairs, shown here.

Machiavellianism Kuzi is a young bank manager in Taiwan. He's had three promotions in the past 4 years. Kuzi makes no apologies for the aggressive tactics he's used to propel his career upward. "I'm prepared to do whatever I have to do to get ahead," he says. Kuzi would properly be called Machiavellian. Shawna led her St. Louis–based company last year in sales performance. She's assertive and persuasive, and she's effective at manipulating customers to buy her product line. Many of her colleagues, including her boss, also consider Shawna as Machiavellian.

The personality characteristic of **Machiavellianism** (often abbreviated Mach) is named after Niccolo Machiavelli, who wrote in the sixteenth century on how to gain and use power. An individual high in Machiavellianism is pragmatic, maintains emotional distance, and believes that ends can justify means. "If it works, use it" is consistent with a high-Mach perspective. A considerable amount of research has been directed toward relating high- and low-Mach personalities to certain behavioral outcomes.[29] High Machs manipulate more, win more, are persuaded less, and persuade others more than do low Machs.[30] Yet high-Mach outcomes are moderated by situational factors. It has been found that high Machs flourish (1) when they interact face-to-face with others rather than indirectly; (2) when the situation has a minimal number of rules and regulations, thus allowing latitude for improvisation; and (3) when emotional involvement with details irrelevant to winning distracts low Machs.[31] Thus, whether high Machs make good employees depends on the type of job. In jobs that require bargaining skills (such as labor negotiation) or that offer substantial rewards for winning (such as commissioned sales), high Machs will be productive. But if ends can't justify the means, if there are absolute standards of behavior, or if the three situational factors we noted are not in evidence, our ability to predict a high Mach's performance will be severely curtailed.

Narcissism Hans likes to be the center of attention. He likes to look at himself in the mirror a lot. He has extravagant dreams and seems to consider himself a person of many talents. Hans is a narcissist. The term is from the Greek myth of Narcissus, the story of a man so vain and proud that he fell in love with his own image. In psychology, **narcissism** describes a person who has a grandiose sense of self-importance, requires excessive admiration, has a sense of entitlement, and is arrogant. An example of narcissistic personality might be Linda Wachner, former CEO of Warnaco. Designer Calvin Klein sued Warnaco for violating a licensing agreement. He described Wachner as having a "vulgar and unprofessional management style." Although Klein and Wachner later settled, Wachner was fired after the company's stock dropped 87 percent in a year, all the way to $1.30 per share. After her firing, Wachner sued Warnaco for $25 million in back pay, and said confidently, "I'm a visionary, and I know it."[32]

A study found that while narcissists thought they were *better* leaders than their colleagues, their supervisors actually rated them as *worse* leaders. For example, an Oracle executive described that company's CEO Larry Ellison as follows: "The difference between God and Larry is that God does not believe he is Larry."[33] Because narcissists often want to gain the admiration of others and receive affirmation of their superiority, they tend to "talk down" to those who threaten them, treating others as if they were inferior. Narcissists also tend to be selfish and exploitive, and they often carry the attitude that others exist for their benefit.[34] Studies indicate that narcissists are rated by their bosses as less effective at their jobs than others, particularly when it comes to helping other people.[35]

Self-Monitoring Joyce McIntyre is always in trouble at work. Though she's competent, hardworking, and productive, her performance reviews tend to rate her no better than average, and she seems to have made a career of irritating bosses. Joyce's problem is that she's politically inept. She's unable to adjust her

Real estate developer Donald Trump is willing to take chances. His risk-taking personality enables him to thrive in situations that others find perilous and stressful. Undeterred by financial setbacks, Trump continues to build his net worth by developing new projects such as the Trump International Hotel and Tower in Chicago, shown here, co-producing and starring in *The Apprentice*, marketing lines of clothing and furniture, and authoring best-selling books.

behavior to fit changing situations. As she puts it, "I'm true to myself. I don't remake myself to please others." We would be correct in describing Joyce as a low self-monitor.

Self-monitoring refers to an individual's ability to adjust his or her behavior to external, situational factors.[36] Individuals high in self-monitoring show considerable adaptability in adjusting their behavior to external situational factors. They are highly sensitive to external cues and can behave differently in different situations. High self-monitors are capable of presenting striking contradictions between their public persona and their private self. Low self-monitors, like Joyce, can't disguise themselves in that way. They tend to display their true dispositions and attitudes in every situation; hence, there is high behavioral consistency between who they are and what they do.

The evidence indicates that high self-monitors tend to pay closer attention to the behavior of others and are more capable of conforming than are low self-monitors.[37] They also receive better performance ratings, are more likely to emerge as leaders, and show less commitment to their organizations.[38] In addition, high self-monitoring managers tend to be more mobile in their careers, receive more promotions (both internal and cross-organizational), and are more likely to occupy central positions in an organization.[39]

Risk Taking   Donald Trump stands out for his willingness to take risks. He started with almost nothing in the 1960s. By the mid-1980s, he had made a fortune by betting on a resurgent New York City real estate market. Then, trying to

Machiavellianism   *The degree to which an individual is pragmatic, maintains emotional distance, and believes that ends can justify means.*

narcissism   *The tendency to be arrogant, have a grandiose sense of self-importance, require excessive admiration, and have a sense of entitlement.*

self-monitoring   *A personality trait that measures an individual's ability to adjust his or her behavior to external, situational factors.*

capitalize on his previous successes, Trump overextended himself. By 1994, he had a *negative* net worth of $850 million. Never fearful of taking chances, "The Donald" leveraged the few assets he had left on several New York, New Jersey, and Caribbean real estate ventures. He hit it big again. In 2007, *Forbes* estimated his net worth at $2.9 billion.

People differ in their willingness to take chances. This propensity to assume or avoid risk has been shown to have an impact on how long it takes managers to make a decision and how much information they require before making a choice. For instance, 79 managers worked on simulated personnel exercises that required them to make hiring decisions.[40] High risk-taking managers made more rapid decisions and used less information in making their choices than did the low risk-taking managers. Interestingly, decision accuracy was the same for both groups.

Although previous studies have shown managers in large organizations to be more risk averse than growth-oriented entrepreneurs who actively manage small businesses, recent findings suggest that managers in large organizations may actually be more willing to take risks than entrepreneurs.[41] For the work population as a whole, there are also differences in risk propensity.[42] As a result, it makes sense to recognize these differences and even to consider aligning risk-taking propensity with specific job demands. For instance, a high risk-taking propensity may lead to more effective performance for a stock trader in a brokerage firm because that type of job demands rapid decision making. On the other hand, a willingness to take risks might prove a major obstacle to an accountant who performs auditing activities. The latter job might be better filled by someone with a low risk-taking propensity.

Type A Personality   Do you know people who are excessively competitive and always seem to be experiencing a sense of time urgency? If you do, it's a good bet those people have **Type A personalities**. A person with a Type A personality is "aggressively involved in a chronic, incessant struggle to achieve more and more in less and less time, and, if required to do so, against the opposing efforts of other things or other persons."[43] In the North American culture, such characteristics tend to be highly prized and positively associated with ambition and the successful acquisition of material goods. Type A's:

1. are always moving, walking, and eating rapidly;
2. feel impatient with the rate at which most events take place;
3. strive to think or do two or more things at once;
4. cannot cope with leisure time;
5. are obsessed with numbers, measuring their success in terms of how many or how much of everything they acquire.

In contrast to the Type A personality is the Type B, who is exactly opposite. Type B's are "rarely harried by the desire to obtain a wildly increasing number of things or participate in an endless growing series of events in an ever-decreasing amount of time."[44] Type B's never suffer from a sense of time urgency with its accompanying impatience, can relax without guilt, and so on.

Type A's operate under moderate to high levels of stress. They subject themselves to more or less continuous time pressure, creating for themselves a life of deadlines. These characteristics result in some rather specific behavioral outcomes. For example, Type A's are fast workers because they emphasize quantity over quality. In managerial positions, Type A's demonstrate their competitiveness by working long hours and, not infrequently, making poor decisions   to new problems. They rarely vary in their responses to specific challenges in their milieu; hence, their behavior is easier to predict than that of Type B's.

MYTH OR SCIENCE?   *"Entrepreneurs Are a Breed Apart"*

*t*his statement is true. A review of 23 studies on the personality of entrepreneurs revealed significant differences between entrepreneurs and managers on four of the Big Five: Entrepreneurs scored significantly higher on conscientiousness, emotional stability, and openness to experience, and they scored significantly lower on agreeableness. Though of course not every entrepreneur achieves these scores, the results clearly suggest that entrepreneurs are different from managers in key ways.

A fascinating study of MBA students provides one explanation for how entrepreneurs are different from others. Studying male MBA students with either some or no prior entrepreneurial experience, the authors found that those with prior experience had significantly higher levels of testosterone (measured by taking a saliva swab at the beginning of the study) and also scored higher on risk propensity. The authors of this study concluded that testosterone, because it is associated with social dominance and aggressiveness, energizes individuals to take entrepreneurial risks. Because individual differences in testosterone are 80 percent inherited, this study adds more weight to the conclusion that entrepreneurs are different from others.

What's the upshot of all this? An individual who is considering a career as an entrepreneur or a business owner might consider how she scores on the Big Five. To the extent that she is high in conscientiousness, emotional stability, and openness and low in agreeableness, such a career might be for her.[45] ■

Do Type A's differ from Type B's in their ability to get hired? The answer appears to be "yes."[46] Type A's do better than Type B's in job interviews because they are more likely to be judged as having desirable traits such as high drive, competence, aggressiveness, and success motivation.

Proactive Personality   Did you ever notice that some people actively take the initiative to improve their current circumstances or create new ones while others sit by passively reacting to situations? The former individuals have been described as having **proactive personalities**.[47] Proactives identify opportunities, show initiative, take action, and persevere until meaningful change occurs. They create positive change in their environment, regardless of or even in spite of constraints or obstacles.[48] Not surprisingly, proactives have many desirable behaviors that organizations covet. For instance, evidence indicates that proactives are more likely than others to be seen as leaders and more likely to act as change agents within an organization.[49] Other actions of proactives can be positive or negative, depending on the organization and the situation. For example, proactives are more likely to challenge the status quo or voice their displeasure when situations aren't to their liking.[50] If an organization requires people with entrepreneurial initiative, proactives make good candidates; however, these are people who are also more likely to leave an organization to start their own businesses.[51] As individuals, proactives are more likely than others to achieve career success.[52] They select, create, and influence work situations in

Type A personality   *Aggressive involvement in a chronic, incessant struggle to achieve more and more in less and less time and, if necessary, against the opposing efforts of other things or other people.*

proactive personality   *People who identify opportunities, show initiative, take action, and persevere until meaningful change occurs.*

International OB

A Global Personality

Determining which employees will succeed on overseas business assignments is often difficult for an organization's managers because the same qualities that predict success in one culture may not in another. However, researchers are naming personality traits that can help managers zero in on which employees would be suited for foreign assignments.

You might think that of the Big Five traits, openness to experience would be most important to effectiveness in international assignments. Open people are more likely to be culturally flexible—to "go with the flow" when things are different in another country. Although research is not fully consistent on the issue, most does suggest that managers who score high on openness perform better than others in international assignments.

James Eyring, Dell's director of learning and development for Asia, agrees that personality is important for success in overseas assignments. "I've seen people fail the openness test—they worked exactly as they would in the U.S. They just weren't open to understanding how things work in a different culture," says Eyring.

What does the research mean for organizations? When it comes to choosing employees for global assignments, personality can make a difference.

Source: Based on M. A. Shaffer, D. A. Harrison, and H. Gregersen, "You Can Take It with You: Individual Differences and Expatriate Effectiveness," *Journal of Applied Psychology*, January 2006, pp. 109–125; and E. Silverman, "The Global Test," *Human Resource Executive Online*, June 16, 2006, www.hreonline.com/HRE/story.jsp?storyId=5669803.

their favor. Proactives are more likely than others to seek out job and organizational information, develop contacts in high places, engage in career planning, and demonstrate persistence in the face of career obstacles.

Having discussed personality traits—the enduring characteristics that describe a person's behavior—we now turn to values. Although personality and values are related, they're not the same. Values are often very specific and describe belief systems rather than behavioral tendencies. Some beliefs or values don't say much about a person's personality, and we don't always act in ways that are consistent with our values.

Values

6 *Define values, demonstrate the importance of values, and contrast terminal and instrumental values.*

Is capital punishment right or wrong? If a person likes power, is that good or bad? The answers to these questions are value laden. Some might argue, for example, that capital punishment is right because it is an appropriate retribution for crimes such as murder and treason. Others might argue, just as strongly, that no government has the right to take anyone's life.

Values represent basic convictions that "a specific mode of conduct or end-state of existence is personally or socially preferable to an opposite or converse mode of conduct or end-state of existence."[53] They contain a judgmental element in that they carry an individual's ideas as to what is right, good, or desirable. Values have both content and intensity attributes. The content attribute says that a mode of conduct or an end-state of existence is *important*. The intensity attribute specifies *how important* it is. When we rank an individual's values in terms of their intensity, we obtain that person's **value system**. All of us have a hierarchy of values that forms our value system. This system is identified by the relative importance we assign to values such as freedom, pleasure, self-respect, honesty, obedience, and equality.

Are values fluid and flexible? Generally speaking, no. They tend to be relatively stable and enduring.[54] A significant portion of the values we hold is established in our early years—from parents, teachers, friends, and others. As children, we are told that certain behaviors or outcomes are *always* desirable or *always* undesirable, with few gray areas. You were told, for example, that you should be honest and responsible. You were never taught to be just a little bit honest or a little bit responsible. It is this absolute, or "black-or-white," learning of values that more or less ensures their stability and endurance. The process of questioning our values, of course, may result in a change. More often, our questioning merely acts to reinforce the values we hold.

The Importance of Values

Values are important to the study of organizational behavior because they lay the foundation for our understanding of people's attitudes and motivation and because they influence our perceptions. Individuals enter an organization with preconceived notions of what "ought" and "ought not" to be. Of course, these notions are not value free. On the contrary, they contain interpretations of right and wrong. Furthermore, they imply that certain behaviors or outcomes are preferred over others. As a result, values cloud objectivity and rationality.

Values generally influence attitudes and behavior.[55] Suppose you enter an organization with the view that allocating pay on the basis of performance is right, while allocating pay on the basis of seniority is wrong. How are you going to react if you find that the organization you've just joined rewards seniority and not performance? You're likely to be disappointed—and this can lead to job dissatisfaction and a decision not to exert a high level of effort because "it's probably not going to lead to more money anyway." Would your attitudes and behavior be different if your values aligned with the organization's pay policies? Most likely.

Terminal Versus Instrumental Values

Can we classify values? Yes. In this section, we review two approaches to developing value typologies.

Rokeach Value Survey   Milton Rokeach created the Rokeach Value Survey (RVS).[56] It consists of two sets of values, each containing 18 individual value items. One set, called **terminal values**, refers to desirable end-states. These are the goals a person would like to achieve during his or her lifetime. The other set, called **instrumental values**, refers to preferable modes of behavior, or means of achieving the terminal values. Exhibit 4-3 gives common examples for each of these sets.

---

values *Basic convictions that a specific mode of conduct or end-state of existence is personally or socially preferable to an opposite or converse mode of conduct or end-state of existence.*

value system *A hierarchy based on a ranking of an individual's values in terms of their intensity.*

terminal values *Desirable end-states of existence; the goals a person would like to achieve during his or her lifetime.*

instrumental values *Preferable modes of behavior or means of achieving one's terminal values.*

Exhibit 4-3	Terminal and Instrumental Values in the Rokeach Value Survey

Terminal Values	Instrumental Values
A comfortable life (a prosperous life)	Ambitious (hardworking, aspiring)
An exciting life (a stimulating, active life)	Broad-minded (open-minded)
A sense of accomplishment (lasting contribution)	Capable (competent, efficient)
A world at peace (free of war and conflict)	Cheerful (lighthearted, joyful)
A world of beauty (beauty of nature and the arts)	Clean (neat, tidy)
Equality (brotherhood, equal opportunity for all)	Courageous (standing up for your beliefs)
Family security (taking care of loved ones)	Forgiving (willing to pardon others)
Freedom (independence, free choice)	Helpful (working for the welfare of others)
Happiness (contentedness)	Honest (sincere, truthful)
Inner harmony (freedom from inner conflict)	Imaginative (daring, creative)
Mature love (sexual and spiritual intimacy)	Independent (self-reliant, self-sufficient)
National security (protection from attack)	Intellectual (intelligent, reflective)
Pleasure (an enjoyable, leisurely life)	Logical (consistent, rational)
Salvation (saved, eternal life)	Loving (affectionate, tender)
Self-respect (self-esteem)	Obedient (dutiful, respectful)
Social recognition (respect, admiration)	Polite (courteous, well-mannered)
True friendship (close companionship)	Responsible (dependable, reliable)
Wisdom (a mature understanding of life)	Self-controlled (restrained, self-disciplined)

Source: Reprinted with the permission of The Free Press, a Division of Simon & Schuster Adult Publishing Group, from The Nature of Human Values by Milton Rokeach. Copyright © 1973 by The Free Press. Copyright renewed © 2001 by Sandra J. Ball-Rokeach. All rights reserved.

Several studies confirm that RVS values vary among groups.[57] People in the same occupations or categories (for example, corporate managers, union members, parents, students) tend to hold similar values. For instance, one study compared corporate executives, members of the steelworkers' union, and members of a community activist group. Although there was a good deal of overlap among the three groups,[58] there were also some very significant differences (see Exhibit 4-4). The activists had value preferences that were quite different from those of the other two groups. They ranked "equality" as their most important terminal value; executives and union members ranked this value 12 and 13, respectively. Activists ranked "helpful" as their second-highest instrumental value. The other two groups both ranked it 14. These differences are important, because executives, union members, and activists all have a vested interest in what corporations do. These differences make things difficult for groups that have to negotiate with each other and can create serious conflicts when they contend with each other over an organization's economic and social policies.[59]

Exhibit 4-4	Mean Value Ranking of Executives, Union Members, and Activists (Top Five Only)

EXECUTIVES		UNION MEMBERS		ACTIVISTS	
Terminal	Instrumental	Terminal	Instrumental	Terminal	Instrumental
1. Self-respect	1. Honest	1. Family security	1. Responsible	1. Equality	1. Honest
2. Family security	2. Responsible	2. Freedom	2. Honest	2. A world of peace	2. Helpful
3. Freedom	3. Capable	3. Happiness	3. Courageous	3. Family security	3. Courageous
4. A sense of accomplishment	4. Ambitious	4. Self-respect	4. Independent	4. Self-respect	4. Responsible
5. Happiness	5. Independent	5. Mature love	5. Capable	5. Freedom	5. Capable

Source: Based on W. C. Frederick and J. Weber, "The Values of Corporate Managers and Their Critics: An Empirical Description and Normative Implications," in W. C. Frederick and L. E. Preston (eds.), *Business Ethics: Research Issues and Empirical Studies* (Greenwich, CT: JAI Press, 1990), pp. 123–144.

7 *Compare generational differences in values and identify the dominant values in today's workforce.*

Generational Values

Contemporary Work Cohorts   Researchers have integrated several recent analyses of work values into four groups that attempt to capture the unique values of different cohorts or generations in the U.S. workforce.[60] Exhibit 4-5 proposes that employees can be segmented by the era in which they entered the workforce. Because most people start work between the ages of 18 and 23, the eras also correlate closely with the chronological age of employees.

Before going any further, let's look at some limitations of this analysis. First, we make no assumption that the framework would apply universally across all cultures. Second, while there is a steady stream of press coverage, there is very little rigorous research on generational values, so we have to rely on an intuitive framework. Finally, these are imprecise categories. There is no law that someone born in 1985 can't have similar values to someone born in 1955. You may see your values better reflected in other generations than in your own. Despite these limitations, values do change over generations,[61] and we can gain some useful insights from analyzing values this way.

Workers who grew up influenced by the Great Depression, World War II, the Andrews Sisters, and the Berlin blockade entered the workforce through the 1950s and early 1960s, believing in hard work, the status quo, and authority figures. We call them *Veterans* (some use the label *Traditionalists*). Once hired, Veterans tended to be loyal to their employer and respectful of authority, hard-working, and practical. These are the people Tom Brokaw wrote about in his book *The Greatest Generation*. In terms of terminal values on the RVS, these employees are likely to place the greatest importance on a comfortable life and family security.

Boomers (*Baby Boomers*) are a large cohort born after World War II when veterans returned to their families and times were good. Boomers entered the workforce from the mid-1960s through the mid-1980s. This cohort was influenced heavily by the civil rights movement, the women's movement, the Beatles, the Vietnam War, and baby boom competition. They brought with them a large measure of the "hippie ethic" and distrust of authority. But they place a great deal of emphasis on achievement and material success. They work hard and want to enjoy the fruits of their labors. They're pragmatists who believe that ends can justify means. Boomers see the organizations that employ them merely as vehicles for their careers. Terminal

Exhibit 4-5	Dominant Work Values in Today's Workforce		
Cohort	**Entered the Workforce**	**Approximate Current Age**	**Dominant Work Values**
Veterans	1950s or early 1960s	65+	Hardworking, conservative, conforming; loyalty to the organization
Boomers	1965–1985	Mid-40s to mid-60s	Success, achievement, ambition, dislike of authority; loyalty to career
Xers	1985–2000	Late 20s to early 40s	Work/life balance, team-oriented, dislike of rules; loyalty to relationships
Nexters	2000 to present	Under 30	Confident, financial success, self-reliant but team-oriented; loyalty to both self and relationships

Companies such as Patagonia, Inc., a marketer of outdoor clothing and equipment, understand the dominant work values of young people in the workforce who value work/life balance and relationships. Patagonia was one of the first U.S. firms to offer employees flexible working hours, maternity and paternity leave, and on-site day care. Through an internship program, employees can leave their jobs for up to 2 months to work full time for the environmental group of their choice while Patagonia continues to pay their salaries and benefits.

values such as a sense of accomplishment and social recognition rank high with them.

The lives of *Xers* (*Generation Xers*) have been shaped by globalization, two-career parents, MTV, AIDS, and computers. They value flexibility, life options, and the achievement of job satisfaction. Family and relationships are very important to this cohort. Unlike Veterans, Xers are skeptical, particularly of authority. They also enjoy team-oriented work. Money is important as an indicator of career performance, but Xers are willing to trade off salary increases, titles, security, and promotions for increased leisure time and expanded lifestyle options. In search of balance in their lives, Xers are less willing to make personal sacrifices for the sake of their employer than previous generations were. On the RVS, they rate high on true friendship, happiness, and pleasure.

The most recent entrants to the workforce, the *Nexters* (also called *Netters*, *Millennials*, *Generation Yers*, and *Generation Nexters*) grew up during prosperous times. They have high expectations and seek meaning in their work. Nexters have life goals more oriented toward becoming rich (81 percent) and famous (51 percent) than do Generation Xers (62 percent and 29 percent, respectively). Nexters are at ease with diversity and are the first generation to take technology for granted. They've lived much of their lives with ATMs, DVDs, cellphones, laptops, and the Internet. More than other generations, they tend to be questioning, socially conscious, and entrepreneurial. At the same time, some have described Nexters as needy. One employer said, "This is the most high-maintenance workforce in the history of the world. The good news is they're also going to be the most high-performing."[62]

An understanding that individuals' values differ but tend to reflect the societal values of the period in which they grew up can be a valuable aid in explaining and predicting behavior. Employees in their late 60s, for instance, are more likely to accept authority than their coworkers who are 10 or 15 years younger. And workers in their 30s are more likely than their parents to balk at having to work weekends and more prone to leave a job in mid-career to pursue another that provides more leisure time.

OB *In the News*

Are U.S. Values Different?

People in the United States are used to being criticized. After all, it was more than a century ago when the Irish playwright George Barnard Shaw wrote, "Americans adore me and will go on adoring me until I say something nice about them."

But as a result of the Iraq War and the fact that the United States is the world's lone remaining superpower, its citizens are taking unprecedented criticism abroad. One critic sneered, "The American pursuit of wealth, size, and abundance—as material surrogates for happiness—is aesthetically unpleasing and ecologically catastrophic." And many Europeans think that U.S. adults are obsessed with work. Some have even argued that the United States and Europe are becoming increasingly polarized.

Overall, the United States is wealthier than Europe and has higher productivity. But what's wrong with that? Well, some stats are not very positive. For example, compared to Europe, the United States is much more violent; it has 685 prisons for every 100,000 people, compared to 87 in the European Union. The United States has also increasingly seemed to reward power with money. For example, in 1980, the average CEO in the United States earned 40 times the annual income of the average manufacturing employee. Today, that ratio is 475:1! By comparison, the ratios are 24:1 in the U.K., 15:1 in France, and 13:1 in Sweden. Finally, the United States contains 5 percent of the world's population, but it is responsible for 25 percent of the world's greenhouse gas output—which is, many scientists argue, responsible for global warming.

Values may account for some of these differences. For example, in a study of people in 14 countries, those in the United States were more likely than others to see natural resources as elements at their disposal. And compared to Europeans, U.S. adults are more likely to believe that war is often necessary, that it is right to kill to defend property, and that physical punishment of children is necessary.

Do you think U.S. values are an underlying factor behind some of these social phenomena? Or is this academic U.S. bashing?

Source: Based on: T. Judt, "Europe vs. America," *New York Review of Books*, February 20, 2005, www.nybooks.com/articles/17726; P. W. Schultz and L. Zelezny, "Values as Predictors of Environmental Attitudes: Evidence for Consistency Across 14 Countries," *Journal of Environmental Psychology*, September 1999, pp. 255–265; and A. McAlister, P. Sandström, P. Puska, A. Veijo, R. Chereches, and L. Heidmets, "Attitudes Towards War, Killing, and Punishment of Children Among Young People in Estonia, Finland, Romania, the Russian Federation, and the USA," *Bulletin of the World Health Organization* 79, no. 5 (2001), pp. 382–387.

Linking an Individual's Personality and Values to the Workplace

Thirty years ago, organizations were concerned only with personality because their primary focus was to match individuals to specific jobs. That concern still exists. But, in recent years, that interest has expanded to include how well the individual's personality *and* values match the *organization*. Why? Because managers today are less interested in an applicant's ability to perform a *specific* job than with the *flexibility* to meet changing situations and commitment to the organization.

We'll now discuss person–job fit and person–organization fit in more detail.

Person–Job Fit

The effort to match job requirements with personality characteristics is best articulated in John Holland's **personality–job fit theory**.[63] Holland presents six

personality–job fit theory *A theory that identifies six personality types and proposes that the fit between personality type and occupational environment determines satisfaction and turnover.*

Exhibit 4-6	Holland's Typology of Personality and Congruent Occupations	
Type	**Personality Characteristics**	**Congruent Occupations**
Realistic: Prefers physical activities that require skill, strength, and coordination	Shy, genuine, persistent, stable, conforming, practical	Mechanic, drill press operator, assembly-line worker, farmer
Investigative: Prefers activities that involve thinking, organizing, and understanding	Analytical, original, curious, independent	Biologist, economist, mathematician, news reporter
Social: Prefers activities that involve helping and developing others	Sociable, friendly, cooperative, understanding	Social worker, teacher, counselor, clinical psychologist
Conventional: Prefers rule-regulated, orderly, and unambiguous activities	Conforming, efficient, practical, unimaginative, inflexible	Accountant, corporate manager, bank teller, file clerk
Enterprising: Prefers verbal activities in which there are opportunities to influence others and attain power	Self-confident, ambitious, energetic, domineering	Lawyer, real estate agent, public relations specialist, small business manager
Artistic: Prefers ambiguous and unsystematic activities that allow creative expression	Imaginative, disorderly, idealistic, emotional, impractical	Painter, musician, writer, interior decorator

personality types and proposes that satisfaction and the propensity to leave a position depend on the degree to which individuals successfully match their personalities to a job. Each one of the six personality types has a congruent occupation. Exhibit 4-6 describes the six types and their personality characteristics and gives examples of congruent occupations.

Holland developed the Vocational Preference Inventory questionnaire, which contains 160 occupational titles. Respondents indicate which of these occupations they like or dislike, and their answers form personality profiles. Research strongly supports the resulting hexagonal diagram shown in Exhibit 4-7.[64] The closer two fields or orientations are in the hexagon, the more compatible they are. Adjacent categories are quite similar, whereas diagonally opposite ones are highly dissimilar.

What does all this mean? The theory argues that satisfaction is highest and turnover is lowest when personality and occupation are in agreement. Social individuals should be in social jobs, conventional people in conventional jobs, and so forth. A realistic person in a realistic job is in a more congruent situation

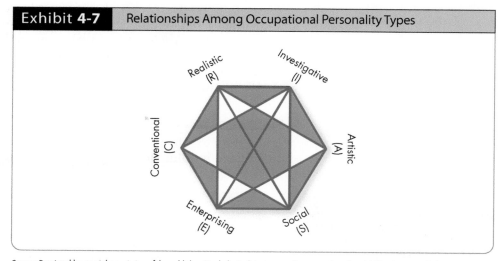

Exhibit 4-7	Relationships Among Occupational Personality Types

than a realistic person in an investigative job. A realistic person in a social job is in the most incongruent situation possible. The key points of this model are that (1) there do appear to be intrinsic differences in personality among individuals, (2) there are different types of jobs, and (3) people in jobs congruent with their personality should be more satisfied and less likely to voluntarily resign than people in incongruent jobs.

Person–Organization Fit

We've noted that researchers in recent years have looked at matching people to *organizations* as well as to jobs. If an organization faces a dynamic and changing environment and requires employees who are able to readily change tasks and move easily between teams, it's more important that employees' personalities fit with the overall organization's culture than with the characteristics of any specific job.

The person–organization fit essentially argues that people are attracted to and selected by organizations that match their values, and they leave organizations that are not compatible with their personalities.[65] Using the Big Five terminology, for instance, we could expect that people high on extraversion fit well with aggressive and team-oriented cultures, that people high on agreeableness match up better with a supportive organizational climate than one that focuses on aggressiveness, and that people high on openness to experience fit better into organizations that emphasize innovation rather than standardization.[66] Following these guidelines at the time of hiring should lead to selecting new employees who fit better with the organization's culture, which should, in turn, result in higher employee satisfaction and reduced turnover. Research on person–organization fit has also looked at people's values and whether they match the organization's culture. The fit of employees' values with the culture of their organization predicts job satisfaction, commitment to the organization, and low turnover.[67]

Global Implications

Personality

Do personality frameworks, such as the Big Five model, transfer across cultures? Are dimensions such as the Type A personality relevant in all cultures? Let's try to answer these questions.

8 *Identify Hofstede's five value dimensions of national culture.*

The five personality factors identified in the Big Five model appear in almost all cross-cultural studies.[68] These studies have included a wide variety of diverse cultures—such as China, Israel, Germany, Japan, Spain, Nigeria, Norway, Pakistan, and the United States. Differences tend to be in the emphasis on dimensions and whether countries are predominantly individualistic or collectivistic. For example, Chinese managers use the category of conscientiousness more often and the category of agreeableness less often than do U.S. managers. And the Big Five appear to predict a bit better in individualistic than in collectivist cultures.[69] But there is a surprisingly high amount of agreement, especially among individuals from developed countries. As a case in point, a comprehensive review of studies covering people from the 15-nation European Community found that conscientiousness was a valid predictor of performance across jobs and occupational groups.[70] This is exactly what U.S. studies have found.

Values

Because values differ across cultures, an understanding of these differences should be helpful in explaining and predicting behavior of employees from different countries.

Hofstede's Framework for Assessing Cultures   One of the most widely referenced approaches for analyzing variations among cultures was done in the late 1970s by Geert Hofstede.[71] He surveyed more than 116,000 IBM employees in 40 countries about their work-related values and found that managers and employees vary on five value dimensions of national culture:

- *Power distance.*   **Power distance** describes the degree to which people in a country accept that power in institutions and organizations is distributed unequally. A high rating on power distance means that large inequalities of power and wealth exist and are tolerated in the culture, as in a class or caste system that discourages upward mobility of its citizens. A low power distance rating characterizes societies that stress equality and opportunity.
- *Individualism versus collectivism.*   **Individualism** is the degree to which people prefer to act as individuals rather than as members of groups and believe in individual rights above all else. **Collectivism** emphasizes a tight social framework in which people expect others in groups of which they are a part to look after them and protect them.
- *Masculinity versus femininity.*   Hofstede's construct of **masculinity** is the degree to which the culture favors traditional masculine roles such as achievement, power, and control, as opposed to viewing men and women as equals. A high masculinity rating indicates the culture has separate roles for men and women, with men dominating the society. A high **femininity** rating means the culture sees little differentiation between male and female roles and treats women as the equals of men in all respects.
- *Uncertainty avoidance.*   The degree to which people in a country prefer structured over unstructured situations defines their uncertainty avoidance. In cultures that score high on uncertainty avoidance, people have an increased level of anxiety about uncertainty and ambiguity and use laws and controls to reduce uncertainty. Cultures low on **uncertainty avoidance** are more accepting of ambiguity and are less rule oriented, take more risks, and more readily accept change.
- *Long-term versus short-term orientation.*   This is the newest addition to Hofstede's typology. It focuses on the degree of a society's long-term devotion to traditional values. People in a culture with **long-term orientation** look to the future and value thrift, persistence, and tradition. In a **short-term orientation**, people value the here and now; they accept change more readily and don't see commitments as impediments to change.

How do different countries score on Hofstede's dimensions? Exhibit 4-8 shows the ratings for the countries for which data are available. For example, power distance is higher in Malaysia than in any other country. The United States is very individualistic. In fact, it's the most individualistic nation of all (closely followed by Australia and Great Britain). The United States also tends to be short term in orientation and is low in power distance (people in the United States tend not to accept built-in class differences between people). The United States is also relatively low on uncertainty avoidance, meaning that most adults are relatively tolerant of uncertainty and ambiguity. The United States scores relatively high on masculinity, meaning that most people emphasize traditional gender roles (at least relative to countries such as Denmark, Finland, Norway, and Sweden).

You'll notice regional differences. Western and Northern nations such as Canada and the Netherlands tend to be more individualistic. Compared with other countries, poorer countries such as Mexico and the Philippines tend to be higher on power distance. South American nations tend to be higher than other countries on uncertainty avoidance, and Asian countries tend to have a long-term orientation.

Hofstede's culture dimensions have been enormously influential on OB researchers and managers. Nevertheless, his research has been criticized. First, although the data have since been updated, the original work is more than 30 years old and was based on a single company (IBM). A lot has happened on the world scene since then. Some of the most obvious changes include the fall of the Soviet Union, the transformation of central and eastern Europe, the end of apartheid in South Africa, the spread of Islam throughout the world today, and the rise of China as a global power. Second, few researchers have read the details of Hofstede's methodology closely and are therefore unaware of the many decisions and judgment calls he had to make (for example, reducing the number of cultural values to just five). Some results are unexpected. For example, Japan, which is often considered a highly collectivist nation, is considered only average on collectivism under Hofstede's dimensions.[72] Despite these concerns, Hofstede has been one of the most widely cited social scientists ever, and his framework has left a lasting mark on OB.

The GLOBE Framework for Assessing Cultures   Begun in 1993, the Global Leadership and Organizational Behavior Effectiveness (GLOBE) research program is an ongoing cross-cultural investigation of leadership and national culture. Using data from 825 organizations in 62 countries, the GLOBE team identified nine dimensions on which national cultures differ.[73] Some of these—such as power distance, individualism/collectivism, uncertainty avoidance, gender differentiation (similar to masculinity versus femininity), and future orientation (similar to long-term versus short-term orientation)—resemble the Hofstede dimensions. The main difference in the GLOBE framework is that it added dimensions, such as humane orientation (the degree to which a society rewards individuals for being altruistic, generous, and kind to others) and performance orientation (the degree to which a society encourages and rewards group members for performance improvement and excellence).

Which framework is better? That's hard to say, and each has its adherents. We give more emphasis to Hofstede's dimensions here because they have stood the test of time and the GLOBE study confirmed them. However, researchers continue to debate the differences between these frameworks, and future studies may, in time, favor the more nuanced perspective of the GLOBE study.[74]

---

power distance   *A national culture attribute that describes the extent to which a society accepts that power in institutions and organizations is distributed unequally.*

individualism   *A national culture attribute that describes the degree to which people prefer to act as individuals rather than as members of groups.*

collectivism   *A national culture attribute that describes a tight social framework in which people expect others in groups of which they are a part to look after them and protect them.*

masculinity   *A national culture attribute that describes the extent to which the culture favors traditional masculine work roles of achievement, power, and control. Societal values are characterized by assertiveness and materialism.*

femininity   *A national culture attribute that has little differentiation between male and female roles, where women are treated as the equals of men in all aspects of the society.*

uncertainty avoidance   *A national culture attribute that describes the extent to which a society feels threatened by uncertain and ambiguous situations and tries to avoid them.*

long-term orientation   *A national culture attribute that emphasizes the future, thrift, and persistence.*

short-term orientation   *A national culture attribute that emphasizes the past and present, respect for tradition, and fulfillment of social obligations.*

Exhibit 4-8	Hofstede's Cultural Values by Nation

Country	Power Distance Index	Power Distance Rank	Individualism Versus Collectivism Index	Individualism Versus Collectivism Rank	Masculinity Versus Femininity Index	Masculinity Versus Femininity Rank	Uncertainty Avoidance Index	Uncertainty Avoidance Rank	Long-Versus Short-Term Orientation Index	Long-Versus Short-Term Orientation Rank
Argentina	49	35–36	46	22–23	56	20–21	86	10–15		
Australia	36	41	90	2	61	16	51	37	31	22–24
Austria	11	53	55	18	79	2	70	24–25	31	22–24
Belgium	65	20	75	8	54	22	94	5–6	38	18
Brazil	69	14	38	26–27	49	27	76	21–22	65	6
Canada	39	39	80	4–5	52	24	48	41–42	23	30
Chile	63	24–25	23	38	28	46	86	10–15		
Colombia	67	17	13	49	64	11–12	80	20		
Costa Rica	35	42–44	15	46	21	48–49	86	10–15		
Denmark	18	51	74	9	16	50	23	51	46	10
Ecuador	78	8–9	8	52	63	13–14	67	28		
El Salvador	66	18–19	19	42	40	40	94	5–6		
Finland	33	46	63	17	26	47	59	31–32	41	14
France	68	15–16	71	10–11	43	35–36	86	10–15	39	17
Germany	35	42–44	67	15	66	9–10	65	29	31	22–24
Great Britain	35	42–44	89	3	66	9–10	35	47–48	25	28–29
Greece	60	27–28	35	30	57	18–19	112	1		
Guatemala	95	2–3	6	53	37	43	101	3		
Hong Kong	68	15–16	25	37	57	18–19	29	49–50	96	2
India	77	10–11	48	21	56	20–21	40	45	61	7
Indonesia	78	8–9	14	47–48	46	30–31	48	41–42		
Iran	58	29–30	41	24	43	35–36	59	31–32		
Ireland	28	49	70	12	68	7–8	35	47–48	43	13
Israel	13	52	54	19	47	29	81	19		
Italy	50	34	76	7	70	4–5	75	23	34	19
Jamaica	45	37	39	25	68	7–8	13	52		
Japan	54	33	46	22–23	95	1	92	7	80	4
Korea (South)	60	27–28	18	43	39	41	85	16–17	75	5
Malaysia	104	1	26	36	50	25–26	36	46		
Mexico	81	5–6	30	32	69	6	82	18		
The Netherlands	38	40	80	4–5	14	51	53	35	44	11–12
New Zealand	22	50	79	6	58	17	49	39–40	30	25–26
Norway	31	47–48	69	13	8	52	50	38	44	11–12
Pakistan	55	32	14	47–48	50	25–26	70	24–25	0	34
Panama	95	2–3	11	51	44	34	86	10–15		
Peru	64	21–23	16	45	42	37–38	87	9		
Philippines	94	4	32	31	64	11–12	44	44	19	31–32
Portugal	63	24–25	27	33–35	31	45	104	2	30	25–26
Singapore	74	13	20	39–41	48	28	8	53	48	9
South Africa	49	35–36	65	16	63	13–14	49	39–40		
Spain	57	31	51	20	42	37–38	86	10–15	19	31–32
Sweden	31	47–48	71	10–11	5	53	29	49–50	33	20
Switzerland	34	45	68	14	70	4–5	58	33	40	15–16
Taiwan	58	29–30	17	44	45	32–33	69	26	87	3
Thailand	64	21–23	20	39–41	34	44	64	30	56	8
Turkey	66	18–19	37	28	45	32–33	85	16–17		
United States	40	38	91	1	62	15	46	43	29	27
Uruguay	61	26	36	29	38	42	100	4		
Venezuela	81	5–6	12	50	73	3	76	21–22		
Yugoslavia	76	12	27	33–35	21	48–49	88	8		
Regions:										
Arab countries	80	7	38	26–27	53	23	68	27		
East Africa	64	21–23	27	33–35	41	39	52	36	25	28–29
West Africa	77	10–11	20	39–41	46	30–31	54	34	16	33

Scores range from 0 = extremely low on dimension to 100 = extremely high.

Note: 1 = highest rank. LTO ranks: 1 = China; 15-16 = Bangladesh; 21 = Poland; 34 = lowest.

Source: Copyright Geert Hofstede BV, hofstede@bovt.nl. Reprinted with permission.

Summary and Implications for Managers

Personality What value, if any, does the Big Five model provide to managers? From the early 1900s through the mid-1980s, researchers sought to find a link between personality and job performance. "The outcome of those 80-plus years of research was that personality and job performance were not meaningfully related across traits or situations."[75] However, the past 20 years have been more promising, largely due to the findings surrounding the Big Five. Screening candidates for jobs who score high on conscientiousness—as well as the other Big Five traits, depending on the criteria an organization finds most important— should pay dividends. Each of the Big Five traits has numerous implications for important OB criteria. Of course, managers still need to take situational factors into consideration.[76] Factors such as job demands, the degree of required interaction with others, and the organization's culture are examples of situational variables that moderate the personality–job performance relationship. You need to evaluate the job, the work group, and the organization to determine the optimal personality fit. Other traits, such as core self-evaluation or narcissism, may be relevant in certain situations, too.

Although the MBTI has been widely criticized, it may have a place in organizations. In training and development, it can help employees to better understand themselves, and it can help team members to better understand each other. And it can open up communication in work groups and possibly reduce conflicts.

Values Why is it important to know an individual's values? Values often underlie and explain attitudes, behaviors, and perceptions. So knowledge of an individual's value system can provide insight into what "makes the person tick."

Employees' performance and satisfaction are likely to be higher if their values fit well with the organization. For instance, the person who places great importance on imagination, independence, and freedom is likely to be poorly matched with an organization that seeks conformity from its employees. Managers are more likely to appreciate, evaluate positively, and allocate rewards to employees who "fit in," and employees are more likely to be satisfied if they perceive that they do fit in. This argues for management to strive during the selection of new employees to find job candidates who have not only the ability, experience, and motivation to perform but also a value system that is compatible with the organization's.

Point   Counterpoint

TRAITS ARE POWERFUL PREDICTORS OF BEHAVIOR[77]

*t*he essence of trait approaches in OB is that employees possess stable personality characteristics that significantly influence their attitudes toward, and behavioral reactions to, organizational settings. People with particular traits tend to be relatively consistent in their attitudes and behavior over time and across situations.

Of course, trait theorists recognize that all traits are not equally powerful. They tend to put them into one of three categories. *Cardinal traits* are those so strong and generalized that they influence every act a person performs. *Primary traits* are generally consistent influences on behavior, but they may not show up in all situations. Finally, *secondary traits* are attributes that do not form a vital part of the personality but come into play only in particular situations. For the most part, trait theories have focused on the power of primary traits to predict employee behavior.

Trait theorists do a fairly good job of meeting the average person's face-validity test. Think of friends, relatives, and acquaintances you have known for a number of years. Do they have traits that have remained essentially stable over time? Most of us would answer that question in the affirmative. If Cousin Anne was shy and nervous when we last saw her 10 years ago, we would be surprised to find her outgoing and relaxed now.

Managers seem to have a strong belief in the power of traits to predict behavior. If managers believed that situations determined behavior, they would hire people almost at random and structure the situation properly. But the employee selection process in most organizations places a great deal of emphasis on how applicants perform in interviews and on tests. Assume that you're an interviewer and ask yourself "What am I looking for in job candidates?" If you answered with terms such as *conscientious, hardworking, persistent, confident*, and *dependable*, you're a trait theorist.

*f*ew people would dispute that some stable individual attributes affect reactions to the workplace. But trait theorists go beyond that and argue that individual behavior consistencies are widespread and account for much of the differences in behavior among people.

Two problems with using traits to explain a large proportion of behavior in organizations are that the evidence isn't all that impressive, and individuals are highly adaptive so that personality traits change in response to organizational situations.

First, though personality does influence workplace attitudes and behaviors, the effects aren't all that strong; traits explain a minority of the variance in attitudes and behavior. Why is this so? The effects of traits are likely to be strongest in relatively weak situations and weakest in relatively strong situations. Organizational settings tend to be strong situations because they have rules and other formal regulations that define acceptable behavior and punish deviant behavior; and they have informal norms that dictate appropriate behaviors. These formal and informal constraints minimize the effects of personality traits.

By arguing that employees possess stable traits that lead to cross-situational consistencies in behaviors, trait theorists imply that individuals don't really adapt to different situations. But a growing body of evidence suggests that an individual's traits are changed by the organizations the individual participates in. If the individual's personality changes as a result of exposure to organizational settings, in what sense can that individual be said to have traits that persistently and consistently affect his or her reactions to those very settings? Moreover, people typically belong to multiple organizations that often include very different kinds of members. And they adapt to those different situations, too. Instead of being prisoners of a rigid and stable personality framework, as trait theorists propose, people regularly adjust their behavior to reflect the requirements of various situations.

Questions for Review

1 What is personality? How do we typically measure it? What factors determine personality?

2 What is the Myers-Briggs Type Indicator (MBTI), and what does it measure?

3 What are the Big Five personality traits?

4 How do the Big Five traits predict work behavior?

5 Besides the Big Five, what other personality traits are relevant to OB?

6 What are values, why are they important, and what is the difference between terminal and instrumental values?

7 Do values differ across generations? How so?

8 Do values differ across cultures? How so?

Experiential Exercise

WHAT ORGANIZATIONAL CULTURE DO YOU PREFER?

The Organizational Culture Profile (OCP) can help assess whether an individual's values match the organization's.[78] The OCP helps individuals sort their characteristics in terms of importance, which indicates what a person values.

1. Working on your own, complete the OCP below.
2. Your instructor may ask you the following questions individually or as group of three or four students (with a spokesperson appointed to speak to the class for each group):

   a. What were your most preferred and least preferred values? Do you think your most preferred and least preferred values are similar to those of other class or group members?

   b. Do you think there are generational differences in the most preferred and least preferred values?

   c. Research has shown that individuals tend to be happier, and perform better, when their OCP values match those of their employer. How important do you think a "values match" is when you're deciding where you want to work?

Ethical Dilemma

HIRING BASED ON BODY ART

Leonardo's Pizza in Gainesville, Florida, regularly employs heavily tattooed workers. Tina Taladge and Meghan Dean, for example, are covered from their shoulders to their ankles in colorful tattoos. So many of the employees at Leonardo's sport tattoos that body art could almost be a qualification for the job. Many employers, however, are not that open to tattoos. Consider Russell Parrish, 29, who lives near Orlando, Florida, and has dozens of tattoos on his arms, hands, torso, and neck. In searching for a job, Parrish walked into 100 businesses, and in 60 cases, he was refused an application. "I want a career," Parrish says, "I want same the shot as everybody else."

Parrish isn't alone. Many employers, including Walt Disney World, GEICO, SeaWorld, the U.S. Postal Service, and Wal-Mart, have policies against visible tattoos. A survey of employers revealed that 58 percent indicated that they would be less likely to hire someone with visible tattoos or body piercings. "Perception is everything when it comes to getting a job," says Elaine Stover, associate director of career services at Arizona State University. "Some employers and clients could perceive body art negatively."

However, other employers—such as Bank of America, Allstate, and IBM—allow tattoos. Bank of America goes so far as to have a policy against using tattoos as a factor in hiring decisions.

Policies toward tattoos vary because, legally, employers can do as they wish. As long as the rule is applied equally to everyone (it would not be permissible to allow tattoos on men but not on women, for example), policies against tattoos are perfectly legal. Though not hiring people with tattoos is discrimination, "it's legal discrimination," said Gary Wilson, a Florida employment lawyer.

Thirty-six percent of those aged 18 to 25, and 40 percent of those aged 26 to 40, have at least one tattoo, whereas only 15 percent of those over 40 do, according to a fall 2006 survey by the Pew Research Center. One study in *American Demographics* suggested that 57 percent of senior citizens viewed visible tattoos as "freakish."

Clint Womack, like most other people with multiple tattoos, realizes there's a line that is dangerous to cross. While the 33-year-old hospital worker's arms, legs, and much of his torso are covered with tattoos, his hands, neck, and face are clear. "Tattoos are a choice you make," he says, "and you have to live with your choices."

Sources: R. R. Hastings, "Survey: The Demographics of Tattoos and Piercings," *HRWeek*, February 2007, www.shrm.org; and H. Wessel, "Taboo of Tattoos in the Workplace," *Orlando (Florida) Sentinel*, May 28, 2007, www.tmcnet.com/usubmit/2007/05/28/2666555.htm.

Questions

1. Why do some employers ban tattoos while others don't mind them?

2. Is it fair for employers to reject applicants who have tattoos? Is it fair to require employees, if hired, to conceal their tattoos?

3. Should it be illegal to allow tattoos to be a factor at all in the hiring process?

Case Incident 1

THE RISE OF THE NICE CEO?

If asked to describe the traits of an effective CEO, most people would probably use adjectives such as *driven*, *competitive*, and *tough*. While it's clear that some hard-nosed CEOs, like Blackstone chief executive Stephen Schwarzman (see the chapter opener), are successful, recently some authors have suggested that being "nice" is really important in today's workplace, even in the CEO suite. In a recent book titled *The No A–hole Rule: Building a Civilized Workplace and Surviving One That Isn't*, Stanford management professor Robert Sutton argues that getting along well with others is important to the successful functioning of organizations.

Many companies, such as Google, have developed policies to weed out those who habitually behave in an uncivil manner. Lars Dalgaard, CEO of SuccessFactors, a business software company, identifies himself as a recovering Fortune 500 "a-hole." Now, Dalgaard has implemented a strict "no a-hole" rule in his company. Job interviews are lengthy and feature probing questions designed to uncover any browbeating tendencies. Last year, Dalgaard took candidates vying for a chief financial officer vacancy to lunch at a local restaurant to see how they treated the wait staff. Some got a free lunch but nothing more. When managers and employees are hired, they get a welcome letter from Dalgaard that spells out 15 corporate values, the last of which is "I will not be an a-hole."

Although it's not clear whether they've read Sutton's book, some CEOs of Fortune 500 companies do seem to project the image of a "kinder, gentler CEO." Let's consider three examples, all of whom were protégés of Jack Welch when he was CEO of General Electric (GE) and were candidates to be his successor: Bob Nardelli, James McNerney, and Jeff Immelt.

Bob Nardelli, former CEO, Home Depot

When Bob Nardelli wasn't chosen to be CEO of GE, he demanded to know why. Didn't he have the best numbers? His bitterness was palpable, say GE insiders. When Nardelli became CEO of Home Depot, in his first few months on the job, he became notorious for his imperious manner and explosive temper. At one meeting, he yelled, "You guys don't know how to run a f--ing business." When Nardelli was fired as CEO in 2006, it was due to a combination of factors, including Home Depot's lackluster stock price, but his abrasive personality played no small part. *BusinessWeek* wrote: "With the stock price recently stuck at just over 40, roughly the same as when Nardelli arrived 6 years ago, he could no longer rely on other sterile metrics to assuage the quivering anger his arrogance provoked within every one of his key constituencies: employees, customers, and shareholders."

James McNerney, CEO, Boeing

These are heady days at Boeing, which commands record levels of new orders and dominates its European rival Airbus as never before. Most CEOs would take credit for this success. Not James McNerney, who gives the credit to Boeing's engineers and employees. "I view myself as a value-added facilitator here more than as someone who's crashing through the waves on the bridge of a frigate," he says. A former GE colleague compared Nardelli and McNerney, saying, "Jim's problems have been as tough, or tougher, than the ones that Bob had to face. But he has tried to solve them in a much more pleasant way. The guy is loved over there at Boeing."

Jeff Immelt, CEO, General Electric

Although Jeff Immelt is the first to point out that the nickname "Neutron Jack" for his predecessor Jack Welch was misleading, and that the differences between him and Welch are not as dramatic as some claim, Immelt is noted for his calm demeanor and trusting approach. In speaking of his approach, he said, "I want to believe the best in terms of what people can do. And if you want to make a growth culture, you've got to have a way to nurture people and not make them fight so goddamn hard to get any idea through the door."

Questions

1. Do you think Sutton is wrong and that the contrasting fortunes, and personalities, of Nardelli, McNerney, and Immelt are coincidental? Why or why not?

2. Do you think the importance of being "nice" varies by industry or type of job? How so?

3. How comfortable would you be working in a culture like that of SuccessFactors, where a certain level of "niceness" is part of the job description?

4. Do you think being "nice" is the same as the Big Five trait of agreeableness? If so, do you think companies should screen out those who score low on agreeableness?

5. Earlier we discussed the fact that entrepreneurs score significantly lower than managers on agreeableness. How would you reconcile this finding with Sutton's point?

Sources: D. Brady, "Being Mean Is So Last Millennium," *BusinessWeek,* January 15, 2007, p. 61; G. Colvin, "How One CEO Learned to Fly," *Fortune,* October 16, 2006; B. Grow, "Out at Home Depot," *BusinessWeek,* January 9, 2007; J. Guynn, "Crusade Against the Jerk at Work," *San Francisco (California) Chronicle,* February 24, 2007; and "The Fast Company Interview: Jeff Immelt," *Fast Company,* July 2005, p. 60.

Case Incident 2

A DIAMOND PERSONALITY

Ask Oscar Rodriguez about the dot-com burst, and he may grin at you as if to say, "What burst?" Rodriguez, a 38-year-old entrepreneur, owns an Internet business that sells loose diamonds to various buyers. Business is booming. In 2004, Rodriguez had sales of $2.06 million—a 140 percent increase from 2003. Rodriguez's database of almost 60,000 available diamonds is one of the largest in the industry and is valued, according to him, at over $350 million. Needless to say, he's optimistic about his business venture.

The future wasn't always so bright. In 1985, Rodriguez moved from his native Puerto Rico to Gainesville, Florida, with little ability to speak English. There, he attended community college and worked at a local mall to support himself. After graduation, his roommate's girlfriend suggested that he work at a local jeweler. "I thought she was crazy. I didn't know anything about jewelry," says Rodriguez, but he took her advice. Though he worked hard and received his Diamonds and Diamonds Grading certification from the Gemological Institute of America, he wasn't satisfied with his progress. "I quickly realized that working there, I was just going to get a salary with a raise here and there. I would never become anything. That drove me to explore other business ventures. I also came to really know diamonds—their pricing and their quality."

In 1997, tired of working for someone else, Rodriguez decided to open his own jewelry store. However, business didn't boom. "Some of my customers were telling me they could find diamonds for less on the Internet. It blew my mind." Rodriguez recognized an opportunity and began contacting well-known diamond dealers to see whether they would be interested in selling their gems online. Rodriguez recalls one conversation with a prominent dealer who told him, "You cannot sell diamonds on the Internet. You will not survive." Discouraged, Rodriguez says he then made a mistake. "I stopped working on it. If you have a dream, you have to keep working harder at it."

A year later, Rodriguez did work harder at his dream and found a dealer who agreed to provide him with some diamonds. Says Rodriguez, "Once I had one, I could approach others. Business started to build. The first three months I sold $200,000 worth of diamonds right off the bat. And that was just me. I started to add employees and eventually closed the jewelry store and got out of retail." Although Rodriquez does have some diamonds in inventory, he primarily acts as a connection point between buyers and suppliers, giving his customers an extraordinary selection from which to choose.

Rodriguez is now a savvy entrepreneur, and his company, Abazias.com, went public in October 2003.

Why is Rodriguez successful? Just ask two people who have known him over the years. Gary Schneider, a realtor who helped build Rodriguez's building, says, "Oscar is a very ambitious young man. I am not surprised at all how successful he is. He is an entrepreneur in the truest sense of the word." One of Rodriguez's former real-estate instructors, Howard Freeman, concurs. "I am not surprised at all at his success," says Freeman. "Oscar has always been an extremely motivated individual with a lot of resources. He has a wonderful personality and pays close attention to detail. He also has an ability to stick to things. You could tell from the beginning that he was going to persevere, and I am proud of him."

Rodriguez is keeping his success in perspective, but he also realizes his business's potential: "I take a very small salary, and our overhead is $250,000 a year. I am not in debt, and the business is breaking even. I care about the company. I want to keep everything even until we take off, and then it may be another ball game."

Questions

1. What factors do you think have contributed to Rodriguez's success? Was he merely "in the right place at the right time," or are there characteristics about him that contribute to his success?

2. How do you believe Rodriguez would score on the Big Five dimensions of personality (extraversion, agreeableness, conscientiousness, emotional stability, openness to experience)? Which ones would he score high on? Which ones might he score low on?

3. Do you believe that Rodriguez is high or low on core self-evaluation? On what information did you base your decision?

4. What information about Rodriguez suggests that he has a proactive personality?

Source: Based on M. Blombert, "Cultivating a Career," *The Gainesville (Florida) Sun,* May 9, 2005, p. D1.

Endnotes

1. N. D. Schwartz, "Wall Street's Man of the Moment," *Fortune,* February 21, 2007, http://money.cnn.com/magazines/fortune/fortune_archive/2007/03/05/8401261; and H. Sender and M. Langley, "How Blackstone's Chief Became $7 Billion Man," *Wall Street Journal,* June 13, 2007, pp. A1, A13.

2. G. W. Allport, *Personality: A Psychological Interpretation* (New York: Holt, Rinehart & Winston, 1937), p. 48. For a brief critique of current views on the meaning of personality, see R. T. Hogan and B. W. Roberts, "Introduction: Personality and Industrial and Organizational Psychology," in B. W. Roberts and R. Hogan (eds.), *Personality Psychology in the Workplace* (Washington, DC: American Psychological Association, 2001), pp. 11–12.

3. K. I. van der Zee, J. N. Zaal, and J. Piekstra, "Validation of the Multicultural Personality Questionnaire in the Context of Personnel Selection," *European Journal of Personality* 17 (2003), pp. S77–S100.

4. T. A. Judge, C. A. Higgins, C. J. Thoresen, and M. R. Barrick, "The Big Five Personality Traits, General Mental Ability, and Career Success Across the Life Span," *Personnel Psychology* 52, no. 3 (1999), pp. 621–652.

5. See, for instance, M. B. Stein, K. L. Jang, and W. J. Livesley, "Heritability of Social Anxiety-Related Concerns and Personality Characteristics: A Twin Study," *Journal of Nervous and Mental Disease,* April 2002, pp. 219–224; and S. Pinker, *The Blank Slate: The Modern Denial of Human Nature* (New York: Viking, 2002).

6. See R. D. Arvey and T. J. Bouchard, Jr., "Genetics, Twins, and Organizational Behavior," in B. M. Staw and L. L. Cummings (eds.), *Research in Organizational Behavior,* vol. 16 (Greenwich, CT: JAI Press, 1994), pp. 65–66; W. Wright, *Born That Way: Genes, Behavior, Personality* (New York: Knopf, 1998); and T. J. Bouchard, Jr., and J. C. Loehlin, "Genes, Evolution, and Personality," *Behavior Genetics,* May 2001, pp. 243–273.

7. S. Srivastava, O. P. John, and S. D. Gosling, "Development of Personality in Early and Middle Adulthood: Set Like Plaster or Persistent Change?" *Journal of Personality and Social Psychology,* May 2003, pp. 1041–1053.

8. See A. H. Buss, "Personality as Traits," *American Psychologist,* November 1989, pp. 1378–1388; R. R. McCrae, "Trait Psychology and the Revival of Personality and Culture Studies," *American Behavioral Scientist,* September 2000, pp. 10–31; and L. R. James and M. D. Mazerolle, *Personality in Work Organizations* (Thousand Oaks, CA: Sage, 2002).

9. See, for instance, G. W. Allport and H. S. Odbert, "Trait Names, A Psycholexical Study," *Psychological Monographs,* no. 47 (1936); and R. B. Cattell, "Personality Pinned Down," *Psychology Today,* July 1973, pp. 40–46.

10. R. B. Kennedy and D. A. Kennedy, "Using the Myers-Briggs Type Indicator in Career Counseling," *Journal of Employment Counseling,* March 2004, pp. 38–44.

11. G. N. Landrum, *Profiles of Genius* (New York: Prometheus, 1993).

12. See, for instance, D. J. Pittenger, "Cautionary Comments Regarding the Myers-Briggs Type Indicator," *Consulting Psychology Journal: Practice and Research,* Summer 2005, pp. 210–221; L. Bess and R. J. Harvey, "Bimodal Score Distributions and the Myers-Briggs Type Indicator: Fact or Artifact?" *Journal of Personality Assessment,* February 2002, pp. 176–186; R. M. Capraro and M. M. Capraro, "Myers-Briggs Type Indicator Score Reliability Across Studies: A Meta-analytic Reliability Generalization Study," *Educational & Psychological Measurement,* August 2002, pp. 590–602; and R. C. Arnau, B. A. Green, D. H. Rosen, D. H. Gleaves, and J. G. Melancon, "Are Jungian Preferences Really Categorical? An Empirical Investigation Using Taxometric Analysis," *Personality & Individual Differences,* January 2003, pp. 233–251.

13. See, for example, J. M. Digman, "Personality Structure: Emergence of the Five-Factor Model," in M. R. Rosenzweig and L. W. Porter (eds.), *Annual Review of Psychology,* vol. 41 (Palo Alto, CA: Annual Reviews, 1990), pp. 417–440; R. R. McCrae, "Special Issue: The Five-Factor Model: Issues and Applications," *Journal of Personality,* June 1992; D. B. Smith, P. J. Hanges, and M. W. Dickson, "Personnel Selection and the Five-Factor Model: Reexamining the Effects of Applicant's Frame of Reference," *Journal of Applied Psychology,* April 2001, pp. 304–315; and M. R. Barrick and M. K. Mount, "Yes, Personality Matters: Moving on to More Important Matters," *Human Performance* 18, no. 4 (2005), pp. 359–372.

14. See, for instance, M. R. Barrick and M. K. Mount, "The Big Five Personality Dimensions and Job Performance: A Meta-analysis," *Personnel Psychology*, Spring 1991, pp. 1–26; G. M. Hurtz and J. J. Donovan, "Personality and Job Performance: The Big Five Revisited," *Journal of Applied Psychology*, December 2000, pp. 869–879; J. Hogan and B. Holland, "Using Theory to Evaluate Personality and Job-Performance Relations: A Socioanalytic Perspective," *Journal of Applied Psychology*, February 2003, pp. 100–112; and M. R. Barrick and M. K. Mount, "Select on Conscientiousness and Emotional Stability," in E. A. Locke (ed.), *Handbook of Principles of Organizational Behavior* (Malden, MA: Blackwell, 2004), pp. 15–28.

15. M. K. Mount, M. R. Barrick, and J. P. Strauss, "Validity of Observer Ratings of the Big Five Personality Factors," *Journal of Applied Psychology*, April 1994, p. 272. Additionally confirmed by G. M. Hurtz and J. J. Donovan, "Personality and Job Performance: The Big Five Revisited"; and M. R. Barrick, M. K. Mount, and T. A. Judge, "The FFM Personality Dimensions and Job Performance: Meta-analysis of Meta-analyses," *International Journal of Selection and Assessment* 9 (2001), pp. 9–30.

16. F. L. Schmidt and J. E. Hunter, "The Validity and Utility of Selection Methods in Personnel Psychology: Practical and Theoretical Implications of 85 Years of Research Findings," *Psychological Bulletin*, September 1998, p. 272.

17. M. Tamir and M. D. Robinson, "Knowing Good from Bad: The Paradox of Neuroticism, Negative Affect, and Evaluative Processing," *Journal of Personality & Social Psychology* 87, no. 6 (2004), pp. 913–925.

18. R. J. Foti and M. A. Hauenstein, "Pattern and Variable Approaches in Leadership Emergence and Effectiveness," *Journal of Applied Psychology*, March 2007, pp. 347–355.

19. L. I. Spirling and R. Persaud, "Extraversion as a Risk Factor," *Journal of the American Academy of Child & Adolescent Psychiatry* 42, no. 2 (2003), p. 130.

20. J. A. LePine, J. A. Colquitt, and A. Erez, "Adaptability to Changing Task Contexts: Effects of General Cognitive Ability, Conscientiousness, and Openness to Experience," *Personnel Psychology* 53 (2000), pp. 563–595.

21. B. Laursen, L. Pulkkinen, and R. Adams, "The Antecedents and Correlates of Agreeableness in Adulthood," *Developmental Psychology* 38, no. 4 (2002), pp. 591–603.

22. B. Barry and R. A. Friedman, "Bargainer Characteristics in Distributive and Integrative Negotiation," *Journal of Personality and Social Psychology*, February 1998, pp. 345–359.

23. T. Bogg and B. W. Roberts, "Conscientiousness and Health-Related Behaviors: A Meta-Analysis of the Leading Behavioral Contributors to Mortality," *Psychological Bulletin* 130, no. 6 (2004), pp. 887–919.

24. S. Lee and H. J. Klein, "Relationships Between Conscientiousness, Self-Efficacy, Self-Deception, and Learning over Time," *Journal of Applied Psychology* 87, no. 6 (2002), pp. 1175–1182; G. J. Feist, "A Meta-analysis of Personality in Scientific and Artistic Creativity," *Personality and Social Psychology Review* 2, no. 4 (1998), pp. 290–309.

25. T. A. Judge and J. E. Bono, "A Rose by Any Other Name . . . Are Self-Esteem, Generalized Self-Efficacy, Neuroticism, and Locus of Control Indicators of a Common Construct?" in B. W. Roberts and R. Hogan (eds.), *Personality Psychology in the Workplace* (Washington, DC: American Psychological Association), pp. 93–118.

26. A. Erez and T. A. Judge, "Relationship of Core Self-Evaluations to Goal Setting, Motivation, and Performance," *Journal of Applied Psychology* 86, no. 6 (2001), pp. 1270–1279.

27. U. Malmendier and G. Tate, "CEO Overconfidence and Corporate Investment," *Journal of Finance* 60, no. 6 (December 2005), pp. 2661–2700.

28. R. Sandomir, "Star Struck," *New York Times*, January 12, 2007, pp. C10, C14.

29. R. G. Vleeming, "Machiavellianism: A Preliminary Review," *Psychological Reports*, February 1979, pp. 295–310.

30. R. Christie and F. L. Geis, *Studies in Machiavellianism* (New York: Academic Press, 1970), p. 312; and N. V. Ramanaiah, A. Byravan, and F. R. J. Detwiler, "Revised Neo Personality Inventory Profiles of Machiavellian and Non-Machiavellian People," *Psychological Reports*, October 1994, pp. 937–938.

31. Christie and Geis, *Studies in Machiavellianism*.

32. "Linda Wachner, 61," *Fortune*, April 16, 2007, p. 106.

33. M. Maccoby, "Narcissistic Leaders: The Incredible Pros, the Inevitable Cons," *The Harvard Business Review*, January–February 2000, pp. 69–77, www.maccoby.com/Articles/NarLeaders.shtml.

34. W. K. Campbell and C. A. Foster, "Narcissism and Commitment in Romantic Relationships: An Investment Model Analysis," *Personality and Social Psychology Bulletin* 28, no. 4 (2002), pp. 484–495.

35. T. A. Judge, J. A. LePine, and B. L. Rich, "The Narcissistic Personality: Relationship with Inflated Self-Ratings of Leadership and with Task and Contextual Performance," *Journal of Applied Psychology* 91, no. 4 (2006), pp. 762–776.

36. See M. Snyder, *Public Appearances/Private Realities: The Psychology of Self-Monitoring* (New York: W. H. Freeman, 1987); and S. W. Gangestad and M. Snyder, "Self-Monitoring: Appraisal and Reappraisal," *Psychological Bulletin*, July 2000, pp. 530–555.

37. Snyder, *Public Appearances/Private Realities*.

38. D. V. Day, D. J. Shleicher, A. L. Unckless, and N. J. Hiller, "Self-Monitoring Personality at Work: A Meta-analytic Investigation of Construct Validity," *Journal of Applied Psychology*, April 2002, pp. 390–401.

39. M. Kilduff and D. V. Day, "Do Chameleons Get Ahead? The Effects of Self-Monitoring on Managerial Careers," *Academy of Management Journal*, August 1994, pp. 1047–1060; and A. Mehra, M. Kilduff, and D. J. Brass, "The Social Networks of High and Low Self-Monitors: Implications for Workplace Performance," *Administrative Science Quarterly*, March 2001, pp. 121–146.

40. R. N. Taylor and M. D. Dunnette, "Influence of Dogmatism, Risk-Taking Propensity, and Intelligence on Decision-Making Strategies for a Sample of Industrial Managers," *Journal of Applied Psychology*, August 1974, pp. 420–423.

41. I. L. Janis and L. Mann, *Decision Making: A Psychological Analysis of Conflict, Choice, and Commitment* (New York: The Free Press, 1977); W. H. Stewart, Jr., and L. Roth, "Risk Propensity Differences Between Entrepreneurs and Managers: A Meta-analytic Review," *Journal of Applied*

Psychology, February 2001, pp. 145–153; J. B. Miner and N. S. Raju, "Risk Propensity Differences Between Managers and Entrepreneurs and Between Low- and High-Growth Entrepreneurs: A Reply in a More Conservative Vein," *Journal of Applied Psychology* 89, no. 1 (2004), pp. 3–13; and W. H. Stewart, Jr., and P. L. Roth, "Data Quality Affects Meta-analytic Conclusions: A Response to Miner and Raju (2004) Concerning Entrepreneurial Risk Propensity," *Journal of Applied Psychology* 89, no. 1 (2004), pp. 14–21.

42. N. Kogan and M. A. Wallach, "Group Risk Taking as a Function of Members' Anxiety and Defensiveness," *Journal of Personality*, March 1967, pp. 50–63.

43. M. Friedman and R. H. Rosenman, *Type A Behavior and Your Heart* (New York: Alfred A. Knopf, 1974), p. 84.

44. Ibid., pp. 84–85.

45. R. E. White, S. Thornhill, and E. Hampson, "Entrepreneurs and Evolutionary Biology: The Relationship Between Testosterone and New Venture Creation," *Organizational Behavior and Human Decision Processes* 100 (2006), pp. 21–34; and H. Zhao and S. E. Seibert, "The Big Five Personality Dimensions and Entrepreneurial State: A Meta-analytical Review," *Journal of Applied Psychology* 91, no. 2 (2006), pp. 259–271.

46. K. W. Cook, C. A. Vance, and E. Spector, "The Relation of Candidate Personality with Selection-Interview Outcomes," *Journal of Applied Social Psychology* 30 (2000), pp. 867–885.

47. J. M. Crant, "Proactive Behavior in Organizations," *Journal of Management* 26, no. 3 (2000), p. 436.

48. S. E. Seibert, M. L. Kraimer, and J. M. Crant, "What Do Proactive People Do? A Longitudinal Model Linking Proactive Personality and Career Success," *Personnel Psychology*, Winter 2001, p. 850.

49. T. S. Bateman and J. M. Crant, "The Proactive Component of Organizational Behavior: A Measure and Correlates," *Journal of Organizational Behavior*, March 1993, pp. 103–118; and J. M. Crant and T. S. Bateman, "Charismatic Leadership Viewed from Above: The Impact of Proactive Personality," *Journal of Organizational Behavior*, February 2000, pp. 63–75.

50. Crant, "Proactive Behavior in Organizations," p. 436.

51. See, for instance, R. C. Becherer and J. G. Maurer, "The Proactive Personality Disposition and Entrepreneurial Behavior Among Small Company Presidents," *Journal of Small Business Management*, January 1999, pp. 28–36.

52. S. E. Seibert, J. M. Crant, and M. L. Kraimer, "Proactive Personality and Career Success," *Journal of Applied Psychology*, June 1999, pp. 416–427; Seibert, Kraimer, and Crant, "What Do Proactive People Do?" p. 850; and J. D. Kammeyer-Mueller, and C. R. Wanberg, "Unwrapping the Organizational Entry Process: Disentangling Multiple Antecedents and Their Pathways to Adjustment," *Journal of Applied Psychology* 88, no. 5 (2003), pp. 779–794.

53. M. Rokeach, *The Nature of Human Values* (New York: The Free Press, 1973), p. 5.

54. M. Rokeach and S. J. Ball-Rokeach, "Stability and Change in American Value Priorities, 1968–1981," *American Psychologist* 44, no. 5 (1989), pp. 775–784; and B. M. Meglino and E. C. Ravlin, "Individual Values in Organizations: Concepts, Controversies, and Research," *Journal of Management* 24, no. 3 (1998), p. 355.

55. See, for instance, Meglino and Ravlin, "Individual Values in Organizations," pp. 351–389.

56. Rokeach, *The Nature of Human Values*, p. 6.

57. J. M. Munson and B. Z. Posner, "The Factorial Validity of a Modified Rokeach Value Survey for Four Diverse Samples," *Educational and Psychological Measurement*, Winter 1980, pp. 1073–1079; and W. C. Frederick and J. Weber, "The Values of Corporate Managers and Their Critics: An Empirical Description and Normative Implications," in W. C. Frederick and L. E. Preston (eds.), *Business Ethics: Research Issues and Empirical Studies* (Greenwich, CT: JAI Press, 1990), pp. 123–144.

58. Frederick and Weber, "The Values of Corporate Managers and Their Critics," pp. 123–144.

59. Ibid., p. 132.

60. See, for example, J. Levitz, "Pitching 401(k)s to Generation Y Is a Tough Sell," *Wall Street Journal*, September 27, 2006, pp. B1, B2; P. Paul, "Global Generation Gap," *American Demographics*, March 2002, pp. 18–19; and N. Watson, "Generation Wrecked," *Fortune*, October 14, 2002, pp. 183–190.

61. K. W. Smola and C. D. Sutton, "Generational Differences: Revisiting Generational Work Values for the New Millennium," *Journal of Organizational Behavior* 23 (2002), pp. 363–382; and K. Mellahi and C. Guermat, "Does Age Matter? An Empirical Examination of the Effect of Age on Managerial Values and Practices in India," *Journal of World Business* 39, no. 2 (2004), pp. 199–215.

62. N. A. Hira, "You Raised Them, Now Manage Them," *Fortune*, May 28, 2007, pp. 38–46; R. R. Hastings, "Surveys Shed Light on Generation Y Career Goals," *SHRM Online*, March 2007, www. shrm. org; and S. Jayson, "The 'Millennials' Come of Age," *USA Today*, June 29, 2006, pp. 1D, 2D.

63. J. L. Holland, *Making Vocational Choices: A Theory of Vocational Personalities and Work Environments* (Odessa, FL: Psychological Assessment Resources, 1997).

64. See, for example, J. L. Holland and G. D. Gottfredson, "Studies of the Hexagonal Model: An Evaluation (or, The Perils of Stalking the Perfect Hexagon)," *Journal of Vocational Behavior*, April 1992, pp. 158–170; T. J. Tracey and J. Rounds, "Evaluating Holland's and Gati's Vocational-Interest Models: A Structural Meta-Analysis," *Psychological Bulletin*, March 1993, pp. 229–246; J. L. Holland, "Exploring Careers with a Typology: What We Have Learned and Some New Directions," *American Psychologist*, April 1996, pp. 397–406; and S. X. Day and J. Rounds, "Universality of Vocational Interest Structure Among Racial and Ethnic Minorities," *American Psychologist*, July 1998, pp. 728–736.

65. See B. Schneider, "The People Make the Place," *Personnel Psychology*, Autumn 1987, pp. 437–453; B. Schneider, H. W. Goldstein, and D. B. Smith, "The ASA Framework: An Update," *Personnel Psychology*, Winter 1995, pp. 747–773; A. L. Kristof, "Person–Organization Fit: An Integrative Review of Its Conceptualizations, Measurement, and Implications," *Personnel Psychology*, Spring 1996, pp. 1–49; B. Schneider, D. B. Smith, S. Taylor, and J. Fleenor, "Personality and Organizations: A Test of the Homogeneity of Personality Hypothesis," *Journal of Applied Psychology*, June 1998, pp. 462–470; W. Arthur, Jr., S. T. Bell, A. J. Villado, and D. Doverspike, "The Use of Person-Organization Fit in Employment Decision-Making: An Assessment of Its

Criterion-Related Validity," *Journal of Applied Psychology* 91, no. 4 (2006), pp. 786–801; and J. R. Edwards, D. M. Cable, I. O. Williamson, L. S. Lambert, and A. J. Shipp, "The Phenomenology of Fit: Linking the Person and Environment to the Subjective Experience of Person–Environment Fit," *Journal of Applied Psychology* 91, no. 4 (2006), pp. 802–827.

66. Based on T. A. Judge and D. M. Cable, "Applicant Personality, Organizational Culture, and Organization Attraction," *Personnel Psychology*, Summer 1997, pp. 359–394.

67. M. L. Verquer, T. A. Beehr, and S. E. Wagner, "A Meta-analysis of Relations Between Person–Organization Fit and Work Attitudes," *Journal of Vocational Behavior* 63, no. 3 (2003), pp. 473–489.

68. See, for instance, J. E. Williams, J. L. Saiz, D. L. Formy-Duval, M. L. Munick, E. E. Fogle, A. Adom, A. Haque, F. Neto, and J. Yu, "Cross-Cultural Variation in the Importance of Psychological Characteristics: A Seven-Country Study," *International Journal of Psychology*, October 1995, pp. 529–550; R. R. McCrae and P. T. Costa, Jr., "Personality Trait Structure as a Human Universal," *American Psychologist*, May 1997, pp. 509–516; R. R. McCrae, "Trait Psychology and the Revival of Personality-and-Culture Studies," *American Behavioral Scientist*, September 2000, pp. 10–31; S. V. Paunonen, M. Zeidner, H. A. Engvik, P. Oosterveld, and R. Maliphant, "The Nonverbal Assessment of Personality in Five Cultures," *Journal of Cross-Cultural Psychology*, March 2000, pp. 220–239; H. C. Triandis and E. M. Suh, "Cultural Influences on Personality," in S. T. Fiske, D. L. Schacter, and C. Zahn-Waxler (eds.), *Annual Review of Psychology*, vol. 53 (Palo Alto, CA: Annual Reviews, 2002), pp. 133–160; R. R. McCrae and J. Allik, *The Five-Factor Model of Personality Across Cultures* (New York: Kluwer Academic/Plenum, 2002); and R. R. McCrae, P. T. Costa, Jr., T. A. Martin, V. E. Oryol, A. A. Rukavishnikov, I. G. Senin, M. Hrebickova, and T. Urbanek, "Consensual Validation of Personality Traits Across Cultures," *Journal of Research in Personality* 38, no. 2 (2004), pp. 179–201.

69. A. T. Church and M. S. Katigbak, "Trait Psychology in the Philippines," *American Behavioral Scientist*, September 2000, pp. 73–94.

70. J. F. Salgado, "The Five Factor Model of Personality and Job Performance in the European Community," *Journal of Applied Psychology*, February 1997, pp. 30–43.

71. G. Hofstede, *Culture's Consequences: International Differences in Work-Related Values* (Beverly Hills, CA: Sage, 1980); G. Hofstede, *Cultures and Organizations: Software of the Mind* (London: McGraw-Hill, 1991); G. Hofstede, "Cultural Constraints in Management Theories," *Academy of Management Executive* 7, no. 1 (1993), pp. 81–94; G. Hofstede and M. F. Peterson, "National Values and Organizational Practices," in N. M. Ashkanasy, C. M. Wilderom, and M. F. Peterson (eds.), *Handbook of Organizational Culture and Climate* (Thousand Oaks, CA: Sage, 2000), pp. 401–416; and G. Hofstede, *Culture's Consequences: Comparing Values, Behaviors, Institutions, and Organizations Across Nations*, 2nd ed.

(Thousand Oaks, CA: Sage, 2001). For criticism of this research, see B. McSweeney, "Hofstede's Model of National Cultural Differences and Their Consequences: A Triumph of Faith—A Failure of Analysis," *Human Relations* 55, no. 1 (2002), pp. 89–118.

72. M. H. Bond, "Reclaiming the Individual from Hofstede's Ecological Analysis—A 20-Year Odyssey: Comment on Oyserman et al. (2002). *Psychological Bulletin* 128, no. 1 (2002), pp. 73–77; G. Hofstede, "The Pitfalls of Cross-National Survey Research: A Reply to the Article by Spector et al. on the Psychometric Properties of the Hofstede Values Survey Module 1994," *Applied Psychology: An International Review* 51, no. 1 (2002), pp. 170–178; and T. Fang, "A Critique of Hofstede's Fifth National Culture Dimension," *International Journal of Cross-Cultural Management* 3, no. 3 (2003), pp. 347–368.

73. M. Javidan and R. J. House, "Cultural Acumen for the Global Manager: Lessons from Project GLOBE," *Organizational Dynamics* 29, no. 4 (2001), pp. 289–305; and R. J. House, P. J. Hanges, M. Javidan, and P. W. Dorfman (eds.), *Leadership, Culture, and Organizations: The GLOBE Study of 62 Societies* (Thousand Oaks, CA: Sage, 2004).

74. P. C. Early, "Leading Cultural Research in the Future: A Matter of Paradigms and Taste," *Journal of International Business Studies*, September 2006, pp. 922–931; G. Hofstede, "What Did GLOBE Really Measure? Researchers' Minds Versus Respondents' Minds," *Journal of International Business Studies*, September 2006, pp. 882–896; and M. Javidan, R. J. House, P. W. Dorfman, P. J. Hanges, and M. S. de Luque, "Conceptualizing and Measuring Cultures and Their Consequences: A Comparative Review of GLOBE's and Hofstede's Approaches," *Journal of International Business Studies*, September 2006, pp. 897–914.

75. L. A. Witt, "The Interactive Effects of Extraversion and Conscientiousness on Performance," *Journal of Management* 28, no. 6 (2002), p. 836.

76. R. P. Tett and D. D. Burnett, "A Personality Trait–Based Interactionist Model of Job Performance," *Journal of Applied Psychology*, June 2003, pp. 500–517.

77. R. Hogan, "In Defense of Personality Measurement: New Wine for Old Whiners," *Human Performance* 18, no. 4 (2005), pp. 331–341; and N. Schmitt, "Beyond the Big Five: Increases in Understanding and Practical Utility," *Human Performance* 17, no. 3 (2004), pp. 347–357.

78. B. Adkins and D. Caldwell, "Firm or Subgroup Culture: Where Does Fitting in Matter Most?" *Journal of Organizational Behavior* 25, no. 8 (2004), pp. 969–978; H. D. Cooper-Thomas, A. van Vianen, and N. Anderson, "Changes in Person–Organization Fit: The Impact of Socialization Tactics on Perceived and Actual P–O Fit," *European Journal of Work & Organizational Psychology* 13, no. 1 (2004), pp. 52–78; and C. A. O'Reilly, J. Chatman, and D. F. Caldwell, "People and Organizational Culture: A Profile Comparison Approach to Assessing Person–Organization Fit," *Academy of Management Journal* 34, no. 3 (1991), pp. 487–516.

Perception and Individual Decision Making

Indecision may or may not be my problem.

—Jimmy Buffett

LEARNING OBJECTIVES

After studying this chapter, you should be able to:

1 Define *perception* and explain the factors that influence it.

2 Explain attribution theory and list the three determinants of attribution.

3 Identify the shortcuts individuals use in making judgments about others.

4 Explain the link between perception and decision making.

5 Apply the rational model of decision making and contrast it with bounded rationality and intuition.

6 List and explain the common decision biases or errors.

7 Explain how individual differences and organizational constraints affect decision making.

8 Contrast the three ethical decision criteria.

9 Define *creativity* and discuss the three-component model of creativity.

a rental car company employee was told she couldn't wear a head scarf during Ramadan and then was fired for complaining. Hotel employees were cursed at and nicknamed "Osama" and "Taliban."

Among the many ramifications of the September 11, 2001, terrorist attacks are heightened negative perceptions of Muslims and Arabs, including those living and working in the United States. More than 6 years after the attacks, 4 of 10 U.S. adults admitted they still harbored

Muslim Americans: Perception and Reality

Source: Joyce Dopkeen/The New York Times

negative feelings or prejudices against Muslims living in the United States, according to a *USA Today*/Gallup poll. A poll of Muslim Americans revealed that 53 percent perceived that life has been more difficult for them since the 9/11 terrorist attacks.

There are 2.35 million Muslims in the United States. *BusinessWeek* concluded, "as a group, they offer a model of assimilation and material success." Although estimates differ, one study suggested that Muslim Americans (59 percent) are twice as likely as the general U.S. population (28 percent) to have a college degree. The median family income of Muslim Americans exceeds the national average of $55,800. In a 2007 poll, 71 percent of American Muslims agreed with the statement "most people who want to get ahead can make it if they work hard," compared to 64 percent of the general U.S. population. Forty percent of U.S. Muslims attend mosque weekly, compared to 45 percent of U.S. Christians who say they attend church weekly. Overall, U.S. Muslims are much more like typical U.S. citizens than Muslims in other Western democracies, such as France, Spain, or the United Kingdom, where the typical Muslim is more likely to be less educated and have a lower income.

There are, however, areas of divergence and concern. Roughly one in four U.S. Muslims under 30 said they believed suicide bombings to defend their religion are acceptable, at least in some circumstances. (Only 9 percent of U.S. Muslims over 30 believed that suicide bombings were ever justified.) And accommodation of Islamic practices is not always easy for U.S. employers. For example, a devout Muslim corrections officer sued the state of New York when he was ordered to remove his kufi, or skullcap; the state eventually settled the suit. A group of female Muslim employees won their challenge against the uniform policy of the in-flight catering company LSG Sky Chefs, which required pants and sports shirts. USAir kept a Muslim flight attendant from working after she chose to wear a hijab (a Muslim head scarf), and Dunkin' Donuts fired a Muslim employee after she refused to remove her hijab. Recently, Aicha Baha sued Walt Disney World, alleging that she was fired because she wouldn't remove her hijab at work.

For the average U.S. citizen, reconciling the two perceptions of Muslim Americans—that most are much like the typical U.S. citizen, while a few clearly are not—often proves difficult. Moreover, for employers, establishing dress codes, attendance policies, and other workplace standards is often difficult. UPS, for example, has a policy that its drivers be clean shaven, but it makes an exception for religious accommodation.

But there are positive signs. The Equal Employment Opportunity Commission (EEOC) witnessed a significant spike in discrimination claims by Muslim Americans in the year after the 9/11 attacks. Since that time, discrimination claims have "slowed considerably and declined in frequency," according to EEOC spokesman David Ginsburg. Moreover, negative attitudes and distrust are less evident in the workplace. But according to a recent survey by the Society for Human Resource Management, 75 percent of U.S. HR professionals thought negative attitudes toward Muslim employees have stayed the same since 9/11, while 16 percent thought they've increased, and 9 percent thought they've decreased.

It's not easy to be an American Muslim. Born and raised in Philadelphia, and now living in Kansas, Mahnaz Shabbir is president of Shabbir Advisors, an integrated strategic management consulting company. Shabbir says, "For most of my life, my identification as a first generation American Muslim has been a struggle."[1] ■

*t*he chapter-opening story considers perceptions, in this case of Muslim Americans. In the following Self-Assessment Library, consider your perceptions of appropriate gender roles.

Self Assessment Library ➤➤

WHAT ARE MY GENDER ROLE PERCEPTIONS?

In the Self-Assessment Library (available on CD or online), take assessment IV.C.2 (What Are My Gender Role Perceptions?) and answer the following questions.

1. *Did you score as high as you thought you would?*
2. *Do you think a problem with measures like this is that people aren't honest in responding?*
3. *If others, such as friends, classmates, and family members, rated you, would they rate you differently? Why or why not?*
4. *Research has shown that people's gender role perceptions are becoming less traditional over time. Why do you suppose this is so?*

What Is Perception?

1 *Define* perception *and explain the factors that influence it.*

Perception is a process by which individuals organize and interpret their sensory impressions in order to give meaning to their environment. However, what we perceive can be substantially different from objective reality. For example, all employees in a firm may view it as a great place to work—favorable working conditions, interesting job assignments, good pay, excellent benefits, understanding and responsible management—but, as most of us know, it's very unusual to find such agreement.

Why is perception important in the study of OB? Simply because people's behavior is based on their perception of what reality is, not on reality itself. *The world as it is perceived is the world that is behaviorally important.*

Factors That Influence Perception

How do we explain the fact that individuals may look at the same thing yet perceive it differently? A number of factors operate to shape and sometimes distort perception. These factors can reside in the *perceiver*, in the object, or *target*, being perceived; or in the context of the *situation* in which the perception is made (see Exhibit 5-1).

---

perception *A process by which individuals organize and interpret their sensory impressions in order to give meaning to their environment.*

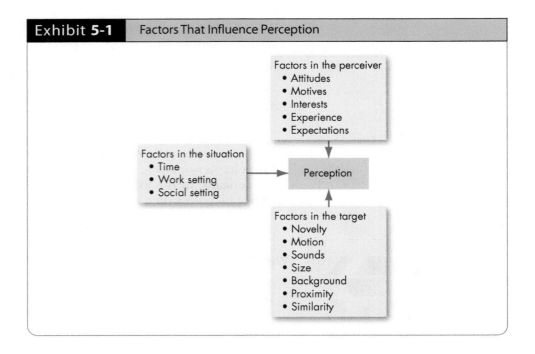

Exhibit 5-1   Factors That Influence Perception

When an individual looks at a target and attempts to interpret what he or she sees, that interpretation is heavily influenced by the personal characteristics of the individual perceiver. Personal characteristics that affect perception include a person's attitudes, personality, motives, interests, past experiences, and expectations. For instance, if you expect police officers to be authoritative, young people to be lazy, or individuals holding public office to be unscrupulous, you may perceive them as such, regardless of their actual traits.

Characteristics of the target we observe can affect what we perceive. Loud people are more likely to be noticed in a group than quiet ones. So, too, are extremely attractive or unattractive individuals. Because we don't look at targets in isolation, the relationship of a target to its background also influences perception, as does our tendency to group close things and similar things together. For instance, women, people of color, or members of any other group that has clearly distinguishable characteristics are often perceived as alike in other, unrelated ways as well.

The context in which we see objects or events is also important. The time at which we see an object or event can influence attention, as can location, light, heat, or any number of situational factors. For example, at a nightclub on Saturday night, you may not notice a young guest "dressed to the nines." Yet that same person so attired for your Monday morning management class would certainly catch your attention (and that of the rest of the class). Neither the perceiver nor the target changed between Saturday night and Monday morning, but the situation is different.

Person Perception: Making Judgments About Others

2 *Explain attribution theory and list the three determinants of attribution.*

Now we turn to the most relevant application of perception concepts to OB. This is the issue of *person perception*, or the perceptions people form about each other.

Attribution Theory

Nonliving objects such as desks, machines, and buildings are subject to the laws of nature, but they have no beliefs, motives, or intentions. People do. That's why when we observe people, we attempt to develop explanations of why they behave in certain ways. Our perception and judgment of a person's actions, therefore, will be significantly influenced by the assumptions we make about that person's internal state.

Attribution theory tries to explain the ways in which we judge people differently, depending on the meaning we attribute to a given behavior.[2] It suggests that when we observe an individual's behavior, we attempt to determine whether it was internally or externally caused. That determination, however, depends largely on three factors: (1) distinctiveness, (2) consensus, and (3) consistency. First, let's clarify the differences between internal and external causation and then we'll elaborate on each of the three determining factors.

Internally caused behaviors are those we believe to be under the personal control of the individual. *Externally* caused behavior is what we imagine the situation forced the individual to do. For example, if one of your employees is late for work, you might attribute his lateness to his partying into the wee hours of the morning and then oversleeping. This is an internal attribution. But if you attribute his arriving late to an automobile accident that tied up traffic, then you are making an external attribution.

Now let's discuss each of the three determining factors. *Distinctiveness* refers to whether an individual displays different behaviors in different situations. Is the employee who arrives late today also the one coworkers say regularly "blows off" commitments? What we want to know is whether this behavior is unusual. If it is, we are likely to give it an external attribution. If it's not unusual, we will probably judge the behavior to be internal.

If everyone who faces a similar situation responds in the same way, we can say the behavior shows *consensus*. The behavior of our tardy employee meets this criterion if all employees who took the same route to work were also late. From an attribution perspective, if consensus is high, you would probably give an external attribution to the employee's tardiness, whereas if other employees who took the same route made it to work on time, you would attribute his lateness to an internal cause.

Finally, an observer looks for *consistency* in a person's actions. Does the person respond the same way over time? Coming in 10 minutes late for work is not perceived in the same way for an employee for whom it is an unusual case (she hasn't been late for several months) as it is for an employee for whom it is part of a routine pattern (she is late two or three times a week). The more consistent the behavior, the more we are inclined to attribute it to internal causes.

Exhibit 5-2 summarizes the key elements in attribution theory. It tells us, for instance, that if an employee, Kim Randolph, generally performs at about the same level on other related tasks as she does on her current task (low distinctiveness), if other employees frequently perform differently—better or worse—than Kim does on that current task (low consensus), and if Kim's performance

attribution theory *An attempt to determine whether an individual's behavior is internally or externally caused.*

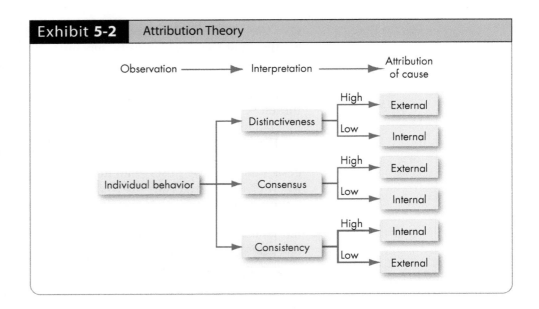

Exhibit 5-2   Attribution Theory

on this current task is consistent over time (high consistency), you or anyone else judging Kim's work will be likely to hold her primarily responsible for her task performance (internal attribution).

One of the most interesting findings from attribution theory is that errors or biases distort attributions. For instance, substantial evidence suggests that when we make judgments about the behavior of other people, we tend to underestimate the influence of external factors and overestimate the influence of internal or personal factors.[3] This **fundamental attribution error** can explain why a sales manager is prone to attribute the poor performance of her sales agents to laziness rather than to the innovative product line introduced by a competitor. Individuals and organizations also tend to attribute their own successes to internal factors such as ability or effort, while putting the blame for failure on external factors such as bad luck or unproductive coworkers. This is the **self-serving bias**.[4] For example, when former (and now deceased) Enron CEO Ken Lay was tried for fraud, he blamed former Chief Financial Officer Andrew Fastow, saying, "I think the primary reason for Enron's collapse was Andy Fastow and his little group of people and what they did."

Frequently Used Shortcuts in Judging Others

We use a number of shortcuts when we judge others. These techniques are frequently valuable: They allow us to make accurate perceptions rapidly and provide valid data for making predictions. However, they are not foolproof. They can and do get us into trouble. Understanding these shortcuts can help you recognize when they can result in significant distortions.

3 Identify the shortcuts individuals use in making judgments about others.

Selective Perception   Any characteristic that makes a person, an object, or an event stand out will increase the probability that we will perceive it. Why? Because it is impossible for us to assimilate everything we see; we can take in only certain stimuli. This tendency explains why you're more likely to notice cars like your own or why a boss may reprimand some people and not others who are doing the same thing. Because we can't observe everything going on about us, we engage in **selective perception**. A classic example shows how vested interests can significantly influence which problems we see.

Dearborn and Simon performed a perceptual study in which 23 business executives read a comprehensive case describing the organization and activities of a steel company.[5] Six were in sales, 5 in production, 4 in accounting, and 8 in miscellaneous functions. Each manager was asked to write down the most important problem he found in the case. Eighty-three percent of the sales executives rated sales important; only 29 percent of the others did so. The researchers concluded that participants perceived as important the aspects of a situation specifically related to their own unit's activities and goals. A group's perception of organizational activities is selectively altered to align with the vested interests they represent.

Because we cannot assimilate all that we observe, we take in bits and pieces. But we don't choose them randomly; rather, we select them according to our interests, background, experience, and attitudes. Selective perception allows us to "speed-read" others, but not without the risk of drawing an inaccurate picture. Because we see what we want to see, we can draw unwarranted conclusions from an ambiguous situation.

Halo Effect   When we draw a general impression about an individual on the basis of a single characteristic, such as intelligence, sociability, or appearance, a **halo effect** is operating.[6] Consider former HP CEO Carly Fiorina. Early in her tenure, she was lauded as articulate, decisive, charismatic, savvy, and visionary. At the time of her appointment, *BusinessWeek* said, "She has it all." After Fiorina was fired, though, she was described as unproven, egotistical, inflexible, and uncompromising. *BusinessWeek* faulted her for her unwillingness to delegate and her inability to execute.[7] So, when Fiorina was deemed effective, everything about her was good. But when she was fired for supposed ineffectiveness, the same people who lauded her before now saw few if any redeeming features. That's both sides of the halo (halo or horns, you might say).

The reality of the halo effect was confirmed in a classic study in which subjects were given a list of traits such as intelligent, skillful, practical, industrious, determined, and warm and asked to evaluate the person to whom those traits applied.[8] Subjects judged the person to be wise, humorous, popular, and imaginative. When the same list was modified to include "cold" instead of "warm," a completely different picture emerged. Clearly, the subjects were allowing a single trait to influence their overall impression of the person they were judging.

Contrast Effects   An old adage among entertainers says, "Never follow an act that has kids or animals in it." Why? Audiences love children and animals so much that you'll look bad in comparison. This example demonstrates how **contrast effects** can distort perceptions. We don't evaluate a person in isolation. Our reaction to a person is influenced by other persons we have recently encountered.

In a series of job interviews, for instance, interviewers can make distortions in any given candidate's evaluation as a result of his place in the interview

---

fundamental attribution error   *The tendency to underestimate the influence of external factors and overestimate the influence of internal factors when making judgments about the behavior of others.*

self-serving bias   *The tendency for individuals to attribute their own successes to internal factors and put the blame for failures on external factors.*

selective perception   *The tendency to selectively interpret what one sees on the basis of one's interests, background, experience, and attitudes.*

halo effect   *The tendency to draw a general impression about an individual on the basis of a single characteristic.*

contrast effects   *Evaluation of a person's characteristics that is affected by comparisons with other people recently encountered who rank higher or lower on the same characteristics.*

International OB

Can Negative Perceptions Dampen International Business Relations?

Japan and China would seem to be natural economic partners, given that they're geographically so close to each other. However, Japanese companies currently lag behind both the United States and Europe in terms of trade with China. Although the Japanese auto industry has had enormous success in other countries, including the United States, the top-selling foreign cars in China are produced by GM (a U.S. company) and Volkswagen (a German company). Also, Japan's booming electronics industry currently captures only 5 percent of the Chinese market.

But who or what is to blame for the dismal business relationship between Japan and China? The perceptions of the public—in both countries—may be the answer. For example, many Chinese citizens are still angered about a report that employees of a Japanese construction company hired Chinese prostitutes for a corporate party. And many Japanese citizens believe that Chinese immigrants are to blame for many of the violent crimes taking place in Japan. In addition to these recent events, historically, relations between the two countries have been strained. Beijing is still upset about Japan's military invasion of China in the 1930s and 1940s, for which Japan refuses to make amends.

These negative perceptions may be difficult to reverse if perceptual errors such as fundamental attribution error and the halo effect are operating. That is, both countries blame each other for their behaviors (internal attribution), and both countries tend to view each other's actions as negative (negative halo effect). Because of these errors, future behaviors, even if they are ambiguous, may be perceived negatively by the other country.

Source: Based on C. Chandler, "Business Is Hot, Relations Are Not," *Fortune (Europe),* April 19, 2004, pp. 20–21; and "China Urges Japan to Do More to Improve Ties," The Associated Press, March 14, 2005.

schedule. A candidate is likely to receive a more favorable evaluation if preceded by mediocre applicants and a less favorable evaluation if preceded by strong applicants.

Stereotyping   When we judge someone on the basis of our perception of the group to which he or she belongs, we are using the shortcut called

Jin, an Asian American rapper, performs at the Garden of Eden in Hollywood, hoping for a hit song in an industry that lacks Asian American pop stars. But Asian American artists and scholars argue that racial stereotyping inaccurately generalizes Asian Americans as studious geeks and that someone who looks Asian must be a foreigner. This stereotyping doesn't fit the "cool" image and born-in-the-U.S.A. authenticity required for musicians like Jin who aspire to become American pop stars.
Source: Misha Erwitt/ The New York Times

stereotyping.[9] We saw the problems stereotyping can create at the opening of this chapter: All Muslims are not terrorists!

We rely on generalizations every day because they help us make decisions quickly. They are a means of simplifying a complex world. It's less difficult to deal with an unmanageable number of stimuli if we use heuristics or stereotypes. The problem occurs, of course, when we generalize inaccurately or too much. In organizations, we frequently hear comments that represent stereotypes based on gender, age, race, religion, ethnicity, and even weight:[10] "Women won't relocate for a promotion," "men aren't interested in child care," "older workers can't learn new skills," "Asian immigrants are hardworking and conscientious," "overweight people lack discipline." Stereotypes can be so deeply ingrained and powerful that they influence life-and-death decisions. One study showed that, controlling for a wide array of factors (such as aggravating or mitigating circumstances), the degree to which black defendants in murder trails looked stereotypically black essentially doubled their odds of receiving a death sentence if convicted.[11]

One specific manifestation of stereotypes is **profiling**—a form of stereotyping in which a group of individuals is singled out, typically on the basis of race or ethnicity, for intensive inquiry, scrutiny, or investigation. Since 9/11, ethnic profiling has become the subject of much debate.[12] On one side, proponents argue that profiling people of Arab descent is necessary in order to prevent terrorism. After all, a good percentage of the large-scale terrorist attacks that have taken place over the past 30 years have been perpetrated by Muslim terrorists.[13] On the other side, critics argue that profiling is demeaning, discriminatory, and an ineffective way to find potential terrorists and that Muslim Americans are as law abiding as other citizens. The debate is important and implies the need to balance the rights of individuals against the greater good of society. Organizations need to sensitize employees and managers to the damage that profiling can create. Many are expanding their diversity training programs, which we discuss in Chapter 18, to particularly address ethnic stereotyping and profiling.

One of the problems of stereotypes is that they *are* widespread and often useful generalizations, despite the fact that they may not contain a shred of truth when applied to a particular person or situation. So we constantly have to check ourselves to make sure we're not unfairly or inaccurately applying a stereotype in our evaluations and decisions. Stereotypes are an example of the warning, "The more useful, the more danger from misuse."

Specific Applications of Shortcuts in Organizations

People in organizations are always judging each other. Managers must appraise their employees' performances. We evaluate how much effort our coworkers are putting into their jobs. When a new person joins a work team, the other members immediately "size her up." In many cases, our judgments have important consequences for the organization. Let's briefly look at a few of the most obvious applications.

stereotyping   *Judging someone on the basis of one's perception of the group to which that person belongs.*

profiling   *A form of stereotyping in which a group of individuals is singled out—typically on the basis of race or ethnicity—for intensive inquiry, scrutiny, or investigation.*

Employment Interview   A major input into who is hired and who is rejected in an organization is the employment interview. It's fair to say that few people are hired without an interview. But evidence indicates that interviewers make perceptual judgments that are often inaccurate.[14] They generally draw early impressions that very quickly become entrenched. Research shows that we form impressions of others within a tenth of a second, based on our first glance at them.[15] If these first impressions are negative, they tend to be more heavily weighted in the interview than if that same information came out later.[16] Most interviewers' decisions change very little after the first 4 or 5 minutes of an interview. As a result, information elicited early in the interview carries greater weight than does information elicited later, and a "good applicant" is probably characterized more by the absence of unfavorable characteristics than by the presence of favorable characteristics.

Performance Expectations   People attempt to validate their perceptions of reality, even when those perceptions are faulty.[17] This characteristic is particularly relevant when we consider performance expectations on the job. The terms **self-fulfilling prophecy** and *Pygmalion effect* have evolved to characterize the fact that an individual's behavior is determined by other people's expectations. In other words, if a manager expects big things from her people, they're not likely to let her down. Similarly, if a manager expects people to perform minimally, they'll tend to behave so as to meet those low expectations. The expectations become reality. The self-fulfilling prophecy has been found to affect the performance of students in school, soldiers in combat, and even accountants.[18]

Performance Evaluation   We'll discuss performance evaluations more fully in Chapter 18, but note for now that they are very much dependent on the perceptual process.[19] An employee's future is closely tied to the appraisal—promotions, pay raises, and continuation of employment are among the most obvious outcomes. Although the appraisal can be objective (for example, a salesperson is appraised on how many dollars of sales he generates in his territory), many jobs are evaluated in subjective terms. Subjective evaluations of performance, though often necessary, are problematic because all the errors we've discussed thus far—selective perception, contrast effects, halo effects, and so on—affect them. Ironically, sometimes performance ratings say as much about the evaluator as they do about the employee!

The Link Between Perception and Individual Decision Making

4   Explain the link between perception and decision making.

Individuals in organizations make **decisions**. That is, they make choices from among two or more alternatives. Top managers, for instance, determine their organization's goals, what products or services to offer, how best to finance operations, or where to locate a new manufacturing plant. Middle- and lower-level managers determine production schedules, select new employees, and decide how pay raises are to be allocated. Of course, making decisions is not the sole province of managers. Nonmanagerial employees also make decisions that affect their jobs and the organizations for which they work. They decide whether to come to work on

Symantec CEO John Thompson made a decision in reaction to the problem of an explosion of Internet viruses. Thompson said, "About every 15 to 18 months, there's a new form of attack that makes old technologies less effective." So he decided to acquire 13 companies that specialize in products such as personal firewalls, intrusion detection, and early warning systems that protect everything from corporate intranets to consumer e-mail inboxes.

any given day, how much effort to put forth at work, and whether to comply with a request made by the boss. In recent years, organizations have been empowering their nonmanagerial employees with job-related decision-making authority that was historically reserved for managers alone. Individual decision making, therefore, is an important part of organizational behavior. But how individuals in organizations make decisions and the quality of their final choices are largely influenced by their perceptions.

Decision making occurs as a reaction to a **problem**.[20] That is, a discrepancy exists between the current state of affairs and some desired state, requiring us to consider alternative courses of action. For example, if your car breaks down and you rely on it to get to work, you have a problem that requires a decision on your part. Unfortunately, most problems don't come neatly packaged and labeled "problem." One person's *problem* is another person's *satisfactory state of affairs*. One manager may view her division's 2 percent decline in quarterly sales to be a serious problem requiring immediate action on her part. In contrast, her counterpart in another division of the same company, who also had a 2 percent sales decrease, might consider that percentage quite acceptable. So the awareness that a problem exists and whether a decision needs to be made is a perceptual issue.

Moreover, every decision requires us to interpret and evaluate information. We typically receive data from multiple sources and need to screen, process, and interpret it. Which data, for instance, are relevant to the decision and which are not? The perceptions of the decision maker will answer that question. We also need to develop alternatives and evaluate the strengths and weaknesses of each. Again, because alternatives don't come with their strengths and weaknesses clearly marked, an individual decision maker's perceptual process will have a large bearing on the final outcome. Finally, throughout the entire decision-making process, perceptual distortions often surface that can bias analysis and conclusions.

Decision Making in Organizations

5 *Apply the rational model of decision making and contrast it with bounded rationality and intuition.*

Business schools generally train students to follow rational decision-making models. While these models have considerable merit, they don't always describe how people actually make decisions. This is where OB enters the picture: If we are to improve how we make decisions in organizations, we need to understand the decision-making errors that people commit (in addition to the perception errors just discussed). In the sections that follow, we describe these errors, and we begin with a brief overview of the rational decision-making model.

The Rational Model, Bounded Rationality, and Intuition

Rational Decision Making   We often think the best decision maker is **rational** and makes consistent, value-maximizing choices within specified constraints.[21]

---

self-fulfilling prophecy   *A situation in which a person inaccurately perceives a second person, and the resulting expectations cause the second person to behave in ways consistent with the original perception.*

decisions   *Choices made from among two or more alternatives.*

problem   *A discrepancy between the current state of affairs and some desired state.*

rational   *Characterized by making consistent, value-maximizing choices within specified constraints.*

Exhibit **5-3**	Steps in the Rational Decision-Making Model

1. Define the problem.
2. Identify the decision criteria.
3. Allocate weights to the criteria.
4. Develop the alternatives.
5. Evaluate the alternatives.
6. Select the best alternative.

These decisions follow a six-step **rational decision-making model**.[22] The six steps are listed in Exhibit 5-3.

The rational decision-making model relies on a number of assumptions, including that the decision maker has complete information, is able to identify all the relevant options in an unbiased manner, and chooses the option with the highest utility.[23] As you might imagine, most decisions in the real world don't follow the rational model. For instance, people are usually content to find an acceptable or reasonable solution to a problem rather than an optimal one. Choices tend to be limited to the neighborhood of the problem symptom and of the current alternative. As one expert in decision making put it, "Most significant decisions are made by judgment, rather than by a defined prescriptive model."[24] What's more, people are remarkably unaware of making suboptimal decisions.[25]

Bounded Rationality   Most people respond to a complex problem by reducing it to a level at which they can readily understand it. The limited information-processing capability of human beings makes it impossible to assimilate and understand all the information necessary to optimize.[26] So people *satisfice*; that is, they seek solutions that are satisfactory and sufficient.

Operating within the confines of bounded rationality, Rose Marie Bravo revitalized the British retailer Burberry Group PLC when she became CEO. Bravo's decisions during her 10 years as CEO transformed a dormant brand into a profitable luxury label. Based on her retail experience at Saks in the United States, Bravo decided to capitalize on Burberry's quality heritage and trademark plaid design as the solution to the company's stagnant growth. She repositioned Burberry as a global luxury brand by running a celebrity ad campaign to redefine the brand's image as hip for the younger generation and by using the plaid design on new lines of swimwear and children's clothing. Bravo stepped down in July 2005 when her contract expired.

When you considered which college to attend, did you look at every viable alternative? Did you carefully identify all the criteria that were important in your decision? Did you evaluate each alternative against the criteria in order to find the optimal college? The answers are probably "no." Well, don't feel bad. Few people made their college choice this way. Instead of optimizing, you probably satisficed.

Because the human mind cannot formulate and solve complex problems with full rationality, we operate within the confines of **bounded rationality**. We construct simplified models that extract the essential features from problems without capturing all their complexity.[27] We can then behave rationally within the limits of the simple model.

How does bounded rationality work for the typical individual? Once we've identified a problem, we begin to search for criteria and alternatives. But the list of criteria is likely to be far from exhaustive. We identify a limited list of the most conspicuous choices, both easy to find and highly visible, that usually represent familiar criteria and tried-and-true solutions. Next, we begin reviewing them, but our review will not be comprehensive. Instead, we focus on alternatives that differ only in a relatively small degree from the choice currently in effect. Following familiar and well-worn paths, we review alternatives only until we identify one that is "good enough"—that meets an acceptable level of performance. That ends our search. So the solution represents a satisficing choice—the first *acceptable* one we encounter—rather than an optimal one.

Intuition   Perhaps the least rational way of making decisions is to rely on intuition. **Intuitive decision making** is a nonconscious process created from distilled experience.[28] Its defining qualities are that it occurs outside conscious thought; it relies on holistic associations, or links between disparate pieces of information; it's fast; and it's affectively charged, meaning that it usually engages the emotions.[29]

Intuition is not rational, but that doesn't necessarily make it wrong. And intuition doesn't necessarily operate in opposition to rational analysis; rather, the two can complement each other. And intuition can be a powerful force in decision making. Research on chess playing provides an excellent illustration of how intuition works.[30]

Novice chess players and grand masters were shown an actual, but unfamiliar, chess game with about 25 pieces on the board. After 5 or 10 seconds, the pieces were removed, and each subject was asked to reconstruct the pieces by position. On average, the grand master could put 23 or 24 pieces in their correct squares, while the novice was able to replace only 6. Then the exercise was changed. This time, the pieces were placed randomly on the board. Again, the novice got only about 6 correct, but so did the grand master! The second exercise demonstrated that the grand master didn't have any better memory than the novice. What the grand master *did* have was the ability, based on the experience of having played thousands of chess games, to recognize patterns and clusters of pieces that occur on chessboards in the course of games. Studies also show

rational decision-making model   *A decision-making model that describes how individuals should behave in order to maximize some outcome.*

bounded rationality   *A process of making decisions by constructing simplified models that extract the essential features from problems without capturing all their complexity.*

intuitive decision making   *An unconscious process created out of distilled experience.*

that chess professionals can play 50 or more games simultaneously, making decisions in seconds, and exhibit only a moderately lower level of skill than when playing 1 game under tournament conditions, where decisions take half an hour or longer. The expert's experience allows him or her to recognize the pattern in a situation and draw on previously learned information associated with that pattern to arrive at a decision choice quickly. The result is that the intuitive decision maker can decide rapidly based on what appears to be very limited information.

For most of the twentieth century, experts believed that decision makers' use of intuition was irrational or ineffective. That's no longer the case.[31] There is growing recognition that rational analysis has been overemphasized and that, in certain instances, relying on intuition can improve decision making.[32] But while intuition can be invaluable in making good decisions, we can't rely on it too much. Because it is so unquantifiable, it's hard to know when our hunches are right or wrong. The key is not to either abandon or rely solely on intuition but to supplement it with evidence and good judgment.

Common Biases and Errors in Decision Making

Decision makers engage in bounded rationality, but an accumulating body of research tells us that decision makers also allow systematic biases and errors to creep into their judgments.[33] These come from attempts to shortcut the decision process. To minimize effort and avoid difficult trade-offs, people tend to rely too heavily on experience, impulses, gut feelings, and convenient rules of thumb. In many instances, these shortcuts are helpful. However, they can lead to severe distortions of rationality. Following are the most common biases in decision making.

6 List and explain the common decision biases or errors.

Overconfidence Bias   It's been said that "no problem in judgment and decision making is more prevalent and more potentially catastrophic than overconfidence."[34] When we're given factual questions and asked to judge the probability that our answers are correct, we tend to be far too optimistic. For instance, studies have found that, when people say they're 65 to 70 percent confident that they're right, they are actually correct only about 50 percent of the time.[35] And when they say they're 100 percent sure, they tend to be 70 to 85 percent correct.[36] Here's another interesting example. In one random-sample national poll, 90 percent of U.S. adults said they expected to go to heaven. But in another random-sample national poll, only 86 percent thought Mother Theresa was in heaven. Talk about an overconfidence bias!

From an organizational standpoint, one of the most interesting findings related to overconfidence is that those individuals whose intellectual and interpersonal abilities are *weakest* are most likely to overestimate their performance and ability.[37] So as managers and employees become more knowledgeable about an issue, they become less likely to display overconfidence.[38] And overconfidence is most likely to surface when organizational members are considering issues or problems that are outside their area of expertise.[39]

Anchoring Bias   The anchoring bias is a tendency to fixate on initial information and fail to adequately adjust for subsequent information.[40] The anchoring bias occurs because our mind appears to give a disproportionate amount of emphasis to the first information it receives.[41] Anchors are widely used by people in professions where persuasion skills are important—such as advertising, management, politics, real estate, and law. For instance, in a mock jury trial, the plaintiff's attorney asked one set of jurors to make an award in the range of $15 million to $50 million. The plaintiff's attorney asked another set of jurors for an award in the range of $50 million to $150 million. Consistent with the anchoring bias, the median awards were $15 million and $50 million, respectively.[42]

Consider the role of anchoring in negotiations. Any time a negotiation takes place, so does anchoring. As soon as someone states a number, your ability to ignore that number has been compromised. For instance, when a prospective employer asks how much you were making in your prior job, your answer typically anchors the employer's offer. You may want to keep this in mind when you negotiate your salary, but remember to set the anchor only as high as you realistically can.

Confirmation Bias   The rational decision-making process assumes that we objectively gather information. But we don't. We *selectively* gather it. The **confirmation bias** represents a specific case of selective perception. We seek out information that reaffirms our past choices, and we discount information that contradicts them.[43] We also tend to accept at face value information that confirms our preconceived views, while we are critical and skeptical of information that challenges these views. Therefore, the information we gather is typically biased toward supporting views we already hold. This confirmation bias influences where we go to collect evidence because we tend to seek out sources most likely to tell us what we want to hear. It also leads us to give too much weight to supporting information and too little to contradictory information.

Availability Bias   Many more people fear flying than fear driving in a car. But if flying on a commercial airline were as dangerous as driving, the equivalent of two 747s filled to capacity would have to crash every week, killing all aboard, to match the risk of being killed in a car accident. Yet the media gives much more attention to air accidents, so we tend to overstate the risk of flying and understate the risk of driving.

This illustrates the **availability bias**, which is the tendency for people to base their judgments on information that is readily available to them.[44] Events that evoke emotions, that are particularly vivid, or that have occurred more recently tend to be more available in our memory. As a result, we tend to overestimate the chances of unlikely events such as an airplane crash. The availability bias can also explain why managers, when doing annual performance appraisals, tend to give more weight to recent employee behaviors than to behaviors of 6 or 9 months ago.

Escalation of Commitment   Another distortion that creeps into decisions in practice is a tendency to escalate commitment when making a series of decisions.[45] **Escalation of commitment** refers to staying with a decision even when

---

anchoring bias *A tendency to fixate on initial information, from which one then fails to adequately adjust for subsequent information.*

confirmation bias *The tendency to seek out information that reaffirms past choices and to discount information that contradicts past judgments.*

availability bias *The tendency for people to base their judgments on information that is readily available to them.*

escalation of commitment *An increased commitment to a previous decision in spite of negative information.*

MYTH OR SCIENCE?

"No One Thinks They're Biased"

*t*his statement is mostly true. Few of us are truly objective. Consider Verizon and its CEO, Ivan G. Seidenberg. Even though Verizon's earnings dropped by more than 5 percent and its stock price fell by more than 25 percent, Seidenberg received a nearly 50 percent increase in compensation. The consulting firm that Verizon used to set Seidenberg's pay said it adhered to "strict policies in place to ensure the independence and objectivity of our consultants."

Or take the case of Lawrence M. Small, former head of the Smithsonian Institution. Small was appointed for his money-raising prowess, but external funding for the Smithsonian actually fell during his tenure. His pay, however, rose dramatically—to $915,698 in 2007. Small's deputy, Sheila P. Burke, also earned a handsome salary, accumulated more than $10 million in outside income from 2000 to 2007, and was absent for 400 business days. When confronted with these points, Burke replied, "There is every indication that I am in fact an extraordinary individual with a very strong work ethic."

These may be extreme examples. But they point to an alarming human tendency that may characterize all of us: Not only do we think we're objective when we evaluate ourselves or others, we don't recognize our biases and lack of objectivity. As one author noted, "Much of what happens in the brain is not evident in the brain itself, and thus people are better at playing these sorts of tricks on themselves than at catching themselves in the act."

A study of doctors, who are often lavished with gifts from pharmaceutical sales representatives, showed this tendency all too well. When asked about whether gifts might influence their prescribing practices, 84 percent thought that their colleagues were influenced by gifts, but only 16 percent thought that they were similarly influenced.[46] It may well be that we think others are *less* truthful or objective than they really are and that we think we are *more* truthful or objective than we really are. The lesson? We should recognize the self-serving biases that contaminate our evaluations of others—and of ourselves. ■

there is clear evidence that it's wrong. For example, consider a friend who has been dating his girlfriend for several years. Although he admits to you that things aren't going too well in the relationship, he says he is still going to marry her. His justification: "I have a lot invested in the relationship!"

It has been well documented that individuals escalate commitment to a failing course of action when they view themselves as responsible for the failure.[47] That is, they "throw good money after bad" to demonstrate that their initial decision wasn't wrong and to avoid having to admit that they made a mistake.[48] Escalation of commitment has obvious implications for managerial decisions. Many an organization has suffered large losses because a manager was determined to prove his original decision was right by continuing to commit resources to what was a lost cause from the beginning.

Randomness Error   Human beings have a lot of difficulty dealing with chance. Most of us like to believe we have some control over our world and our destiny. Although we undoubtedly can control a good part of our future through rational decision making, the truth is that the world will always contain random events. Our tendency to believe we can predict the outcome of random events is the **randomness error**.

Decision making becomes impaired when we try to create meaning out of random events. One of the most serious impairments occurs when we turn imaginary patterns into superstitions.[49] These can be completely contrived ("I never make important decisions on Friday the 13th") or evolve from a certain pattern of behavior that has been reinforced previously (Tiger Woods often wears a red shirt during the final round of a golf tournament because he won many junior golf tournaments while wearing red shirts). Although many of us engage in some superstitious behavior, it can be debilitating when it affects daily judgments or biases major decisions. At the extreme, some decision makers become controlled by their superstitions—making it nearly impossible for them to change routines or objectively process new information.

Winner's Curse   The **winner's curse** argues that the winning participants in a competitive auction typically pay too much for the item. Some buyers will underestimate the value of an item, and others will overestimate it, and the highest bidder (the winner) will be the one who overestimated the most. Therefore, unless the bidders dramatically undervalue, there is a good chance that the "winner" will pay too much.

Logic predicts that the winner's curse gets stronger as the number of bidders increases. The more bidders there are, the more likely that some of them have greatly overestimated the good's value. So, beware of auctions with an unexpectedly large number of bidders.

Hindsight Bias   The **hindsight bias** is the tendency to believe falsely, after the outcome of an event is actually known, that we'd have accurately predicted that outcome.[50] When something happens and we have accurate feedback on the outcome, we seem to be pretty good at concluding that the outcome was relatively obvious. Do you think the 9/11 terrorist attacks should have been prevented? We'll never know, but we have to realize that things always seem much clearer when we know all the facts (or the connections among the facts). As Malcolm Gladwell, author of *Blink* and *The Tipping Point*, writes, "What is clear in hindsight is rarely clear before the fact. It's an obvious point, but one that nonetheless bears repeating, particularly when we're in the midst of assigning blame for the surprise attack of September 11th."[51]

The hindsight bias reduces our ability to learn from the past. It permits us to think that we're better at making predictions than we really are and can result in our being more confident about the accuracy of future decisions than we have a right to be. If, for instance, your actual predictive accuracy is only 40 percent, but you think it's 90 percent, you're likely to become falsely overconfident and less vigilant in questioning your predictive skills.

AM I A DELIBERATE DECISION MAKER?

In the Self-Assessment Library (available on CD or online), take assessment IV.A.2 (Am I a Deliberate Decision Maker?). Would it be better to be a more deliberate decision maker? Why or why not?

Influences on Decision Making: Individual Differences and Organizational Constraints

7   *Explain how individual differences and organizational constraints affect decision making.*

Having examined the rational decision-making model, bounded rationality, and some of the most salient biases and errors in decision making, we turn here to a discussion of factors that influence how people make decisions and the degree to which they are susceptible

---

randomness error   *The tendency of individuals to believe that they can predict the outcome of random events.*

winner's curse   *A decision-making dictum which argues that the winning participants in an auction typically pay too much for the winning item.*

hindsight bias   *The tendency to believe falsely, after an outcome of an event is actually known, that one would have accurately predicted that outcome.*

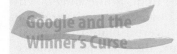

OB In the News

Google and the Winner's Curse

One way the winner's curse is revealed is in initial public offering (IPO) pricing schemes. IPOs occur when a company decides to "go public"—offer itself for sale to investors. In such a case, potential investors need to estimate what the market value of a company's stock will be, lest they pay too much for the company's stock. Here's how the winner's curse operated, so some thought, with the pricing of Google.

Google auctioned off a portion of its stock, with the shares sold to those who paid the most per share. Google explicitly warned potential investors of the winner's curse in its SEC registration statement (the company wrote: "The auction process for our public offering may result in a phenomenon known as the 'winner's curse,' and, as a result, investors may experience significant losses"). Despite this warning, the winning investors paid more than 10 times the estimated pre-IPO value for Google shares, often as much as $200/share. Yet, even 2 years after Google's IPO, its stock price was well above $200 and was trading for more than $600 in June 2007.

Clearly, the Google IPO turned out not to be the winner's curse many thought. So, how can we know when we have the winner's curse and avoid it?

There is no surefire way to avoid the winner's curse without knowing the future value of a good, and of course that's impossible. But bidders can reduce the odds of the winner's curse by doing their homework so they can forecast future value as accurately as possible and by bid shading, or placing a bid below what they believe the good is worth. This may make it less likely the bidder will win the auction, but it will protect her from overpaying when she does win. Savvy bidders know they don't want to win if it means they'll pay more than a good is worth.

Sources: Based on J. D. Miller, "Google's 'Winner's Curse,'" May 4, 2004; G. Deltas and R. Engelbrecht-Wiggans, "Naive Bidding," *Management Science*, March 2005, pp. 328–338; G. P. Zachary, "Google's Dirty Little Secrets: Investors May Suffer from Winner's Curse," August 8, 2004, p. E3; and D. Marasco, "The Winner's Curse—Oil Field Economics and Baseball," http://economics.about.com/cs/baseballeconomics/a/winners_curse.htm.

to errors and biases. We discuss individual differences and organizational constraints.

Individual Differences

Decision making in practice is characterized by bounded rationality, common biases and errors, and the use of intuition. In addition, individual differences create deviations from the rational model. In this section, we look at two differences: personality and gender.

Personality   There hasn't been much research on personality and decision making. One possible reason is that most researchers who conduct decision-making research aren't trained to investigate personality. However, the studies that have been conducted suggest that personality does influence decision making. Research has considered conscientiousness and self-esteem (both of which we discussed in Chapter 4). Let's look at each in the context of decision making.

Some research has shown that specific facets of conscientiousness—rather than the broad trait itself—affect escalation of commitment (see p. 151).[52] Interestingly, one study revealed that two facets of conscientiousness—achievement striving and dutifulness—actually had opposite effects on escalation of commitment. For example, achievement-striving people were more likely to escalate their commitment, whereas dutiful people were less likely. Why might this be the case? Generally, achievement-oriented people hate to fail, so they escalate their commitment, hoping to forestall failure. Dutiful people, however, are more inclined to do what they see as best for the organization. Second, achievement-striving individuals appear to be more susceptible to the hindsight bias, perhaps because they have a greater need to justify the appropriateness of their actions.[53] Unfortunately, we don't have evidence on whether dutiful people are immune to the hindsight bias.

Finally, people with high self-esteem appear to be especially susceptible to the self-serving bias. Why? Because they are strongly motivated to maintain their self-esteem, so they use the self-serving bias to preserve it. That is, they blame others for their failures while taking credit for successes.[54]

Gender Recent research on rumination offers insights into gender differences in decision making.[55] Overall, the evidence indicates that women analyze decisions more than men do.

Rumination refers to reflecting at length. In terms of decision making, it means overthinking problems. Women, in general, are more likely than men to engage in rumination. Twenty years of study find that women spend much more time than men analyzing the past, present, and future. They're more likely to overanalyze problems before making a decision and to rehash a decision once it has been made. On the positive side, this is likely to lead to more careful consideration of problems and choices. However, it can make problems harder to solve, increase regret over past decisions, and increase depression. On this last point, women are nearly twice as likely as men to develop depression.[56]

Why women ruminate more than men is not clear. Several theories have been suggested. One view is that parents encourage and reinforce the expression of sadness and anxiety more in girls than in boys. Another theory is that women, more than men, base their self-esteem and well-being on what others think of them. A third theory is that women are more empathetic and more affected by events in others' lives, so they have more to ruminate about.

Gender differences surface early. By age 11, for instance, girls are ruminating more than boys. But this gender difference seems to lessen with age. Differences are largest during young adulthood and smallest after age 65, when both men and women ruminate the least.[57]

Organizational Constraints

Organizations can constrain decision makers, creating deviations from the rational model. For instance, managers shape their decisions to reflect the organization's performance evaluation and reward system, to comply with the organization's formal regulations, and to meet organizationally imposed time constraints. Previous organizational decisions also act as precedents to constrain current decisions.

Performance Evaluation Managers are strongly influenced in their decision making by the criteria on which they are evaluated. If a division manager believes the manufacturing plants under his responsibility are operating best when he hears nothing negative, we shouldn't be surprised to find his plant managers spending a good part of their time ensuring that negative information doesn't reach him.

Reward Systems The organization's reward system influences decision makers by suggesting to them what choices are preferable in terms of personal payoff. For example, if the organization rewards risk aversion, managers are more likely to make conservative decisions. From the 1930s through the mid-1980s, General Motors consistently gave out promotions and bonuses to managers who kept a low profile and avoided controversy. The result was that GM managers became very adept at dodging tough issues and passing controversial decisions on to committees.

Formal Regulations David Gonzalez, a shift manager at a Taco Bell restaurant in San Antonio, Texas, describes constraints he faces on his job: "I've got rules and regulations covering almost every decision I make—from how to

At McDonald's restaurants throughout the world, formal regulations shape employee decisions by standardizing the behavior of restaurant crew members. McDonald's requires that employees follow rules and regulations for food preparation and service to meet the company's standards of food quality and safety and reliable and friendly service. For example, McDonald's requires 72 safety protocols to be conducted every day in each restaurant as part of a daily monitoring routine for restaurant managers.

make a burrito to how often I need to clean the restrooms. My job doesn't come with much freedom of choice." David's situation is not unique. All but the smallest of organizations create rules and policies to program decisions, which are intended to get individuals to act in the intended manner. And of course, in so doing, they limit the decision maker's choices.

System-Imposed Time Constraints Organizations impose deadlines on decisions. For instance, a report on new-product development may have to be ready for the executive committee to review by the first of the month. Almost all important decisions come with explicit deadlines. These conditions create time pressures on decision makers and often make it difficult, if not impossible, to gather all the information they might like to have before making a final choice.

Historical Precedents Decisions aren't made in a vacuum. They have a context. In fact, individual decisions are accurately characterized as points in a stream of decisions. Decisions made in the past are ghosts that continually haunt current choices—that is, commitments that have already been made constrain current options. It's common knowledge that the largest determinant of the size of any given year's budget is last year's budget.[58] Choices made today, therefore, are largely a result of choices made over the years.

What About Ethics in Decision Making?

8 *Contrast the three ethical decision criteria.*

Ethical considerations should be an important criterion in organizational decision making. This is certainly more true today than at any time in the recent past, given the increasing scrutiny business is under to behave in an ethical and socially responsible way. In this section, we present three different ways to frame decisions ethically.

Three Ethical Decision Criteria

An individual can use three different criteria in making ethical choices.[59] The first is the *utilitarian* criterion, in which decisions are made solely on the basis of their outcomes or consequences. The goal of **utilitarianism** is to provide the greatest good for the greatest number. This view tends to dominate business decision making. It is consistent with goals such as efficiency, productivity, and high profits. By maximizing profits, for instance, a business executive can argue that he is securing the greatest good for the greatest number—as he hands out dismissal notices to 15 percent of his employees.

Another ethical criterion is to focus on *rights*. This calls on individuals to make decisions consistent with fundamental liberties and privileges, as set forth in documents such as the Bill of Rights. An emphasis on rights in decision making means respecting and protecting the basic rights of individuals, such as the right to privacy, to free speech, and to due process. For instance, this criterion protects **whistle-blowers** when they reveal unethical practices by their organization to the press or government agencies, on the grounds of their right to free speech.

A third criterion is to focus on *justice*. This requires individuals to impose and enforce rules fairly and impartially so that there is an equitable distribution of benefits and costs. Union members typically favor this view. It justifies paying people the same wage for a given job, regardless of performance differences, and using seniority as the primary determination in making layoff decisions.

Each of these criteria has advantages and liabilities. A focus on utilitarianism promotes efficiency and productivity, but it can result in ignoring the rights of some individuals, particularly those with minority representation in the organization. The use of rights as a criterion protects individuals from injury and is consistent with freedom and privacy, but it can create an overly legalistic work environment that hinders productivity and efficiency. A focus on justice protects the interests of the underrepresented and less powerful, but it can encourage a sense of entitlement that reduces risk taking, innovation, and productivity.

Decision makers, particularly in for-profit organizations, tend to feel safe and comfortable when they use utilitarianism. A lot of questionable actions can be justified when framed as being in the best interests of "the organization" and stockholders. But many critics of business decision makers argue that this perspective needs to change.[60] Increased concern in society about individual rights and social justice suggests the need for managers to develop ethical standards based on nonutilitarian criteria. This presents a solid challenge to today's managers because making decisions using criteria such as individual rights and social justice involves far more ambiguities than using utilitarian criteria such as effects on efficiency and profits. This helps to explain why managers are increasingly criticized for their actions. Raising prices, selling products with questionable effects on consumer health, closing down inefficient plants, laying off large numbers of employees, moving production overseas to cut costs, and similar decisions can be justified in utilitarian terms. But that may no longer be the single criterion by which good decisions should be judged.

utilitarianism   *A system in which decisions are made to provide the greatest good for the greatest number.*

whistle-blowers   *Individuals who report unethical practices by their employer to outsiders.*

Unleashing the creative potential of employees is paramount to the continued success of videogame maker Electronic Arts in developing innovative entertainment software. Designed to stimulate employees' creativity, EA's work environment is casual and fun, and employees are given the freedom to manage their own work time. To recharge their creativity, they can take a break from their projects and relax at a serenity pool, work out in a state-of-the-art fitness center, play pool or table tennis in a games room, or play basketball, soccer, or beach volleyball in an outdoor recreation area.

Improving Creativity in Decision Making

Although following the steps of the rational decision-making model will often improve decisions, a rational decision maker also needs **creativity**, that is, the ability to produce novel and useful ideas.[61] These are ideas that are different from what's been done before but that are appropriate to the problem or opportunity presented.

9 Define creativity and discuss the three-component model of creativity.

Why is creativity important to decision making? It allows the decision maker to more fully appraise and understand the problem, including seeing problems others can't see. Such thinking is becoming more important. Experts estimate that the United States alone will add 10 million "creative class" jobs—in science, technology, entertainment, design, and entrepreneurship—over the next decade. And both companies and business schools are trying to increase the creative potential of their employees and graduates.[62] L'Oréal puts its managers through creative exercises such as cooking or making music, and University of Chicago's business school has added a requirement for MBA students to make short movies about their experiences.

Creative Potential   Most people have creative potential they can use when confronted with a decision-making problem. But to unleash that potential, they have to get out of the psychological ruts many of us fall into and learn how to think about a problem in divergent ways.

People differ in their inherent creativity, and exceptional creativity is scarce. We all know of creative geniuses in science (Albert Einstein), art (Pablo Picasso), and business (Steve Jobs). But what about the typical individual? People who score high on openness to experience (see Chapter 4), for example, are more likely than others to be creative. Intelligent people also are more likely than others to be creative.[63] Other traits associated with creative people include independence, self-confidence, risk taking, an internal locus of control, tolerance for ambiguity, a low need for structure, and perseverance in the face of frustration.[64]

A study of the lifetime creativity of 461 men and women found that fewer than 1 percent were exceptionally creative.[65] But 10 percent were highly creative and about 60 percent were somewhat creative. This suggests that most of us have creative potential; we just need to learn to unleash it.

Three-Component Model of Creativity   Given that most people have the capacity to be at least somewhat creative, what can individuals and organizations do to stimulate employee creativity? The best answer to this question lies in the **three-component model of creativity**.[66] Based on an extensive body of research, this model proposes that individual creativity essentially requires expertise, creative thinking skills, and intrinsic task motivation (see Exhibit 5-4). Studies confirm that the higher the level of each of these three components, the higher the creativity.

Expertise is the foundation for all creative work. The film writer, producer, and director Quentin Tarantino spent his youth working in a video rental store, where he built up an encyclopedic knowledge of movies. The potential for creativity is enhanced when individuals have abilities, knowledge, proficiencies, and similar expertise in their field of endeavor. For example, you wouldn't expect someone with a minimal knowledge of programming to be very creative as a software engineer.

The second component is *creative-thinking skills.* This encompasses personality characteristics associated with creativity, the ability to use analogies, and the talent to see the familiar in a different light.

Research suggests that we are more creative when we're in good moods, so if we need to be creative, we should do things that make us happy, such as listening to music we enjoy, eating foods we like, watching funny movies, or socializing with others.[67]

Evidence also suggests that being around others who are creative can actually make us more inspired, especially if we're creatively "stuck."[68] One study found that "weak ties" to creative people—knowing creative people but not all that closely—facilitates creativity because the people are there as a resource if

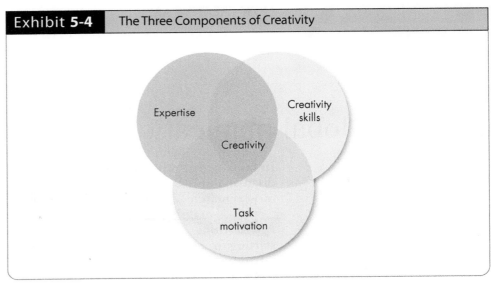

| Exhibit **5-4** | The Three Components of Creativity |

Source: Copyright © 1997, by The Regents of the University of California. Reprinted from *The California Management Review* 40, no. 1. By permission of The Regents.

---

creativity   *The ability to produce novel and useful ideas.*

three-component model of creativity   *The proposition that individual creativity requires expertise, creative thinking skills, and intrinsic task motivation.*

we need them, but they are not so close as to stunt our own independent thinking.[69]

The effective use of analogies allows decision makers to apply an idea from one context to another. One of the most famous examples in which analogy resulted in a creative breakthrough was Alexander Graham Bell's observation that it might be possible to apply the way the ear operates to his "talking box." He noticed that the bones in the ear are operated by a delicate, thin membrane. He wondered why, then, a thicker and stronger piece of membrane shouldn't be able to move a piece of steel. From that analogy, the telephone was conceived.

Some people have developed their creative skills because they are able to see problems in a new way. They're able to make the strange familiar and the familiar strange.[70] For instance, most of us think of hens laying eggs. But how many of us have considered that a hen is only an egg's way of making another egg?

The final component in the three-component model of creativity is *intrinsic task motivation*. This is the desire to work on something because it's interesting, involving, exciting, satisfying, or personally challenging. This motivational component is what turns creativity *potential* into *actual* creative ideas. It determines the extent to which individuals fully engage their expertise and creative skills. Creative people often love their work, to the point of seeming obsession. Our work environment can have a significant effect on intrinsic motivation. Stimulants that foster creativity include a culture that encourages the flow of ideas; fair and constructive judgment of ideas; rewards and recognition for creative work; sufficient financial, material, and information resources; freedom to decide what work is to be done and how to do it; a supervisor who communicates effectively, shows confidence in others, and supports the work group; and work group members who support and trust each other.[71]

HOW CREATIVE AM I?

In the Self-Assessment Library (available on CD or online), take assessment I.A.5 (How Creative Am I?).

Global Implications

In considering whether there are global differences in the concepts we've discussed in this chapter, let's consider the three areas that have attracted the most research: (1) attributions, (2) decision making, and (3) ethics.

Attributions   Although research on cultural differences in perception is just starting to accumulate, there has been some research on cultural differences in attributions. The evidence is mixed, but most of it suggests that there *are* cultural differences across cultures in the attributions people make.[72] For instance, a study of Korean managers found that, contrary to the self-serving bias, they tended to accept responsibility for group failure "because I was not a capable leader" instead of attributing failure to group members.[73] Attribution theory was developed largely based on experiments with U.S. and western European workers. But the Korean study suggests caution in making attribution theory predictions in non-Western societies, especially in countries with strong collectivist traditions.

Decision Making   The rational model makes no acknowledgment of cultural differences, nor does the bulk of OB research literature on decision making. A 2007 review of cross-cultural OB research covered 25 areas, but cultural influence on decision making was not among them. Another 2007 review identified 15 topics, but the result was the same: no research on culture and decision making.[74] It seems that most OB research assumes that culture doesn't matter to decision making.

But Indonesians, for instance, don't necessarily make decisions the same way Australians do. Therefore, we need to recognize that the cultural background of a decision maker can have a significant influence on the selection of problems, the depth of analysis, the importance placed on logic and rationality, and whether organizational decisions should be made autocratically by an individual manager or collectively in groups.[75]

Cultures differ, for example, in terms of time orientation, the importance of rationality, their belief in the ability of people to solve problems, and their preference for collective decision making. Differences in time orientation help us understand why managers in Egypt make decisions at a much slower and more deliberate pace than their U.S. counterparts. While rationality is valued in North America, that's not true elsewhere in the world. A North American manager might make an important decision intuitively but know it's important to appear to proceed in a rational fashion because rationality is highly valued in the West. In countries such as Iran, where rationality is not as paramount as other factors, efforts to appear rational are not necessary.

Some cultures emphasize solving problems, while others focus on accepting situations as they are. The United States falls in the first category; Thailand and Indonesia are examples of the second. Because problem-solving managers believe they can and should change situations to their benefit, U.S. managers might identify a problem long before their Thai or Indonesian counterparts would choose to recognize it as such. Decision making by Japanese managers is much more group oriented than in the United States. The Japanese value conformity and cooperation. So before Japanese CEOs make an important decision, they collect a large amount of information, which they use in consensus-forming group decisions.

In short, we have reason to believe there are important cultural differences in decision making. Unfortunately, though, there is not yet much research to substantiate these beliefs. OB is a research-based discipline, but research does not always respond quickly to important practical concerns.

Ethics   What is seen as an ethical decision in China may not be seen as such in Canada. The reason is that there are no global ethical standards.[76] Contrasts between Asia and the West provide an illustration.[77] Because bribery is commonplace in countries such as China, a Canadian working in China might face a dilemma: Should I pay a bribe to secure business if it is an accepted part of that country's culture? A manager of a large U.S. company operating in China caught an employee stealing. Following company policy, she fired him and turned him over to the local authorities. Later, she was horrified to learn that the employee had been summarily executed.[78]

Although ethical standards may seem ambiguous in the West, criteria defining right and wrong are actually much clearer in the West than in Asia. Few issues are black and white there; most are gray. The need for global organizations to establish ethical principles for decision makers in countries such as India and China and to modify them to reflect cultural norms may be critical if high standards are to be upheld and if consistent practices are to be achieved.

Summary and Implications for Managers

Perception   Individuals base their behavior not on the way their external environment actually is but rather on what they see or believe it to be. Whether a manager successfully plans and organizes the work of employees and actually helps them to structure their work more efficiently and effectively is far less important than how employees perceive the manager's efforts. Similarly, employees judge issues such as fair pay for work performed, the validity of performance appraisals, and the adequacy of working conditions in very individual ways; we cannot be assured that they will interpret conditions about their jobs in a favorable light. Therefore, to influence productivity, it's necessary to assess how workers perceive their jobs.

Absenteeism, turnover, and job satisfaction are also reactions to an individual's perceptions. Dissatisfaction with working conditions and the belief that an organization lacks promotion opportunities are judgments based on attempts to create meaning out of the job. The employee's conclusion that a job is good or bad is an interpretation. Managers must spend time understanding how each individual interprets reality and, when there is a significant difference between what someone sees and what exists, try to eliminate the distortions.

Individual Decision Making   Individuals think and reason before they act. This is why an understanding of how people make decisions can be helpful for explaining and predicting their behavior.

In some decision situations, people follow the rational decision-making model. But few important decisions are simple or unambiguous enough for the rational model's assumptions to apply. So we find individuals looking for solutions that satisfice rather than optimize, injecting biases and prejudices into the decision process, and relying on intuition.

Given the evidence we've described on how decisions are actually made in organizations, what can managers do to improve their decision making? We offer four suggestions.

First, analyze the situation. Adjust your decision-making approach to the national culture you're operating in and to the criteria your organization evaluates and rewards. For instance, if you're in a country that doesn't value rationality, don't feel compelled to follow the rational decision-making model or even to try to make your decisions appear rational. Similarly, organizations differ in terms of the importance they place on risk, the use of groups, and the like. Adjust your decision approach to ensure that it's compatible with the organization's culture.

Second, be aware of biases. Then try to minimize their impact. Exhibit 5-5 offers some suggestions.

Third, combine rational analysis with intuition. These are not conflicting approaches to decision making. By using both, you can actually improve your decision-making effectiveness. As you gain managerial experience, you should feel increasingly confident in imposing your intuitive processes on top of your rational analysis.

Finally, try to enhance your creativity. Actively look for novel solutions to problems, attempt to see problems in new ways, and use analogies. In addition, try to remove work and organizational barriers that might impede your creativity.

Exhibit **5-5**	Reducing Biases and Errors

Focus on Goals. Without goals, you can't be rational, you don't know what information you need, you don't know which information is relevant and which is irrelevant, you'll find it difficult to choose between alternatives, and you're far more likely to experience regret over the choices you make. Clear goals make decision making easier and help you eliminate options that are inconsistent with your interests.

Look for Information That Disconfirms Your Beliefs. One of the most effective means for counteracting overconfidence and the confirmation and hindsight biases is to actively look for information that contradicts your beliefs and assumptions. When we overtly consider various ways we could be wrong, we challenge our tendencies to think we're smarter than we actually are.

Don't Try to Create Meaning out of Random Events. The educated mind has been trained to look for cause-and-effect relationships. When something happens, we ask why. And when we can't find reasons, we often invent them. You have to accept that there are events in life that are outside your control. Ask yourself if patterns can be meaningfully explained or whether they are merely coincidence. Don't attempt to create meaning out of coincidence.

Increase Your Options. No matter how many options you've identified, your final choice can be no better than the best of the option set you've selected. This argues for increasing your decision alternatives and for using creativity in developing a wide range of diverse choices. The more alternatives you can generate, and the more diverse those alternatives, the greater your chance of finding an outstanding one.

Source: S. P. Robbins, *Decide & Conquer: Making Winning Decisions and Taking Control of Your Life* (Upper Saddle River, NJ: Financial Times/Prentice Hall, 2004), pp. 164–168.

Point ⟩⟩ ⟨⟨ Counterpoint

WHEN IN DOUBT, DO!

*l*ife is full of decisions and choices. The real question is not "To be, or not to be" but rather "To do, or not to do?" For example, should I confront my professor about my midterm grade? Should I buy a new car? Should I accept a new job? Should I choose this major? Very often, we are unsure of our decision. In such cases, it is almost always better to choose action over inaction. In life, people more often regret inaction than action. Take the following simple example:

Act	State	
	RAIN	*SHINE*
Carry umbrella	Dry (except your feet!)	Inconvenience
Don't carry umbrella	Miserable drenching	Unqualified bliss

Say you carry an umbrella and it doesn't rain, or you don't carry an umbrella and it does rain. In which situation are you worse off? Would you rather experience the mild inconvenience of the extra weight of the umbrella or get drenched? Chances are you'll regret inaction more than action. Research shows that after we make a decision, we regret inaction more than action. Although we often regret actions in their immediate aftermath, over time, regrets over actions decline markedly, whereas regrets over missed opportunities increase. For example, you finally decide to take a trip to Europe. You have an amazing time, but a few weeks after you get back, your credit card bill arrives—and it isn't pretty. Unfortunately, you have to work overtime and miss a few dinners out with friends to pay off the bills. A few months down the road, however, you decide to reminisce by looking through your photos from the trip, and you can't imagine not having gone. So, when in doubt, just do!

*i*t's just silly to think that when in doubt, you should always act. People will undoubtedly make mistakes following such simple advice. For example, you're out of work, but you still decide to purchase your dream car—a BMW, fully loaded. Not the smartest idea. So why is the motto "just do it" dangerous? Because there are two types of regrets: hot regret, in which an individual kicks herself for having caused something bad, and wistful regret, in which she fantasizes about how else things might have turned out. The danger is that actions are more likely to lead to anguish or hot regret, and inaction is more likely to lead to wistful regret. So the bottom line is that we can't apply simple rules such as "just do it" to important decisions.[79]

Questions for Review

1 What is perception, and what factors influence our perception?

2 What is attribution theory? What are the three determinants of attribution? What are its implications for explaining organizational behavior?

3 What shortcuts do people frequently use in making judgments about others?

4 What is the link between perception and decision making? How does one affect the other?

5 What is the rational model of decision making? How is it different from bounded rationality and intuition?

6 What are some of the common decision biases or errors that people make?

7 What are the influences of individual differences, organizational constraints, and culture on decision making?

8 Are unethical decisions more a function of an individual decision maker or the decision maker's work environment? Explain.

9 What is creativity, and what is the three-component model of creativity?

Experiential Exercise

BIASES IN DECISION MAKING

Step 1

Answer each of the following problems.

1. *Fortune* magazine ranked the following 10 corporations as being among the 500 largest United States–based firms according to sales volume for 2005:

   Group A: Apple Computer, Hershey Foods, Hilton Hotels, Mattel, Levi Strauss

   Group B: American International Group, Cardinal Health, Conagra Foods, Ingram Micro, Valero Energy

   Which group would you say (A or B) had the larger total sales volume? By what percentage (10 percent, 50 percent, 100 percent)?

2. The best student in your introductory MBA class this past semester writes poetry and is rather shy and small in stature. What was the student's undergraduate major: Chinese studies or psychology?

3. Which of the following causes more deaths in the United States each year?

   a. Stomach cancer

   b. Motor vehicle accidents

4. Which would you choose?

   a. A sure gain of $240

   b. A 25 percent chance of winning $1,000 and a 75 percent chance of winning nothing

5. Which would you choose?

   a. A sure loss of $750

   b. A 75 percent chance of losing $1,000 and a 25 percent chance of losing nothing

6. Which would you choose?

   a. A sure loss of $3,000

   b. An 80 percent chance of losing $4,000 and a 20 percent chance of losing nothing

Step 2

Break into groups of three to five students. Compare your answers. Explain why you chose the answers you did.

Step 3

Your instructor will give you the correct answers to each problem. Now discuss the accuracy of your decisions; the biases evident in the decisions you reached; and how you might improve your decision making to make it more accurate.

Source: These problems are based on examples provided in M. H. Bazerman, *Judgment in Managerial Decision Making*, 3rd ed. (New York: Wiley, 1994).

Ethical Dilemma

FIVE ETHICAL DECISIONS: WHAT WOULD YOU DO?

How would you respond to each of the following situations?

1. Assume that you're a middle manager in a company with about 1,000 employees. You're negotiating a contract with a very large potential customer whose representative has hinted that you could almost certainly be assured of getting his business if you gave him and his wife an all-expenses-paid cruise to the Caribbean. You know the representative's employer wouldn't approve of such a "payoff," but you have the discretion to authorize such an expenditure. What would you do?

2. You have an autographed CD by Sean Combs (signed "PuffD"). You have put the CD up for sale on eBay. So far, the highest bid is $74.50. A friend has offered you $100 for the CD, commenting that he could get $150 for the CD on eBay in a year. You know this is highly unlikely. Should you sell your friend the CD for what he offered ($100)? Do you have an obligation to tell your friend you have listed your CD on eBay?

3. Your company's policy on reimbursement for meals while traveling on business is that you will be repaid for your out-of-pocket costs, not to exceed $80 per day. You don't need receipts for these expenses—the company will take your word. When traveling, you tend to eat at fast-food places and rarely spend in excess of $20 a day. Most of your colleagues put in reimbursement requests in the range of $55 to $60 per day, regardless of what their actual expenses are. How much would you request for your meal reimbursements?

4. You work for a company that manufactures, markets, and distributes various products, including nutritional supplements, to health food and nutrition stores. One of the company's best-selling products is an herbal supplement called Rosalife. The company advertises that Rosalife "achieves all the gains of estrogen hormone replacement therapy without any of the side effects." One day, a research assistant stops by your office with some troubling information. She tells you that while researching another product, she came across a recent study that suggests Rosalife does not offer the benefits the company claims it does. You show this study to your supervisor, who says, "We're not responsible for validating non-FDA-controlled products, and nobody's hurt anyway." Indeed, you know this is not the case. What is your ethical responsibility?

5. Assume that you're the manager at a gaming company, and you're responsible for hiring a group to outsource the production of a highly anticipated new game. Because your company is a giant in the industry, numerous companies are trying to get the bid. One of them offers you some kickbacks if you give that firm the bid, but ultimately, it is up to your bosses to decide on the company. You don't mention the incentive, but you push upper management to give the bid to the company that offered you the kickback. Is withholding the truth as bad as lying? Why or why not?

Case Incident 1

NATURAL DISASTERS AND THE DECISIONS THAT FOLLOW

Jeff Rommel's introduction to Florida could be described as trial by hurricane. Rommel took over Florida operations in 2004 for Nationwide Insurance. Over a 2-month period in 2004, Florida experienced its worst hurricane season in history—four major hurricanes (Charley, Frances, Ivan, and Jeanne) slammed the state, causing an estimated $40 billion in damage. In the hurricanes' wake, Nationwide received more than 119,000 claims, collectively worth $850 million.

Although dealing with those claims was difficult, even more difficult was Rommel's later decision to cancel approximately 40,000 homeowners' policies. Nationwide received a huge amount of media attention as a result, almost all negative. In reflecting on the decision, Rommel said, "Pulling out was a sound business decision. Was it good for the individual customer? No, I can't say it was. But the rationale was sound."

Hurricanes aren't the only weapons in nature's arsenal, and the insurance industry is hardly the only industry affected by nature. Consider the airline industry. American Airlines has 80,000 employees, 4 of whom make decisions to cancel flights. One of them is Danny Burgin. When weather systems approach, Burgin needs to consider a host of factors in deciding which flights to cancel and how to reroute affected passengers. He argues that of two major weather factors, winter snowstorms and summer thunderstorms, snowstorms are easier to handle because they are more predictable.

Don't tell that to JetBlue, however. On February 14, 2007, JetBlue was unprepared for a snowstorm that hit the East Coast. Due to the lack of planning, JetBlue held hundreds of passengers on its planes at JFK, in some cases for as long as 10 hours (with bathrooms closed!). To the stranded travelers, JetBlue's tepid offer of a refund was just as outrageous. For an airline that prided itself on customer service and had regularly been rated as the top U.S. airline in customer satisfaction, it was a public relations disaster. Linda Hirneise, an analyst at J.D. Power, said, "It did not appear JetBlue had a plan." In defending the airline, JetBlue's founder and CEO, David Neeleman, said, "Is our good will gone? No, it isn't. We fly 30 million people a year. Ten thousand were affected by this." In responding to another interviewer, he said, "You're overdoing it. Delta screwed people for two days, and we did it for three and a half, okay? So go ask Delta what they did about it. Why don't you grill them?" Eventually, though, Neeleman himself was affected by it, and he stepped down.

Questions

1. Insurance companies in the state of Florida earned record profits in 2006, suggesting that Nationwide's decision to cancel policies in light of the calm hurricane seasons (in Florida) in 2005–2007 may have cost the company potential revenue and customer goodwill. Do you think Rommel's quote about making a "sound business decision" reveals any perceptual or decision-making biases? Why or why not?

2. Review the section on common biases and errors in decision making. For companies such as Nationwide, American Airlines, and JetBlue that must respond to natural events, which of these biases and errors are relevant and why?

3. In each of the three cases discussed here, which organizational constraints were factors in the decisions that were made?

4. How do you think people like Rommel, Burgin, and Neeleman factor ethics into their decisions? Do you think the welfare of policy owners and passengers enter into their decisions?

Sources: M. Blomberg, "Insuring the Nation," *Gainesville (Florida) Sun*, February 27, 2006, pp. 1D, 8D; M. Trottman, "Choices in Stormy Weather," *Wall Street Journal*, February 14, 2006, pp. B1, B2; C. Salter, "Lessons from the Tarmac," *Fast Company*, May 2007, pp. 31–32; and D. Q. Wilber, "Tale of Marooned Passengers Galvanizes Airline Opponents," *Washington Post*, February 16, 2007, p. D1.

Case Incident 2

WHISTLE-BLOWERS: SAINTS OR SINNERS?

Corporate whistle-blowers, individuals who report company wrongdoings, are often lauded for their courage and integrity. For example, Jeffrey Wigand is well known (especially after the docudrama starring Russell Crowe) for exposing the Big Tobacco scandal. Similarly, Sherron Watkins is credited for bringing the Enron scandal to light. Given that whistle-blowers face unemployment, and, often, ridicule from their company, many people do not come forward to report illegal activity. To encourage whistle-blowers, a whistle-blower law adopted in 1986 pays informants as much as 30 percent of legal fines reaped during lawsuits. With settlements often exceeding $100 million, whistle-blowers can sometimes see huge payoffs. Some experts are concerned that these payoffs are creating a culture in which employees quickly report wrongdoings instead of trying to rectify the situation internally.

For example, Douglas Durand was a former vice president of sales at TAP Pharmaceutical Products. In 1995, he began to suspect that TAP was conspiring with doctors to defraud Medicare. Pharmaceutical companies routinely provide doctors with free samples of the latest drugs; however, Durand believed that TAP was working with doctors to bill Medicare for the free drugs, a practice that is against federal law. Later that same year, Durand became more worried when he discovered that TAP had decided to pay a 2 percent fee to individual doctors to cover "administrative costs"—a kickback in Durand's opinion. Durand then began preparing to blow the whistle on TAP and its affiliates. "I wanted to do the right thing," he says. After being referred to attorney Elizabeth Ainslie by one of his colleagues, Durand started keeping notes and collecting company documents, while his lawyer attempted to get the federal government involved.

In February 1996, Durand received a $35,000 bonus from TAP and then quit the company. Three months later, he and Ainslie filed suits against TAP. For the next 5 years, Durand and Ainslie built their case against TAP. At one point, Durand even obtained some of his former coworkers' home phone numbers and called them while the FBI listened in. During one call to a former TAP colleague, Durand lied, saying that he had been subpoenaed, in an attempt to get his former colleague to incriminate himself. All in all, more than 500 boxes of documents were collected, containing evidence against TAP. Although TAP fought the lawsuit, it finally settled in April 2001. Durand's take was a cool $126 million.

On the day TAP settled, prosecutors filed criminal fraud charges against the company. One of those prosecutors, Michael Sullivan, said the charges were filed to send "a very strong signal to the pharmaceutical industry." However, as the trial progressed, holes in Durand's story began to appear. The kickbacks that Durand claimed TAP paid to doctors never occurred, the company didn't over-charge Medicare, and a conference that Durand believed TAP used to bribe doctors into using its drugs was actually paid for by the doctors themselves. Finally, in July 2002, a federal jury in Boston cleared TAP of the charges, but not before the company had incurred over $1 billion in legal fees. Durand is now retired and lives with his wife and daughter in Florida.

Supporters of whistle-blowing, such as Senator Charles Grassley (R-Iowa), say that having informants report on company wrongdoings is the best way to prevent illegal activity. "There can never be enough bureaucrats to dis-courage fraudulent use of taxpayers' money, but know-ing colleagues might squeal can be a deterrent," he states. However, others disagree. According to David Stetler, defense attorney for TAP, "It's absolutely a form of extortion." Whatever position you take, it seems clear that whistle-blowing is a strong means to deter corporate wrongdoing. However, when this right is abused, whistle-blowers can become as unethical as the companies that they are blowing the whistle on.

Questions

1. Do you believe whistle-blowing is good for organiza-tions and its members, or is it, as David Stetler believes, often a means to extort large financial gains from companies?

2. How might self-fulfilling prophecy affect a whistle-blower's search for incriminating evidence against a company?

3. When frivolous lawsuits occur, how might these cases affect future whistle-blowers who have a valid legal claim against their company? Would they be more or less likely to come forward? How might their claims be evaluated? What should companies and the gov-ernment do to prevent frivolous lawsuits?

4. Do you believe employees of a company have an ethi-cal obligation to first attempt to report wrongdoing to members of the company itself, or should they go straight to the authorities when they suspect illegal activity? What are some advantages and disadvantages of both actions?

Source: Based on N. Weinberg, "The Dark Side of Whistle-blowing," *Forbes,* March 14, 2005, pp. 90–95.

Endnotes

1. P. Babcock, "Discriminatory Backlash Lingers After Sept. 11," *SHRM Online,* September 5, 2006, www.shrm.org/hrnews_published; "Muslim Americans: Middle Class and Mostly Mainstream," Pew Research Center, May 22, 2007, http://pewresearch.org/assets/pdf/muslim-americans.pdf; and "They're Muslims, and Yankees, Too," *BusinessWeek,* January 15, 2007, www.businessweek.com/magazine/.

2. H. H. Kelley, "Attribution in Social Interaction," in E. Jones et al. (eds.), *Attribution: Perceiving the Causes of Behavior* (Morristown, NJ: General Learning Press, 1972).

3. See L. Ross, "The Intuitive Psychologist and His Short-comings," in L. Berkowitz (ed.), *Advances in Experimental Social Psychology,* vol. 10 (Orlando, FL: Academic Press, 1977), pp. 174–220; and A. G. Miller and T. Lawson, "The Effect of an Informational Option on the Fundamental Attribution Error," *Personality and Social Psychology Bulletin,* June 1989, pp. 194–204.

4. See, for instance, G. Johns, "A Multi-Level Theory of Self-Serving Behavior in and by Organizations," in R. I. Sutton and B. M. Staw (eds.), *Research in Organizational Behavior,* vol. 21 (Stamford, CT: JAI Press, 1999), pp. 1–38; N. Epley and D. Dunning, "Feeling 'Holier Than Thou': Are Self-Serving Assessments Produced by Errors in Self- or Social Prediction?" *Journal of Personality and Social Psychology,* December 2000, pp. 861–875; and M. Goerke, J. Moller, S. Schulz-Hardt, U. Napiersky, and D. Frey, "'It's Not My Fault—But Only I Can Change It': Counterfactual and Prefactual Thoughts of Managers," *Journal of Applied Psychology,* April 2004, pp. 279–292.

5. D. C. Dearborn and H. A. Simon, "Selective Perception: A Note on the Departmental Identification of Executives," *Sociometry,* June 1958, pp. 140–144. Some of the conclusions in this classic study have recently been challenged in J. Walsh, "Selectivity and Selective Perception: An Investigation of Managers' Belief Structures and Information Processing," *Academy of Management Journal,* December 1988, pp. 873–896; M. J. Waller, G. Huber, and W. H. Glick, "Functional Background as a Determinant of Executives' Selective Perception," *Academy of Management Journal,* August 1995, pp. 943–974; and J. M. Beyer, P. Chattopadhyay, E. George, W. H. Glick, D. T. Ogilvie, and D. Pugliese, "The Selective Perception of Managers Revisited," *Academy of Management Journal,* June 1997, pp. 716–737.

6. See K. R. Murphy and R. L. Anhalt, "Is Halo a Property of the Rater, the Ratees, or the Specific Behaviors Observed?" *Journal of Applied Psychology,* June 1992, pp. 494–500; K. R. Murphy, R. A. Jako, and R. L. Anhalt, "Nature and Consequences of Halo Error: A Critical Analysis," *Journal of Applied Psychology,* April 1993, pp. 218–225; P. Rosenzweig, *The Halo Effect* (New York: The Free Press, 2007); and C. E. Naquin and R. O. Tynan, "The Team Halo Effect: Why Teams Are Not Blamed for Their Failures," *Journal of Applied Psychology,* April 2003, pp. 332–340.

7. P. Burrows, "HP's Carly Fiorina: The Boss" *BusinessWeek,* August 2, 1999; J. D. Markman, "Lessons of Carly Fiorina's Fall," *TheStreet.com,* February 10, 2005; and C. Edwards, "Where Fiorina Went Wrong," *BusinessWeek,* February 9, 2005.

8. S. E. Asch, "Forming Impressions of Personality," *Journal of Abnormal and Social Psychology,* July 1946, pp. 258–290.

9. J. L. Hilton and W. von Hippel, "Stereotypes," in J. T. Spence, J. M. Darley, and D. J. Foss (eds.), *Annual Review of*

Psychology, vol. 47 (Palo Alto, CA: Annual Reviews, 1996), pp. 237–271.

10. See, for example, G. N. Powell, "The Good Manager: Business Students' Stereotypes of Japanese Managers Versus Stereotypes of American Managers," *Group & Organizational Management*, March 1992, pp. 44–56; W. C. K. Chiu, A. W. Chan, E. Snape, and T. Redman, "Age Stereotypes and Discriminatory Attitudes Towards Older Workers: An East–West Comparison," *Human Relations*, May 2001, pp. 629–661; C. Ostroff and L. E. Atwater, "Does Whom You Work with Matter? Effects of Referent Group Gender and Age Composition on Managers' Compensation," *Journal of Applied Psychology*, August 2003, pp. 725–740; and M. E. Heilman, A. S. Wallen, D. Fuchs, and M. M. Tamkins, "Penalties for Success: Reactions to Women Who Succeed at Male Gender-Typed Tasks," *Journal of Applied Psychology*, June 2004, pp. 416–427.

11. J. L. Eberhardt, P. G. Davies, V. J. Purdic-Vaughns, and S. L. Johnson, "Looking Deathworthy: Perceived Stereotypicality of Black Defendants Predicts Capital-Sentencing Outcomes," *Psychological Science* 17, no. 5 (2006), pp. 383–386.

12. See, for example, J. Wilgoren, "Struggling to Be Both Arab and American," *New York Times*, November 4, 2001, p. B1; J. Q. Wilson and H. R. Higgins, "Profiles in Courage," *Wall Street Journal*, January 10, 2002, p. A12; and P. R. Sullivan, "Profiling," *America*, March 18, 2002, pp. 12–14.

13. See the List of Terrorist Incidents Information Resource, http://www.localcolorart.com/search/encyclopedia/List_of_terrorist_incidents/.

14. H. G. Heneman III and T. A. Judge, *Staffing Organizations* (Middleton, WI: Mendota House, 2006).

15. J. Willis and A. Todorov, "First Impressions: Making Up Your Mind After a 100ms Exposure to a Face," *Psychological Science*, July 2006, pp. 592–598.

16. See, for example, E. C. Webster, *Decision Making in the Employment Interview* (Montreal: McGill University, Industrial Relations Center, 1964).

17. See, for example, D. Eden, *Pygmalion in Management* (Lexington, MA: Lexington Books, 1990); D. Eden, "Leadership and Expectations: Pygmalion Effects and Other Self-Fulfilling Prophecies," *Leadership Quarterly*, Winter 1992, pp. 271–305; D. B. McNatt, "Ancient Pygmalion Joins Contemporary Management: A Meta-analysis of the Result," *Journal of Applied Psychology*, April 2000, pp. 314–322; O. B. Davidson and D. Eden, "Remedial Self-Fulfilling Prophecy: Two Field Experiments to Prevent Golem Effects Among Disadvantaged Women," *Journal of Applied Psychology*, June 2000, pp. 386–398; and D. Eden, "Self-Fulfilling Prophecies in Organizations," in J. Greenberg (ed.), *Organizational Behavior: The State of the Science*, 2nd ed. (Mahwah, NJ: Lawrence Erlbaum, 2003), pp. 91–122.

18. D. Eden and A. B. Shani, "Pygmalion Goes to Boot Camp: Expectancy, Leadership, and Trainee Performance," *Journal of Applied Psychology*, April 1982, pp. 194–199; and D. B. McNatt and T. A. Judge, "Boundary Conditions of the Galatea Effect: A Field Experiment and Constructive Replication," *Academy of Management Journal*, August 2004, pp. 550–565.

19. See, for example, R. D. Bretz, Jr., G. T. Milkovich, and W. Read, "The Current State of Performance Appraisal Research and Practice: Concerns, Directions, and Implications," *Journal of Management*, June 1992, pp. 323–324; and S. E. DeVoe and S. S. Iyengar, "Managers' Theories of Subordinates: A Cross-Cultural Examination of Manager Perceptions of Motivation and Appraisal of Performance," *Organizational Behavior and Human Decision Processes*, January 2004, pp. 47–61.

20. R. Sanders, *The Executive Decisionmaking Process: Identifying Problems and Assessing Outcomes* (Westport, CT: Quorum, 1999).

21. See H. A. Simon, "Rationality in Psychology and Economics," *Journal of Business*, October 1986, pp. 209–224; and E. Shafir and R. A. LeBoeuf, "Rationality," in S. T. Fiske, D. L. Schacter, and C. Zahn-Waxler, eds., *Annual Review of Psychology*, vol. 53 (Palo Alto, CA: Annual Reviews, 2002), pp. 491–517.

22. For a review of the rational model, see E. F. Harrison, *The Managerial Decision-Making Process*, 5th ed. (Boston: Houghton Mifflin, 1999), pp. 75–102.

23. J. G. March, *A Primer on Decision Making* (New York: The Free Press, 1994), pp. 2–7; and D. Hardman and C. Harries, "How Rational Are We?" *Psychologist*, February 2002, pp. 76–79.

24. M. Bazerman, *Judgment in Managerial Decision Making*, 3rd ed. (New York: Wiley, 1994), p. 5.

25. J. E. Russo, K. A. Carlson, and M. G. Meloy, "Choosing an Inferior Alternative," *Psychological Science* 17, no. 10 (2006), pp. 899–904.

26. D. Kahneman, "Maps of Bounded Rationality: Psychology for Behavioral Economics," *The American Economic Review* 93, no. 5 (2003), pp. 1449–1475; J. Zhang, C. K. Hsee, and Z. Xiao, "The Majority Rule in Individual Decision Making," *Organizational Behavior and Human Decision Processes* 99 (2006), pp. 102–111.

27. See H. A. Simon, *Administrative Behavior*, 4th ed. (New York: The Free Press, 1997); and M. Augier, "Simon Says: Bounded Rationality Matters," *Journal of Management Inquiry*, September 2001, pp. 268–275.

28. See T. Gilovich, D. Griffin, and D. Kahneman, *Heuristics and Biases: The Psychology of Intuitive Judgment* (New York: Cambridge University Press, 2002).

29. E. Dane and M. G. Pratt, "Exploring Intuition and Its Role in Managerial Decision Making," *Academy of Management Review* 32, no. 1 (2007), pp. 33–54.

30. As described in H. A. Simon, "Making Management Decisions: The Role of Intuition and Emotion," *Academy of Management Executive*, February 1987, pp. 59–60.

31. See, for instance, L. A. Burke and M. K. Miller, "Taking the Mystery Out of Intuitive Decision Making," *Academy of Management Executive*, November 1999, pp. 91–99; N. Khatri and H. A. Ng, "The Role of Intuition in Strategic Decision Making," *Human Relations*, January 2000, pp. 57–86; J. A. Andersen, "Intuition in Managers: Are Intuitive Managers More Effective?" *Journal of Managerial Psychology* 15, no. 1–2 (2000), pp. 46–63; D. Myers, *Intuition: Its Powers and Perils* (New Haven, CT: Yale University Press, 2002); and L. Simpson, "Basic Instincts," *Training*, January 2003, pp. 56–59.

32. See, for instance, Burke and Miller, "Taking the Mystery Out of Intuitive Decision Making," pp. 91–99.

33. S. P. Robbins, *Decide & Conquer: Making Winning Decisions and Taking Control of Your Life* (Upper Saddle River, NJ: Financial Times/Prentice Hall, 2004), p. 13.

34. S. Plous, *The Psychology of Judgment and Decision Making* (New York: McGraw-Hill, 1993), p. 217.

35. S. Lichtenstein and B. Fischhoff, "Do Those Who Know More Also Know More About How Much They Know?" *Organizational Behavior and Human Performance*, December 1977, pp. 159–183.

36. B. Fischhoff, P. Slovic, and S. Lichtenstein, "Knowing with Certainty: The Appropriateness of Extreme Confidence," *Journal of Experimental Psychology: Human Perception and Performance*, November 1977, pp. 552–564.

37. J. Kruger and D. Dunning, "Unskilled and Unaware of It: How Difficulties in Recognizing One's Own Incompetence Lead to Inflated Self-Assessments," *Journal of Personality and Social Psychology*, November 1999, pp. 1121–1134.

38. B. Fischhoff, P. Slovic, and S. Lichtenstein, "Knowing with Certainty: The Appropriateness of Extreme Confidence," *Journal of Experimental Psychology* 3 (1977), pp. 552–564.

39. Kruger and Dunning, "Unskilled and Unaware of It: How Difficulties in Recognizing One's Own Incompetence Lead to Inflated Self-Assessments."

40. See, for instance, A. Tversky and D. Kahneman, "Judgment Under Uncertainty: Heuristics and Biases," *Science*, September 1974, pp. 1124–1131.

41. J. S. Hammond, R. L. Keeney, and H. Raiffa, *Smart Choices* (Boston: HBS Press, 1999), p. 191.

42. R. Hastie, D. A. Schkade, and J. W. Payne, "Juror Judgments in Civil Cases: Effects of Plaintiff's Requests and Plaintiff's Identity on Punitive Damage Awards," *Law and Human Behavior*, August 1999, pp. 445–470.

43. See R. S. Nickerson, "Confirmation Bias: A Ubiquitous Phenomenon in Many Guises," *Review of General Psychology*, June 1998, pp. 175–220; and E. Jonas, S. Schultz-Hardt, D. Frey, and N. Thelen, "Confirmation Bias in Sequential Information Search After Preliminary Decisions," *Journal of Personality and Social Psychology*, April 2001, pp. 557–571.

44. See A. Tversky and D. Kahneman, "Availability: A Heuristic for Judging Frequency and Probability," in D. Kahneman, P. Slovic, and A. Tversky (eds.), *Judgment Under Uncertainty: Heuristics and Biases* (Cambridge, UK: Cambridge University Press, 1982), pp. 163–178; and B. J. Bushman and G. L. Wells, "Narrative Impressions of Literature: The Availability Bias and the Corrective Properties of Meta-analytic Approaches," *Personality and Social Psychology Bulletin*, September 2001, pp. 1123–1130.

45. See B. M. Staw, "The Escalation of Commitment to a Course of Action," *Academy of Management Review*, October 1981, pp. 577–587; K. Fai, E. Wong, M. Yik, and J. Y. Y. Kwong, "Understanding the Emotional Aspects of Escalation of Commitment: The Role of Negative Affect," *Journal of Applied Psychology* 91, no. 2 (2006), pp. 282–297; H. Moon, "Looking Forward and Looking Back: Integrating Completion and Sunk-Cost Effects Within an Escalation-of-Commitment Progress Decision," *Journal of Applied Psychology*, February 2001, pp. 104–113; and A. Zardkoohi, "Do Real Options Lead to Escalation of Commitment? Comment," *Academy of Management Review*, January 2004, pp. 111–119.

46. D. Gilbert, "I'm O.K., You're Biased," *New York Times*, April 16, 2006, p. 12; and J. Dana and G. Loewenstein "A Social Science Perspective on Gifts to Physicians from Industry" *Journal of the American Medical Association*, July 2003, pp. 252–255.

47. B. M. Staw, "Knee-Deep in the Big Muddy: A Study of Escalating Commitment to a Chosen Course of Action," *Organizational Behavior and Human Performance* 16 (1976), pp. 27–44.

48. K. F. E. Wong and J. Y. Y. Kwong, "The Role of Anticipated Regret in Escalation of Commitment," *Journal of Applied Psychology* 92, no. 2 (2007), pp. 545–554.

49. See, for instance, A. James and A. Wells, "Death Beliefs, Superstitious Beliefs and Health Anxiety," *British Journal of Clinical Psychology*, March 2002, pp. 43–53.

50. R. L. Guilbault, F. B. Bryant, J. H. Brockway, and E. J. Posavac, "A Meta-analysis of Research on Hindsight Bias," *Basic and Applied Social Psychology*, September 2004, pp. 103–117; and L. Werth, F. Strack, and J. Foerster, "Certainty and Uncertainty: The Two Faces of the Hindsight Bias," *Organizational Behavior and Human Decision Processes*, March 2002, pp. 323–341.

51. M. Gladwell, "Connecting the Dots," *The New Yorker*, March 10, 2003.

52. H. Moon, J. R. Hollenbeck, S. E. Humphrey, and B. Maue, "The Tripartite Model of Neuroticism and the Suppression of Depression and Anxiety within an Escalation of Commitment Dilemma," *Journal of Personality* 71 (2003), pp. 347–368; and H. Moon, "The Two Faces of Conscientiousness: Duty and Achievement Striving in Escalation of Commitment Dilemmas," *Journal of Applied Psychology* 86 (2001), pp. 535–540.

53. J. Musch, "Personality Differences in Hindsight Bias," *Memory* 11 (2003), pp. 473–489.

54. W. K. Campbell and C. Sedikides, "Self-Threat Magnifies the Self-Serving Bias: A Meta-analytic Integration," *Review of General Psychology* 3 (1999), pp. 23–43.

55. This section is based on S. Nolen-Hoeksema, J. Larson, and C. Grayson, "Explaining the Gender Difference in Depressive Symptoms," *Journal of Personality & Social Psychology*, November 1999, pp. 1061–1072; S. Nolen-Hoeksema and S. Jackson, "Mediators of the Gender Difference in Rumination," *Psychology of Women Quarterly*, March 2001, pp. 37–47; S. Nolen-Hoeksema, "Gender Differences in Depression," *Current Directions in Psychological Science*, October 2001, pp. 173–176; and S. Nolen-Hoeksema, *Women Who Think Too Much* (New York: Henry Holt, 2003).

56. H. Connery, and K. M. Davidson, "A Survey of Attitudes to Depression in the General Public: A Comparison of Age and Gender Differences," *Journal of Mental Health* 15, no. 2 (April 2006), pp. 179–189.

57. M. Elias, "Thinking It Over, and Over, and Over," *USA Today*, February 6, 2003, p. 10D.

58. A. Wildavsky, *The Politics of the Budgetary Process* (Boston: Little, Brown, 1964).

59. G. F. Cavanagh, D. J. Moberg, and M. Valasquez, "The Ethics of Organizational Politics," *Academy of Management Journal*, June 1981, pp. 363–374.

60. See, for example, T. Machan, ed., *Commerce and Morality* (Totowa, NJ: Rowman and Littlefield, 1988).

61. T. M. Amabile, "A Model of Creativity and Innovation in Organizations," in B. M. Staw and L. L. Cummings (eds.), *Research in Organizational Behavior*, vol. 10 (Greenwich, CT: JAI Press, 1988), p. 126; and J. E. Perry-Smith and C. E.

Shalley, "The Social Side of Creativity: A Static and Dynamic Social Network Perspective," *Academy of Management Review*, January 2003, pp. 89–106.

62. R. Florida, "A Search for Jobs in Some of the Wrong Places," *USA Today*, February 13, 2006, p. 11A; and R. Alsop, "Schools Find Fun a Worthy Teacher to Foster Creativity," *Wall Street Journal*, September 12, 2006, p. B8.

63. G. J. Feist and F. X. Barron, "Predicting Creativity from Early to Late Adulthood: Intellect, Potential, and Personality," *Journal of Research in Personality*, April 2003, pp. 62–88.

64. R. W. Woodman, J. E. Sawyer, and R. W. Griffin, "Toward a Theory of Organizational Creativity," *Academy of Management Review*, April 1993, p. 298; J. M. George and J. Zhou, "When Openness to Experience and Conscientiousness Are Related to Creative Behavior: An Interactional Approach," *Journal of Applied Psychology*, June 2001, pp. 513–524; and E. F. Rietzschel, C. K. W. de Dreu, and B. A. Nijstad, "Personal Need for Structure and Creative Performance: The Moderating Influence of Fear of Invalidity," *Personality and Social Psychology Bulletin*, June 2007, pp. 855–866.

65. Cited in C. G. Morris, *Psychology: An Introduction*, 9th ed. (Upper Saddle River, NJ: Prentice Hall, 1996), p. 344.

66. This section is based on T. M. Amabile, "Motivating Creativity in Organizations: On Doing What You Love and Loving What You Do," *California Management Review* 40, no. 1 (Fall 1997), pp. 39–58.

67. A. M. Isen, "Positive Affect," in T. Dalgleish and M. J. Power (eds.), *Handbook of Cognition and Emotion* (New York: Wiley, 1999), pp. 521–539.

68. J. Zhou, "When the Presence of Creative Coworkers Is Related to Creativity: Role of Supervisor Close Monitoring, Developmental Feedback, and Creative Personality," *Journal of Applied Psychology* 88, no. 3 (June 2003), pp. 413–422.

69. J. E. Perry-Smith, "Social yet Creative: The Role of Social Relationships in Facilitating Individual Creativity," *Academy of Management Journal* 49, no. 1 (2006), pp. 85–101.

70. W. J. J. Gordon, *Synectics* (New York: Harper & Row, 1961).

71. See T. M. Amabile, *KEYS: Assessing the Climate for Creativity* (Greensboro, NC: Center for Creative Leadership, 1995); N. Madjar, G. R. Oldham, and M. G. Pratt, "There's No Place Like Home? The Contributions of Work and Nonwork Creativity Support to Employees' Creative Performance," *Academy of Management Journal*, August 2002, pp. 757–767; and C. E. Shalley, J. Zhou, and G. R. Oldham, "The Effects of

Personal and Contextual Characteristics on Creativity: Where Should We Go from Here?" *Journal of Management*, November 2004, pp. 933–958.

72. See, for instance, G. R. Semin, "A Gloss on Attribution Theory," *British Journal of Social and Clinical Psychology*, November 1980, pp. 291–230; M. W. Morris and K. Peng, "Culture and Cause: American and Chinese Attributions for Social and Physical Events," *Journal of Personality and Social Psychology*, December 1994, pp. 949–971; and D. S. Krull, M. H.-M. Loy, J. Lin, C.-F. Wang, S. Chen, and X. Zhao, "The Fundamental Attribution Error: Correspondence Bias in Individualistic and Collectivist Cultures," *Personality & Social Psychology Bulletin*, October 1999, pp. 1208–1219.

73. S. Nam, "Cultural and Managerial Attributions for Group Performance," unpublished doctoral dissertation; University of Oregon. Cited in R. M. Steers, S. J. Bischoff, and L. H. Higgins, "Cross-Cultural Management Research," *Journal of Management Inquiry*, December 1992, pp. 325–326.

74. M. J. Gelfand, M. Erez, and Z. Aycan, "Cross-Cultural Organizational Behavior," *Annual Review of Psychology*, January 2007, pp. 479–514; and A. S. Tsui, S. S. Nifadkar, and A. Y. Ou, "Cross-National, Cross-Cultural Organizational Behavior Research: Advances, Gaps, and Recommendations," *Journal of Management*, June 2007, pp. 426–478.

75. N. J. Adler, *International Dimensions of Organizational Behavior*, 4th ed. (Cincinnati, OH: SouthWestern Publishing, 2002), pp. 182–189.

76. T. Jackson, "Cultural Values and Management Ethics: A 10-Nation Study," *Human Relations*, October 2001, pp. 1267–1302; see also J. B. Cullen, K. P. Parboteeah, and M. Hoegl, "Cross-National Differences in Managers' Willingness to Justify Ethically Suspect Behaviors: A Test of Institutional Anomie Theory," *Academy of Management Journal*, June 2004, pp. 411–421.

77. W. Chow Hou, "To Bribe or Not to Bribe?" *Asia, Inc.*, October 1996, p. 104.

78. P. Digh, "Shades of Gray in the Global Marketplace," *HRMagazine*, April 1997, p. 91.

79. Based on T. Gilovich, V. H. Medvec, and D. Kahneman, "Varieties of Regret: A Debate and Partial Resolution," *Psychological Review* 105 (1998), pp. 602–605; see also M. Tsiros and V. Mittal, "Regret: A Model of Its Antecedents and Consequences in Consumer Decision Making," *Journal of Consumer Research*, March 2000, pp. 401–417.

Motivation Concepts

Luke: "I don't believe it."

Yoda: "That is why you fail."

—*The Empire Strikes Back*

After studying this chapter, you should be able to:

1 Describe the three key elements of motivation.

2 Identify four early theories of motivation and evaluate their applicability today.

3 Apply the predictions of cognitive evaluation theory to intrinsic and extrinsic rewards.

4 Compare and contrast goal-setting theory and management by objectives.

5 Contrast reinforcement theory and goal-setting theory.

6 Demonstrate how organizational justice is a refinement of equity theory.

7 Apply the key tenets of expectancy theory to motivating employees.

8 Compare contemporary theories of motivation.

9 Explain to what degree motivation theories are culture bound.

n 1982, Chris Gardner was homeless, raising a 20-month-old son in San Francisco and peddling medical devices few wanted to buy. Unable to afford both housing and child care, Gardner boarded himself and his son where he could—in cheap hotels in Oakland, in a church shelter when they couldn't afford that, and even in the bathroom at the Bay Area Rapid Transit office when the shelter was full. A happy ending was nowhere in sight.

Chris Gardner's Pursuit of Happyness

A turning point in Gardner's life came in a parking lot, when he met a man driving a red Ferrari. "He was looking for a parking space. I said, 'You can have mine, but I gotta ask you two questions.' The two questions were: What do you do? And how do you do that? Turns out this guy was a stockbroker and he was making $80,000 a month." From that moment, Gardner resolved that he'd be a stockbroker, too. A while later, he looked up the offices of Dean Witter, then one of the largest investment banking firms (it later merged with Morgan Stanley). Gardner was able to line up an interview for a spot in the firm's internship program.

The night before his interview, Gardner was taken to jail for a backlog of parking tickets he couldn't afford to pay. So he went to his interview unshaven, disheveled, in yesterday's clothes. He explained his situation, and Dean Witter took a chance on him. The firm advised him it was only a trial program and that only a few of the most promising prospects would be hired to full-time positions. Gardner remembered advice his mother had given him: "You can only depend on yourself. The cavalry ain't coming."

At Dean Witter, Gardner made 200 calls a day. "Every time I picked up the phone," he said, "I knew I was getting closer to digging myself out of the hole." Gardner made it at Dean Witter, spent 1983–1987 at Bear Stearns & Co., where he became a top earner, and 5 years later, opened his own brokerage firm in Chicago. Named Gardner Rich, it's still thriving today. Now 14 people work at the firm's offices, a few blocks from the Sears Tower in Chicago. Not that Gardner is coasting. Sitting in his Chicago office, dressed in Bermuda shorts, sandals, and two watches (which he always wears to make sure he's never late), Gardner says he's a bit tired of talking about himself and how far he's come.

No wonder. He's given scores of interviews and has been featured on most major TV shows (including *20/20*, *Oprah*, *Today Show*, and *The View*, among others). His life story was made into a best-selling book and a Columbia Pictures film, which he helped produce and which starred Will Smith. When he's not working at his investment bank, Gardner is a motivational speaker and helps various charities in Chicago and San Francisco. For example, with the Cara Program, which assists the homeless and at-risk populations in Chicago with comprehensive job training and placement, Gardner speaks at counseling sessions and assists with permanent job placement. A table in his office is piled high with letters from people inspired by his story. On occasion, he'll call one of the letter writers. He says: "I find myself saying over and over: 'Baby steps count.'"[1] ■

*W*hat motivates people like Chris Gardner to excel? Is there anything organizations can do to encourage that sort of motivation in their employees? Before we answer that question, try a self-assessment of your confidence in your ability to succeed.

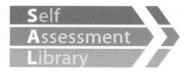

HOW CONFIDENT AM I IN MY ABILITIES TO SUCCEED?

In the Self-Assessment Library (available on CD or online), take assessment IV.A.3 (How Confident Am I in My Abilities to Succeed?) and answer the following questions.

1. *How did you score relative to other class members? Does that surprise you?*
2. *Do you think self-confidence is critical to success? Can a person be too confident?*

Motivation is one of the most frequently researched topics in OB.[2] One reason for its popularity is revealed in a recent Gallup poll, which found that a majority of U.S. employees—55 percent—have no enthusiasm for their work.[3] Moreover, another study suggested that, by workers' own reports, they waste roughly 2 hours per day, not counting lunch and scheduled breaks (the biggest time-wasters were Internet surfing and talking with coworkers).[4] Clearly, motivation seems to be an issue. The good news is that all this research provides us with considerable insights into how to improve motivation.

In this chapter, we'll review the basics of motivation, assess a number of motivation theories, and provide an integrative model that shows how the best of these theories fit together.

Defining *Motivation*

What is motivation? It's the result of the interaction between an individual and a situation. Certainly, some individuals, such as Chris Gardner, seem to be driven to succeed. But the same student who finds it difficult to read a textbook for more than 20 minutes may devour a Harry Potter book in a day. For this student, the difference in motivation is driven by the situation. So as we analyze the concept of motivation, keep in mind that the level of motivation varies both between individuals and within individuals at different times.

1 Describe the three key three elements of motivation.

We define **motivation** as the processes that account for an individual's intensity, direction, and persistence of effort toward attaining a goal.[5] While general motivation is concerned with effort toward *any* goal, we'll narrow the focus to *organizational* goals in order to reflect our singular interest in work-related behavior.

The three key elements in our definition are intensity, direction, and persistence. *Intensity* is concerned with how hard a person tries. This is the element most of us focus on when we talk about motivation. However, high intensity is unlikely to lead to favorable job-performance outcomes unless the effort is channeled in a *direction* that benefits the organization. Therefore, we have to consider the quality of effort as well as its intensity. Effort that is directed toward, and consistent with, the organization's goals is the kind of effort that we should be seeking. Finally, motivation has a *persistence* dimension. This is a measure of how long a person can maintain effort. Motivated individuals stay with a task long enough to achieve their goal.

Early Theories of Motivation

2 Identify four early theories of motivation and evaluate their applicability today.

The 1950s were a fruitful period in the development of motivation concepts. Four specific theories were formulated during this period, which although heavily attacked and now questionable in terms of validity, are probably still the best-known explanations for employee motivation. As you'll see later in this chapter, we have

motivation *The processes that account for an individual's intensity, direction, and persistence of effort toward attaining a goal.*

since developed more valid explanations of motivation, but you should know these early theories for at least two reasons: (1) They represent a foundation from which contemporary theories have grown, and (2) practicing managers still regularly use these theories and their terminology in explaining employee motivation.

Hierarchy of Needs Theory

It's probably safe to say that the most well-known theory of motivation is Abraham Maslow's **hierarchy of needs**.[6] Maslow hypothesized that within every human being, there exists a hierarchy of five needs:

1. **Physiological.**   Includes hunger, thirst, shelter, sex, and other bodily needs
2. **Safety.**   Security and protection from physical and emotional harm
3. **Social.**   Affection, belongingness, acceptance, and friendship
4. **Esteem.**   Internal factors such as self-respect, autonomy, and achievement, and external factors such as status, recognition, and attention
5. **Self-actualization.**   Drive to become what one is capable of becoming; includes growth, achieving one's potential, and self-fulfillment

As each of these needs becomes substantially satisfied, the next need becomes dominant. In terms of Exhibit 6-1, the individual moves up the steps of the hierarchy. From the standpoint of motivation, the theory would say that, although no need is ever fully gratified, a substantially satisfied need no longer motivates. So if you want to motivate someone, according to Maslow, you need to understand what level of the hierarchy that person is currently on and focus on satisfying the needs at or above that level.

Maslow separated the five needs into higher and lower orders. Physiological and safety needs were described as **lower-order needs** and social, esteem, and **self-actualization** as **higher-order needs**. The differentiation between the two orders was made on the premise that higher-order needs are satisfied internally (within the person), whereas lower-order needs are predominantly satisfied externally (by things such as pay, union contracts, and tenure).

Maslow's needs theory has received wide recognition, particularly among practicing managers. This can be attributed to the theory's intuitive logic and ease of understanding. Unfortunately, however, research does not validate the theory. Maslow provided no empirical substantiation, and several studies that sought to validate the theory found no support for it.[7]

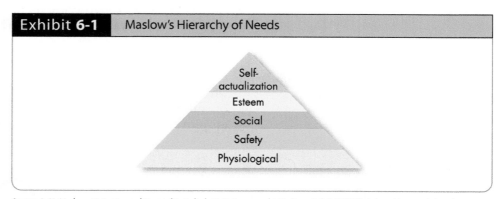

Exhibit 6-1   Maslow's Hierarchy of Needs

Self-actualization
Esteem
Social
Safety
Physiological

Source: A. H. Maslow, *Motivation and Personality*, 3rd ed., R. D. Frager and J. Fadiman (eds.). © 1997. Adapted by permission of Pearson Education, Inc., Upper Saddle River, New Jersey.

Clayton Alderfer attempted to rework Maslow's need hierarchy to align it more closely with empirical research. His revised need hierarchy is labeled **ERG theory**.[8] Alderfer argued that there are three groups of core needs— *existence* (similar to Maslow's physiological and safety needs), *relatedness* (similar to Maslow's social and status needs), and *growth* (similar to Maslow's esteem needs and self-actualization). Unlike Maslow, Alderfer didn't assume that these needs existed in a rigid hierarchy. An individual could be focusing on all three need categories simultaneously. Despite these differences, empirical research hasn't been any more supportive of ERG theory than of the need hierarchy.[9]

Old theories, especially ones that are intuitively logical, apparently die hard. Although the need hierarchy theory and its terminology have remained popular with practicing managers, there is little evidence that need structures are organized along the dimensions proposed by Maslow or Alderfer, that unsatisfied needs motivate, or that a satisfied need activates movement to a new need level.[10]

Theory X and Theory Y

Douglas McGregor proposed two distinct views of human beings: one basically negative, labeled **Theory X**, and the other basically positive, labeled **Theory Y**.[11] After viewing the way in which managers dealt with employees, McGregor concluded that managers' views of the nature of human beings are based on a certain grouping of assumptions and that managers tend to mold their behavior toward employees according to these assumptions.

Under Theory X, managers believe that employees inherently dislike work and must therefore be directed or even coerced into performing it. In contrast to these negative views about the nature of human beings, under Theory Y, managers assume that employees can view work as being as natural as rest or play, and therefore the average person can learn to accept, and even seek, responsibility.

To understand Theory X and Theory Y more fully, think in terms of Maslow's hierarchy. Theory Y assumes that higher-order needs dominate individuals. McGregor himself held to the belief that Theory Y assumptions were more valid than Theory X. Therefore, he proposed such ideas as participative decision making, responsible and challenging jobs, and good group relations as approaches that would maximize an employee's job motivation.

Unfortunately, there is no evidence to confirm that either set of assumptions is valid or that accepting Theory Y assumptions and altering one's actions accordingly will lead to more motivated workers. OB theories need to have empirical support before we can accept them. Such empirical support is lacking for Theory X and Theory Y as it is for the hierarchy of needs theories.

---

hierarchy of needs theory *A hierarchy of five needs—physiological, safety, social, esteem, and self-actualization— in which, as each need is substantially satisfied, the next need becomes dominant.*

lower-order needs *Needs that are satisfied externally, such as physiological and safety needs.*

self-actualization *The drive to become what a person is capable of becoming.*

higher-order needs *Needs that are satisfied internally, such as social, esteem, and self-actualization needs.*

ERG theory *A theory that posits three groups of core needs: existence, relatedness, and growth.*

Theory X *The assumption that employees dislike work, are lazy, dislike responsibility, and must be coerced to perform.*

Theory Y *The assumption that employees like work, are creative, seek responsibility, and can exercise self-direction.*

MYTH OR SCIENCE?

"Women Are More Motivated to Get Along, and Men Are More Motivated to Get Ahead"

this statement is generally true. Compared with women, men are relatively more motivated to excel at tasks and jobs. Compared with men, women are more motivated to maintain relationships.

Before proceeding any further, though, it is important to note that these gender differences do not mean that every man is more motivated by his career than every woman. There are differences, but think of it like gender and longevity. Women, on average, live longer than men, but in a significant percentage of couples (roughly 45 percent), a husband will outlive his wife. So, there are differences, but you need to resist the human tendency to turn a group difference into a universal generalization or stereotype.

Research indicates that men are more likely to be described by what are called "agentic traits," such as *active*, *decisive*, and *competitive*. Women are more likely to be described by what are termed "communal" traits, such as *caring*, *emotional*, and *considerate*. This evidence, however, might reflect gender stereotypes. We might hold stereotypes of the traits of men and women, but that doesn't necessarily prove that men and women are motivated by different things.

Other evidence, though, suggests that this is not just a gender stereotype. A study of 1,398 working Germans revealed that men were more motivated by agentic strivings and women more by communal strivings, and these gender differences did not change over the 17-month course of the study. As a result of these differences, men had higher levels of "objective" career success (income, occupational status) than women. Women, however, were more involved in their families than were men.

We don't know whether these differences are ingrained or socialized. If they are socialized, though, evidence suggests that it begins early. A study of the stories that children aged 4 through 9 told about their lives revealed that girls were more likely to emphasize communion (friendships, helping others, affectionate contact) than were boys.[12] ■

Two-Factor Theory

Psychologist Frederick Herzberg proposed the **two-factor theory**—also called *motivation-hygiene theory*.[13] Believing that an individual's relation to work is basic and that one's attitude toward work can very well determine success or failure, Herzberg investigated the question "What do people want from their jobs?" He asked people to describe, in detail, situations in which they felt exceptionally *good* or *bad* about their jobs. The responses were then tabulated and categorized.

From the categorized responses, Herzberg concluded that the replies people gave when they felt good about their jobs were significantly different from the replies given when they felt bad. As shown in Exhibit 6-2, certain characteristics tend to be consistently related to job satisfaction and others to job dissatisfaction. Intrinsic factors such as advancement, recognition, responsibility, and achievement seem to be related to job satisfaction. Respondents who felt good about their work tended to attribute these factors to themselves. On the other hand, dissatisfied respondents tended to cite extrinsic factors, such as supervision, pay, company policies, and working conditions.

The data suggest, said Herzberg, that the opposite of satisfaction is not dissatisfaction, as was traditionally believed. Removing dissatisfying characteristics from a job does not necessarily make the job satisfying. As illustrated in Exhibit 6-3, Herzberg proposed that his findings indicated the existence of a dual continuum: The opposite of "satisfaction" is "no satisfaction," and the opposite of "dissatisfaction" is "no dissatisfaction."

According to Herzberg, the factors that lead to job satisfaction are separate and distinct from those that lead to job dissatisfaction. Therefore, managers who seek to eliminate factors that can create job dissatisfaction may bring about

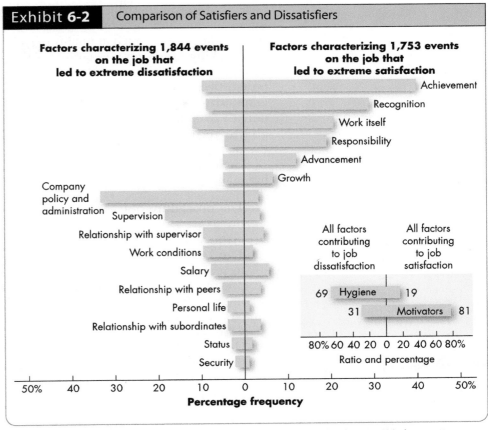

| Exhibit **6-2** | Comparison of Satisfiers and Dissatisfiers |

| Exhibit **6-3** | Contrasting Views of Satisfaction and Dissatisfaction |

Traditional view

Satisfaction — Dissatisfaction

Herzberg's view

Motivators

Satisfaction — No satisfaction

Hygiene factors

No dissatisfaction — Dissatisfaction

two-factor theory *A theory that relates intrinsic factors to job satisfaction and associates extrinsic factors with dissatisfaction. Also called* motivation-hygiene *theory.*

peace but not necessarily motivation. They will be placating their workforce rather than motivating workers. As a result, Herzberg characterized conditions surrounding the job such as quality of supervision, pay, company policies, physical working conditions, relations with others, and job security as **hygiene factors**. When they're adequate, people will not be dissatisfied; neither will they be satisfied. If we want to motivate people on their jobs, Herzberg suggested emphasizing factors associated with the work itself or with outcomes directly derived from it, such as promotional opportunities, opportunities for personal growth, recognition, responsibility, and achievement. These are the characteristics that people find intrinsically rewarding.

The two-factor theory has not been well supported in the literature, and it has many detractors.[14] The criticisms of the theory include the following:

1. The procedure that Herzberg used is limited by its methodology. When things are going well, people tend to take credit themselves. Contrarily, they blame failure on the extrinsic environment.
2. The reliability of Herzberg's methodology is questioned. Raters have to make interpretations, so they may contaminate the findings by interpreting one response in one manner while treating a similar response differently.
3. No overall measure of satisfaction was utilized. A person may dislike part of a job yet still think the job is acceptable overall.
4. Herzberg assumed a relationship between satisfaction and productivity, but the research methodology he used looked only at satisfaction and not at productivity. To make such research relevant, one must assume a strong relationship between satisfaction and productivity.

Regardless of the criticisms, Herzberg's theory has been widely read, and few managers are unfamiliar with its recommendations.

It's important to realize that even though we may intuitively *like* a theory, that does not mean that we should accept it. Many managers find need theories intuitively appealing, but remember that at one time the world seemed intuitively flat. Sometimes science backs up intuition, and sometimes it doesn't. In the case of the two-factor theory—as with the need hierarchy and Theory X/Theory Y—it doesn't.

McClelland's Theory of Needs

You have one beanbag, and there are five targets set up in front of you. Each one is progressively farther away and, hence, more difficult to hit. Target A is a cinch. It sits almost within arm's reach. If you hit it, you get $2. Target B is a bit farther out, but about 80 percent of the people who try can hit it. It pays $4. Target C pays $8, and about half the people who try can hit it. Very few people can hit Target D, but the payoff is $16 for those who do. Finally, Target E pays $32, but it's almost impossible to achieve. Which target would you try for? If you selected C, you're likely to be a high achiever. Why? Read on.

McClelland's theory of needs was developed by David McClelland and his associates.[15] The theory focuses on three needs, defined as follows:

- **Need for achievement (nAch)** is the drive to excel, to achieve in relation to a set of standards, to strive to succeed.
- **Need for power (nPow)** is the need to make others behave in a way in which they would not have behaved otherwise.
- **Need for affiliation (nAff)** is the desire for friendly and close interpersonal relationships.

Anne Sweeney is a high achiever. Since joining The Walt Disney Company in 1996, Sweeney has led the transition of the struggling Disney Channel from a premium cable service to a basic network, quintupling the channel's subscriber base. As co-chair of Disney's Media Networks, Sweeney is trying to achieve a turnaround for Disney's ABC Family channel. In addition, when Sweeney became president of ABC Television in 2004, she accepted the challenging goal of lifting the network from its last-place position.

Of the three needs, McClelland and subsequent researchers focused most of their attention on nAch. High achievers perform best when they perceive their probability of success as 0.5—that is, when they estimate that they have a 50–50 chance of success. They dislike gambling with high odds because they get no achievement satisfaction from success that comes by pure chance. Similarly, they dislike low odds (high probability of success) because then there is no challenge to their skills. They like to set goals that require stretching themselves a little.

Relying on an extensive amount of research, we can make some reasonably well-supported predictions of the relationship between achievement need and job performance. Although less research has been done on power and affiliation needs, there are consistent findings there, too. First, when jobs have a high degree of personal responsibility and feedback and an intermediate degree of risk, high achievers are strongly motivated. High achievers, for example, are successful in entrepreneurial activities such as running their own businesses and managing self-contained units within large organizations.[16] Second, a high need to achieve does not necessarily make someone a good manager, especially in large organizations. People with a high achievement need are interested in how well they do personally and not in influencing others to do well. High-nAch salespeople do not necessarily make good sales managers, and the good general manager in a large organization does not typically have a high need to achieve.[17] Third, the needs for affiliation and power tend to be closely related to managerial success. The best managers are high in their need for power and low in their need for affiliation.[18] In fact, a high power motive may be a requirement for managerial effectiveness.[19]

As you might have gathered, of the early theories of motivation, McClelland's has had the best research support. Unfortunately, it has less practical effect than the others. Because McClelland argued that the three needs are subconscious—meaning that we may be high on these needs but not know it—measuring them is not easy. In the most common approach, a trained expert presents pictures to individuals, asks them to tell a story about each, and then scores their responses in terms of the three needs. However, because measuring the needs is time-consuming and expensive, few organizations have been willing to invest time and resources in measuring McClelland's concept.

Contemporary Theories of Motivation

The previously described theories are well known but, unfortunately, have either not held up well under close examination or fallen out of favor. However, there are a number of contemporary theories, and they have one thing in common: Each has a reasonable degree of valid supporting documentation.

hygiene factors *Factors—such as company policy and administration, supervision, and salary—that, when adequate in a job, placate workers. When these factors are adequate, people will not be dissatisfied.*

McClelland's theory of needs *A theory which states that achievement, power, and affiliation are three important needs that help explain motivation.*

need for achievement (nAch) *The drive to excel, to achieve in relationship to a set of standards, and to strive to succeed.*

need for power (nPow) *The need to make others behave in a way in which they would not have behaved otherwise.*

need for affiliation (nAff) *The desire for friendly and close interpersonal relationships.*

Of course, this doesn't mean that the theories we are about to introduce are unquestionably right. We call them "contemporary theories" not because they were all developed recently but because they represent the current state of thinking in explaining employee motivation.

Cognitive Evaluation Theory

"It's strange," said Marcia. "I started work at the Humane Society as a volunteer. I put in 15 hours a week helping people adopt pets. And I loved coming to work. Then, 3 months ago, they hired me full-time at $11 an hour. I'm doing the same work I did before. But I'm not finding it near as much fun."

3 Apply the predictions of cognitive evaluation theory to intrinsic and extrinsic rewards.

There's an explanation for Marcia's reaction. It's called **cognitive evaluation theory**, which proposes that the introduction of extrinsic rewards, such as pay, for work effort that was previously intrinsically rewarding due to the pleasure associated with the content of the work itself tends to decrease overall motivation.[20] Cognitive evaluation theory has been extensively researched, and a large number of studies have supported it.[21] As we'll show, the major implications of this theory relate to work rewards.

Historically, motivation theorists generally assumed that intrinsic rewards such as interesting work were independent of extrinsic rewards such as high pay. But cognitive evaluation theory suggests otherwise. It argues that when extrinsic rewards are used by organizations as payoffs for superior performance, the intrinsic rewards, which are derived from individuals doing what they like, are reduced. In other words, when extrinsic rewards are given to someone for performing an interesting task, it causes intrinsic interest in the task itself to decline.

Why would such an outcome occur? The popular explanation is that an individual experiences a loss of control over her own behavior so that the previous

Paying Employees Not to Work

There is no better illustration of the woes of the Detroit automakers than the fact that each of "Big Three" has been forced to pay employees for work they *don't* do. This pay has taken two major forms.

First, Ford and General Motors have offered employees cash payments to leave their jobs. The employees are unionized, and their labor agreements guarantee full employment, so the companies must offer buyout deals that workers will accept. Because, in the words of a labor relations specialist, employees "almost see their job as a property right," the cash payments have been

substantial—often in the six-figures range. Ford and GM also pay workers to go to college, paying half their salary and up to $15,000 per year in tuition, as long as they quit when they're done.

A second, more controversial, policy is the "Jobs Bank" in which Ford and GM have paid more than 15,000 employees full salary and benefits to produce nothing. Although some of these employees are paid to perform some company-approved activity, such as volunteer work, many report to what is called "the rubber room"—a windowless old storage shed—where their job is to, literally, do nothing. The Jobs Bank is estimated to cost Ford and GM between $1.4 and $2 billion each year. Why does it exist? It was negotiated as part of the automakers' agreement to full employment policies in the 1980s.

As expensive as the Jobs Bank has proven to be for the automakers, it is not exactly motivating for some employees. Jerry Mellon said time in the rubber room "makes you want to bang your head against the wall." Others, though, love it. Tom Adams said, "The Jobs Bank has been wonderful for me. It's doing what it is supposed to do, which is make it so I won't be a burden on society."

In 2007 GM and Ford entered into new contracts with the UAW. Despite some restrictions, the jobs banks lives on.

Sources: M. Maynard and J. W. Peters, "Getting Auto Workers to Leave a Golden Job," *New York Times*, March 22, 2006, pp. C1, C8; and J. McCracken, "Detroit's Symbol of Dysfunction: Paying Employees Not to Work," *Wall Street Journal*, March 1, 2006, pp. A1, A12.

intrinsic motivation diminishes. Furthermore, the elimination of extrinsic rewards can produce a shift—from an external to an internal explanation—in an individual's perception of causation of why she works on a task. If you're reading a novel a week because your English literature instructor requires you to, you can attribute your reading behavior to an external source. However, after the course is over, if you find yourself continuing to read a novel a week, your natural inclination is to say, "I must enjoy reading novels because I'm still reading one a week."

If the cognitive evaluation theory is valid, it should have major implications for managerial practices. It has been a truism among compensation specialists for years that if pay or other extrinsic rewards are to be effective motivators, they should be made contingent on an individual's performance. But cognitive evaluation theorists would argue that this will only tend to decrease the internal satisfaction that the individual receives from doing the job. In fact, if cognitive evaluation theory is correct, it would make sense to make an individual's pay *noncontingent* on performance in order to avoid decreasing intrinsic motivation.

We noted earlier that the cognitive evaluation theory has been supported in a number of studies. Yet it has also been met with attacks, specifically on the

---

Exhibit 6-4

THE WALL STREET JOURNAL

"**What do you *mean* money isn't everything? This is a bank!**"

Source: From the *Wall Street Journal*, February 8, 1995. Reprinted with permission of Cartoon Features Syndicate.

---

cognitive evaluation theory   *A theory that states that allocating extrinsic rewards for behavior that had been previously intrinsically rewarding tends to decrease the overall level of motivation.*

methodology used in these studies[22] and in the interpretation of the findings.[23] But where does this theory stand today? Can we say that when organizations use extrinsic motivators such as pay and promotions and verbal rewards to stimulate workers' performance, they do so at the expense of reducing intrinsic interest and motivation in the work being done? The answer is not a simple "yes" or a simple "no."

Extrinsic rewards that are verbal (for example, receiving praise from a supervisor or coworker) or tangible (for example, money) can actually have different effects on individuals' intrinsic motivation. That is, verbal rewards increase intrinsic motivation, whereas tangible rewards undermine it. When people are told they will receive a tangible reward, they come to count on it and focus more on the reward than on the task.[24] Verbal rewards, however, seem to keep people focused on the task and encourage them to do it better.

A recent outgrowth of the cognitive evaluation theory is **self-concordance**, which considers the degree to which peoples' reasons for pursuing goals are consistent with their interests and core values. For example, if individuals pursue goals because of an intrinsic interest, they are more likely to attain their goals and are happy even if they do not attain them. Why? Because the process of striving toward them is fun. In contrast, people who pursue goals for extrinsic reasons (money, status, or other benefits) are less likely to attain their goals and are less happy even when they do achieve them. Why? Because the goals are less meaningful to them.[25] OB research suggests that people who pursue work goals for intrinsic reasons are more satisfied with their jobs, feel like they fit into their organizations better, and may perform better.[26]

International OB

How Managers Evaluate Their Employees Depends on Culture

A recent study found interesting differences in managers' perceptions of employee motivation. The study examined managers from three distinct cultural regions: North America, Asia, and Latin America. The results of the study revealed that North American managers perceive their employees as being motivated more by extrinsic factors (for example, pay) than intrinsic factors (for example, doing meaningful work). Asian managers perceive their employees as being motivated by both extrinsic and intrinsic factors, while Latin American managers perceive their employees as being motivated by intrinsic factors.

Even more interesting, these differences affected evaluations of employee performance. As expected, Asian managers focused on both types of motivation when evaluating their employees' performance, and Latin American managers focused on intrinsic motivation. Oddly, North American managers, though believing that employees are motivated primarily by extrinsic factors, actually focused more on *intrinsic* factors when evaluating employee performance. Why the paradox? One explanation is that North Americans value uniqueness, so any deviation from the norm—such as being perceived as being unusually high in intrinsic motivation—is rewarded.

Latin American managers' focus on intrinsic motivation when evaluating employees may be related to a cultural norm termed *simpatía*, a tradition that compels employees to display their internal feelings. Consequently, Latin American managers are more sensitized to these displays and can more easily notice their employees' intrinsic motivation.

So, from an employee perspective, the cultural background of your manager can play an important role in how you are evaluated.

Source: Based on S. E. DeVoe and S. S. Iyengar, "Managers' Theories of Subordinates: A Cross-Cultural Examination of Manager Perceptions of Motivation and Appraisal of Performance," *Organizational Behavior and Human Decision Processes,* January 2004, pp. 47–61.

What does all of this mean? It means choose your job carefully. Make sure you're choosing to do something for reasons other than extrinsic rewards. For organizations, managers need to provide intrinsic rewards in addition to extrinsic incentives. In other words, managers need to make the work interesting, provide recognition, and support employee growth and development. Employees who feel that what they do is within their control and a result of free choice are likely to be more motivated by their work and committed to their employers.[27]

Goal-Setting Theory

4 *Compare and contrast goal-setting theory and management by objectives.*

Gene Broadwater, coach of the Hamilton High School cross-country team, gave his squad these last words before they approached the starting line for the league championship race: "Each one of you is physically ready. Now, get out there and do your best. No one can ever ask more of you than that."

You've heard the sentiment a number of times yourself: "Just do your best. That's all anyone can ask for." But what does "do your best" mean? Do we ever know if we've achieved that vague goal? Would the cross-country runners have recorded faster times if Coach Broadwater had given each a specific goal to shoot for? Might you have done better in your high school English class if your parents had said, "You should strive for 85 percent or higher on all your work in English" rather than telling you to "do your best"? The research on **goal-setting theory** addresses these issues, and the findings, as you'll see, are impressive in terms of the effect that goal specificity, challenge, and feedback have on performance.

In the late 1960s, Edwin Locke proposed that intentions to work toward a goal are a major source of work motivation.[28] That is, goals tell an employee what needs to be done and how much effort will need to be expended.[29] The evidence strongly supports the value of goals. More to the point, we can say that specific goals increase performance; that difficult goals, when accepted, result in higher performance than do easy goals; and that feedback leads to higher performance than does nonfeedback.[30]

Specific goals produce a higher level of output than does the generalized goal of "do your best." Why? The specificity of the goal itself seems to act as an internal stimulus. For instance, when a trucker commits to making 12 round-trip hauls between Toronto and Buffalo, New York, each week, this intention gives him a specific objective to try to attain. We can say that, all things being equal, the trucker with a specific goal will outperform a counterpart operating with no goals or the generalized goal of "do your best."

If factors such as acceptance of the goals are held constant, we can also state that the more difficult the goal, the higher the level of performance. Of course, it's logical to assume that easier goals are more likely to be accepted. But once a hard task is accepted, the employee can be expected to exert a high level of effort to try to achieve it.

But why are people motivated by difficult goals?[31] First, difficult goals direct our attention to the task at hand and away from irrelevant distractions. Challenging goals get our attention and thus tend to help us focus. Second, difficult goals energize us because we have to work harder to attain them. For

self-concordance *The degree to which a person's reasons for pursuing a goal is consistent with the person's interests and core values.*

goal-setting theory *A theory that says that specific and difficult goals, with feedback, lead to higher performance.*

example, think of your study habits. Do you study as hard for an easy exam as you do for a difficult one? Probably not. Third, when goals are difficult, people persist in trying to attain them. Finally, difficult goals lead us to discover strategies that help us perform the job or task more effectively. If we have to struggle for a way to solve a difficult problem, we often think of a better way to go about it.

People do better when they get feedback on how well they are progressing toward their goals because feedback helps to identify discrepancies between what they have done and what they want to do; that is, feedback acts to guide behavior. But all feedback is not equally potent. Self-generated feedback—for which employees are able to monitor their own progress—has been shown to be a more powerful motivator than externally generated feedback.[32]

If employees have the opportunity to participate in the setting of their own goals, will they try harder? The evidence is mixed regarding the superiority of participative over assigned goals.[33] In some cases, participatively set goals elicited superior performance, while in other cases, individuals performed best when assigned goals by their boss. But a major advantage of participation may be in increasing acceptance of the goal itself as a desirable one toward which to work.[34] As we'll note shortly, commitment is important. If participation isn't used, then the individual assigning the goal needs to clearly explain the purpose and importance of the goal.[35]

Are there any contingencies in goal-setting theory, or can we take it as a universal truth that difficult and specific goals will *always* lead to higher performance? In addition to feedback, three other factors have been found to influence the goals–performance relationship: goal commitment, task characteristics, and national culture.

Goal-setting theory presupposes that an individual is committed to the goal; that is, an individual is determined not to lower or abandon the goal. Behaviorally, this means that an individual (1) believes he or she can achieve the goal and (2) wants to achieve it.[36] Goal commitment is most likely to occur when goals are made public, when the individual has an internal locus of control (see Chapter 4), and when the goals are self-set rather than assigned.[37] Research indicates that goal-setting theory doesn't work equally well on all tasks. The evidence suggests that goals seem to have a more substantial effect on performance when tasks are simple rather than complex, well learned rather than novel, and independent rather than interdependent.[38] On interdependent tasks, group goals are preferable.

Finally, goal-setting theory is culture bound. It's well adapted to countries such as the United States and Canada because its key components align reasonably well with North American cultures. It assumes that employees will be reasonably independent (that is, not too high a score on power distance), that managers and employees will seek challenging goals (that is, low in uncertainty avoidance), and that performance is considered important by both (that is, high in achievement). So we can't expect goal setting to necessarily lead to higher employee performance in countries such as Portugal or Chile, where the opposite conditions exist.

Our overall conclusion is that intentions—as articulated in terms of difficult and specific goals—are a potent motivating force. The motivating power of goal-setting theory has been demonstrated on more than 100 tasks involving more than 40,000 participants in many different kinds of industries—from lumber, to insurance, to automobiles. Basically, setting specific, challenging goals for employees is the best thing managers can do to improve performance.

Hasso Plattner, co-founder of the German software firm SAP, motivates employees by setting stretch goals. Plattner set a shockingly optimistic goal of 15 percent annual growth for SAP's software license revenues. Employees responded by achieving an even higher growth rate of 18 percent. Plattner set another stretch goal by announcing a bonus plan that would pay $381 million to hundreds of managers and key employees if they could double the company's market capitalization, from a starting point of $57 billion, by the end of 2010. For Plattner, setting stretch goals is a way to inject entrepreneurial energy into the 35-year-old company.

Self Assessment Library

WHAT ARE MY COURSE PERFORMANCE GOALS?

In the Self-Assessment Library (available on CD or online), take assessment I.C.5 (What Are My Course Performance Goals?).

Implementing Goal-Setting Goal-setting theory has an impressive base of research support. But as a manager, how do you make it operational? That's often left up to the individual manager or leader. Some managers explicitly set aggressive performance targets—what General Electric called "stretch goals." For example, some CEOs, such as Procter & Gamble's A. G. Laffey and SAP's Hasso Plattner, are known for the demanding performance goals they set. The problem with leaving it up to the individual manager is that, in many cases, managers don't set goals. A recent survey revealed that when asked whether their job had clearly defined goals, only a minority of employees agreed.[39]

A more systematic way to utilize goal setting is with a management by objectives program. **Management by objectives (MBO)** emphasizes participatively set goals that are tangible, verifiable, and measurable. As depicted in Exhibit 6-5, the organization's overall objectives are translated into specific objectives for each succeeding level (that is, divisional, departmental, individual) in the organization. But because lower-unit managers jointly participate in setting their own goals,

management by objectives (MBO) *A program that encompasses specific goals, participatively set, for an explicit time period, with feedback on goal progress.*

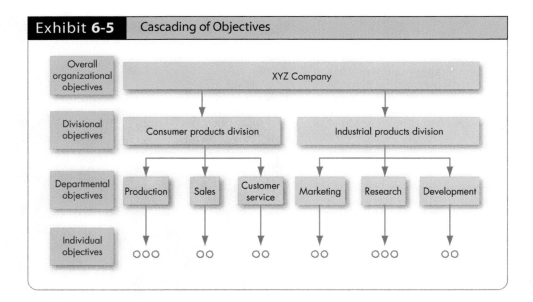

Exhibit **6-5**   Cascading of Objectives

MBO works from the "bottom up" as well as from the "top down." The result is a hierarchy that links objectives at one level to those at the next level. And for the individual employee, MBO provides specific personal performance objectives.

Four ingredients are common to MBO programs: goal specificity, participation in decision making (including participation in the setting of goals or objectives), an explicit time period, and performance feedback.[40] Many of the elements in MBO programs match propositions of goal-setting theory. For example, having an explicit time period to accomplish objectives matches goal-setting theory's emphasis on goal specificity. Similarly, we noted earlier that feedback about goal progress is a critical element of goal-setting theory. The only area of possible disagreement between MBO and goal-setting theory relates to the issue of participation: MBO strongly advocates it, whereas goal-setting theory demonstrates that managers assigning goals is usually just as effective.

You'll find MBO programs in many business, health care, educational, government, and nonprofit organizations.[41] MBO's popularity should not be construed to mean that it always works. There are a number of documented cases in which MBO has been implemented but failed to meet management's expectations.[42] When MBO doesn't work, the culprits tend to be factors such as unrealistic expectations regarding results, lack of commitment by top management, and an inability or unwillingness of management to allocate rewards based on goal accomplishment. Failures can also arise out of cultural incompatibilities. For instance, Fujitsu recently scrapped its MBO-type program because management found it didn't fit well with the Japanese culture's emphasis on minimizing risk and emphasizing long-term goals.

Self-Efficacy Theory

Self-efficacy (also known as *social cognitive theory* or *social learning theory*) refers to an individual's belief that he or she is capable of performing a task.[43] The higher your self-efficacy, the more confidence you have in your ability to succeed in a task. So, in difficult situations, people with low self-efficacy are more likely to lessen their effort or give up altogether, while those with high self-efficacy will try harder to master the challenge.[44] In addition, individuals high in self-efficacy seem to respond to negative feedback with increased effort and motivation, while those low in self-efficacy are likely to

5 Contrast reinforcement theory and goal-setting theory.

Exhibit 6-6	Joint Effects of Goals and Self-Efficacy on Performance

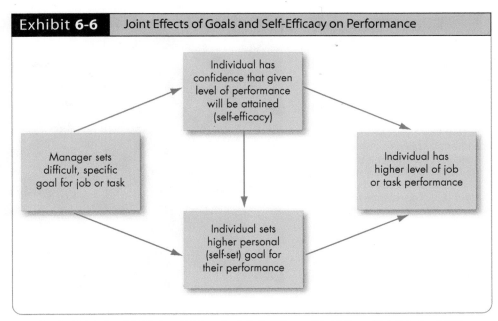

Source: Based on E. A. Locke and G. P. Latham, "Building a Practically Useful Theory of Goal Setting and Task Motivation: A 35-Year Odyssey," *American Psychologist,* September 2002, pp. 705–717.

lessen their effort when given negative feedback.[45] How can managers help their employees achieve high levels of self-efficacy? By bringing together goal-setting theory and self-efficacy theory.

Goal-setting theory and self-efficacy theory don't compete with one another; rather, they complement each other. As Exhibit 6-6 shows, when a manager sets difficult goals for employees, this leads employees to have a higher level of self-efficacy and also leads them to set higher goals for their own performance. Why is this the case? Research has shown that setting difficult goals for people communicates confidence. For example, imagine that your boss sets a high goal for you, and you learn it is higher than the goals she has set for your coworkers. How would you interpret this? As long as you didn't feel you were being picked on, you would probably think, "Well, I guess my boss thinks I'm capable of performing better than others." This then sets into motion a psychological process in which you're more confident in yourself (higher self-efficacy) and you set higher personal goals, causing you to perform better both in the workplace and outside it.

The researcher who developed self-efficacy theory, Albert Bandura, argues that there are four ways self-efficacy can be increased:[46]

1. Enactive mastery
2. Vicarious modeling
3. Verbal persuasion
4. Arousal

According to Bandura, the most important source of increasing self-efficacy is what he calls *enactive mastery*—that is, gaining relevant experience with the task

self-efficacy *An individual's belief that he or she is capable of performing a task.*

The U.S. Coast Guard illustrates the importance of enactive mastery in increasing self-efficacy. Since the September 11 terrorist attacks, the duties of the Coast Guard have expanded in protecting U.S. ports, ships, and waterways. The Coast Guard men and women shown here participate in a tactical law enforcement training program by playing out a hostage scenario. Practicing and building their skills in boarding ships helps the Coast Guard personnel increase their confidence to succeed at their task.

or job. If you've been able to do the job successfully in the past, then you're more confident you'll be able to do it in the future.

The second source is *vicarious modeling*—or becoming more confident because you see someone else doing the task. For example, if your friend loses weight, then it increases your confidence that you can lose weight, too. Vicarious modeling is most effective when you see yourself as similar to the person you are observing. Watching Tiger Woods play a difficult golf shot might not increase your confidence in being able to play the shot yourself, but if you watch a golfer with a handicap similar to yours, it's persuasive.

The third source is *verbal persuasion,* which is becoming more confident because someone convinces you that you have the skills necessary to be successful. Motivational speakers use this tactic a lot.

Finally, Bandura argues that *arousal* increases self-efficacy. Arousal leads to an energized state, which drives a person to complete a task. The person gets "psyched up" and performs better. But when arousal is not relevant, then arousal hurts performance. In other words, if the task is something that requires a steady, lower-key perspective (say, carefully editing a manuscript), arousal may in fact hurt performance.

What are the OB implications of self-efficacy theory? Well, it's a matter of applying Bandura's sources of self-efficacy to the work setting. Training programs often make use of enactive mastery by having people practice and build their skills. In fact, one of the reasons training works is because it increases self-efficacy.[47]

The best way for a manager to use verbal persuasion is through the *Pygmalion effect* or the *Galatea effect.* As discussed in Chapter 5, the Pygmalion effect is a form of a self-fulfilling prophecy in which believing something to be true can make it true. In the Pygmalion effect, self-efficacy is increased by communicating to an individual's teacher or supervisor that the person is of high ability. For example, studies were done in which teachers were told their students had very high IQ scores (when in fact they had a range of IQs—some high, some low, and some in between). Consistent with a Pygmalion effect, the teachers spent more time with the students they *thought* were smart, gave them more challenging assignments, and expected more of them—all of which led to higher student self-efficacy and better student grades.[48] This also has been used in the workplace.[49] The Galatea effect occurs when high performance expectations are communicated directly to an employee. For example, sailors who were told, in a convincing manner, that they would not get seasick in fact were much less likely to get seasick.[50]

Note that intelligence and personality are absent from Bandura's list. A lot of research shows that intelligence and personality (especially conscientiousness and emotional stability) can increase self-efficacy.[51] Those individual traits are so strongly related to self-efficacy (people who are intelligent, conscientiousness, and emotionally stable are much more likely to have high self-efficacy than those who score low on these characteristics) that some researchers would argue that self-efficacy does not exist.[52] What this means is that self-efficacy may simply be a by-product in a smart person with a confident personality, and the term *self-efficacy* is superfluous and unnecessary. Although Bandura strongly disagrees with this conclusion, more research on the issue is needed.

Reinforcement Theory

A counterpoint to goal-setting theory is **reinforcement theory**. The former is a cognitive approach, proposing that an individual's purposes direct his action.

6 *Demonstrate how organizational justice is a refinement of equity theory.*

Reinforcement theory takes a behavioristic approach, arguing that reinforcement conditions behavior. The two theories are clearly at odds philosophically. Reinforcement theorists see behavior as being environmentally caused. You need not be concerned, they would argue, with internal cognitive events; what controls behavior is reinforcers—any consequences that, when immediately following responses, increase the probability that the behavior will be repeated.

Reinforcement theory ignores the inner state of the individual and concentrates solely on what happens to a person when he or she takes some action. Because it does not concern itself with what initiates behavior, it is not, strictly speaking, a theory of motivation. But it does provide a powerful means of analysis of what controls behavior, and for this reason it is typically considered in discussions of motivation.[53]

We discussed the reinforcement process in detail in Chapter 2. Although it's clear that so-called reinforcers such as pay can motivate people, it's just as clear that for people the process is much more complicated than stimulus–response. In its pure form, reinforcement theory ignores feelings, attitudes, expectations, and other cognitive variables that are known to affect behavior. In fact, some researchers look at the same experiments that reinforcement theorists use to support their position and interpret the findings in a cognitive framework.[54]

Reinforcement is undoubtedly an important influence on behavior, but few scholars are prepared to argue that it is the only influence. The behaviors you engage in at work and the amount of effort you allocate to each task are affected by the consequences that follow from your behavior. For instance, if you're consistently reprimanded for outproducing your colleagues, you'll likely reduce your productivity. But your lower productivity may also be explained in terms of goals, inequity, or expectancies.

reinforcement theory *A theory that says that behavior is a function of its consequences.*

In perceiving inequity in pay, American Airlines flight attendants used an *other–inside* referent comparison when comparing their pay to that of the airline's managers. Flight attendants marched in protest after the company earned a profit of $230 million and decided to give 874 executives more than $200 million in bonuses. But almost 80,000 other employees received no bonuses and continued to receive reduced pay and benefits per an agreement the flight attendants had made 3 years earlier to keep the company from declaring bankruptcy.

Equity Theory

Jane Pearson graduated last year from the State University with a degree in accounting. After interviews with a number of organizations on campus, she accepted a position with a top public accounting firm and was assigned to the firm's Boston office. Jane was very pleased with the offer she received: challenging work with a prestigious firm, an excellent opportunity to gain valuable experience, and the highest salary any accounting major at State was offered last year—$4,550 per month. But Jane was the top student in her class; she was articulate and mature, and she fully expected to receive a commensurate salary.

8 *Apply the key tenets of expectancy theory to motivating employees.*

Twelve months have passed since Jane joined her employer. The work has proved to be as challenging and satisfying as she had hoped. Her employer is extremely pleased with her performance; in fact, Jane recently received a $200-per-month raise. However, Jane's motivational level has dropped dramatically in the past few weeks. Why? Her employer has just hired a fresh college graduate out of State University, who lacks the 1-year experience Jane has gained, for $4,800 per month—$50 more than Jane now makes! Jane is irate. She is even talking about looking for another job.

Jane's situation illustrates the role that equity plays in motivation. Employees make comparisons of their job inputs (for example, effort, experience, education, competence) and outcomes (for example, salary levels, raises, recognition) relative to those of others. We perceive what we get from a job situation (outcomes) in relation to what we put into it (inputs), and then we compare our outcome–input ratio with the outcome–input ratios of relevant others. This is shown in Exhibit 6-7. If we perceive our ratio to be equal to that of the relevant others with whom we compare ourselves, a state of equity is said to exist; we perceive our situation as fair and that justice prevails. When we see the ratio as unequal, we experience equity tension. When we see ourselves as underrewarded, the tension creates anger; when we see ourselves as overrewarded, the tension creates guilt. J. Stacy Adams has proposed that this negative state of tension provides the motivation to do something to correct it.[55]

Exhibit **6-7**	Equity Theory

Ratio Comparisons*	Perception
$\dfrac{O}{I_A} < \dfrac{O}{I_B}$	Inequity due to being underrewarded
$\dfrac{O}{I_A} = \dfrac{O}{I_B}$	Equity
$\dfrac{O}{I_A} > \dfrac{O}{I_B}$	Inequity due to being overrewarded

*Where $\dfrac{O}{I_A}$ represents the employee; and $\dfrac{O}{I_B}$ represents relevant others

The referent that an employee selects adds to the complexity of **equity theory**.[56] There are four referent comparisons that an employee can use:

1. *Self–inside.* An employee's experiences in a different position inside the employee's current organization
2. *Self–outside.* An employee's experiences in a situation or position outside the employee's current organization
3. *Other–inside.* Another individual or group of individuals inside the employee's organization
4. *Other–outside.* Another individual or group of individuals outside the employee's organization

Employees might compare themselves to friends, neighbors, coworkers, or colleagues in other organizations or compare their present job with past jobs they themselves have had. Which referent an employee chooses will be influenced by the information the employee holds about referents as well as by the attractiveness of the referent. This has led to focusing on four moderating variables: gender, length of tenure, level in the organization, and amount of education or professionalism.[57]

Research shows that both men and women prefer same-sex comparisons. The research also demonstrates that women are typically paid less than men in comparable jobs and have lower pay expectations than men for the same work.[58] So a woman who uses another woman as a referent tends to calculate a lower comparative standard. This leads us to conclude that employees in jobs that are not sex segregated will make more cross-sex comparisons than those in jobs that are either male or female dominated. This also suggests that if women are tolerant of lower pay, it may be due to the comparative standard they use. Of course, employers' stereotypes about women (for example, the belief that women are less committed to the organization or that "women's work" is less valuable) also may contribute to the pay gap.[59]

Employees with short tenure in their current organizations tend to have little information about others inside the organization, so they rely on their own personal experiences. However, employees with long tenure rely more heavily on coworkers for comparison. Upper-level employees, those in the professional

---

equity theory *A theory that says that individuals compare their job inputs and outcomes with those of others and then respond to eliminate any inequities.*

ranks, and those with higher amounts of education tend to have better information about people in other organizations. Therefore, these types of employees will make more other–outside comparisons.

Based on equity theory, when employees perceive inequity, they can be predicted to make one of six choices:[60]

1. Change their inputs (for example, exert less effort)
2. Change their outcomes (for example, individuals paid on a piece-rate basis can increase their pay by producing a higher quantity of units of lower quality)
3. Distort perceptions of self (for example, "I used to think I worked at a moderate pace, but now I realize that I work a lot harder than everyone else.")
4. Distort perceptions of others (for example, "Mike's job isn't as desirable as I previously thought it was.")
5. Choose a different referent (for example, "I may not make as much as my brother-in-law, but I'm doing a lot better than my Dad did when he was my age.")
6. Leave the field (for example, quit the job)

The theory establishes the following propositions relating to inequitable pay:

A. *Given payment by time, overrewarded employees will produce more than will equitably paid employees.* Hourly and salaried employees will generate high quantity or quality of production in order to increase the input side of the ratio and bring about equity.
B. *Given payment by quantity of production, overrewarded employees will produce fewer, but higher-quality, units than will equitably paid employees.* Individuals paid on a piece-rate basis will increase their effort to achieve equity, which can result in greater quality or quantity. However, increases in quantity will only increase inequity because every unit produced results in further overpayment. Therefore, effort is directed toward increasing quality rather than increasing quantity.
C. *Given payment by time, underrewarded employees will produce less or poorer quality of output.* Effort will be decreased, which will bring about lower productivity or poorer-quality output than equitably paid subjects.
D. *Given payment by quantity of production, underrewarded employees will produce a large number of low-quality units in comparison with equitably paid employees.* Employees on piece-rate pay plans can bring about equity because trading off quality of output for quantity will result in an increase in rewards, with little or no increase in contributions.

Some of these propositions have been supported, but others haven't.[61] First, inequities created by overpayment do not seem to have a very significant impact on behavior in most work situations. Apparently, people have a great deal more tolerance of overpayment inequities than of underpayment inequities or are better able to rationalize them. It's pretty damaging to a theory when one-half of the equation (how people respond to overreward) falls apart. Second, not all people are equity sensitive.[62] For example, there is a small part of the working population who actually prefer that their outcome–input ratios be less than the referent comparison's. Predictions from equity theory are not likely to be very accurate with these "benevolent types."

It's also important to note that while most research on equity theory has focused on pay, employees seem to look for equity in the distribution of other organizational rewards. For instance, it has been shown that the use of high-status job titles as well as large and lavishly furnished offices may function as outcomes for some employees in their equity equation.[63]

Finally, recent research has been directed at expanding what is meant by *equity*, or *fairness*.[64] Historically, equity theory focused on **distributive justice**, which is the employee's perceived fairness of the *amount and allocation* of rewards among individuals. But increasingly equity is thought of from the standpoint of **organizational justice**, which we define as an overall perception of what is fair in the workplace. Employees perceive their organizations as just when they believe the outcomes they have received and the way in which the outcomes were received are fair. One key element of organizational justice is an individual's *perception* of justice. In other words, under organizational justice, fairness or equity can be subjective, and it resides in the perception of the person. What one person may see as unfair another may see as perfectly appropriate. In general, people have an egocentric, or self-serving, bias. They see allocations or procedure favoring themselves as fair.[65] For example, in a recent poll, 61 percent of respondents said that they are personally paying their fair share of taxes, but an almost equal number (54 percent) of those polled felt the system as a whole is unfair, saying that some people skirt the system.[66] Fairness often resides in the eye of the beholder, and we tend to be fairly self-serving about what we see as fair.

Beyond its focus on perceptions of fairness, the other key element of organizational justice is the view that justice is multidimensional. Organizational justice argues that distributive justice is important. For example, how much we get paid relative to what we think we should be paid (distributive justice) is obviously important. But, according to justice researchers, *how* we get paid is just as important. Exhibit 6-8 shows a model of organizational justice.

Beyond distributive justice, the key addition under organizational justice was **procedural justice**—which is the perceived fairness of the *process* used to determine the distribution of rewards. Two key elements of procedural justice are process control and explanations. *Process control* is the opportunity to present one's point of view about desired outcomes to decision makers. *Explanations* are clear reasons for the outcome that management gives to a person. Thus, for employees to see a process as fair, they need to feel that they have some control over the outcome and feel that they were given an adequate explanation about why the outcome occurred. Also, for procedural fairness, it's important that a manager is *consistent* (across people and over time), is *unbiased*, makes decisions based on *accurate information*, and is *open to appeals*.[67]

Research shows that the effects of procedural justice become more important when distributive justice is lacking. This makes sense. If we don't get what we want, we tend to focus on *why*. For example, if your supervisor gives a cushy office to a coworker instead of to you, you're much more focused on your supervisor's treatment of you than if you had gotten the office. Explanations are beneficial when they take the form of post hoc excuses (for example, admitting that the act is unfavorable but denying sole responsibility for it) rather than justifications (for example, accepting full responsibility but denying that the outcome is unfavorable or inappropriate).[68] In the office example, an excuse would be "I know this is bad. I wanted to give you

---

distributive justice *Perceived fairness of the amount and allocation of rewards among individuals.*

organizational justice *An overall perception of what is fair in the workplace, composed of distributive, procedural, and interactional justice.*

procedural justice *The perceived fairness of the process used to determine the distribution of rewards.*

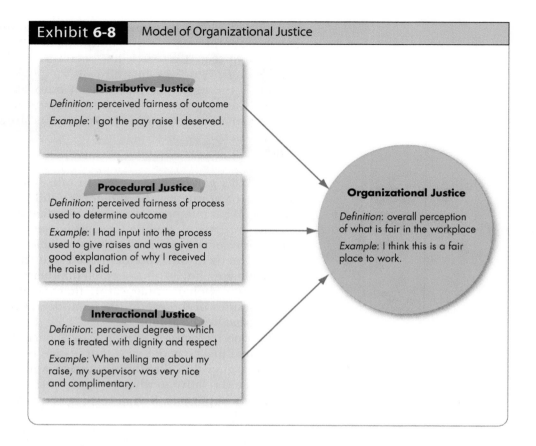

Exhibit 6-8   Model of Organizational Justice

Distributive Justice

Definition: perceived fairness of outcome

Example: I got the pay raise I deserved.

Procedural Justice

Definition: perceived fairness of process used to determine outcome

Example: I had input into the process used to give raises and was given a good explanation of why I received the raise I did.

Interactional Justice

Definition: perceived degree to which one is treated with dignity and respect

Example: When telling me about my raise, my supervisor was very nice and complimentary.

Organizational Justice

Definition: overall perception of what is fair in the workplace

Example: I think this is a fair place to work.

the office, but it was not my decision" and a justification would be "Yes, I decided to give the office to Sam, but having the corner office is not that big of a deal."

A recent addition to research on organizational justice is **interactional justice**, which is an individual's perception of the degree to which she is treated with dignity, concern, and respect. When people are treated in an unjust manner (at least in their own eyes), they respond by retaliating (for example, bad-mouthing a supervisor).[69] Because interactional justice or injustice is intimately tied to the conveyer of the information (usually one's supervisor), whereas procedural injustice often results from impersonal policies, we would expect perceptions of injustice to be more closely related to one's supervisor. Generally, that's what the evidence suggests.[70]

Of these three forms of justice, distributive justice is most strongly related to satisfaction with outcomes (for example, satisfaction with pay) and organizational commitment. Procedural justice relates most strongly to job satisfaction, employee trust, withdrawal from the organization, job performance, and citizenship behaviors. There is less evidence on interactional justice.[71]

Managers can take several steps to foster employees' perceptions of fairness. First, they should realize that employees are especially sensitive to unfairness in procedures when bad news has to be communicated (that is, when distributive justice is low). Thus, when managers have bad news to communicate, it's especially important to openly share information about how allocation decisions are made, follow consistent and unbiased procedures, and engage in similar practices to increase the perception of procedural justice. Second, when addressing perceived injustices, managers need to focus their actions on the source of the problem. For example, in one weekend in June 2007, Northwest Airlines was forced to cancel 352 flights because many pilots and flight attendants called in sick to protest their pay. The pilot's union instructed the pilots: "Fly safe. Fly the contract. Don't fly sick. Don't fly fatigued. Don't fly hungry." In a situation like this, Northwest should realize that the remedy needs to be tangible rather than apologies or changes in procedures.[72]

Expectancy Theory

8 *Compare contemporary theories of motivation.*

Currently, one of the most widely accepted explanations of motivation is Victor Vroom's **expectancy theory**.[73] Although it has its critics, most of the evidence supports the theory.[74]

Expectancy theory argues that the strength of a tendency to act in a certain way depends on the strength of an expectation that the act will be followed by a given outcome and on the attractiveness of that outcome to the individual. In more practical terms, expectancy theory says that employees will be motivated to exert a high level of effort when they believe that effort will lead to a good performance appraisal; that a good appraisal will lead to organizational rewards such as bonuses, salary increases, or promotions; and that the rewards will satisfy the employees' personal goals. The theory, therefore, focuses on three relationships (see Exhibit 6-9):

1. *Effort–performance relationship.* The probability perceived by the individual that exerting a given amount of effort will lead to performance.
2. *Performance–reward relationship.* The degree to which the individual believes that performing at a particular level will lead to the attainment of a desired outcome.
3. *Rewards–personal goals relationship.* The degree to which organizational rewards satisfy an individual's personal goals or needs and the attractiveness of those potential rewards for the individual.[75]

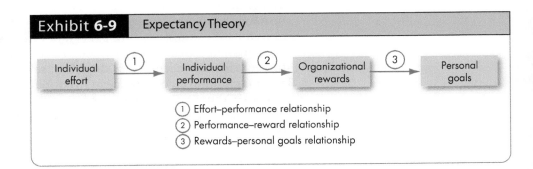

Exhibit **6-9**	Expectancy Theory

Individual effort → (1) → Individual performance → (2) → Organizational rewards → (3) → Personal goals

(1) Effort–performance relationship
(2) Performance–reward relationship
(3) Rewards–personal goals relationship

interactional justice *The perceived degree to which an individual is treated with dignity, concern, and respect.*

expectancy theory *A theory that says that the strength of a tendency to act in a certain way depends on the strength of an expectation that the act will be followed by a given outcome and on the attractiveness of that outcome to the individual.*

Expectancy theory helps explain why a lot of workers aren't motivated on their jobs and do only the minimum necessary to get by. This is evident when we look at the theory's three relationships in a little more detail. We present them as questions employees need to answer in the affirmative if their motivation is to be maximized.

First, *if I give a maximum effort, will it be recognized in my performance appraisal?* For a lot of employees, the answer is "no." Why? Their skill level may be deficient, which means that no matter how hard they try, they're not likely to be high performers. The organization's performance appraisal system may be designed to assess nonperformance factors such as loyalty, initiative, or courage, which means more effort won't necessarily result in a higher evaluation. Another possibility is that employees, rightly or wrongly, perceive that the boss doesn't like them. As a result, they expect to get a poor appraisal, regardless of level of effort. These examples suggest that one possible source of low employee motivation is the belief by employees that, no matter how hard they work, the likelihood of getting a good performance appraisal is low.

Second, *if I get a good performance appraisal, will it lead to organizational rewards?* Many employees see the performance–reward relationship in their job as weak. The reason is that organizations reward a lot of things besides just performance. For example, when pay is allocated to employees based on factors such as seniority, being cooperative, or "kissing up" to the boss, employees are likely to see the performance–reward relationship as being weak and demotivating.

Finally, *if I'm rewarded, are the rewards ones that I find personally attractive?* The employee works hard in the hope of getting a promotion but gets a pay raise instead. Or the employee wants a more interesting and challenging job but receives only a few words of praise. Or the employee puts in extra effort to be relocated to the company's Paris office but instead is transferred to Singapore. These examples illustrate the importance of the rewards being tailored to individual employee needs. Unfortunately, many managers are limited in the rewards they can distribute, which makes it difficult to individualize rewards. Moreover, some managers incorrectly assume that all employees want the same thing, thus overlooking the motivational effects of differentiating rewards. In either case, employee motivation is submaximized.

As a vivid example of how expectancy theory can work, consider the case of stock analysts. Analysts make their living by trying to forecast the future of a stock's price; the accuracy of their buy, sell, or hold recommendations is what keeps them in work or gets them fired. But it's not quite that simple. For example, Mike Mayo, 42, is one of the few Wall Street analysts willing to put sell recommendations on stocks. Why do analysts place so few sell ratings on stocks? After all, in a steady market, by definition, as many stocks are falling as are rising. Expectancy theory provides an explanation: Analysts who place a sell rating on a company's stock have to balance the benefits they receive by being accurate against the risks they run by drawing the company's ire. What are these risks? They include public rebuke, professional blackballing, and exclusion from information. As Mayo said, "There is no recourse for analysts." When analysts place a buy rating on a stock, they face no such trade-off because, obviously, companies love that they are recommending that investors buy their stock. So, the incentive structure suggests that the expected outcome of buy ratings is higher than the expected outcome of sell ratings, and that's why buy ratings vastly outnumber sell ratings.[76]

Does expectancy theory work? Attempts to validate the theory have been complicated by methodological, criterion, and measurement problems. As a result, many published studies that purport to support or negate the theory must be viewed with caution. Importantly, most studies have failed to replicate the methodology as it was originally proposed. For example, the theory proposes to explain different levels of effort from the same person under different circumstances, but almost all replication studies have looked at different people. Correcting for this flaw has greatly improved support for the validity of expectancy theory.[77] Some critics suggest that the theory has only limited use, arguing that it tends to be more valid for predicting in situations in which effort–performance and performance–reward linkages are clearly perceived by the individual.[78] Because few individuals perceive a high correlation between performance and rewards in their jobs, the theory tends to be idealistic. If organizations actually rewarded individuals for performance rather than according to criteria such as seniority, effort, skill level, and job difficulty, then the theory's validity might be considerably greater. However, rather than invalidating expectancy theory, this criticism can be used in support of the theory because it explains why a significant segment of the workforce exerts low levels of effort in carrying out job responsibilities.

Integrating Contemporary Theories of Motivation

9 *Explain to what degree motivation theories are culture bound.*

We've looked at a lot of motivation theories in this chapter. The fact that a number of these theories have been supported only complicates the matter. It would be simpler if, after presenting half a dozen theories, only one was found valid. But the theories we presented are not all in competition with one another. Because one is valid doesn't automatically make the others invalid. In fact, many of the theories presented in this chapter are complementary. The challenge is now to tie these theories together to help you understand their interrelationships.[79]

Exhibit 6-10 presents a model that integrates much of what we know about motivation. Its basic foundation is the expectancy model shown in Exhibit 6-9. Let's work through Exhibit 6-10. (We will look at job design closely in Chapter 7.)

We begin by explicitly recognizing that opportunities can either aid or hinder individual effort. The individual effort box also has another arrow leading into it. This arrow flows out of the person's goals. Consistent with goal-setting theory, this goals–effort loop is meant to remind us that goals direct behavior.

Expectancy theory predicts that employees will exert a high level of effort if they perceive that there is a strong relationship between effort and performance, performance and rewards, and rewards and satisfaction of personal goals. Each of these relationships, in turn, is influenced by certain factors. For effort to lead to good performance, the individual must have the requisite ability to perform, and the performance appraisal system that measures the individual's performance must be perceived as being fair and objective. The performance–reward relationship will be strong if the individual perceives that it is performance (rather than seniority, personal favorites, or other criteria) that is rewarded. If cognitive evaluation theory were fully valid in the actual

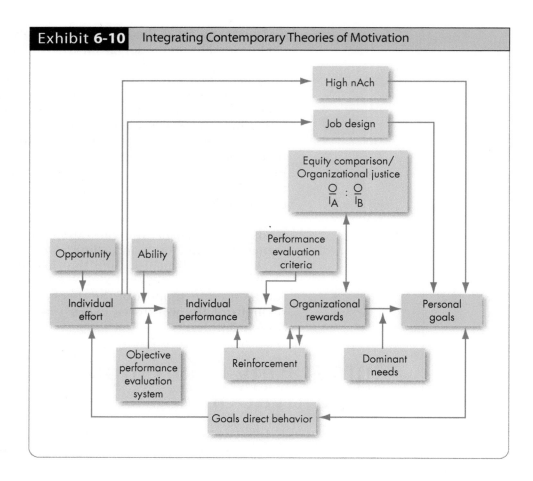

Exhibit 6-10 Integrating Contemporary Theories of Motivation

workplace, we would predict here that basing rewards on performance should decrease the individual's intrinsic motivation. The final link in expectancy theory is the rewards–goals relationship. Motivation would be high to the degree that the rewards an individual received for high performance satisfied the dominant needs consistent with individual goals.

A closer look at Exhibit 6-10 also reveals that the model considers achievement motivation, job design, reinforcement, and equity theories/organizational justice. A high achiever is not motivated by an organization's assessment of performance or organizational rewards, hence the jump from effort to personal goals for those with a high nAch. Remember, high achievers are internally driven as long as the jobs they are doing provide them with personal responsibility, feedback, and moderate risks. They are not concerned with the effort–performance, performance–rewards, or rewards–goal linkages.

Reinforcement theory enters the model by recognizing that the organization's rewards reinforce the individual's performance. If management has designed a reward system that is seen by employees as "paying off" for good performance, the rewards will reinforce and encourage continued good performance. Rewards also play the key part in organizational justice research. Individuals will judge the favorability of their outcomes (for example, their pay) relative to what others receive but also with respect to how they are treated: When people are disappointed in their rewards, they are likely to be sensitive to the perceived fairness of the procedures used and the consideration given to them by their supervisor.

Global Implications

In our discussion of goal-setting theory, we said that care needs to be taken in applying this theory because it assumes cultural characteristics that are not universal. This is true for many of the theories presented in this chapter because most current motivation theories were developed in the United States by and about U.S. adults.[80] For instance, both goal-setting and expectancy theories emphasize goal accomplishment as well as rational and individual thought—characteristics consistent with U.S. culture. Let's take a look at several motivation theories and consider their cross-cultural transferability.

Maslow's needs hierarchy argues that people start at the physiological level and then move progressively up the hierarchy in this order: physiological, safety, social, esteem, and self-actualization. This hierarchy, if it has any application at all, aligns with U.S. culture. In countries such as Japan, Greece, and Mexico, where uncertainty-avoidance characteristics are strong, security needs would be on top of the need hierarchy. Countries that score high on nurturing characteristics—such as Denmark, Sweden, Norway, the Netherlands, and Finland—would have social needs on top.[81] We would predict, for instance, that group work will motivate employees more when the country's culture scores high on the nurturing criterion.

Another motivation concept that clearly has a U.S. bias is the achievement need. The view that a high achievement need acts as an internal motivator presupposes two cultural characteristics—a willingness to accept a moderate degree of risk (which excludes countries with strong uncertainty avoidance characteristics) and a concern with performance (which applies almost singularly to countries with strong achievement characteristics). This combination is found in Anglo-American countries such as the United States, Canada, and Great Britain.[82] However, these characteristics are relatively absent in countries such as Chile and Portugal.

U.S. firms expanding their operations in China are learning that motivation concepts that succeed in the United States don't always apply to Chinese employees. For example, compensation for salespeople in China is based on seniority, not on performance. And most Chinese firms do not offer any nonmonetary motivation such as employee recognition programs. For the Chinese salesperson shown here assisting a customer interested in GM's Cadillac CTS, motivation may come from satisfying her economic and achievement needs.

Equity theory has gained a relatively strong following in the United States. That's not surprising because U.S.-style reward systems are based on the assumption that workers are highly sensitive to equity in reward allocations. And in the United States equity is meant to closely tie pay to performance. However, evidence suggests that in collectivist cultures, especially in the former socialist countries of central and eastern Europe, employees expect rewards to reflect their individual needs as well as their performance.[83] Moreover, consistent with a legacy of communism and centrally planned economies, employees exhibited an entitlement attitude—that is, they expected outcomes to be *greater* than their inputs.[84] These findings suggest that U.S.-style pay practices may need modification, especially in Russia and former communist countries, in order to be perceived as fair by employees.

But don't assume there are *no* cross-cultural consistencies. For instance, the desire for interesting work seems important to almost all workers, regardless of their national culture. In a study of seven countries, employees in Belgium, Britain, Israel, and the United States ranked "interesting work" number one among 11 work goals. And workers in Japan, the Netherlands, and Germany ranked this factor either second or third.[85] Similarly, in a study comparing job-preference outcomes among graduate students in the United States, Canada, Australia, and Singapore, growth, achievement, and responsibility were rated the top three and had identical rankings.[86] Both of these studies suggest some universality to the importance of intrinsic factors in the two-factor theory.

Summary and Implications for Managers

The theories we've discussed in this chapter address different outcome variables. Some, for instance, are directed at explaining turnover, while others emphasize productivity. The theories also differ in their predictive strength. In this section, we (1) review the most established motivation theories to determine their relevance in explaining the dependent variables, and (2) assess the predictive power of each.[87]

Need Theories   We introduced four theories that focused on needs: Maslow's hierarchy, ERG, McClelland's needs, and the two-factor theory. None of these theories has found widespread support, although the strongest of them is probably McClelland's theory, particularly regarding the relationship between achievement and productivity. In general, need theories (Maslow and ERG) are not very valid explanations of motivation.

Goal-Setting Theory   There is little dispute that clear and difficult goals lead to higher levels of employee productivity. This evidence leads us to conclude that goal-setting theory provides one of the most powerful explanations of this dependent variable. The theory, however, does not address absenteeism, turnover, or satisfaction.

Reinforcement Theory   This theory has an impressive record for predicting factors such as quality and quantity of work, persistence of effort, absenteeism, tardiness, and accident rates. It does not offer much insight into employee satisfaction or the decision to quit.

Equity Theory/Organizational Justice   Equity theory deals with productivity, satisfaction, absence, and turnover variables. However, its strongest legacy probably is that it provided the spark for research on organizational justice, which has more support in the literature.

Expectancy Theory   Our final theory, expectancy theory, focuses on performance variables. It has proved to offer a relatively powerful explanation of employee productivity, absenteeism, and turnover. But expectancy theory assumes that employees have few constraints on their decision discretion. It makes many of the same assumptions that the rational model makes about individual decision making (see Chapter 5), and this limits its applicability. Expectancy theory has some validity because for many behaviors people consider expected outcomes. However, the rational model goes only so far in explaining behavior.

Point ⟫⟪ Counterpoint

FAILURE MOTIVATES!

*i*t's sad but true that many of the best lessons we learn in life are from our failures. Often when we're riding on the wings of success, we coast—until we crash to earth.

Take the example of Dan Doctoroff. Doctoroff is a successful New York investment banker who spent 5 years obsessed with bringing the 2012 Olympics to New York. In his efforts, he used $4 million of his own money, traveled half a million miles, worked 100-hour weeks, and staked his reputation on achieving a goal many thought was foolhardy.

What happened? New York wasn't selected, and all Doctoroff's efforts were in vain. His immediate reaction? He felt "emotionally paralyzed." But Doctoroff is not sorry he made the effort. He said he learned a lot about himself in trying to woo Olympic decision makers in 78 countries. Colleagues had once described him as brash and arrogant. As a result of his efforts, Doctoroff said, he learned to listen more and talk less. He also said that losing made him realize how supportive his wife and three teenage children could be.

Not only does failure bring perspective to people such as Doctoroff, it often provides important feedback on how to improve. The important thing is to learn from the failure and to persist. As Doctoroff says, "The only way to ensure you'll lose is not to try."

One of the reasons successful people fail so often is that they set their own bars so high. Harvard's Rosabeth Moss Kanter, who has spent her career studying executives, says, "Many successful people set the bar so high that they don't achieve the distant goal. But they do achieve things that wouldn't have been possible without that bigger goal."[88]

*d*o people learn from failure? We've seen that one of the decision-making errors people make is escalation of commitment: They persist in a failed venture just because they think persistence is a virtue or because their ego is involved, even when logic suggests they should move on. One research study found that managers often illogically persist in launching new products, even when the evidence becomes clear that the product is going nowhere. As the authors note, "It sometimes takes more courage to kill a product that's going nowhere than to sustain it." So, the thought of learning from failure is a nice ideal, but most people are too defensive to do that.

Moreover, there is ample evidence that when people fail they often rationalize their failures to preserve their self-esteem and thus don't learn at all. Although the example of Dan Doctoroff is interesting, it's not clear he's done anything but rationalize his failure. It's human nature. Research shows that when we fail, we often engage in external attributions—blaming the failure on bad luck or powerful others—or we devalue what we failed to get ("It wasn't that important to me anyway," we may tell ourselves). These rationalizations may not be correct, but that's not the point. We engage in them not to be right but to preserve our often fragile self-esteem. We need to believe in ourselves to motivate ourselves, and because failing undermines that self-belief, we have to do what we can to recover our self-confidence.[89]

In sum, although it is a nice story that failure is actually good, as one songwriter wrote, "the world is not a song." Failure hurts, and to either protect ourselves or recover from the pain, we often do *not* learn from failure—we rationalize it away.

Questions for Review

1. Define *motivation.* What are the key elements of motivation?

2. What are the early theories of motivation? How well have they been supported by research?

3. What is cognitive evaluation theory? What does it assume about the effects of intrinsic and extrinsic rewards on behavior?

4. What are the major predictions of goal-setting theory? Have these predictions been supported by research?

5. What is reinforcement theory? How is it related to goal-setting theory? Has research supported reinforcement theory?

6. What is equity theory? Why has it been supplanted by organizational justice?

7. What are the key tenets of expectancy theory? What has research had to say about this theory?

8. How do the contemporary theories of work motivation complement one another?

9. Do you think motivation theories are often culture bound? Why or why not?

Experiential Exercise

GOAL-SETTING TASK

Purpose
This exercise will help you learn how to write tangible, verifiable, measurable, and relevant goals that might evolve from an MBO program.

Time
Approximately 20 to 30 minutes.

Instructions

1. Break into groups of three to five.

2. Spend a few minutes discussing your class instructor's job. What does he or she do? What defines good performance? What behaviors lead to good performance?

3. Each group is to develop a list of five goals that, although not established participatively with your instructor, you believe might be developed in an MBO program at your college. Try to select goals that seem most critical to the effective performance of your instructor's job.

4. Each group will select a leader who will share the group's goals with the entire class. For each group's goals, class discussion should focus on the goals' (a) specificity, (b) ease of measurement, (c) importance, and (d) motivational properties.

Ethical Dilemma

IS GOAL-SETTING MANIPULATION?

Managers are interested in the subject of motivation because they're concerned with learning how to get the most effort from their employees. Is this ethical? For example, when managers set hard, specific goals for employees, aren't they manipulating them?

Manipulate is defined as "(1) to handle, manage, or use, especially with skill, in some process of treatment or performance; (2) to manage or influence by artful skill; (3) to adapt or change to suit one's purpose or advantage."

Aren't these definitions compatible with the notion of managers skillfully seeking to influence employee productivity for the benefit of the manager and the organization?

Do managers have the right to seek control over their employees? Does anyone, for that matter, have the right to control others? Does control imply manipulation? And if so, is there anything wrong with managers manipulating employees through goal setting or other motivational techniques?

Case Incident 1

DO U.S. WORKERS "LIVE TO WORK"?

Many people around the world believe that U.S. adults live only to work. Do we really work that much harder than people in other countries? To answer this question, we turn to data collected by OECD, an organization that does research on economic development issues. The following figures represent the average hours worked per week (total number of hours an average employee works per year, divided by 52), averaged over the more recent 5 years available, for countries that are members of the OECD:

1.	South Korea	46.7
2.	Greece	39.9
3.	Hungary	38.6
4.	Czech Republic	38.2
5.	Poland	38.1
6.	Mexico	36.0
7.	Italy	35.2
8.	Iceland	34.9
9.	New Zealand	34.9
10.	Japan	34.5
11.	Canada	33.6
12.	Slovak Republic	33.5
13.	Australia	33.4
14.	Finland	33.2
15.	United States	33.0
16.	Spain	32.7
17.	Portugal	32.5
18.	United Kingdom	32.4
19.	Ireland	31.8
20.	Switzerland	31.7
21.	Austria	31.6
22.	Luxembourg	30.5
23.	Sweden	30.4
24.	Denmark	29.8
25.	France	29.8
26.	Belgium	29.6
27.	Germany	27.8
28.	Netherlands	26.1
29.	Norway	26.0

Questions

1. Do these results surprise you? Why or why not?

2. Why do you think U.S. employees have a reputation for "living to work"?

3. Do these results prove that Koreans, for example, are more motivated to work than their U.S. counterparts? Why or why not?

4. A research study has suggested that changes in hours worked over time are due, in part, to changes in tax rates. "If taxes and [government expenditures] are high, that may lead to less work," said one of the researchers. Supporting this theory, since 2001, workers in the United States have increased their hours worked while tax rates have dropped. What theory or theories of motivation might support such a change?

Sources: L. Ohanian, A. Raffo, and R. Rogerson, *Long-Term Changes in Labor Supply and Taxes: Evidence from OECD Countries, 1956–2004,* NBER working paper 12786, December 2006; and J. J. Smith, "Taxes Likely Causing Some Countries' Workers to Labor Fewer Hours," *SHRM Online,* May 2007, www.shrm.org.

Case Incident 2

BULLYING BOSSES

"It got to where I was twitching, literally, on the way into work," states Carrie Clark, a 52-year-old retired teacher and administrator. After enduring 10 months of repeated insults and mistreatment from her supervisor, she finally quit her job. "I had to take care of my health."

Although many individuals recall bullies from their elementary school days, some are realizing that bullies can exist in the workplace as well. And these bullies do not just pick on the weakest in the group; rather, any subordinate in their path may fall prey to their torment, according to Dr. Gary Namie, director of the Workplace Bullying and Trauma Institute. Dr. Namie further says

workplace bullies are not limited to men—women are at least as likely to be bullies. However, gender discrepancies are found in victims of bullying, as women are more likely to be targets.

What motivates a boss to be a bully? Dr. Harvey Hornstein, a retired professor from Teachers College at Columbia University, suggests that supervisors may use bullying as a means to subdue a subordinate who poses a threat to the supervisor's status. In addition, supervisors may bully individuals to vent frustrations. Many times, however, the sheer desire to wield power may be the primary reason for bullying.

What is the impact of bullying on employee motivation and behavior? Surprisingly, even though victims of workplace bullies may feel less motivated to go to work every day, it does not appear that they discontinue performing their required job duties. However, it does appear that victims of bullies are less motivated to perform extra-role or citizenship behaviors. Helping others, speaking positively about the organization, and going beyond the call of duty are behaviors that are reduced as a result of bullying. According to Dr. Bennett Tepper of the University of North Carolina, fear may be the reason that many workers continue to perform their job duties. And not all individuals reduce their citizenship behaviors. Some continue to engage in extra-role behaviors to make themselves look better than their colleagues.

What should you do if your boss is bullying you? Don't necessarily expect help from coworkers. As Emelise Aleandri, an actress and a producer from New York who left her job after being bullied, stated, "Some people were afraid to do anything. But others didn't mind what was happening at all, because they wanted my job." Moreover, according to Dr. Michelle Duffy of the University of Kentucky, coworkers often blame victims of bullying in order to resolve their guilt. "They do this by wondering whether maybe the person deserved the treatment, that he or she has been annoying, or lazy, they did something to earn it," states Dr. Duffy. One example of an employee who observed this phenomenon firsthand is Sherry Hamby, who was frequently verbally abused by her boss and then eventually fired. She stated, "This was a man who insulted me, who insulted my family, who would lay into me while everyone else in the office just sat there and let it happen. The people in my office eventually started blaming me."

What can a bullied employee do? Dr. Hornstein suggests that employees try to ignore the insults and respond only to the substance of the bully's gripe. "Stick with the substance, not the process, and often it won't escalate," he states. Of course, that is easier said than done.

Questions

1. Of the three types of organizational justice, which one does workplace bullying most closely resemble?

2. What aspects of motivation might workplace bullying reduce? For example, are there likely to be effects on an employee's self-efficacy? If so, what might those effects be?

3. If you were a victim of workplace bullying, what steps would you take to try to reduce its occurrence? What strategies would be most effective? What strategies might be ineffective? What would you do if one of your colleagues were a victim of an abusive supervisor?

4. What factors do you believe contribute to workplace bullying? Are bullies a product of the situation, or do they have flawed personalities? What situations and what personality factors might contribute to the presence of bullies?

Source: Based on C. Benedict, "The Bullying Boss," *New York Times,* June 22, 2004, p. F1.

Endnotes

1. J. L. Yang, "'Happyness' for Sale," *Fortune,* September 18, 2006, pp. 56–58.

2. C. A. O'Reilly III, "Organizational Behavior: Where We've Been, Where We're Going," in M. R. Rosenzweig and L. W. Porter (eds.), *Annual Review of Psychology,* vol. 42 (Palo Alto, CA: Annual Reviews, 1991), p. 431. See also M. L. Ambrose and C. T. Kulik, "Old Friends, New Faces: Motivation Research in the 1990s," *Journal of Management* 25, no. 3 (1999), pp. 231–292.

3. Cited in D. Jones, "Firms Spend Billions to Fire Up Workers—With Little Luck," *USA Today,* May 10, 2001, p. 1A.

4. "Wasted Time at Work Costs Employers Billions," *IPMA-HR Bulletin,* August 11, 2006, pp. 1–7.

5. See, for instance, T. R. Mitchell, "Matching Motivational Strategies with Organizational Contexts," in L. L. Cummings and B. M. Staw (eds.), *Research in Organizational Behavior,* vol. 19 (Greenwich, CT: JAI Press, 1997), pp. 60–62.

6. A. Maslow, *Motivation and Personality* (New York: Harper & Row, 1954).

7. See, for example, E. E. Lawler III and J. L. Suttle, "A Causal Correlation Test of the Need Hierarchy Concept," *Organizational Behavior and Human Performance,* April 1972, pp. 265–287; D. T. Hall and K. E. Nougaim, "An Examination of Maslow's Need Hierarchy in an Organizational Setting," *Organizational Behavior and Human Performance,* February 1968, pp. 12–35; A. K. Korman, J. H. Greenhaus, and I. J. Badin, "Personnel Attitudes and Motivation," in M. R. Rosenzweig and L. W. Porter (eds.), *Annual Review of Psychology* (Palo Alto, CA: Annual Reviews, 1977), pp. 178–179; and J. Rauschenberger, N. Schmitt, and J. E. Hunter, "A Test of the Need Hierarchy Concept by a Markov Model of Change in Need Strength," *Administrative Science Quarterly,* December 1980, pp. 654–670.

8. C. P. Alderfer, "An Empirical Test of a New Theory of Human Needs," *Organizational Behavior and Human Performance,* May 1969, pp. 142–175.

9. C. P. Schneider and C. P. Alderfer, "Three Studies of Measures of Need Satisfaction in Organizations," *Administrative Science Quarterly,* December 1973, pp. 489–505; and I. Borg and M. Braun, "Work Values in East and West Germany: Different Weights, but Identical Structures," *Journal of Organizational Behavior* 17, special issue (1996), pp. 541–555.

10. M. A. Wahba and L. G. Bridwell, "Maslow Reconsidered: A Review of Research on the Need Hierarchy Theory," *Organizational Behavior and Human Performance*, April 1976, pp. 212–240.

11. D. McGregor, *The Human Side of Enterprise* (New York: McGraw-Hill, 1960). For an updated analysis of Theory X and Theory Y constructs, see R. J. Summers and S. F. Cronshaw, "A Study of McGregor's Theory X, Theory Y and the Influence of Theory X, Theory Y Assumptions on Causal Attributions for Instances of Worker Poor Performance," in S. L. McShane (ed.), Organizational Behavior, *ASAC 1988 Conference Proceedings*, vol. 9, Part 5. Halifax, Nova Scotia, 1988, pp. 115–123.

12. A. E. Abele, "The Dynamics of Masculine-Agentic and Feminine-Communal Traits: Findings from a Prospective Study," *Journal of Personality and Social Psychology*, October 2003, pp. 768–776; and R. Ely, G. Melzi, and L. Hadge, "Being Brave, Being Nice: Themes of Agency and Communion in Children's Narratives," *Journal of Personality*, April 1998, pp. 257–284.

13. F. Herzberg, B. Mausner, and B. Snyderman, *The Motivation to Work* (New York: Wiley, 1959).

14. R. J. House and L. A. Wigdor, "Herzberg's Dual-Factor Theory of Job Satisfaction and Motivations: A Review of the Evidence and Criticism," *Personnel Psychology*, Winter 1967, pp. 369–389; D. P. Schwab and L. L. Cummings, "Theories of Performance and Satisfaction: A Review," *Industrial Relations*, October 1970, pp. 403–430; and J. Phillipchuk and J. Whittaker, "An Inquiry into the Continuing Relevance of Herzberg's Motivation Theory," *Engineering Management Journal* 8 (1996), pp. 15–20.

15. D. C. McClelland, *The Achieving Society* (New York: Van Nostrand Reinhold, 1961); J. W. Atkinson and J. O. Raynor, *Motivation and Achievement* (Washington, DC: Winston, 1974); D. C. McClelland, *Power: The Inner Experience* (New York: Irvington, 1975); and M. J. Stahl, *Managerial and Technical Motivation: Assessing Needs for Achievement, Power, and Affiliation* (New York: Praeger, 1986).

16. D. C. McClelland and D. G. Winter, *Motivating Economic Achievement* (New York: The Free Press, 1969); and J. B. Miner, N. R. Smith, and J. S. Bracker, "Role of Entrepreneurial Task Motivation in the Growth of Technologically Innovative Firms: Interpretations from Follow-up Data," *Journal of Applied Psychology*, October 1994, pp. 627–630.

17. D. C. McClelland, *Power*; D. C. McClelland and D. H. Burnham, "Power Is the Great Motivator," *Harvard Business Review*, March–April 1976, pp. 100–110; and R. E. Boyatzis, "The Need for Close Relationships and the Manager's Job," in D. A. Kolb, I. M. Rubin, and J. M. McIntyre, *Organizational Psychology: Readings on Human Behavior in Organizations*, 4th ed. (Upper Saddle River, NJ: Prentice Hall, 1984), pp. 81–86.

18. D. G. Winter, "The Motivational Dimensions of Leadership: Power, Achievement, and Affiliation," in R. E. Riggio, S. E. Murphy, and F. J. Pirozzolo (eds.), *Multiple Intelligences and Leadership* (Mahwah, NJ: Lawrence Erlbaum, 2002), pp. 119–138.

19. J. B. Miner, *Studies in Management Education* (New York: Springer, 1965).

20. R. de Charms, *Personal Causation: The Internal Affective Determinants of Behavior* (New York: Academic Press, 1968).

21. E. L. Deci, *Intrinsic Motivation* (New York: Plenum, 1975); J. Cameron and W. D. Pierce, "Reinforcement, Reward, and Intrinsic Motivation: A Meta-analysis," *Review of Educational Research*, Fall 1994, pp. 363–423; S. Tang and V. C. Hall, "The Overjustification Effect: A Meta-analysis," *Applied Cognitive Psychology*, October 1995, pp. 365–404; E. L. Deci, R. Koestner, and R. M. Ryan, "A Meta-analytic Review of Experiments Examining the Effects of Extrinsic Rewards on Intrinsic Motivation," *Psychological Bulletin* 125, no. 6 (1999), pp. 627–668; R. M. Ryan and E. L. Deci, "Intrinsic and Extrinsic Motivations: Classic Definitions and New Directions," *Contemporary Educational Psychology*, January 2000, pp. 54–67; and N. Houlfort, R. Koestner, M. Joussemet, A. Nantel-Vivier, and N. Lekes, "The Impact of Performance-Contingent Rewards on Perceived Autonomy and Competence," *Motivation & Emotion* 26, no. 4 (2002), pp. 279–295.

22. W. E. Scott, "The Effects of Extrinsic Rewards on 'Intrinsic Motivation': A Critique," *Organizational Behavior and Human Performance*, February 1976, pp. 117–119; B. J. Calder and B. M. Staw, "Interaction of Intrinsic and Extrinsic Motivation: Some Methodological Notes," *Journal of Personality and Social Psychology*, January 1975, pp. 76–80; and K. B. Boal and L. L. Cummings, "Cognitive Evaluation Theory: An Experimental Test of Processes and Outcomes," *Organizational Behavior and Human Performance*, December 1981, pp. 289–310.

23. G. R. Salancik, "Interaction Effects of Performance and Money on Self-Perception of Intrinsic Motivation," *Organizational Behavior and Human Performance*, June 1975, pp. 339–351; and F. Luthans, M. Martinko, and T. Kess, "An Analysis of the Impact of Contingency Monetary Rewards on Intrinsic Motivation," *Proceedings of the Nineteenth Annual Midwest Academy of Management*, St. Louis, 1976, pp. 209–221.

24. Deci, Koestner, and Ryan, "A Meta-analytic Review of Experiments Examining the Effects of Extrinsic Rewards on Intrinsic Motivation," pp. 627–668.

25. K. M. Sheldon, A. J. Elliot, and R. M. Ryan, "Self-Concordance and Subjective Well-being in Four Cultures," *Journal of Cross-Cultural Psychology* 35, no. 2 (2004), pp. 209–223.

26. J. E. Bono and T. A. Judge, "Self-Concordance at Work: Toward Understanding the Motivational Effects of Transformational Leaders," *Academy of Management Journal* 46, no. 5 (2003), pp. 554–571.

27. J. P. Meyer, T. E. Becker, and C. Vandenberghe, "Employee Commitment and Motivation: A Conceptual Analysis and Integrative Model," *Journal of Applied Psychology* 89, no. 6 (2004), pp. 991–1007.

28. E. A. Locke, "Toward a Theory of Task Motivation and Incentives," *Organizational Behavior and Human Performance*, May 1968, pp. 157–189.

29. P. C. Earley, P. Wojnaroski, and W. Prest, "Task Planning and Energy Expended: Exploration of How Goals Influence Performance," *Journal of Applied Psychology*, February 1987, pp. 107–114.

30. See M. E. Tubbs "Goal Setting: A Meta-analytic Examination of the Empirical Evidence," *Journal of Applied Psychology*, August 1986, pp. 474–483; E. A. Locke and G. P. Latham, "Building a Practically Useful Theory of Goal Setting and Task Motivation," *American Psychologist*, September 2002, pp. 705–717; and E. A. Locke and G. P. Latham, "New

Directions in Goal-Setting Theory," *Current Directions in Psychological Science* 15, no. 5 (2006), pp. 265–268.

31. E. A. Locke and G. P. Latham, "Building a Practically Useful Theory of Goal Setting and Task Motivation: A 35-Year Odyssey," *American Psychologist* 57, no. 9 (2002), pp. 705–717.

32. J. M. Ivancevich and J. T. McMahon, "The Effects of Goal Setting, External Feedback, and Self-Generated Feedback on Outcome Variables: A Field Experiment," *Academy of Management Journal*, June 1982, pp. 359–372; and E. A. Locke, "Motivation through Conscious Goal Setting," *Applied and Preventive Psychology* 5 (1996), pp. 117–124.

33. See, for example, G. P. Latham, M. Erez, and E. A. Locke, "Resolving Scientific Disputes by the Joint Design of Crucial Experiments by the Antagonists: Application to the Erez-Latham Dispute Regarding Participation in Goal Setting," *Journal of Applied Psychology*, November 1988, pp. 753–772; T. D. Ludwig and E. S. Geller, "Assigned Versus Participative Goal Setting and Response Generalization: Managing Injury Control among Professional Pizza Deliverers," *Journal of Applied Psychology*, April 1997, pp. 253–261; and S. G. Harkins and M. D. Lowe, "The Effects of Self-Set Goals on Task Performance," *Journal of Applied Social Psychology*, January 2000, pp. 1–40.

34. M. Erez, P. C. Earley, and C. L. Hulin, "The Impact of Participation on Goal Acceptance and Performance: A Two-Step Model," *Academy of Management Journal*, March 1985, pp. 50–66.

35. E. A. Locke, "The Motivation to Work: What We Know," *Advances in Motivation and Achievement* 10 (1997), pp. 375–412; and Latham, Erez, and Locke, "Resolving Scientific Disputes by the Joint Design of Crucial Experiments by the Antagonists," pp. 753–772.

36. H. J. Klein, M. J. Wesson, J. R. Hollenbeck, P. M. Wright, and R. D. DeShon, "The Assessment of Goal Commitment: A Measurement Model Meta-analysis," *Organizational Behavior and Human Decision Processes* 85, no. 1 (2001), pp. 32–55.

37. J. R. Hollenbeck, C. R. Williams, and H. J. Klein, "An Empirical Examination of the Antecedents of Commitment to Difficult Goals," *Journal of Applied Psychology*, February 1989, pp. 18–23. See also J. C. Wofford, V. L. Goodwin, and S. Premack, "Meta-analysis of the Antecedents of Personal Goal Level and of the Antecedents and Consequences of Goal Commitment," *Journal of Management*, September 1992, pp. 595–615; M. E. Tubbs, "Commitment as a Moderator of the Goal-Performance Relation: A Case for Clearer Construct Definition," *Journal of Applied Psychology*, February 1993, pp. 86–97; and J. E. Bono and A. E. Colbert, "Understanding Responses to Multi-Source Feedback: The Role of Core Self-evaluations," *Personnel Psychology*, Spring 2005, pp. 171–203.

38. See R. E. Wood, A. J. Mento, and E. A. Locke, "Task Complexity as a Moderator of Goal Effects: A Meta-analysis," *Journal of Applied Psychology*, August 1987, pp. 416–425; R. Kanfer and P. L. Ackerman, "Motivation and Cognitive Abilities: An Integrative/Aptitude-Treatment Interaction Approach to Skill Acquisition," *Journal of Applied Psychology* (monograph), vol. 74, 1989, pp. 657–690; T. R. Mitchell and W. S. Silver, "Individual and Group Goals When Workers Are Interdependent: Effects on Task Strategies and Performance," *Journal of Applied Psychology*, April 1990, pp. 185–193; and A. M. O'Leary-Kelly, J. J. Martocchio, and D. D. Frink, "A Review of

the Influence of Group Goals on Group Performance," *Academy of Management Journal*, October 1994, pp. 1285–1301.

39. "KEYGroup Survey Finds Nearly Half of All Employees Have No Set Performance Goals," *IPMA-HR Bulletin*, March 10, 2006, p. 1; S. Hamm, "SAP Dangles a Big, Fat Carrot," *BusinessWeek*, May 22, 2006, pp. 67–68; and "P&G CEO Wields High Expectations but No Whip," *USA Today*, February 19, 2007, p. 3B.

40. See, for instance, S. J. Carroll and H. L. Tosi, *Management by Objectives: Applications and Research* (New York: Macmillan, 1973); and R. Rodgers and J. E. Hunter, "Impact of Management by Objectives on Organizational Productivity," *Journal of Applied Psychology*, April 1991, pp. 322–336.

41. See, for instance, R. C. Ford, F. S. MacLaughlin, and J. Nixdorf, "Ten Questions About MBO," *California Management Review*, Winter 1980, p. 89; T. J. Collamore, "Making MBO Work in the Public Sector," *Bureaucrat*, Fall 1989, pp. 37–40; G. Dabbs, "Nonprofit Businesses in the 1990s: Models for Success," *Business Horizons*, September–October 1991, pp. 68–71; R. Rodgers and J. E. Hunter, "A Foundation of Good Management Practice in Government: Management by Objectives," *Public Administration Review*, January–February 1992, pp. 27–39; T. H. Poister and G. Streib, "MBO in Municipal Government: Variations on a Traditional Management Tool," *Public Administration Review*, January/February 1995, pp. 48–56; and C. Garvey, "Goalsharing Scores," *HRMagazine*, April 2000, pp. 99–106.

42. See, for instance, C. H. Ford, "MBO: An Idea Whose Time Has Gone?" *Business Horizons*, December 1979, p. 49; R. Rodgers and J. E. Hunter, "Impact of Management by Objectives on Organizational Productivity," *Journal of Applied Psychology*, April 1991, pp. 322–336; R. Rodgers, J. E. Hunter, and D. L. Rogers, "Influence of Top Management Commitment on Management Program Success," *Journal of Applied Psychology*, February 1993, pp. 151–155; and M. Tanikawa, "Fujitsu Decides to Backtrack on Performance-Based Pay," *New York Times*, March 22, 2001, p. W1.

43. A. Bandura, *Self-Efficacy: The Exercise of Control* (New York: Freeman, 1997).

44. A. D. Stajkovic and F. Luthans, "Self-Efficacy and Work-Related Performance: A Meta-analysis," *Psychological Bulletin*, September 1998, pp. 240–261; and A. Bandura, "Cultivate Self-Efficacy for Personal and Organizational Effectiveness," in E. Locke (ed.), *Handbook of Principles of Organizational Behavior* (Malden, MA: Blackwell, 2004), pp. 120–136.

45. A. Bandura and D. Cervone, "Differential Engagement in Self-Reactive Influences in Cognitively-Based Motivation," *Organizational Behavior and Human Decision Processes*, August 1986, pp. 92–113.

46. A. Bandura, *Self-Efficacy: The Exercise of Control* (New York: Freeman, 1997).

47. C. L. Holladay and M. A. Quiñones, "Practice Variability and Transfer of Training: The Role of Self-Efficacy Generality," *Journal of Applied Psychology* 88, no. 6 (2003), pp. 1094–1103.

48. R. C. Rist, "Student Social Class and Teacher Expectations: The Self-Fulfilling Prophecy in Ghetto Education," *Harvard Educational Review* 70, no. 3 (2000), pp. 266–301.

49. D. Eden, "Self-Fulfilling Prophecies in Organizations," in J. Greenberg (ed.), *Organizational Behavior: The State of the Science*, 2nd ed. (Mahwah, NJ: Erlbaum, 2003), pp. 91–122.

50. Ibid.

51. T. A. Judge, C. L. Jackson, J. C. Shaw, B. Scott, and B. L. Rich, "Self-Efficacy and Work-Related Performance: The Integral Role of Individual Differences," *Journal of Applied Psychology* 92, no. 1 (2007), pp. 107–127.

52. Ibid.

53. J. L. Komaki, T. Coombs, and S. Schepman, "Motivational Implications of Reinforcement Theory," in R. M. Steers, L. W. Porter, and G. Bigley (eds.), *Motivation and Work Behavior*, 6th ed. (New York: McGraw-Hill, 1996), pp. 87–107.

54. E. A. Locke, "Latham vs. Komaki: A Tale of Two Paradigms," *Journal of Applied Psychology*, February 1980, pp. 16–23.

55. J. S. Adams, "Inequity in Social Exchanges," in L. Berkowitz (ed.), *Advances in Experimental Social Psychology* (New York: Academic Press, 1965), pp. 267–300.

56. P. S. Goodman, "An Examination of Referents Used in the Evaluation of Pay," *Organizational Behavior and Human Performance*, October 1974, pp. 170–195; S. Ronen, "Equity Perception in Multiple Comparisons: A Field Study," *Human Relations*, April 1986, pp. 333–346; R. W. Scholl, E. A. Cooper, and J. F. McKenna, "Referent Selection in Determining Equity Perception: Differential Effects on Behavioral and Attitudinal Outcomes," *Personnel Psychology*, Spring 1987, pp. 113–127; and T. P. Summers and A. S. DeNisi, "In Search of Adams' Other: Reexamination of Referents Used in the Evaluation of Pay," *Human Relations*, June 1990, pp. 497–511.

57. C. T. Kulik and M. L. Ambrose, "Personal and Situational Determinants of Referent Choice," *Academy of Management Review*, April 1992, pp. 212–237.

58. C. Ostroff and L. E. Atwater, "Does Whom You Work with Matter? Effects of Referent Group Gender and Age Composition on Managers' Compensation," *Journal of Applied Psychology* 88, no. 4 (2003), pp. 725–740.

59. Ibid.

60. See, for example, E. Walster, G. W. Walster, and W. G. Scott, *Equity: Theory and Research* (Boston: Allyn & Bacon, 1978); and J. Greenberg, "Cognitive Reevaluation of Outcomes in Response to Underpayment Inequity," *Academy of Management Journal*, March 1989, pp. 174–184.

61. P. S. Goodman and A. Friedman, "An Examination of Adams' Theory of Inequity," *Administrative Science Quarterly*, September 1971, pp. 271–288; R. P. Vecchio, "An Individual-Differences Interpretation of the Conflicting Predictions Generated by Equity Theory and Expectancy Theory," *Journal of Applied Psychology*, August 1981, pp. 470–481; J. Greenberg, "Approaching Equity and Avoiding Inequity in Groups and Organizations," in J. Greenberg and R. L. Cohen (eds.), *Equity and Justice in Social Behavior* (New York: Academic Press, 1982), pp. 389–435; R. T. Mowday, "Equity Theory Predictions of Behavior in Organizations," in R. Steers, L. W. Porter, and G. Bigley (eds.), *Motivation and Work Behavior*, 6th ed. (New York: McGraw-Hill, 1996), pp. 111–131; S. Werner and N. P. Mero, "Fair or Foul? The Effects of External, Internal, and Employee Equity on Changes in Performance of Major League Baseball Players," *Human Relations*, October 1999, pp. 1291–1312; R. W. Griffeth and S. Gaertner, "A Role for Equity Theory in the Turnover Process: An Empirical Test," *Journal of Applied Social Psychology*, May 2001, pp. 1017–1037; and L. K. Scheer, N. Kumar, and J.-B. E. M. Steenkamp, "Reactions to Perceived Inequity in U.S.

and Dutch Interorganizational Relationships," *Academy of Management* 46, no. 3 (2003), pp. 303–316.

62. See, for example, R. C. Huseman, J. D. Hatfield, and E. W. Miles, "A New Perspective on Equity Theory: The Equity Sensitivity Construct," *Academy of Management Journal*, April 1987, pp. 222–234; K. S. Sauley and A. G. Bedeian, "Equity Sensitivity: Construction of a Measure and Examination of Its Psychometric Properties," *Journal of Management* 26, no. 5 (2000), pp. 885–910; M. N. Bing and S. M. Burroughs, "The Predictive and Interactive Effects of Equity Sensitivity in Teamwork-Oriented Organizations," *Journal of Organizational Behavior*, May 2001, pp. 271–290; and J. A. Colquitt, "Does the Justice of One Interact with the Justice of Many? Reactions to Procedural Justice in Teams," *Journal of Applied Psychology* 89, no. 4 (2004), pp. 633–646.

63. J. Greenberg and S. Ornstein, "High Status Job Title as Compensation for Underpayment: A Test of Equity Theory," *Journal of Applied Psychology*, May 1983, pp. 285–297; and J. Greenberg, "Equity and Workplace Status: A Field Experiment," *Journal of Applied Psychology*, November 1988, pp. 606–613.

64. See, for instance, J. Greenberg, *The Quest for Justice on the Job* (Thousand Oaks, CA: Sage, 1996); R. Cropanzano and J. Greenberg, "Progress in Organizational Justice: Tunneling through the Maze," in C. L. Cooper and I. T. Robertson (eds.), *International Review of Industrial and Organizational Psychology*, vol. 12 (New York: Wiley, 1997); J. A. Colquitt, D. E. Conlon, M. J. Wesson, C. O. L. H. Porter, and K. Y. Ng, "Justice at the Millennium: A Meta-Analytic Review of the 25 Years of Organizational Justice Research," *Journal of Applied Psychology*, June 2001, pp. 425–445; T. Simons and Q. Roberson, "Why Managers Should Care About Fairness: The Effects of Aggregate Justice Perceptions on Organizational Outcomes," *Journal of Applied Psychology*, June 2003, pp. 432–443; and G. P. Latham and C. C. Pinder, "Work Motivation Theory and Research at the Dawn of the Twenty-First Century," *Annual Review of Psychology* 56 (2005), pp. 485–516.

65. K. Leung, K. Tong, and S. S. Ho, "Effects of Interactional Justice on Egocentric Bias in Resource Allocation Decisions," *Journal of Applied Psychology* 89, no. 3 (2004), pp. 405–415.

66. "Americans Feel They Pay Fair Share of Taxes, Says Poll," *NewsTarget.com*, May 2, 2005, www.newstarget.com/007297.html.

67. G. S. Leventhal, "What Should Be Done with Equity Theory? New Approaches to the Study of Fairness in Social Relationships," in K. Gergen, M. Greenberg, and R. Willis (eds.), *Social Exchange: Advances in Theory and Research* (New York: Plenum, 1980), pp. 27–55.

68. J. C. Shaw, E. Wild, and J. A. Colquitt, "To Justify or Excuse? A Meta-Analytic Review of the Effects of Explanations," *Journal of Applied Psychology* 88, no. 3 (2003), pp. 444–458.

69. D. P. Skarlicki and R. Folger, "Retaliation in the Workplace: The Roles of Distributive, Procedural, and Interactional Justice," *Journal of Applied Psychology* 82, no. 3 (1997), pp. 434–443.

70. R. Cropanzano, C. A. Prehar, and P. Y. Chen, "Using Social Exchange Theory to Distinguish Procedural from Interactional Justice," *Group & Organization Management* 27, no. 3 (2002), pp. 324–351; and S. G. Roch and L. R. Shanock, "Organizational Justice in an Exchange Framework: Clarifying

Organizational Justice Dimensions," *Journal of Management*, April 2006, pp. 299–322.

71. Colquitt, Conlon, Wesson, Porter, and Ng, "Justice at the Millennium," pp. 425–445.

72. J. Reb, B. M. Goldman, L. J. Kray, and R. Cropanzano, "Different Wrongs, Different Remedies? Reactions to Organizational Remedies After Procedural and Interactional Injustice," *Personnel Psychology* 59 (2006), pp. 31–64; and "Northwest Airlines Flight Cancellations Mount as Labor Woes Continue," *Aero-News.net*, June 26, 2007, www.aero-news.net.

73. V. H. Vroom, *Work and Motivation* (New York: Wiley, 1964).

74. For criticism, see H. G. Heneman III and D. P. Schwab, "Evaluation of Research on Expectancy Theory Prediction of Employee Performance," *Psychological Bulletin*, July 1972, pp. 1–9; T. R. Mitchell, "Expectancy Models of Job Satisfaction, Occupational Preference and Effort: A Theoretical, Methodological and Empirical Appraisal," *Psychological Bulletin*, November 1974, pp. 1053–1077; and W. Van Eerde and H. Thierry, "Vroom's Expectancy Models and Work-Related Criteria: A Meta-analysis," *Journal of Applied Psychology*, October 1996, pp. 575–586. For support, see L. W. Porter and E. E. Lawler III, *Managerial Attitudes and Performance* (Homewood, IL: Irwin, 1968); and J. J. Donovan, "Work Motivation," in N. Anderson et al (eds.), *Handbook of Industrial, Work & Organizational Psychology*, vol. 2 (Thousand Oaks, CA: Sage, 2001), pp. 56–59.

75. Vroom refers to these three variables as expectancy, instrumentality, and valence, respectively.

76. J. Nocera, "The Anguish of Being an Analyst," *New York Times*, March 4, 2006, pp. B1, B12.

77. P. M. Muchinsky, "A Comparison of Within- and Across-Subjects Analyses of the Expectancy-Valence Model for Predicting Effort," *Academy of Management Journal*, March 1977, pp. 154–158; and C. W. Kennedy, J. A. Fossum, and B. J. White, "An Empirical Comparison of Within-Subjects and Between-Subjects Expectancy Theory Models," *Organizational Behavior and Human Decision Process*, August 1983, pp. 124–143.

78. R. J. House, H. J. Shapiro, and M. A. Wahba, "Expectancy Theory as a Predictor of Work Behavior and Attitudes: A Re-evaluation of Empirical Evidence," *Decision Sciences*, January 1974, pp. 481–506.

79. For other examples of models that seek to integrate motivation theories, see H. J. Klein, "An Integrated Control Theory Model of Work Motivation," *Academy of Management Review*, April 1989, pp. 150–172; E. A. Locke, "The Motivation Sequence, the Motivation Hub, and the Motivation Core," *Organizational Behavior and Human Decision Processes*, December 1991, pp. 288–299; and T. R. Mitchell, "Matching Motivational Strategies with Organizational Contexts," pp. 60–62.

80. N. J. Adler, *International Dimensions of Organizational Behavior*, 4th ed. (Cincinnati, OH: South-Western Publishing, 2002), p. 174.

81. G. Hofstede, "Motivation, Leadership, and Organization: Do American Theories Apply Abroad?" *Organizational Dynamics*, Summer 1980, p. 55.

82. Ibid.

83. J. K. Giacobbe-Miller, D. J. Miller, and V. I. Victorov, "A Comparison of Russian and U.S. Pay Allocation Decisions, Distributive Justice Judgments, and Productivity Under Different Payment Conditions," *Personnel Psychology*, Spring 1998, pp. 137–163.

84. S. L. Mueller and L. D. Clarke, "Political-Economic Context and Sensitivity to Equity: Differences Between the United States and the Transition Economies of Central and Eastern Europe," *Academy of Management Journal*, June 1998, pp. 319–329.

85. I. Harpaz, "The Importance of Work Goals: An International Perspective," *Journal of International Business Studies*, First Quarter 1990, pp. 75–93.

86. G. E. Popp, H. J. Davis, and T. T. Herbert, "An International Study of Intrinsic Motivation Composition," *Management International Review*, January 1986, pp. 28–35.

87. This section is based on F. J. Landy and W. S. Becker, "Motivation Theory Reconsidered," in L. L. Cummings and B. M. Staw (eds.), *Research in Organizational Behavior*, vol. 9 (Greenwich, CT: JAI Press, 1987), pp. 24–35.

88. J. Zaslow, "Losing Well: How a Successful Man Deal with a Rare and Public Failure," *Wall Street Journal*, March 2, 2006, p. D1.

89. E. Biyalogorsky, W. Boulding, and R. Staelin, "Stuck in the Past: Why Managers Persist with New Product Failures," *Journal of Marketing*, April 2006, pp. 108–121.

Motivation: From Concepts to Applications

Money is better than poverty,

if only for financial reasons.

—Woody Allen

LEARNING OBJECTIVES

After studying this chapter, you should be able to:

1 Describe the job characteristics model and evaluate the way it motivates by changing the work environment.

2 Compare and contrast the three main ways jobs can be redesigned.

3 Identify three alternative work arrangements and show how they might motivate employees.

4 Give examples of employee involvement measures and show how they can motivate employees.

5 Demonstrate how the different types of variable-pay programs can increase employee motivation.

6 Show how flexible benefits turn benefits into motivators.

7 Identify the motivational benefits of intrinsic rewards.

*h*ow would you like to work wherever you want, whenever you want? Although Best Buy, the big-box retailer based in Minnesota, does not run its headquarters with quite that degree of flexibility, it's close.

One afternoon last year, Chap Allen, who oversees online orders at Best Buy, turned off his computer at 2 P.M. and told his staff, "See you tomorrow. I'm going to a matinee." Steve Hance has taken to going hunting on

Free as a Bird at Best Buy

workdays, his 12-gauge shotgun in one hand, his Verizon LG in the other. Best Buy e-learning specialist Mark Wells has been spending some workdays following the Dave Matthews Band around the country. Single parent Kelly McDevitt, an online promotions manager, has started leaving work at 2:30 P.M. to pick up her daughter from school. Scott Jauman began spending one-third of his work schedule at his Northwoods cabin.

What is going on at Best Buy? Is this any way to run a business?

For most jobs, lack of flexibility is still the norm, and flexibility is often dictated by the nature of the business. For example, if you are a manager with Kohl's Department Stores, your schedule needs to conform to the hours the store is open. With changes in technology, though, more managerial jobs place no such restrictions on managers' time.

This is what caused Best Buy HR managers Jody Thompson and Cali Ressler to wonder whether there was a better way to do business. In 2003, two senior managers complained to them that their top performers were under an unsustainable level of stress. They also knew from survey data that employees gave Best Buy low marks for jobs with high demands and low control. They asked Best Buy's senior management to partake in an experiment—allow managers to set their own schedules and abolish meetings, as long as managers' performance evaluation was based on output.

There was some resistance. Senior VP John Thompson, a former GE executive, was highly skeptical. But even he was won over by the results of the experiment. Best Buy found that in the three divisions that implemented the program—dot-com, logistics, and sourcing—voluntary turnover dropped 90 percent, 52 percent, and 75 percent, respectively. Thompson and Ressler also estimate that productivity has increased 35 percent in these departments over the same time span. They argue that morale and engagement are higher than they have ever been in the company.

Best Buy is not alone. One survey of employers revealed that 85 percent expect a large increase in the number of "unleashed" workers at their companies. The changes at some of the biggest U.S. corporations have already been dramatic. IBM estimates that 40 percent of its workforce has no formal office. One-third of AT&T's managers also don't have any dedicated office space. Sun Microsystems allows its employees to work anywhere they want.

It's possible that such programs are a fad. However, as Ressler says, "The old way of managing and looking at work isn't going to work anymore."[1] ■

*a*s the Best Buy experiment shows, companies vary a lot in the practical approach they take to motivating employees. Best Buy's approach assumes that employees do their best work when given a lot of autonomy in deciding how (and where and when) they go about doing it. The following self-assessment will provide some information on how motivating *your* job might be.

WHAT'S MY JOB'S MOTIVATING POTENTIAL?

In the Self-Assessment Library (available on CD or online), take assessment I.C.9 (What's My Job's Motivating Potential?) and answer the following questions. If you currently do not have a job, answer the questions for your most recent job.

1. *How did you score relative to your classmates?*
2. *Did your score surprise you? Why or why not?*
3. *How might your results affect your career path?*

Self
Assessment
Library

In Chapter 6, we focused on motivation theories. In this chapter, we focus on applying motivation concepts. We link motivation theories to practices such as employee involvement and skill-based pay. Why? Because it's one thing to be able to know specific motivation theories; it's quite another to see how, as a manager, you can use them.

Motivating by Job Design: The Job Characteristics Model

Increasingly, research on motivation is focused on approaches that link motivational concepts to changes in the way work is structured.

1 Describe the job characteristics model and evaluate the way it motivates by changing the work environment.

Research in **job design** provides stronger evidence that the way the elements in a job are organized can act to increase or decrease effort. This research also offers detailed insights into what those elements are. We'll first review the job characteristics model and then discuss some ways jobs can be redesigned. Finally, we'll explore some alternative work arrangements.

The Job Characteristics Model

Developed by J. Richard Hackman and Greg Oldham, the **job characteristics model (JCM)** proposes that any job can be described in terms of five core job dimensions:[2]

1. **Skill variety.**   **Skill variety** is the degree to which a job requires a variety of different activities so the worker can use a number of different skills and talent. For instance, an example of a job scoring high on skill variety would be the job of an owner-operator of a garage who does electrical repairs, rebuilds engines, does body work, and interacts with customers. A job scoring low on this dimension would be the job of a body shop worker who sprays paint 8 hours a day.
2. **Task identity.**   **Task identity** is the degree to which a job requires completion of a whole and identifiable piece of work. An example of a job scoring high on identity would be the job of a cabinetmaker who designs a piece of furniture, selects the wood, builds the object, and finishes it to perfection. A job scoring low on this dimension would be the job of a worker in a furniture factory who operates a lathe solely to make table legs.
3. **Task significance.**   **Task significance** is the degree to which a job has a substantial impact on the lives or work of other people. An example of a job scoring high on significance would be the job of a nurse handling the diverse needs of patients in a hospital intensive care unit. A job scoring low on this dimension would be the job of a janitor sweeping floors in a hospital.

---

job design   *The way the elements in a job are organized.*

job characteristics model (JCM)   *A model that proposes that any job can be described in terms of five core job dimensions: skill variety, task identity, task significance, autonomy, and feedback.*

skill variety   *The degree to which a job requires a variety of different activities.*

task identity   *The degree to which a job requires completion of a whole and identifiable piece of work.*

task significance   *The degree to which a job has a substantial impact on the lives or work of other people.*

4. **Autonomy.** **Autonomy** is the degree to which a job provides substantial freedom, independence, and discretion to the individual in scheduling the work and in determining the procedures to be used in carrying it out. An example of a job scoring high on autonomy is the job of a salesperson who schedules his or her own work each day and decides on the most effective sales approach for each customer without supervision. A job scoring low on this dimension would be the job of a salesperson who is given a set of leads each day and is required to follow a standardized sales script with each potential customer.

5. **Feedback.** **Feedback** is the degree to which carrying out the work activities required by a job results in the individual obtaining direct and clear information about the effectiveness of his or her performance. An example of a job with high feedback is the job of a factory worker who assembles iPods and tests them to see if they operate properly. A job scoring low on feedback would be the job of a factory worker who, after assembling an iPod, is required to route it to a quality-control inspector who tests it for proper operation and makes needed adjustments.

Exhibit 7-1 presents the job characteristics model. Note how the first three dimensions—skill variety, task identity, and task significance—combine to create meaningful work. That is, if these three characteristics exist in a job, the model predicts that the incumbent will view the job as being important, valuable, and worthwhile. Note, too, that jobs with high autonomy give job incumbents a feeling of personal responsibility for the results and that, if a job provides feedback, employees will know how effectively they are performing. From a motivational standpoint, the JCM says that individuals obtain internal rewards when they learn (knowledge of results) that they personally (experienced responsibility) have performed well on a task that they care about (experienced meaningfulness).[3] The more these three psychological states are present, the greater will be employees' motivation, performance, and satisfaction and the lower their absenteeism and likelihood of leaving the organization.

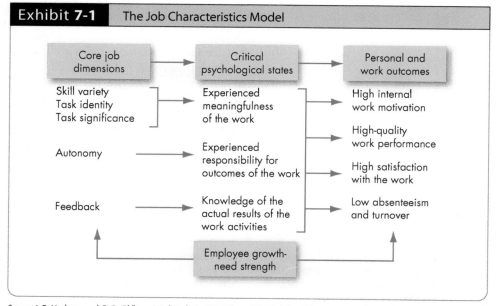

Exhibit 7-1 The Job Characteristics Model

Source: J. R. Hackman and G. R. Oldham, *Work Redesign* © 1980; pp. 78–80. Adapted by permission of Pearson Education, Inc., Upper Saddle River, New Jersey.

As Exhibit 7-1 shows, the links between the job dimensions and the outcomes are moderated or adjusted by the strength of the individual's growth need—that is, by the employee's desire for self-esteem and self-actualization. This means that individuals with a high growth need are more likely to experience the psychological states when their jobs are enriched than are their counterparts with low growth need. Moreover, the individuals with a high growth need will respond more positively to the psychological states when they are present than will individuals with a low growth need.

The core dimensions can be combined into a single predictive index, called the **motivating potential score (MPS)**, which is calculated as follows:

$$\text{MPS} = \frac{\text{Skill variety} + \text{Task identity} + \text{Task significance}}{3} \times \text{Autonomy} \times \text{Feedback}$$

Jobs that are high on motivating potential must be high on at least one of the three factors that lead to experienced meaningfulness, and they must be high on both autonomy and feedback. If jobs score high on motivating potential, the model predicts that motivation, performance, and satisfaction will be positively affected and that the likelihood of absence and turnover will be reduced.

The JCM has been well researched. And most of the evidence supports the general framework of the theory—that is, there is a set of job characteristics, and these characteristics affect behavioral outcomes.[4] But it appears that the MPS model doesn't work—that is, we can better derive motivating potential by adding the characteristics rather than using the complex MPS formula.[5] Beyond employee growth-need strength, other variables, such as the employee's perception of his or her work load compared with that of others, may also moderate the link between the core job dimensions and personal and work outcomes.[6] Overall, though, it appears that jobs that have the intrinsic elements of variety, identity, significance, autonomy, and feedback are more satisfying and generate higher performance from people than jobs that lack these characteristics.

Take some time to think about your job. Do you have the opportunity to work on different tasks, or is your day pretty routine? Are you able to work independently, or do you constantly have a supervisor or coworker looking over your shoulder? What do you think your answers to these questions say about your job's motivating potential? Revisit your answers to the self-assessment at the beginning of this chapter and then calculate your MPS from the job characteristics model.

How Can Jobs Be Redesigned?

2 Compare and contrast the three main ways jobs can be redesigned.

"Every day was the same thing," Frank Greer said. "Stand on that assembly line. Wait for an instrument panel to be moved into place. Unlock the mechanism and drop the panel into the Jeep Liberty as it moved by on the line. Then I plugged in the harnessing wires. I repeated that for eight hours a day. I don't care that they were paying me $24 an hour. I was

---

autonomy   *The degree to which a job provides substantial freedom and discretion to the individual in scheduling the work and in determining the procedures to be used in carrying it out.*

feedback   *The degree to which carrying out the work activities required by a job results in the individual obtaining direct and clear information about the effectiveness of his or her performance.*

motivating potential score (MPS)   *A predictive index that suggests the motivating potential in a job.*

going crazy. I did it for almost a year and a half. Finally, I just said to my wife that this isn't going to be the way I'm going to spend the rest of my life. My brain was turning to Jell-O on that Jeep assembly line. So I quit. Now I work in a print shop and I make less than $15 an hour. But let me tell you, the work I do is really interesting. The job changes all the time, I'm continually learning new things, and the work really challenges me! I look forward every morning to going to work again."

Frank Greer's job at the Jeep plant involved repetitive tasks that provided him with little variety, autonomy, or motivation. In contrast, his job in the print shop is challenging and stimulating. Let's look at some of the ways to put JCM into practice to make jobs more motivating.

Job Rotation   If employees suffer from overroutinization of their work, one alternative is to use **job rotation** (or what many now call *cross-training*). We define this practice as the periodic shifting of an employee from one task to another. When an activity is no longer challenging, the employee is rotated to another job, usually at the same level, that has similar skill requirements. Singapore Airlines, one of the best-rated airlines in the world, uses job rotation extensively. For example, a ticket agent may take on the duties of a baggage handler. Job rotation is one of the reasons Singapore Airlines is rated as a highly desirable place to work. Many manufacturing firms have adopted job rotation as a means of increasing flexibility and avoiding layoffs.[7] For instance, managers at Apex Precision Technologies, a custom-machine shop in Indiana, continually train workers on all of the company's equipment so they can be moved around in response to the requirements of incoming orders. During the 2001 recession, Cleveland-based Lincoln Electric moved some salaried workers to hourly clerical jobs and rotated production workers among various machines. This manufacturer of welding and cutting parts was able to minimize layoffs because of its commitment to continual cross-training and moving workers wherever they're needed.

The strengths of job rotation are that it reduces boredom, increases motivation through diversifying the employee's activities, and helps employees better

Job rotation adds variety to routine assembly tasks at the Autoliv automobile airbag manufacturing plant. Autoliv replaced its assembly line with U-shaped production cells that consist of a group of workstations staffed by a handful of employees. Workers change their jobs every 24 minutes when Autoliv announces a job rotation by piping rock music from the 1970s group Steam through the company's public address system: "Na, na, na, na, hey, hey, hey, good-bye."

MYTH OR SCIENCE?   *"Everyone Wants a Challenging Job"*

t his statement is false. Many employees do want challenging, interesting, complex work. But, despite all the attention focused by the media, academicians, and social scientists on human potential and the needs of individuals, some people prosper in simple, routinized work.[8]

The individual-difference variable that seems to gain the greatest support for explaining who prefers a challenging job and who doesn't is the strength of an individual's higher-order needs.[9] Individuals with high growth needs are more responsive to challenging work. But what percentage of rank-and-file workers actually desires higher-order need satisfaction and will respond positively to challenging jobs? No current data are available, but a study from the 1970s estimated the figure at about 15 percent.[10] Even after adjusting

for technological and economic changes in the nature of work, it seems unlikely that the number today exceeds 40 percent.

Many employees relish challenging work. But this desire has been overgeneralized to all workers. Organizations increasingly have pushed extra responsibilities onto workers, often without knowing whether this is desired or how an employee will handle the increased responsibilities.

Many workers meet their higher-order needs *off* the job. There are 168 hours in every individual's week. Work rarely consumes more than 30 percent of this time. That leaves considerable opportunity, even for individuals with strong growth needs, to find higher-order need satisfaction outside the workplace. ■

understand how their work contributes to the organization. Job rotation also has indirect benefits for the organization because when employees have a wider range of skills give, management has more flexibility in scheduling work, adapting to changes, and filling vacancies.[11] However, job rotation is not without drawbacks. Training costs are increased, and productivity is reduced by moving a worker into a new position just when efficiency at the prior job is creating organizational economies. Job rotation also creates disruptions. Members of the work group have to adjust to the new employee. And supervisors may also have to spend more time answering questions and monitoring the work of recently rotated employees.

Job Enlargement More than 35 years ago, the idea of expanding jobs horizontally, or what we call **job enlargement**, grew in popularity. Increasing the number and variety of tasks that an individual performed resulted in jobs with more diversity. Instead of only sorting the incoming mail by department, for instance, a mail sorter's job could be enlarged to include physically delivering the mail to the various departments or running outgoing letters through the postage meter. The difference between job rotation and job enlargement may seem subtle. However, in job rotation, jobs are not redesigned. Employees simply move from one job to another, but the nature of the work does not change. Job enlargement, however, involves actually changing the job.

Efforts at job enlargement have met with less-than-enthusiastic results.[12] One employee who experienced such a redesign on his job remarked, "Before I had one lousy job. Now, through enlargement, I have three!" However, there have been some successful applications of job enlargement. The housekeeping job in some small hotels, for example, includes not only cleaning bathrooms,

job rotation *The periodic shifting of an employee from one task to another.*

job enlargement *Increasing the number and variety of tasks that an individual performs. Job enlargement results in jobs with more diversity.*

making beds, and vacuuming but also replacing burned-out light bulbs, providing turn-down service, and restocking mini-bars.

Job Enrichment   **Job enrichment** refers to the vertical expansion of jobs. It increases the degree to which the worker controls the planning, execution, and evaluation of the work. An enriched job organizes tasks so as to allow the worker to do a complete activity, increases the employee's freedom and independence, increases responsibility, and provides feedback so individuals will be able to assess and correct their own performance.[13]

How does management enrich an employee's job? Exhibit 7-2 offers suggested guidelines based on the job characteristics model. *Combining tasks* takes existing and fractionalized tasks and puts them back together to form a new and larger module of work. *Forming natural work units* means that the tasks an employee does create an identifiable and meaningful whole. *Establishing client relationships* increases the direct relationships between workers and their clients (these may be an internal customer as well as someone outside the organization). *Expanding jobs vertically* gives employees responsibilities and control that were formerly reserved for management. *Opening feedback channels* lets employees know how well they are performing their jobs and whether their performance is improving, deteriorating, or remaining at a constant level.

One recent study attested to the benefits of establishing direct relationships between employees and the beneficiaries of their work. Researchers found that when university fundraisers briefly interacted with the undergraduate students who would be funded by the scholarships that were the target of the fundraising efforts, they persisted 42 percent longer, and raised nearly twice as much money, as those who didn't interact with the potential scholarship recipients.[14]

To illustrate job enrichment, let's look at what management at Bank One in Chicago did with its international trade banking department.[15] The department's chief product is commercial letters of credit—essentially a bank guarantee to stand behind huge import and export transactions. Prior to enriching jobs, the department's 300 employees processed documents in an assembly-line fashion, with errors creeping in at each handoff. Meanwhile, employees did little to hide the boredom they were experiencing from doing narrow and specialized tasks. Management enriched these jobs by making each clerk a trade expert who was able to handle a customer from start to finish. After 200 hours

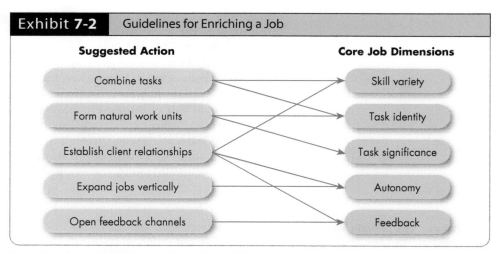

Exhibit **7-2**   Guidelines for Enriching a Job

Suggested Action

Combine tasks

Form natural work units

Establish client relationships

Expand jobs vertically

Open feedback channels

Core Job Dimensions

Skill variety

Task identity

Task significance

Autonomy

Feedback

Source: J. R. Hackman and J. L. Suttle (eds.), *Improving Life at Work* (Glenview, IL: Scott Foresman, 1977), p. 138. Reprinted by permission of Richard Hackman and J. Lloyd Suttle.

of training in finance and law, the clerks became full-service advisers who could turn around documents in a day while advising clients on such arcane matters as bank procedures in Turkey and U.S. munitions' export controls. The results? Department productivity more than tripled, employee satisfaction soared, and transaction volume rose more than 10 percent per year.

The overall evidence on job enrichment generally shows that it reduces absenteeism and turnover costs and increases satisfaction, but on the critical issue of productivity, the evidence is inconclusive.[16] Some recent evidence suggests that job enrichment works best when it compensates for poor feedback and reward systems.[17]

Alternative Work Arrangements

Beyond redesigning the nature of the work itself and involving employees in decisions, another approach to making the work environment more motivating is to alter work arrangements. We'll discuss three alternative work arrangements: flextime, job sharing, and telecommuting. With the increasing advances in technology, all these alternative work arrangements have become more popular.

3 Identify three alternative work arrangements and show how they might motivate employees.

Flextime Susan Ross is the classic "morning person." She rises each day at 5 A.M. sharp and full of energy. However, as she puts it, "I'm usually ready for bed right after the 7 P.M. news."

Susan's work schedule as a claims processor at The Hartford Financial Services Group is flexible. It allows her some degree of freedom as to when she comes to work and when she leaves. Her office opens at 6 A.M. and closes at

Research scientists and other employees at Eli Lilly and Company, a pharmaceutical firm, are offered flexible work options, with the approval of management. With Lilly's daily flextime option, full-time employees may arrive at work from 6 to 9 A.M. and leave work from 3 to 6 P.M. Lilly also provides employees a flexweek option that includes four 10-hour days or four 9-hour days followed by one half day.
Source: Tom Strattman/ The New York Times

job enrichment *The vertical expansion of jobs, which increases the degree to which the worker controls the planning, execution, and evaluation of the work.*

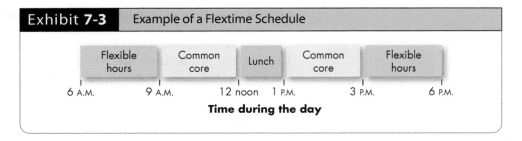

Exhibit 7-3 | Example of a Flextime Schedule

| Flexible hours | Common core | Lunch | Common core | Flexible hours |

6 A.M.   9 A.M.   12 noon   1 P.M.   3 P.M.   6 P.M.

Time during the day

7 P.M. It's up to her how she schedules her 8-hour day within this 13-hour period. Because Susan is a morning person and also has a 7-year-old son who gets out of school at 3 P.M. every day, she opts to work from 6 A.M. to 3 P.M. "My work hours are perfect. I'm at the job when I'm mentally most alert, and I can be home to take care of my son after he gets out of school."

Susan Ross's work schedule at The Hartford is an example of **flextime**. The term is short for "flexible work time." It allows employees some discretion over when they arrive at work and when they leave. Employees have to work a specific number of hours a week, but they are free to vary the hours of work within certain limits. As shown in Exhibit 7-3, each day consists of a common core, usually 6 hours, with a flexibility band surrounding the core. For example, exclusive of a 1-hour lunch break, the core may be 9 A.M. to 3 P.M., with the office actually opening at 6 A.M. and closing at 6 P.M. All employees are required to be at their jobs during the common core period, but they are allowed to accumulate their other 2 hours before and/or after the core time. Some flextime programs allow extra hours to be accumulated and turned into a free day off each month.

Flextime has become an extremely popular scheduling option. The proportion of full-time U.S. employees on flextime more than doubled between the late 1980s and 2005. Approximately 43 percent of the U.S. full-time workforce now has flexibility in their daily arrival and departure times.[18] And this is not just a U.S. phenomenon. In Germany, for instance, 29 percent of businesses have flextime for their employees.[19]

The benefits claimed for flextime are numerous. They include reduced absenteeism, increased productivity, reduced overtime expenses, reduced hostility toward management, reduced traffic congestion around work sites, elimination of tardiness, and increased autonomy and responsibility for employees that may increase employee job satisfaction.[20] But beyond the claims, what's flextime's record?

Most of the performance evidence stacks up favorably. Flextime tends to reduce absenteeism and frequently improves worker productivity,[21] probably for several reasons. Employees can schedule their work hours to align with personal demands, thus reducing tardiness and absences, and employees can adjust their work activities to those hours in which they are individually most productive.

Flextime's major drawback is that it's not applicable to every job. It works well with clerical tasks for which an employee's interaction with people outside his or her department is limited. It is not a viable option for receptionists, sales personnel in retail stores, or similar jobs for which comprehensive service demands that people be at their workstations at predetermined times.

Job Sharing   A recent work scheduling innovation is **job sharing**. It allows two or more individuals to split a traditional 40-hour-a-week job. So, for example, one person might perform the job from 8 A.M. to noon, while another performs the same job from 1 P.M. to 5 P.M.; or the two could work full, but alternate, days. As a case in point, Sue Manix and Charlotte Schutzman share the title of vice president of employee communications in the Philadelphia office of Verizon.[22] Schutzman works Monday and Tuesday, Manix works Thursday and Friday, and they alternate Wednesdays. The two women have job-shared for 10 years, acquiring promotions, numerous bonuses, and a 20-person staff along the way. With each having children at home, this arrangement allows them the flexibility to better balance their work and family responsibilities.

Approximately 31 percent of large organizations now offer their employees job sharing.[23] However, despite its availability, it doesn't seem to be widely adopted by employees. This is probably because of the difficulty of finding compatible partners to share a job and the negative perceptions historically held of individuals not completely committed to their job and employer.

Job sharing allows an organization to draw on the talents of more than one individual in a given job. A bank manager who oversees two job sharers describes it as an opportunity to get two heads but "pay for one."[24] It also opens up the opportunity to acquire skilled workers—for instance, women with young children and retirees—who might not be available on a full-time basis.[25] Many Japanese firms are increasingly considering job sharing—but for a very different reason.[26] Because Japanese executives are extremely reluctant to fire people, job sharing is seen as a potentially humanitarian means for avoiding layoffs due to overstaffing.

From the employee's perspective, job sharing increases flexibility. As such, it can increase motivation and satisfaction for those to whom a 40-hour-a-week job is just not practical. But the major drawback from management's perspective is finding compatible pairs of employees who can successfully coordinate the intricacies of one job.[27]

Telecommuting   It might be close to the ideal job for many people. No commuting, flexible hours, freedom to dress as you please, and few or no interruptions from colleagues. It's called **telecommuting**, and it refers to employees who do their work at home at least 2 days a week on a computer that is linked to their office.[28] (A closely related term—*the virtual office*—is increasingly being used to describe employees who work out of their home on a relatively permanent basis.)

Recent estimates indicate that between 9 million and 24 million people telecommute in the United States, depending on exactly how the term is defined.[29] This translates to about 10 percent or more of the workforce. Well-known organizations that actively encourage telecommuting include AT&T, IBM, Merrill Lynch, American Express, Hewlett-Packard, and a number of U.S. government agencies.[30] The concept is also catching on elsewhere in the world. In Finland, Sweden, Britain, and Germany, telecommuters represent 17, 15, 8, and 6 percent of their workforces, respectively.[31]

What kinds of jobs lend themselves to telecommuting? Three categories have been identified as most appropriate: routine information-handling tasks, mobile activities, and professional and other knowledge-related tasks.[32] Writers, attorneys, analysts, and employees who spend the majority of their time on computers or the telephone are natural candidates for telecommuting. For instance, telemarketers, customer-service representatives, reservation agents, and product-support specialists spend most of their time on the phone.

---

job sharing   *An arrangement that allows two or more individuals to split a traditional 40-hour-a-week job.*

telecommuting   *Working from home at least two days a week on a computer that is linked to the employee's office.*

flextime   *Flexible work hours.*

Telecommuting is appropriate for the knowledge-based work of employees at KPMG, a global network of professional firms that provides audit, tax, and advisory services. Kelvin Brown, a senior manager in KPMG's research and development tax concession section, works on his laptop at his beef cattle farm near Harden, Australia, a 4-hour drive away from the company's office in Sydney. For Brown, working from home increases his productivity and allows him more time to spend with his family.

As telecommuters, they can access information on their computers at home as easily as in the company's office.

There are numerous stories of telecommuting's success.[33] For instance, 3,500 Merrill Lynch employees telecommute. And after the program was in place just a year, management reported an increase in productivity of between 15 and 20 percent among their telecommuters, 3.5 fewer sick days a year, and a 6 percent decrease in turnover. Putnam Investments, located in Boston, has found telecommuting to be an attractive recruitment tool. The company was having difficulty attracting new hires. But after introducing telecommuting, the number of its applicants grew 20-fold. And Putnam's management calculates that the 12 percent of its employees who telecommute have substantially higher productivity than in-office staff and about one-tenth the attrition rate.

The potential pluses of telecommuting for management include a larger labor pool from which to select, higher productivity, less turnover, improved morale, and reduced office-space costs. The major downside for management is less direct supervision of employees. In addition, in today's team-focused workplace, telecommuting may make it more difficult for management to coordinate teamwork.[34] From the employee's standpoint, telecommuting offers a considerable increase in flexibility. But not without costs. For employees with a high social need, telecommuting can increase feelings of isolation and reduce job satisfaction. And all telecommuters potentially suffer from the "out of sight, out of mind" effect. Employees who aren't at their desks, who miss meetings, and who don't share in day-to-day informal workplace interactions may be at a disadvantage when it comes to raises and promotions. It can be easy for bosses to overlook or undervalue the contribution of employees whom they don't see regularly.

Ability and Opportunity

Robin and Chris both graduated from college a couple years ago, with degrees in elementary education. They both took jobs as first-grade teachers but in different school districts. Robin immediately confronted a number of obstacles on the job: a large class (42 students), a small and dingy classroom, and inadequate supplies.

Chris's situation couldn't have been more different. He had only 15 students in his class, plus a teaching aide for 15 hours each week, a modern and well-lighted room, a well-stocked supply cabinet, an iMac computer for every student, and a highly supportive principal. Not surprisingly, at the end of their first school year, Chris had been considerably more effective as a teacher than had Robin.

The preceding episode illustrates an obvious but often overlooked fact. Success on a job is facilitated or hindered by the existence or absence of support resources.

A popular, although arguably simplistic, way of thinking about employee performance is as a function (f) of the interaction of ability (A) and motivation (M); that is, Performance $= f(A \times M)$. If either ability or motivation is inadequate, performance will be negatively affected. This helps to explain, for instance, a hard-working athlete or student with modest abilities who consistently outperforms a more gifted, but lazy, rival. So, as noted in Chapter 2, an individual's intelligence and skills (subsumed under the label *ability*) must be considered in addition to motivation if we are to accurately explain and predict employee performance. But a piece of the puzzle is still missing. We need to add **opportunity to perform** (O) to our equation: Performance $= f(A \times M \times O)$.[35] Even though an individual may be willing and able, there may be obstacles that constrain performance.

When you attempt to assess why an employee is not performing to the level at which you believe he or she is capable of performing, take a look at the work environment to see if it's supportive. Does the employee have adequate tools, equipment, materials, and supplies? Does the employee have favorable working conditions, helpful coworkers, supportive work rules and procedures, sufficient information to make job-related decisions, adequate time to do a good job, and the like? If not, performance will suffer.

Employee Involvement

4 *Give examples of employee involvement measures and show how they can motivate employees.*

What specifically do we mean by **employee involvement**? We define it as a participative process that uses the input of employees to increase their commitment to the organization's success. The underlying logic is that if we involve workers in the decisions that affect them and increase their autonomy and control over their work lives, employees will become more motivated, more committed to the organization, more productive, and more satisfied with their jobs.[36]

Examples of Employee Involvement Programs

Let's look at the three major forms of employee involvement—participative management, representative participation, and quality circles—in more detail.

Participative Management The distinct characteristic common to all **participative management** programs is the use of joint decision making. That is,

---

opportunity to perform *Absence of obstacles that constrain the employee. High levels of performance are partially a function of the opportunity to perform.*

employee involvement *A participative process that uses the input of employees and is intended to increase employee commitment to an organization's success.*

participative management *A process in which subordinates share a significant degree of decision-making power with their immediate superiors.*

subordinates actually share a significant degree of decision-making power with their immediate superiors. Participative management has, at times, been promoted as a panacea for poor morale and low productivity. But for it to work, the issues in which employees get involved must be relevant to their interests so they'll be motivated, employees must have the competence and knowledge to make a useful contribution, and there must be trust and confidence between all parties involved.[37]

Dozens of studies have been conducted on the participation–performance relationship. The findings, however, are mixed.[38] A careful review of the research seems to show that participation typically has only a modest influence on variables such as employee productivity, motivation, and job satisfaction. Of course, this doesn't mean that the use of participative management can't be beneficial under the right conditions. What it says, however, is that the use of participation is not a sure means for improving employee performance.

Representative Participation   Almost every country in western Europe has some type of legislation that requires companies to practice **representative participation**. That is, rather than participating directly in decisions, workers are represented by a small group of employees who actually participate. Representative participation has been called "the most widely legislated form of employee involvement around the world."[39] The goal of representative participation is to redistribute power within an organization, putting labor on a more equal footing with the interests of management and stockholders.

The two most common forms representative participation takes are works councils and board representatives.[40] Works councils are groups of nominated or elected employees who must be consulted when management makes decisions involving personnel. Board representatives are employees who sit on a company's board of directors and represent the interests of the firm's employees.

The overall influence of representative participation on working employees seems to be minimal.[41] For instance, the evidence suggests that works councils are dominated by management and have little impact on employees or the organization. And although this form of employee involvement might increase the motivation and satisfaction of the individuals who are doing the representing, there is little evidence that this trickles down to the operating employees whom they represent. Overall, "the greatest value of representative participation is symbolic. If one is interested in changing employee attitudes or in improving organizational performance, representative participation would be a poor choice."[42]

Quality Circles   **Quality circles** became popular in North America and Europe during the 1980s.[43] Companies such as Hewlett-Packard, General Electric, Xerox, Procter & Gamble, IBM, Motorola, and American Airlines used quality circles. A quality circle is defined as a work group of 8 to 10 employees and supervisors who have a shared area of responsibility and who meet regularly—typically once a week, on company time and on company premises—to discuss their quality problems, investigate causes of the problems, recommend solutions, and take corrective actions.

A review of the evidence on quality circles indicates that they tend to show little or no effect on employee satisfaction, and although many studies report positive results from quality circles on productivity, these results are by no means guaranteed.[44] The failure of many quality circle programs to produce

Wegmans grocery stores involve their employees in making decisions that affect their work and please their customers. For example, Wegmans bakery employee Maria Benjamin, shown here, persuaded the company president to sell her chocolate meatball cookies that were made using a recipe passed down from Benjamins's Italian ancestors. Wegmans encourages employees to make on-the-spot decisions without consulting their immediate supervisors. That could include an employee's decision to cook customers' Thanksgiving turkeys because the ones they bought were too big for their home ovens.

measurable benefits has also led to a large number of them being discontinued. One of the reasons for their failure is that managers deal with employee involvement in only a limited way. "At most, these programs operate for one hour per week, with the remaining 39 hours unchanged. Why should changes in 2.5 percent of a person's job have a major impact?"[45] Basically, quality circles were an easy way for management to get on the employee involvement bandwagon without really involving employees.

Linking Employee Involvement Programs and Motivation Theories

Employee involvement draws on a number of the motivation theories discussed in Chapter 6. For instance, Theory Y is consistent with participative management, and Theory X aligns with the more traditional autocratic style of managing people. In terms of two-factor theory, employee involvement programs could provide employees with intrinsic motivation by increasing opportunities for growth, responsibility, and involvement in the work itself. Similarly, the opportunity to make and implement decisions—and then seeing them work out—can help satisfy an employee's needs for responsibility, achievement, recognition, growth, and enhanced self-esteem. So employee involvement is compatible with ERG theory and efforts to stimulate the achievement need. And extensive employee involvement programs clearly have the potential to increase employee intrinsic motivation in work tasks.

Using Rewards to Motivate Employees

5 *Demonstrate how the different types of variable-pay programs can increase employee motivation.*

As we saw in Chapter 3, pay is not a primary factor driving job satisfaction. However, it does motivate people, and companies often underestimate the importance of pay in keeping top talent. A 2006 study found that whereas only 45 percent of employers thought that pay was a key factor in losing top talent, 71 percent of top performers indicated that it was a top reason.[46]

Given that pay is so important, we need to understand what to pay employees and how to pay them. To do that, management must make some strategic decisions. Will the organization lead, match, or lag the market in pay? How will individual contributions be recognized? In this section, we consider four major strategic rewards decisions that need to be made: (1) what to pay employees (which is decided by establishing a pay structure); (2) how to pay individual employees (which is decided through

---

representative participation   *A system in which workers participate in organizational decision making through a small group of representative employees.*

quality circle   *A work group of employees who meet regularly to discuss their quality problems, investigate causes, recommend solutions, and take corrective actions.*

variable pay plans and skill-based pay plans); (3) what benefits to offer, especially whether to offer employees choice in benefits (flexible benefits); and (4) how to construct employee recognition programs.

What to Pay: Establishing a Pay Structure

There are many ways to pay employees. The process of initially setting pay levels can be rather complex and entails balancing *internal equity*—the worth of the job to the organization (usually established through a technical process called job evaluation)—and *external equity*—the external competitiveness of an organization's pay relative to pay elsewhere in its industry (usually established through pay surveys). Obviously, the best pay system pays the job what it is worth (internal equity) while also paying competitively relative to the labor market.

Some organizations prefer to be pay leaders by paying above the market, while some may lag the market because they can't afford to pay market rates, or they are willing to bear the costs of paying below market (namely, higher turnover as people are lured to better-paying jobs). Wal-Mart, for example, pays less than its competitors and often outsources jobs overseas. Chinese workers in Shenzhen earn $120 a month (that's $1,440 per year) to make stereos for Wal-Mart. Of the 6,000 factories that are worldwide suppliers to Wal-Mart, 80 percent are located in China. In fact, one-eighth of all Chinese exports to the United States go to Wal-Mart.[47]

Pay more, and you may get better-qualified, more highly motivated employees who will stay with the organization longer. But pay is often the highest single operating cost for an organization, which means that paying too much can make the organization's products or services too expensive. It's a strategic decision an organization must make, with clear trade-offs.

How to Pay: Rewarding Individual Employees Through Variable-Pay Programs

"Why should I put any extra effort into this job?" asked Anne Garcia, a fourth-grade elementary schoolteacher in Denver, Colorado. "I can excel or I can do the bare minimum. It makes no difference. I get paid the same. Why do anything above the minimum to get by?"

Comments similar to Anne's have been voiced by schoolteachers for decades because pay increases were tied to seniority. Recently, however, a number of schools have begun revamping their compensation systems to motivate people like Anne to strive for excellence in their jobs. For instance, Arizona, Florida, Iowa, and Kentucky have introduced state programs that tie teacher pay to the performance of the students in their classrooms.[48] In California, some teachers are now eligible for performance bonuses as high as $25,000 per year.[49]

A number of organizations—business firms as well as school districts and other government agencies—are moving away from paying people based solely on credentials or length of service and toward using variable-pay programs. Piece-rate plans, merit-based pay, bonuses, profit-sharing, gainsharing, and employee stock ownership plans are all forms of **variable-pay programs**. Instead of paying a person only for time on the job or seniority, a variable-pay program bases a portion of an employee's pay on some individual and/or organizational measure of performance. Earnings therefore fluctuate up and down with the measure of performance.[50] Variable-pay plans have long been used to compensate salespeople and executives. Recently they have begun to be applied to other employees. IBM, Wal-Mart, Pizza Hut, Cigna Corp., and John Deere are

Science teacher John Roper-Batker at Seward Montessori School in Minneapolis supports the variable-pay initiative being adopted by many school districts in Minnesota. The new pay plan motivates teachers by basing their pay on their performance in raising student achievement rather than on seniority or degrees. The move toward rewarding teachers with bonuses for their individual performance follows the widespread adoption of variable-pay plans in many businesses and government agencies.

Source: Ben Garvin/ The New York Times

just a few examples of companies using variable pay with rank-and-file employees.[51] Today, more than 70 percent of U.S. companies have some form of variable-pay plan, up from only about 5 percent in 1970.[52] Unfortunately, recent survey data indicate that most employees still don't see a strong connection between pay and performance. Only 29 percent say that when they do a good job, their performance is rewarded.[53]

It is precisely the fluctuation in variable pay that has made these programs attractive to management. It turns part of an organization's fixed labor costs into a variable cost, thus reducing expenses when performance declines. So when the U.S. economy encountered a recession in 2001, companies with variable pay were able to reduce their labor costs much faster than companies that had maintained non-performance-based compensation systems.[54] In addition, when pay is tied to performance, the employee's earnings recognize contribution rather than being a form of entitlement. Low performers find, over time, that their pay stagnates, while high performers enjoy pay increases commensurate with their contributions.

Let's examine the different types of variable-pay programs in more detail.

Piece-Rate Pay   Piece-rate wages have been popular for more than a century as a means of compensating production workers. In **piece-rate pay plans**, workers are paid a fixed sum for each unit of production completed. When an employee gets no base salary and is paid only for what he or she produces, this is a pure piece-rate plan. People who work in ballparks selling peanuts and soda are frequently paid this way. If they sell only 40 bags of peanuts, their take

variable-pay program   *A pay plan that bases a portion of an employee's pay on some individual and/or organizational measure of performance.*

piece-rate pay plan   *A pay plan in which workers are paid a fixed sum for each unit of production completed.*

is only $40. The harder they work and the more peanuts they sell, the more they earn. The limitation of these plans is that they're not feasible for many jobs. For example, Alabama college football coach Nick Saban earns $4 million per year. That salary is paid regardless of how many games he wins. Would it be better to pay Saban, for example, $400,000 for each win? It seems unlikely he would accept such a deal, and it may cause unanticipated consequences as well (such as cheating). So, although incentives are motivating and relevant for some jobs, it is unrealistic to think they can constitute the only piece of some employees' pay.

Merit-Based Pay   Merit-based pay plans pay for individual performance. However, unlike piece-rate plans, which pay based on objective output, **merit-based pay plans** are based on performance appraisal ratings. A main advantage of merit pay plans is that they allow employers to differentiate pay based on performance so that those people thought to be high performers are given bigger raises. The plans can be motivating because, if they are designed correctly, individuals perceive a strong relationship between their performance and the rewards they receive. The evidence supports the importance of this linkage.[55]

Most large organizations have merit pay plans, especially for salaried employees. IBM's merit pay plan, for example, provides increases to employees' base salary based on their annual performance evaluation. Since the 1990s, when the economy stumbled badly, an increasing number of Japanese companies have abandoned seniority-based pay in favor of merit-based pay. Koichi Yanashita, of Takeda Chemical Industries, commented, "The merit-based salary system is an important means to achieve goals set by the company's top management, not just a way to change wages."[56]

In an effort to motivate and retain top performers, more companies are increasing the differential between top and bottom performers. The consulting firm Hewitt Associates found that, in 2006, employers gave their best performers roughly 10 percent raises, compared to 3.6 percent for average performers and 1.3 percent for below-average performers. They've also found that these differences have increased over time. Martyn Fisher of Imperial Chemical in the United Kingdom said that his company has widened the merit pay gap between top and average performers because, "as much as we would regret our average performers leaving, we'd regret more an above-target performer leaving."[57]

Despite the intuitive appeal of pay for performance, merit pay plans have several limitations. One of them is that, typically, such plans are based on an annual performance appraisal. Thus, the merit pay is as valid or invalid as the performance ratings on which it is based. Another limitation of merit pay is that sometimes the pay raise pool fluctuates based on economic conditions or other factors that have little to do with an individual employee's performance. One year, a colleague at a top university who performed very well in teaching and research was given a pay raise of $300. Why? Because the pay raise pool was very small. Yet that is hardly pay-for-performance. Finally, unions typically resist merit pay plans. Because the largest teachers' unions have generally resisted it, relatively few teachers are covered by merit pay. Instead, seniority-based pay, where all employees get the same raises, predominates.

Bonuses   For many jobs, annual bonuses are a significant component of the total compensation. Among Fortune 100 CEOs, the bonus (with a mean of $1.01 million) generally exceeds the base salary (with a mean of $863,000). Increasingly, bonus plans are casting a larger net within organizations to include lower-ranking employees. Many companies now routinely reward production employees with bonuses in the thousands of dollars when company profits improve. Steel company Nucor, for example, guarantees its employees only about $10/hour, but its bonuses can be substantial; the average Nucor worker made roughly $91,000 last year. One advantage of bonuses over merit pay is that **bonuses** reward employees for recent performance rather than historical performance. The incentive effects of performance should be higher because, rather than paying people for performance that may have occurred years ago (and was rolled into their base pay), bonuses reward only recent performance. The downside of bonuses is that employees may view them as pay—after all, any worker would choose a $5,000 raise rolled into her base pay over a one-time payment of $5,000. KeySpan Corp., a 9,700-employee utility company in New York, tried to manage this trade-off by combining yearly bonuses with a smaller merit-pay raise. Elaine Weinstein, KeySpan's senior vice president of HR, credits the plan with changing the culture from "entitlement to meritocracy."[58]

Skill-Based Pay   **Skill-based pay** is an alternative to job-based pay. Rather than having an individual's job title define his or her pay category, skill-based pay (also called *competency-based* or *knowledge-based pay*) sets pay levels on the basis of how many skills employees have or how many jobs they can do.[59] For instance, employees at American Steel & Wire can boost their annual salaries by up to $12,480 by acquiring as many as 10 new skills. Frito-Lay Corporation ties its compensation for frontline operations managers to developing their skills in leadership, workforce development, and functional excellence. For employers, the lure of skill-based pay plans is that they increase the flexibility of the workforce: Filling staffing needs is easier when employee skills are interchangeable. Skill-based pay also facilitates communication across the organization because people gain a better understanding of each others' jobs.

What about the downside of skill-based pay? People can "top out"—that is, they can learn all the skills the program calls for them to learn. This can frustrate employees after they've become challenged by an environment of learning, growth, and continual pay raises. There is also a problem created by paying people for acquiring skills for which there may be no immediate need. This happened at IDS Financial Services.[60] The company found itself paying people more money even though there was little immediate use for their new skills. IDS eventually dropped its skill-based pay plan and replaced it with one that equally balances individual contribution and gains in work-team productivity. Finally, skill-based plans don't address the level of performance. They deal only with whether someone can perform the skill.

Profit-Sharing Plans   **Profit-sharing plans** are organizationwide programs that distribute compensation based on some established formula designed around a company's profitability. These can be direct cash outlays or, particularly

---

merit-based pay plan   *A pay plan based on performance appraisal ratings.*

bonus   *A pay plan that rewards employees for recent performance rather than historical performance.*

skill-based pay   *A pay plan that sets pay levels on the basis of how many skills employees have or how many jobs they can do.*

profit-sharing plan   *An organizationwide program that distributes compensation based on some established formula designed around a company's profitability.*

Continental Airlines President Jeff Smisek (center) celebrates with employees after distributing $111 million in profit-sharing checks to the company's 44,000 employees who helped return the airline to profitability. In addition, employees received stock options valued at about $250 million.

in the case of top managers, allocations of stock options. When you read about executives like Reuben Mark, the CEO at Colgate-Palmolive, earning $148 million in a year, almost all this comes from cashing in stock options previously granted based on company profit performance. Not all profit-sharing plans, though, need be so grand in scale. Jacob Luke, 13, started his own lawn-mowing business after getting a mower from his uncle. Jacob employs his brother, Isaiah, and friend, Marcel Monroe, and pays them each 25 percent of the profits he makes on each yard.

Gainsharing A variable-pay program that has gotten a great deal of attention in recent years is **gainsharing**.[61] This is a formula-based group incentive plan. Improvements in group productivity from one period to another determine the total amount of money that is to be allocated. Gainsharing's popularity seems to be narrowly focused among large manufacturing companies such as Champion Spark Plug and Mead Paper. For instance, approximately 45 percent of Fortune 1000 firms have implemented gainsharing plans.[62] Gainsharing is different from profit-sharing in that rewards are tied to productivity gains rather than on profits. Employees in a gainsharing plan can receive incentive awards even when the organization isn't profitable.

Employee Stock Ownership Plans Employee stock ownership plans **(ESOPs)** are company-established benefit plans in which employees acquire stock, often at below-market prices, as part of their benefits. Companies as varied as Publix Supermarkets and W.L. Gore & Associates are now over 50 percent employee owned.[63] But most of the 10,000 or so ESOPs in the United States are in small, privately held companies.[64]

The research on ESOPs indicates that they increase employee satisfaction.[65] But their impact on performance is less clear. ESOPs have the potential to increase employee job satisfaction and work motivation. But for this potential to be realized, employees need to psychologically experience ownership.[66] That is, in addition to merely having a financial stake in the company, employees

OB *In the News*

Motivating with Performance Reviews

The past few years have witnessed some pretty dramatic changes in the ways employers are reviewing employees' performance. Traditionally, almost all employees participated in a yearly performance review, where performance was thoroughly reviewed in a sit-down with their immediate supervisor, a written letter or form was completed, and the employee was given an annual raise.

Although a lot of companies still do it this way, increasingly employers are turning to more frequent and less formal performance reviews. Whirlpool has switched from an annual performance review to a quarterly review. Jeffrey Davidoff, a marketing manager at Whirlpool, reviews each of his eight immediate subordinates for 45 minutes each quarter. When asked about the new program, Davidoff commented, "I'm noticing much better results. I am pleasantly surprised at how many day-to-day behaviors have changed."

In today's business environment, short-term results matter, and performance varies too much on a day-to-day basis to leave it to an annual review. For these reasons, many other employers besides Whirlpool are conducting more frequent performance reviews. National Cooperative Bank in Washington, DC, now conducts more frequent reviews, as does forest products company Weyerhauser.

Whirlpool's Davidoff has found that the more frequent appraisal process has changed his behavior, too. Rather than doing the marketing work himself, he now focuses more on coaching and developing his employees to take on some of his responsibilities. "This is how work gets done," he says. "If you believe in your people, the time with them is literally the best way to spend your time."

Source: Based on E. White, "For Relevance, Firms Revamp Worker Reviews," *Wall Street Journal,* July 17, 2006, pp. B1, B5.

need to be kept regularly informed of the status of the business and also have the opportunity to exercise influence over it. The evidence consistently indicates that it takes ownership and a participative style of management to achieve significant improvements in an organization's performance.[67]

Evaluation of Variable Pay   Do variable-pay programs increase motivation and productivity? The answer is a qualified "yes." For example, studies generally support the idea that organizations with profit-sharing plans have higher levels of profitability than those without them.[68] Similarly, gainsharing has been found to improve productivity in a majority of cases and often has a positive impact on employee attitudes.[69] Another study found that whereas piece-rate pay-for-performance plans stimulated higher levels of productivity, this positive affect was not observed for risk-averse employees. Thus, in general, what economist Ed Lazear has said seems generally right: "Workers respond to prices just as economic theory predicts. Claims by sociologists and others that monetizing incentives may actually reduce output are unambiguously refuted by the data." But that doesn't mean everyone responds positively to variable-pay plans.[70]

Flexible Benefits: Developing a Benefits Package

6 *Show how flexible benefits turn benefits into motivators.*

Todd Evans and Allison Murphy both work for Citigroup, but they have very different needs in terms of employee benefits. Todd is married and has three young children and a wife who is at home full time. Allison, too, is married, but her husband has a high-paying job with the federal

gainsharing   *A formula-based group incentive plan.*

employee stock ownership plan (ESOP)   *A company-established benefits plan in which employees acquire stock, often at below-market prices, as part of their benefits.*

Software developer Oracle Corporation in Redwood City, California, provides employees with basic benefits and then enables them to choose coverage levels and additional benefits that meet their individual needs and those of their dependents. Flexible benefits are consistent with the expectancy theory thesis that links rewards to individual employees' goals. The OracleFlex plan gives employees flex credits they can use to purchase benefits so they can control the amount they spend for each benefit option. Employees with remaining credits may direct them toward taxable income or to their 401(k) savings plan, health care reimbursement, or dependent care reimbursement accounts.

government, and they have no children. Todd is concerned about having a good medical plan and enough life insurance to support his family in case it's needed. In contrast, Allison's husband already has her medical needs covered on his plan, and life insurance is a low priority for both Allison and her husband. Allison is more interested in extra vacation time and long-term financial benefits such as a tax-deferred savings plan.

A standardized benefits package for all employees at Citigroup would be unlikely to satisfactorily meet the needs of both Todd and Allison. Citigroup could, however, cover both sets of needs if it offered flexible benefits.

Flexible benefits allow each employee to put together a benefits package individually tailored to his or her own needs and situation. It replaces the traditional "one-benefit-plan-fits-all" programs that dominated organizations for more than 50 years.[71] Consistent with expectancy theory's thesis that organizational rewards should be linked to each individual employee's goals, flexible benefits individualize rewards by allowing each employee to choose the compensation package that best satisfies his or her current needs. The average organization provides fringe benefits worth approximately 40 percent of an employee's salary. Traditional benefits programs were designed for the typical employee of the 1950s—a male with a wife and two children at home. Less than 10 percent of employees now fit this stereotype. About 25 percent of today's employees are single, and one-third are part of two-income families with no children. Traditional programs don't meet their diverse needs, but flexible benefits do. They can be uniquely tailored to accommodate differences in employee needs based on age, marital status, spouses' benefit status, number and age of dependents, and the like.

The three most popular types of benefits plans are modular plans, core-plus options, and flexible spending accounts.[72] *Modular plans* are predesigned packages of benefits, with each module put together to meet the needs of a specific group of employees. So a module designed for single employees with no dependents might include only essential benefits. Another, designed for single parents, might have additional life insurance, disability insurance, and expanded health coverage. *Core-plus plans* consist of a core of essential benefits and a menu-like selection of other benefit options from which employees can select and add to the core. Typically, each employee is given "benefit credits," which allow the "purchase" of additional benefits that uniquely meet his or her needs. *Flexible spending plans* allow employees to set aside up to the dollar amount offered in the plan to pay for particular services. It's a convenient way, for example, for employees to pay for health care and dental premiums. Flexible spending accounts can increase employee take-home pay because employees don't have to pay taxes on the dollars they spend out of these accounts.

Intrinsic Rewards: Employee Recognition Programs

Laura Schendell makes only $8.50 per hour working at her fast-food job in Pensacola, Florida, and the job isn't very challenging or interesting. Yet Laura talks enthusiastically about her job, her boss, and the company that employs her. "What I like is the fact that Guy [her supervisor] appreciates the effort I make. He compliments me regularly in front of the other people on my shift, and I've been chosen Employee of the Month twice in the past six months. Did you see my picture on that plaque on the wall?"

Organizations are increasingly recognizing what Laura Schendell knows: Important work rewards can be both intrinsic and extrinsic. Rewards are intrinsic in the form of employee recognition programs and extrinsic in the form of compensation systems. In this section,

7 *Identify the motivational benefits of intrinsic rewards.*

Exhibit 7-4

THE WALL STREET JOURNAL

Source: From the *Wall Street Journal*, October 21, 1997. Reprinted by permission of Cartoon Features Syndicate.

we deal with ways in which managers can reward and motivate employee performance.

Employee recognition programs range from a spontaneous and private "thank you" up to widely publicized formal programs in which specific types of behavior are encouraged and the procedures for attaining recognition are clearly identified. Some research has suggested that whereas financial incentives may be more motivating in the short term, in the long run, nonfinancial incentives are more motivating.[73]

Nichols Foods Ltd., a British bottler of soft drinks and syrups, has a comprehensive recognition program.[74] The central hallway in its production area is lined with "bragging boards," where the accomplishments of various individuals and teams are regularly updated. Monthly awards are presented to people who have been nominated by peers for extraordinary effort on the job. And monthly award winners are eligible for further recognition at an annual off-site meeting for all employees. In contrast, most managers use a far more informal approach. Julia Stewart, president of Applebee's restaurants, frequently leaves sealed notes on the chairs of employees after everyone has gone home.[75] These notes explain how critical Stewart thinks the person's work is or how much she appreciates the completion of a recent project. Stewart also relies heavily on voice mail messages left after office hours to tell employees how appreciative she is for a job well done.

A few years ago, 1,500 employees were surveyed in a variety of work settings to find out what they considered to be the most powerful workplace motivator. Their response? Recognition, recognition, and more recognition.[76] As illustrated in Exhibit 7-5, Phoenix Inn, a West Coast chain of small hotels, encourages employees to smile by letting customers identify this desirable behavior

flexible benefits   *A benefits plan that allows each employee to put together a benefits package individually tailored to his or her own needs and situation.*

Exhibit 7-5

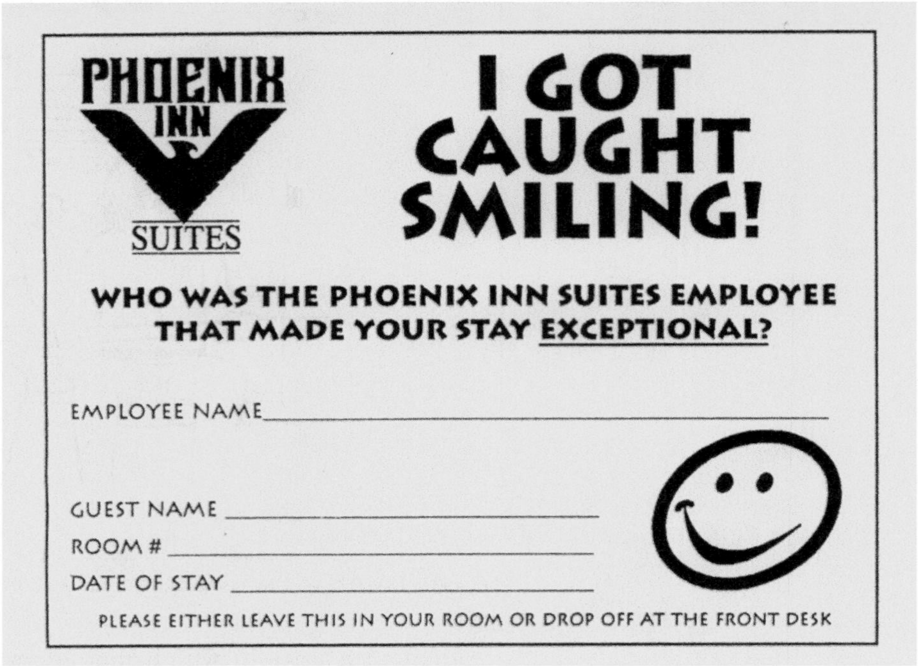

PHOENIX INN SUITES

I GOT CAUGHT SMILING!

WHO WAS THE PHOENIX INN SUITES EMPLOYEE THAT MADE YOUR STAY <u>EXCEPTIONAL</u>?

EMPLOYEE NAME_____

GUEST NAME _____

ROOM # _____

DATE OF STAY _____

PLEASE EITHER LEAVE THIS IN YOUR ROOM OR DROP OFF AT THE FRONT DESK

---

and then recognizing employees who are identified smiling most often by giving them rewards and publicity.

An obvious advantage of recognition programs is that they are inexpensive (praise, of course, is free!).[77] It shouldn't be surprising, therefore, to find that employee recognition programs have grown in popularity. A 2002 survey of 391 companies found that 84 percent had some program to recognize worker achievements and that 4 in 10 said they were doing more to foster employee recognition than they had been just a year earlier.[78]

Despite the increased popularity of employee recognition programs, critics argue that these programs are highly susceptible to political manipulation by management.[79] When applied to jobs where performance factors are relatively objective, such as sales, recognition programs are likely to be perceived by employees as fair. However, in most jobs, the criteria for good performance aren't self-evident, which allows managers to manipulate the system and recognize their favorite employees. Abuse of such a system can undermine the value of recognition programs and lead to demoralizing employees.

Global Implications

Do the motivational approaches discussed in this chapter vary by culture? Because we've discussed some very different approaches in this chapter, let's break down our analysis by approach. Not every approach has been studied by cross-cultural researchers, so we don't discuss every motivational approach. However, we consider cross-cultural differences in the following approaches: (1) job characteristics and job enrichment, (2) telecommuting, (3) variable pay, (4) flexible benefits, and (5) employee involvement.

International OB

Cultural Differences in Job Characteristics and Job Satisfaction

How do various factors of one's job contribute to satisfaction in different cultures? A recent study attempted to answer this question in a survey of about 50 countries. The authors of the study distinguished between intrinsic job characteristics (for example, having a job that allows one to use one's skills, frequently receiving recognition from one's supervisor) and extrinsic job characteristics (for example, receiving pay that is competitive within a given industry, working in an environment

that has comfortable physical conditions) and assessed differences between the two in predicting employee job satisfaction.

The study found that, across all countries, extrinsic job characteristics were consistently and positively related to satisfaction with one's job. However, countries differed in the extent to which intrinsic job characteristics predicted job satisfaction. Wealthier countries, countries with stronger social security, countries that stress individualism rather than collectivism, and countries with a smaller power distance (those that value a more equal distribution of power in organizations and institutions) showed a stronger relationship between the presence of intrinsic job characteristics and job satisfaction.

What explains these findings? One explanation is that in countries with greater wealth and social security, concerns over survival are taken for granted, and thus employees have the freedom to place greater importance on intrinsic aspects of the job. Another explanation is that cultural norms that emphasize the individual and have less power asymmetry socialize individuals to focus on the intrinsic aspects of their job. In other words, such norms tell individuals that it is okay to want jobs that are intrinsically rewarding.

Source: Based on X. Huang and E. Van De Vliert, "Where Intrinsic Job Satisfaction Fails to Work: National Moderators of Intrinsic Motivation," *Journal of Organizational Behavior* 24, no. 2 (2003), pp. 159–179.

Job Characteristics and Job Enrichment Although a few studies have tested the job characteristics model in different cultures, the results aren't very consistent. One study suggested that when employees are "other-oriented" (that is, concerned with the welfare of others at work), the relationship between intrinsic job characteristics and job satisfaction was weaker. As the authors note, because the job characteristics model is relatively individualistic (considering the relationship between the employee and his or her work), this suggests that job enrichment strategies may not have the same effects in more collectivistic cultures that they do in individualistic cultures (as in the United States).[80] However, another study suggested that the degree to which jobs had intrinsic job characteristics predicted job satisfaction and job involvement equally well for U.S., Japanese, and Hungarian employees.[81]

Telecommuting Does the degree to which employees telecommute vary by nation? Does it effectiveness depend on culture? First, one study suggests that telecommuting is more common in the United States than in all the European Union (EU) nations except the Netherlands. In the study, 24.6 percent of U.S. employees engaged in telecommuting, compared to only 13.0 percent of EU employees. Of the EU countries, the Netherlands had the highest rate of telecommuting (26.4 percent); the lowest rates were in Spain (4.9 percent) and Portugal (3.4 percent). Thus, telecommuting appears to be more common in the United States than in Europe. What about the rest of the world? Unfortunately, there are very little data comparing telecommuting rates in other parts of the world. Similarly, we don't really know whether telecommuting works better in the United States than in other countries. However, the same study that compared telework rates between the United States and the EU determined that employees in Europe appeared to have the same level of interest in telework: Regardless of country, interest is higher among employees than among employers.[82]

Variable Pay   You'd probably think that individual pay systems (such as merit pay or pay-for-performance) would work better in individualistic cultures like the United States than in collectivistic cultures like China or Venezuela. Similarly, you'd probably hypothesize that group-based rewards such as gainsharing or profit-sharing would work better in collectivistic cultures than in individualistic cultures. Unfortunately, there isn't much research on the issue. One recent study did suggest, though, that beliefs about the fairness of a group incentive plan were more predictive of pay satisfaction for employees in the United States than for employees in Hong Kong. One interpretation of these findings is that U.S. employees are more critical in appraising a group pay plan, and therefore it's more critical that the plan be communicated clearly and administered fairly.[83]

Flexible Benefits   Today, almost all major corporations in the United States offer flexible benefits. And they're becoming the norm in other countries, too. For instance, a recent survey of 136 Canadian organizations found that 93 percent have adopted or will adopt flexible benefits in the near term.[84] And a similar survey of 307 firms in the United Kingdom found that while only 16 percent have flexible benefits programs in place, another 60 percent are either in the process of implementing them or are seriously considering it.[85]

Employee Involvement   Employee involvement programs differ among countries.[86] For instance, a study comparing the acceptance of employee involvement programs in four countries, including the United States and India, confirmed the importance of modifying practices to reflect national culture.[87] Specifically, while U.S. employees readily accepted these programs, managers in India who tried to empower their employees through employee involvement programs were rated low by those employees. Employee satisfaction also decreased. These reactions are consistent with India's high power–distance culture, which accepts and expects differences in authority.

Summary and Implications for Managers

We've presented a number of motivation theories and applications in Chapter 6 and in this chapter. Although it's always dangerous to synthesize a large number of complex ideas into a few simple guidelines, the following suggestions summarize the essence of what we know about motivating employees in organizations.

Recognize Individual Differences   Managers should be sensitive to individual differences. For example, employees from Asian cultures prefer not to be singled out as special because it makes them uncomfortable.

Employees have different needs. Don't treat them all alike. Moreover, spend the time necessary to understand what's important to each employee. This allows you to individualize goals, level of involvement, and rewards to align with individual needs. Also, design jobs to align with individual needs and therefore maximize the motivation potential in jobs.

Use Goals and Feedback   Employees should have firm, specific goals, and they should get feedback on how well they are faring in pursuit of those goals.

Allow Employees to Participate in Decisions That Affect Them   Employees can contribute to a number of decisions that affect them: setting work goals, choosing their own benefits packages, solving productivity and quality problems, and the like. This can increase employee productivity, commitment to work goals, motivation, and job satisfaction.

Link Rewards to Performance   Rewards should be contingent on performance. Importantly, employees must perceive a clear linkage between performance and rewards. Regardless of how closely rewards are actually correlated to performance criteria, if individuals perceive this relationship to be low, the results will be low performance, a decrease in job satisfaction, and an increase in turnover and absenteeism.

Check the System for Equity   Employees should perceive rewards as equating with the inputs they bring to the job. At a simplistic level, this should mean that experience, skills, abilities, effort, and other obvious inputs should explain differences in performance and, hence, pay, job assignments, and other obvious rewards.

Point

Counterpoint

PRAISE MOTIVATES

Some of the most memorable, and meaningful, words we've ever heard have probably been words of praise. Genuine compliments mean a lot to people—and can go a long way toward inspiring the best performance. Numerous research studies show that students who receive praise from their teachers are more motivated, and often this motivation lasts well after the praise is given. Too often we assume that simple words of praise mean little, but most of us yearn for genuine praise from people who are in a position to evaluate us.

Companies are starting to learn this lesson. Walt Disney, Lands' End, and Hallmark have worked on how to use praise as a work reward to motivate employees. The 1,000-employee Scooter Store even has a "celebrations assistant" whose job is to celebrate employee successes. The Container Store estimates that 1 of its 4,000 employees receives praise every 20 seconds. Bank of America also believes in the power of praise. It "encourage[s] managers to start every meeting with informal recognition," says Bank of American VP Kevin Cronin.

Praise even seems to be important to long-term relationships. The Gottman Institute, a relationship research and training firm in Seattle, says its research suggests that the happiest marriages are those in which couples make five times as many positive statements to and about each other as negative ones. Of course, praise is not everything, but it is a very important and often underutilized motivator. And best of all, it's free.

Praise is highly overrated. Sure, in theory, it's nice to receive compliments, but in practice, praise has some real pitfalls.

First, a lot of praise is not genuine. Falsely praising people breeds narcissism. Jean Twenge, a researcher who studies narcissism, has said that scores on narcissism have risen steadily since 1982. As she notes, lavishing praise may be the culprit. Told we're wonderful time after time, we start to believe it, even when we aren't.

Second, praise is paradoxical in that the more it's given, the less meaningful it is. If we go around telling everyone they're special, soon it means nothing to those who do achieve something terrific. In the animated film *The Incredibles*, a superhero's mom tells her son, "Everyone's special!" His reply, "Which is another way of saying no one is."

Third, some of the most motivating people are those who are difficult to please. Think of Jack Welch, former CEO of GE, or A. G. Lafley, current CEO of Procter & Gamble. They are known for being difficult to please, which means most people will work harder to meet their expectations. Conversely, what happens when you dish out kudos for an employee who just shows up? What you've done is send a message that simply showing up is enough. Praise may seem like it's free, but when it's "dumbing down" performance expectations—so that employees think mediocrity is okay—the price may be huge.

Often what people really need is a gentle kick in the pants. As Steve Smolinsky of the Wharton School at the University of Pennsylvania says, "You have to tell students, 'It's not as good as you can do. . . . You can do better.' "

As one management consultant says, "People want to know how they're doing. Don't sugarcoat it. Just give them the damn data."[88]

Questions for Review

1 What is the job characteristics model? How does it motivate employees?

2 What are the three major ways that jobs can be redesigned? In your view, in what situations would one of the methods be favored over the others?

3 What are the three alternative work arrangements of flextime, job sharing, and telecommuting? What are the advantages and disadvantages of each?

4 What are employee involvement programs? How might they increase employee motivation?

5 What is variable pay? What are the variable-pay programs that are used to motivate employees? What are their advantages and disadvantages?

6 How can flexible benefits motivate employees?

7 What are the motivational benefits of intrinsic rewards?

Experiential Exercise

ASSESSING EMPLOYEE MOTIVATION AND SATISFACTION USING THE JOB CHARACTERISTICS MODEL

Purpose
This exercise will help you examine outcomes of the job characteristics model for different professions.

Time
Approximately 30 to 45 minutes.

Background
Data were collected on 6,930 employees in 56 different organizations in the United States, using the Job Diagnostic Survey. The following table contains data on the five core job dimensions of the job characteristics model for several professions. Also included are growth-needs strength, internal motivation, and pay satisfaction for each profession. The values are averages based on a 7-point scale.

Instructions
1. Break into groups of three to five.
2. Calculate the MPS score for each of the professions and compare them. Discuss whether you think these scores accurately reflect your perceptions of the motivating potential of these professions.
3. Graph the relationship between each profession's core job dimensions and its corresponding value for internal motivation and for pay satisfaction, using the core job dimensions as independent variables. What conclusions can you draw about motivation and satisfaction of employees in these professions?

Job Characteristics Averages for Six Professions

	Profession					
Variable	*Professional/ Technical*	*Managerial*	*Sales*	*Service*	*Clerical*	*Machine Trades*
Skill variety	5.4	5.6	4.8	5.0	4.0	5.1
Task identity	5.1	4.7	4.4	4.7	4.7	4.9
Task significance	5.6	5.8	5.5	5.7	5.3	5.6
Autonomy	5.4	5.4	4.8	5.0	4.5	4.9
Feedback	5.1	5.2	5.4	5.1	4.6	4.9
Growth-needs strength	5.6	5.3	5.7	5.4	5.0	4.8
Internal motivation	5.8	5.8	5.7	5.7	5.4	5.6
Pay satisfaction	4.4	4.6	4.2	4.1	4.0	4.2

Source: J. R. Hackman and G. R. Oldham, *Work Redesign* (Reading, MA: Addison-Wesley, 1980).

Ethical Dilemma

ARE U.S. EXECUTIVES PAID TOO MUCH?

There is no question that executive pay is growing. From 1999 to 2003, the pay of the top five executives from the 1,500 largest companies in the United States amounted to $122 billion, compared with $68 billion from 1993 to 1997. In comparison, from 2001 to 2003, top executive compensation amounted to 9.8 percent of the companies' net income, and the figure was 5 percent from 1993 to 1995. Perks, bonuses, and stock options are often particularly controversial. Ford's CEO Alan Mulally pulled in $28.2 million in 2006, including a bonus of $18.5 million, and free corporate jet travel for his wife, Nicki (which cost Ford $172,974 for the first quarter of 2006). Verizon's CEO Ivan Seidenberg received stock options worth $27 million in 2005, despite the fact that the company's stock dropped 25 percent that year. One of the members of Verizon's board of directors argued that the options were granted to make up for the fact that Seidenberg had been underpaid in the past.

The value of stock options is boosted when companies grant executive stock options when prices are low. You've probably heard of backdating, a practice in which executives are given the right to purchase their company's stock at some prior price, generally when the price of the stock was low. For example, when the stock market tanked after the 9/11 terrorist attacks, many companies granted executives stock options (Home Depot issued $19.2 million worth of options to its top five executives on September 17, and Merrill Lynch gave $14.4 million to its CEO on September 27) even though September is usually a month in which stock options are rarely issued. Some companies, such as Apple, went even further and backdated stock options so that a stock could be purchased at some retroactive lower price.

Even though bonuses, perks, and stock options have caused the ratio of executive pay to employee pay to grow dramatically over the past 25 years, some say this represents a classic economic response with a situation in which the demand is great for high-quality top executive talent and the supply is low. Ira Kay, a compensation consultant, says: "It's not fair to compare [executives] with hourly workers. Their market is the global market for executives." However, executive pay is considerably higher in the United States than in most other countries. U.S. CEOs are paid more than twice as much as Canadian CEOs, nearly three times as much as British CEOs, and four times as much as German CEOs. This difference is even greater when compared with what average workers make. U.S. CEOs make 531 times the pay of their average hourly employees. In contrast, British CEOs make 25 times as much as their workers, Canadians 21 times as much, and Germans 11 times as much.

Critics of executive pay practices in the United States argue that CEOs choose board members whom they can count on to support ever-increasing pay (including lucrative bonus and stock-option plans) for top management. If board members fail to "play along," they risk losing their positions, their fees, and the prestige and power inherent in board membership. Mutual funds own a significant percentage of the stock of publicly traded companies. So you would think they would reign in excessive pay to executives. Mutual fund companies, however, vote in favor of management pay plans 76 percent of the time, while they vote for shareholder proposals only 28 percent of the time. Don Phillips of the research firm Morningstar, commented, "Most asset managers are reluctant to pick fights with management because these big corporations are the ones who can write big checks to money-management firms for business."

Is high compensation of U.S. executives a problem? If so, does the blame for the problem lie with CEOs or with the shareholders and boards that knowingly allow the practice? Are U.S. CEOs greedy? Are they acting unethically? What do you think?

Sources: J. S. Lublin, "For CEO Spouses, Corporate Jets Are the Perfect Perk," *Wall Street Journal,* June 30, 2007, p. A1, A8; J. Levitz, "Do Mutual Funds Back CEO Pay? *Wall Street Journal,* March 28, 2006, pp. C1, C4; and J. Eisinger, "Lavish Pay Puts a Bit on Profits," *Wall Street Journal,* November 11, 2006, pp. C1, C7.

Case Incident 1

REDUCING TRAVEL COSTS AT APPLEBEE'S

Applebee's International is a large restaurant chain—with roughly 2,000 restaurants in the United States and 16 other countries—headquartered in the Kansas City area. Applebee's has been growing over time, opening roughly 100 new restaurants per year. As it has grown, the chain has found that its travel expenses have grown as well.

Although much of the roughly $6 million Applebee's was spending on travel was money well spent, the firm was interested in finding ways to contain the costs. Andrew Face, Applebee's senior manager of human resources, was asked by his boss, the senior vice president of HR, to redesign Applebee's travel system. Face's job was to eliminate non-essential travel costs at the same time that he increased corporate travel benefits.

Face's first idea was to outsource—to look to an off-site call center, through which he would be able to negotiate group discounts for travel costs. But Face's boss thought outsourcing to a vendor wouldn't offer the type of support Applebee's needed for its employee travelers. For example, managers' plans would often change, and they needed flexibility in the travel system to accommodate that.

Face eventually decided on QualityAgent, a Web-based system that offered employee support. Because Applebee's was concerned about weaning users off the old system (using travel agents), participation was voluntary. But Face got an e-mail every time an employee used QualityAgent to make an airline reservation that didn't fall within the Applebee's travel policy, so he could send an e-mail before the employee purchased the ticket to remind the person of the policy. He also got weekly reports on travel usage to control costs and usage patterns better.

Although these elements alone saved Applebee's money, Face wasn't finished. He decided to provide incentives for using the system. To employees who followed travel policy and took six or more trips per year, Face promised a pair of domestic airline tickets if the company saved $100,000 in costs that first year. Eventually he got usage up to 55 percent to 60 percent of employee travel.

Questions

1. Consider the variable-pay programs discussed in this chapter. Of which type of program is Applebee's program an example? Explain.

2. If you were asked to revise the Applebee's program to include more individual incentives, how might you do that?

3. How would you react to such a program? Explain your reactions.

4. Why do you think more companies do not use these sorts of incentives?

Source: L. Thornburg, "Applebee's International Cuts Travel Costs," *SHRM Online*, February 9, 2007, www.shrm.org.

Case Incident 2

THANKS FOR NOTHING

Although it may seem fairly obvious that receiving praise and recognition from one's company is a motivating experience, sadly, many companies are failing miserably when it comes to saying thanks to their employees. According to Curt Coffman, global practice leader at Gallup, 71 percent of U.S. workers are "disengaged," essentially meaning that they couldn't care less about their organization. Coffman states, "We're operating at one-quarter of the capacity in terms of managing human capital. It's alarming." Employee recognition programs, which became more popular as the U.S. economy shifted from industrial to knowledge based, can be an effective way to motivate employees and make them feel valued. In many cases, however, recognition programs are doing "more harm than good," according to Coffman.

Take Ko, a 50-year-old former employee of a dot-com in California. Her company proudly instituted a rewards program designed to motivate employees. What were the rewards for a job well done? Employees would receive a badge that read "U Done Good" and, each year, would receive a T-shirt as a means of annual recognition. Once an employee received 10 "U Done Good" badges, he or she could trade them in for something bigger and better—a paperweight. Ko states that she would have preferred a raise. "It was patronizing. There wasn't any deep thought involved in any of this." To make matters worse, she says, the badges were handed out arbitrarily and were

not tied to performance. And what about those T-shirts? Ko states that the company instilled a strict dress code, so employees couldn't even wear the shirts if they wanted to. Needless to say, the employee recognition program seemed like an empty gesture rather than a motivator.

Even programs that provide employees with more expensive rewards can backfire, especially if the rewards are given insincerely. Eric Lange, an employee of a trucking company, recalls a time when one of the company's vice presidents achieved a major financial goal for the company. The vice president, who worked in an office next to Lange, received a Cadillac Seville as his company car and a new Rolex wristwatch that cost the company $10,000. Both were lavish gifts, but the way they were distributed left a sour taste in the vice president's mouth. He entered his office to find the Rolex in a cheap cardboard box sitting on his desk, along with a brief letter explaining that he would be receiving a 1099 tax form in order to pay taxes on the watch. Lange states of the vice president, "He came into my office, which was right next door, and said, 'Can you believe this?'" A mere 2 months later, the vice president pawned the watch. Lange explains, "It had absolutely no meaning for him."

Such experiences resonate with employees who may find more value in a sincere pat on the back than in gifts from management that either are meaningless or aren't conveyed with respect or sincerity. However, sincere pats on the back may be hard to come by. Gallup's poll found that 61 percent of employees stated that they haven't received a sincere "thank you" from management in the past year. Findings such as these are troubling, as verbal rewards are not only inexpensive for companies to hand out but also quick and easy to distribute. Of course, verbal rewards do need to be paired sometimes with tangible benefits that employees value—after all, money talks. In addition, when praising employees for a job well done, managers need to ensure that the praise is given in conjunction with the specific accomplishment. In this way, employees may not only feel valued by their organization but will also know what actions to take to be rewarded in the future.

Questions

1. If praising employees for doing a good job seems to be a fairly easy and obvious motivational tool, why do you think companies and managers don't often do it?

2. As a manager, what steps would you take to motivate your employees after observing them perform well?

3. Are there any downsides to giving employees too much verbal praise? What might these downsides be and how could you alleviate them as a manager?

4. As a manager, how would you ensure that recognition given to employees is distributed fairly and justly?

Source: Based on J. Sandberg, "Been Here 25 Years and All I Got Was This Lousy T-Shirt," *Wall Street Journal,* January 28, 2004, p. B1.

Endnotes

1. M. Conlin, "Smashing the Clock," *BusinessWeek,* December 11, 2006, pp. 60–68.

2. J. R. Hackman and G. R. Oldham, "Motivation Through the Design of Work: Test of a Theory," *Organizational Behavior and Human Performance,* August 1976, pp. 250–279; and J. R. Hackman and G. R. Oldham, *Work Redesign* (Reading, MA: Addison-Wesley, 1980).

3. J. R. Hackman, "Work Design," in J. R. Hackman and J. L. Suttle (eds.), *Improving Life at Work* (Santa Monica, CA: Goodyear, 1977), p. 129.

4. See "Job Characteristics Theory of Work Redesign," in J. B. Miner, *Theories of Organizational Behavior* (Hinsdale, IL: Dryden Press, 1980), pp. 231–266; B. T. Loher, R. A. Noe, N. L. Moeller, and M. P. Fitzgerald, "A Meta-analysis of the Relation of Job Characteristics to Job Satisfaction," *Journal of Applied Psychology,* May 1985, pp. 280–289; W. H. Glick, G. D. Jenkins, Jr., and N. Gupta, "Method Versus Substance: How Strong Are Underlying Relationships Between Job haracteristics and Attitudinal Outcomes?" *Academy of Management Journal,* September 1986, pp. 441–464; Y. Fried and G. R. Ferris, "The Validity of the Job Characteristics Model: A Review and Meta-analysis," *Personnel Psychology,* Summer 1987, pp. 287–322; S. J. Zaccaro and E. F. Stone, Incremental Validity of an Empirically Based Measure of Job haracteristics," *Journal of Applied Psychology,* May 1988, pp. 245–252; J. R. Rentsch and R. P. Steel, "Testing the Durability of Job Characteristics as Predictors of Absenteeism over a Six-Year Period," *Personnel Psychology,* Spring 1998, pp. 165–190; S. J. Behson, E. R. Eddy, and S. J. Lorenzet, "The Importance of the Critical Psychological States in the Job Characteristics Model: A Meta-analytic and Structural Equations Modeling Examination," *Current Research in Social Psychology,* May 2000, pp. 170–189; and T. A. Judge, "Promote Job atisfaction Through Mental Challenge," in E. A. Locke (ed.), *Handbook of Principles of Organizational Behavior,* pp. 75–89.

5. T. A. Judge, S. K. Parker, A. E. Colbert, D. Heller, and R. Ilies, "Job Satisfaction: A Cross-Cultural Review," in N. Anderson, D. S. Ones (eds.), *Handbook of Industrial, Work and Organizational Psychology,* vol. 2 (Thousand Oaks, CA: Sage Publications, 2002), pp. 25–52.

6. C. A. O'Reilly and D. F. Caldwell, "Informational Influence as a Determinant of Perceived Task Characteristics and Job Satisfaction," *Journal of Applied Psychology,* April 1979, pp. 157–165; R. V. Montagno, "The Effects of Comparison [to] Others and Prior Experience on Responses to Task Design," *Academy of Management Journal,* June 1985, pp. 491–498; and P. C. Bottger and I. K.-H. Chew, "The Job Characteristics Model and Growth Satisfaction: Main Effects of Assimilation of Work Experience and Context Satisfaction," *Human Relations,* June 1986, pp. 575–594.

7. C. Ansberry, "In the New Workplace, Jobs Morph to Suit Rapid Pace of Change," *Wall Street Journal,* March 22, 2002, p. A1.

8. Hackman, "Work Design," pp. 115–120.

9. J. P. Wanous, "Individual Differences and Reactions to Job Characteristics," *Journal of Applied Psychology,* October 1974, pp. 616–622; and H. P. Sims and A. D. Szilagyi, "Job Characteristic Relationships: Individual and Structural Moderators," *Organizational Behavior and Human Performance,* June 1976, pp. 211–230.

10. M. Fein, "The Real Needs and Goals of Blue-Collar Workers," *The Conference Board Record,* February 1972, pp. 26–33.

11. J. Ortega, "Job Rotation as a Learning Mechanism," *Management Science,* October 2001, pp. 1361–1370.

12. See, for instance, data on job enlargement described in M. A. Campion and C. L. McClelland, "Follow-up and Extension of the Interdisciplinary Costs and Benefits of Enlarged Jobs," *Journal of Applied Psychology,* June 1993, pp. 339–351.

13. Hackman and Oldham, *Work Redesign.*

14. A. M. Grant, E. M. Campbell, G. Chen, K. Cottone, D. Lapedis, and K. Lee, "Impact and the Art of Motivation Maintenance: The Effects of Contact with Beneficiaries on Persistence Behavior," *Organizational Behavior and Human Decision Processes* 103 (2007), pp. 53–67.

15. Cited in *U.S. News & World Report,* May 31, 1993, p. 63.

16. See, for example, Hackman and Oldham, *Work Redesign;* Miner, *Theories of Organizational Behavior,* pp. 231–266;

R. W. Griffin, "Effects of Work Redesign on Employee Perceptions, Attitudes, and Behaviors: A Long-Term Investigation," *Academy of Management Journal* 34, no. 2 (1991), pp. 425–435; and J. L. Cotton, *Employee Involvement* (Newbury Park, CA: Sage, 1993), pp. 141–172.

17. F. P. Morgeson, M. D. Johnson, M. A. Campion, G. J. Medsker, and T. V. Mumford, "Understanding Reactions to Job Redesign: A Quasi-Experimental Investigation of the Moderating Effects of Organizational Contact on Perceptions of Performance Behavior," *Personnel Psychology* 39 (2006), pp. 333–363.

18. From the National Study of the Changing Workforce, cited in S. Shellenbarger, "Number of Women Managers Rise," *Wall Street Journal,* September 30, 2003, p. D2.

19. Cited in "Flextime Gains in Popularity in Germany," *Manpower Argus,* September 2000, p. 4.

20. D. R. Dalton and D. J. Mesch, "The Impact of Flexible Scheduling on Employee Attendance and Turnover," *Administrative Science Quarterly,* June 1990, pp. 370–387; K. S. Kush and L. K. Stroh, "Flextime: Myth or Reality," *Business Horizons,* September–October 1994, p. 53; and L. Golden, "Flexible Work Schedules: What Are We Trading Off to Get Them?" *Monthly Labor Review,* March 2001, pp. 50–55.

21. See, for example, D. A. Ralston and M. F. Flanagan, "The Effect of Flextime on Absenteeism and Turnover for Male and Female Employees," *Journal of Vocational Behavior,* April 1985, pp. 206–217; D. A. Ralston, W. P. Anthony, and D. J. Gustafson, "Employees May Love Flextime, but What Does It Do to the Organization's Productivity?" *Journal of Applied Psychology,* May 1985, pp. 272–279; J. B. McGuire and J. R. Liro, "Flexible Work Schedules, Work Attitudes, and Perceptions of Productivity," *Public Personnel Management,* Spring 1986, pp. 65–73; P. Bernstein, "The Ultimate in Flextime: From Sweden, by Way of Volvo," *Personnel,* June 1988, pp. 70–74; Dalton and Mesch, "The Impact of Flexible Scheduling on Employee Attendance and Turnover," pp. 370–387; and B. B. Baltes, T. E. Briggs, J. W. Huff, J. A. Wright, and G. A. Neuman, "Flexible and Compressed Workweek Schedules: A Meta-analysis of Their Effects on Work-Related Criteria," *Journal of Applied Psychology* 84, no. 4 (1999), pp. 496–513.

22. Cited in S. Caminiti, "Fair Shares," *Working Woman,* November 1999, pp. 52–54.

23. Ibid., p. 54.

24. S. Shellenbarger, "Two People, One Job: It Can Really Work," *Wall Street Journal,* December 7, 1994, p. B1.

25. "Job-Sharing: Widely Offered, Little Used," *Training,* November 1994, p. 12.

26. C. Dawson, "Japan: Work-Sharing Will Prolong the Pain," *BusinessWeek,* December 24, 2001, p. 46.

27. Shellenbarger, "Two People, One Job," p. B1.

28. See, for example, T. H. Davenport and K. Pearlson, "Two Cheers for the Virtual Office," *Sloan Management Review,* Summer 1998, pp. 61–65; E. J. Hill, B. C. Miller, S. P. Weiner, and J. Colihan, "Influences of the Virtual Office on Aspects of Work and Work/Life Balance," *Personnel Psychology,* Autumn 1998, pp. 667–683; K. E. Pearlson and C. S. Saunders, "There's No Place Like Home: Managing Telecommuting Paradoxes," *Academy of Management Executive,* May 2001,

pp. 117–128; S. J. Wells, "Making Telecommuting Work," *HRMagazine,* October 2001, pp. 34–45; and E. J. Hill, M. Ferris, and V. Martinson, "Does It Matter Where You Work? A Comparison of How Three Work Venues (Traditional Office, Virtual Office, and Home Office) Influence Aspects of Work and Personal/Family Life," *Journal of Vocational Behavior* 63, no. 2 (2003), pp. 220–241.

29. N. B. Kurland and D. E. Bailey, "Telework: The Advantages and Challenges of Working Here, There, Anywhere, and Anytime," *Organizational Dynamics,* Autumn 1999, pp. 53–68; and Wells, "Making Telecommuting Work," p. 34.

30. See, for instance, J. D. Glater, "Telecommuting's Big Experiment," *New York Times,* May 9, 2001, p. C1; and S. Shellenbarger, "Telework Is on the Rise, but It Isn't Just Done from Home Anymore, " *Wall Street Journal,* January 23, 2001, p. B1.

31. U. Huws, "Wired in the Country," *People Management,* November 1999, pp. 46–47.

32. Cited in R. W. Judy and C. D'Amico, *Workforce 2020* (Indianapolis: Hudson Institute, 1997), p. 58.

33. Cited in Wells, "Making Telecommuting Work," pp. 34–45.

34. J. M. Stanton and J. L. Barnes-Farrell, "Effects of Electronic Performance Monitoring on Personal Control, Task Satisfaction, and Task Performance," *Journal of Applied Psychology,* December 1996, pp. 738–745; B. Pappas, "They Spy," *Forbes,* February 8, 1999, p. 47; S. Armour, "More Bosses Keep Tabs on Telecommuters," *USA Today,* July 24, 2001, p. 1B; and D. Buss, "Spies Like Us," *Training,* December 2001, pp. 44–48.

35. L. H. Peters, E. J. O'Connor, and C. J. Rudolf, "The Behavioral and Affective Consequences of Performance-Relevant Situational Variables," *Organizational Behavior and Human Performance,* February 1980, pp. 79–96; M. Blumberg and C. D. Pringle, "The Missing Opportunity in Organizational Research: Some Implications for a Theory of Work Performance," *Academy of Management Review,* October 1982, pp. 560–569; D. A. Waldman and W. D. Spangler, "Putting Together the Pieces: A Closer Look at the Determinants of Job Performance," *Human Performance* 2 (1989), pp. 29–59; and J. Hall, "Americans Know How to Be Productive if Managers Will Let Them," *Organizational Dynamics,* Winter 1994, pp. 33–46.

36. See, for example, the increasing body of literature on empowerment, such as W. A. Randolph, "Re-Thinking Empowerment: Why Is It So Hard to Achieve?" *Organizational Dynamics,* 29, no. 2 (2000), pp. 94–107; K. Blanchard, J. P. Carlos, and W. A. Randolph, *Empowerment Takes More Than a Minute,* 2nd ed. (San Francisco: Berrett-Koehler, 2001); D. P. Ashmos, D. Duchon, R. R. McDaniel, Jr., and J. W. Huonker, "What a Mess! Participation as a Simple Managerial Rule to 'Complexify' Organizations," *Journal of Management Studies,* March 2002, pp. 189–206; and S. E. Seibert, S. R. Silver, and W. A. Randolph, "Taking Empowerment to the Next Level: A Multiple-Level Model of Empowerment, Performance, and Satisfaction" *Academy of Management Journal* 47, no. 3 (2004), pp. 332–349.

37. F. Heller, E. Pusic, G. Strauss, and B. Wilpert, *Organizational Participation: Myth and Reality* (Oxford, UK: Oxford University Press, 1998).

38. See, for instance, K. L. Miller and P. R. Monge, "Participation, Satisfaction, and Productivity: A Meta-analytic Review," *Academy of Management Journal*, December 1986, pp. 727–753; J. A. Wagner III and R. Z. Gooding, "Shared Influence and Organizational Behavior: A Meta-analysis of Situational Variables Expected to Moderate Participation–Outcome Relationships," *Academy of Management Journal*, September 1987, pp. 524–541; J. A. Wagner III, "Participation's Effects on Performance and Satisfaction: A Reconsideration of Research Evidence," *Academy of Management Review*, April 1994, pp. 312–330; C. Doucouliagos, "Worker Participation and Productivity in Labor-Managed and Participatory Capitalist Firms: A Meta-Analysis," *Industrial and Labor Relations Review*, October 1995, pp. 58–77; J. A. Wagner III, C. R. Leana, E. A. Locke, and D. M. Schweiger, "Cognitive and Motivational Frameworks in U.S. Research on Participation: A Meta-analysis of Primary Effects," *Journal of Organizational Behavior* 18 (1997), pp. 49–65; J. S. Black and H. B. Gregersen, "Participative Decision-Making: An Integration of Multiple Dimensions," *Human Relations*, July 1997, pp. 859–878; E. A. Locke, M. Alavi, and J. A. Wagner III, "Participation in Decision Making: An Information Exchange Perspective," in G. R. Ferris (ed.), *Research in Personnel and Human Resource Management*, vol. 15 (Greenwich, CT: JAI Press, 1997), pp. 293–331; and J. A. Wagner III and J. A. LePine, "Effects of Participation on Performance and Satisfaction: Additional Meta-analytic Evidence," *Psychological Reports*, June 1999, pp. 719–725.

39. Cotton, *Employee Involvement*, p. 114.

40. See, for example, M. Gilman and P. Marginson, "Negotiating European Works Council: Contours of Constrained Choice," *Industrial Relations Journal*, March 2002, pp. 36–51; J. T. Addison and C. R. Belfield, "What Do We Know About the New European Works Council? Some Preliminary Evidence from Britain," *Scottish Journal of Political Economy*, September 2002, pp. 418–444; and B. Keller, "The European Company Statute: Employee Involvement—And Beyond," *Industrial Relations Journal*, December 2002, pp. 424–445.

41. Cotton, *Employee Involvement*, pp. 129–130, 139–140.

42. Ibid., p. 140.

43. See, for example, G. W. Meyer and R. G. Stott, "Quality Circles: Panacea or Pandora's Box?" *Organizational Dynamics*, Spring 1985, pp. 34–50; E. E. Lawler III, and S. A. Mohrman, "Quality Circles: After the Honeymoon," *Organizational Dynamics*, Spring 1987, pp. 42–54; T. R. Miller, "The Quality Circle Phenomenon: A Review and Appraisal," *SAM Advanced Management Journal*, Winter 1989, pp. 4–7; K. Buch and R. Spangler, "The Effects of Quality Circles on Performance and Promotions," *Human Relations*, June 1990, pp. 573–582; P. R. Liverpool, "Employee Participation in Decision-Making: An Analysis of the Perceptions of Members and Nonmembers of Quality Circles," *Journal of Business and Psychology*, Summer 1990, pp. 411–422, E. E. Adams, Jr., "Quality Circle Performance," *Journal of Management*, March 1991, pp. 25–39; and L. I. Glassop, "The Organizational Benefits of Teams," *Human Relations* 55, no. 2 (2002), pp. 225–249.

44. T. L. Tang and E. A. Butler, "Attributions of Quality Circles' Problem-Solving Failure: Differences Among Management, Supporting Staff, and Quality Circle Members," *Public Personnel Management*, Summer 1997, pp. 203–225; G. Hammersley and A. Pinnington, "Quality Circles Reach End of the Line at Land Rover," *Human Resource Management International Digest*, May/June 1999, pp. 4–5; and D. Nagar and M. Takore, "Effectiveness of Quality Circles in a Large Public Sector," *Psychological Studies*, January–July 2001, pp. 63–68.

45. Cotton, *Employee Involvement*, p. 87.

46. E. White, "Opportunity Knocks, and It Pays a Lot Better," *Wall Street Journal*, November 13, 2006, p. B3.

47. P. S. Goodman and P. P. Pan, "Chinese Workers Pay for Wal-Mart's Low Prices," *The Washington Post*, February 8, 2004; p. A1.

48. See T. Henry, "States to Tie Teacher Pay to Results," *USA Today*, September 30, 1999, p. 1A.

49. D. Kollars, "Some Educators Win $25,000 Bonus as Test Scores Rise," *Sacramento (California) Bee*, January 8, 2001, p. 1.

50. Based on J. R. Schuster and P. K. Zingheim, "The New Variable Pay: Key Design Issues," *Compensation & Benefits Review*, March–April 1993, p. 28; K. S. Abosch, "Variable Pay: Do We Have the Basics in Place?" *Compensation & Benefits Review*, July–August 1998, pp. 12–22; and K. M. Kuhn and M. D. Yockey, "Variable Pay as a Risky Choice: Determinants of the Relative Attractiveness of Incentive Plans," *Organizational Behavior and Human Decision Processes*, March 2003, pp. 323–341.

51. W. Zellner, "Trickle-Down Is Trickling Down at Work," *BusinessWeek*, March 18, 1996, p. 34; and "Linking Pay to Performance Is Becoming a Norm in the Workplace," *Wall Street Journal*, April 6, 1999, p. A1.

52. L. Wiener, "Paycheck Plus," *U.S. News & World Report*, February 24/March 3, 2003, p. 58.

53. Cited in "Pay Programs: Few Employees See the Pay-for-Performance Connection," *Compensation & Benefits Report*, June 2003, p. 1.

54. B. Wysocki, Jr., "Chilling Reality Awaits Even the Employed," *Wall Street Journal*, November 5, 2001, p. A1.

55. M. Fein, "Work Measurement and Wage Incentives," *Industrial Engineering*, September 1973, pp. 49–51. For updated reviews of the effect of pay on performance, see G. D. Jenkins, Jr., N. Gupta, A. Mitra, and J. D. Shaw, "Are Financial Incentives Related to Performance? A Meta-analytic Review of Empirical Research," *Journal of Applied Psychology*, October 1998, pp. 777–787; and S. L. Rynes, B. Gerhart, and L. Parks, "Personnel Psychology: Performance Evaluation and Pay for Performance," *Annual Review of Psychology* 56, no. 1 (2005), pp. 571–600.

56. E. Arita, "Teething Troubles Aside, Merit-Based Pay Catching On," *Japan Times*, April 23, 2004, http://search.japantimes.co.jp/cgi-bin/nb20040423a3.html.

57. E. White, "The Best vs. the Rest," *Wall Street Journal*, January 30, 2006, pp. B1, B3.

58. E. White, "Employers Increasingly Favor Bonuses to Raises," *Wall Street Journal*, August 28, 2006, p. B3; and J. S. Lublin, "Boards Tie CEO Pay More Tightly to Performance," *Wall Street Journal*, February 21, 2006, pp. A1, A14.

59. G. E. Ledford, Jr., "Paying for the Skills, Knowledge, and Competencies of Knowledge Workers," *Compensation & Benefits Review*, July–August 1995, pp. 55–62; B. Murray and B. Gerhart, "An Empirical Analysis of a Skill-Based Pay Program and Plant Performance Outcomes," *Academy of Management Journal*, February 1998, pp. 68–78; J. R. Thompson and C. W. LeHew, "Skill-Based Pay as an Organizational Innovation," *Review of Public Personnel Administration*, Winter 2000, pp. 20–40; and J. D. Shaw, N. Gupta, A. Mitra, and

G. E. Ledford, Jr., "Success and Survival of Skill-Based Pay Plans," *Journal of Management*, February 2005, pp. 28–49.

60. "Tensions of a New Pay Plan," *New York Times*, May 17, 1992, p. F5.

61. See, for instance, D.-O. Kim, "Determinants of the Survival of Gainsharing Programs," *Industrial & Labor Relations Review*, October 1999, pp. 21–42; "Why Gainsharing Works Even Better Today Than in the Past," *HR Focus*, April 2000, pp. 3–5; L. R. Gomez-Mejia, T. M. Welbourne, and R. M. Wiseman, "The Role of Risk Sharing and Risk Taking Under Gainsharing," *Academy of Management Review*, July 2000, pp. 492–507; W. Atkinson, "Incentive Pay Programs That Work in Textile," *Textile World*, February 2001, pp. 55–57; M. Reynolds, "A Cost-Reduction Strategy That May Be Back," *Healthcare Financial Management*, January 2002, pp. 58–64; and M. R. Dixon, L. J. Hayes, and J. Stack, "Changing Conceptions of Employee Compensation," *Journal of Organizational Behavior Management* 23, no. 2–3 (2003), pp. 95–116.

62. Employment Policy Foundation, *U.S. Wage and Productivity Growth Attainable Through Gainsharing*, May 10, 2000.

63. "The Employee Ownership 100," *National Center for Employee Ownership*, July 2003, www.nceo. org.

64. Cited in K. Frieswick, "ESOPs: Split Personality," *CFO*, July 7, 2003, p. 1.

65. A. A. Buchko, "The Effects of Employee Ownership on Employee Attitudes: A Test of Three Theoretical Perspectives," *Work and Occupations* 19, no. 1 (1992), 59–78.

66. J. L. Pierce and C. A. Furo, "Employee Ownership: Implications for Management," *Organizational Dynamics* 18 no. 3 (1990), pp. 32–43.

67. See data in D. Stamps, "A Piece of the Action," *Training*, March 1996, p. 66.

68. C. G. Hanson and W. D. Bell, *Profit Sharing and Profitability: How Profit Sharing Promotes Business Success* (London: Kogan Page, 1987); M. Magnan and S. St-Onge, "Profit-Sharing and Firm Performance: A Comparative and Longitudinal Analysis," paper presented at the 58th annual meeting of the Academy of Management, San Diego, August 1998; and D. D'Art and T. Turner, "Profit Sharing, Firm Performance, and Union Influence in Selected European Countries," *Personnel Review* 33, no. 3 (2004), pp. 335–350.

69. T. M. Welbourne and L. R. Gomez-Mejia, "Gainsharing: A Critical Review and a Future Research Agenda," *Journal of Management* 21, no. 3 (1995), pp. 559–609.

70. C. B. Cadsby, F. Song, and F. Tapon, "Sorting and Incentive Effects of Pay for Performance: An Experimental Investigation," *Academy of Management Journal* 50, no. 2 (2007), pp. 387–405.

71. See, for instance, M. W. Barringer and G. T. Milkovich, "A Theoretical Exploration of the Adoption and Design of Flexible Benefit Plans: A Case of Human Resource Innovation," *Academy of Management Review*, April 1998, pp. 305–324; D. Brown, "Everybody Loves Flex," *Canadian HR Reporter*, November 18, 2002, p. 1; J. Taggart, "Putting Flex Benefits Through Their Paces," *Canadian HR Reporter*, December 2, 2002, p. G3; and N. D. Cole and D. H. Flint, "Perceptions of Distributive and Procedural Justice in Employee Benefits: Flexible Versus Traditional Benefit Plans," *Journal of Managerial Psychology* 19, no. 1 (2004), pp. 19–40.

72. D. A. DeCenzo and S. P. Robbins, *Human Resource Management*, 7th ed. (New York: Wiley, 2002), pp. 346–348.

73. S. E. Markham, K. D. Scott, and G. H. McKee, "Recognizing Good Attendance: A Longitudinal, Quasi-Experimental Field Study," *Personnel Psychology*, Autumn 2002, p. 641; and S. J. Peterson and F. Luthans, "The Impact of Financial and Nonfinancial Incentives on Business Unit Outcomes over Time," *Journal of Applied Psychology* 91, no. 1 (2006), pp. 156–165.

74. D. Drickhamer, "Best Plant Winners: Nichols Foods Ltd.," *IndustryWeek*, October 1, 2001, pp. 17–19.

75. M. Littman, "Best Bosses Tell All," *Working Woman*, October 2000, p. 54.

76. Cited in S. Caudron, "The Top 20 Ways to Motivate Employees," *IndustryWeek*, April 3, 1995, pp. 15–16. See also B. Nelson, "Try Praise," *INC.*, September 1996, p. 115.

77. A. D. Stajkovic and F. Luthans, "Differential Effects of Incentive Motivators on Work Performance," *Academy of Management Journal*, June 2001, p. 587. See also F. Luthans and A. D. Stajkovic, "Provide Recognition for Performance Improvement," in E. A. Locke (ed.), *Handbook of Principles of Organizational Behavior* (Malden, MA: Blackwell, 2004), pp. 166–180.

78. Cited in K. J. Dunham, "Amid Shrinking Workplace Morale, Employers Turn to Recognition," *Wall Street Journal*, November 19, 2002, p. B8.

79. Ibid.

80. B. M. Meglino and A. M. Korsgaard, "The Role of Other Orientation in Reactions to Job Characteristics," *Journal of Management*, February 2007, pp. 57–83.

81. M. F. Peterson and S. A. Ruiz-Quintanilla, "Cultural Socialization as a Source of Intrinsic Work Motivation," *Group & Organization Management*, June 2003, pp. 188–216.

82. P. Peters and L. den Dulk, "Cross Cultural Differences in Managers' Support for Home-Based Telework: A Theoretical Elaboration," *International Journal of Cross Cultural Management*, December 2003, pp. 329–346.

83. S. C. L. Fong and M. A. Shaffer, "The Dimensionality and Determinants of Pay Satisfaction: A Cross-Cultural Investigation of a Group Incentive Plan," *International Journal of Human Resource Management*, June 2003, pp. 559–580.

84. Brown, "Everybody Loves Flex.," p. 1.

85. E. Unsworth, "U.K. Employers Find Flex Benefits Helpful: Survey," *Business Insurance*, May 21, 2001, pp. 19–20.

86. See, for instance, A. Sagie and Z. Aycan, "A Cross-Cultural Analysis of Participative Decision-Making in Organizations," *Human Relations*, April 2003, pp. 453–473; and J. Brockner, "Unpacking Country Effects: On the Need to Operationalize the Psychological Determinants of Cross-National Differences," in R. M. Kramer and B. M. Staw (eds.), *Research in Organizational Behavior*, vol. 25 (Oxford, UK: Elsevier, 2003), pp. 336–340.

87. C. Robert, T. M. Probst, J. J. Martocchio, R. Drasgow, and J. J. Lawler, "Empowerment and Continuous Improvement in the United States, Mexico, Poland, and India: Predicting Fit on the Basis of the Dimensions of Power Distance and Individualism," *Journal of Applied Psychology*, October 2000, pp. 643–658.

88. "The Most Praised Generation Goes to Work," *Gainesville (Florida) Sun*, April 29, 2007, pp. 5G, 6G; and J. Zaslow, "In Praise of Less Praise," *Wall Street Journal*, May 3, 2007, p. D1.

Emotions and Moods

Time cools, time clarifies; no mood can be maintained quite unaltered through the course of hours.

—Mark Twain

LEARNING OBJECTIVES

After studying this chapter, you should be able to:

1 Differentiate emotions from moods and list the basic emotions and moods.

2 Discuss whether emotions are rational and what functions they serve.

3 Identify the sources of emotions and moods.

4 Show the impact emotional labor has on employees.

5 Describe affective events theory and identify its applications.

6 Contrast the evidence for and against the existence of emotional intelligence.

7 Apply concepts about emotions and moods to specific OB issues.

8 Contrast the experience, interpretation, and expression of emotions across cultures.

Can revenge be a motivator? Absolutely. Consider what Terry Garnett says: "I do hold grudges. Am I motivated by that? Absolutely."

In the 1990s, Garnett was a senior vice president at Oracle, reporting to Oracle CEO Larry Ellison. The two traveled around the world together, rubbed elbows with media and movie moguls, and became friends. The families even vacationed together in Japan. Ellison, an ardent admirer of all things Japanese, invited Garnett to join him in the

Sweet Revenge

famed Philosopher's Walk to the Ginkakuji Temple in Kyoto.

A few weeks after returning from their trip to Japan, Ellison called Garnett into his office and summarily fired him. Feeling numb and lacking a clear explanation for his dismissal, Garnett walked the 30 feet from Ellison's office to his own, packed up his things, and left. "I tried to keep composed," he said. Privately, though, he was seething, telling himself, "There will be a day of reckoning."

Channeling his anger, Garnett started competing directly with Ellison and Oracle by investing in promising start-up projects. A recent example is Ingres, a low-cost software provider that Garnett hopes will compete directly with Oracle's bread-and-butter offering: its high-price database business (together, Oracle and IBM claim 70 percent of the global database business). Garnett has hired away numerous Oracle employees; forming a small army of engineers and managers to help him take the battle to the enemy. In 2004, Garnett and David Helfrich founded Garnett & Helfrich Capital, a $350 million private equity fund for midsized technology spinouts. Rather than focusing on start-ups or buyouts of well-established companies, Garnett & Helfrich focuses on existing technology businesses or product lines that have struggled.

In reflecting on his successes, Garnett says, "The simplest way to create a culture is to pick an enemy. We have an enemy. It's Oracle."[1] ■

*a*s the example of Terry Garnett shows, emotions can spur us to action. Before we delve further into emotions and moods, get an assessment of your mood state right now. Take the following self-assessment to find out what sort of mood you're in.

Self Assessment Library

HOW ARE YOU FEELING RIGHT NOW?

In the Self-Assessment Library (available on CD or online), take assessment IV.D.1 (How Are You Feeling Right Now?) and answer the following questions.

1. *What was higher—your positive mood score or negative mood score? How do these scores compare with those of your classmates?*
2. *Did your score surprise you? Why or why not?*
3. *What sorts of things influence your positive moods? your negative moods?*

Given the obvious role that emotions play in our work and everyday lives, it might surprise you to learn that, until recently, the field of OB has given the topic of emotions little or no attention.[2] How could this be? We can offer two possible explanations.

The first is the *myth of rationality*.[3] From the late nineteenth century and the rise of scientific management until very recently, the protocol of the work world was to keep a damper on emotions. A well-run organization didn't allow employees to express frustration, fear, anger, love, hate, joy, grief, and similar feelings. The prevailing thought was that such emotions were the antithesis of rationality. Even though researchers and managers knew that emotions were an inseparable part of everyday life, they tried to create organizations that were emotion free. That, of course, wasn't possible.

The second explanation is that many believed that emotions of any kind are disruptive.[4] When researchers considered emotions, they looked at strong negative emotions—especially anger—that interfered with an employee's ability to work effectively. They rarely viewed emotions as constructive or contributing to enhanced performance.

Certainly some emotions, particularly when exhibited at the wrong time, can hinder employee performance. But this doesn't change the fact that employees bring their emotional sides with them to work every day and that no study of OB would be comprehensive without considering the role of emotions in workplace behavior.

What Are Emotions and Moods?

1 *Differentiate emotions from moods and list the basic emotions and moods.*

Although we don't want to belabor definitions, before we can proceed with our analysis, we need to clarify three terms that are closely intertwined: *affect, emotions,* and *moods.*

Affect is a generic term that covers a broad range of feelings that people experience. It's an umbrella concept that encompasses both emotions and moods.[5] **Emotions** are intense feelings that are directed at someone or something.[6] **Moods** are feelings that tend to be less intense than emotions and that often (though not always) lack a contextual stimulus.[7]

Most experts believe that emotions are more fleeting than moods.[8] For example, if someone is rude to you, you'll feel angry. That intense feeling of anger probably comes and goes fairly quickly, maybe even in a matter of seconds. When you're in a bad mood, though, you can feel bad for several hours.

Emotions are reactions to a person (for example, seeing a friend at work may make you feel glad) or event (for example, dealing with a rude client may make you feel angry). You show your emotions when you're "happy about something, angry at someone, afraid of something."[9] Moods, in contrast, aren't usually directed at a person or an event. But emotions can turn into moods when you lose focus on the event or object that started the feeling. And, by the same token, good or bad moods can make you more emotional in response to an event. So when a colleague criticizes how you spoke to a client, you might become angry at him. That is, you show emotion (anger) toward a specific object (your colleague). But as the specific emotion dissipates, you might just feel generally dispirited. You can't attribute this feeling to any single event; you're just not your normal self. You might then overreact to other events. This affect state describes a mood. Exhibit 8-1 shows the relationships among affect, emotions, and mood.

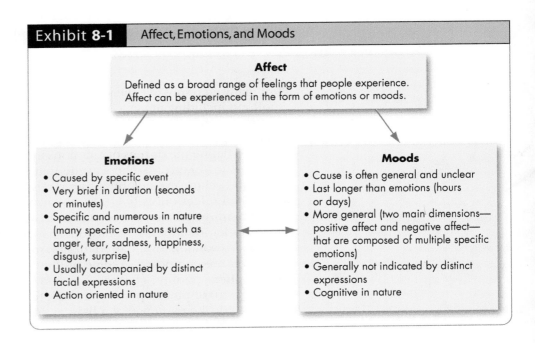

Exhibit 8-1 Affect, Emotions, and Moods

Affect
Defined as a broad range of feelings that people experience. Affect can be experienced in the form of emotions or moods.

Emotions
- Caused by specific event
- Very brief in duration (seconds or minutes)
- Specific and numerous in nature (many specific emotions such as anger, fear, sadness, happiness, disgust, surprise)
- Usually accompanied by distinct facial expressions
- Action oriented in nature

Moods
- Cause is often general and unclear
- Last longer than emotions (hours or days)
- More general (two main dimensions—positive affect and negative affect—that are composed of multiple specific emotions)
- Generally not indicated by distinct expressions
- Cognitive in nature

---

affect *A broad range of feelings that people experience.*

emotions *Intense feelings that are directed at someone or something.*

moods *Feelings that tend to be less intense than emotions and that lack a contextual stimulus.*

First, as the exhibit shows, affect is a broad term that encompasses emotions and moods. Second, there are differences between emotions and moods. Some of these differences—that emotions are more likely to be caused by a specific event, and emotions are more fleeting than moods—we just discussed. Other differences are subtler. For example, unlike moods, emotions tend to be more clearly revealed with facial expressions (for example, anger, disgust). Also, some researchers speculate that emotions may be more action-oriented—they may lead us to some immediate action—while moods may be more cognitive, meaning they may cause us to think or brood for a while.[10]

Finally, the exhibit shows that emotions and moods can mutually influence each other. For example, an emotion, if it's strong and deep enough, can turn into a mood: Getting your dream job may generate the emotion of joy, but it also can put you in a good mood for several days. Similarly, if you're in a good or bad mood, it might make you experience a more intense positive or negative emotion than would otherwise be the case. For example, if you're in a bad mood, you might "blow up" in response to a coworker's comment when normally it would have just generated a mild reaction. Because emotions and moods can mutually influence each other, there will be many points throughout the chapter where emotions and moods will be closely connected.

Although affect, emotions, and moods are separable in theory, in practice the distinction isn't always crystal clear. In fact, in some areas, researchers have studied mostly moods, and in other areas, mainly emotions. So, when we review the OB topics on emotions and moods, you may see more information on emotions in one area and moods in another. This is simply the state of the research.

Also, the terminology can be confusing. For example, the two main mood dimensions are positive affect and negative affect, yet we have defined affect more broadly than mood. So, although the topic can be fairly dense in places, hang in there. The material is interesting—and applicable to OB.

The Basic Emotions

How many emotions are there? In what ways do they vary? There are dozens of emotions, including anger, contempt, enthusiasm, envy, fear, frustration, disappointment, embarrassment, disgust, happiness, hate, hope, jealousy, joy, love, pride, surprise, and sadness. There have been numerous research efforts to limit and define the dozens of emotions into a fundamental or basic set of emotions.[11] But some researchers argue that it makes no sense to think of basic emotions because even emotions we rarely experience, such as shock, can have a powerful effect on us.[12] Other researchers, even philosophers, argue that there are universal emotions common to all of us. René Descartes, often called the founder of modern philosophy, identified six "simple and primitive passions"—wonder, love, hatred, desire, joy, and sadness—and argued that "all the others are composed of some of these six or are species of them."[13] Other philosophers (Hume, Hobbes, Spinoza) identified categories of emotions. Although these philosophers were helpful, the burden to provide conclusive evidence for the existence of a basic set of emotions still rests with contemporary researchers.

In contemporary research, psychologists have tried to identify basic emotions by studying facial expressions.[14] One problem with this approach is that some emotions are too complex to be easily represented on our faces. Take love, for example. Many think of love as the most universal of all emotions,[15] yet it's not easy to express a loving emotion with one's face only. Also, cultures have norms that govern emotional expression, so how we *experience* an emotion isn't always the same as how we *show* it. And many companies today offer anger-management programs to teach people to contain or even hide their inner feelings.[16]

It's unlikely that psychologists or philosophers will ever completely agree on a set of basic emotions, or even whether it makes sense to think of basic emotions. Still, enough researchers have agreed on six essentially universal emotions—anger, fear, sadness, happiness, disgust, and surprise—with most other emotions subsumed under one of these six categories.[17] Some researchers even plot these six emotions along a continuum: happiness—surprise—fear—sadness—anger—disgust.[18] The closer any two emotions are to each other on this continuum, the more likely it is that people will confuse them. For instance, we sometimes mistake happiness for surprise, but rarely do we confuse happiness and disgust. In addition, as we'll see later on, cultural factors can also influence interpretations.

The Basic Moods: Positive and Negative Affect

One way to classify emotions is by whether they are positive or negative.[19] Positive emotions—such as joy and gratitude—express a favorable evaluation or feeling. Negative emotions—such as anger or guilt—express the opposite. Keep in mind that emotions can't be neutral. Being neutral is being nonemotional.[20]

When we group emotions into positive and negative categories, they become mood states because we are now looking at them more generally instead of isolating one particular emotion. In Exhibit 8-2, excited is a specific emotion that is a pure marker of high positive affect, while boredom is a pure marker of low positive affect. Similarly, nervous is a pure marker of high negative affect, while relaxed is a pure marker of low negative affect. Finally, some emotions—such as contentment (a mixture of high positive affect and low negative affect) and sadness (a mixture of low positive affect and high negative affect)—are in between. You'll notice that this model does not include all emotions. There are two reasons. First, we can fit other emotions such as enthusiasm or depression into the model, but we're short on space. Second, some emotions, such as surprise, don't fit well because they're not as clearly positive or negative.

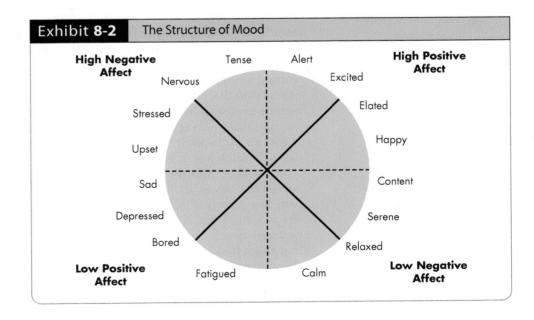

Exhibit 8-2 | The Structure of Mood

So, we can think of **positive affect** as a mood dimension consisting of positive emotions such as excitement, self-assurance, and cheerfulness at the high end and boredom, sluggishness, and tiredness at the low end. **Negative affect** is a mood dimension consisting of nervousness, stress, and anxiety at the high end and relaxation, tranquility, and poise at the low end. (Note that positive and negative affect *are* moods. We're using these labels, rather than *positive mood* and *negative mood* because that's how researchers label them.)

Positive affect and negative affect play out at work (and beyond work, of course) in that they color our perceptions, and these perceptions can become their own reality. For example, one flight attendant posted an anonymous blog on the Web that said: "I work in a pressurized aluminum tube and the environment outside my 'office' cannot sustain human life. That being said, the human life inside is not worth sustaining sometimes . . . in fact, the passengers can be jerks, and idiots. I am often treated with no respect, nobody listens to me . . . until I threaten to kick them off the plane."[21] Clearly, if a flight attendant is in a bad mood, it's going to influence his perceptions of passengers, which will, in turn, influence his behavior.

Importantly, negative emotions are likely to translate into negative moods. People think about events that created strong negative emotions five times as long as they do about events that created strong positive ones.[22] So, we should expect people to recall negative experiences more readily than positive ones. Perhaps one of the reasons is that, for most of us, they're also more unusual. Indeed, research shows that there is a **positivity offset**, meaning that at zero input (when nothing in particular is going on), most individuals experience a mildly positive mood.[23] So, for most people, positive moods are somewhat more common than negative moods. The positivity offset also appears to operate at work. For example, one study of customer-service representatives in a British call center (probably a job where it's pretty difficult to feel positive) revealed that people reported experiencing positive moods 58 percent of the time.[24]

The Function of Emotions

Do Emotions Make Us Irrational?   How often have you heard someone say, "Oh, you're just being emotional"? You might have been offended. The famous astronomer Carl Sagan once wrote, "Where we have strong emotions, we're liable to fool ourselves." These observations suggest that rationality and emotion are in conflict with one another and that if you exhibit emotion you are likely to act irrationally. One team of authors argues that displaying emotions such as sadness, to the point of crying, is so toxic to a career that we should leave the room rather than allow others to witness our emotional display.[25] The author Lois Frankel advises that women should avoid being emotional at work because it will undermine how others rate their competence.[26] These perspectives suggest that the demonstration or even experience of emotions is likely to make us seem weak, brittle, or irrational. However, the research disagrees and is increasingly showing that emotions are actually critical to rational thinking.[27] In fact, there has been evidence of such a link for a long time.

2   *Discuss whether emotions are rational and what functions they serve.*

Take the example of Phineas Gage, a railroad worker in Vermont. One September day in 1848, while Gage was setting an explosive charge at work, a 3'7" iron bar flew into his lower-left jaw and out through the top of his skull. Remarkably, Gage survived his injury. He was still able to read and speak, and he performed well above average on cognitive ability tests. However, it became clear that Gage had lost his ability to experience emotion. He was emotionless at even the saddest misfortunes or the happiest occasions. Gage's inability to express emotion eventually took away his ability to reason. He started making irrational choices about his life, often behaving erratically and against his self-interests. Despite being

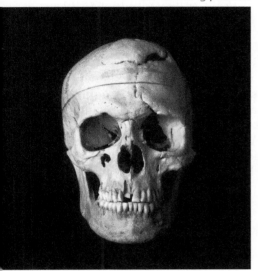

By studying brain injuries, such as the one experienced by Phineas Gage, whose skull is shown here, researchers discovered an important link between emotions and rational thinking. They found that losing the ability to emote led to the loss of the ability to reason. From this discovery, researchers learned that our emotions provide us with valuable information that helps our thinking process.

an intelligent man whose intellectual abilities were unharmed by the accident, Gage drifted from job to job, eventually taking up with a circus. In commenting on Gage's condition, one expert noted, "Reason may not be as pure as most of us think it is or wish it were . . . emotions and feelings may not be intruders in the bastion of reason at all: they may be enmeshed in its networks, for worse *and* for better."[28]

The examples of Phineas Gage and many other brain injury studies show us that emotions are critical to rational thinking. We must have the ability to experience emotions to be rational. Why? Because our emotions provide important information about how we understand the world around us. Although we might think of a computer as intellectually superior, a human so void of emotion would be unable to function. Think about a manager making a decision to fire an employee. Would you really want the manager to make the decision without regarding either his or the employee's emotions? The key to good decision making is to employ both thinking *and* feeling in one's decisions.

What Functions Do Emotions Serve?   Why do we have emotions? What role do they serve? We just discussed one function—that we need them to think rationally. Charles Darwin, however, took a broader approach. In *The Expression of the Emotions in Man and Animals*, Darwin argued that emotions developed over time to help humans solve problems. Emotions are useful, he said, because they motivate people to engage in actions that are important for survival— actions such as foraging for food, seeking shelter, choosing mates, guarding against predators, and predicting others' behaviors. For example, disgust (an emotion) motivates us to avoid dangerous or harmful things (such as rotten foods). Excitement (also an emotion) motivates us to take on situations in which we require energy and initiative (for example, tackling a new career).

Drawing from Darwin are researchers who focus on **evolutionary psychology**. This field of study says we must experience emotions—whether they are positive or negative—because they serve a purpose.[29] For example, you would probably consider jealousy to be a negative emotion. Evolutionary psychologists would argue that it exists in people because it has a useful purpose. Mates may feel jealousy to increase the chance that their genes, rather than a rival's genes, are passed on to the next generation.[30] Although we tend to think of anger as being "bad," it actually can help us protect our rights when we feel they're being violated. For example, a person showing anger when she's double-crossed by a colleague is serving a warning for others not to repeat the same behavior. Consider another example. Rena Weeks was a secretary at a prominent law firm. Her boss wouldn't stop touching and grabbing her. His treatment of her made her angry. So she did more than quit—she sued, and won a multimillion-dollar case.[31] It's not that anger is always good. But as with all other emotions, it exists because it serves a useful purpose. Positive emotions also serve a purpose. For example, a service employee who feels empathy for a customer may provide better customer service than an seemingly unfeeling employee.

But some researchers are not firm believers of evolutionary psychology. Why? Think about fear (an emotion). It's just as easy to think of the harmful effects of

positive affect   *A mood dimension that consists of specific positive emotions such as excitement, self-assurance, and cheerfulness at the high end and boredom, sluggishness, and tiredness at the low end.*

negative affect   *A mood dimension that consists of emotions such as nervousness, stress, and anxiety at the high end and relaxation, tranquility, and poise at the low end.*

positivity offset   *The tendency of most individuals to experience a mildly positive mood at zero input (when nothing in particular is going on).*

evolutionary psychology   *An area of inquiry which argues that we must experience the emotions we do because they serve a purpose.*

fear as it is the beneficial effects. For example, running in fear from a predator increases the likelihood of survival. But what benefit does freezing in fear serve? Evolutionary psychology provides an interesting perspective on the functions of emotions, but it's difficult to know whether this perspective is valid all the time.[32]

Sources of Emotions and Moods

3 *Identify the sources of emotions and moods.*

Have you ever said, "I got up on the wrong side of the bed today"? Have you ever snapped at a coworker or family member for no particular reason? If you have, it probably makes you wonder where emotions and moods come from. Here we discuss some of the primary influences on moods and emotions.

Personality   Moods and emotions have a trait component—most people have built-in tendencies to experience certain moods and emotions more frequently than others do. Moreover, people naturally differ in how intensely they experience the same emotions. Contrast Texas Tech basketball coach Bobby Knight to Microsoft CEO Bill Gates. One is easily moved to anger, while the other is relatively distant and unemotional. Knight and Gates probably differ in **affect intensity**, or how strongly they experience their emotions.[33] Affectively intense people experience both positive and negative emotions more deeply—when they're sad, they're really sad, and when they're happy, they're really happy.

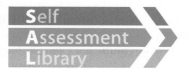

WHAT'S MY AFFECT INTENSITY?

In the Self-Assessment Library (available on CD or online), take assessment IV.D.2 (What's My Affect Intensity?).

Day of the Week and Time of the Day   Are people in their best moods on the weekends? Well, sort of. As Exhibit 8-3 shows, people tend to be in their worst moods (highest negative affect and lowest positive affect) early in the week and in their best moods (highest positive affect and lowest negative affect) late in the week.[34]

What about time of the day? (See Exhibit 8-4.) We often think that people differ, depending on whether they are "morning" or "evening" people. However, the vast majority of us follow the same pattern. Regardless of what time people go to bed at night or get up in the morning, levels of positive affect tend to peak around the halfway point between waking and sleeping. Negative affect, however, shows little fluctuation throughout the day.[35] This basic pattern seems to hold whether people describe themselves as morning people or evening people.[36]

What does this mean for organizational behavior? Monday morning is probably not the best time to ask someone for a favor or convey bad news. Our workplace interactions will probably be more positive from midmorning onward and also later in the week.

Weather   When do you think you would be in a better mood—when it's 70 degrees and sunny or when it's a gloomy, cold, rainy day? Many people believe their mood is tied to the weather. However, evidence suggests that weather has little effect on mood. One expert concluded, "Contrary to the prevailing cultural view, these data indicate that people do not report a better mood on bright and sunny days (or, conversely, a worse mood on dark and rainy days)."[37] *Illusory correlation* explains why people tend to *think* that nice weather improves their mood. **Illusory correlation** occurs when people associate two events but in reality there is no connection.

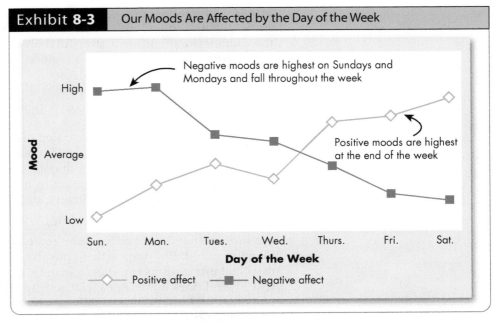

| Exhibit **8-3** | Our Moods Are Affected by the Day of the Week |

Source: D. Watson, *Mood and Temperament* (New York: Guilford Press, 2000).

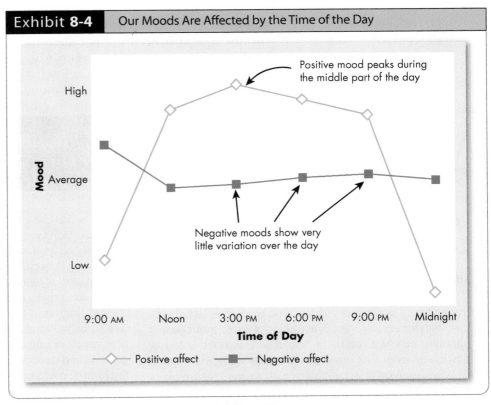

| Exhibit **8-4** | Our Moods Are Affected by the Time of the Day |

Source: D. Watson, *Mood and Temperament* (New York: Guilford Press, 2000).

affect intensity   *Individual differences in the strength with which individuals experience their emotions.*

illusory correlation

The tendency of people to associate two events when in reality there is no connection.

Stress   As you might imagine, stress affects emotions and moods. For example, students have higher levels of fear before an exam, but their fear dissipates once the exam is over.[38] At work, stressful daily events (for example, a nasty e-mail, an impending deadline, the loss of a big sale, being reprimanded by your boss) negatively affect employees' moods. Also, the effects of stress build over time. As the authors of one study note, "a constant diet of even low-level stressful events has the potential to cause workers to experience gradually increasing levels of strain over time."[39] Such mounting levels of stress and strain at work can worsen our moods, and we experience more negative emotions. Consider the following entry from a worker's blog: "i'm in a bit of a blah mood today . . . physically, i feel funky, though and the weather out combined with the amount of personal and work i need to get done are getting to me." Although sometimes we thrive on stress, for most of us, like this blogger, stress takes a toll on our mood.[40]

Social Activities   Do you tend to be happiest when you are out with friends? For most people, social activities increase positive mood and have little effect on negative mood. But do people in positive moods seek out social interactions, or do social interactions cause people to be in good moods? It seems that both are true.[41] And does the *type* of social activity matter? Indeed it does. Research suggests that physical (skiing or hiking with friends), informal (going to a party), or epicurean (eating with others) activities are more strongly associated with increases in positive mood than formal (attending a meeting) or sedentary (watching TV with friends) events.[42]

Sleep   U.S. adults report that they sleep less than they did a generation ago.[43] Do this lack of sleep make people grumpier? Sleep quality does affect mood. Undergraduates and adult workers who are sleep deprived report greater feelings of fatigue, anger, and hostility.[44] One of the reasons less sleep, or poor sleep quality, puts people in a bad mood is that it impairs decision making and

MYTH OR SCIENCE?

"People Can't Accurately Forecast Their Own Emotions"

*t*his statement is essentially true. People tend to do a pretty bad job of predicting how they're going to feel when something happens. The research on this topic—called *affective forecasting*—shows that our poor job of affective forecasting takes two forms.

First, we tend to overestimate the pleasure we'll receive from a future positive event. We tend to think we'll be happier with a new car than is actually the case, that owning our own home will feel better than it actually does once we buy it, and even that marriage will make us happier than it will. Research on affective forecasting shows that we overestimate both the intensity (how happy we'll feel) and the duration (how long we'll feel happy) of future positive events. For example, when Joakim Noah was contemplating being a first-round basketball draft pick, a reporter asked him what he'd most look forward to. Noah said he couldn't wait to have "the best bathroom in the NBA." Noah was a first-round pick (by the Chicago Bulls), so chances are he got his world-class bathroom in Chicago, but chances also are that it didn't make him as happy as he thought it would.

A second area where we are not very good at affective forecasting is negative events. Just as positive events tend not to make us feel as good as we think they will, negative events don't make us feel as bad as we think they will.

Many different studies have supported our poor affective forecasting abilities: College students overestimate how happy or unhappy they'll be after being assigned to a good or bad dormitory, people overestimate how unhappy they'll be 2 months after a break-up, untenured college professors overestimate how happy they will be with tenure, and women overestimate the emotional impact of unwanted results for a pregnancy test.[45]

So, there is good news and bad news in this story: It's true that the highs aren't as high as we think, but it's also true that the lows aren't as low as we fear. Odds are, the future isn't as bright as you hope, but neither is it as bleak as you fear. ■

Sweat therapy enhances the mood of Mark Saunders, senior marketing manager at GlaxoSmithKline, a pharmaceutical firm. Saunders regularly works out with the help of a trainer at the company's fitness center. Saunders says exercise makes him more energetic and sharp and boosts his creativity and productivity. "Especially in winter, this keeps my engine going," he says. Like many other companies that provide fitness centers for employees, GlaxoSmithKline believes that exercise increases positive moods, resulting in happier, healthier, and more productive employees.

makes it difficult to control emotions.[46] A recent study suggests that poor sleep the previous night also impairs peoples' job satisfaction the next day, mostly because people feel fatigued, irritable, and less alert.[47]

Exercise   You often hear that people should exercise to improve their mood. But does "sweat therapy" really work? It appears so. Research consistently shows that exercise enhances peoples' positive mood.[48] It appears that the therapeutic effects of exercise are strongest for those who are depressed. Although the effects of exercise on moods are consistent, they are not terribly strong. So, exercise may help put you in a better mood, but don't expect miracles.

Age   Do you think that young people experience more extreme, positive emotions (so-called "youthful exuberance") than older people do? If you answered "yes," you were wrong. One study of people aged 18 to 94 years revealed that negative emotions seem to occur less as people get older. Periods of highly positive moods lasted longer for older individuals, and bad moods faded for them more quickly than for younger people.[49] The study implies that emotional experience tends to improve with age, so that as we get older, we experience fewer negative emotions.

Gender   The common belief is that women are more emotional than men. Is there any truth to this? The evidence does confirm that women are more emotionally expressive than are men;[50] they experience emotions more intensely, they tend to "hold onto" emotions longer than men, and they display more frequent expressions of both positive and negative emotions, except anger.[51] Although there may be innate differences between the genders, research suggests that emotional differences also are due to the different ways men and women have been socialized.[52] Men are taught to be tough and brave. Showing emotion is inconsistent with this image. Women, in contrast, are socialized to be nurturing. For instance, women are expected to express more positive emotions on the job (shown by smiling) than men, and they do.[53]

Emotional Recognition: Universal or Culture Specific?

Early researchers studying how we understand emotions based on others' expressions believed that all individuals, regardless of their culture, could recognize the same emotion. So, for example, a frown would be recognized as indicating the emotion sadness, no matter where one was from. However, more recent research suggests that this universal approach to the study of emotions is incorrect because there are subtle differences in the degree to which we can tell what emotions people from different cultures are feeling, based on their facial expressions.

One study examined how quickly and accurately we can read the facial expressions of people of different cultural backgrounds. Although individuals were at first faster at recognizing the emotional expression of others from their own culture, when living in a different culture, the speed and accuracy at which they recognized others' emotions increased as they became more familiar with the culture. For example, as Chinese residing in the United States adapted to their surroundings, they were able to recognize the emotions of people native to the United States more quickly. In fact, foreigners are sometimes better at recognizing emotions among the citizens in their non-native country than are those citizens themselves.

Interestingly, these effects begin to occur relatively quickly. For example, Chinese students living in the

United States for an average of 2.4 years were better at recognizing the facial expressions of U.S. citizens than they were at reading the facial expressions of Chinese citizens. Why is this the case? According to the authors of the study, it could be that because they are limited in speaking the language, they rely more on nonverbal communication. What is the upshot for OB? When conducting business in a foreign country, the ability to correctly recognize others' emotions can facilitate interactions and lead to less miscommunication. Otherwise, a slight smile that is intended to communicate disinterest may be mistaken for happiness.

Source: Based on H. A. Elfenbein and N. Ambady, "When Familiarity Breeds Accuracy: Cultural Exposure and Facial Emotion Recognition," *Journal of Personality and Social Psychology,* August 2003, pp. 276–290.

Emotional Labor

If you've ever had a job working in retail sales or waiting on tables in a restaurant, you know the importance of projecting a friendly demeanor and smiling. Even though there were days when you didn't feel cheerful, you knew management expected you to be upbeat when dealing with customers. So you faked it, and in so doing, you expressed emotional labor.

4 *Show the impact emotional labor has on employees.*

Every employee expends physical and mental labor when they put their bodies and cognitive capabilities, respectively, into their job. But jobs also require **emotional labor**. Emotional labor is an employee's expression of organizationally desired emotions during interpersonal transactions at work.[54]

The concept of emotional labor emerged from studies of service jobs. Airlines expect their flight attendants, for instance, to be cheerful; we expect funeral directors to be sad; and we expect doctors to be emotionally neutral. But really, emotional labor is relevant to almost every job. Your managers expect you, for example, to be courteous, not hostile, in interactions with coworkers. The true challenge arises when employees have to project one emotion while simultaneously feeling another.[55] This disparity is **emotional dissonance**, and it can take a heavy toll on employees. Bottled-up feelings of frustration, anger, and resentment can eventually lead to emotional exhaustion and burnout.[56] It's from the increasing importance of emotional labor as a key component of effective job performance that an understanding of emotion has gained heightened relevance within the field of OB.

When Apple's iPhone first went on sale at an Apple Store in San Francisco, employees enthusiastically greeted the first customers. Giving customers a warm reception with smiling faces and applause is an example of displayed emotions, those an organization requires employees to show and considers appropriate in a given job.

Emotional labor creates dilemmas for employees. There are people with whom you have to work that you just plain don't like. Maybe you consider their personality abrasive. Maybe you know they've said negative things about you behind your back. Regardless, your job requires you to interact with these people on a regular basis. So you're forced to feign friendliness.

It can help you, on the job especially, if you separate emotions into *felt* or *displayed emotions.*[57] **Felt emotions** are an individual's actual emotions. In contrast, **displayed emotions** are those that the organization requires workers to show and considers appropriate in a given job. They're not innate; they're learned. "The ritual look of delight on the face of the first runner-up as the new Miss America is announced is a product of the display rule that losers should mask their sadness with an expression of joy for the winner."[58] Similarly, most of us know that we're expected to act sad at funerals, regardless of whether we consider the person's death to be a loss, and to pretend to be happy at weddings, even if we don't feel like celebrating.[59]

Effective managers have learned to be serious when giving an employee a negative performance evaluation and to hide their anger when they've been passed over for promotion. And a salesperson who hasn't learned to smile and appear friendly, regardless of his true feelings at the moment, isn't typically going to last long on most sales jobs. How we *experience* an emotion isn't always the same as how we *show* it.[60]

Yet another point is that displaying fake emotions requires us to suppress the emotions we really feel (not showing anger toward a customer, for example). In other words, the individual has to "act" to keep her job. **Surface acting** is hiding

---

emotional labor A situation in which an employee expresses organizationally desired emotions during interpersonal transactions at work.

emotional dissonance Inconsistencies between the emotions people feel and the emotions they project.

felt emotions An individual's actual emotions.

displayed emotions Emotions that are organizationally required and considered appropriate in a given job.

surface acting Hiding one's inner feelings and forgoing emotional expressions in response to display rules.

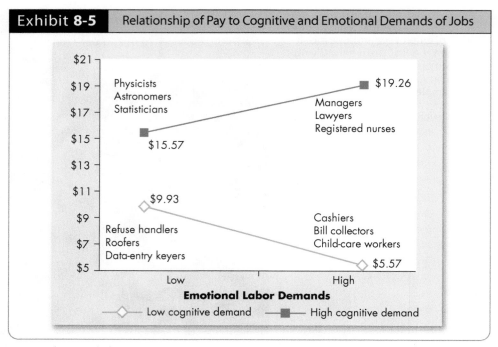

Exhibit 8-5   Relationship of Pay to Cognitive and Emotional Demands of Jobs

Physicists
Astronomers
Statisticians $19.26

Managers
Lawyers
Registered nurses

$15.57

$9.93

Refuse handlers
Roofers
Data-entry keyers

Cashiers
Bill collectors
Child-care workers

$5.57

Low   High

Emotional Labor Demands

◇ Low cognitive demand   ■ High cognitive demand

Source: Based on: T. M. Glomb, J. D. Kammeyer-Mueller, and M. Rotundo, "Emotional Labor Demands and Compensating Wage Differentials," *Journal of Applied Psychology* 89, no. 4 (August 2004), pp. 700–714.

one's inner feelings and forgoing emotional expressions in response to display rules. For example, when a worker smiles at a customer even when he doesn't feel like it, he is surface acting. **Deep acting** is trying to modify one's true inner feelings based on display rules. A health care provider trying to genuinely feel more empathy for her patients is deep acting.[61] Surface acting deals with one's *displayed* emotions, and deep acting deals with one's *felt* emotions. Research shows that surface acting is more stressful to employees than deep acting because it entails feigning one's true emotions.[62]

Interestingly, as important as managing emotions is to many jobs, it seems that the market does not necessarily reward emotional labor. A recent study found that emotional demands matter in setting compensation levels, but only when jobs are already cognitively demanding—such as jobs in law and nursing. But, for instance, child-care workers and waiters—holders of jobs with high emotional demands but relatively low cognitive demands—receive little compensation for the emotional demands of their work.[63] Exhibit 8-5 shows the relationship between cognitive and emotional demands and pay. The model doesn't seem to depict a fair state of affairs. After all, why should emotional demands be rewarded in only cognitively complex jobs? One explanation may be that it's hard to find qualified people who are willing and able to work in such jobs.

Affective Events Theory

5 Describe affective events theory and identify its applications.

As we have seen, emotions and moods are an important part of our lives, especially our work lives. But how do our emotions and moods influence our job performance and satisfaction? A model called **affective events theory (AET)** has increased our understanding of the links.[64] AET demonstrates that employees react emotionally to things that happen to them at work and that this reaction influences their job performance and satisfaction.

Exhibit 8-6   Affective Events Theory

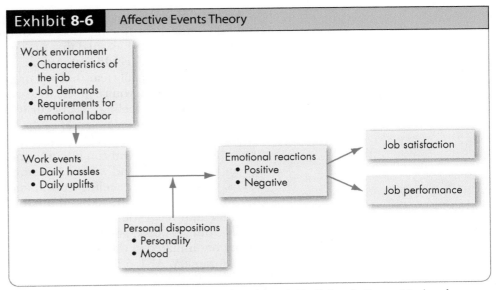

Source: Based on N. M. Ashkanasy and C. S. Daus, "Emotion in the Workplace: The New Challenge for Managers," *Academy of Management Executive,* February 2002, p. 77.

Exhibit 8-6 summarizes AET. The theory begins by recognizing that emotions are a response to an event in the work environment. The work environment includes everything surrounding the job—the variety of tasks and degree of autonomy, job demands, and requirements for expressing emotional labor. This environment creates work events that can be hassles, uplifting events, or both. Examples of hassles are colleagues who refuse to carry their share of work, conflicting directions from different managers, and excessive time pressures. Examples of uplifting events include meeting a goal, getting support from a colleague, and receiving recognition for an accomplishment.[65]

These work events trigger positive or negative emotional reactions. But employees' personalities and moods predispose them to respond with greater or lesser intensity to the event. For instance, people who score low on emotional stability are more likely to react strongly to negative events. And their mood introduces the reality that their general affect cycle creates fluctuations. So a person's emotional response to a given event can change, depending on mood. Finally, emotions influence a number of performance and satisfaction variables, such as organizational citizenship behavior, organizational commitment, level of effort, intentions to quit, and workplace deviance.

In addition, tests of the theory suggest that (1) an emotional episode is actually a series of emotional experiences precipitated by a single event. It contains elements of both emotions and mood cycles. (2) Current emotions influence job satisfaction at any given time, along with the history of emotions surrounding the event. (3) Because moods and emotions fluctuate over time, their effect on performance also fluctuates. (4) Emotion-driven behaviors are typically short in duration and of high variability. (5) Because emotions, even positive ones, tend to be incompatible with behaviors required to do a job, they typically have a negative influence on job performance.[66]

deep acting   *Trying to modify one's true inner feelings based on display rules.*

affective events theory (AET)   *A model that suggests that workplace events cause emotional reactions on the part of employees, which then influence workplace attitudes and behaviors.*

An example might help better explain AET.[67] Say that you work as an aeronautical engineer for Boeing. Because of the downturn in the demand for commercial jets, you've just learned that the company is considering laying off 10,000 employees. This layoff could include you. This event is likely to make you feel negative emotions, especially fear that you might lose your job and primary source of income. And because you're prone to worry a lot and obsess about problems, this event increases your feelings of insecurity. The layoff also puts into place a series of smaller events that create an episode: You talk with your boss, and he assures you that your job is safe; you hear rumors that your department is high on the list to be eliminated; and you run into a former colleague who was laid off 6 months ago and still hasn't found work. These events, in turn, create emotional ups and downs. One day, you're feeling upbeat and that you'll survive the cuts. The next day, you might be depressed and anxious. These emotional swings take your attention away from your work and lower your job performance and satisfaction. Finally, your response is magnified because this is the fourth-largest layoff that Boeing has initiated in the past 3 years.

In summary, AET offers two important messages.[68] First, emotions provide valuable insights into understanding employee behavior. The model demonstrates how workplace hassles and uplifting events influence employee performance and satisfaction. Second, employees and managers shouldn't ignore emotions and the events that cause them, even when they appear to be minor, because they accumulate.

Emotional Intelligence

Diane Marshall is an office manager. Her awareness of her own and others' emotions is almost nil. She's moody and unable to generate much enthusiasm or interest in her employees. She doesn't understand why employees get upset with her. She often overreacts to problems and chooses the most ineffectual responses to emotional situations.[69] Diane Marshall has low emotional intelligence. **Emotional intelligence (EI)** is a person's ability to (1) be self-aware (to recognize her own emotions when she experiences them), (2) detect emotions in others, and (3) manage emotional cues and information. People who know their own emotions and are good at reading emotion cues—for instance, knowing why they're angry and how to express themselves without violating norms—are most likely to be effective.[70]

6 *Contrast the evidence for and against the existence of emotional intelligence.*

Several studies suggest that EI plays an important role in job performance. One study looked at the characteristics of engineers at Lucent Technologies who were rated as stars by their peers. The researchers concluded that stars were better at relating to others. That is, it was EI, not IQ, that characterized high performers. Another illuminating study looked at the successes and failures of 11 American presidents—from Franklin Roosevelt to Bill Clinton. They were evaluated on six qualities—communication, organization, political skill, vision, cognitive style, and emotional intelligence. It was found that the key quality that differentiated the successful (such as Roosevelt, Kennedy, and Reagan) from the unsuccessful (such as Johnson, Carter, and Nixon) was emotional intelligence.[71]

EI has been a controversial concept in OB. It has supporters and detractors. In the following sections, we review the arguments for and against the viability of EI in OB.

The Case for EI

The arguments in favor of EI include its intuitive appeal, the fact that EI predicts criteria that matter, and the idea that EI is biologically based.

Meg Whitman, CEO of eBay, is a leader with high emotional intelligence. Since eBay founder Pierre Omidyar selected Whitman to transform his start-up into a global enterprise, she has emerged as a star performer in a job that demands interacting socially with employees, customers, and political leaders throughout the world. Whitman is described as self-confident yet humble, trustworthy, culturally sensitive, and expert at building teams and leading change. Shown here, Whitman welcomes Gloria Arroyo, president of the Philippine Islands where eBay has an auction site, to eBay headquarters.

Intuitive Appeal   There's a lot of intuitive appeal to the EI concept. Almost everyone would agree that it is good to possess street smarts and social intelligence. People who can detect emotions in others, control their own emotions, and handle social interactions well will have a powerful leg up in the business world, so the thinking goes. As just one example, partners in a multinational consulting firm who scored above the median on an EI measure delivered $1.2 million more in business than did the other partners.[72]

EI Predicts Criteria That Matter   More and more evidence is suggesting that a high level of EI means a person will perform well on the job. One study found that EI predicted the performance of employees in a cigarette factory in China.[73] Another study found that being able to recognize emotions in others' facial expressions and to emotionally "eavesdrop" (that is, pick up subtle signals about peoples' emotions) predicted peer ratings of how valuable those people were to their organization.[74] Finally, a review of 59 studies indicated that, overall, EI correlated moderately with job performance.[75]

EI Is Biologically Based   One study has shown that people with damage to the part of the brain that governs emotional processing (lesions in an area of the prefrontal cortex) score significantly lower than others on EI tests. Even though these brain-damaged people scored no lower on standard measures of intelligence than people without the same brain damage, they were still impaired in normal decision making. Specifically, when people were playing a card game in which there is a reward (money) for picking certain types of cards and a punishment (a loss of money) for picking other types of cards, the

emotional intelligence (EI)

The ability to detect and to manage emotional cues and information.

participants with no brain damage learned to succeed in the game, while the performance of the brain-damaged group worsened over time. This study suggests that EI is neurologically based in a way that's unrelated to standard measures of intelligence and that people who suffer neurological damage score lower on EI and make poorer decisions than people who are healthier in this regard.[76]

The Case Against EI

For all its supporters, EI has just as many critics. Its critics say that EI is vague and impossible to measure, and they question its validity.

EI Is Too Vague a Concept   To many researchers, it's not clear what EI is. Is it a form of intelligence? Most of us wouldn't think that being self-aware or self-motivated or having empathy is a matter of intellect. So, is EI a misnomer? Moreover, many times different researchers focus on different skills, making it difficult to get a definition of EI. One researcher may study self-discipline. Another may study empathy. Another may look at self-awareness. As one reviewer noted, "The concept of EI has now become so broad and the components so variegated that . . . it is no longer even an intelligible concept."[77]

EI Can't Be Measured   Many critics have raised questions about measuring EI. Because EI is a form of intelligence, for instance, there must be right and wrong answers about it on tests, they argue. Some tests do have right and wrong answers, although the validity of some of the questions on these measures is questionable. For example, one measure asks you to associate particular feelings with specific colors, as if purple always makes us feel cool and not warm. Other measures are self-reported, meaning there is no right or wrong answer. For example, an EI test question might ask you to respond to the statement, "I'm good at 'reading' other people." In general, the measures of EI are diverse, and researchers have not subjected them to as much rigorous study as they have measures of personality and general intelligence.[78]

The Validity of EI Is Suspect   Some critics argue that because EI is so closely related to intelligence and personality, once you control for these factors, EI has nothing unique to offer. There is some foundation to this argument. EI appears to be highly correlated with measures of personality, especially emotional stability.[79] But there hasn't been enough research on whether EI adds insight beyond measures of personality and general intelligence in predicting job performance. Still, among consulting firms and in the popular press, EI is wildly popular. For example, one company's promotional materials for an EI measure claimed, "EI accounts for more than 85 percent of star performance in top leaders."[80] To say the least, it's difficult to validate this statement with the research literature.

Weighing the arguments for and against EI, it's still too early to tell whether the concept is useful. It *is* clear, though, that the concept is here to stay.

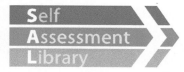

WHAT'S MY EMOTIONAL INTELLIGENCE SCORE?

In the Self-Assessment Library (available on CD or online), take assessment I.E.1 (What's My Emotional Intelligence Score?).

OB Applications of Emotions and Moods

7 *Apply concepts about emotions and moods to specific OB issues.*

In this section, we assess how an understanding of emotions and moods can improve our ability to explain and predict the selection process in organizations, decision making, creativity, motivation, leadership, interpersonal conflict, negotiation, customer service, job attitudes, and deviant workplace behaviors. We also look at how managers can influence our moods.

Selection

One implication from the evidence to date on EI is that employers should consider it a factor in hiring employees, especially in jobs that demand a high degree of social interaction. In fact, more and more employers are starting to use EI measures to hire people. A study of U.S. Air Force recruiters showed that top-performing recruiters exhibited high levels of EI. Using these findings, the Air Force revamped its selection criteria. A follow-up investigation found that future hires who had high EI scores were 2.6 times more successful than those who didn't. At L'Oreal, salespersons selected on EI scores outsold those hired using the company's old selection procedure. On an annual basis, salespeople selected on the basis of emotional competence sold $91,370 more than other salespeople did, for a net revenue increase of $2,558,360.[81]

Decision Making

As you saw in Chapter 5, traditional approaches to the study of decision making in organizations have emphasized rationality. More and more OB researchers, though, are finding that moods and emotions have important effects on decision making.

Positive moods and emotions seem to help decision making. People in good moods or those experiencing positive emotions are more likely than others to use heuristics, or rules of thumb,[82] to help make good decisions quickly. Positive emotions also enhance problem-solving skills so that positive people find better solutions to problems.[83]

The U.S. Air Force uses emotional intelligence as a selection criterion for recruiters, whose jobs demand a high degree of social interaction. By hiring recruiters with high EI scores, the Air Force has reduced turnover rates among new recruiters and decreased hiring and training costs. The recruiter shown here interacts with a new enlistee by teaching her the proper way to salute before she reports to boot camp.

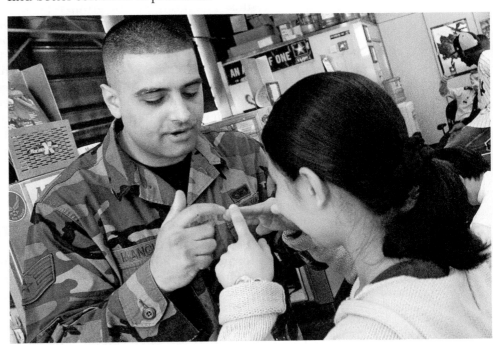

OB researchers continue to debate the role of negative emotions and moods in decision making. Although one often-cited study suggested that depressed people reach more accurate judgments,[84] more recent evidence has suggested that people who are depressed make poorer decisions. Why? Because depressed people are slower at processing information and tend to weigh all possible options rather than the most likely ones.[85] Although it would seem that weighing all possible options is a good thing, the problem is that depressed people search for the perfect solution when rarely is any solution perfect.

Creativity

People who are in good moods tend to be more creative than people in bad moods.[86] They produce more ideas, others think their ideas are original, and they tend to identify more creative options to problems.[87] It seems that people who are experiencing positive moods or emotions are more flexible and open in their thinking, which may explain why they're more creative.[88] Supervisors should actively try to keep employees happy because doing so creates more good moods (employees like their leaders to encourage them and provide positive feedback on a job well done), which in turn leads people to be more creative.[89]

Some researchers, however, do not believe that a positive mood makes people more creative. They argue that when people are in positive moods, they may relax ("If I'm in a good mood, things must be going okay, and I must not need to think of new ideas") and not engage in the critical thinking necessary for some forms of creativity.[90] However, this view is controversial.[91] Until there are more studies on the subject, we can safely conclude that for many tasks, positive moods increase our creativity.

Motivation

Two studies have highlighted the importance of moods and emotions on motivation. The first study had two groups of people solve a number of word puzzles. One group saw a funny video clip, which was intended to put the group in a good mood before having to solve the puzzles. The other group was not shown the clip and just started working on solving the word puzzles right away. The results? The positive-mood group reported higher expectations of being able to solve the puzzles, worked harder at them, and solved more puzzles as a result.[92]

The second study found that giving people feedback—whether real or fake—about their performance influenced their mood, which then influenced their motivation.[93] So a cycle can exist in which positive moods cause people to be more creative, which leads to positive feedback from those observing their work. This positive feedback then further reinforces their positive mood, which may then make them perform even better, and so on.

Both of these studies highlight the effects of mood and emotions on motivation and suggest that organizations that promote positive moods at work are likely to have more motivated workers.

Leadership

Effective leaders rely on emotional appeals to help convey their messages.[94] In fact, the expression of emotions in speeches is often the critical element that makes us accept or reject a leader's message. "When leaders feel excited, enthusiastic, and active, they may be more likely to energize their subordinates and convey a sense of efficacy, competence, optimism, and enjoyment."[95] Politicians, as a case in point, have learned to show enthusiasm when talking about their chances of winning an election, even when polls suggest otherwise.

Corporate executives know that emotional content is critical if employees are to buy into their vision of their company's future and accept change. When higher-ups

Known as an enthusiastic cheerleader for Microsoft, CEO Steve Ballmer travels the world, delivering impassioned speeches to inspire employees and business partners. Through his emotionally charged speeches, Ballmer presents a road map for employees and partners of Microsoft's competitive focus and company vision. "I want everyone to share my passion for our products and services," he says. "I want people to understand the amazing positive way our software can make leisure time more enjoyable and work and businesses more successful."

offer new visions, especially when the visions contain distant or vague goals, it is often difficult for employees to accept those visions and the changes they'll bring. By arousing emotions and linking them to an appealing vision, leaders increase the likelihood that managers and employees alike will accept change.[96]

Negotiation

Negotiation is an emotional process; however, we often say a skilled negotiator has a "poker face." The founder of Britain's Poker Channel, Crispin Nieboer, stated, "It is a game of bluff and there is fantastic human emotion and tension, seeing who can bluff the longest."[97] Several studies have shown that a negotiator who feigns anger has an advantage over the opponent. Why? Because when a negotiator shows anger, the opponent concludes that the negotiator has conceded all that she can, so the opponent gives in.[98]

Displaying a negative emotion (such as anger) can be effective, but feeling bad about your performance appears to impair future negotiations. Individuals who do poorly in a negotiation experience negative emotions, develop negative perceptions of their counterpart, and are less willing to share information or be cooperative in future negotiations.[99] Interestingly, then, while moods and emotions have benefits at work, in negotiation, unless we're putting up a false front (feigning anger), it seems that emotions may impair negotiator performance. In fact, a 2005 study found that people who suffered damage to the emotional centers of their brains (damage to the same part of the brain as Phineas Gage) may be the *best* negotiators because they're not likely to overcorrect when faced with negative outcomes.[100]

Customer Service

A worker's emotional state influences customer service, which influences levels of repeat business and levels of customer satisfaction.[101] Providing quality customer service makes demands on employees because it often puts them in a state of emotional dissonance. Over time, this state can lead to job burnout, declines in job performance, and lower job satisfaction.[102]

In addition, employees' emotions may transfer to the customer. Studies indicate a matching effect between employee and customer emotions, an effect that is called **emotional contagion**—the "catching" of emotions from others.[103] How does emotional contagion work? The primary explanation is that when someone experiences positive emotions and laughs and smiles at you, you begin to copy that person's behavior. So when employees express positive emotions, customers tend to respond positively. Emotional contagion is important because when customers catch the positive moods or emotions of employees they shop longer. But what about negative emotions and moods? Are they contagious, too? Absolutely. When an employee feels unfairly treated by a customer, for example, it's harder for him to display the positive emotions his organization expects of him.[104]

Job Attitudes

Ever hear the advice "Never take your work home with you," meaning that people should forget about their work once they go home? As it turns out, that's easier said than done. Several studies have shown that people who had a good day at work tend to be in a better mood at home that evening. And people who had a bad day tend to be in a bad mood once they're at home.[105] Evidence also suggests that people who have a stressful day at work have trouble relaxing after they get off work.[106]

Even though people do emotionally take their work home with them, by the next day, the effect is usually gone.[107] So, although it may be difficult or even unnatural to "never take your work home with you," it doesn't appear that, for most people, a negative mood resulting from a bad day at work carries over to the next day.

Deviant Workplace Behaviors

Negative emotions can lead to a number of deviant workplace behaviors.

Anyone who has spent much time in an organization realizes that people often behave in ways that violate established norms and that threaten the organization, its members, or both. As we saw in Chapter 1, these actions are called *workplace deviant behaviors*.[108] Many of these deviant behaviors can be traced to negative emotions.

For instance, envy is an emotion that occurs when you resent someone for having something that you don't have but that you strongly desire—such as a better work assignment, larger office, or higher salary.[109] It can lead to malicious deviant behaviors. An envious employee, for example, could then act hostilely by backstabbing another employee, negatively distorting others' successes, and positively distorting his own accomplishments.[110] Evidence suggests that people who feel negative emotions, particularly those who feel angry or hostile, are more likely than people who don't feel negative emotions to engage in deviant behavior at work.[111]

How Managers Can Influence Moods

In general, you can improve peoples' moods by showing them a funny video clip, giving them a small bag of candy, or even having them taste a pleasant beverage.[112] But what can companies do to improve their employees' moods? Managers can use humor and give their employees small tokens of appreciation for work well done. Also, research indicates that when leaders are in good moods, group members are more positive, and as a result, the members cooperate more.[113]

Finally, selecting positive team members can have a contagion effect as positive moods transmit from team member to team member. One study of professional cricket teams (cricket is a sport played in countries such as Great Britain and India that's a little like baseball) found that players' happy moods affected the moods of their team members and also positively influenced their performance.[114] It makes sense, then, for managers to select team members who are predisposed to experience positive moods.

OB In the News

Crying at Work Gains Acceptance

As we have noted, many employers discourage the expression of emotions at work, especially when those emotions are negative. Recently, though, there are signs that situation is starting to change.

One day, only 4 months into her first job, Hannah Seligson, now 24, was called into the big boss's office and told that her immediate supervisor was not happy with her work. She bawled on the spot. "I was just floored," she said. "I had been working so hard."

Kathryn Brady, 34, is a finance manager for a large corporation in Atlanta. Occasionally she has had bosses who have driven her to tears. Brady argues that when she has cried, it has been out of frustration, not weakness. "The misinterpretation that I'm whiny or weak is just not fair," she says.

To many, however, these emotional displays are signs of weakness. On the reality show *The Apprentice*, Martha Stewart warned one of the contestants not to cry. "Cry, and you're out of here," she said. "Women in business don't cry, my dear."

Although that "old school" wisdom still holds true in many places, it is changing in others. George Merkle, CEO of a San Antonio credit company, does not mind if his employees cry. If someone cries, he says, "No apology needed. I know it's upsetting, and we can work our way through it."

Surveys indicate that women are more likely to cry at work than men, but that may be changing, too. When 6'3" 253-pound football tight end Vernon Davis cried after being selected in the first round of the NFL draft, nobody accused him of being a wimp.

Sources: P. Kitchen, "Experts: Crying at Work on the Rise," *Newsday*, June 10, 2007; and S. Shellenbarger, "Read This and Weep," *Wall Street Journal*, April 26, 2007, p. D1.

Global Issues

8 *Contrast the experience, interpretation, and expression of emotions across cultures.*

Does the degree to which people *experience* emotions vary across cultures? Do peoples' *interpretations* of emotions vary across cultures? Finally, do the norms for the *expression* of emotions differ across cultures? Let's tackle each of these questions.

Does the Degree to Which People Experience Emotions Vary Across Cultures?   Yes. In China, for example, people report experiencing fewer positive and negative emotions than people in other cultures, and the emotions they experience are less intense than what other cultures report. Compared with Mainland Chinese, Taiwanese are more like U.S. workers in their experience of emotions: On average, Taiwanese report more positive and fewer negative emotions than their Chinese counterparts.[115] In general, people in most cultures appear to experience certain positive and negative emotions, but the frequency of their experience and their intensity varies to some degree.[116]

Do Peoples' Interpretations of Emotions Vary Across Cultures?   In general, people from all over the world interpret negative and positive emotions the same way. We all view negative emotions, such as hate, terror, and rage, as dangerous and destructive. And we all desire positive emotions, such as joy, love, and happiness. However, some cultures value certain emotions more than others. For example, U.S. culture values enthusiasm, while the Chinese consider negative emotions to be more useful and constructive than do people in the United States. In general, pride is seen as a positive emotion in Western, individualistic cultures such as the United States, but Eastern cultures such as China and Japan tend to view pride as undesirable.[117]

emotional contagion   *The process by which peoples' emotions are caused by the emotions of others.*

Do the Norms for the Expression of Emotions Differ Across Cultures?

Absolutely. For example, Muslims see smiling as a sign of sexual attraction, so women have learned not to smile at men.[118] And research has shown that in collectivist countries people are more likely to believe the emotional displays of another have something to do with their own relationship with the person expressing the emotion, while people in individualistic cultures don't think that another's emotional expressions are directed at them. Evidence indicates that in the United States there's a bias against expressing emotions, especially intense negative emotions. French retail clerks, in contrast, are infamous for being surly toward customers. (A report from the French government itself confirmed this.) There are also reports that serious German shoppers have been turned off by Wal-Mart's friendly greeters and helpful personnel.[119]

In general, and not surprisingly, it's easier for people to accurately recognize emotions within their own culture than in other cultures. For example, a Chinese businessperson is more likely to accurately label the emotions underlying the facial expressions of a fellow Chinese colleague than those of a U.S. colleague.[120]

Interestingly, some cultures lack words for standard U.S. emotional terms such as *anxiety, depression,* and *guilt.* Tahitians, as a case in point, don't have a word directly equivalent to *sadness.* When Tahitians are sad, their peers attribute their state to a physical illness.[121] Our discussion illustrates the need to consider the fact that cultural factors influence what managers think is emotionally appropriate.[122] What's acceptable in one culture may seem extremely unusual or even dysfunctional in another. Managers need to know the emotional norms in each culture they do business in or with so they don't send unintended signals or misread the reactions of others. For example, a U.S. manager in Japan should know that while U.S. culture tends to view smiling positively, the Japanese attribute frequent smiling to a lack of intelligence.[123]

Summary and Implications for Managers

Emotions and moods are similar in that both are affective in nature. But they're also different—moods are more general and less contextual than emotions. And events do matter. The time of day and day of the week, stressful events, social activities, and sleep patterns are some of the factors that influence emotions and moods.

Emotions and moods have proven themselves to be relevant for virtually every OB topic we study. Increasingly, organizations are selecting employees they believe have high levels of emotional intelligence. Emotions, especially positive moods, appear to facilitate effective decision-making and creativity. Although the research is relatively recent, research suggests that mood is linked to motivation, especially through feedback, and that leaders rely on emotions to increase their effectiveness. The display of emotions is important to negotiation and customer service, and the experience of emotions is closely linked to job attitudes and behaviors that follow from attitudes, such as deviant behavior in the workplace.

Can managers control their colleagues' and employees' emotions and moods? Certainly there are limits, practical and ethical. Emotions and moods are a natural part of an individual's makeup. Where managers err is in ignoring their coworkers' and employees' emotions and assessing others' behavior as if it were completely rational. As one consultant aptly put it, "You can't divorce emotions from the workplace because you can't divorce emotions from people."[124] Managers who understand the role of emotions and moods will significantly improve their ability to explain and predict their coworkers' and employees' behavior.

Point >< Counterpoint

THE COSTS AND BENEFITS OF ORGANIZATIONAL DISPLAY RULES

Organizations today realize that good customer service means good business. After all, who wants to end a shopping trip at the grocery store with a surly checker? Research clearly shows that organizations that provide good customer service have higher profits than those with poor customer service.[125] An integral part of customer-service training is to set forth display rules to teach employees to interact with customers in a friendly, helpful, professional way—and evidence indicates that such rules work: Having display rules increases the odds that employees will display the emotions expected of them.[126]

As one Starbucks manager says, "What makes Starbucks different is our passion for what we do. We're trying to provide a great experience for people, with a great product. That's what we all care about."[127] Starbucks may have good coffee, but a big part of the company's growth has been the customer experience. For instance, the cashiers are friendly and will get to know you by name if you are a repeat customer.

Asking employees to act friendly is good for them, too. Research shows that employees of organizations that require them to display positive emotions actually feel better as a result.[128] And, if someone feels that being asked to smile is bad for him, he doesn't belong in the service industry in the first place.

Organizations have no business trying to regulate the emotions of their employees. Companies should not be "the thought police" and force employees to feel and act in ways that serve only organizational needs. Service employees should be professional and courteous, yes, but many companies expect them to take abuse and refrain from defending themselves. That's wrong. As the philosopher Jean Paul Sartre wrote, we have a responsibility to be authentic—true to ourselves—and within reasonable limits organizations have no right to ask us to be otherwise.

Service industries have no business teaching their employees to be smiling punching bags. Most customers might even prefer that employees be themselves. Employees shouldn't be openly nasty or hostile, of course, but who appreciates a fake smile? Think about trying on an outfit in a store and the clerk automatically says it looks "absolutely wonderful" when you know it doesn't and you sense the clerk is lying. Most customers would rather talk with a "real" person than someone enslaved to an organization's display rules. Furthermore, if an employee doesn't feel like slapping on an artificial smile, then it's only going to create dissonance between her and her employer.[129]

Finally, research shows that forcing display rules on employees takes a heavy emotional toll.[130] It's unnatural to expect someone to smile all the time or to passively take abuse from customers, clients, or fellow employees. Organizations can improve their employees' psychological health by encouraging them to be themselves, within reasonable limits.

Questions for Review

1 What are the similarities and differences between emotions and moods? What are the basic emotions and the basic mood dimensions?

2 Are emotions and moods rational? What functions do emotions and moods serve?

3 What are the primary sources of emotions and moods?

4 What is emotional labor, and why is it important to understanding OB?

5 What is affective events theory? Why is it important to understanding emotions?

6 What is emotional intelligence, and what are the arguments for and against its importance?

7 What effect do emotions and moods have on different OB issues? As a manager, what steps would you take to improve your employees' moods?

8 Does the degree to which people *experience* emotions vary across cultures? Do peoples' *interpretations* of emotions vary across cultures, and do different norms across cultures govern the expression of emotions?

Experiential Exercise

WHO CAN CATCH A LIAR?

In this chapter, we discussed how people determine emotions from facial expressions. There has been research on whether people can tell whether someone is lying based on facial expression. Let's see who is good at catching liars. Split up into teams and follow these instructions.

1. Randomly choose someone to be the team organizer. Have this person write down on a piece of paper "T" for truth and "L" for lie. If there are, say, six people in the group (other than the organizer), then three people will get a slip with a "T" and three a slip with an "L." It's important that all team members keep what's on their paper a secret.

2. Each team member who holds a T slip needs to come up with a true statement, and each team member who holds

an L slip needs to come up with a false statement. Try not to make the statement so outrageous that no one would believe it (for example, "I have flown to the moon").

3. The organizer will have each member make his or her statement. Group members should then examine the person making the statement closely to try to determine whether he or she is telling the truth or lying. Once each person has made his or her statement, the organizer will ask for a vote and record the tallies.

4. Each person should now indicate whether the statement was the truth or a lie.

5. How good was your group at catching the liars? Were some people good liars? What did you look for to determine if someone was lying?

Ethical Dilemma

ARE WORKPLACE ROMANCES UNETHICAL?

A large percentage of married individuals first met in the workplace. A 2006 survey revealed that 40 percent of all employees have been in an office romance. Another survey of singles showed that most employees would be open to such a romance. Given the amount of time people spend at work, this isn't terribly surprising. Yet office romances pose sensitive ethical issues for organizations and employees. What rights and responsibilities do organizations have to regulate the romantic lives of their employees?

Take the example of Julie Roehm, senior VP of marketing at Wal-Mart, who began dating Sean Womack, VP of communications architecture. When Wal-Mart learned of

the relationship, it fired both Roehm and Womack, arguing that the undisclosed relationship violated its policy against workplace romances. After her firing, Roehm sued Wal-Mart, claiming that the company breached her contract and damaged her reputation. Wal-Mart then countersued, alleging that Roehm showed favoritism on Womack's behalf. Eventually, Roehm dropped her lawsuit in exchange for Wal-Mart dropping its countersuit.

The Wal-Mart, Julie Roehm, and Sean Womack saga shows that while workplace romances are personal matters, it's hard to keep them out of the political complexities of organizational life.

Questions

1. Nearly three-quarters of organizations have no policies governing workplace romances. Do you think organizations should have such policies in place?

2. Do you agree with Wal-Mart's policy against workplace romantic relationships? Why or why not?

3. Do you think it is ever appropriate for a supervisor to date an employee under his or her supervision? Why or why not?

4. Some companies, such as Nike and Southwest Airlines, openly try to recruit couples. Do you think this is a good idea? How would you feel working in a department with a "couple"?

Sources: J. Geenwald, "Employers Are the Losers in the Dating Game," *Workforce Week,* June 3, 2007, pp. 1–2; and "My Year at Wal-Mart," *Business Week,* February 12, 2007.

Case Incident 1

THE UPSIDE OF ANGER?

A researcher doing a case study on emotions in organizations interviewed Laura, a 22-year-old customer-service representative in Australia. The following is a summary of the interview (with some paraphrasing of the interviewer questions):

Interviewer: How would you describe your workplace?

Laura: *Very cold, unproductive, [a] very, umm, cold environment, atmosphere.*

Interviewer: What kinds of emotions are prevalent in your organization?

Laura: *Anger, hatred towards other people, other staff members.*

Interviewer: So it seems that managers keep employees in line using fear tactics?

Laura: *Yeah. [The General Manager's] favorite saying is, "Nobody's indispensable." So, it's like, "I can't do that because I'll get sacked!"*

Interviewer: How do you survive in this situation?

Laura: *You have to cater your emotions to the sort of situation, the specific situation . . . because it's just such a hostile environment, this is sort of the only way you can survive.*

Interviewer: Are there emotions you have to hide?

Laura: *Managers don't like you to show your emotions. . . . They don't like to show that there is anything wrong or anything emotional in the working environment.*

Interviewer: Why do you go along?

Laura: *I feel I have to put on an act because . . . to show your true emotions, especially towards my managers [Laura names two of her senior managers], it would be hatred sometimes. So, you just can't afford to do that because it's your job and you need the money.*

Interviewer: Do you ever rebel against this system?

Laura: *You sort of put on a happy face just so you can annoy [the managers]. I find that they don't like people being happy, so you just annoy them by being happy. So, yeah. It just makes you laugh. You just "put it on" just because you know it annoys [management]. It's pretty vindictive and manipulative but you just need to do that.*

Interviewer: Do you ever find that this gets to you?

Laura: *I did care in the beginning and I think it just got me into more trouble. So now I just tell myself, "I don't care." If you tell yourself something for long enough, eventually you believe it. Yeah, so now I just go "Oh well."*

Interviewer: Do you intend to keep working here?

Laura: *It's a means to an end now. So every time I go [to work] and every week I just go, "Well, one week down, one week less until I go away." But if I knew that I didn't have this goal, I don't know if I could handle it, or if I would even be there now.*

Interviewer: Is there an upside to working here?

Laura: *I'm so much better at telling people off now than I ever used to be. I can put people in place in about three sentences. Like, instead of, before I would walk away from it. But now I just stand there and fight. . . . I don't know if that's a good thing or a bad thing.*

Questions

1. Do you think Laura is justified in her responses to her organization's culture? Why or why not?

2. Do you think Laura's strategic use and display of emotions serve to protect her?

3. Assuming that Laura's description is accurate, how would *you* react to the organization's culture?

4. Research shows that acts of coworkers (37 percent) and management (22 percent) cause more negative emotions for employees than do acts of customers (7 percent).[131] What can Laura's company do to change its emotional climate?

Source: J. Perrone and M. H. Vickers, "Emotions as Strategic Game in a Hostile Workplace: An Exemplar Case," *Employee Responsibilities and Rights Journal* 16, no. 3 (2004), pp. 167–178.

Case Incident 2

ABUSIVE CUSTOMERS CAUSE EMOTIONS TO RUN HIGH

Telephone customer-service representatives have a tough time these days. With automated telephone systems that create a labyrinth for customers, result in long hold times, and make it difficult for them to speak to an actual human being, a customer's frustration often settles in before the representative has had time to say "hello." Says Donna Earl, an owner of a customer-service consulting firm in San Francisco, "By the time you get to the person you need to talk to, you're mad."

Erin Calabrese knows all too well just how mad customers can get. A customer-service representative at a financial services company, she still vividly recalls one of her worst experiences—with a customer named Jane. Jane called Calabrese over some charges on her credit card and began "ranting and raving." "Your #%#% company, who do you think you are?" yelled Jane. Though Calabrese tried to console the irate customer by offering a refund, Jane only called Calabrese an "idiot." The heated conversation continued for almost 10 minutes before Calabrese, shaking, handed the phone to her supervisor and left her desk.

Sometimes customers can be downright racist. One customer-service representative finally quit her job at a New Jersey company because she constantly heard racial remarks from customers after, she contends, they heard her Spanish accent. "By the time you leave, your head is spinning with all the complaints," she said.

Unfortunately, these employees have little choice but to take the abuse. Many companies require customer-service employees to display positive emotions at all times to maintain satisfied customers. But the result could be an emotional nightmare that doesn't necessarily end once the calls stop. Calabrese stated that she would frequently take her negative emotions home. The day after she received the abusive call from Jane, Calabrese went home and started a fight with her roommate. It was "an all-out battle," recalls Calabrese, "I just blew up." The former customer-service representative who worked in New Jersey also recalls the effects of the abusive calls on her family. "My children would say, 'Mom, stop talking about your work. You're home.' My husband would say the same thing," she said.

Emma Parsons, who quit her job as a customer-service representative for the travel industry, was frustrated by the inability to do anything about abusive customers and the mood they'd put her in. "Sometimes you'd finish a call and you'd want to smash somebody's face. I had no escape, no way of releasing." She said that if she did retaliate toward an abusive customer, her boss would punish her.

Some companies train their representatives to defuse a customer's anger and to avoid taking abuse personally, but the effort isn't enough. Liz Aherarn of Radclyffe Group, a consulting firm in Lincoln Park, New Jersey, says customer-service employees who work the phones are absent more frequently, are more prone to illness, and are more likely to make stress-related disability claims than other employees. Thus, it is apparent that in the world of customer service, particularly when interactions take place over the phone, emotions can run high, and the effects can be damaging. Although the adage "the customer comes first" has been heard by many, companies should empower employees to decide when it is appropriate to put the customer second. Otherwise, employees are forced to deal with abusive customers, the effects of which can be detrimental to both the individual and the company.

Questions

1. From an emotional labor perspective, how does dealing with an abusive customer lead to stress and burnout?

2. If you were a recruiter for a customer-service call center, what personality types would you prefer to hire and why? In other words, what individual differences are likely to affect whether an employee can handle customer abuse on a day-to-day basis?

3. Emotional intelligence is one's ability to detect and manage emotional cues and information. How might emotional intelligence play a role in responding to

abusive customers? What facets of emotional intelligence might employees who are able to handle abusive customers possess?

4. What steps should companies take to ensure that their employees are not victims of customer abuse?

Should companies allow a certain degree of abuse if that abuse results in satisfied customers and perhaps greater profit? What are the ethical implications of this?

Source: Based on S. Shellenbarger, "Domino Effect: The Unintended Results of Telling Off Customer-Service Staff," *Wall Street Journal,* February 5, 2004, p. D.1.

Endnotes

1. Based on J. McGregor, "Sweet Revenge," *BusinessWeek,* January 22, 2007, pp. 64–70.
2. See, for instance, C. D. Fisher and N. M. Ashkanasy, "The Emerging Role of Emotions in Work Life: An Introduction," *Journal of Organizational Behavior,* Special Issue 2000, pp. 123–129; N. M. Ashkanasy, C. E. J. Hartel, and W. J. Zerbe (eds.), *Emotions in the Workplace: Research, Theory, and Practice* (Westport, CT: Quorum Books, 2000); N. M. Ashkanasy and C. S. Daus, "Emotion in the Workplace: The New Challenge for Managers," *Academy of Management Executive,* February 2002, pp. 76–86; and N. M. Ashkanasy, C. E. J. Hartel, and C. S. Daus, "Diversity and Emotion: The New Frontiers in Organizational Behavior Research," *Journal of Management* 28, no. 3 (2002), pp. 307–338.
3. See, for example, L. L. Putnam and D. K. Mumby, "Organizations, Emotion and the Myth of Rationality," in S. Fineman (ed.), *Emotion in Organizations* (Thousand Oaks, CA: Sage, 1993), pp. 36–57; and J. Martin, K. Knopoff, and C. Beckman, "An Alternative to Bureaucratic Impersonality and Emotional Labor: Bounded Emotionality at the Body Shop," *Administrative Science Quarterly,* June 1998, pp. 429–469.
4. B. E. Ashforth and R. H. Humphrey, "Emotion in the Workplace: A Reappraisal," *Human Relations,* February 1995, pp. 97–125.
5. S. G. Barsade and D. E. Gibson, "Why Does Affect Matter in Organizations?" *Academy of Management Perspectives,* February 2007, pp. 36–59.
6. See N. H. Frijda, "Moods, Emotion Episodes and Emotions," in M. Lewis and J. M. Haviland (eds.), *Handbook of Emotions* (New York: Guilford Press, 1993), pp. 381–403.
7. H. M. Weiss and R. Cropanzano, "Affective Events Theory: A Theoretical Discussion of the Structure, Causes and Consequences of Affective Experiences at Work," in B. M. Staw and L. L. Cummings (eds.), *Research in Organizational Behavior,* vol. 18 (Greenwich, CT: JAI Press, 1996), pp. 17–19.
8. See P. Ekman and R. J. Davidson (eds.), *The Nature of Emotions: Fundamental Questions* (Oxford, UK: Oxford University Press, 1994).
9. Frijda, "Moods, Emotion Episodes and Emotions," p. 381.
10. See Ekman and Davidson (eds.), *The Nature of Emotions.*
11. See, for example, P. Ekman, "An Argument for Basic Emotions," *Cognition and Emotion,* May/July 1992, pp. 169–200; C. E. Izard, "Basic Emotions, Relations Among Emotions, and Emotion–Cognition Relations," *Psychological Bulletin,* November 1992, pp. 561–565; and J. L. Tracy and R. W. Robins, "Emerging Insights into the Nature and Function of Pride," *Current Directions in Psychological Science* 16, no. 3 (2007), pp. 147–150.
12. R. C. Solomon, "Back to Basics: On the Very Idea of 'Basic Emotions,'" *Journal for the Theory of Social Behaviour* 32, no. 2 (June 2002), pp. 115–144.
13. R. Descartes, *The Passions of the Soul* (Indianapolis: Hackett, 1989).
14. P. Ekman, *Emotions Revealed: Recognizing Faces and Feelings to Improve Communication and Emotional Life* (New York: Times Books/Henry Holt and Co., 2003).
15. P. R. Shaver, H. J. Morgan, and S. J. Wu, "Is Love a 'Basic' emotion?" *Personal Relationships* 3, no. 1 (March 1996), pp. 81–96.
16. Solomon, "Back to Basics."
17. Weiss and Cropanzano, "Affective Events Theory," pp. 20–22.
18. Cited in R. D. Woodworth, *Experimental Psychology* (New York: Holt, 1938).
19. D. Watson, L. A. Clark, and A. Tellegen, "Development and Validation of Brief Measures of Positive and Negative Affect: The PANAS Scales," *Journal of Personality and Social Psychology,* 1988, pp. 1063–1070.
20. A. Ben-Ze'ev, *The Subtlety of Emotions* (Cambridge, MA: MIT Press, 2000), p. 94.
21. "Flight Attendant War Stories . . . Stewardess," *AboutMyJob.com,* www.aboutmyjob.com/main.php3?action=displayarticle&artid=2111.
22. Cited in Ibid., p. 99.
23. J. T. Cacioppo and W. L. Gardner, "Emotion," in *Annual Review of Psychology,* vol. 50 (Palo Alto, CA: Annual Reviews, 1999), pp. 191–214.
24. D. Holman, "Call Centres," in D. Holman, T. D. Wall, C. Clegg, P. Sparrow, and A. Howard (eds.), *The Essentials of the New Work Place: A Guide to the Human Impact of Modern Working Practices* (Chichester, UK: Wiley, 2005), pp. 111–132.
25. L. M. Poverny and S. Picascia, "There Is No Crying in Business," *Womensmedia.com,* www.womensmedia.com/new/Crying-at-Work.shtml.
26. L. P. Frankel, *Nice Girls Don't Get the Corner Office* (New York: Warner Book, 2004).
27. A. R. Damasio, *Descartes' Error: Emotion, Reason, and the Human Brain* (New York: Quill, 1994).
28. Ibid.
29. L. Cosmides and J. Tooby, "Evolutionary Psychology and the Emotions," in M. Lewis and J. M. Haviland-Jones (eds.), *Handbook of Emotions,* 2nd ed. (New York: Guilford Press, 2000), pp. 91–115.
30. D. M. Buss, "Cognitive Biases and Emotional Wisdom in the Evolution of Conflict Between the Sexes," *Current Directions in Psychological Science* 10, no. 6 (December 2001), pp. 219–223.

31. K. Hundley, "An Unspoken Problem: Two-Thirds of Female Lawyers Say They Have Experienced or Seen Harassment at Work. But Few Want to Talk About It," *St. Petersburg (Florida) Times*, April 25, 2004, www.sptimes.com/2005/04/24/Business/An_unspoken_problem.shtml.

32. K. N. Laland and G. R. Brown, *Sense and Nonsense: Evolutionary Perspectives on Human Behaviour* (Oxford, UK: Oxford University Press, 2002).

33. R. J. Larsen and E. Diener, "Affect Intensity as an Individual Difference Characteristic: A Review," *Journal of Research in Personality* 21 (1987), pp. 1–39.

34. D. Watson, *Mood and Temperament* (New York: Guilford Press, 2000).

35. Ibid.

36. Ibid.

37. Ibid., p. 100.

38. Ibid., p. 73.

39. J. A. Fuller, J. M. Stanton, G. G. Fisher, C. Spitzmüller, S. S. Russell, and P. C. Smith, "A Lengthy Look at the Daily Grind: Time Series Analysis of Events, Mood, Stress, and Satisfaction," *Journal of Applied Psychology* 88, no. 6 (December 2003), pp. 1019–1033.

40. See "Monday Blahs," May 16, 2005, www.ashidome.com/blogger/housearrest.asp?c=809&m=5&y=2005.

41. A. M. Isen, "Positive Affect as a Source of Human Strength," in L. G. Aspinwall and U. Staudinger (eds.), *The Psychology of Human Strengths* (Washington, DC: American Psychological Association, 2003), pp. 179–195.

42. Watson, *Mood and Temperament* (2000).

43. *Sleep in America Poll* (Washington, DC: National Sleep Foundation, 2005).

44. M. Lavidor, A. Weller, and H. Babkoff, "How Sleep Is Related to Fatigue," *British Journal of Health Psychology* 8 (2003), pp. 95–105; and J. J. Pilcher and E. Ott, "The Relationships Between Sleep and Measures of Health and Well-Being in College Students: A Repeated Measures Approach," *Behavioral Medicine* 23 (1998), pp. 170–178.

45. T. D. Wilson and D. T. Gilbert, "Affective Forecasting: Knowing What to Want," *Current Directions in Psychological Science*, June 2005, pp. 131–134.

46. E. K. Miller and J. D. Cohen, "An Integrative Theory of Prefrontal Cortex Function," *Annual Review of Neuroscience* 24 (2001), pp. 167–202.

47. B. A. Scott and T. A. Judge, "Tired and Cranky? The Effects of Sleep Quality on Employee Emotions and Job Satisfaction," working paper, Department of Management, University of Florida, 2005.

48. P. R. Giacobbi, H. A. Hausenblas, and N. Frye, "A Naturalistic Assessment of the Relationship Between Personality, Daily Life Events, Leisure-Time Exercise, and Mood," *Psychology of Sport & Exercise* 6, no. 1 (January 2005), pp. 67–81.

49. L. L. Carstensen, M. Pasupathi, M. Ulrich, and J. R. Nesselroade, "Emotional Experience in Everyday Life Across the Adult Life Span," *Journal of Personality and Social Psychology* 79, no. 4 (2000), pp. 644–655.

50. K. Deaux, "Sex Differences," in M. R. Rosenzweig and L. W. Porter (eds.), *Annual Review of Psychology*, vol. 26 (Palo Alto, CA: Annual Reviews, 1985), pp. 48–82; M. LaFrance and M. Banaji, "Toward a Reconsideration of the Gender–Emotion Relationship," in M. Clark (ed.), *Review of Personality and Social*

Psychology, vol. 14 (Newbury Park, CA: Sage, 1992), pp. 178–197; and A. M. Kring and A. H. Gordon, "Sex Differences in Emotion: Expression, Experience, and Physiology," *Journal of Personality and Social Psychology*, March 1998, pp. 686–703.

51. L. R. Brody and J. A. Hall, "Gender and Emotion," in M. Lewis and J. M. Haviland (eds.), *Handbook of Emotions* (New York: Guilford Press, 1993), pp. 447–460; M. G. Gard and A. M. Kring, "Sex Differences in the Time Course of Emotion," *Emotion* 7, no. 2 (2007), pp. 429–437; and M. Grossman and W. Wood, "Sex Differences in Intensity of Emotional Experience: A Social Role Interpretation," *Journal of Personality and Social Psychology*, November 1992, pp. 1010–1022.

52. N. James, "Emotional Labour: Skill and Work in the Social Regulations of Feelings," *Sociological Review*, February 1989, pp. 15–42; A. Hochschild, *The Second Shift* (New York: Viking, 1989); and F. M. Deutsch, "Status, Sex, and Smiling: The Effect of Role on Smiling in Men and Women," *Personality and Social Psychology Bulletin*, September 1990, pp. 531–540.

53. A. Rafaeli, "When Clerks Meet Customers: A Test of Variables Related to Emotional Expression on the Job," *Journal of Applied Psychology*, June 1989, pp. 385–393; and LaFrance and Banaji, "Toward a Reconsideration of the Gender–Emotion Relationship."

54. See J. A. Morris and D. C. Feldman, "Managing Emotions in the Workplace," *Journal of Managerial Issues* 9, no. 3 (1997), pp. 257–274; S. Mann, *Hiding What We Feel, Faking What We Don't: Understanding the Role of Your Emotions at Work* (New York: HarperCollins, 1999); and S. M. Kruml and D. Geddes, "Catching Fire Without Burning Out: Is There an Ideal Way to Perform Emotion Labor?" in N. M. Ashkansay, C. E. J. Hartel, and W. J. Zerbe, *Emotions in the Workplace* (New York: Quorum Books, 2000), pp. 177–188.

55. P. Ekman, W. V. Friesen, and M. O'sullivan, "Smiles When Lying," in P. Ekman and E. L. Rosenberg (eds.), *What the Face Reveals: Basic and Applied Studies of Spontaneous Expression Using the Facial Action Coding System (FACS)* (London: Oxford University Press, 1997), pp. 201–216.

56. A. Grandey, "Emotion Regulation in the Workplace: A New Way to Conceptualize Emotional Labor," *Journal of Occupational Health Psychology* 5, no. 1 (2000), pp. 95–110; and R. Cropanzano, D. E. Rupp, and Z. S. Byrne, "The Relationship of Emotional Exhaustion to Work Attitudes, Job Performance, and Organizational Citizenship Behavior," *Journal of Applied Psychology*, February 2003, pp. 160–169.

57. A. R. Hochschild, "Emotion Work, Feeling Rules, and Social Structure," *American Journal of Sociology*, November 1979, pp. 551–575; W.-C. Tsai, "Determinants and Consequences of Employee Displayed Positive Emotions," *Journal of Management* 27, no. 4 (2001), pp. 497–512; M. W. Kramer and J. A. Hess, "Communication Rules for the Display of Emotions in Organizational Settings," *Management Communication Quarterly*, August 2002, pp. 66–80; and J. M. Diefendorff and E. M. Richard, "Antecedents and Consequences of Emotional Display Rule Perceptions," *Journal of Applied Psychology*, April 2003, pp. 284–294.

58. B. M. DePaulo, "Nonverbal Behavior and Self-Presentation," *Psychological Bulletin*, March 1992, pp. 203–243.

59. C. S. Hunt, "Although I Might Be Laughing Loud and Hearty, Deep Inside I'm Blue: Individual Perceptions Regarding Feeling and Displaying Emotions at Work," paper

presented at the Academy of Management Conference, Cincinnati, August 1996, p. 3.

60. Solomon, "Back to Basics."

61. C. M. Brotheridge and R. T. Lee, "Development and Validation of the Emotional Labour Scale," *Journal of Occupational & Organizational Psychology* 76, no. 3 (September 2003), pp. 365–379.

62. A. A. Grandey, "When 'the Show Must Go On': Surface Acting and Deep Acting as Determinants of Emotional Exhaustion and Peer-Rated Service Delivery," *Academy of Management Journal*, February 2003, pp. 86–96; and A. A. Grandey, D. N. Dickter, and H. Sin, "The Customer Is Not Always Right: Customer Aggression and Emotion Regulation of Service Employees," *Journal of Organizational Behavior* 25, no. 3 (May 2004), pp. 397–418.

63. T. M. Glomb, J. D. Kammeyer-Mueller, and M. Rotundo, "Emotional Labor Demands and Compensating Wage Differentials," *Journal of Applied Psychology* 89, no. 4 (August 2004), pp. 700–714.

64. H. M. Weiss and R. Cropanzano, "An Affective Events Approach to Job Satisfaction," *Research in Organizational Behavior* 18 (1996), pp. 1–74.

65. J. Basch and C. D. Fisher, "Affective Events–Emotions Matrix: A Classification of Work Events and Associated Emotions," in N. M. Ashkanasy, C. E. J. Hartel, and W. J. Zerbe, (eds.), *Emotions in the Workplace* (Westport, CT: Quorum Books, 2000), pp. 36–48.

66. See, for example, H. M. Weiss and R. Cropanzano, "Affective Events Theory"; and C. D. Fisher, "Antecedents and Consequences of Real-Time Affective Reactions at Work," *Motivation and Emotion*, March 2002, pp. 3–30.

67. Based on H. M. Weiss and R. Cropanzano, "Affective Events Theory," p. 42.

68. N. M. Ashkanasy, C. E. J. Hartel, and C. S. Daus, "Diversity and Emotion: The New Frontiers in Organizational Behavior Research," *Journal of Management* 28, no. 3 (2002), p. 324.

69. Based on D. R. Caruso, J. D. Mayer, and P. Salovey, "Emotional Intelligence and Emotional Leadership," in R. E. Riggio, S. E. Murphy, and F. J. Pirozzolo (eds.), *Multiple Intelligences and Leadership* (Mahwah, NJ: Lawrence Erlbaum, 2002), p. 70.

70. This section is based on Daniel Goleman, *Emotional Intelligence* (New York: Bantam, 1995); P. Salovey and D. Grewal, "The Science of Emotional Intelligence," *Current Directions in Psychological Science* 14, no. 6 (2005), pp. 281–285; M. Davies, L. Stankov, and R. D. Roberts, "Emotional Intelligence: In Search of an Elusive Construct," *Journal of Personality and Social Psychology*, October 1998, pp. 989–1015; D. Geddes and R. R. Callister, "Crossing the Line(s): A Dual Threshold Model of Anger in Organizations," *Academy of Management Review* 32, no. 3 (2007), pp. 721–746; and J. Ciarrochi, J. P. Forgas, and J. D. Mayer (eds.), *Emotional Intelligence in Everyday Life* (Philadelphia: Psychology Press, 2001).

71. F. I. Greenstein, *The Presidential Difference: Leadership Style from FDR to Clinton* (Princeton, NJ: Princeton University Press, 2001).

72. C. Cherniss, "The Business Case for Emotional Intelligence," *Consortium for Research on Emotional Intelligence in Organizations*, 1999, www.eiconsortium.org/research/business_case_for_ei.pdf.

73. K. S. Law, C. Wong, and L. J. Song, "The Construct and Criterion Validity of Emotional Intelligence and Its Potential Utility for Management Studies," *Journal of Applied Psychology* 89, no. 3 (2004), pp. 483–496.

74. H. A. Elfenbein and N. Ambady, "Predicting Workplace Outcomes from the Ability to Eavesdrop on Feelings," *Journal of Applied Psychology* 87, no. 5 (October 2002), pp. 963–971.

75. D. L. Van Rooy and C. Viswesvaran, "Emotional Intelligence: A Meta-analytic Investigation of Predictive Validity and Nomological Net," *Journal of Vocational Behavior* 65, no. 1 (August 2004), pp. 71–95.

76. R. Bar-On, D. Tranel, N. L. Denburg, and A. Bechara, "Exploring the Neurological Substrate of Emotional and Social Intelligence," *Brain* 126, no. 8 (August 2003), pp. 1790–1800.

77. E. A. Locke, "Why Emotional Intelligence Is an Invalid Concept," *Journal of Organizational Behavior* 26, no. 4 (June 2005), pp. 425–431.

78. J. M. Conte, "A Review and Critique of Emotional Intelligence Measures," *Journal of Organizational Behavior* 26, no. 4 (June 2005), pp. 433–440; and M. Davies, L. Stankov, and R. D. Roberts, "Emotional Intelligence: In Search of an Elusive Construct," *Journal of Personality and Social Psychology* 75, no. 4 (1998), pp. 989–1015.

79. T. Decker, "Is Emotional Intelligence a Viable Concept?" *Academy of Management Review* 28, no. 2 (April 2003), pp. 433–440; and Davies, Stankov, and Roberts, "Emotional Intelligence: In Search of an Elusive Construct."

80. F. J. Landy, "Some Historical and Scientific Issues Related to Research on Emotional Intelligence," *Journal of Organizational Behavior* 26, no. 4 (June 2005), pp. 411–424.

81. L. M. J. Spencer, D. C. McClelland, and S. Kelner, *Competency Assessment Methods: History and State of the Art* (Boston: Hay/McBer, 1997).

82. J. Park and M. R. Banaji, "Mood and Heuristics: The Influence of Happy and Sad States on Sensitivity and Bias in Stereotyping," *Journal of Personality and Social Psychology* 78, no. 6 (2000), pp. 1005–1023.

83. See A. M. Isen, "Positive Affect and Decision Making," in M. Lewis and J. M. Haviland-Jones (eds.), *Handbook of Emotions*, 2nd ed. (New York: Guilford, 2000), pp. 261–277.

84. L. B. Alloy and L. Y. Abramson, "Judgement of Contingency in Depressed and Nondepressed Students: Sadder but Wiser?" *Journal of Experimental Psychology: General* 108 (1979), pp. 441–485.

85. N. Ambady and H. M. Gray, "On Being Sad and Mistaken: Mood Effects on the Accuracy of Thin-Slice Judgments," *Journal of Personality and Social Psychology* 83, no. 4 (2002), pp. 947–961.

86. A. M. Isen, "On the Relationship Between Affect and Creative Problem Solving," in S. W. Russ (ed.), *Affect, Creative Experience and Psychological Adjustment* (Philadelphia, PA: Brunner/Mazel, 1999), pp. 3–17; and S. Lyubomirsky, L. King, and E. Diener, "The Benefits of Frequent Positive Affect: Does Happiness Lead to Success?" *Psychological Bulletin* 131, no. 6 (2005), pp. 803–855.

87. M. J. Grawitch, D. C. Munz, and E. K. Elliott, "Promoting Creativity in Temporary Problem-Solving Groups: The Effects of Positive Mood and Autonomy in Problem

Definition on Idea-Generating Performance," *Group Dynamics* 7, no. 3 (September 2003), pp. 200–213.

88. S. Lyubomirsky, L. King, and E. Diener, "The Benefits of Frequent Positive Affect: Does Happiness Lead to Success?" *Psychological Bulletin* 131, no. 6 (2005), pp. 803–855.

89. N. Madjar, G. R. Oldham, and M. G. Pratt, "There's No Place Like Home? The Contributions of Work and Nonwork Creativity Support to Employees' Creative Performance," *Academy of Management Journal* 45, no. 4 (2002), pp. 757–767.

90. J. M. George and J. Zhou, "Understanding When Bad Moods Foster Creativity and Good Ones Don't: The Role of Context and Clarity of Feelings," *Journal of Applied Psychology* 87, no. 4 (August 2002), pp. 687–697; and J. P. Forgas and J. M. George, "Affective Influences on Judgments and Behavior in Organizations: An Information Processing Perspective," *Organizational Behavior and Human Decision Processes* 86, no. 1 (2001), pp. 3–34.

91. L. L. Martin, "Mood as Input: A Configural View of Mood Effects," in L. L. Martin and G. L. Clore (eds.), *Theories of Mood and Cognition: A User's Guidebook* (Mahwah, NJ: Lawrence Erlbaum, 2001), pp. 135–157.

92. A. Erez and A. M. Isen, "The Influence of Positive Affect on the Components of Expectancy Motivation," *Journal of Applied Psychology* 87, no. 6 (2002), pp. 1055–1067.

93. R. Ilies and T. A. Judge, "Goal Regulation Across Time: The Effect of Feedback and Affect," *Journal of Applied Psychology* 90, no. 3 (May 2005), pp. 453–467.

94. K. M. Lewis, "When Leaders Display Emotion: How Followers Respond to Negative Emotional Expression of Male and Female Leaders," *Journal of Organizational Behavior*, March 2000, pp. 221–234; and J. M. George, "Emotions and Leadership: The Role of Emotional Intelligence," *Human Relations*, August 2000, pp. 1027–1055.

95. George, "Trait and State Affect," p. 162.

96. Ashforth and Humphrey, "Emotion in the Workplace," p. 116.

97. N. Reynolds, "Whiz-Kids Gamble on TV Channel for Poker," *telegraph.co.uk*, April 16, 2005, www.telegraph.co.uk.

98. G. A. Van Kleef, C. K. W. De Dreu, and A. S. R. Manstead, "The Interpersonal Effects of Emotions in Negotiations: A Motivated Information Processing Approach," *Journal of Personality and Social Psychology* 87, no. 4 (2004), pp. 510–528; and G. A. Van Kleef, C. K. W. De Dreu, and A. S. R. Manstead, "The Interpersonal Effects of Anger and Happiness in Negotiations," *Journal of Personality and Social Psychology* 86, no. 1 (2004), pp. 57–76.

99. K. M. O'Connor and J. A. Arnold, "Distributive Spirals: Negotiation Impasses and the Moderating Role of Disputant Self-Efficacy," *Organizational Behavior and Human Decision Processes* 84, no. 1 (2001), pp. 148–176.

100. B. Shiv, G. Loewenstein, A. Bechara, H. Damasio, and A. R. Damasio, "Investment Behavior and the Negative Side of Emotion," *Psychological Science* 16, no. 6 (2005), pp. 435–439.

101. W.-C. Tsai and Y.-M. Huang, "Mechanisms Linking Employee Affective Delivery and Customer Behavioral Intentions," *Journal of Applied Psychology*, October 2002, pp. 1001–1008.

102. Grandey, "When 'the Show Must Go On.'"

103. See P. B. Barker and A. A. Grandey, "Service with a Smile and Encounter Satisfaction: Emotional Contagion and Appraisal Mechanisms," *Academy of Management Journal* 49, no. 6 (2006), pp. 1229–1238; and S. D. Pugh, "Service with a Smile: Emotional Contagion in the Service Encounter," *Academy of Management Journal*, October 2001, pp. 1018–1027.

104. D. E. Rupp and S. Spencer, "When Customers Lash Out: The Effects of Customer Interactional Injustice on Emotional Labor and the Mediating Role of Emotions," *Journal of Applied Psychology* 91, no. 4 (2006), pp. 971–978; and Tsai and Huang, "Mechanisms Linking Employee Affective Delivery and Customer Behavioral Intentions."

105. R. Ilies and T. A. Judge, "Understanding the Dynamic Relationships Among Personality, Mood, and Job Satisfaction: A Field Experience Sampling Study," *Organizational Behavior and Human Decision Processes* 89 (2002), pp. 1119–1139.

106. R. Rau, "Job Strain or Healthy Work: A Question of Task Design," *Journal of Occupational Health Psychology* 9, no. 4 (October 2004), pp. 322–338; and R. Rau and A. Triemer, "Overtime in Relation to Blood Pressure and Mood During Work, Leisure, and Night Time," *Social Indicators Research* 67, no. 1–2 (June 2004), pp. 51–73.

107. T. A. Judge and R. Ilies, "Affect and Job Satisfaction: A Study of Their Relationship at Work and at Home," *Journal of Applied Psychology* 89 (2004), pp. 661–673.

108. See R. J. Bennett and S. L. Robinson, "Development of a Measure of Workplace Deviance," *Journal of Applied Psychology*, June 2000, pp. 349–360. See also P. R. Sackett and C. J. DeVore, "Counterproductive Behaviors at Work," in N. Anderson, D. S. Ones, H. K. Sinangil, and C. Viswesvaran (eds.), *Handbook of Industrial, Work & Organizational Psychology*, vol. 1 (Thousand Oaks, CA: Sage, 2001), pp. 145–164.

109. A. G. Bedeian, "Workplace Envy," *Organizational Dynamics*, Spring 1995, p. 50; and Ben-Ze'ev, *The Subtlety of Emotions*, pp. 281–326.

110. Bedeian, "Workplace Envy," p. 54.

111. K. Lee and N. J. Allen, "Organizational Citizenship Behavior and Workplace Deviance: The Role of Affect and Cognition," *Journal of Applied Psychology* 87, no. 1 (2002), pp. 131–142; and T. A. Judge, B. A. Scott, and R. Ilies, "Hostility, Job Attitudes, and Workplace Deviance: Test of a Multilevel Model," *Journal of Applied Psychology* 91, no. 1 (2006) 126–138.

112. A. M. Isen, A. A. Labroo, and P. Durlach, "An Influence of Product and Brand Name on Positive Affect: Implicit and Explicit Measures," *Motivation & Emotion* 28, no. 1 (March 2004), pp. 43–63.

113. T. Sy, S. Côté, and R. Saavedra, "The Contagious Leader: Impact of the Leader's Mood on the Mood of Group Members, Group Affective Tone, and Group Processes," *Journal of Applied Psychology* 90, no. 2 (2005), pp. 295–305.

114. P. Totterdell, "Catching Moods and Hitting Runs: Mood Linkage and Subjective Performance in Professional Sports Teams," *Journal of Applied Psychology* 85, no. 6 (2000), pp. 848–859.

115. M. Eid and E. Diener, "Norms for Experiencing Emotions in Different Cultures: Inter- and International Differences," *Journal of Personality & Social Psychology* 81, no. 5 (2001), pp. 869–885.

116. S. Oishi, E. Diener, and C. Napa Scollon, "Cross-Situational Consistency of Affective Experiences Across Cultures," *Journal of Personality & Social Psychology* 86, no. 3 (2004), pp. 460–472.

117. Eid and Diener, "Norms for Experiencing Emotions in Different Cultures."

118. Ibid.

119. Ashforth and Humphrey, "Emotion in the Workplace," p. 104; B. Plasait, "Accueil des Touristes Dans les Grands Centres de Transit Paris," *Rapport du Bernard Plasait*, October 4, 2004, www.tourisme.gouv.fr/fr/navd/presse/dossiers/att00005767/dp_plasait.pdf; B. Mesquita, "Emotions in Collectivist and Individualist Contexts," *Journal of Personality and Social Psychology* 80, no. 1 (2001), pp. 68–74; and D. Rubin, "Grumpy German Shoppers Distrust the Wal-Mart Style," *Seattle Times*, December 30, 2001, p. A15.

120. H. A. Elfenbein and N. Ambady, "When Familiarity Breeds Accuracy: Cultural Exposure and Facial Emotional Recognition," *Journal of Personality and Social Psychology* 85, no. 2 (2003), pp. 276–290.

121. R. I. Levy, *Tahitians: Mind and Experience in the Society Islands* (Chicago: University of Chicago Press, 1973).

122. B. Mesquita and N. H. Frijda, "Cultural Variations in Emotions: A Review," *Psychological Bulletin*, September 1992, pp. 179–204; and B. Mesquita, "Emotions in Collectivist and Individualist Contexts," *Journal of Personality and Social Psychology*, January 2001, pp. 68–74.

123. D. Matsumoto, "Cross-Cultural Psychology in the 21st Century," http://teachpsych.lemoyne.edu/teachpsych/faces/script/Ch05.htm.

124. S. Nelton, "Emotions in the Workplace," *Nation's Business*, February 1996, p. 25.

125. H. Liao and A. Chuang, "A Multilevel Investigation of Factors Influencing Employee Service Performance and Customer Outcomes," *Academy of Management Journal* 47, no. 1 (2004), pp. 41–58.

126. D. J. Beal, J. P. Trougakos, H. M. Weiss, and S. G. Green, "Episodic Processes in Emotional Labor: Perceptions of Affective Delivery and Regulation Strategies," *Journal of Applied Psychology* 91, no. 5 (2006), pp. 1057–1065.

127. *Starbucks.com*, May 16, 2005, www.starbucks.com.

128. D. Zapf and M. Holz, "On the Positive and Negative Effects of Emotion Work in Organizations," *European Journal of Work and Organizational Psychology* 15, no. 1 (2006), pp. 1–28.

129. D. Zapf, "Emotion Work and Psychological Well-Being: A Review of the Literature and Some Conceptual Considerations," *Human Resource Management Review* 12, no. 2 (2002), pp. 237–268.

130. J. E. Bono and M. A. Vey, "Toward Understanding Emotional Management at Work: A Quantitative Review of Emotional Labor Research," in C. E. Härtel and W. J. Zerbe (eds.), *Emotions in Organizational Behavior* (Mahwah, NJ: Lawrence Erlbaum, 2005), pp. 213–233.

131. Kruml and Geddes, "Catching Fire Without Burning Out."

Foundations of Group Behavior

Madness is the exception in individuals but the rule in groups.

—Friedrich Nietzsche

9

LEARNING OBJECTIVES

After studying this chapter, you should be able to:

1 Define *group* and differentiate between different types of groups.

2 Identify the five stages of group development.

3 Show how role requirements change in different situations.

4 Demonstrate how norms and status exert influence on an individual's behavior.

5 Show how group size affects group performance.

6 Contrast the benefits and disadvantages of cohesive groups.

7 Contrast the strengths and weaknesses of group decision making.

8 Compare the effectiveness of interacting, brainstorming, nominal, and electronic meeting groups.

9 Evaluate evidence for cultural differences in group status and social loafing as well as the effects of diversity in groups.

You know the drill. Gather a small group of people together. Appoint someone to write the ideas on an easel with paper (or type them on a laptop). It's called brainstorming, and it's been around for a long time.

Some brainstorming sessions founder because group members are afraid of saying something stupid. Joe Polidoro, a manager who has worked at several banks, says of brainstorming sessions, "We sit there looking embarrassed like we're all new to a nudist colony."

Brainstorming: A Lousy Idea for Ideas?

Others struggle with the scheduled nature of such sessions. Some feel as if they're put in a room and told, "Okay, be creative now." "I'm more mercurial than that," says Kate Lee, a former manager at GE.

Others think the whole idea of brainstorming is fatally flawed, that such sessions rarely produce the creative ideas they are meant to produce. Martha McGuire, senior VP of a bank, argued that the majority of recommendations resulting from brainstorming sessions are obvious. "You end up with a more pedestrian solution than you would have had, had you not held the session," she says.

Some argue that the real purpose of brainstorming sessions is not to produce the best idea. Rather, it's to

283

get buy-in for decisions that have already been made. Christopher Holland, a policy analyst for the Australian government, said, "These things are usually designed to give people the idea that they have input into decisions when the decisions have already been decided."

One researcher argues that the problems of brainstorming demonstrate the problems of groups. "If you leave groups to their own devices," he says, "they're going to do a very miserable job."[1] ■

*f*rom what you just read, you might think groups are hopeless, but that's not the case. Groups have their place—and their pitfalls. Before we launch into a discussion of these issues, first examine your own attitude toward working in groups. Take the following self-assessment and answer the accompanying questions.

Self Assessment Library

DO I HAVE A NEGATIVE ATTITUDE TOWARD WORKING IN GROUPS?

In the Self-Assessment Library (available on CD or online), take assessment IV.E.1 (Do I Have a Negative Attitude Toward Working in Groups?) and answer the following questions.

1. *Are you surprised by your results? If yes, why? If not, why not?*
2. *Do you think it is important to always have a positive attitude toward working in groups? Why or why not?*

The objectives of this chapter and Chapter 10 are to introduce you to basic group concepts, provide you with a foundation for understanding how groups work, and show you how to create effective teams. Let's begin by defining *group* and explaining why people join groups.

Defining and Classifying Groups

A **group** is defined as two or more individuals, interacting and interdependent, who have come together to achieve particular objectives. Groups can be either formal or informal. By **formal groups**, we mean those defined by the organization's structure, with designated work assignments establishing tasks. In formal groups,

1 Define group and differentiate between different types of groups.

the behaviors that team members should engage in are stipulated by and directed toward organizational goals. The six members making up an airline flight crew are an example of a formal group. In contrast, **informal groups** are alliances that are neither formally structured nor organizationally determined. These groups are natural formations in the work environment that appear in response to the need for social contact. Three employees from different departments who regularly eat lunch or have coffee together are an example of an informal group. These types of interactions among individuals, even though informal, deeply affect their behavior and performance.

It's possible to further subclassify groups as command, task, interest, or friendship groups. Command and task groups are dictated by formal organization, whereas interest and friendship groups are informal alliances.

A **command group** is determined by the organization chart. It is composed of the individuals who report directly to a given manager. An elementary school principal and her 18 teachers form a command group, as do a director of postal audits and his five inspectors.

Task groups, also organizationally determined, represent individuals working together to complete a job task. However, a task group's boundaries are not limited to its immediate hierarchical superior. It can cross command relationships. For instance, if a college student is accused of a campus crime, dealing with the problem might require communication and coordination among the dean of academic affairs, the dean of students, the registrar, the director of security, and the student's advisor. Such a formation would constitute a task group. It should be noted that all command groups are also task groups, but because task groups can cut across the organization, the reverse need not be true.

People who may or may not be aligned into common command or task groups may affiliate to attain a specific objective with which each is concerned. This is an **interest group**. Employees who band together to have their vacation schedules altered, to support a peer who has been fired, or to seek improved working conditions represent the formation of a united body to further their common interest.

Groups often develop because the individual members have one or more common characteristics. We call these formations **friendship groups**. Social alliances, which frequently extend outside the work situation, can be based on similar age or ethnic heritage, support for Notre Dame football, interest in the same alternative rock band, or the holding of similar political views, to name just a few such characteristics.

There is no single reason why individuals join groups. Because most people belong to a number of groups, it's obvious that different groups provide different benefits to their members. Exhibit 9-1 summarizes the most popular reasons people have for joining groups.

Exhibit **9-1**	Why Do People Join Groups?

Security.   By joining a group, individuals can reduce the insecurity of "standing alone." People feel stronger, have fewer self-doubts, and are more resistant to threats when they are part of a group.

Status.   Inclusion in a group that is viewed as important by others provides recognition and status for its members.

Self-esteem.   Groups can provide people with feelings of self-worth. That is, in addition to conveying status to those outside the group, membership can also give increased feelings of worth to the group members themselves.

Affiliation.   Groups can fulfill social needs. People enjoy the regular interaction that comes with group membership. For many people, these on-the-job interactions are their primary source for fulfilling their needs for affiliation.

Power.   What cannot be achieved individually often becomes possible through group action. There is power in numbers.

Goal achievement.   There are times when it takes more than one person to accomplish a particular task—there is a need to pool talents, knowledge, or power in order to complete a job. In such instances, management will rely on the use of a formal group.

group   *Two or more individuals, interacting and interdependent, who have come together to achieve particular objectives.*

formal group   *A designated work group defined by an organization's structure.*

informal group   *A group that is neither formally structured nor organizationally determined; such a group appears in response to the need for social contact.*

command group   *A group composed of the individuals who report directly to a given manager.*

task group   *People working together to complete a job task.*

interest group   *People working together to attain a specific objective with which each is concerned.*

friendship group   *People brought together because they share one or more common characteristics.*

Stages of Group Development

2   Identify the five stages of group development.

Groups generally pass through a standardized sequence in their evolution. We call this sequence the five-stage model of group development. Although research indicates that not all groups follow this pattern,[3] it is a useful framework for understanding group development. In this section, we describe the five-stage general model and an alternative model for temporary groups with deadlines.

The Five-Stage Model

As shown in Exhibit 9-2, the **five-stage group-development model** characterizes groups as proceeding through five distinct stages: forming, storming, norming, performing, and adjourning.[4]

The first stage, **forming**, is characterized by a great deal of uncertainty about the group's purpose, structure, and leadership. Members "test the waters" to determine what types of behaviors are acceptable. This stage is complete when members have begun to think of themselves as part of a group.

The **storming stage** is one of intragroup conflict. Members accept the existence of the group, but there is resistance to the constraints that the group imposes on individuality. Furthermore, there is conflict over who will control the group. When this stage is complete, there will be a relatively clear hierarchy of leadership within the group.

The third stage is one in which close relationships develop and the group demonstrates cohesiveness. There is now a strong sense of group identity and camaraderie. This **norming stage** is complete when the group structure solidifies and the group has assimilated a common set of expectations of what defines correct member behavior.

The fourth stage is **performing**. The structure at this point is fully functional and accepted. Group energy has moved from getting to know and understand each other to performing the task at hand.

For permanent work groups, performing is the last stage in the group development. However, for temporary committees, teams, task forces, and similar groups that have a limited task to perform, there is an **adjourning stage**. In this stage, the group prepares for its disbandment. High task performance is no longer the group's top priority. Instead, attention is directed toward wrapping up activities. Responses of group members vary in this stage. Some are upbeat, basking in the group's accomplishments. Others may be depressed over the loss of camaraderie and friendships gained during the work group's life.

Many interpreters of the five-stage model have assumed that a group becomes more effective as it progresses through the first four stages. Although this assumption may be generally true, what makes a group effective is more complex than this model acknowledges.[5] Under some conditions, high levels of conflict may be conducive to high group performance. So we might expect to find situations in

---

Exhibit 9-2   Stages of Group Development

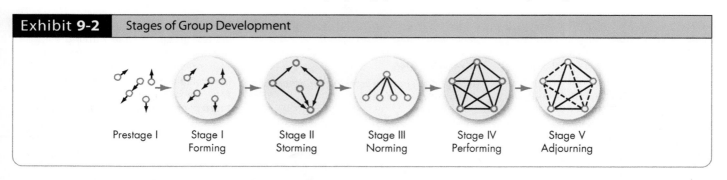

| Prestage I | Stage I Forming | Stage II Storming | Stage III Norming | Stage IV Performing | Stage V Adjourning |

Having passed through the forming, storming, and norming phases of group development, this group of women at a Delphi Delco Electronics factory in Mexico now function as a permanent work group in the performing stage. Their structure is functional and accepted, and each day they begin their work with a small shift meeting before performing their tasks.

which groups in Stage II outperform those in Stage III or IV. Similarly, groups do not always proceed clearly from one stage to the next. Sometimes, in fact, several stages go on simultaneously, as when groups are storming and performing at the same time. Groups even occasionally regress to previous stages. Therefore, even the strongest proponents of this model do not assume that all groups follow its five-stage process precisely or that Stage IV is always the most preferable.

Another problem with the five-stage model, in terms of understanding work-related behavior, is that it ignores organizational context.[6] For instance, a study of a cockpit crew in an airliner found that within 10 minutes three strangers assigned to fly together for the first time had become a high-performing group. What allowed for this speedy group development was the strong organizational context surrounding the tasks of the cockpit crew. This context provided the rules, task definitions, information, and resources needed for the group to perform. They didn't need to develop plans, assign roles, determine and allocate resources, resolve conflicts, and set norms the way the five-stage model predicts.

An Alternative Model for Temporary Groups with Deadlines

Temporary groups with deadlines don't seem to follow the usual five-stage model. Studies indicate that they have their own unique sequencing of actions (or inaction): (1) Their first meeting sets the group's direction; (2) this first phase of group activity is one of inertia; (3) a transition takes place at the end of this first phase, which occurs exactly when the group has used up half its allotted time; (4) a transition initiates major changes; (5) a second phase of inertia

five-stage group-development model   *The five distinct stages groups go through: forming, storming, norming, performing, and adjourning.*

forming stage   *The first stage in group development, characterized by much uncertainty.*

storming stage   *The second stage in group development, characterized by intragroup conflict.*

norming stage   *The third stage in group development, characterized by close relationships and cohesiveness.*

performing stage   *The fourth stage in group development, during which the group is fully functional.*

adjourning stage   *The final stage in group development for temporary groups, characterized by concern with wrapping up activities rather than task performance.*

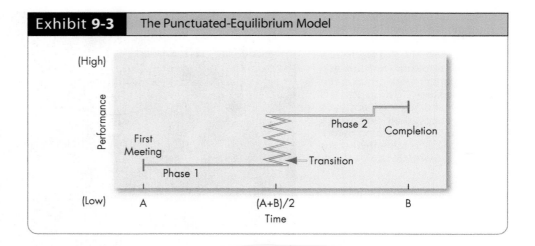

Exhibit 9-3   The Punctuated-Equilibrium Model

follows the transition; and (6) the group's last meeting is characterized by markedly accelerated activity.[7] This pattern, called the **punctuated-equilibrium model**, is shown in Exhibit 9-3.

The first meeting sets the group's direction. A framework of behavioral patterns and assumptions through which the group will approach its project emerges in this first meeting. These lasting patterns can appear as early as the first few seconds of the group's existence. Once set, the group's direction becomes "written in stone" and is unlikely to be reexamined throughout the first half of the group's life. This is a period of inertia—that is, the group tends to stand still or become locked into a fixed course of action. Even if it gains new insights that challenge initial patterns and assumptions, the group is incapable of acting on these new insights in Phase 1.

One of the most interesting discoveries made in studies of groups[8] was that each group experienced its transition at the same point in its calendar— precisely halfway between its first meeting and its official deadline—despite the fact that some groups spent as little as an hour on their project while others spent 6 months. It was as if the groups universally experienced a midlife crisis at this point. The midpoint appears to work like an alarm clock, heightening members' awareness that their time is limited and that they need to "get moving." This transition ends Phase 1 and is characterized by a concentrated burst of changes, dropping of old patterns, and adoption of new perspectives. The transition sets a revised direction for Phase 2. Phase 2 is a new equilibrium or period of inertia. In this phase, the group executes plans created during the transition period.

The group's last meeting is characterized by a final burst of activity to finish its work. In summary, the punctuated-equilibrium model characterizes groups as exhibiting long periods of inertia interspersed with brief revolutionary changes triggered primarily by their members' awareness of time and deadlines. Keep in mind, however, that this model doesn't apply to all groups. It's essentially limited to temporary task groups who are working under a time-constrained completion deadline.[9]

Group Properties: Roles, Norms, Status, Size, and Cohesiveness

Work groups are not unorganized mobs. Work groups have properties that shape the behavior of members and make it possible to explain and predict a large portion of individual behavior within the group as well as the perfor-

Trumpeter Wynton Marsalis plays a number of diverse roles. As artistic director of the Jazz at Lincoln Center Orchestra, Marsalis serves on the senior management team in leading the world's largest not-for-profit arts organization dedicated to jazz. He is also a composer, performer, music teacher, fundraiser, and goodwill ambassador as a United Nations Messenger of Peace. Each of these positions imposes different role requirements on Marsalis. This photo shows Marsalis joining Chef Emeril Lagasse at a free educational event for schoolchildren in New Orleans that explored two aspects of the city's culture: jazz and food.

mance of the group itself. Some of these properties are roles, norms, status, group size, and the degree of group cohesiveness.

Group Property 1: Roles

3 Show how role requirements change in different situations.

Shakespeare said, "All the world's a stage, and all the men and women merely players." Using the same metaphor, all group members are actors, each playing a **role**. By this term, we mean a set of expected behavior patterns attributed to someone occupying a given position in a social unit. The understanding of role behavior would be dramatically simplified if each of us chose one role and "played it out" regularly and consistently. Unfortunately, we are required to play a number of diverse roles, both on and off our jobs. As we'll see, one of the tasks in understanding behavior is grasping the role that a person is currently playing.

For example, Bill Patterson is a plant manager with EMM Industries, a large electrical equipment manufacturer in Phoenix. He has a number of roles that he fulfills on that job—for instance, EMM employee, member of middle management, electrical engineer, and primary company spokesperson in the community. Off the job, Bill Patterson finds himself in still more roles: husband, father, Catholic, Rotarian, tennis player, member of the Thunderbird Country Club, and president of his homeowners' association. Many of these roles are compatible; some create conflicts. For instance, how does his religious involvement influence his managerial decisions regarding layoffs, expense account padding, and provision of accurate information to government agencies? A recent offer of promotion requires Bill to relocate, yet his family very much wants to stay in Phoenix. Can the role demands of his job be reconciled with the demands of his husband and father roles?

punctuated-equilibrium model *A set of phases that temporary groups go through that involves transitions between inertia and activity.*

role *A set of expected behavior patterns attributed to someone occupying a given position in a social unit.*

The issue should be clear: Like Bill Patterson, we are all required to play a number of roles, and our behavior varies with the role we are playing. Bill's behavior when he attends church on Sunday morning is different from his behavior on the golf course later that same day. So different groups impose different role requirements on individuals.

Role Identity   Certain attitudes and actual behaviors are consistent with a role, and they create the **role identity**. People have the ability to shift roles rapidly when they recognize that a situation and its demands clearly require major changes. For instance, when union stewards were promoted to supervisory positions, it was found that their attitudes changed from pro-union to pro-management within a few months of their promotion. When these promotions had to be rescinded later because of economic difficulties in the firm, it was found that the demoted supervisors had once again adopted their pro-union attitudes.[10]

Role Perception   Our view of how we're supposed to act in a given situation is a **role perception**. Based on an interpretation of how we believe we are supposed to behave, we engage in certain types of behavior. Where do we get these perceptions? We get them from stimuli all around us—friends, books, television. For example, we may form an impression of the work of doctors from watching *Grey's Anatomy*. Of course, the primary reason apprenticeship programs exist in many trades and professions is to allow beginners to watch an "expert" so they can learn to act as they are supposed to.

Role Expectations   **Role expectations** are defined as the way others believe you should act in a given situation. How you behave is determined to a large extent by the role defined in the context in which you are acting. For instance, the role of a U.S. federal judge is viewed as having propriety and dignity, while a football coach is seen as aggressive, dynamic, and inspiring to his players.

In the workplace, it can be helpful to look at the topic of role expectations through the perspective of the **psychological contract**—an unwritten agreement that exists between employees and their employer. This psychological contract sets out mutual expectations—what management expects from workers and vice versa.[11] In effect, this contract defines the behavioral expectations that go with every role. For instance, management is expected to treat employees justly, provide acceptable working conditions, clearly communicate what is a fair day's work, and give feedback on how well an employee is doing. Employees are expected to respond by demonstrating a good attitude, following directions, and showing loyalty to the organization.

What happens when role expectations as implied in the psychological contract are not met? If management is derelict in keeping up its part of the bargain, we can expect negative repercussions on employee performance and satisfaction. When employees fail to live up to expectations, the result is usually some form of disciplinary action up to and including firing.

Role Conflict   When an individual is confronted by divergent role expectations, the result is **role conflict**. It exists when an individual finds that compliance with one role requirement may make it difficult to comply with another.[12] At the extreme, it would include situations in which two or more role expectations are mutually contradictory.

Our previous discussion of the many roles Bill Patterson had to deal with included several role conflicts—for instance, Bill's attempt to reconcile the expectations placed on him as a husband and father with those placed on him as an executive with EMM Industries. The former, as you will remember, emphasizes stability and concern for the desire of his wife and children to remain in Phoenix. EMM, on the other hand, expects its employees to be responsive to the needs and requirements of the company. Although it might be in Bill's financial and career interests to accept a relocation, the conflict comes down to choosing between family and career role expectations.

An Experiment: Zimbardo's Prison Experiment   One of the most illuminating role experiments was done a number of years ago by Stanford University psychologist Philip Zimbardo and his associates.[13] They created a "prison" in the basement of the Stanford psychology building, hired at $15 a day two dozen emotionally stable, physically healthy, law-abiding students who scored "normal average" on extensive personality tests, randomly assigned them the role of either "guard" or "prisoner," and established some basic rules.

To get the experiment off to a "realistic" start, Zimbardo got the cooperation of the local police department. The police went, unannounced, to each future prisoners' home, arrested and handcuffed them, put them in a squad car in front of friends and neighbors, and took them to police headquarters, where they were booked and fingerprinted. From there, they were taken to the Stanford prison.

At the start of the planned 2-week experiment, there were no measurable differences between the individuals assigned to be guards and those chosen to be prisoners. In addition, the guards received no special training in how to be prison guards. They were told only to "maintain law and order" in the prison and not to take any nonsense from the prisoners. Physical violence was forbidden. To simulate further the realities of prison life, the prisoners were allowed visits from relatives and friends. And although the mock guards worked 8-hour shifts, the mock prisoners were kept in their cells around the clock and were allowed out only for meals, exercise, toilet privileges, head-count lineups, and work details.

It took the "prisoners" little time to accept the authority positions of the guards or the mock guards to adjust to their new authority roles. After the guards crushed a rebellion attempt on the second day, the prisoners became increasingly passive. Whatever the guards "dished out," the prisoners took. The prisoners actually began to believe and act as if they were, as the guards constantly reminded them, inferior and powerless. And every guard, at some time during the simulation, engaged in abusive, authoritative behavior. For example, one guard said, "I was surprised at myself. . . . I made them call each other names and clean the toilets out with their bare hands. I practically considered the prisoners cattle, and I kept thinking: 'I have to watch out for them in case they try something.'" Another guard added, "I was tired of seeing the prisoners in their rags and smelling the strong odors of their bodies that filled the cells. I watched them tear at each other on orders given by us. They didn't see it as an experiment. It was real and they were fighting to keep their identity. But we were always there to show them who was boss." Surprisingly, during the entire experiment—even after days of abuse—not one prisoner said, "Stop this. I'm a student like you. This is just an experiment!"

The simulation actually proved *too successful* in demonstrating how quickly individuals learn new roles. The researchers had to stop it after only 6 days

---

role identity   *Certain attitudes and behaviors consistent with a role.*

role perception   *An individual's view of how he or she is supposed to act in a given situation.*

role expectations   *How others believe a person should act in a given situation.*

psychological contract   *An unwritten agreement that sets out what management expects from an employee and vice versa.*

role conflict   *A situation in which an individual is confronted by divergent role expectations.*

because of the participants' pathological reactions. And remember, these were individuals chosen precisely for their normalcy and emotional stability.

What can we conclude from this prison simulation? The participants in this experiment had, like the rest of us, learned stereotyped conceptions of guard and prisoner roles from the mass media and their own personal experiences in power and powerlessness relationships gained at home (parent–child), in school (teacher–student), and in other situations. This, then, allowed them easily and rapidly to assume roles that were very different from their inherent personalities. In this case, we saw that people with no prior personality pathology or training in their roles could execute extreme forms of behavior consistent with the roles they were playing.

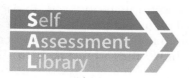

DO I TRUST OTHERS?

In the Self-Assessment Library (available on CD or online), take assessment II.B.3 (Do I Trust Others?). You can also check out assessment II.B.4 (Do Others See Me as Trusting?).

Group Properties 2 and 3: Norms and Status

Did you ever notice that golfers don't speak while their partners are putting on the green or that employees don't criticize their bosses in public? Why? The answer is norms.

> 4 *Demonstrate how norms and status exert influence on an individual's behavior.*

All groups have established **norms**—that is, acceptable standards of behavior that are shared by the group's members. Norms tell members what they ought and ought not to do under certain circumstances. From an individual's standpoint, they tell what is expected of you in certain situations. When agreed to and accepted by the group, norms act as a means of influencing the behavior of group members with a minimum of external controls. Different groups, communities, and societies have different norms, but they all have them.[14]

Norms can cover virtually any aspect of group behavior.[15] Probably the most common group norm is a *performance norm*. Work groups typically provide their members with explicit cues to how hard they should work, how to get the job done, what their level of output should be, what level of tardiness is appropriate, and the like. These norms are extremely powerful in affecting an individual employee's performance—they are capable of significantly modifying a performance prediction that was based solely on the employee's ability and level of personal motivation. Although arguably the most important, performance norms aren't the only kind. Other types include *appearance norms* (for example, dress codes, unspoken rules about when to look busy), *social arrangement norms* (for example, with whom group members eat lunch, whether to form friendships on and off the job), and *resource allocation norms* (for example, assignment of difficult jobs, distribution of resources like pay or equipment).

The Hawthorne Studies   Behavioral scientists generally agree that full-scale appreciation of the importance norms play in influencing worker behavior did not occur until the early 1930s. This enlightenment grew out of a series of studies undertaken at Western Electric Company's Hawthorne Works in Chicago between 1924 and 1932.[16] Originally initiated by Western Electric officials and later overseen by Harvard professor Elton Mayo, the Hawthorne studies concluded that a worker's behavior and sentiments were closely related, that group influences were significant in affecting individual behavior, that

From the Hawthorne studies, observers gained valuable insights into how individual behavior is influenced by group norms. The group of workers determined the level of fair output and established norms for individual work rates that conformed to the output. To enforce the group norms, workers used sarcasm, ridicule, and even physical force to influence individual behaviors that were not acceptable to the group.

group standards were highly effective in establishing individual worker output, and that money was less a factor in determining worker output than were group standards, sentiments, and security. Let us briefly discuss the Hawthorne investigations and demonstrate the importance of these findings in explaining group behavior.

The Hawthorne researchers began by examining the relationship between the physical environment and productivity. Illumination and other working conditions were selected to represent this physical environment. The researchers' initial findings contradicted their anticipated results.

They began with illumination experiments with various groups of workers. The researchers manipulated the intensity of illumination upward and downward, while at the same time noting changes in group output. Results varied, but one thing was clear: In no case was the increase or decrease in output in proportion to the increase or decrease in illumination. So the researchers introduced a control group: An experimental group was presented with varying intensity of illumination, while the controlled unit worked under a constant illumination intensity. Again, the results were bewildering to the Hawthorne researchers. As the light level was increased in the experimental unit, output rose for both the control group and the experimental group. But to the surprise of the researchers, as the light level was dropped in the experimental group, productivity continued to increase in both groups. In fact, a productivity decrease was observed in the experimental group only when the light intensity had been reduced to that of moonlight. The Hawthorne researchers concluded that illumination intensity was only a minor influence among the many influences that affected an employee's productivity, but they could not explain the behavior they had witnessed.

As a follow-up to the illumination experiments, the researchers began a second set of experiments in the relay assembly test room at Western Electric.

norms *Acceptable standards of behavior within a group that are shared by the group's members.*

A small group of women was isolated from the main work group so that their behavior could be more carefully observed. They went about their job of assembling small telephone relays in a room laid out similarly to their normal department. The only significant difference was the placement in the room of a research assistant who acted as an observer—keeping records of output, rejects, working conditions, and a daily log sheet describing everything that happened. Observations covering a multiyear period found that this small group's output increased steadily. The number of personal absences and those due to sickness was approximately one-third of those recorded by women in the regular production department. What became evident was that this group's performance was significantly influenced by its status of being a "special" group. The women in the test room thought that being in the experimental group was fun, that they were in sort of an elite group, and that management was concerned with their interest by engaging in such experimentation. In essence, workers in both the illumination and assembly-test-room experiments were reacting to the increased attention they were receiving.

A third study, in the bank wiring observation room, was introduced to ascertain the effect of a sophisticated wage incentive plan. The assumption was that individual workers would maximize their productivity when they saw that it was directly related to economic rewards. The most important finding to come out of this study was that employees did not individually maximize their outputs. Rather, their output became controlled by a group norm that determined what was a proper day's work. Output was not only being restricted, but individual workers were giving erroneous reports. The total for a week would check with the total week's output, but the daily reports showed a steady level of output, regardless of actual daily production. What was going on?

Interviews determined that the group was operating well below its capability and was leveling output in order to protect itself. Members were afraid that if they significantly increased their output, the unit incentive rate would be cut, the expected daily output would be increased, layoffs might occur, or slower workers would be reprimanded. So the group established its idea of a fair output—neither too much nor too little. They helped each other out to ensure that their reports were nearly level.

The norms the group established included a number of "don'ts." *Don't* be a rate-buster, turning out too much work. *Don't* be a chiseler, turning out too little work. *Don't* be a squealer on any of your peers. How did the group enforce these norms? Their methods were neither gentle nor subtle. They included sarcasm, name-calling, ridicule, and even physical punches to the upper arm of any member who violated the group's norms. Members would also ostracize individuals whose behavior was against the group's interest.

The Hawthorne studies made an important contribution to our understanding of group behavior—particularly the significant place that norms have in determining individual work behavior.

Conformity   As a member of a group, you desire acceptance by the group. Because of your desire for acceptance, you are susceptible to conforming to the group's norms. There is considerable evidence that groups can place strong pressures on individual members to change their attitudes and behaviors to conform to the group's standard.[17]

Do individuals conform to the pressures of all the groups to which they belong? Obviously not, because people belong to many groups, and their norms vary. In some cases, they may even have contradictory norms. So what do people do? They conform to the important groups to which they belong or hope to belong. The important groups have been called **reference groups**, and they're characterized as ones in which a person is aware of other members,

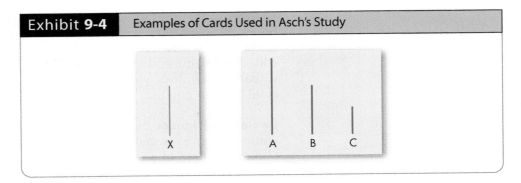

defines himself or herself as a member or would like to be a member, and feels that the group members are significant to him or her.[18] The implication, then, is that all groups do not impose equal conformity pressures on their members.

The impact that group pressures for **conformity** can have on an individual member's judgment and attitudes was demonstrated in the now-classic studies by Solomon Asch.[19] Asch made up groups of seven or eight people, who sat around a table and were asked to compare two cards held by the experimenter. One card had one line, and the other had three lines of varying length. As shown in Exhibit 9-4, one of the lines on the three-line card was identical to the line on the one-line card. Also as shown in Exhibit 9-4, the difference in line length was quite obvious; in fact, under ordinary conditions, subjects made fewer than 1 percent errors. The object was to announce aloud which of the three lines matched the single line. But what happens if the members in the group begin to give incorrect answers? Will the pressures to conform result in an unsuspecting subject (USS) altering an answer to align with the others? That was what Asch wanted to know. So he arranged the group so that only the USS was unaware that the experiment was "fixed." The seating was prearranged: The USS was placed so as to be one of the last to announce a decision.

The experiment began with several sets of matching exercises. All the subjects gave the right answers. On the third set, however, the first subject gave an obviously wrong answer—for example, saying "C" in Exhibit 9-4. The next subject gave the same wrong answer, and so did the others until it got to the unknowing subject. He knew "B" was the same as "X," yet everyone else had said "C." The decision confronting the USS was this: Do you publicly state a perception that differs from the preannounced position of the others in your group? Or do you give an answer that you strongly believe is incorrect in order to have your response agree with that of the other group members?

The results obtained by Asch demonstrated that over many experiments and many trials 75 percent of the subjects gave at least one answer that conformed—that is, that they knew was wrong but that was consistent with the replies of other group members—and the average for conformers was 37 percent. What meaning can we draw from these results? They suggest that there are group norms that press us toward conformity. That is, we desire to be one of the group and avoid being visibly different.

The preceding conclusions are based on research that was conducted 50 years ago. Has time altered their validity? And should we consider these findings generalizable across cultures? The evidence indicates that there have been

---

reference groups *Important groups to which individuals belong or hope to belong and with whose norms individuals are likely to conform.*

conformity *The adjustment of one's behavior to align with the norms of the group.*

changes in the level of conformity over time; and Asch's findings are culture bound.[20] Specifically, levels of conformity have steadily declined since Asch's studies in the early 1950s. In addition, conformity to social norms is higher in collectivist cultures than in individualistic cultures. Nevertheless, even in individualistic countries, you should consider conformity to norms to still be a powerful force in groups.

Deviant Workplace Behavior   Ted Vowinkel is frustrated by a coworker who constantly spreads malicious and unsubstantiated rumors about him. Debra Hundley is tired of a member of her work team who, when confronted with a problem, takes out his frustration by yelling and screaming at her and other work team members. And Rhonda Lieberman recently quit her job as a dental hygienist after being constantly sexually harassed by her employer.

What do these three episodes have in common? They represent employees being exposed to acts of *deviant workplace behavior*.[21] **Deviant workplace behavior** (also called *antisocial behavior* or *workplace incivility*) is voluntary behavior that violates significant organizational norms and, in doing so, threatens the well-being of the organization or its members. Exhibit 9-5 provides a typology of deviant workplace behaviors, with examples of each.

Few organizations will admit to creating or condoning conditions that encourage and maintain deviant norms. Yet they exist. Employees report, for example, an increase in rudeness and disregard toward others by bosses and coworkers in recent years. And nearly half of employees who have suffered this incivility report that it has led them to think about changing jobs, with 12 percent actually quitting because of it.[22]

As with norms in general, individual employees' antisocial actions are shaped by the group context within which they work. Evidence demonstrates that the antisocial behavior exhibited by a work group is a significant predictor of an individual's antisocial behavior at work.[23] In other words, deviant workplace behavior is likely to flourish where it's supported by group norms. What this means for managers is that when deviant workplace norms surface, employee cooperation, commitment, and motivation are likely to suffer. This, in turn, can lead to reduced employee productivity and job satisfaction and increased turnover.

In addition, just being part of a group can increase an individual's deviant behavior. In other words, someone who ordinarily wouldn't engage in deviant

Exhibit 9-5	Typology of Deviant Workplace Behavior
Category	**Examples**
Production	Leaving early
	Intentionally working slowly
	Wasting resources
Property	Sabotage
	Lying about hours worked
	Stealing from the organization
Political	Showing favoritism
	Gossiping and spreading rumors
	Blaming coworkers
Personal aggression	Sexual harassment
	Verbal abuse
	Stealing from coworkers

Source: Adapted from S. L. Robinson and R. J. Bennett, "A Typology of Deviant Workplace Behaviors: A Multidimensional Scaling Study," *Academy of Management Journal*, April 1995, p. 565.

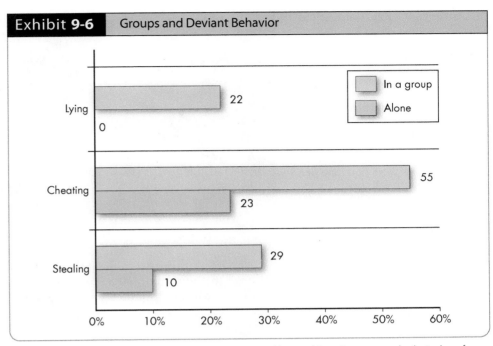

Exhibit 9-6   Groups and Deviant Behavior

Source: A. Erez, H. Elms, and E. Fong, "Lying, Cheating, Stealing: Groups and the Ring of Gyges," paper presented at the Academy of Management Annual Meeting, Honolulu, HI, August 8, 2005.

behavior might be more likely to do so when working in a group. In fact, a recent study suggests that, compared with individuals working alone, those working in a group were more likely to lie, cheat, and steal. As shown in Exhibit 9-6, in this study, no individual working alone lied, but 22 percent of those working in groups did. Moreover, individuals working in groups also were more likely to cheat (55 percent of individuals working in a group cheated on a task versus 23 percent of individuals working alone) and steal (29 percent of individuals working in a group stole compared to only 10 percent working alone).[24] Groups provide a shield of anonymity so that someone who ordinarily might be afraid of getting caught for stealing can rely on the fact that other group members had the same opportunity or reason to steal. This creates a false sense of confidence that may result in more aggressive behavior. Thus, deviant behavior depends on the accepted norms of the group—or even whether an individual is part of a group.[25]

Status

Status—that is, a socially defined position or rank given to groups or group members by others—permeates every society. Even the smallest group will develop roles, rights, and rituals to differentiate its members. Status is an important factor in understanding human behavior because it is a significant motivator and has major behavioral consequences when individuals perceive a disparity between what they believe their status to be and what others perceive it to be.

deviant workplace behavior   *Voluntary behavior that violates significant organizational norms and, in so doing, threatens the well-being of the organization or its members. Also called* antisocial behavior *or* workplace incivility.

status   *A socially defined position or rank given to groups or group members by others.*

Otsuka Yuriko has high status at the Canon manufacturing plant in Ami, Japan. As an employee in a cell-manufacturing unit, she wears a badge on the sleeve of her work uniform labeled Eiji Meister. Yuriko earned the badge by completing an apprenticeship program and becoming proficient in all the tasks required to assemble a machine. Because she has mastered all the tasks, Yuriko can train other employees in her work unit, and her contributions are critical to her group's success.

What Determines Status?   According to **status characteristics theory**, status tends to be derived from one of three sources:[26]

1. **The power a person wields over others.**   Because they likely control the group's resources, people who control the outcomes of a group through their power tend to be perceived as high status.
2. **A person's ability to contribute to a group's goals.**   People whose contributions are critical to the group's success tend to have high status. (For example, some thought NBA star Kobe Bryant had more say over player decisions than his coaches [though not as much as Bryant wanted!].)
3. **An individual's personal characteristics.**   Someone whose personal characteristics are positively valued by the group (for example, good looks, intelligence, money, or a friendly personality) typically has higher status than someone who has fewer valued attributes.

Status and Norms   Status has been shown to have some interesting effects on the power of norms and pressures to conform. For instance, high-status members of groups are often given more freedom to deviate from norms than are other group members.[27] High-status people are also better able to resist conformity pressures than their lower-status peers. An individual who is highly valued by a group but who doesn't much need or care about the social rewards the group provides is particularly able to pay minimal attention to conformity norms.[28]

The previous findings explain why many star athletes, celebrities, top-performing salespeople, and outstanding academics seem oblivious to appearance or social norms that constrain their peers. As high-status individuals, they're given a wider range of discretion. But this is true only as long as the high-status person's activities aren't severely detrimental to group goal achievement.[29]

Status and Group Interaction   Interaction among members of groups is influenced by status. We find, for instance, that high-status people tend to be more assertive.[30] They speak out more often, criticize more, state more commands, and interrupt others more often. But status differences actually inhibit diversity of ideas and creativity in groups because lower-status members tend to be less active participants in group discussions. In situations in which lower-status members possess expertise and insights that could aid the group, their expertise and insights are not likely to be fully utilized, thus reducing the group's overall performance.

Status Inequity   It is important for group members to believe that the status hierarchy is equitable. Perceived inequity creates disequilibrium, which results in various types of corrective behavior.[31]

The concept of equity presented in Chapter 6 applies to status. People expect rewards to be proportionate to costs incurred. If Dana and Anne are the two finalists for the head nurse position in a hospital, and it is clear that Dana has more seniority and better preparation for assuming the promotion, Anne will view the selection of Dana to be equitable. However, if Anne is chosen because she is the daughter-in-law of the hospital director, Dana will believe an injustice has been committed.

Groups generally agree within themselves on status criteria and, hence, there is usually high concurrence in group rankings of individuals. However, individuals can find themselves in a conflict situation when they move between groups whose status criteria are different or when they join groups whose members have heterogeneous backgrounds. For instance, business executives may use personal income or the growth rate of their companies as determinants of status. Government bureaucrats may use the size of their budgets. Blue-collar workers may use years of seniority. In groups made up of heterogeneous individuals or when heterogeneous groups are forced to be interdependent, status differences may initiate conflict as the group attempts to reconcile and align the differing hierarchies. As we'll see in Chapter 10, this can be a particular problem when management creates teams made up of employees from across varied functions within the organization.

Group Property 4: Size

Does the size of a group affect the group's overall behavior? The answer to this question is a definite "yes," but the effect is contingent on what dependent variables you look at.[32] The evidence indicates, for instance, that smaller groups are faster at completing tasks than are larger ones and that individuals perform better in smaller groups than in larger ones.[33] However, for groups engaged in problem solving, large groups consistently get better marks than their smaller counterparts.[34] Translating these results into specific numbers is a bit more hazardous, but we can offer some parameters. Large groups—those with a dozen or more members—are good for gaining diverse input. So if the goal of the group is fact-finding, larger groups should be more effective. On the other hand, smaller groups are better at doing something productive with that input. Groups of approximately seven members tend to be more effective for taking action.

One of the most important findings related to the size of a group has been labeled **social loafing**. Social loafing is the tendency for individuals to expend less effort when working collectively than when working individually.[35] It directly challenges the logic that the productivity of the group as a whole should at least equal the sum of the productivity of the individuals in that group.

5 *Show how group size affects group performance.*

---

status characteristics theory   *A theory that states that differences in status characteristics create status hierarchies within groups.*

social loafing   *The tendency for individuals to expend less effort when working collectively than when working individually.*

Studies indicate that these employees in Miles, China, collecting harvest grapes for the production of red wine, perform better in a group than when working alone. In collectivist societies such as China, employees show less propensity to engage in social loafing. Unlike individualistic cultures such as the United States, where people are dominated by self-interest, the Chinese are motivated by in-group goals.

A common stereotype about groups is that the sense of team spirit spurs individual effort and enhances the group's overall productivity. But that stereotype may be wrong. In the late 1920s, a German psychologist named Max Ringelmann compared the results of individual and group performance on a rope-pulling task.[36] He expected that the group's effort would be equal to the sum of the efforts of individuals within the group. That is, three people pulling together should exert three times as much pull on the rope as one person, and eight people should exert eight times as much pull. Ringelmann's results, however, didn't confirm his expectations. One person pulling on a rope alone exerted an average of 63 kilograms of force. In groups of three, the per-person force dropped to 53 kilograms. And in groups of eight, it fell to only 31 kilograms per person.

Replications of Ringelmann's research with similar tasks have generally supported his findings.[37] Group performance increases with group size, but the addition of new members to the group has diminishing returns on productivity. So more may be better in the sense that the total productivity of a group of four is greater than that of three people, but the individual productivity of each group member declines.

What causes this social loafing effect? It may be due to a belief that others in the group are not carrying their fair share. If you see others as lazy or inept, you can reestablish equity by reducing your effort. Another explanation is the dispersion of responsibility. Because the results of the group cannot be attributed to any single person, the relationship between an individual's input and the group's output is clouded. In such situations, individuals may be tempted to become "free riders" and coast on the group's efforts. In other words, there will be a reduction in efficiency when individuals think that their contribution cannot be measured.

The implications for OB of this effect on work groups are significant. When managers use collective work situations to enhance morale and teamwork, they must also provide means by which they can identify individual efforts. If this isn't done, management must weigh the potential losses in productivity from using groups against any possible gains in worker satisfaction.[38]

There are several ways to prevent social loafing : (1) Set group goals so that the group has a common purpose to strive toward; (2) increase intergroup competition, which again focuses the group on the shared outcome; (3) engage in peer evaluation so that each person's contribution to the group is evaluated by each group member; and (4) if possible, distribute group rewards, in part, based on each member's unique contributions.[39] Although none of these actions is a "magic bullet" that will prevent social loafing in all cases, they should help minimize its effect.

Group Property 5: Cohesiveness

6 *Contrast the benefits and disadvantages of cohesive groups.*

Groups differ in their **cohesiveness**—that is, the degree to which members are attracted to each other and are motivated to stay in the group.[40] For instance, some work groups are cohesive because the members have spent a great deal of time together, or the group's small size facilitates high interaction, or the group has experienced external threats that have brought members close together. Cohesiveness is important because it has been found to be related to group productivity.[41]

Studies consistently show that the relationship between cohesiveness and productivity depends on the performance-related norms established by the group.[42] If performance-related norms are high (for example, high output, quality work, cooperation with individuals outside the group), a cohesive group will be more productive than will a less cohesive group. But if cohesiveness is high and performance norms are low, productivity will be low. If cohesiveness is low and performance norms are high, productivity increases, but it increases less than in the high-cohesiveness/high-norms situation. When cohesiveness and performance-related norms are both low, productivity tends to fall into the low-to-moderate range. These conclusions are summarized in Exhibit 9-7.

What can you do to encourage group cohesiveness? You might try one or more of the following suggestions: (1) Make the group smaller, (2) encourage agreement with group goals, (3) increase the time members spend together, (4) increase the status of the group and the perceived difficulty of attaining membership in the group, (5) stimulate competition with other groups, (6) give rewards to the group rather than to individual members, and (7) physically isolate the group.[43]

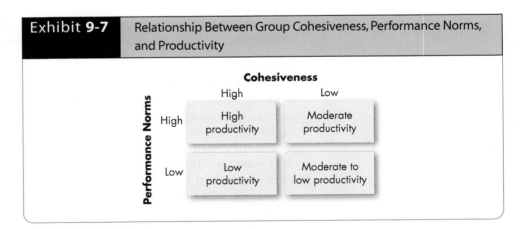

| Exhibit 9-7 | Relationship Between Group Cohesiveness, Performance Norms, and Productivity |

cohesiveness *The degree to which group members are attracted to each other and are motivated to stay in the group.*

International OB

Group Cohesiveness Across Cultures

A recent study attempted to determine whether motivating work groups by giving them more complex tasks and greater autonomy resulted in increased group cohesiveness. Researchers studied bank teams in the United States, an individualist culture, and in Hong Kong, a collectivist culture. Both teams were composed of individuals from each respective country. The results

showed that, regardless of what culture the teams were from, giving teams difficult tasks and more freedom to accomplish those tasks created a more tight-knit group. Consequently, team performance was enhanced.

However, the teams differed in the extent to which increases in task complexity and autonomy resulted in greater group cohesiveness. Teams in individualist cultures responded more strongly than did teams in collectivist cultures, became more united and committed, and, as a result, received higher performance ratings from their supervisors than teams from collectivist cultures.

Why do these cultural differences exist? One explanation is that collectivist teams already have a strong predisposition to work together as a group, so there's less need for increased teamwork. What's the lesson? Managers in individualist cultures may need to work harder to increase team cohesiveness. One way to do this is to give teams more challenging assignments and provide them with more independence.

Source: Based on D. Man and S. S. K. Lam, "The Effects of Job Complexity and Autonomy on Cohesiveness in Collectivist and Individualistic Work Groups: A Cross-Cultural Analysis," *Journal of Organizational Behavior*, December 2003, pp. 979–1001.

Group Decision Making

7 Contrast the strengths and weaknesses of group decision making.

The belief—characterized by juries—that two heads are better than one has long been accepted as a basic component of North American and many other countries' legal systems. This belief has expanded to the point that, today, many decisions in organizations are made by groups, teams, or committees.[44] In this section, we discuss group decision making.

Groups Versus the Individual

Decision-making groups may be widely used in organizations, but does that imply that group decisions are preferable to those made by an individual alone? The answer to this question depends on a number of factors. Let's begin by looking at the strengths and weaknesses of group decision making.[45]

Strengths of Group Decision Making Groups generate *more complete information and knowledge.* By aggregating the resources of several individuals, groups bring more input into the decision process. In addition to more input, groups can bring heterogeneity to the decision process. They offer *increased diversity of views.* This opens up the opportunity for more approaches and alternatives to be considered. Finally, groups lead to increased *acceptance of a solution.* Many decisions fail after the final choice is made because people don't accept the solution. Group members who participated in making a decision are likely to enthusiastically support the decision and encourage others to accept it.

Weaknesses of Group Decision Making In spite of the pluses noted, group decisions have their drawbacks. They're time-consuming because groups typically take more time to reach a solution than would be the case if an individual were making the decision. There are *conformity pressures in groups.* The desire by group members to be accepted and considered an asset to the group can result in squashing any overt disagreement. Group discussion can be *dominated by one* *or a few members.* If this dominant coalition is composed of low- and medium-ability members, the group's overall effectiveness will suffer. Finally, group decisions suffer from *ambiguous responsibility.* In an individual decision, it's clear who is accountable for the final outcome. In a group decision, the responsibility of any single member is watered down.

Effectiveness and Efficiency   Whether groups are more effective than individuals depends on the criteria you use to define effectiveness. In terms of *accuracy,* group decisions are generally more accurate than the decisions of the average individual in a group, but they are less accurate than the judgments of the most accurate group member.[46] If decision effectiveness is defined in terms of *speed,* individuals are superior. If *creativity* is important, groups tend to be more effective than individuals. And if effectiveness means the degree of *acceptance* the final solution achieves, the nod again goes to the group.[47]

But effectiveness cannot be considered without also assessing efficiency. In terms of efficiency, groups almost always stack up as a poor second to the individual decision maker. With few exceptions, group decision making consumes more work hours than if an individual were to tackle the same problem alone. The exceptions tend to be the instances in which, to achieve comparable quantities of diverse input, the single decision maker must spend a great deal of time reviewing files and talking to people. Because groups can include members from diverse areas, the time spent searching for information can be reduced. However, as we noted, these advantages in efficiency tend to be the exception. Groups are generally less efficient than individuals. In deciding whether to use groups, then, consideration should be given to assessing whether increases in effectiveness are more than enough to offset the reductions in efficiency.

Summary   In summary, groups offer an excellent vehicle for performing many of the steps in the decision-making process. They are a source of both breadth and depth of input for information gathering. If the group is composed of individuals with diverse backgrounds, the alternatives generated should be more extensive and the analysis more critical. When the final solution is agreed on, there are more people in a group decision to support and implement it. These pluses, however, can be more than offset by the time

MYTH OR SCIENCE?   *"Are Two Heads Better Than One?"*

two heads are not necessarily always better than one. In fact, the evidence generally confirms the superiority of individuals over groups when brainstorming. The best individual in a group also makes better decisions than groups as a whole, though groups do tend to do better than the average group member.[48]

Research also indicates that groups are superior only when they meet certain criteria.[49] These criteria include:

1. **The group must have diversity among members.**   To get benefits from "two heads," the heads must differ in relevant skills and abilities.

2. **The group members must be able to communicate their ideas freely and openly.**   This requires an absence of hostility and intimidation.

3. **The task being undertaken must be complex.**   Relative to individuals, groups do better on complex rather than simple tasks. ■

consumed by group decisions, the internal conflicts they create, and the pressures they generate toward conformity. Therefore, in some cases, individuals can be expected to make better decisions than groups.

Groupthink and Groupshift

Two byproducts of group decision making have received a considerable amount of attention from researchers in OB. As we'll show, these two phenomena have the potential to affect a group's ability to appraise alternatives objectively and to arrive at quality decision solutions.

The first phenomenon, called **groupthink**, is related to norms. It describes situations in which group pressures for conformity deter the group from critically appraising unusual, minority, or unpopular views. Groupthink is a disease that attacks many groups and can dramatically hinder their performance. The second phenomenon we shall discuss is called **groupshift**. It indicates that, in discussing a given set of alternatives and arriving at a solution, group members tend to exaggerate the initial positions they hold. In some situations, caution dominates, and there is a conservative shift. More often, however, the evidence indicates that groups tend toward a risky shift. Let's look at each of these phenomena in more detail.

Groupthink   Have you ever felt like speaking up in a meeting, a classroom, or an informal group but decided against it? One reason may have been shyness. On the other hand, you may have been a victim of groupthink, a phenomenon that occurs when group members become so enamored of seeking concurrence that the norm for consensus overrides the realistic appraisal of alternative courses of action and the full expression of deviant, minority, or unpopular views. It describes a deterioration in an individual's mental efficiency, reality testing, and moral judgment as a result of group pressures.[50]

We have all seen the symptoms of the groupthink phenomenon:

1. Group members rationalize any resistance to the assumptions they have made. No matter how strongly the evidence may contradict their basic assumptions, members behave so as to reinforce those assumptions continually.
2. Members apply direct pressures on those who momentarily express doubts about any of the group's shared views or who question the validity of arguments supporting the alternative favored by the majority.
3. Members who have doubts or hold differing points of view seek to avoid deviating from what appears to be group consensus by keeping silent about misgivings and even minimizing to themselves the importance of their doubts.
4. There appears to be an illusion of unanimity. If someone doesn't speak, it's assumed that he or she is in full accord. In other words, abstention becomes viewed as a "yes" vote.[51]

In studies of historic American foreign policy decisions, these symptoms were found to prevail when government policy-making groups failed—unpreparedness at Pearl Harbor in 1941, the U.S. invasion of North Korea, the Bay of Pigs fiasco, and the escalation of the Vietnam War.[52] More recently, the *Challenger* and *Columbia* space shuttle disasters and the failure of the main mirror on the *Hubble* telescope have been linked to decision processes at NASA in which groupthink symptoms were evident.[53] And groupthink was found to be a primary factor leading to setbacks at both British Airways and retailer Marks & Spencer as they tried to implement globalization strategies.[54]

Groupthink appears to be closely aligned with the conclusions Asch drew in his experiments with a lone dissenter. Individuals who hold a position that is different from that of the dominant majority are under pressure to suppress,

OB In the News

Groupthink for an Enron Jury?

Although most of us view Enron as the very symbol of corporate corruption, not every Enron employee behaved unethically. Twenty former Enron employees—most notably Ken Lay, Jeff Skilling, and Andrew Fastow—were either convicted of or pleaded guilty to fraudulent behavior. The conviction of another Enron executive you've probably never heard of—former broadband finance chief Kevin Howard—provides a fascinating,

and disturbing, glimpse into how juries use group pressure to reach decisions.

Howard's first trial ended in a hung jury. In the second trial, he was found guilty of conspiracy, fraud, and falsifying records. However, shortly after his conviction, two jurors and two alternate jurors said they were pressured by other jurors to reach a unanimous decision even though they believed Howard was innocent. Juror Ann Marie Campbell said, in a sworn statement, "There was just so much pressure to change my vote that I felt like we had to compromise and give in to the majority because I felt like there was no other choice." Campbell said at one point a male juror tried to "grab her by the

shoulders" to convince her, and another "banged his first on the table during deliberations." Another jury member said, "There was an atmosphere of 'let's fry them.'"

On appeal, a judge threw out Howard's conviction, based, in part, on the earlier judge's instruction to the convicting jury which pressured them to reach a unanimous decision. The Kevin Howard case shows how strong groupthink pressures can be and the degree to which individuals can be pressured to give in to the majority.

Source: K. Hays, "Judge Dismisses Enron Convictions," *Houston (Texas) Chronicle,* February 1, 2007.

---

withhold, or modify their true feelings and beliefs. As members of a group, we find it more pleasant to be in agreement—to be a positive part of the group—than to be a disruptive force, even if disruption is necessary to improve the effectiveness of the group's decisions.

Does groupthink attack all groups? No. It seems to occur most often when there is a clear group identity, when members hold a positive image of their group that they want to protect, and when the group perceives a collective threat to this positive image.[55] So groupthink is not a dissenter-suppression mechanism as much as it's a means for a group to protect its positive image. For NASA, its problems stem from its attempt to confirm its identity as "the elite organization that could do no wrong."[56]

What can managers do to minimize groupthink?[57] First, they can monitor group size. People grow more intimidated and hesitant as group size increases, and, although there is no magic number that will eliminate groupthink, individuals are likely to feel less personal responsibility when groups get larger than about 10. Managers should also encourage group leaders to play an impartial role. Leaders should actively seek input from all members and avoid expressing their own opinions, especially in the early stages of deliberation. In addition, managers should appoint one group member to play the role of devil's advocate; this member's role is to overtly challenge the majority position and offer divergent perspectives. Still another suggestion is to use exercises that stimulate active discussion of diverse alternatives without threatening the group and intensifying identity protection. One such exercise is to have group members talk about dangers or risks involved in a decision and delaying discussion of any

---

groupthink *A phenomenon in which the norm for consensus overrides the realistic appraisal of alternative courses of action.*

groupshift *A change in decision risk between a group's decision and an individual decision that a member within the group would make; the shift can be toward either conservatism or greater risk.*

potential gains. Requiring members to first focus on the negatives of a decision alternative makes the group less likely to stifle dissenting views and more likely to gain an objective evaluation.

Groupshift   In comparing group decisions with the individual decisions of members within the group, evidence suggests that there are differences.[58] In some cases, group decisions are more conservative than individual decisions. More often, the shift is toward greater risk.[59]

What appears to happen in groups is that the discussion leads to a significant shift in the positions of members toward a more extreme position in the direction in which they were already leaning before the discussion. So conservative types become more cautious, and more aggressive types take on more risk. The group discussion tends to exaggerate the initial position of the group.

Groupshift can be viewed as actually a special case of groupthink. The decision of the group reflects the dominant decision-making norm that develops during the group's discussion. Whether the shift in the group's decision is toward greater caution or more risk depends on the dominant prediscussion norm.

The greater occurrence of the shift toward risk has generated several explanations for the phenomenon.[60] It's been argued, for instance, that discussion creates familiarization among the members. As they become more comfortable with each other, they also become more bold and daring. Another argument is that most societies in developed nations value risk, that they admire individuals who are willing to take risks, and that group discussion motivates members to show that they are at least as willing as their peers to take risks. The most plausible explanation of the shift toward risk, however, seems to be that the group diffuses responsibility. Group decisions free any single member from accountability for the group's final choice. Greater risk can be taken because even if the decision fails no one member can be held wholly responsible.

So how should you use the findings on groupshift? You should recognize that group decisions exaggerate the initial position of the individual members, that the shift has been shown more often to be toward greater risk, and that whether a group will shift toward greater risk or caution is a function of the members' prediscussion inclinations.

Having discussed group decision making and its pros and cons, we now turn to the techniques by which groups make decisions. These techniques reduce some of the dysfunctional aspects of group decision making.

Group Decision-Making Techniques

The most common form of group decision making takes place in **interacting groups**. In these groups, members meet face-to-face and rely on both verbal and nonverbal interaction to communicate with each other. But as our discussion of groupthink demonstrated, interacting groups often censor themselves and pressure individual members toward conformity of opinion. Brainstorming, the nominal group technique, and electronic meetings have been proposed as ways to reduce many of the problems inherent in the traditional interacting group.

8 Compare the effectiveness of interacting, brainstorming, nominal, and electronic meeting groups.

Brainstorming is meant to overcome pressures for conformity in an interacting group that retard the development of creative alternatives.[61] It does this by utilizing an idea-generation process that specifically encourages any and all alternatives while withholding any criticism of those alternatives.

In a typical brainstorming session, a half-dozen to a dozen people sit around a table. The group leader states the problem in a clear manner so that it is understood by all participants. Members then "freewheel" as many alternatives as they can in a given length of time. No criticism is allowed, and all the

Exhibit **9-8**

Source: S. Adams, *Build a Better Life by Stealing Office Supplies* (Kansas City, MO: Andrews & McMeal, 1991), p. 31. Dilbert reprinted with permission of United Features Syndicate, Inc.

alternatives are recorded for later discussion and analysis. One idea stimulates others, and judgments of even the most bizarre suggestions are withheld until later to encourage group members to "think the unusual."

Brainstorming may indeed generate ideas—but not in a very efficient manner. Research consistently shows that individuals working alone generate more ideas than a group in a brainstorming session. Why? One of the primary reasons is because of "production blocking." In other words, when people are generating ideas in a group, there are many people talking at once, which blocks the thought process and eventually impedes the sharing of ideas.[62] The following two techniques go further than brainstorming by offering methods that help groups arrive at a preferred solution.[63]

The **nominal group technique** restricts discussion or interpersonal communication during the decision-making process, hence the term *nominal*. Group members are all physically present, as in a traditional committee meeting, but members operate independently. Specifically, a problem is presented and then the group takes the following steps:

1. Members meet as a group, but before any discussion takes place, each member independently writes down ideas on the problem.
2. After this silent period, each member presents one idea to the group. Each member takes a turn, presenting a single idea, until all ideas have been

---

interacting groups   *Typical groups in which members interact with each other face-to-face.*

brainstorming   *An idea-generation process that specifically encourages any and all alternatives while withholding any criticism of those alternatives.*

nominal group technique   *A group decision-making method in which individual members meet face-to-face to pool their judgments in a systematic but independent fashion.*

presented and recorded. No discussion takes place until all ideas have been recorded.

3. The group discusses the ideas for clarity and evaluates them.
4. Each group member silently and independently rank-orders the ideas. The idea with the highest aggregate ranking determines the final decision.

The chief advantage of the nominal group technique is that it permits a group to meet formally but does not restrict independent thinking, as does an interacting group. Research generally shows that nominal groups outperform brainstorming groups.[64]

The most recent approach to group decision making blends the nominal group technique with sophisticated computer technology.[65] It's called a computer-assisted group, or an **electronic meeting**. Once the required technology is in place, the concept is simple. Up to 50 people sit around a horseshoe-shaped table, empty except for a series of computer terminals. Issues are presented to participants, who type their responses into their computers. Individual comments, as well as aggregate votes, are displayed on a projection screen. The proposed advantages of electronic meetings are anonymity, honesty, and speed. Participants can anonymously type any message they want, and it flashes on the screen for all to see at the push of a participant's keyboard key. This technique also allows people to be brutally honest without penalty. And it's supposedly fast because chitchat is eliminated, discussions don't digress, and many participants can "talk" at once without stepping on one another's toes. The early evidence, however, indicates that electronic meetings don't achieve most of their proposed benefits. Evaluations of numerous studies found that electronic meetings actually led to *decreased* group effectiveness, required *more* time to complete tasks, and resulted in *reduced* member satisfaction compared with face-to-face groups.[66] Nevertheless, current enthusiasm for computer-mediated communications suggests that this technology is here to stay and is likely to increase in popularity in the future.

Each of these four group decision techniques has its own set of strengths and weaknesses. The choice of one technique over another depends on what criteria you want to emphasize and the cost–benefit trade-off. For instance, as Exhibit 9-9 indicates, an interacting group is good for achieving commitment to a solution, brainstorming develops group cohesiveness, the nominal group technique is an inexpensive means for generating a large number of ideas, and electronic meetings minimize social pressures and conflicts.

Exhibit **9-9**	Evaluating Group Effectiveness			

| Effectiveness Criteria | Type of Group | | | |
	Interacting	Brainstorming	Nominal	Electronic
Number and quality of ideas	Low	Moderate	High	High
Social pressure	High	Low	Moderate	Low
Money costs	Low	Low	Low	High
Speed	Moderate	Moderate	Moderate	Moderate
Task orientation	Low	High	High	High
Potential for interpersonal conflict	High	Low	Moderate	Low
Commitment to solution	High	Not applicable	Moderate	Moderate
Development of group cohesiveness	High	High	Moderate	Low

Global Implications

Evaluate evidence for cultural differences in group status and social loafing, as well as the effects of diversity in groups.

As in most other areas of OB, most of the research on groups has been conducted in North America, but that situation is changing quickly. There are three areas of groups research where cross-cultural issues are particularly important.

Status and Culture   Do cultural differences affect status? The answer is a resounding "yes."[67]

The importance of status does vary between cultures. The French, for example, are highly status conscious. Countries also differ on the criteria that create status. For instance, status for Latin Americans and Asians tends to be derived from family position and formal roles held in organizations. In contrast, although status is still important in countries such as the United States and Australia, it is often bestowed more for accomplishments than on the basis of titles and family trees.[68]

The message here is to make sure you understand who and what holds status when interacting with people from a culture different from your own. A U.S. manager who doesn't understand that physical office size is not a measure of a Japanese executive's position or who fails to grasp the importance the British place on family genealogy and social class is likely to unintentionally offend his overseas counterparts and, in so doing, lessen his interpersonal effectiveness.

Social Loafing   Social loafing appears to have a Western bias. It's consistent with individualistic cultures, such as the United States and Canada, that are dominated by self-interest. It is *not* consistent with collective societies, in which individuals are motivated by in-group goals. For instance, in studies comparing employees from the United States with employees from the People's Republic of China and Israel (both collectivist societies), the Chinese and Israelis showed no propensity to engage in social loafing. In fact, the Chinese and Israelis actually performed better in a group than when working alone.

Group Diversity   More and more research is being done on how diversity influences group performance. Some of this research looks at cultural diversity, and some of it considers diversity on other characteristics (such as race or gender). Collectively, the research points to both benefits and costs from group diversity.

In terms of costs, diversity appears to lead to increased group conflict, especially in the early stages of a group's tenure. This conflict often results in lower group morale and group members dropping out. One study of groups that were either culturally diverse (composed of people from different countries) or homogeneous (composed of people from the same country) found that, on a wilderness survival exercise (not unlike the Experiential Exercise in this chapter), the diverse and homogenous groups performed equally well, but the diverse groups were less satisfied with their groups, were less cohesive, and had more conflict.[69]

In terms of the benefits to diversity, more evidence is accumulating that, over time, culturally and demographically diverse groups may perform better, if they can get over their initial conflicts. Why might this be the case?

electronic meeting   *A meeting in which members interact on computers, allowing for anonymity of comments and aggregation of votes.*

Research shows that surface-level diversity—observable characteristics such as national origin, race, and gender—actually cues people to possible differences in deep-level diversity—underlying attitudes, values, and opinions. One researcher argues, "The mere presence of diversity you can see, such as a person's race or gender, actually cues a team that there's likely to be differences of opinion." Although those differences of opinion can lead to conflict, they also provide an opportunity to solve problems in unique ways.

One study of jury behavior, for example, found that diverse juries were more likely to deliberate longer, share more information, and make fewer factual errors when discussing evidence. Interestingly, two studies of MBA student groups found that surface-level diversity led to greater openness even when there was no deep-level diversity. In such cases, the surface-level diversity of a group may subconsciously cue team members to be more open-minded in their views.[70]

In sum, the impact of cultural diversity on groups is a mixed bag. It is difficult to be in a diverse group in the short term. However, if the group members can weather their differences, over time, diversity may help them be more open-minded and creative, thus allowing them to do better in the long run. However, we should realize that even when there are positive effects of diversity on group performance, they are unlikely to be especially strong. As one review stated, "the business case (in terms of demonstrable financial results) for diversity remains hard to support based on the extant research."[71]

Summary and Implications for Managers

Performance   A number of group properties show a relationship with performance. Among the most prominent are role perception, norms, status differences, size of the group, and cohesiveness.

There is a positive relationship between role perception and an employee's performance evaluation.[72] The degree of congruence that exists between an employee and the boss in the perception of the employee's job influences the degree to which the boss will judge that employee as an effective performer. To the extent that the employee's role perception fulfills the boss's role expectations, the employee will receive a higher performance evaluation.

Norms control group member behavior by establishing standards of right and wrong. The norms of a given group can help to explain the behaviors of its members for managers. When norms support high output, managers can expect individual performance to be markedly higher than when group norms aim to restrict output. Similarly, norms that support antisocial behavior increase the likelihood that individuals will engage in deviant workplace activities.

Status inequities create frustration and can adversely influence productivity and the willingness to remain with an organization. Among individuals who are equity sensitive, incongruence is likely to lead to reduced motivation and an increased search for ways to bring about fairness (for example, taking another job). In addition, because lower-status people tend to participate less in group discussions, groups characterized by high status differences among members are likely to inhibit input from the lower-status members and to underperform their potential.

The impact of size on a group's performance depends on the type of task in which the group is engaged. Larger groups are more effective at fact-finding activities. Smaller groups are more effective at action-taking tasks. Our knowledge of social loafing suggests that, if management uses larger groups, efforts should be made to provide measures of individual performance within the group.

Cohesiveness can play an important function in influencing a group's level of productivity. Whether it does depends on the group's performance-related norms.

Satisfaction   As with the role perception–performance relationship, high congruence between a boss and an employee as to the perception of the employee's job shows a significant association with high employee satisfaction.[73] Similarly, role conflict is associated with job-induced tension and job dissatisfaction.[74]

Most people prefer to communicate with others at their own status level or a higher one rather than with those below them.[75] As a result, we should expect satisfaction to be greater among employees whose job minimizes interaction with individuals who are lower in status than themselves.

The group size–satisfaction relationship is what one would intuitively expect: Larger groups are associated with lower satisfaction.[76] As size increases, opportunities for participation and social interaction decrease, as does the ability of members to identify with the group's accomplishments. At the same time, having more members also prompts dissension, conflict, and the formation of subgroups, which all act to make the group a less pleasant entity of which to be a part.

Point × Counterpoint

ALL JOBS SHOULD BE DESIGNED AROUND GROUPS

*g*roups, not individuals, are the ideal building blocks for an organization. There are several reasons for designing all jobs around groups.

First, in general, groups make better decisions than the average individual acting alone.

Second, with the growth in technology, society is becoming more intertwined. Look at the growth of social networking sites such as MySpace, Facebook, and YouTube. People are connected anyway, so why not design work in the same way?

Third, small groups are good for people. They can satisfy social needs and provide support for employees in times of stress and crisis. Evidence indicates that social support—both when they provide it and when they receive it—makes people happier and even allows them to live longer.

Fourth, groups are very effective tools for implementation for decisions. Groups gain commitment from their members so that group decisions are likely to be willingly and more successfully carried out.

Fifth, groups can control and discipline individual members in ways that are often extremely difficult through impersonal quasi-legal disciplinary systems. Group norms are powerful control devices.

Sixth, groups are a means by which large organizations can fend off many of the negative effects of increased size. Groups help prevent communication lines from growing too long, the hierarchy from growing too steep, and individuals from getting lost in the crowd.

The rapid growth of team-based organizations in recent years suggests that we may well be on our way toward a day when almost all jobs are designed around groups.

*c*apitalistic countries such as the United States, Canada, Australia, and the United Kingdom value the individual. Designing jobs around groups is inconsistent with the economic values of these countries. Moreover, as capitalism and entrepreneurship have spread throughout eastern Europe, Asia, and other more collective societies, we should expect to see *less* emphasis on groups and *more* on the individual in workplaces throughout the world. Let's look at the United States to see how cultural and economic values shape employee attitudes toward groups.

The United States was built on the ethic of the individual. Its culture strongly values individual achievement and encourages competition. Even in team sports, people want to identify individuals for recognition. U.S. adults enjoy being part of a group in which they can maintain a strong individual identity. They don't enjoy sublimating their identity to that of the group. When they are assigned to groups, all sorts of bad things happen, including conflict, groupthink, social loafing, and deviant behavior.

The U.S. worker likes a clear link between individual effort and a visible outcome. It's not by chance that the United States, as a nation, has a considerably larger proportion of high achievers than exists in most of the rest of the world. It breeds achievers, and achievers seek personal responsibility. They would be frustrated in job situations in which their contribution was commingled and homogenized with the contributions of others.

U.S. workers want to be hired, evaluated, and rewarded on their individual achievements. They are not likely to accept a group's decision on such issues as their job assignments and wage increases, nor are they comfortable in a system in which the sole basis for their promotion or termination is the performance of their group.

Though teams have grown in popularity as a device for employers to organize people and tasks, we should expect resistance to any effort to treat individuals solely as members of a group—especially among workers raised in capitalistic economies.

Questions for Review

1 Define *group*? What are the different types of groups?

2 What are the five stages of group development?

3 Do role requirements change in different situations? If so, how?

4 How do group norms and status influence an individual's behavior?

5 How does group size affect group performance?

6 What are the advantages and limitations of cohesive groups?

7 What are the strengths and weaknesses of group (versus individual) decision making?

8 How effective are interacting, brainstorming, nominal, and electronic meeting groups?

9 What is the evidence for the effect of culture on group status and social loafing? How does diversity affect groups and their effectiveness over time?

Experiential Exercise

WILDERNESS SURVIVAL

You are a member of a hiking party. After reaching base camp on the first day, you decide to take a quick sunset hike by yourself. After a few exhilarating miles, you decide to return to camp. On your way back, you realize that you are lost. You have shouted for help, to no avail. It is now dark. And getting cold.

Your Task

Without communicating with anyone else in your group, read the following scenarios and choose the best answer. Keep track of your answers on a sheet of paper. You have 10 minutes to answer the 10 questions.

1. The first thing you decide to do is to build a fire. However, you have no matches, so you use the bow-and-drill method. What is the bow-and-drill method?

   a. A dry, soft stick is rubbed between one's hands against a board of supple green wood.

   b. A soft green stick is rubbed between one's hands against a hardwood board.

   c. A straight stick of wood is quickly rubbed back-and-forth against a dead tree.

   d. Two sticks (one being the bow, the other the drill) are struck to create a spark.

2. It occurs to you that you can also use the fire as a distress signal. When signaling with fire, how do you form the international distress signal?

   a. 2 fires

   b. 4 fires in a square

   c. 4 fires in a cross

   d. 3 fires in a line

3. You are very thirsty. You go to a nearby stream and collect some water in the small metal cup you have in your backpack. How long should you boil the water?

   a. 15 minutes

   b. A few seconds

   c. 1 hour

   d. It depends on the altitude.

4. You are very hungry, so you decide to eat what appear to be edible berries. When performing the universal edibility test, what should you do?

   a. Do not eat for 2 hours before the test.

   b. If the plant stings your lip, confirm the sting by holding it under your tongue for 15 minutes.

   c. If nothing bad has happened 2 hours after digestion, eat half a cup of the plant and wait again.

   d. Separate the plant into its basic components and eat each component, one at a time.

5. Next, you decide to build a shelter for the evening. In selecting a site, what do you *not* have to consider?

   a. It must contain material to make the type of shelter you need.

   b. It must be free of insects, reptiles, and poisonous plants.

   c. It must be large enough and level enough for you to lie down comfortably.

   d. It must be on a hill so you can signal rescuers and keep an eye on your surroundings.

6. In the shelter that you built, you notice a spider. You heard from a fellow hiker that black widow spiders populate the area. How do you identify a black widow spider?

   a. Its head and abdomen are black; its thorax is red.

   b. It is attracted to light.

   c. It runs away from light.

   d. It is a dark spider with a red or orange marking on the female's abdomen.

7. After getting some sleep, you notice that the night sky has cleared, so you decide to try to find your way back to base camp. You believe you should travel north and can use the North Star for navigation. How do you locate the North Star?

   a. Hold your right hand up as far as you can and look between your index and middle fingers.

   b. Find Sirius and look 60 degrees above it and to the right.

   c. Look for the Big Dipper and follow the line created by its cup end.

   d. Follow the line of Orion's belt.

8. You come across a fast-moving stream. What is the best way to cross it?

   a. Find a spot downstream from a sandbar, where the water will be calmer.

   b. Build a bridge.

   c. Find a rocky area, as the water will be shallow and you will have hand- and footholds.

   d. Find a level stretch where it breaks into a few channels.

9. After walking for about an hour, you feel several spiders in your clothes. You don't feel any pain, but you know some spider bites are painless. Which of these spider bites is painless?

   a. Black widow   c. Wolf spider

   b. Brown recluse   d. Harvestman (daddy longlegs)

10. You decide to eat some insects. Which insects should you avoid?

    a. Adults that sting or bite

    b. Caterpillars and insects that have a pungent odor

    c. Hairy or brightly colored ones

    d. All the above

Group Task

Break into groups of five or six people. Now imagine that your whole group is lost. Answer each question as a group, employing a consensus approach to reach each decision. Once the group comes to an agreement, write the decision down on the same sheet of paper that you used for your individual answers. You will have approximately 20 minutes for the group task.

Scoring Your Answers

Your instructor will provide you with the correct answers, which are based on expert judgments in these situations. Once you have received the answers, calculate (A) your individual score; (B) your group's score; (C) the average individual score in the group; (D) the best individual score in the group. Write these down and consult with your group to ensure that these scores are accurate.

(A) Your individual score _____

(B) Your group's score _____

(C) Average individual score in group _____

(D) Best individual score in group _____

Discussion Questions

1. How did your group (B) perform relative to yourself (A)?

2. How did your group (B) perform relative to the average individual score in the group (C)?

3. How did your group (B) perform relative to the best individual score in the group (D)?

4. Compare your results with those of other groups. Did some groups do a better job of outperforming individuals than others?

5. What do these results tell you about the effectiveness of group decision making?

6. What can groups do to make group decision-making more effective?

Ethical Dilemma

DEALING WITH SHIRKERS

We've noted that one of the most common problems in groups is social loafing, which means group members contribute less than if they were working on their own. We might call such individuals "shirkers"—those who are contributing far less than other group members.

Most of us have experienced social loafing, or shirking, in groups. And we may even admit to times when we shirked ourselves. We discussed earlier in the chapter some ways of discouraging social loafing, such as limiting group size, holding individuals responsible for their contributions, and setting group goals. While these tactics may be effective, in our experience, many students simply work around shirkers. "We just did it ourselves—it was easier that way," says one group member.

Consider the following questions for dealing with shirking in groups:

1. If group members end up "working around" shirkers, do you think this information should be communicated to the instructor so that individual's contribution to the project is judged more fairly? If so, does the group have an ethical responsibility to communicate this to the shirking group member? If not, isn't the shirking group member unfairly reaping the rewards of a "free ride"?

2. Do you think confronting the shirking group member is justified? Does this depend on the skills of the shirker (whether he is capable of doing good-quality work)?

3. Social loafing has been found to be higher in Western, more individualist nations, than in other countries. Do you think this means we should tolerate shirking on the part of U.S. workers to a greater degree than if it occurred with someone from Asia?

Case Incident 1

"IF TWO HEADS ARE BETTER THAN ONE, ARE FOUR EVEN BETTER?"

Maggie Becker, 24, is a marketing manager for Kavu, a small chain of coffee shops in eastern Ohio. Recently, Maggie's wealthy uncle passed away and left to Maggie, his only niece, $100,000. Maggie considers her current salary to be adequate to meet her current living expenses, so she'd like to invest the money so that when she buys a house she'll have a nice nest egg on which to draw.

One of Maggie's neighbors, Brian, is a financial advisor. Brian told Maggie there was a virtually endless array of investment options. She asked him to present her with two of the best options, and this is what he came up with:

1. **A very low-risk AAA municipal bond fund.** With this option, based on the information Brian provided, Maggie estimates that after 5 years she stands virtually zero chance of losing money, with an expected gain of approximately $7,000.

2. **A moderate-risk mutual fund.** Based on the information Brian provided her, Maggie estimates that with this option she stands a 50 percent chance of making $40,000 but also a 50 percent chance of losing $20,000.

Maggie prides herself on being rational and objective in her thinking. However, she's unsure of what to do in this case. Brian refuses to help her, telling her that she's already limited herself by asking for only two options. While driving to her parents' house for the weekend, Maggie finds herself vacillating between the two options. Her older brother is also visiting the folks this weekend, so Maggie decides to gather her family around the table after dinner, lay out the two options, and go with their decision. "You know the old saying—two heads are better than one," she says to herself, "so four heads should be even better."

Questions

1. Has Maggie made a good decision about the way she is going to make the decision?

2. Which investment would you choose? Why?

3. Which investment do you think most people would choose?

4. Based on what you have learned about groupshift, which investment do you think Maggie's family will choose?

Case Incident 2

THE DANGERS OF GROUPTHINK

Sometimes, the desire to maintain group harmony overrides the importance of making sound decisions. When that occurs, team members are said to engage in groupthink. Here are some examples:

- A civilian worker at a large Air Force base recalls a time that groupthink overcame her team's decision-making ability. She was a member of a process improvement team that an Air Force general had formed to develop a better way to handle the base's mail, which included important letters from high-ranking military individuals. The team was composed mostly of civilians, and it took almost a month to come up with a plan. The problem: The plan was not a process improvement. Recalls the civilian worker, "I was horrified. What used to be 8 steps; now there were 19." The team had devised a new system that resulted in each piece of mail being read by several middle managers before reaching its intended recipient. The team's new plan slowed down the mail considerably, with an average delay of 2 weeks. Even though the team members all knew that the new system was worse than its predecessor, no one wanted to question the team's solidarity. The problems lasted for almost an entire year. It wasn't until the general who formed the team complained about the mail that the system was changed.

- During the dot-com boom of the late 1990s, Virginia Turezyn, managing director of Infinity Capital, states that she was a victim of groupthink. At first, Turezyn was skeptical about the stability of the boom. But after continually reading about start-ups turning into multimillion-dollar payoffs, she felt different. Turezyn decided to invest millions in several dot-coms, including I-drive, a company that provided electronic data storage. The problem was that I-drive was giving the storage away for free, and as a result, the company was losing money. Turezyn recalls one board meeting at I-drive where she spoke up to no avail. "We're spending way too much money," she screamed. The younger executives shook their heads and replied that if they charged for storage they would lose their customers. Says Turezyn, "I started to think, 'Maybe I'm just too old. Maybe I really don't get it.'" Unfortunately, Turezyn did get it. I-drive later filed for bankruptcy.

- Steve Blank, an entrepreneur, also fell victim to groupthink. Blank was a dot-com investor, and he participated on advisory boards of several Internet start-ups. During meetings for one such start-up, a Web photo finisher, Blank tried to persuade his fellow board members to change the business model to be more traditional. Recalls Blank, "I went to those meetings and started saying things like 'Maybe you should spend that $10 million you just raised on acquiring a customer base rather than building a brand.' The CEO told me, 'Steve, you just don't get it—all the rules have changed.'" The team didn't take Blank's advice, and Blank says that he lost hundreds of thousands of dollars on the deal.

According to Michael Useem, a professor at the University of Pennsylvania's Wharton College of Business, one of the main reasons that groupthink occurs is a lack of conflict. "A single devil's advocate or whistle-blower faces a really uphill struggle," he states. "But if you [the naysayer] have one ally that is enormously strengthening."

Questions

1. What are some factors that led to groupthink in the cases described here? What can teams do to attempt to prevent groupthink from occurring?

2. How might differences in status among group members contribute to groupthink? For example, how might lower-status members react to a group's decision? Are lower-status members more or less likely to be dissenters? Why might higher-status group members be more effective dissenters?

3. Microsoft CEO Steve Ballmer says that he encourages dissent. Can such norms guard against the occurrence of groupthink? As a manager, how would you try to cultivate norms that prevent groupthink?

4. How might group characteristics such as size and cohesiveness affect groupthink?

Source: Based on C. Hawn, "Fear and Posing," *Forbes,* March 25, 2002, pp. 22–25; and J. Sandberg, "Some Ideas Are So Bad That Only Team Efforts Can Account for Them," *Wall Street Journal,* September 29, 2004, p. B1.

Endnotes

1. J. Sandberg, "Brainstorming Works Best if People Scramble for Ideas on Their Own," *Wall Street Journal,* June 13, 2006, p. B1.
2. L. R. Sayles, "Work Group Behavior and the Larger Organization," in C. Arensburg, et al. (eds.), *Research in Industrial Relations* (New York: Harper & Row, 1957), pp. 131–145.
3. J. F. McGrew, J. G. Bilotta, and J. M. Deeney, "Software Team Formation and Decay: Extending the Standard Model for Small Groups," *Small Group Research* 30, no. 2, (1999), pp. 209–234.
4. B. W. Tuckman, "Developmental Sequences in Small Groups," *Psychological Bulletin,* June 1965, pp. 384–399; B. W. Tuckman and M. C. Jensen, "Stages of Small-Group Development Revisited," *Group and Organizational Studies,* December 1977, pp. 419–427; and M. F. Maples, "Group Development: Extending Tuckman's Theory," *Journal for Specialists in Group Work,* Fall 1988, pp. 17–23; and K. Vroman and J. Kovacich, "Computer-Mediated Interdisciplinary Teams: Theory and Reality," *Journal of Interprofessional Care* 16, no. 2 (2002), pp. 159–170.
5. J. F. George and L. M. Jessup, "Groups over Time: What Are We Really Studying?" *International Journal of Human-Computer Studies* 47, no. 3 (1997), pp. 497–511.
6. R. C. Ginnett, "The Airline Cockpit Crew," in J. R. Hackman (ed.), *Groups That Work (and Those That Don't)* (San Francisco: Jossey-Bass, 1990).
7. C. J. G. Gersick, "Time and Transition in Work Teams: Toward a New Model of Group Development," *Academy of Management Journal,* March 1988, pp. 9–41; C. J. G. Gersick, "Marking Time: Predictable Transitions in Task Groups," *Academy of Management Journal,* June 1989, pp. 274–309; M. J. Waller, J. M. Conte, C. B. Gibson, and M. A. Carpenter,

"The Effect of Individual Perceptions of Deadlines on Team Performance," *Academy of Management Review*, October 2001, pp. 586–600; and A. Chang, P. Bordia, and J. Duck, "Punctuated Equilibrium and Linear Progression: Toward a New Understanding of Group Development," *Academy of Management Journal*, February 2003, pp. 106–117; see also H. Arrow, M. S. Poole, K. B. Henry, S. Wheelan, and R. Moreland, "Time, Change, and Development: The Temporal Perspective on Groups," *Small Group Research*, February 2004, pp. 73–105.

8. Gersick, "Time and Transition in Work Teams;" and Gersick, "Marking Time."

9. A. Seers and S. Woodruff, "Temporal Pacing in Task Forces: Group Development or Deadline Pressure?" *Journal of Management* 23, no. 2 (1997), pp. 169–187.

10. S. Lieberman, "The Effects of Changes in Roles on the Attitudes of Role Occupants," *Human Relations*, November 1956, pp. 385–402.

11. See D. M. Rousseau, *Psychological Contracts in Organizations: Understanding Written and Unwritten Agreements* (Thousand Oaks, CA: Sage, 1995); E. W. Morrison and S. L. Robinson, "When Employees Feel Betrayed: A Model of How Psychological Contract Violation Develops," *Academy of Management Review*, April 1997, pp. 226–256; D. Rousseau and R. Schalk (eds.), *Psychological Contracts in Employment: Cross-Cultural Perspectives* (San Francisco: Jossey-Bass, 2000); L. Sels, M. Janssens, and I. Van den Brande, "Assessing the Nature of Psychological Contracts: A Validation of Six Dimensions," *Journal of Organizational Behavior*, June 2004, pp. 461–488; and C. Hui, C. Lee, and D. M. Rousseau, "Psychological Contract And Organizational Citizenship Behavior in China: Investigating Generalizability and Instrumentality," *Journal of Applied Psychology*, April 2004, pp. 311–321.

12. See M. F. Peterson et al., "Role Conflict, Ambiguity, and Overload: A 21-Nation Study," *Academy of Management Journal*, April 1995, pp. 429–452; and I. H. Settles, R. M. Sellers, and A. Damas, Jr., "One Role or Two? The Function of Psychological Separation in Role Conflict," *Journal of Applied Psychology*, June 2002, pp. 574–582.

13. P. G. Zimbardo, C. Haney, W. C. Banks, and D. Jaffe, "The Mind Is a Formidable Jailer: A Pirandellian Prison," *New York Times*, April 8, 1973, pp. 38–60; and C. Haney and P. G. Zimbardo, "Social Roles and Role-Playing: Observations from the Stanford Prison Study," *Behavioral and Social Science Teacher*, January 1973, pp. 25–45.

14. For a review of the research on group norms, see J. R. Hackman, "Group Influences on Individuals in Organizations," in M. D. Dunnette and L. M. Hough (eds.), *Handbook of Industrial & Organizational Psychology*, 2nd ed., vol. 3 (Palo Alto, CA: Consulting Psychologists Press, 1992), pp. 235–250. For a more recent discussion, see M. G. Ehrhart and S. E. Naumann, "Organizational Citizenship Behavior in Work Groups: A Group Norms Approach," *Journal of Applied Psychology*, December 2004, pp. 960–974.

15. Adapted from P. S. Goodman, E. Ravlin, and M. Schminke, "Understanding Groups in Organizations," in L. L. Cummings and B. M. Staw (eds.), *Research in Organizational Behavior*, vol. 9 (Greenwich, CT: JAI Press, 1987), p. 159.

16. E. Mayo, *The Human Problems of an Industrial Civilization* (New York: Macmillan, 1933); and F. J. Roethlisberger and W. J. Dickson, *Management and the Worker* (Cambridge, MA: Harvard University Press, 1939).

17. C. A. Kiesler and S. B. Kiesler, *Conformity* (Reading, MA: Addison-Wesley, 1969).

18. Ibid., p. 27.

19. S. E. Asch, "Effects of Group Pressure upon the Modification and Distortion of Judgments," in H. Guetzkow (ed.), *Groups, Leadership and Men* (Pittsburgh: Carnegie Press, 1951), pp. 177–190; and S. E. Asch, "Studies of Independence and Conformity: A Minority of One Against a Unanimous Majority," *Psychological Monographs: General and Applied* 70, no. 9 (1956), pp. 1–70.

20. R. Bond and P. B. Smith, "Culture and Conformity: A Meta-analysis of Studies Using Asch's (1952, 1956) Line Judgment Task," *Psychological Bulletin*, January 1996, pp. 111–137.

21. See S. L. Robinson and R. J. Bennett, "A Typology of Deviant Workplace Behaviors: A Multidimensional Scaling Study," *Academy of Management Journal*, April 1995, pp. 555–572; S. L. Robinson and A. M. O'Leary-Kelly, "Monkey See, Monkey Do: The Influence of Work Groups on the Antisocial Behavior of Employees," *Academy of Management Journal*, December 1998, pp. 658–672; and R. J. Bennett and S. L. Robinson, "The Past, Present, and Future of Workplace Deviance," in J. Greenberg (ed.), *Organizational Behavior: The State of the Science*, 2nd ed. (Mahwah, NJ: Erlbaum, 2003), pp. 237–271.

22. C. M. Pearson, L. M. Andersson, and C. L. Porath, "Assessing and Attacking Workplace Civility," *Organizational Dynamics* 29, no. 2 (2000), p. 130; see also C. Pearson, L. M. Andersson, and C. L. Porath, "Workplace Incivility," in S. Fox and P. E. Spector (eds.), *Counterproductive Work Behavior: Investigations of Actors and Targets* (Washington, DC American Psychological Association, 2005), pp. 177–200.

23. Robinson and O'Leary-Kelly, "Monkey See, Monkey Do."

24. A. Erez, H. Elms, and E. Fong, "Lying, Cheating, Stealing: It Happens More in Groups," paper presented at the European Business Ethics Network Annual Conference, Budapest, Hungary, August 30, 2003.

25. S. L. Robinson and M. S. Kraatz, "Constructing the Reality of Normative Behavior: The Use of Neutralization Strategies by Organizational Deviants," in R. W. Griffin and A. O'Leary-Kelly (eds.), *Dysfunctional Behavior in Organizations: Violent and Deviant Behavior* (Greenwich, CT: JAI Press, 1998), pp. 203–220.

26. See R. S. Feldman, *Social Psychology*, 3rd ed. (Upper Saddle River, NJ: Prentice Hall, 2001), pp. 464–465.

27. Cited in Hackman, "Group Influences on Individuals in Organizations," p. 236.

28. O. J. Harvey and C. Consalvi, "Status and Conformity to Pressures in Informal Groups," *Journal of Abnormal and Social Psychology*, Spring 1960, pp. 182–187.

29. J. A. Wiggins, F. Dill, and R. D. Schwartz, "On 'Status-Liability,'" *Sociometry*, April–May 1965, pp. 197–209.

30. See J. M. Levine and R. L. Moreland, "Progress in Small Group Research," in J. T. Spence, J. M. Darley, and D. J. Foss (eds.), *Annual Review of Psychology*, vol. 41 (Palo Alto, CA: Annual Reviews, 1990), pp. 585–634; S. D. Silver, B. P. Cohen, and J. H. Crutchfield, "Status Differentiation and Information Exchange in Face-to-Face and Computer-Mediated Idea Generation," *Social Psychology Quarterly*, 1994,

pp. 108–123; and J. M. Twenge, "Changes in Women's Assertiveness in Response to Status and Roles: A Cross-Temporal Meta-analysis, 1931–1993," *Journal of Personality and Social Psychology*, July 2001, pp. 133–145.

31. J. Greenberg, "Equity and Workplace Status: A Field Experiment," *Journal of Applied Psychology*, November 1988, pp. 606–613.

32. E. J. Thomas and C. F. Fink, "Effects of Group Size," *Psychological Bulletin*, July 1963, pp. 371–384; A. P. Hare, *Handbook of Small Group Research* (New York: The Free Press, 1976); and M. E. Shaw, *Group Dynamics: The Psychology of Small Group Behavior*, 3rd ed. (New York: McGraw-Hill, 1981).

33. G. H. Seijts and G. P. Latham, "The Effects of Goal Setting and Group Size on Performance in a Social Dilemma," *Canadian Journal of Behavioural Science* 32, no. 2 (2000), pp. 104–116.

34. Shaw, *Group Dynamics: The Psychology of Small Group Behavior*.

35. See, for instance, D. R. Comer, "A Model of Social Loafing in Real Work Groups," *Human Relations*, June 1995, pp. 647–667; S. M. Murphy, S. J. Wayne, R. C. Liden, and B. Erdogan, "Understanding Social Loafing: The Role of Justice Perceptions and Exchange Relationships," *Human Relations*, January 2003, pp. 61–84; and R. C. Liden, S. J. Wayne, R. A. Jaworski, and N. Bennett, "Social Loafing: A Field Investigation," *Journal of Management*, April 2004, pp. 285–304.

36. W. Moede, "Die Richtlinien der Leistungs-Psychologie," *Industrielle Psychotechnik* 4 (1927), pp. 193–207. See also D. A. Kravitz and B. Martin, "Ringelmann Rediscovered: The Original Article," *Journal of Personality and Social Psychology*, May 1986, pp. 936–941.

37. See, for example, J. A. Shepperd, "Productivity Loss in Performance Groups: A Motivation Analysis," *Psychological Bulletin*, January 1993, pp. 67–81; and S. J. Karau and K. D. Williams, "Social Loafing: A Meta-analytic Review and Theoretical Integration," *Journal of Personality and Social Psychology*, October 1993, pp. 681–706.

38. S. G. Harkins and K. Szymanski, "Social Loafing and Group Evaluation," *Journal of Personality and Social Psychology*, December 1989, pp. 934–941.

39. A. Gunnthorsdottir and A. Rapoport, "Embedding Social Dilemmas in Intergroup Competition Reduces Free-Riding," *Organizational Behavior and Human Decision Processes* 101 (2006), pp. 184–199.

40. For some of the controversy surrounding the definition of cohesion, see J. Keyton and J. Springston, "Redefining Cohesiveness in Groups," *Small Group Research*, May 1990, pp. 234–254.

41. B. Mullen and C. Cooper, "The Relation Between Group Cohesiveness and Performance: An Integration," *Psychological Bulletin*, March 1994, pp. 210–227; P. M. Podsakoff, S. B. MacKenzie, and M. Ahearne, "Moderating Effects of Goal Acceptance on the Relationship Between Group Cohesiveness and Productivity," *Journal of Applied Psychology*, December 1997, pp. 974–983; and D. J. Beal, R. R. Cohen, M. J. Burke, and C. L. McLendon, "Cohesion and Performance in Groups: A Meta-analytic Clarification of Construct Relations," *Journal of Applied Psychology*, December 2003, pp. 989–1004.

42. Ibid.

43. Based on J. L. Gibson, J. M. Ivancevich, and J. H. Donnelly, Jr., *Organizations*, 8th ed. (Burr Ridge, IL: Irwin, 1994), p. 323.

44. N. Foote, E. Matson, L. Weiss, and E. Wenger, "Leveraging Group Knowledge for High-Performance Decision-Making," *Organizational Dynamics* 31, no. 2 (2002), pp. 280–295.

45. See N. R. F. Maier, "Assets and Liabilities in Group Problem Solving: The Need for an Integrative Function," *Psychological Review*, April 1967, pp. 239–249; G. W. Hill, "Group Versus Individual Performance: Are N+1 Heads Better Than One?" *Psychological Bulletin*, May 1982, pp. 517–539; A. E. Schwartz and J. Levin, "Better Group Decision Making," *Supervisory Management*, June 1990, p. 4; and R. F. Martell and M. R. Borg, "A Comparison of the Behavioral Rating Accuracy of Groups and Individuals," *Journal of Applied Psychology*, February 1993, pp. 43–50.

46. D. Gigone and R. Hastie, "Proper Analysis of the Accuracy of Group Judgments," *Psychological Bulletin*, January 1997, pp. 149–167; and B. L. Bonner, S. D. Sillito, and M. R. Baumann, "Collective Estimation: Accuracy, Expertise, and Extroversion as Sources of Intra-Group Influence," *Organizational Behavior and Human Decision Processes* 103 (2007), pp. 121–133.

47. See, for example, W. C. Swap and Associates, *Group Decision Making* (Newbury Park, CA: Sage, 1984).

48. D. D. Henningsen, M. G. Cruz, and M. L. Miller, "Role of Social Loafing in Predeliberation Decision Making," *Group Dynamics: Theory, Research, and Practice* 4, no. 2 (June 2000), pp. 168–175.

49. J. H. Davis, *Group Performance* (Reading, MA: Addison-Wesley, 1969); J. P. Wanous and M. A. Youtz, "Solution Diversity and the Quality of Group Decisions," *Academy of Management Journal*, March 1986, pp. 149–159; and R. Libby, K. T. Trotman, and I. Zimmer, "Member Variation, Recognition of Expertise, and Group Performance," *Journal of Applied Psychology*, February 1987, pp. 81–87.

50. I. L. Janis, *Groupthink* (Boston: Houghton Mifflin, 1982); W. Park, "A Review of Research on Groupthink," *Journal of Behavioral Decision Making*, July 1990, pp. 229–245; J. N. Choi and M. U. Kim, "The Organizational Application of Groupthink and Its Limits in Organizations," *Journal of Applied Psychology*, April 1999, pp. 297–306; and W. W. Park, "A Comprehensive Empirical Investigation of the Relationships Among Variables of the Groupthink Model," *Journal of Organizational Behavior*, December 2000, pp. 873–887.

51. Janis, *Groupthink*.

52. Ibid.

53. G. Moorhead, R. Ference, and C. P. Neck, "Group Decision Fiascos Continue: Space Shuttle Challenger and a Revised Groupthink Framework," *Human Relations*, May 1991, pp. 539–550; E. J. Chisson, *The Hubble Wars* (New York: HarperPerennial, 1994); and C. Covault, "*Columbia* Revelations Alarming E-Mails Speak for Themselves. But Administrator O'Keefe Is More Concerned About Board Findings on NASA Decision-Making," *Aviation Week & Space Technology*, March 3, 2003, p. 26.

54. J. Eaton, "Management Communication: The Threat of Groupthink," *Corporate Communication* 6, no. 4 (2001), pp. 183–192.

55. M. E. Turner and A. R. Pratkanis, "Mitigating Groupthink by Stimulating Constructive Conflict," in C. De Dreu and E. Van de Vliert (eds.), *Using Conflict in Organizations* (London: Sage, 1997), pp. 53–71.

56. Ibid., p. 68.

57. See N. R. F. Maier, *Principles of Human Relations* (New York: Wiley, 1952); I. L. Janis, *Groupthink: Psychological Studies of Policy Decisions and Fiascoes*, 2nd ed. (Boston: Houghton Mifflin, 1982); C. R. Leana, "A Partial Test of Janis' Groupthink Model: Effects of Group Cohesiveness and Leader Behavior on Defective Decision Making," *Journal of Management*, Spring 1985, pp. 5–17; and N. Richardson Ahlfinger and J. K. Esser, "Testing the Groupthink Model: Effects of Promotional Leadership and Conformity Predisposition," *Social Behavior & Personality* 29, no. 1 (2001), pp. 31–41.

58. See D. J. Isenberg, "Group Polarization: A Critical Review and Meta-Analysis," *Journal of Personality and Social Psychology*, December 1986, pp. 1141–1151; J. L. Hale and F. J. Boster, "Comparing Effect Coded Models of Choice Shifts," *Communication Research Reports*, April 1988, pp. 180–186; and P. W. Paese, M. Bieser, and M. E. Tubbs, "Framing Effects and Choice Shifts in Group Decision Making," *Organizational Behavior and Human Decision Processes*, October 1993, pp. 149–165.

59. See, for example, N. Kogan and M. A. Wallach, "Risk Taking as a Function of the Situation, the Person, and the Group," in *New Directions in Psychology*, vol. 3 (New York: Holt, Rinehart and Winston, 1967); and M. A. Wallach, N. Kogan, and D. J. Bem, "Group Influence on Individual Risk Taking," *Journal of Abnormal and Social Psychology* 65 (1962), pp. 75–86.

60. R. D. Clark III, "Group-Induced Shift Toward Risk: A Critical Appraisal," *Psychological Bulletin*, October 1971, pp. 251–270.

61. A. F. Osborn, *Applied Imagination: Principles and Procedures of Creative Thinking*, 3rd ed. (New York: Scribner, 1963). See also T. Rickards, "Brainstorming Revisited: A Question of Context," *International Journal of Management Reviews*, March 1999, pp. 91–110; and R. P. McGlynn, D. McGurk, V. S. Effland, N. L. Johll, and D. J. Harding, "Brainstorming and Task Performance in Groups Constrained by Evidence," *Organizational Behavior and Human Decision Processes*, January 2004, pp. 75–87.

62. N. L. Kerr and R. S. Tindale, "Group Performance and Decision-Making," *Annual Review of Psychology* 55 (2004), pp. 623–655.

63. See A. L. Delbecq, A. H. Van deVen, and D. H. Gustafson, *Group Techniques for Program Planning: A Guide to Nominal and Delphi Processes* (Glenview, IL: Scott, Foresman, 1975); and P. B. Paulus and H.-C. Yang, "Idea Generation in Groups: A Basis for Creativity in Organizations," *Organizational Behavior and Human Decision Processing*, May 2000, pp. 76–87.

64. C. Faure, "Beyond Brainstorming: Effects of Different Group Procedures on Selection of Ideas and Satisfaction with the Process," *Journal of Creative Behavior* 38 (2004), pp. 13–34.

65. See, for instance, A. B. Hollingshead and J. E. McGrath, "Computer-Assisted Groups: A Critical Review of the Empirical Research," in R. A. Guzzo and E. Salas (eds.), *Team Effectiveness and Decision Making in Organizations* (San Francisco: Jossey-Bass, 1995), pp. 46–78.

66. B. B. Baltes, M. W. Dickson, M. P. Sherman, C. C. Bauer, and J. LaGanke, "Computer-Mediated Communication and Group Decision Making: A Meta-Analysis," *Organizational Behavior and Human Decision Processes*, January 2002, pp. 156–179.

67. See G. Hofstede, *Cultures and Organizations: Software of the Mind* (New York, McGraw-Hill, 1991).

68. This section is based on P. R. Harris and R. T. Moran, *Managing Cultural Differences*, 5th ed. (Houston: Gulf Publishing, 1999).

69. D. S. Staples and L. Zhao, "The Effects of Cultural Diversity in Virtual Teams Versus Face-to-Face Teams," *Group Decision and Negotiation*, July 2006, pp. 389–406.

70. K. W. Phillips and D. L. Loyd, "When Surface and Deep-Level Diversity Collide: The Effects on Dissenting Group Members," *Organizational Behavior and Human Decision Processes* 99 (2006), pp. 143–160; and S. R. Sommers, "On Racial Diversity and Group Decision Making: Identifying Multiple Effects of Racial Composition on Jury Deliberations," *Journal of Personality and Social Psychology*, April 2006, pp. 597–612.

71. E. Mannix and M. A. Neale, "What Differences Make a Difference? The Promise and Reality of Diverse Teams in Organizations," *Psychological Science in the Public Interest*, October 2005, pp. 31–55.

72. T. P. Verney, "Role Perception Congruence, Performance, and Satisfaction," in D. J. Vredenburgh and R. S. Schuler (eds.), *Effective Management: Research and Application*, Proceedings of the 20th Annual Eastern Academy of Management, Pittsburgh, PA, May 1983, pp. 24–27.

73. Ibid.

74. A. G. Bedeian and A. A. Armenakis, "A Path-Analytic Study of the Consequences of Role Conflict and Ambiguity," *Academy of Management Journal*, June 1981, pp. 417–424; and P. L. Perrewe, K. L. Zellars, G. R. Ferris, A. M. Rossi, C. J. Kacmar, and D. A. Ralston, "Neutralizing Job Stressors: Political Skill as an Antidote to the Dysfunctional Consequences of Role Conflict," *Academy of Management Journal*, February 2004, pp. 141–152.

75. Shaw, *Group Dynamics*.

76. B. Mullen, C. Symons, L. Hu, and E. Salas, "Group Size, Leadership Behavior, and Subordinate Satisfaction," *Journal of General Psychology*, April 1989, pp. 155–170.

Understanding Work Teams

We're going to turn this team

around 360 degrees.

—Jason Kidd

After studying this chapter, you should be able to:

1 Analyze the growing popularity of using teams in organizations.

2 Contrast groups and teams.

3 Compare and contrast four types of teams.

4 Identify the characteristics of effective teams.

5 Show how organizations can create team players.

6 Decide when to use individuals instead of teams.

7 Show how the understanding of teams differs in a global context.

*i*n the competitive search for top talent, it is not unusual for top employees to be hired away from successful companies. Google, for example, has seen a lot of companies hire away its people.

A new wrinkle in the talent wars is hiring away an entire team. Take Mark Metz, the CEO of Optimus Solutions, a computer systems and services company. When Metz founded Optimus, he brought on board 7 of his former colleagues to help start the company. Even though he was sued for hiring them

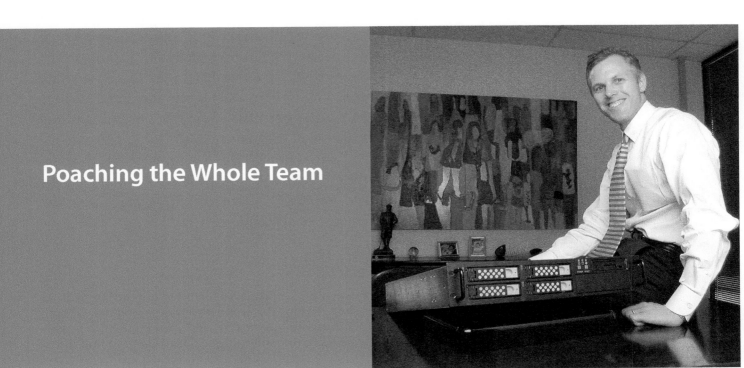

Poaching the Whole Team

away, he wasn't deterred. In 2001, he recruited another team of 10. In 2005, he topped that, hiring away a manager's entire 30-person team. Experience matters in the IT area, and Metz believes he was able to gain valuable experience quickly without having to develop it over time. "You get the dynamics of a functioning team without having to create that yourself," he said.

Although some have accused Metz of raiding, executive recruiters see such "lift-outs" as a growing trend. Although the practice has been around in industries such as financial services and law, it's becoming increasingly common in other sectors, such as IT, management consulting, medical services, and accounting.

"We've even seen it happen between recruiters, which is its own irony," says one expert.

One factor explaining the rise in lift-outs, as Metz recognized, is speed. When organizations need to enter a competitive market ASAP, they don't have time to spend months hiring and then training team members. Hiring an entire team may be the quickest way to enter a new market or launch a product or service.

Another factor is private equity buyouts. Private equity firms seek to turn around a company quickly so that, in most cases, they can resell it for a profit (like "flipping" in real estate). Time is money, and poaching whole teams can reduce the time necessary to return the company to profitability.

Hiring away whole teams does have disadvantages. One is legality: Most companies have noncompete clauses in place, and some lift-outs run the risk of drawing a lawsuit from the company whose team was poached. Another challenge is that the team may act like a team and use its cohesion against the new employer. Metz found that after he recruited one of his teams to Optimus, the team started to negotiate en masse for better benefits. "You think you're just hiring many people," Metz said, "But they turn into mini acquisitions."[1] ∎

*t*eams are increasingly becoming the primary means for organizing work in contemporary business firms. In fact, this trend is so widespread that companies such as Optimus are hiring whole teams. What do you think of your skills in leading and building a team? Take the following self-assessment to find out.

HOW GOOD AM I AT BUILDING AND LEADING A TEAM?

In the Self-Assessment Library (available on CD or online), take assessment II.B.6 (How Good Am I at Building and Leading a Team?) and answer the following questions.

1. *Did you score as high as you thought you would? Why or why not?*
2. *Do you think you can improve your score? If so, how? If not, why not?*
3. *Do you think there is such a thing as team players? If yes, what are their behaviors?*

Why Have Teams Become So Popular?

1   Analyze the growing popularity of using teams in organizations.

Decades ago, when companies such as W. L. Gore, Volvo, and General Foods introduced teams into their production processes, it made news because no one else was doing it. Today, it's just the opposite. It's the organization that *doesn't* use teams that has become newsworthy. Teams are everywhere.

How do we explain the current popularity of teams? As organizations have restructured themselves to compete more effectively and efficiently, they have turned to teams as a better way to use employee talents. Management has found that teams are more flexible and responsive to changing events than are traditional departments or other forms of permanent groupings. Teams have the capability to quickly assemble, deploy, refocus, and disband. But don't overlook the motivational properties of teams. Consistent with our discussion in Chapter 7 of the role of employee involvement as a motivator, teams facilitate employee participation in operating decisions. So another explanation for the popularity of teams is that they are an effective means for management to democratize their organizations and increase employee motivation.

The fact that organizations have turned to teams doesn't necessarily mean they're always effective. Decision makers, as humans, can be swayed by fads and herd mentality. Are teams truly effective? What conditions affect their potential? How do teams work together? These are some of the questions we'll answer in this chapter.

Differences Between Groups and Teams

2 Contrast groups and teams.

Groups and teams are not the same thing. In this section, we define and clarify the difference between work groups and work teams.[2]

In Chapter 9, we defined a *group* as two or more individuals, interacting and interdependent, who have come together to achieve particular objectives. A **work group** is a group that interacts primarily to share information and to make decisions to help each member perform within his or her area of responsibility.

Work groups have no need or opportunity to engage in collective work that requires joint effort. So their performance is merely the summation of each group member's individual contribution. There is no positive synergy that would create an overall level of performance that is greater than the sum of the inputs.

A **work team** generates positive synergy through coordinated effort. The individual efforts result in a level of performance that is greater than the sum of those individual inputs. Exhibit 10-1 highlights the differences between work groups and work teams.

These definitions help clarify why so many organizations have recently restructured work processes around teams. Management is looking for positive synergy that will allow the organizations to increase performance. The extensive use of teams creates the *potential* for an organization to generate greater outputs with no increase in inputs. Notice, however, that we said *potential.* There is nothing inherently magical in the creation of teams that ensures the achievement of positive synergy. Merely calling a *group* a *team* doesn't automatically increase its performance. As we show later in this chapter, effective teams have certain common characteristics. If management hopes to gain increases in organizational performance through the use of teams, it needs to ensure that its teams possess these characteristics.

work group   *A group that interacts primarily to share information and to make decisions to help each group member perform within his or her area of responsibility.*

work team   *A group whose individual efforts result in performance that is greater than the sum of the individual inputs.*

Exhibit 10-1 | Comparing Work Groups and Work Teams

Work Groups		Work Teams
Share information	←— Goal —→	Collective performance
Neutral (sometimes negative)	←— Synergy —→	Positive
Individual	←— Accountability —→	Individual and mutual
Random and varied	←— Skills —→	Complementary

Types of Teams

3 *Compare and contrast four types of teams.*

Teams can do a variety of things. They can make products, provide services, negotiate deals, coordinate projects, offer advice, and make decisions.[3] In this section, we'll describe the four most common types of teams you're likely to find in an organization: *problem-solving teams, self-managed work teams, cross-functional teams,* and *virtual teams* (see Exhibit 10-2).

Problem-Solving Teams

Twenty years ago or so, teams were just beginning to grow in popularity, and most of those teams took similar form. They were typically composed of 5 to 12 hourly employees from the same department who met for a few hours each week to discuss ways of improving quality, efficiency, and the work environment.[4] We call these **problem-solving teams**.

In problem-solving teams, members share ideas or offer suggestions on how work processes and methods can be improved; they rarely have the authority to unilaterally implement any of their suggested actions. For instance, Merrill Lynch created a problem-solving team to specifically figure out ways to reduce the number of days it took to open up a new cash management account.[5] By suggesting cuts in the number of steps in the process from 46 to 36, the team was able to reduce the average number of days from 15 to 8.

Self-Managed Work Teams

Although problem-solving teams involve employees in decisions, they "only" make recommendations. Some organizations have gone further and created teams that can not only solve problems but implement solutions and take responsibility for outcomes.

Exhibit 10-2 | Four Types of Teams

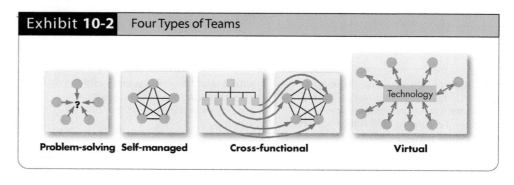

Problem-solving Self-managed Cross-functional Virtual

At the Louis Vuitton factory in Ducey, France, all employees work in problem-solving teams, with each team focusing on one product at a time. Team members are encouraged to suggest improvements in manufacturing work methods and processes as well as product quality. When a team was asked to make a test run on a prototype of a new handbag, team members discovered that decorative studs were causing the bag's zipper to bunch up. The team alerted managers, who had technicians move the studs away from the zipper, which solved the problem.

Self-managed work teams are groups of employees (typically 10 to 15 in number) who perform highly related or interdependent jobs and take on many of the responsibilities of their former supervisors.[6] Typically, these tasks are involved in planning and scheduling work, assigning tasks to members, making operating decisions, taking action on problems, and working with suppliers and customers. Fully self-managed work teams even select their own members and have the members evaluate each other's performance. As a result, supervisory positions take on decreased importance and may even be eliminated.

Business periodicals have been chock-full of articles describing successful applications of self-managed teams. But a word of caution needs to be offered: The overall research on the effectiveness of self-managed work teams has not been uniformly positive.[7] Moreover, although individuals on these teams do tend to report higher levels of job satisfaction compared to other individuals, they also sometimes have higher absenteeism and turnover rates. Inconsistency in findings suggests that the effectiveness of self-managed teams depends on the strength and make-up of team norms, the type of tasks the team undertakes, and the reward structure the team operates under—each of which can significantly influence how well the team performs.

Cross-Functional Teams

The Boeing Company created a team made up of employees from production, planning, quality, tooling, design engineering, and information systems to automate shims on the company's C-17 program. The team's suggestions

---

problem-solving teams   *Groups of 5 to 12 employees from the same department who meet for a few hours each week to discuss ways of improving quality, efficiency, and the work environment.*

self-managed work teams   *Groups of 10 to 15 people who take on responsibilities of their former supervisors.*

resulted in drastically reduced cycle time and cost as well as improved quality on the C-17 program.[8]

This Boeing example illustrates the use of **cross-functional teams**. These are teams made up of employees from about the same hierarchical level but from different work areas, who come together to accomplish a task.

Many organizations have used horizontal, boundary-spanning groups for decades. For example, IBM created a large task force in the 1960s—made up of employees from across departments in the company—to develop its highly successful System 360. But today cross-functional teams are so widely used that it is hard to imagine a major organizational initiative without one. For instance, all the major automobile manufacturers—including Toyota, Honda, Nissan, BMW, GM, Ford, and Chrysler—currently use this form of team to coordinate complex projects. And Harley-Davidson relies on specific cross-functional teams to manage each line of its motorcycles. These teams include Harley employees from design, manufacturing, and purchasing as well as representatives from key outside suppliers.[9]

Cross-functional teams are an effective means for allowing people from diverse areas within an organization (or even between organizations) to exchange information, develop new ideas and solve problems, and coordinate complex projects. Of course, cross-functional teams are no picnic to manage. Their early stages of development are often very time-consuming, as members learn to work with diversity and complexity. It takes time to build trust and teamwork, especially among people from different backgrounds with different experiences and perspectives.

Virtual Teams

The previously described types of teams do their work face-to-face. **Virtual teams** use computer technology to tie together physically dispersed members in order to achieve a common goal.[10] They allow people to collaborate online—using communication links such as wide-area networks, video conferencing, or e-mail—whether they're only a room away or continents apart. Virtual teams are so pervasive, and technology has advanced so far, that it's probably a bit of a misnomer to call these teams "virtual." Nearly all teams today do at least some of their work remotely.

Despite their ubiquity, virtual teams face special challenges. They may suffer because there is less social rapport and less direct interaction among members. They aren't able to duplicate the normal give-and-take of face-to-face discussion. Especially when members haven't personally met, virtual teams tend to be more task oriented and exchange less social–emotional information than face-to-face teams. Not surprisingly, virtual team members report less satisfaction with the group interaction process than do face-to-face teams. For virtual teams to be effective, management should ensure that (1) trust is established among team members (research has shown that one inflammatory remark in a team member e-mail can severely undermine team trust); (2) team progress is monitored closely (so the team doesn't lose sight of its goals and no team member "disappears"); and (3) the efforts and products of the virtual team are publicized throughout the organization (so the team does not become invisible).[11]

Creating Effective Teams

Many have tried to identify factors related to team effectiveness.[12] However, recent studies have organized what was once a "veritable laundry list of characteristics"[13] into a relatively focused model.[14] Exhibit 10-3 summarizes what we currently know

International OB

Global Virtual Teams

Years ago, before the vast working public ever dreamed of e-mail, instant messaging, or live video conferencing, work teams used to be in the same locations, with possibly one or two members a train or plane ride away. Today, however, the reach of corporations spans many countries, so the need for teams to work together across international lines has increased. To deal with this challenge, multinationals use global virtual teams to gain a competitive advantage.

Global virtual teams have advantages and disadvantages. On the positive side, because team members come from different countries with different knowledge and points of view, they may develop creative ideas and solutions to problems that work for multiple cultures. On the negative side, global virtual teams face more challenges than traditional teams that meet face-to-face. For one thing, miscommunication can lead to misunderstandings, which can create stress and conflict among team members. Also, members who do not accept individuals from different cultures may hesitate to share information openly, which can create problems of trust.

To create and implement effective global virtual teams, managers must carefully select employees whom they believe will thrive in such an environment. Employees must be comfortable with communicating electronically with others, and they must be open to different ideas. When dealing with team members in other countries, speaking multiple languages may also be necessary. Team members also must realize that the values they hold may be vastly different from their teammates' values. For instance, an individual from a country that values relationships and sensitivity, such as Sweden, might face a challenge when interacting with someone from Spain, which values assertiveness and competitiveness.

Although global virtual teams face many challenges, companies that implement them effectively can realize tremendous rewards through the diverse knowledge they gain.

Source: Based on N. Zakaria, A. Amelinckx, and D. Wilemon, "Working Together Apart? Building a Knowledge-Sharing Culture for Global Virtual Teams," *Creativity and Innovation Management*, March 2004, pp. 15–29.

---

4 *Identify the characteristics of effective teams.*

about what makes teams effective. As you'll see, it builds on many of the group concepts introduced in Chapter 9.

The following discussion is based on the model in Exhibit 10-3. Keep in mind two caveats before we proceed. First, teams differ in form and structure. Because the model we present attempts to generalize across all varieties of teams, you need to be careful not to rigidly apply the model's predictions to all teams.[15] You should use the model as a guide. Second, the model assumes that it's already been determined that teamwork is preferable to individual work. Creating "effective" teams in situations in which individuals can do the job better is equivalent to solving the wrong problem perfectly.

The key components of effective teams can be subsumed into four general categories. First are the resources and other *contextual* influences that make teams effective. The second relates to the team's *composition*. The third category is *work design*. Finally, *process* variables reflect those things that go on in the team that influences effectiveness. What does *team effectiveness* mean in this model? Typically, it has included objective measures of the team's productivity, managers' ratings of the team's performance, and aggregate measures of member satisfaction.

---

cross-functional teams *Employees from about the same hierarchical level, but from different work areas, who come together to accomplish a task.*

virtual teams *Teams that use computer technology to tie together physically dispersed members in order to achieve a common goal.*

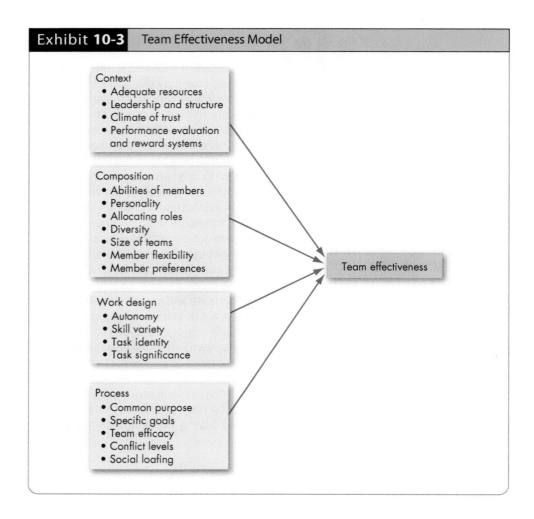

Exhibit 10-3   Team Effectiveness Model

Context
• Adequate resources
• Leadership and structure
• Climate of trust
• Performance evaluation and reward systems

Composition
• Abilities of members
• Personality
• Allocating roles
• Diversity
• Size of teams
• Member flexibility
• Member preferences

Work design
• Autonomy
• Skill variety
• Task identity
• Task significance

Process
• Common purpose
• Specific goals
• Team efficacy
• Conflict levels
• Social loafing

Team effectiveness

Context: What Factors Determine Whether Teams Are Successful

The four contextual factors that appear to be most significantly related to team performance are the presence of adequate resources, effective leadership, a climate of trust, and a performance evaluation and reward system that reflects team contributions.

Adequate Resources   Teams are part of a larger organization system. As such, every work team relies on resources outside the group to sustain it. A scarcity of resources directly reduces the ability of a team to perform its job effectively. As one set of researchers concluded, after looking at 13 factors potentially related to group performance, "perhaps one of the most important characteristics of an effective work group is the support the group receives from the organization."[16] This support includes timely information, proper equipment, adequate staffing, encouragement, and administrative assistance. Teams must receive the necessary support from management and the larger organization if they are to succeed in achieving their goals.

Leadership and Structure   Teams can't function if they can't agree on who is to do what and ensure that all members contribute equally in sharing the work load. Agreeing on the specifics of work and how they fit together to integrate individual skills requires team leadership and structure. This can be provided directly by management or by the team members themselves. Although you might think there is no role for leaders in self-managed teams, that couldn't be further from the truth. It is true that, in self-managed teams, team members absorb many of the duties typically assumed by managers. However, a manager's job becomes managing *outside* (rather than inside) the team.

Leadership is especially important in **multi-team systems**—where different teams need to coordinate their efforts to produce a desired outcome. In such systems, leaders need to empower teams by delegating responsibility to them, and they need to play the role of facilitator, making sure the teams are coordinating their efforts so that they work together rather than against one another.[17]

Climate of Trust   Members of effective teams trust each other. And they also exhibit trust in their leaders.[18] Interpersonal trust among team members facilitates cooperation, reduces the need to monitor each others' behavior, and bonds members around the belief that others on the team won't take advantage of them. Team members, for instance, are more likely to take risks and expose vulnerabilities when they believe they can trust others on their team. Similarly, as discussed in Chapter 13, trust is the foundation of leadership. Trust in leadership is important in that it allows a team to be willing to accept and commit to its leader's goals and decisions.

Performance Evaluation and Reward Systems   How do you get team members to be both individually and jointly accountable? The traditional, individually oriented evaluation and reward system must be modified to reflect team performance.[19] Individual performance evaluations and incentives may interfere with the development of high-performance teams. So in addition to evaluating and rewarding employees for their individual contributions, management should consider group-based appraisals, profit-sharing, gainsharing, small-group incentives, and other system modifications that reinforce team effort and commitment.

Surgical Teams Lack Teamwork

Surgery is almost always performed by a team, but in many cases, it's a team in name only. So says a new study of more than 2,100 surgeons, anesthesiologists, and nurses.

When the researchers surveyed these surgery team members, they asked them to "describe the quality of communication and collaboration you have experienced" with other members of the surgical unit. Perhaps not surprisingly, surgeons were given the lowest ratings for teamwork and nurses the highest ratings. "The study is somewhat humbling to me," said Martin Makary, the lead author on the study and a surgeon at Johns Hopkins. "There's a lot of pride in the surgical community. We need to balance out the captain-of-the-ship doctrine."

The researchers attribute many operating room errors, such as sponges left in patients and operations performed on the wrong part of the body, to poor teamwork. But improving the system is easier said than done. One recent study in Pennsylvania found that, over an 18-month period, there were 174 cases of surgeons operating on the wrong limb or body part. For its part, Johns Hopkins is modeling surgical team training after airline crew training. "Teamwork is an important component of patient safety," says Makary.

Sources: E. Nagourney, "Surgical Teams Found Lacking, in Teamwork," *New York Times,* May 9, 2006, p. D6; and "Nurses Give Surgeons Poor Grades on Teamwork in OR," *Forbes,* May 5, 2006.

---

multi-team systems   *Systems in which different teams need to coordinate their efforts to produce a desired outcome.*

Team Composition

The team composition category includes variables that relate to how teams should be staffed. In this section, we address the ability and personality of team members, allocation of roles and diversity, size of the team, and members' preference for teamwork.

Abilities of Members   Part of a team's performance depends on the knowledge, skills, and abilities of its individual members.[20] It's true that we occasionally read about an athletic team composed of mediocre players who, because of excellent coaching, determination, and precision teamwork, beats a far more talented group of players. But such cases make the news precisely because they represent an aberration. As the old saying goes, "The race doesn't always go to the swiftest nor the battle to the strongest, but that's the way to bet." A team's performance is not merely the summation of its individual members' abilities. However, these abilities set parameters for what members can do and how effectively they will perform on a team.

To perform effectively, a team requires three different types of skills. First, it needs people who have *technical expertise.* Second, it needs people who have the *problem-solving and decision-making skills* to be able to identify problems, generate alternatives, evaluate those alternatives, and make competent choices. Finally, teams need people who have good listening, feedback, conflict resolution, and other *interpersonal skills.*[21] No team can achieve its performance potential without developing all three types of skills. The right mix is crucial. Too much of one at the expense of others will result in lower team performance. But teams don't need to have all the complementary skills in place at their beginning. It's not uncommon for one or more members to take responsibility for learning the skills in which the group is deficient, thereby allowing the team to reach its full potential.

Research on the abilities of team members has revealed some interesting insights into team composition and performance. First, when the task entails considerable thought (for example, solving a complex problem such as reengineering an assembly line), high-ability teams (that is, teams composed of mostly

Senior product scientists Syed Abbas and Albert Post and technology team manager Laurie Coyle functioned as a high-ability team in developing Unilever's new Dove Nutrium bar soap. In solving the complex problems involved in product innovation, the intelligent members of Unilever's research and development teams have advanced science degrees, the ability to think creatively, and the interpersonal skills needed to perform effectively with other team members.

Source: Ruth Fremson/The New York Times

intelligent members) do better than lower-ability teams, especially when the work load is distributed evenly. (That way, team performance does not depend on the weakest link.) High-ability teams are also more adaptable to changing situations in that they can more effectively adapt prior knowledge to suit a set of new problems.

Second, although high-ability teams generally have an advantage over lower-ability teams, this is not always the case. For example, when tasks are simple (for example, tasks that individual team members might be able to solve on their own), high-ability teams do not perform as well, perhaps because, in such tasks, high-ability teams become bored and turn their attention to other activities that are more stimulating, whereas low-ability teams stay on task. High-ability teams should be "saved" for tackling the tough problems. So matching team ability to the task is important.

Finally, the ability of the team's leader also matters. Research shows that smart team leaders help less intelligent team members when they struggle with a task. But a less intelligent leader can neutralize the effect of a high-ability team.[22]

Personality of Members   We demonstrated in Chapter 4 that personality has a significant influence on individual employee behavior. This can also be extended to team behavior. Many of the dimensions identified in the Big Five personality model have been shown to be relevant to team effectiveness. A recent review of the literature suggested that three of the Big Five traits were especially important for team performance.[23] Specifically, teams that rate higher on mean levels of conscientiousness and openness to experience tend to perform better. Moreover, the minimum level of team member agreeableness also matters: Teams did worse when they had one or more highly disagreeable members. Perhaps one bad apple *can* spoil the whole bunch!

Research has also provided us with a good idea about why these personality traits are important to teams. Conscientious people are valuable in teams because they're good at backing up other team members, and they're also good at sensing when that support is truly needed. Open team members communicate better with one another and throw out more ideas, which leads teams composed of open people to be more creative and innovative.[24]

Even if an organization does a really good job of selecting individuals for team roles, most likely they'll find there aren't enough, say, conscientious people to go around. Suppose an organization needs to create 20 teams of 4 people each and has 40 highly conscientious people and 40 who score low on conscientiousness. Would the organization be better off (A) putting all the conscientious people together (forming 10 teams with the highly conscientious people and 10 teams of members low on conscientiousness) or (B) "seeding" each team with 2 people who scored high and 2 who scored low on conscientiousness?

Perhaps surprisingly, the evidence tends to suggest that option A is the best choice; performance across the teams will be higher if the organization forms 10 highly conscientious teams and 10 teams low in conscientiousness. "This may be because, in such teams, members who are highly conscientious not only must perform their own tasks but also must perform or re-do the tasks of low-conscientious members. It may also be because such diversity leads to feelings of contribution inequity."[25]

Allocation of Roles   Teams have different needs, and people should be selected for a team to ensure that all the various roles are filled.

We can identify nine potential team roles (see Exhibit 10-4). Successful work teams have people to fill all these roles and have selected people to play these roles based on their skills and preferences.[26] (On many teams, individuals will play multiple roles.) Managers need to understand the individual strengths that

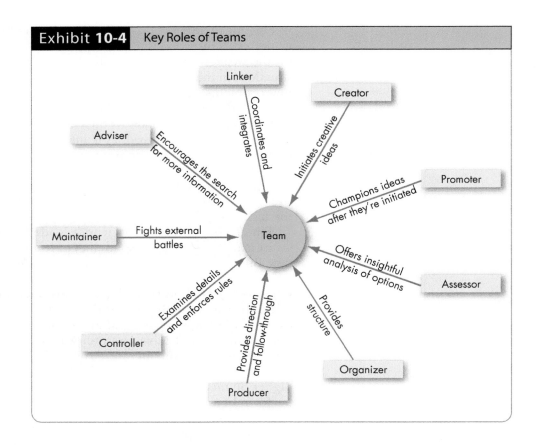

Exhibit 10-4   Key Roles of Teams

each person can bring to a team, select members with their strengths in mind, and allocate work assignments that fit with members' preferred styles. By matching individual preferences with team role demands, managers increase the likelihood that the team members will work well together.

Diversity of Members   In Chapter 9, we discussed research on the effect of diversity on groups. How does *team* diversity affect *team* performance?

Many of us hold the optimistic view that diversity should be a good thing—diverse teams should benefit from differing perspectives and do better. Unfortunately, the evidence appears to favor the pessimists. One review concluded, "Studies on diversity in teams from the last 50 years have shown that surface-level social-category differences such as race/ethnicity, gender, and age tend to... have negative effects" on the performance of teams.[27] As in the literature on groups, there is some evidence that the disruptive effects of diversity decline over time, but unlike in the groups literature, there is less evidence that diverse teams perform better eventually.

One of the pervasive problems with teams is that while diversity may have real potential benefits, a team is deeply focused on commonly held information. But if diverse teams are to realize their creative potential, they need to focus not on their similarities but on their differences. There is some evidence, for example, that when team members believe others have more expertise, they will work to support those members, leading to higher levels of effectiveness.[28] The key is for diverse teams to communicate what they uniquely know and also what they don't know.

An offshoot of the diversity issue has received a great deal of attention from group and team researchers. This is the degree to which members of a work unit (group, team, or department) share a common demographic

Many team members share the common demographic of age at Yahoo!, where more than half of employees are age 34 or younger. Young team members of Yahoo!'s oneSearch team shown here, grew up during the information revolution, are well educated, and are results driven. The sharing of these attributes should result in better communication among team members, low turnover, and few power struggles.

Source: Jim Wilson/ The New York Times

attribute, such as age, sex, race, educational level, or length of service in the organization, and the impact of that attribute on turnover. We call this variable **organizational demography**. Organizational demography suggests that attributes such as age or the date that someone joins a specific work team or organization should help us to predict turnover. Essentially, the logic goes like this: Turnover will be greater among those with dissimilar experiences because communication is more difficult. Conflict and power struggles are more likely, and they are more severe when they occur. The increased conflict makes unit membership less attractive, so employees are more likely to quit. Similarly, the losers in a power struggle are more apt to leave voluntarily or to be forced out.[29]

Size of Teams   The president of AOL Technologies says the secret to a great team is to "think small. Ideally, your team should have seven to nine people."[30] His advice is supported by evidence.[31] Generally speaking, the most effective teams have five to nine members. And experts suggest using the smallest number of people who can do the task. Unfortunately, there is a pervasive tendency for managers to err on the side of making teams too large. While a minimum of four or five may be necessary to develop diversity of views and skills, managers seem to seriously underestimate how coordination problems can exponentially increase as team members are added. When teams have excess members, cohesiveness and mutual accountability decline, social loafing increases, and more and more people do less talking relative to others. Moreover, large teams have trouble coordinating with one another, especially when under time pressure.

organizational demography   *The degree to which members of a work unit share a common demographic attribute, such as age, sex, race, educational level, or length of service in an organization, and the impact of this attribute on turnover.*

MYTH OR SCIENCE?

"Old Teams Can't Learn New Tricks"

*t*his statement is true for some types of teams and false for others. Let's look at why.

To study this question, researchers at Michigan State University composed 80 four-person teams from undergraduate business students. The teams engaged in a networked computer simulation that was developed for the Department of Defense. In the simulation, teams played a command-and-control simulation in which each team member sat at a networked computer connected to his or her other team members' computers. The team's mission was to monitor a geographic area, keep unfriendly forces from moving in, and support friendly forces. Performance was measured by both speed (how quickly they identified targets and friendly forces) and accuracy (the number of friendly fire errors and missed opportunities).

Teams were rewarded either cooperatively (in which case team members shared rewards equally) or competitively (in which case team members were rewarded based on their individual contributions). After playing a few rounds, the reward structures were switched so that the cooperatively rewarded teams were switched to competitive rewards and the competitively rewarded teams were now cooperatively rewarded.

The researchers found that the initially cooperatively rewarded teams easily adapted to the competitive reward conditions and learned to excel. However, the formerly competitively rewarded teams could not adapt to cooperative rewards. As the authors note, their results may shed light on the intelligence failures of the CIA and FBI; when these formerly separate organizations were asked to cooperate, they found it very difficult to do so.

If the results of this study generalize to actual teams, it seems that teams that "cut their teeth" being cooperative can learn to be competitive, but competitive teams find it much harder to learn to cooperate.

Source: M. D. Johnson, S. E. Humphrey, D. R. Ilgen, D. Jundt, and C. J. Meyer, "Cutthroat Cooperation: Asymmetrical Adaptation to Changes in Team Reward Structures," *Academy of Management Journal* 49, vol. 1 (2006), pp. 103–119. ∎

So in designing effective teams, managers should try to keep them at nine or fewer members. If a natural working unit is larger and you want a team effort, consider breaking the group into subteams.[32]

Member Preferences   Not every employee is a team player. Given the option, many employees will select themselves *out* of team participation. When people who would prefer to work alone are required to team up, there is a direct threat to the team's morale and to individual member satisfaction.[33] This suggests that, when selecting team members, individual preferences should be considered as along with abilities, personalities, and skills. High-performing teams are likely to be composed of people who prefer working as part of a group.

Work Design

Effective teams need to work together and take collective responsibility for completing significant tasks. An effective team must be more than a "team in name only."[34] Based on terminology introduced in Chapter 7, the work-design category includes variables such as freedom and autonomy, the opportunity to use different skills and talents (skill variety), the ability to complete a whole and identifiable task or product (task identity), and work on a task or project that has a substantial impact on others (task significance). The evidence indicates that these characteristics enhance member motivation and increase team effectiveness.[35] These work-design characteristics motivate because they increase members' sense of responsibility and ownership of the work and because they make the work more interesting to perform.[36]

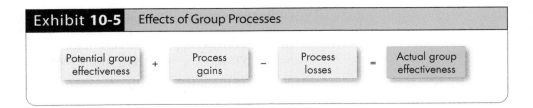

Exhibit **10-5**   Effects of Group Processes

Potential group effectiveness $+$ Process gains $-$ Process losses $=$ Actual group effectiveness

Team Processes

The final category related to team effectiveness is process variables. These include member commitment to a common purpose, establishment of specific team goals, team efficacy, a managed level of conflict, and minimization of social loafing.

Why are processes important to team effectiveness? One way to answer this question is to return to the topic of social loafing. We found that $1 + 1 + 1$ doesn't necessarily add up to 3. In team tasks for which each member's contribution is not clearly visible, there is a tendency for individuals to decrease their effort. Social loafing, in other words, illustrates a process loss as a result of using teams. But team processes should produce positive results. That is, teams should create outputs greater than the sum of their inputs. The development of creative alternatives by a diverse group would be one such instance. Exhibit 10-5 illustrates how group processes can have an impact on a group's actual effectiveness.[37] Research teams are often used in research laboratories because they can draw on the diverse skills of various individuals to produce more meaningful research as a team than could be generated by all the researchers working independently. That is, they produce positive synergy. Their process gains exceed their process losses.

Common Plan and Purpose   An effective team has a common plan and purpose that provides direction, momentum, and commitment for members.[38] This purpose is a vision, or master plan. It's broader than specific goals.

Members of successful teams put a tremendous amount of time and effort into discussing, shaping, and agreeing on a purpose that belongs to them both

Employee teams at New Balance share the common purpose of continuously improving their work processes. In the company's stitching department, shown here, sharing the purpose of quality improvement motivated members of team CS-39 to develop a cross-training program so all members could learn and perform each other's job skills.

collectively and individually. This common purpose, when accepted by the team, becomes the equivalent of what celestial navigation is to a ship captain: It provides direction and guidance under any and all conditions. Like the proverbial ship following the wrong course, teams that don't have good planning skills are doomed; perfectly executing the wrong plan is a lost cause.[39] Effective teams also show **reflexivity**, meaning that they reflect on and adjust their master plan when necessary. A team has to have a good plan, but it also has to be willing and able to adapt when condition call for it.[40]

Specific Goals   Successful teams translate their common purpose into specific, measurable, and realistic performance goals. Just as we demonstrated in Chapter 6 how goals lead individuals to higher performance, goals also energize teams. Specific goals facilitate clear communication. They also help teams maintain their focus on getting results.

Also, consistent with the research on individual goals, team goals should be challenging. Difficult goals have been found to raise team performance on those criteria for which they're set. So, for instance, goals for quantity tend to raise quantity, goals for speed tend to raise speed, goals for accuracy raise accuracy, and so on.[41]

Team Efficacy   Effective teams have confidence in themselves. They believe they can succeed. We call this *team efficacy*.[42] Success breeds success. Teams that have been successful raise their beliefs about future success, which, in turn, motivates them to work harder. What, if anything, can management do to increase team efficacy? Two possible options are helping the team to achieve small successes and providing skill training. Small successes build team confidence. As a team develops an increasingly stronger performance record, it also increases the collective belief that future efforts will lead to success. In addition, managers should consider providing training to improve members' technical and interpersonal skills. The greater the abilities of team members, the greater the likelihood that the team will develop confidence and the capability to deliver on that confidence.

Mental Models   Effective teams have accurate and common **mental models**—knowledge and beliefs (a "psychological map") about how the work gets done. If team members have the wrong mental models, which is particularly likely to happen with teams under acute stress, their performance suffers.[43] For example, in the Iraq war, many military leaders said they underestimated the power of the insurgency and the infighting among Iraqi religious sects. The similarity of team members' mental models matters, too. If team members have different ideas about how to do things, the teams will fight over how to do things rather than focus on what needs to be done.[44]

WHAT IS MY TEAM EFFICACY?

In the Self-Assessment Library (available on CD or online), take assessment IV.E.2 (What Is My Team Efficacy?).

Conflict Levels   Conflict on a team isn't necessarily bad. As discussed in more depth in Chapter 15, teams that are completely void of conflict are likely to become apathetic and stagnant. So conflict can actually improve team effectiveness.[45] But not all types of conflict. Relationship conflicts—those based on interpersonal incompatibilities, tension, and animosity toward others—are almost always dysfunctional. However, on teams performing nonroutine activities, disagreements among members about task content (called *task conflicts*) is not detrimental. In fact, it is often beneficial because it reduces the likelihood of groupthink. Task conflicts stimulate discussion, promote critical assessment of problems and options, and can lead to better team decisions. So effective teams can be characterized as having an appropriate level of conflict.

Social Loafing   We talked in Chapter 9 about the fact that individuals can hide inside a group. They can engage in social loafing and coast on the group's effort because their individual contributions can't be identified. Effective teams undermine this tendency by holding themselves accountable at both the individual and team levels. Successful teams make members individually and jointly accountable for the team's purpose, goals, and approach.[46] Therefore, members should be clear on what they are individually responsible for and what they are jointly responsible for.

Turning Individuals into Team Players

To this point, we've made a strong case for the value and growing popularity of teams. But many people are not inherently team players. There are also

> **5** *Show how organizations can create team players.*

many organizations that have historically nurtured individual accomplishments. Finally, countries differ in terms of how they rate on individualism and collectivism. Teams fit well with countries that score high on collectivism. But what if an organization wants to introduce teams into a work population that is made up largely of individuals born and raised in an individualistic society? A veteran employee of a large company, who had done well working in an individualistic company in an individualist country, described the experience of joining a team: "I'm learning my lesson. I just had my first negative performance appraisal in 20 years."[47]

So what can organizations do to enhance team effectiveness—to turn individual contributors into team members? The following are the primary options managers have for trying to turn individuals into team players.

Selection: Hiring Team Players   Some people already possess the interpersonal skills to be effective team players. When hiring team members, in addition to the technical skills required to fill the job, care should be taken to ensure that candidates can fulfill their team roles as well as technical requirements.[48]

Many job candidates don't have team skills. This is especially true for those socialized around individual contributions. When faced with such candidates, managers basically have three options. The candidates can undergo training to "make them into team players." If this isn't possible or doesn't work, the other two options are to transfer the individual to another unit within the organization that does not have teams (if this possibility exists) or not to hire the candidate. In established organizations that decide to redesign jobs around teams, it should be expected that some employees will resist being team players

---

reflexivity   *A team characteristic of reflecting on and adjusting the master plan when necessary.*

mental models   *Team members' knowledge and beliefs about how the work gets done by the team.*

Whole Foods Markets uses a team structure throughout its entire organization, with each store averaging 10 self-managed teams. Team members participate in both the interview and selection processes. After new hires are trained during an orientation period, other team members vote on whether to add the candidate to their team, based on criteria such as positive job performance, adherence to policies and procedures, customer-service skills, and teamwork. The team voting process empowers team members to share in the building of a quality team.

and may be untrainable. Unfortunately, such people typically become casualties of the team approach.

Training: Creating Team Players   A large proportion of people raised on the importance of individual accomplishments can be trained to become team players. Training specialists conduct exercises that allow employees to experience the satisfaction that teamwork can provide. They typically offer workshops to help employees improve their problem-solving, communication, negotiation, conflict-management, and coaching skills. Employees also learn the five-stage group development model described in Chapter 9. At Verizon, for example, trainers focus on how a team goes through various stages before it finally gels. And employees are reminded of the importance of patience—because teams take longer to make decisions than do employees acting alone.[49]

Emerson Electric's Specialty Motor Division in Missouri, for instance, has achieved remarkable success in getting its 650-member workforce not only to accept but to welcome team training.[50] Outside consultants were brought in to give workers practical skills for working in teams. After less than a year, employees were enthusiastically accepting the value of teamwork.

Rewarding: Providing Incentives to Be a Good Team Player   An organization's reward system needs to be reworked to encourage cooperative efforts rather than competitive ones.[51] For instance, Hallmark Cards, Inc., added to its basic individual-incentive system an annual bonus based on achievement of team goals. Trigon Blue Cross/Blue Shield changed its system to reward an even split between individual goals and team-like behaviors.[52]

Promotions, pay raises, and other forms of recognition should be given to individuals who work effectively as collaborative team members. This doesn't mean individual contributions should be ignored; rather, they should be balanced with selfless contributions to the team. Examples of behaviors that should be rewarded include training new colleagues, sharing information with teammates, helping to resolve team conflicts, and mastering new skills that the team needs but in which it is deficient.

Finally, don't forget the intrinsic rewards that employees can receive from teamwork. Teams provide camaraderie. It's exciting and satisfying to be an integral part of a successful team. The opportunity to engage in personal development and to help teammates grow can be a very satisfying and rewarding experience for employees.

Beware! Teams Aren't Always the Answer

6 Decide when to use individuals instead of teams.

Teamwork takes more time and often more resources than individual work. For instance, teams have increased communication demands, conflicts to be managed, and meetings to be run. So the benefits of using teams have to exceed the costs. And that's not always the case.[53]

In the excitement to enjoy the benefits of teams, some managers have introduced them into situations in which the work is better done by individuals. So before you rush to implement teams, you should carefully assess whether the work requires or will benefit from a collective effort.

How do you know if the work of your group would be better done in teams? It's been suggested that three tests be applied to see if a team fits the situation.[54] First, can the work be done better by more than one person? A good indicator is the complexity of the work and the need for different perspectives. Simple tasks that don't require diverse input are probably better left to individuals. Second, does the work create a common purpose or set of goals for the people in the group that is more than the aggregate of individual goals? For instance, many new-car dealer service departments have introduced teams that link customer-service personnel, mechanics, parts specialists, and sales representatives. Such teams can better manage collective responsibility for ensuring that customer needs are properly met. The final test to assess whether teams fit the situation is to determine whether the members of the group are interdependent. Using teams makes sense when there is interdependence between tasks—when the success of the whole depends on the success of each one *and* the success of each one depends on the success of the others. Soccer, for instance, is an obvious *team* sport. Success requires a great deal of coordination between interdependent players. Conversely, except possibly for relays, swim teams are not really teams. They're groups of individuals, performing individually, whose total performance is merely the aggregate summation of their individual performances.

Global Implications

7 Show how the understanding of teams differs in a global context.

Although research on global considerations in the use of teams is just beginning, three areas are particularly worth mentioning: the extent of teamwork, self-managed teams, and team cultural diversity.

Extent of Teamwork   Although the use of work teams is pervasive in the United States, some evidence suggests that the extent of teamwork—the degree to which U.S. teams deeply affect the way work is done—is not as significant in the United States as in other countries. One study comparing U.S. workers to Canadian and Asian workers revealed that 51 percent of workers in Asia-Pacific and 48 percent of Canadian employees report high levels of teamwork. But only about one-third (32 percent) of U.S. employees say their organization has a high level of teamwork.[55] Thus, although teamwork is widely used in the United States, this evidence suggests that there still is a heavy role for individual contributions. Given that U.S. culture is highly individualistic, that may continue to be true for quite some time.

Self-Managed Teams   Although self-managed teams have not proven to be the panacea many thought they would be, special care needs to be taken when introducing self-managed teams globally. For instance, evidence suggests that these types of teams have not fared well in Mexico, largely due to that culture's low tolerance of ambiguity and uncertainty and employees' strong respect for hierarchical authority.[56] Thus, in countries that are relatively high in power distance—meaning that roles of leaders and followers are clearly delineated—a team may need to be structured so that leadership roles are spelled out and power relationships are identified.

Team Cultural Diversity and Team Performance   Earlier, we discussed research on team diversity in terms of factors such as race or gender. But what about diversity created by national differences? Like the earlier research, evidence indicates that these elements of diversity interfere with team processes, at least in the short term.[57] Cultural diversity does seem to be an asset for tasks that call for a variety of viewpoints. But culturally heterogeneous teams have more difficulty learning to work with each other and solving problems. The good news is that these difficulties seem to dissipate with time. Although newly formed culturally diverse teams underperform newly formed culturally homogeneous teams, the differences disappear after about 3 months.[58] The reason is that it takes culturally diverse teams a while to learn how to work through disagreements and different approaches to solving problems.

Summary and Implications for Managers

Few trends have influenced jobs as much as the massive movement to introduce teams into the workplace. The shift from working alone to working on teams requires employees to cooperate with others, share information, confront differences, and sublimate personal interests for the greater good of the team.

Effective teams have common characteristics. They have adequate resources, effective leadership, a climate of trust, and a performance evaluation and reward system that reflects team contributions. These teams have individuals with technical expertise as well as problem-solving, decision-making, and interpersonal skills and the right traits, especially conscientiousness and openness. Effective teams also tend to be small—with fewer than 10 people, preferably of diverse backgrounds. They have members who fill role demands and who prefer to be part of a group. And the work that members do provides freedom and autonomy, the opportunity to use different skills and talents, the ability to complete a whole and identifiable task or product, and work that has a substantial impact on others. Finally, effective teams have members who believe in the team's capabilities and are committed to a common plan and purpose, an accurate shared mental model of what is to be accomplished, specific team goals, a manageable level of conflict, and a minimal degree of social loafing.

Because individualistic organizations and societies attract and reward individual accomplishments, it is can be difficult to create team players in these environments. To make the conversion, management should try to select individuals who have the interpersonal skills to be effective team players, provide training to develop teamwork skills, and reward individuals for cooperative efforts.

Point ➤ ✕ Counterpoint

SPORTS TEAMS ARE GOOD MODELS FOR WORKPLACE TEAMS

Studies from football, soccer, basketball, hockey, and baseball have found a number of elements of successful sports teams that can be extrapolated to successful work teams.

Successful teams integrate cooperation and competition. Sports teams with the best win–loss record had coaches who promote a strong spirit of cooperation and a high level of healthy competition among their players.

Successful teams score early wins. Early successes build teammates' faith in themselves and their capacity as a team. Research on hockey teams of relatively equal ability found that 72 percent of the time, the team that was ahead at the end of the first period went on to win. So managers should provide teams with early tasks that are simple and provide "easy wins."

Successful teams avoid losing streaks. A couple failures can lead to a downward spiral if a team becomes demoralized. Managers need to instill confidence in team members that they can turn things around when they encounter setbacks.

Practice makes perfect. Successful sport teams execute on game day but learn from their mistakes in practice. Practice should be used to try new things and fail. A wise manager encourages work teams to experiment and learn.

Successful teams use half-time breaks. The best coaches in basketball and football use half-time during a game to reassess what is working and what isn't. Managers of work teams should similarly build in assessments at the approximate halfway point in a team project to evaluate what it can do to improve.

Winning teams have stable membership. Stability improves performance. Studies of professional basketball teams have found that when teammates have more time together they are more able to anticipate one another's moves, and they are clearer about one another's roles.

Successful teams debrief after failures and successes. The best sports teams study the game video. Similarly, work teams should routinely assess their successes and failures and should learn from them.

Sports metaphors are useful. For example, a recent *Harvard Business Review* issue had as the lead story "Playing to Win . . . Five Killer Strategies for Trouncing the Competition." The article argues that winners in business play hardball, which means they pick their shots, seek out competitive encounters, set the pace of innovation, and test the edges of the possible. Like sports teams, in business you have to play hardball, which means playing to win. That is what the sports model can teach us.

There are flaws in using sports as a model for developing effective work teams. Here are just four caveats.

All sport teams aren't alike. In baseball, for instance, there is little interaction among teammates. Rarely are more than two or three players directly involved in a play. The performance of the team is largely the sum of the performance of its individual players. In contrast, basketball has much more interdependence among players. Geographic distribution is dense. Usually all players are involved in every play, team members have to be able to switch from offense to defense at a moment's notice, and there is continuous movement by all, not just the player who has the ball. The performance of the team is more than the sum of its individual players. So when using sports teams as a model for work teams, you have to make sure you're making the correct comparison. As one expert noted, "The problem with sports metaphors is that the meaning you extract from a sports metaphor is entirely dependent on the sport you pick."

Work teams are more varied and complex than sports teams. In an athletic league, the design of the task, the design of the team, and the team's context vary relatively little from team to team. But these variables can vary tremendously between work teams. As a result, coaching plays a much more significant part of a sports team's performance than in that of a work team. Performance of work teams is a function of getting the team's structural and design variables right. So, in contrast to sports, managers of work teams should focus more on getting the team set up for success than on coaching.

A lot of employees can't relate to sports metaphors. Not everyone on work teams is conversant in sports. Some people aren't as interested in sports as "sports hounds" and aren't as savvy about sports terminology. And team members from different cultures may not know the sports metaphors you're using. Most Americans, for instance, are unfamiliar with the rules and terminology of Australian Rules football.

Work team outcomes aren't easily defined in terms of wins and losses. Sports teams typically measure success in terms of wins and losses. Such measures of success are rarely as clear for work teams. When managers try to define success in wins and losses, it tends to infer that the workplace is ethically no more complex than the playing field, which is rarely true.

Source: See N. Katz, "Sports Teams as a Model for Workplace Teams: Lessons and Liabilities," *Academy of Management Executive*, August 2001, pp. 56–67; "Talent Inc.," *The New Yorker Online Only*, July 22, 2002, www.newyorker.com/online; and D. Batstone, "HBR Goes CG?," *Worthwhile.com*, April 14, 2004 www.worthwhilemag.com.

Questions for Review

1 How do you explain the growing popularity of teams in organizations?

2 What is the difference between a group and a team?

3 What are the four types of teams?

4 What conditions or context factors determine whether teams are effective?

5 How can organizations create team players?

6 When is work performed by individuals preferred over work performed by teams?

7 What are three ways in which our understanding of teams differs in a global context?

Experiential Exercise

FIXED VERSUS VARIABLE FLIGHT CREWS

Break into teams of five. Assume that you've been hired by AJet, a start-up airline based in St. Louis. Your team has been formed to consider the pros and cons of using variable flight crews and to arrive at a recommendation on whether to follow this industry practice at AJet.

Variable flight crews are crews formed when pilots, copilots, and flight attendants typically bid for schedules on specific planes (for instance, Boeing 737s, 757s, or 767s) based on seniority. Then they're given a monthly schedule made up of 1- to 4-day trips. So any given flight crew on a plane is rarely together for more than a few days at a time. A complicated system is required to complete the schedules. Because of this system, it's not unusual for a senior pilot at a large airline to fly with a different copilot on every trip during any given month. And a pilot and copilot who work together for 3 days in January may never work together again the rest of the year. (In contrast, a fixed flight crew consists of the same group of pilots and attendants who fly together for a period of time.)

In considering whether to use variable flight crews, your team is to answer the following questions:

1. What are the primary advantages of variable flight crews?
2. If you were to recommend some version of fixed flight crews, drawing from the material in this chapter, on what criteria would you assign AJet crews?

When your team has considered the advantages and disadvantages of variable flight crews and answered these questions, be prepared to present to the class your recommendations and justification.

Ethical Dilemma

PRESSURE TO BE A TEAM PLAYER

"Okay, I admit it. I'm not a team player. I work best when I work alone and am left alone," says Zachery Sanders.

Zach's employer, Broad's Furniture, an office furniture manufacturer, recently reorganized around teams. All production in the company's Michigan factory is now done in teams. And Zach's design department has been broken up into three design teams. To Zach's dismay, he was assigned to the modular-office design (MOD) team, which does work that Zach finds less interesting and challenging than other work he's done. What's worse, Zach believes that some low-performing individuals have been put in the team. Maddie Saunders, MOD's new team leader, seems to agree with Zach. She told him, "Zach, listen, I know you're not wild about the work MOD is doing, and it's true some weaker individual contributors have been assigned to the team. But that's why we formed the team. We really think that when we work together, the strengths of the team will be magnified and the weaknesses limited."

Although Zach respects Maggie, he's not convinced. "I've worked here for 4 years. I'm very good at what I do. And my performance reviews confirm that. I've been rated in the highest performance category every year I've been here. But now everything is changing. My evaluations and pay raises are going to depend on how well the team does. And, get this, 50 percent of my evaluation will depend on how well the team does—and this isn't a great team. I'm really frustrated and demoralized. They hired me for my design skills. They knew I wasn't a social type. Now they're forcing me to be a team player. This doesn't play to my strengths at all."

Is it unethical for Zach's employer to force him to be a team leader? Is his firm breaking an implied contract that it made with him at the time he was hired? Does this employer have any responsibility to provide Zach with an alternative that would allow him to continue to work independently? If you were Zach, how would you respond?

Case Incident 1

TEAMWORK: ONE COMPANY'S APPROACH TO HIGH PERFORMANCE

At ICU Medical Inc., teams haven't always been the answer. A maker of medical devices, the San Clemente, California, company was founded in 1984 by current chief executive officer Dr. George Lopez. At first, most of the major decisions were made by Lopez. Business was good—so good, in fact—that the company was ready for a public offering by the early 1990s. The company's products were in high demand, but dealing with that demand "was an overwhelming task for one entrepreneur CEO," states Lopez.

A solution to dealing with the increasing growth came to Lopez while watching his son play hockey. During a game, the opposing team had a star player who dominated his teammates and tried to make most of the plays himself. His son's team, however, worked together as a group and overwhelmed the star player. Lopez clearly saw that "the team was better than one player." He decided to reorganize his company to rely on teams that would not merely share in the decision-making process, but instead would have full autonomy to make their own decisions—setting their own meeting times, assigning their own tasks, and creating their own deadlines, and even deciding whether to form a team in the first place.

At that time, his company employed around 100 employees, but they weren't used to making decisions for themselves. Lopez put his new plan in place, telling his employees to form teams to come up with ideas to handle the increasing demand. At first, it didn't work as expected. Angered by the new team-based approach, the chief financial officer of the company quit. The new teams weren't faring well either. According to Lopez, "nothing was getting done, except people were spending a lot of time talking." Confident that teams were the answer, Lopez persisted and instructed teams to elect leaders. Team guidelines were put in place (e.g., "Challenge the issue, not the person"), and the company began using group rewards to motivate teamwork.

The new strategies paid off. Employees began to enjoy working together and making decisions for themselves, and ICU was able to easily handle the increasing demand. Since then, ICU has continued to prosper. Currently, the company employs close to 1,500 individuals. The company's stock price is six times higher than it was when the company first went public, and in 2006, revenue increased 28% to over $200 million. Each year, nearly 60 different teams, usually composed of five to seven members, finish projects. Those teams that are successful share in the $300,000 in team bonuses that the company allots annually.

Although teams at ICU have largely been beneficial, they are not without their problems. In particular, the team-based reward structure has sometimes created competitiveness and tension among employees. Colleen Wilder, who has worked on many teams at ICU over the years, recounts an incident where she refused to share a reward with coworkers who were not pulling their share. "You did nothing, and I propose you get nothing," she informed them. The team members evaluated what each person had contributed to the project and agreed that those who did not contribute should not receive a bonus. In addition, although Dr. Lopez's original vision was of teams that are completely autonomous, over the years the company has instituted more rules and policies, such as a 25-page handbook that tells teams how to operate. Although the goal of these rules is to help teams work together more smoothly, they take away some of the ability of teams to completely make their own decisions.

Despite these potential downsides, Dr. Lopez isn't about to change his reliance on teams. His reason is simple: "Top-down decisions are frequently wrong."

Questions

1. Using the terms from this chapter, how would you characterize the teams at ICU Medical Inc.? What are some advantages and disadvantages of giving teams a lot of autonomy to make decisions?

2. Four contextual factors (adequate resources, leadership and structure, climate of trust, and performance evaluation and reward systems) influence team performance. Which of these appear to be present in the above case? If present, are they supportive or unsupportive? How?

3. If you were to compose a team that will be given decision-making responsibility to solve complex problems, what types of members would you select in terms of abilities and personalities?

4. What are some processes losses that are likely to occur in teams such as those at ICU Medical Inc? How can these processes losses be avoided?

Source: Based on E. White, "How a Company Made Everyone a Team Player," *Wall Street Journal,* August 13, 2007, p. B.1

Case Incident 2

TEAM-BUILDING RETREATS

Team-building retreats are big business. Companies believe such retreats, where team members participate in activities ranging from mountain climbing, to trust-building exercises (where team members let themselves fall backwards into their colleagues' arms), to *Iron Chef*–inspired cooking contests (used by UBS, Hewlett-Packard, and Verizon) can foster effective teamwork. But why do organizations have teammates participate in activities that seem irrelevant to the organization's primary activities? Howard Atkins, chief financial officer at Wells Fargo, believes that corporate retreats aid team building, which in turn improves company performance. At a luxury hotel in Sonoma, California, Atkins—along with several other corporate executives—participated in an exercise in which he and his team had to build a bridge out of boxes and unstable wooden planks. To the delight of his colleagues, Atkins was able to make it across the bridge. The team succeeded. According to Atkins, "What I have been trying to do is get them to see the power of acting more like a team. It's really a terrific success."

Part of the success that Atkins is referring to is the double-digit gains in earnings by Wells Fargo—gains that he says are one of the effects of the corporate retreats. "Success more often than not is a function of execution, and execution is really about people, so we invest pretty heavily into our people." How heavy is the investment? Wells Fargo paid $50,000 for the retreat in Sonoma.

Given the level of expense, some companies are now discontinuing their team-building activities outside the organization. According to Susan Harper, a business psychologist, "team-building has definitely gone down. People are reluctant to spend money on what they think is not an absolute necessity." Atkins believes otherwise: "I know intuitively the payback here is huge. It's a very small investment to make for the payback we are going to get."

Hard drive maker Seagate takes it even further. Every year, Seagate flies roughly 200 managers to New Zealand to participate in "Eco Seagate," its annual team-building exercise. The tab? $9,000 per manager. Chief Financial Officer Charles Pope says it's one of the last things he's cut from Seagate's budget.

It's clear that companies that invest in team-building retreats think they're worth the investment. Sometimes, though, they have unintended consequences. In 2001, a dozen Burger King employees burned themselves while participating in a "fire walk"—a team-building exercise that requires teammates to walk barefoot across an 8-foot pit of burning-hot coals. The results were injured employees and

some very negative publicity for Burger King. In 2006, an employee of security systems company Alarm One was award $1.7 million in damages in a lawsuit in which she claimed she had been spanked on the job as part of a camaraderie-building exercise. One observer of these retreats said, "Most of the time, people asking for these activities aren't interested in real teamwork building. What they really want is entertainment."

Some companies are taking team-building exercises in a different direction, having their employees engage in hands-on volunteer work. When the breweries Coors and Molson merged, they wanted to use a team-building exercise to acquaint the executive teams, but they didn't want to go the route of the typical golf outings or ropes course. So they helped Habitat for Humanity build a home. UPS has new managers participate in various community projects, such as distributing secondhand medical equipment in developing countries.

It is questionable whether team-building exercises such as mountain climbing, cooking contests, and fire walks result in improved company financial performance, and it may be better to think of such activities as morale boosters. According to Merianne Liteman, a professional corporate retreat organizer, "Where good retreats have a quantifiable effect is on retention, on morale, on productivity." Daryl Jesperson, CEO of RE/MAX International, says, "There is a productivity boost anytime you have one of these. People feel better about themselves, they feel better about the company, and as a result will do a better job."

Questions

1. Do you believe that team-building activities increase productivity? Why or why not? What other factors might be responsible for increases in profitability following a corporate retreat?

2. What are some other ways besides those described here to build effective teams and increase teamwork among company employees? How might these alternatives be better or worse than corporate retreats?

3. What should companies do about employees who lack athletic talent but are still pressured to participate in physical activities with their colleagues? How might poor performance by those with low athletic ability affect their status within the organization?

4. How might you increase teamwork when team members are not often in direct contact with one another? Can you think of any "electronic" team-building exercises?

Sources: Based on C. Dahle, "How to Avoid a Rout at the Company Retreat," *New York Times*, October 31, 2004, p. 10; S. Max, "Seagate's Morale-athon," *BusinessWeek*, April 3, 2006, pp. 110–112; M. C. White, "Doing Good on Company Time," *New York Times*, May 8, 2007, p. C6; and N. H. Woodward, "Making the Most of Team Building," *HRMagazine*, September 2006, pp. 73–76.

Endnotes

1. J. McGregor, "I Can't Believe They Took the Whole Team," *BusinessWeek*, December 18, 2006, pp. 120–122.

2. This section is based on J. R. Katzenbach and D. K. Smith, *The Wisdom of Teams* (Cambridge, MA: Harvard University Press, 1993), pp. 21, 45, 85; and D. C. Kinlaw, *Developing Superior Work Teams* (Lexington, MA: Lexington Books, 1991), pp. 3–21.

3. See, for instance, E. Sunstrom, K. DeMeuse, and D. Futrell, "Work Teams: Applications and Effectiveness," *American Psychologist*, February 1990, pp. 120–133.

4. J. H. Shonk, *Team-Based Organizations* (Homewood, IL: Business One Irwin, 1992); and M. A. Verespej, "When Workers Get New Roles," *IndustryWeek*, February 3, 1992, p. 11.

5. G. Bodinson and R. Bunch, "AQP's National Team Excellence Award: Its Purpose, Value and Process," *The Journal for Quality and Participation*, Spring 2003, pp. 37–42.

6. See, for example, S. G. Cohen, G. E. Ledford, Jr., and G. M. Spreitzer, "A Predictive Model of Self-Managing Work Team Effectiveness," *Human Relations*, May 1996, pp. 643–676; C. E. Nicholls, H. W. Lane, and M. Brehm Brechu, "Taking Self-Managed Teams to Mexico," *Academy of Management Executive*, August 1999, pp. 15–27; and A. Erez, J. A. LePine, and H. Elms, "Effects of Rotated Leadership and Peer Evaluation on the Functioning and Effectiveness of Self-Managed Teams: A Quasi-experiment," *Personnel Psychology*, Winter 2002, pp. 929–948.

7. See, for instance, J. L. Cordery, W. S. Mueller, and L. M. Smith, "Attitudinal and Behavioral Effects of Autonomous Group Working: A Longitudinal Field Study," *Academy of Management Journal*, June 1991, pp. 464–476; R. A. Cook and J. L. Goff, "Coming of Age with Self-Managed Teams: Dealing with a Problem Employee," *Journal of Business and Psychology*, Spring 2002, pp. 485–496; and C. W. Langfred, "Too Much of a Good Thing? Negative Effects of High Trust and Individual Autonomy in Self-Managing Teams," *Academy of Management Journal*, June 2004, pp. 385–399.

8. Bodinson and Bunch, "AQP's National Team Excellence Award."

9. M. Brunelli, "How Harley-Davidson Uses Cross-Functional Teams," *Purchasing Online*, November 4, 1999, www.purchasing. com/article/CA147865.html.

10. See, for example, J. Lipnack and J. Stamps, *Virtual Teams: People Working Across Boundaries and Technology*, 2nd ed. (New York: Wiley, 2000); C. B. Gibson and S. G. Cohen (eds.), *Virtual Teams That Work* (San Francisco: Jossey-Bass, 2003); and L. L. Martins, L. L. Gilson, and M. T. Maynard, "Virtual Teams: What Do We Know and Where Do We Go from Here?" *Journal of Management*, November 2004, pp. 805–835.

11. A. Malhotra, A. Majchrzak, and B. Rosen, "Leading Virtual Teams," *Academy of Management Perspectives*, February 2007, pp. 60–70; and J. M. Wilson, S. S. Straus, and B. McEvily, "All in Due Time: The Development of Trust in Computer-Mediated and Face-to-Face Teams," *Organizational Behavior and Human Decision Processes* 19 (2006), pp. 16–33.

12. See, for instance, J. R. Hackman, "The Design of Work Teams," in J. W. Lorsch (ed.), *Handbook of Organizational Behavior* (Upper Saddle River, NJ: Prentice Hall, 1987), pp. 315–342;

and M. A. Campion, G. J. Medsker, and C. A. Higgs, "Relations Between Work Group Characteristics and Effectiveness: Implications for Designing Effective Work Groups," *Personnel Psychology*, Winter 1993, pp. 823–850.

13. D. E. Hyatt and T. M. Ruddy, "An Examination of the Relationship Between Work Group Characteristics and Performance: Once More into the Breech," *Personnel Psychology*, Autumn 1997, p. 555.

14. This model is based on M. A. Campion, E. M. Papper, and G. J. Medsker, "Relations Between Work Team Characteristics and Effectiveness: A Replication and Extension," *Personnel Psychology*, Summer 1996, pp. 429–452; D. E. Hyatt and T. M. Ruddy, "An Examination of the Relationship Between Work Group Characteristics and Performance," pp. 553–585; S. G. Cohen and D. E. Bailey, "What Makes Teams Work: Group Effectiveness Research from the Shop Floor to the Executive Suite," *Journal of Management* 23, no. 3 (1997), pp. 239–290; L. Thompson, *Making the Team* (Upper Saddle River, NJ: Prentice Hall, 2000), pp. 18–33; and J. R. Hackman, *Leading Teams: Setting the Stage for Great Performance* (Boston: Harvard Business School Press, 2002).

15. See M. Mattson, T. V. Mumford, and G. S. Sintay, "Taking Teams to Task: A Normative Model for Designing or Recalibrating Work Teams," paper presented at the National Academy of Management Conference, Chicago, August 1999; and G. L. Stewart and M. R. Barrick, "Team Structure and Performance: Assessing the Mediating Role of Intrateam Process and the Moderating Role of Task Type," *Academy of Management Journal*, April 2000, pp. 135–148.

16. Hyatt and Ruddy, "An Examination of the Relationship Between Work Group Characteristics and Performance," p. 577.

17. P. Balkundi and D. A. Harrison, "Ties, Leaders, and Time in Teams: Strong Inference About Network Structure's Effects on Team Viability and Performance," *Academy of Management Journal* 49, no. 1 (2006), pp. 49–68; G. Chen, B. L. Kirkman, R. Kanfer, D. Allen, and B. Rosen, "A Multilevel Study of Leadership, Empowerment, and Performance in Teams," *Journal of Applied Psychology* 92, no. 2 (2007), pp. 331–346; L. A. DeChurch and M. A. Marks, "Leadership in Multiteam Systems," *Journal of Applied Psychology* 91, no. 2 (2006), pp. 311–329; A. Srivastava, K. M. Bartol, and E. A. Locke, "Empowering Leadership in Management Teams: Effects on Knowledge Sharing, Efficacy, and Performance," *Academy of Management Journal* 49, no. 6 (2006), pp. 1239–1251; and J. E. Mathieu, K. K. Gilson, and T. M. Ruddy, "Empowerment and Team Effectiveness: An Empirical Test of an Integrated Model," *Journal of Applied Psychology* 91, no. 1 (2006), pp. 97–108.

18. K. T. Dirks, "Trust in Leadership and Team Performance: Evidence from NCAA Basketball," *Journal of Applied Psychology*, December 2000, pp. 1004–1012; and M. Williams, "In Whom We Trust: Group Membership as an Affective Context for Trust Development," *Academy of Management Review*, July 2001, pp. 377–396.

19. See S. T. Johnson, "Work Teams: What's Ahead in Work Design and Rewards Management," *Compensation & Benefits Review*, March–April 1993, pp. 35–41; and L. N. McClurg, "Team Rewards: How Far Have We Come?" *Human Resource Management*, Spring 2001, pp. 73–86.

20. R. R. Hirschfeld, M. H. Jordan, H. S. Feild, W. F. Giles, and A. A. Armenakis, "Becoming Team Players: Team Members' Mastery of Teamwork Knowledge as a Predictor of Team Task Proficiency and Observed Teamwork Effectiveness," *Journal of Applied Psychology* 91, no. 2 (2006), pp. 467–474.

21. For a more detailed breakdown of team skills, see M. J. Stevens and M. A. Campion, "The Knowledge, Skill, and Ability Requirements for Teamwork: Implications for Human Resource Management," *Journal of Management,* Summer 1994, pp. 503–530.

22. H. Moon, J. R. Hollenbeck, and S. E. Humphrey, "Asymmetric Adaptability: Dynamic Team Structures as One-Way Streets," *Academy of Management Journal* 47, no. 5 (October 2004), pp. 681–695; A. P. J. Ellis, J. R. Hollenbeck, and D. R. Ilgen, "Team Learning: Collectively Connecting the Dots," *Journal of Applied Psychology* 88, no. 5 (October 2003), pp. 821–835; C. L. Jackson and J. A. LePine, "Peer Responses to a Team's Weakest Link: A Test and Extension of LePine and Van Dyne's Model," *Journal of Applied Psychology* 88, no. 3 (June 2003), pp. 459–475; and J. A. LePine, "Team Adaptation and Postchange Performance: Effects of Team Composition in Terms of Members' Cognitive Ability and Personality," *Journal of Applied Psychology* 88, no. 1 (February 2003), pp. 27–39.

23. S. T. Bell, "Deep-Level Composition Variables as Predictors of Team Performance: A Meta-analysis," *Journal of Applied Psychology* 92, no. 3 (2007), pp. 595–615; and M. R. Barrick, G. L. Stewart, M. J. Neubert, and M. K. Mount, "Relating Member Ability and Personality to Work-Team Processes and Team Effectiveness," *Journal of Applied Psychology,* June 1998, pp. 377–391.

24. Ellis, Hollenbeck, and Ilgen, "Team Learning"; C. O. L. H. Porter, J. R. Hollenbeck, and D. R. Ilgen, "Backing Up Behaviors in Teams: The Role of Personality and Legitimacy of Need," *Journal of Applied Psychology* 88, no. 3 (June 2003), pp. 391–403; A. Colquitt, J. R. Hollenbeck, and D. R. Ilgen, "Computer-Assisted Communication and Team Decision-Making Performance: The Moderating Effect of Openness to Experience," *Journal of Applied Psychology* 87, no. 2 (April 2002), pp. 402–410; J. A. LePine, J. R. Hollenbeck, D. R. Ilgen, and J. Hedlund, "The Effects of Individual Differences on the Performance of Hierarchical Decision Making Teams: Much More Than G," *Journal of Applied Psychology* 82 (1997), pp. 803–811; Jackson and LePine, "Peer Responses to a Team's Weakest Link"; and LePine, "Team Adaptation and Postchange Performance."

25. Barrick, Stewart, Neubert, and Mount, "Relating Member Ability and Personality to Work-Team Processes and Team Effectiveness," p. 388; and S. E. Humphrey, J. R. Hollenbeck, C. J. Meyer, and D. R. Ilgen, "Trait Configurations in Self-Managed Teams: A Conceptual Examination of the Use of Seeding for Maximizing and Minimizing Trait Variance in Teams," *Journal of Applied Psychology* 92, no. 3 (2007), pp. 885–892.

26. C. Margerison and D. McCann, *Team Management: Practical New Approaches* (London: Mercury Books, 1990).

27. E. Mannix and M. A. Neale, "What Differences Make a Difference: The Promise and Reality of Diverse Teams in Organizations," *Psychological Science in the Public Interest,* October 2005, pp. 31–55.

28. G. S. Van Der Vegt, J. S. Bunderson, and A. Oosterhof, "Expertness Diversity and Interpersonal Helping in Teams: Why Those Who Need the Most Help End Up Getting the Least," *Academy of Management Journal* 49, no. 5 (2006), pp. 877–893.

29. K. Y. Williams and C. A. O'Reilly III, "Demography and Diversity in Organizations: A Review of 40 Years of Research," in B. M. Staw and L. L. Cummings (eds.), *Research in Organizational Behavior,* vol. 20, pp. 77–140; and A. Joshi, "The Influence of Organizational Demography on the External Networking Behavior of Teams," *Academy of Management Review,* July 2006, pp. 583–595.

30. J. Katzenbach, "What Makes Teams Work?" *Fast Company,* November 2000, p. 110.

31. The evidence in this section is described in Thompson, *Making the Team,* pp. 65–67. See also L. A. Curral, R. H. Forrester, and J. F. Dawson, "It's What You Do and the Way That You Do It: Team Task, Team Size, and Innovation-Related Group Processes," *European Journal of Work & Organizational Psychology* 10, no. 2 (June 2001), pp. 187–204; R. C. Liden, S. J. Wayne, and R. A. Jaworski, "Social Loafing: A Field Investigation," *Journal of Management* 30, no. 2 (2004), pp. 285–304; and J. A. Wagner, "Studies of Individualism–Collectivism: Effects on Cooperation in Groups," *Academy of Management Journal* 38, no. 1 (February 1995), pp. 152–172.

32. "Is Your Team Too Big? Too Small? What's the Right Number? *Knowledge@Wharton,* June 14, 2006, pp. 1–5.

33. Hyatt and Ruddy, "An Examination of the Relationship Between Work Group Characteristics and Performance"; J. D. Shaw, M. K. Duffy, and E. M. Stark, "Interdependence and Preference for Group Work: Main and Congruence Effects on the Satisfaction and Performance of Group Members," *Journal of Management* 26, no. 2 (2000), pp. 259–279; and S. A. Kiffin-Peterson and J. L. Cordery, "Trust, Individualism, and Job Characteristics of Employee Preference for Teamwork," *International Journal of Human Resource Management,* February 2003, pp. 93–116.

34. R. Wageman, "Critical Success Factors for Creating Superb Self-Managing Teams," *Organizational Dynamics,* Summer 1997, p. 55.

35. Campion, Papper, and Medsker, "Relations Between Work Team Characteristics and Effectiveness," p. 430; B. L. Kirkman and B. Rosen, "Powering Up Teams," *Organizational Dynamics,* Winter 2000, pp. 48–66; and D. C. Man and S. S. K. Lam, "The Effects of Job Complexity and Autonomy on Cohesiveness in Collectivist and Individualist Work Groups: A Cross-Cultural Analysis," *Journal of Organizational Behavior,* December 2003, pp. 979–1001.

36. Campion, Papper, and Medsker, "Relations Between Work Team Characteristics and Effectiveness," p. 430.

37. I. D. Steiner, *Group Processes and Productivity* (New York: Academic Press, 1972).

38. K. Hess, *Creating the High-Performance Team* (New York: Wiley, 1987); Katzenbach and Smith, *The Wisdom of Teams,* pp. 43–64; K. D. Scott and A. Townsend, "Teams: Why Some Succeed and Others Fail," *HRMagazine,* August 1994, pp. 62–67; and K. Blanchard, D. Carew, and E. Parisi-Carew, "How to Get Your Group to Perform Like a Team," *Training and Development,* September 1996, pp. 34–37.

39. J. E. Mathieu and W. Schulze, "The Influence of Team Knowledge and Formal Plans on Episodic Team Process—Performance Relationships," *Academy of Management Journal* 49, no. 3 (2006), pp. 605–619.

40. A. Gurtner, F. Tschan, N. K. Semmer, and C. Nagele, "Getting Groups to Develop Good Strategies: Effects of Reflexivity Interventions on Team Process, Team Performance, and Shared Mental Models," *Organizational Behavior and Human Decision Processes* 102 (2007), pp. 127–142; M. C. Schippers, D. N. Den Hartog, and P. L. Koopman, "Reflexivity in Teams: A Measure and Correlates," *Applied Psychology: An International Review* 56, no. 2 (2007), pp. 189–211; and C. S. Burke, K. C. Stagl, E. Salas, L. Pierce, and D. Kendall, "Understanding Team Adaptation: A Conceptual Analysis and Model," *Journal of Applied Psychology* 91, no. 6 (2006), pp. 1189–1207.

41. E. Weldon and L. R. Weingart, "Group Goals and Group Performance," *British Journal of Social Psychology*, Spring 1993, pp. 307–334. See also R. P. DeShon, S. W. J. Kozlowski, A. M. Schmidt, K. R. Milner, and D. Wiechmann, "A Multiple-Goal, Multilevel Model of Feedback Effects on the Regulation of Individual and Team Performance," *Journal of Applied Psychology*, December 2004, pp. 1035–1056.

42. K. Tasa, S. Taggar, and G. H. Seijts, "The Development of Collective Efficacy in Teams: A Multilevel and Longitudinal Perspective," *Journal of Applied Psychology* 92, no. 1 (2007), pp. 17–27; C. B. Gibson, "The Efficacy Advantage: Factors Related to the Formation of Group Efficacy," *Journal of Applied Social Psychology*, October 2003, pp. 2153–2086; and D. I. Jung and J. J. Sosik, "Group Potency and Collective Efficacy: Examining Their Predictive Validity, Level of Analysis, and Effects of Performance Feedback on Future Group Performance," *Group & Organization Management*, September 2003, pp. 366–391.

43. A. P. J. Ellis, "System Breakdown: The Role of Mental Models and Transactive Memory on the Relationships Between Acute Stress and Team Performance," *Academy of Management Journal* 49, no. 3 (2006), pp. 576–589.

44. S. W. J. Kozlowski and D. R. Ilgen, "Enhancing the Effectiveness of Work Groups and Teams," *Psychological Science in the Public Interest*, December 2006, pp. 77–124; and B. D. Edwards, E. A. Day, W. Arthur, Jr., and S. T. Bell, "Relationships Among Team Ability Composition, Team Mental Models, and Team Performance," *Journal of Applied Psychology* 91, no. 3 (2006), pp. 727–736.

45. K. A. Jehn, "A Qualitative Analysis of Conflict Types and Dimensions in Organizational Groups," *Administrative Science Quarterly*, September 1997, pp. 530–557. See also R. S. Peterson and K. J. Behfar, "The Dynamic Relationship Between Performance Feedback, Trust, and Conflict in Groups: A Longitudinal Study," *Organizational Behavior and Human Decision Processes*, September–November 2003, pp. 102–112.

46. K. H. Price, D. A. Harrison, and J. H. Gavin, "Withholding Inputs in Team Contexts: Member Composition, Interaction Processes, Evaluation Structure, and Social Loafing," *Journal of Applied Psychology* 91, no. 6 (2006), pp. 1375–1384.

47. See, for instance, B. L. Kirkman and D. L. Shapiro, "The Impact of Cultural Values on Employee Resistance to Teams: Toward a Model of Globalized Self-Managing Work Team Effectiveness," *Academy of Management Review*, July 1997, pp. 730–757; and B. L. Kirkman, C. B. Gibson, and D. L. Shapiro, "'Exporting' Teams: Enhancing the Implementation and Effectiveness of Work Teams in Global Affiliates," *Organizational Dynamics* 30, no. 1 (2001), pp. 12–29.

48. G. Hertel, U. Konradt, and K. Voss, "Competencies for Virtual Teamwork: Development and Validation of a Web-Based Selection Tool for Members of Distributed Teams," *European Journal of Work and Organizational Psychology* 15, no. 4 (2006), pp. 477–504.

49. T. D. Schellhardt, "To Be a Star Among Equals, Be a Team Player," *Wall Street Journal*, April 20, 1994, p. B1.

50. "Teaming Up for Success," *Training*, January 1994, p. s41.

51. J. S. DeMatteo, L. T. Eby, and E. Sundstrom, "Team-Based Rewards: Current Empirical Evidence and Directions for Future Research," in B. M. Staw and L. L. Cummings (eds.), *Research in Organizational Behavior*, vol. 20, pp. 141–183.

52. B. Geber, "The Bugaboo of Team Pay," *Training*, August 1995, pp. 27, 34.

53. C. E. Naquin and R. O. Tynan, "The Team Halo Effect: Why Teams Are Not Blamed for Their Failures," *Journal of Applied Psychology*, April 2003, pp. 332–340.

54. A. B. Drexler and R. Forrester, "Teamwork—Not Necessarily the Answer," *HRMagazine*, January 1998, pp. 55–58. See also R. Saavedra, P. C. Earley, and L. Van Dyne, "Complex Interdependence in Task-Performing Groups," *Journal of Applied Psychology*, February 1993, pp. 61–72; and K. A. Jehn, G. B. Northcraft, and M. A. Neale, "Why Differences Make a Difference: A Field Study of Diversity, Conflict, and Performance in Workgroups," *Administrative Science Quarterly*, December 1999, pp. 741–763.

55. "Watson Wyatt's Global Work Studies." *WatsonWyatt.com*, www.watsonwyatt.com/research/featured/workstudy.asp

56. Nicholls, Lane, and Brehm Brechu, "Taking Self-Managed Teams to Mexico."

57. W. E. Watson, K. Kumar, and L. K. Michaelsen, "Cultural Diversity's Impact on Interaction Process and Performance: Comparing Homogeneous and Diverse Task Groups," *Academy of Management Journal*, June 1993, pp. 590–602; P. C. Earley and E. Mosakowski, "Creating Hybrid Team Cultures: An Empirical Test of Transnational Team Functioning," *Academy of Management Journal*, February 2000, pp. 26–49; and S. Mohammed and L. C. Angell, "Surface- and Deep-Level Diversity in Workgroups: Examining the Moderating Effects of Team Orientation and Team Process on Relationship Conflict," *Journal of Organizational Behavior*, December 2004, pp. 1015–1039.

58. Watson, Kumar, and Michaelsen, "Cultural Diversity's Impact on Interaction Process and Performance: Comparing Homogeneous and Diverse Task Groups."

Communication

Constantly talking isn't necessarily communicating.

—Joel in *Eternal Sunshine of the Spotless Mind*

After studying this chapter, you should be able to:

1 Identify the main functions of communication.

2 Describe the communication process and distinguish between formal and informal communication.

3 Contrast downward, upward, and lateral communication and provide examples of each.

4 Contrast oral, written, and nonverbal communication.

5 Contrast formal communication networks and the grapevine.

6 Analyze the advantages and challenges of electronic communication.

7 Show how channel richness underlies the choice of communication channel.

8 Identify common barriers to effective communication.

9 Show how to overcome the potential problems in cross-cultural communication.

Although gossip often seems benign, it can have some pretty serious consequences. Just ask four former employees of the town of Hooksett, New Hampshire (population 11,721), who were fired by the town council for gossiping about their boss. (Pictured below: from left, Sandra Piper, Joann Drewniak, Jessica Skorupski, and Michelle Bonsteel.)

The longtime employees—two administrative assistants and two department heads—were fired because one had referred to the town administrator in derogatory

Gossip at Work: The Hooksett Four

terms and because all four had discussed a rumor that he was having an affair with a female subordinate. One of the employees supposedly referred to the town administrator, David Jodoin, as "a little f_____." The fired employees (all of whom are female) also acknowledged feeling resentment toward the woman, who worked in a specially created position and was paid more than two of the employees, despite having less experience and seniority.

The four employees appealed their dismissal. The Hooksett council denied the appeal and issued a statement arguing "These employees do not represent the best interests of the town of Hooksett and the false rumors, gossip and derogatory statements have contributed to a negative working environment and malcontent among their fellow employees."

B. J. Branch, an attorney representing the four women, said his clients were "legitimately questioning the conduct of their supervisor, and whether the female subordinate was getting preferential treatment. It almost cheapens it to call it gossip. It might have been idle, not particularly thoughtful, talk. But there was no harm intended."

The fired employees—Michelle Bonsteel (code enforcement officer), Sandra Piper (tax assessor), and Jessica Skorupski and Joann Drewniak (both administrative assistants)—who have come to be known as the "Hooksett Four," also claimed they heard the rumor of the affair from a town resident, who questioned the late hours shared by the administrator and his female subordinate.

Some employers have policies against office gossip. Balliet's, an Oklahoma City department store, recently added a malicious-gossip paragraph to the store's personnel policies and procedures manual. It reads: "Malicious gossip by employees about other employees or customers is strictly forbidden, as is researching personal information about employees or customers on the Internet or other records. Violation of this policy may result in immediate termination of employment." The policy grew out of two incidents that occurred recently—one in which after-hours socializing led to things being said about people at work, and the other in which three employees went online to check out a situation about a coworker. "Both created enormous tension in the store," owner Bob Benham said. "Someone wouldn't talk to someone else, creating a mood customers could feel."

Since they were fired, the Hooksett Four have appeared on *Good Morning America*, and they are considering their legal options. A petition calling for their reinstatement was signed by 419 Hooksett residents and forwarded to the town council. "If we didn't fire them, we would have been sued for sexual harassment and malicious slander. We would have been liable for a lawsuit if we had done nothing," said George Longfellow, town council chair. "I'm definitely not going away, that's for sure," Drewniak said. "They wrongfully fired me, and I shouldn't be out of work."

Whatever the legal merits of the Hooksett Four's claim, it's clear that what may have seemed like benign gossip had pretty malignant consequences.[1] ■

the preceding examples illustrate the profound consequences of communication. In this chapter, we'll analyze the power of communication and ways in which it can be made more effective. One of the topics we'll discuss is gossip. Consider the following self-assessment and how you score on your attitudes toward gossip at work.

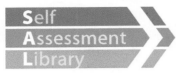

AM I A GOSSIP?

In the Self-Assessment Library (available on CD or online), take assessment IV.E.3 (Am I a Gossip?) and answer the following questions.

1. *How did you score relative to your classmates?*
2. *Do you think gossiping is morally wrong? Why or why not?*

Gossip is one communication issue. There are many others. Research indicates that poor communication is probably the most frequently cited source of interpersonal conflict.[2] Because individuals spend nearly 70 percent of their waking hours communicating—writing, reading, speaking, listening—it seems reasonable to conclude that one of the most inhibiting forces to successful group performance is a lack of effective communication. And good communication skills are very important to your career success. A 2007 study of recruiters found that they rated communication skills as *the* most important characteristic of an ideal job candidate.[3]

No individual, group, or organization can exist without communication: the transfer of meaning among its members. It is only through transmitting meaning from one person to another that information and ideas can be conveyed. Communication, however, is more than merely imparting meaning. It must also be understood. In a group in which one member speaks only German and the others do not know German, the individual speaking German will not be fully understood. Therefore, **communication** must include both the *transfer and the understanding of meaning.*

An idea, no matter how great, is useless until it is transmitted and understood by others. Perfect communication, if there were such a thing, would exist when a thought or an idea was transmitted so that the mental picture perceived by the receiver was exactly the same as that envisioned by the sender. Although elementary in theory, perfect communication is never achieved in practice, for reasons we shall expand on later in the chapter.

Before making too many generalizations concerning communication and problems in communicating effectively, we need to review briefly the functions that communication performs and describe the communication process.

Functions of Communication

Communication serves four major functions within a group or organization: control, motivation, emotional expression, and information.[4]

Communication acts to *control* member behavior in several ways. Organizations have authority hierarchies and formal guidelines that employees are required to follow. For instance, when employees are required to communicate any job-related grievance to their immediate boss, to follow their job description, or to comply with company policies, communication is performing a control function. But informal communication also controls behavior. When work groups tease or harass a member who produces too much (and makes the rest of the group look bad), they are informally communicating with, and controlling, the member's behavior.

1   *Identify the main functions of communication.*

communication   *The transfer and understanding of meaning.*

Globalization has changed the way Toyota Motor Corporation provides employees with the information they need for decision making. In the past, Toyota transferred employee knowledge on the job from generation to generation through "tacit understanding," a common communication method used in the conformist and subdued Japanese culture. Today, however, as a global organization, Toyota transfers knowledge of its production methods to overseas employees by bringing them to its training center in Japan, shown here, to teach them production methods by using how-to manuals, practice drills, and lectures.

Communication fosters *motivation* by clarifying to employees what is to be done, how well they are doing, and what can be done to improve performance if it's subpar. We saw this operating in our review of goal-setting and reinforcement theories in Chapter 6. The formation of specific goals, feedback on progress toward the goals, and reinforcement of desired behavior all stimulate motivation and require communication.

For many employees, their work group is a primary source for social interaction. The communication that takes place within the group is a fundamental mechanism by which members show their frustrations and feelings of satisfaction. Communication, therefore, provides a release for the *emotional expression* of feelings and for fulfillment of social needs.

The final function that communication performs relates to its role in facilitating decision making. It provides the *information* that individuals and groups need to make decisions by transmitting the data to identify and evaluate alternative choices.

No one of these four functions should be seen as being more important than the others. For groups to perform effectively, they need to maintain some form of control over members, stimulate members to perform, provide a means for emotional expression, and make decision choices. You can assume that almost every communication interaction that takes place in a group or an organization performs one or more of these four functions.

The Communication Process

2   *Describe the communication process and distinguish between formal and informal communication.*

Before communication can take place, a purpose, expressed as a message to be conveyed, is needed. It passes between a sender and a receiver. The message is encoded (converted to a symbolic form) and passed by way of some medium (channel) to the receiver, who retranslates (decodes) the message initiated by the sender. The result is transfer of meaning from one person to another.[5]

Exhibit **11-1** The Communication Process

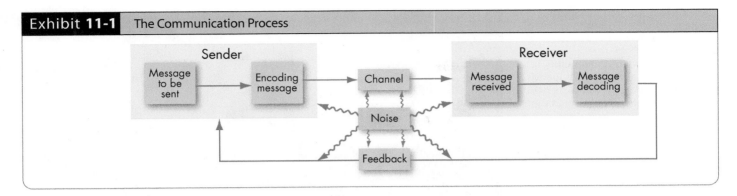

Exhibit 11-1 depicts this **communication process**. The key parts of this model are: (1) the sender, (2) encoding, (3) the message, (4) the channel, (5) decoding, (6) the receiver, (7) noise, and (8) feedback.

The *sender* initiates a message by encoding a thought. The *message* is the actual physical product from the sender's *encoding*. When we speak, the speech is the message. When we write, the writing is the message. When we gesture, the movements of our arms and the expressions on our faces are the message. The *channel* is the medium through which the message travels. It is selected by the sender, who must determine whether to use a formal or informal channel. **Formal channels** are established by the organization and transmit messages that are related to the professional activities of members. They traditionally follow the authority chain within the organization. Other forms of messages, such as personal or social, follow **informal channels** in the organization. These informal channels are spontaneous and emerge as a response to individual choices.[6] The *receiver* is the object to whom the message is directed. But before the message can be received, the symbols in it must be translated into a form that can be understood by the receiver. This step is the *decoding* of the message. *Noise* represents communication barriers that distort the clarity of the message. Examples of possible noise sources include perceptual problems, information overload, semantic difficulties, or cultural differences. The final link in the communication process is a feedback loop. *Feedback* is the check on how successful we have been in transferring our messages as originally intended. It determines whether understanding has been achieved.

Direction of Communication

3 *Contrast downward, upward, and lateral communication and provide examples of each.*

Communication can flow vertically or laterally. The vertical dimension can be further divided into downward and upward directions.[7]

Downward Communication

Communication that flows from one level of a group or organization to a lower level is downward communication. When we think of managers communicating with employees, the downward pattern is the one we are usually thinking of.

---

communication process *The steps between a source and a receiver that result in the transfer and understanding of meaning.*

formal channels *Communication channels established by an organization to transmit messages related to the professional activities of members.*

informal channels *Communication channels that are created spontaneously and that emerge as responses to individual choices.*

After AT&T acquired BellSouth and Cingular Wireless, Ed Whitacre, then CEO of AT&T, used downward communication to inform the former BellSouth and Cingular employees about the company's acquisition strategy. Whitacre held meetings to assure employees that he understood the changes resulting from the acquisition caused turmoil and confusion in the short term and asked them to continually provide excellent customer service during the transitional period. The face-to-face meetings gave employees the opportunity to ask questions.
Source: Erik S. Lesser/ The New York Times

It's used by group leaders and managers to assign goals, provide job instructions, inform employees of policies and procedures, point out problems that need attention, and offer feedback about performance. But downward communication doesn't have to be oral or face-to-face contact. When management sends letters to employees' homes to advise them of the organization's new sick leave policy, it's using downward communication. Another example of downward communication is an e-mail from a team leader to the members of her team, reminding them of an upcoming deadline.

When engaging in downward communication, managers must explain the reasons *why* a decision was made. One study found that employees were twice as likely to be committed to changes when the reasons behind them were fully explained. Although this may seem like common sense, many managers feel they are too busy to explain things, or that explanations will "open up a big can of worms." Evidence clearly indicates, though, that explanations increase employee commitment and support of decisions.[8]

Another problem in downward communication is its one-way nature; generally, managers inform employees but rarely solicit their advice or opinions. A 2006 study revealed that nearly two-thirds of employees say their boss rarely or never asks their advice. The author of the study noted, "Organizations are always striving for higher employee engagement, but evidence indicates they unnecessarily create fundamental mistakes. People need to be respected and listened to." Anne Mulcahy, CEO of Xerox, finds that listening takes work: "Listening is one of those things that is easy to talk about, difficult to do."[9]

The best communicators are those who explain the reasons behind their downward communications, but also solicit upward communication from the employees they supervise. That leads us to the next direction: upward communication.

Upward Communication

Upward communication flows to a higher level in the group or organization. It's used to provide feedback to higher-ups, inform them of progress toward goals, and relay current problems. Upward communication keeps managers aware of how employees feel about their jobs, coworkers, and the organization in general. Managers also rely on upward communication for ideas on how things can be improved.

Given that job responsibilities of most managers and supervisors have expanded, upward communication is increasingly difficult because managers are overwhelmed and easily distracted. To engage in effective upward communication, try to reduce distractions (meet in a conference room if you can, rather than your boss's office or cubicle), communicate in headlines not paragraphs (your job is to get your boss's attention, not to engage in a meandering discussion), support your headlines with actionable items (what you believe should happen), and prepare an agenda to make sure you use your boss's attention well.[10]

Lateral Communication

When communication takes place among members of the same work group, among members of work groups at the same level, among managers at the same level, or among any other horizontally equivalent personnel, we describe it as lateral communications.

Why would there be a need for horizontal communications if a group or an organization's vertical communications are effective? The answer is that horizontal communication is often necessary to save time and facilitate coordination. In some cases, such lateral relationships are formally sanctioned. More often, they are informally created to short-circuit the vertical hierarchy and expedite action. So lateral communications can, from management's viewpoint, be good or bad. Because strict adherence to the formal vertical structure for all communications can impede the efficient and accurate transfer of information, lateral communications can be beneficial. In such cases, they occur with the knowledge and support of superiors. But they can create dysfunctional conflicts when the formal vertical channels are breached, when members go above or around their superiors to get things done, or when bosses find out that actions have been taken or decisions have been made without their knowledge.

Interpersonal Communication

4 *Contrast oral, written, and nonverbal communication.*

How do group members transfer meaning between and among each other? There are three basic methods. People essentially rely on oral, written, and nonverbal communication.

Oral Communication

The chief means of conveying messages is oral communication. Speeches, formal one-on-one and group discussions, and the informal rumor mill, or grapevine, are popular forms of oral communication.

The advantages of oral communication are speed and feedback. A verbal message can be conveyed and a response received in a minimal amount of time. If the receiver is unsure of the message, rapid feedback allows for early detection by the sender and, hence, allows for early correction. As one professional put it, "Face-to-face communication on a consistent basis is still the best way to get information to and from employees."[11]

The major disadvantage of oral communication surfaces whenever a message has to be passed through a number of people. The more people a message must pass through, the greater the potential distortion. If you've ever played the game "telephone," you know the problem. Each person interprets the message in his or her own way. The message's content, when it reaches its destination, is often

MYTH OR SCIENCE?

"People Are Good at Catching Liars at Work"

this statement is essentially false. The core purpose of communication in the workplace may be to convey business-related information. However, in the workplace, we also communicate in order to manage impressions others form of us. Some of this impression management is unintentional and harmless (for example, complimenting your boss on his clothing). However, sometimes people manage impressions through outright lies, such as making up an excuse for missing work or failing to make a deadline.

One of the reasons people lie—in the workplace and elsewhere—is that it works. Although most of us think we're good at detecting a lie, research shows that most people perform no better than chance at detecting whether someone is lying or telling the truth.

A recent review of 108 studies revealed that people detect lies at a rate, on average, only 4.2 percent better than chance. This study also found that people's confidence in their judgments of whether someone was lying bore almost no relationship to their actual accuracy; we think we're a lot better at catching people lying than we really are. What's even more discouraging is that so-called experts—police officers, parole officers, detectives, judges, and psychologists—perform no better than other people. As the authors of this review conclude, "People are not good detectors of deception regardless of their age, sex, confidence, and experience."

The point? Don't believe everything you hear and don't place too much weight on your ability to catch a liar based just on your intuition. When someone makes a claim that it's reasonable to doubt, ask her or him to back it up with evidence. ∎

Source: M. G. Aamodt and H. Custer, "Who Can Best Catch a Liar? A Meta-analysis of Individual Differences in Detecting Deception," *The Forensic Examiner*, Spring 2006, pp. 6–11.

---

very different from that of the original. In an organization, where decisions and other communiqués are verbally passed up and down the authority hierarchy, there are considerable opportunities for messages to become distorted.

Written Communication

Written communications include memos, letters, fax transmissions, e-mail, instant messaging, organizational periodicals, notices placed on bulletin boards, or any other device that is transmitted via written words or symbols.

Why would a sender choose to use written communications? They're often tangible and verifiable. When they're printed, both the sender and receiver have a record of the communication; and the message can be stored for an indefinite period. If there are questions concerning the content of the message, it is physically available for later reference. This feature is particularly important for complex and lengthy communications. The marketing plan for a new product, for instance, is likely to contain a number of tasks spread out over several months. By putting it in writing, those who have to initiate the plan can readily refer to it over the life of the plan. A final benefit of all written communication comes from the process itself. People are usually more careful with the written word than with the oral word. They're forced to think more thoroughly about what they want to convey in a written message than in a spoken one. Thus, written communications are more likely to be well thought out, logical, and clear.

Of course, written messages have drawbacks. They're time-consuming. You could convey far more information to a college instructor in a 1-hour oral exam than in a 1-hour written exam. In fact, you could probably say the same thing in 10 to 15 minutes that it would take you an hour to write. So, although writing may be more precise, it also consumes a great deal of time. The other major disadvantage is feedback, or lack of it. Oral communication allows the receiver to respond rapidly to what he thinks he hears. Written communication, however, does not have a built-in feedback mechanism. The result is that the mailing of a memo is no assurance that it has been received, and, if received, there is no guarantee the recipient will interpret it as the sender intended. The latter point is also relevant in oral communiqués, except it's easy in such cases merely to ask the receiver to summarize what you've said. An accurate summary presents feedback evidence that the message has been received and understood.

Nonverbal Communication

Every time we verbally give a message to someone, we also impart a nonverbal message.[12] In some instances, the nonverbal component may stand alone. For example, in a singles bar, a glance, a stare, a smile, a frown, and a provocative body movement all convey meaning. Therefore, no discussion of communication would be complete without consideration of *nonverbal communication*—which includes body movements, the intonations or emphasis we give to words, facial expressions, and the physical distance between the sender and receiver.

It can be argued that every *body movement* has a meaning, and no movement is accidental. For example, through body language, we say, "Help me, I'm lonely"; "Take me, I'm available"; and "Leave me alone, I'm depressed." Rarely do we send our messages consciously. We act out our state of being with nonverbal body language. We lift one eyebrow for disbelief. We rub our noses for puzzlement. We clasp our arms to isolate ourselves or to protect ourselves. We shrug our shoulders for indifference, wink one eye for intimacy, tap our fingers for impatience, slap our forehead for forgetfulness.[13]

The two most important messages that body language conveys are (1) the extent to which an individual likes another and is interested in his or her views and (2) the relative perceived status between a sender and receiver.[14] For instance, we're more likely to position ourselves closer to people we like and touch them more often. Similarly, if you feel that you're of higher status than another, you're more likely to display body movements—such as crossed legs or a slouched seated position—that reflect a casual and relaxed manner.[15]

Body language adds to, and often complicates, verbal communication. A body position or movement does not by itself have a precise or universal meaning, but when it is linked with spoken language, it gives fuller meaning to a sender's message.

If you read the verbatim minutes of a meeting, you wouldn't grasp the impact of what was said in the same way you would if you had been there or if you saw the meeting on video. Why? There is no record of nonverbal communication. The emphasis given to words or phrases is missing. Exhibit 11-2

Exhibit **11-2**	Intonations: It's the Way You Say It!

Change your tone and you change your meaning:

Placement of the emphasis	What it means
Why don't I take **you** to dinner tonight?	I was going to take someone else.
Why don't **I** take you to dinner tonight?	Instead of the guy you were going with.
Why **don't** I take you to dinner tonight?	I'm trying to find a reason why I **shouldn't** take you.
Why don't I take you to dinner tonight?	Do you have a problem with me?
Why don't I **take** you to dinner tonight?	Instead of going on your own.
Why don't I take you to **dinner** tonight?	Instead of lunch tomorrow.
Why don't I take you to dinner **tonight**?	Not tomorrow night.

Source: Based on M. Kiely, "When 'No' Means 'Yes,'" *Marketing*, October 1993, pp. 7–9. Reproduced in A. Huczynski and D. Buchanan, *Organizational Behavior*, 4th ed. (Essex, UK: Pearson Education, 2001), p. 194.

illustrates how *intonations* can change the meaning of a message. *Facial expressions* also convey meaning. A snarling face says something different from a smile. Facial expressions, along with intonations, can show arrogance, aggressiveness, fear, shyness, and other characteristics that would never be communicated if you read a transcript of what had been said.

The way individuals space themselves in terms of *physical distance* also has meaning. What is considered proper spacing is largely dependent on cultural norms. For example, what is considered a businesslike distance in some European countries would be viewed as intimate in many parts of North America. If someone stands closer to you than is considered appropriate, it may indicate aggressiveness or sexual interest; if farther away than usual, it may mean disinterest or displeasure with what is being said.

It's important for the receiver to be alert to these nonverbal aspects of communication. You should look for nonverbal cues as well as listen to the literal meaning of a sender's words. You should particularly be aware of contradictions between the messages. Your boss may say she is free to talk to you about a pressing budget problem, but you may see nonverbal signals suggesting that this is not the time to discuss the subject. Regardless of what is being said, an individual who frequently glances at her wristwatch is giving the message that she would prefer to terminate the conversation. We misinform others when we express one message verbally, such as trust, but nonverbally communicate a contradictory message that reads, "I don't have confidence in you."

Organizational Communication

5 *Contrast formal communication networks and the grapevine.*

In this section, we move from interpersonal communication to organizational communication. Our first focus will be to describe and distinguish formal networks and the grapevine. In the following section, we discuss technological innovations in communication.

Formal Small-Group Networks

Formal organizational networks can be very complicated. They can, for instance, include hundreds of people and a half-dozen or more hierarchical levels. To simplify our discussion, we've condensed these networks into three common small groups of five people each (see Exhibit 11-3). These three networks are the

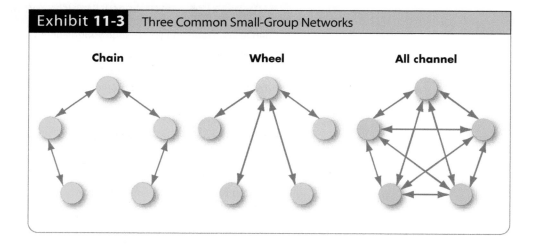

Exhibit 11-3   Three Common Small-Group Networks

Chain   Wheel   All channel

| | Exhibit 11-4 | Small-Group Networks and Effective Criteria | | |

| | | Networks | | |
Criteria	Chain	Wheel	All Channel
Speed	Moderate	Fast	Fast
Accuracy	High	High	Moderate
Emergence of a leader	Moderate	High	None
Member satisfaction	Moderate	Low	High

chain, wheel, and all channel. Although these three networks have been extremely simplified, they allow us to describe the unique qualities of each.

The *chain* rigidly follows the formal chain of command. This network approximates the communication channels you might find in a rigid three-level organization. The *wheel* relies on a central figure to act as the conduit for all of the group's communication. It simulates the communication network you would find on a team with a strong leader. The *all-channel* network permits all group members to actively communicate with each other. The all-channel network is most often characterized in practice by self-managed teams, in which all group members are free to contribute and no one person takes on a leadership role.

As Exhibit 11-4 demonstrates, the effectiveness of each network depends on the dependent variable you're concerned about. For instance, the structure of the wheel facilitates the emergence of a leader, the all-channel network is best if you are concerned with having high member satisfaction, and the chain is best if accuracy is most important. Exhibit 11-4 leads us to the conclusion that no single network will be best for all occasions.

The Grapevine

The formal system is not the only communication network in a group or organization. There is also an informal one, called the **grapevine**.[16] Although the grapevine may be informal, it's still an important source of information. For instance, a survey found that 75 percent of employees hear about matters first through rumors on the grapevine.[17]

The grapevine has three main characteristics.[18] First, it is not controlled by management. Second, it is perceived by most employees as being more believable and reliable than formal communiqués issued by top management. Finally, it is largely used to serve the self-interests of the people within it.

One of the most famous studies of the grapevine investigated the communication pattern among 67 managerial personnel in a small manufacturing firm.[19] The basic approach used was to learn from each communication recipient how he or she first received a given piece of information and then trace it back to its source. It was found that, while the grapevine was an important source of information, only 10 percent of the executives acted as liaison individuals (that is, passed the information on to more than one other person). For example, when one executive decided to resign to enter the insurance business, 81 percent of the executives knew about it, but only 11 percent transmitted this information to others.

grapevine *An organization's informal communication network.*

Exhibit 11-5	Suggestions for Reducing the Negative Consequences of Rumors

1. Announce timetables for making important decisions.
2. Explain decisions and behaviors that may appear inconsistent or secretive.
3. Emphasize the downside, as well as the upside, of current decisions and future plans.
4. Openly discuss worst-case possibilities—it is almost never as anxiety provoking as the unspoken fantasy.

Source: Adapted from L. Hirschhorn, "Managing Rumors," in L. Hirschhorn (ed.), *Cutting Back* (San Francisco: Jossey-Bass, 1983), pp. 54–56. Used with permission.

Is the information that flows along the grapevine accurate? The evidence indicates that about 75 percent of what is carried is accurate.[20] But what conditions foster an active grapevine? What gets the rumor mill rolling?

It's frequently assumed that rumors start because they make titillating gossip. This is rarely the case. Rumors emerge as a response to situations that are *important* to us, when there is *ambiguity*, and under conditions that arouse *anxiety*.[21] The fact that work situations frequently contain these three elements explains why rumors flourish in organizations. The secrecy and competition that typically prevail in large organizations—around issues such as the appointment of new bosses, the relocation of offices, downsizing decisions, and the realignment of work assignments—create conditions that encourage and sustain rumors on the grapevine. A rumor will persist either until the wants and expectations creating the uncertainty underlying the rumor are fulfilled or until the anxiety is reduced.

What can we conclude from the preceding discussion? Certainly the grapevine is an important part of any group or organization communication network and is well worth understanding. It gives managers a feel for the morale of their organization, identifies issues that employees consider important, and helps tap into employee anxieties. The grapevine also serves employees' needs: Small talk serves to create a sense of closeness and friendship among those who share information, although research suggests that it often does so at the expense of those in the "out" group.[22]

Can management entirely eliminate rumors? No. What management should do, however, is minimize the negative consequences of rumors by limiting their range and impact. Exhibit 11-5 offers a few suggestions for minimizing those negative consequences.

Electronic Communications

6 Analyze the advantages and challenges of electronic communication.

An indispensable—and in 71 percent of cases, the primary—medium of communication in today's organizations is electronic. Electronic communications include e-mail, text messaging, networking software, Internet or Web logs (blogs), and video conferencing. Let's discuss each.

E-mail   E-mail uses the Internet to transmit and receive computer-generated text and documents. Its growth has been spectacular, and its use is now so pervasive that it's hard to imagine life without it.

When Bill Gates goes to work, he has three screens synchronized, two of which are for e-mail (the other is Internet Explorer). As a communication tool, e-mail has a long list of benefits. E-mail messages can be quickly written, edited, and stored. They can be distributed to one person or thousands with a click of a mouse. They can be read, in their entirety, at the convenience of the recipient. And the cost of sending formal e-mail messages to employees is a fraction of the cost of printing, duplicating, and distributing a comparable letter or brochure.[23]

E-mail, of course, is not without drawbacks. The following are some of the most significant limitations of e-mail and what organizations should do to reduce or eliminate these problems:

- *Misinterpreting the message.* It's true that we often misinterpret verbal messages, but the potential for misinterpretation with e-mail is even greater. One research team at New York University found that we can accurately decode an e-mail's intent and tone only 50 percent of the time, yet most of us vastly overestimate our ability to send and interpret clear messages. If you're sending an important message, make sure you reread it for clarity. And if you're upset about the presumed tone of someone else's message, keep in mind that you may be misinterpreting it.[24]

- *Communicating negative messages.* When companies have negative information to communicate, managers need to think carefully. E-mail may not be the best way to communicate the message. When Radio Shack decided to lay off 400 employees, it drew down an avalanche of scorn inside and outside the company by doing it via e-mail. Employees need to be careful communicating negative messages via e-mail, too. Justen Deal, 22, wrote an e-mail critical of some strategic decisions made by his employer, pharmaceutical giant Kaiser Permanente. In the e-mail, he criticized the "misleadership" of Kaiser CEO George Halvorson and questioned the financing of several information technology projects. Within hours, Deal's computer was seized; he was later fired.[25]

- *Overuse of e-mail.* An estimated 6 trillion e-mails are sent every year, and someone has to answer all those messages! As people become established in their careers and their responsibilities expand, so do their inboxes. A survey of Canadian managers revealed that 58 percent spent 2 to 4 hours per day reading and responding to e-mails. Some people, such as venture capitalist Fred Wilson, have become so overwhelmed by e-mail that they've declared "e-mail bankruptcy." Recording artist Moby sent an e-mail to all those in his address book announcing that he was taking a break from e-mail for the rest of the year. Although you probably don't want to declare e-mail bankruptcy, or couldn't get away with it even if you did, you should use e-mail judiciously, especially when you're contacting people inside the organization who may already be wading through lots of e-mail messages every day.[26]

- *E-mail emotions.* We tend to think of e-mail as a sort of sterile, faceless form of communication. But that doesn't mean it's unemotional. As you no doubt know, e-mails are often highly emotional. One CEO said, "I've seen people not talk to each other, turf wars break out and people quit their jobs as a result of e-mails." E-mail tends to have a disinhibiting effect on people; senders write things they'd never be comfortable saying in person. Facial expressions tend to temper our emotional expressions, but in e-mail, there is no other face to look at, and so many of us fire away. An increasingly common way of communicating emotions in e-mail is with emoticons. For example, Yahoo!'s e-mail software allows the user to pick from 32 emoticons. Although emoticons used to be considered for personal use only, increasingly adults are using them in business e-mails. Still, some see them as too informal for business use.

    When others send flaming messages, remain calm and try not to respond in kind. Also, when writing new e-mails, try to temper your own tendencies to quickly fire off messages.[27]

- *Privacy concerns.* There are two privacy issues with e-mail. First, you need to be aware that your e-mails may be, and often are, monitored. Also, you can't always trust that the recipient of your e-mail will keep it confidential. For these reasons, you shouldn't write anything you wouldn't want made public. Before Wal-Mart fired marketing VP Julie Roehm, its managers examined her e-mails for evidence of an inappropriate romantic relationship. Second, you need to exercise caution in forwarding e-mail from your company's e-mail account to a personal, or "public," (for example, Gmail, Yahoo!, MSN) e-mail account. These accounts often aren't as secure as corporate accounts, so when you forward a company e-mail to them, you may be violating your organization's policy or unintentionally disclosing confidential data. Many employers hire vendors that sift through e-mails, using software to catch not only the obvious ("insider trading") but the vague ("that thing we talked about") or guilt ridden ("regret"). Another survey revealed that nearly 40 percent of companies have employees whose only job is to read other employees' e-mail. You are being watched—so be careful what you e-mail![28]

Instant Messaging and Text Messaging   Like e-mail, instant messaging (IM) and text messaging (TM) use electronic messages. Unlike e-mail, though, IM and TM are either in "real" time (IM) or use portable communication devices (TM). In just a few years, IM/TM has become pervasive. As you no doubt know from experience, IM is usually sent via desktop or laptop computer, whereas TM is transmitted via cellphones or handheld devices such as Blackberrys.

The growth of TM has been spectacular. In 2001, for instance, just 8 percent of U.S. employees were using it. Now that number is more than 50 percent.[29] Why? Because IM and TM represent fast and inexpensive means for managers to stay in touch with employees and for employees to stay in touch with each other. In an increasing number of cases, this isn't just a luxury, it's a business imperative. For example, Bill Green, CEO of the consulting firm Accenture, doesn't have a permanent office. Since he's on the road all the time, visiting Accenture's 100 locations scattered across the globe, TM is essential for him keep in touch. Although there aren't many other examples so dramatic, the great advantage of TM is that it is flexible; with it, you can be reached almost anywhere, anytime.[30]

Despite their advantages, IM and TM aren't going to replace e-mail. E-mail is still probably a better device for conveying long messages that need to be saved. IM is preferable for one- or two-line messages that would just clutter up an e-mail inbox. On the downside, some IM/TM users find the technology intrusive and distracting. Their continual presence can make it hard for employees to concentrate and stay focused. For example, a survey of managers revealed that in 86 percent of meetings, at least some participants checked TM. Finally, because instant messages can be intercepted easily, many organizations are concerned about the security of IM/TM.[31]

One other point: It's important to not let the informality of text messaging ("omg! r u serious? brb") spill over into business e-mails. Many prefer to keep business communication relatively formal. A survey of employers revealed that 58 percent rate grammar, spelling, and punctuation as "very important" in e-mail messages.[32] By making sure your professional communications are, well, professional, you'll show yourself to be mature and serious. That doesn't mean, of course, that you have to give up TM or IM; you just need to maintain the boundaries between how you communicate with your friends and how you communicate professionally.

Networking Software   Nowhere has communication been transformed more than in the area of networking. You are doubtless familiar with and perhaps a user of social networking platforms such as Facebook and MySpace.

Rather than being one huge site, Facebook, which has 30 million active users, is actually composed of separate networks based on schools, companies, or regions. It might surprise you to learn that individuals over 25 are the fastest-growing users of Facebook.

Facebook founder and CEO Mark Zuckerberg continues to transform communication. He announced a new platform strategy that allows third parties to develop services on the Facebook site, which allows communication opportunities for business entrepreneurs. For Zuckerberg, Facebook is more than a social networking site. He describes it as a communication tool that facilitates the flow of information between users and their friends, family members, and professional connections.

Source: Noah Berger/ The New York Times

More than 100 million users have created accounts at MySpace. This site averages more than 40 billion hits per month. MySpace profiles contain two "blurbs": "About Me" and "Who I'd Like to Meet" sections. Profiles can also contain "Interests" and "Details" sections, photos, blog entries, and other details. Compared to Facebook, MySpace is relatively more likely to be used for purely personal reasons, as illustrated by the "Friends Space" portion of a user's account.

Amid the growth of Facebook and MySpace, professional networking sites have entered the marketplace and expanded as well. LinkedIn, Ziggs, and ZoomInfo are all professional Web sites that allow users to set up lists of contacts and do everything from casually "pinging" them with updates to hosting chat rooms for all or some of the users' contacts. Some companies, such as IBM, have their own social networks (IBM's is called BluePages); IBM is selling the BluePages tool to companies and individual users. Microsoft is doing the same thing with its SharePoint tool.

To get the most out of social networks, while avoiding irritating your contacts, use them "for high-value items only"—not as an everyday or even every-week tool. Also, remember that a prospective employer might check your MySpace or Facebook entry. In fact, some entrepreneurs have developed software that mines such Web sites for companies (or individuals) that want to check up on a job applicant (or potential date). So keep in mind that what you post may be read by people other than your intended contacts.[33]

Web Logs (Blogs)   Sun Microsystems CEO Jonathan Schwartz is a big fan of Web logs (**blogs**), Web sites about a single person or company that are usually updated daily. He encourages his employees to have them and has one himself (http://blogs.sun.com/jonathan). Schwartz's blog averages 400,000 hits per

blog (Web log)   *A Web site where entries are written, generally displayed in reverse chronological order, about news, events, and personal diary entries.*

month, and Schwartz, like Apple's managers, allows Sun customers to post comments about the company's products on its Web site.

Obviously, Schwartz is not the only fan of blogs. Experts estimate that more than 10 million U.S. workers have blogs, and nearly 40 million people read blogs on a regular basis. Thousands of Microsoft employees have blogs. Google, GM, Nike, IBM, and many other large organizations also have corporate blogs.

So what's the downside? Although some companies have policies in place governing the content of blogs, many don't, and 39 percent of individual bloggers say they have posted comments that could be construed as harmful to their company's reputation. Many bloggers think their personal blogs are outside their employer's purview, but if someone else in a company happens to read a blog entry, there is nothing to keep him or her from sharing that information with others, and the employee could be dismissed as a result. Schwartz says that Sun would not fire an employee over any blog entry short of one that broke the law. "Our blogging policy is 'Be authentic. Period,'" he says. But most organizations are unlikely to be so forgiving of any blog entry that might cast a negative light on them.

When Andrew McDonald landed an internship with Comedy Central, his first day at work, he started a blog. His supervisors asked him to change various things about the blog, essentially removing all specific references to his employer. Kelly Kreth was fired from her job as a marketing director for blogging about her coworkers. So was Jessa Werner, who later said, "I came to the realization that I probably shouldn't have been blogging about work."

One legal expert notes, "Employee bloggers mistakenly believe that First Amendment gives them the right to say whatever they want on their personal blogs. Wrong!" Also, beware of posting personal blog entries at work. More than three-quarters of employers actively monitor employees' Web site connections. In short, if you are going to have a personal blog, maintain a strict work–personal "firewall."[34]

Video Conferencing   *Video conferencing* permits employees in an organization to have meetings with people at different locations. Live audio and video images of members allow them to see, hear, and talk with each other. Video conferencing technology, in effect, allows employees to conduct interactive meetings without the necessity of all being physically in the same location.

In the late 1990s, video conferencing was basically conducted from special rooms equipped with television cameras, located at company facilities. More recently, cameras and microphones are being attached to individual computers, allowing people to participate in video conferences without leaving their desks. As the cost of this technology drops, video conferencing is likely to be increasingly seen as an alternative to expensive and time-consuming travel.

Knowledge Management

Our final topic under organizational communication is **knowledge management (KM)**. This is a process of organizing and distributing an organization's collective wisdom so the right information gets to the right people at the right time. When done properly, KM provides an organization with both a competitive edge and improved organizational performance because it makes its employees smarter. It can also help control leaks of vital company information so that an organization's competitive advantage is preserved for as long as possible. Despite its importance, KM gets low marks from most business leaders. When consulting firm Bain & Co. asked 960 executives about the effectiveness of 25 management tools, KM ranked near the bottom of the list. One expert concluded, "Most organizations are still managing as if we were in the industrial era."[35]

OB In the News

Starbucks' Great Communicator

Jim Donald seems to do nothing but communicate. Donald, 52, has been president and CEO of Starbucks since 2005. Donald tracks how he spends his time carefully, and on a typical month, this is how it breaks down:

As you can see, Donald spends almost all his time communicating with people. What's more, he even does his own e-mail. He says, "If anyone in our company e-mails me or leaves me a voicemail, they get a response, quickly. I'm fanatical about communicating."

In a typical morning, Donald will leave 6 A.M. voice mail messages for up to 100 managers, write 25 thank-you notes to "partners" (Starbucks lingo for employees), sign birthday cards, and check his Treo portable communication device and/or e-mail. As you might imagine, he is big on brevity—he limits meetings to 45 minutes, and his e-mail and voice mail messages are usually short. He notes, "I'm brief, but that's better than not responding."

The best part of Donald's job? The store visits. "Whenever I go into a Starbucks, I walk into the back of the counter, put on an apron, and start talking to our partners."

Source: J. Donald, "A Double Shot of Productivity," *Fortune,* October 16, 2006, p. 51.

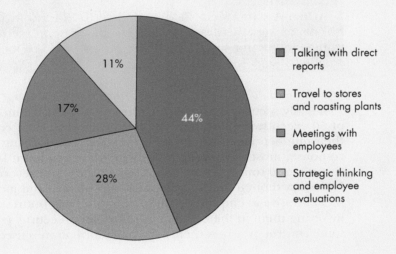

- ■ Talking with direct reports
- ■ Travel to stores and roasting plants
- ■ Meetings with employees
- □ Strategic thinking and employee evaluations

Effective KM begins by identifying what knowledge matters to the organization.[36] Management needs to review processes to identify those that provide the most value. Then it can develop computer networks and databases that can make that information readily available to the people who need it the most. But KM won't work unless the culture supports sharing of information.[37] As we'll show in Chapter 14, information that is important and scarce can be a potent source of power. And people who hold that power are often reluctant to share it with others. So KM requires an organizational culture that promotes, values, and rewards sharing knowledge. Finally, KM must provide the mechanisms and the motivation for employees to share knowledge that employees find useful on the job and enables them to achieve better performance.[38] *More* knowledge isn't necessarily *better* knowledge. Information overload needs to be avoided by designing the system to capture only pertinent information and then organizing it so it can be quickly accessed by the people whom it can help.

knowledge management (KM) *The process of organizing and distributing an organization's collective wisdom so the right information gets to the right people at the right time.*

With the average age of its aerospace engineers at 54, defense contractor Northrop Grumman has developed a knowledge-based system to transfer knowledge from older to younger employees. Northrop has created a culture of knowledge sharing by forming "communities of practice," groups from different divisions that meet in person and online to share information. Aerospace engineer Tamra Johnson, shown here, started a community of practice for new engineers so they could learn from retired project managers and older employees.

Finally, security is a huge concern with any KM system. A Merrill Lynch survey of 50 executives found that 52 percent rated leaks of company information as their number-one information security concern, topping viruses and hackers. In response, most companies actively monitor employee Internet use and e-mail records, and some even use video surveillance and record phone conversations. Necessary though they may be, such surveillance and monitoring practices may seem invasive to employees. An organization can buttress employee concerns by involving them in the creation of information-security policies and giving them some control over how their personal information is used.[39]

Choice of Communication Channel

> 7   *Show how channel richness underlies the choice of communication channel.*

Neal L. Patterson, CEO at medical software maker Cerner Corp., likes e-mail. Maybe too much so. Upset with his staff's work ethic, he recently sent a seething e-mail to his firm's 400 managers.[40] Here are some of that e-mail's highlights:

Hell will freeze over before this CEO implements ANOTHER EMPLOYEE benefit in this Culture. . . . We are getting less than 40 hours of work from a large number of our Kansas City-based employees. The parking lot is sparsely used at 8 A.M.; likewise at 5 P.M. As managers—you either do not know what your EMPLOYEES are doing; or YOU do not CARE. . . . You have a problem and you will fix it or I will replace you. . . . What you are doing, as managers, with this company makes me SICK.

Patterson's e-mail additionally suggested that managers schedule meetings at 7 A.M., 6 P.M., and Saturday mornings; promised a staff reduction of 5 percent and institution of a time-clock system; and Patterson's intention to charge unapproved absences to employees' vacation time.

Within hours of this e-mail, copies of it had made its way onto a Yahoo! Web site. And within 3 days, Cerner's stock price had plummeted 22 percent.

Although one can argue whether such harsh criticism should be communicated at all, one thing is certainly clear: Patterson erred by selecting the wrong channel for his message. Such an emotional and sensitive message would likely have been better received in a face-to-face meeting.

Why do people choose one channel of communication over another—for instance, a phone call instead of a face-to-face talk? Is there any general insight we might be able to provide regarding choice of communication channel? The answer to the latter question is a qualified "yes." A model of media richness has been developed to explain channel selection among managers.[41]

Research has found that channels differ in their capacity to convey information. Some are rich in that they have the ability to (1) handle multiple cues simultaneously, (2) facilitate rapid feedback, and (3) be very personal. Others are lean in that they score low on these three factors. As Exhibit 11-6 illustrates, face-to-face conversation scores highest in terms of **channel richness** because it provides for the maximum amount of information to be transmitted during a communication episode. That is, it offers multiple information cues (words, postures, facial expressions, gestures, intonations), immediate feedback (both verbal and nonverbal), and the personal touch of "being there." Impersonal written media such as formal reports and bulletins rate lowest in richness.

The choice of one channel over another depends on whether the message is routine or nonroutine. The former types of messages tend to be straightforward and have a minimum of ambiguity. The latter are likely to be complicated and have the potential for misunderstanding. Managers can communicate routine messages efficiently through channels that are lower in richness. However, they can communicate nonroutine messages effectively only by selecting rich channels. Referring back to the Cerner Corp. example, it appears that Neal Patterson used a channel relatively low in richness (e-mail) to convey a

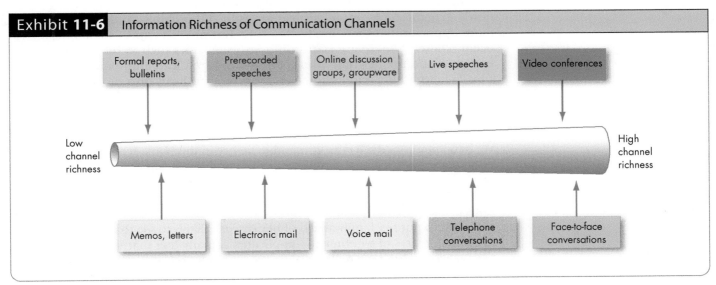

Exhibit 11-6   Information Richness of Communication Channels

Low channel richness — Formal reports, bulletins; Prerecorded speeches; Online discussion groups, groupware; Live speeches; Video conferences; Memos, letters; Electronic mail; Voice mail; Telephone conversations; Face-to-face conversations — High channel richness

Source: Based on R. H. Lengel and R. L. Daft, "The Selection of Communication Media as an Executive Skill," *Academy of Management Executive*, August 1988, pp. 225–232; and R. L. Daft and R. H. Lengel, "Organizational Information Requirements, Media Richness, and Structural Design," *Managerial Science*, May 1996, pp. 554–572. Reproduced from R. L. Daft and R. A. Noe, *Organizational Behavior* (Fort Worth, TX: Harcourt, 2001), p. 311.

channel richness   *The amount of information that can be transmitted during a communication episode.*

message that, because of its nonroutine nature and complexity, should have been conveyed using a rich communication medium.

Evidence indicates that high-performing managers tend to be more media sensitive than low-performing managers.[42] That is, they're better able to match appropriate media richness with the ambiguity involved in the communication.

The media richness model is consistent with organizational trends and practices of the past decade. It is not just coincidence that more and more senior managers have been using meetings to facilitate communication and regularly leaving the isolated sanctuary of their executive offices to manage by walking around. These executives are relying on richer channels of communication to transmit the more ambiguous messages they need to convey. The past decade has been characterized by organizations closing facilities, imposing large layoffs, restructuring, merging, consolidating, and introducing new products and services at an accelerated pace—all nonroutine messages high in ambiguity and requiring the use of channels that can convey a large amount of information. It is not surprising, therefore, to see the most effective managers expanding their use of rich channels.

Barriers to Effective Communication

8   *Identify common barriers to effective communication.*

A number of barriers can retard or distort effective communication. In this section, we highlight the most important of these barriers.

Filtering

Filtering refers to a sender's purposely manipulating information so it will be seen more favorably by the receiver. For example, when a manager tells his boss what he feels his boss wants to hear, he is filtering information.

The major determinant of filtering is the number of levels in an organization's structure. The more vertical levels in the organization's hierarchy, the more opportunities there are for filtering. But you can expect some filtering to occur wherever there are status differences. Factors such as fear of conveying bad news and the desire to please one's boss often lead employees to tell their superiors what they think those superiors want to hear, thus distorting upward communications.

Selective Perception

We have mentioned selective perception before in this book. It appears again here because the receivers in the communication process selectively see and hear based on their needs, motivations, experience, background, and other personal characteristics. Receivers also project their interests and expectations into communications as they decode them. An employment interviewer who expects a female job applicant to put her family ahead of her career is likely to see that in female applicants, regardless of whether the applicants actually feel that way. As we said in Chapter 5, we don't see reality; we interpret what we see and call it reality.

Information Overload

Individuals have a finite capacity for processing data. When the information we have to work with exceeds our processing capacity, the result is **information overload**. And with e-mails, IM, phone calls, faxes, meetings, and the need to keep current in one's field, the potential for today's managers and professionals to suffer from information overload is high.

What happens when individuals have more information than they can sort out and use? They tend to select, ignore, pass over, or forget information. Or

Call-center operators at Wipro Spectramind in New Delhi, India, speak English in serving their customers from the United States and the United Kingdom. But even though the operators and customers speak a common language, communication barriers exist because of differences in the countries' cultures and language accents. To overcome these barriers, the operators receive training in American and British pop culture so they can make small talk and are taught to speak with Western accents so they can be more easily understood by the calling clients.

they may put off further processing until the overload situation is over. In any case, the result is lost information and less effective communication.

Emotions

How the receiver feels at the time of receipt of a communication influences how he or she interprets it. The same message received when you're angry or distraught is often interpreted differently than it is when you're happy. Extreme emotions such as jubilation or depression are most likely to hinder effective communication. In such instances, we are most prone to disregard our rational and objective thinking processes and substitute emotional judgments.

Language

Even when we're communicating in the same language, words mean different things to different people. Age and context are two of the biggest factors that influence the language a person uses and the definitions he or she gives to words.

When Michael Schiller, a business consultant, was talking with his 15-year-old daughter about where she was going with her friends, he told her, "You need to recognize your ARAs and measure against them." Schiller said that in response, his daughter "looked at him like he was from outer space." (For the record, ARA stands for accountability, responsibility, and authority.) Those of you new to corporate lingo may find acronyms such as ARA, words such as "skeds" (schedules), or phrases such as "bake your noodle" (provide a service) to be bewildering, much in the same way that your parents may be mystified by the slang of your generation.[43]

The point is that although you and I probably speak a common language—English—our use of that language is far from uniform. If we knew how each of us modified the language, communication difficulties would be minimized.

filtering   *A sender's manipulation of information so that it will be seen more favorably by the receiver.*

information overload   *A condition in which information inflow exceeds an individual's processing capacity.*

The problem is that members in an organization usually don't know how those with whom they interact have modified the language. Senders tend to assume that the words and terms they use mean the same to the receiver as they do to them. This assumption is often incorrect.

Communication Apprehension

Another major barrier to effective communication is that some people—an estimated 5 to 20 percent of the population[44]—suffer from debilitating **communication apprehension**, or anxiety. Lots of people dread speaking in front of a group, but communication apprehension is a more serious problem because it affects a whole category of communication techniques. People who suffer from it experience undue tension and anxiety in oral communication, written communication, or both.[45] For example, oral apprehensives may find it extremely difficult to talk with others face-to-face or may become extremely anxious when they have to use the telephone. As a result, they may rely on memos or faxes to convey messages when a phone call would be not only faster but more appropriate.

Studies demonstrate that oral-communication apprehensives avoid situations that require them to engage in oral communication.[46] We should expect to find some self-selection in jobs so that such individuals don't take positions, such as teacher, for which oral communication is a dominant requirement.[47] But almost all jobs require some oral communication. And of greater concern is the evidence that high-oral-communication apprehensives distort the communication demands of their jobs in order to minimize the need for communication.[48] So we need to be aware that there is a set of people in organizations who severely limit their oral communication and rationalize this practice by telling themselves that more communication isn't necessary for them to do their job effectively.

Gender Differences

Gender differences are sometimes a barrier to effective communication. Deborah Tannen's research shows that men tend to use talk to emphasize status, whereas women tend to use it to create connections. These tendencies, of course, don't apply to *every* man and *every* woman. As Tannen puts it, her generalization means "a larger percentage of women or men *as a group* talk in a particular way, or individual women and men *are more likely* to talk one way or the other."[49] She has found that women speak and hear a language of connection and intimacy; men speak and hear a language of status, power, and independence. So, for many men, conversations are primarily a means to preserve independence and maintain status in a hierarchical social order. For many women, conversations are negotiations for closeness in which people try to seek and give confirmation and support.

For example, men frequently complain that women talk on and on about their problems. Women criticize men for not listening. What's happening is that when men hear a problem, they frequently assert their desire for independence and control by offering solutions. Many women, on the other hand, view telling a problem as a means to promote closeness. The women present the problem to gain support and connection, not to get advice. Mutual understanding is symmetrical. But giving advice is asymmetrical—it sets up the advice giver as more knowledgeable, more reasonable, and more in control. This contributes to distancing men and women in their efforts to communicate.

"Politically Correct" Communication

A final barrier to effective communication is politically correct communication, communication so concerned with being inoffensive that meaning and simplicity are lost or free expression is hampered. When Don Imus used inappropriate

Exhibit 11-7

THE FAR SIDE® BY GARY LARSON

© 1994 FarWorks, Inc. All Rights Reserved/Dist. by Creators Syndicate

"Well, actually, Doreen, I rather resent being called a 'swamp thing.' ... I prefer the term 'wetlands-challenged mutant.'"

Source: The Far Side by Gary Larson © 1994 Far Works, Inc. All rights reserved. Used with permission.

language to describe the Rutgers women's basketball team, he lost his job. There is no doubt that what Imus said was wrong. But is one consequence of his downfall that people will become even more politically correct in what they say, at least in certain company?

There are plenty of words and phrases we can use that invoke neither racial slur nor politically correct language. But there are also situations in which our desire to avoid offense blocks communication (by keeping us from saying what's really on our mind) or alters our communication in such a way as to make it unclear. When does being respectful turn into being politically correct? Consider a few examples:[50]

- The *Los Angeles Times* allows its journalists to use the term *old age* but cautions that the onset of old age varies from "person to person," so a group of 75-year-olds aren't necessarily all old.
- CNN has fined its broadcasters for using the word *foreign* instead of *international.*
- Little People of America (LPA) association prefers the term *little people* to *dwarfs* or *midgets.*

Certain words can and do stereotype, intimidate, and insult individuals. In an increasingly diverse workforce, we must be sensitive to how words might offend others. But there's a downside to political correctness: It can complicate

communication apprehension
Undue tension and anxiety about oral communication, written communication, or both.

our vocabulary, making it more difficult for people to communicate. To illustrate, you probably know what these three terms mean: *garbage, quotas,* and *women.* But each of these words also has been found to offend one or more groups. They've been replaced with terms such as *postconsumer waste materials, educational equity,* and *people of gender.* The problem is that this latter group of terms is much less likely to convey a uniform message than the words they replaced. By removing certain words from our vocabulary, we make it harder to communicate accurately. When we further replace these words with new terms whose meanings are less well understood, we reduce the likelihood that our messages will be received as we intended them.

We must be sensitive to how our choice of words might offend others. But we also have to be careful not to sanitize our language to the point at which it clearly restricts clarity of communication. There is no simple solution to this dilemma. However, you should be aware of the trade-offs and the need to find a proper balance.

Global Implications

9 Show how to overcome the potential problems in cross-cultural communication.

Effective communication is difficult under the best of conditions. Cross-cultural factors clearly create the potential for increased communication problems. This is illustrated in Exhibit 11-8. A gesture that is well understood and acceptable in one culture can be meaningless or lewd in another. Unfortunately, as business has become more global, companies' communication approaches have not kept pace. Only 18 percent of

Exhibit 11-8	Hand Gestures Mean Different Things in Different Countries

The A-OK Sign

In the United States, this is just a friendly sign for "All right!" or "Good going." In Australia and Islamic countries, it is equivalent to what generations of high school students know as "flipping the bird."

The "Hook'em Horns" Sign

This sign encourages University of Texas athletes, and it's a good luck gesture in Brazil and Venezuela. In parts of Africa, it is a curse. In Italy, it is signaling to another that "your spouse is being unfaithful."

"V" for Victory Sign

In many parts of the world, this means "victory" or "peace." In England, if the palm and fingers face inward, it means "Up yours!" especially if executed with an upward jerk of the fingers.

Finger-Beckoning Sign

This sign means "come here" in the United States. In Malaysia, it is used only for calling animals. In Indonesia and Australia, it is used for beckoning "ladies of the night."

Source: "What's A-O-K in the U.S.A. Is Lewd and Worthless Beyond," New York Times, August 18, 1996, p. E7. From Roger E. Axtell, GESTURES: The Do's and Taboos of Body Language Around the World. Copyright © 1991. This material is used by permission of Wiley.

International OB

Lost in Translation?

In global commerce, language can be a barrier to conducting business effectively. Many U.S. companies have overseas parents, including DaimlerChrysler AG, Bertelsmann, Diageo PLC, and Anglo-Dutch Unilever PLC. Similarly, U.S. companies have an overseas presence; for example, Ford has manufacturing plants in Belgium, Germany, Spain, Sweden, Turkey, and the United Kingdom. To make matters more complicated, as a result of mergers and acquisitions, companies are often owned by multiple overseas parents, creating an even greater strain on communication. Although English is the dominant language

at many multinational companies, failing to speak a host country's language can make it tougher for managers to do their jobs well, especially if they are misinterpreted or if they misinterpret what others are saying. Such communication problems make it tougher to conduct business effectively and efficiently and may result in lost business opportunities.

To avoid communication problems, many companies require their managers to learn the local language. For example, German-based Siemens requires its managers to learn the language of their host country. Ernst Behrens, the head of Siemens's China operations, learned to speak Mandarin fluently. Robert Kimmett, a former Siemens board member, believes that learning a host country's language gives managers "a better grasp of what is going on inside a company . . . not just the

facts and figures but also texture and nuance."

However, learning a foreign language can be difficult for managers. The challenge for North Americans is often deepened when the language is Asian, such as Japanese or Mandarin, because it is so different. To compensate, U.S. managers sometimes rely solely on body language and facial expressions to communicate. The problem? Cultural differences in these nonverbal forms of communication may result in serious misunderstandings. To avoid this pitfall, managers should to familiarize themselves with their host country's culture.

Source: Based on K. Kanhold, D. Bilefsky, M. Karnitschnig, and G. Parker, "Lost in Translation? Managers at Multinationals May Miss the Job's Nuances If They Speak Only English," *Wall Street Journal*, May 18, 2004, p. B.1.

companies have documented strategies for communicating with employees across cultures, and only 31 percent of companies require that corporate messages be customized for consumption in other cultures. P&G seems to be an exception; more than half of the company's employees don't speak English as their first language, so the company focuses on simple messages to make sure everyone knows what's important.[51]

Cultural Barriers   One author has identified four specific problems related to language difficulties in cross-cultural communications.[52]

First, there are *barriers caused by semantics.* As we've noted previously, words mean different things to different people. This is particularly true for people from different national cultures. Some words, for instance, don't translate between cultures. Understanding the word *sisu* will help you in communicating with people from Finland, but this word is untranslatable into English. It means something akin to "guts" or "dogged persistence." Similarly, the new capitalists in Russia may have difficulty communicating with their British or Canadian counterparts because English terms such as *efficiency, free market,* and *regulation* are not directly translatable into Russian.

Second, there are *barriers caused by word connotations.* Words imply different things in different languages. Negotiations between Americans and Japanese executives, for instance, can be difficult because the Japanese word *hai* translates as "yes," but its connotation is "yes, I'm listening" rather than "yes, I agree."

Third are *barriers caused by tone differences.* In some cultures, language is formal, and in others, it's informal. In some cultures, the tone changes, depending on the context: People speak differently at home, in social situations, and at work. Using a personal, informal style in a situation in which a more formal style is expected can be embarrassing and off-putting.

Fourth, there are *barriers caused by differences among perceptions.* People who speak different languages actually view the world in different ways. Eskimos perceive snow

Exhibit **11-9**

High- Versus Low-Context Cultures

High context	Chinese
	Korean
	Japanese
	Vietnamese
	Arab
	Greek
	Spanish
	Italian
	English
	North American
	Scandinavian
Low context	Swiss
	German

differently because they have many words for it. Thais perceive "no" differently than do Americans because the former have no such word in their vocabulary.

Cultural Context   A better understanding of the cultural barriers just discussed and their implications for communicating across cultures can be achieved by considering the concepts of high- and low-context cultures.[53]

Cultures tend to differ in the importance to which context influences the meaning that individuals take from what is actually said or written in light of who the other person is. Countries such as China, Korea, Japan, and Vietnam are **high-context cultures**. They rely heavily on nonverbal and subtle situational cues in communicating with others. What is *not* said may be more significant than what *is* said. A person's official status, place in society, and reputation carry considerable weight in communications. In contrast, people from Europe and North America reflect their **low-context cultures**. They rely essentially on words to convey meaning. Body language and formal titles are secondary to spoken and written words (see Exhibit 11-9).

What do these contextual differences mean in terms of communication? Actually, quite a lot. Communication in high-context cultures implies considerably more trust by both parties. What may appear, to an outsider, as casual and insignificant conversation is important because it reflects the desire to build a relationship and create trust. Oral agreements imply strong commitments in high-context cultures. And who you are—your age, seniority, rank in the organization—is highly valued and heavily influences your credibility. But in low-context cultures, enforceable contracts tend to be in writing, precisely worded, and highly legalistic. Similarly, low-context cultures value directness. Managers are expected to be explicit and precise in conveying intended meaning. It's quite different in high-context cultures, in which managers tend to "make suggestions" rather than give orders.

A Cultural Guide   When communicating with people from a different culture, what can you do to reduce misperceptions, misinterpretations, and misevaluations? You can begin by trying to assess the cultural context. You're likely to have fewer difficulties if people come from a similar cultural context to you. In addition, the following four rules can be helpful:[54]

1. *Assume differences until similarity is proven.*   Most of us assume that others are more similar to us than they actually are. But people from different countries are often very different from us. You are therefore far less likely to make an error if you assume that others are different from you rather than assume similarity until difference is proven.

2. *Emphasize description rather than interpretation or evaluation.*   Interpreting or evaluating what someone has said or done, in contrast to description, is based more on the observer's culture and background than on the observed situation. As a result, delay judgment until you've had sufficient time to observe and interpret the situation from the differing perspectives of all the cultures involved.

3. *Practice empathy.*   Before sending a message, put yourself in the recipient's shoes. What are his or her values, experiences, and frames of reference? What do you know about his or her education, upbringing, and background that can give you added insight? Try to see the other person as he or she really is.

4. *Treat your interpretations as a working hypothesis.*   Once you've developed an explanation for a new situation or think you empathize with someone from a foreign culture, treat your interpretation as a hypothesis that needs further testing rather than as a certainty. Carefully assess the feedback provided by recipients to see if it confirms your hypothesis. For important decisions or communiqués, you can also check with other foreign and home-country colleagues to make sure that your interpretations are on target.

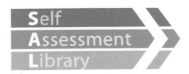

Summary and Implications for Managers

A careful review of this chapter yields a common theme regarding the relationship between communication and employee satisfaction: The less the uncertainty, the greater the satisfaction. Distortions, ambiguities, and incongruities in communications all increase uncertainty and, hence, they have a negative impact on satisfaction.[55]

The less distortion that occurs in communication, the more that goals, feedback, and other management messages to employees will be received as they were intended.[56] This, in turn, should reduce ambiguities and clarify the group's task. Extensive use of vertical, lateral, and informal channels will increase communication flow, reduce uncertainty, and improve group performance and satisfaction. We should also expect incongruities between verbal and nonverbal communiqués to increase uncertainty and to reduce satisfaction.

Findings in the chapter further suggest that the goal of perfect communication is unattainable. Yet there is evidence that demonstrates a positive relationship between effective communication (which includes factors such as perceived trust, perceived accuracy, desire for interaction, top-management receptiveness, and upward information requirements) and worker productivity.[57] Choosing the correct channel, being an effective listener, and using feedback may, therefore, make for more effective communication. But the human factor generates distortions that can never be fully eliminated. The communication process represents an exchange of messages, but the outcome is meanings that may or may not approximate those that the sender intended. Whatever the sender's expectations, the decoded message in the mind of the receiver represents his or her reality. And it is this "reality" that will determine performance, along with the individual's level of motivation and degree of satisfaction.

Paying close attention to communication effectiveness is all the more important given the ways in which communication technology has transformed the workplace. Despite the great advantages of electronic communication formats, the pitfalls are numerous. Because we gather so much meaning from how a message is communicated (voice tone, facial expressions, body language), the potential for misunderstandings in electronic communication is great. E-mail, IM and TM, and networking software are vital aspects of organizational communication, but we need to use these tools wisely, or we'll not be as effective as managers as we might be.

Finally, there are a lot of barriers to effective communication, such as gender and culture. By keeping these barriers in mind, we can overcome them and increase our communication effectiveness.

high-context cultures *Cultures that rely heavily on nonverbal and subtle situational cues in communication.*

low-context cultures *Cultures that rely heavily on words to convey meaning in communication.*

Point   Counterpoint

KEEP IT A SECRET

We're better off keeping more things to ourselves.[58] Workplace gossip is out of control, and very often, we can't trust people with secrets. Tell a friend never, ever to tell something to someone else, and you've aroused in them an irresistible desire to share the "juicy news" with others. A good rule of thumb is that if you're sure a confidante has told no one else, that probably means he or she has told only three other people. You might think this is a paranoid reaction, but research suggests that so-called confidantes rarely keep secrets, even when they swear they will.

Keeping our own secrets is normal, and most children learn to do it at any early age. People survive by protecting themselves, and when someone is keeping a secret, he usually has a good reason for doing so.

Even when we feel like confiding in someone else, it's prudent to keep confidential information to ourselves. Research shows that few of us are able to keep secrets and that if we fear certain negative consequences of telling our secrets (for example, our confidante will think less of us or will tell others), those fears not only don't keep us from blabbing, they are often justified.

Organizational secrets are all the more important to keep quiet. Organizations are rumor mills, and we can permanently damage our careers and the organizations for which we work by disclosing confidential information. Improper disclosure of organizational proprietary information is a huge cost and concern for organizations. Look at the HP debacle when board chair Patricia Dunn lost her job and two other board members resigned. The cause of this disaster? Board members telling reporters secrets they had no business telling.

The problem with keeping secrets is that they're expensive to maintain.

One social psychologist found that when people are instructed not to disclose certain information, it becomes more distracting and difficult for them to do so. In fact, the more people are instructed to keep something to themselves, the more they see the secret in everything they do. "We don't realize that in keeping it secret we've created an obsession in a jar," he says. So keeping things hidden takes a toll on our psyche—it (usually unnecessarily) adds to the mental burdens we carry with us.

Another psychologist has found that these costs are real. This researcher found that young people who experienced a traumatic experience often had more health problems later in life. As he researched the topic further, he found out why. Generally, these people conceal the event from others. He even did an experiment which showed that when people who have experienced traumatic events shared them, they later had fewer health problems than people who hadn't shared them. There isn't one identifiable reason why sharing these traumatic events seems to help people, but the result has been found repeatedly.

Thus, for mental and physical health reasons, we're better off not keeping secrets from others.

Questions for Review

1 What are the primary functions of the communication process in organizations?

2 What are the key parts of the communication process, and how do you distinguish formal and informal communication?

3 What are the differences among downward, upward, and lateral communication?

4 What are the unique challenges to oral, written, and nonverbal communication?

5 How are formal communication networks and the grapevine similar and different?

6 What are the main forms of electronic communication? What are their unique benefits and challenges?

7 Why is channel richness fundamental to the choice of communication channels?

8 What are some common barriers to effective communication?

9 What unique problems underlie cross-cultural communication?

Experiential Exercise

AN ABSENCE OF NONVERBAL COMMUNICATION

This exercise will help you to see the value of nonverbal communication to interpersonal relations.

1. The class is to split up into pairs (Party A and Party B).

2. Party A is to select a topic from the following list:

   a. Managing in the Middle East is significantly different from managing in North America.

   b. Employee turnover in an organization can be functional.

   c. Some conflict in an organization is good.

   d. Whistle-blowers do more harm than good for an organization.

   e. An employer has a responsibility to provide every employee with an interesting and challenging job.

   f. Everyone should register to vote.

   g. Organizations should require all employees to undergo regular drug tests.

   h. Individuals who have majored in business or economics make better employees than those who have majored in history or English.

   i. The place where you get your college degree is more important in determining your career success than what you learn while you're there.

   j. It's unethical for a manager to purposely distort communications to get a favorable outcome.

3. Party B is to choose a position on this topic (for example, arguing *against* the view that "some conflict in an organization is good"). Party A now must automatically take the opposite position.

4. The two parties have 10 minutes in which to debate their topic. The catch is that the individuals can only communicate verbally. They may *not* use gestures, facial movements, body movements, or any other nonverbal communication. It may help for each party to sit on their hands to remind them of their restrictions and to maintain an expressionless look.

5. After the debate is over, form groups of six to eight and spend 15 minutes discussing the following:

   a. How effective was communication during these debates?

   b. What barriers to communication existed?

   c. What purposes does nonverbal communication serve?

   d. Relate the lessons learned in this exercise to problems that might occur when communicating on the telephone or through e-mail.

Ethical Dilemma

DEFINING THE BOUNDARIES OF TECHNOLOGY

You work for a company that has no specific policies regarding non-work-related uses of computers and the Internet. It also has no electronic monitoring devices to determine what employees are doing on their computers. Are any of the following actions unethical? Explain your position on each.

a. Using the company's e-mail system for personal reasons during the workday

b. Playing computer games during the workday

c. Using your office computer for personal use (to check ESPN.com, shop online) during the workday

d. Looking for a mate on an Internet dating service Web site during the workday

e. Visiting "adult" Web sites on your office computer during the workday

f. Using your employer's portable communication device (Blackberry) for personal use

g. Conducting any of the above activities at work but before or after normal work hours

h. For telecommuters working from home, using a computer and Internet access line paid for by your employer to visit online shopping or dating-service sites during normal working hours

Case Incident 1

DIANNA ABDALA

To illustrate how precious e-mail is, consider the case of Dianna Abdala. In 2005, Abdala was a recent graduate of Suffolk University's law school, and she passed the bar exam. She then interviewed with and was offered a job at a law firm started by William Korman, a former state prosecutor.

The following is a summary of their e-mail communications:

- - - - -Original Message- - - - -
From: Dianna Abdala
Sent: Friday, February 03, 2006 9:23 p.m.
To: William A. Korman
Subject: Thank you

Dear Attorney Korman,

At this time, I am writing to inform you that I will not be accepting your offer. After careful consideration, I have come to the conclusion that the pay you are offering would neither fulfill me nor support the lifestyle I am living in light of the work I would be doing for you. I have decided instead to work for myself, and reap 100% of the benefits that I sew [sic].

Thank you for the interviews.

Dianna L. Abdala, Esq.

- - - - -Original Message- - - - -
From: William A. Korman
To: Dianna Abdala
Sent: Monday, February 06, 2006 12:15 p.m.
Subject: RE: Thank you

Dianna- -

Given that you had two interviews, were offered and accepted the job (indeed, you had a definite start date), I am surprised that you chose an e-mail and a 9:30 p.m. voicemail message to convey this information to me. It smacks of immaturity and is quite unprofessional. Indeed, I did rely upon your acceptance by ordering stationary [sic] and business cards with your name, reformatting a computer and setting up both internal and external e-mails for you here at the office. While I do not quarrel with your reasoning, I am extremely disappointed in the way this played out. I sincerely wish you the best of luck in your future endeavors.

Will Korman

- - - - -Original Message- - - - -
From: Dianna Abdala
Sent: Monday, February 06, 2006 4:01 p.m.
To: William A. Korman
Subject: Re: Thank you

A real lawyer would have put the contract into writing and not exercised any such reliance until he did so.

Again, thank you.

- - - - -Original Message- - - - -
From: William A. Korman
To: Dianna Abdala
Sent: Monday, February 06, 2006 4:18 p.m.
Subject: RE: Thank you

Thank you for the refresher course on contracts. This is not a bar exam question. You need to realize that this is a very small legal community, especially the criminal defense bar. Do you really want to start pissing off more experienced lawyers at this early stage of your career?

- - - - -Original Message- - - - -
From: Dianna Abdala
To: William A. Korman
Sent: Monday, February 06, 2006 4:28 p.m.
Subject: Re: Thank you

bla bla bla

After this e-mail exchange, Korman forwarded the correspondence to several colleagues, and it quickly spread exponentially.

Questions

1. With whom do you side here—Abdala or Korman?

2. What mistakes do you think each party made?

3. Do you think this exchange will damage Abdala's career? Korman's firm?

4. What does this exchange tell you about the limitations of e-mail?

Sources: "Dianna Abdala," *Wikipedia* (http://en.wikipedia.org/wiki/Dianna_Abdala); and J. Sandberg, "Infamous Email Writers Aren't Always Killing Their Careers After All," *Wall Street Journal,* February 21, 2006, p. B1.

Case Incident 2

DO YOU NEED A SPEECH COACH?

Speech coaching is a growing business. In a way, this is surprising. As noted earlier, more and more communication is electronic, seemingly making the quality of one's speaking skills less important. Although electronic forms of communication clearly have grown exponentially, that doesn't mean that oral communication no longer matters, especially for some jobs.

Consider Michael Sipe, president of Private Equities, a small mergers and acquisitions firm in Silicon Valley. Sipe worked with a communications coach to give him the edge when pitching his company's services relative to competitors. "If a customer can't determine who is any better or different or worse, then they are left with a conversation about price," says Snipe. "And as a business owner, if you're only in a price conversation, that's a losing conversation. It is really important to paint a picture of why should do business with them in a very compelling way." Snipe felt a speech coach helped him do that.

To look at it another way, you can have all the expertise in the world, but if you can't effectively communicate that expertise, then you're not getting the most from your talents. R. W. Armstrong & Associates, an Indianapolis-based engineering project management company, has used speech coaches to refine its pitches. Although the investment wasn't small—the company estimates it paid $8,000 to $10,000 per day to train 25 employees—the firm believes it helped land several lucrative contracts.

Asset manager David Freeman agrees. "We may fly across the country to present for 45 minutes to a pension fund or consulting firm that can be worth $25 million, $50 million, or $100 million in the amount of money we are being given to manage," he says. "You want to increase the probability that you are going to be remembered."

So what do these coaches do? Some of their training is oriented around speech—how to communicate with excitement, how to use inflection effectively—and body language. One of the big areas is to teach people to use short sentences, to speak in sound bites, and to pause so listeners can absorb what's been said.

Questions

1. What do you think explains the growth of speech coaches in business?

2. Do you think hiring a speech coach is a good investment for managers to make?

3. Do you think you would benefit from the help of a speech coach? Why or why not?

Source: H. Chura, "Um, Uh, Like Call in the Speech Coach," *New York Times,* January 11, 2007, p. C7.

Endnotes

1. P. B. Erickson, "Drawing the Line Between Gossip, Watercooler Chat," *NewsOK.com* (June 15, 2007); and G. Cuyler, "'Hooksett 4' to Seek Judge's Aid in Getting Jobs Back," *Union Leader* (June 25, 2007).

2. See, for example, K. W. Thomas and W. H. Schmidt, "A Survey of Managerial Interests with Respect to Conflict," *Academy of Management Journal,* June 1976, p. 317.

3. "Employers Cite Communication Skills, Honesty/Integrity as Key for Job Candidates," *IPMA-HR Bulletin* (March 23, 2007), p. 1.

4. W. G. Scott and T. R. Mitchell, *Organization Theory: A Structural and Behavioral Analysis* (Homewood, IL: Irwin, 1976).

5. D. K. Berlo, *The Process of Communication* (New York: Holt, Rinehart & Winston, 1960), pp. 30–32.

6. J. Langan-Fox, "Communication in Organizations: Speed, Diversity, Networks, and Influence on Organizational Effectiveness, Human Health, and Relationships," in N. Anderson, D. S. Ones, H. K. Sinangil, and C. Viswesvaran (eds.), *Handbook of Industrial, Work and Organizational Psychology*, vol. 2 (Thousand Oaks, CA: Sage, 2001), p. 190.

7. R. L. Simpson, "Vertical and Horizontal Communication in Formal Organizations," *Administrative Science Quarterly*, September 1959, pp. 188–196; B. Harriman, "Up and Down the Communications Ladder," *Harvard Business Review*, September–October 1974, pp. 143–151; A. G. Walker and J. W. Smither, "A Five-Year Study of Upward Feedback: What Managers Do with Their Results Matter," *Personnel Psychology*, Summer 1999, pp. 393–424; and J. W. Smither and A. G. Walker, "Are the Characteristics of Narrative Comments Related to Improvement in Multirater Feedback Ratings Over Time?" *Journal of Applied Psychology* 89, no. 3 (June 2004), pp. 575–581.

8. P. Dvorak, "How Understanding the 'Why' of Decisions Matters," *Wall Street Journal* (March 19, 2007), p. B3.

9. K. Gurchiek, "Employers Show 'Top-Down Bias' on Employee Input," *HRWeek*, September 26, 2006, p. 1; and A. Pomeroy, "CEOs Emphasize Listening to Employees," *HRMagazine*, January 2007, p. 14.

10. E. Nichols, "Hyper-Speed Managers," *HRMagazine*, April 2007, pp. 107–110.

11. L. Dulye, "Get Out of Your Office," *HRMagazine*, July 2006, pp. 99–101.

12. L. S. Rashotte, "What Does That Smile Mean? The Meaning of Nonverbal Behaviors in Social Interaction," *Social Psychology Quarterly*, March 2002, pp. 92–102.

13. J. Fast, *Body Language* (Philadelphia: M. Evan, 1970), p. 7.

14. A. Mehrabian, *Nonverbal Communication* (Chicago: Aldine-Atherton, 1972).

15. N. M. Henley, "Body Politics Revisited: What Do We Know Today?" in P. J. Kalbfleisch and M. J. Cody (eds.), *Gender, Power, and Communication in Human Relationships* (Hillsdale, NJ: Erlbaum, 1995), pp. 27–61.

16. See, for example, N. B. Kurland and L. H. Pelled, "Passing the Word: Toward a Model of Gossip and Power in the Workplace," *Academy of Management Review*, April 2000, pp. 428–438; and N. Nicholson, "The New Word on Gossip," *Psychology Today*, June 2001, pp. 41–45.

17. Cited in "Heard It Through the Grapevine," *Forbes*, February 10, 1997, p. 22.

18. See, for instance, J. W. Newstrom, R. E. Monczka, and W. E. Reif, "Perceptions of the Grapevine: Its Value and Influence," *Journal of Business Communication*, Spring 1974, pp. 12–20; and S. J. Modic, "Grapevine Rated Most Believable," *IndustryWeek*, May 15, 1989, p. 14.

19. K. Davis, "Management Communication and the Grapevine," *Harvard Business Review*, September–October 1953, pp. 43–49.

20. K. Davis, cited in R. Rowan, "Where Did That Rumor Come From?" *Fortune*, August 13, 1979, p. 134.

21. R. L. Rosnow and G. A. Fine, *Rumor and Gossip: The Social Psychology of Hearsay* (New York: Elsevier, 1976).

22. J. K. Bosson, A. B. Johnson, K. Niederhoffer, and W. B. Swann, Jr., "Interpersonal Chemistry Through Negativity: Bonding by Sharing Negative Attitudes About Others," *Personal Relationships* 13 (2006), pp. 135–150.

23. B. Gates, "How I Work," *Fortune*, April 17, 2006, http://money.cnn.com/2006/03/30/news/newsmakers/gates_howiwork_fortune/.

24. D. Brady, "*!#?@ the E-mail. Can We Talk?" *BusinessWeek*, December 4, 2006, p. 109.

25. E. Binney, "Is E-mail the New Pink Slip?" *HR Magazine*, November 2006, pp. 32–33; and R. L. Rundle, "Critical Case: How an Email Rant Jolted a Big HMO," *Wall Street Journal*, April 24, 2007, pp. A1, A16.

26. "Some Email Recipients Say 'Enough Already'," *Gainesville (Florida) Sun*, June 3, 2007, p. 1G.

27. D. Goleman, "Flame First, Think Later: New Clues to E-mail Misbehavior," *New York Times*, February 20, 2007, p. D5; and E. Krell, "The Unintended Word," *HRMagazine*, August 2006, pp. 50–54.

28. R. Zeidner, "Keeping E-mail in Check," *HRMagazine*, June 2007, pp. 70–74; "E-mail May Be Hazardous to Your Career," *Fortune*, May 14, 2007, p. 24; "More Firms Fire Employees for E-mail Violations," *Gainesville (Florida) Sun*, June 6, 2006, p. B1.

29. Cited in C. Y. Chen, "The IM Invasion," *Fortune*, May 26, 2003, pp. 135–138.

30. C. Hymowitz, "Have Advice, Will Travel," *Wall Street Journal*, June 5, 2006, pp. B1, B3.

31. "Survey Finds Mixed Reviews on Checking E-mail During Meetings," *IPMA-HR Bulletin*, April 27, 2007, p. 1.

32. K. Gurchiek, "Shoddy Writing Can Trip Up Employees, Organizations," *SHRM Online*, April 27, 2006, pp. 1–2.

33. D. Lidsky, "It's Not Just Who You Know," *Fast Company*, May 2007, p. 56.

34. A. Bahney, "Interns? No Bloggers Need Apply," *New York Times*, May 25, 2006, pp. 1–2; "Bosses Battle Risk by Firing E-mail, IM & Blog Violators," *IPMA-HR Bulletin*, January 12, 2007, pp. 1–2; G. Krants, "Blogging with a Vendetta," *Workforce Week* 8, no. 25 (June 10, 2007), www.workforce.com/section/quick_takes/49486_3.html. D. Jones, "Sun CEO Sees Competitive Advantage in Blogging," *USA Today*, June 26, 2006, p. 7B; and B. Leonard, "Blogs Can Present New Challenges to Employers," *SHRM Online*, March 13, 2006, pp. 1–2.

35. P. R. Carlile, "Transferring, Translating, and Transforming: An Integrative Framework for Managing Knowledge Across Boundaries," *Organization Science* 15, no. 5 (September–October 2004), pp. 555–568; and S. Thurm, "Companies Struggle to Pass on Knowledge That Workers Acquire," *Wall Street Journal*, January 23, 2006, p. B1.

36. B. Fryer, "Get Smart," *INC*, September 15, 1999, p. 63.

37. E. Truch, "Managing Personal Knowledge: The Key to Tomorrow's Employability," *Journal of Change Management*, December 2001, pp. 102–105; and D. Mason and D. J. Pauleen, "Perceptions of Knowledge Management: A Qualitative Analysis," *Journal of Knowledge Management* 7, no. 4 (2003), pp. 38–48.

38. J. Gordon, "Intellectual Capital and You," *Training*, September 1999, p. 33.

39. "At Many Companies, Hunt for Leakers Expands Arsenal of Monitoring Tactics," *Wall Street Journal* September 11, 2006, pp. B1, B3; and B. J. Alge, G. A. Ballinger, S. Tangirala, and J. L.

Oakley, "Information Privacy in Organizations: Empowering Creative and Extrarole Performance," *Journal of Applied Psychology* 91, no. 1 (2006), pp. 221–232.

40. T. M. Burton and R. E. Silverman, "Lots of Empty Spaces in Cerner Parking Lot Get CEO Riled Up," *Wall Street Journal*, March 30, 2001, p. B3; and E. Wong, "A Stinging Office Memo Boomerangs," *New York Times*, April 5, 2001, p. C1.

41. See R. L. Daft and R. H. Lengel, "Information Richness: A New Approach to Managerial Behavior and Organization Design," in B. M. Staw and L. L. Cummings (eds.), *Research in Organizational Behavior*, vol. 6 (Greenwich, CT: JAI Press, 1984), pp. 191–233; R. L. Daft and R. H. Lengel, "Organizational Information Requirements, Media Richness, and Structural Design," *Managerial Science*, May 1986, pp. 554–572; R. E. Rice, "Task Analyzability, Use of New Media, and Effectiveness," *Organization Science*, November 1992, pp. 475–500; S. G. Straus and J. E. McGrath, "Does the Medium Matter? The Interaction of Task Type and Technology on Group Performance and Member Reaction," *Journal of Applied Psychology*, February 1994, pp. 87–97; L. K. Trevino, J. Webster, and E. W. Stein, "Making Connections: Complementary Influences on Communication Media Choices, Attitudes, and Use," *Organization Science*, March–April 2000, pp. 163–182; and N. Kock, "The Psychobiological Model: Towards a New Theory of Computer-Mediated Communication Based on Darwinian Evolution," *Organization Science* 15, no. 3 (May–June 2004), pp. 327–348.

42. R. L. Daft, R. H. Lengel, and L. K. Trevino, "Message Equivocality, Media Selection, and Manager Performance: Implications for Information Systems," *MIS Quarterly*, September 1987, pp. 355–368.

43. J. Sandberg, "The Jargon Jumble," *Wall Street Journal*, October 24, 2006, p. B1.

44. J. C. McCroskey, J. A. Daly, and G. Sorenson, "Personality Correlates of Communication Apprehension," *Human Communication Research*, Spring 1976, pp. 376–380.

45. See, for instance, B. H. Spitzberg and M. L. Hecht, "A Competent Model of Relational Competence," *Human Communication Research*, Summer 1984, pp. 575–599; and S. K. Opt and D. A. Loffredo, "Rethinking Communication Apprehension: A Myers-Briggs Perspective," *Journal of Psychology*, September 2000, pp. 556–570.

46. See, for example, L. Stafford and J. A. Daly, "Conversational Memory: The Effects of Instructional Set and Recall Mode on Memory for Natural Conversations," *Human Communication Research*, Spring 1984, pp. 379–402; and T. L. Rodebaugh, "I Might Look OK, But I'm Still Doubtful, Anxious, and Avoidant: The Mixed Effects of Enhanced Video Feedback on Social Anxiety Symptoms," *Behaviour Research & Therapy* 42, no. 12 (December 2004), pp. 1435–1451.

47. J. A. Daly and J. C. McCroskey, "Occupational Desirability and Choice as a Function of Communication Apprehension," *Journal of Counseling Psychology* 22, no. 4 (1975), pp. 309–313.

48. J. A. Daly and M. D. Miller, "The Empirical Development of an Instrument of Writing Apprehension," *Research in the Teaching of English*, Winter 1975, pp. 242–249.

49. D. Tannen, *Talking from 9 to 5: Men and Women at Work* (New York: Harper, 2001), p. 15.

50. Cited in J. Leo, "Falling for Sensitivity," *U.S. News & World Report*, December 13, 1993, p. 27.

51. R. E. Axtell, *Gestures: The Do's and Taboos of Body Language Around the World* (New York: Wiley, 1991); "Effective Communication: A Leading Indicator of Financial Performance," Watson Wyatt 2006, www.watsonwyatt.com; and A. Markels, "Turning the Tide at P&G," *U.S. News & World Report*, October 30, 2006, p. 69.

52. See M. Munter, "Cross-Cultural Communication for Managers," *Business Horizons*, May–June 1993, pp. 75–76.

53. See E. T. Hall, *Beyond Culture* (Garden City, NY: Anchor Press/Doubleday, 1976); E. T. Hall, "How Cultures Collide," *Psychology Today*, July 1976, pp. 67–74; E. T. Hall and M. R. Hall, *Understanding Cultural Differences* (Yarmouth, ME: Intercultural Press, 1990); R. E. Dulek, J. S. Fielden, and J. S. Hill, "International Communication: An Executive Primer," *Business Horizons*, January–February 1991, pp. 20–25; D. Kim, Y. Pan, and H. S. Park, "High- Versus Low-Context Culture: A Comparison of Chinese, Korean, and American Cultures," *Psychology and Marketing*, September 1998, pp. 507–521; M. J. Martinko and S. C. Douglas, "Culture and Expatriate Failure: An Attributional Explication," *International Journal of Organizational Analysis*, July 1999, pp. 265–293; and W. L. Adair, "Integrative Sequences and Negotiation Outcome in Same- and Mixed-Culture Negotiations," *International Journal of Conflict Management* 14, no. 3–4 (2003), pp. 1359–1392.

54. N. Adler, *International Dimensions of Organizational Behavior*, 4th ed. (Cincinnati, OH: South-Western Publishing, 2002), p. 94.

55. See, for example. R. S. Schuler, "A Role Perception Transactional Process Model for Organizational Communication-Outcome Relationships," *Organizational Behavior and Human Performance*, April 1979, pp. 268–291.

56. J. P. Walsh, S. J. Ashford, and T. E. Hill, "Feedback Obstruction: The Influence of the Information Environment on Employee Turnover Intentions," *Human Relations*, January 1985, pp. 23–46.

57. S. A. Hellweg and S. L. Phillips, "Communication and Productivity in Organizations: A State-of-the-Art Review," in *Proceedings of the 40th Annual Academy of Management Conference*, Detroit, 1980, pp. 188–192. See also B. A. Bechky, "Sharing Meaning Across Occupational Communities: The Transformation of Understanding on a Production Floor," *Organization Science* 14, no. 3 (May–June 2003), pp. 312–330.

58. Based on E. Jaffe, "The Science Behind Secrets," *APS Observer*, July 2006, pp. 20–22.

Basic Approaches to Leadership

I am more afraid of an army of 100 sheep led by a lion than an army of 100 lions led by a sheep.

—Talleyrand

12

After studying this chapter, you should be able to:

1 Define *leadership* and contrast leadership and management.

2 Summarize the conclusions of trait theories.

3 Identify the central tenets and main limitations of behavioral theories.

4 Assess contingency theories of leadership by their level of support.

5 Contrast the interactive theories path-goal and leader–member exchange.

6 Identify the situational variables in the leader-participation model.

7 Show how U.S. managers might need to adjust their leadership approaches in Brazil, France, Egypt, and China.

*i*t probably doesn't surprise you to learn that Wrigley has been making chewing gum for more than a century. What may surprise you is that until 2006, the firm had always been run by Wrigleys. Bill Wrigley, Jr., great-grandson of Wrigley founder William Wrigley, Jr., is still executive chairman of the board and actively involved in the company. However, when Wrigley, who had been CEO since 1999, shifted roles from CEO to chairman and hired William Perez, both moves surprised industry insiders.

The First Wrigley CEO Whose Name Isn't Wrigley

Perez, after all, had recently been unceremoniously dumped by Nike founder and Chairman Philip Knight. Knight claimed that Perez had failed to "wrap his arms around" Nike's culture and replaced him with a long-time Nike company veteran. Bob Nardelli (fired at Home Depot, now CEO of Chrysler) notwithstanding, fired CEOs are usually not prime candidates to become CEOs of other large companies, especially ones that had such a strong family lineage as Wrigley.

Adding to the surprise is that Perez hardly seems to fit the profile of a CEO. He is a self-described introvert who, some say, prefers numbers to people. As we'll learn in this chapter, extraversion tends to be a good predictor of leadership, especially of whether a leader will emerge. So how did Perez emerge as the first non-Wrigley to be CEO, and can an introvert really lead a Fortune 500 company?

As it turns out, Perez has been down this road before. Before joining Nike, he was CEO of S.C. Johnson, the large household products company. When Perez took over, S.C. Johnson was in the hands of Samuel C. Johnson who, like Bill Wrigley, Jr., was a fourth-generation CEO. Despite being an outsider, Perez worked so well with Johnson that staffers couldn't tell whether directives had come from Johnson or Perez.

Moreover, Wrigley's culture bears striking similarities to S.C. Johnson's. Though Wrigley is a publicly traded company and S.C. Johnson is private, both have low-key cultures and are reluctant to share many details with Wall Street investors or the business press. Since becoming CEO, Perez has worked as closely with Wrigley as he did with Johnson. The two exchange emails three or four times a day.

It's too soon to tell whether Perez will thrive as Wrigley's first outside CEO. However, it's clear that his personality and leadership style are a fit with the company's culture, even if his introverted nature doesn't fit the CEO prototype. Speaking of Perez, Wrigley said he is a "unique fit and brings in some tremendous skills."[1] ■

*a*s Wrigley's hiring of William Perez shows, leadership is all about finding managers with "the right stuff"—the qualities to successfully lead work groups or organizations. But what is the right stuff? Personality traits, discussed in Chapter 4 and elsewhere in the text, are only some of the qualities we might associate with effective leadership. To assess yourself on another set of qualities that we'll discuss shortly, take the following self-assessment.

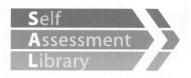

WHAT'S MY LEADERSHIP STYLE?

In the Self-Assessment Library (available on CD and online) take assessment II.B.1 (What's My Leadership Style?) and answer the following questions.

1. *How did you score on the two scales?*
2. *Do you think a leader can be both task oriented and people oriented? Do you think there are situations in which a leader has to make a choice between the two styles?*
3. *Do you think your leadership style will change over time? Why or why not?*

In this chapter, we'll look at the basic approaches to determining what makes an effective leader and what differentiates leaders from nonleaders. First, we'll present trait theories, which dominated the study of leadership up to the late 1940s. Then we'll discuss behavioral theories, which were popular until the late 1960s. Next, we'll introduce contingency theories and interactive theories. But before we review these approaches, let's first clarify what we mean by the term *leadership*.

What Is Leadership?

1 *Define* leadership *and contrast* leadership and management.

Leadership and *management* are two terms that are often confused. What's the difference between them?

John Kotter of the Harvard Business School argues that management is about coping with complexity.[2] Good management brings about order and consistency by drawing up formal plans, designing rigid organization structures, and monitoring results against the plans. Leadership, in contrast, is about coping with change. Leaders establish direction by developing a vision of the future; then they align people by communicating this vision and inspiring them to overcome hurdles.

Robert House of the Wharton School at the University of Pennsylvania basically concurs when he says that managers use the authority inherent in their designated formal rank to obtain compliance from organizational members.[3] Management consists of implementing the vision and strategy provided by leaders, coordinating and staffing the organization, and handling day-to-day problems.

Although Kotter and House provide separate definitions of the two terms, both researchers and practicing managers frequently make no such distinctions. So we need to present leadership in a way that can capture how it is used in theory and practice.

We define **leadership** as the ability to influence a group toward the achievement of a vision or set of goals. The source of this influence may be formal, such as that provided by the possession of managerial rank in an organization. Because management positions come with some degree of formally designated authority, a person may assume a leadership role simply because of the position

The personal qualities of Richard Branson, chairman of Virgin Group, make him a great leader. Branson is described as fun loving, sensitive to the needs of others, hard working, innovative, charismatic, enthusiastic, energetic, decisive, and risk taking. These traits helped the British entrepreneur build one of the most recognized and respected brands in the world.

leadership   *The ability to influence a group toward the achievement of a vision or set of goals.*

he or she holds in the organization. But not all leaders are managers, nor, for that matter, are all managers leaders. Just because an organization provides its managers with certain formal rights is no assurance that they will be able to lead effectively. We find that nonsanctioned leadership—that is, the ability to influence that arises outside the formal structure of the organization—is often as important or more important than formal influence. In other words, leaders can emerge from within a group as well as by formal appointment to lead a group.

One last comment before we move on: Organizations need strong leadership *and* strong management for optimal effectiveness. In today's dynamic world, we need leaders to challenge the status quo, to create visions of the future, and to inspire organizational members to want to achieve the visions. We also need managers to formulate detailed plans, create efficient organizational structures, and oversee day-to-day operations.

Trait Theories

2   *Summarize the conclusions of trait theories.*

Throughout history, strong leaders—Buddha, Napoleon, Mao, Churchill, Roosevelt, Thatcher, Reagan—have all been described in terms of their traits. For example, when Margaret Thatcher was prime minister of Great Britain, she was regularly described as confident, iron willed, determined, and decisive.

Trait theories of leadership differentiate leaders from nonleaders by focusing on personal qualities and characteristics. Individuals such as Margaret Thatcher, South Africa's Nelson Mandela, Virgin Group CEO Richard Branson, Apple co-founder Steve Jobs, and American Express chairman Ken Chenault are recognized as leaders and described in terms such as *charismatic, enthusiastic,* and *courageous.* The search for personality, social, physical, or intellectual attributes that would describe leaders and differentiate them from nonleaders goes back to the earliest stages of leadership research.

Research efforts at isolating leadership traits resulted in a number of dead ends. For instance, a review in the late 1960s of 20 different studies identified nearly 80 leadership traits, but only 5 of these traits were common to 4 or more of the investigations.[4] By the 1990s, after numerous studies and analyses, about the best thing that could be said was that most "leaders are not like other people," but the particular traits that were isolated varied a great deal from review to review.[5] It was a pretty confusing state of affairs.

A breakthrough, of sorts, came when researchers began organizing traits around the Big Five personality framework (see Chapter 4).[6] It became clear that most of the dozens of traits emerging in various leadership reviews could be subsumed under one of the Big Five and that this approach resulted in consistent and strong support for traits as predictors of leadership. For instance, ambition and energy—two common traits of leaders—are part of extraversion. Rather than focus on these two specific traits, it is better to think of them in terms of the more general trait of extraversion.

A comprehensive review of the leadership literature, when organized around the Big Five, has found that extraversion is the most important trait of effective leaders.[7] But results show that extraversion is more strongly related to leader emergence than to leader effectiveness. This is not totally surprising since sociable and dominant people are more likely to assert themselves in group situations. While the assertive nature of extraverts is a positive, leaders need to make sure they're not too assertive—one study found that leaders who scored very high on assertiveness were less effective than those who were moderately high.[8]

Conscientiousness and openness to experience also showed strong and consistent relationships to leadership, though not quite as strong as extraversion. The traits of agreeableness and emotional stability weren't as strongly correlated with leadership. Overall, it does appear that the trait approach does have something to offer. Leaders who are extraverted (individuals who like being around people and are able to assert themselves), conscientious (individuals who are disciplined and keep commitments they make), and open (individuals who are creative and flexible) do seem to have an advantage when it comes to leadership, suggesting that good leaders do have key traits in common.

Recent studies are indicating that another trait that may indicate effective leadership is emotional intelligence (EI), which we discussed in Chapter 8. Advocates of EI argue that without it, a person can have outstanding training, a highly analytical mind, a compelling vision, and an endless supply of terrific ideas but still not make a great leader. This may be especially true as individuals move up in an organization.[9] But why is EI so critical to effective leadership? A core component of EI is empathy. Empathetic leaders can sense others' needs, listen to what followers say (and don't say), and are able to read the reactions of others. As one leader noted, "The caring part of empathy, especially for the people with whom you work, is what inspires people to stay with a leader when the going gets rough. The mere fact that someone cares is more often than not rewarded with loyalty."[10]

Despite these claims for its importance, the link between EI and leadership effectiveness is much less investigated than other traits. One reviewer noted, "Speculating about the practical utility of the EI construct might be premature.

OB *In the News*

Bad Bosses Abound

Although much is expected of leaders, what's surprising is how rarely they seem to meet the most basic definitions of effectiveness. A recent study of 700 workers by Florida State University revealed that many employees believe their supervisors don't give credit when it's due, gossip about them behind their backs, and don't keep their word. The situation is so bad that for many employees, the study's lead author says, "they don't leave their company, they leave their boss."

Among the other findings of the study:

- 39 percent said their supervisor failed to keep promises.
- 37 percent said their supervisor failed to give credit when due.
- 31 percent said their supervisor gave them the "silent treatment" in the past year.
- 27 percent said their supervisor made negative comments about them to other employees or managers.
- 24 percent said their supervisor invaded their privacy.
- 23 percent said their supervisor blames others to cover up mistakes or minimize embarrassment.

Why do companies promote such people into leadership positions? One reason may be the Peter Principle. When people are promoted into one job (say, as a supervisor or coach) based on how well they did another (say, salesperson or player), that assumes that the skills of one role are the same as the other. The only time such people stop being promoted is when they reach their level of incompetence. Judging from the results of this study, that level of leadership incompetence is reached all too often.

Another study of CEOs revealed that while, on average, the performance of companies led by narcissistic CEOs was not worse, it was significantly more variable. The authors of this study argue this is because narcissistic CEOs encourage excessive risk-taking, noting: "They changed the rules so as to encourage more extremism, more flamboyance, go-for-broke types."

Sources: D. Fost, "Survey Finds Many Workers Mistrust Bosses," *San Francisco Chronicle,* January 3, 2007,www.SFGate.com. T. Weiss, "The Narcissistic CEO," Forbes (Aug. 29, 2006); http://www.forbes.com/.

trait theories of leadership   *Theories that consider personal qualities and characteristics that differentiate leaders from nonleaders.*

MYTH OR SCIENCE?

"Narcissists Make Better Leaders"

*t*his statement is false. Narcissism—the tendency to be self-absorbed, to be exploitive of others, and to have a grandiose self-regard—has sometimes been argued to be a necessary condition for effective leadership. If you don't admire yourself, the thinking goes, who else will? A recent research effort, however, suggests that narcissistic self-admiration is toxic to effective leadership.

The authors conducted two studies—one of lifeguards on the East Coast and another of MBA students in the Southeast. In these studies, the authors first used a standard measure of narcissism, containing items such as "I am more capable than other people," to assess participants' level of narcissism. Then they asked the participants to describe their leadership effectiveness and, independently and confidentially, they asked the participants' peers for their views of the participants' leadership effectiveness.

The authors found, for both lifeguards and MBA students, that those who scored high on narcissism thought they were better-than-average leaders. However, their peers not only disagreed, they rated them as *worse* than average. So narcissists tend to think they're very good leaders when, in the eyes of others, they are very bad leaders. It's ironic that narcissism may cause people to want to be leaders and to believe they can be good leaders when in fact they are the very people who should *not* be leaders.

This study arouses particular concern because we all may be becoming more narcissistic. Some researchers who have studied narcissism over time have found that narcissism levels in the population are rising. Poet Tony Hoagland argues that "American culture encourages self-involvement to a degree that makes it difficult for us to pay attention to anything but ourselves." Whether that statement is true is debatable, but thoughts of Paris Hilton or presidential candidate John Edwards' haircut make one wonder.[11] ■

Despite such warnings, EI is being viewed as a panacea for many organizational malaises with recent suggestions that EI is essential for leadership effectiveness."[12] But until more rigorous evidence accumulates, we can't be confident about the connection.

Based on the latest findings, we offer two conclusions. First, traits can predict leadership. Twenty years ago, the evidence suggested otherwise. But this was probably due to the lack of a valid framework for classifying and organizing traits. The Big Five seems to have rectified that. Second, traits do a better job at predicting the emergence of leaders and the appearance of leadership than in actually distinguishing between *effective* and *ineffective* leaders.[13] The fact that an individual exhibits the traits and others consider that person to be a leader does not necessarily mean that the leader is successful at getting his or her group to achieve its goals.

Behavioral Theories

The failures of early trait studies led researchers in the late 1940s through the 1960s to go in a different direction. They began looking at the behaviors exhibited by specific leaders. They wondered if there was something unique in the way that effective leaders behave. To use contemporary examples, Siebel Systems Chairman Tom Siebel and Oracle CEO Larry Ellison have been very successful in leading their companies through difficult times.[14] And they both rely on a common leadership style that is tough-talking, intense, and autocratic. Does this suggest that autocratic behavior is a preferred style for all leaders? In this section, we look at three different **behavioral theories of leadership** to answer that question. First, however, let's consider the practical implications of the behavioral approach.

3 *Identify the central tenets and main limitations of behavioral theories.*

If the behavioral approach to leadership were successful, it would have implications quite different from those of the trait approach. Trait research provides a basis for *selecting* the "right" persons to assume formal positions in groups and organizations requiring leadership. In contrast, if behavioral studies were to turn up critical behavioral determinants of leadership, we could *train* people to be leaders. The difference between trait and behavioral theories, in terms of application, lies in their underlying assumptions. Trait theories assume that leaders are born rather than made. However, if there were specific behaviors that identified leaders, then we could teach leadership; we could design programs that implanted these behavioral patterns in individuals who desired to be effective leaders. This was surely a more exciting avenue, for it meant that the supply of leaders could be expanded. If training worked, we could have an infinite supply of effective leaders.

Ohio State Studies

The most comprehensive and replicated of the behavioral theories resulted from research that began at Ohio State University in the late 1940s.[15] Researchers at Ohio State sought to identify independent dimensions of leader behavior. Beginning with over 1,000 dimensions, they eventually narrowed the list to two categories that substantially accounted for most of the leadership behavior described by employees. They called these two dimensions *initiating structure* and *consideration*.

Initiating structure refers to the extent to which a leader is likely to define and structure his or her role and those of employees in the search for goal attainment. It includes behavior that attempts to organize work, work relationships, and goals. A leader characterized as high in initiating structure could be described as someone who "assigns group members to particular tasks," "expects workers to maintain definite standards of performance," and "emphasizes the meeting of deadlines."

Consideration is described as the extent to which a person is likely to have job relationships that are characterized by mutual trust, respect for employees' ideas, and regard for their feelings. We could describe a leader high in consideration as one who helps employees with personal problems, is friendly and approachable, treats all employees as equals, and expresses appreciation and support. A recent survey of employees revealed that, when asked to indicate the factors that most motivated them at work, 66 percent mentioned appreciation. This speaks to the motivating potential of considerate leadership behavior.[16]

At one time, the results of the Ohio State studies were thought to be disappointing. One 1992 review concluded, "Overall, the research based on a two-factor conceptualization of leadership behavior has added little to our knowledge about effective leadership."[17] However, a more recent review suggests that this two-factor conceptualization was given a premature burial. A review of 160 studies found that both initiating structure and consideration were associated with effective leadership. Specifically, consideration was more strongly related to the individual. In other words, the followers of leaders who

---

behavioral theories of leadership *Theories proposing that specific behaviors differentiate leaders from nonleaders.*

initiating structure *The extent to which a leader is likely to define and structure his or her role and those of subordinates in the search for goal attainment.*

consideration *The extent to which a leader is likely to have job relationships characterized by mutual trust, respect for subordinates' ideas, and regard for their feelings.*

were high in consideration were more satisfied with their jobs and more motivated and also had more respect for their leader. Initiating structure, however, was more strongly related to higher levels of group and organization productivity and more positive performance evaluations.

University of Michigan Studies

Leadership studies undertaken at the University of Michigan's Survey Research Center at about the same time as those being done at Ohio State had similar research objectives: to locate behavioral characteristics of leaders that appeared to be related to measures of performance effectiveness.

The Michigan group also came up with two dimensions of leadership behavior that they labeled *employee oriented* and *production oriented*.[18] The **employee-oriented leaders** were described as emphasizing interpersonal relations; they took a personal interest in the needs of their employees and accepted individual differences among members. The **production-oriented leaders**, in contrast, tended to emphasize the technical or task aspects of the job; their main concern was in accomplishing their group's tasks, and the group members were a means to that end. These dimensions—employee oriented and production oriented—are closely related to the Ohio State dimensions. Employee-oriented leadership is similar to consideration, and production-oriented leadership is similar to initiating structure. In fact, most leadership researchers use the terms synonymously.[19]

The conclusions the Michigan researchers arrived at strongly favored the leaders who were employee oriented in their behavior. Employee-oriented leaders were associated with higher group productivity and greater job satisfaction. Production-oriented leaders tended to be associated with low group productivity and lower job satisfaction. Although the Michigan studies emphasized employee-oriented leadership (or consideration) over production-oriented leadership (or initiating structure), the Ohio State studies garnered more research attention and suggested that *both* consideration and initiating structure are important to effective leadership.

Drawing from the Ohio State and Michigan studies, Blake and Mouton proposed a **managerial grid** (sometimes called the *leadership grid*) based on the styles of "concern for people" and "concern for production," which essentially represent the Ohio State dimensions of consideration and initiating structure or the Michigan dimensions of employee oriented and production oriented.[20]

The grid, depicted in Exhibit 12-1, has 9 possible positions along each axis, creating 81 different positions in which the leader's style may fall. The grid does not show results produced; rather, it shows the dominating factors in a leader's thinking in regard to getting results. Based on the findings of Blake and Mouton, managers were found to perform best under a 9,9 style, as contrasted, for example, with a 9,1 (authority type) or 1,9 (laissez-faire type) style.[21] Unfortunately, the grid offers a better framework for conceptualizing leadership style than for presenting any tangible new information in clarifying the leadership quandary because it doesn't really convey any new information in addition to the Ohio State and the University of Michigan research.[22]

Summary of Trait Theories and Behavioral Theories

Judging from the evidence, the behavioral theories, like the trait theories, add to our understanding of leadership effectiveness. Leaders who have certain traits and who display consideration and structuring behaviors, do appear to be more effective. Perhaps trait theories and behavioral theories should be

Sally Jewell, CEO of Recreational Equipment, Inc., is an employee-oriented leader. During her tenure as CEO, Jewell has turned a struggling company into one with record sales. But she credits REI's success to the work of employees, stating that she doesn't believe in "hero CEOs." Jewell respects each employee's contribution to the company and includes in her leadership people who are very different from herself. Described as a leader high in consideration, she listens to employees' ideas and empowers them in performing their jobs.

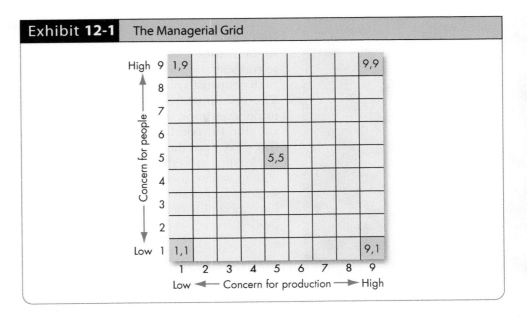

Exhibit 12-1   The Managerial Grid

integrated. For example, you would think that conscientious leaders (conscientiousness is a trait) are more likely to be structuring (structuring is a behavior). And maybe extraverted leaders (extraversion is a trait) are more likely to be considerate (consideration is a behavior). Unfortunately, we can't be sure there is a connection. Future research is needed to integrate these approaches.

Trait theories and behavioral theories aren't the last word on leadership. Missing is consideration of the situational factors that influence success or failure. Some leaders may have the right traits or display the right behaviors and still fail. For example, former Hewlett-Packard CEO Carly Fiorina seemed to have "the right stuff" but still was ousted after HP failed to perform up to expectations. As important as trait theories and behavioral theories are in determining effective versus ineffective leaders, they do not guarantee a leader's success. The context matters, too.

Contingency Theories: Fiedler Model and Situational Leadership Theory

4 *Assess contingency theories of leadership by their level of support.*

Some tough-minded leaders—such as former Home-Depot CEO Bob Nardelli or former Warnaco CEO Linda Wachner—seem to gain a lot of admirers when they take over struggling companies and help lead them out of the doldrums. However, these tough-minded leaders don't seem to "wear" well. Both Nardelli and Wachner were ousted after they had successfully transformed their companies, and Nardelli was later picked to lead another turnaround, this time at Chrysler.

employee-oriented leader   *A leader who emphasizes interpersonal relations, takes a personal interest in the needs of employees, and accepts individual differences among members.*

production-oriented leader   *A leader who emphasizes technical or task aspects of the job.*

managerial grid   *A nine-by-nine matrix outlining 81 different leadership styles.*

When Home Depot hired Robert Nardelli as CEO, the company believed he was "the right guy" to improve the company's performance. Under his leadership, Home Depot's profits, sales, and number of stores doubled. But shareholders criticized his leadership because he failed to improve the company's stock price relative to his huge pay package. After leaving Home Depot, Nardelli was hired as "the right guy" to revitalize Chrysler based on his turnaround expertise. Predicting the effectiveness of Nardelli's leadership as CEO of Home Depot and Chrysler illustrates the premise of contingency theories that leadership effectiveness is dependent on situational influences.

The rise and fall of Nardelli and Wachner illustrates that predicting leadership success is more complex than isolating a few traits or preferable behaviors. In their cases, what worked in very bad times and in very good times didn't seem to translate into long-term success. The failure by researchers in the mid-twentieth century to obtain consistent results led to a focus on situational influences. The relationship between leadership style and effectiveness suggested that under condition *a*, style *x* would be appropriate, whereas style *y* would be more suitable for condition *b*, and style *z* would be more suitable for condition *c*. But what were the conditions *a*, *b*, *c*, and so forth? It was one thing to say that leadership effectiveness was dependent on the situation and another to be able to isolate those situational conditions. Several approaches to isolating key situational variables have proven more successful than others and, as a result, have gained wider recognition. We shall consider three of these: the Fiedler model, Hersey and Blanchard's situational theory, and the path-goal theory.

Fiedler Model

The first comprehensive contingency model for leadership was developed by Fred Fiedler.[23] The **Fiedler contingency model** proposes that effective group performance depends on the proper match between the leader's style and the degree to which the situation gives control to the leader.

Identifying Leadership Style   Fiedler believes a key factor in leadership success is the individual's basic leadership style. So he begins by trying to find out what that basic style is. Fiedler created the **least preferred coworker (LPC) questionnaire** for this purpose; it purports to measure whether a person is task- or relationship-oriented. The LPC questionnaire contains sets of 16 contrasting adjectives (such as pleasant–unpleasant, efficient–inefficient, open–guarded, supportive–hostile). It asks respondents to think of all the coworkers they have ever had and to describe the one person they *least enjoyed* working with by rating that person on a scale of 1 to 8 for each of the 16 sets of contrasting adjectives. Fiedler believes that based on the respondents' answers to this LPC questionnaire, he can determine their basic leadership style. If the least preferred coworker is described in relatively positive terms (a high LPC score), then the respondent is primarily interested in good personal relations with this coworker. That is, if you essentially describe the person you are least able to work with in favorable terms, Fiedler would label you *relationship oriented*. In contrast, if the least preferred coworker is seen in relatively unfavorable terms (a low LPC score), the respondent is primarily interested in productivity and thus would be labeled *task oriented*. About 16 percent of respondents score in the middle range.[24] Such individuals cannot be classified as either relationship oriented or task oriented and thus fall outside the theory's predictions. The rest of our discussion, therefore, relates to the 84 percent who score in either the high or low range of the LPC questionnaire.

Fiedler assumes that an individual's leadership style is fixed. As we'll show, this is important because it means that if a situation requires a task-oriented

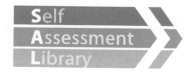

WHAT'S MY LPC SCORE?

In the Self-Assessment Library (available on CD and online) take assessment IV.E.5 (What's My LPC Score?).

leader and the person in that leadership position is relationship oriented, either the situation has to be modified or the leader has to be
replaced in order to achieve optimal effectiveness.

Defining the Situation   After an individual's basic leadership style has
been assessed through the LPC questionnaire, it is necessary to match
the leader with the situation. Fiedler has identified three contingency
dimensions that, he argues, define the key situational factors that determine leadership effectiveness. These are leader–member relations, task
structure, and position power. They are defined as follows:

1. **Leader–member relations** is the degree of confidence, trust, and
   respect members have in their leader.
2. **Task structure** is the degree to which the job assignments are procedurized (that is, structured or unstructured).
3. **Position power** is the degree of influence a leader has over power
   variables such as hiring, firing, discipline, promotions, and salary
   increases.

The next step in the Fiedler model is to evaluate the situation in terms
of these three contingency variables. Leader–member relations are either
good or poor, task structure is either high or low, and position power is
either strong or weak.

Fiedler states that the better the leader–member relations, the more
highly structured the job, and the stronger the position power, the more
control the leader has. For example, a very favorable situation (in which
the leader would have a great deal of control) might involve a payroll
manager who is well respected and whose employees have confidence in
her (good leader–member relations), for which the activities to be
done—such as wage computation, check writing, and report filing—are
specific and clear (high task structure), and the job provides considerable freedom for her to reward and punish her employees (strong position power). However, an unfavorable situation might be the disliked
chairperson of a voluntary United Way fundraising team. In this job, the
leader has very little control. Altogether, by mixing the three contingency dimensions, there are potentially eight different situations or categories in which leaders could find themselves (see Exhibit 12-2).

Matching Leaders and Situations   With knowledge of an individual's
LPC score and an assessment of the three contingency dimensions, the
Fiedler model proposes matching them up to achieve maximum leadership effectiveness.[25] Based on his research, Fiedler concluded that
task-oriented leaders tend to perform better in situations that were very

---

Fiedler contingency model   *The theory
that effective groups depend on a
proper match between a leader's style
of interacting with subordinates and
the degree to which the situation gives
control and influence to the leader.*

**least preferred coworker (LPC)
questionnaire**   *An instrument that
purports to measure whether a person
is task or relationship oriented.*

leader–member relations   *The degree
of confidence, trust, and respect
subordinates have in their leader.*

task structure   *The degree to which
job assignments are procedurized.*

position power   *Influence derived from
one's formal structural position in the
organization; includes power to hire,
fire, discipline, promote, and give
salary increases.*

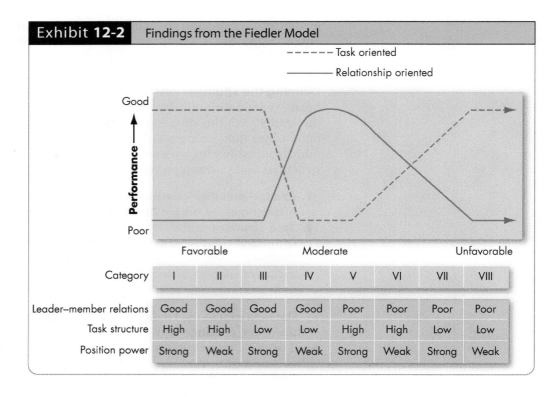

Exhibit 12-2   Findings from the Fiedler Model

Category	I	II	III	IV	V	VI	VII	VIII
Leader–member relations	Good	Good	Good	Good	Poor	Poor	Poor	Poor
Task structure	High	High	Low	Low	High	High	Low	Low
Position power	Strong	Weak	Strong	Weak	Strong	Weak	Strong	Weak

favorable to them and in situations that were very unfavorable (see Exhibit 12-2). So Fiedler would predict that when faced with a category I, II, III, VII, or VIII situation, task-oriented leaders perform better. Relationship-oriented leaders, however, perform better in moderately favorable situations—categories IV through VI. In recent years, Fiedler has condensed these eight situations down to three.[26] He now says that task-oriented leaders perform best in situations of high and low control, while relationship-oriented leaders perform best in moderate control situations.

How would you apply Fiedler's findings? You would seek to match leaders and situations. Individuals' LPC scores would determine the type of situation for which they were best suited. That "situation" would be defined by evaluating the three contingency factors of leader–member relations, task structure, and position power. But remember that Fiedler views an individual's leadership style as being fixed. Therefore, there are really only two ways in which to improve leader effectiveness.

First, you can change the leader to fit the situation—as in a baseball game, where a manager can put a right-handed pitcher or a left-handed pitcher into the game, depending on the situational characteristics of the hitter. So, for example, if a group situation rates as highly unfavorable but is currently led by a relationship-oriented manager, the group's performance could be improved by replacing that manager with one who is task oriented. The second alternative would be to change the situation to fit the leader. That could be done by restructuring tasks or increasing or decreasing the power that the leader has to control factors such as salary increases, promotions, and disciplinary actions.

Evaluation   As a whole, reviews of the major studies that have tested the overall validity of the Fiedler model lead to a generally positive conclusion. That is, there is considerable evidence to support at least substantial parts of the model.[27] If predictions from the model use only three categories rather than the original eight, there is ample evidence to support Fiedler's conclusions.[28] But there are problems with the LPC questionnaire and the practical use of the model that need to be addressed. For instance, the logic underlying the LPC questionnaire is not well understood, and studies have shown that respondents' LPC scores are not stable.[29] Also, the contingency variables are complex and difficult for practitioners to assess. It's often difficult in practice to determine how good the leader–member relations are, how structured the task is, and how much position power the leader has.[30]

Cognitive Resource Theory   More recently, Fiedler has reconceptualized his original theory.[31] In this refinement, called **cognitive resource theory**, he focuses on the role of stress as a form of situational unfavorableness and how a leader's intelligence and experience influence his or her reaction to stress.

The essence of the new theory is that stress is the enemy of rationality. It's difficult for leaders (or anyone else, for that matter) to think logically and analytically when they're under stress. Moreover, the importance of a leader's intelligence and experience to effectiveness differs under low- and high-stress situations. Fiedler and associates found that a leader's intellectual abilities correlate positively with performance under low stress but negatively under high stress. And, conversely, a leader's experience correlates negatively with performance under low stress but positively under high stress. So, it's the level of stress in the situation that determines whether an individual's intelligence or experience will contribute to leadership performance.

In spite of its newness, cognitive resource theory is developing a solid body of research support.[32] In fact, a study confirmed that when the stress level was low and the leader was directive (that is, when the leader was willing to tell people what to do), intelligence was important to a leader's effectiveness.[33] And in high-stress situations, intelligence was of little help because the leader was too cognitively taxed to put smarts to good use. Similarly, if a leader is nondirective, intelligence is of little help because the leader is afraid to put these smarts to use to tell people what to do. These results are exactly what cognitive resource theory predicts.

Hersey and Blanchard's Situational Theory

Paul Hersey and Ken Blanchard have developed a leadership model that has gained a strong following among management development specialists.[34] This model—called **situational leadership theory (SLT)**—has been incorporated into leadership training programs at more than 400 of the Fortune 500 companies; and more than 1 million managers per year from a wide variety of organizations are being taught its basic elements.[35]

Situational leadership is a contingency theory that focuses on the followers. Successful leadership is achieved by selecting the right leadership style, which Hersey and Blanchard argue is contingent on the level of the followers' readiness. Before we proceed, we should clarify two points: Why focus on the followers? And what do they mean by the term *readiness*?

The emphasis on the followers in leadership effectiveness reflects the reality that it is the followers who accept or reject the leader. Regardless of what the

cognitive resource theory   *A theory of leadership that states that stress unfavorably affects a situation and that intelligence and experience can reduce the influence of stress on the leader.*

situational leadership theory (SLT)   *A contingency theory that focuses on followers' readiness.*

These researchers at Cytos Biotechnology in Zurich, Switzerland, are developing anti-smoking and anti-obesity vaccines. The biologists and chemists at Cytos use their expertise in immunology and biotechnology in developing vaccines to treat the cause and progression of common chronic diseases that afflict millions of people worldwide. They have a high level of follower readiness. As highly educated, experienced, and responsible employees, they are able and willing to complete their tasks under leadership that gives them freedom to make and implement decisions. This leader–follower relationship is consistent with Hersey and Blanchard's situational leadership theory.

leader does, effectiveness depends on the actions of the followers. This is an important dimension that has been overlooked or underemphasized in most other leadership theories. The term *readiness*, as defined by Hersey and Blanchard, refers to the extent to which people have the ability and willingness to accomplish a specific task.

SLT essentially views the leader–follower relationship as analogous to that between a parent and a child. Just as a parent needs to relinquish control as a child becomes more mature and responsible, so too should leaders. Hersey and Blanchard identify four specific leader behaviors—from highly directive to highly laissez-faire. The most effective behavior depends on a follower's ability and motivation. SLT says that if followers are *unable* and *unwilling* to do a task, the leader needs to give clear and specific directions; if followers are *unable* and *willing*, the leader needs to display high task orientation to compensate for the followers' lack of ability and high relationship orientation to get the followers to "buy into" the leader's desires; if followers are *able* and *unwilling*, the leader needs to use a supportive and participative style; and if the employee is both *able* and *willing*, the leader doesn't need to do much.

SLT has an intuitive appeal. It acknowledges the importance of followers and builds on the logic that leaders can compensate for ability and motivational limitations in their followers. Yet research efforts to test and support the theory have generally been disappointing.[36] Why? Possible explanations include internal ambiguities and inconsistencies in the model itself as well as problems with research methodology in tests of the theory. So despite its intuitive appeal and wide popularity, any enthusiastic endorsement, at least at this time, has to be cautioned against.

Path-Goal Theory

Developed by Robert House, path-goal theory extracts elements from the Ohio State leadership research on initiating structure and consideration and the expectancy theory of motivation.[37]

The Theory   The essence of **path-goal theory** is that it's the leader's job to provide followers with the information, support, or other resources necessary for them to achieve their goals. The term *path-goal* is derived from the belief that effective leaders clarify the path to help their followers get from where they are to the achievement of their work goals and to make the journey along the path easier by reducing roadblocks.

Leader Behaviors   House identified four leadership behaviors. The *directive leader* lets followers know what is expected of them, schedules work to be done, and gives specific guidance as to how to accomplish tasks. The *supportive leader* is friendly and shows concern for the needs of followers. The *participative leader* consults with followers and uses their suggestions before making a decision. The *achievement-oriented leader* sets challenging goals and expects followers to perform at their highest level. In contrast to Fiedler, House assumes leaders are flexible and that the same leader can display any or all of these behaviors depending on the situation.

Path-Goal Variables and Predictions

As Exhibit 12-3 illustrates, path-goal theory proposes two classes of contingency variables that moderate the leadership behavior–outcome relationship: those in the environment that are outside the control of the employee (task structure, the formal authority system, and the work group) and those that are part of the personal characteristics of the employee (locus of control, experience, and perceived ability). Environmental factors determine the type of leader behavior required as a complement if follower outcomes are to be maximized, while personal characteristics of the employee determine how the environment and leader behavior are interpreted. So the theory proposes that leader behavior

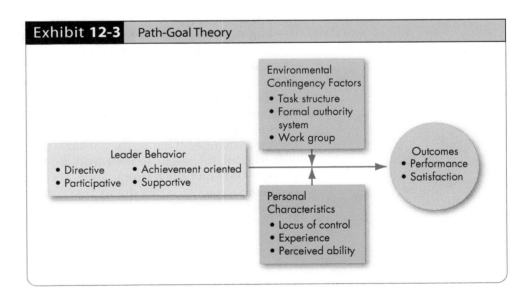

Exhibit 12-3   Path-Goal Theory

path-goal theory   *A theory that states that it is the leader's job to assist followers in attaining their goals and to provide the necessary direction and/or support to ensure that their goals are compatible with the overall objectives of the group or organization.*

will be ineffective when it is redundant with sources of environmental structure or incongruent with employee characteristics. For example, the following are illustrations of predictions based on path-goal theory:

- Directive leadership leads to greater satisfaction when tasks are ambiguous or stressful than when they are highly structured and well laid out.
- Supportive leadership results in high employee performance and satisfaction when employees are performing structured tasks.
- Directive leadership is likely to be perceived as redundant among employees with high perceived ability or with considerable experience.
- Employees with an internal locus of control will be more satisfied with a participative style.
- Achievement-oriented leadership will increase employees' expectancies that effort will lead to high performance when tasks are ambiguously structured.

Evaluation   Due to the complexity of the theory, testing path-goal theory has not proven to be easy. A review of the evidence suggests mixed support. As the authors of this review commented, "These results suggest that either effective leadership does not rest in the removal of roadblocks and pitfalls to employee path instrumentalities as path-goal theories propose or that the nature of these hindrances is not in accord with the proposition of the theories." Another review concluded that the lack of support was "shocking and disappointing."[38] These conclusions have been challenged by others who argue that adequate tests of the theory have yet to be conducted.[39] Thus, it is safe to say that the jury is still out regarding the validity of path-goal theory. Because it is so complex to test, that may remain the case for some time to come.

Summary of Contingency Theories

It's fair to say that none of the contingency theories have panned out as well as their developers had hoped. In particular, results for situational leadership theory and path-goal theory have been disappointing. Fiedler's LPC theory has fared better in the research literature.

One limitation of the contingency theories, and indeed of all the theories we've covered so far, is that they ignore the followers. Yet, as one leadership scholar noted, "leaders do not exist in a vacuum"; leadership is a symbiotic relationship between leaders and followers.[40] But the leadership theories we've covered to this point have largely assumed that leaders treat all their followers in the same manner. That is, they assume that leaders use a fairly homogeneous style with all the people in their work unit. But think about your experiences in groups. Did you notice that leaders often act very differently toward different people? Next we look at a theory that considers differences in the relationships leaders form with different followers.

Leader–Member Exchange (LMX) Theory

Think of a leader you know. Did this leader tend to have favorites who made up his or her "in-group"? If you answered "yes," you're acknowledging the foundation of leader–member exchange theory.[41] The **leader–member exchange (LMX) theory** argues that, because of time pressures, leaders establish a special relationship with a small group of their followers. These individuals make up the in-group—they are trusted, get a disproportionate amount of the leader's attention, and are more likely to

5   Contrast the interactive theories path-goal and leader–member exchange.

receive special privileges. Other followers fall into the out-group. They get less of the leader's time, get fewer of the preferred rewards that the leader controls, and have leader–follower relations based on formal authority interactions.

The theory proposes that early in the history of the interaction between a leader and a given follower, the leader implicitly categorizes the follower as an "in" or an "out," and that relationship is relatively stable over time. Leaders induce LMX by rewarding those employees with whom they want a closer linkage and punishing those with whom they do not.[42] But for the LMX relationship to remain intact, the leader and the follower must invest in the relationship.

Just precisely how the leader chooses who falls into each category is unclear, but there is evidence that leaders tend to choose in-group members because they have demographic, attitude, and personality characteristics that are similar to the leader's or a higher level of competence than out-group members[43] (see Exhibit 12-4). For example, leaders of the same gender tend to have closer (higher LMX) relationships than when leaders and followers are of different genders.[44] The key point to note here is that, even though it is the leader who is doing the choosing, it is the follower's characteristics that are driving the leader's categorizing decision.

Research to test LMX theory has been generally supportive. More specifically, the theory and research surrounding it provide substantive evidence that leaders do differentiate among followers; that these disparities are far from random; and that followers with in-group status will have higher performance ratings, engage in more helping or "citizenship" behaviors at work, and report greater satisfaction with their superior.[45] These positive findings for in-group members shouldn't be totally surprising, given our knowledge of self-fulfilling prophecy (see Chapter 5). Leaders invest their resources with those they expect to perform best. And "knowing" that in-group members are the most competent, leaders treat them as such and unwittingly fulfill their prophecy.[46]

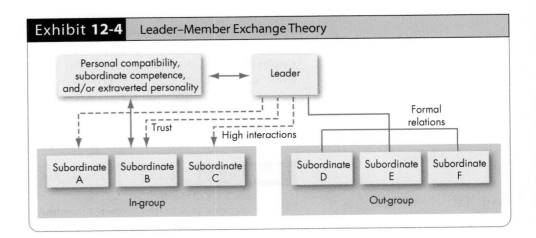

Exhibit 12-4   Leader–Member Exchange Theory

leader–member exchange (LMX) theory   *A theory that supports leaders' creation of in-groups and out-groups; subordinates with in-group status will have higher performance ratings, less turnover, and greater job satisfaction.*

Decision Theory: Vroom and Yetton's Leader-Participation Model

6 Identify the situational variables in the leader-participation model.

The final theory we'll cover in this chapter argues that *the way* the leader makes decisions is as important as *what* she or he decides. Victor Vroom and Phillip Yetton developed a **leader-participation model** that relates leadership behavior and participation in decision making.[47] Recognizing that task structures have varying demands for routine and nonroutine activities, these researchers argued that leader behavior must adjust to reflect the task structure. Vroom and Yetton's model is normative—it provides a sequential set of rules that should be followed in determining the form and amount of participation in decision making, as determined by different types of situations. The model is a decision tree incorporating seven contingencies (whose relevance can be identified by making "yes" or "no" choices) and five alternative leadership styles. More recent work by Vroom and Arthur Jago has resulted in a revision of this model.[48] The revised model retains the same five alternative leadership styles—from the leader's making the decision completely alone to sharing the problem with the group and developing a consensus decision—but adds a set of problem types and expands the contingency variables to 12. The 12 contingency variables are listed in Exhibit 12-5.

Research testing both the original and revised leader-participation models has not been encouraging, although the revised model rates higher in effectiveness.[49] Criticism has tended to focus on variables that have been omitted and on the model's overall complexity.[50] Other contingency theories demonstrate that stress, intelligence, and experience are important situational variables. Yet the leader-participation model fails to include them. But more important, at least from a practical point of view, is the fact that the model is far too complicated for the typical manager to use on a regular basis. Although Vroom and Jago have developed a computer program to guide managers through all the decision branches in the revised model, it's not very realistic to expect practicing managers to consider 12 contingency variables, eight problem types, and five leadership styles in trying to select the appropriate decision process for a specific problem.

We obviously haven't done justice in this discussion to the model's sophistication. So what can you gain from this brief review? Additional insights into relevant contingency variables. Vroom and his associates have provided us with some specific, empirically supported contingency variables that you should consider when choosing your leadership style.

Exhibit 12-5	Contingency Variables in the Revised Leader-Participation Model

1. Importance of the decision
2. Importance of obtaining follower commitment to the decision
3. Whether the leader has sufficient information to make a good decision
4. How well structured the problem is
5. Whether an autocratic decision would receive follower commitment
6. Whether followers "buy into" the organization's goals
7. Whether there is likely to be conflict among followers over solution alternatives
8. Whether followers have the necessary information to make a good decision
9. Time constraints on the leader that may limit follower involvement
10. Whether costs to bring geographically dispersed members together is justified
11. Importance to the leader of minimizing the time it takes to make the decision
12. Importance of using participation as a tool for developing follower decision skills

International OB

Cultivating an International Perspective: A Necessity for Leaders

Accounting and consulting firm PricewaterhouseCoopers (PwC) is serious about expanding the worldview of its up-and-coming leaders. So the company started the Ulysses Program, which sends the company's potential leaders to foreign countries to gain knowledge and experience in cultural diversity.

For example, PwC sent one group of managers on an 8-week consulting assignment in the Namibian outback. Their job? To help village leaders deal with the growing AIDS crisis. Without PowerPoint presentations and e-mail, the managers quickly learned to communicate in a more traditional way—face-to-face. The managers were forced to rely less on quick technologies and more on forging connections by cultivating relationships with diverse clients. By experiencing diversity firsthand at what is perhaps its extreme, PwC hopes that its managers will be better equipped to handle issues in any culture in which they conduct business. The company says that the program gives its future leaders a broad, international perspective on business issues and makes it more likely that they will find creative, unconventional solutions to complex problems.

In addition, participants can realize what they are able to accomplish when they do not have access to their usual resources. In essence, they are forced to become leaders.

The jury is still out on whether the program is effective at increasing the global leadership skills of those who participate. Nevertheless, participants of the Ulysses Program tout its benefits, and other companies have taken notice; Johnson & Johnson and Cisco Systems are just two of several companies that have adopted similar programs.

Source: Based on J. Hempel, and S. Porges, "It Takes a Village—And a Consultant," *BusinessWeek*, September 6, 2004, p. 76.

Global Implications

7 *Show how U.S. managers might need to adjust their leadership approaches in Brazil, France, Egypt, and China.*

Most of the research on the leadership theories discussed in this chapter has been conducted in English-speaking countries. Thus, we know very little about how culture might influence their validity, particularly in Eastern cultures. However, a recent analysis of the Global Leadership and Organizational Behavior Effectiveness (GLOBE) research project (see Chapter 4 for more details on this study) has produced some useful, if preliminary, insights into cultural issues that leaders need to consider.[51]

In this article, the authors sought to answer the practical question of how culture might affect a U.S. manager if he or she had been given two years to lead a project in four prototypical countries whose cultures diverged from that of the United States in different ways: Brazil, France, Egypt, and China. Let's consider each case in turn.

Brazil   Based on the GLOBE study findings of the values of Brazilian employees, a U.S. manager leading a team in Brazil would need to be team oriented, participative, and humane. This would suggest that leaders who are high on consideration, who emphasize participative decision making, and who have

leader-participation model *A leadership theory that provides a set of rules to determine the form and amount of participative decision making in different situations.*

high LPC scores would be best suited to managing employees in this culture. As one Brazilian manager said in the study, "We do not prefer leaders who take self-governing decisions and act alone without engaging the group. That's part of who we are."

France   Compared to U.S. employees, the French tend to have a more bureaucratic view of leaders and are less likely to expect them to be humane and considerate. Thus, a leader who is high on initiating structure, or relatively task oriented, will do best, and she can make decisions in a relatively autocratic manner. A manager who scores high on consideration (people-oriented) leadership may find that style backfiring in France.

Egypt   Like those in Brazil, employees in Egypt are more likely to value team-oriented and participative leadership than U.S. employees. However, Egypt is also a relatively high-power-distance culture, meaning that status differences between leaders and followers are expected. How would a U.S. manager be participative and yet act in a manner that shows his or her high level of status? According to the authors, the leaders should ask employees for their opinions, try to minimize conflicts, but also not be afraid to take charge and make the final decision (after consulting team members).

China   According to the GLOBE study, Chinese culture emphasizes being polite, considerate, and unselfish. But the culture also has a high performance orientation. These two factors suggest that both consideration and initiating structure may be important. Although Chinese culture is relatively participative compared to that of the United States, there are also status differences between leaders and employees. This suggests that, as in Egypt, a moderately participative style may work best.

Though we have little research to confirm the conclusions of this study, and of course there will always be variation across employees (not every Brazilian is more collective than every U.S. employee), the GLOBE study suggests that leaders need to take culture into account whenever they are managing employees from different cultures.

Summary and Implications for Managers

Leadership plays a central part in understanding group behavior, for it's the leader who usually provides the direction toward goal attainment. Therefore, a more accurate predictive capability should be valuable in improving group performance.

The early search for a set of universal leadership traits failed. However, recent efforts using the Big Five personality framework have generated much more encouraging results. Specifically, the traits of extraversion, conscientiousness, and openness to experience show strong and consistent relationships to leadership.

The behavioral approach's major contribution was narrowing leadership into task-oriented (initiating structure) and people-oriented (consideration) styles. As with the trait approach, results from the behavioral school were initially dismissed. But recent efforts have confirmed the importance of task- and people-oriented leadership styles.

A major shift in leadership research came when we recognized the need to develop contingency theories that included situational factors. At present, the evidence indicates that relevant situational variables include the task structure of the job; level of situational stress; level of group support; leader's intelligence and experience; and follower characteristics, such as personality, experience, ability, and motivation. Although contingency theories haven't lived up to their initial promise, the literature has provided basic support for Fiedler's LPC theory.

Finally, two other theories—leader–member exchange (LMX) theory and the leader-participation model—also contribute to our understanding of leadership. LMX theory has proved influential for its analysis of followers—whether they are included in the leader's "in-group" or were relegated to the "out group." Vroom's leader-participation model focuses on the leader's role as decision maker and considers *how* leaders make decisions (such as whether to involve followers in their decision making).

As a group, these traditional theories have enhanced our understanding of effective leadership. As we'll discover in the next chapter, however, more recent theories have shown even more promise in describing effective leadership.

Point ▶◀ Counterpoint

LEADERS ARE BORN, NOT MADE

*i*n the United States, people are socialized to believe they can be whoever they want to be—and that includes being a leader. While that makes for a nice children's tale (think *The Little Engine That Could*—"I think I can, I think I can"), the world's affairs and people's lives are not always wrapped in pretty little packages, and this is one example. Being an effective leader has more to do with what you're born with than what you do with what you have.

That leaders are born, not made, isn't a new idea. The Victorian-era historian Thomas Carlyle wrote, "History is nothing but the biography of a few great men." Although today we should modify this to include women, his point still rings true: Great leaders are what make teams, companies, and even countries great. Can anyone disagree that people like Abraham Lincoln and Franklin Roosevelt were gifted political leaders? Or that Joan of Arc and George Patton were brilliant and courageous military leaders? Or that Henry Ford, Jack Welch, Steve Jobs, and Rupert Murdoch are gifted business leaders? As one reviewer of the literature put it, "Leaders are not like other people." These leaders are great leaders because they have the right stuff—stuff the rest of us don't have, or have in lesser quantities.

If you're not yet convinced, there is new evidence to support this position. A recent study of several hundred identical twins separated at birth found an amazing correlation in their ascendance into leadership roles. These twins were raised in totally different environments—some rich, some poor, some by educated parents, others by relatively uneducated parents, some in cities, others in small towns. But the researchers found that, despite their different environments, each pair of twins had striking similarities in terms of whether they became leaders.

Other research has found that shared environment—being raised in the same household, for example—has very little influence on leadership emergence. Despite what we might like to believe, the evidence is clear: A substantial part of leadership is a product of our genes. If we have the right stuff, we're destined to be effective leaders. If we have the wrong stuff, we're unlikely to excel in that role. Leadership cannot be for everyone, and we make a mistake in thinking that everyone is equally capable of being a good leader.[52]

---

*O*f course, personal qualities and characteristics matter to leadership, as they do to most other behaviors. But the real key is what you do with what you have.

First, if great leadership were merely the possession of a few key traits—say intelligence and personality—we could simply give people a test and select the most intelligent, extraverted, and conscientious people to be leaders. But that would be a disaster. It helps to have these traits, but leadership is much too complex to be reduced to a simple formula of traits. As smart as Steve Jobs is, there are smarter and more extraverted people out there—thousands of them. That isn't the essence of what makes him, or political or military leaders, great. It is a combination of factors—upbringing, early business experiences, learning from failure, and driving ambition.

Second, great leaders tell us that the key to their leadership success is not the characteristics they had at birth but what they learned along the way.

Take Warren Buffett, who is admired not only for his investing prowess but also as a leader and boss. Being a great leader, according to Buffett, is a matter of acquiring the right habits. "The chains of habit are too light to be noticed until they are too heavy to be broken," he says. Buffett argues that characteristics or habits such as intelligence, trustworthiness, and integrity are the most important to leadership—and at least the latter two can be developed. He says, "You need integrity, intelligence and energy to succeed. Integrity is totally a matter of choice—and it is habit-forming."

Finally, this focus on "great men and great women" is not very productive. Even if it were true that great leaders were born, it's a very impractical approach to leadership. People need to believe in something, and one of those things is that they can improve themselves. If we walked around thinking we were just some accumulation of genetic markers and our entire life was just a stage in which our genes played themselves out who would want to live that way? People like the optimistic story of *The Little Engine That Could* because we have a choice to think positively (we can become good leaders) or negatively (leaders are predetermined), and it's better to be positive.[53]

Questions for Review

1 Are leadership and management different from one another? If so, how?

2 What is the premise of trait theories? What traits are associated with leadership?

3 What are the central tenets and main limitations of behavioral theories?

4 What is Fiedler's contingency model? Has it been supported in research?

5 What are the main tenets of path-goal theory? What about leader–member exchange theory?

6 What are the predictions of the leader-participation model?

7 How specifically might an American leader need to adapt to the Brazilian, French, Egyptian, and Chinese cultures?

Experiential Exercise

WHAT IS A LEADER?

1. Working on your own, write down 12 adjectives that describe an effective business leader.
2. Break into groups of four or five people each. Appoint a note-taker and spokesperson. Compare your lists, making a new list of adjectives common across two or more persons' list. (Count synonyms—decisive and forceful, for example—as the same.)
3. Each spokesperson should present the group's list to the class.
4. Across the lists, are there many similarities? What does this tell you about the nature of leadership?

Ethical Dilemma

DO ENDS JUSTIFY THE MEANS?

The power that comes from being a leader can be used for evil as well as for good. When you assume the benefits of leadership, you also assume ethical burdens. But many highly successful leaders have relied on questionable tactics to achieve their ends. These include manipulation, verbal attacks, physical intimidation, lying, fear, and control. Consider a few examples:

- Jack Welch, former head of General Electric, provided the leadership that made GE the most valuable company in the United States. He also earned the label "Neutron Jack" by firing the lowest-performing 10 percent of the company's employees every year.
- Apple CEO Steve Jobs received backdated stock options: He was allowed to purchase shares of Apple at prices well below their market price at the time he was given the options. In fact, the options were backdated so that he could buy the shares at the lowest possible price. Former Apple CFO Fred Anderson argues that he warned Jobs about the accounting problems produced by backdating but says he (Anderson) is the one who took the fall.
- Cisco Systems CEO John Chambers commented that the tough times were "likely to be just a speed bump." Tell that to the 17,000 workers—nearly 20 percent of the company's workforce—he laid off. And yet Cisco has returned to profitability.

Questions

1. What is more important in judging a leader—his or her actions or the outcomes? Which *should* be more important?
2. How much of leadership success is due to luck or other factors beyond a leader's control?
3. Are employees, shareholders, and society too quick to excuse leaders who use questionable means if they are successful in achieving their goals?
4. Is it impossible for leaders to be both ethical *and* successful?

Case Incident 1

MOVING FROM COLLEAGUE TO SUPERVISOR

Cheryl Kahn, Rob Carstons, and Linda McGee have something in common. They all were promoted within their organizations into management positions. And each found the transition a challenge.

Cheryl Kahn was promoted to director of catering for the Glazier Group of restaurants in New York City. With the promotion, she realized that things would never be the same again. No longer would she be able to participate in water-cooler gossip or shrug off an employee's chronic lateness. She says she found her new role to be daunting. "At first I was like a bulldozer knocking everyone over, and that was not well received. I was saying, 'It's my way or the highway.' And was forgetting that my friends were also in transition." She admits that this style alienated just about everyone with whom she worked.

Rob Carstons, a technical manager at IBM in California, talks about the uncertainty he felt after being promoted to being a manager from being a junior programmer: "It was a little bit challenging to be suddenly giving directives to peers, when just the day before you were one of them. You try to be careful not to offend anyone. It's strange walking into a room and the whole conversation changes. People

don't want to be as open with you when you become the boss."

Linda McGee is now president of Medex Insurance Services in Baltimore, Maryland. She started as a customer service representative with the company and then leapfrogged over colleagues in a series of promotions. Her fast rise created problems. She says colleagues "would say, 'Oh, here comes the big cheese now.' God only knows what they talked about behind my back."

Questions

1. A lot of new managers err in selecting the right leadership style when they move into management. Why do you think this happens?

2. What does this say about leadership and leadership training?

3. Which leadership theories, if any, could help new leaders deal with this type of transition?

4. Do you think it's easier or harder to be promoted internally into a formal leadership position than to come into it as an outsider? Explain.

Source: Based on D. Koeppel, "A Tough Transition: Friend to Supervisor," *New York Times*, March 16, 2003, p. BU-12.

Case Incident 2

THE KINDER, GENTLER LEADER?

The stereotypical view of a CEO—tough-minded, dominant, and hyper-aggressive—may be giving way to a more sensitive image. Nowhere is this shifting standard more apparent than at General Electric. There may be no CEO more revered for his leadership style than former CEO Jack Welch, a "tough guy" in his own words. Yet his hand-picked successor, Jeff Immelt, is remarkable for his very different leadership style. Whereas Welch was intense, brash, and directive, Immelt was described by *Financial Times* as "unshakably polite, self-deprecating and relaxed."

Of course, Immelt is only one leader, and his success at GE is hardly assured. But he's far from alone in the set of seemingly sensitive CEOs. Colgate-Palmolive CEO Reuben Mark says of his leadership credo: "I have made it my business to be sure that nothing important or creative at Colgate-Palmolive is perceived as my idea." In an interesting contrast to Chrysler CEO Bob Nardelli, Chrysler President Jim Press (formerly president of Toyota of America) embraces "servant leadership" and says one of

his main functions is to "get out of the way" and support those who work with him.

A recent study of CEOs seems to suggest that this trend is spreading. The CEOs in its sample scored, on average, 12 points *below* average on tough-mindedness. Yes, that's *below* average. As one observer of the corporate world concludes, "The Jack Welch approach appears to be on the wane."

You might think a kinder, gentler approach works only for Fortune 500 CEOs, whose very job security might rely on glowing press coverage. In the United States, though, you don't get much further from Wall Street than the Hanford, Washington, nuclear cleanup site, and there's evidence that the "nice" approach to leadership is taking hold there, too. Jerry Long, VP of operations for CH2MHILL's cleanup of the Hanford site, argues that a central part of his job is "showing them you care."

Consider the meteoric rise of Barack Obama—all the way from state senator to serious presidential contender in just 3 years. While a student at Harvard Law School, Obama was famous attorney Laurence Tribe's research assistant. Tribe said of Obama, "I've known senators, presidents. I've never known anyone with what seems to me more raw political talent. He just seems to have the surest way of calmly reaching across what are impenetrable barriers to many people." Although some have argued that Obama's campaign represents an emphasis of style over substance, it may be that after years of acrimonious political wars, people consider the *how* as important as the *what*. Regardless of whether Obama makes it to the White House, it seems clear that part of his incredible rise reflects people's desire for a kinder, gentler leader.

Questions

1. Do you think the kinder, gentler leader image is just a fad?

2. Do you think the kinder, gentler leadership approach works better in some situations than others? It is possible that Welch and Immelt are *both* effective leaders?

3. Do you think the leadership style of people like Immelt and Obama is a result of nature, nurture, or both? What factors can you think of to support your answer?

Sources: Based on J. Hollon, "Leading Well Is Simple," *Workforce Management*, November 6, 2006, p. 50; A. Pomeroy, "CEOs Show Sensitive Side," *HRMagazine*, August 2006, p. 14; P. Bacon, Jr., "Barack Obama," *Time*, April 18, 2005, p. 60–61; J. Marquez, "Kindness Pays . . . Or Does It?" *Workforce Management*, June 25, 2007, pp. 40–41; and C. Woodyard, "Press: 'I was in love with cars every second,'" *USA Today*, January 23, 2006, p. 5B.

Endnotes

1. J. Weber and P. Gogoi "Why Wrigley and Perez Need Each Other," *BusinessWeek*, October 23, 2006, pp. 1–2; and D. Carpenter, "Wrigley Hires Perez to Serve as Its CEO," *Washington Post*, October 23, 2006,

2. J. P. Kotter, "What Leaders Really Do," *Harvard Business Review*, May–June 1990, pp. 103–111; and J. P. Kotter, *A Force for Change: How Leadership Differs from Management* (New York: The Free Press, 1990).

3. R. J. House and R. N. Aditya, "The Social Scientific Study of Leadership: Quo Vadis?" *Journal of Management* 23, no. 3 (1997), p. 445.

4. J. G. Geier, "A Trait Approach to the Study of Leadership in Small Groups," *Journal of Communication*, December 1967, pp. 316–323.

5. S. A. Kirkpatrick and E. A. Locke, "Leadership: Do Traits Matter?" *Academy of Management Executive*, May 1991, pp. 48–60; and S. J. Zaccaro, R. J. Foti, and D. A. Kenny, "Self-Monitoring and Trait-Based Variance in Leadership: An Investigation of Leader Flexibility Across Multiple Group Situations," *Journal of Applied Psychology*, April 1991, pp. 308–315.

6. See T. A. Judge, J. E. Bono, R. Ilies, and M. Werner, "Personality and Leadership: A Review," paper presented at the 15th Annual Conference of the Society for Industrial and Organizational Psychology, New Orleans, 2000; and T. A. Judge, J. E. Bono, R. Ilies, and M. W. Gerhardt, "Personality and Leadership: A Qualitative and Quantitative Review," *Journal of Applied Psychology*, August 2002, pp. 765–780.

7. Judge, Bono, Ilies, and Gerhardt, "Personality and Leadership."

8. D. R. Ames and F. J. Flynn, "What Breaks a Leader: The Curvilinear Relation Between Assertiveness and Leadership," *Journal of Personality and Social Psychology* 92, no. 2 (2007), pp. 307–324.

9. This section is based on D. Goleman, "What Makes a Leader?" *Harvard Business Review*, November–December 1998, pp. 93–102; J. M. George, "Emotions and Leadership: The Role of Emotional Intelligence," *Human Relations*, August 2000, pp. 1027–55; C.-S. Wong and K. S. Law, "The Effects of Leader and Follower Emotional Intelligence on Performance and Attitude: An Exploratory Study," *Leadership Quarterly*, June 2002, pp. 243–274; and D. R. Caruso, and C. J. Wolfe, "Emotional Intelligence and Leadership Development" in D. David and S. J. Zaccaro (eds.), *Leader Development for Transforming Organizations: Growing Leaders for Tomorrow* (Mahwah, NJ: Lawrence Erlbaum, 2004) pp. 237–263.

10. J. Champy, "The Hidden Qualities of Great Leaders," *Fast Company* 76 (November 2003), p. 135.

11. T. A. Judge, J. A. LePine, and B. L. Rich, "Loving Yourself Abundantly: Relationship of the Narcissistic Personality to Self- and Other Perceptions of Workplace Deviance, Leadership, and Task and Contextual Performance," *Journal of Applied Psychology* 91, no. 4 (2006), pp. 762–776.

12. J. Antonakis, "Why 'Emotional Intelligence' Does Not Predict Leadership Effectiveness: A Comment on Prati, Douglas, Ferris, Ammeter, and Buckley (2003)," *International Journal of Organizational Analysis* 11 (2003), pp. 355–361; see also M. Zeidner, G. Matthews, and R. D. Roberts, "Emotional Intelligence in the Workplace: A Critical Review," *Applied Psychology: An International Review* 53 (2004), pp. 371–399.

13. Ibid.; Ibid 7; R. G. Lord, C. L. DeVader, and G. M. Alliger, "A Meta-analysis of the Relation Between Personality Traits and Leadership Perceptions: An Application of Validity Generalization Procedures," *Journal of Applied Psychology*, August 1986, pp. 402–410; and J. A. Smith and R. J. Foti, "A Pattern Approach to the Study of Leader Emergence," *Leadership Quarterly*, Summer 1998, pp. 147–160.

14. See S. Hansen, "Stings Like a Bee," *INC.*, November 2002, pp. 56–64; J. Greenbaum, "Is Ghengis on the Hunt Again?" *internetnews.com*, January 14, 2005, www.internetnews.com/commentary/article.php/3459771.

15. R. M. Stogdill and A. E. Coons (eds.), *Leader Behavior: Its Description and Measurement*, Research Monograph no. 88 (Columbus: Ohio State University, Bureau of Business Research, 1951). This research is updated in C. A. Schriesheim, C. C. Cogliser, and L. L. Neider, "Is It 'Trustworthy'? A Multiple-Levels-of-Analysis Reexamination of an Ohio State Leadership Study, with Implications for Future Research," *Leadership Quarterly*, Summer 1995,

pp. 111–145; and T. A. Judge, R. F. Piccolo, and R. Ilies, "The Forgotten Ones? The Validity of Consideration and Initiating Structure in Leadership Research," *Journal of Applied Psychology*, February 2004, pp. 36–51.

16. D. Akst, "The Rewards of Recognizing a Job Well Done," *Wall Street Journal*, January 31, 2007, p. D9.

17. G. Yukl, and D. D. Van Fleet, "Theory and Research on Leadership in Organizations," in M. D. Dunnette and L. M. Hough (eds.), *Handbook of Industrial and Organizational Psychology*, vol. 2 (Palo Alto, CA: Consulting Psychologists Press, 1992), pp. 147–197.

18. R. Kahn and D. Katz, "Leadership Practices in Relation to Productivity and Morale," in D. Cartwright and A. Zander (eds.), *Group Dynamics: Research and Theory*, 2nd ed. (Elmsford, NY: Row, Paterson, 1960).

19. Judge, Piccolo, and Ilies, "The Forgotten Ones?"

20. R. R. Blake and J. S. Mouton, *The Managerial Grid* (Houston: Gulf, 1964).

21. See, for example, R. R. Blake and J. S. Mouton, "A Comparative Analysis of Situationalism and 9,9 Management by Principle," *Organizational Dynamics*, Spring 1982, pp. 20–43.

22. See, for example, L. L. Larson, J. G. Hunt, and R. N. Osborn, "The Great Hi-Hi Leader Behavior Myth: A Lesson from Occam's Razor," *Academy of Management Journal*, December 1976, pp. 628–641; and P. C. Nystrom, "Managers and the Hi-Hi Leader Myth," *Academy of Management Journal*, June 1978, pp. 325–331.

23. F. E. Fiedler, *A Theory of Leadership Effectiveness* (New York: McGraw-Hill, 1967).

24. S. Shiflett, "Is There a Problem with the LPC Score in LEADER MATCH?" *Personnel Psychology*, Winter 1981, pp. 765–769.

25. F. E. Fiedler, M. M. Chemers, and L. Mahar, *Improving Leadership Effectiveness: The Leader Match Concept* (New York: Wiley, 1977).

26. Cited in House and Aditya, "The Social Scientific Study of Leadership," p. 422.

27. L. H. Peters, D. D. Hartke, and J. T. Pohlmann, "Fiedler's Contingency Theory of Leadership: An Application of the Meta-Analysis Procedures of Schmidt and Hunter," *Psychological Bulletin*, March 1985, pp. 274–285; C. A. Schriesheim, B. J. Tepper, and L. A. Tetrault, "Least Preferred Coworker Score, Situational Control, and Leadership Effectiveness: A Meta-Analysis of Contingency Model Performance Predictions," *Journal of Applied Psychology*, August 1994, pp. 561–573; and R. Ayman, M. M. Chemers, and F. Fiedler, "The Contingency Model of Leadership Effectiveness: Its Levels of Analysis," *Leadership Quarterly*, Summer 1995, pp. 147–167.

28. House and Aditya, "The Social Scientific Study of Leadership," p. 422.

29. See, for instance, R. W. Rice, "Psychometric Properties of the Esteem for the Least Preferred Coworker (LPC) Scale," *Academy of Management Review*, January 1978, pp. 106–118; C. A. Schriesheim, B. D. Bannister, and W. H. Money, "Psychometric Properties of the LPC Scale: An Extension of Rice's Review," *Academy of Management Review*, April 1979, pp. 287–290; and J. K. Kennedy, J. M. Houston, M. A. Korgaard, and D. D. Gallo, "Construct Space of the Least Preferred

Coworker (LPC) Scale," *Educational & Psychological Measurement*, Fall 1987, pp. 807–814.

30. See E. H. Schein, *Organizational Psychology*, 3rd ed. (Upper Saddle River, NJ: Prentice Hall, 1980), pp. 116–117; and B. Kabanoff, "A Critique of Leader Match and Its Implications for Leadership Research," *Personnel Psychology*, Winter 1981, pp. 749–764.

31. F. E. Fiedler and J. E. Garcia, *New Approaches to Effective Leadership: Cognitive Resources and Organizational Performance* (New York: Wiley, 1987).

32. See F. E. Fiedler, "Cognitive Resources and Leadership Performance," *Applied Psychology—An International Review*, January 1995, pp. 5–28; and F. E. Fiedler, "The Curious Role of Cognitive Resources in Leadership," in R. E. Riggio, S. E. Murphy, F. J. Pirozzolo (eds.), *Multiple Intelligences and Leadership* (Mahwah, NJ: Lawrence Erlbaum, 2002), pp. 91–104.

33. T. A. Judge, A. E. Colbert, and R. Ilies, "Intelligence and Leadership: A Quantitative Review and Test of Theoretical Propositions," *Journal of Applied Psychology*, June 2004, pp. 542–552.

34. P. Hersey and K. H. Blanchard, "So You Want to Know Your Leadership Style?" *Training and Development Journal*, February 1974, pp. 1–15; and P. Hersey, K. H. Blanchard, and D. E. Johnson, *Management of Organizational Behavior: Leading Human Resources*, 8th ed. (Upper Saddle River, NJ: Prentice Hall, 2001).

35. Cited in C. F. Fernandez and R. P. Vecchio, "Situational Leadership Theory Revisited: A Test of an Across-Jobs Perspective," *Leadership Quarterly* 8, no. 1 (1997), p. 67.

36. See, for instance, ibid., pp. 67–84; C. L. Graeff, "Evolution of Situational Leadership Theory: A Critical Review," *Leadership Quarterly* 8, no. 2 (1997), pp. 153–170; and R. P. Vecchio and K. J. Boatwright, "Preferences for Idealized Styles of Supervision," *Leadership Quarterly*, August 2002, pp. 327–342.

37. R. J. House, "A Path-Goal Theory of Leader Effectiveness," *Administrative Science Quarterly*, September 1971, pp. 321–338; R. J. House and T. R. Mitchell, "Path-Goal Theory of Leadership," *Journal of Contemporary Business*, Autumn 1974, pp. 81–97; and R. J. House, "Path-Goal Theory of Leadership: Lessons, Legacy, and a Reformulated Theory," *Leadership Quarterly*, Fall 1996, pp. 323–352.

38. J. C. Wofford and L. Z. Liska, "Path-Goal Theories of Leadership: A Meta-Analysis," *Journal of Management*, Winter 1993, pp. 857–876; and P. M. Podsakoff, S. B. MacKenzie, and M. Ahearne, "Searching for a Needle in a Haystack: Trying to Identify the Illusive Moderators of Leadership Behaviors," *Journal of Management* 21 (1995), pp. 423–470.

39. J. R. Villa, J. P. Howell, and P. W. Dorfman, "Problems with Detecting Moderators in Leadership Research Using Moderated Multiple Regression," *Leadership Quarterly* 14 (2003), pp. 3–23; C. A. Schriesheim, and L. Neider, "Path-Goal Leadership Theory: The Long and Winding Road," *Leadership Quarterly* 7 (1996), pp. 317–321; and M. G. Evans, "R. J. House's 'A Path-Goal Theory of Leader Effectiveness.'" *Leadership Quarterly* 7 (1996), pp. 305–309.

40. W. Bennis, "The Challenges of Leadership in the Modern World," *American Psychologist*, January 2007, pp. 2–5.

41. R. M. Dienesch and R. C. Liden, "Leader–Member Exchange Model of Leadership: A Critique and Further

Development," *Academy of Management Review,* July 1986, pp. 618–634; G. B. Graen and M. Uhl-Bien, "Relationship-Based Approach to Leadership: Development of Leader–Member Exchange (LMX) Theory of Leadership Over 25 Years: Applying a Multi-Domain Perspective," *Leadership Quarterly,* Summer 1995, pp. 219–247; R. C. Liden, R. T. Sparrowe, and S. J. Wayne, "Leader–Member Exchange Theory: The Past and Potential for the Future," in G. R. Ferris (ed.), *Research in Personnel and Human Resource Management,* vol. 15 (Greenwich, CT: JAI Press, 1997), pp. 47–119; and C. A. Schriesheim, S. L. Castro, X. Zhou, and F. J. Yammarino, "The Folly of Theorizing 'A' but Testing 'B': A Selective Level-of-Analysis Review of the Field and a Detailed Leader–Member Exchange Illustration," *Leadership Quarterly,* Winter 2001, pp. 515–551.

42. R. Liden and G. Graen, "Generalizability of the Vertical Dyad Linkage Model of Leadership," *Academy of Management Journal,* September 1980, pp. 451–465; R. C. Liden, S. J. Wayne, and D. Stilwell, "A Longitudinal Study of the Early Development of Leader–Member Exchanges," *Journal of Applied Psychology,* August 1993, pp. 662–674; S. J. Wayne, L. M. Shore, W. H. Bommer, and L. E. Tetrick, "The Role of Fair Treatment and Rewards in Perceptions of Organizational Support and Leader–Member Exchange," *Journal of Applied Psychology* 87, no. 3 (June 2002), pp. 590–598; and S. S. Masterson, K. Lewis, and B. M. Goldman, "Integrating Justice and Social Exchange: The Differing Effects of Fair Procedures and Treatment on Work Relationships," *Academy of Management Journal* 43, no. 4 (August 2000), pp. 738–748.

43. D. Duchon, S. G. Green, and T. D. Taber, "Vertical Dyad Linkage: A Longitudinal Assessment of Antecedents, Measures, and Consequences," *Journal of Applied Psychology,* February 1986, pp. 56–60; Liden, Wayne, and Stilwell, "A Longitudinal Study on the Early Development of Leader–Member Exchanges"; and M. Uhl-Bien, "Relationship Development as a Key Ingredient for Leadership Development," in S. E. Murphy and R. E. Riggio (eds.), *Future of Leadership Development* (Mahwah, NJ: Lawrence Erlbaum, 2003) pp. 129–147.

44. R. Vecchio and D. M. Brazil, "Leadership and Sex-Similarity: A Comparison in a Military Setting," *Personnel Psychology* 60 (2007), pp. 303–335.

45. See, for instance, C. R. Gerstner and D. V. Day, "Meta-analytic Review of Leader–Member Exchange Theory: Correlates and Construct Issues," *Journal of Applied Psychology,* December 1997, pp. 827–844; R. Ilies, J. D. Nahrgang, and F. P. Morgeson, "Leader–Member Exchange and Citizenship Behaviors: A Meta-Analysis," *Journal of Applied Psychology* 92, no. 1 (2007), pp. 269–277; and Z. Chen, W. Lam, and J. A. Zhong, "Leader–Member Exchange and Member Performance: A New Look at Individual-Level Negative Feedback-Seeking Behavior and Team-Level Empowerment Culture," *Journal of Applied Psychology* 92, no. 1 (2007), pp. 202–212.

46. D. Eden, "Leadership and Expectations: Pygmalion Effects and Other Self-fulfilling Prophecies in Organizations," *Leadership Quarterly,* Winter 1992, pp. 278–279.

47. See V. H. Vroom and P. W. Yetton, *Leadership and Decision-Making* (Pittsburgh: University of Pittsburgh Press, 1973); and V. H. Vroom and A. G. Jago, "The Role of the Situation in Leadership," *American Psychologist,* January 2007, pp. 17–24.

48. V. H. Vroom and A. G. Jago, *The New Leadership: Managing Participation in Organizations* (Englewood Cliffs, NJ: Prentice Hall, 1988). See also V. H. Vroom and A. G. Jago, "Situation Effects and Levels of Analysis in the Study of Leader Participation," *Leadership Quarterly,* Summer 1995, pp. 169–181.

49. See, for example, R. H. G. Field, "A Test of the Vroom-Yetton Normative Model of Leadership," *Journal of Applied Psychology,* October 1982, pp. 523–532; C. R. Leana, "Power Relinquishment Versus Power Sharing: Theoretical Clarification and Empirical Comparison of Delegation and Participation," *Journal of Applied Psychology,* May 1987, pp. 228–233; J. T. Ettling and A. G. Jago, "Participation Under Conditions of Conflict: More on the Validity of the Vroom-Yetton Model," *Journal of Management Studies,* January 1988, pp. 73–83; R. H. G. Field and R. J. House, "A Test of the Vroom-Yetton Model Using Manager and Subordinate Reports," *Journal of Applied Psychology,* June 1990, pp. 362–366; and R. H. G. Field and J. P. Andrews, "Testing the Incremental Validity of the Vroom-Jago Versus Vroom-Yetton Models of Participation in Decision Making," *Journal of Behavioral Decision Making,* December 1998, pp. 251–261.

50. House and Aditya, "The Social Scientific Study of Leadership," p. 428.

51. M. Javidan, P. W. Dorfman, M. S. de Luque, and R. J. House, "In the Eye of the Beholder: Cross Cultural Lessons in Leadership from Project GLOBE," *Academy of Management Perspectives,* February 2006, pp. 67–90.

52. R. D. Arvey, Z. Zhang, and B. J. Avolio, "Developmental and Genetic Determinants of Leadership Role Occupancy Among Women," *Journal of Applied Psychology,* May 2007, pp. 693–706.

53. M. Pandya, "Warren Buffett on Investing and Leadership: I'm Wired for This Game," *Wharton Leadership Digest* 3, no. 7 (April 1999), http://leadership.wharton.upenn.edu/digest/04-99.shtml.

Contemporary Issues in Leadership

There's nothing more demoralizing than a leader who can't clearly articulate why we're doing what we're doing.

—James Kouzes and Barry Posner

13

LEARNING OBJECTIVES

After studying this chapter, you should be able to:

1 Show how framing influences leadership effectiveness.

2 Define *charismatic leadership* and show how it influences followers.

3 Contrast transformational leadership and transactional leadership and discuss how transformational leadership works.

4 Define *authentic leadership* and show why ethics and trust are vital to effective leadership.

5 Identify the three types of trust.

6 Demonstrate the importance of mentoring, self-leadership, and virtual leadership to our understanding of leadership.

7 Identify when leadership may not be necessary.

8 Explain how to find and create effective leaders.

9 Assess whether charismatic and transformational leadership generalize across cultures.

Conventional wisdom suggests that visionary leaders are optimists. Patagonia's founder, Yvon Chouinard, is living proof that that conventional wisdom isn't always right.

Patagonia is famous for its outdoor gear. But it's also famous for its eco-friendly ethic. Much of the credit for this balance goes to Chouinard, who has embraced David Brower's call, "There is no business to be done on a dead planet." But like the ethos of all successful leaders, Chouinard's values—favoring environmentalism, infor-

Patagonia's Pessimistic Visionary

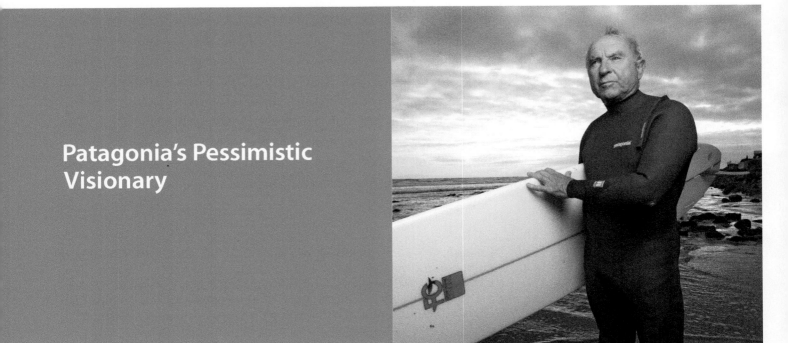

mality, and a love of the outdoors—have become engrained in the company's culture. Its corporate offices are unlike any others: filled with wandering pets, surfboards, barefoot employees, and a shed full of convalescing owls and hawks.

While Chouinard's values seem remarkably prescient, given today's corporate focus on sustainability, just as remarkable is Chouinard's ever-present pessimism. He says, "I don't think we're going to be here 100 years from now as a society, or maybe even as a species." In another forum, he wrote, "Patagonia will never be completely socially responsible. It will never make a totally sustainable, nondamaging product."

Some business model, you might think. Preach doom and gloom and be the worst critic of your own products. But that's how Chouinard's vision works. By portraying the future of mankind in its darkest terms, Patagonia builds the case for its way of doing business. If humans are on the verge of extinguishing themselves, then it becomes all the more important to buy from environmentally conscious companies. Patagonia's mission statement, featured prominently on its Web site, is *Build the best product, do no unnecessary harm, use business to inspire and implement solutions to the environmental crisis.*

Chouinard's pessimistic vision seems to be working. The company continues to grow, Chouinard regularly declines offers to buy the firm ("I don't want some Wall Street greaseball running my company," he says), and Patagonia receives 900 applications for every position it fills. Although Patagonia is not as large as some retailers, its use of environmentalism to its advantage has influenced other retailers—such as The Gap, Levi Strauss, and, most recently, Wal-Mart—to follow in its footsteps.

You would think all this would make Chouinard optimistic about the future. Not a chance. "I know everything's going to hell," he says.[1] ■

*a*lthough he's uncharacteristic of leaders in some ways, Yvon Chouinard embodies the qualities of an inspirational leader—that is, he has a vision, sticks with it, and inspires followers to transcend their own self-interests in pursuing it. One form of inspirational leadership is charismatic leadership. Take the following self-assessment to see how you score on charismatic leadership.

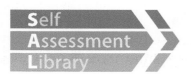

HOW CHARISMATIC AM I?

In the Self-Assessment Library (available on CD and online), take assessment II.B.2 (How Charismatic Am I?) and answer the following questions.

1. *How did you score compared to your classmates? Do you think your score is accurate?*
2. *Why do you think you scored as you did? Do you think the reason is in your genes? Are your parents charismatic? Or do you think your score has to do with your environment? Were there factors in your upbringing or early life experiences that affected your charisma?*
3. *Based on the material presented in the chapter, do you think you could become more charismatic? If yes, how might you go about it?*

Inspirational Approaches to Leadership

1 Show how framing influences leadership effectiveness.

Traditional approaches to leadership—those we considered in Chapter 12—ignore the importance of the leader as a communicator. **Framing** is a way of communicating to shape meaning. It's a way for leaders to influence how others see and understand events. It includes selecting and highlighting one or more aspects of a subject while excluding others.

Framing is especially important to an aspect of leadership ignored in the traditional theories: the ability of the leader to inspire others to act beyond their immediate self-interests.

In this section, we present two contemporary leadership theories with a common theme. They view leaders as individuals who inspire followers through their words, ideas, and behaviors. These theories are charismatic leadership and transformational leadership.

Charismatic Leadership

2   Define charismatic leadership and show how it influences followers.

John F. Kennedy, Martin Luther King, Jr., Ronald Reagan, Bill Clinton, Mary Kay Ash (founder of Mary Kay Cosmetics), and Steve Jobs (cofounder of Apple Computer) are individuals frequently cited as being charismatic leaders. So what do they have in common?

What Is Charismatic Leadership?   Max Weber, a sociologist, was the first scholar to discuss charismatic leadership. More than a century ago, he defined *charisma* (from the Greek for "gift") as "a certain quality of an individual personality, by virtue of which he or she is set apart from ordinary people and treated as endowed with supernatural, superhuman, or at least specifically exceptional powers or qualities. These are not accessible to the ordinary person, but are regarded as of divine origin or as exemplary, and on the basis of them the individual concerned is treated as a leader."[2] Weber argued that charismatic leadership was one of several ideal types of authority.

The first researcher to consider charismatic leadership in terms of OB was Robert House. According to House's **charismatic leadership theory**, followers make attributions of heroic or extraordinary leadership abilities when they observe certain behaviors.[3] There have been a number of studies that have attempted to identify the characteristics of the charismatic leader. One of the best reviews of the literature has documented four—they have a vision, they are willing to take personal risks to achieve that vision, they are sensitive to follower needs, and they exhibit behaviors that are out of the ordinary.[4] These characteristics are described in Exhibit 13-1.

Are Charismatic Leaders Born or Made?   Are charismatic leaders born with their qualities? Or can people actually learn how to be charismatic leaders? The answer to both questions is yes.

Exhibit **13-1**   Key Characteristics of Charismatic Leaders
1. *Vision and articulation.* Has a vision—expressed as an idealized goal—that proposes a future better than the status quo; and is able to clarify the importance of the vision in terms that are understandable to others.
2. *Personal risk.* Willing to take on high personal risk, incur high costs, and engage in self-sacrifice to achieve the vision.
3. *Sensitivity to follower needs.* Perceptive of others' abilities and responsive to their needs and feelings.
4. *Unconventional behavior.* Engages in behaviors that are perceived as novel and counter to norms.

Source: Based on J. A. Conger and R. N. Kanungo, *Charismatic Leadership in Organizations* (Thousand Oaks, CA: Sage, 1998), p. 94.

framing   *A way of using language to manage meaning.*

charismatic leadership theory   *A leadership theory that states that followers make attributions of heroic or extraordinary leadership abilities when they observe certain behaviors.*

It is true that individuals are born with traits that make them charismatic. In fact, studies of identical twins have found that they score similarly on charismatic leadership measures, even if they were raised in different households and had never met. Research suggests that personality is also related to charismatic leadership. Charismatic leaders are likely to be extraverted, self-confident, and achievement oriented.[5] Consider CNN co-founder Ted Turner. When referring to himself, he has said, "A full moon blanks out all the stars around it" and "If I only had humility, I'd be perfect." Although not all charismatic leaders are as bold or colorful as Turner, most of them do have an alluring, interesting, and dynamic nature.

Although a small minority thinks that charisma is inherited and therefore cannot be learned, most experts believe that individuals also can be trained to exhibit charismatic behaviors and can thus enjoy the benefits that accompany being labeled "a charismatic leader."[6] After all, just because we inherit certain tendencies doesn't mean that we can't learn to change. One set of authors proposes that a person can learn to become charismatic by following a three-step process.[7] First, an individual needs to develop an aura of charisma by maintaining an optimistic view; using passion as a catalyst for generating enthusiasm; and communicating with the whole body, not just with words. Second, an individual draws others in by creating a bond that inspires others to follow. Third, the individual brings out the potential in followers by tapping into their emotions.

The three-step approach seems to work, as evidenced by researchers who have succeeded in actually scripting undergraduate business students to "play" charismatic.[8] The students were taught to articulate an overarching goal, communicate high performance expectations, exhibit confidence in the ability of followers to meet these expectations, and empathize with the needs of their followers; they learned to project a powerful, confident, and dynamic presence; and they practiced using a captivating and engaging voice tone. To further capture the dynamics and energy of charisma, the leaders were trained to evoke charismatic nonverbal characteristics: They alternated between pacing and sitting on the edges of their desks, leaned toward the subjects, maintained direct

The inspiring vision of Apple's charismatic co-founder and CEO Steve Jobs is to make state-of-the-art technology easy for people to use. Through this vision, Jobs inspires, motivates, and leads employees to develop products such as McIntosh computers, iPod music players, and iPhones. "The iPhone is like having your life in your pocket," says Jobs; Apple's entry into the mobile phone market includes an iPod, a camera, an alarm clock, and Internet communication capabilities with an easy-to-use touch-screen design.

eye contact, and had relaxed postures and animated facial expressions. These researchers found that the students could learn how to project charisma. Moreover, followers of these leaders had higher task performance, task adjustment, and adjustment to the leader and to the group than did followers who worked under groups led by noncharismatic leaders.

How Charismatic Leaders Influence Followers How do charismatic leaders actually influence followers? The evidence suggests a four-step process.[9] It begins by the leader articulating an appealing **vision**. A vision is a long-term strategy for how to attain a goal or goals. The vision provides a sense of continuity for followers by linking the present with a better future for the organization. For example, at Apple, Steve Jobs championed the iPod, noting, "It's as Apple as anything Apple has ever done." The creation of the iPod achieved Apple's goal of offering groundbreaking and easy-to-use-technology. Apple's strategy was to create a product that had a user-friendly interface where songs could be quickly uploaded and easily organized. It was the first major-market device to link data storage capabilities with music downloading.

A vision is incomplete unless it has an accompanying vision statement. A **vision statement** is a formal articulation of an organization's vision or mission. Charismatic leaders may use vision statements to "imprint" on followers an overarching goal and purpose. Once a vision and vision statement are established, the leader then communicates high performance expectations and expresses confidence that followers can attain them. This enhances follower self-esteem and self-confidence.

Next, the leader conveys, through words and actions, a new set of values and, by his or her behavior, sets an example for followers to imitate. One study of Israeli bank employees showed, for example, that charismatic leaders were more effective because their employees personally identified with the leaders. Finally, the charismatic leader engages in emotion-inducing and often unconventional behavior to demonstrate courage and convictions about the vision. There is an emotional contagion in charismatic leadership whereby followers "catch" the emotions their leader is conveying.[10] The next time you see Martin Luther King, Jr.'s "I Have a Dream" speech, focus on the reactions of the crowd, and it will bring to light how a charismatic leader can spread his emotion to his followers.

Because the vision is such a critical component of charismatic leadership, we should clarify exactly what we mean by the term, identify specific qualities of an effective vision, and offer some examples.[11]

A review of various definitions finds that a vision differs from other forms of direction setting in several ways: "A vision has clear and compelling imagery that offers an innovative way to improve, which recognizes and draws on traditions, and connects to actions that people can take to realize change. Vision taps people's emotions and energy. Properly articulated, a vision creates the enthusiasm that people have for sporting events and other leisure-time activities, bringing this energy and commitment to the workplace."[12]

The key properties of a vision seem to be inspirational possibilities that are value centered, realizable, with superior imagery and articulation.[13] Visions should be able to create possibilities that are inspirational and unique and that offer a new order that can produce organizational distinction. A vision is likely to fail if it doesn't offer a view of the future that is clearly and demonstrably better for the organization and its members. Desirable visions fit the times and

---

vision *A long-term strategy for attaining a goal or goals.*

vision statement *A formal articulation of an organization's vision or mission.*

circumstances and reflect the uniqueness of the organization. People in the organization must also believe that the vision is attainable. It should be perceived as challenging yet doable. Also, visions that have clear articulation and powerful imagery are more easily grasped and accepted.

What are some examples of visions? Rupert Murdoch had a vision of the future of the communication industry by combining entertainment and media. Through News Corporation, Murdoch has successfully integrated a broadcast network, TV stations, movie studio, publishing, and global satellite distribution. John Malone of Liberty Media calls News Corporation "the best run, most strategically positioned vertically integrated media company in the world."[14] The late Mary Kay Ash's vision of women as entrepreneurs selling products that improved their self-image gave impetus to her cosmetics company. And Michael Dell has created a vision of a business that allows Dell Computer to sell and deliver a finished PC directly to a customer in fewer than 8 days.

Does Effective Charismatic Leadership Depend on the Situation?   There is an increasing body of research that shows impressive correlations between charismatic leadership and high performance and satisfaction among followers.[15] People working for charismatic leaders are motivated to exert extra work effort and, because they like and respect their leader, express greater satisfaction. It also appears that organizations with charismatic CEOs are more profitable. And charismatic college professors enjoy higher course evaluations.[16] However, there is a growing body of evidence indicating that charisma may not always be generalizable; that is, its effectiveness may depend on the situation. Charisma appears to be most successful when the follower's task has an ideological component or when the environment involves a high degree of stress and uncertainty.[17] This may explain why, when charismatic leaders surface, it's likely to be in politics, religion, wartime, or when a business firm is in its infancy or facing a life-threatening crisis. For example, in the 1930s, Franklin D. Roosevelt offered a vision to get Americans out of the Great Depression. In the early 1970s, when Chrysler Corp. was on the brink of bankruptcy, it needed a charismatic leader with unconventional ideas like Lee Iacocca to reinvent the

Sony Corporation chose a charismatic leader to inspire the company to return to its innovative roots. As Sony's first CEO and chairman from outside Japan, Howard Stringer, from Wales, is reorganizing the company to lead the change in making the Sony brand more relevant to digital-age consumers. Stringer's strong sense of humor, optimism, boundless energy, and confidence are motivating employees worldwide, from engineers to executives. One top manager says, "Howard's personality and his character and the way he communicates have been good for the company." In this photo, the fun-loving Stringer jokes with Sony top executives about the color of their ties during a press conference announcing his new job as CEO.

company. In 1997, when Apple Computer was floundering and lacking direction, the board persuaded charismatic co-founder Steve Jobs to return as interim CEO and to inspire the company to return to its innovative roots.

In addition to ideology and uncertainty, another situational factor limiting charisma appears to be level in the organization. Remember that the creation of a vision is a key component of charisma. But visions typically apply to entire organizations or major divisions. They tend to be created by top executives. Charisma therefore probably has more direct relevance to explaining the success and failures of chief executives than of lower-level managers. So even though an individual may have an inspiring personality, it's more difficult to utilize the person's charismatic leadership qualities in lower-level management jobs. Lower-level managers *can* create visions to lead their units. It's just harder to define such visions and align them with the larger goals of the organization as a whole.

Finally, charismatic leadership may affect some followers more than others. Research suggests, for example, that people are especially receptive to charismatic leadership when they sense a crisis, when they are under stress, or when they fear for their lives. More generally, some peoples' personalities are especially susceptible to charismatic leadership.[18] Consider self-esteem. If an individual lacks self-esteem and questions his self-worth, he is more likely to absorb a leader's direction rather than establish his own way of leading or thinking.

The Dark Side of Charismatic Leadership   Charismatic business leaders like AIG's Hank Greenberg, GE's Jack Welch, Tyco's Dennis Kozlowski, Southwest Airlines's Herb Kelleher, Disney's Michael Eisner, and HP's Carly Fiorina became celebrities on the order of David Beckham and Madonna. Every company wanted a charismatic CEO. And to attract these people, boards of directors gave them unprecedented autonomy and resources. They had private jets at their beck and call, use of $30 million penthouses, interest-free loans to buy beach homes and artwork, security staffs provided by their companies, and similar benefits befitting royalty. One study showed that charismatic CEOs were able to use their charisma to leverage higher salaries even when their performance was mediocre.[19]

Unfortunately, charismatic leaders who are larger-than-life don't necessarily act in the best interests of their organizations.[20] Many of these leaders used their power to remake their companies in their own image. These leaders often completely blurred the boundary separating their personal interests from their organization's interests. The perils of this ego-driven charisma at its worst are leaders who allow their self-interest and personal goals to override the goals of the organization. Intolerant of criticism, they surround themselves with yes-people who are rewarded for pleasing the leader and create a climate where people are afraid to question or challenge the "king" or "queen" when they think he or she is making a mistake. The results at companies such as Enron, Tyco, Worldcom, and HealthSouth were leaders who recklessly used organizational resources for their personal benefit and executives who broke laws and crossed ethical lines to generate financial numbers that temporarily inflated stock prices and allowed leaders to cash in millions of dollars in stock options.

A study of 29 companies that went from good to great (based on the fact that their cumulative stock returns were all at least three times better than the general stock market over 15 years) found an *absence* of ego-driven charismatic leaders. Although the leaders of these firms were fiercely ambitious and driven, their ambition was directed toward their company rather than themselves. They generated extraordinary results but with little fanfare or hoopla. They took responsibility for mistakes and poor results and gave credit for successes to other people. They prided themselves on developing strong leaders inside the firm who could direct the company to greater heights after they were gone. These individuals have been called **level-5 leaders** because they have four basic leadership qualities—individual capability, team skills, managerial competence, and the ability to stimulate others to high performance—plus a fifth dimension: a paradoxical blend of personal humility and professional will. Level-5 leaders channel their ego needs away from themselves and into the goal of building a great company. So while level-5 leaders are highly effective, they tend to be people you've never heard of and who get little notoriety in the business press—people like Orin Smith at Starbucks, Kristine McDivitt of Patagonia, John Whitehead of Goldman Sachs, and Jack Brennan of Vanguard. This study is important because it confirms that leaders don't necessarily need to be charismatic to be effective, especially where charisma is enmeshed with an outsized ego.[21]

We don't mean to suggest that charismatic leadership isn't effective. Overall, its effectiveness is well supported. The point is that a charismatic leader isn't always the answer. Yes, an organization with a charismatic leader at the helm is more likely to be successful, but that success depends, to some extent, on the situation and on the leader's vision. Some charismatic leaders—Hitler, for example—are all too successful at convincing their followers to pursue a vision that can be disastrous.

Transformational Leadership

3 Contrast transformational leadership and transactional leadership and discuss how transformational leadership works.

A stream of research has focused on differentiating transformational leaders from transactional leaders.[22] Most of the leadership theories presented in Chapter 12—for instance, the Ohio State studies, Fiedler's model, and path-goal theory—have concerned **transactional leaders**. These kinds of leaders guide or motivate their followers in the direction of established goals by clarifying role and task requirements. **Transformational leaders** inspire followers to transcend their own self-interests for the good of the organization and are capable of having a profound and extraordinary effect on their followers. Andrea Jung at Avon, Richard Branson of the Virgin Group, and Jim McNerney of Boeing are all

A. G. Lafley is a transformational leader. Since joining Procter & Gamble as CEO in 2000, he has brought flexibility and creativity to a slow-growing company. He expanded core brands like Crest toothpaste to innovations such as teeth whiteners and toothbrushes. He shifted P&G's focus from in-house innovation by setting a goal that 50 percent of new products be developed with outside partners. With more than half of P&G's business outside the United States, Lafley recast his top management group to be 50 percent non-American. These changes have raised P&G's revenues, profits, and stock price. Shown here with Iams pet-food mascot Euka, Lafley helped move the brand from the No. 5 position in the United States to the No. 1 spot and doubled worldwide sales of Iams.

Exhibit 13-2	Characteristics of Transactional and Transformational Leaders

Transactional Leader

Contingent Reward: Contracts exchange of rewards for effort, promises rewards for good performance, recognizes accomplishments.

Management by Exception (active): Watches and searches for deviations from rules and standards, takes correct action.

Management by Exception (passive): Intervenes only if standards are not met.

Laissez-Faire: Abdicates responsibilities, avoids making decisions.

Transformational Leader

Idealized Influence: Provides vision and sense of mission, instills pride, gains respect and trust.

Inspirational Motivation: Communicates high expectations, uses symbols to focus efforts, expresses important purposes in simple ways.

Intellectual Stimulation: Promotes intelligence, rationality, and careful problem solving.

Individualized Consideration: Gives personal attention, treats each employee individually, coaches, advises.

Source: B. M. Bass, "From Transactional to Transformational Leadership: Learning to Share the Vision," *Organizational Dynamics*, Winter 1990, p. 22. Reprinted by permission of the publisher, American Management Association, New York. All rights reserved.

examples of transformational leaders. They pay attention to the concerns and developmental needs of individual followers; they change followers' awareness of issues by helping them to look at old problems in new ways; and they are able to excite, arouse, and inspire followers to put out extra effort to achieve group goals. Exhibit 13-2 briefly identifies and defines the characteristics that differentiate these two types of leaders.

Transactional and transformational leadership shouldn't be viewed as opposing approaches to getting things done.[23] Transformational and transactional leadership complement each other, but that doesn't mean they're equally important. Transformational leadership builds *on top of* transactional leadership and produces levels of follower effort and performance that go beyond what would occur with a transactional approach alone. But the reverse isn't true. So if you are a good transactional leader but do not have transformational qualities, you'll likely only be a mediocre leader. The best leaders are transactional *and* transformational.

Full Range of Leadership Model   Exhibit 13-3 shows the full range of leadership model. Laissez-faire is the most passive and therefore the least effective of the leader behaviors. Leaders using this style are rarely viewed as effective. Management by exception—regardless of whether it is active or passive—is slightly better than laissez-faire, but it's still considered ineffective leadership. Leaders who practice management by exception leadership tend to be available only when there is a problem, which is often too late. Contingent reward leadership can be an effective style of leadership. However, leaders will not get their employees to go above and beyond the call of duty when practicing this style of leadership. Only with the four remaining leadership styles—which are all

level-5 leaders *Leaders who are fiercely ambitious and driven but whose ambition is directed toward their company rather than themselves.*

transactional leaders *Leaders who guide or motivate their followers in the direction of established goals by clarifying role and task requirements.*

transformational leaders *Leaders who inspire followers to transcend their own self-interests and who are capable of having a profound and extraordinary effect on followers.*

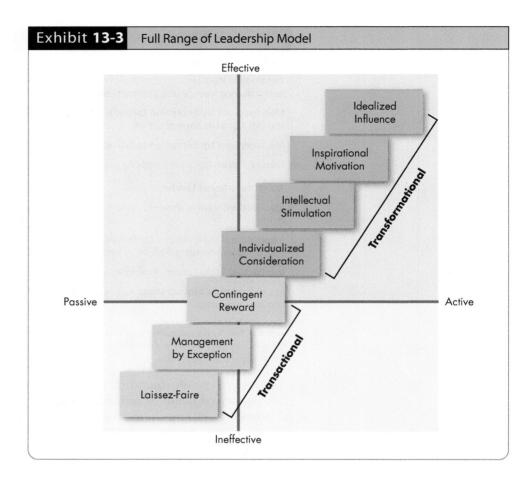

Exhibit 13-3 Full Range of Leadership Model

aspects of transformational leadership—are leaders able to motivate followers to perform above expectations and transcend their own self-interest for the sake of the organization. Individualized consideration, intellectual stimulation, inspirational motivation, and idealized influence all result in extra effort from workers, higher productivity, higher morale and satisfaction, higher organizational effectiveness, lower turnover, lower absenteeism, and greater organizational adaptability. Based on this model, leaders are generally most effective when they regularly use each of the four transformational behaviors.

How Transformational Leadership Works In the past few years, a great deal of research has been conducted to explain how transformational leadership works. Transformational leaders encourage their followers to be more innovative and creative.[24] For example, Army Colonel Leonard Wong found that, in the Iraq war, the Army was encouraging "reactive instead of proactive thought, compliance instead of creativity, and adherence instead of audacity." In response, Colonel Leonard Wong is working to empower junior officers to be creative and to take more risks.[25] Transformational leaders are more effective because they themselves are more creative, but they're also more effective because they encourage those who follow them to be creative, too.

Goals are another key mechanism that explains how transformational leadership works. Followers of transformational leaders are more likely to pursue ambitious goals, be familiar with and agree on the strategic goals of the organization, and believe that the goals they are pursuing are personally important.[26] VeriSign's CEO, Stratton Sclavos, says, "It comes down to charting a course—having the ability to articulate for your employees where you're headed and how you're going to get there. Even more important is choosing people to work with who have that same level of passion, commitment, fear, and competitiveness to drive toward those same goals."

Sclavos's remark about goals brings up vision. Just as research has shown that vision is important in explaining how charismatic leadership works, research has also shown that vision explains part of the effect of transformational leadership. Indeed, one study found that vision was even more important than a charismatic (effusive, dynamic, lively) communication style in explaining the success of entrepreneurial firms.[27] Finally, transformational leadership also engenders commitment on the part of followers and instills in them a greater sense of trust in the leader.[28]

Evaluation of Transformational Leadership   The evidence supporting the superiority of transformational leadership over transactional leadership is impressive. Transformational leadership has been supported in disparate occupations (for example, school principals, marine commanders, ministers, presidents of MBA associations, military cadets, union shop stewards, school teachers, sales reps) and at various job levels. One recent study of R&D firms found, for example, that teams led by project leaders who scored high on transformational leadership produced better-quality products as judged 1 year later and were more profitable 5 years later.[29] A review of 87 studies testing transformational leadership found that it was related to the motivation and satisfaction of followers and to the higher performance and perceived effectiveness of leaders.[30]

Transformational leadership theory is not perfect. There are concerns about whether contingent reward leadership is strictly a characteristic of transactional leaders only. And contrary to the full range of leadership model, contingent reward leadership is sometimes more effective than transformational leadership.

In summary, the overall evidence indicates that transformational leadership is more strongly correlated than transactional leadership with lower turnover rates, higher productivity, lower employee stress and burnout, and higher employee satisfaction.[31] Like charisma, it appears that transformational leadership can be learned. One study of Canadian bank managers found that those managers who underwent transformational leadership training had bank branches that performed significantly better than branches with managers who did not undergo training. Other studies show similar results.[32]

Transformational Leadership Versus Charismatic Leadership   There is some debate about whether transformational leadership and charismatic leadership are the same. The researcher most responsible for introducing charismatic leadership to OB, Robert House, considers them synonymous, calling the differences "modest" and "minor." However, the individual who first researched transformational leadership, Bernard Bass, considers charisma to be part of transformational leadership but argues that transformational leadership is broader than charisma, suggesting that charisma is, by itself, insufficient to "account for the transformational process."[33] Another researcher commented, "The purely charismatic [leader] may want followers to adopt the charismatic's world view and go no further; the transformational leader will attempt to instill in followers the ability to question not only established views but eventually those established by the leader."[34] Although many researchers believe that transformational leadership is broader than charismatic leadership, studies show that in reality a leader who scores high on transformational leadership is also likely to score high on charisma. Therefore, in practice, measures of charisma and transformational leadership may be roughly equivalent.

Authentic Leadership: Ethics and Trust Are the Foundation of Leadership

4 *Define* authentic leadership *and show why ethics and trust are vital to effective leadership.*

Although charismatic leadership theories and transformational leadership theories have added greatly to our understanding of effective leadership, they do not explicitly deal with the role of ethics and trust. Some scholars have argued that a consideration of ethics and trust is essential to complete the picture of effective leadership. Here we consider these two concepts under the rubric of authentic leadership.[35]

What Is Authentic Leadership?

Douglas R. Conant is not your typical CEO. His style is decidedly understated. When asked to reflect on the strong performance of Campbell Soup, he demurs, "We're hitting our stride a little bit more (than our peers)." He regularly admits mistakes and often says, "I can do better." Conant appears to be a good exemplar of authentic leadership.[36]

Authentic leaders know who they are, know what they believe in and value, and act on those values and beliefs openly and candidly. Their followers would consider them to be ethical people. The primary quality, therefore, produced by authentic leadership is trust. How does authentic leadership build trust? Authentic leaders share information, encourage open communication, and stick to their ideals. The result: People come to have faith in authentic leaders.

Because the concept is so recent, there hasn't been a lot of research on authentic leadership. However, we believe it's a promising way to think about ethics and trust in leadership because it focuses on the moral aspects of being a leader. Transformational or charismatic leaders can have a vision, and communicate it persuasively, but sometimes the vision is wrong (as in the case of Hitler), or the leader is more concerned with his own needs or pleasures, as in the case with business leaders Dennis Kozlowski (ex-CEO of Tyco) and Jeff Skilling (ex-CEO of Enron).[37]

Campbell Soup CEO Douglas Conant exemplifies authentic leadership. In leading the company to becoming one of the best performers in the food industry, Conant motivates employees by giving them credit for innovation while deflecting praise of himself. During his 6 years as CEO, Conant has written 16,000 thank-you notes to employees, from the receptionist to the chief investment officer. Campbell's chairman says, "He's an extraordinary leader who behaves with the utmost integrity. People follow him and believe in him. He's an Eagle Scout."

Self
Assessment
Library

AM I AN ETHICAL LEADER?

In the Self-Assessment Library (available on CD and online), take assessment IV.E.4 (Am I an Ethical Leader?).

Ethics and Leadership

The topic of ethics and leadership has received surprisingly little attention. Only recently have ethicists and leadership researchers begun to consider the ethical implications in leadership.[38] Why now? One reason may be the growing general interest in ethics throughout the field of management. Another reason may be the discovery by probing biographers that many of our past leaders—such as Martin Luther King, Jr., John F. Kennedy, and Thomas Jefferson—suffered from ethical shortcomings. Ethical lapses by business leaders are never absent from the headlines. Some companies, like Boeing, are even tying executive compensation to ethics. They've done so to reinforce the idea that "there's no compromise between doing things the right way and performance," in the words of Boeing's CEO Jim McNerney.[39]

Ethics touches on leadership at a number of junctures. Transformational leaders, for instance, have been described by one authority as fostering moral virtue when they try to change the attitudes and behaviors of followers.[40] Charisma, too, has an ethical component. Unethical leaders are more likely to use their charisma to enhance *power over* followers, directed toward self-serving ends. Ethical leaders are considered to use their charisma in a socially constructive way to serve others.[41] There is also the issue of abuse of power by leaders, for example, when they give themselves large salaries, bonuses, and stock options while, at the same time, they seek to cut costs by laying off long-time employees. Because top executives set the moral tone for an organization, they need to set high ethical standards, demonstrate those standards through their own behavior, and encourage and reward integrity in others.

Leadership effectiveness needs to address the *means* a leader uses in trying to achieve goals, as well as the content of those goals. Recently, scholars have tried to integrate ethical and charismatic leadership by advancing the idea of **socialized charismatic leadership**—leadership that conveys values that are other-centered versus self-centered by leaders who model ethical conduct.[42]

Leadership is not value free. Before we judge any leader to be effective, we should consider both the means used by the leader to achieve goals and the moral content of those goals.

Now let's examine the issue of trust and its role in shaping strong leaders.

What Is Trust?

Trust, or lack of trust, is an increasingly important leadership issue in today's organizations.[43] In this section, we define *trust* and provide you with some guidelines for helping build credibility and trust.

authentic leaders *Leaders who know who they are, know what they believe in and value, and act on those values and beliefs openly and candidly. Their followers would consider them to be ethical people.*

socialized charismatic leadership *A leadership concept that states that leaders convey values that are other-centered versus self-centered and who role model ethical conduct.*

Trust is a positive expectation that another will not—through words, actions, or decisions—act opportunistically.[44] The two most important elements of our definition are that it implies familiarity and risk.

The phrase *positive expectation* in our definition assumes knowledge and familiarity about the other party. Trust is a history-dependent process based on relevant but limited samples of experience.[45] It takes time to form, building incrementally and accumulating. Most of us find it hard, if not impossible, to trust someone immediately if we don't know anything about them. At the extreme, in the case of total ignorance, we can gamble, but we can't trust.[46] But as we get to know someone and the relationship matures, we gain confidence in our ability to form a positive expectation.

The term *opportunistic* refers to the inherent risk and vulnerability in any trusting relationship. Trust involves making oneself vulnerable as when, for example, we disclose intimate information or rely on another's promises.[47] By its very nature, trust provides the opportunity for disappointment or to be taken advantage of.[48] But trust is not taking risk per se; rather, it is a *willingness* to take risk.[49] So when I trust someone, I expect that they will not take advantage of me. This willingness to take risks is common to all trust situations.[50]

What are the key dimensions that underlie the concept of trust? Evidence has identified five: integrity, competence, consistency, loyalty, and openness[51] (see Exhibit 13-4).

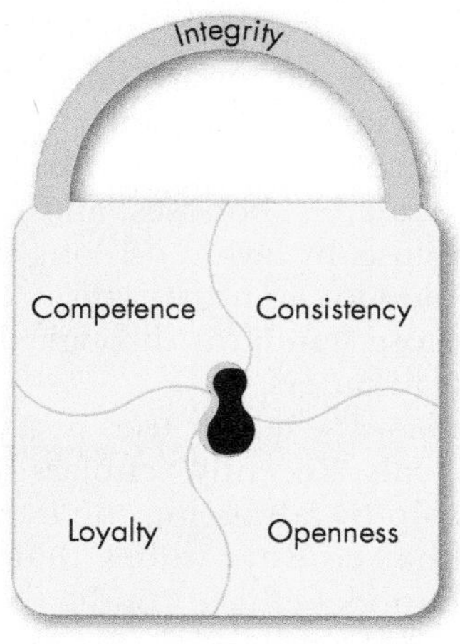

Integrity refers to honesty and truthfulness. Of the five dimensions, this one seems to be most critical when someone assesses another's trustworthiness.[52] For instance, when 570 white-collar employees were recently given a list of 28 attributes related to leadership, honesty was rated the most important by far.[53]

Competence encompasses an individual's technical and interpersonal knowledge and skills. Does the person know what he or she is talking about? You're unlikely to listen to or depend on someone whose abilities you don't respect. You need to believe that the person has the skills and abilities to carry out what he or she says they will do.

Consistency relates to an individual's reliability, predictability, and good judgment in handling situations. "Inconsistencies between words and action decrease trust."[54] This dimension is particularly relevant for managers. "Nothing is noticed more quickly... than a discrepancy between what executives preach and what they expect their associates to practice."[55]

Loyalty is the willingness to protect and save face for another person. Trust requires that you can depend on someone not to act opportunistically.

The final dimension of trust is *openness*. Can you rely on the person to give you the full truth?

Exhibit 13-4

Trust Dimensions

Integrity

Competence   Consistency

Loyalty   Openness

Trust and Leadership

As we have shown in discussing ethical and authentic leadership, trust is a primary attribute associated with leadership; and when this trust is broken, it can have serious adverse effects on a group's performance.[56] As one author noted: "Part of the leader's task has been, and continues to be, working with people to find and solve problems, but whether leaders gain access to the knowledge and creative thinking they need to solve problems depends on how much people trust them. Trust and trust-worthiness modulate the leader's access to knowledge and cooperation."[57]

When followers trust a leader, they are willing to be vulnerable to the leader's actions—confident that their rights and interests will not be abused.[58] People are unlikely to look up to or follow someone whom they perceive as dishonest or who is likely to take advantage of them. Honesty, for instance, consistently ranks at the top of most people's list of characteristics they admire in their leaders. "Honesty is absolutely essential to leadership. If people are going to follow someone willingly, whether it be into battle or into the boardroom, they first want to assure themselves that the person is worthy of their trust."[59]

Three Types of Trust

5 *Identify the three types of trust.*

There are three types of trust in organizational relationships: *deterrence* based, *knowledge* based, and *identification* based.[60]

Deterrence-Based Trust The most fragile relationships are contained in **deterrence-based trust.** One violation or inconsistency can destroy the relationship. This form of trust is based on fear of reprisal if the trust is violated. Individuals who are in this type of relationship do what they do because they fear the consequences from not following through on their obligations.

Deterrence-based trust will work only to the degree that punishment is possible, consequences are clear, and the punishment is actually imposed if the trust is violated. To be sustained, the potential loss of future interaction with the other party must outweigh the profit potential that comes from violating expectations. Moreover, the potentially harmed party must be willing to introduce harm (for example, "I have no qualms about speaking badly of you if you betray my trust") to the person acting distrustingly.

Most new relationships begin on a base of deterrence. Take, as an illustration, a situation in which you're selling your car to a friend of a friend. You don't know the buyer. You might be motivated to refrain from telling this buyer all the problems with the car that you know about. Such behavior would increase your chances of selling the car and securing the highest price. But you don't withhold information. You openly share the car's flaws. Why? Probably because of fear of reprisal. If the buyer later thinks you deceived him, he is likely to share this with your mutual friend. If you knew that the buyer would never say anything to the mutual friend, you might be tempted to take advantage of the opportunity. If it's clear that the buyer would tell and that your mutual friend would think considerably less of you for taking advantage of this buyer-friend, your honesty could be explained in deterrence terms.

Another example of deterrence-based trust is a new manager–employee relationship. As an employee, you typically trust a new boss even though you have little experience on which to base that trust. The bond that creates this trust lies in the authority held by the boss and the punishment he or she can impose if you fail to fulfill your job-related obligations.

Knowledge-Based Trust Most organizational relationships are rooted in **knowledge-based trust**—that is, trust is based on the behavioral predictability that comes from a history of interaction. It exists when you have adequate information about someone to understand them well enough to be able to accurately predict his or her behavior.

Knowledge-based trust relies on information rather than deterrence. Knowledge of the other party and predictability of his or her behavior replaces the contracts, penalties, and legal arrangements more typical of deterrence-based trust. This knowledge develops over time, largely as a function of experience that builds confidence of trustworthiness and predictability. The better you know someone, the more accurately you can predict what he or she will do.

---

trust *A positive expectation that another will not act opportunistically.*

deterrence-based trust *Trust based on fear of reprisal if the trust is violated.*

knowledge-based trust *Trust based on behavioral predictability that comes from a history of interaction.*

Organizational relationships with Shelly Lazarus, CEO and chairman of Ogilvy & Mather Worldwide, are founded on knowledge-based trust. With the advertising agency for more than 30 years, Lazarus has earned a reputation for being honest, passionate about her work, intelligent, loyal, an excellent communicator, and respectful of employees' ideas. Lazarus believes her job as a leader is to be a role model for ethical behavior and to influence everyone at the agency to move productively in the same direction. Her vision is credited with the agency serving some of the world's most recognizable brands, including American Express and IBM.

Predictability enhances trust—even if the other is predictably untrustworthy—because the ways that the other will violate the trust can be predicted! The more communication and regular interaction you have with someone else, the more this form of trust can be developed and depended on.

Interestingly, at the knowledge-based level, trust is not necessarily broken by inconsistent behavior. If you believe you can adequately explain or understand another's apparent violation, you can accept it, forgive the person, and move on in the relationship. However, the same inconsistency at the deterrence level is likely to irrevocably break the trust.

In an organizational context, most manager–employee relationships are knowledge based. Both parties have enough experience working with each other that they know what to expect. A long history of consistently open and honest interactions, for instance, is not likely to be permanently destroyed by a single violation.

Identification-Based Trust   The highest level of trust is achieved when there is an emotional connection between the parties. It allows one party to act as an agent for the other and substitute for that person in interpersonal transactions. This is called **identification-based trust**. Trust exists because the parties understand each other's intentions and appreciate each other's wants and desires. This mutual understanding is developed to the point that each can effectively act for the other. Controls are minimal at this level. You don't need to monitor the other party because there exists unquestioned loyalty.

The best example of identification-based trust is a long-term, happily married couple. A husband comes to learn what's important to his wife and anticipates those actions. She, in turn, trusts that he will anticipate what's important to her without having to ask. Increased identification enables each to think like the other, feel like the other, and respond like the other.

You see identification-based trust occasionally in organizations among people who have worked together for long periods of time and have a depth of experience that allows them to know each other inside and out. This is also the type of trust that managers ideally seek in teams. Team members are comfortable with and trusting of each other that they can anticipate each other and act freely in each other's absence. In the current work world, it's probably accurate to say that most large corporations have broken the bonds of identification trust that were built with long-term employees. Broken promises have led to a breakdown in what was, at one time, a bond of unquestioned loyalty. It's likely to have been replaced with knowledge-based trust.

Basic Principles of Trust

Research allows us to offer some principles for better understanding the creation of both trust and mistrust.[61]

Mistrust Drives Out Trust   People who are trusting demonstrate their trust by increasing their openness to others, disclosing relevant information, and expressing their true intentions. People who mistrust do not reciprocate. They conceal information and act opportunistically to take advantage of others. To defend against repeated exploitation, trusting people are driven to mistrust. A few mistrusting people can poison an entire organization.

Trust Begets Trust   In the same way that mistrust drives out trust, exhibiting trust in others tends to encourage reciprocity. Effective leaders increase trust in small increments and allow others to respond in kind. By offering trust in only small increments, leaders limit penalty or loss that might occur if their trust is exploited.

Trust Can Be Regained   Once it is violated, trust can be regained, but only in certain situations. When an individual's trust in another is broken because the other party failed to do what was expected of him, it can be restored when the individual observes a consistent pattern of trustworthy behaviors by the transgressor. However, when the same untrustworthy behavior occurs with deception, trust never fully recovers, even when the deceived is given apologies, promises, or a consistent pattern of trustworthy actions.[62]

Mistrusting Groups Self-destruct   The corollary to the previous principle is that when group members mistrust each other, they repel and separate. They pursue their own interests rather than the group's. Members of mistrusting groups tend to be suspicious of each other, are constantly on guard against exploitation, and restrict communication with others in the group. These actions tend to undermine and eventually destroy the group.

Mistrust Generally Reduces Productivity   Although we cannot say that trust necessarily *increases* productivity, though it usually does, mistrust almost always *reduces* productivity. Mistrust focuses attention on the differences in member interests, making it difficult for people to visualize common goals. People respond by concealing information and secretly pursuing their own interests. When employees encounter problems, they avoid calling on others, fearing that those others will take advantage of them. A climate of mistrust tends to stimulate dysfunctional forms of conflict and retard cooperation.

identification-based trust   *Trust based on a mutual understanding of each other's intentions and appreciation of each other's wants and desires.*

Contemporary Leadership Roles

6 *Demonstrate the importance of mentoring, self-leadership, and virtual leadership to our understanding of leadership.*

Why are many effective leaders also active mentors? How can leaders develop self-leadership skills in their employees? And how does leadership work when face-to-face interaction is gone? In this section, we briefly address these three leadership role issues.

Mentoring

Many leaders create mentoring relationships. A **mentor** is a senior employee who sponsors and supports a less-experienced employee (a protégé). Successful mentors are good teachers. They can present ideas clearly, listen well, and empathize with the problems of their protégés. Mentoring relationships have been described in terms of two broad categories of functions—career functions and psychosocial functions:

Career Functions
- Lobbying to get the protégé challenging and visible assignments
- Coaching the protégé to help develop her skills and achieve work objectives
- Assisting the protégé by providing exposure to influential individuals within the organization
- Protecting the protégé from possible risks to her reputation
- Sponsoring the protégé by nominating her for potential advances or promotions
- Acting as a sounding board for ideas that the protégé might be hesitant to share with her direct supervisor

Psychosocial Functions
- Counseling the protégé about anxieties and uncertainty to help bolster her self-confidence
- Sharing personal experiences with the protégé
- Providing friendship and acceptance
- Acting as a role model[63]

Narayana Murtha (right in photo), one of the founders of Infosys Technologies in Bangalore, India, stepped down as CEO to serve the firm as chief mentor. In this role, Murtha shares his experiences, knowledge, and lessons learned while he built the company he started in 1981 and grew to 75,000 employees with sales of $3 billion. In mentoring Infosys's core management team, he wants to provide next-generation leadership for the firm. His goal is to build leadership qualities among Infosys employees by spending time at various corporate campuses and discussing issues that add value to the company. Murtha is shown here mentoring the new Infosys CEO, Nandan Nilekani.

Some organizations, such as Edward Jones, a financial services firm with 24,000 employees, have formal mentoring programs that officially assign mentors to new or high-potential employees. However, in contrast to Edward Jones's formal system, most organizations rely on informal mentoring—with senior managers personally selecting an employee and taking on that employee as a protégé. Informal mentoring is the most effective mentoring relationship outside the immediate boss–subordinate interface.[64] The boss–subordinate context has an inherent conflict of interest and tension, mostly attributable to managers' directly evaluating the performance of subordinates, limiting openness and meaningful communication.

Why would a leader want to be a mentor? There are personal benefits to the leader as well as benefits for the organization. The mentor–protégé relationship gives the mentor unfiltered access to the attitudes and feelings of lower-ranking employees, and protégés can be an excellent source of early warning signals that identify potential problems. Research suggests that mentor commitment to a program is key to its effectiveness, so if a program is to be successful, it's critical that mentors be on board and see the relationship as beneficial to themselves and the protégé. It's also important that the protégé feel that he has input into the relationship; if it's something he feels is foisted on him, he'll just go through the motions, too.[65]

Are all employees in an organization equally likely to participate in a mentoring relationship? Unfortunately, the answer is no.[66] Evidence indicates that minorities and women are less likely to be chosen as protégés than are white males and thus are less likely to accrue the benefits of mentorship. Mentors tend to select protégés who are similar to themselves in terms of criteria such as background, education, gender, race, ethnicity, and religion. "People naturally move to mentor and can more easily communicate with those with whom they most closely identify."[67] In the United States, for instance, upper-management positions in most organizations have been traditionally staffed by white males, so it is hard for minorities and women to be selected as protégés. In addition, in terms of cross-gender mentoring, senior male managers may select male protégés to minimize problems such as sexual attraction or gossip. Organizations have responded to this dilemma by increasing formal mentoring programs and providing training and coaching for potential mentors of special groups such as minorities and women.[68]

You might assume that mentoring is important, but the research has been fairly disappointing. Two large-scale reviews suggest that the benefits are primarily psychological rather than tangible. Based on these reviews, it appears that the objective outcomes of mentoring, in terms of career success (compensation, job performance), are very small. One of these reviews concluded, "Though mentoring may not be properly labeled an utterly useless concept to careers, neither can it be argued to be as important as the main effects of other influences on career success such as ability and personality."[69] It may *feel* nice to have a mentor, but it does not appear that having a mentor, or even having a good mentor who provides both support and advice, is important to one's career.

Some managers seem to recognize the limits of mentoring. When Scott Flanders became CEO of Freedom Communications, he told his managers to *limit* the time they spent mentoring their staffs. Tom Mattia, a manager at Coca-Cola who oversees 90 direct reports, finds that he has to practice "mentoring on the go."[70]

mentor *A senior employee who sponsors and supports a less-experienced employee, called a protégé.*

Self-Leadership

Is it possible for people to lead themselves? An increasing body of research suggests that many can.[71] Proponents of **self-leadership** propose that there are a set of processes through which individuals control their own behavior. And effective leaders (or what advocates like to call *superleaders*) help their followers to lead themselves. They do this by developing leadership capacity in others and nurturing followers so they no longer need to depend on formal leaders for direction and motivation.

The underlying assumptions behind self-leadership are that people are responsible, capable, and able to exercise initiative without the external constraints of bosses, rules, or regulations. Given the proper support, individuals can monitor and control their own behavior. The importance of self-leadership has increased with the expanded popularity of teams. Empowered, self-managed teams need individuals who are themselves self-directed. Management can't expect individuals who have spent their organizational lives under boss-centered leadership to suddenly adjust to self-managed teams. Therefore, training in self-leadership is an excellent means to help employees make the transition from dependence to autonomy.

To engage in effective self-leadership: (1) make your mental organizational chart horizontal rather than vertical (although vertical reporting relationships matter, often your most trusted colleagues and people of greatest possible impact are peers); (2) focus on influence and not control (do your job *with* your colleagues, not *for* them or *to* them); and (3) don't wait for the right time to make your mark; create your opportunities rather than wait for them.[73]

MYTH OR SCIENCE?

"Men Make Better Leaders Than Women"

this statement is false. There is little evidence to support the belief that men make better leaders than women; indeed, though the differences are small, evidence suggests just the opposite.

From the dawn of the "great man" theory through the late 1980s, the common belief regarding gender and leadership effectiveness was that men made better leaders than women. This stereotype was predicated on the belief that men were inherently better skilled for leadership due to having a stronger task focus, lower emotionality, and a greater propensity to be directive.

The most recent assessment of the evidence concludes that women actually have a leadership advantage. Although the differences are fairly small, meaning that there is a great deal of overlap between males and females in their leadership styles, women do have, on average, a slight edge over men. A recent review of 45 companies found that female leaders were more transformational than male leaders. The authors concluded, "These data attest to the ability of women to perform very well in leadership roles in contemporary organizations."

It is true that men continue to dominate leadership positions. Only 2 percent of the CEOs of Fortune 500 companies are women. But being chosen as leader is not the same as performing well once selected. Research suggests that more individuals prefer male leaders. Given the evidence we've reviewed here, those preferences deserve serious reexamination.[72] ■

self-leadership   *A set of processes through which individuals control their own behavior.*

Exhibit 13-5

"So, does anyone in the group feel like responding to what Richard has just shared with us?"

Online Leadership

How do you lead people who are physically separated from you and with whom your interactions are basically reduced to written digital communications? This is a question that, to date, has received minimal attention from OB researchers.[74] Leadership research has been directed almost exclusively to face-to-face and verbal situations. But we can't ignore the reality that today's managers and their employees are increasingly being linked by networks rather than geographic proximity. Obvious examples include managers who regularly use e-mail to communicate with their staff, managers who oversee virtual projects or teams, and managers whose telecommuting employees are linked to the office by a computer and an Internet connection.

If leadership is important for inspiring and motivating dispersed employees, we need to offer some guidance as to how leadership might function in this context. Keep in mind, however, that there is limited research on this topic. So our intention here is not to provide definitive guidelines for leading online. Rather, it's to introduce you to an increasingly important issue and get you to think about how leadership changes when relationships are defined by network interactions.

In face-to-face communications, harsh *words* can be softened by nonverbal action. A smile and comforting gesture, for instance, can lessen the blow behind strong words like *disappointed, unsatisfactory, inadequate,* or *below expectations.* That nonverbal component doesn't exist with online interactions. The *structure* of words in a digital communication also has the power to motivate or demotivate the receiver. A manager who inadvertently sends a message in short phrases and in all caps may get a very different response than if she sent that same message in full sentences using mixed case.

We know that messages convey more than surface information. From a leadership standpoint, messages can convey trust or lack of trust, status, task directives, or emotional warmth. Concepts such as task structure, supportive behavior, and vision can be conveyed in written form as well as verbally. It may even be possible for leaders to convey charisma through the written word. But to effectively convey online leadership, managers must recognize that they have choices in the words and structure of their digital communications. They also need to develop the skills of "reading between the lines" in the messages they receive. In the same way that emotional intelligence taps an individual's ability to monitor and assess others' emotions, effective online leaders need to develop the skill of deciphering the emotional components of messages.

We propose that online leaders have to think carefully about what actions they want their digital messages to initiate. Networked communication is a powerful channel. When used properly, it can build and enhance an individual's leadership effectiveness. But when misused, it has the potential to undermine a great deal of what a leader has been able to achieve through his or her verbal actions.

In addition, online leaders confront unique challenges, the greatest of which appears to be developing and maintaining trust. Identification-based trust, for instance, is particularly difficult to achieve when there is a lack of intimacy and face-to-face interaction.[75] And online negotiations have also been found to be hindered because parties express lower levels of trust.[76] At this time, it's not clear whether it's even possible for employees to identify with or trust leaders with whom they only communicate electronically.[77]

This discussion leads us to the tentative conclusion that, for an increasing number of managers, good interpersonal skills may include the abilities to communicate support and leadership through written words on a computer screen and to read emotions in others' messages. In this "new world" of communications, writing skills are likely to become an extension of interpersonal skills.

Challenges to the Leadership Construct

7 *Identify when leadership may not be necessary.*

A noted management expert takes issue with the omnipotent role that academicians, practicing managers, and the general public have given to the concept of leadership. He says, "In the 1500s, people ascribed all events they didn't understand to God. Why did the crops fail? God. Why did someone die? God. Now our all-purpose explanation is leadership."[78] He notes that when a company succeeds, people need someone to give the credit to. And that's typically the firm's CEO. Similarly, when a company does poorly, people need someone to blame. CEOs also play this role. But much of an organization's success or failure is due to factors outside the influence of leadership. In many cases, success or failure is just a matter of being in the right or wrong place at a given time.

In this section, we present two perspectives that challenge the widely accepted belief in the importance of leadership. The first argument proposes that leadership is more about appearances than reality. You don't have to *be* an effective leader as long as you *look* like one. The second argument directly attacks the notion that some leadership *will always be effective*, regardless of the situation. This argument contends that in many situations, whatever actions leaders exhibit are irrelevant.

Leadership as an Attribution

We introduced attribution theory in Chapter 5. As you may remember, it deals with the ways in which people try to make sense out of cause-and-effect relationships. We said that when something happens, we want to attribute it to something else. The **attribution theory of leadership** says that leadership is merely an attribution that people make about other individuals.[79] The attribution theory has shown that people characterize leaders as having such traits as intelligence, outgoing personality, strong verbal skills, aggressiveness, understanding, and industriousness.[80] At the organizational level, the attribution framework accounts for the conditions under which people use leadership to explain organizational outcomes. Those conditions are extremes in organizational performance. When an organization has either extremely negative or extremely positive performance, people are prone to make leadership attributions to explain the performance.[81] As noted earlier, this tendency helps to account for the vulnerability of CEOs (and high-ranking state officials) when their organizations suffer a major financial setback, regardless of whether they had much to do with it, and it also accounts for why CEOs tend to be given credit for extremely positive financial results—again, regardless of how much or how little they contributed.

One longitudinal study of 128 major U.S. corporations provided important support for the attributional approach. Analyzing top management team members' perceptions of the charisma of their CEOs and their companies' objective performance, this study found that, whereas perceptions of CEO charisma did not lead to objective company performance, company performance did lead to perceptions of charisma.[82]

Following the attribution theory of leadership, we'd say that what's important in being characterized as an "effective leader" is projecting the *appearance* of being a leader rather than focusing on *actual accomplishments*. Leader-wannabes can attempt to shape the perception that they're smart, personable, verbally adept, aggressive, hardworking, and consistent in their style. By doing so, they increase the probability that their bosses, colleagues, and employees will *view* them as an effective leader.

International **OB**

Cultural Variation in Charismatic Attributions

Do people from different cultures make different attributions about their leaders' charisma? One recent study attempted to answer this question.

A team of researchers conducted a study in which individuals from the United States and Turkey read short stories about a hypothetical leader. Each story portrayed the leader's behaviors and the performance of the leader's company differently. In both cultures, individuals believed that the leader possessed more charisma when displaying behaviors such as promoting the company's vision and involving subordinates *and* when the leader's company performed well. However, the participants from the United States, who are more individualistic, focused on the leader's behaviors when attributing charisma. In contrast, the participants from Turkey, who are more collectivistic, focused on the company's performance when attributing charisma.

Why do these differences exist? The researchers speculated that people from individualistic cultures place more emphasis on the person than on the situation and so they attribute charisma when a leader displays certain traits. People from collectivistic cultures, in contrast, place more emphasis on the situation and assume that the leader is charismatic when the company performs well. So whether others see you as charismatic may, in part, depend on what culture you work in.

Source: Based on N. Ensari and S. E. Murphy, "Cross-Cultural Variations in Leadership Perceptions and Attribution of Charisma to the Leader," *Organizational Behavior and Human Decision Processes,* September 2003, pp. 52–66.

attribution theory of leadership *A leadership theory that says that leadership is merely an attribution that people make about other individuals.*

Substitutes for and Neutralizers of Leadership

Contrary to the arguments made throughout this chapter and Chapter 12, leadership may not always be important. A theory of leadership suggests that, in many situations, whatever actions leaders exhibit are irrelevant. Certain individual, job, and organizational variables can act as *substitutes* for leadership or *neutralize* the leader's influence on his or her followers.[83]

Neutralizers make it impossible for leader behavior to make any difference to follower outcomes. They negate the leader's influence. Substitutes, however, make a leader's influence not only impossible but also unnecessary. They act as a replacement for the leader's influence. For instance, characteristics of employees such as their experience, training, "professional" orientation, or indifference toward organizational rewards can substitute for, or neutralize the effect of, leadership. Experience and training can replace the need for a leader's support or ability to create structure and reduce task ambiguity. Jobs that are inherently unambiguous and routine or that are intrinsically satisfying may place fewer demands on the leadership variable. Organizational characteristics such as explicit, formalized goals, rigid rules and procedures, and cohesive work groups can also replace formal leadership (see Exhibit 13-6).

This recognition that leaders don't always have an impact on follower outcomes should not be that surprising. After all, we have introduced a number of variables in this text—attitudes, personality, ability, and group norms, to name but a few—that have been documented as having an effect on employee performance and satisfaction. Yet supporters of the leadership concept place an undue burden on this variable for explaining and predicting behavior. It's too simplistic to consider employees as guided to goal accomplishments solely by the actions of their leader. It's important, therefore, to recognize explicitly that leadership is merely another independent variable in our overall OB model. In some situations, it may contribute a lot to explaining employee productivity, absence, turnover, satisfaction, and citizenship behavior, but in other situations, it may contribute little toward that end.

Before and After

In case you're tempted to dismiss the attribution theory of leadership as another esoteric theory that lacks real-world relevance, consider the case of former Home Depot CEO Bob Nardelli (now head of Chrysler).

In March 2006, Nardelli was featured on *BusinessWeek*'s cover. The article noted that Home Depot was "thriving" under Nardelli's "diamond-cut" leadership style. The article went on to argue that "Nardelli's feisty spirit is rekindling stellar financial performance."

Just 10 months later, in January 2007, Nardelli was back on *BusinessWeek*'s cover. Confronted with a languishing stock price that had never performed up to the level of rival Lowe's, Home Depot's board asked Nardelli to restructure his pay package so that it was more closely tied to the company's stock price. When Nardelli refused, he was out.

What is striking, though, is how, in the same publication, things had changed so quickly after only a few months. In this article, Nardelli was described as "notoriously imperious," "arrogant," "autocratic," and "stubborn." The article explained his dismissal as evidence that "he could no longer rely on other sterile metrics

to assuage the quivering anger his arrogance provoked within every one of his constituencies."

Are these two articles, by the same writer, really describing the same person? Sure they are. What changed was the results. Just as the attribution theory would predict, the same leader's behavior is attributed differently, depending on the results. In reflecting on the Nardelli saga, we might paraphrase Shakespeare and conclude, "There is no good or bad leader, but success makes it so."

Sources: B. Grow, "Renovating Home Depot," *BusinessWeek*, March 6, 2006, pp. 50–58; and B. Grow, "Out at Home Depot," *BusinessWeek*, January 15, 2007, pp. 56–62.

Exhibit **13-6**	Substitutes for Neutralizers of Leadership	
Defining Characteristics	**Relationship-Oriented Leadership**	**Task-Oriented Leadership**
Individual		
Experience/training	No effect on	Substitutes for
Professionalism	Substitutes for	Substitutes for
Indifference to rewards	Neutralizes	Neutralizes
Job		
Highly structured task	No effect on	Substitutes for
Provides its own feedback	No effect on	Substitutes for
Intrinsically satisfying	Substitutes for	No effect on
Organization		
Explicit formalized goals	No effect on	Substitutes for
Rigid rules and procedures	No effect on	Substitutes for
Cohesive work groups	Substitutes for	Substitutes for

Source: Based on S. Kerr and J. M. Jermier, "Substitutes for Leadership: Their Meaning and Measurement," *Organizational Behavior and Human Performance,* December 1978, p. 378.

The validity of substitutes and neutralizers is controversial. One of the problems is that the theory is very complicated: There are many possible substitutes for and neutralizers of many different types of leader behaviors across many different situations. Moreover, sometimes the difference between substitutes and neutralizers is fuzzy. For example, if I'm working on a task that's intrinsically enjoyable, the theory predicts that leadership will be less important because the task itself provides enough motivation. But does that mean that intrinsically enjoyable tasks neutralize leadership effects, or substitute for them, or both? Another problem that this review points out is that substitutes for leadership (such as employee characteristics, the nature of the task, and so forth) matter, but it does not appear that they substitute for or neutralize leadership.[84]

Finding and Creating Effective Leaders

8 Explain how to find and create effective leaders.

We have covered a lot of ground in these two chapters on leadership. But the ultimate goal of our review is to answer this question: How can organizations find or create effective leaders? Let's try to answer that question.

Selecting Leaders

The entire process that organizations go through to fill management positions is essentially an exercise in trying to identify individuals who will be effective leaders. Your search might begin by reviewing the specific requirements for the position to be filled. What knowledge, skills, and abilities are needed to do the job effectively? You should try to analyze the situation to find candidates who will make a proper match.

Testing is useful for identifying and selecting leaders. Personality tests can be used to look for traits associated with leadership—extraversion, conscientiousness, and openness to experience. Testing to find a leadership-candidate's score on self-monitoring also makes sense. High self-monitors are likely to outperform their low-scoring counterparts because the former are better at reading situations and adjusting their behavior accordingly. You can also assess candidates for emotional intelligence. Given the importance of social skills to

The French couturier Chanel developed an ascension plan for selecting a global CEO, a new position the firm created to manage the intense competition in the luxury-goods business. Selection criteria included a combination of business analytical skills and the ability to think creatively, a requirement for articulating the vision of Chanel's creative leaders. After interviewing 10 executives from the retailing, consumer-goods, and luxury-goods industries, Chanel selected Maureen Chiquet, an American who was president of The Gap's Banana Republic. Chiquet spent a year in Paris learning Chanel's culture and then served as president of Chanel's U.S. division before she became the firm's global CEO.

managerial effectiveness, candidates with a high EI should have an advantage, especially in situations requiring transformational leadership.[85]

Interviews also provide an opportunity to evaluate leadership candidates. For instance, we know that experience is a poor predictor of leader effectiveness, but situation-specific experience is relevant. You can use an interview to determine whether a candidate's prior experience fits with the situation you're trying to fill. Similarly, the interview is a reasonably good vehicle for identifying the degree to which a candidate has leadership traits such as extraversion, self-confidence, a vision, the verbal skills to frame issues, or a charismatic physical presence.

The most important event organizations need to plan for is leadership changes. Nothing lasts forever, so it's always simply a matter of *when* a leader exits, not whether. University of Florida athletic director Jeremy Foley always keeps a list of replacements. He has in place a successful football coach (Urban Meyer) and basketball coach (Billy Donovan). When Donovan surprised Foley in 2007 by announcing that he would coach an NBA team, the same day, Foley put his list in action and was about to offer the job to another candidate before Donovan had a change of heart and decided to stay. Unfortunately, some companies just aren't prepared. Frank Lanza is the 75-year-old chairman and CEO of L-3 Communications Holdings, and even though he recently underwent serious surgery, he's engaged in no planning for his successor. "I don't go for that," he said. That means when Lanza is no longer CEO, his replacement will have to be selected quickly and perhaps haphazardly.[86]

Training Leaders

Organizations, in aggregate, spend billions of dollars, yen, and euros on leadership training and development.[87] These efforts take many forms—from $50,000 executive leadership programs offered by universities such as Harvard to sailing experiences at the Outward Bound school. Business schools, including some elite programs, such as Dartmouth, MIT, and Stanford, are placing renewed emphasis on leadership development. Some companies, too, place a lot of emphasis on leadership development. For example, Goldman Sachs is well known for developing leaders, so much so that *BusinessWeek* called it the "Leadership Factory."[88]

Although much of the money spent on training may provide dubious benefits, our review suggests that there are some things managers can do to get the maximum effect from their leadership-training budgets.[89]

First, let's recognize the obvious. People are not equally trainable. Leadership training of any kind is likely to be more successful with individuals who are high self-monitors than with low self-monitors. Such individuals have the flexibility to change their behavior.

What kinds of things can individuals learn that might be related to higher leader effectiveness? It may be a bit optimistic to believe that we can teach "vision creation," but we can teach implementation skills. We can train people to develop "an understanding about content themes critical to effective visions."[90] We can also teach skills such as trust building and mentoring. And leaders can be taught situational-analysis skills. They can learn how to evaluate situations, how to modify situations to make them fit better with their style, and how to assess which leader behaviors might be most effective in given situations. A number of companies have recently turned to executive coaches to help senior managers improve their leadership skills.[91] For instance, Charles Schwab, eBay, Pfizer, Unilever, and American Express have hired executive coaches to provide specific one-on-one training for their top executives to help them improve their interpersonal skills and to learn to act less autocratically.[92]

On an optimistic note, there is evidence suggesting that behavioral training through modeling exercises can increase an individual's ability to exhibit charismatic leadership qualities. The success of the researchers mentioned earlier (see "Are Charismatic Leaders Born or Made?" on page 413) in actually scripting undergraduate business students to "play" charismatic is a case in point.[93] Finally, there is accumulating research showing that leaders can be trained in transformational leadership skills. Once learned, these skills have bottom-line results, whether in the financial performance of Canadian banks or the training effectiveness of soldiers in the Israeli Defense Forces.[94]

Global Implications

9 *Assess whether charismatic and transformational leadership generalize across cultures.*

We noted in Chapter 12 that while there is little cross-cultural research on the traditional theories of leadership, there is reason to believe that certain types of leadership behaviors work better in some cultures than in others. What about the more contemporary leadership roles covered in this chapter? Is there cross-cultural research on charismatic/transformational leadership? Does it generalize across cultures? Yes and yes. There has been cross-cultural research on charismatic/transformational leadership, and it seems to suggest that the leadership style works in different cultures.

The GLOBE research program, which we introduced in Chapter 4, has gathered data on approximately 18,000 middle managers in 825 organizations, covering 62 countries. It's the most comprehensive cross-cultural study of leadership ever undertaken. So its findings should not be quickly dismissed. It's illuminating that one of the results coming from the GLOBE program is that there *are* some universal aspects to leadership. Specifically, a number of the elements making up transformational leadership appear to be associated with effective leadership, regardless of what country the leader is in.[95] This conclusion is very important because it flies in the face of the contingency view that leadership style needs to adapt to cultural differences.

What elements of transformational leadership appear universal? Vision, foresight, providing encouragement, trustworthiness, dynamism, positiveness, and proactiveness. The results led two members of the GLOBE team to conclude that "effective business leaders in any country are expected by their subordinates to provide a powerful and proactive vision to guide the company into the future, strong motivational skills to stimulate all employees to fulfill the vision, and excellent planning skills to assist in implementing the vision."[96]

What might explain the universal appeal of these transformational leader attributes? It's been suggested that pressures toward common technologies and management practices, as a result of global competition and multinational influences, may make some aspects of leadership universally accepted. If that's true, we may be able to select and train leaders in a universal style and thus significantly raise the quality of leadership worldwide.

None of this is meant to suggest that a certain cultural sensitivity or adaptation in styles might not be important when leading teams in different cultures. A vision is important in any culture, but how that vision is formed and communicated may still need to vary by culture. This is true even for companies that are known worldwide for their emphasis on vision. For example, a GE executive recalls the following of using his U.S. leadership style in Japan: "Nothing happened. I quickly realized that I had to adapt my approach, to act more as a consultant to my colleagues and to adopt a team-based motivational decision-making process rather than the more vocal style which tends to be common in the West. In Japan the silence of a leader means far more than a thousand words uttered by somebody else."[97]

Summary and Implications for Managers

Organizations are increasingly searching for managers who can exhibit transformational leadership qualities. They want leaders with vision and the charisma to carry out their vision. And although true leadership effectiveness may be a result of exhibiting the right behaviors at the right time, the evidence is quite strong that people have a relatively uniform perception of what a leader should look like. They attribute "leadership" to people who are smart, personable, verbally adept, and the like. To the degree that managers project these qualities, others are likely to deem them leaders. There is increasing evidence that the effectiveness of charismatic and transformational leadership crosses cultural boundaries.

Effective managers today must develop trusting relationships with those they seek to lead because, as organizations have become less stable and predictable, strong bonds of trust are likely to be replacing bureaucratic rules in defining expectations and relationships. Managers who aren't trusted aren't likely to be effective leaders.

For managers concerned with how to fill key positions in their organization with effective leaders, we have shown that tests and interviews help to identify people with leadership qualities. In addition to focusing on leadership selection, managers should also consider investing in leadership training. Many individuals with leadership potential can enhance their skills through formal courses, workshops, rotating job responsibilities, coaching, and mentoring.

Point ▶◀ Counterpoint

KEEP LEADERS ON A SHORT LEASH

a company's leaders need to be managed just like everyone else. Often they cause more harm than good. There is a long list of CEOs who practically drove their companies into the ground: Carly Fiorina (HP), Harry Stonecipher (Boeing), Raymond Gilmartin (Merck), Will McGuire (UnitedHealth), Franklin Raines (Fannie Mae), Henry McKinnell (Pfizer), Peter Dolan (Bristol-Myers Squibb), and the list could go on and on. Although the names always change, this sad fact never does: CEOs are often given the "run of the house" and are reined in only after the damage is done. So what happens? A new CEO is hired, and all too often, the same pattern repeats itself.

The key is not who the leader is but how he or she is managed. CEOs are given far too much influence and treated with kid gloves by their board of directors (who generally end up selecting, and rewarding, one another). They make nice while they're being interviewed, but once hired, most turn into autocrats, running their empires with little room for participation, dissent, and, heaven forbid, any limits on their power. When ex-Pfizer CEO Henry McKinnell was forced out, he complained about the "war against the corporation." Actually, the war was against his out-of-control pay package. After he was forced out, Hank Greenberg groused, "If I were starting over, I'd move to China or India." Poor Hank just didn't have enough room to run his empire with those darned stakeholders to answer to.

Yes, CEOs need to be hired carefully, but there are limits to how well we can see the "real" CEO. Much more important is having an autonomous board that will limit the CEO's powers and make him strongly accountable based on performance metrics.

y es, some CEOs fail, but that's business. If everyone succeeded, why would you need a CEO in the first place? The key to leading companies is to choose wisely.

Select poorly, and you need to put systems in place to manage the leader. But this is a losing game. It you're stuck with a dog as CEO, you'll never be able to manage all aspects of her job. Blessed with a good one, and you won't need to worry about managing her performance—the CEO will do that job quite well on her own. Take the example of Boeing's CEO Jim McNerney. He is the first to point out the limits of his own power. "I'm just one of eleven with a point of view," he says. "I have to depend on my power to persuade."

To treat him as if he were some child to be rewarded and punished at every step is to eliminate any benefits of the job altogether. Boeing hired well, and though every CEO needs some metrics, mostly the board should stay out of his way and focus on the big picture—strategic planning, meeting long-term objectives, and so on. It is fine and good to pay CEOs based on performance, but the devil is often in the details. Link all of a CEO's pay to stock price, and what do you think will happen? Some good CEOs won't take the job because they realize they can't perfectly control stock price. Others will take the job only to cynically manipulate it to their short-term advantage. Either way, in the long run, the company loses.

Some companies have limited the leader's authority by slicing up the leader's job and micromanaged him or her at every turn. For example, when Citigroup's Chairman and CEO Charles Prince was forced out in late 2007, many argued in favor of separating the role of Chairman and CEO because the CEO couldn't and shouldn't be trusted to do the job. What company, and what leader, can excel under such a handicap?

There is nothing better than hiring the right CEO. There is nothing worse than hiring the wrong one.[98]

Questions for Review

1 How does framing influence leadership effectiveness?

2 What is charismatic leadership and how does it work?

3 What is transformational leadership? How is it different from transactional and charismatic leadership?

4 What is authentic leadership? Why do ethics and trust matter to leadership?

5 What are the three types of trust?

6 What are the importance of mentoring, self-leadership, and virtual leadership?

7 Are there situations in which leadership is not necessary?

8 How can organizations select and develop effective leaders?

9 Do charismatic and transformational leadership generalize across cultures?

Experiential Exercise

YOU BE THE JUDGE: WHICH VISION STATEMENT IS EFFECTIVE

There has been a lot of research about what makes an effective vision statement. A good vision statement is said to have the following qualities:

a. Identifies values and beliefs.
b. Is idealistic or utopian.
c. Represents broad and overarching (versus narrow and specific) goals.
d. Is inspiring.
e. Is future oriented.
f. Is bold and ambitious.
g. Reflects the uniqueness of the organization.
h. Is well articulated and easily understood.

Now that you know what makes a good vision statement, you can rate vision statements from actual companies.

1. Break into groups of four or five people each.
2. Each group member should rate each of the following vision statements—based on the eight qualities listed here—on a scale from 1 = very poor to 10 = excellent.
3. Compare your ratings. Did your group agree or disagree?
4. What do you think caused the agreement or disagreement?
5. How would you improve these vision statements?

Vision Statements

- *DuPont.* Our vision is to be the world's most dynamic science company, creating sustainable solutions essential to a better, safer and healthier life for people everywhere.
- *Nucor.* Nucor Corporation is made up of 11,900 teammates whose goal is to "Take Care of Our Customers." We are accomplishing this by being the safest, highest quality, lowest cost, most productive and most profitable steel and steel products company in the world. We are committed to doing this while being cultural and environmental stewards in our communities where we live and work. We are succeeding by working together.
- *Toshiba.* Toshiba delivers technology and products remarkable for their innovation and artistry—contributing to a safer, more comfortable, more productive life. We bring together the spirit of innovation with our passion and conviction to shape the future and help protect the global environment—our shared heritage. We foster close relationships, rooted in trust and respect, with our customers, business partners and communities around the world.
- *University of Northern Iowa.* The University of Northern Iowa offers a world-class university education, providing personalized experiences and creating a lifetime of opportunities. Hallmarks of UNI's success include: (1) An environment that places "Students First," (2) A commitment to Great Learning through Great Teaching, and (3) A broad range of services designed to enhance the lives and livelihoods of Iowans.
- *Nissan.* Call us zealous, even overzealous, but at Nissan we know that settling for just any solution is just that. Settling. And, not to mention, the fastest way to go from being an automotive company fueled by imagination to just another automotive company, period. That's why we think beyond the answer. And ask. Because only through this process of constant challenge can real change occur. One question at a time.

Source: The vision attributes are based on S. A. Kirkpatrick, E. A. Locke, and G. P. Latham, "Implementing the Vision: How Is It Done?" *Polish Psychological Bulletin* 27 (1996), pp. 93–106.

Ethical Dilemma

WHOLE FOODS'S RAHODEB

Whole Foods, a fast-growing chain of upscale grocery stores, has long been a Wall Street and business press favorite. It regularly appears high on *Fortune*'s list of *100 Best Companies to Work For* (it was 5th in 2007), and it has spawned its share of competitors, including Fresh Market, Trader Joe's, and Wild Oats.

Given that most industry analysts see a bright future for upscale, organic markets like Whole Foods, it's no surprise that the market has attracted its share of investor blogs. One of the prominent bloggers (filing hundreds of blog entries), "Rahodeb" has consistently extolled the virtues of Whole Foods's stock and derided Wild Oats. Rahodeb predicted that Wild Oats would eventually be forced into bankruptcy and that the stock price of Whole Foods would grow at an annual rate of 18 percent. Rahodeb's Yahoo! Finance blog entries were widely read because he seemed to have special insights into the industry and into Whole Foods in particular.

Would it surprise you to learn that in 2007, Rahodeb was exposed as Whole Foods co-founder and CEO John Mackey? ("Rahodeb" is an anagram of "Deborah," Mackey's wife.) What's more, while Rahodeb was talking down Wild Oats's stock, Whole Foods was in the process of acquiring Wild Oats, and talking down the company may have made the acquisition easier, and cheaper. Because the companies often have stores in the same cities, the Federal Trade Commission (FTC) is attempting to block the acquisition, and the FTC was responsible for "outing" Mackey.

It's not clear that Mackey's behavior was illegal. Mackey said, "I posted on Yahoo! under a pseudonym because I had fun doing it. Many people post on bulletin boards using pseudonyms. The views articulated by rahodeb sometimes represented what I believed and sometimes they didn't."

Do you think it is unethical for a company leader like Mackey to pose as an investor, talking up his or her company's stock price while talking down his competitor's? Would Mackey's behavior affect your willingness to work for or invest in Whole Foods?

Source: D. Kesmodel and J. R. Wilke, "Whole Foods Is Hot, Wild Oats a Dud—So Said 'Rahodeb,'" *Wall Street Journal,* July 12, 2007, pp. A1, A10; and G. Farrell and P. Davidson, "Whole Foods' CEO Was Busy Guy Online," *USA Today,* July 13, 2007, p. 4B.

Case Incident 1

THE MAKING OF A GREAT PRESIDENT

What does it take to be a great U.S. president? A survey of 78 history, political science, and law scholars rated the U.S. presidents from George Washington to Bill Clinton. Here are the presidents who were rated "great" and "near great."

Great
George Washington
Abraham Lincoln
Franklin D. Roosevelt (FDR)

Near Great
Thomas Jefferson
Theodore Roosevelt
Ronald Reagan
Harry Truman
Dwight Eisenhower
James Polk
Andrew Jackson

Among recent presidents, Presidents Nixon, Ford, and Carter were rated "Below Average," and Presidents G. H. W. Bush and Clinton were rated "Average."

What about George W. Bush? Given his relative unpopularity, you might think that he will go down in history as a failure. However, popularity is not a perfect indicator of whether a president's accomplishments stand the test of time. Harry Truman left office with an approval rating in the low 30s, whereas Bill Clinton left office with an approval rating in the mid-60s. Yet historians have judged Truman the more effective president.

Questions

1. Would you rate George W. Bush as a charismatic or transformational leader? What about Bill Clinton?

2. Do you think leaders in other contexts (for example, business, sports, religion) exhibit the same qualities as great or near-great U.S. presidents?

3. Do you think being in the right place at the right time could influence presidential greatness?

Source: "Presidential Leadership: The Rankings," *OpinionJournal.com,* September 12, 2005, www.opinionjournal.com/extra/?id=110007243.

Case Incident 2

GENERATION GAP: MENTORS AND PROTÉGÉS

As the baby boom generation nears retirement, many Boomers are mentoring their future work replacements—Generation Xers. Some Boomers have found the process difficult. William Slater, a 47-year-old computer engineer who participates in his company's formal mentoring program, has had negative experiences with three protégés. He recalls that one tried, unsuccessfully, to take his job, while another repeatedly spoke badly about him to his boss. "I have an ax to grind with Generation X. They're stabbing aging Baby Boomers in the back," says Slater.

It is not only Baby Boomers who have had bad experiences. Joel Bershok, a 24-year-old, was optimistic about the prospects of having a mentor. However, his mentor dissolved the relationship after only 3 weeks. Says Bershok: "He just wanted it for his resume." To Bershok, one of the major problems with a mentoring relationship is a lack of trust. With an uncertain economy and companies making frequent layoff announcements, Boomers are wary of teaching their younger counterparts too much for fear that those counterparts, who usually make less—and so cost the company less than Boomers—may replace them.

The fear may be justified. For example, Janet Wheeler, a 49-year-old broker, saw her job replaced by two younger workers after her company let her go. Wheeler thinks that other Boomers are beginning to notice the risks of mentoring and are responding by not teaching their protégés as much as they could. "You see young people being brought along just enough to get the job done, but not so much that they'll take your job," she states.

Given that some studies have demonstrated the beneficial effects of mentoring on employee outcomes such as performance, job satisfaction, and employee retention, many analysts are concerned that Baby Boomers are failing to see mentoring as a responsibility. According to a study by Menttium Corporation, a firm that aids companies in installing mentoring programs, almost 90 percent of formal mentoring relationships end prematurely. The primary reasons include poor matching of mentors to protégés and a lack of effort to keep the relationship going.

But some workers have strongly benefited from mentoring programs and are trying to maintain mentoring programs in their companies. Three years after joining Dell, Lynn Tyson, 41, helped start a formal mentoring program open to all of Dell's 42,000 employees. "I never had a formal mentor in my entire career. Most of the time I was shaking in my shoes," says Tyson. Her program has been successful so far—and she mentors 40 protégés. "I'm not trying to make this sound sappy, but I have the ability to make a difference in somebody's career, and that excites me every day." The benefits are especially apparent for women and minorities who, historically, have had greater difficulty than white males in climbing to top management positions. According to a study by Harvard University professor David A. Thomas, the most successful racial minorities at three different corporations had a strong network of mentors. In addition, research has shown that women also benefit from having positive mentoring experiences in that they have greater career success and career satisfaction.

With the right amount of effort, protégés, mentors, and the companies that sponsor such relationships can realize tremendous benefits. However, individuals in mentoring relationships may need to look past generational and other individual differences to achieve such benefits. Though Slater has had his share of bad mentoring experiences, he is still optimistic. "Mentoring is a time-honored concept. Those of us who've been mentored should mentor others. Otherwise, we've short-circuited the process and the future," he says.

Questions

1. What factors do you believe lead to successful mentoring programs? If you were designing a mentoring program, what might it look like?

2. In what ways might a protégé benefit from having a mentor? In what ways might a mentor benefit from having a protégé?

3. Of the three types of trust discussed in the chapter, which one may be the primary type in mentoring relationships and why?

4. What types of leaders, in terms of personality traits and behavioral tendencies, would most likely be good mentors? What types of leaders might be poor mentors?

Source: Based on J. Zaslow, "Moving On: Don't Trust Anyone Under 30: Boomers Struggle with Their New Role as Mentors," *Wall Street Journal,* June 5, 2003, p. D1; P. Garfinkel, "Putting a Formal Stamp on Mentoring," *New York Times,* January 18, 2004, p. 10; and J. E. Wallace, "The Benefits of Mentoring for Female Lawyers," *Journal of Vocational Behavior,* June 2001, pp. 366–391.

Endnotes

1. "Endless Summer," *Fortune*, April 2, 2007, pp. 63–70.

2. M. Weber, *The Theory of Social and Economic Organization*, A. M. Henderson and T. Parsons (trans.) (New York: The Free Press, 1947).

3. J. A. Conger and R. N. Kanungo, "Behavioral Dimensions of Charismatic Leadership," in J. A. Conger, R. N. Kanungo and Associates (eds.), *Charismatic Leadership* (San Francisco: Jossey-Bass, 1988), p. 79.

4. J. A. Conger and R. N. Kanungo, *Charismatic Leadership in Organizations* (Thousand Oaks, CA: Sage, 1998); and R. Awamleh and W. L. Gardner, "Perceptions of Leader Charisma and Effectiveness: The Effects of Vision Content, Delivery, and Organizational Performance," *Leadership Quarterly*, Fall 1999, pp. 345–373.

5. R. J. House and J. M. Howell, "Personality and Charismatic Leadership," *Leadership Quarterly* 3 (1992), pp. 81–108; D. N. Den Hartog and P. L., "Leadership in Organizations," in N. Anderson and D. S. Ones (eds.), *Handbook of Industrial, Work and Organizational Psychology*, vol. 2 (Thousand Oaks, CA: Sage, 2002), pp. 166–187.

6. See J. A. Conger and R. N. Kanungo, "Training Charismatic Leadership: A Risky and Critical Task," *Charismatic Leadership* (San Francisco: Jossey-Bass, 1988), pp. 309–323; A. J. Towler, "Effects of Charismatic Influence Training on Attitudes, Behavior, and Performance," *Personnel Psychology*, Summer 2003, pp. 363–381; and M. Frese, S. Beimel, and S. Schoenborn, "Action Training for Charismatic Leadership: Two Evaluations of Studies of a Commercial Training Module on Inspirational Communication of a Vision," *Personnel Psychology*, Autumn 2003, pp. 671–697.

7. R. J. Richardson and S. K. Thayer, *The Charisma Factor: How to Develop Your Natural Leadership Ability* (Upper Saddle River, NJ: Prentice Hall, 1993).

8. J. M. Howell and P. J. Frost, "A Laboratory Study of Charismatic Leadership," *Organizational Behavior and Human Decision Processes*, April 1989, pp. 243–269. See also Frese, Beimel, and Schoenborn, "Action Training for Charismatic Leadership."

9. B. Shamir, R. J. House, and M. B. Arthur, "The Motivational Effects of Charismatic Leadership: A Self-Concept Theory," *Organization Science*, November 1993, pp. 577–594.

10. B. Kark, R. Gan, and B. Shamir, "The Two Faces of Transformational Leadership: Empowerment and Dependency," *Journal of Applied Psychology*, April 2003, pp. 246–255; and P. D. Cherlunik, K. A. Donley, T. S. R. Wiewel, and S. R. Miller, "Charisma Is Contagious: The Effect of Leaders' Charisma on Observers' Affect," *Journal of Applied Social Psychology*, October 2001, pp. 2149–2159.

11. For reviews on the role of vision in leadership, see S. J. Zaccaro, "Visionary and Inspirational Models of Executive Leadership: Empirical Review and Evaluation," in S. J. Zaccaro (ed.), *The Nature of Executive Leadership: A Conceptual and Empirical Analysis of Success* (Washington, DC: American Psychological Assoc., 2001), pp. 259–278; and M. Hauser and R. J. House, "Lead Through Vision and Values," in E. A. Locke (ed.), *Handbook of Principles of Organizational Behavior* (Malden, MA: Blackwell, 2004), pp. 257–273.

12. P. C. Nutt and R. W. Backoff, "Crafting Vision," *Journal of Management Inquiry*, December 1997, p. 309.

13. Ibid., pp. 312–314.

14. J. L. Roberts, "A Mogul's Migraine," *Newsweek*, November 29, 2004, pp. 38–40.

15. D. A. Waldman, B. M. Bass, and F. J. Yammarino, "Adding to Contingent-Reward Behavior: The Augmenting Effect of Charismatic Leadership," *Group & Organization Studies*, December 1990, pp. 381–394; and S. A. Kirkpatrick and E. A. Locke, "Direct and Indirect Effects of Three Core Charismatic Leadership Components on Performance and Attitudes," *Journal of Applied Psychology*, February 1996, pp. 36–51.

16. A. H. B. de Hoogh, D. N. den Hartog, P. L. Koopman, H. Thierry, P. T. van den Berg, and J. G. van der Weide, "Charismatic Leadership, Environmental Dynamism, and Performance," *European Journal of Work & Organizational Psychology*, December 2004, pp. 447–471; S. Harvey, M. Martin, and D. Stout, "Instructor's Transformational Leadership: University Student Attitudes and Ratings," *Psychological Reports*, April 2003, pp. 395–402; and D. A. Waldman, M. Javidan, and P. Varella, "Charismatic Leadership at the Strategic Level: A New Application of Upper Echelons Theory," *Leadership Quarterly*, June 2004, pp. 355–380.

17. R. J. House, "A 1976 Theory of Charismatic Leadership," in J. G. Hunt and L. L. Larson (eds.), *Leadership: The Cutting Edge* (Carbondale, IL: Southern Illinois University Press, 1977), pp. 189–207; and Robert J. House and Ram N. Aditya, "The Social Scientific Study of Leadership," *Journal of Management* 23, no. 3 (1997), p. 441.

18. F. Cohen, S. Solomon, M. Maxfield, T. Pyszczynski, and J. Greenberg, "Fatal Attraction: The Effects of Mortality Salience on Evaluations of Charismatic, Task-Oriented, and Relationship-Oriented Leaders," *Psychological Science*, December 2004, pp. 846–851; and M. G. Ehrhart and K. J. Klein, "Predicting Followers' Preferences for Charismatic Leadership: The Influence of Follower Values and Personality," *Leadership Quarterly*, Summer 2001, pp. 153–179.

19. H. L. Tosi, V. Misangyi, A. Fanelli, D. A. Waldman, and F. J. Yammarino, "CEO Charisma, Compensation, and Firm Performance," *Leadership Quarterly*, June 2004, pp. 405–420.

20. See, for instance, R. Khurana, *Searching for a Corporate Savior: The Irrational Quest for Charismatic CEOs* (Princeton, NJ: Princeton University Press, 2002); and J. A. Raelin, "The Myth of Charismatic Leaders," *Training & Development*, March 2003, pp. 47–54.

21. J. Collins, "Level 5 Leadership: The Triumph of Humility and Fierce Resolve," *Harvard Business Review*, January 2001, pp. 67–76; J. Collins, "Good to Great," *Fast Company*, October 2001, pp. 90–104; J. Collins, "The Misguided Mix-up," *Executive Excellence*, December 2002, pp. 3–4; and Tosi et al., "CEO Charisma, Compensation, and Firm Performance."

22. See, for instance, B. M. Bass, B. J. Avolio, D. I. Jung, and Y. Berson, "Predicting Unit Performance by Assessing Transformational and Transactional Leadership," *Journal of Applied Psychology*, April 2003, pp. 207–218; and T. A. Judge, and R. F. Piccolo, "Transformational and Transactional Leadership: A Meta-analytic Test of Their Relative Validity," *Journal of Applied Psychology*, October 2004, pp. 755–768.

23. B. M. Bass, "Leadership: Good, Better, Best," *Organizational Dynamics*, Winter 1985, pp. 26–40; and J. Seltzer and B. M. Bass, "Transformational Leadership: Beyond Initiation and Consideration," *Journal of Management*, December 1990, pp. 693–703.

24. D. I. Jung, C. Chow, and A. Wu, "The Role of Transformational Leadership in Enhancing Organizational Innovation: Hypotheses and Some Preliminary Findings," *Leadership Quarterly*, August–October 2003, pp. 525–544; D. I. Jung, "Transformational and Transactional Leadership and Their Effects on Creativity in Groups," *Creativity Research Journal* 13, no. 2 (2001), pp. 185–195; and S. J. Shin and J. Zhou, "Transformational Leadership, Conservation, and Creativity: Evidence from Korea," *Academy of Management Journal*, December 2003, pp. 703–714.

25. D. Baum, "Battle Lessons: What the Generals Don't Know," *New Yorker*, January 17, 2005, pp. 42–48.

26. J. E. Bono and T. A. Judge, "Self-Concordance at Work: Toward Understanding the Motivational Effects of Transformational Leaders," *Academy of Management Journal*, October 2003, pp. 554–571; Y. Berson and B. J. Avolio, "Transformational Leadership and the Dissemination of Organizational Goals: A Case Study of a Telecommunication Firm," *Leadership Quarterly*, October 2004, pp. 625–646; and S. Shinn, "21st-Century Engineer," *BizEd*, January/February, 2005, pp. 18–23.

27. J. R. Baum, E. A. Locke, and S. A. Kirkpatrick, "A Longitudinal Study of the Relation of Vision and Vision Communication to Venture Growth in Entrepreneurial Firms," *Journal of Applied Psychology*, February 2000, pp. 43–54.

28. B. J. Avolio, W. Zhu, W. Koh, and P. Bhatia, "Transformational Leadership and Organizational Commitment: Mediating Role of Psychological Empowerment and Moderating Role of Structural Distance," *Journal of Organizational Behavior*, December 2004, pp. 951–968; and T. Dvir, Taly, N. Kass, and B. Shamir, "The Emotional Bond: Vision and Organizational Commitment Among High-Tech Employees," *Journal of Organizational Change Management* 17, no. 2 (2004), pp. 126–143.

29. R. T. Keller, "Transformational Leadership, Initiating Structure, and Substitutes for Leadership: A Longitudinal Study of Research and Development Project Team Performance," *Journal of Applied Psychology* 91, no. 1 (2006), pp. 202–210.

30. Judge and Piccolo, "Transformational and Transactional Leadership."

31. H. Hetland, G. M. Sandal, and T. B. Johnsen, "Burnout in the Information Technology Sector: Does Leadership matter?" *European Journal of Work and Organizational Psychology* 16, no. 1 (2007), pp. 58–75; and K. B. Lowe, K. G. Kroeck, and N. Sivasubramaniam, "Effectiveness Correlates of Transformational and Transactional Leadership: A Meta-Analytic Review of the MLQ Literature," *Leadership Quarterly*, Fall 1996, pp. 385–425.

32. See, for instance, J. Barling, T. Weber, and E. K. Kelloway, "Effects of Transformational Leadership Training on Attitudinal and Financial Outcomes: A Field Experiment," *Journal of Applied Psychology*, December 1996, pp. 827–832; and T. Dvir, D. Eden, and B. J. Avolio, "Impact of Transformational Leadership on Follower Development and Performance: A Field Experiment," *Academy of Management Journal*, August 2002, pp. 735–744.

33. R. J. House and P. M. Podsakoff, "Leadership Effectiveness: Past Perspectives and Future Directions for Research," in J. Greenberg (ed.), *Organizational Behavior: The State of the Science* (Hillsdale, NJ: Erlbaum, 1994), pp. 45–82; and B. M. Bass, *Leadership and Performance Beyond Expectations* (New York: The Free Press, 1985).

34. B. J. Avolio and B. M. Bass, "Transformational Leadership, Charisma and Beyond," working paper, School of management, State University of New York, Binghamton, 1985, p. 14.

35. See B. J. Avolio, W. L. Gardner, F. O. Walumbwa, F. Luthans, and D. R. May, "Unlocking the Mask: A Look at the Process by Which Authentic Impact Follower Attitudes and Behaviors," *Leadership Quarterly*, December 2004, pp. 801–823; W. L. Gardner and J. R. Schermerhorn, Jr., "Performance Gains Through Positive Organizational Behavior and Authentic Leadership," *Organizational Dynamics*, August 2004, pp. 270–281; and M. M. Novicevic, M. G. Harvey, M. R. Buckley, J. A. Brown-Radford, and R. Evans, "Authentic Leadership: A Historical Perspective," *Journal of Leadership and Organizational Behavior* 13, no. 1 (2006), pp. 64–76.

36. A. Carter, "Lighting a Fire Under Campbell," *BusinessWeek*, December 4, 2006, pp. 96–101.

37. R. Ilies, F. P. Morgeson, and J. D. Nahrgang, "Authentic Leadership and Eudaemonic Wellbeing: Understanding Leader-Follower Outcomes," *Leadership Quarterly* 16 (2005), pp. 373–394.

38. This section is based on E. P. Hollander, "Ethical Challenges in the Leader–Follower Relationship," *Business Ethics Quarterly*, January 1995, pp. 55–65; J. C. Rost, "Leadership: A Discussion About Ethics," *Business Ethics Quarterly*, January 1995, pp. 129–142; L. K. Treviño, M. Brown, and L. P. Hartman, "A Qualitative Investigation of Perceived Executive Ethical Leadership: Perceptions from Inside and Outside the Executive Suite," *Human Relations*, January 2003, pp. 5–37; and R. M. Fulmer, "The Challenge of Ethical Leadership," *Organizational Dynamics* 33, no. 3 (2004), pp. 307–317.

39. J. L. Lunsford, "Piloting Boeing's New Course," *Wall Street Journal*, June 13, 2006, pp. B1, B3.

40. J. M. Burns, *Leadership* (New York: Harper & Row, 1978).

41. J. M. Howell and B. J. Avolio, "The Ethics of Charismatic Leadership: Submission or Liberation?" *Academy of Management Executive*, May 1992, pp. 43–55.

42. M. E. Brown and L. K. Treviño, "Socialized Charismatic Leadership, Values Congruence, and Deviance in Work Groups," *Journal of Applied Psychology* 91, no. 4 (2006), pp. 954–962.

43. See, for example, K. T. Dirks and D. L. Ferrin, "Trust in Leadership: Meta-Analytic Findings and Implications for Research and Practice," *Journal of Applied Psychology*, August 2002, pp. 611–628; the special issue on trust in an organizational context, B. McEvily, V. Perrone, A. Zaheer, guest editors, *Organization Science*, January–February 2003; and R. Galford and A. S. Drapeau, *The Trusted Leader* (New York: The Free Press, 2003).

44. Based on S. D. Boon and J. G. Holmes, "The Dynamics of Interpersonal Trust: Resolving Uncertainty in the Face of

Risk," in R. A. Hinde and J. Groebel (eds.), *Cooperation and Prosocial Behavior* (Cambridge, UK: Cambridge University Press, 1991), p. 194; D. J. McAllister, "Affect- and Cognition-Based Trust as Foundations for Interpersonal Cooperation in Organizations," *Academy of Management Journal*, February 1995, p. 25; and D. M. Rousseau, S. B. Sitkin, R. S. Burt, and C. Camerer, "Not So Different After All: A Cross-Discipline View of Trust," *Academy of Management Review*, July 1998, pp. 393–404.

45. J. B. Rotter, "Interpersonal Trust, Trustworthiness, and Gullibility," *American Psychologist*, January 1980, pp. 1–7.

46. J. D. Lewis and A. Weigert, "Trust as a Social Reality," *Social Forces*, June 1985, p. 970.

47. J. K. Rempel, J. G. Holmes, and M. P. Zanna, "Trust in Close Relationships," *Journal of Personality and Social Psychology*, July 1985, p. 96.

48. M. Granovetter, "Economic Action and Social Structure: The Problem of Embeddedness," *American Journal of Sociology*, November 1985, p. 491.

49. R. C. Mayer, J. H. Davis, and F. D. Schoorman, "An Integrative Model of Organizational Trust," *Academy of Management Review*, July 1995, p. 712.

50. C. Johnson-George and W. Swap, "Measurement of Specific Interpersonal Trust: Construction and Validation of a Scale to Assess Trust in a Specific Other," *Journal of Personality and Social Psychology*, September 1982, p. 1306.

51. P. L. Schindler and C. C. Thomas, "The Structure of Interpersonal Trust in the Workplace," *Psychological Reports*, October 1993, pp. 563–573.

52. H. H. Tan and C. S. F. Tan, "Toward the Differentiation of Trust in Supervisor and Trust in Organization," *Genetic, Social, and General Psychology Monographs*, May 2000, pp. 241–260.

53. Cited in D. Jones, "Do You Trust Your CEO?" *USA Today*, February 12, 2003, p. 7B.

54. D. McGregor, *The Professional Manager* (New York: McGraw-Hill, 1967), p. 164.

55. B. Nanus, *The Leader's Edge: The Seven Keys to Leadership in a Turbulent World* (Chicago: Contemporary Books, 1989), p. 102.

56. See, for instance, Dirks and Ferrin, "Trust in Leadership"; D. I. Jung and B. J. Avolio, "Opening the Black Box: An Experimental Investigation of the Mediating Effects of Trust and Value Congruence on Transformational and Transactional Leadership," *Journal of Organizational Behavior*, December 2000, pp. 949–964; and A. Zacharatos, J. Barling, and R. D. Iverson, "High-Performance Work Systems and Occupational Safety," *Journal of Applied Psychology*, January 2005, pp. 77–93.

57. D. E. Zand, *The Leadership Triad: Knowledge, Trust, and Power* (New York: Oxford University Press, 1997), p. 89.

58. Based on L. T. Hosmer, "Trust: The Connecting Link Between Organizational Theory and Philosophical Ethics," *Academy of Management Review*, April 1995, p. 393; and R. C. Mayer, J. H. Davis, and F. D. Schoorman, "An Integrative Model of Organizational Trust," *Academy of Management Review*, July 1995, p. 712.

59. J. M. Kouzes and B. Z. Posner, *Credibility: How Leaders Gain and Lose It, and Why People Demand It* (San Francisco: Jossey-Bass, 1993), p. 14.

60. D. Shapiro, B. H. Sheppard, and L. Cheraskin, "Business on a Handshake," *Negotiation Journal*, October 1992, pp. 365–377; R. J. Lewicki, E. C. Tomlinson, and N. Gillespie, "Models of Interpersonal Trust Development: Theoretical Approaches, Empirical Evidence, and Future Directions," *Journal of Management*, December 2006, pp. 991–1022; and J. Child, "Trust—The Fundamental Bond in Global Collaboration," *Organizational Dynamics* 29, no. 4 (2001), pp. 274–288.

61. This section is based on Zand, *The Leadership Triad*, pp. 122–134; and A. M. Zak, J. A. Gold, R. M. Ryckman, and E. Lenney, "Assessments of Trust in Intimate Relationships and the Self-Perception Process," *Journal of Social Psychology*, April 1998, pp. 217–228.

62. M. E. Schweitzer, J. C. Hershey, and E. T. Bradlow, "Promises and Lies: Restoring Violated Trust," *Organizational Behavior and Human Decision Processes* 101 (2006), pp. 1–19.

63. See, for example, M. Murray, *Beyond the Myths and Magic of Mentoring: How to Facilitate an Effective Mentoring Process*, rev. ed. (New York: Wiley, 2001); K. E. Kram, "Phases of the Mentor Relationship," *Academy of Management Journal*, December 1983, pp. 608–625; R. A. Noe, "An Investigation of the Determinants of Successful Assigned Mentoring Relationships," *Personnel Psychology*, Fall 1988, pp. 559–580; and L. Eby, M. Butts, and A. Lockwood, "Protégés' Negative Mentoring Experiences: Construct Development and Nomological Validation," *Personnel Psychology*, Summer 2004, pp. 411–447.

64. J. A. Wilson and N. S. Elman, "Organizational Benefits of Mentoring," *Academy of Management Executive*, November 1990, p. 90; and J. Reingold, "Want to Grow as a Leader? Get a Mentor?" *Fast Company*, January 2001, pp. 58–60.

65. T. D. Allen, E. T. Eby, and E. Lentz, "The Relationship Between Formal Mentoring Program Characteristics and Perceived Program Effectiveness," *Personnel Psychology* 59 (2006), pp. 125–153; and T. D. Allen, L. T. Eby, and E. Lentz, "Mentorship Behaviors and Mentorship Quality Associated with Formal Mentoring Programs: Closing the Gap Between Research and Practice," *Journal of Applied Psychology* 91, no. 3 (2006), pp. 567–578.

66. See, for example, K. E. Kram and D. T. Hall, "Mentoring in a Context of Diversity and Turbulence," in E. E. Kossek and S. A. Lobel (eds.), *Managing Diversity* (Cambridge, MA: Blackwell, 1996), pp. 108–136; B. R. Ragins and J. L. Cotton, "Mentor Functions and Outcomes: A Comparison of Men and Women in Formal and Informal Mentoring Relationships," *Journal of Applied Psychology*, August 1999, pp. 529–550; and D. B. Turban, T. W. Dougherty, and F. K. Lee, "Gender, Race, and Perceived Similarity Effects in Developmental Relationships: The Moderating Role of Relationship Duration," *Journal of Vocational Behavior*, October 2002, pp. 240–262.

67. Wilson and Elman, "Organizational Benefits of Mentoring," p. 90.

68. See, for instance, K. Houston-Philpot, "Leadership Development Partnerships at Dow Corning Corporation," *Journal of Organizational Excellence*, Winter 2002, pp. 13–27.

69. T. D. Allen, L. T. Eby, M. L. Poteet, Mark L., E. Lentz, and L. Lizzette, "Career Benefits Associated with Mentoring for Protégés: A Meta-Analysis," *Journal of Applied Psychology*,

February 2004, pp. 127–136; and J. D. Kammeyer-Mueller and T. A. Judge, "A Quantitative Review of the Mentoring Literature: Test of a Model," Working paper, University of Florida, 2005.

70. C. Hymowitz, "Today's Bosses Find Mentoring Isn't Worth the Time and Risks," *Wall Street Journal*, March 13, 2006, p. B1.

71. See C. C. Manz, "Self-Leadership: Toward an Expanded Theory of Self-Influence Processes in Organizations," *Academy of Management Review*, July 1986, pp. 585–600; C. C. Manz and H. P. Sims, Jr., *The New Superleadership: Leading Others to Lead Themselves* (San Francisco: Berrett-Koehler, 2001); C. L. Dolbier, M. Soderstrom, M. A. Steinhardt, "The Relationships Between Self-Leadership and Enhanced Psychological, Health, and Work Outcomes," *Journal of Psychology*, September 2001, pp. 469–485; and J. D. Houghton, T. W. Bonham, C. P. Neck, and K. Singh, "The Relationship Between Self-Leadership and Personality: A Comparison of Hierarchical Factor Structures," *Journal of Managerial Psychology* 19, no. 4 (2004), pp. 427–441.

72. A. H. Eagly, "Female Leadership Advantage and Disadvantage: Resolving the Contradictions," *Psychology of Women Quarterly*, March 2007, pp. 1–12; and A. H. Eagly, M. C. Johannesen-Schmidt, and M. L. van Engen, "Transformational, Transactional, and Laissez-Faire Leadership Styles: A Meta-analysis Comparing Women and Men," *Psychological Bulletin*, July 2003, pp. 569–591.

73. J. Kelly and S. Nadler, "Leading from Below," *Wall Street Journal*, March 3, 2007, pp. R4, R10.

74. L. A. Hambley, T. A. O'Neill, and T. J. B. Kline, "Virtual Team Leadership: The Effects of Leadership Style and Communication Medium on Team Interaction Styles and Outcomes," *Organizational Behavior and Human Decision Processes* 103 (2007), pp. 1–20; and B. J. Avolio and S. S. Kahai, "Adding the 'E' to E-Leadership: How it May Impact Your Leadership," *Organizational Dynamics* 31, no. 4 (2003), pp. 325–338.

75. S. J. Zaccaro and P. Bader, "E-Leadership and the Challenges of Leading E-Teams: Minimizing the Bad and Maximizing the Good," *Organizational Dynamics* 31, no. 4 (2003), pp. 381–385.

76. C. E. Naquin and G. D. Paulson, "Online Bargaining and Interpersonal Trust," *Journal of Applied Psychology*, February 2003, pp. 113–120.

77. B. Shamir, "Leadership in Boundaryless Organizations: Disposable or Indispensable?" *European Journal of Work and Organizational Psychology* 8, no. 1 (1999), pp. 49–71.

78. Comment by Jim Collins and cited in J. Useem, "Conquering Vertical Limits," *Fortune*, February 19, 2001, p. 94.

79. See, for instance, J. R. Meindl, "The Romance of Leadership as a Follower-Centric Theory: A Social Constructionist Approach," *Leadership Quarterly*, Fall 1995, pp. 329–341; and S. A. Haslam, M. J. Platow, J. C. Turner, K. J. Reynolds, C. McGarty, P. J. Oakes, S. Johnson, M. K. Ryan, and K. Veenstra, "Social Identity and the Romance of Leadership: The Importance of Being Seen to Be 'Doing It for Us,'" *Group Processes & Intergroup Relations*, July 2001, pp. 191–205.

80. R. G. Lord, C. L. DeVader, and G. M. Alliger, "A Meta-analysis of the Relation Between Personality Traits and Leadership Perceptions: An Application of Validity Generalization Procedures," *Journal of Applied Psychology*, August 1986, pp. 402–410.

81. J. R. Meindl, S. B. Ehrlich, and J. M. Dukerich, "The Romance of Leadership," *Administrative Science Quarterly*, March 1985, pp. 78–102.

82. B. R. Agle, N. J. Nagarajan, J. A. Sonnenfeld, and D. Srinivasan, "Does CEO Charisma Matter?" *Academy of Management Journal* 49, no. 1 (2006), pp. 161–174.

83. S. Kerr and J. M. Jermier, "Substitutes for Leadership: Their Meaning and Measurement," *Organizational Behavior and Human Performance*, December 1978, pp. 375–403; J. M. Jermier and S. Kerr, "Substitutes for Leadership: Their Meaning and Measurement—Contextual Recollections and Current Observations," *Leadership Quarterly* 8, no. 2 (1997), pp. 95–101; and E. de Vries Reinout, R. A. Roe, and T. C. B. Taillieu, "Need for Leadership as a Moderator of the Relationships Between Leadership and Individual Outcomes," *Leadership Quarterly*, April 2002, pp. 121–138.

84. S. D. Dionne, F. J. Yammarino, L. E. Atwater, and L. R. James, "Neutralizing Substitutes for Leadership Theory: Leadership Effects and Common-Source Bias," *Journal of Applied Psychology*, 87 (2002), pp. 454–464; and J. R. Villa, J. P. Howell, P. W. Dorfman, and D. L. Daniel, "Problems with Detecting Moderators in Leadership Research Using Moderated Multiple Regression," *Leadership Quarterly* 14 (2002), pp. 3–23.

85. B. M. Bass, "Cognitive, Social, and Emotional Intelligence of Transformational Leaders," in R. E. Riggio, S. E. Murphy, and F. J. Pirozzolo (eds.), *Multiple Intelligences and Leadership* (Mahwah, NJ: Erlbaum, 2002), pp. 113–114.

86. J. Karp, "Tough Question for L-3's CEO: Who's Next?" *Wall Street Journal*, May 8, 2006, pp. B1, B3.

87. See, for instance, P. Dvorak, "M.B.A. Programs Hone 'Soft Skills,'" *Wall Street Journal*, February 12, 2007, p. B3.

88. J. Weber, "The Leadership Factor," *BusinessWeek*, June 12, 2006, pp. 60–64.

89. See, for instance, Barling, Weber, and Kelloway, "Effects of Transformational Leadership Training on Attitudinal and Financial Outcomes"; and D. V. Day, "Leadership Development: A Review in Context," *Leadership Quarterly*, Winter 2000, pp. 581–613.

90. M. Sashkin, "The Visionary Leader," in J. A. Conger, R. N. Kanungo et al. (eds.), *Charismatic Leadership* (San Francisco: Jossey-Bass, 1988), p. 150.

91. D. V. Day, "Leadership Development: A Review in Context," *Leadership Quarterly*, Winter 2000, pp. 590–593.

92. M. Conlin, "CEO Coaches," *BusinessWeek*, November 11, 2002, pp. 98–104.

93. Howell and Frost, "A Laboratory Study of Charismatic Leadership."

94. Dvir, Eden, and Avolio, "Impact of Transformational Leadership on Follower Development and Performance"; B. J. Avolio and B. M. Bass, *Developing Potential Across a Full Range of Leadership: Cases on Transactional and Transformational Leadership* (Mahwah, NJ: Lawrence Erlbaum, 2002); A. J. Towler, "Effects of Charismatic Influence Training on Attitudes, Behavior, and Performance," *Personnel Psychology*, Summer 2003, pp. 363–381; and Barling, Weber, and Kelloway, "Effects of Transformational Leadership Training on Attitudinal and Financial Outcomes."

95. R. J. House, M. Javidan, P. Hanges, and P. Dorfman, "Understanding Cultures and Implicit Leadership Theories Across the Globe: An Introduction to Project GLOBE," *Journal of World Business*, Spring 2002, pp. 3–10.

96. D. E. Carl and M. Javidan, "Universality of Charismatic Leadership: A Multi-Nation Study," paper presented at the National Academy of Management Conference, Washington, DC, August 2001, p. 29.

97. N. Beccalli, "European Business Forum Asks: Do Companies Get the Leaders They Deserve?" *European Business Forum*, 2003, www.pwcglobal.com/extweb/pwcpublications.nsf/DocID/D1EC3380F589844585256D7300346A1B.

98. A. Murray, "After the Revolt, Creating a New CEO," *Wall Street Journal*, May 5, 2007, pp. A1, A18.

Power and Politics

Power is not revealed by
striking hard or often, but by
striking true.

—Honoré de Balzac

LEARNING OBJECTIVES

After studying this chapter, you should be able to:

1 Define *power* and contrast leadership and power.

2 Contrast the five bases of power.

3 Identify nine power or influence tactics and their contingencies.

4 Show the connection between sexual harassment and the abuse of power.

5 Distinguish between legitimate and illegitimate political behavior.

6 Identify the causes and consequences of political behavior.

7 Apply impression management techniques.

8 Determine whether a political action is ethical.

9 Show the influence of culture on the uses and perceptions of politics.

*y*ou would think investment analysts are nothing if not objective. After all, if an analyst's buy, sell, or hold ratings are tainted by personal relationships, power plays, or office politics, the very credibility the analyst depends on is undermined. Analysts, though, are finding that they're coming under increasing pressure from companies whose stock they're evaluating, and by shareholders themselves.

"You Better Change It"

Consider Michael Krensavage, who has been an analyst for more than 11 years and is senior vice president of Equity Research for Raymond James & Associates. Although a veteran like Krensavage has seen his share of disappointed and angry managers, a recent phone message he received was particularly nasty. "Hey, ah, Mike," the caller said. "Let me tell you something right now. I am going to have an SEC investigation into your company for you downgrading the Bentley Pharmaceutical. You took a stock, your company is putting a short in and manipulating the stock down. I know about it; I'm going to get to the bottom of it. You better, you better upgrade that goddamn thing. Because let me tell you something right now my friend, you're going to go to jail. That stock had 90 percent better earnings this year than last year and then you hit it down. We know what you're doing, and I am going to get the S.E.C. to investigate you and your company. You better believe it. You better change it."

What spawned this phone message was a report Krensavage had filed a few days earlier about Bentley, noting that the company's stock continued to underperform and urging investors to consider selling their Bentley shares.

Sometimes the threats come not from individual investors but from the companies themselves. When Krensavage downgraded his rating of AAIPharmia, a drug development company, the company bad-mouthed him at every opportunity. At one point, it launched an effort to get him fired, calling several of Krensavage's bosses. Although Krensavage wasn't fired, the situation reveals the political pressures many analysts face and succumb to.

"It's not easy putting a sell rating on a stock," Krensavage said. "You often face significant repercussions."[1] ■

*P*ower and *politics* have been described as the last dirty words. It is easier for most of us to talk about sex or money than it is to talk about power or political behavior. People who have power deny it, people who want it try not to look like they're seeking it, and those who are good at getting it are secretive about how they do so.[2] To see whether you think your work environment is political, take the following self-assessment.

Self Assessment Library

IS MY WORKPLACE POLITICAL?

In the Self-Assessment Library (available on CD and online), take assessment IV.F.1 (Is My Workplace Political?); if you don't currently have a job, answer for your most recent job. Then answer the following questions.

1. *How does your score relate to those of your classmates? Do you think your score is accurate? Why or why not?*
2. *Do you think a political workplace is a bad thing? If yes, why? If no, why not?*
3. *What factors cause your workplace to be political?*

A major theme of this chapter is that power and political behavior are natural processes in any group or organization. Given that, you need to know how power is acquired and exercised if you are to fully understand organizational behavior. Although you may have heard the phrase "power corrupts and absolute power corrupts absolutely," power is not always bad. As one author has noted, most medicines can kill if taken in the wrong amount, and thousands die each year in automobile accidents, but we don't abandon chemicals or cars because of the dangers associated with them. Rather, we consider danger an incentive to get training and information that will help us to use these forces productively.[3] The same applies to power. It's a reality of organizational life, and it's not going to go away. Moreover, by learning how power works in organizations, you'll be better able to use your knowledge to become a more effective manager.

A Definition of *Power*

1 Define power and contrast leadership and power.

Power refers to a capacity that *A* has to influence the behavior of *B* so that *B* acts in accordance with *A*'s wishes.[4] This definition implies a *potential* that need not be actualized to be effective, and a *dependency* relationship.

Power may exist but not be used. It is, therefore, a capacity or potential. Someone can have power but not impose it. Probably the most important aspect of power is that it is a function of **dependency**. The greater *B*'s dependence on *A*, the greater is *A*'s power in the relationship. Dependence, in turn, is based on alternatives that *B* perceives and the importance that *B* places on the alternative(s) that *A* controls. A person can have power over you only if he or she controls something you desire. If you want a college degree and have to pass a certain course to get it, and your current instructor is the only faculty member in the college who teaches that course, he or she has power over you. Your alternatives are highly limited, and you place a high degree of importance on obtaining a passing grade. Similarly, if you're attending college on funds totally provided by your parents, you probably recognize the power that they hold over you. You're dependent on them for financial support. But once you're out of school, have a job, and are making a good income, your parents' power is reduced significantly. Who among us, though, has not known or heard of a rich relative who is able to control a large number of family members merely through the implicit or explicit threat of "writing them out of the will"?

Contrasting Leadership and Power

A careful comparison of our description of power with our description of leadership in Chapters 12 and 13 reveals that the concepts are closely intertwined. Leaders use power as a means of attaining group goals. Leaders achieve goals, and power is a means of facilitating their achievement.

What differences are there between the two terms? One difference relates to goal compatibility. Power does not require goal compatibility, merely dependence. Leadership, on the other hand, requires some congruence between the goals of the leader and those being led. A second difference relates to the direction of influence. Leadership focuses on the downward influence on one's followers. It minimizes the importance of lateral and upward influence patterns. Power does not. Still another difference deals with research emphasis. Leadership research, for the most part, emphasizes style. It seeks answers to questions such as: How supportive should a leader be? How much decision making should be shared with followers? In contrast, the research on power has tended to encompass a broader area and to focus on tactics for gaining compliance. It has gone beyond the individual as the exerciser of power because power can be used by groups as well as by individuals to control other individuals or groups.

---

power *A capacity that A has to influence the behavior of B so that B acts in accordance with A's wishes.*

dependency *B's relationship to A when A possesses something that B requires.*

Bases of Power

Where does power come from? What is it that gives an individual or a group influence over others? We answer these questions by dividing the bases or sources of power into two general groupings—formal and personal—and then breaking each of these down into more specific categories.[5]

Formal Power

Formal power is based on an individual's position in an organization. Formal power can come from the ability to coerce or reward, or it can come from formal authority.

Coercive Power   The **coercive power** base is dependent on fear. A person reacts to this power out of fear of the negative results that might occur if she failed to comply. It rests on the application, or the threat of application, of physical sanctions such as the infliction of pain, the generation of frustration through restriction of movement, or the controlling by force of basic physiological or safety needs.

At the organizational level, A has coercive power over B if A can dismiss, suspend, or demote B, assuming that B values his or her job. Similarly, if A can assign B work activities that B finds unpleasant or treat B in a manner that B finds embarrassing, A possesses coercive power over B. Coercive power can also come from withholding key information. People in an organization who have data or knowledge that others need can make those others dependent on them.

Reward Power   The opposite of coercive power is **reward power**. People comply with the wishes or directives of another because doing so produces positive benefits; therefore, one who can distribute rewards that others view as valuable will have power over those others. These rewards can be either financial—such as controlling pay rates, raises, and bonuses; or nonfinancial—including recognition, promotions, interesting work assignments, friendly colleagues, and preferred work shifts or sales territories.[6]

Coercive power and reward power are actually counterparts of each other. If you can remove something of positive value from another or inflict something of negative value, you have coercive power over that person. If you can give someone something of positive value or remove something of negative value, you have reward power over that person.

Dr. Julie Gerberding, director of the Centers for Disease Control and Prevention, has both legitimate power and expert power. As director of the CDC, she has formal authority to use the government agency's resources in protecting the health and safety of the U.S. population. Gerberding is able to wield power because of her expertise in infectious diseases gained through her education and work experience. She earned under-graduate degrees in biology and chemistry and an M.D. degree. Before becoming the CDC director, Gerberding was acting deputy director of the National Center for Infectious Diseases.

Legitimate Power   In formal groups and organizations, probably the most frequent access to one or more of the power bases is one's structural position. This is called **legitimate power**. It represents the formal authority to control and use organizational resources.

Positions of authority include coercive and reward powers. Legitimate power, however, is broader than the power to coerce and reward. Specifically, it includes acceptance by members in an organization of the authority of a position. When school principals, bank presidents, or army captains speak (assuming that their directives are viewed to be within the authority of their positions), teachers, tellers, and first lieutenants listen and usually comply.

Personal Power

You don't have to have a formal position in an organization to have power. Many of the most competent and productive chip designers at Intel, for instance, have power, but they aren't managers and have no formal power.

What they have is personal power—power that comes from an individual's unique characteristics. In this section, we look at two bases of personal power—expertise and the respect and admiration of others.

Expert Power   **Expert power** is influence wielded as a result of expertise, special skill, or knowledge. Expertise has become one of the most powerful sources of influence as the world has become more technologically oriented. As jobs become more specialized, we become increasingly dependent on experts to achieve goals. It is generally acknowledged that physicians have expertise and hence expert power—most of us follow the advice that our doctors give us. But it's also important to recognize that computer specialists, tax accountants, economists, industrial psychologists, and other specialists are able to wield power as a result of their expertise.

Referent Power   **Referent power** is based on identification with a person who has desirable resources or personal traits. If I like, respect, and admire you, you can exercise power over me because I want to please you.

Referent power develops out of admiration of another and a desire to be like that person. It helps explain, for instance, why celebrities are paid millions of dollars to endorse products in commercials. Marketing research shows that people such as LeBron James and Tom Brady have the power to influence your choice of athletic shoes and credit cards. With a little practice, you and I could probably deliver as smooth a sales pitch as these celebrities, but the buying public doesn't identify with you and me. One of the ways in which individuals acquire referent power is through charisma. Some people have referent power who, while not in formal leadership positions, nevertheless are able to exert influence over others because of their charismatic dynamism, likability, and emotional effects on us.

Which Bases of Power Are Most Effective?

Of the three bases of formal power (coercive, reward, legitimate) and two bases of personal power (expert, referent), which is most important to have? Interestingly, research suggests pretty clearly that the personal sources of power are most effective. Both expert and referent power are positively related to employees' satisfaction with supervision, their organizational commitment, and their performance, whereas reward and legitimate power seem to be unrelated to these outcomes. Moreover, one source of formal power—coercive power—actually can backfire in that it is negatively related to employee satisfaction and commitment.[7]

Consider Steve Stoute's company, Translation, which matches pop-star spokespersons with corporations that want to promote their brands. Stoute has paired Gwen Stefani with HP, Justin Timberlake with McDonald's, Beyoncé Knowles with Tommy Hilfiger, and Jay-Z with Reebok. Stoute's business seems to be all about referent power. As one record company executive commented when reflecting on Stoute's successes, "He's the right guy for guiding brands in using the record industry to reach youth culture in a credible way."[8] In other

---

coercive power   *A power base that is dependent on fear.*

reward power   *Compliance achieved based on the ability to distribute rewards that others view as valuable.*

legitimate power   *The power a person receives as a result of his or her position in the formal hierarchy of an organization.*

expert power   *Influence based on special skills or knowledge.*

referent power   *Influence based on possession by an individual of desirable resources or personal traits.*

Exhibit **14-1**

"*I was just going to say 'Well, I don't make the rules.' But, of course, I do make the rules.*"

Source: Drawing by Leo Cullum in *The New Yorker*, copyright © 1986 *The New Yorker Magazine*. Reprinted by permission.

words, using pop stars to market products works because of referent power: People buy products associated with cool figures because they wish to identify with these figures and emulate them.

Dependency: The Key to Power

Earlier in this chapter we said that probably the most important aspect of power is that it is a function of dependency. In this section, we show how having an understanding of dependency is central to furthering your understanding of power itself.

The General Dependency Postulate

Let's begin with a general postulate: *The greater B's dependency on A, the greater the power A has over B.* When you possess anything that others require but that you alone control, you make them dependent on you, and, therefore, you gain power over them.[9] Dependency, then, is inversely proportional to the alternative sources of supply. If something is plentiful, possession of it will not increase your power. If everyone is intelligent, intelligence gives no special advantage. Similarly, among the superrich, money is no longer power. But, as the old saying goes, "In the land of the blind, the one-eyed man is king!" If you can create a monopoly by controlling information, prestige, or anything else that others crave, they become dependent on you. Conversely, the more that you can

Because Xerox Corporation has staked its future on development and innovation, Sophie Vandebroek is in a position of power at Xerox. As the company's chief technology officer, she leads the Xerox Innovation Group of 5,000 scientists and engineers at the company's global research centers. The group's mission is "to pioneer high-impact technologies that enable us to lead in our core markets and to create future markets for Xerox." Xerox depends on Vandebroek to make that mission a reality.

expand your options, the less power you place in the hands of others. This explains, for example, why most organizations develop multiple suppliers rather than give their business to only one. It also explains why so many of us aspire to financial independence. Financial independence reduces the power that others can have over us.

What Creates Dependency?

Dependency is increased when the resource you control is important, scarce, and nonsubstitutable.[10]

Importance If nobody wants what you have, it's not going to create dependency. To create dependency, the thing(s) you control must be perceived as being important. Organizations, for instance, actively seek to avoid uncertainty.[11] We should, therefore, expect that the individuals or groups who can absorb an organization's uncertainty will be perceived as controlling an important resource. For instance, a study of industrial organizations found that the marketing departments in these firms were consistently rated as the most powerful.[12] The researcher concluded that the most critical uncertainty facing these firms was selling their products. This might suggest that engineers, as a group, would be more powerful at Matsushita than at Procter & Gamble. These inferences appear to be generally valid. An organization such as Matsushita, which is heavily technologically oriented, is highly dependent on its engineers to maintain its products' technical advantages and quality. And, at Matsushita, engineers are clearly a powerful group. At Procter & Gamble, marketing is the name of the game, and marketers are the most powerful occupational group.

Scarcity As noted previously, if something is plentiful, possession of it will not increase your power. A resource needs to be perceived as scarce to create dependency. This can help explain how low-ranking members in an organization who have important knowledge not available to high-ranking members gain power over the high-ranking members. Possession of a scarce resource—in this case, important knowledge—makes the high-ranking member dependent on the low-ranking member. This also helps to make sense out of behaviors of low-ranking members that otherwise might seem illogical, such as destroying the procedure manuals that describe how a job is done, refusing to train people in their jobs or even to show others exactly what they do, creating specialized language and terminology that inhibit others from understanding their jobs, or operating in secrecy so an activity will appear more complex and difficult than it really is. Ferruccio Lamborghini, the guy who created the exotic supercars that continue to carry his name, understood the importance of scarcity and used it to his advantage during World War II. Lamborghini was in Rhodes with the Italian army. His superiors were impressed with his mechanical skills, as he demonstrated an almost uncanny ability to repair tanks and cars that no one else could fix. After the war, he admitted that his ability was largely due to having been the first person on the island to receive the repair manuals, which he memorized and then destroyed so as to become indispensable.[13]

The scarcity–dependency relationship can further be seen in the power of occupational categories. Individuals in occupations in which the supply of personnel is low relative to demand can negotiate compensation and benefits packages that are far more attractive than can those in occupations for which there is an abundance of candidates. College administrators have no problem today finding English instructors. The market for network systems analysts, in contrast, is extremely tight, with the demand high and the supply limited. The result is that the bargaining power of computer-engineering faculty allows them to negotiate higher salaries, lighter teaching loads, and other benefits.

Nonsubstitutability   The fewer viable substitutes for a resource, the more power the control over that resource provides. Higher education again provides an excellent example. At universities in which there are strong pressures for the faculty to publish, we can say that a department head's power over a faculty member is inversely related to that member's publication record. The more recognition the faculty member receives through publication, the more mobile he or she is; that is, because other universities want faculty who are highly published and visible, there is an increased demand for that person's services. Although the concept of tenure can act to alter this relationship by restricting the department head's alternatives, faculty members who have few or no publications have the least mobility and are subject to the greatest influence from their superiors.

Power Tactics

3 *Identify nine power or influence tactics and their contingencies.*

What **power tactics** do people use to translate power bases into specific action? That is, what options do individuals have for influencing their bosses, coworkers, or employees? And are some of these options more effective than others? In this section, we review popular tactical options and the conditions under which one may be more effective than another. Research has identified nine distinct influence tactics:[14]

- *Legitimacy.*   Relying on one's authority position or stressing that a request is in accordance with organizational policies or rules.
- *Rational persuasion.*   Presenting logical arguments and factual evidence to demonstrate that a request is reasonable.

- *Inspirational appeals.*   Developing emotional commitment by appealing to a target's values, needs, hopes, and aspirations.
- *Consultation.*   Increasing the target's motivation and support by involving him or her in deciding how the plan or change will be accomplished.
- *Exchange.*   Rewarding the target with benefits or favors in exchange for following a request.
- *Personal appeals.*   Asking for compliance based on friendship or loyalty.
- *Ingratiation.*   Using flattery, praise, or friendly behavior prior to making a request.
- *Pressure.*   Using warnings, repeated demands, and threats.
- *Coalitions.*   Enlisting the aid of other people to persuade the target or using the support of others as a reason for the target to agree.

Some tactics are more effective than others. Specifically, evidence indicates that rational persuasion, inspirational appeals, and consultation tend to be the most effective. On the other hand, pressure tends to frequently backfire and is typically the least effective of the nine tactics.[15] You can also increase your chance of success by using more than one type of tactic at the same time or sequentially, as long as your choices are compatible.[16] For instance, using both ingratiation and legitimacy can lessen the negative reactions that might come from the appearance of being "dictated to" by the boss.

To see how these tactics can work in practice, let's consider the most effective way of getting a raise. You can start with rational persuasion. That means doing your homework and carefully thinking through the best way to build your case: Figure out how your pay compares to that of peers, or land a competing job offer, or show objective results that testify to your performance. For example, Kitty Dunning, a vice president at Don Jagoda Associates, landed a 16 percent raise when she emailed her boss numbers showing she had increased sales.[17] You can also make good use of salary calculators such as Salary.com to compare your pay with comparable other.

But the effectiveness of some influence tactics depends on the direction of influence.[18] As shown in Exhibit 14-2, studies have found that rational persuasion is the only tactic that is effective across organizational levels. Inspirational appeals work best as a downward-influencing tactic with subordinates. When pressure works, it's generally only to achieve downward influence. And the use of personal appeals and coalitions are most effective with lateral influence attempts. In addition to the direction of influence, a number of other factors

Exhibit **14-2**	Preferred Power Tactics by Influence Direction	
Upward Influence	**Downward Influence**	**Lateral Influence**
Rational persuasion	Rational persuasion	Rational persuasion
	Inspirational appeals	Consultation
	Pressure	Ingratiation
	Consultation	Exchange
	Ingratiation	Legitimacy
	Exchange	Personal appeals
	Legitimacy	Coalitions

power tactics *Ways in which individuals translate power bases into specific actions.*

International **OB**

Influence Tactics in China

Researchers usually examine cross-cultural influences in business by comparing two very different cultures, such as those from Eastern and Western societies. However, it is also important to examine differences within a given culture because those differences can sometimes be greater than differences between cultures.

For example, although we might view all Chinese people as being alike due to their shared heritage and appearance, China is a big country, housing different cultures and traditions. A recent study examining Mainland Chinese, Taiwanese, and Hong Kong managers explored how the three cultural subgroups differ according to the influence tactics they prefer to use.

Though managers from all three places believe that rational persuasion and exchange are the most effective influence tactics, managers in Taiwan tend to use inspirational appeals and ingratiation more than managers from either Mainland China or Hong Kong. The study also found that managers from Hong Kong rate pressure as more effective in influencing others than do managers in Taiwan or Mainland China. Such differences have implications for business relationships. For example, Taiwanese or Mainland Chinese managers may be taken aback by the use of pressure tactics by a Hong Kong manager. Likewise, managers from Hong Kong may not be persuaded by managers from Taiwan, who tend to use ingratiating tactics. Such differences in influence tactics may make business dealings difficult. Companies should address these issues, perhaps making their managers aware of the differences within cultures.

Managers need to know what variations exist within their local cultures so they can be better prepared to deal with others. Managers who fail to realize these differences may miss out on opportunities to deal effectively with others.

Source: Based on P. P. Fu, T. K. Peng, J. C. Kennedy, and G. Yukl, "A Comparison of Chinese Managers in Hong Kong, Taiwan, and Mainland China," *Organizational Dynamics*, February 2004, pp. 32–46.

have been found to affect which tactics work best. These include the sequencing of tactics, a person's skill in using the tactic, and the culture of the organization.

You're more likely to be effective if you begin with "softer" tactics that rely on personal power such as personal and inspirational appeals, rational persuasion, and consultation. If these fail, you can move to "harder" tactics (which emphasize formal power and involve greater costs and risks), such as exchange, coalitions, and pressure.[19] Interestingly, it's been found that using a single soft tactic is more effective than using a single hard tactic and that combining two soft tactics or a soft tactic and rational persuasion is more effective than any single tactic or a combination of hard tactics.[20]

Recently, research has shown that people differ in their **political skill**, or the ability to influence others in such a way as to enhance their own objectives. Those who are politically skilled are more effective in their use of influence tactics, regardless of the tactics they're using. Political skill also appears to be more effective when the stakes are high—such as when the individual is accountable for important organizational outcomes. That's also why Tiger Woods sticks to the majors and other big tournaments. Finally, the politically skilled are able to exert their influence without others detecting it, which is a key element in being effective (it's damaging to be labeled political).[21]

Finally, we know that cultures within organizations differ markedly—for example, some are warm, relaxed, and supportive; others are formal and conservative. The organizational culture in which a person works, therefore, will have a bearing on defining which tactics are considered appropriate. Some cultures encourage the use of participation and consultation, some encourage reason, and still others rely on pressure. So the organization itself will influence which subset of power tactics is viewed as acceptable for use.

Sexual Harassment: Unequal Power in the Workplace

4 *Show the connection between sexual harassment and the abuse of power.*

This employee was one of 90 workers who filed a sexual harassment lawsuit against Dial Corporation. The female employees alleged that male coworkers and supervisors at a Dial soap factory in Illinois fostered a "permissive culture" that condoned groping, sexual insults, and displays of pornography and that women who reported harassment faced retaliation or inaction by upper management. Although Dial denied wrongdoing, the company agreed to pay $10 million to settle the lawsuit, to revise its harassment policies and procedures, and to comply with federal compliance monitoring at its plant for 2½ years.

Sexual harassment is wrong. It can also be costly to employers. Just ask executives at Philip Morris, Dial, and UPS.[22] A Kentucky jury awarded $2 million to a Philip Morris plant supervisor who suffered through more than a year of sexual harassment by men she supervised. Dial agreed to pay $10 million to resolve widespread sexual harassment practices at its soap factory in Aurora, Illinois. And a former UPS manager won an $80 million suit against UPS for fostering a hostile work environment when it failed to listen to her complaints of sexual harassment.

Not only are there legal dangers to sexual harassment, it obviously can have a negative impact on the work environment, too. Research shows that sexual harassment negatively affects job attitudes and leads those who feel harassed to withdraw from the organization. Moreover, in many cases, reporting sexual harassment doesn't improve the situation because the organization responds in a negative or unhelpful way. When organizational leaders make honest efforts to stop the harassment, the outcomes are much more positive.[23]

Sexual harassment is defined as any unwanted activity of a sexual nature that affects an individual's employment and creates a hostile work environment. The U.S. Supreme Court helped to clarify this definition by adding that the key test for determining if sexual harassment has occurred is whether comments or behavior in a work environment "would reasonably be perceived, and [are] perceived, as hostile or abusive."[24] But there continues to be disagreement as to what *specifically* constitutes sexual harassment. Organizations have generally made considerable progress in the past decade toward limiting overt forms of sexual harassment. This includes unwanted physical touching, recurring requests for dates when it is made clear the person isn't interested, and coercive threats that a person will lose the job if he or she refuses a sexual proposition. The problems today are likely to surface around more subtle forms of sexual harassment—unwanted looks or comments, off-color jokes, sexual artifacts like pin-ups posted in the workplace, or misinterpretations of where the line between being friendly ends and harassment begins.

A recent review concluded that 58 percent of women report having experienced potentially harassing behaviors and 24 percent report having experienced sexual harassment at work.[25] One problem with sexual harassment is that it is, to some degree, in the eye of the beholder. For example, women are more likely than men to see a given behavior or sets of behaviors as constituting sexual harassment. Men are less likely to see as harassment such behaviors as kissing someone, asking for a date, or making sex-stereotyped jokes. As the authors of this study note, "Although progress has been made at defining sexual harassment, it is still unclear as to whose perspective should be taken."[26] Thus, although some behaviors indisputably constitute harassment, men and women continue to differ to some degree on what constitutes harassment. For you, the best approach is to be careful—refrain from any behavior that may be taken as harassing, even if that was not your intent. Realize that what you see as an innocent joke or hug may be seen as harassment by the other party.

Most studies confirm that the concept of power is central to understanding sexual harassment.[27] This seems to be true whether the harassment comes from a

political skill   *The ability to influence others in such a way as to enhance one's objectives.*

sexual harassment   *Any unwanted activity of a sexual nature that affects an individual's employment and creates a hostile work environment.*

supervisor, a coworker, or an employee. And sexual harassment is more likely to occur when there are large power differentials. The supervisor–employee dyad best characterizes an unequal power relationship, where formal power gives the supervisor the capacity to reward and coerce. Because employees want favorable performance reviews, salary increases, and the like, it's clear that supervisors control resources that most employees consider important and scarce. Because of power inequities, sexual harassment by one's boss typically creates the greatest difficulty for those who are being harassed. If there are no witnesses, it is the victim's word against the harasser's. Are there others this boss has harassed, and, if so, will they come forward? Because of the supervisor's control over resources, many of those who are harassed are afraid of speaking out for fear of retaliation by the supervisor.

Although coworkers don't have legitimate power, they can have influence and use it to sexually harass peers. In fact, although coworkers appear to engage in somewhat less severe forms of harassment than do supervisors, coworkers are the most frequent perpetrators of sexual harassment in organizations. How do coworkers exercise power? Most often it's by providing or withholding information, cooperation, and support. For example, the effective performance of most jobs requires interaction and support from coworkers. This is especially true today because work is often assigned to teams. By threatening to withhold or delay providing information that's necessary for the successful achievement of your work goals, coworkers can exert power over you.

Although it doesn't get nearly as much attention as harassment by a supervisor, as seen in the lawsuit against Philip Morris, women in positions of power can be subjected to sexual harassment from males who occupy less powerful positions within the organization. This is usually achieved by the employee devaluing the woman through highlighting traditional gender stereotypes (such as helplessness, passivity, lack of career commitment) that reflect negatively on the woman in power. An employee may engage in such practices to attempt to gain some power over the higher-ranking female or to minimize power differentials. Increasingly, too, there are cases of women in positions of power harassing male employees.

The topic of sexual harassment is about power. It's about an individual controlling or threatening another individual. It's wrong. And whether perpetrated against women or men, it's illegal. But you can understand how sexual harassment surfaces in organizations if you analyze it in terms of power.

A recent review of the literature shows the damage caused by sexual harassment. As you would expect, individuals who are sexually harassed report more negative job attitudes (lower job satisfaction, diminished organizational commitment) as a result. This review also revealed that sexual harassment undermines the victims' mental and physical health. However, sexual harassment also negatively affects the group in which the victim works, lowering its level of productivity. The authors of this study conclude that sexual harassment "is significantly and substantively associated with a host of harms."[28]

We have seen how sexual harassment can wreak havoc on an organization, not to mention on the victims themselves. But it can be avoided. A manager's role in preventing sexual harassment is critical. Some ways managers can protect themselves and their employees from sexual harassment follow:

1. Make sure a policy is in place that defines what constitutes sexual harassment, that informs employees that they can be fired for sexually harassing another employee, and that establishes procedures for how complaints can be made.
2. Ensure employees that they will not encounter retaliation if they issue a complaint.
3. Investigate every complaint and include the legal and human resource departments.
4. Make sure that offenders are disciplined or terminated.

5. Set up in-house seminars to raise employee awareness of the issues surrounding sexual harassment.

The bottom line is that managers have a responsibility to protect their employees from a hostile work environment, but they also need to protect themselves. Managers may be unaware that one of their employees is being sexually harassed. But being unaware does not protect them or their organization. If investigators believe a manager could have known about the harassment, both the manager and the company can be held liable.

Politics: Power in Action

5 *Distinguish between legitimate and illegitimate political behavior.*

When people get together in groups, power will be exerted. People want to carve out a niche from which to exert influence, to earn rewards, and to advance their careers.[29] When employees in organizations convert their power into action, we describe them as being engaged in politics. Those with good political skills have the ability to use their bases of power effectively.[30]

Definition of *Organizational Politics*

There has been no shortage of definitions of *organizational politics*. Essentially, however, they have focused on the use of power to affect decision making in an organization or on behaviors by members that are self-serving and organizationally nonsanctioned.[31] For our purposes, we shall define **political behavior** in organizations as activities that are not required as part of one's formal role in the organization but that influence, or attempt to influence, the distribution of advantages and disadvantages within the organization.[32] This definition encompasses key elements from what most people mean when they talk about organizational politics. Political behavior is outside one's specified job requirements. The behavior requires some attempt to use one's power bases. In addition, our definition encompasses efforts to influence the goals, criteria, or processes used for *decision making* when we state that politics is concerned with "the distribution of advantages and disadvantages within the organization." Our definition is broad enough to include varied political behaviors such as withholding key information from decision makers, joining a coalition, whistle-blowing, spreading rumors, leaking confidential information about organizational activities to the media, exchanging favors with others in the organization for mutual benefit, and lobbying on behalf of or against a particular individual or decision alternative.

A final comment relates to what has been referred to as the "legitimate–illegitimate" dimension in political behavior.[33] **Legitimate political behavior** refers to normal everyday politics—complaining to your supervisor, bypassing the chain of command, forming coalitions, obstructing organizational policies or decisions through inaction or excessive adherence to rules, and developing contacts outside the organization through one's professional activities. On the other hand, there are also **illegitimate political behaviors** that violate the

---

political behavior *Activities that are not required as part of a person's formal role in the organization but that influence, or attempt to influence, the distribution of advantages and disadvantages within the organization.*

legitimate political behavior *Normal everyday politics.*

illegitimate political behavior *Extreme political behavior that violates the implied rules of the game.*

In 2002, David Welch, chief financial officer of Bank of Floyd in Virginia, blew the whistle on the bank's president, alleging that he had engaged in the unethical business practice of buying stocks before the announcement of a bank merger. As a result, Welch was fired. Since then, Welch has compiled piles of documents supporting his allegation. He was the first whistle- blower the government ordered to be reinstated to a job under the Sarbanes-Oxley Act, but the reinstatement order was overturned by a Labor Department judge. Welch continues his legal battle in an appeal to a circuit court.

implied rules of the game. Those who pursue such extreme activities are often described as individuals who "play hardball." Illegitimate activities include sabotage, whistle-blowing, and symbolic protests such as wearing unorthodox dress or protest buttons and groups of employees simultaneously calling in sick.

The vast majority of all organizational political actions are of the legitimate variety. The reasons are pragmatic: The extreme illegitimate forms of political behavior pose a very real risk of loss of organizational membership or extreme sanctions against those who use them and then fall short in having enough power to ensure that they work.

The Reality of Politics

Politics is a fact of life in organizations. People who ignore this fact of life do so at their own peril. But why, you may wonder, must politics exist? Isn't it possible for an organization to be politics free? It's *possible* but unlikely.

Organizations are made up of individuals and groups with different values, goals, and interests.[34] This sets up the potential for conflict over resources. Departmental budgets, space allocations, project responsibilities, and salary adjustments are just a few examples of the resources about whose allocation organizational members will disagree.

Resources in organizations are also limited, which often turns potential conflict into real conflict.[35] If resources were abundant, then all the various constituencies within the organization could satisfy their goals. But because they are limited, not everyone's interests can be provided for. Furthermore, whether true or not, gains by one individual or group are often *perceived* as being at the expense of others within the organization. These forces create competition among members for the organization's limited resources.

Maybe the most important factor leading to politics within organizations is the realization that most of the "facts" that are used to allocate the limited resources are open to interpretation. What, for instance, is *good* performance? What's an *adequate* improvement? What constitutes an *unsatisfactory* job? One person's view that an act is a "selfless effort to benefit the organization" is seen by another as a "blatant attempt to further one's interest."[36] The manager of any major league baseball team knows a .400 hitter is a high performer and a .125 hitter is a poor performer. You don't need to be a baseball genius to know you should play your .400 hitter and send the .125 hitter back to the minors. But what if you have to choose between players who hit .280 and .290? Then other factors—less objective ones—come into play: fielding expertise, attitude, potential, ability to perform in a clutch, loyalty to the team, and so on. More managerial decisions resemble choosing between a .280 and a .290 hitter than deciding between a .125 hitter and a .400 hitter. It is in this large and ambiguous middle ground of organizational life—where the facts *don't* speak for themselves—that politics flourish (see Exhibit 14-3).

Finally, because most decisions have to be made in a climate of ambiguity—where facts are rarely fully objective and thus are open to interpretation—people within organizations will use whatever influence they can to taint the facts to support their goals and interests. That, of course, creates the activities we call *politicking*.

Therefore, to answer the earlier question of whether it is possible for an organization to be politics free, we can say "yes," if all members of that organization hold the same goals and interests, if organizational resources are not scarce, and if performance outcomes are completely clear and objective. But that doesn't describe the organizational world that most of us live in.

Exhibit **14-3**	Politics Is in the Eye of the Beholder

A behavior that one person labels as "organizational politics" is very likely to be characterized as an instance of "effective management" by another. The fact is not that effective management is necessarily political, although in some cases it might be. Rather, a person's reference point determines what he or she classifies as organizational politics. Take a look at the follwing labels used to describe the same phenomenon. These suggest that politics, like beauty, is in the eye of the beholder.

"Political" Label		"Effective Management" Label
1. Blaming others	vs.	Fixing responsibility
2. "Kissing up"	vs.	Developing working relationships
3. Apple polishing	vs.	Demonstrating loyalty
4. Passing the buck	vs.	Delegating authority
5. Covering your rear	vs.	Documenting decisions
6. Creating conflict	vs.	Encouraging change and innovation
7. Forming coalitions	vs.	Facilitating teamwork
8. Whistle-blowing	vs.	Improving efficiency
9. Scheming	vs.	Planning ahead
10. Overachieving	vs.	Competent and capable
11. Ambitious	vs.	Career minded
12. Opportunistic	vs.	Astute
13. Cunning	vs.	Practical minded
14. Arrogant	vs.	Confident
15. Perfectionist	vs.	Attentive to detail

Source: Based on T. C. Krell, M. E. Mendenhall, and J. Sendry, "Doing Research in the Conceptual Morass of Organizational Politics," paper presented at the Western Academy of Management Conference, Hollywood, CA, April 1987.

Causes and Consequences of Political Behavior

6 *Identify the causes and consequences of political behavior.*

Factors Contributing to Political Behavior

Not all groups or organizations are equally political. In some organizations, for instance, politicking is overt and rampant, while in others, politics plays a small role in influencing outcomes. Why is there this variation? Recent

MYTH OR SCIENCE?   "*Power Breeds Contempt*"

*t*his statement appears to be true. When people have power bestowed on them, they appear to be inclined to ignore the perspectives and interests of those without power, so says a study completed by a team of researchers from Northwestern, Stanford, and New York University.[37]

In this study, researchers made one group of participants feel powerful by asking them to recall and write about a situation in which they had power over another person. Another group of participants was instructed to recall and write about an incident in which someone had power over them. When the groups were then asked to work together on a problem, participants in the powerful group were much more likely to ignore the perspectives of those in the less powerful group, were less able to accurately read their emotional expressions, and were less interested in understanding how other individuals see things. The authors of this study conclude that power leads to "the tendency to view other people only in terms of qualities that serve one's personal goals and interests, while failing to consider those features of others that define their humanity."

So, while power has perks, it also appears to have costs—especially in terms of seeing things from the perspective of those with less of it. ■

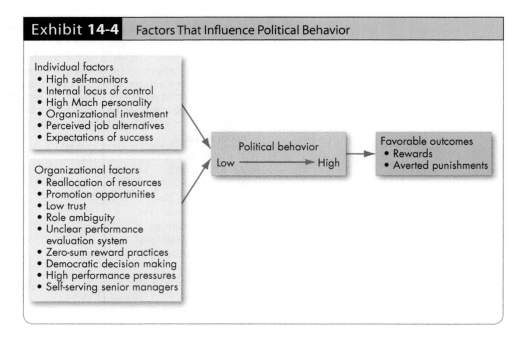

Exhibit 14-4   Factors That Influence Political Behavior

Individual factors
- High self-monitors
- Internal locus of control
- High Mach personality
- Organizational investment
- Perceived job alternatives
- Expectations of success

Organizational factors
- Reallocation of resources
- Promotion opportunities
- Low trust
- Role ambiguity
- Unclear performance evaluation system
- Zero-sum reward practices
- Democratic decision making
- High performance pressures
- Self-serving senior managers

Political behavior
Low ———————→ High

Favorable outcomes
- Rewards
- Averted punishments

research and observation have identified a number of factors that appear to encourage political behavior. Some are individual characteristics, derived from the unique qualities of the people the organization employs; others are a result of the organization's culture or internal environment. Exhibit 14-4 illustrates how both individual and organizational factors can increase political behavior and provide favorable outcomes (increased rewards and averted punishments) for both individuals and groups in the organization.

Individual Factors   At the individual level, researchers have identified certain personality traits, needs, and other factors that are likely to be related to political behavior. In terms of traits, we find that employees who are high self-monitors, possess an internal locus of control, and have a high need for power are more likely to engage in political behavior.[38] The high self-monitor is more sensitive to social cues, exhibits higher levels of social conformity, and is more likely to be skilled in political behavior than the low self-monitor. Individuals with an internal locus of control, because they believe they can control their environment, are more prone to take a proactive stance and attempt to manipulate situations in their favor. Not surprisingly, the Machiavellian personality—characterized by the will to manipulate and the desire for power—is comfortable using politics as a means to further his or her self-interest.

In addition, an individual's investment in the organization, perceived alternatives, and expectations of success will influence the degree to which he or she will pursue illegitimate means of political action.[39] The more a person has invested in the organization in terms of expectations of increased future benefits, the more that person has to lose if forced out and the less likely he or she is to use illegitimate means. The more alternative job opportunities an individual has—due to a favorable job market or the possession of scarce skills or knowledge, a prominent reputation, or influential contacts outside the organization—the more likely that individual is to risk illegitimate political actions. Finally, if an individual has a low expectation of success in using illegitimate means, it is unlikely that he or she will attempt to do so. High expectations of success in the use of illegitimate means are most likely to be the province of both experienced and powerful individuals with polished political skills and inexperienced and naive employees who misjudge their chances.

Politicking is more likely to surface when organizational resources are declining. From 2000 to 2006, Delta Airlines suffered losses of $14.5 billion and then filed for bankruptcy protection. To address the company's severe financial problems, the airline devised a $3 billion cost-cutting plan that included eliminating jobs and reducing pay for pilots and frontline employees. These actions stimulated conflict and increased politicking, such as the informational picketing shown here, as the pilots wanted to safeguard their pay.

Organizational Factors   Political activity is probably more a function of an organization's characteristics than of individual difference variables. Why? Because many organizations have a large number of employees with the individual characteristics we listed, yet the extent of political behavior varies widely.

Although we acknowledge the role that individual differences can play in fostering politicking, the evidence more strongly supports the idea that certain situations and cultures promote politics. Specifically, when an organization's resources are declining, when the existing pattern of resources is changing, and when there is opportunity for promotions, politicking is more likely to surface.[40] In addition, cultures characterized by low trust, role ambiguity, unclear performance evaluation systems, zero-sum reward allocation practices, democratic decision making, high pressures for performance, and self-serving senior managers will create breeding grounds for politicking.[41]

When organizations downsize to improve efficiency, reductions in resources have to be made. Threatened with the loss of resources, people may engage in political actions to safeguard what they have. But any changes, especially those that imply significant reallocation of resources within the organization, are likely to stimulate conflict and increase politicking.

Promotion decisions have consistently been found to be one of the most political actions in organizations. The opportunity for promotions or advancement encourages people to compete for a limited resource and to try to positively influence the decision outcome.

The less trust there is within the organization, the higher the level of political behavior and the more likely that the political behavior will be of the illegitimate kind. So high trust should suppress the level of political behavior in general and inhibit illegitimate actions in particular.

Role ambiguity means that the prescribed behaviors of the employee are not clear. There are fewer limits, therefore, to the scope and functions of the employee's political actions. Because political activities are defined as those not required as part of one's formal role, the greater the role ambiguity, the more one can engage in political activity with little chance of it being visible.

The practice of performance evaluation is far from a perfect science. The more that organizations use subjective criteria in the appraisal, emphasize a single outcome measure, or allow significant time to pass between the time of an action and its appraisal, the greater the likelihood that an employee can get away with politicking. Subjective performance criteria create ambiguity. The use of a single outcome measure encourages individuals to do whatever is necessary to "look good" on that measure, but often at the expense of performing well on other important parts of the job that are not being appraised. The amount of time that elapses between an action and its appraisal is also a relevant factor. The longer the time, the more unlikely that the employee will be held accountable for his political behaviors.

The more that an organization's culture emphasizes the zero-sum or win/lose approach to reward allocations, the more employees will be motivated to engage in politicking. The zero-sum approach treats the reward "pie" as fixed so that any gain one person or group achieves has to come at the expense of another person or group. If I win, you must lose! If $15,000 in annual raises is to be distributed among five employees, then any employee who gets more than $3,000 takes money away from one or more of the others. Such a practice encourages making others look bad and increasing the visibility of what you do.

In the past 25 years, there has been a general move in North America and among most developed nations toward making organizations less autocratic. Managers in these organizations are being asked to behave more democratically. They're told that they should allow employees to advise them on decisions and that they should rely to a greater extent on group input into the decision process. Such moves toward democracy, however, are not necessarily embraced by all individual managers. Many managers sought their positions in order to have legitimate power so as to be able to make unilateral decisions. They fought hard and often paid high personal costs to achieve their influential positions. Sharing their power with others runs directly against their desires. The result is that managers, especially those who began their careers in the 1960s and 1970s, may use the required committees, conferences, and group meetings in a superficial way, as arenas for maneuvering and manipulating.

The more pressure that employees feel to perform well, the more likely they are to engage in politicking. When people are held strictly accountable for outcomes, this puts great pressure on them to "look good." If a person perceives that his or her entire career is riding on next quarter's sales figures or next month's plant productivity report, there is motivation to do whatever is necessary to make sure the numbers come out favorably.

Finally, when employees see the people on top engaging in political behavior, especially when they do so successfully and are rewarded for it, a climate is created that supports politicking. Politicking by top management, in a sense, gives permission to those lower in the organization to play politics by implying that such behavior is acceptable.

How Do People Respond to Organizational Politics?

Trish O'Donnell loves her job as a writer on a weekly television comedy series but hates the internal politics. "A couple of the writers here spend more time kissing up to the executive producer than doing any work. And our head writer clearly has his favorites. While they pay me a lot and I get to really use my creativity, I'm sick of having to be on alert for backstabbers and constantly having to self-promote my contributions. I'm tired of doing most of the work and getting little of the credit." Are Trish O'Donnell's comments typical of people who work in highly politicized workplaces? We all know of friends or relatives who

Exhibit **14-5**	Employee Responses to Organizational Politics

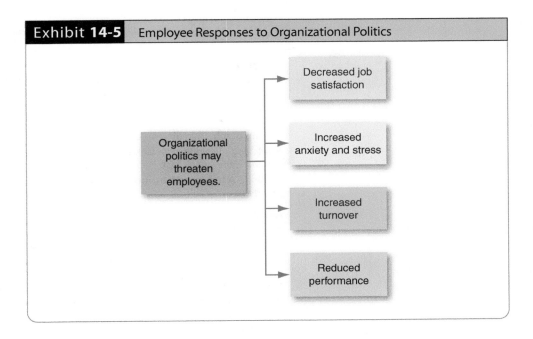

regularly complain about the politics at their job. But how do people in general react to organizational politics? Let's look at the evidence.

In our discussion earlier in this chapter of factors that contribute to political behavior, we focused on the favorable outcomes for individuals who successfully engage in politicking. But for most people—who have modest political skills or are unwilling to play the politics game—outcomes tend to be predominantly negative. Exhibit 14-5 summarizes the extensive research on the relationship between organizational politics and individual outcomes.[42] There is, for instance, very strong evidence indicating that perceptions of organizational politics are negatively related to job satisfaction.[43] The perception of politics also tends to increase job anxiety and stress. This seems to be due to the perception that, by not engaging in politics, a person may be losing ground to others who are active politickers; or, conversely, because of the additional pressures individuals feel because of having entered into and competing in the political arena.[44] Not surprisingly, when politicking becomes too much to handle, it can lead to employees quitting.[45] Finally, there is preliminary evidence suggesting that politics leads to self-reported declines in employee performance. This may occur because employees perceive political environments to be unfair, which demotivates them.[46]

In addition to these conclusions, several interesting qualifiers have been noted. First, the politics–performance relationship appears to be moderated by an individual's understanding of the "hows" and "whys" of organizational politics. "An individual who has a clear understanding of who is responsible for making decisions and why they were selected to be the decision makers would have a better understanding of how and why things happen the way they do than someone who does not understand the decision-making process in the organization."[47] When both politics and understanding are high, performance is likely to increase because the individual will see political actions as an opportunity. This is consistent with what you might expect among individuals with well-honed political skills. But when understanding is low, individuals are more likely to see politics as a threat, which would have a negative effect on job performance.[48] Second, when politics is seen as a threat and consistently responded to with defensiveness, negative outcomes are almost sure to surface eventually. When people perceive politics as a threat rather than as an opportunity, they

Exhibit **14-6**	Defensive Behaviors

Avoiding Action

Overconforming. Strictly interpreting your responsibility by saying things like, "The rules clearly state . . . " or "This is the way we've always done it."

Buck passing. Transferring responsibility for the execution of a task or decision to someone else.

Playing dumb. Avoiding an unwanted task by falsely pleading ignorance or inability.

Stretching. Prolonging a task so that one person appears to be occupied—for example, turning a two-week task into a four-month job.

Stalling. Appearing to be more or less supportive publicly while doing little or nothing privately.

Avoiding Blame

Buffing. This is a nice way to refer to "covering your rear." It describes the practice of rigorously documenting activity to project an image of competence and thoroughness.

Playing safe. Evading situations that may reflect unfavorably. It includes taking on only projects with a high probability of success, having risky decisions approved by superiors, qualifying expressions of judgment, and taking neutral positions in conflicts.

Justifying. Developing explanations that lessen one's responsibility for a negative outcome and/or apologizing to demonstrate remorse.

Scapegoating. Placing the blame for a negative outcome on external factors that are not entirely blameworthy.

Misrepresenting. Manipulation of information by distortion, embellishment, deception, selective presentation, or obfuscation.

Avoiding Change

Prevention. Trying to prevent a threatening change from occurring.

Self-protection. Acting in ways to protect one's self-interest during change by guarding information or other resources.

often respond with **defensive behaviors**—reactive and protective behaviors to avoid action, blame, or change.[49] (Exhibit 14-6 provides some examples of these defensive behaviors.) And defensive behaviors are often associated with negative feelings toward the job and work environment.[50] In the short run, employees may find that defensiveness protects their self-interest. But in the long run, it wears them down. People who consistently rely on defensiveness find that, eventually, it is the only way they know how to behave. At that point, they lose the trust and support of their peers, bosses, employees, and clients.

Are our conclusions about responses to politics globally valid? Should we expect employees in Israel, for instance, to respond the same way to workplace politics that employees in the United States do? Almost all our conclusions on employee reactions to organizational politics are based on studies conducted in North America. The few studies that have included other countries suggest some minor modifications.[51] Israelis and Brits, for instance, seem to generally respond as do North Americans. That is, the perception of organizational politics among employees in these countries is related to decreased job satisfaction and increased turnover.[52] But in countries that are more politically unstable, such as Israel, employees seem to demonstrate greater tolerance of intense political processes in the workplace. This is likely to be because people in these countries are used to power struggles and have more experience in coping with them.[53] This suggests that people from politically turbulent countries in the Middle East or Latin America might be more accepting of organizational politics, and even more willing to use aggressive political tactics in the workplace, than people from countries such as Great Britain or Switzerland.

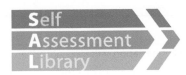

Impression Management

7 *Apply impression management techniques.*

We know that people have an ongoing interest in how others perceive and evaluate them. For example, North Americans spend billions of dollars on diets, health club memberships, cosmetics, and plastic surgery—all intended to make them more attractive to others.[54] Being perceived positively by others should have benefits for people in organizations. It might, for instance, help them initially to get the jobs they want in an organization and, once hired, to get favorable evaluations, superior salary increases, and more rapid promotions. In a political context, it might help sway the distribution of advantages in their favor. The process by which individuals attempt to control the impression others form of them is called **impression management (IM)**.[55] It's a subject that has gained the attention of OB researchers only recently.[56]

Is everyone concerned with IM? No! Who, then, might we predict to engage in IM? No surprise here. It's our old friend, the high self-monitor.[57] Low self-monitors tend to present images of themselves that are consistent with their personalities, regardless of the beneficial or detrimental effects for them. In contrast, high self-monitors are good at reading situations and molding their appearances and behavior to fit each situation. If you want to control the impression others form of you, what techniques can you use? Exhibit 14-7 summarizes some of the most popular IM techniques and provides an example of each.

Keep in mind that IM does not imply that the impressions people convey are necessarily false (although, of course, they sometimes are).[58] Excuses, for instance, may be offered with sincerity. Referring to the example used in Exhibit 14-7, you can *actually* believe that ads contribute little to sales in your region. But misrepresentation can have a high cost. If the image claimed is false, you may be discredited.[59] If you "cry wolf" once too often, no one is likely to believe you when the wolf really comes. So the impression manager must be cautious not to be perceived as insincere or manipulative.[60]

Are there *situations* in which individuals are more likely to misrepresent themselves or more likely to get away with it? Yes—situations that are characterized by high uncertainty or ambiguity provide relatively little information for challenging a fraudulent claim and reduce the risks associated with misrepresentation.[61]

Most of the studies undertaken to test the effectiveness of IM techniques have related it to two criteria: interview success and performance evaluations. Let's consider each of these.

The evidence indicates that most job applicants use IM techniques in interviews[62] and that, when IM behavior is used, it works.[63] In one study, for instance, interviewers felt that applicants for a position as a customer service representative who used IM techniques performed better in the interview, and they seemed somewhat more inclined to hire these people.[64] Moreover, when the researchers considered applicants' credentials, they concluded that it was the IM techniques alone that influenced the interviewers. That is, it didn't seem

defensive behaviors *Reactive and protective behaviors to avoid action, blame, or change.*

impression management (IM) *The process by which individuals attempt to control the impression others form of them.*

Exhibit **14-7**	Impression Management (IM) Techniques

Conformity

Agreeing with someone else's opinion in order to gain his or her approval.

Example: A manager tells his boss, "You're absolutely right on your reorganization plan for the western regional office. I couldn't agree with you more."

Excuses

Explanations of a predicament-creating event aimed at minimizing the apparent severity of the predicament.

Example: Sales manager to boss, "We failed to get the ad in the paper on time, but no one responds to those ads anyway."

Apologies

Admitting responsibility for an undesirable event and simultaneously seeking to get a pardon for the action.

Example: Employee to boss, "I'm sorry I made a mistake on the report. Please forgive me."

Self-Promotion

Highlighting one's best qualities, downplaying one's deficits, and calling attention to one's achievements.

Example: A salesperson tells his boss: "Matt worked unsuccessfully for three years to try to get that account. I sewed it up in six weeks. I'm the best closer this company has."

Flattery

Complimenting others about their virtues in an effort to make oneself appear perceptive and likeable.

Example: New sales trainee to peer, "You handled that client's complaint so tactfully! I could never have handled that as well as you did."

Favors

Doing something nice for someone to gain that person's approval.

Example: Salesperson to prospective client, "I've got two tickets to the theater tonight that I can't use. Take them. Consider it a thank-you for taking the time to talk with me."

Association

Enhancing or protecting one's image by managing information about people and things with which one is associated.

Example: A job applicant says to an interviewer, "What a coincidence. Your boss and I were roommates in college."

Source: Based on B. R. Schlenker, *Impression Management* (Monterey, CA: Brooks/Cole, 1980); W. L. Gardner and M. J. Martinko, "Impression Management in Organizations," *Journal of Management*, June 1988, p. 332; and R. B. Cialdini, "Indirect Tactics of Image Management Beyond Basking," in R. A. Giacalone and P. Rosenfeld (eds.), *Impression Management in the Organization* (Hillsdale, NJ: Lawrence Erlbaum, 1989), pp. 45–71.

to matter if applicants were well or poorly qualified. If they used IM techniques, they did better in the interview.

Research indicates that some IM techniques work better than others in the interview. Researchers have compared applicants who used IM techniques that focused on promoting one's accomplishments (called *self-promotion*) to applicants who used techniques that focused on complimenting the interviewer and finding areas of agreement (referred to as *ingratiation*). In general, applicants appear to use self-promotion more than ingratiation.[65] What's more, self-promotion tactics may be more important to interviewing success. Applicants who work to create an appearance of competence by enhancing their accomplishments, taking credit for successes, and explaining away failures do better in interviews. These effects reach beyond the interview: Applicants who use more self-promotion tactics also seem to get more follow-up job-site visits, even after adjusting for grade-point average, gender, and job type. Ingratiation also works well in interviews, meaning

OB In the News

Excuses Are Everywhere

As we've noted, excuses are one means of managing impressions so as to avoid negative repercussions of our actions. However, judging from some recent evidence on absenteeism, excuses are also a chance for workers to engage in their creative side.

A 2007 survey of nearly 7,000 employees and 3,000 hiring managers revealed some pretty creative excuses for being late for work or absent from work:

"Someone was following me and I drove all around town trying to lose them."

"My dog dialed 911 and the police wanted to question me about what really happened."

"My girlfriend got mad and destroyed all of my undergarments."

"A buffalo escaped from a game preserve and kept charging me every time I tried to leave my house."

"A skunk got into my house and sprayed all my uniforms."

"My mother-in-law poisoned me."

"My mother-in-law is in jail."

"I blew my nose so hard my back went out."

"My cow bit me."

"I'm too fat to get into my work pants."

Though you have to give the excuse makers high marks for originality, we seriously doubt supervisors bought these excuses. The making of excuses may be one of the few areas in which creativity is bad.

Sources: Based on K. Gurchiek, "'Sorry I'm Late; A Raccoon Stole My Shoe,'" _HRWeek,_ May 29, 2007, www.shrm.org/hrnews_published/archives/CMS_021684.asp; and K. Gurchiek, "Runaway Horses, Charging Buffalo Kept Workers Home in '06," December 28, 2006, _HRWeek,_ www.shrm.org/hrnews_published/archives/CMS_019743.asp.

---

that applicants who compliment the interviewer, agree with his or her opinions, and emphasize areas of fit do better than those who don't.[66]

In terms of performance ratings, the picture is quite different. Ingratiation is positively related to performance ratings, meaning that those who ingratiate with their supervisors get higher performance evaluations. However, self-promotion appears to backfire: Those who self-promote actually seem to receive _lower_ performance evaluations.[67] Another study of 760 boards of directors found that individuals who ingratiate themselves to current board members (express agreement with the director, point out shared attitudes and opinions, compliment the director) increase their chances of landing on a board.[68]

What explains these results? If you think about them, they make sense. Ingratiating always works because everyone—both interviewers and supervisors—likes to be treated nicely. However, self-promotion may work only in interviews and backfire on the job because, whereas the interviewer has little idea whether you're blowing smoke about your accomplishments, the supervisor knows because it's his or her job to observe you. Thus, if you're going to self-promote, remember that what works in an interview will not always work once you're on the job.

The Ethics of Behaving Politically

8 _Determine whether a political action is ethical._

We conclude our discussion of politics by providing some ethical guidelines for political behavior. Although there are no clear-cut ways to differentiate ethical from unethical politicking, there are some questions you should consider. For example, what is the utility of engaging in politicking? Sometimes we engage in political behaviors for little good reason. For example, major league baseball player Al Martin claimed he played football at USC when in fact he never did. Because Martin was playing baseball, not football, there was little to be gained by his lie. Outright lies like this may be a rather extreme example of impression management, but many of us have distorted information to make a favorable impression. The point is that, before we do so, one thing to keep in mind is whether it's really worth the risk. Another question to ask is an ethical one: How does the utility of engaging in the political behavior balance out any harm (or potential harm) it will do to others? For example, complimenting a supervisor on his or her appearance to curry favor is probably much less harmful than grabbing credit for a project that is deserved by others.

Finally, does the political activity conform to standards of equity and justice? Sometimes it is hard to weigh the costs and benefits of a political action, but its ethicality is clear. The department head who inflates the performance evaluation of a favored employee and deflates the evaluation of a disfavored employee—and then uses these evaluations to justify giving the former a big raise and nothing to the latter—has treated the disfavored employee unfairly.

Unfortunately, the answers to these questions are often argued in ways to make unethical practices seem ethical. Powerful people, for example, can become very good at explaining self-serving behaviors in terms of the organization's best interests. Similarly, they can persuasively argue that unfair actions are really fair and just. Our point is that immoral people can justify almost any behavior. Those who are powerful, articulate, and persuasive are most vulnerable because they are likely to be able to get away with unethical practices successfully. When faced with an ethical dilemma regarding organizational politics, try to consider the preceding issues (is playing politics worth the risk, and will others be harmed in the process?). If you have a strong power base, recognize the ability of power to corrupt. Remember that it's a lot easier for the powerless than the powerful to act ethically, if for no other reason than they typically have very little political discretion to exploit.

Global Implications

9 Show the influence of culture on the uses and perceptions of politics.

Although culture might enter any of the topics we've covered to this point, three questions are particularly important: (1) Does culture influence politics perceptions? (2) Does culture affect the power of influence tactics people prefer to use? and (3) Does culture influence the effectiveness of different tactics?

Politics Perceptions

We noted earlier that when people see their work environment as political, negative consequences in their overall work attitudes and behaviors generally result. Most of the research on politics perceptions has been conducted in the United States. A recent study, however, suggested that politics perceptions have the same negative effects in Nigeria. When employees of two agencies in Nigeria viewed their work environments as political, they reported higher levels of job distress and were less likely to help their coworkers. Thus, although developing countries such as Nigeria are perhaps more ambiguous and more political environments in which to work, the negative consequences appear to be the same as in the United States.[69]

Preference for Power Tactics

Evidence indicates that people in different countries tend to prefer different power tactics.[70] For instance, a study comparing managers in the United States and China found that U.S. managers prefer rational appeal, whereas Chinese managers preferred coalition tactics.[71] These differences tend to be consistent with the values in these two countries. Reason is consistent with the U.S. preference for direct confrontation and the use of rational persuasion to influence others and resolve differences. Similarly, coalition tactics are consistent with the Chinese preference for using indirect approaches for difficult or controversial requests. Research also has shown that individuals in Western, individualistic cultures tend to engage in more self-enhancement (such as self-promotion) behaviors than individuals in Eastern, more collectivistic cultures.[72]

Effectiveness of Power Tactics

Unfortunately, while we know people in different cultures seem to have different preferences for the use of power or influence tactics, there is much less evidence as to whether these tactics work better in some cultures than in others. One study of managers in U.S. culture and three Chinese cultures (People's Republic of China, Hong Kong, Taiwan) found that U.S. managers evaluated "gentle persuasion" tactics such as consultation and inspirational appeal as more effective than did their Chinese counterparts.[73]

Summary and Implications for Managers

If you want to get things done in a group or an organization, it helps to have power. As a manager who wants to maximize your power, you will want to increase others' dependence on you. You can, for instance, increase your power in relation to your boss by developing knowledge or a skill that she needs and for which she perceives no ready substitute. But power is a two-way street. You will not be alone in attempting to build your power bases. Others, particularly employees and peers, will be seeking to make you dependent on them. The result is a continual battle. While you seek to maximize others' dependence on you, you will be seeking to minimize your dependence on others. And, of course, others you work with will be trying to do the same.

Few employees relish being powerless in their job and organization. It's been argued, for instance, that when people in organizations are difficult, argumentative, and temperamental, it may be because they are in positions of powerlessness positions in which the performance expectations placed on them exceed their resources and capabilities.[74]

There is evidence that people respond differently to the various power bases.[75] Expert and referent power are derived from an individual's personal qualities. In contrast, coercion, reward, and legitimate power are essentially organizationally derived. Because people are more likely to enthusiastically accept and commit to an individual whom they admire or whose knowledge they respect (rather than someone who relies on his or her position for influence), the effective use of expert and referent power should lead to higher employee motivation, performance, commitment, and satisfaction.[76] Competence especially appears to offer wide appeal, and its use as a power base results in high performance by group members. The message for managers seems to be "Develop and use your expert power base!"

The power of your boss may also play a role in determining your job satisfaction. "One of the reasons many of us like to work for and with people who are powerful is that they are generally more pleasant—not because it is their native disposition, but because the reputation and reality of being powerful permits them more discretion and more ability to delegate to others."[77]

An effective manager accepts the political nature of organizations. By assessing behavior in a political framework, you can better predict the actions of others and use that information to formulate political strategies that will gain advantages for you and your work unit.

Some people are significantly more "politically astute" than others, meaning that they are aware of the underlying politics and can manage impressions. Those who are good at playing politics can be expected to get higher performance evaluations and, hence, larger salary increases and more promotions than the politically naive or inept.[78] The politically astute are also likely to exhibit higher job satisfaction and be better able to neutralize job stressors.[79] For employees with poor political skills or who are unwilling to play the politics game, the perception of organizational politics is generally related to lower job satisfaction and self-reported performance, increased anxiety, and higher turnover.

Point

Counterpoint

MANAGING IMPRESSIONS IS UNETHICAL

*M*anaging impressions is wrong for both ethical and practical reasons.

First, managing impressions is just another name for lying. Don't we have a responsibility, both to ourselves and to others, to present ourselves as we really are? The Australian philosopher Tony Coady wrote, "Dishonesty has always been perceived in our culture, and in all cultures but the most bizarre, as a central human vice." Immanuel Kant's categorical imperative asks us to consider the following: If you want to know whether telling a lie on a particular occasion is justifiable, you must try to imagine what would happen if everyone were to lie. Surely you would agree that a world in which no one lies is preferable to one in which lying is common because in such a world we could never trust anyone. Thus, we should try to present the truth as best we can. Impression management goes against this virtue.

Practically speaking, impression management generally backfires in the long run. Remember Sir Walter Scott's quote, "Oh what a tangled web we weave, when first we practice to deceive!" Once we start to distort the facts, where do we stop? When George O'Leary was hired as Notre Dame's football coach, he said on his résumé that 30 years before, he had obtained a degree from Stony Brook University that he never earned. Obviously, this information was unimportant to his football accomplishments, and ironically, he had written it on his resume 20 years earlier when hired for a job at Syracuse University; he had simply never corrected the inaccuracy. But when the truth came out, O'Leary was finished.

At Indiana University's Kelley School of Business, the code of ethics instructs students to provide only truthful information on their résumés and obligates them to be honest in interviews.

People are most satisfied with their jobs when their values match the culture of the organizations. If either side misrepresents itself in the interview process, then odds are, people won't fit in the organizations they choose. What's the benefit in this?

This doesn't imply that a person shouldn't put his or her best foot forward. But that means exhibiting qualities that are good no matter the context—being friendly, being positive and self-confident, being qualified and competent, while still being honest.

*O*h, come on. Get off your high horse. *Everybody* fudges to some degree in the process of applying for a job. If you really told the interviewer what your greatest weakness or worst mistake was, you'd never get hired. What if you answered, "I find it hard to get up in the morning and get to work"?

These sorts of "white lies" are expected and act as a kind of social lubricant. If we really knew what people where thinking, we'd go crazy. Moreover, you can quote all the philosophy you want, but sometimes it's necessary to lie. You mean you wouldn't lie to save the life of your family? It's naïve to think we can live in a world without lying.

Sometimes a bit of deception is necessary to get a job. I know a gay applicant who was rejected from a job he really wanted because he told the interviewer he had written two articles for gay magazines. What if he had told the interviewer a little lie? Would harm really have been done? At least he'd have a job.

As another example, when an interviewer asks you what you earned on your previous job, that information will be used against you, to pay you a salary lower than you deserve. Is it wrong to boost your salary a bit? Or would it be better to disclose your actual salary and be taken advantage of?

The same goes for complimenting interviewers, agreeing with their opinions, and so forth. If an interviewer tells you, "We believe in community involvement," are you supposed to tell the interviewer you've never volunteered for anything?

Of course you can go too far. We're not advocating that people totally fabricate their backgrounds. What we are talking about here is a reasonable amount of enhancement. If we can help ourselves without doing any real harm, then impression management is not the same as lying and actually is something we should teach others.

Questions for Review

1 How would you define *power*? How is it different from leadership?

2 What are the five bases of power?

3 What are the nine power or influence tactics?

4 In what way is sexual harassment about the abuse of power?

5 What is political behavior and how would you distinguish between legitimate and illegitimate political behavior?

6 What are the causes and consequences of political behavior?

7 What is impression management and what are the techniques for managing impressions?

8 How can one determine whether a political action is ethical?

9 How does culture influence politics perceptions, preferences for different power or influence tactics, and the effectiveness of those tactics?

Experiential Exercise

UNDERSTANDING POWER DYNAMICS

Create Groups

Each student is to turn in a dollar bill (or similar value of currency) to the instructor, and students are then divided into three groups, based on criteria given by the instructor, assigned to their workplaces, and instructed to read the following rules and tasks. The money is divided into thirds, and two-thirds of it is given to the top group, one-third to the middle group, and none to the bottom group.

Conduct Exercise

Groups go to their assigned workplaces and have 30 minutes to complete their tasks.

Rules

Members of the top group are free to enter the space of either of the other groups and to communicate whatever they wish, whenever they wish. Members of the middle group may enter the space of the lower group when they wish but must request permission to enter the top group's space (which the top group can refuse). Members of the lower group may not disturb the top group in any way unless specifically invited by the top. The lower group does have the right to knock on the door of the middle group and request permission to communicate with them (which can also be refused).

The members of the top group have the authority to make any change in the rules that they wish, at any time, with or without notice.

Tasks

- *Top group.* To be responsible for the overall effectiveness and learning from the exercise and to decide how to use its money.

- *Middle group.* To assist the top group in providing for the overall welfare of the organization and to decide how to use its money.

- *Bottom group.* To identify its resources and to decide how best to provide for learning and the overall effectiveness of the organization.

Debriefing

Each of the three groups chooses two representatives to go to the front of the class and discuss the following:

1. Summarize what occurred within and among the three groups.

2. What are some of the differences between being in the top group and being in the bottom group?

3. What can we learn about power from this experience?

4. How accurate do you think this exercise is in reflecting the reality of resource allocation decisions in large organizations?

Source: Adapted from L. Bolman and T. E. Deal, *Exchange* 3, no. 4 (1979), pp. 38–42. Reprinted by permission of Sage Publications, Inc.

Ethical Dilemma

Jack Grubman was a powerful man on Wall Street. As a star analyst of telecom companies for the Salomon Smith Barney unit of Citigroup, he made recommendations that carried a lot of weight with investors.

For years, Grubman had been negative on the stock of AT&T. But in November 1999, he changed his opinion. Based on e-mail evidence, it appears that Grubman's decision to upgrade AT&T wasn't based on the stock's fundamentals. There were other factors involved.

At the time, his boss at Citigroup, Sanford "Sandy" Weill, was in the midst of a power struggle with co-CEO John Reed to become the single head of the company. Meanwhile, Salomon was looking for additional business to increase its revenues. Getting investment banking business fees from AT&T would be a big plus. And Salomon's chances of getting that AT&T business would definitely be improved if Grubman would upgrade his opinion on the stock. Furthermore, Weill sought Grubman's upgrade to win favor with AT&T CEO Michael Armstrong, who sat on Citigroup's board. Weill wanted Armstrong's backing in his efforts to oust Reed.

Grubman had his own concerns. Though earning tens of millions a year in his job, as the son of a city worker in Philadelphia, he was a man of modest background. He wanted the best for his twin daughters, including entry to an exclusive New York City nursery school (the posh 92nd Street Y)—a school that a year earlier had reportedly turned down Madonna's daughter. Weill made a call to the school on Grubman's behalf and pledged a $1 million donation from Citigroup. At approximately the same time, Weill also asked Grubman to "take a fresh look" at his neutral rating on AT&T. Shortly after being asked to review his rating, Grubman raised it, and AT&T awarded Salomon an investment-banking job worth nearly $45 million. Shares of AT&T soared.

Did Sandy Weill do anything unethical? How about Jack Grubman? What do you think?

Source: Based on C. Gasparino, "Out of School," *Newsweek,* January 17, 2005, pp. 38–39.

Case Incident 1

Jennifer Cohen thought she had a good grip on her company's dress code. She was wrong.

Cohen works for a marketing firm in Philadelphia. Before a meeting, an older colleague pulled 24-year-old Cohen aside and told her that she was dressing inappropriately by wearing Bermuda shorts, sleeveless tops, and Capri pants. Cohen was stunned by the rebuke. "Each generation seems to have a different idea of what is acceptable in the workplace," she said. "In this case, I was highly offended."

What offended Cohen even more was what came next: Cohen wasn't allowed to attend the meeting because her attire was deemed inappropriate.

Cohen's employer is not alone. Although many employers have "casual" days at work, the number of employers who are enforcing more formal dress codes has increased, according to a survey of employers by the Society for Human Resource Management. In 2001, 53 percent of employers allowed casual dress every day. Now that figure is 38 percent. Silicon Valley marketing firm McGrath/Power used to allow casual attire. Now, it enforces a more formal dress code. "The pendulum has swung," says CEO Jonathan Bloom, "We went through a too-causal period.... When we were very casual, the quality of the work wasn't as good."

Ironically, as more employers enforce more formal dress codes, other employers known for their formality are going the other way. IBM, which once had a dress code of business suits with white shirts, has thrown out dress codes altogether. IBM researcher Dan Gruhl typically goes to work at IBM's San Jose, California, office in flip-flops and shorts. "Having a relaxed environment encourages you to think more openly," he says. Although not going quite as far as IBM, other traditional employers, such as Ford, General Motors, and Procter & Gamble, have relaxed dress codes.

Still, for every IBM, there are more companies that have tightened the rules. Even the NBA has adopted an off-court dress code for its players. As for Cohen, she still bristles at the dress code. "When you're comfortable, you don't worry," she says. "You focus on your work."

Questions

1. Do you think Cohen had a right to be offended? Why or why not?

2. In explaining why she was offended, Cohen argued, "People my age are taught to express themselves, and saying something negative about someone's fashion is saying something negative about them." Do you agree with Cohen?

3. Does an employer have an unfettered right to set a company's dress code? Why or why not?

4. How far would you go to conform to an organization's dress code? If your boss dressed in a relatively formal manner, would you feel compelled to dress in a like manner to manage impressions?

Source: Based on S. Armour, "'Business Casual' Causes Confusion," *USA Today,* July 10, 2007, pp. 1B, 2B.

Case Incident 2

THE POLITICS OF BACKSTABBING

Scott Rosen believed that he was making progress as an assistant manager of a financial-services company—until he noticed that his colleague, another assistant manager, was attempting to push him aside. On repeated occasions, Rosen would observe his colleague speaking with their manager behind closed doors. During these conversations, Rosen's colleague would attempt to persuade the supervisor that Rosen was incompetent and mismanaging his job, a practice that Mr. Rosen found out after the fact. Rosen recounts one specific instance of his colleague's backstabbing efforts: When a subordinate asked Rosen a question to which Rosen did not know the answer, his colleague would say to their supervisor, "I can't believe he didn't know something like that." On other occasions, after instructing a subordinate to complete a specific task, Rosen's colleague would say, "I wouldn't make you do something like that." What was the end result of such illegitimate political tactics? Rosen was demoted, an action that led him to resign shortly after, while his colleague was promoted. "Whatever I did, I lost," recounts Rosen.

What leads individuals to behave this way? According to Judith Briles, a management consultant who has extensively studied the practice of backstabbing, a tight job market is often a contributing factor. Fred Nader, another management consultant, believes that backstabbing is the result of "some kind of character disorder."

One executive at a technology company in Seattle admits that blind ambition was responsible for the backstabbing he did. In 1999, he was assigned as an external sales representative, partnered with a colleague who worked internally at their client's office. The executive wanted the internal sales position for himself. To reach this goal, he systematically engaged in backstabbing to shatter his colleague's credibility. Each time he heard a complaint, however small, from the client, he would ask for it in an e-mail and then forward the information to his boss. He'd include a short message about his colleague, such as: "I'm powerless to deal with this. She's not being responsive and the customer is beating on me." In addition, he would fail to share important information with her before presentations with their boss, to convey the impression that she did not know what she was talking about. He even went so far as to schedule meetings with their boss on an electronic calendar but then altered her version so that she was late. Eventually, he convinced his boss that she was overworked. He was transferred to the client's office, while his colleague was moved back to the main office.

Incidents such as these may not be uncommon in the workplace. Given today's competitive work environment, employees may be using political games to move ahead. To guard against backstabbing, Bob McDonald, a management consultant, recommends telling supervisors and other key personnel that the backstabber is not a friend. He states that this may be effective because backstabbers often claim to be friends of their victims and then act as if they are hesitant about sharing negative information with others because of this professed friendship. In any event, it is clear that employees in organizations need to be aware of illegitimate political behavior. Companies may need to adopt formal policies to safeguard employees against such behavior; however, it may be the case that behaviors such as backstabbing and spreading negative rumors are difficult to detect. Thus, both employees and managers should try to verify information to avoid the negative repercussions that can come from backstabbing and other illegitimate behaviors.

Questions

1. What factors, in addition to those cited here, do you believe lead to illegitimate political behaviors such as backstabbing?

2. Imagine that a colleague is engaging in illegitimate political behavior toward you. What steps might you take to reduce or eliminate this behavior?

3. Do you believe that it is ever justifiable to engage in illegitimate political behaviors such as backstabbing? If so, what are some conditions that might justify such behavior?

4. In addition to the obvious negative effects of illegitimate political behavior on victims, such as those described in this case, what might be some negative effects on the perpetrators? on the organization as a whole?

Source: Based on J. Sandberg, "Sabotage 101: The Sinister Art of Backstabbing," *Wall Street Journal*, February 11, 2004, p. B1.

Endnotes

1. G. Morgenson, "Downgrade a Stock, Then Duck and Cover," *New York Times*, March 12, 2006, pp. B1, B9.
2. R. M. Kanter, "Power Failure in Management Circuits," *Harvard Business Review*, July–August 1979, p. 65.
3. J. Pfeffer, "Understanding Power in Organizations," *California Management Review*, Winter 1992, p. 35.
4. Based on B. M. Bass, *Bass & Stogdill's Handbook of Leadership*, 3rd ed. (New York: The Free Press, 1990).
5. J. R. P. French, Jr., and B. Raven, "The Bases of Social Power," in D. Cartwright (ed.), *Studies in Social Power* (Ann Arbor, MI: University of Michigan, Institute for Social Research, 1959), pp. 150–167; B. J. Raven, "The Bases of Power: Origins and Recent Developments," *Journal of Social Issues*, Winter 1993, pp. 227–251; and G. Yukl, "Use Power Effectively," in E. A. Locke (ed.), *Handbook of Principles of Organizational Behavior* (Malden, MA: Blackwell, 2004), pp. 242–247.
6. E. A. Ward, "Social Power Bases of Managers: Emergence of a New Factor," *Journal of Social Psychology*, February 2001, pp. 144–147.
7. P. M. Podsakoff and C. A. Schriesheim, "Field Studies of French and Raven's Bases of Power: Critique, Reanalysis, and Suggestions for Future Research," *Psychological Bulletin*, May 1985, pp. 387–411; T. R. Hinkin and C. A. Schriesheim, "Development and Application of New Scales to Measure the French and Raven (1959) Bases of Social Power," *Journal of Applied Psychology*, August 1989, pp. 561–567; and P. P. Carson, K. D. Carson, and C. W. Roe, "Social Power Bases: A Meta-Analytic Examination of Interrelationships and Outcomes" *Journal of Applied Social Psychology* 23, no. 14 (1993), pp. 1150–1169.
8. J. L. Roberts, "Striking a Hot Match," *Newsweek*, January 24, 2005, pp. 54–55.
9. R. E. Emerson, "Power–Dependence Relations," *American Sociological Review*, February 1962, pp. 31–41.
10. H. Mintzberg, *Power In and Around Organizations* (Upper Saddle River, NJ: Prentice Hall, 1983), p. 24.
11. R. M. Cyert and J. G. March, *A Behavioral Theory of the Firm* (Upper Saddle River, NJ: Prentice Hall, 1963).
12. C. Perrow, "Departmental Power and Perspective in Industrial Firms," in M. N. Zald (ed.), *Power in Organizations* (Nashville, TN: Vanderbilt University Press, 1970).
13. N. Foulkes, "Tractor Boy," *High Life*, October 2002, p. 90.
14. See, for example, D. Kipnis and S. M. Schmidt, "Upward-Influence Styles: Relationship with Performance Evaluations, Salary, and Stress," *Administrative Science Quarterly*, December 1988, pp. 528–542; G. Yukl and J. B. Tracey, "Consequences of Influence Tactics Used with Subordinates, Peers, and the Boss," *Journal of Applied Psychology*, August 1992, pp. 525–535; G. Blickle, "Influence Tactics Used by Subordinates: An Empirical Analysis of the Kipnis and Schmidt Subscales," *Psychological Reports*, February 2000, pp. 143–154; and G. Yukl, "Use Power Effectively," pp. 249–252.
15. G. Yukl, *Leadership in Organizations*, 5th ed. (Upper Saddle River, NJ: Prentice Hall, 2002), pp. 141–174; G. R. Ferris, W. A. Hochwarter, C. Douglas, F. R. Blass, R. W. Kolodinksy, and D. C. Treadway, "Social Influence Processes in Organizations and Human Resource Systems," in G. R. Ferris and J. J. Martocchio (eds.), *Research in Personnel and Human Resources Management*, vol. 21 (Oxford, UK: JAI Press/Elsevier, 2003), pp. 65–127; and C. A. Higgins, T. A. Judge, and G. R. Ferris, "Influence Tactics and Work Outcomes: A Meta-analysis," *Journal of Organizational Behavior*, March 2003, pp. 89–106.
16. C. M. Falbe and G. Yukl, "Consequences for Managers of Using Single Influence Tactics and Combinations of Tactics," *Academy of Management Journal*, July 1992, pp. 638–653.
17. J. Badal, "Getting a Raise from the Boss," *Wall Street Journal*, July 8, 2006, pp. B1, B5.
18. Yukl, *Leadership in Organizations.*
19. Ibid.
20. Falbe and Yukl, "Consequences for Managers of Using Single Influence Tactics and Combinations of Tactics."
21. G. R. Ferris, D. C. Treadway, P. L. Perrewé, R. L. Brouer, C. Douglas, and S. Lux, "Political Skill in Organizations," *Journal of Management*, June 2007, pp. 290–320; K. J. Harris, K. M. Kacmar, S. Zivnuska, and J. D. Shaw, "The Impact of Political Skill on Impression Management Effectiveness," *Journal of Applied Psychology* 92, no. 1 (2007), pp. 278–285; W. A. Hochwarter, G. R. Ferris, M. B. Gavin, P. L. Perrewé, A. T. Hall, and D. D. Frink," Political Skill as Neutralizer of Felt Accountability–Job Tension Effects on Job Performance Ratings: A Longitudinal Investigation," *Organizational Behavior and Human Decision Processes* 102 (2007), pp. 226–239; D. C. Treadway, G. R. Ferris, A. B. Duke, G. L. Adams, and J. B. Tatcher, "The Moderating Role of Subordinate Political Skill on Supervisors' Impressions of Subordinate Ingratiation and Ratings of Subordinate Interpersonal Facilitation," *Journal of Applied Psychology* 92, no. 3 (2007), pp. 848–855.
22. www.chicagolegalnet.com; and S. Ellison and J. S. Lublin, "Dial to Pay $10 Million to Settle a Sexual-Harassment Lawsuit," *Wall Street Journal*, April 30, 2003, p. B4.
23. L. J. Munson, C. Hulin, and F. Drasgow, "Longitudinal Analysis of Dispositional Influences and Sexual Harassment: Effects on Job and Psychological Outcomes," *Personnel Psychology*, Spring 2000, pp. 21–46; T. M. Glomb, L. J. Munson,

C. L. Hulin, M. E. Bergman, and F. Drasgow, "Structural Equation Models of Sexual Harassment: Longitudinal Explorations and Cross-Sectional Generalizations," *Journal of Applied Psychology*, February 1999, pp. 14–28; M. E. Bergman, R. D. Langhout, P. A. Palmieri, L. M. Cortina, and L. F. Fitzgerald, "The (Un)reasonableness of Reporting: Antecedents and Consequences of Reporting Sexual Harassment," *Journal of Applied Psychology*, April 2002, pp. 230–242; L. R. Offermann and A. B. Malamut, "When Leaders Harass: The Impact of Target Perceptions of Organizational Leadership and Climate on Harassment Reporting and Outcomes," *Journal of Applied Psychology*, October 2002, pp. 885–893.

24. S. Silverstein and S. Christian, "Harassment Ruling Raises Free-Speech Issues," *Los Angeles Times*, November 11, 1993, p. D2.

25. R. Ilies, N. Hauserman, S. Schwochau, and J. Stibal, "Reported Incidence Rates of Work-Related Sexual Harassment in the United States: Using Meta-analysis to Explain Reported Rate Disparities," *Personnel Psychology*, Fall 2003, pp. 607–631

26. M. Rotundo, D. Nguyen, and P. R. Sackett, "A Meta-Analytic Review of Gender Differences in Perceptions of Sexual Harassment," *Journal of Applied Psychology*, October 2001, pp. 914–922.

27. Ilies, Hauserman, Schwochau, and Stibal, "Reported Incidence Rates of Work-Related Sexual Harassment in the United States; A. B. Malamut and L. R. Offermann, "Coping with Sexual Harassment: Personal, Environmental, and Cognitive Determinants," *Journal of Applied Psychology*, December 2001, pp. 1152–1166; L. M. Cortina and S. A. Wasti, "Profiles in Coping: Responses to Sexual Harassment Across Persons, Organizations, and Cultures," *Journal of Applied Psychology*, February 2005, pp. 182–192.

28. C. R. Willness, P. Steel, and K. Lee, "A Meta-analysis of the Antecedents and Consequences of Workplace Sexual Harassment," *Personnel Psychology* 60 (2007), pp. 127–162.

29. S. A. Culbert and J. J. McDonough, *The Invisible War: Pursuing Self-Interest at Work* (New York: Wiley, 1980), p. 6.

30. Mintzberg, *Power In and Around Organizations*, p. 26. See also K. M. Kacmar and R. A. Baron, "Organizational Politics: The State of the Field, Links to Related Processes, and an Agenda for Future Research," in G. R. Ferris (ed.), *Research in Personnel and Human Resources Management*, vol. 17 (Greenwich, CT: JAI Press, 1999), pp. 1–39; and G. R. Ferris, D. C. Treadway, R. W. Kolokinsky, W. A. Hochwarter, C. J. Kacmar, and D. D. Frink, "Development and Validation of the Political Skill Inventory," *Journal of Management*, February 2005, pp. 126–152.

31. S. B. Bacharach and E. J. Lawler, "Political Alignments in Organizations," in R. M. Kramer and M. A. Neale (eds.), *Power and Influence in Organizations* (Thousand Oaks, CA: Sage, 1998, pp. 68–69.

32. D. Farrell and J. C. Petersen, "Patterns of Political Behavior in Organizations," *Academy of Management Review,* July 1982, p. 405. For analyses of the controversies underlying the definition of organizational politics, see A. Drory and T. Romm, "The Definition of Organizational Politics: A Review," *Human Relations,* November 1990, pp. 1133–1154; and R. S. Cropanzano, K. M. Kacmar, and D. P. Bozeman,

"Organizational Politics, Justice, and Support: Their Differences and Similarities," in R. S. Cropanzano and K. M. Kacmar (eds.), *Organizational Politics, Justice and Support: Managing Social Climate at Work* (Westport, CT: Quorum Books, 1995), pp. 1–18.

33. Farrell and Peterson, "Patterns of Political Behavior in Organizations," pp. 406–407; and A. Drory, "Politics in Organization and Its Perception Within the Organization," *Organization Studies* 9, no. 2 (1988), pp. 165–179.

34. J. Pfeffer, *Power in Organizations* (Marshfield, MA: Pitman, 1981).

35. Drory and Romm, "The Definition of Organizational Politics."

36. S. M. Rioux and L. A. Penner, "The Causes of Organizational Citizenship Behavior: A Motivational Analysis," *Journal of Applied Psychology*, December 2001, pp. 1306–1314; and M. A. Finkelstein and L. A. Penner, "Predicting Organizational Citizenship Behavior: Integrating the Functional and Role Identity Approaches," *Social Behavior & Personality* 32, no. 4 (2004), pp. 383–398.

37. A. D. Galinsky, J. C. Magee, M. E. Inesi, and D. H. Gruenfeld, "Power and Perspectives Not Taken," *Psychological Science,* December 2006, pp. 1068–1074.

38. See, for example, G. R. Ferris, G. S. Russ, and P. M. Fandt, "Politics in Organizations," in R. A. Giacalone and P. Rosenfeld (eds.), *Impression Management in the Organization* (Hillsdale, NJ: Lawrence Erlbaum, 1989), pp. 155–156; and W. E. O'Connor and T. G. Morrison, "A Comparison of Situational and Dispositional Predictors of Perceptions of Organizational Politics," *Journal of Psychology*, May 2001, pp. 301–312.

39. Farrell and Petersen, "Patterns of Political Behavior in Organizations," p. 408.

40. G. R. Ferris and K. M. Kacmar, "Perceptions of Organizational Politics," *Journal of Management*, March 1992, pp. 93–116.

41. See, for example, P. M. Fandt and G. R. Ferris, "The Management of Information and Impressions: When Employees Behave Opportunistically," *Organizational Behavior and Human Decision Processes*, February 1990, pp. 140–158; Ferris, Russ, and Fandt, "Politics in Organizations," p. 147; and J. M. L. Poon, "Situational Antecedents and Outcomes of Organizational Politics Perceptions," *Journal of Managerial Psychology* 18, no. 2 (2003), pp. 138–155.

42. Ferris, Russ, and Fandt, "Politics in Organizations"; and K. M. Kacmar, D. P. Bozeman, D. S. Carlson, and W. P. Anthony, "An Examination of the Perceptions of Organizational Politics Model: Replication and Extension," *Human Relations*, March 1999, pp. 383–416.

43. W. A. Hochwarter, C. Kiewitz, S. L. Castro, P. L. Perrewe, and G. R. Ferris, "Positive Affectivity and Collective Efficacy as Moderators of the Relationship Between Perceived Politics and Job Satisfaction," *Journal of Applied Social Psychology*, May 2003, pp. 1009–1035; C. C. Rosen, P. E. Levy, and R. J. Hall, "Placing Perceptions of Politics in the Context of Feedback Environment, Employee Attitudes, and Job Performance," *Journal of Applied Psychology* 91, no. 1 (2006), pp. 211–230.

44. G. R. Ferris, D. D. Frink, M. C. Galang, J. Zhou, K. M. Kacmar, and J. L. Howard, "Perceptions of Organizational Politics: Prediction, Stress-Related Implications, and Outcomes," *Human Relations*, February 1996, pp. 233–266;

E. Vigoda, "Stress-Related Aftermaths to Workplace Politics: The Relationships Among Politics, Job Distress, and Aggressive Behavior in Organizations," *Journal of Organizational Behavior*, August 2002, pp. 571–591.

45. C. Kiewitz, W. A. Hochwarter, G. R. Ferris, and S. L. Castro, "The Role of Psychological Climate in Neutralizing the Effects of Organizational Politics on Work Outcomes," *Journal of Applied Social Psychology*, June 2002, pp. 1189–1207; and M. C. Andrews, L. A. Witt, and K. M. Kacmar, "The Interactive Effects of Organizational Politics and Exchange Ideology on Manager Ratings of Retention," *Journal of Vocational Behavior*, April 2003, pp. 357–369.

46. S. Aryee, Z. Chen, and P. S. Budhwar, "Exchange Fairness and Employee Performance: An Examination of the Relationship Between Organizational Politics and Procedural Justice," *Organizational Behavior & Human Decision Processes*, May 2004, pp. 1–14; and Kacmar, Bozeman, Carlson, and Anthony, "An Examination of the Perceptions of Organizational Politics Model."

47. Kacmar, Bozeman, Carlson, and Anthony, "An Examination of the Perceptions of Organizational Politics Model," p. 389.

48. Ibid., p. 409.

49. B. E. Ashforth and R. T. Lee, "Defensive Behavior in Organizations: A Preliminary Model," *Human Relations*, July 1990, pp. 621–648.

50. M. Valle and P. L. Perrewe, "Do Politics Perceptions Relate to Political Behaviors? Tests of an Implicit Assumption and Expanded Model," *Human Relations*, March 2000, pp. 359–386.

51. See T. Romm and A. Drory, "Political Behavior in Organizations: A Cross-Cultural Comparison," *International Journal of Value Based Management* 1 (1988), pp. 97–113; and E. Vigoda, "Reactions to Organizational Politics: A Cross-Cultural Examination in Israel and Britain," *Human Relations*, November 2001, pp. 1483–1518.

52. E. Vigoda, "Reactions to Organizational Politics," p. 1512.

53. Ibid., p. 1510.

54. M. R. Leary and R. M. Kowalski, "Impression Management: A Literature Review and Two-Component Model," *Psychological Bulletin*, January 1990, pp. 34–47.

55. Ibid., p. 34.

56. See, for instance, B. R. Schlenker, *Impression Management: The Self-Concept, Social Identity, and Interpersonal Relations* (Monterey, CA: Brooks/Cole, 1980); W. L. Gardner and M. J. Martinko, "Impression Management in Organizations," *Journal of Management*, June 1988, pp. 321–338; D. P. Bozeman and K. M. Kacmar, "A Cybernetic Model of Impression Management Processes in Organizations," *Organizational Behavior and Human Decision Processes*, January 1997, pp. 9–30; M. C. Bolino and W. H. Turnley, "More Than One Way to Make an Impression: Exploring Profiles of Impression Management," *Journal of Management* 29, no. 2 (2003), pp. 141–160; S. Zivnuska, K. M. Kacmar, L. A. Witt, D. S. Carlson, and V. K. Bratton, "Interactive Effects of Impression Management and Organizational Politics on Job Performance," *Journal of Organizational Behavior*, August 2004, pp. 627–640; and W.-C. Tsai, C.-C. Chen, and S.-F. Chiu, "Exploring Boundaries of the Effects of Applicant Impression Management Tactics in Job Interviews," *Journal of Management*, February 2005, pp. 108–125.

57. M. Snyder and J. Copeland, "Self-monitoring Processes in Organizational Settings," in Giacalone and Rosenfeld (eds.), *Impression Management in the Organization* (Hillsdale, NJ: Lawrence Erlbaum, 1989), p. 11; A. Montagliani and R. A. Giacalone, "Impression Management and Cross-Cultural Adaptation," *Journal of Social Psychology*, October 1998, pp. 598–608; and W. H. Turnley and M. C. Bolino, "Achieved Desired Images While Avoiding Undesired Images: Exploring the Role of Self-Monitoring in Impression Management," *Journal of Applied Psychology*, April 2001, pp. 351–360.

58. Leary and Kowalski, "Impression Management," p. 40.

59. Gardner and Martinko, "Impression Management in Organizations," p. 333.

60. R. A. Baron, "Impression Management by Applicants During Employment Interviews: The 'Too Much of a Good Thing' Effect," in R. W. Eder and G. R. Ferris (eds.), *The Employment Interview: Theory, Research, and Practice* (Newbury Park, CA: Sage Publishers, 1989), pp. 204–215.

61. Ferris, Russ, and Fandt, "Politics in Organizations."

62. A. P. J. Ellis, B. J. West, A. M. Ryan, and R. P. DeShon, "The Use of Impression Management Tactics in Structural Interviews: A Function of Question Type?" *Journal of Applied Psychology*, December 2002, pp. 1200–1208.

63. Baron, "Impression Management by Applicants During Employment Interviews"; D. C. Gilmore and G. R. Ferris, "The Effects of Applicant Impression Management Tactics on Interviewer Judgments," *Journal of Management*, December 1989, pp. 557–564; C. K. Stevens and A. L. Kristof, "Making the Right Impression: A Field Study of Applicant Impression Management During Job Interviews," *Journal of Applied Psychology* 80 (1995), pp. 587–606; and L. A. McFarland, A. M. Ryan, and S. D. Kriska, "Impression Management Use and Effectiveness Across Assessment Methods," *Journal of Management* 29, no. 5 (2003), pp. 641–661; and Tsai, Chen, and Chiu, "Exploring Boundaries of the Effects of Applicant Impression Management Tactics in Job Interviews."

64. Gilmore and Ferris, "The Effects of Applicant Impression Management Tactics on Interviewer Judgments."

65. Stevens and Kristof, "Making the Right Impression: A Field Study of Applicant Impression Management During Job Interviews."

66. C. A. Higgins, T. A. Judge, and G. R. Ferris, "Influence Tactics and Work Outcomes: A Meta-Analysis," *Journal of Organizational Behavior*, March 2003, pp. 89–106.

67. Ibid.

68. J. D. Westphal and I. Stern, "Flattery Will Get You Everywhere (Especially if You Are a Male Caucasian): How Ingratiation, Boardroom Behavior, and Demographic Minority Status Affect Additional Board Appointments of U.S. Companies," *Academy of Management Journal* 50, no. 2 (2007), pp. 267–288.

69. O. J. Labedo, "Perceptions of Organisational Politics: Examination of the Situational Antecedent and Consequences Among Nigeria's Extension Personnel," *Applied Psychology: An International Review* 55, no. 2 (2006), pp. 255–281.

70. P. P. Fu and G. Yukl, "Perceived Effectiveness of Influence Tactics in the United States and China," *Leadership Quarterly*, Summer 2000, pp. 251–266; O. Branzei, "Cultural Explanations

of Individual Preferences for Influence Tactics in Cross-Cultural Encounters," *International Journal of Cross Cultural Management*, August 2002, pp. 203–218; G. Yukl, P. P. Fu, and R. McDonald, "Cross-Cultural Differences in Perceived Effectiveness of Influence Tactics for Initiating or Resisting Change," *Applied Psychology: An International Review*, January 2003, pp. 66–82; and P. P. Fu, T. K. Peng, J. C. Kennedy, and G. Yukl, "Examining the Preferences of Influence Tactics in Chinese Societies: A Comparison of Chinese Managers in Hong Kong, Taiwan, and Mainland China," *Organizational Dynamics* 33, no. 1 (2004), pp. 32–46.

71. Fu and Yukl, "Perceived Effectiveness of Influence Tactics in the United States and China."

72. S. J. Heine, "Making Sense of East Asian Self-Enhancement," *Journal of Cross-Cultural Psychology*, September 2003, pp. 596–602.

73. J. L. T. Leong, M. H. Bond, and P. P. Fu, "Perceived Effectiveness of Influence Strategies in the United States and Three Chinese Societies," *International Journal of Cross Cultural Management*, May 2006, pp. 101–120.

74. R. M. Kanter, *Men and Women of the Corporation* (New York: Basic Books, 1977).

75. See, for instance, Falbe and Yukl, "Consequences for Managers of Using Single Influence Tactics and Combinations of Tactics."

76. See J. G. Bachman, D. G. Bowers, and P. M. Marcus, "Bases of Supervisory Power: A Comparative Study in Five Organizational Settings," in A. S. Tannenbaum (ed.), *Control in Organizations* (New York: McGraw-Hill, 1968), p. 236; M. A. Rahim, "Relationships of Leader Power to Compliance and Satisfaction with Supervision: Evidence from a National Sample of Managers," *Journal of Management*, December 1989, pp. 545–556; P. A. Wilson, "The Effects of Politics and Power on the Organizational Commitment of Federal Executives," *Journal of Management*, Spring 1995, pp. 101–118; and A. R. Elangovan and J. L. Xie, "Effects of Perceived Power of Supervisor on Subordinate Stress and Motivation: The Moderating Role of Subordinate Characteristics," *Journal of Organizational Behavior*, May 1999, pp. 359–373.

77. J. Pfeffer, *Managing with Power: Politics and Influence in Organizations* (Boston: Harvard Business School Press, 1992).

78. G. R. Ferris, P. L. Perrewé, W. P. Anthony, and D. C. Gilmore, "Political Skill at Work," *Organizational Dynamics*, Spring 2000, pp. 25–37; K. K. Ahearn, G. R. Ferris, W. A. Hochwarter, C. Douglas, and A. P. Ammeter, "Leader Political Skill and Team Performance," *Journal of Management* 30, no. 3 (2004), pp. 309–327; and S. E. Seibert, M. L. Kraimer, and J. M. Crant, "What Do Proactive People Do? A Longitudinal Model Linking Proactive Personality and Career Success," *Personnel Psychology*, Winter 2001, pp. 845–874.

79. R. W. Kolodinsky, W. A. Hochwarter, and G. R. Ferris, "Nonlinearity in the Relationship Between Political Skill and Work Outcomes: Convergent Evidence from Three Studies," *Journal of Vocational Behavior*, October 2004, pp. 294–308; W. Hochwarter, "The Interactive Effects of Pro-Political Behavior and Politics Perceptions on Job Satisfaction and Affective Commitment," *Journal of Applied Social Psychology*, July 2003, pp. 1360–1378; and P. L. Perrewé, K. L. Zellars, G. R. Ferris, A. Rossi, C. J. Kacmar, and D. A. Ralston, "Neutralizing Job Stressors: Political Skill as an Antidote to the Dysfunctional Consequences of Role Conflict," *Academy of Management Journal*, February 2004, pp. 141–152.

Conflict and Negotiation

Let us never negotiate out of fear. But let us never fear to negotiate.

—John F. Kennedy

LEARNING OBJECTIVES

After studying this chapter, you should be able to:

1 Define *conflict*.

2 Differentiate between the traditional, human relations, and interactionist views of conflict.

3 Outline the conflict process.

4 Define *negotiation*.

5 Contrast distributive and integrative bargaining.

6 Apply the five steps of the negotiation process.

7 Show how individual differences influence negotiations.

8 Assess the roles and functions of third-party negotiations.

9 Describe cultural differences in negotiations.

_d_espite a storied history and one of the best-known brand names in all of consumer products, H. J. Heinz Co. has had its share of troubles in the past decade. The company's earnings have been flat, and despite a recent upswing, Heinz's stock is well below the price at which it traded 10 years ago.

Enter Nelson Peltz, CEO and founding partner of Trian Fund Management L.P. Peltz thought Heinz's underperforming stock represented an opportunity, so

Ketchup Fight

he gradually acquired 3 percent of Heinz's shares—enough to land a seat on Heinz's board of directors, where he began lobbying for changes.

Peltz's play at Heinz is nothing new to him—he bought a 3 percent share in Kraft, a 2.98 percent stake in Cadbury Schweppes PLC, a 5.54 percent stake in Tiffany & Co., and a 5.5 percent share of Wendy's International, Inc. His goal is to buy a big enough stake to be able to lobby for changes that will raise the company's stock price, at which time he can cash in on his investment. Generally, Peltz targets high-profile consumer products companies whose stock has been underperforming.

When investors such as Peltz, Carl Icahn, or Kirk Kerkorian push for shareholder-led changes in a company, often the CEO chafes. However, in this case, the conflict became personal. Heinz CEO William R. Johnson angrily wrote to Peltz, "Now is not the time for adding a self-interested and divisive voice inside the Heinz boardroom." Peltz retorted, "Maybe they need some adult supervision." Another Heinz director entered the fight, calling Peltz "infuriating."

Like many other conflicts that turn personal, this one started out as a difference in strategies and tactics. Johnson's focus for Heinz's turnaround was on restructuring. He believed Heinz was spread too thin, and he has tried to focus the company on its best-selling brands. Peltz's goal was to cut costs even further and, at the same time, invest more in advertising to make the most of the Heinz brand.

Though it's hard to make cause-and-effect inferences for a single incident, it appears that the conflict has produced some tasty results for Heinz and its stakeholders. Since Heinz's aggressive advertising campaign last fall, the company's stock is up roughly 11 percent.

While you'd think the company's successes would ease tensions between Peltz and Johnson, personality conflicts don't often heal. Recently, when Peltz was told that Johnson claimed ownership of the idea for the advertising campaign, Peltz called that "an utter lie."[1] ■

*a*s we see in the Heinz example, conflict can often turn personal. It can create chaotic conditions that make it nearly impossible for employees to work as a team. However, conflict also has a less-well-known positive side. We'll explain the difference between negative and positive conflicts in this chapter and provide a guide to help you understand how conflicts develop. We'll also present a topic closely akin to conflict: negotiation. But first, gauge how you handle conflict by taking the following self-assessment.

WHAT'S MY PREFERRED CONFLICT-HANDLING STYLE?

In the Self-Assessment Library (available on CD and online), take assessment II.C.5 (What's My Preferred Conflict-Handling Style?) and answer the following questions.

1. *Judging from your highest score, what's your primary conflict-handling style?*
2. *Do you think your style varies, depending on the situation?*
3. *Would you like to change any aspects of your conflict-handling style?*

A Definition of *Conflict*

1 *Define* conflict.

There has been no shortage of definitions of *conflict*.[2] Despite the divergent meanings the term has acquired, several common themes underlie most definitions. Conflict must be perceived by the parties to it; whether or not conflict exists is a perception issue. If no one is aware of a conflict, then it is generally agreed that no conflict exists. Additional commonalities in the definitions are opposition or incompatibility and some form of interaction.[3] These factors set the conditions that determine the beginning point of the conflict process.

We can define **conflict**, then, as a process that begins when one party perceives that another party has negatively affected, or is about to negatively affect, something that the first party cares about.[4] This definition is purposely broad. It describes that point in any ongoing activity when an interaction "crosses over" to become an interparty conflict. It encompasses the wide range of conflicts that people experience in organizations—incompatibility of goals, differences over interpretations of facts, disagreements based on behavioral expectations, and the like. Finally, our definition is flexible enough to cover the full range of conflict levels—from overt and violent acts to subtle forms of disagreement.

Transitions in Conflict Thought

2   Differentiate between the traditional, human relations, and interactionist views of conflict.

It is entirely appropriate to say there has been conflict over the role of conflict in groups and organizations. One school of thought has argued that conflict must be avoided—that it indicates a malfunctioning within the group. We call this the *traditional* view. Another school of thought, the *human relations* view, argues that conflict is a natural and inevitable outcome in any group and that it need not be evil but rather has the potential to be a positive force in determining group performance. The third, and most recent, perspective proposes not only that conflict can be a positive force in a group but explicitly argues that some conflict is *absolutely necessary* for a group to perform effectively. We label this third school the *interactionist* view. Let's take a closer look at each of these views.

The Traditional View of Conflict

The early approach to conflict assumed that all conflict was bad. Conflict was viewed negatively, and it was used synonymously with such terms as *violence*, *destruction*, and *irrationality* to reinforce its negative connotation. Conflict, by definition, was harmful and was to be avoided. The **traditional view of conflict** was consistent with the attitudes that prevailed about group behavior in the 1930s and 1940s. Conflict was seen as a dysfunctional outcome resulting from poor communication, a lack of openness and trust between people, and the failure of managers to be responsive to the needs and aspirations of their employees.

The view that all conflict is bad certainly offers a simple approach to looking at the behavior of people who create conflict. Because all conflict is to be avoided, we need merely direct our attention to the causes of conflict and correct those malfunctions to improve group and organizational performance. Although research studies now provide strong evidence to dispute that this approach to conflict reduction results in high group performance, many of us still evaluate conflict situations using this outmoded standard.

---

conflict   *A process that begins when one party perceives that another party has negatively affected, or is about to negatively affect, something that the first party cares about.*

traditional view of conflict   *The belief that all conflict is harmful and must be avoided.*

The Human Relations View of Conflict

The **human relations view of conflict** argued that conflict was a natural occurrence in all groups and organizations. Because conflict was inevitable, the human relations school advocated acceptance of conflict. Proponents rationalized its existence: It cannot be eliminated, and there are even times when conflict may benefit a group's performance. The human relations view dominated conflict theory from the late 1940s through the mid-1970s.

The Interactionist View of Conflict

Whereas the human relations view accepted conflict, the **interactionist view of conflict** encourages conflict on the grounds that a harmonious, peaceful, tranquil, and cooperative group is prone to becoming static, apathetic, and nonresponsive to needs for change and innovation.[5] The major contribution of the interactionist view, therefore, is encouraging group leaders to maintain an ongoing minimum level of conflict—enough to keep the group viable, self-critical, and creative.

The interactionist view does not propose that all conflicts are good. Rather, some conflicts support the goals of the group and improve its performance; these are **functional**, constructive, forms of conflict. In addition, there are conflicts that hinder group performance; these are **dysfunctional**, or destructive, forms of conflict. What differentiates functional from dysfunctional conflict? The evidence indicates that you need to look at the *type* of conflict.[6] Specifically, there are three types: task, relationship, and process.

Task conflict relates to the content and goals of the work. **Relationship conflict** focuses on interpersonal relationships. **Process conflict** relates to how the work gets done. Studies demonstrate that relationship conflicts are almost always dysfunctional.[7] Why? It appears that the friction and interpersonal hostilities inherent in relationship conflicts increase personality clashes and decrease mutual understanding, which hinders the completion of organizational tasks. Unfortunately, managers spend a lot of their time resolving personality conflicts; one survey indicated that 18 percent of managers' time is spent trying to resolve personality conflicts among staff members.[8]

Unlike with relationship conflict, low levels of process conflict and low to moderate levels of task conflict are functional. For process conflict to be productive, it must be kept low. Intense arguments about who should do what become dysfunctional when they create uncertainty about task roles, increase the time to complete tasks, and lead to members working at cross purposes. Low-to-moderate levels of task conflict consistently demonstrate a positive effect on group performance because it stimulates discussion of ideas that helps groups perform better.

The Conflict Process

3 Outline the conflict process.

The **conflict process** has five stages: potential opposition or incompatibility, cognition and personalization, intentions, behavior, and outcomes. The process is diagrammed in Exhibit 15-1.

Stage I: Potential Opposition or Incompatibility

The first step in the conflict process is the presence of conditions that create opportunities for conflict to arise. They *need not* lead directly to conflict, but one of these conditions is necessary if conflict is to surface. For simplicity's sake, these conditions (which we can also look at as causes or sources of conflict)

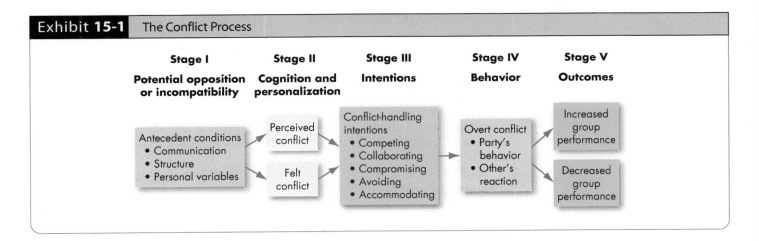

| Exhibit 15-1 | The Conflict Process |

Stage I
Potential opposition or incompatibility

Stage II
Cognition and personalization

Stage III
Intentions

Stage IV
Behavior

Stage V
Outcomes

Antecedent conditions
• Communication
• Structure
• Personal variables

Perceived conflict

Felt conflict

Conflict-handling intentions
• Competing
• Collaborating
• Compromising
• Avoiding
• Accommodating

Overt conflict
• Party's behavior
• Other's reaction

Increased group performance

Decreased group performance

have been condensed into three general categories: communication, structure, and personal variables.

Communication   Susan had worked in supply-chain management at Bristol-Myers Squibb for 3 years. She enjoyed her work in large part because her boss, Tim McGuire, was a great guy to work for. Then Tim got promoted 6 months ago, and Chuck Benson took his place. Susan says her job is a lot more frustrating now. "Tim and I were on the same wavelength. It's not that way with Chuck. He tells me something and I do it. Then he tells me I did it wrong. I think he means one thing but says something else. It's been like this since the day he arrived. I don't think a day goes by when he isn't yelling at me for something. You know, there are some people you just find it easy to communicate with. Well, Chuck isn't one of those!"

Susan's comments illustrate that communication can be a source of conflict.[9] They represent the opposing forces that arise from semantic difficulties, misunderstandings, and "noise" in the communication channels. Much of this discussion can be related to our comments on communication in Chapter 11.

A review of the research suggests that differing word connotations, jargon, insufficient exchange of information, and noise in the communication channel are all barriers to communication and potential antecedent conditions to conflict. Research has further demonstrated a surprising finding: The potential for conflict increases when either too little or too much communication takes place. Apparently, an increase in communication is functional up to a point, whereupon it is possible to overcommunicate, with a resultant increase in the potential for conflict.

Structure   Charlotte and Teri both work at the Portland Furniture Mart—a large discount furniture retailer. Charlotte is a salesperson on the floor, and Teri is the company credit manager. The two women have known each other for

human relations view of conflict   *The belief that conflict is a natural and inevitable outcome in any group.*

interactionist view of conflict   *The belief that conflict is not only a positive force in a group but that it is also an absolute necessity for a group to perform effectively.*

functional conflict   *Conflict that supports the goals of the group and improves its performance.*

dysfunctional conflict   *Conflict that hinders group performance.*

task conflict   *Conflict over content and goals of the work.*

relationship conflict   *Conflict based on interpersonal relationships.*

process conflict   *Conflict over how work gets done.*

conflict process   *A process that has five stages: potential opposition or incompatibility, cognition and personalization, intentions, behavior, and outcomes.*

years and have much in common: They live within two blocks of each other, and their oldest daughters attend the same middle school and are best friends. In reality, if Charlotte and Teri had different jobs, they might be best friends themselves, but these two women are consistently fighting battles with each other. Charlotte's job is to sell furniture, and she does a heck of a job. But most of her sales are made on credit. Because Teri's job is to make sure the company minimizes credit losses, she regularly has to turn down the credit application of a customer with whom Charlotte has just closed a sale. It's nothing personal between Charlotte and Teri; the requirements of their jobs just bring them into conflict.

The conflicts between Charlotte and Teri are structural in nature. The term *structure* is used, in this context, to include variables such as size, degree of specialization in the tasks assigned to group members, jurisdictional clarity, member-goal compatibility, leadership styles, reward systems, and the degree of dependence between groups.

Research indicates that size and specialization act as forces to stimulate conflict. The larger the group and the more specialized its activities, the greater the likelihood of conflict. Tenure and conflict have been found to be inversely related. The potential for conflict tends to be greatest when group members are younger and when turnover is high.

The greater the ambiguity in precisely defining where responsibility for actions lies, the greater the potential for conflict to emerge. Such jurisdictional ambiguities increase intergroup fighting for control of resources and territory. Diversity of goals among groups is also a major source of conflict. When groups within an organization seek diverse ends, some of which—like sales and credit at Portland Furniture Mart—are inherently at odds, there are increased opportunities for conflict. Reward systems, too, are found to create conflict when one member's gain is at another's expense. Finally, if a group is dependent on another group (in contrast to the two being mutually independent) or if interdependence allows one group to gain at another's expense, opposing forces are stimulated.[10]

Personal variables such as personality differences can be the source of conflict among coworkers. To reduce conflict resulting from personality differences, Vertex Pharmaceuticals teaches employees how to identify other people's personality types and then how to communicate effectively with them. At Vertex, innovation is critical to the company's mission of developing drugs that treat life-threatening diseases. By training employees to work harmoniously in spite of personality differences, Vertex hopes to eliminate unproductive conflict that impedes innovation.

Personal Variables Have you ever met someone to whom you took an immediate disliking? You disagreed with most of the opinions they expressed. Even insignificant characteristics—the sound of their voice, the smirk when they smiled, their personality—annoyed you. We've all met people like that. When you have to work with such individuals, there is often the potential for conflict.

Our last category of potential sources of conflict is personal variables, which include personality, emotions, and values. Evidence indicates that certain personality types—for example, individuals who are highly authoritarian and dogmatic—lead to potential conflict. Emotions can also cause conflict. For example, an employee who shows up to work irate from her hectic morning commute may carry that anger with her to her 9 A.M. meeting. The problem? Her anger can annoy her colleagues, which may lead to a tension-filled meeting.[11]

Stage II: Cognition and Personalization

If the conditions cited in Stage I negatively affect something that one party cares about, then the potential for opposition or incompatibility becomes actualized in the second stage.

As we noted in our definition of conflict, perception is required. Therefore, one or more of the parties must be aware of the existence of the antecedent conditions. However, because a conflict is **perceived conflict** does not mean that it is personalized. In other words, "*A* may be aware that *B* and *A* are in serious disagreement . . . but it may not make *A* tense or anxious, and it may have no effect whatsoever on *A*'s affection toward *B*."[12] It is at the **felt conflict** level, when individuals become emotionally involved, that parties experience anxiety, tension, frustration, or hostility.

Keep in mind two points. First, Stage II is important because it's where conflict issues tend to be defined. This is the place in the process where the parties decide what the conflict is about.[13] In turn, this "sense making" is critical because the way a conflict is defined goes a long way toward establishing the sort of outcomes that might settle it. For instance, if I define our salary disagreement as a zero-sum situation (that is, if you get the increase in pay you want, there will be just that amount less for me) I am going to be far less willing to compromise than if I frame the conflict as a potential win/win situation (that is, the dollars in the salary pool might be increased so that both of us could get the added pay we want). So the definition of a conflict is important because it typically delineates the set of possible settlements. Our second point is that emotions play a major role in shaping perceptions.[14] For example, negative emotions have been found to produce oversimplification of issues, reductions in trust, and negative interpretations of the other party's behavior.[15] In contrast, positive feelings have been found to increase the tendency to see potential relationships among the elements of a problem, to take a broader view of the situation, and to develop more innovative solutions.[16]

Stage III: Intentions

Intentions intervene between people's perceptions and emotions and their overt behavior. These intentions are decisions to act in a given way.[17]

Intentions are separated out as a distinct stage because you have to infer the other's intent to know how to respond to that other's behavior. A lot of conflicts

---

perceived conflict *Awareness by one or more parties of the existence of conditions that create opportunities for conflict to arise.*

felt conflict *Emotional involvement in a conflict that creates anxiety, tenseness, frustration, or hostility.*

intentions *Decisions to act in a given way.*

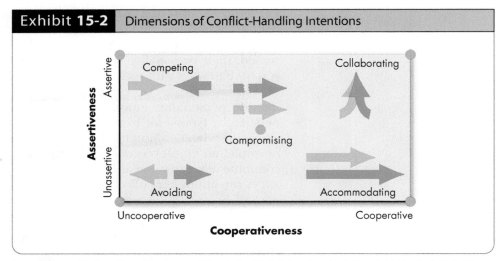

| Exhibit **15-2** | Dimensions of Conflict-Handling Intentions |

Source: K. Thomas, "Conflict and Negotiation Processes in Organizations," in M. D. Dunnette and L. M. Hough (eds.), *Handbook of Industrial and Organizational Psychology*, 2nd ed. vol. 3 (Palo Alto, CA: Consulting Psychologists Press, 1992), p. 668. Used with permission.

are escalated merely by one party attributing the wrong intentions to the other party. In addition, there is typically a great deal of slippage between intentions and behavior, so behavior does not always accurately reflect a person's intentions.

Exhibit 15-2 represents one author's effort to identify the primary conflict-handling intentions. Using two dimensions—*cooperativeness* (the degree to which one party attempts to satisfy the other party's concerns) and *assertiveness* (the degree to which one party attempts to satisfy his or her own concerns)—five conflict-handling intentions can be identified: *competing* (assertive and uncooperative), *collaborating* (assertive and cooperative), *avoiding* (unassertive and uncooperative), *accommodating* (unassertive and cooperative), and *compromising* (midrange on both assertiveness and cooperativeness).[18]

Competing When one person seeks to satisfy his or her own interests, regardless of the impact on the other parties to the conflict, that person is **competing**. Competing is when you, for example, win a bet and your opponent loses.

Collaborating When the parties to conflict each desire to fully satisfy the concerns of all parties, there is cooperation and a search for a mutually beneficial outcome. In **collaborating**, the intention of the parties is to solve a problem by clarifying differences rather than by accommodating various points of view. If you attempt to find a win/win solution that allows both parties' goals to be completely achieved, that's collaborating.

Avoiding A person may recognize that a conflict exists and want to withdraw from it or suppress it. Examples of **avoiding** include trying to just ignore a conflict and avoiding others with whom you disagree.

Accommodating When one party seeks to appease an opponent, that party may be willing to place the opponent's interests above his or her own. In other words, in order for the relationship to be maintained, one party needs to be willing to be self-sacrificing. We refer to this intention as **accommodating**. Supporting someone else's opinion despite your reservations about it, for example, would represent accommodating.

Compromising When each party to a conflict seeks to give up something, sharing occurs, resulting in a compromised outcome. In **compromising**, there is no clear winner or loser. Rather, there is a willingness to ration the object of the conflict and accept a solution that provides incomplete satisfaction of both parties' concerns. The distinguishing characteristic of compromising, therefore, is that each party intends to give up something.

Intentions are not always fixed. During the course of a conflict, they might change because of reconceptualization or because of an emotional reaction to the behavior of the other party. However, research indicates that people have an underlying disposition to handle conflicts in certain ways.[19] Specifically, individuals have preferences among the five conflict-handling intentions just described; these preferences tend to be relied on quite consistently, and a person's intentions can be predicted rather well from a combination of intellectual and personality characteristics.

Stage IV: Behavior

When most people think of conflict situations, they tend to focus on Stage IV because this is where conflicts become visible. The behavior stage includes the statements, actions, and reactions made by the conflicting parties. These conflict behaviors are usually overt attempts to implement each party's intentions. But these behaviors have a stimulus quality that is separate from intentions. As a result of miscalculations or unskilled enactments, overt behaviors sometimes deviate from original intentions.[20]

It helps to think of Stage IV as a dynamic process of interaction. For example, you make a demand on me, I respond by arguing, you threaten me, I threaten you back, and so on. Exhibit 15-3 provides a way of visualizing conflict behavior. All conflicts exist somewhere along this continuum. At the lower part of the continuum are conflicts characterized by subtle, indirect, and highly controlled forms of tension. An illustration might be a student questioning in class a point the instructor has just made. Conflict intensities escalate as they move upward along the continuum until they become highly destructive. Strikes, riots, and wars clearly fall in this upper range. For the most part, you should assume that conflicts that reach the upper ranges of the continuum are almost

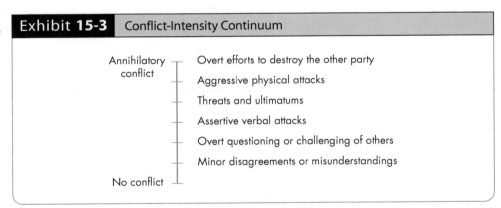

Exhibit **15-3**   Conflict-Intensity Continuum

Annihilatory conflict — Overt efforts to destroy the other party
— Aggressive physical attacks
— Threats and ultimatums
— Assertive verbal attacks
— Overt questioning or challenging of others
— Minor disagreements or misunderstandings
No conflict

Source: Based on S. P. Robbins, *Managing Organizational Conflict: A Nontraditional Approach* (Upper Saddle River, NJ: Prentice Hall, 1974), pp. 93–97; and F. Glasi, "The Process of Conflict Escalation and the Roles of Third Parties," in G. B. J. Bomers and R. Peterson (eds.), *Conflict Management and Industrial Relations* (Boston: Kluwer-Nijhoff, 1982), pp. 119–140.

competing   *A desire to satisfy one's interests, regardless of the impact on the other party to the conflict.*

collaborating   *A situation in which the parties to a conflict each desire to satisfy fully the concerns of all parties.*

avoiding   *The desire to withdraw from or suppress a conflict.*

accommodating   *The willingness of one party in a conflict to place the opponent's interests above his or her own.*

compromising   *A situation in which each party to a conflict is willing to give up something.*

Exhibit **15-4**	Conflict-Management Techniques

Conflict-Resolution Techniques

Problem solving	Face-to-face meeting of the conflicting parties for the purpose of identifying the problem and resolving it through open discusssion.
Superordinate goals	Creating a shared goal that cannot be attained without the cooperation of each of the conflicting parties.
Expansion of resources	When a conflict is caused by the scarcity of a resource—say, money, promotion, opportunities, office space—expansion of the resource can create a win/win solution.
Avoidance	Withdrawal from or suppression of the conflict.
Smoothing	Playing down differences while emphasizing common interests between the conflicting parties.
Compromise	Each party to the conflict gives up something of value.
Authoritative command	Management uses its formal authority to resolve the conflict and then communicates its desires to the parties involved.
Altering the human variable	Using behavioral change techniques such as human relations training to alter attitudes and behaviors that cause conflict.
Altering the structural variables	Changing the formal organization structure and the interaction patterns of conflicting parties through job redesign, transfers, creation of coordinating positions, and the like.

Conflict-Stimulation Techniques

Communication	Using ambiguous or threatening messages to increase conflict levels.
Bringing in outsiders	Adding employees to a group whose backgrounds, values, attitudes, or managerial styles differ from those of present members.
Restructuring the organization	Realigning work groups, altering rules and regulations, increasing interdependence, and making similar structural changes to disrupt the status quo.
Appointing a devil's advocate	Designating a critic to purposely argue against the majority positions held by the group.

Source: Based on S. P. Robbins, Managing Organizational Conflict: A Nontraditional Approach (Upper Saddle River, NJ: Prentice Hall, 1974), pp. 59–89.

always dysfunctional. Functional conflicts are typically confined to the lower range of the continuum.

If a conflict is dysfunctional, what can the parties do to de-escalate it? Or, conversely, what options exist if conflict is too low and needs to be increased? This brings us to **conflict-management** techniques. Exhibit 15-4 lists the major resolution and stimulation techniques that allow managers to control conflict levels. Note that several of the resolution techniques were described earlier as conflict-handling intentions. This, of course, shouldn't be surprising. Under ideal conditions, a person's intentions should translate into comparable behaviors.

Stage V: Outcomes

The action–reaction interplay between the conflicting parties results in consequences. As our model (see Exhibit 15-1) demonstrates, these outcomes may be functional in that the conflict results in an improvement in the group's performance or dysfunctional in that it hinders group performance.

Functional Outcomes How might conflict act as a force to increase group performance? It is hard to visualize a situation in which open or violent aggression could be functional. But there are a number of instances in which it's possible to envision how low or moderate levels of conflict could improve the effectiveness of a group. Because people often find it difficult to think of instances in which conflict can be constructive, let's consider some examples and then review the research evidence. Note how all these examples focus on task and process conflicts and exclude the relationship variety.

Conflict is constructive when it improves the quality of decisions, stimulates creativity and innovation, encourages interest and curiosity among group

A lack of functional conflict among General Motors management in past decades resulted in concessions to union demands for generous health benefits and pensions. Today, burdened by health costs that GM provides to more than 1 million employees, retirees, and dependents, the automaker is eliminating jobs and closing assembly plants as part of a cost-cutting strategy. The two employees shown here embrace as the last automobile rolls off the assembly line at GM's plant in Linden, New Jersey, which GM closed after 68 years of operation.

members, provides the medium through which problems can be aired and tensions released, and fosters an environment of self-evaluation and change. The evidence suggests that conflict can improve the quality of decision making by allowing all points, particularly the ones that are unusual or held by a minority, to be weighed in important decisions.[21] Conflict is an antidote for groupthink. It doesn't allow the group to passively "rubber-stamp" decisions that may be based on weak assumptions, inadequate consideration of relevant alternatives, or other debilities. Conflict challenges the status quo and therefore furthers the creation of new ideas, promotes reassessment of group goals and activities, and increases the probability that the group will respond to change.

For an example of a company that suffered because it had too little functional conflict, you don't have to look further than automobile behemoth General Motors.[22] Many of GM's problems, from the late 1960s to the present day, can be traced to a lack of functional conflict. GM hired and promoted individuals who were yespeople, loyal to GM to the point of never questioning company actions. Many, like investor Kirk Kekorian, fault GM management's conflict aversion for its acceding to the UAW's demands for generous health care and pension benefits. (GM's labor costs average $73.26 per hour, which is much higher than for its Japanese competitors.) In fairness to GM, Chrysler and Ford also approved similar benefits, but they've struggled mightily as well.

Conflict aversion is not limited to the automakers. Yahoo!'s former CEO Tim Koogle was so conflict averse that a sense of complacency settled in that left managers afraid to challenge the status quo. Even though Yahoo! started out much more successful than Google, it was soon overtaken, and most now believe it will never catch up.

Research studies in diverse settings confirm the functionality of conflict. Consider the following findings. Conflict can also positively relate to productivity.

conflict management   *The use of resolution and stimulation techniques to achieve the desired level of conflict.*

For instance, it was demonstrated that, among established groups, performance tended to improve more when there was conflict among members than when there was fairly close agreement. The investigators observed that when groups analyzed decisions that had been made by the individual members of that group, the average improvement among the high-conflict groups was 73 percent greater than that of those groups characterized by low-conflict conditions.[23] Others have found similar results: Groups composed of members with different interests tend to produce higher-quality solutions to a variety of problems than do homogeneous groups.[24]

The preceding leads us to predict that the increasing cultural diversity of the workforce should provide benefits to organizations. And that's what the evidence indicates. Research demonstrates that heterogeneity among group and organization members can increase creativity, improve the quality of decisions, and facilitate change by enhancing member flexibility.[25] For example, researchers compared decision-making groups composed of all-Caucasian individuals with groups that also contained members from Asian, Hispanic, and black ethnic groups. The ethnically diverse groups produced more effective and more feasible ideas and the unique ideas they generated tended to be of higher quality than the unique ideas produced by the all-Caucasian group.

Dysfunctional Outcomes   The destructive consequences of conflict on a group's or an organization's performance are generally well known. A reasonable summary might state: Uncontrolled opposition breeds discontent, which acts to dissolve common ties and eventually leads to the destruction of the group. And, of course, there is a substantial body of literature to document how conflict—the dysfunctional varieties—can reduce group effectiveness.[26] Among the more undesirable consequences are a retarding of communication, reductions in group cohesiveness, and subordination of group goals to the primacy of infighting among members. At the extreme, conflict can bring group functioning to a halt and potentially threaten the group's survival.

The demise of an organization as a result of too much conflict isn't as unusual as it might first appear. For instance, one of New York's best-known law firms, Shea & Gould, closed down solely because the 80 partners just couldn't get along.[27] As one legal consultant familiar with the organization said: "This was a firm that had basic and principled differences among the partners that were basically irreconcilable." That same consultant also addressed the partners at their last meeting: "You don't have an economic problem," he said. "You have a personality problem. You hate each other!"

Creating Functional Conflict   If managers accept the interactionist view toward conflict, what can they do to encourage functional conflict in their organizations?[28]

There seems to be general agreement that creating functional conflict is a tough job, particularly in large U.S. corporations. As one consultant put it, "A high proportion of people who get to the top are conflict avoiders. They don't like hearing negatives; they don't like saying or thinking negative things. They frequently make it up the ladder in part because they don't irritate people on the way up." Another suggests that at least 7 out of 10 people in U.S. business hush up when their opinions are at odds with those of their superiors, allowing bosses to make mistakes even when they know better.

Such anticonflict cultures may have been tolerable in the past but are not in today's fiercely competitive global economy. Organizations that don't encourage and support dissent may find their survival threatened. Let's look at some approaches organizations are using to encourage their people to challenge the system and develop fresh ideas.

Hewlett-Packard rewards dissenters by recognizing go-against-the-grain types, or people who stay with the ideas they believe in even when those ideas are rejected by management. Herman Miller Inc., an office furniture manufacturer, has a formal system in which employees evaluate and criticize their bosses. IBM also has a formal system that encourages dissension. Employees can question their boss with impunity. If the disagreement can't be resolved, the system provides a third party for counsel. Anheuser-Busch builds devil's advocates into the decision process. When the policy committee considers a major move, such as getting into or out of a business or making a major capital expenditure, it often assigns teams to make the case for each side of the question. This process frequently results in decisions and alternatives that hadn't been considered previously.

One common ingredient in organizations that successfully create functional conflict is that they reward dissent and punish conflict avoiders. The real challenge for managers, however, is when they hear news they don't want to hear. The news may make their blood boil or their hopes collapse, but they can't show it. They have to learn to take the bad news without flinching. No tirades, no tight-lipped sarcasm, no eyes rolling upward, no gritting of teeth. Rather, managers should ask calm, even-tempered questions: "Can you tell me more about what happened?" "What do you think we ought to do?" A sincere "Thank you for bringing this to my attention" will probably reduce the likelihood that managers will be cut off from similar communications in the future.

Having considered conflict—its nature, causes, and consequences—we now turn to negotiation. Negotiation and conflict are closely related because negotiation often resolves conflict.

Negotiation

4 Define negotiation.

Negotiation permeates the interactions of almost everyone in groups and organizations. There's the obvious: Labor bargains with management. There's the not-so-obvious: Managers negotiate with employees, peers, and bosses; salespeople negotiate with customers; purchasing agents negotiate with suppliers. And there's the subtle: An employee agrees to answer a colleague's phone for a few minutes in exchange for some past or future benefit. In today's loosely structured organizations, in which members are increasingly finding themselves having to work with colleagues over whom they have no direct authority and with whom they may not even share a common boss, negotiation skills become critical.

We can define **negotiation** as a process in which two or more parties exchange goods or services and attempt to agree on the exchange rate for them.[29] Note that we use the terms *negotiation* and *bargaining* interchangeably. In this section, we contrast two bargaining strategies, provide a model of the negotiation process, ascertain the role of moods and personality traits on bargaining, review gender and cultural differences in negotiation, and take a brief look at third-party negotiations.

negotiation *A process in which two or more parties exchange goods or services and attempt to agree on the exchange rate for them.*

Bargaining Strategies

There are two general approaches to negotiation—*distributive bargaining* and *integrative bargaining*.[30] As Exhibit 15-5 shows, distributive and integrative bargaining differ in their goal and motivation, focus, interests, information sharing, and duration of relationship. We now define distributive and integrative bargaining and illustrate the differences between these two approaches.

Distributive Bargaining   You see a used car advertised for sale in the newspaper. It appears to be just what you've been looking for. You go out to see the car. It's great, and you want it. The owner tells you the asking price. You don't want to pay that much. The two of you then negotiate over the price. The negotiating strategy you're engaging in is called **distributive bargaining**. Its most identifying feature is that it operates under zero-sum conditions. That is, any gain I make is at your expense and vice versa. In the used-car example, every dollar you can get the seller to cut from the car's price is a dollar you save. Conversely, every dollar more the seller can get from you comes at your expense. So the essence of distributive bargaining is negotiating over who gets what share of a fixed pie. By **fixed pie**, we mean that the bargaining parties believe there is only a set amount of goods or services to be divvied up. Therefore, fixed pies are zero-sum games in that every dollar in one party's pocket is a dollar out of their counterpart's pocket. When parties believe the pie is fixed, they tend to bargain distributively.

Probably the most widely cited example of distributive bargaining is in labor-management negotiations over wages. Typically, labor's representatives come to the bargaining table determined to get as much money as possible out of management. Because every cent more that labor negotiates increases management's costs, each party bargains aggressively and treats the other as an opponent who must be defeated.

The essence of distributive bargaining is depicted in Exhibit 15-6. Parties *A* and *B* represent two negotiators. Each has a *target point* that defines what he or she would like to achieve. Each also has a *resistance point,* which marks the lowest outcome that is acceptable—the point below which they would break off negotiations rather than accept a less-favorable settlement. The area between these two points makes up each one's aspiration range. As long as there is some overlap between *A*'s and *B*'s aspiration ranges, there exists a settlement range in which each one's aspirations can be met.

Exhibit 15-5	Distributive Versus Integrative Bargaining	
Bargaining Characteristic	**Distributive Bargaining**	**Integrative Bargaining**
Goal	Get as much of the pie as possible	Expand the pie so that both parties are satisfied
Motivation	Win/lose	Win/win
Focus	Positions ("I can't go beyond this point on this issue.")	Interests ("Can you explain why this issue is so important to you?")
Interests	Opposed	Congruent
Information sharing	Low (sharing information will only allow other party to take advantage)	High (sharing information will allow each party to find ways to satisfy interests of each party)
Duration of relationship	Short term	Long term

Exhibit **15-6**	Staking Out the Bargaining Zone

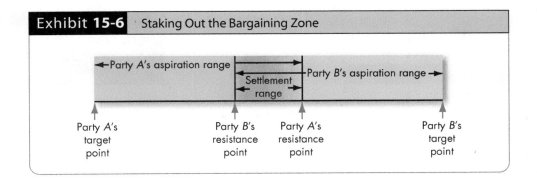

When engaged in distributive bargaining, one of the best things you can do is to make the first offer, and to make it an aggressive one. Research consistently shows that the best negotiators are those who make the first offer, and whose initial offer has very favorable terms. Why is this so? One reason is that making the first offer shows power; research shows that individuals in power are much more likely to make initial offers, speak first at meetings, and thereby gain the advantage. Another reason was mentioned in Chapter 5. Recall that we discussed the anchoring bias, which is the tendency for people to fixate on initial information. Once that anchoring point is set, people fail to adequately adjust it based on subsequent information. A savvy negotiator sets an anchor with the initial offer, and scores of negotiation studies show that such anchors greatly favor the person who sets it.[31]

For example, say you have a job offer, and your prospective employer asks you what sort of starting salary you'd be looking for. You need to realize that you've just been given a great gift—you have a chance to set the anchor, meaning that you should ask for the highest salary that you think the employer could reasonably offer. For most of us, asking for a million dollars is only going to make us look ridiculous, which is why we suggest being on the high end of what you think is reasonable. Too often, we err on the side of caution, being afraid of scaring off the employer and thus settling for too little. It *is* possible to scare off an employer, and it's true that employers don't like candidates to be assertive in salary negotiations, but liking isn't the same as respect or doing what it takes to hire or retain someone.[32] You should realize that what happens much more often is that we ask for less than what we could have gotten.

Another distributive bargaining tactic is revealing a deadline. Consider the following example. Erin is a human resources manager. She is negotiating salary with Ron, who is a highly sought after new hire. Because Ron knows the company needs him, he decides to play hardball and ask for an extraordinary salary and many benefits. Erin tells Ron that the company can't meet his requirements. Ron tells Erin he is going to have to think things over. Worried the company is going to lose Ron to a competitor, Erin decides to tell Ron that she is under time pressure and that she needs to reach an agreement with him immediately, or she will have to offer the job to another candidate. Would you consider Erin to be a savvy negotiator? Well, she is. Why? Negotiators who reveal deadlines speed concessions from their negotiating counterparts, making them reconsider their position. And even though negotiators don't *think* this tactic works, in reality, negotiators who reveal deadlines do better.[33]

distributive bargaining *Negotiation that seeks to divide up a fixed amount of resources; a win/lose situation.*

fixed pie *The belief that there is only a set amount of goods or services to be divvied up between the parties.*

MYTH OR SCIENCE?

"When Selling in an Auction, Start the Bidding High"

*t*his statement is false. That might surprise you, given that we just reviewed evidence on anchoring bias, which would seem suggest that if I'm selling something in an auction, I should set the initial bid as high as possible. Research shows that, while this generally is true, for auctions, this would be a mistake. In fact, the opposite strategy is better.

Analyzing auction results on eBay, a group of researchers found that *lower* starting bids generated higher final prices. As just one example, Nikon digital cameras with ridiculously low starting bids (one penny) sold for an average of $312,

whereas those with higher starting prices went for an average of $204.[34]

What explains such a counterintuitive result? The researchers found that low starting bids attract more bidders, and the increased traffic generates more competing bidders so that in the end, the price is higher. Although this may seem irrational, negotiation and bidding behavior aren't always rational, and as you've probably experienced firsthand, once you start bidding for something, you want to "win," forgetting that for many auctions, the one with the highest bid is often the loser (the so-called winner's curse). ■

Integrative Bargaining A sales representative for a women's sportswear manufacturer has just closed a $15,000 order from a small clothing retailer. The sales rep calls in the order to her firm's credit department. She is told that the firm can't approve credit to this customer because of a past slow-payment record. The next day, the sales rep and the firm's credit manager meet to discuss the problem. The sales rep doesn't want to lose the business. Neither does the credit manager, but he also doesn't want to get stuck with an uncollectible debt. The two openly review their options. After considerable discussion, they agree on a solution that meets both their needs: The credit manager will approve the sale, but the clothing store's owner will provide a bank guarantee that will ensure payment if the bill isn't paid within 60 days. This sales-credit

United Auto Workers President Ron Gettelfinger (left) shakes hands with Ford Motor Company Executive Chairman Bill Ford at the opening of negotiations for a new union contract. Both the union and Ford say they are committed to integrative bargaining in finding mutually acceptable solutions to issues such as funding retiree health care and pensions that will boost Ford's competitiveness with Japanese automakers.

negotiation is an example of **integrative bargaining**. In contrast to distributive bargaining, integrative bargaining operates under the assumption that there are one or more settlements that can create a win/win solution.

In terms of intraorganizational behavior, all things being equal, integrative bargaining is preferable to distributive bargaining. Why? Because the former builds long-term relationships. It bonds negotiators and allows them to leave the bargaining table feeling that they have achieved a victory. Distributive bargaining, however, leaves one party a loser. It tends to build animosities and deepen divisions when people have to work together on an ongoing basis. Research shows that over repeated bargaining episodes, when the "losing" party feels positive about the negotiation outcome, he is much more likely to bargain cooperatively in subsequent negotiations. This points to the important advantage of integrative negotiations: Even when you "win," you want your opponent to feel positively about the negotiation.[35]

Why, then, don't we see more integrative bargaining in organizations? The answer lies in the conditions necessary for this type of negotiation to succeed. These include parties who are open with information and candid about their concerns, a sensitivity by both parties to the other's needs, the ability to trust one another, and a willingness by both parties to maintain flexibility.[36] Because these conditions often don't exist in organizations, it isn't surprising that negotiations often take on a win-at-any-cost dynamic.

There are some ways to achieve more integrative outcomes. For example, individuals who bargain in teams reach more integrative agreements than those who bargain individually. This happens because more ideas are generated when more people are at the bargaining table. So try bargaining in teams.[37] Another way to achieve higher joint-gain settlements is to put more issues on the table. The more negotiable issues that are introduced into a negotiation, the more opportunity there is for "logrolling" where issues are traded because of differences in preferences. This creates better outcomes for each side than if each issue were negotiated individually.[38]

Finally, you should realize that compromise may be your worst enemy in negotiating a win/win agreement. This is because compromising reduces the pressure to bargain integratively. After all, if you or your opponent caves in easily, it doesn't require anyone to be creative to reach a settlement. Thus, people end up settling for less than they could have obtained if they had been forced to consider the other party's interests, trade off issues, and be creative.[39] Think of the classic example where two sisters are arguing over who gets an orange. Unbeknownst to each other, one sister wants the orange to drink the juice, whereas the other sister wants the orange peel to bake a cake. If one sister simply capitulates and gives the other sister the orange, then they will not be forced to explore their reasons for wanting the orange, and thus they will never find the win/win solution: They could *each* have the orange because they want different parts of it!

The Negotiation Process

6   *Apply the five steps of the negotiation process.*

Exhibit 15-7 provides a simplified model of the negotiation process. It views negotiation as made up of five steps: (1) preparation and planning, (2) definition of ground rules, (3) clarification and justification, (4) bargaining and problem solving, and (5) closure and implementation.[40]

integrative bargaining   *Negotiation that seeks one or more settlements that can create a win/win solution.*

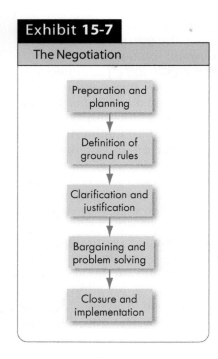

Exhibit 15-7

The Negotiation

- Preparation and planning
- Definition of ground rules
- Clarification and justification
- Bargaining and problem solving
- Closure and implementation

Preparation and Planning Before you start negotiating, you need to do your homework. What's the nature of the conflict? What's the history leading up to this negotiation? Who's involved and what are their perceptions of the conflict? What do you want from the negotiation? What are *your* goals? If you're a supply manager at Dell Computer, for instance, and your goal is to get a significant cost reduction from your supplier of keyboards, make sure that this goal stays paramount in your discussions and doesn't get overshadowed by other issues. It often helps to put your goals in writing and develop a range of outcomes—from "most hopeful" to "minimally acceptable"—to keep your attention focused.

You also want to prepare an assessment of what you think the other party's goals are. What are they likely to ask for? How entrenched are they likely to be in their position? What intangible or hidden interests may be important to them? What might they be willing to settle on? When you can anticipate your opponent's position, you are better equipped to counter arguments with the facts and figures that support your position.

Once you've gathered your information, use it to develop a strategy. For example, expert chess players have a strategy. They know ahead of time how they will respond to any given situation. As part of your strategy, you should determine yours and the other side's *best alternative to a negotiated agreement* (**BATNA**).[41] Your BATNA determines the lowest value acceptable to you for a negotiated agreement. Any offer you receive that is higher than your BATNA is better than an impasse. Conversely, you shouldn't expect success in your negotiation effort unless you're able to make the other side an offer they find more attractive than their BATNA. If you go into your negotiation having a good idea of what the other party's BATNA is, even if you're not able to meet theirs, you might be able to get them to change it.

Definition of Ground Rules Once you've done your planning and developed a strategy, you're ready to begin defining the ground rules and procedures with the other party over the negotiation itself. Who will do the negotiating? Where will it take place? What time constraints, if any, will apply? To what issues will negotiation be limited? Will there be a specific procedure to follow if an impasse is reached? During this phase, the parties will also exchange their initial proposals or demands.

Clarification and Justification When initial positions have been exchanged, both you and the other party will explain, amplify, clarify, bolster, and justify your original demands. This needn't be confrontational. Rather, it's an opportunity for educating and informing each other on the issues, why they are important, and how each arrived at their initial demands. This is the point at which you might want to provide the other party with any documentation that helps support your position.

Bargaining and Problem Solving The essence of the negotiation process is the actual give-and-take in trying to hash out an agreement. This is where both parties will undoubtedly need to make concessions.

Closure and Implementation The final step in the negotiation process is formalizing the agreement that has been worked out and developing any procedures that are necessary for implementation and monitoring. For major negotiations—which would include everything from labor-management negotiations to bargaining over lease terms to buying a piece of real estate to negotiating a job offer for a senior management position—this requires hammering out the specifics in a formal contract. For most cases, however, closure of the negotiation process is nothing more formal than a handshake.

Individual Differences in Negotiation Effectiveness

7 *Show how individual differences influence negotiations.*

Are some people better negotiators than others? Though the answer to this question might seem obvious, as it turns out the answers are more complex than you might think. Here we discuss three factors that influence how effectively individuals negotiate: personality, mood/emotions, and gender.

Personality Traits in Negotiation   Can you predict an opponent's negotiating tactics if you know something about his or her personality? It's tempting to answer "yes" to this question. For instance, you might assume that high-risk takers would be more aggressive bargainers who make fewer concessions. Surprisingly, the evidence hasn't always supported this intuition.[42]

Assessments of the personality–negotiation relationship have been that personality traits have no significant direct effect on either the bargaining process or the negotiation outcomes. However, recent research has started to question the theory that personality and the negotiation process aren't connected. In fact, it appears that several of the Big Five traits are related to negotiation outcomes. For example, negotiators who are agreeable or extraverted are not very successful when it comes to distributive bargaining. Why? Because extraverts are outgoing and friendly, they tend to share more information than they should. And agreeable people are more interested in finding ways to cooperate rather than butt heads. These traits, while slightly helpful in integrative negotiations, are liabilities when interests are opposed. So the best distributive bargainer appears to be a disagreeable introvert—that is, someone who is interested in his own outcomes versus pleasing the other party and having a pleasant social exchange. Research also suggests that intelligence predicts negotiation effectiveness, but, as with personality, the effects aren't especially strong.[43]

Though personality and intelligence do appear to have some influence on negotiation, it's not a strong effect. In a sense, that's good news because it means even if you're an agreeable extrovert, you're not severely disadvantaged when it comes time to negotiate. We all can learn to be better negotiators.

Moods/Emotions in Negotiation   Do moods and emotions influence negotiation? They do, but the way they do appears to depend on the type of negotiation. In distributive negotiations, it appears that negotiators who show anger negotiate better outcomes, because their anger induces concessions from their opponents. This appears to hold true even when the negotiators are instructed to show anger despite not being truly angry.

In integrative negotiations, in contrast, positive moods and emotions appear to lead to more integrative agreements (higher levels of joint gain). This may happen because, as we noted in Chapter 5, positive mood is related to creativity.[44]

Gender Differences in Negotiations   Do men and women negotiate differently? And does gender affect negotiation outcomes? The answer to the first question appears to be no.[45] The answer to the second is a qualified yes.[46]

A popular stereotype is that women are more cooperative and pleasant in negotiations than are men. The evidence doesn't support this belief. However, men have been found to negotiate better outcomes than women, although the

BATNA   *The best alternative to a negotiated agreement; the least the individual should accept.*

Respected for her intelligence, confident negotiating skills, and successful outcomes, Christine Lagarde was appointed by French President Nicholas Sarkozy to the powerful position of minister for the economy, finance, and employment. As the first female finance minister of a G-8 nation, Lagarde brings to her new post experience as the trade minister of France, where she used her negotiating skills in boosting French exports by 10 percent. Before that, Lagarde was a noted labor and antitrust lawyer for the global law firm Baker & McKenzie. Among her tasks, Lagarde must negotiate with France's trade unions to change the country's labor laws, including raising the 35-hour workweek, to help boost the nation's sluggish economy.

difference is relatively small. It's been postulated that this difference might be due to men and women placing divergent values on outcomes. "It is possible that a few hundred dollars more in salary or the corner office is less important to women than forming and maintaining an interpersonal relationship."[47]

The belief that women are "nicer" than men in negotiations is probably due to a confusion between gender and the lower degree of power women typically hold in most large organizations. Because women are expected to be "nice" and men "tough," research shows that, relative to men, women are penalized when they initiate negotiations.[48] What's more, when women and men actually do conform to these stereotypes—women act "nice" and men "tough"—it becomes a self-fulfilling prophecy, reinforcing the stereotypical gender differences between male and female negotiators.[49] Thus, one of the reasons why negotiations favor men is that women are "damned if they do, damned if they don't." Negotiate tough and they are penalized for violating a gender stereotype. Negotiate nice and it only reinforces the stereotype (and is taken advantage of).

Self Assessment Library

WHAT'S MY NEGOTIATING STYLE?

In the Self-Assessment Library (available on CD and online), take assessment II.C.6 (What's My Negotiating Style?).

In addition to the other party's attitudes and behaviors, the evidence also suggests that women's own attitudes and behaviors hurt them in negotiations. Managerial women demonstrate less confidence in anticipation of negotiating and are less satisfied with their performance after the process is complete, even when their performance and the outcomes they achieve are similar to those for men.[50] This latter conclusion suggests that women may unduly penalize themselves by failing to engage in negotiations when such action would be in their best interests.

International OB

Negotiating Across Cultures

Obtaining a favorable outcome in a negotiation may in part depend on the cultural characteristics of your opponent. A study of negotiators in the United States, China, and Japan found that culture plays an important role in successful negotiation. The study found that, overall, negotiators who had both a self-serving "egoistic" orientation and a high goal level fared the best overall compared with negotiators with an other-serving "prosocial" orientation and low goal level. In other words, the strategy combining a self-serving negotiation position, where one is focused only on maximizing one's

own outcomes, coupled with a strong desire to obtain the best outcomes, led to the most favorable negotiation results.

However, the degree to which this particular strategy resulted in better outcomes depended on the negotiating partner. The results showed that being self-serving and having a high negotiation goal level resulted in higher outcomes (in this case, profits) only when the negotiating opponent was other-serving. Negotiators from the United States are more likely to be self-serving and have high goal levels. In China and Japan, however, there is a greater likelihood that negotiators are other-serving and thus are more concerned with others' outcomes. Consequently, negotiators from the United States are likely to obtain better outcomes for themselves when negotiating with individuals

from China and Japan because American negotiators tend to be more concerned with their own outcomes, sometimes at the expense of the other party.

Though this study suggests that being self-serving can be beneficial in some situations, negotiators should be wary of being too self-serving. U.S. negotiators may benefit from a self-serving negotiation position and a high goal level when negotiating with individuals from China or Japan, but being too self-serving may result in damaged relationships, leading to less favorable outcomes in the long run.

Source: Based on Y. Chen, E. A. Mannix, and T. Okumura, "The Importance of Who You Meet: Effects of Self- Versus Other-Concerns Among Negotiators in the United States, the People's Republic of China, and Japan," *Journal of Experimental Social Psychology*, January, 2003, pp. 1–15.

Third-Party Negotiations

8 Assess the roles and functions of third-party negotiations.

To this point, we've discussed bargaining in terms of direct negotiations. Occasionally, however, individuals or group representatives reach a stalemate and are unable to resolve their differences through direct negotiations. In such cases, they may turn to a third party to help them find a solution. There are four basic third-party roles: mediator, arbitrator, conciliator, and consultant.[51]

A **mediator** is a neutral third party who facilitates a negotiated solution by using reasoning and persuasion, suggesting alternatives, and the like. Mediators are widely used in labor-management negotiations and in civil court disputes. The overall effectiveness of mediated negotiations is fairly impressive. The settlement rate is approximately 60 percent, with negotiator satisfaction at about 75 percent. But the situation is the key to whether or not mediation will succeed; the conflicting parties must be motivated to bargain and resolve their conflict. In addition, conflict intensity can't be too high; mediation is most effective under moderate levels of conflict. Finally, perceptions of the mediator are important; to be effective, the mediator must be perceived as neutral and noncoercive.

An **arbitrator** is a third party with the authority to dictate an agreement. Arbitration can be voluntary (requested by the parties) or compulsory (forced on the parties by law or contract). The big plus of arbitration over mediation is

mediator *A neutral third party who facilitates a negotiated solution by using reasoning, persuasion, and suggestions for alternatives.*

arbitrator *A third party to a negotiation who has the authority to dictate an agreement.*

OB In the News

"Marriage Counseling" for the Top Bosses

That the two top executives of a company conflicted with one another is no surprise. What's surprising is what they did about it.

When Watermark, a struggling maker of kayaks and car racks, brought in a new executive team, the top two executives came from very different backgrounds. CEO Jim Clark, 43, was an avid hunter and outdoorsman. COO Thomas Fumarelli, 50, was an urbane professional used to high finance in New York and Paris. Because the organization was struggling, with anxious employees who

were playing them off one another, the two executives knew their differences were likely to overwhelm them. So they headed off personality conflicts at the pass with 2 ½ years of joint executive-coaching sessions.

Although such joint coaching sessions are highly unusual, both Clark and Fumarelli (it was his idea) credit the weekly sessions for helping them work through their differences. "It was like marriage counseling," said Clark. "You get all the issues on the table."

Early on, the coaches asked Clark and Fumarelli what they needed from another. Clark said that he needed Fumarelli to be his eyes and ears for the company and to "cover his back." Fumarelli replied that he needed Clark to support him. "I can check my ego at the door," he recalls saying, "But I

need validation and support from you for the role I'm playing to support you."

The two discovered a conflict, though, when the coaches asked them separately how much time they should spend on various corporate activities. Both Clark and Fumarelli thought that development of the annual budget was his responsibility. After getting this out in the open, Clark realized the budget should primarily be Fumarelli's responsibility. "Very early on, we knew we were going to be stepping on each other's toes," Clark said.

When a private equity company bought Watermark, both left the company. But even then, the two used coaches to handle what they called their "divorce."

Source: Based on P. Dvorak, "CEO and COO Try 'Marriage Counseling,'" *Wall Street Journal*, July 31, 2006, p. B1, B3.

that it always results in a settlement. Whether or not there is a negative side depends on how "heavy-handed" the arbitrator appears. If one party is left feeling overwhelmingly defeated, that party is certain to be dissatisfied and unlikely to graciously accept the arbitrator's decision. Therefore, the conflict may resurface at a later time.

A **conciliator** is a trusted third party who provides an informal communication link between the negotiator and the opponent. This role was made famous by Robert Duval in the first *Godfather* film. As Don Corleone's adopted son and a lawyer by training, Duval acted as an intermediary between the Corleone family and the other Mafioso families. Comparing its effectiveness to mediation has proven difficult because the two overlap a great deal. In practice, conciliators typically act as more than mere communication conduits. They also engage in fact-finding, interpreting messages, and persuading disputants to develop agreements.

A **consultant** is a skilled and impartial third party who attempts to facilitate problem solving through communication and analysis, aided by a knowledge of conflict management. In contrast to the previous roles, the consultant's role is not to settle the issues, but, rather, to improve relations between the conflicting parties so that they can reach a settlement themselves. Instead of putting forward specific solutions, the consultant tries to help the parties learn to understand and work with each other. Therefore, this approach has a longer-term focus: to build new and positive perceptions and attitudes between the conflicting parties.

Global Implications

9 *Describe cultural differences in negotiations.*

Conflict and Culture

Although there is relatively little research on cross-cultural differences in conflict resolution strategies, some research suggests differences between U.S. and Asian managers. Some research indicates that individuals in

Japan and in the United States view conflict differently. Compared to Japanese negotiators, their U.S. counterparts are more likely to see offers from their counterparts as unfair and to reject them. Another study revealed that whereas U.S. managers were more likely to use competing tactics in the face of conflicts, compromising and avoiding are the most preferred methods of conflict management in China.[52]

Cultural Differences in Negotiations

Compared to the research on conflict, there is a lot more research on how negotiating styles vary across national cultures.[53] One study compared U.S. and Japanese negotiators. These researchers found that the Japanese negotiators tended to communicate indirectly and adapt their behaviors to the situation. A follow-up study showed that whereas among U.S. managers making early offers led to the anchoring effect we noted when discussing distributive negotiation, for Japanese negotiators, early offers led to more information sharing and better integrative outcomes.[54]

Another study compared North American, Arab, and Russian negotiators.[55] North Americans tried to persuade by relying on facts and appealing to logic. They countered opponents' arguments with objective facts. They made small concessions early in the negotiation to establish a relationship and usually reciprocated opponents' concessions. North Americans treated deadlines as very important. The Arabs tried to persuade by appealing to emotion. They countered opponents' arguments with subjective feelings. They made concessions throughout the bargaining process and almost always reciprocated opponents' concessions. Arabs approached deadlines very casually. The Russians based their arguments on asserted ideals. They made few, if any, concessions. Any concession offered by an opponent was viewed as a weakness and almost never reciprocated. Finally, the Russians tended to ignore deadlines.

Another study looked at verbal and nonverbal negotiation tactics exhibited by North Americans, Japanese, and Brazilians during half-hour bargaining sessions.[56] Some of the differences were particularly interesting. For instance, the Brazilians on average said "no" 83 times, compared to 5 times for the Japanese and 9 times for the North Americans. The Japanese displayed more than 5 periods of silence lasting longer than 10 seconds during the 30-minute sessions. North Americans averaged 3.5 such periods; the Brazilians had none. The Japanese and North Americans interrupted their opponent about the same number of times, but the Brazilians interrupted 2.5 to 3 times more often than the North Americans and the Japanese. Finally, the Japanese and the North Americans had no physical contact with their opponents during negotiations except for handshaking, but the Brazilians touched each other almost 5 times every half hour.

Summary and Implications for Managers

Many people automatically assume that conflict is related to lower group and organizational performance. This chapter has demonstrated that this assumption is frequently incorrect. Conflict can be either constructive or destructive to the functioning of a group or unit. As shown in Exhibit 15-8, levels of conflict

conciliator   *A trusted third party who provides an informal communication link between the negotiator and the opponent.*

consultant   *An impartial third party, skilled in conflict management, who attempts to facilitate creative problem solving through communication and analysis.*

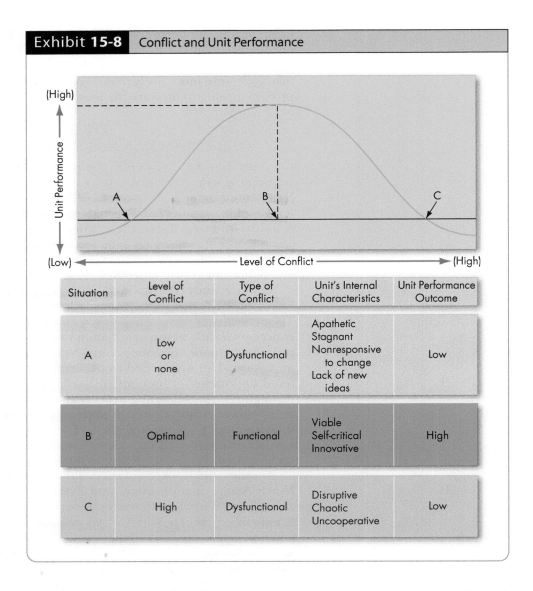

Exhibit 15-8 | Conflict and Unit Performance

Situation	Level of Conflict	Type of Conflict	Unit's Internal Characteristics	Unit Performance Outcome
A	Low or none	Dysfunctional	Apathetic Stagnant Nonresponsive to change Lack of new ideas	Low
B	Optimal	Functional	Viable Self-critical Innovative	High
C	High	Dysfunctional	Disruptive Chaotic Uncooperative	Low

can be either too high or too low. Either extreme hinders performance. An optimal level is one at which there is enough conflict to prevent stagnation, stimulate creativity, allow tensions to be released, and initiate the seeds for change, yet not so much as to be disruptive or to deter coordination of activities.

What advice can we give managers faced with excessive conflict and the need to reduce it? Don't assume that one conflict-handling intention will always be best! You should select an intention appropriate for the situation. The following are some guidelines:[57]

- Use *competition* when quick, decisive action is vital (in emergencies), on important issues, where unpopular actions need to be implemented (in cost cutting, enforcing unpopular rules, discipline), on issues vital to the organization's welfare when you know you're right, and against people who take advantage of noncompetitive behavior.
- Use *collaboration* to find an integrative solution when both sets of concerns are too important to be compromised, when your objective is to learn, to merge insights from people with different perspectives, to gain commitment by incorporating concerns into a consensus, and to work through feelings that have interfered with a relationship.

- Use *avoidance* when an issue is trivial or when more important issues are pressing, when you perceive no chance of satisfying your concerns, when potential disruption outweighs the benefits of resolution, to let people cool down and regain perspective, when gathering information supersedes immediate decision, when others can resolve the conflict more effectively, and when issues seem tangential or symptomatic of other issues.
- Use *accommodation* when you find that you're wrong and to allow a better position to be heard, to learn, and to show your reasonableness; when issues are more important to others than to yourself and to satisfy others and maintain cooperation; to build social credits for later issues; to minimize loss when you are outmatched and losing; when harmony and stability are especially important; and to allow employees to develop by learning from mistakes.
- Use *compromise* when goals are important but not worth the effort of potential disruption of more assertive approaches; when opponents with equal power are committed to mutually exclusive goals; to achieve temporary settlements to complex issues; to arrive at expedient solutions under time pressure; and as a backup when collaboration or competition is unsuccessful.

Negotiation is an ongoing activity in groups and organizations. Distributive bargaining can resolve disputes, but it often negatively affects the satisfaction of one or more negotiators because it is focused on the short term and because it is confrontational. Integrative bargaining, in contrast, tends to provide outcomes that satisfy all parties and that build lasting relationships. When engaged in negotiation, make sure you set aggressive goals and try to find creative ways to achieve the goals of both parties, especially when you value the long-term relationship with the other party. That doesn't mean "giving in" on your self-interest; rather, it means trying to find creative solutions that give both parties what they really want.

Point   Counterpoint

CONFLICT BENEFITS ORGANIZATIONS

*l*et's briefly review how stimulating conflict can provide benefits to the organization:

- **Conflict is a means to solve problems and bring about radical change.** It's an effective device by which management can drastically change the existing power structure, current inter-action patterns, and entrenched attitudes. If there is no conflict, it means the real problems aren't being addressed.
- **Conflict facilitates group cohesiveness.** Whereas conflict increases hostility between groups, external threats tend to cause a group to pull together as a unit. Conflict with another group brings together those within each group. Such intragroup cohesion is a critical resource that groups draw on in good and especially in bad times.
- **Conflict improves group and organizational effectiveness.** Groups or organizations devoid of conflict are likely to suffer from apathy, stagnation, groupthink, and other debilitating diseases. In fact, more organizations probably fail because they have *too little* conflict, not because they have too much. Stagnation is the biggest threat to organizations, but since it occurs slowly, its ill effects often go unnoticed until it's too late. Conflict can break complacency—though most of us don't like conflict, it often is the last best hope of saving an organization.

*i*n general, conflicts are dysfunctional, and it is one of manage-ment's major responsibilities to keep conflict intensity as low as humanly possible. A few points support this case:

- **The negative consequences from conflict can be devastating.** The list of negatives associated with conflict is awesome. The most obvious negatives are increased turnover, decreased employee satisfaction, inefficiencies between work units, sabo-tage, and labor grievances and strikes. One study estimated that managing conflict at work costs the average employer nearly 450 days of management time a year.[58]
- **Effective managers build teamwork.** A good manager builds a coordinated team. Conflict works against such an objective. When a team works well, the whole becomes greater than the sum of the parts. Management creates teamwork by minimizing internal conflicts and facilitating internal coordination.
- **Conflict is avoidable.** It may be true that conflict is inevitable when an organization is in a downward spiral, but the goal of good leadership and effective management is to avoid the spiral to begin with. You don't see Warren Buffett getting into a lot of conflicts with his board of directors. It's possible they're com-placent, but we think it's more likely because Berkshire Hathaway is a well-run company, doing what it should, and avoiding conflict as a result.

Questions for Review

1 What is conflict?

2 What are the differences among the traditional, human relations, and interactionist views of conflict?

3 What are the steps of the conflict process?

4 What is negotiation?

5 What are the differences between distributive and integrative bargaining?

6 What are the five steps in the negotiation process?

7 How do the individual differences of personality and gender influence negotiations?

8 What are the roles and functions of third-party negotiations?

9 How does culture influence negotiations?

Experiential Exercise

A NEGOTIATION ROLE PLAY

This role-play is designed to help you develop your negotiating skills. The class is to break into pairs. One person will play the role of Alex, the department supervisor. The other person will play C. J., Alex's boss. Both participants should read "The Situation," "The Negotiation," and then their role only.

The Situation

Alex and C. J. work for Nike in Portland, Oregon. Alex supervises a research laboratory. C.J. is the manager of research and development. Alex and C.J. are former college runners who have worked for Nike for more than 6 years. C.J. has been Alex's boss for 2 years. One of Alex's employees has greatly impressed Alex. This employee is Lisa Roland. Lisa was hired 11 months ago. She is 24 years old and holds a master's degree in mechanical engineering. Her entry-level salary was $47,500 per year. Alex told her that, in accordance with corporation policy, she would receive an initial perfor-mance evaluation at 6 months and a comprehensive review after 1 year. Based on her performance record, Lisa was told she could expect a salary adjustment at the time of the 1-year evaluation.

Alex's evaluation of Lisa after 6 months was very positive. Alex commented on the long hours Lisa was putting in, her cooperative spirit, the fact that others in the lab enjoyed working with her, and that she was making an immediate positive impact on the project she had been assigned. Now that Lisa's first anniversary is coming up, Alex has again reviewed Lisa's perfor-mance. Alex thinks Lisa may be the best new person the R&D group has ever hired. After only a year, Alex has ranked Lisa as the number-three performer in a department of 11.

Salaries in the department vary greatly. Alex, for instance, has a base salary of $76,000, plus eligibility for a bonus that might add another $7,000 to $12,000 a year. The salary range of the 11 department members is $38,400 to $66,350. The individual with the lowest salary is a recent hire with a bachelor's degree in physics. The two people whom Alex has rated above Lisa earn base salaries of $59,200 and $66,350. They're both 27 years old and have been at Nike for 3 and 4 years, respectively. The median salary in Alex's department is $54,960.

Alex's Role

You want to give Lisa a big raise. Although she's young, she has proven to be an excellent addition to the depart-ment. You don't want to lose her. More importantly, she knows in general what other people in the department are earning and she thinks she's underpaid. The com-pany typically gives 1-year raises of 5 percent, although 10 percent is not unusual, and 20 to 30 percent increases have been approved on occasion. You'd like to get Lisa as large an increase as C.J. will approve.

C.J.'s Role

All your supervisors typically try to squeeze you for as much money as they can for their people. You under-stand this because you did the same thing when you were a supervisor, but your boss wants to keep a lid on costs. He wants you to keep raises for recent hires generally in the 5 to 8 percent range. In fact, he's sent a memo to all managers and supervisors saying this. He also said that managers will be evaluated on their ability to maintain budgetary control. However, your boss is also concerned with equity and paying people what they're worth. You feel assured that he will support any salary recommenda-tion you make, as long as it can be justified. Your goal, consistent with cost reduction, is to keep salary increases as low as possible.

The Negotiation

Alex has a meeting scheduled with C.J. to discuss Lisa's performance review and salary adjustment. Take a couple minutes to think through the facts in this exercise and to prepare a strategy. Then you have up to 15 minutes to conduct your negotiation. When your negotiation is complete, the class will compare the various strategies used and pair outcomes.

Ethical Dilemma

IS IT UNETHICAL TO LIE, DECEIVE, OR COLLUDE DURING NEGOTIATIONS?

In Chapter 11, we addressed lying in the context of communication. Here we return to the topic of lying but specifically as it relates to negotiation. We think this issue is important because, for many people, there is no such thing as lying when it comes to negotiating.

It's been said that the whole notion of negotiation is built on ethical quicksand: To succeed, you must deceive. Is this true? Apparently, a lot of people think so. For instance, one study found that 28 percent of negotiators lied about at least one issue during negotiations, while another study found that 100 percent of negotiators either failed to reveal a problem or actively lied about it during negotiations if they were not directly asked about the issue. Why do you think these numbers are so high? The research on negotiation provides numerous examples of lying giving the negotiator a strategic advantage.[59]

We can probably agree that bald-faced lies during negotiation are wrong. At least most ethicists would probably agree. The universal dilemma surrounds the little lies: The omissions, evasions, and concealments that are often necessary to best an opponent.

During negotiations, when is a lie a *lie*? Is exaggerating benefits, downplaying negatives, ignoring flaws, or saying "I don't know" when in reality you do considered lying? Is declaring "this is my final offer and nonnegotiable" (even when you're posturing) a lie? Is pretending to bend over backward to make meaningful concessions lying? Rather than being considered unethical, the use of these "lies" is considered by many as an indicator that a negotiator is strong, smart, and savvy.

Or consider the issue of colluding, as when two bidders agree not to bid against one another in a (concealed) effort to keep the bids down. In some cases, such collusion is illegal, but even when it isn't illegal, is it ethical?

Questions

1. When are deception, evasiveness, or collusion out of bounds?
2. Can such tactics be legal and still be unethical?
3. Is it naive to be completely honest and bare your soul during negotiations?
4. Are the rules of negotiations unique? Is any tactic that will improve your chance of winning acceptable?

Source: Based on R. Cohen, "Bad Bidness," *New York Times Magazine*, September 2, 2006, p. 22; M. E. Schweitzer, "Deception in Negotiations," in S. J. Hoch and H. C. Kunreuther (eds.), *Wharton on Making Decisions* (New York: Wiley, 2001), pp. 187–200; and M. Diener, "Fair Enough," *Entrepreneur*, January 2002, pp. 100–102.

Case Incident 1

DAVID OUT-NEGOTIATING GOLIATH: APOTEX AND BRISTOL-MYERS SQUIBB

Peter Dolan survived many crises in his five-year tenure as CEO of drug giant Bristol-Myers Squibb. There were a corporate accounting scandal, allegations of insider trading, FBI raids of his office, and a stock price that dropped 60 percent during his tenure. But in the end, what may have done Dolan in was his negotiation performance against the head of Apotex, a Canadian drug company founded by Dr. Barry Sherman.

At its peak, Plavix—a drug to prevent heart attacks—was Bristol-Myers's best-selling drug and accounted for a staggering one-third of its profits. So when Apotex developed a generic Plavix knockoff, Dolan sought to negotiate an agreement that would pay Apotex in exchange for a delayed launch of Apotex's generic competitor. Dolan sent one of his closest lieutenants, Andrew Bodnar, to negotiate with Sherman. Bodnar and Sherman developed a good rapport, and at several points in their negotiations asked their attorneys to leave them alone. At one key point in the negotiations, Bodnar flew to Toronto alone, without Bristol-Myers's attorneys, as a "gesture of goodwill. The thinking was that the negotiations would be more effective this way."

As Dolan, Bodnar, and Bristol-Myers became increasingly concerned with reaching an agreement with Sherman and Apotex, they developed a blind spot. Privately, Sherman was betting that the Federal Trade Commission (FTC) wouldn't approve the noncompete agreement the two parties were negotiating, and his goal in the negotiation was to extract an agreement from Bristol-Myers that would position Apotex favorably should the FTC reject the deal. Indeed, he nonchalantly inserted a clause in the deal that would require Bristol-Myers to pay Apotex $60 million if the FTC rejected the deal. "I thought the FTC would turn it down, but I didn't let on that I did," Sherman said. "They seemed blind to it."

In the meantime, Apotex covertly began shipping its generic equivalent, and it quickly became the best-selling generic drug ever. Thus, Sherman also managed to launch the generic equivalent without Bristol-Myers's even considering the possibility that he would do so while still engaged in negotiations.

"It looks like a much smaller generic private company completely outmaneuvered two of the giants of the pharmaceutical industry," said Gbola Amusa, European pharmaceutical analyst for Sanford C. Bernstein & Company. "It's not clear how or why that happened. The reaction from investors and analysts has ranged from shock to outright anger." Within a few months, Dolan was out at Bristol-Myers.

Questions

1. What principles of distributive negotiation did Sherman use to gain his advantage?

2. Do you think Sherman behaved ethically? Why or why not?

3. What does this incident tell you about the role of deception in negotiation?

Source: Based on J. Carreyrou and J. S. Lublin, "How Bristol-Myers Fumbled Defense of $4 Billion Drug," *Wall Street Journal,* September 2, 2006, pp. A1, A7; and S. Saul, "Marketers of Plavix Outfoxed on a Deal," *New York Times,* August 9, 2006.

Case Incident 2

NEGOTIATION PUTS HOCKEY IN THE PENALTY BOX

Not every negotiation ends on a good note. Just ask National Hockey League (NHL) Commissioner Gary Bettman, who, on February 16, 2005, cancelled all the games remaining in the season following a 5-month lockout by the owners. Though professional sports such as hockey and baseball have had close calls with losing an entire season, Bettman's decision was a first: The whole schedule was lost. Said Bettman, "This is a sad, regrettable day."

On the other side of the dispute, Bob Goodenow, executive director of the NHL Player's Association, similarly regretted the impasse. He said, "Yes, we apologize to the fans." Though the repercussions to the league and its players are obvious, canceling the season also had ramifications on a broader level, including lost revenues for local businesses and NHL game merchandise sales.

So, why did Bettman cancel the season? The primary issue was a salary cap, but Goodenow said, "The players never asked for more money. They didn't want to be locked out. Gary owes the apology. He started the lockout.

We've done an awful lot to try to get to a fair resolution." According to reports, negotiations began when the league attempted to lower the average salary from $1.8 million per year to $1.3 million per year—a 28 percent decrease. The league's reason? Although the NHL's total revenue had reached $2.1 billion a year, players were paid 75 percent of this revenue. According to the league, this high percentage kept the league from being profitable and directly contributed to the league's loss of $479 million over the past two seasons. The player's union then countered with an offer to reduce salaries by 24 percent rather than the 28 percent the league wanted. Bettman then tried an alternative solution: to persuade the union to accept a salary percentage of no more than 55 percent of league revenues. Instead of reducing pay to an average level, this proposal would link players' pay to the leagues' revenues, which could fluctuate up or down. The league's players opposed both ideas until Bettman and the NHL team owners offered a salary cap that did not link payroll and revenue. At this point, negotiations looked promising.

However, neither party could agree on an amount. The owners offered a cap of $40 million per team and then increased it to $42.5 million. But the players wanted a cap of $52 million per team and then lowered their proposal to $49 million. Although the dollar difference in this round of negotiations amounted to only 6.5 million, neither side could agree, negotiations stopped, and the season was cancelled.

Said Goodenow, "Gary gave us a final offer, a take-it-or-leave-it offer. We made a counterproposal and events ground to a halt." A reporter asked both sides whether they would have accepted a compromise of around $45 million per team. Such a compromise may have saved the season. Bettman stated, "If they wanted $45 million, I'm not saying we would have gone there, but they sure should have told us." Goodenow, however, wouldn't speculate: "The what-ifs aren't for real."

So how did the two sides eventually get the players back on the ice? They agreed to a 6-year deal that set a salary cap of $39 million per team for the 2005–2006 season. (Remember that the players wanted a cap of $49 million.) Many players were unhappy with the terms of the deal but felt that fighting the salary cap was a waste of time that did nothing but alienate the fans. Many players spoke out against Goodenow, arguing that he put the players in a no-win situation. Less than a week after the lockout ended, Goodenow resigned as executive director of the NHL Player's Association. He denied

that his resignation was in response to the players' complaints. The lack of an agreement in the NHL negotiations was a loss to everyone—the league and businesses connected to the league, the owners, the players, and, of course, the fans.

Questions

1. How would you characterize the NHL negotiation—as distributive or integrative? From what perspective (distributive or integrative) did the parties approach the negotiation? How might this approach have affected the outcome?

2. What factors do you believe led to the lack of a settlement in the NHL negotiations? How might you have handled the negotiation if you were a representative of the league? of the player's union?

3. Negotiating parties are often reluctant to reveal their BATNA (best alternative to a negotiated agreement) to the opposing party. Do you believe that parties in the NHL negotiation were aware of each other's BATNA? How might this knowledge have affected the negotiation?

4. It appears that a point of compromise (a $45 million-per-team salary cap, for example) may have existed. What steps could both parties have taken to reach this point of compromise?

Source: Based on J. Lapointe, and R. Westhead, "League Cancels Hockey Season in Labor Battle," *New York Times,* February 17, 2005, p. A1.

Endnotes

1. S. Gray, "Ketchup Fight: Peltz, Heinz CEO Go at It," *Wall Street Journal,* August 4, 2006, pp. C1, C5.
2. See, for instance, C. F. Fink, "Some Conceptual Difficulties in the Theory of Social Conflict," *Journal of Conflict Resolution,* December 1968, pp. 412–460; and E. Infante, "On the Definition of Interpersonal Conflict: Cluster Analysis Applied to the Study of Semantics," *Revista de Psicologia Social* 13, no. 3 (1998), pp. 485–493.
3. L. L. Putnam and M. S. Poole, "Conflict and Negotiation," in F. M. Jablin, L. L. Putnam, K. H. Roberts, and L. W. Porter (eds.), *Handbook of Organizational Communication: An Interdisciplinary Perspective* (Newbury Park, CA: Sage, 1987), pp. 549–599.
4. K. W. Thomas, "Conflict and Negotiation Processes in Organizations," in M. D. Dunnette and L. M. Hough (eds.),

Handbook of Industrial and Organizational Psychology, 2nd ed., vol. 3 (Palo Alto, CA: Consulting Psychologists Press, 1992), pp. 651–717.
5. For a comprehensive review of the interactionist approach, see C. De Dreu and E. Van de Vliert (eds.), *Using Conflict in Organizations* (London: Sage, 1997).
6. See K. A. Jehn, "A Multimethod Examination of the Benefits and Detriments of Intragroup Conflict," *Administrative Science Quarterly,* June 1995, pp. 256–282; K. A. Jehn, "A Qualitative Analysis of Conflict Types and Dimensions in Organizational Groups," *Administrative Science Quarterly,* September 1997, pp. 530–557; K. A. Jehn and E. A. Mannix, "The Dynamic Nature of Conflict: A Longitudinal Study of Intragroup Conflict and Group Performance," *Academy of Management Journal,* April 2001, pp. 238–251; and C. K. W. De Dreu and L. R. Weingart, "Task Versus Relationship Conflict, Team Performance, and Team Member Satisfaction: A Meta-Analysis," *Journal of Applied Psychology,* August 2003, pp. 741–749.

7. J. Yang and K. W. Mossholder, "Decoupling Task and Relationship Conflict: The Role of Intragroup Emotional Processing," *Journal of Organizational Behavior* 25, no. 5 (August 2004), pp. 589–605.

8. "Survey Shows Managers Have Their Hands Full Resolving Staff Personality Conflicts," *IPMA-HR Bulletin*, November 3, 2006.

9. R. S. Peterson and K. J. Behfar, "The Dynamic Relationship Between Performance Feedback, Trust, and Conflict in Groups: A Longitudinal Study," *Organizational Behavior & Human Decision Processes*, September–November 2003, pp. 102–112.

10. Jehn, "A Multimethod Examination of the Benefits and Detriments of Intragroup Conflict."

11. R. Friedman, C. Anderson, J. Brett, M. Olekalns, N. Goates, and C. C. Lisco, "The Positive and Negative Effects of Anger on Dispute Resolution: Evidence from Electronically Mediated Disputes," *Journal of Applied Psychology*, April 2004, pp. 369–376.

12. L. R. Pondy, "Organizational Conflict: Concepts and Models," *Administrative Science Quarterly*, September 1967, p. 302.

13. See, for instance, R. L. Pinkley, "Dimensions of Conflict Frame: Disputant Interpretations of Conflict," *Journal of Applied Psychology*, April 1990, pp. 117–126; and R. L. Pinkley and G. B. Northcraft, "Conflict Frames of Reference: Implications for Dispute Processes and Outcomes," *Academy of Management Journal*, February 1994, pp. 193–205.

14. A. M. Isen, A. A. Labroo, and P. Durlach, "An Influence of Product and Brand Name on Positive Affect: Implicit and Explicit Measures," *Motivation & Emotion*, March 2004, pp. 43–63.

15. Ibid.

16. P. J. D. Carnevale and A. M. Isen, "The Influence of Positive Affect and Visual Access on the Discovery of Integrative Solutions in Bilateral Negotiations," *Organizational Behavior and Human Decision Processes*, February 1986, pp. 1–13.

17. Thomas, "Conflict and Negotiation Processes in Organizations."

18. Ibid.

19. See R. A. Baron, "Personality and Organizational Conflict: Effects of the Type A Behavior Pattern and Self-monitoring," *Organizational Behavior and Human Decision Processes*, October 1989, pp. 281–296; R. J. Volkema and T. J. Bergmann, "Conflict Styles as Indicators of Behavioral Patterns in Interpersonal Conflicts," *Journal of Social Psychology*, February 1995, pp. 5–15; and J. A. Rhoades, J. Arnold, and C. Jay, "The Role of Affective Traits and Affective States in Disputants' Motivation and Behavior During Episodes of Organizational Conflict," *Journal of Organizational Behavior*, May 2001, pp. 329–345.

20. Thomas, "Conflict and Negotiation Processes in Organizations."

21. See, for instance, K. A. Jehn, "Enhancing Effectiveness: An Investigation of Advantages and Disadvantages of Value-Based Intragroup Conflict," *International Journal of Conflict Management*, July 1994, pp. 223–238; R. L. Priem, D. A. Harrison, and N. K. Muir, "Structured Conflict and Consensus Outcomes in Group Decision Making," *Journal of Management* 21, no. 4 (1995), pp. 691–710; and K. A. Jehn and E. A. Mannix, "The Dynamic Nature of Conflict: A Longitudinal Study of Intragroup Conflict and Group Performance," *Academy of Management Journal*, April 2001, pp. 238–251.

22. See, for instance, C. J. Loomis, "Dinosaurs?" *Fortune*, May 3, 1993, pp. 36–42.

23. J. Hall and M. S. Williams, "A Comparison of Decision-Making Performances in Established and Ad-hoc Groups," *Journal of Personality and Social Psychology*, February 1966, p. 217.

24. R. L. Hoffman, "Homogeneity of Member Personality and Its Effect on Group Problem-Solving," *Journal of Abnormal and Social Psychology*, January 1959, pp. 27–32; R. L. Hoffman and N. R. F. Maier, "Quality and Acceptance of Problem Solutions by Members of Homogeneous and Heterogeneous Groups," *Journal of Abnormal and Social Psychology*, March 1961, pp. 401–407; and P. Pitcher and A. D. Smith, "Top Management Team Heterogeneity: Personality, Power, and Proxies," *Organization Science*, January–February 2001, pp. 1–18.

25. See T. H. Cox, S. A. Lobel, and P. L. McLeod, "Effects of Ethnic Group Cultural Differences on Cooperative Behavior on a Group Task," *Academy of Management Journal*, December 1991, pp. 827–847; L. H. Pelled, K. M. Eisenhardt, and K. R. Xin, "Exploring the Black Box: An Analysis of Work Group Diversity, Conflict, and Performance," *Administrative Science Quarterly*, March 1999, pp. 1–28; and D. van Knippenberg, C. K. W. De Dreu, and A. C. Homan, "Work Group Diversity and Group Performance: An Integrative Model and Research Agenda," *Journal of Applied Psychology*, December 2004, pp. 1008–1022.

26. For example, see J. A. Wall, Jr., and R. R. Callister, "Conflict and Its Management," pp. 523–526 for evidence supporting the argument that conflict is almost uniformly dysfunctional; see also P. J. Hinds, and D. E. Bailey, "Out of Sight, Out of Sync: Understanding Conflict in Distributed Teams," *Organization Science*, November–December 2003, pp. 615–632.

27. M. Geyelin and E. Felsenthal, "Irreconcilable Differences Force Shea & Gould Closure," *Wall Street Journal*, January 31, 1994, p. B1.

28. This section is based on F. Sommerfield, "Paying the Troops to Buck the System," *Business Month*, May 1990, pp. 77–79; W. Kiechel III, "How to Escape the Echo Chamber," *Fortune*, June 18, 1990, pp. 129–130; E. Van de Vliert and C. De Dreu, "Optimizing Performance by Stimulating Conflict," *International Journal of Conflict Management*, July 1994, pp. 211–222; E. Van de Vliert, "Enhancing Performance by Conflict-Stimulating Intervention," in C. De Dreu and E. Van de Vliert (eds.), *Using Conflict in Organizations*, pp. 208–222; K. M. Eisenhardt, J. L. Kahwajy, and L. J. Bourgeois III, "How Management Teams Can Have a Good Fight," *Harvard Business Review*, July–August 1997, pp. 77–85; S. Wetlaufer, "Common Sense and Conflict," *Harvard Business Review*, January–February 2000, pp. 114–124; and G. A. Okhuysen and K. M. Eisenhardt,

"Excel Through Group Process," in E. A. Locke (ed.), *Handbook of Principles of Organizational Behavior* (Malden, MA: Blackwell, 2004), pp. 216–218.

29. J. A. Wall, Jr., *Negotiation: Theory and Practice* (Glenview, IL: Scott, Foresman, 1985).

30. R. E. Walton and R. B. McKersie, *A Behavioral Theory of Labor Negotiations: An Analysis of a Social Interaction System* (New York: McGraw-Hill, 1965).

31. J. C. Magee, A. D. Galinsky, and D. H. Gruenfeld, "Power, Propensity to Negotiate, and Moving First in Competitive Interactions," *Personality and Social Psychology Bulletin*, February 2007, pp. 200–212.

32. H. R. Bowles, L. Babcock, and L. Lei, "Social Incentives for Gender Differences in the Propensity to Initiative Negotiations: Sometimes It Does Hurt to Ask," *Organizational Behavior and Human Decision Processes* 103 (2007), pp. 84–103.

33. D. A. Moore, "Myopic Prediction, Self-Destructive Secrecy, and the Unexpected Benefits of Revealing Final Deadlines in Negotiation," *Organizational Behavior & Human Decision Processes*, July 2004, pp. 125–139.

34. G. Ku, A. D. Galinsky, and J. K. Murnighan, "Starting Low but Ending High: A Reversal of the Anchoring Effect in Auctions," *Journal of Personality and Social Psychology* 90 (June 2006), pp. 975–986.

35. J. R. Curhan, H. A. Elfenbein, and H. Xu, "What Do People Value When They Negotiate? Mapping the Domain of Subjective Value in Negotiation," *Journal of Personality and Social Psychology* 91, no. 3 (year), pp. 493–512.

36. Thomas, "Conflict and Negotiation Processes in Organizations."

37. P. M. Morgan and R. S. Tindale, "Group vs. Individual Performance in Mixed-Motive Situations: Exploring an Inconsistency," *Organizational Behavior & Human Decision Processes*, January 2002, pp. 44–65.

38. C. E. Naquin, "The Agony of Opportunity in Negotiation: Number of Negotiable Issues, Counterfactual Thinking, and Feelings of Satisfaction," *Organizational Behavior & Human Decision Processes*, May 2003, pp. 97–107.

39. C. K. W. De Dreu, L. R. Weingart, and S. Kwon, "Influence of Social Motives on Integrative Negotiation: A Meta-analytic Review and Test of Two Theories," *Journal of Personality & Social Psychology*, May 2000, pp. 889–905.

40. This model is based on R. J. Lewicki, "Bargaining and Negotiation," *Exchange: The Organizational Behavior Teaching Journal* 6, no. 2 (1981), pp. 39–40.

41. M. H. Bazerman and M. A. Neale, *Negotiating Rationally* (New York: The Free Press, 1992), pp. 67–68.

42. J. A. Wall, Jr., and M. W. Blum, "Negotiations," *Journal of Management*, June 1991, pp. 278–282.

43. B. Barry and R. A. Friedman, "Bargainer Characteristics in Distributive and Integrative Negotiation," *Journal of Personality & Social Psychology*, February 1998, pp. 345–359.

44. S. Kopelman, A. S. Rosette, and L. Thompson, "The Three Faces of Eve: Strategic Displays of Positive, Negative, and Neutral Emotions in Negotiations," *Organizational Behavior and Human Decision Processes* 99 (2006), pp. 81–101; and J. M. Brett, M. Olekalns, R. Friedman, N. Goates, C. Anderson, C. C. Lisco, "Sticks and Stones: Language, Face, and Online Dispute Resolution," *Academy of Management Journal* 50, no. 1 (2007), pp. 85–99.

45. C. Watson and L. R. Hoffman, "Managers as Negotiators: A Test of Power Versus Gender as Predictors of Feelings, Behavior, and Outcomes," *Leadership Quarterly*, Spring 1996, pp. 63–85.

46. A. E. Walters, A. F. Stuhlmacher, and L. L. Meyer, "Gender and Negotiator Competitiveness: A Meta-analysis," *Organizational Behavior and Human Decision Processes*, October 1998, pp. 1–29; and A. F. Stuhlmacher and A. E. Walters, "Gender Differences in Negotiation Outcome: A Meta-analysis," *Personnel Psychology*, Autumn 1999, pp. 653–677.

47. Stuhlmacher and Walters, "Gender Differences in Negotiation Outcome," p. 655.

48. Bowles, Babcock, and Lei, "Social Incentives for Gender Differences in the Propensity to Initiative Negotiations."

49. L. J. Kray, A. D. Galinsky, and L. Thompson, "Reversing the Gender Gap in Negotiations: An Exploration of Stereotype Regeneration," *Organizational Behavior & Human Decision Processes*, March 2002, pp. 386–409.

50. C. K. Stevens, A. G. Bavetta, and M. E. Gist, "Gender Differences in the Acquisition of Salary Negotiation Skills: The Role of Goals, Self-Efficacy, and Perceived Control," *Journal of Applied Psychology* 78, no. 5 (October 1993), pp. 723–735.

51. Wall and Blum, "Negotiations," pp. 283–287.

52. M. J. Gelfand, M. Higgins, L. H. Nishii, J. L. Raver, A. Dominguez, F. Murakami, S. Yamaguchi, and M. Toyama, "Culture and Egocentric Perceptions of Fairness in Conflict and Negotiation," *Journal of Applied Psychology*, October 2002, pp. 833–845; Z. Ma, "Chinese Conflict Management Styles and Negotiation Behaviours: An Empirical Test," *International Journal of Cross Cultural Management*, April 2007, pp. 101–119.

53. Gelfand et al., "Culture and Egocentric Perceptions of Fairness in Conflict and Negotiation," pp. 833–845; and X. Lin and S. J. Miller, "Negotiation Approaches: Direct and Indirect Effect of National Culture," *International Marketing Review* 20, no. 3 (2003), pp. 286–303.

54. W. L. Adair, T. Okumura, and J. M. Brett, "Negotiation Behavior When Cultures Collide: The United States and Japan," *Journal of Applied Psychology*, June 2001, pp. 371–385; and W. L. Adair, L. Weingart, and J. Brett, "The Timing and Function of Offers in U.S. and Japanese Negotiations," *Journal of Applied Psychology* 92, no. 4 (2007), pp. 1056–1068.

55. E. S. Glenn, D. Witmeyer, and K. A. Stevenson, "Cultural Styles of Persuasion," *Journal of Intercultural Relations*, Fall 1977, pp. 52–66.

56. J. Graham, "The Influence of Culture on Business Negotiations," *Journal of International Business Studies*, Spring 1985, pp. 81–96.

57. K. W. Thomas, "Toward Multidimensional Values in Teaching: The Example of Conflict Behaviors," *Academy of Management Review,* July 1977, p. 487.

58. Q. Reade, "Workplace Conflict Is Time-consuming Problem for Business," *PersonnelToday.com,* September 30, 2004, www.personneltoday.co.uk.

59. K. O'Connor and P. Carnevale, "A Nasty but Effective Negotiation Strategy: Misrepresentation of a Common-Value Issue," *Personality and Social Psychology Bulletin,* May 1997, pp. 504–515.

Foundations of Organization Structure

Every revolution evaporates and leaves behind only the slime of a new bureaucracy.

—Franz Kafka

16

LEARNING OBJECTIVES

After studying this chapter, you should be able to:

1 Identify the six elements of an organization's structure.

2 Identify the characteristics of a bureaucracy.

3 Describe a matrix organization.

4 Identify the characteristics of a virtual organization.

5 Show why managers want to create boundaryless organizations.

6 Demonstrate how organizational structures differ, and contrast mechanistic and organic structural models.

7 Analyze the behavioral implications of different organizational designs.

8 Show how globalization affects organizational structure.

*f*ord is in trouble, and everyone knows it. It lost $12.7 billion in 2006. Its stock price plummeted from $27.63 in September 2005 to $6.97 in December 2007. There have been whispers of bankruptcy.

When Bill Ford (great-grandson of founder Henry Ford) became CEO in 2001, he started closing Ford plants at a rate of about one per year. That wasn't enough. So in 2006, Ford announced plans to close 14 more plants, at a rate of more than two per year,

Fixing Ford

through 2012. When even that proved inadequate, Ford hired former Boeing executive Alan Mulally to become CEO while Ford remained as executive chairman.

Ford has come to realize, too slowly for some critics, that the new global business environment won't support Ford's current product line or organizational structure. Ford's market share has fallen steadily since 2000, when it commanded 25 percent of the market. By 2012, it may be half that. But Mulally and Ford recognize that the only way to survive is by shrinking, and Ford's painful efforts to shrink will affect every aspect of its business, including, obviously, its workforce. "Ford's always been good to me," says Dick Holland, a long-time Ford factory worker. "But things have changed."

In addition to closing plants and cutting costs, Mulally has targeted Ford's organizational structure. Mulally argues that the structure has been archaic for a long time. "We have been going out of business for 40 years," he says to every employee group he addresses. Among the structural changes Mulally wishes to make are to centralize its operations. In the past, Ford has had regional fiefdoms, where every global market has its own strategy and products. Mulally wants to break down these structural divisions and create a single worldwide organization.

While Ford was geographically decentralized, it also was highly bureaucratic within its divisions. An elaborate system of pay grades clearly established the pecking order within divisions. Managers were not encouraged to socialize with people outside their pay grade. "The bureaucracy at Ford grew, and managers took refuge in the structure when things got tough, rather than innovate or try ideas that seemed risky," said a retired Ford executive.

This decentralization also affected communication among divisions. In the past, Ford held monthly division chief meetings, during which there was little sharing of information. Mulally has changed that to weekly meetings, and he's tried to increase information sharing.

It's not clear that Mulally can transform this structure—what *BusinessWeek* called a "balkanized mess." It does seem clear, though, that without major structural changes, Ford is unlikely to survive. "There's no global company I know of that can succeed with the level of complexity we have at Ford," he says.[1] ■

Structural decisions are arguably the most fundamental ones a leader, such as Ford's Alan Mulally, has to make. Before we delve into the elements of an organization's structure and how they can affect behavior, consider how you might react to one type of organizational structure—the bureaucratic structure—by taking the following self-assessment.

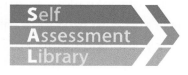

DO I LIKE BUREAUCRACY?

In the Self-Assessment Library (available on CD and online), take assessment IV.F.2 (Do I Like Bureaucracy?) and answer the following questions.

1. *Judging from the results, how willing are you to work in a bureaucratic organization?*
2. *Do you think scores on this measure matter? Why or why not?*
3. *Do you think people who score very low (or even very high) on this measure should try to adjust their preferences based on where they are working?*

What Is Organizational Structure?

An **organizational structure** defines how job tasks are formally divided, grouped, and coordinated. There are six key elements that managers need to address when they design their organization's structure: work specialization, departmentalization, chain of command, span of control, centralization and decentralization, and formalization.[2] Exhibit 16-1 presents each of these elements as answers to an important structural question. The following sections describe these six elements of structure.

1 **Identify the six elements of an organization's structure.**

Work Specialization

Early in the twentieth century, Henry Ford became rich and famous by building automobiles on an assembly line. Every Ford worker was assigned a specific, repetitive task. For instance, one person would just put on the right-front wheel, and someone else would install the right-front door. By breaking jobs up into small standardized tasks, which could be performed over and over again, Ford was able to produce cars at the rate of one every 10 seconds, while using employees who had relatively limited skills.

Ford demonstrated that work can be performed more efficiently if employees are allowed to specialize. Today we use the term **work specialization**, or *division of labor*, to describe the degree to which activities in the organization are subdivided into separate jobs. The essence of work specialization is that rather than an entire job being done by one individual, it is broken down into a number of steps, with each step being completed by a separate individual. In essence, individuals specialize in doing part of an activity rather than the entire activity.

By the late 1940s, most manufacturing jobs in industrialized countries were being done with high work specialization. Because not all employees in an organization have the same skills, management saw specialization as a means to

Exhibit 16-1	Key Design Questions and Answers for Designing the Proper Organizational Structure
The Key Question	**The Answer Is Provided By**
1. To what degree are activities subdivided into separate jobs?	Work specialization
2. On what basis will jobs be grouped together?	Departmentalization
3. To whom do individuals and groups report?	Chain of command
4. How many individuals can a manager efficiently and effectively direct?	Span of control
5. Where does decision-making authority lie?	Centralization and decentralization
6. To what degree will there be rules and regulations to direct employees and managers?	Formalization

organizational structure   *The way in which job tasks are formally divided, grouped, and coordinated.*

work specialization   *The degree to which tasks in an organization are subdivided into separate jobs.*

Work is specialized at the Russian factories that manufacture the wooden nesting dolls called matryoshkas. At this factory outside Moscow, individuals specialize in doing part of the doll production, from the craftsmen who carve the dolls to the painters who decorate them. Work specialization brings efficiency to doll production, as some 50 employees can make 100 matryoshkas every 2 days.

make the most efficient use of its employees' skills. Managers also saw other efficiencies that could be achieved through work specialization. Employee skills at performing a task successfully increase through repetition. Less time is spent in changing tasks, in putting away one's tools and equipment from a prior step in the work process, and in getting ready for another. Equally important, training for specialization is more efficient from the organization's perspective. It's easier and less costly to find and train workers to do specific and repetitive tasks. This is especially true of highly sophisticated and complex operations. For example, could Cessna produce one Citation jet a year if one person had to build the entire plane alone? Not likely! Finally, work specialization increases efficiency and productivity by encouraging the creation of special inventions and machinery.

For much of the first half of the twentieth century, managers viewed work specialization as an unending source of increased productivity. And they were probably right. Because specialization was not widely practiced, its introduction almost always generated higher productivity. But by the 1960s, there came increasing evidence that a good thing can be carried too far. The point had been reached in some jobs at which the human diseconomies from specialization—which surfaced as boredom, fatigue, stress, low productivity, poor quality, increased absenteeism, and high turnover—more than offset the economic advantages (see Exhibit 16-2). In such cases, productivity could be increased by enlarging, rather than narrowing, the scope of job activities. In addition, a number of companies found that by giving employees a variety of activities to do, allowing them to do a whole and complete job, and putting them into teams with interchangeable skills, they often achieved significantly higher output, with increased employee satisfaction.

Most managers today see work specialization as neither obsolete nor an unending source of increased productivity. Rather, managers recognize the economies it provides in certain types of jobs and the problems it creates when it's carried too far. You'll find, for example, high work specialization being used by McDonald's to efficiently make and sell hamburgers and fries and by medical specialists in most health maintenance organizations. On the other hand,

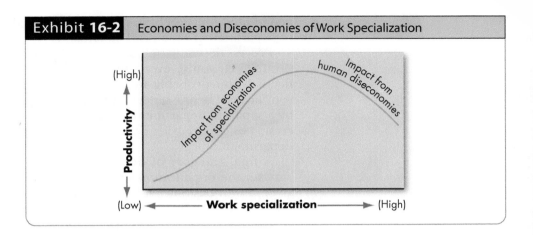

Exhibit 16-2 Economies and Diseconomies of Work Specialization

companies such as Saturn Corporation have had success by broadening the scope of jobs and reducing specialization.

Departmentalization

Once you've divided jobs up through work specialization, you need to group these jobs together so that common tasks can be coordinated. The basis by which jobs are grouped together is called **departmentalization**.

One of the most popular ways to group activities is by *functions* performed. A manufacturing manager might organize a plant by separating engineering, accounting, manufacturing, personnel, and supply specialists into common departments. Of course, departmentalization by function can be used in all types of organizations. Only the functions change to reflect the organization's objectives and activities. A hospital might have departments devoted to research, patient care, accounting, and so forth. A professional football franchise might have departments entitled Player Personnel, Ticket Sales, and Travel and Accommodations. The major advantage to this type of grouping is obtaining efficiencies from putting like specialists together. Functional departmentalization seeks to achieve economies of scale by placing people with common skills and orientations into common units.

Jobs can also be departmentalized by the type of *product* the organization produces. Procter & Gamble, for instance, is organized along these lines. Each major product—such as Tide, Pampers, Charmin, and Pringles—is placed under the authority of an executive who has complete global responsibility for that product. The major advantage to this type of grouping is increased accountability for product performance since all activities related to a specific product are under the direction of a single manager. If an organization's activities were service related rather than product related, each service would be autonomously grouped.

Another way to departmentalize is on the basis of *geography*, or territory. The sales function, for instance, may have Western, Southern, Midwestern, and Eastern regions. Each of these regions is, in effect, a department organized around geography. If an organization's customers are scattered over a large

departmentalization *The basis by which jobs in an organization are grouped together.*

geographic area and have similar needs based on their location, then this form of departmentalization can be valuable.

Process departmentalization can be used for processing customers as well as products. If you've ever been to a state motor vehicle office to get a driver's license, you probably went through several departments before receiving your license. In one state, applicants must go through three steps, each handled by a separate department: (1) validation by motor vehicles division; (2) processing by the licensing department; and (3) payment collection by the treasury department.

A final category of departmentalization is to use the particular type of *customer* the organization seeks to reach. Microsoft, for instance, is organized around four customer markets: consumers, large corporations, software developers, and small businesses. The assumption underlying customer departmentalization is that customers in each department have a common set of problems and needs that can best be met by having specialists for each.

Large organizations may use all of the forms of departmentalization that we've described. A major Japanese electronics firm, for instance, organizes each of its divisions along functional lines and its manufacturing units around processes; it departmentalizes sales around seven geographic regions and divides each sales region into four customer groupings. Across organizations of all sizes, one strong trend has developed over the past decade. Rigid, functional departmentalization is being increasingly complemented by teams that cross over traditional departmental lines. As we described in Chapter 10, as tasks have become more complex and more diverse skills are needed to accomplish those tasks, management has turned to cross-functional teams.

Chain of Command

Thirty-five years ago, the chain-of-command concept was a basic cornerstone in the design of organizations. As you'll see, it has far less importance today.[3] But contemporary managers should still consider its implications when they decide how best to structure their organizations. The **chain of command** is an unbroken line of authority that extends from the top of the organization to the lowest echelon and clarifies who reports to whom. It answers questions for employees such as "To whom do I go if I have a problem?" and "To whom am I responsible?"

You can't discuss the chain of command without discussing two complementary concepts: *authority* and *unity of command*. **Authority** refers to the rights inherent in a managerial position to give orders and expect the orders to be obeyed. To facilitate coordination, each managerial position is given a place in the chain of command, and each manager is given a degree of authority in order to meet his or her responsibilities. The **unity-of-command** principle helps preserve the concept of an unbroken line of authority. It states that a person should have one and only one superior to whom that person is directly responsible. If the unity of command is broken, an employee might have to cope with conflicting demands or priorities from several superiors.

Times change, and so do the basic tenets of organizational design. The concepts of chain of command, authority, and unity of command have substantially less relevance today because of advancements in information technology and the trend toward empowering employees. For instance, a low-level employee today can access information in seconds that 35 years ago was available only to top managers. Similarly, networked computers increasingly allow employees anywhere in an organization to communicate with anyone else without going through formal channels. Moreover, the concepts of authority and maintaining the chain of command are increasingly less relevant as operating employees are being empowered to make decisions that previously were reserved for management. Add to this the popularity of self-managed and cross-functional teams and the creation of new structural designs that include multiple bosses, and the unity-of-command concept takes on less relevance. There are, of course, still many organizations that find they can be most productive by enforcing the chain of command. There just seem to be fewer of them today.

Span of Control

How many employees can a manager efficiently and effectively direct? This question of **span of control** is important because, to a large degree, it determines the number of levels and managers an organization has. All things being equal, the wider or larger the span, the more efficient the organization. An example can illustrate the validity of this statement.

Assume that we have two organizations, each of which has approximately 4,100 operative-level employees. As Exhibit 16-3 illustrates, if one has a uniform span of four and the other a span of eight, the wider span would have two fewer levels and approximately 800 fewer managers. If the average manager made $50,000 a year, the wider span would save $40 million a year in management salaries! Obviously, wider spans are more efficient in terms of cost. However, at some point, wider spans reduce effectiveness. That is, when the span becomes too large, employee performance suffers because supervisors no longer have the time to provide the necessary leadership and support.

Narrow, or small, spans have their advocates. By keeping the span of control to five or six employees, a manager can maintain close control.[4] But narrow spans have three major drawbacks. First, as already described, they're expensive

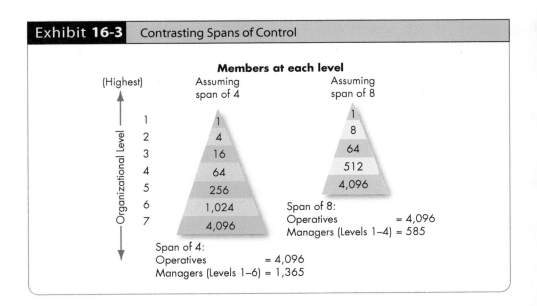

Exhibit 16-3 Contrasting Spans of Control

Members at each level

Organizational level	(Highest)	Assuming span of 4	Assuming span of 8
1		1	1
2		4	8
3		16	64
4		64	512
5		256	4,096
6		1,024	
7		4,096	

Span of 8:
Operatives = 4,096
Managers (Levels 1–4) = 585

Span of 4:
Operatives = 4,096
Managers (Levels 1–6) = 1,365

---

chain of command *The unbroken line of authority that extends from the top of the organization to the lowest echelon and clarifies who reports to whom.*

authority *The rights inherent in a managerial position to give orders and to expect the orders to be obeyed.*

unity of command *The idea that a subordinate should have only one superior to whom he or she is directly responsible.*

span of control *The number of subordinates a manager can efficiently and effectively direct.*

because they add levels of management. Second, they make vertical communication in the organization more complex. The added levels of hierarchy slow down decision making and tend to isolate upper management. Third, narrow spans of control encourage overly tight supervision and discourage employee autonomy.

The trend in recent years has been toward wider spans of control.[5] They're consistent with recent efforts by companies to reduce costs, cut overhead, speed up decision making, increase flexibility, get closer to customers, and empower employees. However, to ensure that performance doesn't suffer because of these wider spans, organizations have been investing heavily in employee training. Managers recognize that they can handle a wider span when employees know their jobs inside and out or can turn to their coworkers when they have questions.

Centralization and Decentralization

In some organizations, top managers make all the decisions. Lower-level managers merely carry out top management's directives. At the other extreme, there are organizations in which decision making is pushed down to the managers who are closest to the action. The former organizations are highly centralized; the latter are decentralized.

The term **centralization** refers to the degree to which decision making is concentrated at a single point in the organization. The concept includes only formal authority—that is, the rights inherent in one's position. Typically, it's said that if top management makes the organization's key decisions with little or no input from lower-level personnel, then the organization is centralized. In contrast, the more that lower-level personnel provide input or are actually given the discretion to make decisions, the more decentralization there is. An organization characterized by centralization is an inherently different structural animal from one that is decentralized. In a decentralized organization, action can be taken more quickly to solve problems, more people provide input into decisions, and employees are less likely to feel alienated from those who make the decisions that affect their work lives.

Consistent with recent management efforts to make organizations more flexible and responsive, there has been a marked trend toward decentralizing decision making. In large companies, lower-level managers are closer to "the action" and typically have more detailed knowledge about problems than do top managers. For instance, big retailers such as Sears and JCPenney have given their store managers considerably more discretion in choosing what merchandise to stock. This allows those stores to compete more effectively against local merchants.

HOW WILLING AM I TO DELEGATE?

In the Self-Assessment Library (available on CD and online), take assessment III.A.2 (How Willing Am I to Delegate?).

Formalization

Formalization refers to the degree to which jobs within the organization are standardized. If a job is highly formalized, then the job incumbent has a minimum amount of discretion over what is to be done, when it is to be done, and how it is to be done. Employees can be expected always to handle the same input in exactly the same way, resulting in a consistent and uniform output. There are explicit job descriptions, lots of organizational rules, and clearly defined procedures covering work processes in organizations in which there is high formalization. Where formalization is low, job behaviors are relatively nonprogrammed, and employees have a great deal of freedom to exercise discretion in their work. Because an individual's discretion on the job is inversely related to the amount of behavior in that job that is preprogrammed by the organization, the greater the standardization, the less input the employee has into how the work is to be done. Standardization not only eliminates the possibility of employees engaging in alternative behaviors, but it even removes the need for employees to consider alternatives.

The degree of formalization can vary widely between organizations and within organizations. Certain jobs, for instance, are well known to have little formalization. College book travelers—the representatives of publishers who call on professors to inform them of their company's new publications—have a great deal of freedom in their jobs. They have no standard sales "spiel," and the extent of rules and procedures governing their behavior may be little more than the requirement that they submit a weekly sales report and some suggestions on what to emphasize for the various new titles. At the other extreme, there are clerical and editorial positions in the same publishing houses for which employees are required to be at their desks by 8:00 A.M. or be docked a half-hour's pay and, once at that desk, to follow a set of precise procedures dictated by management.

Siemens Simple Structure—Not

There is perhaps no tougher task for an executive than to restructure a European organization. Ask former Siemens CEO Klaus Kleinfeld.

Siemens, with $114 billion in revenues in 2006 and branches in 190 countries, is one of the largest electronics companies in the world. Although the company has long been respected for its engineering prowess, it's also derided for its sluggishness and mechanistic structure. So when Kleinfeld took over as CEO, he sought to restructure the company along the lines of what Jack Welch did at General Electric. He has tried to make the structure less bureaucratic so that decisions are made

faster. He spun off underperforming businesses. And he simplified the company's structure.

Kleinfeld's efforts drew angry protests from employee groups, with constant picket lines outside his corporate offices. One of the challenges of transforming European organizations is the active participation of employees in executive decisions. Half the seats on the Seimens board of directors are allocated to labor representatives. Not surprisingly, the labor groups did not react positively to Kleinfeld's GE-like restructuring efforts. In his efforts to speed those efforts, labor groups alleged, Kleinfeld secretly bankrolled a business-friendly workers' group to try to undermine Germany's main industrial union.

Due to this and other allegations, Kleinfeld was forced out in June 2007 and replaced by Peter Löscher. Löscher has found the same tensions between inertia and the need for restructuring. Only a

month after becoming CEO, Löscher was faced with a decision whether to spin off its underperforming $14 billion auto parts unit, VDO. Löscher had to weigh the forces for stability, who wish to protect worker interests, with U.S.-style pressures for financial performance. One of VDO's possible buyers is a U.S. company, TRW, the controlling interest of which is held by U.S. private equity firm Blackstone. Private equity firms have been called "locusts" by German labor representatives, so, more than most CEOs, Löscher had to balance worker interests with pressure for financial performance. When Löscher decided to sell VDO to German tire giant Continental Corporation, Continental promptly began to downsize and restructure operations.

Source: Based on M. Esterl and D. Crawford, "Siemens CEO Put to Early Test," *Wall Street Journal,* July 23, 2007, p. A8; and J. Ewing, "Siemens' Culture Clash," *BusinessWeek,* January 29, 2007, pp. 42–46.

centralization   *The degree to which decision making is concentrated at a single point in an organization.*

formalization   *The degree to which jobs within an organization are standardized.*

Common Organizational Designs

We now turn to describing three of the more common organizational designs found in use: the *simple structure*, the *bureaucracy*, and the *matrix structure*.

The Simple Structure

What do a small retail store, an electronics firm run by a hard-driving entrepreneur, and an airline in the midst of a companywide pilot's strike have in common? They probably all use the **simple structure**.

The simple structure is said to be characterized most by what it is not rather than by what it is. The simple structure is not elaborate.[6] It has a low degree of departmentalization, wide spans of control, authority centralized in a single person, and little formalization. The simple structure is a "flat" organization; it usually has only two or three vertical levels, a loose body of employees, and one individual in whom the decision-making authority is centralized.

The simple structure is most widely practiced in small businesses in which the manager and the owner are one and the same. This, for example, is illustrated in Exhibit 16-4, an organization chart for a retail men's store. Jack Gold owns and manages this store. Although he employs five full-time salespeople, a cashier, and extra personnel for weekends and holidays, he "runs the show." But large companies, in times of crisis, often simplify their structures as a means of focusing their resources. For example, when Anne Mulcahy took over Xerox, its product mix and management structure were overly complex. She simplified both, cutting corporate overhead by 26 percent. In such times of crisis, she says, "It's a case of placing your bets in a few areas."[7]

The strength of the simple structure lies in its simplicity. It's fast, flexible, and inexpensive to maintain, and accountability is clear. One major weakness is that it's difficult to maintain in anything other than small organizations. It becomes increasingly inadequate as an organization grows because its low formalization and high centralization tend to create information overload at the top. As size increases, decision making typically becomes slower and can eventually come to a standstill as the single executive tries to continue making all the decisions. This often proves to be the undoing of many small businesses. When an organization begins to employ 50 or 100 people, it's very difficult for the owner-manager to make all the choices. If the structure isn't changed and made more elaborate, the firm often loses momentum and can eventually fail. The simple structure's other weakness is that it's risky—everything depends on one person. One heart attack can literally destroy the organization's information and decision-making center.

Exhibit 16-4	A Simple Structure (Jack Gold's Men's Store)

The Internal Revenue Service relies on standardized work processes for coordination and control. IRS service-center employees follow formalized rules and regulations in performing their routine operating tasks. The bureaucracy of the IRS enables employees to perform standardized activities in an efficient way. The IRS employees shown here open about 19 million federal tax returns and check for missing documents or information.

The Bureaucracy

2 Identify the characteristics of a bureaucracy.

Standardization! That's the key concept that underlies all bureaucracies. Take a look at the bank where you keep your checking account, the department store where you buy your clothes, or the government offices that collect your taxes, enforce health regulations, or provide local fire protection. They all rely on standardized work processes for coordination and control.

The **bureaucracy** is characterized by highly routine operating tasks achieved through specialization, very formalized rules and regulations, tasks that are grouped into functional departments, centralized authority, narrow spans of control, and decision making that follows the chain of command. As the opening quote to this chapter attests, *bureaucracy* is a dirty word in many people's minds. However, it does have its advantages. The primary strength of the bureaucracy lies in its ability to perform standardized activities in a highly efficient manner. Putting like specialties together in functional departments results in economies of scale, minimum duplication of personnel and equipment, and employees who have the opportunity to talk "the same language" among their peers. Furthermore, bureaucracies can get by nicely with less talented—and, hence, less costly—middle- and lower-level managers. The

simple structure *A structure characterized by a low degree of departmentalization, wide spans of control, authority centralized in a single person, and little formalization.*

bureaucracy *A structure with highly routine operating tasks achieved through specialization, very formalized rules and regulations, tasks that are grouped into functional departments, centralized authority, narrow spans of control, and decision making that follows the chain of command.*

pervasiveness of rules and regulations substitutes for managerial discretion. Standardized operations, coupled with high formalization, allow decision making to be centralized. There is little need, therefore, for innovative and experienced decision makers below the level of senior executives.

One of the major weaknesses of a bureaucracy is illustrated in the following dialogue among four executives in one company: "Ya know, nothing happens in this place until we *produce* something," said the production executive. "Wrong," commented the research and development manager. "Nothing happens until we *design* something!" "What are you talking about?" asked the marketing executive. "Nothing happens here until we *sell* something!" Finally, the exasperated accounting manager responded, "It doesn't matter what you produce, design, or sell. No one knows what happens until we *tally up the results!*" This conversation points up the fact that specialization creates subunit conflicts. Functional unit goals can override the overall goals of the organization.

The other major weakness of a bureaucracy is something we've all experienced at one time or another when having to deal with people who work in these organizations: obsessive concern with following the rules. When cases arise that don't precisely fit the rules, there is no room for modification. The bureaucracy is efficient only as long as employees confront problems that they have previously encountered and for which programmed decision rules have already been established.

International OB

Structural Considerations in Multinationals

When bringing out a business innovation in any country, trudging through corporate bureaucracy can cause delays that result in a competitive disadvantage. This is especially true in China, one of the world's fastest-growing economies. Successful multinational corporations operating in China are realizing that the optimal structure is decentralized with a relatively high degree of managerial autonomy. Given that more than 1.3 billion people live in China, the opportunity for businesses is tremendous, and as a result, competition is increasing. To take advantage of this opportunity, companies must be able to

respond to changes before their competitors.

For example, Tyson Foods gives its vice president and head of the company's China operations, James Rice, the freedom to build the company's business overseas. While walking past a food vendor in Shanghai, Rice got the idea for cumin-flavored chicken strips. Without the need to obtain approval from upper management, Rice and his team immediately developed the recipe, tested it, and, after receiving a 90 percent customer-approval rating, began selling the product within 2 months of coming up with the idea.

Other companies that have implemented more formalized, bureaucratic structures have fared less well. One manager of a consumer electronics company who wanted to reduce the package size of a product to lower its cost and attract lower-income Chinese customers had to

send the idea to his boss. His boss, the vice president of Asian operations, then sent the idea to the vice president of international operations, who in turn sent the idea to upper management in the United States. Although the idea was approved, the process took 5 months, during which a competitor introduced a similarly packaged product.

So, when it comes to innovating in a dynamic, fast-paced economy such as China, decentralization and autonomy can be major competitive advantages for multinational companies. To gain this competitive advantage, companies like Tyson are empowering their overseas managers to make their own decisions.

Source: Based on C. Hymowitz, "Executives in China Need Both Autonomy and Fast Access to Boss," *Wall Street Journal,* May 10, 2005, p. B1.

The Matrix Structure

Another popular organizational design option is the **matrix structure**. You'll find it being used in advertising agencies, aerospace firms, research and development laboratories, construction companies, hospitals, government agencies, universities, management consulting firms, and entertainment companies.[8] Essentially, the matrix combines two forms of departmentalization: functional and product departmentalization.

3 *Describe a matrix organization.*

The strength of functional departmentalization lies in putting like specialists together, which minimizes the number necessary while allowing the pooling and sharing of specialized resources across products. Its major disadvantage is the difficulty of coordinating the tasks of diverse functional specialists so that their activities are completed on time and within budget. Product departmentalization, on the other hand, has exactly the opposite benefits and disadvantages. It facilitates coordination among specialties to achieve on-time completion and to meet budget targets. Furthermore, it provides clear responsibility for all activities related to a product, but with duplication of activities and costs. The matrix attempts to gain the strengths of each, while avoiding their weaknesses.

The most obvious structural characteristic of the matrix is that it breaks the unity-of-command concept. Employees in the matrix have two bosses—their functional department managers and their product managers. Therefore, the matrix has a dual chain of command.

Exhibit 16-5 shows the matrix form as used in a college of business administration. The academic departments of accounting, decision and information systems, marketing, and so forth are functional units. In addition, specific programs (that is, products) are overlaid on the functions. In this way, members in a matrix structure have a dual assignment—to their functional department and to their product groups. For instance, a professor of accounting who is teaching

| Exhibit **16-5** | Matrix Structure for a College of Business Administration |

Academic Departments \ Programs	Undergraduate	Master's	Ph.D.	Research	Executive Development	Community Service
Accounting						
Finance						
Decision and Information Systems						
Management						
Marketing						

matrix structure *A structure that creates dual lines of authority and combines functional and product departmentalization.*

an undergraduate course may report to the director of undergraduate programs as well as to the chairperson of the accounting department.

The strength of the matrix lies in its ability to facilitate coordination when the organization has a multiplicity of complex and interdependent activities. As an organization gets larger, its information-processing capacity can become overloaded. In a bureaucracy, complexity results in increased formalization. The direct and frequent contact between different specialties in the matrix can make for better communication and more flexibility. Information permeates the organization and more quickly reaches the people who need to take account of it. Furthermore, the matrix reduces "bureaupathologies"—the dual lines of authority reduce the tendencies of departmental members to become so busy protecting their little worlds that the organization's overall goals become secondary.

There is another advantage to the matrix. It facilitates the efficient allocation of specialists. When individuals with highly specialized skills are lodged in one functional department or product group, their talents are monopolized and underused. The matrix achieves the advantages of economies of scale by providing the organization with both the best resources and an effective way of ensuring their efficient deployment.

The major disadvantages of the matrix lie in the confusion it creates, its propensity to foster power struggles, and the stress it places on individuals.[9] When you dispense with the unity-of-command concept, ambiguity is significantly increased, and ambiguity often leads to conflict. For example, it's frequently unclear who reports to whom, and it is not unusual for product managers to fight over getting the best specialists assigned to their products. Confusion and ambiguity also create the seeds of power struggles. Bureaucracy reduces the potential for power grabs by defining the rules of the game. When those rules are "up for grabs," power struggles between functional and product managers result. For individuals who desire security and absence from ambiguity, this work climate can produce stress. Reporting to more than one boss introduces role conflict, and unclear expectations introduce role ambiguity. The comfort of bureaucracy's predictability is absent, replaced by insecurity and stress.

New Design Options

Over the past decade or two, senior managers in a number of organizations have been working to develop new structural options that can better help their firms to compete effectively. In this section, we'll describe two such structural designs: the *virtual organization* and the *boundaryless organization*.

The Virtual Organization

Why own when you can rent? That question captures the essence of the **virtual organization** (also sometimes called the *network*, or *modular*, organization), typically a small, core organization that outsources major business functions.[10] In structural terms, the virtual organization is highly centralized, with little or no departmentalization.

4 Identify the characteristics of a virtual organization.

The prototype of the virtual structure is today's movie-making organization. In Hollywood's golden era, movies were made by huge, vertically integrated corporations. Studios such as MGM, Warner Brothers, and 20th Century Fox owned large movie lots and employed thousands of full-time specialists—set designers, camera people, film editors, directors, and even actors.

The Boeing Company outsourced the production of about 70 percent of the components of its new 787 Dreamliner passenger jet aircraft. For example, the Italian firm Alenia Aeronautica produced the plane's rear fuselage and horizontal stabilizer, and Tokyo-based Mitsubishi Motors Corporation created the wings. Global outsourcing helped Boeing reduce the plane's development and production costs, enabling it to offer the plane at a price attractive to buyers. Before the Dreamliner's maiden flight, Boeing had a record-breaking 500 orders for the plane, many of which came from the countries that made parts for the aircraft that was assembled at Boeing's Everett, Washington, plant.

Today, most movies are made by a collection of individuals and small companies who come together and make films project by project.[11] This structural form allows each project to be staffed with the talent most suited to its demands, rather than having to choose just from the people employed by the studio. It minimizes bureaucratic overhead because there is no lasting organization to maintain. And it lessens long-term risks and their costs because there is no long term—a team is assembled for a finite period and then disbanded.

Ancle Hsu and David Ji run a virtual organization. Their firm, California-based Apex Digital, is one of the world's largest producers of DVD players, yet the company neither owns a factory nor employs an engineer. They contract everything out to firms in China. With minimal investment, Apex has grown from nothing to annual sales of over $500 million in just 3 years. Similarly, Paul Newman's food products company, Newman's Own, sells over $120 million in food every year yet employs only 19 people. This is possible because it outsources almost everything—manufacturing, procurement, shipping, and quality control.

Almost all large organizations have increased their outsourcing. Boeing, for example, assembles all its planes in the Seattle area, but it outsources the production of many of its components. Other companies may outsource their entire information systems to organizations like EDS or IBM. Still others, such as Cingular, Dell, and Time Warner, outsource entire operations—such as customer service or technical support—to other (often overseas) organizations.

What's going on here? A quest for maximum flexibility. These virtual organizations have created networks of relationships that allow them to contract out manufacturing, distribution, marketing, or any other business function for which

virtual organization *A small, core organization that outsources major business functions.*

Exhibit **16-6**	A Virtual Organization

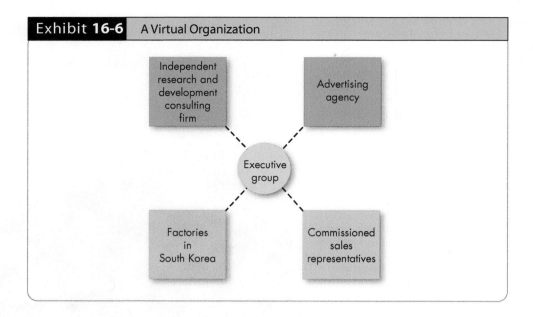

management feels that others can do better or more cheaply. The virtual organization stands in sharp contrast to the typical bureaucracy that has many vertical levels of management and where control is sought through ownership. In such organizations, research and development are done in-house, production occurs in company-owned plants, and sales and marketing are performed by the company's own employees. To support all this, management has to employ extra staff, including accountants, human resource specialists, and lawyers. The virtual organization, however, outsources many of these functions and concentrates on what it does best. For most U.S. firms, that means focusing on design or marketing.

Exhibit 16-6 shows a virtual organization in which management outsources all of the primary functions of the business. The core of the organization is a small group of executives whose job is to oversee directly any activities that are done in-house and to coordinate relationships with the other organizations that manufacture, distribute, and perform other crucial functions for the virtual organization. The dotted lines in Exhibit 16-6 represent the relationships typically maintained under contracts. In essence, managers in virtual structures spend most of their time coordinating and controlling external relations, typically by way of computer-network links.

The major advantage to the virtual organization is its flexibility. For instance, it allows individuals with an innovative idea and little money, such as Ancle Hsu and David Ji, to successfully compete against the likes of Sony, Hitachi, and Sharp Electronics. The primary drawback to this structure is that it reduces management's control over key parts of its business.

The Boundaryless Organization

General Electric's former chairman, Jack Welch, coined the term **boundaryless organization** to describe his idea of what he wanted GE to become. Welch wanted to turn his company into a "family grocery store."[12] That is, in spite of its monstrous size (2006 revenues were $163 billion), he wanted to eliminate *vertical* and *horizontal* boundaries within GE and break down *external* barriers between the company and its customers and suppliers. The boundaryless organization seeks to eliminate the chain of command, have limitless spans of control, and replace departments with empowered teams. And because it relies so heavily on information technology, some

5 *Show why managers want to create boundaryless organizations.*

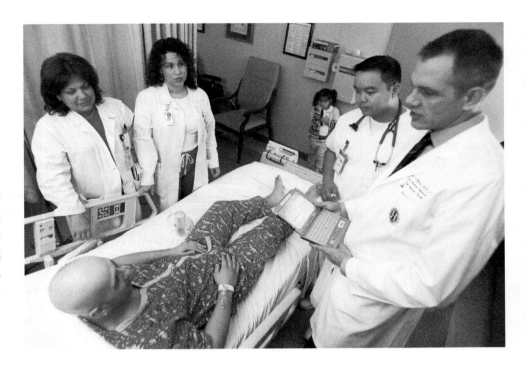

Information technology is transforming hospitals from bureaucracies to boundaryless operations. At Hackensack University Medical Center, a computerized clinical information system allows multidisciplinary teams of doctors, nurses, social workers, pharmacists, nutritionists, and other medical staff members to communicate, coordinate, and implement patients' care plans. Doctors and nurses use wireless laptop computers to input patient information and medicine orders and to review lab tests and scans. The IT system improves decision making, helps ensure patient safety, and enables staff members to check patient records from remote locations.

have turned to calling this structure the *T-form* (or technology-based) organization.[13] Although GE has not yet achieved this boundaryless state—and probably never will—it has made significant progress toward that end. So have other companies, such as Hewlett-Packard, AT&T, Motorola, and 3M. Let's take a look at what a boundaryless organization would look like and what some firms are doing to try to make it a reality.[14]

By removing vertical boundaries, management flattens the hierarchy. Status and rank are minimized. Cross-hierarchical teams (which include top executives, middle managers, supervisors, and operative employees), participative decision-making practices, and the use of 360-degree performance appraisals (in which peers and others above and below the employee evaluate performance) are examples of what GE is doing to break down vertical boundaries. At Oticon A/S, a $160-million-per-year Danish hearing aid manufacturer, all traces of hierarchy have disappeared. Everyone works at uniform mobile workstations. And project teams, not functions or departments, coordinate work.

Functional departments create horizontal boundaries. And these boundaries stifle interaction between functions, product lines, and units. The way to reduce these barriers is to replace functional departments with cross-functional teams and to organize activities around processes. For instance, Xerox now develops new products through multidisciplinary teams that work in a single process instead of around narrow functional tasks. Similarly, some AT&T units are now doing annual budgets based not on functions or departments but on processes such as the maintenance of a worldwide telecommunications network. Another way management can cut through horizontal barriers is to use lateral transfers, rotating people into and out of different functional areas. This approach turns specialists into generalists.

boundaryless organization *An organization that seeks to eliminate the chain of command, have limitless spans of control, and replace departments with empowered teams.*

Why Do Structures Differ?

6 Demonstrate how organizational structures differ, and contrast mechanistic and organic structural models.

In the previous sections, we described a variety of organizational designs ranging from the highly structured and standardized bureaucracy to the loose and amorphous boundaryless organization. The other designs we discussed tend to exist somewhere between these two extremes.

Exhibit 16-7 reconceptualizes our previous discussions by presenting two extreme models of organizational design. One extreme we'll call the **mechanistic model**. It's generally synonymous with the bureaucracy in that it has extensive departmentalization, high formalization, a limited information network (mostly downward communication), and little participation by low-level members in decision making. At the other extreme is the **organic model**. This model looks a lot like the boundaryless organization. It's flat, uses cross-hierarchical and cross-functional teams, has low formalization, possesses a comprehensive information network (using lateral and upward communication as well as downward), and involves high participation in decision making.[15]

With these two models in mind, we're now prepared to address a couple questions: Why are some organizations structured along more mechanistic lines whereas others follow organic characteristics? What are the forces that influence the design that is chosen? In the following pages, we present the major forces that have been identified as causes or determinants of an organization's structure.[16]

Strategy

An organization's structure is a means to help management achieve its objectives. Because objectives are derived from the organization's overall strategy, it's only logical that strategy and structure should be closely linked. More specifically, structure should follow strategy. If management makes a significant change in its organization's strategy, the structure will need to be modified to accommodate and support this change.[17]

Most current strategy frameworks focus on three strategy dimensions—innovation, cost minimization, and imitation—and the structural design that works best with each.[18]

Exhibit 16-7   Mechanistic Versus Organic Models

The Mechanistic Model

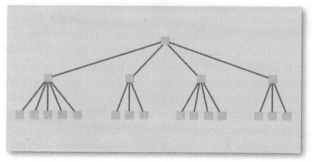

- High specialization
- Rigid departmentalization
- Clear chain of command
- Narrow spans of control
- Centralization
- High formalization

The Organic Model

- Cross-functional teams
- Cross-hierarchical teams
- Free flow of information
- Wide spans of control
- Decentralization
- Low formalization

Exhibit **16-8**	The Strategy–Structure Relationship
Strategy	**Structural Option**
Innovation	**Organic:** A loose structure; low specialization, low formalization, decentralized
Cost minimization	**Mechanistic:** Tight control; extensive work specialization, high formalization, high centralization
Imitation	**Mechanistic and organic:** Mix of loose with tight properties; tight controls over current activities and looser controls for new undertakings

To what degree does an organization introduce major new products or services? An **innovation strategy** does not mean a strategy merely for simple or cosmetic changes from previous offerings but rather one for meaningful and unique innovations. Obviously, not all firms pursue innovation. This strategy may appropriately characterize 3M and Apple, but it's not a strategy pursued by conservative retailer Marks & Spencer.

An organization that is pursuing a **cost-minimization strategy** tightly controls costs, refrains from incurring unnecessary innovation or marketing expenses, and cuts prices in selling a basic product. This would describe the strategy pursued by Wal-Mart or the makers of generic grocery products.

Organizations following an **imitation strategy** try to capitalize on the best of both of the previous strategies. They seek to minimize risk and maximize opportunity for profit. Their strategy is to move into new products or new markets only after viability has been proven by innovators. They take the successful ideas of innovators and copy them. Manufacturers of mass-marketed fashion goods that are rip-offs of designer styles follow the imitation strategy. This label probably also characterizes well-known firms such as HP and Caterpillar. They essentially follow their smaller and more innovative competitors with superior products, but only after their competitors have demonstrated that the market is there.

Exhibit 16-8 describes the structural option that best matches each strategy. Innovators need the flexibility of the organic structure, whereas cost minimizers seek the efficiency and stability of the mechanistic structure. Imitators combine the two structures. They use a mechanistic structure in order to maintain tight controls and low costs in their current activities, while at the same time they create organic subunits in which to pursue new undertakings.

Organization Size

There is considerable evidence to support the idea that an organization's size significantly affects its structure.[19] For instance, large organizations—those that typically employ 2,000 or more people—tend to have more specialization, more

---

mechanistic model *A structure characterized by extensive departmentalization, high formalization, a limited information network, and centralization.*

organic model *A structure that is flat, uses cross-hierarchical and cross-functional teams, has low formalization, possesses a comprehensive information network, and relies on participative decision making.*

innovation strategy *A strategy that emphasizes the introduction of major new products and services.*

cost-minimization strategy *A strategy that emphasizes tight cost controls, avoidance of unnecessary innovation or marketing expenses, and price cutting.*

imitation strategy *A strategy that seeks to move into new products or new markets only after their viability has already been proven.*

The degree of routineness differentiates technologies. At Wallstrip.com, nonroutineness characterizes the customized work of employees who create an entertaining daily Web video show and accompanying blog about the stock market. The show relies heavily on the knowledge of specialists such as host Lindsay Campbell and writer/producer Adam Elend, who are shown here in the production studio, where they're getting ready to film an episode of their show.

Source: Dima Gavrysh/ The New York Times

departmentalization, more vertical levels, and more rules and regulations than do small organizations. However, the relationship isn't linear. Rather, size affects structure at a decreasing rate. The impact of size becomes less important as an organization expands. Why is this? Essentially, once an organization has around 2,000 employees, it's already fairly mechanic. An additional 500 employees will not have much impact. On the other hand, adding 500 employees to an organization that has only 300 members is likely to result in a significant shift toward a more mechanistic structure.

Technology

The term **technology** refers to how an organization transfers its inputs into outputs. Every organization has at least one technology for converting financial, human, and physical resources into products or services. The Ford Motor Co., for instance, predominantly uses an assembly-line process to make its products. On the other hand, colleges may use a number of instruction technologies—the ever-popular formal lecture method, the case-analysis method, the experiential exercise method, the programmed learning method, and so forth. In this section we want to show that organizational structures adapt to their technology.

Numerous studies have been carried out on the technology–structure relationship.[20] The details of those studies are quite complex, so we'll go straight to "the bottom line" and attempt to summarize what we know.

The common theme that differentiates technologies is their *degree of routineness*. By this we mean that technologies tend toward either routine or nonroutine activities. The former are characterized by automated and standardized operations. Nonroutine activities are customized. They include varied operations such as furniture restoring, custom shoemaking, and genetic research.

What relationships have been found between technology and structure? Although the relationship is not overwhelmingly strong, we find that routine tasks are associated with taller and more departmentalized structures. The relationship between technology and formalization, however, is stronger. Studies consistently show routineness to be associated with the presence of rule manuals, job descriptions, and other formalized documentation. Finally, an interesting relationship has been found between technology and centralization. It seems logical that routine technologies would be associated with a centralized structure, while nonroutine technologies, which rely more heavily on the knowledge of specialists, would be characterized by delegated decision authority. This position has met with some support. However, a more generalizable conclusion is that the technology-centralization relationship is moderated by the degree of formalization. Formal regulations and centralized decision making are both control mechanisms and management can substitute one for the other. Routine technologies should be associated with centralized control if there is a minimum of rules and regulations. However, if formalization is high, routine technology can be accompanied by decentralization. So we would predict that routine technology would lead to centralization, but only if formalization is low.

Environment

An organization's **environment** is composed of institutions or forces outside the organization that potentially affect the organization's performance. These typically include suppliers, customers, competitors, government regulatory agencies, public pressure groups, and the like.

Why should an organization's structure be affected by its environment? Because of environmental uncertainty. Some organizations face relatively static environments—few forces in their environment are changing. There are, for example, no new competitors, no new technological breakthroughs by current competitors, or little activity by public pressure groups to influence the organization. Other organizations face very dynamic environments—rapidly changing government regulations affecting their business, new competitors, difficulties in acquiring raw materials, continually changing product preferences by customers, and so on. Static environments create significantly less uncertainty for managers than do dynamic ones. And because uncertainty is a threat to an organization's effectiveness, management will try to minimize it. One way to reduce environmental uncertainty is through adjustments in the organization's structure.[21]

Recent research has helped clarify what is meant by environmental uncertainty. It's been found that there are three key dimensions to any organization's environment: capacity, volatility, and complexity.[22]

The *capacity* of an environment refers to the degree to which it can support growth. Rich and growing environments generate excess resources, which can buffer the organization in times of relative scarcity.

The degree of instability in an environment is captured in the *volatility* dimension. When there is a high degree of unpredictable change, the environment is dynamic. This makes it difficult for management to predict accurately the probabilities associated with various decision alternatives. Because information technology changes at such a rapid place, more organizations' environments are becoming volatile.

technology *The way in which an organization transfers its inputs into outputs.*

environment *Institutions or forces outside an organization that potentially affect the organization's performance.*

MYTH OR SCIENCE?   *"People Are Our Most Important Asset"*

though this bromide has been expressed so often it arouses a cynical smirk on the faces of many, there is evidence that for most companies, it's true.

When we separate the U.S. economy into hard or tangible (manufacturing, real estate, etc.) and soft or intangible (medical care, communications, education) sectors, the soft industries provide 79 percent of all jobs and 76 percent of all U.S. GDP. Although this separation is far from perfect, it does suggest that the so-called knowledge worker is an increasingly important part of the economy. Yet many organizational structures tend to be based on physical assets rather than intellectual resources.

For example, to return to the auto industry example, U.S. auto manufacturers focus their structure along physical assets—product lines or component systems—and outsource part-making or assembly to a small degree.

Japanese auto manufacturers like Toyota or Honda, conversely, focus on developing the intellectual products in-house (design and engineering), and outsource some or most of manufacturing and assembly to the countries where they sell their products. It has been argued that these structural differences account for the intangible advantages (design, engineering) enjoyed by Japanese over U.S. automakers.

The authors of a recent study note: "While managing professional intellect is clearly the key to value creation and profitability for most companies, few have arrived at a systematic structures for developing, focusing, leveraging, and measure their intellectual capabilities."

So, even if most organizations argue that people are their most important asset, they aren't structured to make the maximum use of that asset.[23] ■

Finally, the environment needs to be assessed in terms of *complexity*—that is, the degree of heterogeneity and concentration among environmental elements. Simple environments—like in the tobacco industry—are homogeneous and concentrated. In contrast, environments characterized by heterogeneity and dispersion—think of companies in the broadband industry, such as Verizon—are called complex, meaning the environment is diverse and the competitors numerous.

Exhibit 16-9 summarizes our definition of the environment along its three dimensions. The arrows in this figure are meant to indicate movement toward higher uncertainty. So organizations that operate in environments characterized as scarce, dynamic, and complex face the greatest degree of uncertainty. Why? Because they have little room for error, high unpredictability, and a diverse set of elements in the environment to monitor constantly.

| **Exhibit 16-9** | Three-Dimensional Model of the Environment |

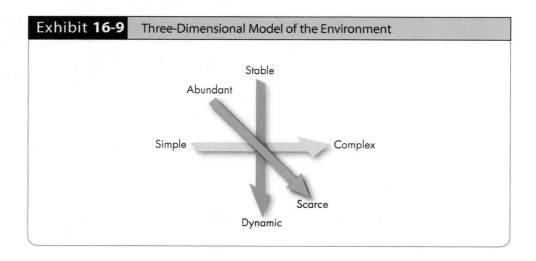

Given this three-dimensional definition of *environment*, we can offer some general conclusions. There is evidence that relates the degrees of environmental uncertainty to different structural arrangements. Specifically, the more scarce, dynamic, and complex the environment, the more organic a structure should be. The more abundant, stable, and simple the environment, the more the mechanistic structure will be preferred.

Organizational Designs and Employee Behavior

Analyze the behavioral implications of different organizational designs.

We opened this chapter by implying that an organization's structure can have significant effects on its members. In this section, we want to assess directly just what those effects might be.

A review of the evidence linking organizational structures to employee performance and satisfaction leads to a pretty clear conclusion—you can't generalize! Not everyone prefers the freedom and flexibility of organic structures. Some people are most productive and satisfied when work tasks are standardized and ambiguity is minimized—that is, in mechanistic structures. So any discussion of the effect of organizational design on employee behavior has to address individual differences. To illustrate this point, let's consider employee preferences for work specialization, span of control, and centralization.[24]

The evidence generally indicates that *work specialization* contributes to higher employee productivity but at the price of reduced job satisfaction. However, this statement ignores individual differences and the type of job tasks people do. As we noted previously, work specialization is not an unending source of higher productivity. Problems start to surface, and productivity begins to suffer, when the human diseconomies of doing repetitive and narrow tasks overtake the economies of specialization. As the workforce has become more highly educated and desirous of jobs that are intrinsically rewarding, the point at which productivity begins to decline seems to be reached more quickly than in decades past.

Although more people today are undoubtedly turned off by overly specialized jobs than were their parents or grandparents, it would be naive to ignore the reality that there is still a segment of the workforce that prefers the routine and repetitiveness of highly specialized jobs. Some individuals want work that makes minimal intellectual demands and provides the security of routine. For these people, high work specialization is a source of job satisfaction. The empirical question, of course, is whether this represents 2 percent of the workforce or 52 percent. Given that there is some self-selection operating in the choice of careers, we might conclude that negative behavioral outcomes from high specialization are most likely to surface in professional jobs occupied by individuals with high needs for personal growth and diversity.

A review of the research indicates that it is probably safe to say there is no evidence to support a relationship between *span of control* and employee performance. Although it is intuitively attractive to argue that large spans might lead to higher employee performance because they provide more distant supervision and more opportunity for personal initiative, the research fails to support this notion. At this point it's impossible to state that any particular span of control is best for producing high performance or high satisfaction among employees. Again, the reason is probably individual differences. That is, some people like to be left alone, while others prefer the security of a boss who is quickly available at

The tasks of these women making cookies at a factory in South Korea are highly standardized. Individual differences influence how these employees respond to their high work specialization. For these women, specialization may be a source of job satisfaction because it provides the security of routine and gives them the chance to socialize on the job because they work closely with coworkers.

all times. Consistent with several of the contingency theories of leadership discussed in Chapter 12, we would expect factors such as employees' experiences and abilities and the degree of structure in their tasks to explain when wide or narrow spans of control are likely to contribute to their performance and job satisfaction. However, there is some evidence indicating that a manager's job satisfaction increases as the number of employees supervised increases.

We find fairly strong evidence linking *centralization* and job satisfaction. In general, organizations that are less centralized have a greater amount of autonomy. And the evidence suggests that autonomy is positively related to job satisfaction. But, again, individual differences surface. While one employee may value her freedom, another may find autonomous environments frustratingly ambiguous.

Our conclusion: To maximize employee performance and satisfaction, individual differences, such as experience, personality, and the work task, should be taken into account. As we'll note shortly, culture needs to be taken into consideration, too.

One obvious insight needs to be made before we leave this topic: People don't select employers randomly. There is substantial evidence that individuals are attracted to, selected by, and stay with organizations that suit their personal characteristics.[25] Job candidates who prefer predictability, for instance, are likely to seek out and take employment in mechanistic structures, and those who want autonomy are more likely to end up in an organic structure. So the effect of structure on employee behavior is undoubtedly reduced when the selection process facilitates proper matching of individual characteristics with organizational characteristics.

Global Implications

8   Show how globalization affects organizational structure.

When we think about how culture influences how organizations are to be structured, several questions come to mind. First, does culture really matter to organizational structure? Second, do employees in different countries vary in their perceptions of different types of organizational structures? Finally, how do cultural considerations fit with our discussion of the boundaryless organization? Let's tackle each of these questions in turn.

Culture and Organizational Structure   Does culture really affect organizational structure? The answer might seem obvious—yes!—but there are reasons culture may not matter as much as you think. The U.S. model of business has been very influential, so much so that the organizational structures in other countries may mirror those of U.S. organizations. Moreover, U.S. structures themselves have been influenced by structures in other countries (especially Japan, Great Britain, and Germany). However, cultural concerns still might be important. Bureaucratic structures still dominate in many parts of Europe and Asia. Moreover, one management expert argues that U.S. management often places too much emphasis on individual leadership, which may be jarring in countries where decision making is more decentralized.[26]

Culture and Employee Structure Preferences   Although there isn't a great deal of research out there, it does suggest that national culture influences the preference for structure, so it, too, needs to be considered.[27] For instance, organizations that operate with people from high power distance cultures, such as those found in Greece, France, and most of Latin America, find employees much more accepting of mechanistic structures than where employees come from low power distance countries. So you need to consider cultural differences along with individual differences when making predictions on how structure will affect employee performance and satisfaction.

Culture and the Boundaryless Organization   When fully operational, the boundaryless organization also breaks down barriers created by geography. Most large U.S. companies today see themselves as global corporations, and may well do as much business overseas as in the United States (Coca-Cola, for example). As a result, many companies struggle with the problem of how to incorporate geographic regions into their structure. The boundaryless organization provides one solution to this problem because geography is considered more of a tactical, logistical issue than a structural issue. In short, the goal of the boundaryless organization is to break down cultural barriers.

One way to break down barriers is through strategic alliances. Firms such as NEC Corp., Boeing, and Apple Computer each have strategic alliances or joint partnerships with dozens of companies. These alliances blur the distinction between one organization and another as employees work on joint projects. And some companies are allowing customers to perform functions that previously were done by management. For instance, some AT&T units are receiving bonuses based on customer evaluations of the teams that serve them. Finally, telecommuting is blurring organizational boundaries. The security analyst with Merrill Lynch who does his job from his ranch in Montana or the software designer who works for a San Francisco company but does her job in Boulder, Colorado, are just two examples of the millions of workers who are now doing their jobs outside the physical boundaries of their employers' premises.

Summary and Implications for Managers

The theme of this chapter has been that an organization's internal structure contributes to explaining and predicting behavior. That is, in addition to individual and group factors, the structural relationships in which people work has a bearing on employee attitudes and behavior.

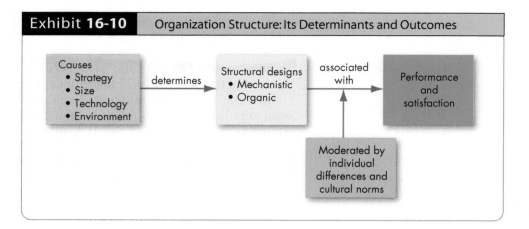

Exhibit **16-10**   Organization Structure: Its Determinants and Outcomes

What's the basis for the argument that structure has an impact on both attitudes and behavior? To the degree that an organization's structure reduces ambiguity for employees and clarifies concerns such as "What am I supposed to do?" "How am I supposed to do it?" "To whom do I report?" and "To whom do I go if I have a problem?" it shapes their attitudes and facilitates and motivates them to higher levels of performance.

Of course, structure also constrains employees to the extent that it limits and controls what they do. For example, organizations structured around high levels of formalization and specialization, strict adherence to the chain of command, limited delegation of authority, and narrow spans of control give employees little autonomy. Controls in such organizations are tight, and behavior tends to vary within a narrow range. In contrast, organizations that are structured around limited specialization, low formalization, wide spans of control, and the like provide employees greater freedom and, thus, are characterized by greater behavioral diversity.

Exhibit 16-10 visually summarizes what we've discussed in this chapter. Strategy, size, technology, and environment determine the type of structure an organization will have. For simplicity's sake, we can classify structural designs around one of two models: mechanistic or organic. The specific effect of structural designs on performance and satisfaction is moderated by employees' individual preferences and cultural norms.

Finally, increasingly, technology is reshaping work such that organizational structures may be increasingly amorphous. This allows a manager the flexibility of taking into account things like employee preferences, experience, and culture so as to design work systems that truly motivate employees.

Point ❯❯ ❮❮ Counterpoint

DOWNSIZING IMPROVES ORGANIZATIONAL PERFORMANCE

*t*here aren't many leaders who like to downsize. Doing so always means inflicting pain on employees and enduring attacks by politicians, labor groups, and the media. But if there is one thing we have learned in the past 20 years, it's that downsizing has been an indispensable factor in making companies more competitive.

In the 1970s and 1980s, most companies in established countries such as the United States were overstaffed. That made them vulnerable to foreign competition from companies with lower labor costs and a better ability to quickly adapt to new economic conditions and technologies. It's perhaps inevitable that companies do this: Success breeds complacency; and, when business is good, companies tend to overstaff and become bloated. Like the patient with a heart condition, they find the remedy is often painful; but fail to address it, and the eventual harm may be much worse.

Nearly all major U.S. companies that were around in the 1970s have shrunk their workforces and streamlined their operations. Look at IBM. Once one of the largest employers in the world, it often touted its no-layoff policy. But in the 1980s and 1990s, it became quite clear that IBM was too big, too complex, and spread too thin. Today, IBM is profitable again, but only after it shed nearly 100,000 jobs. Here is what former IBM CEO Lou Gerstner said about the need to restructure the company:

> It got stuck because it fell victim to what I call the success syndrome. The more successful enterprises are the more they try to replicate, duplicate, codify what makes us great. And suddenly they're inward thinking. They're thinking how can we continue to do what we've done in the past without understanding that what made them successful is to take risks, to change and to adapt and to be responsive. And so in a sense success breeds its own failure. And I think it's true of a lot of successful businesses.

Layoffs and restructuring are rarely the popular things to do. But without them, most organizations would not survive, much less remain competitive.[28]

*d*ownsizing has become a sort of rite of passage for business leaders: You're not a real leader unless you've downsized a company. However, to separate fact from myth, let's look at the evidence. Do companies that have downsized perform better as a result?

To study this, a research team looked at *Standard & Poor's 500* (S&P 500) companies over 20 years. They asked whether reductions in employment at one period of time were associated with higher levels of financial performance at a later period in time.

What did they find? In analyzing 6,418 occurrences of changes in employment among the S&P 500, they found that downsizing strategies did *not* result in improved long-term financial performance (as measured by industry-adjusted return on assets). It's important to remember that the results control for prior financial performance and reflect financial performance after the downsizing efforts occurred.

The authors of this study don't argue that downsizing is always a bad strategy. Rather, the upshot is that managers shouldn't assume layoffs are a quick fix to what ails a company. In general, downsizing does *not* improve performance, so the key is to do it only when needed and to do it in the right way.

What are some ways organizations can do this? First, they should use downsizing only as a last resort. Second, and related, they should inform employees about the problem, and give them a chance to contribute alternative restructuring solutions. Third, organizations need to bend over backward to ensure that employees see the layoff process as fair, including making sure the layoff criteria *are* fair (and ideally result from employee involvement), advance notice is given, and job relocation assistance is provided. Finally, make sure downsizing is done to good effect—not just to cut costs, but to reallocate resources to where they can be most effective.[29]

Questions for Review

1 What are the six key elements that define an organization's structure?

2 What is a bureaucracy, and how does it differ from a simple structure?

3 What is a matrix organization?

4 What are the characteristics of a virtual organization?

5 How can managers create a boundaryless organization?

6 Why do organizational structures differ, and what is the difference between a mechanistic structure and an organic structure?

7 What are the behavioral implications of different organizational designs?

8 How does globalization affect organizational structure?

Experiential Exercise

AUTHORITY FIGURES

Purpose
To learn about one's experiences with and feelings about authority.

Time
Approximately 75 minutes.

Procedure

1. Your instructor will separate class members into groups based on their birth order. Groups are formed consisting of "only children," "eldest," "middle," and "youngest," according to placement in families. Larger groups will be broken into smaller ones, with four or five members, to allow for freer conversation.

2. Each group member should talk about how he or she "typically reacts to the authority of others." Focus should be on specific situations that offer general information about how individuals deal with authority

figures (for example, bosses, teachers, parents, or coaches). The group has 25 minutes to develop a written list of how the group generally deals with others' authority. Be sure to separate tendencies that group members share and those they do not.

3. Repeat step 2, except this time, discuss how group members "typically are as authority figures." Again make a list of shared characteristics.

4. Each group will share its general conclusions with the entire class.

5. Class discussion will focus on questions such as:

   a. What patterned differences have surfaced between the groups?

   b. What may account for these differences?

   c. What hypotheses might explain the connection between how individuals react to the authority of others and how they are as authority figures?

Source: This exercise is adapted from W. A. Kahn, "An Exercise of Authority," *Organizational Behavior Teaching Review* 14, no. 2 (1989–1990), pp. 28–42. Reprinted with permission.

Ethical Dilemma

HOW MUCH SHOULD DIRECTORS DIRECT?

One critical structural element of most corporations is the board of directors. Nearly any organization of appreciable size has a board of directors. And formally at least, chief executives often report to the directors. Informally, however, many boards defer to the CEO and *advise* more than *direct*.

There is some evidence, though, that this cozy relationship is starting to change. Some directors are mingling with employees to get the 411 on any problems that are brewing. Others are opening communication channels with investors to hear their complaints. Some are even

taking over responsibilities that used to be handled by the CEO, such as nominating new board members.

You might think an active board is always good for an organization. However, like most structural decisions, it has downsides and risks. When directors are empowered, they can become "free agents" who pursue their own agendas, including some that may be conflict with the CEO's. Or they may make statements or disclose information that goes against company interests. For example, when the AFL-CIO union secured a meeting with Home Depot director Bonnie Hill, some executives in the company were concerned that she might disclose private information.

Though that didn't appear to be the case with Ms. Hill, one can envision some rogue board members undermining a CEO strategy they don't like through such communiqués. A final danger is the possibility that board members will micromanage a CEO's strategy. For example, when top management of one company went to the board with a proposal for executive bonuses, the board hired its own pay consultants. Such actions don't go over well with CEOs. As one said, "You don't need someone guiding your hand."

Questions

1. How active do you think boards should be?

2. Should directors mix with employees to obtain company information from the ranks? Why or why not?

3. When is the line between representing shareholders' interests and micromanaging or second-guessing the CEO?

Source: Based on K. Whitehouse, "Move Over, CEO: Here Come the Directors," *Wall Street Journal,* October 9, 2006, pp. R1, R4.

Case Incident 1

CAN A STRUCTURE BE *TOO* FLAT?

Steelmaker Nucor likes to think it has management figured out. And with good reason. It is the darling of the business press. Its management practices are often favorably reviewed in management texts. And it's been effective by nearly any business metric.

There's one fundamental management practice that Nucor doesn't appear to have mastered—how to structure itself.

Nucor has always prided itself on having just three levels of management separating the CEO from factory workers. With Nucor's structure, plant managers report directly to CEO Dan DiMicco. As Nucor continues to grow, though, DiMicco is finding it increasingly hard to maintain this simple structure. So, in 2006, DiMicco added another layer of management, creating a new layer of five executive vice presidents. "I needed to be free to make decisions on trade battles," he said.

Still, even with the new layer in its structure, Nucor is remarkably lean and simple. U.S. Steel Corp. employs 1,200 people at its corporate headquarters, compared to a scant 66 at Nucor's. At Nucor, managers still answer their own phone calls and e-mails, and the firm has no corporate jet. Even comparatively lean companies like Toyota appear fat and complicated compared to Nucor. "You're going to get at least ten layers at Toyota before you get to the president," says a former Toyota engineer.

Questions

1. How does the Nucor case illustrate the limitations of the simple organizational structure?

2. Do you think other organizations should attempt to replicate Nucor's structure? Why or why not?

3. Why do you think other organizations have developed much more complex structures than Nucor?

4. Generally, organizational structures tend to reflect the views of the CEO. As more and more "new blood" comes into Nucor, do you think the structure will begin to look like that of other organizations?

Source: P. Glader, "It's Not Easy Being Lean," *Wall Street Journal,* June 19, 2006, pp. B1, B3.

Case Incident 2

NO BOSSES AT W. L. GORE & ASSOCIATES

You've probably bought a garment made of W. L. Gore & Associates's flagship product, Gore-Tex, a fabric that blocks wind and water yet is highly breathable, thanks to Gore's patented technology. But you might not know that the company offers a host of other products, from heart patches and synthetic blood vessels to air pollution filters and fuel cells. In fact, W. L. Gore & Associates makes more than 1,000 products. Though its financial data are not publicly available, a spokesperson for the company said that Gore had double-digit revenue growth the past 3 years. With this type of performance and extensive product line, you might expect Gore to be structured like big companies such as General Electric, Microsoft, or 3M. But it's not, and it never was.

Wilbert L. Gore founded W. L. Gore & Associates in 1958. Gore believed that too much hierarchy and bureaucracy stifled creativity and adaptation, a view he formed during his 17-year career as a DuPont engineer. He stated once that "communication really happens in the car pool," meaning that informal arenas allow employees to share their ideas openly, without fear of criticism from management. So Gore decided to eliminate the hierarchy found in most organizations. Instead, he instructed everyone to communicate openly, with little regard to status differences. In fact, Gore eliminated status differences altogether.

At W. L. Gore & Associates, there are no job titles. Each employee works on projects collaboratively and has the freedom to develop new ideas. Ideas that are deemed worthy of pursuing by team members are then developed.

In addition to the lack of bureaucracy, Gore also kept his facilities staffed with a small number of employees to promote information sharing and foster teamwork. For example, he limited staffing at manufacturing plants to 200 employees, which is smaller than typical manufacturing firms. Gore believed the number was low enough for employees to get to know one another, allowing them to talk freely about their knowledge and ideas. The result of such a corporate structure has been tremendous growth and profit. Gore also has been an industry leader in innovation.

Gore's unique structure does take some getting used to, particularly for new employees. Diane Davidson recalls that the lack of a formal hierarchy was bewildering at first. As a sales executive in the apparel industry, Davidson was hired by Gore to promote its fabrics to designers such as Prada and Hugo Boss. States Davidson, "I came from a very traditional, male-dominated business—the men's shoe business. When I arrived at Gore, I didn't know who did what. I wondered how anything got done here. It was driving me crazy." Instead of a formal supervisor, Davidson was assigned to a "starting sponsor." As opposed to a traditional supervisor, the sponsor at Gore helps new hires learn the ropes—which primarily consist of getting to know one's team.

"Who's my boss?" she repeatedly asked her sponsor. Her sponsor would reply, "Stop using the b-word."

Davidson eventually got used to Gore's structure. "Your team is your boss, because you don't want to let them down.

Everyone's your boss, and no one's your boss," she explains. Not only are there no formal supervisors at Gore, but employees' job descriptions are conspicuously absent as well. Employees at Gore perform multiple tasks to create a new product. Davidson, for example, is involved in marketing, sales, and sponsorship—roles that typically are separated in other organizations. As John Morgan, an employee of Gore for more than 20 years, states, "You join a team and you're an idiot. It takes 18 months to build credibility. Early on, it's really frustrating. In hindsight, it makes sense. As a sponsor, I tell new hires, 'Your job for the first 6 months is to get to know the team,' but they have trouble believing it—and not contributing when other people are."

Questions

1. How would you characterize Gore's organizational structure using terms from this chapter? For example, is it mechanistic or organic? How might this structure influence Gore's strategy?

2. Considering what you know about individual differences such as personality, what types of employees might respond more and less favorably to Gore's lack of hierarchy?

3. What are some advantages and disadvantages of Gore's structure from a company perspective? What about from an employee perspective?

4. How might Gore's organizational design affect its relationships with external companies that are more hierarchical in nature?

Source: Based on A. Deutschman, "The Fabric of Creativity," *Fast Company,* December 2004, pp. 54–62.

Endnotes

1. D. Kiley, "The New Heat on Ford," *BusinessWeek,* June 4, 2007, pp. 32–38; and J. W. Peters, "Many Workers, Few Shifts," *New York Times,* January 24, 2006, pp. C1, C6.
2. See, for instance, R. L. Daft, *Organization Theory and Design,* 8th ed. (Cincinnati, OH: South-Western Publishing, 2004).
3. C. Hymowitz, "Managers Suddenly Have to Answer to a Crowd of Bosses," *Wall Street Journal,* August 12, 2003, p. B1.
4. See, for instance, L. Urwick, *The Elements of Administration* (New York: Harper & Row, 1944), pp. 52–53; and J. H. Gittell, "Supervisory Span, Relational Coordination, and Flight Departure Performance: A Reassessment of Postbureaucracy Theory," *Organization Science,* July–August 2001, pp. 468–483.
5. J. Child and R. G. McGrath, "Organizations Unfettered: Organizational Form in an Information-Intensive Economy," *Academy of Management Journal,* December 2001, pp. 1135–1148.
6. H. Mintzberg, *Structure in Fives: Designing Effective Organizations* (Upper Saddle River, NJ: Prentice Hall, 1983), p. 157.
7. W. M. Bulkeley, "Back from the Brink," *Wall Street Journal,* April 24, 2006, pp. B1, B3.
8. L. R. Burns and D. R. Wholey, "Adoption and Abandonment of Matrix Management Programs: Effects of Organizational

Characteristics and Interorganizational Networks," *Academy of Management Journal,* February 1993, pp. 106–138.
9. See, for instance, S. M. Davis and P. R. Lawrence, "Problems of Matrix Organization," *Harvard Business Review,* May–June 1978, pp. 131–142; and T. Sy and S. Cote, "Emotional Intelligence: A Key Ability to Succeed in the Matrix Organization," *Journal of Management Development* 23, no. 5 (2004), pp. 437–455.
10. See, for instance, R. E. Miles and C. C. Snow, "The New Network Firm: A Spherical Structure Built on Human Investment Philosophy," *Organizational Dynamics,* Spring 1995, pp. 5–18; D. Pescovitz, "The Company Where Everybody's a Temp," *New York Times Magazine,* June 11, 2000, pp. 94–96; W. F. Cascio, "Managing a Virtual Workplace," *Academy of Management Executive,* August 2000, pp. 81–90; B. Hedberg, G. Dahlgren, J. Hansson, and N. Olve, *Virtual Organizations and Beyond* (New York: Wiley, 2001); J. Gertner, "Newman's Own: Two Friends and a Canoe Paddle," *New York Times,* November 16, 2003, p. 4BU; and Y. Shin, "A Person-Environment Fit Model for Virtual Organizations," *Journal of Management,* October 2004, pp. 725–743.
11. J. Bates, "Making Movies and Moving On," *Los Angeles Times,* January 19, 1998, p. A1.
12. "GE: Just Your Average Everyday $60 Billion Family Grocery Store," *IndustryWeek,* May 2, 1994, pp. 13–18.

13. H. C. Lucas Jr., *The T-Form Organization: Using Technology to Design Organizations for the 21st Century* (San Francisco: Jossey-Bass, 1996).

14. This section is based on D. D. Davis, "Form, Function and Strategy in Boundaryless Organizations," in A. Howard (ed.), *The Changing Nature of Work* (San Francisco: Jossey-Bass, 1995), pp. 112–138; P. Roberts, "We Are One Company, No Matter Where We Are. Time and Space Are Irrelevant," *Fast Company*, April–May 1998, pp. 122–128; R. L. Cross, A. Yan, and M. R. Louis, "Boundary Activities in 'Boundaryless' Organizations: A Case Study of a Transformation to a Team-Based Structure," *Human Relations*, June 2000, pp. 841–868; and R. Ashkenas, D. Ulrich, T. Jick, and S. Kerr, *The Boundaryless Organization: Breaking the Chains of Organizational Structure*, revised and updated (San Francisco: Jossey-Bass, 2002).

15. T. Burns and G. M. Stalker, *The Management of Innovation* (London: Tavistock, 1961); and J. A. Courtright, G. T. Fairhurst, and L. E. Rogers, "Interaction Patterns in Organic and Mechanistic Systems," *Academy of Management Journal*, December 1989, pp. 773–802.

16. This analysis is referred to as a contingency approach to organization design. See, for instance, J. M. Pennings, "Structural Contingency Theory: A Reappraisal," in B. M. Staw and L. L. Cummings (eds.), *Research in Organizational Behavior*, vol. 14 (Greenwich, CT: JAI Press, 1992), pp. 267–309; J. R. Hollenbeck, H. Moon, A. P. J. Ellis, B. J. West, D. R. Ilgen, L. Sheppard, C. O. L. H. Porter, and J. A. Wagner III, "Structural Contingency Theory and Individual Differences: Examination of External and Internal Person-Team Fit," *Journal of Applied Psychology*, June 2002, pp. 599–606; and H. Moon, J. R. Hollenbeck, S. E. Humphrey, D. R. Ilgen, B. West, A. P. J. Ellis, and C. O. L. H. Porter, "Asymmetric Adaptability: Dynamic Team Structures as One-Way Streets," *Academy of Management Journal*, October 2004, pp. 681–695.

17. The strategy–structure thesis was originally proposed in A. D. Chandler, Jr., *Strategy and Structure: Chapters in the History of the Industrial Enterprise* (Cambridge, MA: MIT Press, 1962). For an updated analysis, see T. L. Amburgey and T. Dacin, "As the Left Foot Follows the Right? The Dynamics of Strategic and Structural Change," *Academy of Management Journal*, December 1994, pp. 1427–1452.

18. See R. E. Miles and C. C. Snow, *Organizational Strategy, Structure, and Process* (New York: McGraw-Hill, 1978); D. Miller, "The Structural and Environmental Correlates of Business Strategy," *Strategic Management Journal*, January–February 1987, pp. 55–76; D. C. Galunic and K. M. Eisenhardt, "Renewing the Strategy–Structure–Performance Paradigm," in B. M. Staw and L. L. Cummings (eds.), *Research in Organizational Behavior*, vol. 16 (Greenwich, CT: JAI Press, 1994), pp. 215–255; and I. C. Harris and T. W. Ruefli, "The Strategy/Structure Debate: An Examination of the Performance Implications," *Journal of Management Studies*, June 2000, pp. 587–603.

19. See, for instance, P. M. Blau and R. A. Schoenherr, *The Structure of Organizations* (New York: Basic Books, 1971); D. S. Pugh, "The Aston Program of Research: Retrospect and Prospect," in A. H. Van de Ven and W. F. Joyce (eds.), *Perspectives on Organization Design and Behavior* (New York: Wiley, 1981), pp. 135–166; R. Z. Gooding and J. A. Wagner III, "A Meta-Analytic Review of the Relationship Between Size and Performance: The Productivity and Efficiency of Organizations and Their Subunits," *Administrative Science Quarterly*, December 1985, pp. 462–481; and A. C. Bluedorn, "Pilgrim's Progress: Trends and Convergence in Research on Organizational Size and Environments," *Journal of Management*, Summer 1993, pp. 163–192.

20. See J. Woodward, *Industrial Organization: Theory and Practice* (London: Oxford University Press, 1965); C. Perrow, "A Framework for the Comparative Analysis of Organizations," *American Sociological Review*, April 1967, pp. 194–208; J. D. Thompson, *Organizations in Action* (New York: McGraw-Hill, 1967); J. Hage and M. Aiken, "Routine Technology, Social Structure, and Organizational Goals," *Administrative Science Quarterly*, September 1969, pp. 366–377; C. C. Miller, W. H. Glick, Y. Wang, and G. P. Huber, "Understanding Technology-Structure Relationships: Theory Development and Meta-analytic Theory Testing," *Academy of Management Journal*, June 1991, pp. 370–399; and K. H. Roberts and M. Grabowski, "Organizations, Technology, and Structuring," in S. R. Clegg, C. Hardy, and W. R. Nord (eds.), *Managing Organizations: Current Issues* (Thousand Oaks, CA: Sage, 1999), pp. 159–171.

21. See F. E. Emery and E. Trist, "The Causal Texture of Organizational Environments," *Human Relations*, February 1965, pp. 21–32; P. Lawrence and J.W. Lorsch, *Organization and Environment: Managing Differentiation and Integration* (Boston: Harvard Business School, Division of Research, 1967); M. Yasai-Ardekani, "Structural Adaptations to Environments," *Academy of Management Review*, January 1986, pp. 9–21; Bluedorn, "Pilgrim's Progress"; and M. Arndt, and B. Bigelow, "Presenting Structural Innovation in an Institutional Environment: Hospitals' Use of Impression Management," *Administrative Science Quarterly*, September 2000, pp. 494–522.

22. G. G. Dess and D. W. Beard, "Dimensions of Organizational Task Environments," *Administrative Science Quarterly*, March 1984, pp. 52–73; E. A. Gerloff, N. K. Muir, and W. D. Bodensteiner, "Three Components of Perceived Environmental Uncertainty: An Exploratory Analysis of the Effects of Aggregation," *Journal of Management*, December 1991, pp. 749–768; and O. Shenkar, N. Aranya, and T. Almor, "Construct Dimensions in the Contingency Model: An Analysis Comparing Metric and Non-metric Multivariate Instruments," *Human Relations*, May 1995, pp. 559–580.

23. J. B. Quinn, P. Anderson, and S. Finkelstein, "Leveraging intellect," *Academy of Management Executive*, November 2005, pp. 78–94.

24. See, for instance, L. W. Porter and E. E. Lawler III, "Properties of Organization Structure in Relation to Job Attitudes and Job Behavior," *Psychological Bulletin*, July 1965, pp. 23–51; L. R. James and A. P. Jones, "Organization Structure: A Review of Structural Dimensions and Their Conceptual Relationships with Individual Attitudes and Behavior," *Organizational Behavior and Human Performance*, June 1976, pp. 74–113; D. R. Dalton, W. D. Todor, M. J. Spendolini, G. J. Fielding, and L. W. Porter, "Organization Structure and Performance: A Critical Review," *Academy of Management Review*, January 1980, pp. 49–64; and D. B. Turban and T. L. Keon, "Organizational Attractiveness: An Interactionist Perspective," *Journal of Applied Psychology*, April 1994, pp. 184–193.

25. See, for instance, B. Schneider, H. W. Goldstein, and D. B. Smith, "The ASA Framework: An Update," *Personnel Psychology* 48, no. 4 (1995), pp. 747–773.

26. P. Dvorak, "Making U.S. Management Ideas Work Elsewhere," *Wall Street Journal*, May 22, 2006, p. B3.

27. See, for example, P. R. Harris and R. T. Moran, *Managing Cultural Differences*, 5th ed. (Houston: Gulf Publishing, 1999).

28. "In Focus: Lou Gerstner," *CNN World Business*, July 2, 2004, www. cnn. com.

29. W. F. Cascio, "Strategies for Responsible Restructuring," *Academy of Management Executive* 19, no. 4 (2005), pp. 39–50.

Organizational Culture

When I hear the word culture,
I reach for my Browning.

—Hanns Johst

LEARNING OBJECTIVES

After studying this chapter, you should be able to:

1 Relate institutionalization culture to organizational culture.

2 Define *organizational culture* and describe its common characteristics.

3 Compare the functional and dysfunctional effects of organizational culture on people and the organization.

4 Explain the factors that create and sustain an organization's culture.

5 Show how culture is transmitted to employees.

6 Demonstrate how an ethical culture can be created.

7 Describe a positive organizational culture.

8 Identify characteristics of a spiritual culture.

9 Show how national culture may affect the way organizational culture is transported to a different country.

S ilicon Valley has established an outpost, and it's not on the "other" coast, it's on another continent—London. The move has been going on for several years, but lately it's picked up speed. In 2006 alone, some 30 California companies opened offices in London. One of every three U.S. companies in London is now from California, including Silicon Valley fixtures Apple, Google, Sun Microsystems, Amgen, and Cisco. If California were a country, it would rank *second* (behind the rest of the United States and

California Moves to London

ahead of Canada) as place of origin for foreign countries in London.

You don't need to know much about Silicon Valley or London to see a culture clash in the making here. London is famous (or notorious, depending on your point of view) for its formality—business suits, formal lunches, conservative offices, and polite, proper communication. California is renowned for just the opposite culture. So what gives? Which culture wins?

So far, it seems, California. At Google's London offices, the California touches include foosball tables, bean bag chairs, giant games, and catered sandwiches (rather than a three-course meal). The dress code is business casual, even though most of the employees at Google's

London headquarters are British. "You can be serious without a suit," says one Google Londoner who has grown accustomed to the California style.

When another Londoner, Nigel Thornton, was hired by Amgen, he was surprised by the number of e-mails soliciting his opinion and by the different customs. "The funny thing about Americans in our office is that they are always eating or drinking something," said Thornton. "Brits are still used to just breakfast, lunch, and dinner."

When British visit the offices of DVS Shoe Co. (based in Torrance, California), they are often surprised by the informal dress and low-key atmosphere. "They'll see us dressed casual," says Erik Ecklund, a DVS manager, "and say, 'Man, you guys should have told us.' "[1] ■

*a*s the chapter-opening example shows, organizational culture is often so strong that it transcends national boundaries. A strong culture provides stability to an organization. But for some organizations, it can also be a major barrier to change. In this chapter, we show that every organization has a culture and, depending on its strength, it can have a significant influence on the attitudes and behaviors of organization members. Before doing so, let's figure out what kind of organizational culture you prefer. Take the self-assessment to find out.

Self Assessment Library

WHAT'S THE RIGHT ORGANIZATIONAL CULTURE FOR ME?

In the Self-Assessment Library (available on CD and online), take assessment III.B.1 (What's the Right Organizational Culture for Me?) and answer the following questions.

1. *Judging from your results, do you fit better in a more formal and structured culture or in a more informal and unstructured culture?*
2. *Did your results surprise you? Why do you think you scored as you did?*
3. *How might your results affect your career path?*

Institutionalization: A Forerunner of Culture

1 *Relate institutionalization culture to organizational culture.*

The idea of viewing organizations as cultures—where there is a system of shared meaning among members—is a relatively recent phenomenon. Until the mid-1980s, organizations were, for the most part, simply thought of as rational means by which to coordinate and control a group of people. They had vertical levels, departments, authority relationships, and so forth. But organizations are more. They have personalities, too, just like individuals. They can be rigid or flexible, unfriendly or supportive, innovative or conservative. GM offices and people *are* different from the offices and people at Wachovia. Organizational theorists now acknowledge this by recognizing the important role that culture plays in the lives of organization members. Interestingly, though, the origin of culture as an independent variable affecting an employee's attitudes and behavior can be traced back more than 50 years ago to the notion of **institutionalization**.[2]

When an organization becomes institutionalized, it takes on a life of its own, apart from its founders or any of its members. Ross Perot created Electronic Data Systems (EDS) in the early 1960s, but he left in 1987 to found a new company, Perot Systems. EDS has continued to thrive despite the departure of its founder. Sony, Gillette, McDonald's, and Disney are examples of organizations that have existed beyond the life of their founder or any one member.

When an organization becomes institutionalized, it becomes valued for itself, not merely for the goods or services it produces. It acquires immortality. If its original goals are no longer relevant, it doesn't go out of business. Rather, it redefines itself. A classic example is the March of Dimes. It was originally created to fund the battle against polio. When polio was essentially eradicated in the 1950s, the March of Dimes didn't close down. It merely redefined its objectives as funding research for reducing birth defects and lowering infant mortality.

Institutionalization operates to produce common understandings among members about what is appropriate and, fundamentally, meaningful behavior.[3] So when an organization takes on institutional permanence, acceptable modes of behavior become largely self-evident to its members. As we'll see, this is essentially the same thing that organizational culture does. So an understanding of what makes up an organization's culture and how it is created, sustained, and learned will enhance our ability to explain and predict the behavior of people at work.

What Is Organizational Culture?

A number of years back, an executive was asked what he thought *organizational culture* meant. He gave essentially the same answer that a Supreme Court justice once gave in attempting to define pornography: "I can't define it, but I know it when I see it." This executive's approach to defining organizational culture isn't acceptable for our purposes. We need a basic definition to provide a point of departure for our quest to better understand the phenomenon. In this section, we propose a specific definition and review several peripheral issues that revolve around this definition.

> **2** *Define* organizational culture *and describe its common characteristics.*

A Definition of *Organizational Culture*

There seems to be wide agreement that **organizational culture** refers to a system of shared meaning held by members that distinguishes the organization from other organizations.[4] This system of shared meaning is, on closer examination, a set of key characteristics that the organization values. The research suggests that there are seven primary characteristics that, in aggregate, capture the essence of an organization's culture:[5]

1. *Innovation and risk taking.* The degree to which employees are encouraged to be innovative and take risks.
2. *Attention to detail.* The degree to which employees are expected to exhibit precision, analysis, and attention to detail.

institutionalization *A condition that occurs when an organization takes on a life of its own, apart from any of its members, and acquires immortality.*

organizational culture *A system of shared meaning held by members that distinguishes the organization from other organizations.*

Southwest Airlines has a people-oriented culture based on company values of concern, respect, and caring for employees and customers. Southwest empowers its employees to make decisions from the heart that will provide positive benefits to customers. In hiring new employees, Southwest looks for "a servant's heart" in job candidates. The source of Southwest's caring and fun-loving culture is Herb Kelleher, co-founder and chairman, shown here with employees during a ceremony celebrating the inauguration of Southwest's service at the Philadelphia International Airport.

3. *Outcome orientation.*   The degree to which management focuses on results or outcomes rather than on the techniques and processes used to achieve those outcomes.

4. *People orientation.*   The degree to which management decisions take into consideration the effect of outcomes on people within the organization.

5. *Team orientation.*   The degree to which work activities are organized around teams rather than individuals.

6. *Aggressiveness.*   The degree to which people are aggressive and competitive rather than easygoing.

7. *Stability.*   The degree to which organizational activities emphasize maintaining the status quo in contrast to growth.

Each of these characteristics exists on a continuum from low to high. Appraising the organization on these seven characteristics, then, gives a composite picture of the organization's culture. This picture becomes the basis for feelings of shared understanding that members have about the organization, how things are done in it, and the way members are supposed to behave. Exhibit 17-1 demonstrates how these characteristics can be mixed to create highly diverse organizations.

Culture Is a Descriptive Term

Organizational culture is concerned with how employees perceive the characteristics of an organization's culture, not with whether they like them. That is, it's a descriptive term. This is important because it differentiates this concept from job satisfaction.

Research on organizational culture has sought to measure how employees see their organization: Does it encourage teamwork? Does it reward innovation? Does it stifle initiative? In contrast, job satisfaction seeks to measure affective responses to the work environment. It's concerned with how employees feel about the organization's expectations, reward practices, and the like. Although the two terms undoubtedly have overlapping characteristics, keep in mind that the term *organizational culture* is descriptive, whereas *job satisfaction* is evaluative.

Exhibit **17-1**	Contrasting Organizational Cultures

Organization A

This organization is a manufacturing firm. Managers are expected to fully document all decisions, and "good managers" are those who can provide detailed data to support their recommendations. Creative decisions that incur significant change or risk are not encouraged. Because managers of failed projects are openly criticized and penalized, managers try not to implement ideas that deviate much from the status quo. One lower-level manager quoted an often-used phrase in the company: "If it ain't broke, don't fix it."

There are extensive rules and regulations in this firm that employees are required to follow. Managers supervise employees closely to ensure there are no deviations. Management is concerned with high productivity, regardless of the impact on employee morale or turnover.

Work activities are designed around individuals. There are distinct departments and lines of authority, and employees are expected to minimize formal contact with other employees outside their functional area or line of command. Performance evaluations and rewards emphasize individual effort, although seniority tends to be the primary factor in the determination of pay raises and promotions.

Organization B

This organization is also a manufacturing firm. Here, however, management encourages and rewards risk taking and change. Decisions based on intuition are valued as much as those that are well rationalized. Management prides itself on its history of experimenting with new technologies and its success in regularly introducing innovative products. Managers or employees who have a good idea are encouraged to "run with it." And failures are treated as "learning experiences." The company prides itself on being market-driven and rapidly responsive to the changing needs of its customers.

There are few rules and regulations for employees to follow, and supervision is loose because management believes that its employees are hardworking and trustworthy. Management is concerned with high productivity, but believes that this comes through treating its people right. The company is proud of its reputation as being a good place to work.

Job activities are designed around work teams, and team members are encouraged to interact with people across functions and authority levels. Employees talk positively about the competition between teams. Individuals and teams have goals, and bonuses are based on achievement of these outcomes. Employees are given considerable autonomy in choosing the means by which the goals are attained.

Do Organizations Have Uniform Cultures?

Organizational culture represents a common perception held by the organization's members. This was made explicit when we defined culture as a system of *shared* meaning. We should expect, therefore, that individuals with different backgrounds or at different levels in the organization will tend to describe the organization's culture in similar terms.[6]

Acknowledgment that organizational culture has common properties does not mean, however, that there cannot be subcultures within any given culture. Most large organizations have a dominant culture and numerous sets of subcultures.[7] A **dominant culture** expresses the core values that are shared by a majority of the organization's members. When we talk about an organization's culture, we are referring to its dominant culture. It is this macro view of culture that gives an organization its distinct personality.[8] **Subcultures** tend to develop

dominant culture   *A culture that expresses the core values that are shared by a majority of the organization's members.*

subcultures   *Minicultures within an organization, typically defined by department designations and geographical separation.*

in large organizations to reflect common problems, situations, or experiences that members face. These subcultures are likely to be defined by department designations and geographical separation. The purchasing department, for example, can have a subculture that is uniquely shared by members of that department. It will include the **core values** of the dominant culture plus additional values unique to members of the purchasing department. Similarly, an office or unit of the organization that is physically separated from the organization's main operations may take on a different personality. Again, the core values are essentially retained, but they are modified to reflect the separated unit's distinct situation.

If organizations had no dominant culture and were composed only of numerous subcultures, the value of organizational culture as an independent variable would be significantly lessened because there would be no uniform interpretation of what represented appropriate and inappropriate behavior. It is the "shared meaning" aspect of culture that makes it such a potent device for guiding and shaping behavior. That's what allows us to say, for example, that Microsoft's culture values aggressiveness and risk taking[9] and then to use that information to better understand the behavior of Microsoft executives and employees. But we cannot ignore the reality that many organizations also have subcultures that can influence the behavior of members.

Strong Versus Weak Cultures

It has become increasingly popular to differentiate between strong and weak cultures.[10] The argument here is that strong cultures have a greater impact on employee behavior and are more directly related to reduced turnover.

In a **strong culture**, the organization's core values are both intensely held and widely shared.[11] The more members who accept the core values and the greater their commitment to those values is, the stronger the culture is. Consistent with this definition, a strong culture will have a great influence on the behavior of its members because the high degree of sharedness and intensity creates an internal climate of high behavioral control. For example, Seattle-based Nordstrom has developed one of the strongest service cultures in the retailing industry. Nordstrom employees know in no uncertain terms what is expected of them, and these expectations go a long way in shaping their behavior.

One specific result of a strong culture should be lower employee turnover. A strong culture demonstrates high agreement among members about what the organization stands for. Such unanimity of purpose builds cohesiveness, loyalty, and organizational commitment. These qualities, in turn, lessen employees' propensity to leave the organization.[12]

Culture Versus Formalization

A strong organizational culture increases behavioral consistency. In this sense, we should recognize that a strong culture can act as a substitute for formalization.[13]

In the previous chapter, we discussed how formalization's rules and regulations act to regulate employee behavior. High formalization in an organization creates predictability, orderliness, and consistency. Our point here is that a strong culture achieves the same end without the need for written documentation. Therefore, we should view formalization and culture as two different roads to a common destination. The stronger an organization's culture, the less management need be concerned with developing formal rules and regulations to guide employee behavior. Those guides will be internalized in employees when they accept the organization's culture.

International OB

A Good Organizational Culture Knows No Boundaries

In a study of 230 organizations from different industries around the world, and from regions including North America, Asia, Europe, the Middle East, and Africa, having a strong and positive organizational culture was associated with increased organizational effectiveness.

The study, published in the journal *Organizational Dynamics*, found that the strong and positive aspects of organizational culture most criti-

cal to success across regions generally included

- Empowering employees
- Having a team orientation
- Having a clear strategic direction and intent
- Possessing a strong and recognizable vision

Though there were similarities when comparing regions in terms of organizational culture and effectiveness, there were some differences when researchers compared individual countries. An organizational culture that stresses empowerment, for example, appears to be more important for performance in countries such as the United States and Brazil and less important in countries such as Japan because of the

former two countries' focus on the individual. Also, a focus on creating change within the organization appears to be a strong predictor of organizational effectiveness in South Africa but a relatively weak predictor in Jamaica, but it currently is unclear as to why this is the case.

Overall, the study confirms that having a strong, productive organizational culture is associated with increased sales growth, profitability, employee satisfaction, and overall organizational performance regardless of where the organization is physically located.

Source: Based on D. R. Denison, S. Haaland, and P. Goelzer, "Corporate Culture and Organizational Effectiveness: Is Asia Different from the Rest of the World?" *Organizational Dynamics*, February 2004, pp. 98–109.

What Do Cultures Do?

3 *Compare the functional and dysfunctional effects of organizational culture on people and the organization.*

We've alluded to the impact of organizational culture on behavior. We've also explicitly argued that a strong culture should be associated with reduced turnover. In this section, we will more carefully review the functions that culture performs and assess whether culture can be a liability for an organization.

Culture's Functions

Culture performs a number of functions within an organization. First, it has a boundary-defining role; that is, it creates distinctions between one organization and others. Second, it conveys a sense of identity for organization members. Third, culture facilitates the generation of commitment to something larger than one's individual self-interest. Fourth, it enhances the stability of the social system. Culture is the social glue that helps hold the organization together by providing appropriate standards for what employees should say and do. Finally, culture serves as a sense-making and control mechanism that guides and shapes the attitudes and behavior of employees. It is this last function that is of

core values *The primary or dominant values that are accepted throughout the organization.*

strong culture *A culture in which the core values are intensely held and widely shared.*

Organizational culture guides and shapes the attitudes of employees at New Zealand Air. One of the airline's guiding principles is to champion and promote New Zealand and its national heritage both within the country and overseas. In this photo, a cabin crew member dressed in traditional Maori clothing and a pilot touch noses to represent the sharing of a single breath following a ceremony for the airline's purchase of a Boeing airplane in Everett, Washington. This expression of representing their country with pride creates a strong bond among employees.

particular interest to us.[14] As the following quote makes clear, culture defines the rules of the game:

> Culture by definition is elusive, intangible, implicit, and taken for granted. But every organization develops a core set of assumptions, understandings, and implicit rules that govern day-to-day behavior in the workplace.... Until newcomers learn the rules, they are not accepted as full-fledged members of the organization. Transgressions of the rules on the part of high-level executives or front-line employees result in universal disapproval and powerful penalties. Conformity to the rules becomes the primary basis for reward and upward mobility.[15]

The role of culture in influencing employee behavior appears to be increasingly important in today's workplace.[16] As organizations have widened spans of control, flattened structures, introduced teams, reduced formalization, and empowered employees, the *shared meaning* provided by a strong culture ensures that everyone is pointed in the same direction.

As we show later in this chapter, who receives a job offer to join the organization, who is appraised as a high performer, and who gets a promotion are strongly influenced by the individual–organization "fit"—that is, whether the applicant's or employee's attitudes and behavior are compatible with the culture. It's not a coincidence that employees at Disney theme parks appear to be almost universally attractive, clean, and wholesome looking, with bright smiles. That's the image Disney seeks. The company selects employees who will maintain that image. And once on the job, a strong culture, supported by formal rules and regulations, ensures that Disney theme-park employees will act in a relatively uniform and predictable way.

Culture as a Liability

We are treating culture in a nonjudgmental manner. We haven't said that it's good or bad, only that it exists. Many of its functions, as outlined, are valuable for both the organization and the employee. Culture enhances organizational commitment and increases the consistency of employee behavior. These are clearly benefits to an organization. From an employee's standpoint, culture is valuable because it reduces ambiguity. It tells employees how things are done and what's important. But we shouldn't ignore the potentially dysfunctional aspects of culture, especially a strong one, on an organization's effectiveness.

Barriers to Change   Culture is a liability when the shared values are not in agreement with those that will further the organization's effectiveness. This is most likely to occur when an organization's environment is dynamic.[17] When an environment is undergoing rapid change, an organization's entrenched culture may no longer be appropriate. So consistency of behavior is an asset to an organization when it faces a stable environment. It may, however, burden the organization and make it difficult to respond to changes in the environment. This helps to explain the challenges that executives at organizations like Mitsubishi, Eastman Kodak, Boeing, and the U.S. Federal Bureau of Investigation have had in recent years in adapting to upheavals in their environment.[18] These organizations have strong cultures that worked well for them in the past. But these strong cultures become barriers to change when "business as usual" is no longer effective.

Barriers to Diversity   Hiring new employees who, because of race, age, gender, disability, or other differences, are not like the majority of the organization's members creates a paradox.[19] Management wants new employees to accept the organization's core cultural values. Otherwise, these employees are unlikely to fit in or be accepted. But at the same time, management wants to openly acknowledge and demonstrate support for the differences that these employees bring to the workplace.

Strong cultures put considerable pressure on employees to conform. They limit the range of values and styles that are acceptable. In some instances, such as the widely publicized Texaco case (which was settled on behalf of 1,400 employees for $176 million) in which senior managers made disparaging remarks about minorities, a strong culture that condones prejudice can even undermine formal corporate diversity policies.[20] Organizations seek out and hire diverse individuals because of the alternative strengths these people bring to the workplace. Yet these diverse behaviors and strengths are likely to diminish in strong cultures as people attempt to fit in. Strong cultures, therefore, can be liabilities when they effectively eliminate the unique strengths that people of different backgrounds bring to the organization. Moreover, strong cultures can also be liabilities when they support institutional bias or become insensitive to people who are different.

Barriers to Acquisitions and Mergers   Historically, the key factors that management looked at in making acquisition or merger decisions were related to financial advantages or product synergy. In recent years, cultural compatibility has become the primary concern.[21] While a favorable financial statement or product line may be the initial attraction of an acquisition candidate, whether the acquisition actually works seems to have more to do with how well the two organizations' cultures match up.

Many acquisitions fail shortly after their consummation. A survey by consulting firm A.T. Kearney revealed that 58 percent of mergers failed to reach the value goals set by top managers.[22] The primary cause of failure is conflicting organizational cultures. As one expert commented, "Mergers have an unusually high failure rate, and it's always because of people issues." For instance, the 2001 $183 billion merger between America Online (AOL) and Time Warner

MYTH OR SCIENCE?   *"People Socialize Themselves"*

*t*his statement is true to a significant degree. Although we generally think of socialization as the process in which a person is shaped by his environment—and indeed that is the major focus of socialization research—more evidence is accumulating that many people socialize themselves, or at least substantially mold their socialization experiences.

Research has shown that people with a proactive personality are much better at learning the ropes than are newcomers. (As we noted in Chapter 4, people with a proactive personality identify opportunities, show initiative, and take action.) That's because they are more likely to ask questions, seek out help, and solicit feedback—in short, they learn more because they seek out more information and feedback.

Research indicates that individuals with a proactive personality are also better at networking when they join an organization, and achieve a closer fit with the culture of their organizations—in short, they build their own "social capital." As a result of being more effectively socialized into the organization, proactive people tend to like their jobs more, perform them better, and show less propensity to quit. Proactive people, it seems, do a lot to socialize *themselves* into the culture of an organization.

None of this is meant to deny that socialization matters. The point is that people are not passive actors in being socialized. It may well be that how well someone is socialized into a new culture depends more on her personality than anything else.[23] ■

was the largest in corporate history. The merger has been a disaster—only 2 years later, the stock had fallen an astounding 90 percent. Culture clash is commonly argued to be one of the causes of AOL Time Warner's problems. As one expert noted, "In some ways the merger of AOL and Time Warner was like the marriage of a teenager to a middle-aged banker. The cultures were vastly different. There were open collars and jeans at AOL. Time Warner was more buttoned-down."[24]

Creating and Sustaining Culture

4 Explain the factors that create and sustain an organization's culture.

An organization's culture doesn't pop out of thin air. Once established, it rarely fades away. What forces influence the creation of a culture? What reinforces and sustains these forces once they're in place? We answer both of these questions in this section.

How a Culture Begins

An organization's current customs, traditions, and general way of doing things are largely due to what it has done before and the degree of success it has had with those endeavors. This leads us to the ultimate source of an organization's culture: its founders.[25]

The founders of an organization traditionally have a major impact on that organization's early culture. They have a vision of what the organization should be. They are unconstrained by previous customs or ideologies. The small size that typically characterizes new organizations further facilitates the founders' imposition of their vision on all organizational members. Culture creation occurs in three ways.[26] First, founders hire and keep only employees who think and feel the same way they do. Second, they indoctrinate and socialize these employees to their way of thinking and feeling. And finally, the founders' own behavior acts as a role model that encourages employees to identify with them

The source of Cranium's culture is co-founder and CEO Richard Tait, shown here at a toy fair demonstrating the toys and games his company makes. Tait created a culture of fun and collaboration at Cranium so employees can work in an environment that stimulates creativity and innovation in developing new products. At Cranium, employees choose their own titles. Tait chose Grand Poo Bah, and the chief financial officer selected Professor Profit. The office walls at Cranium are painted in bright primary colors, and music plays everywhere.

and thereby internalize their beliefs, values, and assumptions. When the organization succeeds, the founders' vision becomes seen as a primary determinant of that success. At this point, the founders' entire personality becomes embedded in the culture of the organization.

The culture at Hyundai, the giant Korean conglomerate, is largely a reflection of its founder Chung Ju Yung. Hyundai's fierce, competitive style and its disciplined, authoritarian nature are the same characteristics often used to describe Chung. Other contemporary examples of founders who have had an immeasurable impact on their organization's culture would include Bill Gates at Microsoft, Ingvar Kamprad at IKEA, Herb Kelleher at Southwest Airlines, Fred Smith at FedEx, and Richard Branson at the Virgin Group.

Keeping a Culture Alive

Once a culture is in place, there are practices within the organization that act to maintain it by giving employees a set of similar experiences.[27] For example, many of the human resource practices we discuss in the next chapter reinforce the organization's culture. The selection process, performance evaluation criteria, training and development activities, and promotion procedures ensure that those hired fit in with the culture, reward those who support it, and penalize (and even expel) those who challenge it. Three forces play a particularly important part in sustaining a culture: selection practices, the actions of top management, and socialization methods. Let's take a closer look at each.

Selection   The explicit goal of the selection process is to identify and hire individuals who have the knowledge, skills, and abilities to perform the jobs within the organization successfully. Typically, more than one candidate will be identified who meets any given job's requirements. When that point is reached, it would be naive to ignore the fact that the final decision as to who is hired will be significantly influenced by the decision-maker's judgment of how well the candidates will fit into the organization. This attempt to ensure a proper match, whether purposely or inadvertently, results in the hiring of people who have values essentially consistent with those of the organization, or at least a good portion of those values.[28]

In addition, the selection process provides information to applicants about the organization. Candidates learn about the organization, and, if they perceive a conflict between their values and those of the organization, they can self-select themselves out of the applicant pool. Selection, therefore, becomes a two-way street, allowing employer or applicant to abrogate a marriage if there appears to be a mismatch. In this way, the selection process sustains an organization's culture by selecting out those individuals who might attack or undermine its core values.

For instance, W. L. Gore & Associates, the maker of Gore-Tex fabric used in outerwear, prides itself on its democratic culture and teamwork. There are no job titles at Gore, nor bosses nor chains of command. All work is done in teams. In Gore's selection process, teams of employees put job applicants through extensive interviews to ensure that candidates who can't deal with the level of uncertainty, flexibility, and teamwork that employees have to deal with in Gore plants are selected out.[29]

Top Management   The actions of top management also have a major impact on the organization's culture.[30] Through what they say and how they behave, senior executives establish norms that filter down through the organization as to whether risk taking is desirable; how much freedom managers should give their employees; what is appropriate dress; what actions will pay off in terms of pay raises, promotions, and other rewards; and the like.

For example, Robert A. Keirlin has been called "the cheapest CEO in America."[31] Keirlin is chairman and CEO of Fastenal Co., the largest specialty retailer of nuts and bolts in the United States, with 6,500 employees. He takes a salary of only $60,000 a year. He owns only three suits, each of which he bought used. He clips grocery coupons, drives a Toyota, and stays in low-priced motels when he travels on business. Does Keirlin need to pinch pennies? No. The market value of his stock in Fastenal is worth about $300 million. But the man prefers a modest personal lifestyle. And he prefers the same for his company. Keirlin argues that his behavior should send a message to all his employees: We don't waste things in this company. Keirlin sees himself as a role model for frugality, and employees at Fastenal have learned to follow his example.

New employees at Broad Air Conditioning in Changsha, China, are indoctrinated in the company's military-style culture by going through a 10-day training session of boot camp, where they are divided into platoons and live in barracks. Boot camp prepares new hires for the military formality that prevails at Broad, where employees begin their work week standing in formation during a flag-raising ceremony of two company flags and the flag of China. All employees live in dorms on the company campus and receive free food and lodging. To motivate its workers, Broad has scattered throughout the campus 43 life-size bronze statues of inspirational leaders from Confucius to Jack Welch, the former CEO of General Electric.

Socialization   No matter how good a job the organization does in recruiting and selection, new employees are not fully indoctrinated in the organization's culture. Because they are unfamiliar with the organization's culture, new employees are potentially likely to disturb the beliefs and customs that are in place. The organization will, therefore, want to help new employees adapt to its culture. This adaptation process is called **socialization**.[32]

All Marines must go through boot camp, where they "prove" their commitment. Of course, at the same time, the Marine trainers are indoctrinating new recruits in the "Marine way." All new employees at Neumann Homes in Warrenville, Illinois, go through a 40-hour orientation program.[33] They're introduced to the company's values and culture through a variety of activities—including a customer service lunch, an interactive departmental roundtable fair, and presentations made by groups of new hires to the CEO regarding the company's core values. For new incoming employees in the upper ranks, companies often put considerably more time and effort into the socialization process. At Limited Brands, newly hired vice presidents and regional directors go through an intensive 1-month program, called "onboarding," designed to immerse these executives in the culture of Limited Brands.[34] During this month, they have no direct responsibilities for tasks associated with their new positions. Instead, they spend all their work time meeting with other senior leaders and mentors, working the floors of retail stores, evaluating employee and customer habits, investigating the competition, and studying Limited Brands' past and current operations.

As we discuss socialization, keep in mind that the most critical socialization stage is at the time of entry into the organization. This is when the organization seeks to mold the outsider into an employee "in good standing." Employees who fail to learn the essential or pivotal role behaviors risk being labeled "nonconformists" or "rebels," which often leads to expulsion. But the organization will be socializing every employee, though maybe not as explicitly, throughout his or her entire career in the organization. This further contributes to sustaining the culture.

Socialization can be conceptualized as a process made up of three stages: prearrival, encounter, and metamorphosis.[35] The first stage encompasses all the learning that occurs before a new member joins the organization. In the second stage, the new employee sees what the organization is really like and confronts the possibility that expectations and reality may diverge. In the third stage, the relatively long-lasting changes take place. The new employee masters the skills required for the job, successfully performs the new roles, and makes the adjustments to the work group's values and norms.[36] This three-stage process has an impact on the new employee's work productivity, commitment to the organization's objectives, and eventual decision to stay with the organization. Exhibit 17-2 depicts this process.

The **prearrival stage** explicitly recognizes that each individual arrives with a set of values, attitudes, and expectations. These cover both the work to be done and the organization. For instance, in many jobs, particularly professional work, new members will have undergone a considerable degree of prior socialization in training and in school. One major purpose of a business school, for example, is to socialize business students to the attitudes and behaviors that business firms want. If business executives believe that successful employees value the profit ethic, are loyal, will work hard, and desire to achieve, they can hire individuals out of business schools who have been premolded in this pattern.

socialization   *A process that adapts employees to the organization's culture.*

prearrival stage   *The period of learning in the socialization process that occurs before a new employee joins the organization.*

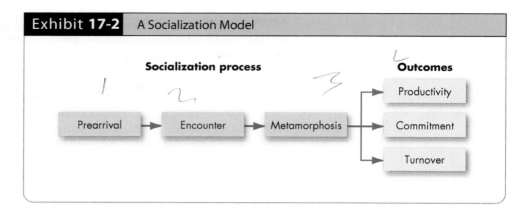

Exhibit **17-2**   A Socialization Model

Moreover, most people in business realize that no matter how well they think they can socialize newcomers, the most important predictor of newcomers' future behavior is their past behavior. Research shows that what people know before they join the organization, and how proactive their personality is, are critical predictors of how well they adjust to a new culture.[37]

One way to capitalize on the importance of prehire characteristics in socialization is to select employees with the "right stuff" and to use the selection process to inform prospective employees about the organization as a whole. In addition, as noted previously, the selection process also acts to ensure the inclusion of the "right type"—those who will fit in. "Indeed, the ability of the individual to present the appropriate face during the selection process determines his ability to move into the organization in the first place. Thus, success depends on the degree to which the aspiring member has correctly anticipated the expectations and desires of those in the organization in charge of selection."[38]

On entry into the organization, the new member enters the **encounter stage**. Here the individual confronts the possible dichotomy between expectations—about the job, the coworkers, the boss, and the organization in general—and reality. If expectations prove to have been more or less accurate, the encounter stage merely provides a reaffirmation of the perceptions gained earlier. However, this is often not the case. Where expectations and reality differ, the new employee must undergo socialization that will detach her from her previous assumptions and replace them with another set that the organization deems desirable. At the extreme, a new member may become totally disillusioned with the actualities of the job and resign. Proper selection should significantly reduce the probability of the latter occurrence. Also, an employee's network of friends and coworkers can play a critical role in helping them "learn the ropes." Newcomers are more committed to the organization when their friendship networks are large and diverse. So organizations can help newcomers socialize by encouraging friendship ties in organizations.[39]

Finally, the new member must work out any problems discovered during the encounter stage. This may mean going through changes—hence, we call this the **metamorphosis stage**. The options presented in Exhibit 17-3 are alternatives designed to bring about the desired metamorphosis. Note, for example, that the more management relies on socialization programs that are formal, collective, fixed, serial, and emphasize divestiture, the greater the likelihood that newcomers' differences and perspectives will be stripped away and replaced by standardized and predictable behaviors. Careful selection by management of newcomers' socialization experiences can—at the extreme—create conformists who maintain traditions and customs, or inventive and creative individualists who consider no organizational practice sacred.

We can say that metamorphosis and the entry socialization process is complete when new members have become comfortable with the organization and their job.

Exhibit **17-3**	Entry Socialization Options

Formal vs. Informal The more a new employee is segregated from the ongoing work setting and differentiated in some way to make explicit his or her newcomer's role, the more formal socialization is. Specific orientation and training programs are examples. Informal socialization puts the new employee directly into the job, with little or no special attention.

Individual vs. Collective New members can be socialized individually. This describes how it's done in many professional offices. They can also be grouped together and processed through an identical set of experiences, as in military boot camp.

Fixed vs. Variable This refers to the time schedule in which newcomers make the transition from outsider to insider. A fixed schedule establishes standardized stages of transition. This characterizes rotational training programs. It also includes probationary periods, such as the 8- to 10-year "associate" status used by accounting and law firms before deciding on whether or not a candidate is made a partner. Variable schedules give no advance notice of their transition timetable. Variable schedules describe the typical promotion system, in which one is not advanced to the next stage until one is "ready."

Serial vs. Random Serial socialization is characterized by the use of role models who train and encourage the newcomer. Apprenticeship and mentoring programs are examples. In random socialization, role models are deliberately withheld. New employees are left on their own to figure things out.

Investiture vs. Divestiture Investiture socialization assumes that the newcomer's qualities and qualifications are the necessary ingredients for job success, so these qualities and qualifications are confirmed and supported. Divestiture socialization tries to strip away certain characteristics of the recruit. Fraternity and sorority "pledges" go through divestiture socialization to shape them into the proper role.

They have internalized the norms of the organization and their work group, and understand and accept those norms. New members feel accepted by their peers as trusted and valued individuals. They are self-confident that they have the competence to complete the job successfully. They understand the system—not only their own tasks but the rules, procedures, and informally accepted practices as well. Finally, they know how they will be evaluated; that is, what criteria will be used to measure and appraise their work. They know what is expected of them and what constitutes a job "well done." As Exhibit 17-2 shows, successful metamorphosis should have a positive impact on new employees' productivity and their commitment to the organization and reduce their propensity to leave the organization.

Summary: How Cultures Form

Exhibit 17-4 summarizes how an organization's culture is established and sustained. The original culture is derived from the founder's philosophy. This, in turn, strongly influences the criteria used in hiring. The actions of the current top management set the general climate of what is acceptable behavior and what is not. How employees are to be socialized will depend both on the degree of success achieved in matching new employees' values to those of the organization's in the selection process and on top management's preference for socialization methods.

encounter stage   *The stage in the socialization process in which a new employee sees what the organization is really like and confronts the possibility that expectations and reality may diverge.*

metamorphosis stage   *The stage in the socialization process in which a new employee changes and adjusts to the job, work group, and organization.*

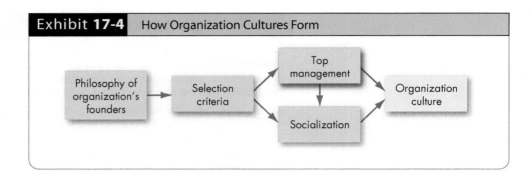

During the days when Henry Ford II was chairman of the Ford Motor Co., you

How Employees Learn Culture

5   *Show how culture is transmitted to employees.*

Culture is transmitted to employees in a number of forms, the most potent being stories, rituals, material symbols, and language.

Stories

During the days when Henry Ford II was chairman of the Ford Motor Co., you would have been hard pressed to find a manager who hadn't heard the story about Mr. Ford reminding his executives, when they got too arrogant, that "it's my name that's on the building." The message was clear: Henry Ford II ran the company.

Nike has a number of senior executives who spend much of their time serving as corporate storytellers. And the stories they tell are meant to convey what Nike is about.[40] When they tell the story of how co-founder (and Oregon track coach) Bill Bowerman went to his workshop and poured rubber into his wife's waffle iron to create a better running shoe, they're talking about Nike's spirit of innovation. When new hires hear tales of Oregon running star Steve Prefontaine's battles to make running a professional sport and to attain better-performance equipment, they learn of Nike's commitment to helping athletes.

Stories such as these circulate through many organizations. They typically contain a narrative of events about the organization's founders, rule breaking, rags-to-riches successes, reductions in the workforce, relocation of employees, reactions to past mistakes, and organizational coping.[41] These stories anchor the present in the past and provide explanations and legitimacy for current practices.

Rituals

Rituals are repetitive sequences of activities that express and reinforce the key values of the organization—what goals are most important, which people are important, and which people are expendable.[42] One of the better-known corporate rituals is Wal-Mart's company chant. Begun by the company's founder, Sam Walton, as a way to motivate and unite his workforce, "Gimme a W, gimme an A, gimme an L, gimme a squiggle, give me an M, A, R, T!" has become a company ritual that bonds Wal-Mart workers and reinforces Sam Walton's belief in the importance of his employees to the company's success. Similar corporate chants are used by IBM, Ericsson, Novell, Deutsche Bank, and PricewaterhouseCoopers.[43]

Material Symbols

The headquarters of Alcoa doesn't look like your typical head-office operation. There are few individual offices, even for senior executives. It is essentially made up of cubicles, common areas, and meeting rooms. This informal corporate

At Wal-Mart, culture is transmitted to employees through the daily ritual of the "Wal-Mart cheer." Shown here is the manager of a Wal-Mart store leading employees in the motivational chant that helps preserve a small-family spirit and work environment within the world's largest retailer.

headquarters conveys to employees that Alcoa values openness, equality, creativity, and flexibility. Some corporations provide their top executives with chauffeur-driven limousines and, when they travel by air, unlimited use of the corporate jet. Others may not get to ride in limousines or private jets, but they might still get a car and air transportation paid for by the company. Only the car is a Chevrolet (with no driver), and the jet seat is in the economy section of a commercial airliner.

The layout of corporate headquarters, the types of automobiles top executives are given, and the presence or absence of corporate aircraft are a few examples of material symbols. Others include the size of offices, the elegance of furnishings, executive perks, and attire.[44] These material symbols convey to employees who is important, the degree of egalitarianism desired by top management, and the kinds of behavior (for example, risk taking, conservative, authoritarian, participative, individualistic, social) that are appropriate.

Language

Many organizations and units within organizations use language as a way to identify members of a culture or subculture. By learning this language, members attest to their acceptance of the culture and, in so doing, help to preserve it. The following are examples of terminology used by employees at Knight-Ridder Information, a California-based data redistributor: *accession number* (a number assigned to each individual record in a database), *KWIC* (a set of key-words-in-context), and *relational operator* (searching a database for names or key terms in some order). If you're a new employee at Boeing, you'll find yourself learning a whole unique vocabulary of acronyms, including *BOLD* (Boeing online data), *CATIA* (computer-graphics-aided three-dimensional interactive application),

rituals *Repetitive sequences of activities that express and reinforce the key values of the organization, which goals are most important, which people are important, and which are expendable.*

OB In the News

Change Jobs, and You May Be in for a Culture Shock

When Lyria Charles, a project manager, changed jobs, she didn't check her e-mail on weekends. Eventually, a fellow manager pulled her aside and told her that managers were expected to read e-mail over the weekend. "I didn't know," Charles said. "No one told me."

Employees have to learn the ropes when they change jobs. But unlike many aspects of business, organizational culture has few written rules. Very often, people learn the new culture only after stumbling into barriers and violating unwritten rules. "It's like going to a different country," says Michael Kanazawa of Dissero Partners, a management consulting firm.

There are myriad ways in which one organization's culture differs from another. To paraphrase Tolstoy, in certain ways, organizations are all alike, but each develops its culture in its own way.

Some of the differences—such as dress codes—are pretty easy to detect. Others are much harder to discern. In addition to weekend e-mails, another unwritten rule Charles learned was that she shouldn't have meetings with subordinates in her own office. How did she learn that? When Charles asked to meet with them, her assistant kept scheduling the meetings in the subordinates' cubicles.

When Charles asked why, her assistant told her, "That's how it's done."

One way to decode the maze is to astutely observe unwritten rules and customs and to ask lots of questions. Some learning of an organization's culture, though, is pure trial and error. When Kevin Hall started a new job as a mortgage banker, he had to make his own travel arrangements because the first person he asked said it wasn't part of her job. When he observed colleagues getting help, though, he asked someone else, who was happy to oblige. "You feel your way as you go," Hall said.

Source: Based on E. White, "Culture Shock: Learning Customs of a New Office," *Wall Street Journal,* November 28, 2006, p. B6.

MAIDS (manufacturing assembly and installation data system), *POP* (purchased outside production), and *SLO* (service-level objectives).[45]

Organizations, over time, often develop unique terms to describe equipment, offices, key personnel, suppliers, customers, or products that relate to its business. New employees are frequently overwhelmed with acronyms and jargon that, after 6 months on the job, have become fully part of their language. Once assimilated, this terminology acts as a common denominator that unites members of a given culture or subculture.

Creating an Ethical Organizational Culture

6 *Demonstrate how an ethical culture can be created.*

The content and strength of a culture influence an organization's ethical climate and the ethical behavior of its members.[46] An organizational culture most likely to shape high ethical standards is one that's high in risk tolerance, low to moderate in aggressiveness, and focuses on means as well as outcomes. Managers in such a culture are supported for taking risks and innovating, are discouraged from engaging in unbridled competition, and will pay attention to *how* goals are achieved as well as to *what* goals are achieved.

A strong organizational culture will exert more influence on employees than a weak one. If the culture is strong and supports high ethical standards, it should have a very powerful and positive influence on employee behavior. Johnson & Johnson, for example, has a strong culture that has long stressed corporate obligations to customers, employees, the community, and shareholders, in that order. When poisoned Tylenol (a Johnson & Johnson product) was found on store shelves, employees at Johnson & Johnson across the United States independently pulled the product from these stores before management had even issued a statement concerning the tamperings. No one had to tell these individuals what was morally right; they knew what Johnson & Johnson would expect them to do. On the other hand, a strong culture that encourages pushing the limits can be a powerful force in shaping unethical behavior. For instance, Enron's aggressive culture, with unrelenting pressure on executives to rapidly expand earnings, encouraged ethical corner-cutting and eventually contributed to the company's collapse.[47]

What can management do to create a more ethical culture? We suggest a combination of the following practices:

- *Be a visible role model.*   Employees will look to the behavior of top management as a benchmark for defining appropriate behavior. When senior management is seen as taking the ethical high road, it provides a positive message for all employees.
- *Communicate ethical expectations.*   Ethical ambiguities can be minimized by creating and disseminating an organizational code of ethics. It should state the organization's primary values and the ethical rules that employees are expected to follow.
- *Provide ethical training.*   Set up seminars, workshops, and similar ethical training programs. Use these training sessions to reinforce the organization's standards of conduct, to clarify what practices are and are not permissible, and to address possible ethical dilemmas.
- *Visibly reward ethical acts and punish unethical ones.*   Performance appraisals of managers should include a point-by-point evaluation of how his or her decisions measure up against the organization's code of ethics. Appraisals must include the means taken to achieve goals as well as the ends themselves. People who act ethically should be visibly rewarded for their behavior. Just as importantly, unethical acts should be conspicuously punished.
- *Provide protective mechanisms.*   The organization needs to provide formal mechanisms so that employees can discuss ethical dilemmas and report unethical behavior without fear of reprimand. This might include creation of ethical counselors, ombudsmen, or ethical officers.

Creating a Positive Organizational Culture

7 *Describe a positive organizational culture.*

It's often difficult to separate management fads from lasting changes in management thinking, especially early. In this book, we try to keep current while staying away from fads. There is one early trend, though, that we think is here to stay: creating a positive organizational culture.

At first blush, creating a positive culture may sound hopelessly naïve, or like a Dilbert-style conspiracy. The one thing that makes us believe this trend is here to stay is that there are signs that management practice and OB research are converging.

A **positive organizational culture** is defined as a culture that emphasizes building on employee strengths, rewards more than it punishes, and emphasizes individual vitality and growth.[48] Let's consider each of these areas.

Building on Employee Strengths   A lot of OB, and management practice, is concerned with how to fix employee problems. Although a positive organizational culture does not ignore problems, it does emphasize showing workers how they can capitalize on their strengths. As management guru Peter Drucker said, "Most Americans do not know what their strengths are. When you ask

positive organizational culture   *A culture that emphasizes building on employee strengths, rewards more than it punishes, and emphasizes individual vitality and growth.*

them, they look at you with a blank stare, or they respond in terms of subject knowledge, which is the wrong answer." Do you know what your strengths are? Wouldn't it be better to be in an organizational culture that helped you discover those, and learn ways to make the most of them?

Larry Hammond used this approach—finding and exploiting employee strengths—at a time when you'd least expect it: during the darkest days of the business. Hammond is CEO of Auglaize Provico, an agribusiness company based in Ohio. The company was in the midst of its worst financial struggles and had to lay off one-quarter of its workforce. At that nadir, Hammond decided to try a different approach. Rather than dwell on what was wrong, he decided to take advantage of what was right. "If you really want to [excel], you have to know yourself—you have to know what you're good at, and you have to know what you're not so good at," says Hammond. With the help of Gallup consultant Barry Conchie, Auglaize Provico focused on discovering and using employee strengths. Hammond and Auglaize Provico turned the company around. "You ask Larry [Hammond] what the difference is, and he'll say that it's individuals using their natural talents," says Conchie.[49]

Rewarding More Than Punishing   There is, of course, a time and place for punishment, but there is also a time and place for rewards. Although most organizations are sufficiently focused on extrinsic rewards like pay and promotions, they often forget about the power of smaller (and cheaper) rewards like praise. Creating a positive organizational culture means that managers "catch employees doing something right." Part of creating a positive culture is articulating praise. Many managers withhold praise either because they're afraid employees will coast, or because they think praise is not valued. Failing to praise can become a "silent killer" like escalating blood pressure. Because employees generally don't ask for praise, managers usually don't realize the costs of failing to do it.

Take the example of Elżbieta Górska-Kołodziejczyk, a plant manager for International Paper's facility in Kwidzyn, Poland. The job environment at the plant is bleak and difficult. Employees work in a windowless basement. Staffing is only roughly one-third of its prior level, while production has tripled. These challenges had done in the previous three managers. So, when Górska-Kołodziejczyk took over, she knew she had her work cut out for her. Although she had many items on her list of ways to transform the organization, at the top of her list was recognition and praise. She initially found it difficult to give praise to those who weren't used to it, especially men, but she found over time that they valued it, too. "They were like cement at the beginning," she said. "Like cement." Górska-Kołodziejczyk has found that giving praise is often reciprocated. One day a department supervisor pulled her over to tell her she was doing a good job. "This I do remember, yes," she said.[50]

Emphasizing Vitality and Growth   A positive organizational culture emphasizes not only organizational effectiveness, but individuals' growth as well. No organization will get the best out of employees if the employees see themselves as mere tools or parts of the organization. A positive culture realizes the difference between a job and a career, and shows an interest not only in what the employee does to contribute to organizational effectiveness, but in what the organization does it has have assessed over thousands of organizations, fully one-third feel they are not learning and growing on their job. The figure is even higher in some industries, such as banking, manufacturing, communications, and utilities. Although it may take more creativity to encourage employee growth in some types of industries, it can happen in the fast-paced food service industry. Consider the case of Philippe Lescornez and Didier Brynaert.

Employees at Genentech, a biotechnology pioneer, work within a positive organizational culture that promotes individuals' vitality and growth. Genentech provides training opportunities and the resources and equipment needed to get work done and offers courses to help each employee develop the skills they need on their current job as well as for their future work. To discover talent within the company, Genentech allows employees to grow their careers both within departments and across them. An internal transfer program encourages employees to apply for jobs that can help them advance their careers. Scientists and engineers are also allowed to spend 20 percent of each workweek pursuing their favorite projects.

Philippe Lescornez leads a team of employees at Masterfoods in Belgium. One of his team members is Didier Brynaert, who works in Luxembourg, nearly 150 miles from Masterfoods's Belgian headquarters. Brynaert was considered a good sales promoter who was meeting expectations. Lescornez decided that Brynaert's job could be made more important if he were seen less as just another sales promoter and more as an expert on the unique features of the Luxembourg market. So Lescornez asked Brynaert for information he could share with the home office. He hoped that by raising Brynaert's profile in Brussels, he could create in him a greater sense of ownership for his remote sales territory. "I started to communicate much more what he did to other people [within the company], because there's quite some distance between the Brussels office and the section he's working in. So I started to communicate, communicate, communicate. The more I communicated, the more he started to provide material," says Lescornez. As a result, "Now he's recognized as the specialist for Luxembourg—the guy who is able to build a strong relationship with the Luxembourg clients," says Lescornez. What's good for Brynaert, of course, is also good for Lescornez, who gets credit for helping Brynaert grow and develop.[51]

Limits of Positive Culture   Is a positive culture a panacea? Cynics (or should we say realists?) may be skeptical about the benefits of positive organizational culture. To be sure, even though some companies such as GE, Xerox, Boeing, and 3M have embraced aspects of a positive organizational culture, it is a new enough area that there is some uncertainty about how and when it works best. Moreover, any OB scholar or manager needs to make sure he is objective about the benefits—and risks—of cultivating a positive organizational culture.

Not all cultures value being positive as much as U.S. culture does, and, even within U.S. culture, there surely are limits to how far we should go to preserve a positive culture. For example, Admiral, a British insurance company, has established a Ministry of Fun in its call centers to organize such events as poem writings, foosball, conker competitions (a British game involving chestnuts), and fancy dress days. When does the pursuit of a positive culture start to seem coercive or even Orwellian? As one critic notes, "Promoting a social orthodoxy of positiveness focuses on a particular constellation of desirable states and traits but, in so doing, can stigmatize those who fail to fit the template."[52]

Our point is that there may be benefits to establishing a positive culture, but an organization also needs to be careful to be objective, and not pursue it past the point of effectiveness.

Spirituality and Organizational Culture

8 *Identify characteristics of a spiritual culture.*

What do Southwest Airlines, Hewlett-Packard, The Men's Wearhouse, Ford, Wetherill Associates, and Tom's of Maine have in common? They're among a growing number of organizations that have embraced workplace spirituality.

What Is Spirituality?

Workplace spirituality is *not* about organized religious practices. It's not about God or theology. **Workplace spirituality** recognizes that people have an inner life that nourishes and is nourished by meaningful work that takes place in the context of community.[53] Organizations that promote a spiritual culture recognize that people have both a mind and a spirit, seek to find meaning and purpose in their work, and desire to connect with other human beings and be part of a community.

Why Spirituality Now?

Historical models of management and organizational behavior had no room for spirituality. As we noted in our discussion of emotions in Chapter 8, the myth of rationality assumed that the well-run organization eliminated feelings. Similarly, concern about an employee's inner life had no role in the perfectly rational model. But just as we've now come to realize that the study of emotions improves our understanding of organizational behavior, an awareness of spirituality can help you to better understand employee behavior in the twenty-first century.

Of course, employees have always had an inner life. So why has the search for meaning and purposefulness in work surfaced now? There are a number of reasons. We summarize them in Exhibit 17-5.

Characteristics of a Spiritual Organization

The concept of workplace spirituality draws on our previous discussions of topics such as values, ethics, motivation, leadership, and work/life balance. Spiritual organizations are concerned with helping people develop and reach their full

Exhibit **17-5**	Reasons for the Growing Interest in Spirituality

- As a counterbalance to the pressures and stress of a turbulent pace of life. Contemporary lifestyles—single-parent families, geographic mobility, the temporary nature of jobs, new technologies that create distance between people—underscore the lack of community many people feel and increase the need for involvement and connection.

- Formalized religion hasn't worked for many people, and they continue to look for anchors to replace lack of faith and to fill a growing feeling of emptiness.

- Job demands have made the workplace dominant in many people's lives, yet they continue to question the meaning of work.

- The desire to integrate personal life values with one's professional life.

- An increasing number of people are finding that the pursuit of more material acquisitions leaves them unfulfilled.

Mark Trang, an employee of Salesforce.com, teaches business basics to fifth-grade students at an elementary school. Salesforce.com encourages every employee to donate 1 percent of his or her working time to the community. Through volunteer work, Salesforce.com gives employees the opportunity to experience the joy and satisfaction that comes from helping others. Employees give to the community by feeding the homeless, tutoring kids, gardening in community parks, lending computer expertise to nonprofit organizations, and providing disaster relief.

potential. Similarly, organizations that are concerned with spirituality are more likely to directly address problems created by work/life conflicts. What differentiates spiritual organizations from their nonspiritual counterparts? Although research on this question is only preliminary, our review identified four cultural characteristics that tend to be evident in spiritual organizations:[54]

- *Strong sense of purpose.* Spiritual organizations build their cultures around a meaningful purpose. Although profits may be important, they're not the primary values of the organization. People want to be inspired by a purpose that they believe is important and worthwhile.
- *Trust and respect.* Spiritual organizations are characterized by mutual trust, honesty, and openness. Managers aren't afraid to admit mistakes. The president of Wetherill Associates, a highly successful auto parts distribution firm, says: "We don't tell lies here, and everyone knows it. We are specific and honest about quality and suitability of the product for our customers' needs, even if we know they might not be able to detect any problem."[55]
- *Humanistic work practices.* These practices embraced by spiritual organizations include flexible work schedules, group- and organization-based rewards, narrowing of pay and status differentials, guarantees of individual worker rights, employee empowerment, and job security. Hewlett-Packard, for instance, has handled temporary downturns through voluntary attrition and shortened workweeks (shared by all), and it has handled longer-term declines through early retirements and buyouts.
- *Toleration of employee expression.* The final characteristic that differentiates spiritually based organizations is that they don't stifle employee emotions.

workplace spirituality *The recognition that people have an inner life that nourishes and is nourished by meaningful work that takes place in the context of community.*

They allow people to be themselves—to express their moods and feelings without guilt or fear of reprimand. Employees at Southwest Airlines, for instance, are encouraged to express their sense of humor on the job, to act spontaneously, and to make their work fun.

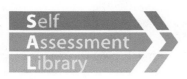

HOW SPIRITUAL AM I?

In the Self-Assessment Library (available on CD and online), take assessment IV.A.4 (How Spiritual Am I?). Note: People's scores on this measure vary from time to time, so take that into account when interpreting the results.

Criticisms of Spirituality

Critics of the spirituality movement in organizations have focused on three issues. First is the question of scientific foundation. What really is workplace spirituality? Is it just a new management buzzword? Second, are spiritual organizations legitimate? Specifically, do organizations have the right to impose spiritual values on their employees? Third is the question of economics: Are spirituality and profits compatible?

First, as you might imagine, there is very little research on workplace spirituality. We don't know whether the concept will have staying power. Do the cultural characteristics just identified really separate spiritual organizations? What is a nonspiritual organization, anyway? Do employees of so-called spiritual organizations perceive that they work in spiritual organizations? Although there is some research suggesting support for workplace spirituality (as we discuss later), before the concept of spirituality gains full credence, the questions we've just posed need to be answered.

On the second question, there is clearly the potential for an emphasis on spirituality to make some employees uneasy. Critics might argue that secular institutions, especially business firms, have no business imposing spiritual values on employees. This criticism is undoubtedly valid when spirituality is defined as bringing religion and God into the workplace.[56] However, the criticism seems less stinging when the goal is limited to helping employees find meaning in their work lives. If the concerns listed in Exhibit 17-5 truly characterize a growing segment of the workforce, then perhaps the time is right for organizations to help employees find meaning and purpose in their work and to use the workplace as a source of community.

Finally, the issue of whether spirituality and profits are compatible objectives is certainly relevant for managers and investors in business. The evidence, although limited, indicates that the two objectives may be very compatible. A recent research study by a major consulting firm found that companies that introduced spiritually based techniques improved productivity and significantly reduced turnover.[57] Another study found that organizations that provide their employees with opportunities for spiritual development outperformed those that didn't.[58] Other studies also report that spirituality in organizations was positively related to creativity, employee satisfaction, team performance, and organizational commitment.[59] And if you're looking for a single case to make the argument for spirituality, it's hard to beat Southwest Airlines. Southwest has one of the lowest employee turnover rates in the airline industry; it consistently has the lowest labor costs per miles flown of any major airline; it regularly outpaces its competitors for achieving on-time arrivals and fewest customer complaints; and it has proven itself to be the most consistently profitable airline in the United States.[60]

Global Implications

9 *Show how national culture may affect the way organizational culture is transported to a different country.*

We considered global cultural values (collectivism–individualism, power distance, and so on) in Chapter 4. Here our focus is a bit narrower: How is organizational culture affected by a global context? As the opening vignette suggests, organizational cultures are so powerful that they often transcend national boundaries. But that doesn't mean that organizations should, or could, be blissfully ignorant of local culture.

This is becoming a bigger issue. In 2007, half of GE's revenue came from outside the United States. GE even moved the headquarters of its health care division to the United Kingdom, and the number of non-U.S. citizens among GE's top 500 managers has tripled since 2001. GE is hardly alone. Large and small organizations alike are often heavily dependent on foreign product markets, labor markets, or both.

As we noted in Chapter 4, national cultures differ. Organizational cultures often reflect national culture. For example, the culture at AirAsia, a Malaysian-based airline, emphasizes informal dress so as not to create status differences. The carrier has lots of parties, participative management, and no private offices. This organizational culture reflects Malaysia's relatively collectivistic culture. However, the culture of USAirways does not reflect the same degree of informality. If USAirways were to set up operations in Malaysia, or merge with AirAsia, it would need to take these cultural differences into account. So when an organization opens up operations in another country, it ignores the local culture to its own risk.

One of the primary things U.S. managers can do is to be culturally sensitive. The United States is a dominant force in business and in culture, and with that influence comes a reputation. "We are broadly seen throughout the world as arrogant people, totally self-absorbed and loud," says one U.S. executive. Companies such as American Airlines, Lowe's, Novell, ExxonMobil, and Microsoft have implemented training programs to sensitize their managers to cultural differences. Some ways in which U.S. managers can be culturally sensitive include talking in a low tone of voice, speaking slowly, listening more, and avoiding discussions of religion and politics.

U.S. employees are not the only ones who need to be culturally sensitive. For example, three times a week, employees at the Canadian unit of Japanese video game maker Koei begin each day standing next to their desks, facing their boss, and saying in unison, "Good morning." That is followed by employees delivering short speeches on topics that range from corporate principles to 3D game engines. Koei also has employees punch a time clock. And Koei asks women to serve tea to top executive guests. Although these practices are consistent with Koei's culture, they do not fit Canadian culture very well. "It's kind of like school," says one Canadian employee.[61]

Summary and Implications for Managers

Exhibit 17-6 depicts organizational culture as an intervening variable. Employees form an overall subjective perception of the organization based on factors such as degree of risk tolerance, team emphasis, and support of people. This overall perception becomes, in effect, the organization's culture or personality. These favorable or unfavorable perceptions then affect employee performance and satisfaction, with the impact being greater for stronger cultures.

Just as people's personalities tend to be stable over time, so too do strong cultures. This makes strong cultures difficult for managers to change. When a

Exhibit 17-6 How Organizational Cultures Have an Impact on Employee Performance and Satisfaction

culture becomes mismatched to its environment, management will want to change it. But as the Point/Counterpoint demonstrates, changing an organization's culture is a long and difficult process. The result, at least in the short term, is that managers should treat their organization's culture as relatively fixed.

One of the most important managerial implications of organizational culture relates to selection decisions. Hiring individuals whose values don't align with those of the organization is likely to lead to employees who lack motivation and commitment and who are dissatisfied with their jobs and the organization.[62] Not surprisingly, employee "misfits" have considerably higher turnover rates than individuals who perceive a good fit.[63]

We should also not overlook the influence socialization has on employee performance. An employee's performance depends to a considerable degree on knowing what he should or should not do. Understanding the right way to do a job indicates proper socialization.

As a manager, you can shape the culture of your work environment. That is particularly the case with some of the cultural aspects we discussed in the latter part of the chapter—all managers can do their part to create an ethical culture, and spirituality and a positive organizational culture should be considered, too. Often you can do as much to shape your organizational culture as the culture of the organization shapes you.

Point ⟫⟪ Counterpoint

ORGANIZATIONAL CULTURES CAN'T BE CHANGED

*a*n organization's culture is made up of relatively stable characteristics. It develops over many years and is rooted in deeply held values to which employees are strongly committed. In addition, there are a number of forces continually operating to maintain a given culture. These include written statements about the organization's mission and philosophy, the design of physical spaces and buildings, the dominant leadership style, hiring criteria, past promotion practices, entrenched rituals, popular stories about key people and events, the organization's historic performance evaluation criteria, and the organization's formal structure.

Selection and promotion policies are particularly important devices that work against cultural change. Employees chose the organization because they perceived their values to be a "good fit" with the organization. They become comfortable with that fit and will strongly resist efforts to disturb the equilibrium. The terrific difficulties that organizations such as Ford, VW, and the U.S. Postal Service have had in trying to reshape their cultures attest to this dilemma. These organizations historically tended to attract individuals who desired situations that were stable and highly structured. Those in control in organizations will also select senior managers who will continue the current culture. Even attempts to change a culture by going outside the organization to hire a new chief executive are unlikely to be effective. The evidence indicates that the culture is more likely to change the executive than the other way around.

Our argument should not be viewed as saying that culture can *never* be changed. In the unusual case in which an organization confronts a survival-threatening crisis, members of the organization will be responsive to efforts at cultural change. However, anything less than that is unlikely to be effective in bringing about cultural change.

*c*hanging an organization's culture is extremely difficult, but cultures *can* be changed. The evidence suggests that cultural change is most likely to take place when most or all of the following conditions exist:

- **A dramatic crisis.** This is a shock that undermines the status quo and calls into question the relevance of the current culture. Examples are a surprising financial setback, the loss of a major customer, and a dramatic technological breakthrough by a competitor.
- **Turnover in leadership.** New top leadership, which can provide an alternative set of key values, may be perceived as more capable of responding to the crisis (as when Mark Hurd replaced Carly Fiorina at HP).
- **Young and small organizations.** The younger the organization, the less entrenched its culture will be. Similarly, it's easier for management to communicate its new values when the organization is small.
- **Weak culture.** The more widely held a culture is and the higher the agreement among members on its values, the more difficult it will be to change. Conversely, weak cultures are more amenable to change than strong ones.

If all or most of these conditions exist, the following management actions may lead to change: initiating new stories and rituals, selecting and promoting employees who espouse the new values, changing the reward system to support the new values, and undermining current subcultures through transfers, job rotation, and terminations.

Under the best of conditions, these actions won't result in an immediate or dramatic shift in the culture. In the final analysis, cultural change is a lengthy process—measured in years rather than in months. But cultures can be changed. The success that new leadership had in turning around the cultures at companies like IBM, 3M, and GE attests to this claim.

Questions for Review

1 What is institutionalization and how does it affect organizational culture?

2 What is organizational culture and what are its common characteristics?

3 What are the functional and dysfunctional effects of organizational culture?

4 What factors create and sustain an organization's culture?

5 How is culture transmitted to employees?

6 How can an ethical culture be created?

7 What is a positive organizational culture?

8 What are the characteristics of a spiritual culture?

9 How does national culture affect how organizational culture is transported to a different country?

Experiential Exercise

RATE YOUR CLASSROOM CULTURE

Listed here are 14 statements. Using the 5-item scale (from Strongly Agree to Strongly Disagree), respond to each statement by circling the number that best represents your opinion.

	Strongly Agree	Agree	Neutral	Disagree	Strongly Disagree
1. I feel comfortable challenging statements made by my instructor.	5	4	3	2	1
2. My instructor heavily penalizes assignments that are not turned in on time.	1	2	3	4	5
3. My instructor believes that "it's final results that count."	1	2	3	4	5
4. My instructor is sensitive to my personal needs and problems.	5	4	3	2	1
5. A large portion of my grade depends on how well I work with others in the class.	5	4	3	2	1
6. I often feel nervous and tense when I come to class.	1	2	3	4	5
7. My instructor seems to prefer stability over change.	1	2	3	4	5
8. My instructor encourages me to develop new and different ideas.	5	4	3	2	1
9. My instructor has little tolerance for sloppy thinking.	1	2	3	4	5
10. My instructor is more concerned with how I came to a conclusion than with the conclusion itself.	5	4	3	2	1
11. My instructor treats all students alike.	1	2	3	4	5
12. My instructor frowns on class members helping each other with assignments.	1	2	3	4	5
13. Aggressive and competitive people have a distinct advantage in this class.	1	2	3	4	5
14. My instructor encourages me to see the world differently.	5	4	3	2	1

Calculate your total score by adding up the numbers you circled. Your score will fall between 14 and 70.

A high score (49 or above) describes an open, risk-taking, supportive, humanistic, team-oriented, easy-going, growth-oriented culture. A low score (35 or below) describes a closed, structured, task-oriented, individualistic, tense, and stability-oriented culture. Note that differences count, so a score of 60 is a more open culture than

one that scores 50. Also, realize that one culture isn't preferable over another. The "right" culture depends on you and your preferences for a learning environment.

Form teams of five to seven members each. Compare your scores. How closely do they align? Discuss and resolve any discrepancies. Based on your team's analysis, what type of student do you think would perform best in this class?

Ethical Dilemma

IS THERE ROOM FOR SNOOPING IN AN ORGANIZATION'S CULTURE?

Although some of the spying Hewlett-Packard performed on some members of its board of directors appeared to violate California law, much of it was legal. Moreover, many companies spy on their employees—sometimes with and sometimes without their knowledge or consent. Organizations differ in their culture of surveillance. Some differences are due to the type of business. A Department of Defense contractor has more reason—perhaps even obligation—to spy on its employees than does an orange juice producer.

However, surveillance in most industries is on the upswing. There are several reasons for this, including the huge growth of two sectors with theft and security problems (services and information technology, respectively) and the increased availability of surveillance technology.

Consider the following surveillance actions and, for each action, decide whether it would never be ethical (mark N), would sometimes be ethical (mark S), or would always be ethical (mark A). For those you mark S, indicate on what factors your judgment would depend.

1. Sifting through an employee's trash for evidence of wrongdoing
2. Periodically reading e-mail messages for disclosure of confidential information or inappropriate use
3. Conducting video surveillance of workspace
4. Monitoring Web sites visited by employees and determining the appropriateness and work-relatedness of those visited
5. Taping phone conversations
6. Posing as a job candidate, an investor, a customer, or a colleague (when the real purpose is to solicit information)

Would you be less likely to work for an employer that engaged in some of these methods? Why or why not? Do you think use of surveillance says something about an organization's culture?

Case Incident 1

MERGERS DON'T ALWAYS LEAD TO CULTURE CLASHES

A lot of mergers lead to culture clashes and, ultimately, failure. So in 2005 when banking giant Bank of America (BOA) announced its $35 billion acquisition of credit card giant MBNA, many thought that in a few years, this merger would join for heap of those done in by cultural differences.

MBNA's culture was characterized by a free-wheeling, entrepreneurial spirit that was also quite secretive. MBNA employees also were accustomed to the high life. Their corporate headquarters in Wilmington, Delaware, could be described as lavish, and employees throughout the company enjoyed high salaries and generous perks—from the private golf course at its headquarters, to its fleet of corporate jets and private yachts.

Bank of America, in contrast, grew by thrift. It was a low-cost, no-nonsense operation. Unlike MBNA, it believed that size and smarts were more important than speed. It was an acquisition machine that some likened to *Star Trek's* relentless Borg collective.

In short, the cultures in the two companies were very, very different.

Although these cultural differences seemed a recipe for disaster, it appears, judging from the reactions of BOA and MBNA employees, that the merger has worked. How can this be?

BOA had the foresight to know which MBNA practices to attempt to change, and which to keep in place. Especially critical was BOA's appreciation and respect for MBNA's culture. "On Day 1, I was directed that this was not like the ones you are used to," said Clifford Skelton, who had helped manage BOA's acquisition of FleetBoston Financial before moving on to MBNA.

To try to manage the cultural transition, executives of both companies began by comparing thousands of practices covering everything from hiring to call-center operations. In many cases, BOA chose to keep MBNA's cultural practices in place. In other cases, BOA did impose its will on MBNA. For example, because MBNA's pay rates were well above market, many MBNA managers were forced to swallow a steep pay cut. Some MBNA employees have left, but most have remained.

In other cases, the cultures co-adapted. For example, MBNA's dress code was much more formal than BOA's business casual approach. In the end, a hybrid code was adopted, where business suits were expected in the credit-card division's corporate offices and in front of clients, but business causal was the norm otherwise.

While most believe the merger has been successful, there are tensions. Some BOA managers see MBNA managers as arrogant and autocratic. Some MBNA managers see their BOA counterparts as bureaucratic.

What about those famous MBNA perks? As you might have guessed, most of those have gone away. All but one of the corporate jets is gone. The golf course was donated to the state of Delaware. Gone too, are most of the works of art that hung in MBNA's corporate offices.

Questions

1. In what ways were the cultures of Bank of America and MBNA incompatible?

2. Why do you think their cultures appeared to mesh rather than clash?

3. Do you think culture is important to the success of a merger/acquisition? Why or why not?

4. How much of the smooth transition, if any, do you think comes from both companies glossing over real differences in an effort to make the merger work?

Source: Based on E. Dash, "A Clash of Cultures, Averted," *New York Times,* February 20, 2007, pp. B1, B3.

Case Incident 2

WEGMANS

Amid corporate giants such as Microsoft, GM, and General Electric stands a relatively small grocery store that has appeared at the top (number 1 in 2005) or near the top (number 3 in 2007) of *Fortune*'s "Best Companies to Work For."

Typically, grocery stores are not thought of as great places to work. Hours are anything but 9 to 5, and the pay is low compared with other occupations. The result is an industry that sees high annual turnover rates. Employees at Wegmans, however, view working for a grocer a bit differently. Instead of viewing their job as a temporary setback on the way to a more illustrious career, many employees at Wegmans view working for the grocer as their career. And given Wegmans's high profitability (it had sales in 2004 of $3.4 billion from 67 stores, giving it one of the highest profit-per-store ratios in the industry), it looks like the grocer will be around long enough to make such careers a reality for those who pursue them.

Why is Wegmans so effective? One reason is its culture. The chain began in 1930 when brothers John and Walter Wegman opened their first grocery store in Rochester, New York. One of its distinguishing features was a café that seated 300 customers. The store's immediate focus on fine foods quickly separated it from other grocers—a focus that is maintained by the company's employees, many of whom are hired based on their interest in food.

In 1950, Walter's son, Robert, became president and immediately added a generous number of employee benefits such as profit sharing and medical coverage, completely paid for by the company. What was Robert's reason for offering such great benefits? "I was no different from them," he said, referring to the company's employees. Though the benefits are still generous at Wegmans, the rising cost of health care has forced it to have all employees contribute for coverage.

Now, Robert's son, Danny, is president of the company, and he has continued the Wegmans tradition of taking care of its employees. To date, Wegmans has paid more than $54 million in college scholarships for its employees, both full time and part time. In addition to benefits, employees receive pay that is well above the market average. As a result, annual turnover at Wegmans for full-time employees is a mere 6 percent, according to the Food Marketing Institute, when is it is 24 percent in the industry overall.

The culture that has developed at Wegmans is an important part of the company's success. Employees are proud to say they work at Wegmans. For example, Sara Goggins, a 19-year-old college student who works part time at Wegmans, recalls when Danny Wegman personally complimented her on a store display that she helped set up. "I love this place," she says. "If teaching doesn't work out, I would so totally work at Wegmans." And Kelly Schoeneck, a store manager, recounts that a few years ago, her supervisor asked her to analyze a frequent-shopper program that a competitor had recently adopted. Though she assumed that her supervisor would take credit for her findings, Schoeneck's supervisor had her present her findings directly to Robert Wegman.

Maintaining a culture of driven, happy, and loyal employees who are eager to help one another is not easy. Wegmans carefully selects each employee, and growth is often slow and meticulous, with only two new stores opened each year. When a new store is opened, employees from existing stores are brought in to the new store to maintain the culture. The existing employees are then able to transmit their knowledge and the store's values to new employees.

Managers especially are ingrained in the Wegmans culture. More than half started working at Wegmans when they were teenagers. Says Edward McLaughlin, director of Cornell's Food Industry Management Program, "When you're a 16-year-old kid, the last thing you want to do is wear a geeky shirt and work for a supermarket. But at Wegman's, it's a badge of honor. You are not a geeky cashier. You are part of the social fabric."

Employees at Wegmans are not selected based on intellectual ability or experience alone. "Just about everybody in the store has some genuine interest in food," states Jeff Burris, a supervisor at the Dulles, Virginia, store. Those employees who do not express this interest may not fit in and are sometimes not hired. The result is a culture that "is bigger than Danny in the same way that Wal-Mart's became bigger than Sam [Walton]," says Darrell Rigby, a consultant at Bain & Co.

Questions

1. Would you characterize Wegmans's culture as strong or weak? Why? How is the strength of the culture at

Wegmans likely to affect its employees, particularly new hires?

2. Wegmans attempts to maintain its core cultural values by hiring individuals who are passionate about the food industry and by staffing new stores partly with existing employees. What are some advantages and

disadvantages of trying to impose a similar culture throughout different areas of a company?

3. What is the primary source of Wegmans's culture, and what are some ways that it has been able to sustain itself?

4. How might stories and rituals play a role in maintaining Wegmans's corporate culture?

Source: Based on E. Iwata, "Businesses Grow More Socially Conscious," *USA Today*, June 14, 2007, p. 3B; and M. Boyle and E. F. Kratz, "The Wegman's Way," *Fortune*, January 24, 2005, pp. 62–66.

Endnotes

1. C. Ricketts, "When in London, Do as the Californians Do," *Wall Street Journal*, January 23, 2007, p. B5.

2. P. Selznick, "Foundations of the Theory of Organizations," *American Sociological Review*, February 1948, pp. 25–35.

3. See L. G. Zucker, "Organizations as Institutions," in S. B. Bacharach (ed.), *Research in the Sociology of Organizations* (Greenwich, CT: JAI Press, 1983), pp. 1–47; A. J. Richardson, "The Production of Institutional Behaviour: A Constructive Comment on the Use of Institutionalization Theory in Organizational Analysis," *Canadian Journal of Administrative Sciences*, December 1986, pp. 304–316; L. G. Zucker, *Institutional Patterns and Organizations: Culture and Environment* (Cambridge, MA: Ballinger, 1988); R. L. Jepperson, "Institutions, Institutional Effects, and Institutionalism," in W. W. Powell and P. J. DiMaggio (eds.), *The New Institutionalism in Organizational Analysis* (Chicago: University of Chicago Press, 1991), pp. 143–163; and T. B. Lawrence, M. K. Mauws, B. Dyck, and R. F. Kleysen, "The Politics of Organizational Learning: Integrating Power into the 4I Framework," *Academy of Management Review*, January 2005, pp. 180–191.

4. See, for example, H. S. Becker, "Culture: A Sociological View," *Yale Review*, Summer 1982, pp. 513–527; and E. H. Schein, *Organizational Culture and Leadership* (San Francisco: Jossey-Bass, 1985), p. 168.

5. This seven-item description is based on C. A. O'Reilly III, J. Chatman, and D. F. Caldwell, "People and Organizational Culture: A Profile Comparison Approach to Assessing Person-Organization Fit," *Academy of Management Journal*, September 1991, pp. 487–516; and J. A. Chatman and K. A. Jehn, "Assessing the Relationship between Industry Characteristics and Organizational Culture: How Different Can You Be?" *Academy of Management Journal*, June 1994, pp. 522–553.

6. The view that there will be consistency among perceptions of organizational culture has been called the "integration" perspective. For a review of this perspective and conflicting approaches, see D. Meyerson and J. Martin, "Cultural Change: An Integration of Three Different Views," *Journal of Management Studies*, November 1987, pp. 623–647; and P. J. Frost, L. F. Moore, M. R. Louis, C. C. Lundberg, and J. Martin (eds.), *Reframing Organizational Culture* (Newbury Park, CA: Sage Publications, 1991).

7. See J. M. Jermier, J. W. Slocum, Jr., L. W. Fry, and J. Gaines, "Organizational Subcultures in a Soft Bureaucracy: Resistance Behind the Myth and Facade of an Official Culture," *Organization Science*, May 1991, pp. 170–194; and S. A.

Sackmann, "Culture and Subcultures: An Analysis of Organizational Knowledge," *Administrative Science Quarterly*, March 1992, pp. 140–161; G. Hofstede, "Identifying Organizational Subcultures: An Empirical Approach," *Journal of Management Studies*, January 1998, pp. 1–12.

8. T. A. Timmerman, "Do Organizations Have Personalities?" paper presented at the 1996 National Academy of Management Conference; Cincinnati, OH, August 1996.

9. S. Hamm, "No Letup—And No Apologies," *BusinessWeek*, October 26, 1998, pp. 58–64; and C. Carlson, "Former Intel Exec Slams Microsoft Culture," *eWEEK.com*, March 26, 2002, www.eweek.com/article2/0,1759,94976,00.asp.

10. See, for example, G. G. Gordon and N. DiTomaso, "Predicting Corporate Performance from Organizational Culture," *Journal of Management Studies*, November 1992, pp. 793–798; J. B. Sorensen, "The Strength of Corporate Culture and the Reliability of Firm Performance," *Administrative Science Quarterly*, March 2002, pp. 70–91; and J. Rosenthal and M. A. Masarech, "High-Performance Cultures: How Values Can Drive Business Results," *Journal of Organizational Excellence*, Spring 2003, pp. 3–18.

11. Y. Wiener, "Forms of Value Systems: A Focus on Organizational Effectiveness and Cultural Change and Maintenance," *Academy of Management Review*, October 1988, p. 536.

12. R. T. Mowday, L. W. Porter, and R. M. Steers, *Employee–Organization Linkages: The Psychology of Commitment, Absenteeism, and Turnover* (New York: Academic Press, 1982); and C. Vandenberghe, "Organizational Culture, Person-Culture Fit, and Turnover: A Replication in the Health Care Industry," *Journal of Organizational Behavior*, March 1999, pp. 175–184.

13. S. L. Dolan and S. Garcia, "Managing by Values: Cultural Redesign for Strategic Organizational Change at the Dawn of the Twenty-First Century," *Journal of Management Development* 21, no. 2 (2002), pp. 101–117.

14. See C. A. O'Reilly and J. A. Chatman, "Culture as Social Control: Corporations, Cults, and Commitment," in B. M. Staw and L. L. Cummings (eds.), *Research in Organizational Behavior*, vol. 18 (Greenwich, CT: JAI Press, 1996), pp. 157–200. See also M. Pinae Cunha, "The 'Best Place to Be': Managing Control and Employee Loyalty in a Knowledge-Intensive Company," *Journal of Applied Behavioral Science*, December 2002, pp. 481–495.

15. T. E. Deal and A. A. Kennedy, "Culture: A New Look Through Old Lenses," *Journal of Applied Behavioral Science*, November 1983, p. 501.

16. J. Case, "Corporate Culture," *INC.*, November 1996, pp. 42–53.

17. Sorensen, "The Strength of Corporate Culture and the Reliability of Firm Performance."

18. See, for instance, P. L. Moore, "She's Here to Fix the Xerox," *BusinessWeek*, August 6, 2001, pp. 47–48; and C. Ragavan, "FBI Inc.," *U.S. News & World Report*, June 18, 2001, pp. 15–21.

19. See C. Lindsay, "Paradoxes of Organizational Diversity: Living Within the Paradoxes," in L. R. Jauch and J. L. Wall (eds.), *Proceedings of the 50th Academy of Management Conference* (San Francisco, 1990), pp. 374–378; T. Cox, Jr., *Cultural Diversity in Organizations: Theory, Research & Practice* (San Francisco: Berrett-Koehler, 1993), pp. 162–170; and L. Grensing-Pophal, "Hiring to Fit Your Corporate Culture," *HRMagazine*, August 1999, pp. 50–54.

20. K. Labich, "No More Crude at Texaco," *Fortune*, September 6, 1999, pp. 205–212; and "Rooting Out Racism," *BusinessWeek*, January 10, 2000, p. 66.

21. A. F. Buono and J. L. Bowditch, *The Human Side of Mergers and Acquisitions: Managing Collisions Between People, Cultures, and Organizations* (San Francisco: Jossey-Bass, 1989); S. Cartwright and C. L. Cooper, "The Role of Culture Compatibility in Successful Organizational Marriages," *Academy of Management Executive*, May 1993, pp. 57–70; E. Krell, "Merging Corporate Cultures," *Training*, May 2001, pp. 68–78; and R. A. Weber and C. F. Camerer, "Cultural Conflict and Merger Failure: An Experimental Approach," *Management Science*, April 2003, pp. 400–412.

22. P. Gumbel, "Return of the Urge to Merge," *Time Europe Magazine*, July 13, 2003, www.time.com/time/europe/magazine/article/0,13005,901030721-464418,00.html.

23. T. A. Lambert, L. T. Eby, and M. P. Reeves, "Predictors of Networking Intensity and Network Quality Among White-Collar Job Seekers," *Journal of Career Development*, June 2006, pp. 351–365; and J. A. Thompson, "Proactive Personality and Job Performance: A Social Capital Perspective," *Journal of Applied Psychology*, September 2005, pp. 1011–1017.

24. S. F. Gale, "Memo to AOL Time Warner: Why Mergers Fail—Case Studies," *Workforce*, February 2003, www.workforce.com; and W. Bock, "Mergers, Bubbles, and Steve Case," *Wally Bock's Monday Memo*, January 20, 2003, www.mondaymemo.net/030120feature.htm.

25. E. H. Schein, "The Role of the Founder in Creating Organizational Culture," *Organizational Dynamics*, Summer 1983, pp. 13–28.

26. E. H. Schein, "Leadership and Organizational Culture," in F. Hesselbein, M. Goldsmith, and R. Beckhard (eds.), *The Leader of the Future* (San Francisco: Jossey-Bass, 1996), pp. 61–62.

27. See, for example, J. R. Harrison and G. R. Carroll, "Keeping the Faith: A Model of Cultural Transmission in Formal Organizations," *Administrative Science Quarterly*, December 1991, pp. 552–582; see also G. George, R. G. Sleeth, and M. A. Siders, "Organizational Culture: Leader Roles, Behaviors, and Reinforcement Mechanisms," *Journal of Business & Psychology*, Summer 1999, pp. 545–560.

28. B. Schneider, "The People Make the Place," *Personnel Psychology*, Autumn 1987, pp. 437–453; D. E. Bowen, G. E. Ledford, Jr., and B. R. Nathan, "Hiring for the Organization, Not the Job," *Academy of Management Executive*, November 1991, pp. 35–51; B. Schneider, H. W. Goldstein, and D. B. Smith, "The ASA Framework: An Update," *Personnel Psychology*, Winter 1995, pp. 747–773; A. L. Kristof, "Person–Organization Fit: An Integrative Review of Its Conceptualizations, Measurement, and Implications," *Personnel Psychology*, Spring 1996, pp. 1–49;

D. M. Cable and T. A. Judge, "Interviewers' Perceptions of Person-Organization Fit and Organizational Selection Decisions," *Journal of Applied Psychology*, August 1997, pp. 546–561; and M. L. Verquer, T. A. Beehr, and S. H. Wagner, "A Meta-Analysis of Relations Between Person-Organization Fit and Work Attitudes," *Journal of Vocational Behavior*, December 2003, pp. 473–489.

29. L. Grensing-Pophal, "Hiring to Fit Your Corporate Culture," *HRMagazine*, August 1999, pp. 50–54.

30. D. C. Hambrick and P. A. Mason, "Upper Echelons: The Organization as a Reflection of Its Top Managers," *Academy of Management Review*, April 1984, pp. 193–206; B. P. Niehoff, C. A. Enz, and R. A. Grover, "The Impact of Top-Management Actions on Employee Attitudes and Perceptions," *Group & Organization Studies*, September 1990, pp. 337–352; and H. M. Trice and J. M. Beyer, "Cultural Leadership in Organizations," *Organization Science*, May 1991, pp. 149–169.

31. J. S. Lublin, "Cheap Talk," *Wall Street Journal*, April 11, 2002, p. B14.

32. See, for instance, J. P. Wanous, *Organizational Entry*, 2nd ed. (New York: Addison-Wesley, 1992); G. T. Chao, A. M. O'Leary-Kelly, S. Wolf, H. J. Klein, and P. D. Gardner, "Organizational Socialization: Its Content and Consequences," *Journal of Applied Psychology*, October 1994, pp. 730–743; B. E. Ashforth, A. M. Saks, and R. T. Lee, "Socialization and Newcomer Adjustment: The Role of Organizational Context," *Human Relations*, July 1998, pp. 897–926; D. A. Major, "Effective Newcomer Socialization into High-Performance Organizational Cultures," in N. M. Ashkanasy, C. P. M. Wilderom, and M. F. Peterson (eds.), *Handbook of Organizational Culture & Climate*, pp. 355–368; D. M. Cable and C. K. Parsons, "Socialization Tactics and Person-Organization Fit," *Personnel Psychology*, Spring 2001, pp. 1–23; and K. Rollag, "The Impact of Relative Tenure on Newcomer Socialization Dynamics," *Journal of Organizational Behavior*, November 2004, pp. 853–872.

33. J. Schettler, "Orientation ROI," *Training*, August 2002, p. 38.

34. K. Rhodes, "Breaking in the Top Dogs," *Training*, February 2000, pp. 67–74.

35. J. Van Maanen and E. H. Schein, "Career Development," in J. R. Hackman and J. L. Suttle (eds.), *Improving Life at Work* (Santa Monica, CA: Goodyear, 1977), pp. 58–62.

36. D. C. Feldman, "The Multiple Socialization of Organization Members," *Academy of Management Review*, April 1981, p. 310.

37. G. Chen and R. J. Klimoski, "The Impact of Expectations on Newcomer Performance in Teams as Mediated by Work Characteristics, Social Exchanges, and Empowerment," *Academy of Management Journal* 46 (2003), pp. 591–607; C. R. Wanberg and J. D. Kammeyer-Mueller, "Predictors and Outcomes of Proactivity in the Socialization Process," *Journal of Applied Psychology* 85 (2000), pp. 373–385; J. D. Kammeyer-Mueller and C. R. Wanberg, "Unwrapping the Organizational Entry Process: Disentangling Multiple Antecedents and Their Pathways to Adjustment," *Journal of Applied Psychology* 88 (2003), pp. 779–794; and E. W. Morrison, "Longitudinal Study of the Effects of Information Seeking on Newcomer Socialization," *Journal of Applied Psychology* 78 (2003), pp. 173–183.

38. Van Maanen and Schein, "Career Development," p. 59.

39. E. W. Morrison, "Newcomers' Relationships: The Role of Social Network Ties During Socialization," *Academy of Management Journal* 45 (2002), pp. 1149–1160.

40. E. Ransdell, "The Nike Story? Just Tell It!" *Fast Company*, January–February 2000, pp. 44–46.

41. D. M. Boje, "The Storytelling Organization: A Study of Story Performance in an Office-Supply Firm," *Administrative Science Quarterly*, March 1991, pp. 106–126; C. H. Deutsch, "The Parables of Corporate Culture," *New York Times*, October 13, 1991, p. F25; and M. Ricketts and J. G. Seiling, "Language, Metaphors, and Stories: Catalysts for Meaning Making in Organizations," *Organization Development Journal*, Winter 2003, pp. 33–43.

42. See K. Kamoche, "Rhetoric, Ritualism, and Totemism in Human Resource Management," *Human Relations*, April 1995, pp. 367–385.

43. V. Matthews, "Starting Every Day with a Shout and a Song," *Financial Times*, May 2, 2001, p. 11; and M. Gimein, "Sam Walton Made Us a Promise," *Fortune*, March 18, 2002, pp. 121–130.

44. A. Rafaeli and M. G. Pratt, "Tailored Meanings: On the Meaning and Impact of Organizational Dress," *Academy of Management Review*, January 1993, pp. 32–55; and J. M. Higgins and C. McAllaster, "Want Innovation? Then Use Cultural Artifacts That Support It," *Organizational Dynamics*, August 2002, pp. 74–84.

45. *DCACronyms* (Seattle: Boeing, April 1997).

46. See B. Victor and J. B. Cullen, "The Organizational Bases of Ethical Work Climates," *Administrative Science Quarterly*, March 1988, pp. 101–125; L. K. Trevino, "A Cultural Perspective on Changing and Developing Organizational Ethics," in W. A. Pasmore and R. W. Woodman (eds.), *Research in Organizational Change and Development*, vol. 4 (Greenwich, CT: JAI Press, 1990); M. W. Dickson, D. B. Smith, M. W. Grojean, and M. Ehrhart, "An Organizational Climate Regarding Ethics: The Outcome of Leader Values and the Practices That Reflect Them," *Leadership Quarterly*, Summer 2001, pp. 197–217; and R. L. Dufresne, "An Action Learning Perspective on Effective Implementation of Academic Honor Codes," *Group & Organization Management*, April 2004, pp. 201–218.

47. J. A. Byrne, "The Environment Was Ripe for Abuse," *BusinessWeek*, February 25, 2002, pp. 118–120; and A. Raghavan, K. Kranhold, and A. Barrionuevo, "How Enron Bosses Created a Culture of Pushing Limits," *Wall Street Journal*, August 26, 2002, p. A1.

48. D. L. Nelson and C. L. Cooper (eds.), *Positive Organizational Behavior* (London: Sage, 2007); K. S. Cameron, J. E. Dutton, and R. E. Quinn (eds.), *Positive Organizational Scholarship: Foundations of a New Discipline* (San Francisco: Berrett-Koehler, 2003); and F. Luthans and C. M. Youssef, "Emerging Positive Organizational Behavior," *Journal of Management*, June 2007, pp. 321–349.

49. J. Robison, "Great Leadership Under Fire," *Gallup Leadership Journal*, March 8, 2007, pp. 1–3.

50. R. Wagner and J. K. Harter, *12: The Elements of Great Managing* (New York: Gallup Press, 2006).

51. R. Wagner and J. K. Harter, "Performance Reviews Without the Anxiety," *Gallup Leadership Journal*, July 12, 2007, pp. 1–4; and Wagner and Harter, *12: The Elements of Great Managing*.

52. S. Fineman, "On Being Positive: Concerns and Counterpoints," *Academy of Management Review* 31, no. 2 (2006), pp. 270–291.

53. D. P. Ashmos and D. Duchon, "Spirituality at Work: A Conceptualization and Measure," *Journal of Management Inquiry*, June 2000, p. 139. For a comprehensive review of definitions of workplace spirituality, see R. A. Giacalone and C. L. Jurkiewicz, "Toward a Science of Workplace Spirituality," in R. A. Giacalone and C. L. Jurkiewicz (eds.), *Handbook of Workplace Spirituality and Organizational Performance* (Armonk, NY: M. E. Sharpe, 2003), pp. 6–13.

54. This section is based on C. Ichniowski, D. L. Kochan, C. Olson, and G. Strauss, "What Works at Work: Overview and Assessment," *Industrial Relations*, 1996, pp. 299–333; I. A. Mitroff and E. A. Denton, *A Spiritual Audit of Corporate America: A Hard Look at Spirituality, Religion, and Values in the Workplace* (San Francisco: Jossey-Bass, 1999); J. Milliman, J. Ferguson, D. Trickett, and B. Condemi, "Spirit and Community at Southwest Airlines: An Investigation of a Spiritual Values-Based Model," *Journal of Organizational Change Management* 12, no. 3 (1999), pp. 221–233; and E. H. Burack, "Spirituality in the Workplace," *Journal of Organizational Change Management* 12, no. 3 (1999), pp. 280–291.

55. Cited in Wagner-Marsh and Conley, "The Fourth Wave," p. 295.

56. M. Conlin, "Religion in the Workplace: The Growing Presence of Spirituality in Corporate America," *BusinessWeek*, November 1, 1999, pp. 151–158; and P. Paul, "A Holier Holiday Season," *American Demographics*, December 2001, pp. 41–45.

57. Cited in Conlin, "Religion in the Workplace," p. 153.

58. C. P. Neck and J. F. Milliman, "Thought Self-Leadership: Finding Spiritual Fulfillment in Organizational Life," *Journal of Managerial Psychology* 9, no. 8 (1994), p. 9; for a recent review, see J.-C. Garcia-Zamor, "Workplace Spirituality and Organizational Performance," *Public Administration Review*, May–June 2003, pp. 355–363.

59. D. W. McCormick, "Spirituality and Management," *Journal of Managerial Psychology* 9, no. 6 (1994), p. 5; E. Brandt, "Corporate Pioneers Explore Spiritual Peace," *HRMagazine* 41, no. 4 (1996), p. 82; P. Leigh, "The New Spirit at Work," *Training and Development* 51, no. 3 (1997), p. 26; P. H. Mirvis, "Soul Work in Organizations," *Organization Science* 8, no. 2 (1997), p. 193; and J. Milliman, A. Czaplewski, and J. Ferguson, "An Exploratory Empirical Assessment of the Relationship Between Spirituality and Employee Work Attitudes," paper presented at the National Academy of Management Meeting, Washington, DC, August 2001.

60. Cited in Milliman et al., "Spirit and Community at Southwest Airlines."

61. P. Dvorak, "A Firm's Culture Can Get Lost in Translation," *Wall Street Journal*, April 3, 2006, pp. B1, B3; K. Kranhold, "The Immelt Era, Five Years Old, Transforms GE," *Wall Street Journal*, September 11, 2006, pp. B1, B3; and S. McCartney, "Teaching Americans How to Behave Abroad," *Wall Street Journal*, April 11, 2006, pp. D1, D4.

62. J. A. Chatman, "Matching People and Organizations: Selection and Socialization in Public Accounting Firms," *Administrative Science Quarterly*, September 1991, pp. 459–484; and A. E. M. Van Vianen, "Person-Organization Fit: The Match Between Newcomers' and Recruiters Preferences for Organizational Cultures," *Personnel Psychology*, Spring 2000, pp. 113–149.

63. J. E. Sheridan, "Organizational Culture and Employee Retention," *Academy of Management Journal*, December 1992, pp. 1036–1056; and Ibid., p. 68.

Human Resource Policies and Practices

To manage people well, companies should... elevate HR to a position of power and primacy in the organization.

—Jack Welch

18

After studying this chapter, you should be able to:

1 Define *initial selection* and identify the most useful methods.

2 Define *substantive selection* and identify the most useful methods.

3 Define *contingent selection* and contrast the arguments for and against drug testing.

4 Compare the four main types of training.

5 Contrast formal and informal training methods and contrast on-the-job and off-the-job training.

6 Describe the purposes of performance evaluation and list the methods by which it can be done.

7 Show how managers can improve performance evaluations.

8 Explain how diversity can be managed in organizations.

9 Show how a global context affects human resource management.

*i*t may surprise you to learn that scores on a 12-minute paper-and-pencil test are one of the very best predictors of corporate job performance. We're talking about the Wonderlic Personnel Test, one of the most extensively validated tests ever. We first met the test in Chapter 2. Here we're going to discuss one of the most interesting things about it: It works in the National Football League (NFL).

Making the Cut in the NFL

As NFL fans know, prior to the NFL draft every year, potential draftees go through a "combine" where their skills are tested: They run, they bench press, they scrimmage—and they also take the Wonderlic. Although players and members of the media often express skepticism about the validity of the test, evidence suggests it works.

Scores on the Wonderlic range from 0 to 50, with the average being about 19. The average chemist scores 31, compared to 26 for a journalist, 22 for a bank teller, and 15 for a warehouse worker.

Wonderlic scores vary by football position. Offensive linemen and quarterbacks, on average, have much higher scores than running backs, cornerbacks, or middle linebackers.

Most NFL experts will tell you that intelligence is most important for the positions of quarterback and offensive lineman, in large part because of the extensive playbook they have to learn and remember. Here's a sample of how some quarterbacks who have recently played in the NFL have fared on the Wonderlic:*

Very Smart: 30 and Higher   Alex Smith: 40, Eli Manning: 39, Charlie Frye: 38, Matt Leinart: 35, Tom Brady: 33, J.P. Losman: 31, Josh McCown: 30, Philip Rivers: 30, Tony Romo: 30, Matt Schaub: 30

Smart: 25–29   Marc Bulger: 29, Rex Grossman: 29, Matt Hasselbeck: 29, Brady Quinn: 29, Drew Brees: 28, Peyton Manning: 28, Jason Campbell: 27, Jay Cutler: 26, Carson Palmer: 26, Damon Huard: 25, Byron Leftwich: 25, Chad Pennington: 25, Ben Roethlisberger: 25

Above Average: 20–24   JaMarcus Russell: 24, Brett Favre: 22, Michael Vick: 20

It's clear that NFL quarterbacks are smart—they score well above average relative to the U.S. population. Do differences among the quarterbacks predict success? You might have your own opinion, but it doesn't appear that there is much of a relationship between how the quarterbacks scored on the Wonderlic and how they performed during the 2006-2007 season. (Scores for some NFL quarterbacks, such as Trent Green, were not available.) So, it appears that a certain level of intellect is required to make it as an NFL quarterback, but after a certain point, your arm (and legs) are as important as your brains.

Some complain that the Wonderlic gets more weight than it deserves. Things have come a long way since former Harvard player and Rhodes scholar Pat McInally's perfect score cost him in the draft because he was seen as *too* smart. McInally spent 10 years in the NFL and now works for Wonderlic.[1] ▪

*t*he message of this chapter is that human resource (HR) policies and practices—such as employee selection, training, and performance management—influence an organization's effectiveness.[2] However, studies show that many managers—even HR managers—often don't know which HR practices work and which don't. To see how much you know (before learning the right answers in the chapter!), take the self-assessment.

*Note: The players listed are 2006 starters and top picks from the 2007 draft. Some players (such as Michael Vick) did not play or start in the 2007–2008 NFL season.

Selection Practices

It's been said the most important HR decision you can make is who you hire. That makes sense—if you can figure out who the right people are. The objective of effective selection is to figure out who these right people are, by matching individual characteristics (ability, experience, and so on) with the requirements of the job.[3] When management fails to get a proper match, both employee performance and satisfaction suffer.

How the Selection Process Works

Exhibit 18-1 shows how the selection process works in most organizations. Having decided to apply for a job, applicants go through several stages—three are shown in the exhibit—during which they can be rejected at any time. In practice, some organizations forgo some of these steps in the interests of time. A meat-packing plant may hire someone who walks in the door (there is not a long line of people who want to "thread" a pig's intestines for a living). But most organizations follow a process that looks something like this. Let's go into a bit more detail about each of the stages.

Initial Selection

Initial selection devices are the first information applicants submit and are used for preliminary "rough cuts" to decide whether an applicant meets the basic qualifications for a job. Application forms (including letters of recommendation) are initial selection devices. We list background checks as either an initial selection device or a contingent selection device, depending on how the organization does it. Some organizations prefer to check into an applicant's background right away. Others wait until the applicant is about ready to be hired, contingent on everything checking out.

1 Define initial selection and identify the most useful methods.

Application Forms   You've no doubt submitted your fair share of applications. By itself, the information submitted on an application form is not a very useful predictor of performance. However, it can be a good initial screen. For example, there's no sense in spending time interviewing an applicant for a registered nurse position if he or she doesn't have the proper credentials (education, certification, experience). More and more organizations encourage applicants to submit an application online. It takes only a few minutes, and the form can be forwarded to the people responsible for making the hiring decision. For example, Starbucks (www.starbucks.com) has a career center page where you can search for available positions by location or job type and then apply online.

It's important that organizations be careful about the questions they ask on applications. It's pretty obvious that questions about race, gender, and nationality

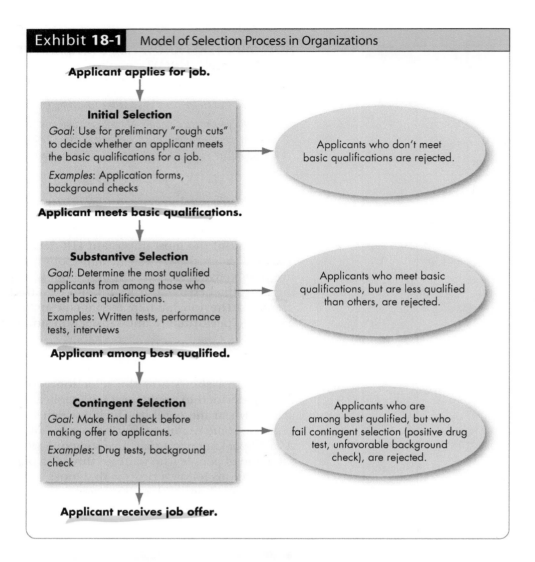

Exhibit 18-1   Model of Selection Process in Organizations

Applicant applies for job.

Initial Selection

Goal: Use for preliminary "rough cuts" to decide whether an applicant meets the basic qualifications for a job.

Examples: Application forms, background checks

→ Applicants who don't meet basic qualifications are rejected.

Applicant meets basic qualifications.

Substantive Selection

Goal: Determine the most qualified applicants from among those who meet basic qualifications.

Examples: Written tests, performance tests, interviews

→ Applicants who meet basic qualifications, but are less qualified than others, are rejected.

Applicant among best qualified.

Contingent Selection

Goal: Make final check before making offer to applicants.

Examples: Drug tests, background check

→ Applicants who are among best qualified, but who fail contingent selection (positive drug test, unfavorable background check), are rejected.

Applicant receives job offer.

are disallowed. However, it might surprise you to learn that other questions also put companies in legal jeopardy. For example, it generally is not permissible to ask about prior arrest records or even convictions unless the answer is job related.

Background Checks   More than 80 percent of employers conduct reference checks on applicants at some point in the hiring process. The reason is obvious: They want to know how an applicant did in past jobs and whether former employers would recommend hiring the person. The problem is that rarely do former employers provide useful information. In fact, nearly two-thirds of employers refuse to provide detailed reference information on applicants. Why? They are afraid of being sued for saying something bad about a former employee. Although this concern is often unfounded (employers are safe as long as they stick to documented facts), in our litigious society, most employers play it safe. The result is a paradox: Most employers want reference information, but few will give it out.

Letters of recommendation are another form of background check. These also aren't as useful as they may seem. Applicants self-select those who will write good letters, so almost all letters of recommendation are positive. In the end, readers of such letters either ignore them altogether or read "between the lines" to try to find hidden meaning there.

Finally, some employers do background checks on credit history or on criminal records. A bank hiring tellers, for example, would probably want to know about an applicant's criminal and credit histories. Because of the invasive nature of such checks, employers need to be sure there is a need for them. However, not checking can carry a legal cost. Manor Park Nursing Home in Texas failed to do a criminal background check of an employee who later sexually assaulted a resident of the nursing home. The jury awarded the plaintiff $1.1 million, concluding that the nursing home was negligent for failing to conduct a background check.[4]

Substantive Selection

2 *Define* substantive selection *and identify the most useful methods.*

If an applicant passes the initial screens, next are substantive selection methods. These are the heart of the selection process and include written tests, performance tests, and interviews.

Written Tests Long popular as selection devices, written tests ("paper-and-pencil" tests—though most are now available online) suffered a decline in use between the late 1960s and mid-1980s, especially in the United States. They were frequently characterized as discriminatory, and many organizations had not validated them as job-related. The past 20 years, however, have seen a resurgence in their use. It's been estimated that today more than 60 percent of all U.S. organizations and most of the Fortune 1000 use some type of employment test.[5] Managers have come to recognize that there are valid tests available and they can be helpful in predicting who will be successful on the job.[6] Applicants, however, tend to view written tests as less valid and fair than interviews or performance tests.[7]

Typical written tests include (1) intelligence or cognitive ability tests, (2) personality tests, (3) integrity tests, and (4) interest inventories.

Tests of intellectual ability, spatial and mechanical ability, perceptual accuracy, and motor ability have proven to be valid predictors for many skilled, semiskilled, and unskilled operative jobs in industrial organizations.[8] Intelligence tests have proven to be particularly good predictors for jobs that include cognitively complex tasks.[9] Many experts argue that intelligence tests are the *single best* selection measure across jobs. A recent review of the literature suggested that intelligence tests are at least as valid in European Economic Community (EEC) nations as in the United States.[10]

The use of personality tests has grown in the past decade. Japanese automakers, when staffing plants in the United States, have relied heavily on written tests to identify candidates who will be high performers.[11] Getting a job with Toyota can require up to 3 days of testing and interviewing. Organizations use numerous measures of the Big Five traits in selection decisions. The traits that best predict job performance are conscientiousness and positive self-concept.[12] This makes sense in that conscientious people tend to be motivated and dependable, and positive people are "can-do" oriented and persistent. Personality tests are relatively inexpensive and simple to use and administer.

As ethical problems have increased in organizations, integrity tests have gained popularity. These are paper-and-pencil tests that measure factors such as dependability, carefulness, responsibility, and honesty. The evidence is impressive that these tests are powerful in predicting supervisory ratings of job performance and counterproductive employee behavior on the job, such as theft, discipline problems, and excessive absenteeism.[13]

You may wonder why applicants would respond truthfully to personality and integrity tests. After all, who would answer "strongly disagree" to the question "I always show up on time," even if they were generally late? Research shows that

Written tests are the heart of the selection process at Cabela's, a specialty retailer of hunting, fishing, camping, and other outdoor merchandise. Job applicants for the Cabela's contact center and retail stores are given a difficult 150-question test that measures the depth of their outdoor sport expertise. Cabela's management believes that the tests are helpful in determining who will succeed in providing customers with exceptional service and product knowledge.

although applicants can "fake good" if they are motivated to do so, it doesn't appear that this fakery undermines the validity of personality and integrity tests.[14] Why? One speculation is that if faking does exist, those who "fake good" on selection tests also probably continue to present themselves in a desirable light once on the job. Thus, this sort of impression management not only helps get people hired but it helps them perform better on the job, at least unless taken to pathological degrees.

Performance-Simulation Tests   What better way to find out whether applicants can do a job successfully than by having them do it? That's precisely the logic of performance-simulation tests.

Although they are more complicated to develop and more difficult to administer than written tests, performance-simulation tests have increased in popularity during the past several decades. This appears to be due to the fact that they have higher "face validity" than do most written tests.

The two best-known performance-simulation tests are work samples and assessment centers. The former are suited to routine jobs, while the latter are relevant for the selection of managerial personnel.

Work sample tests are hands-on simulations of part or all of the job that must be performed by applicants. By carefully devising work samples based on specific job tasks, management determines the knowledge, skills, and abilities needed for each job. Then each work sample element is matched with a corresponding job performance element. Work samples are widely used in the hiring of skilled workers, such as welders, machinists, carpenters, and electricians. For instance, job candidates for production jobs at BMW's factory in South Carolina have 90 minutes to perform a variety of typical work tasks on a specially built simulated assembly line.[15] Work samples yield validities superior to written aptitude and personality tests.[16]

A more elaborate set of performance-simulation tests, specifically designed to evaluate a candidate's managerial potential, are administered in **assessment centers**. In these tests, line executives, supervisors, and/or trained psychologists evaluate candidates as they go through 1 to several days of exercises that simulate real problems they would confront on the job.[17] For instance, a candidate might be required to play the role of a manager who must decide how to respond to 10 memos in an in-basket within a 2-hour period.

Interviews   Of all the selection devices organizations around the globe use to differentiate candidates, the interview continues to be the most common.[18] Not only is the interview widely used, it also seems to carry a great deal of weight. That is, the results tend to have a disproportionate amount of influence on the selection decision. The candidate who performs poorly in the employment interview is likely to be cut from the applicant pool regardless of experience, test scores, or letters of recommendation. Conversely, "all too often, the person most polished in job-seeking techniques, particularly those used in the interview process, is the one hired, even though he or she may not be the best candidate for the position."[19]

These findings are important because of the unstructured manner in which the selection interview is frequently conducted.[20] The unstructured interview—short in duration, casual, and made up of random questions—is not a very effective selection device.[21] The data gathered from such interviews are typically biased and often only modestly related to future job performance. Still, managers are reluctant to use structured interviews in place of their favorite pet questions (such as "If you could be any animal, what would you be, and why?").[22]

Without structure, a number of biases can distort interview results. These biases include interviewers tending to favor applicants who share their

MYTH OR SCIENCE?

"It's First Impressions That Count"

*t*his statement is true. When we meet someone for the first time, we notice a number of things about that person: physical characteristics, clothes, firmness of handshake, gestures, tone of voice, and the like. We then use these impressions to fit the person into ready-made categories. And these first impressions tend to hold greater weight than information received later.

The best evidence about first impressions comes from research on employment interviews. Findings clearly demonstrate that first impressions count. A recent study suggested that interviewers often know whether they will hire someone soon after the opening handshake and small talk.[23]

Research on applicant appearance confirms the power of first impressions.[24] Attractive applicants fare better in interviews and overweight applicants are penalized.

Another study revealed just how superficial interviewer judgments often are. These researchers responded to employment ads in Chicago and Boston. In their responses, they submitted fake résumés of high and low quality, and used names that were traditionally African American (Kenya and Hakim) and Caucasian (Allison and Brad). The researchers found that the résumés with Caucasian names received 50 percent more callbacks than those with African American names. Moreover, while 27 percent of the high-quality résumés with Caucasian names received callbacks, only 8 percent of the high-quality résumés with African American names did.[25]

A final body of confirming research finds that interviewers' post-interview evaluations of applicants conform, to a substantial degree, to their pre-interview impressions.[26] That is, those first impressions carry considerable weight in shaping the interviewers' final evaluations, assuming that the interview elicits no highly negative information. ■

attitudes, giving unduly high weight to negative information, and allowing the order in which applicants are interviewed to influence evaluations.[27] Using a standardized set of questions, providing interviewers with a uniform method of recording information, and standardizing the rating of the applicant's qualifications reduce the variability of results across applicants and enhance the validity of the interview as a selection device. The effectiveness of the interview also improves when employers use behavioral structured interviews.[28] This interview technique requires applicants to describe how they handled specific problems and situations in previous jobs. It's built on the assumption that past behavior offers the best predictor of future behavior.

In practice, most organizations use interviews for more than a "prediction-of-performance" device.[29] Companies as diverse as Southwest Airlines, Disney, Bank of America, Microsoft, Procter & Gamble, and Harrah's Entertainment use the interview to assess applicant–organization fit. So in addition to specific, job-relevant skills, organizations are looking at candidates' personality characteristics, personal values, and the like to find individuals who fit with the organization's culture and image.

Contingent Selection

If applicants pass the substantive selection methods, they are basically ready to be hired, contingent on a final check. One common contingent method is a drug test. For example, Publix grocery stores make a tentative offer to

work sample test *A test that is a miniature replica of a job that is used to evaluate the performance abilities of job candidates.*

assessment centers *A set of performance-simulation tests designed to evaluate a candidate's managerial potential.*

Wheeler Landscaping in Chagrin Falls, Ohio, uses the contingent selection method of drug testing before hiring new employees. A growing number of small businesses like Wheeler, which has 76 employees, are using drug tests to help reduce insurance costs, workers' compensation claims due to workplace accidents, absenteeism, and employee theft.

Source: Amy E. Voigt/ The New York Times

3 *Define* contingent selection *and contrast the arguments for and against drug testing.*

applicants, contingent on their passing a drug test. This means Publix is ready to make an offer to the applicant as long as the person checks out to be drug free.

Drug testing is controversial. Many applicants think it is unfair or invasive to test them without reasonable suspicion. Such individuals likely believe that drug use is a private matter and applicants should be tested on factors that directly bear on job performance, not lifestyle issues that may or may not be job relevant. Drug tests typically screen out individuals who have used marijuana but not alcohol (for both legal and practical reasons—alcohol is legal and leaves the system in 24 hours).

Employers might counter this view with the argument that drug use and abuse are extremely costly, not just in terms of financial resources but in terms of people's safety. Moreover, employers have the law on their side. The Supreme Court has concluded that drug tests are "minimally invasive" selection procedures that as a rule do not violate individuals' rights.

Drug tests are not cheap. If the first test (typically a urine test) turns up positive, then the result is reanalyzed to make sure. Contrary to popular claims, the tests generally are quite accurate, and results are not easily faked. They tend to be quite precise, telling the employer what specific kind of drug appeared to be in the applicant's system. Despite the controversy over drug testing, it's probably here to stay.

Training and Development Programs

Competent employees don't remain competent forever. Skills deteriorate and can become obsolete and new skills need to be learned. That's why organizations spend billions of dollars each year on formal training. For instance, it was reported that U.S. corporations with 100 or more employees spent more than $51 billion on formal training in a recent year.[30] For example, IBM, Accenture, Intel, and Lockheed Martin each spend in excess of $300 million per year on employee training.[31]

Types of Training

Training can include everything from teaching employees basic reading skills to conducting advanced courses in executive leadership. Here we discuss four general skill categories—basic literacy and technical, interpersonal, and problem-solving skills. In addition, we briefly discuss ethics training.

4   Compare the four main types of training.

Basic Literacy Skills   Statistics show that nearly 40 percent of the U.S. labor force and more than 50 percent of high school graduates don't possess the basic work skills needed to perform in today's workplace.[32] The National Institute of Learning estimates that this literacy problem costs corporate America about $60 billion per year in lost productivity.[33] This problem, of course, isn't unique to the United States. It's a worldwide problem—from the most developed countries to the least.[34] For many undeveloped countries, where few workers can read or have gone beyond the equivalent of the third grade, widespread illiteracy means there is almost no hope of competing in a global economy.

Organizations increasingly have to teach basic reading and math skills to their employees. For instance, jobs at gun manufacturer Smith & Wesson have become more complex.[35] A literacy audit showed that employees needed to have at least an eighth-grade reading level to do typical workplace tasks. Yet 30 percent of the company's 676 workers with no degree scored below eighth-grade levels in either reading or math. These employees were told that they wouldn't lose their jobs, but they had to take basic skill classes, paid for by the company and provided on company time. After the first round of classes, 70 percent of attendees brought their skills up to the target level. And these improved skills allowed employees to do a better job. They displayed greater ease in writing and reading charts, graphs, and bulletin boards, increased abilities to use fractions and decimals, better overall communication, and a significant increase in confidence.

Emerging technology in the mobile-phone industry drives the need for technical-skill training at TSI Telecommunications Services. TSI trained customer-service employees to troubleshoot number-transfer orders when consumers were allowed to change their telecommunications service provider while keeping their existing telephone number. Improving employees' technical skills enables TSI to provide valuable services for its wireless carrier customers that operate in a complicated and rapidly changing industry.

Source: David Kadlubowski/ The New York Times

Technical Skills   Most training is directed at upgrading and improving an employee's technical skills. Technical training has become increasingly important today for two reasons—new technology and new structural designs in the organization.

Jobs change as a result of new technologies and improved methods. For instance, many auto repair personnel have had to undergo extensive training to fix and maintain recent models with computer-monitored engines, electronic stabilizing systems, GPS, keyless remote entry, and other innovations. Similarly, computer-controlled equipment has required millions of production employees to learn a whole new set of skills.[36]

In addition, technical training has become increasingly important because of changes in organization design. As organizations flatten their structures, expand their use of teams, and break down traditional departmental barriers, employees need mastery of a wider variety of tasks and increased knowledge of how their organization operates. For instance, the restructuring of jobs at Miller Brewing Co. around empowered teams has led management to introduce a comprehensive business literacy program to help employees better understand competition, the state of the beer industry, where the company's revenues come from, how costs are calculated, and where employees fit into the company's value chain.[37]

Interpersonal Skills   Almost all employees belong to a work unit, and their work performance depends to some degree on their ability to effectively interact with their coworkers and their boss. Some employees have excellent interpersonal skills, but others require training to improve theirs. This includes learning how to be a better listener, how to communicate ideas more clearly, and how to be a more effective team player.

Problem-Solving Skills   Managers, as well as many employees who perform nonroutine tasks, have to solve problems on their jobs. When people require these skills but are deficient in them, they can participate in problem-solving training. This can include activities to sharpen their logic, reasoning, and problem-defining skills as well as their abilities to assess causation, develop and analyze alternatives, and select solutions. Problem-solving training has become a basic part of almost every organizational effort to introduce self-managed teams or implement quality-management programs.

What About Ethics Training?   A recent survey found that about 75 percent of employees working in the 1,000 largest U.S. corporations receive ethics training.[38] This training may be included in a newly hired employee's orientation program, made part of an ongoing developmental training program, or provided to all employees as a periodic reinforcement of ethical principles.[39] But the jury is still out on whether you can actually teach ethics.[40]

Critics argue that ethics are based on values, and value systems are fixed at an early age. By the time employers hire people, their ethical values have already been established. The critics also claim that ethics cannot be formally "taught" but must be learned by example.

Supporters of ethics training argue that values can be learned and changed after early childhood. And even if they couldn't, ethics training would be effective because it helps employees to recognize ethical dilemmas and become more aware of the ethical issues underlying their actions. Another argument is that ethics training reaffirms an organization's expectations that members will act ethically.

International OB

Cultural Training

In a global economy, employee training is no longer limited to the specific tasks of the job. As more and more positions in the information technology and service industries move to India from the United States, many companies are training their Indian employees to improve their cultural skills when dealing with American clients.

For example, the Hyderabad offices of Sierra Atlantic, a California-based software company, trains its Indian employees in various aspects of U.S. culture, including addressing colleagues as Mr. or Ms., learning how to interact with others during a conference call, and even how to sip wine. According to Lu Ellen Schafer, executive director at Global Savvy, a consulting firm based in California, "The training in American culture is not to make Indian software professionals less Indian. It is to make them more globally competent."

Some companies are benefiting from cultural training. Sierra Atlantic's offices in Hyderabad, for example, won a bid with an American firm over an Indian competitor because the Sierra employees were viewed as a better cultural fit. Such successes make it likely that companies with foreign clients will either adopt or continue to use cultural training.

Source: Based on S. Rai, "Indian Companies Are Adding Western Flavor," *New York Times,* August 19, 2003, p. W1.

Training Methods

Training methods are most readily classified as formal or informal and as on-the-job or off-the-job training.

5   *Contrast formal and informal training methods and contrast on-the-job and off-the-job training.*

Historically, training meant *formal training*. It's planned in advance and has a structured format. However, recent evidence indicates that 70 percent of workplace learning is made up of *informal training*—unstructured, unplanned, and easily adapted to situations and individuals—for teaching skills and keeping employees current.[41] In reality, most informal training is nothing other than employees helping each other out. They share information and solve work-related problems with one another. Perhaps the most important outcome of this realization is that many managers are now supportive of what used to be considered "idle chatter." At a Siemens plant in North Carolina, for instance, management now recognizes that people needn't be on the production line to be working.[42] Discussions around the water cooler or in the cafeteria weren't, as managers thought, about nonwork topics such as sports or politics. They largely focused on solving work-related problems. So now Siemens's management encourages such casual meetings.

On-the-job training includes job rotation, apprenticeships, understudy assignments, and formal mentoring programs. But the primary drawback of these on-the-job training methods is that they often disrupt the workplace. So organizations invest in *off-the-job training*. The $51 billion figure we cited earlier for training costs was largely spent on the formal off-the-job variety. What types of training might this include? The most popular continues to be live classroom lectures. But it also encompasses videotapes, public seminars, self-study programs, Internet courses, satellite-beamed television classes, and group activities that use role-plays and case studies.

In recent years, the fastest-growing means for delivering training is probably computer-based training, or e-training.[43] Kinko's, for instance, has created an internal network that allows its 20,000 employees to take online courses covering everything from products to policies.[44] Cisco Systems provides a curriculum of

At Ito Yokado, the largest supermarket chain in Japan, week-long training for new employees includes role-playing exercises. The group of young men shown here is learning the proper techniques of guiding blind, disabled, and elderly people. This off-the-job training technique of role-playing is effective because employees become sensitive to the special needs of shoppers who require assistance.

training courses on its corporate intranet, organized by job titles, specific technologies, and products.[45] Although more than 5,000 companies now offer all or some of their employee training online, it's unclear how effective it actually is. On the positive side, e-training increases flexibility by allowing organizations to deliver materials anywhere and at any time. It also seems to be fast and efficient. On the other hand, it's expensive to design self-paced online materials, many employees miss the social interaction provided by a classroom environment, online learners are often more susceptible to distractions, and "clicking through" training is no assurance that employees have actually learned anything.[46]

Individualizing Formal Training to Fit the Employee's Learning Style

The way you process, internalize, and remember new and difficult material isn't necessarily the same way others do. This fact means that effective formal training should be individualized to reflect the learning style of the employee.[47]

Some examples of different learning styles are reading, watching, listening, and participating. Some people absorb information better when they read about it. They're the kind of people who can learn to use computers by sitting in their study and reading manuals. Some people learn best by observation. They watch others and then imitate the behaviors they've seen. Such people can watch someone use a computer for a while and then copy what they've done. Listeners rely heavily on their auditory senses to absorb information. They would prefer to learn how to use a computer, for instance, by listening to an audiotape. People who prefer a participating style learn by doing. They want to sit down, turn on the computer, and gain hands-on experience by practicing.

You can translate these styles into different learning methods. To maximize learning, readers should be given books or other reading material to review; watchers should get the opportunity to observe individuals modeling the new skills either in person or on video; listeners will benefit from hearing lectures or audiotapes; and participants will benefit most from experiential opportunities in which they can simulate and practice the new skills.

These different learning styles are obviously not mutually exclusive. In fact, good teachers recognize that their students learn differently and, therefore, provide multiple learning methods. They assign readings before class; give lectures; use visual aids to illustrate concepts; and have students participate in group projects, case analyses, role-plays, and experiential learning exercises. If you know the preferred style of an employee, you can design a formal training program to take advantage of this preference. If you don't have that information, it's probably best to design the program to use a variety of learning styles. Over-reliance on a single style places individuals who don't learn well from that style at a disadvantage.

Evaluating Effectiveness

Most training programs work rather well in that the majority of people who undergo training learn more than those who do not, react positively to the training experience, and after the training engage in the behaviors targeted by the program. Still, some factors make certain programs work better than others. For example, although lecture styles have a poor reputation, they are surprisingly effective training methods. On the other hand, conducting a needs assessment prior to training was relatively unimportant in predicting the success of a training program.[48]

The success of training also depends on the individual. If individuals are unmotivated to learn, they will benefit very little. What factors determine training motivation? Personality is important: Those with an internal locus of control, high conscientiousness, high cognitive ability, and high self-efficacy learn more in training programs. The training climate also is important: When trainees believe that there are opportunities on the job to apply their newly learned skills and enough resources to apply what they have learned, they are more motivated to learn and do better in training programs.[49]

Performance Evaluation

Would you study differently or exert a different level of effort for a college course graded on a pass–fail basis than for one that awarded letter grades from A to F? Students typically tell us they study harder when letter grades are at stake. In addition, when they take a course on a pass–fail basis, they tend to do just enough to ensure a passing grade.

This finding illustrates how performance evaluation systems influence behavior. Major determinants of your in-class behavior and out-of-class studying effort in college are the criteria and techniques your instructor uses to evaluate your performance. What applies in the college context also applies to employees at work. In this section, we show how the choice of a performance evaluation system and the way it's administered can be an important force influencing employee behavior.

Purposes of Performance Evaluation

6 Describe the purposes of performance evaluation and list the methods by which it can be done.

Performance evaluation serves a number of purposes.[50] One purpose is to help management make general *human resource decisions*. Evaluations provide input into important decisions such as promotions, transfers, and terminations. Evaluations also *identify training and development needs*. They pinpoint employee skills and competencies that are currently inadequate but for which remedial programs can be developed. Evaluations also fulfill the purpose of *providing feedback to employees* on how the organization views their performance. Furthermore, performance evaluations are the *basis for reward allocations*. Decisions as to who gets merit pay increases and other rewards are frequently determined by performance evaluations.

Each of these functions of performance evaluation is valuable. Yet their importance to us depends on the perspective we're taking. Several are clearly relevant to human resource management decisions. But our interest is in organizational behavior. As a result, we shall be emphasizing performance evaluation as a mechanism for providing feedback and as a determinant of reward allocations.

What Do We Evaluate?

The criteria that management chooses to evaluate when appraising employee performance will have a major influence on what employees do. The three most popular sets of criteria are individual task outcomes, behaviors, and traits.

Individual Task Outcomes   If ends count, rather than means, then management should evaluate an employee's task outcomes. Using task outcomes, a plant manager could be judged on criteria such as quantity produced, scrap generated, and cost per unit of production. Similarly, a salesperson could be assessed on overall sales volume in the territory, dollar increase in sales, and number of new accounts established.

General Electric Company evaluates the performance of its corporate managers, including the group of GE's top executives in India shown here, on five "growth traits." The traits are inclusiveness, imagination/ courage, expertise, external focus, and clear thinking/decisiveness. By evaluating its 5,000 top managers on these traits, GE believes it will generate corporate leaders who will help the company achieve its goal of building the revenue growth of its business units that operate throughout the world.

Behaviors In many cases, it's difficult to identify specific outcomes that can be directly attributed to an employee's actions. This is particularly true of personnel in advisory or support positions and individuals whose work assignments are intrinsically part of a group effort. We may readily evaluate the group's performance but have difficulty distinguishing clearly the contribution of each group member. In such instances, it's not unusual for management to evaluate the employee's behavior. Using the previous examples, behaviors of a plant manager that could be used for performance evaluation purposes might include promptness in submitting monthly reports or the leadership style the manager exhibits. Pertinent salesperson behaviors could be the average number of contact calls made per day or sick days used per year.

Note that these behaviors needn't be limited to those directly related to individual productivity.[51] As we pointed out in our previous discussion on organizational citizenship behavior (see specifically Chapters 1 and 4), helping others, making suggestions for improvements, and volunteering for extra duties make work groups and organizations more effective and often are incorporated into evaluations of employee performance.

Traits The weakest set of criteria, yet one that is still widely used by organizations, is individual traits.[52] We say they're weaker than either task outcomes or behaviors because they're farthest removed from the actual performance of the job itself. Traits such as having a good attitude, showing confidence, being dependable, looking busy, or possessing a wealth of experience may or may not be highly correlated with positive task outcomes, but only the naive would ignore the reality that such traits are frequently used as criteria for assessing an employee's level of performance.

Who Should Do the Evaluating?

Who should evaluate an employee's performance? By tradition, the task has fallen to the manager, on the grounds that managers are held responsible for their employees' performance. But that logic may be flawed. Others may actually be able to do the job better.

With many of today's organizations using self-managed teams, telecommuting, and other organizing devices that distance bosses from their employees, an employee's immediate superior may not be the most reliable judge of that employee's performance. Thus, in more and more cases, peers and even subordinates are being asked to participate in the performance evaluation process. Also, increasingly, employees are participating in their own performance evaluation. For instance, a recent survey found that about half of executives and 53 percent of employees now have input into their performance evaluations.[53] As you might surmise, self-evaluations often suffer from overinflated assessment and self-serving bias. Moreover, self-evaluations are often low in agreement with superiors' ratings.[54] Because of these drawbacks, self-evaluations are probably better suited to developmental than evaluative purposes and should be combined with other sources of information to reduce rating errors.

In most situations, in fact, it is highly advisable to use multiple sources of ratings. Any individual performance rating may say as much about the rater as about the person being evaluated. By averaging across raters, we can obtain a more reliable, unbiased, and accurate performance evaluation.

The latest approach to performance evaluation is the use of 360-degree evaluations.[55] It provides for performance feedback from the full circle of daily contacts that an employee might have, ranging from mailroom personnel to customers to bosses to peers (see Exhibit 18-2). The number of appraisals can be as few as 3 or 4 or as many as 25, with most organizations collecting 5 to 10 per employee.

More and more employers are using 360-degree programs. Some of them are Alcoa, DuPont, Levi Strauss, Honeywell, UPS, Sprint, AT&T, and W. L. Gore & Associates. What's their appeal? By relying on feedback from coworkers, customers, and subordinates, these organizations are hoping to give everyone more of a sense of participation in the review process and gain more accurate readings on employee performance.

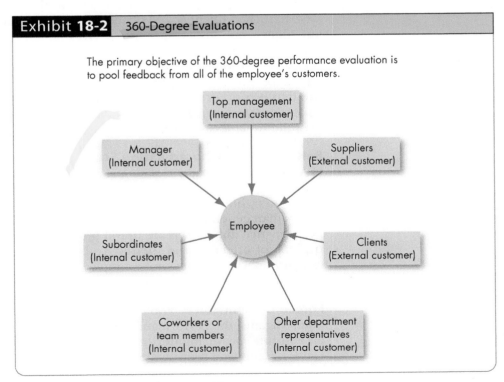

Exhibit 18-2   360-Degree Evaluations

The primary objective of the 360-degree performance evaluation is to pool feedback from all of the employee's customers.

- Top management (Internal customer)
- Manager (Internal customer)
- Suppliers (External customer)
- Subordinates (Internal customer)
- Employee
- Clients (External customer)
- Coworkers or team members (Internal customer)
- Other department representatives (Internal customer)

Source: Adapted from *Personnel Journal*, November 1994, p. 100.

The evidence on the effectiveness of 360-degree evaluations, however, is mixed.[56] It provides employees with a wider perspective of their performance. But it also has the potential for being misused. For instance, to minimize costs, many organizations don't spend the time to train evaluators in giving constructive criticism. Some organizations allow employees to choose the peers and subordinates who evaluate them, which can artificially inflate feedback. Problems also arise from the difficulty of reconciling disagreements and contradictions between rater groups.

Methods of Performance Evaluation

The previous sections explained *what* we evaluate and *who* should do the evaluating. Now we ask: *How* do we evaluate an employee's performance? That is, what are the specific techniques for evaluation?

Written Essays   Probably the simplest method of evaluation is to write a narrative describing an employee's strengths, weaknesses, past performance, potential, and suggestions for improvement. The written essay requires no complex forms or extensive training to complete. But in this method a good or bad appraisal may be determined as much by the evaluator's writing skill as by the employee's actual level of performance.

Critical Incidents   **Critical incidents** focus the evaluator's attention on the behaviors that are key in making the difference between executing a job effectively and executing it ineffectively. That is, the appraiser writes down anecdotes that describe what the employee did that was especially effective or ineffective. The key here is to cite only specific behaviors, not vaguely defined personality traits. A list of critical incidents provides a rich set of examples from which the employee can be shown the behaviors that are desirable and those that call for improvement.

Graphic Rating Scales   One of the oldest and most popular methods of evaluation is the use of **graphic rating scales**. In this method, a set of performance factors, such as quantity and quality of work, depth of knowledge, cooperation, attendance, and initiative, is listed. The evaluator then goes down the list and rates each on incremental scales. The scales may specify five points, so a factor such as *job knowledge* might be rated 1 ("poorly informed about work duties") to 5 ("has complete mastery of all phases of the job"). Although they don't provide the depth of information that essays or critical incidents do, graphic rating scales are less time-consuming to develop and administer. They also allow for quantitative analysis and comparison.

Behaviorally Anchored Rating Scales   **Behaviorally anchored rating scales (BARS)** combine major elements from the critical incident and graphic rating scale approaches: The appraiser rates the employees based on items along a continuum, but the points are examples of actual behavior on the given job rather than general descriptions or traits. Examples of job-related behavior and performance dimensions are found by asking participants to give specific illustrations of effective and ineffective behavior regarding each performance dimension. These behavioral examples are then translated into a set of performance dimensions, each dimension having varying levels of performance.

Forced Comparisons   Forced comparisons evaluate one individual's performance against the performance of another or others. It is a relative rather than an absolute measuring device. The two most popular comparisons are group order ranking and individual ranking.

The **group order ranking** requires the evaluator to place employees into a particular classification, such as top one-fifth or second one-fifth. This method is often used in recommending students to graduate schools. Evaluators are asked whether the student ranks in the top 5 percent of the class, the next 5 percent, the next 15 percent, and so forth. But in this type of performance appraisal, managers deal with all their subordinates. Therefore, if a rater has 20 employees, only 4 can be in the top fifth and, of course, 4 must also be relegated to the bottom fifth. The **individual ranking** approach rank-orders employees from best to worst. If the manager is required to appraise 30 employees, this approach assumes that the difference between the first and second employee is the same as that between the twenty-first and twenty-second. Even though some of the employees may be closely grouped, no ties are permitted. The result is a clear ordering of employees, from the highest performer down to the lowest.

One parallel to the use of forced ranking systems is a forced distribution in the giving of college grades. Why would universities do this?

As shown in Exhibit 18-3, the average GPA of a Princeton University undergraduate has gotten much higher over time.[57]

It's not just Princeton. For example, the average student GPA at Wheaton College was 2.75 in 1962. Now it's 3.40. At Pomona College, the average GPA was 3.06 in 1970. Now it's 3.43. About half the grades at Duke, Harvard, and Columbia are in the "A" range. At Harvard, 91 percent of seniors graduated with some sort of honors in 2001. These are just randomly selected examples.

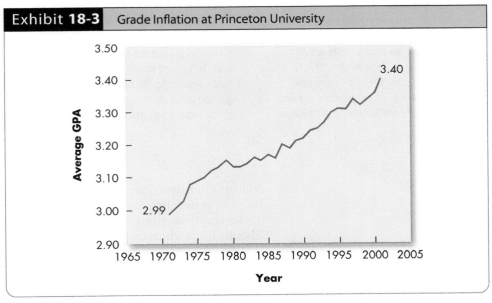

| Exhibit **18-3** | Grade Inflation at Princeton University |

Source: www.gradeinflation.com.

---

critical incidents   *A way of evaluating the behaviors that are key in making the difference between executing a job effectively and executing it ineffectively.*

graphic rating scales   *An evaluation method in which the evaluator rates performance factors on an incremental scale.*

behaviorally anchored rating scales (BARS)   *Scales that combine major elements from the critical incident and graphic rating scale approaches: The appraiser rates the employees based on items along a continuum, but the points are examples of actual behavior on the given job rather than general descriptions or traits.*

group order ranking   *An evaluation method that places employees into a particular classification, such as quartiles.*

individual ranking   *An evaluation method that rank-orders employees from best to worst.*

OB *In the News*

The Rise and Fall of Forced Ranking

Forced ranking was once one of the fastest-growing trends in performance evaluation. Companies like Ford, GE, Microsoft, Sun Microsystems, H&R Block, and Sprint were among the 33 percent of U.S. companies that were ranking their employees from best to worst and then using those rankings to compensate, manage, and fire.

Forced ranking, or what has derisively been called "rank and yank" by its critics, was created because many top executives had become frustrated by managers who rated all their employees "above average." In addition, executives wanted a system that would increase the organization's competitiveness—one that would reward the very best performers and encourage poor performers to leave.

For instance, all 18,000 of Ford Motor's managers underwent the forced ranking process. These managers were divided into groups of 30 to 50 and then rated. For each group, 10 percent had to get an A, 80 percent a B, and 10 percent a C. Anyone receiving a C was barred from a pay raise, and 2 consecutive years of a C rating resulted in either a demotion or a termination.

The best-known "rank and yank" program is GE's "20–70–10 plan." The company forces the heads of each of its divisions to review all managers and professional employees and to identify their top 20 percent, middle 70 percent, and bottom 10 percent. GE then does everything possible to keep and reward its top performers and fires all bottom-group performers.

Forced ranking grew in popularity because it was seen as a means to continually improve an organization's workforce and to reward those who are most deserving. Research has suggested that forced ranking systems yield initial improvements in productivity, but

that their benefits diminished over time as the poor performers are weeded out.

Although forced ranking systems are still in use, many companies that adopted the system, like Hallmark Cards, have recently dropped it. They found it undermined employee morale and created a "zero-sum game" that discouraged cooperation and teamwork. In addition, several companies have been hit with age discrimination suits by older workers who claim the system has adversely affected them. Several large companies, including Ford and Capital One, settled class-action suits in which former employees claimed that forced ranking systems discriminated against employees based on sex, age, or race.

Sources: Based on K. Holland, "Performance Reviews: Many Need Improvement," *New York Times*, September 10, 2006, www.nytimes.com/2006/09/10/business/yourmoney/10mgmt.html; D. Stafford, "Forced Rankings Are No Cure," *Kansas City Star*, January 27, 2005; and S. E. Scullen, P. K. Bergey, and L. Aiman-Smith, "Forced Distribution Rating Systems and the Improvement of Workforce Potential: A Baseline Simulation," *Personnel Psychology*, Spring 2005, pp. 1–32.

Almost all universities have seen considerable grade inflation, although, interestingly, it may be more severe at prestigious institutions.

In response to grade inflation, some colleges have instituted forced grade distributions whereby professors must give a certain percentage of students A's, B's, and C's. This is exactly what Princeton recently did; each department can now give A's to no more than 35 percent of its students. Natasha Gopaul, a senior at Princeton, commented, "You do feel you might be one of the ones they just cut off."

Suggestions for Improving Performance Evaluations

7   Show how managers can improve performance evaluations.

The performance evaluation process is a potential minefield of problems. For instance, evaluators can unconsciously inflate evaluations (positive leniency), understate performance (negative leniency), or allow the assessment of one characteristic to unduly influence the assessment of others (the halo error). Some appraisers bias their evaluations by unconsciously favoring people who have qualities and traits similar to their own (the similarity error). And, of course, some evaluators see the evaluation process as a political opportunity to overtly reward or punish employees they like or dislike. Although there are no protections that will *guarantee* accurate performance evaluations, the following suggestions can significantly help to make the process more objective and fair.

Use Multiple Evaluators   As the number of evaluators increases, the probability of attaining more accurate information increases. If rater error tends to follow a normal curve, an increase in the number of appraisers will tend to find the majority congregating about the middle. We often see multiple evaluators in competitions in such sports as diving and gymnastics. A set of evaluators judges a performance, the highest and lowest scores are dropped, and the final evaluation is made up of those remaining. The logic of multiple evaluators applies to organizations as well.

If an employee has had 10 supervisors, 9 having rated her excellent and 1 poor, we can safely discount the one poor evaluation. Therefore, by moving employees about within the organization so as to gain a number of evaluations or by using multiple assessors (as provided in 360-degree appraisals), we increase the probability of achieving more valid and reliable evaluations.

Evaluate Selectively   Appraisers should evaluate only in areas in which they have some expertise.[58] This precaution increases the interrater agreement and makes the evaluation a more valid process. It also recognizes that different organizational levels often have different orientations toward those being rated and observe them in different settings. In general, therefore, appraisers should be as close as possible, in terms of organizational level, to the individual being evaluated. Conversely, the more levels that separate the evaluator and the person being evaluated, the less opportunity the evaluator has to observe the individual's behavior and, not surprisingly, the greater the possibility for inaccuracies.

Train Evaluators   If you can't *find* good evaluators, the alternative is to *make* good evaluators. There is substantial evidence that training evaluators can make them more accurate raters.[59]

Common errors such as halo and leniency have been minimized or eliminated in workshops where managers practice observing and rating behaviors. These workshops typically run from 1 to 3 days, but allocating many hours to training may not always be necessary. One case has been cited in which both halo and leniency errors were decreased immediately after exposing evaluators to explanatory training sessions lasting only 5 minutes.[60] But the effects of training appear to diminish over time.[61] This suggests the need for regular refresher sessions.

Provide Employees with Due Process   The concept of *due process* can be applied to appraisals to increase the perception that employees are being treated fairly.[62] Three features characterize due process systems: (1) Individuals are provided with adequate notice of what is expected of them; (2) all evidence relevant to a proposed violation is aired in a fair hearing so the individuals affected can respond; and (3) the final decision is based on the evidence and free of bias.

There is considerable evidence that evaluation systems often violate employees' due process by providing them with infrequent and relatively general performance feedback, allowing them little input into the appraisal process, and knowingly introducing bias into performance ratings. However, when due process has been part of the evaluation system, employees report positive reactions to the appraisal process, perceive the evaluation results as more accurate, and express increased intent to remain with the organization.

Providing Performance Feedback

For many managers, few activities are more unpleasant than providing performance feedback to employees.[63] In fact, unless pressured by organizational policies and controls, managers are likely to ignore this responsibility.[64]

Why the reluctance to give performance feedback? There seem to be at least three reasons. First, managers are often uncomfortable discussing performance weaknesses directly with employees. Even though almost every employee could stand to improve in some areas, managers fear a confrontation when presenting negative feedback. This apprehension apparently applies even when people give negative feedback to a computer! Bill Gates reports that Microsoft conducted a project requiring users to rate their experience with a computer. "When we had the computer the users had worked with ask for an evaluation of its performance, the responses tended to be positive. But when we had a second computer ask the same people to evaluate their encounters with the first machine, the people were significantly more critical. Their reluctance to criticize the first computer 'to its face' suggested that they didn't want to hurt its feelings, even though they knew it was only a machine."[65]

Second, many employees tend to become defensive when their weaknesses are pointed out. Instead of accepting the feedback as constructive and a basis for improving performance, some employees challenge the evaluation by criticizing the manager or redirecting blame to someone else. A survey of 151 area managers in Philadelphia, for instance, found that 98 percent encountered some type of aggression after giving employees negative appraisals.[66]

Finally, employees tend to have an inflated assessment of their own performance. Statistically speaking, half of all employees must be below-average performers. But the evidence indicates that the average employee's estimate of his or her own performance level generally falls around the 75th percentile.[67] So even when managers are providing good news, employees are likely to perceive it as not good enough.

The solution to the performance feedback problem is not to ignore it, but to train managers to conduct constructive feedback sessions. An effective review—one in which the employee perceives the appraisal as fair, the manager as sincere, and the climate as constructive—can result in the employee's leaving the interview in an upbeat mood, informed about the performance areas needing improvement, and determined to correct the deficiencies.[68] In addition, the performance review should be designed more as a counseling activity than a judgment process. This can best be accomplished by allowing the review to evolve out of the employee's own self-evaluation.

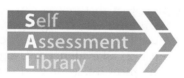

HOW GOOD AM I AT GIVING PERFORMANCE FEEDBACK?

In the Self-Assessment Library (available on CD and online), take assessment III.A.3 (How Good Am I at Giving Performance Feedback?).

Managing Diversity in Organizations

8 *Explain how diversity can be managed in organizations.*

David Morris and his father, Saul, started Habitat International in 1981. Located in Rossville, Georgia, the company manufactures a grasslike indoor/outdoor carpet. From the beginning, the Morrises hired refugees from Cambodia, Bosnia, and Laos, many of whom didn't speak English. But when a social-service worker suggested in 1984 that the company hire mentally challenged people, Saul balked. Hiring someone with a condition such as Down syndrome seemed too chancy. But David thought otherwise. He talked his dad into giving it a try.[69]

Diversity training for police officers in Miami, Florida, includes a program called Building Cultural Competency. Designed to improve police–citizen relationships, the training focuses on developing interpersonal skills such as active listening and understanding the differences in the cultural, religious, and ethnic population in the community.

The first group of eight mentally disabled workers came in with their job coach from the social-services agency and went straight to work boxing mats. Two weeks later, says Saul, employees were coming to him and wondering why the company couldn't "hire more people like this, who care, do their work with pride, and smile?"

Today, 75 percent of Habitat's employees have some kind of disability. People with schizophrenia, for instance, are driving forklifts next to employees with autism or cerebral palsy. Meanwhile, the Morris father-and-son team is doing good things both for these people and for themselves. The disabled employees have enhanced self-esteem and are now self-sufficient enough to be off government aid, and the Morrises enjoy the benefits of a dedicated, hard-working labor force. "We have practically zero absenteeism and very little turnover," says David.

Habitat International illustrates the role of employee selection in increasing diversity. But effective diversity programs go well beyond merely hiring a diverse workforce. They also include managing work–life conflicts and providing diversity training. These seem to be common characteristics among major organizations that have developed reputations as diversity leaders—including Avon, McDonald's, Fannie Mae, PepsiCo, Coca-Cola, Xerox, and Safeway.[70]

Work–Life Conflicts

We introduced work–life balance in Chapter 1 and discussed the forces that are blurring the lines between work life and personal life. In this section we want to elaborate on this issue—specifically focusing on what organizations can do to help employees reduce conflicts.

Work–life conflicts grabbed management's attention in the 1980s, largely as a result of the growing number of women with dependent children entering the workforce. In response, most major organizations took actions to make their workplaces more family friendly.[71] They introduced programs such as on-site child care, summer day camps, flextime, job sharing, leaves for school functions, telecommuting, and part-time employment. But organizations quickly realized that work–life conflicts were not experienced only by female employees with children. Male workers and women without children were also facing this problem. Heavy work loads and increased travel demands, for instance, were making it increasingly hard for a wide range of employees to meet both work and personal responsibilities. A Harvard study found that 82 percent of men between the ages of 20 and 39 said a "family-friendly" schedule was their most important job criterion.[72]

Organizations are modifying their workplaces to accommodate the varied needs of a diverse workforce. This includes providing a wide range of scheduling options and benefits that allow employees more flexibility at work and permit them to better balance or integrate their work and personal lives. For instance, employees at the corporate office of retailer Eddie Bauer are provided with flexible scheduling, plus a full array of on-site services, including dry cleaning pick-up and delivery, an ATM, a gym with personal trainers, flu shots, Weight Watchers classes, and financial seminars.[73] Exhibit 18-4 lists some

Exhibit **18-4**	Work–Life Initiatives	
Strategy	**Program or Policy**	**Example**
Time-based strategies	Flextime Job sharing Part-time work Leave for new parents Telecommuting Closing plants/offices for special occasions	At Mentor Graphics, 98 percent of employees use flextime IBM; gives parents three years of job-guaranteed leave following childbirth J. M. Smuckers shuts down plants in deer country for first day of hunting season
Information-based strategies	Intranet work/life Web site Relocation assistance Eldercare resources	Ernst & Young provides intranet work/life Web sites that include information on how to write flexible work arrangements proposals, find a job share partner, etc.
Money-based strategies	Vouchers for child care Flexible benefits Adoption assistance Discounts for child-care tuition Leave with pay	At Lucent Technologies, employees with 6 months of service receive 52 weeks of childbirth leave at half pay
Direct services	On-site child care Emergency back-up care On-site health/beauty services Concierge services Takeout dinners	S. C. Johnson offers its employees subsidized concierge services for car maintenance, shopping, etc. AFLAC has two on-site child-care centers Genentech has an on-site hair salon Stratus Technologies provides on-site mammograms and skin-cancer testing Every major location of Johnson & Johnson has a fitness center
Culture-change strategies	Training for managers to help employees deal with work/life conflicts Tie manager pay to employee satisfaction Focus on employees' actual performance, not "face time"	Lucent, Marriott, Merck, Pfizer, Prudential, and Xerox, among others, tie manager pay to employee satisfaction

Source: Based on C. A. Thompson, "Managing the Work–Life Balance Act: An Introductory Exercise," *Journal of Management Education*, April 2002, p. 210; and R. Levering and M. Maskowitz, "The Best in the Worst of Times," *Fortune*, February 4, 2002, pp. 60–90.

broader examples of initiatives that organizations provide to help their employees reduce work–life conflicts.

Recent research on work–life conflicts has provided new insights for managers into what works and when. For instance, evidence indicates that time pressures aren't the primary problem underlying work–life conflicts.[74] It's the psychological incursion of work into the family domain and vice versa. People are worrying about personal problems at work and thinking about work problems at home. So dad may physically make it home in time for dinner, but his mind is elsewhere while he's at the dinner table. This suggests that organizations should spend less effort helping employees with time-management issues and more helping them clearly segment their lives. Keeping work loads reasonable, reducing work-related travel, and offering on-site quality child care are examples of practices that can help in this endeavor.

Also, not surprisingly, people have been found to differ in their preference for scheduling options and benefits.[75] Some people prefer organizational initiatives that better segment work from their personal lives. Others prefer initiatives that facilitate integration. For instance, flextime segments because it allows employees to schedule work hours that are less likely to conflict with personal responsibilities. On the other hand, on-site child care integrates by blurring the boundaries between work and family responsibilities. People who prefer segmentation are more likely to be satisfied and committed to their work when offered options such as flextime, job sharing, and part-time hours. People who prefer integration are more likely to respond positively to options such as on-site child care, gym facilities, and company-sponsored family picnics.

Diversity Training

The centerpiece of most diversity programs is training. For instance, a relatively recent survey found that 93 percent of companies with diversity initiatives used training as part of their programs.[76] Diversity training programs are generally intended to provide a vehicle for increasing awareness and examining stereotypes. Participants learn to value individual differences, increase their cross-cultural understanding, and confront stereotypes.[77]

Global Implications

9 Show how a global context affects human resource management.

Many of the human resource policies and practices discussed in this chapter have to be modified to reflect cultural differences.[78] To illustrate this point, let's briefly look at the universality of selection practices and the importance of performance evaluation in different cultures.

Selection

A recent study of 300 large organizations in 22 countries demonstrated that selection practices differ by nation.[79] A few common procedures were found. For instance, the use of educational qualifications in screening candidates seems to be a universal practice. For the most part, however, different countries tend to emphasize different selection techniques. Structured interviews, as a case in point, were popular in some countries and nonexistent in others. The authors of the study suggested that "certain cultures may find structured interviews antithetical to beliefs about how one should conduct an interpersonal interaction or the extent to which one should trust the judgment of the interviewer."[80]

Executives of ImageNet Company (in red jackets), one of Japan's top Internet clothing retailers, conducted job interviews atop Mount Fuji, Japan's highest mountain. Of the 20 candidates who applied for one of four job openings, 11 succeeded in reaching the summit of the 12,388-foot mountain for the interview. ImageNet staged the unique interview setting to identify candidates who are highly motivated, determined to succeed, and prepared for unusual challenges. In the United States and most European nations, this type of interview would run afoul of equal employment opportunity laws.

This study, when combined with earlier research, tells us that there are no universal selection practices. Moreover, global firms that attempt to implement standardized worldwide selection practices can expect to face considerable resistance from local managers. Policies and practices need to be modified to reflect culture-based norms and social values, as well as legal and economic differences.

Performance Evaluation

We've looked at the role performance evaluation plays in motivating and affecting behavior. We must use caution, however, in generalizing across cultures. Why? Because many cultures are not particularly concerned with performance appraisal, or, if they are, they don't look at it the same way as do managers in the United States or Canada.

Let's look at performance evaluation in the context of four cultural dimensions: individualism/collectivism, a person's relationship to the environment, time orientation, and focus of responsibility.

Individual-oriented cultures such as the United States emphasize formal performance evaluation systems more than informal systems. They advocate, for instance, written evaluations performed at regular intervals, the results of which managers share with employees and use in the determination of rewards. On the other hand, the collectivist cultures that dominate Asia and much of Latin America are characterized by more informal systems—downplaying formal feedback and disconnecting reward allocations from performance ratings. Japanese technology giant Fujitsu, for instance, introduced a formal, performance-based evaluation system in Japan in the mid-1990s. But the company recently began to dismantle it, recognizing that it "had proved flawed and a poor fit with Japanese [collectivist] business culture."[81]

U.S. and Canadian organizations hold people responsible for their actions because people in these countries believe they can dominate their environment. In Middle Eastern countries, on the other hand, performance evaluations aren't likely to be widely used because managers in these countries tend to see people as subject to their environment.

Some countries, such as the United States, have a short-term time orientation. Performance evaluations are likely to be frequent in such a culture—at least once a year. In Japan, however, where people hold a long-term time frame, performance appraisals may occur only every 5 or 10 years.

Israel's culture values group activities much more than does the culture of the United States or Canada. So, whereas North American managers traditionally emphasize the individual in performance evaluations, their counterparts in Israel are much more likely to emphasize group contributions and performance.

Summary and Implications for Managers

An organization's human resource policies and practices represent important forces for shaping employee behavior and attitudes. In this chapter, we specifically discussed the influence of selection practices, training and development programs, and performance evaluation systems.

Selection Practices   An organization's selection practices will determine who gets hired. If properly designed, they will identify competent candidates and accurately match them to the job and the organization. The use of the proper selection devices will increase the probability that the right person will be chosen to fill a slot.

Although employee selection is far from a science, some organizations fail to design a selection system that will increase the likelihood of achieving the right person–job fit. When hiring errors are made, the chosen candidate's performance may be less than satisfactory. Training may be necessary to improve the candidate's skills. At worst, the candidate will prove unacceptable, and the firm will need to find a replacement. Similarly, when the selection process results in the hiring of less-qualified candidates or individuals who don't fit into the organization, those chosen are likely to feel anxious, tense, and uncomfortable. This, in turn, is likely to increase dissatisfaction with the job.

Training and Development Programs   Training programs can affect work behavior in two ways. The most obvious is by directly improving the skills necessary for the employee to successfully complete the job. An increase in ability improves the employee's potential to perform at a higher level. Of course, whether that potential becomes realized is largely an issue of motivation.

A second benefit of training is that it increases an employee's self-efficacy. As discussed in Chapter 6, self-efficacy is a person's expectation that she can successfully execute the behaviors required to produce an outcome.[82] For employees, those behaviors are work tasks, and the outcome is effective job performance. Employees with high self-efficacy have strong expectations about their abilities to perform successfully in new situations. They're confident and expect to be successful. Training, then, is a means to positively affect self-efficacy because employees may be more willing to undertake job tasks and exert a high level of effort. Or in expectancy terms (see Chapter 6), individuals are more likely to perceive their effort as leading to performance.

Performance Evaluation   A major goal of performance evaluation is to assess an individual's performance accurately as a basis for making reward allocation decisions. If the performance evaluation process emphasizes the wrong criteria or inaccurately appraises actual job performance, employees will be over-rewarded or under-rewarded. As demonstrated in Chapter 6, in our discussion of equity theory, this can lead to negative consequences such as reduced effort, increases in absenteeism, or a search for alternative job opportunities. In addition, the content of the performance evaluation has been found to influence employee performance and satisfaction.[83] Specifically, performance and satisfaction are increased when the evaluation is based on behavioral, results-oriented criteria, when career issues as well as performance issues are discussed, and when the employee has an opportunity to participate in the evaluation.

Point ⟫ ⟪ Counterpoint

TELECOMMUTING MAKES GOOD BUSINESS SENSE[84]

More and more companies are turning to flexible work schedules, for good reasons.

The first and most obvious reason is changes in how, and where, work is done. Today's virtual organizations realize that where people work is becoming less and less important.

Second, organizations are realizing that offering telecommuting and other flexible schedules allows them to attract and retain the best talent. Best Buy, for example, believes that flexible schedules allows it to get the most out of its people, and it has evidence to prove it (see the opening vignette in Chapter 7). Best Buy is not alone. As a head of one government agency noted, "Telework is not a 'nice to have' anymore; it is critical to agencies' business continuity and productivity, as well as retaining a knowledgeable workforce and appealing to a new generation of employees interested in work/life balance." Companies such as Ernst & Young have ramped up flexible schedules not only to attract and retain knowledge workers, but to be flexible as a business, such as during tax time. Lehman Brothers has done the same: "We're committed to de-stigmatizing flex schedules," says one Lehman employee.

Third, research shows that while managers are a main source of opposition to telework, when managers are exposed to telecommuting, they become much more positive in their attitudes toward it.

There are too many arguments in favor of telecommuting and flexible schedules for organizations to ignore. Nearly half of all organizations now offer flexible schedules; those that do are ahead of the curve.

Telecommuting and other flexible schedules are one of those management fads that sounds good but, like most other fads, don't stand up to close scrutiny and logical analysis.

Managers don't view telecommuters very positively. You can agree or disagree with them, but you would have a hard time advising employees to indulge in flexible work schedules when doing so hurts their career. A recent study gave some interesting support to this argument.

When surveyed, more than two-thirds (68 percent) of employees thought that working at home made them more productive. However, when managers were surveyed, more than one-third (37 percent) thought that if allowed to work at home, staff would use their so-called working hours for personal activities.

Sure, employees want flexible schedules and rationalize their preferences by arguing that it helps them get more done. But a lot of managers know better—that while some of "working at home" does involve work, another part of it involves "goofing off" doing non-work stuff like chores, personal or family activities, and so on. That's exactly why employees want it so much.

If you asked employees, "Would you like to get paid the same for working half as many hours?" most employees would probably say, "Sure!" But that doesn't mean that management should give employees something for nothing. Effective HRM sometimes means not giving employees what they want.

Questions for Review

1 What is initial selection and what are the most useful initial selection methods?

2 What is substantive selection and what are the most useful substantive selection methods?

3 What is contingent selection and what are the arguments for and against drug testing?

4 What are the four main types of training?

5 What are the differences between formal and informal training methods and between on-the-job and off-the-job training?

6 What are the main purposes of performance evaluation?

7 How can performance evaluation be improved?

8 How can diversity be managed in organizations?

9 How is human resource management affected by a global context?

Experiential Exercise

EVALUATING PERFORMANCE AND PROVIDING FEEDBACK

Objective
To experience the assessment of performance and observe the provision of performance feedback.

Time
Approximately 30 minutes.

Procedure
Select a class leader, either a volunteer or someone chosen by your instructor. The class leader will preside over the class discussion and perform the role of manager in the evaluation review.

Your instructor will leave the room. The class leader is then to spend up to 15 minutes helping the class to evaluate your instructor. Your instructor understands that this is only a class exercise and is prepared to accept criticism (and, of course, any praise you may want to convey). Your instructor also recognizes that the leader's evaluation is actually a composite of many students' input. So be open and honest in your evaluation

and have confidence that your instructor will not be vindictive.

Research has identified seven performance dimensions to the college instructor's job: (1) instructor knowledge, (2) testing procedures, (3) student–teacher relations, (4) organizational skills, (5) communication skills, (6) subject relevance, and (7) utility of assignments. The discussion of your instructor's performance should focus on these seven dimensions. The leader may want to take notes for personal use but will not be required to give your instructor any written documentation.

When the 15-minute class discussion is complete, the leader will invite the instructor back into the room. The performance review will begin as soon as the instructor walks through the door, with the class leader becoming the manager and the instructor playing himself or herself.

When completed, class discussion will focus on performance evaluation criteria and how well your class leader did in providing performance feedback.

Ethical Dilemma

IS IT UNETHICAL TO "SHAPE" YOUR RÉSUMÉ?

When does "putting a positive spin" on your accomplishments step over the line to become misrepresentation or lying? Does a résumé have to be 100 percent truthful? Apparently, a lot of people don't think so. Studies have found that nearly half of all résumés contain at least one lie.[85] To help clarify your ethical views on this issue, consider the following three situations and answer the questions for each.

1. Sean left a job for which his title was "credit clerk." When looking for a new job, he lists his previous title as "credit analyst." He thinks it sounds more impressive. Is this "retitling" of a former job wrong? Why or why not?

2. About 8 years ago, Emily took 9 months off between jobs to travel overseas. Afraid that people might consider her unstable or lacking in career motivation, she put down on her résumé that she was engaged in "independent consulting activities" during the period. Was she wrong? How else could she have described this time period on her résumé?

3. David is the 46-year-old CEO of a Fortune 1000 company. He enrolled in Pacific Coast Baptist College 20 years ago, but he never got a degree. Just 9 months after he was appointed CEO, a local newspaper reported that he had lied on his résumé. His résumé

indicated that he had a bachelor's degree in psychology, but neither he nor the college can produce any evidence of that. Should he be terminated? If yes, why, and if not, what should his employer do about David's missing credentials? (This last scenario is based on a true story; to find out more, enter "David Edmondson" and "resume" in your favorite search engine.)

Source: Based on M. Conlin, "You Are What You Post," *BusinessWeek*, March 27, 2006, pp. 52–53.

Case Incident 1

DIGGING UP THE DIRT

On a rainy night in Seattle, Josh Santangelo, 22, was surfing the Internet and came across a Web site called Fray. After reading a post asking whether anyone had been high lately, Santangelo started typing away: "Actually, yes, about 36 hours ago," he wrote. "Two Rolls Royces and four hits of liquor later, I was at a Playboy-themed birthday party... It's hard to say no when a pretty girl is popping things into your mouth."

Posting a blog entry like Santangelo's seems so innocent, and so easy to do. Yet, what takes a few seconds to type can last forever. Santangelo posted his entry, a blogger named Jason Kottke immediately linked to the blog, and Santangelo's entry was on its way to more than 100,000 Google hits.

Although people post blog entries for numerous reasons, it's critical to remember that what seems quick and innocent now can be fodder for prospective employers later. Someone asked Santangelo whether he worried that a future employer would check up on him. He replied, "I might not have made the post if I'd thought of that question beforehand.... As far as future employers go, I'd hope they wouldn't try and dig that deeply into my personal background."

The fact of the matter is a lot of employers *are* checking up on their current and prospective employees. Flight attendant Ellen Simonetti lost her job at Delta after she posted some suggestive pictures of herself in uniform (even though she didn't identify Delta as her employer). She sued Delta and lost.

Heather Armstrong wrote about her job in a blog and was fired. She started a Web site (Dooce.com), which spawned a neologism—"Dooced"—to describe workers who are fired for what they post on the Web.

Such concerns are causing some to be careful. Dave Fonseca, a senior at the University of Massachusetts, recently pulled his Facebook profile. "Employers are looking at these things," he said. Armstrong herself advises bloggers: *BE YE NOT SO STUPID*.

Questions

1. Do you think employers have a right to check into applicants by "Googling" them, or checking out sites like MySpace? What about checking out their current employees?

2. Before posting entries on a blog or Web site like MySpace or Facebook, do you think about whether current or future employers might have access to the information?

3. If you worked for a company that wanted you to examine the feasibility of mining the INTERNET for information about job applicants as a means of background checking, what would you advise? Would your advice depend on the nature of the job?

Source: Based on S. Foss, M. Collin, "You Are What You Post," *Business Week* (March 27, 2006), pp. 52–53.

Case Incident 2

JOB CANDIDATES WITHOUT STRONG SAT SCORES NEED NOT APPLY

Many high school students probably believe that once they get into college, their SAT scores are a thing of the past. However, many job seekers are now discovering that their would-be employers are asking for their SAT scores as part of the selection process. Donna Chan, a 23-year-old graduate of New York's Wagner College, learned that one of the minimum requirements for many of the entry-level financial services jobs she was seeking was a combined SAT score of 1300. How strong of a score is 1300? The maximum score on the old version of the SAT (the new version has added a writing section, in addition to the traditional math and verbal sections) was 1600. According to the College Board, the organization that administers the exam, the average combined math and verbal score of the freshman class of 2005 (the last class to take the old version of the SAT) was 1028. Donna Chan's score was "in the 1200s"—a good score to be sure, but not good enough to obtain any of the positions she was seeking, even though she obtained a 3.9 grade-point average in college. "I think it's asking a bit much," says Chan. "That's something high school kids have to worry about. After four years of working hard, I think you've paid your dues, and unless you're applying to Princeton Review or some math-related, analytical job, I don't see the relevance."

Apparently, however, some recruiters do see the relevance. Alan Sage, a vice president at systems-management software company Configuresoft Inc., states that SAT scores are a good predictor of success in his company and regularly has applicants submit their scores when applying for sales positions. He set the mark at a combined score of 1200—lower than what Donna Chan had to face, but well above average nonetheless. Says Sage, "In my experience, people with high SAT scores tend to do better." Sage himself scored between 1200 and 1300. He adds, however, that "We wouldn't exclude someone from an interview if he or she didn't score high."

Some do not believe there is a connection between high SAT scores and job performance. Seppy Basilli, vice president of Kaplan Inc., one of several companies that provides instruction on taking the SAT, believes that companies are misusing SAT scores. "It's such a maligned instrument," he says. "It's not designed to measure job performance, and the kind of person who performs well on the SATs is not necessarily the kind of person who will perform well sitting at her desk." Morgan Denny, who works as a headhunter in New York, shares a similar opinion. Though his clients typically want to consider only applicants with high SAT scores, Denny often shows his clients applicants he believes are strong candidates for the position despite a lower score. "The SAT is an annoyance for us and an annoyance for our candidates," says Denny.

Some individuals, such as Kristin Carnahan, a spokesperson for the College Board, feel that companies should use other measures of cognitive ability to screen job applicants. Carnahan states that college grades, which are more recent indicators of performance than SAT scores, should be given greater weight. However, critics argue that grades are not "standardized" across different educational institutions, meaning that grades from different colleges cannot be compared like SAT scores can. Grade inflation also may make it more difficult for recruiters to assess the validity of an applicant's GPA. Because research in organizational behavior has shown that cognitive ability is a strong predictor of job performance—and the SAT is supposedly a measure of cognitive ability—many companies may continue to use the SAT as a benchmark for job applicants.

Questions

1. Is it fair for organizations to require minimum scores on standardized tests such as the SAT? Why or why not?

2. As a recruiter, in choosing between two individuals with different SAT scores, would it be difficult for you to give the job to the individual with the lower score? What additional factors might your choice depend on?

3. What are some other indicators of job performance, besides SAT scores, that you could use to screen potential job applicants? What are the advantages and disadvantages of each?

4. Say you worked at a company that uses SAT scores for hiring purposes. How would you handle diverse applicants, such as those from a foreign country who may not have taken the SAT?

Source: Based on S. Foss, "Background Check—Background Search," *American Chronicle*, July 12, 2007; and K. J. Dunham, "Career Journal: More Employers Ask Job Seekers for SAT Scores," *Wall Street Journal*, October 28, 2003, p. B1.

Endnotes

1. Sources: M. Mirabile, "NFL Quarterback Wonderlic Scores," *MacMirabile.com*, March 18, 2004, www.macmirabile.com/Wonderlic.htm; and J. Saraceno, "Who Knows If This Longhorn Is Short on IQ," *USA Today*, March 1, 2006, p. 2C.

2. See B. Becker and B. Gerhart, "The Impact of Human Resource Management on Organizational Performance: Progress and Prospects," *Academy of Management Journal*, August 1996, pp. 779–801; J. T. Delaney and M. A. Huselid, "The Impact of Human Resource Management Practices on the Perceptions of Organizational Performance," *Academy of Management Journal*, August 1996, pp. 949–969; M. A. Huselid, S. E. Jackson, and R. S. Schuler, "Technical and Strategic Human Resource Management Effectiveness as Determinants of Firm Performance," *Academy of Management Journal*, February 1997, pp. 171–188; and G. A. Gelade and M. Ivery, "The Impact of Human Resource Management and Work Climate on Organizational Performance," *Personnel Psychology*, Summer 2003, pp. 383–404; C. J. Collins, and K. D. Clark, "Strategic Human Resource Practices, Top Management Team Social Networks, and Firm Performance: The Role of Human Resource Practices in Creating Organizational Competitive Advantage," *Academy of Management Journal*, December 2003, pp. 740–751; and D. E. Bowen and C. Ostroff, "Understanding HRM–Firm Performance Linkages: The Role of the 'Strength' of the HRM System," *Academy of Management Review*, April 2004, pp. 203–221.

3. See, for instance, C. T. Dortch, "Job–Person Match," *Personnel Journal*, June 1989, pp. 49–57; and S. Rynes and B. Gerhart, "Interviewer Assessments of Applicant 'Fit': An Exploratory Investigation," *Personnel Psychology*, Spring 1990, pp. 13–34.

4. C. Lachnit, "The Cost of Not Doing Background Checks," *Workforce Management*, www.workforce.com/archive/feature/22/16/22/224149.php.

5. Cited in J. H. Prager, "Nasty or Nice: 56-Question Quiz," *Wall Street Journal*, February 22, 2000, p. A4; and H. Wessel,

"Personality Tests Grow Popular," *Seattle Post–Intelligencer*, August 3, 2003, p. G1.

6. G. Nicholsen, "Screen and Glean: Good Screening and Background Checks Help Make the Right Match for Every Open Position," *Workforce*, October 2000, pp. 70–72.

7. J. P. Hausknecht, D. V. Day, and S. C. Thomas, "Applicant Reactions to Selection Procedures: An Updated Model and Meta-analysis," *Personnel Psychology*, September 2004, pp. 639–683.

8. E. E. Ghiselli, "The Validity of Aptitude Tests in Personnel Selection," *Personnel Psychology*, Winter 1973, p. 475.

9. R. J. Herrnstein and C. Murray, *The Bell Curve: Intelligence and Class Structure in American Life* (New York: The Free Press, 1994); and M. J. Ree, J. A. Earles, and M. S. Teachout, "Predicting Job Performance: Not Much More Than g," *Journal of Applied Psychology*, August 1994, pp. 518–524.

10. J. F. Salgado, N. Anderson, S. Moscoso, C. Bertua, F. de Fruyt, and J. P. Rolland, "A Meta-Analytic Study of General Mental Ability Validity for Different Occupations in the European Community," *Journal of Applied Psychology*, December 2003, pp. 1068–1081.

11. J. Flint, "Can You Tell Applesauce from Pickles?" *Forbes*, October 9, 1995, pp. 106–108.

12. M. R. Barrick, M. K. Mount, and T. A. Judge, "Personality and Performance at the Beginning of the New Millennium: What Do We Know and Where Do We Go Next?" *International Journal of Selection & Assessment*, March–June 2001, pp. 9–30; M. R. Barrick, G. L. Stewart, and M. Piotrowski, "Personality and Job Performance: Test of the Mediating Effects of Motivation Among Sales Representatives," *Journal of Applied Psychology*, February 2002, pp. 43–51; and C. J. Thoresen, J. C. Bradley, P. D. Bliese, and J. D. Thoresen, "The Big Five Personality Traits and Individual Job Performance and Growth Trajectories in Maintenance and Transitional Job Stages," *Journal of Applied Psychology*, October 2004, pp. 835–853.

13. D. S. Ones, C. Viswesvaran, and F. L. Schmidt, "Comprehensive Meta-Analysis of Integrity Test Validities: Findings and Implications for Personnel Selection and Theories of Job Performance," *Journal of Applied Psychology*, August 1993, pp. 679–703; P. R. Sackett and J. E. Wanek, "New Developments in the Use of Measures of Honesty, Integrity, Conscientiousness, Dependability, Trustworthiness, and Reliability for Personnel Selection," *Personnel Psychology*, Winter 1996, pp. 787–829; F. L. Schmidt and J. E. Hunter, "The Validity and Utility of Selection Methods in Personnel Psychology: Practical and Theoretical Implications of 85 Years of Research Findings," *Psychological Bulletin*, September 1998, pp. 262–274; and D. S. Ones, C. Viswesvaran, and F. L. Schmidt, "Personality and Absenteeism: A Meta-analysis of Integrity Tests," *European Journal of Personality*, March–April 2003, Supplement 1, pp. S19–S38.

14. See D. B. Smith, P. J. Hanges, and M. W. Dickson, "Personnel Selection and the Five-Factor Model: Reexamining the Effects of Applicant's Frame of Reference," *Journal of Applied Psychology*, April 2001, pp. 304–315; and R. Mueller-Hanson, E. D. Heggestad, and G. C. Thornton III, "Faking and Selection: Considering the Use of Personality from Select-In and Select-Out Perspectives," *Journal of Applied Psychology*, April 2003, pp. 348–355.

15. P. Carbonara, "Hire for Attitude, Train for Skill," *Fast Company*, Greatest Hits, vol. 1, 1997, p. 68.

16. J. J. Asher and J. A. Sciarrino, "Realistic Work Sample Tests: A Review," *Personnel Psychology*, Winter 1974, pp. 519–533; I. T. Robertson and R. S. Kandola, "Work Sample Tests: Validity, Adverse Impact and Applicant Reaction," *Journal of Occupational Psychology*, Spring 1982, pp. 171–182; and M. Callinan and I. T. Robertson, "Work Sample Testing," *International Journal of Selection & Assessment*, December 2000, pp. 248–260.

17. See, for instance, A. C. Spychalski, M. A. Quinones, B. B. Gaugler, and K. Pohley, "A Survey of Assessment Center Practices in Organizations in the United States, *Personnel Psychology*, Spring 1997, pp. 71–90; C. Woodruffe, *Development and Assessment Centres: Identifying and Assessing Competence* (London: Institute of Personnel and Development, 2000); and J. Schettler, "Building Bench Strength," *Training*, June 2002, pp. 55–58.

18. R. A. Posthuma, F. P. Moregeson, and M. A. Campion, "Beyond Employment Interview Validity: A Comprehensive Narrative Review of Recent Research and Trend Over Time," *Personnel Psychology*, Spring 2002, p. 1; and S. L. Wilk and P. Cappelli, "Understanding the Determinants of Employer Use of Selection Methods," *Personnel Psychology*, Spring 2003, p. 111.

19. T. J. Hanson and J. C. Balestreri-Spero, "An Alternative to Interviews," *Personnel Journal*, June 1985, p. 114. See also T. W. Dougherty, D. B. Turban, and J. C. Callender, "Confirming First Impressions in the Employment Interview: A Field Study of Interviewer Behavior," *Journal of Applied Psychology*, October 1994, pp. 659–665.

20. K. I. van der Zee, A. B. Bakker, and P. Bakker, "Why Are Structured Interviews So Rarely Used in Personnel Selection?" *Journal of Applied Psychology*, February 2002, pp. 176–184.

21. See M. A. McDaniel, D. L. Whetzel, F. L. Schmidt, and S. D. Maurer, "The Validity of Employment Interviews: A Comprehensive Review and Meta-Analysis," *Journal of Applied Psychology*, August 1994, pp. 599–616; J. M. Conway, R. A. Jako, and D. F. Goodman, "A Meta-analysis of Interrater and Internal Consistency Reliability of Selection Interviews," *Journal of Applied Psychology*, October 1995, pp. 565–579; M. A. Campion, D. K. Palmer, and J. E. Campion, "A Review of Structure in the Selection Interview," *Personnel Psychology*, Autumn 1997, pp. 655–702; F. L. Schmidt and J. E. Hunter, "The Validity and Utility of Selection Methods in Personnel Psychology: Practical and Theoretical Implications of 85 Years of Research Findings," *Psychological Bulletin*, September 1998, pp. 262–274; and A. I. Huffcutt and D. J. Woehr, "Further Analysis of Employment Interview Validity: A Quantitative Evaluation of Interviewer-Related Structuring Methods," *Journal of Organizational Behavior*, July 1999, pp. 549–560.

22. van der Zee, Bakker, and Bakker, "Why Are Structured Interviews So Rarely Used in Personnel Selection?"

23. "Survey Finds Employers Form Opinions of Job Interviewees Within 10 Minutes," *IPMA-HR Bulletin*, April 21, 2007, p. 1.

24. R. L. Dipboye, *Selection Interviews: Process Perspectives* (Cincinnati, OH: South-Western Publishing, 1992), pp. 42–44; and R. A. Posthuma, F. P. Moregeson, and M. A. Campion, "Beyond Employment Interview Validity," pp. 1–81.

25. K. M. Engemann and M. T. Owyang, "What's in a Name?" *The Regional Economist*, January 2006, pp. 10–11.

26. J. F. Salgado and S. Moscoso, "Validity of the Structured Behavioral Interview," *Revista de Psicología del Trabajo y las Organizaciones* 11 (1995), pp. 9–24; see also S. Moscoso, and

J. F. Salgado, "Psychometric Properties of a Structured Behavioral Interview to Hire Private Security Personnel," *Journal of Business & Psychology*, Fall 2001, pp. 51–59.

27. R. E. Carlson, "Effect of Interview Information in Altering Valid Impressions," *Journal of Applied Psychology*, February 1971, pp. 66–72; M. London and M. D. Hakel, "Effects of Applicant Stereotypes, Order, and Information on Interview Impressions," *Journal of Applied Psychology*, April 1974, pp. 157–162; E. C. Webster, *The Employment Interview: A Social Judgment Process* (Ontario: S.I.P., 1982); and T. W. Dougherty, D. B. Turban, and J. C. Callender, "Confirming First Impressions in the Employment Interview: A Field Study of Interviewer Behavior," *Journal of Applied Psychology*, October 1994, pp. 659–665.

28. N. R. Bardack and F. T. McAndrew, "The Influence of Physical Attractiveness and Manner of Dress on Success in a Simulated Personnel Decision," *Journal of Social Psychology*, August 1985, pp. 777–778; R. Bull and N. Rumsey, *The Social Psychology of Facial Appearance* (London: Springer-Verlag, 1988); and L. M. Watkins, and L. Johnston, "Screening Job Applicants: The Impact of Physical Attractiveness and Application Quality," *International Journal of Selection & Assessment*, June 2000, pp. 76–84.

29. See G. A. Adams, T. C. Elacqua, and S. M. Colarelli, "The Employment Interview as a Sociometric Selection Technique," *Journal of Group Psychotherapy*, Fall 1994, pp. 99–113; R. L. Dipboye, "Structured and Unstructured Selection Interviews: Beyond the Job-Fit Model," *Research in Personnel Human Resource Management* 12 (1994), pp. 79–123; B. Schneider, D. B. Smith, S. Taylor, and J. Fleenor, "Personality and Organizations: A Test of the Homogeneity of Personality Hypothesis," *Journal of Applied Psychology*, June 1998, pp. 462–470; and M. Burke, "Funny Business," *Forbes*, June 9, 2003, p. 173.

30. Cited in *Training*, October 2003, p. 21.

31. Cited in *Training*, March 2003, p. 20.

32. "Basic Skills Training Pays Off for Employers," *HRMagazine*, October 1999, p. 32.

33. Baynton, "America's $60 Billion Problem," p. 51.

34. A. Bernstein, "The Time Bomb in the Workforce: Illiteracy," *BusinessWeek*, February 25, 2002, p. 122.

35. D. Baynton, "America's $60 Billion Problem," *Training*, May 2001, p. 52.

36. C. Ansberry, "A New Blue-Collar World," *Wall Street Journal*, June 30, 2003, p. B1.

37. J. Barbarian, "Mark Spear: Director of Management and Organizational Development, Miller Brewing Co.," *Training*, October 2001, pp. 34–38.

38. G. R. Weaver, L. K. Trevino, and P. L. Cochran, "Corporate Ethics Practices in the Mid-1990's: An Empirical Study of the Fortune 1000," *Journal of Business Ethics*, February 1999, pp. 283–294.

39. M. B. Wood, *Business Ethics in Uncertain Times* (Upper Saddle River, NJ: Prentice Hall, 2004), p. 61.

40. See, for example, D. Seligman, "Oxymoron 101," *Forbes*, October 28, 2002, pp. 160–164; and R. B. Schmitt, "Companies Add Ethics Training; Will It Work?" *Wall Street Journal*, November 4, 2002, p. B1.

41. K. Dobbs, "The U.S. Department of Labor Estimates that 70 Percent of Workplace Learning Occurs Informally," *Sales & Marketing Management*, November 2000, pp. 94–98.

42. S. J. Wells, "Forget the Formal Training. Try Chatting at the Water Cooler," *New York Times*, May 10, 1998, p. BU-11.

43. See, for instance, K. G. Brown, "Using Computers to Deliver Training: Which Employees Learn and Why?" *Personnel Psychology*, Summer 2001, pp. 271–296; "The Delivery: How U.S. Organizations Use Classrooms and Computers in Training," *Training*, October 2001, pp. 66–72; and L. K. Long, and R. D. Smith, "The Role of Web-Based Distance Learning in HR Development," *Journal of Management Development* 23, no. 3 (2004), pp. 270–284.

44. "Web Smart 50: Kinko's," *BusinessWeek*, November 24, 2003, p. 101.

45. A. Muoio, "Cisco's Quick Study," *Fast Company*, October 2000, pp. 287–295.

46. E. A. Ensher, T. R. Nielson, and E. Grant-Vallone, "Tales from the Hiring Line: Effects of the Internet and Technology on HR Processes," *Organizational Dynamics* 31, no. 3 (2002), pp. 232–233.

47. D. A. Kolb, "Management and the Learning Process," *California Management Review*, Spring 1976, pp. 21–31; and B. Filipczak, "Different Strokes: Learning Styles in the Classroom," *Training*, March 1995, pp. 43–48.

48. W. J. Arthur, Jr., W. Bennett, Jr., P. S. Edens, and S. T. Bell, "Effectiveness of Training in Organizations: A Meta-Analysis of Design and Evaluation Features," *Journal of Applied Psychology*, April 2003, pp. 234–245.

49. J. A. Colquitt, J. A. LePine, and R. A. Noe, "Toward an Integrative Theory of Training Motivation: A Meta-Analytic Path Analysis of 20 Years of Research," *Journal of Applied Psychology*, October 2000, pp. 678–707.

50. W. F. Cascio, *Applied Psychology in Human Resource Management*, 5th ed. (Upper Saddle River, NJ: Prentice Hall, 1998), p. 59.

51. See W. C. Borman and S. J. Motowidlo, "Expanding the Criterion Domain to Include Elements of Contextual Performance," in N. Schmitt and W. C. Borman (eds.), *Personnel Selection in Organizations* (San Francisco, CA: Jossey-Bass, 1993), pp. 71–98; W. H. Bommer, J. L. Johnson, G. A. Rich, P. M. Podsakoff, and S. B. MacKenzie, "On the Interchangeability of Objective and Subjective Measures of Employee Performance: A Meta-Analysis," *Personnel Psychology*, Autumn 1995, pp. 587–605; and S. E. Scullen, M. K. Mount, and T. A. Judge, "Evidence of the Construct Validity of Developmental Ratings of Managerial Performance," *Journal of Applied Psychology*, February 2003, pp. 50–66.

52. A. H. Locher and K. S. Teel, "Appraisal Trends," *Personnel Journal*, September 1988, pp. 139–145.

53. Cited in S. Armour, "Job Reviews Take on Added Significance in Down Times," *USA Today*, July 23, 2003, p. 4B.

54. See review in R. D. Bretz, Jr., G. T. Milkovich, and W. Read, "The Current State of Performance Appraisal Research and Practice: Concerns, Directions, and Implications," *Journal of Management*, June 1992, p. 326; and P. W. B. Atkins and R. E. Wood, "Self-Versus Others' Ratings as Predictors of Assessment Center Ratings: Validation Evidence for 360-Degree Feedback Programs," *Personnel Psychology*, Winter 2002, pp. 871–904.

55. See, for instance, J. D. Facteau and S. B. Craig, "Are Performance Appraisal Ratings from Different Rating Sources Compatible?" *Journal of Applied Psychology*, April 2001, pp. 215–227; J. F. Brett and L. E. Atwater, "360-Degree Feedback: Accuracy, Reactions, and Perceptions of

Usefulness," *Journal of Applied Psychology*, October 2001, pp. 930–942; F. Luthans and S. J. Peterson, "360 Degree Feedback with Systematic Coaching: Empirical Analysis Suggests a Winning Combination," *Human Resource Management*, Fall 2003, pp. 243–256; and B. I. J. M. van der Heijden, and A. H. J. Nijhof, "The Value of Subjectivity: Problems and Prospects for 360-Degree Appraisal Systems," *International Journal of Human Resource Management*, May 2004, pp. 493–511.

56. Atkins and Wood, "Self- Versus Others' Ratings as Predictors of Assessment Center Ratings"; and B. Pfau, I. Kay, K. M. Nowack, and J. Ghorpade, "Does 360-Degree Feedback Negatively Affect Company Performance?" *HRMagazine* 47, no. 6 (June 2002), pp. 54–59.

57. "Princeton Cracks Down on Grade Inflation," *USA Today*, January 22, 2005, www.usatoday.com/news/education/2005-01-22-princeton-grade-inflation_x.htm.

58. See, for instance, J. W. Hedge and W. C. Borman, "Changing Conceptions and Practices in Performance Appraisal," in A. Howard (ed.), *The Changing Nature of Work* (San Francisco, CA: Jossey-Bass, 1995), pp. 453–459.

59. See, for instance, T. R. Athey and R. M. McIntyre, "Effect of Rater Training on Rater Accuracy: Levels-of-Processing Theory and Social Facilitation Theory Perspectives," *Journal of Applied Psychology*, November 1987, pp. 567–572; and D. J. Woehr, "Understanding Frame-of-Reference Training: The Impact of Training on the Recall of Performance Information," *Journal of Applied Psychology*, August 1994, pp. 525–534.

60. H. J. Bernardin, "The Effects of Rater Training on Leniency and Halo Errors in Student Rating of Instructors," *Journal of Applied Psychology*, June 1978, pp. 301–308.

61. Ibid.; and J. M. Ivancevich, "Longitudinal Study of the Effects of Rater Training on Psychometric Error in Ratings," *Journal of Applied Psychology*, October 1979, pp. 502–508.

62. M. S. Taylor, K. B. Tracy, M. K. Renard, J. K. Harrison, and S. J. Carroll, "Due Process in Performance Appraisal: A Quasi-Experiment in Procedural Justice," *Administrative Science Quarterly*, September 1995, pp. 495–523.

63. J. S. Lublin, "It's Shape-up Time for Performance Reviews," *Wall Street Journal*, October 3, 1994, p. B1.

64. Much of this section is based on H. H. Meyer, "A Solution to the Performance Appraisal Feedback Enigma," *Academy of Management Executive*, February 1991, pp. 68–76.

65. B. Gates, *The Road Ahead* (New York: Viking, 1995), p. 86.

66. T. D. Schelhardt, "It's Time to Evaluate Your Work, and All Involved Are Groaning," *Wall Street Journal*, November 19, 1996, p. A1.

67. R. J. Burke, "Why Performance Appraisal Systems Fail," *Personnel Administration*, June 1972, pp. 32–40.

68. B. D. Cawley, L. M. Keeping, and P. E. Levy, "Participation in the Performance Appraisal Process and Employee Reactions: A Meta-analytic Review of Field Investigations," *Journal of Applied Psychology*, August 1998, pp. 615–633; and P. E. Levy, and J. R. Williams, "The Social Context of Performance Appraisal: A Review and Framework for the Future," *Journal of Management* 30, no. 6 (2004), pp. 881–905.

69. N. B. Henderson, "An Enabling Work Force," *Nation's Business*, June 1998, p. 93.

70. See J. Hickman, "50 Best Companies for Minorities," *Fortune*, June 28, 2004, pp. 136–142.

71. See, for instance, *Harvard Business Review on Work and Life Balance* (Boston: Harvard Business School Press, 2000); and R. Rapoport, L. Bailyn, J. K. Fletcher, and B. H. Pruitt, *Beyond Work-Family Balance* (San Francisco: Jossey-Bass, 2002).

72. "On the Daddy Track," *Wall Street Journal*, May 11, 2000, p. A1.

73. K. Weiss, "Eddie Bauer Uses Time as an Employee Benefit," *Journal of Organizational Excellence*, Winter 2002, pp. 67–72.

74. S. D. Friedman and J. H. Greenhaus, *Work and Family—Allies or Enemies?* (New York: Oxford University Press, 2000).

75. N. P. Rothbard, T. L. Dumas, and K. W. Phillips, "The Long Arm of the Organization: Work-Family Policies and Employee Preferences for Segmentation," paper presented at the 61st Annual Academy of Management Meeting, Washington, DC, August 2001.

76. Cited in "Survey Shows 75% of Large Corporations Support Diversity Programs," *Fortune*, July 6, 1998, p. S14.

77. See, for example, J. K. Ford and S. Fisher, "The Role of Training in a Changing Workplace and Workforce: New Perspectives and Approaches," in E. E. Kossek and S. A. Lobel (eds.), *Managing Diversity* (Cambridge, MA: Blackwell Publishers, 1996), pp. 164–193; and J. Barbian, "Moving Toward Diversity," *Training*, February 2003, pp. 44–48.

78. See, for instance, C. Fletcher and E. L. Perry, "Performance Appraisal and Feedback: A Consideration of National Culture and a Review of Contemporary Research and Future Trends," in N. Anderson, D. S. Ones, H. K. Sinangil, and C. Viswesvaran (eds.), *Handbook of Industrial, Work, & Organizational Psychology*, vol. 1 (Thousand Oaks, CA: Sage, 2001), pp. 127–144.

79. A. M. Ryan, L. McFarland, H. Baron, and R. Page, "An International Look at Selection Practices: Nation and Culture as Explanations for Variability in Practice," *Personnel Psychology*, Summer 1999, pp. 359–392.

80. Ibid., p. 386.

81. M. Tanikawa, "Fujitsu Decides to Backtrack on Performance-Based Pay," *New York Times*, March 22, 2001, p. W1.

82. P. C. Earley, "Self or Group? Cultural Effects of Training on Self-Efficacy and Performance," *Administrative Science Quarterly*, March 1994, pp. 89–117.

83. B. R. Nathan, A. M. Mohrman, Jr., and J. Milliman, "Interpersonal Relations as a Context for the Effects of Appraisal Interviews on Performance and Satisfaction: A Longitudinal Study," *Academy of Management Journal* 34, no. 2 (June 1991), pp. 352–369; and Cawley, Keeping, and Levy, "Participation in the Performance Appraisal Process and Employee Reactions."

84. J. Badal, "To Retain Valued Women Employees, Companies Pitch Flextime as Macho," *Wall Street Journal*, December 11, 2006, pp. B1, B3; "Telework Exchange and Federal Managers Association Study Reveals Only 35% of Managers Believe Their Agencies Support Telework," *IPMA-HR Bulletin*, January 26, 2007, pp. 1–2; and R. Scally, "'Working From Home Today' That's Not What Your Boss Thinks," *Workforce Week*, May 6, 2007, p. 1.

85. C. Soltis, "Eagle-Eyed Employers Scour Résumés for Little White Lies," *Wall Street Journal*, March 21, 2006, p. B7.

Organizational Change and Stress Management

It is not the strongest of the species that survives, nor the most intelligent, but the one most responsive to change.

—Charles Darwin

19

LEARNING OBJECTIVES

After studying this chapter, you should be able to:

1 Identify forces that act as stimulants to change and contrast planned and unplanned change.

2 List the sources for resistance to change.

3 Compare the four main approaches to managing organizational change.

4 Demonstrate two ways of creating a culture for change.

5 Define *stress* and identify its potential sources.

6 Identify the consequences of stress.

7 Contrast the individual and organizational approaches to managing stress.

8 Explain global differences in organizational change and work stress.

*n*ot to be insulting, but Richard Clark is no George Clooney. Short, pudgy, balding, and bespectacled with Dick Cheney–like eyeglasses, Clark is 61 and looks it. He doesn't have an Ivy League pedigree. He's not particularly charismatic. It took him more than 30 takes to tape a short commercial advertisement. "Low key" might be the positive way to describe his personality.

Yet, Clark is CEO of one of America's largest companies.

"A Crisis Is a Terrible Thing to Waste"

We must be writing about Clark here to tell the story of someone who's led his company to greatness against the odds, right? Well, not really.

Financially, the company Richard Clark leads has been a bit of a dog. Its stock price trades at 20 percent below its level 4 years ago and less than *half* what it was in 2000. Its profits have declined for 3 years in a row. And the company has been the target of 27,000 claims and more than 9,200 active lawsuits, all for a single product that has allegedly killed people.

Richard Clark is CEO of Merck, one of the largest drug companies in the world, and also one of the most troubled companies you'll find listed among the Fortune 500 (it was number 99 as of 2007). Clark is noteworthy not because he's leading a successful company but because he's leading a company that's fighting for its survival.

Any drug company is one launch away from instant success—think Viagra or Prozac—or financial ruin. Sometimes they're both, like Merck. When Merck launched the anti-arthritis drug Vioxx in 1999, it quickly rose to sales of $2.5 billion per year. However, problems with the drug soon became apparent, and lawsuits started to accumulate. In 2004, Merck pulled Vioxx from the market, and it now budgets $1 billion per year to fight lawsuits against the product.

Clark's predecessor shrugged off Merck's problems. Not Clark. He's trying to make changes in the company that reach well beyond the Vioxx debacle. He argues to employees that without dramatic changes, Merck will not survive.

Clark's vision for transforming Merck includes streamlining the company—eliminating its hierarchical organizational structure, which he felt worked against innovation—and gathering more input from patients, doctors, and employees. He also set new goals for bringing drugs to market as well as establishing other markers of performance. Increased accountability is a big part of how Clark hopes to change the culture at Merck.

Many analysts have applauded his efforts. "At least we can measure whether the company is meeting its goals or not," said one industry analyst. "It's very important for us to be able to respond and say, 'Here's our scorecard of how we're doing', vs. saying, 'Trust me, in 2010 we'll be there,'" Clark says.

In addition to setting high aspirations, and transforming Merck's structure, Clark has also attacked the complacency that, he argues, has put the entire industry in a rut. "If you ever feel comfortable that your model is the right model, you end up where the industry is today," he says. "It's always going to be continuous improvement. We will never declare victory."

It's not clear whether Clark and Merck will be successful. But it is clear that Clark does not see the status quo as an option. "A crisis is a terrible thing to waste," says the CEO.[1] ■

*t*his chapter is about change and stress. We describe environmental forces that require managers to implement comprehensive change programs. We also consider why people and organizations often resist change and how this resistance can be overcome. We review various processes for managing organizational change. We also discuss contemporary change issues for today's managers. Then we move to the topic of stress. We elaborate on the sources and consequences of stress. Finally, we conclude this chapter with a discussion of what individuals and organizations can do to better manage stress levels.

Before we delve into the subject of change, see how well you handle change by taking the following self-assessment.

HOW WELL DO I RESPOND TO TURBULENT CHANGE?

In the Self-Assessment Library (available on CD and online), take assessment III.C.1 (How Well Do I Respond to Turbulent Change?) and answer the following questions.

1. How did you score? Are you surprised by your score?
2. During what time of your life have you experienced the most change? How did you deal with it? Would you handle these changes in the same way today? Why or why not?
3. Are there ways you might reduce your resistance to change?

Forces for Change

No company today is in a particularly stable environment. Even traditionally stable industries such as energy and utilities have witnessed—and will continue to experience—turbulent change. Companies that occupy a dominant market share in their industries must change, sometimes radically. While Microsoft is struggling with launching its controversial new operating system—Vista—it also is trying to outflank smaller companies such as Google that are increasingly offering free, Web-based software packages. How well Microsoft performs is not simply a function of managing one change but a matter of how well it can manage both short-term and long-term changes.

1 Identify forces that act as stimulants to change and contrast planned and unplanned change.

Thus, the dynamic and changing environments that organizations face today require adaptation, sometimes calling for deep and rapid responses. "Change or die!" is the rallying cry among today's managers worldwide. Exhibit 19-1 summarizes six specific forces that are acting as stimulants for change.

Exhibit 19-1 Forces for Change	
Force	**Examples**
Nature of the workforce	More cultural diversity Aging population Many new entrants with inadequate skills
Technology	Faster, cheaper, and more mobile computers Online music sharing Deciphering of the human genetic code
Economic shocks	Rise and fall of dot-com stocks 2000–2002 stock market collapse Record low interest rates
Competition	Global competitors Mergers and consolidations Growth of e-commerce
Social trends	Internet chat rooms Retirement of baby boomers Rise in discount and "big box" retailers
World politics	Iraq–U.S. war Opening of markets in China War on terrorism following 9/11/01

In a number of places in this book, we've discussed the *changing nature of the workforce*. For instance, almost every organization is having to adjust to a multicultural environment. Demographic changes, immigration, and outsourcing also have transformed the nature of the workforce.

Technology is changing jobs and organizations. Just about the time an organization adapts to one technological change, other technological challenges and opportunities come to the forefront. It is not hard to imagine the very idea of an office becoming an antiquated concept in the near future.

Economic shocks have continued to impose changes on organizations. In recent years, for instance, new dot-com businesses have been created, turned tens of thousands of investors into overnight millionaires, then crashed, and others rose in their wake. And record low interest rates first stimulated a rapid rise in home values, helped sustain consumer spending, and benefited many industries, especially construction and banking. But when the bubble burst, businesses in these same industries suffered.

Competition is changing. The global economy means that competitors are as likely to come from across the ocean as from across town. Heightened competition means that successful organizations will be the ones that can change in response to the competition. They'll be fast on their feet, capable of developing new products rapidly and getting them to market quickly. They'll rely on short production runs, short product cycles, and an ongoing stream of new products. In other words, they'll be flexible. They will require an equally flexible and responsive workforce that can adapt to rapidly and even radically changing conditions.

Social trends don't remain static. For instance, in contrast to just 15 years ago, people are meeting and sharing information in Internet chat rooms; Baby Boomers have begun to retire; and consumers are increasingly doing their shopping at "big box" retailers and online. A company like Liz Claiborne needs to continually adjust its product and marketing strategies to be sensitive to changing social trends, as it did when it sold off brands (like Ellen Tracy), deemphasized large department stores like Macy's as vendors, and streamlined its operations and cut staff.

Throughout this book we have argued strongly for the importance of seeing OB in a global context. Business schools have been preaching a global perspective since the early 1980s, but no one—not even the strongest proponents of globalization—could have imagined how *world politics* would change in recent years. We've seen the breakup of the Soviet Union; the opening up of China and Southeast Asia; political instability in many parts of the world; and, of course, the rise of Muslim fundamentalism. The invasion of Iraq by the United States has led to an expensive postwar rebuilding and an increase in anti-American attitudes in much of the world. The attacks on New York and Washington, DC, on September 11, 2001, and the subsequent war on terrorism have led to changes in business practices related to the creation of backup systems, employee security, employee stereotyping and profiling, and post-terrorist-attack anxiety.

Planned Change

A group of housekeeping employees who work for a small hotel confronted the owner: "It's very hard for most of us to maintain rigid 7-to-4 work hours," said their spokeswoman. "Each of us has significant family and personal responsibilities. And rigid hours don't work for us. We're going to begin looking for someplace else to work if you don't set up flexible work hours." The owner listened thoughtfully to the group's ultimatum and agreed to its request. The next day, the owner introduced a flextime plan for these employees.

A major automobile manufacturer spent several billion dollars to install state-of-the-art robotics. One area that would receive the new equipment was quality control. Sophisticated computer-controlled equipment would be put in place to significantly improve the company's ability to find and correct defects. Because the new equipment would dramatically change the jobs of the people working in the quality-control area, and because management anticipated considerable employee resistance to the new equipment, executives were developing a program to help people become familiar with the equipment and to deal with any anxieties they might be feeling.

Both of the previous scenarios are examples of **change**. That is, both are concerned with making things different. However, only the second scenario describes a **planned change**. Many changes in organizations are like the one that occurred at the hotel—they just happen. Some organizations treat all change as an accidental occurrence. We're concerned with change activities that are proactive and purposeful. In this chapter, we address change as an intentional, goal-oriented activity.

What are the goals of planned change? Essentially there are two. First, it seeks to improve the ability of the organization to adapt to changes in its environment. Second, it seeks to change employee behavior.

If an organization is to survive, it must respond to changes in its environment. When competitors introduce new products or services, government agencies enact new laws, important sources of supplies go out of business, or similar environmental changes take place, the organization needs to adapt. Efforts to stimulate innovation, empower employees, and introduce work teams are examples of planned-change activities directed at responding to changes in the environment.

Because an organization's success or failure is essentially due to the things that its employees do or fail to do, planned change also is concerned with changing the behavior of individuals and groups within the organization. Later in this chapter, we review a number of techniques that organizations can use to get people to behave differently in the tasks they perform and in their interactions with others.

Who in organizations is responsible for managing change activities? The answer is **change agents**.[2] Change agents can be managers or nonmanagers, current employees of the organization, newly hired employees, or outside consultants. A contemporary example of a change agent is Lawrence Summers, former president of Harvard University.[3] When he accepted the presidency in 2001, Summers aggressively sought to shake up the complacent institution by, among other things, leading the battle to reshape the undergraduate curriculum, proposing that the university be more directly engaged with problems in education and public health, and reorganizing to consolidate more power in the president's office. His change efforts generated tremendous resistance, particularly among Harvard faculty. Finally, in 2006, when Summers made comments suggesting that women were less able to excel in science than men, the Harvard faculty revolted, and in a few weeks, Summers was forced to resign. Despite Summer's support among students—a poll shortly before his resignation showed

Fiat Group Automobiles hired an outsider as a change agent to return the ailing company to profitability. As Fiat's new CEO, Sergio Marchionne led a turnaround by changing a hierarchical, status-driven firm into a market-driven one. Marchionne reduced the layers of Fiat's management and fired 10 percent of its 20,000 white-collar employees. He improved relationships with union employees, reduced car-development time, and introduced new car designs. Marchionne is shown here with the redesigned version of the compact Fiat 500, which he hopes will be for the company what the iPod was for Apple.

change   *Making things different.*

planned change   *Change activities that are intentional and goal oriented.*

change agents   *Persons who act as catalysts and assume the responsibility for managing change activities.*

that students supported him by a 3:1 ratio—his efforts at change had ruffled one too many feathers. In 2007, he was replaced with Drew Gilpin Faust, Harvard's first female president, who promised to be less aggressive in instituting changes.[4]

Summers's case shows that many change agents fail because organizational members resist change. In the next section, we discuss resistance to change and what can be done about it.

Resistance to Change

One of the most well-documented findings from studies of individual and organizational behavior is that organizations and their members resist change. One recent study showed that even when employees are shown data that suggests they need to change, they latch onto whatever data they can find that suggests they are okay and don't need to change. Our egos are fragile, and we often see change as threatening.[5]

 List the sources for resistance to change.

In some ways, resistance to change is positive. It provides a degree of stability and predictability to behavior. If there weren't some resistance, organizational behavior would take on the characteristics of chaotic randomness. Resistance to change can also be a source of functional conflict. For example, resistance to a reorganization plan or a change in a product line can stimulate a healthy debate over the merits of the idea and result in a better decision. But there is a definite downside to resistance to change. It hinders adaptation and progress.

Resistance to change doesn't necessarily surface in standardized ways. Resistance can be overt, implicit, immediate, or deferred. It's easiest for management to deal with resistance when it is overt and immediate. For instance, a change is proposed and employees quickly respond by voicing complaints, engaging in a work slowdown, threatening to go on strike, or the like. The greater challenge is managing resistance that is implicit or deferred. Implicit resistance efforts are more subtle—loss of loyalty to the organization, loss of motivation to work, increased errors or mistakes, increased absenteeism due to "sickness"—and hence are more difficult to recognize. Similarly, deferred actions cloud the link between the source of the resistance and the reaction to it. A change may produce what appears to be only a minimal reaction at the time it is initiated, but then resistance surfaces weeks, months, or even years later. Or a single change that in and of itself might have little impact becomes the straw that breaks the camel's back. Reactions to change can build up and then explode in some response that seems totally out of proportion to the change action it follows. The resistance, of course, has merely been deferred and stockpiled. What surfaces is a response to an accumulation of previous changes.

Exhibit 19-2 summarizes major forces for resistance to change, categorized by individual and organizational sources. Individual sources of resistance reside in basic human characteristics such as perceptions, personalities, and needs. Organizational sources reside in the structural makeup of organizations themselves.

Before we move on to ways to overcome resistance to change, it's important to note that not all change is good. Research has shown that sometimes an emphasis on making speedy decisions can lead to bad decisions. Sometimes the line between resisting needed change and falling into a "speed trap" is a fine one indeed. What's more, sometimes in the "fog of change," those who are initiating change fail to realize the full magnitude of the effects they are causing or to estimate their true costs to the organization. Thus, although the perspective generally taken is that rapid, transformational change is good, this is not always

Exhibit **19-2**	Sources of Resistance to Change

Individual Sources

Habit—To copy with life's complexities, we rely on habits or programmed responses. But when confronted with change, this tendency to respond in our accustomed ways becomes a source of resistance.

Security—People with a high need for security are likely to resist change because it threatens their feelings of safety.

Economic factors—Changes in job tasks or established work routines can arouse economic fears if people are concerned that they won't be able to perform the new tasks or routines to their previous standards, especially when pay is closely tied to productivity.

Fear of the unknown—Change substitutes ambiguity and uncertainty for the unknown.

Selective information processing—Individuals are guilty of selectively processing information in order to keep their perceptions intact. They hear what they want to hear and they ignore information that challenges the world they've created.

Organizational Sources

Structural inertia—Organizations have built-in mechanisms—like their selection processes and formalized regulations—to produce stability. When an organization is confronted with change, this structural inertia acts as a counterbalance to sustain stability.

Limited focus of change—Organizations are made up of a number of interdependent subsystems. One can't be changed without affecting the others. So limited changes in subsystems tend to be nullified by the larger system.

Group inertia—Even if individuals want to change their behavior, group norms may act as a constraint.

Threat to expertise—Changes in organizational patterns may threaten the expertise of specialized groups.

Threat to established power relationships—Any redistribution of decision-making authority can threaten long-established power relationships within the organization.

Threat to established resource allocations—Groups in the organization that control sizable resources often see change as a threat. They tend to be content with the way things are.

the case. Some organizations, such as Baring Brothers Bank in the United Kingdom, have collapsed for this reason.[6] Change agents need to carefully think through the full implications.

Overcoming Resistance to Change

Seven tactics have been suggested for use by change agents in dealing with resistance to change.[7] Let's review them briefly.

Education and Communication   Resistance can be reduced through communicating with employees to help them see the logic of a change. Communication can reduce resistance on two levels. First, it fights the effects of misinformation and poor communication: If employees receive the full facts and get any misunderstandings cleared up, resistance should subside. Second, communication can be helpful in "selling" the need for change. Indeed, research shows that the way the need for change is sold matters—change is more likely when the necessity of changing is packaged properly.[8] A study of German companies revealed that changes are most effective when a company communicates its rationale balancing various stakeholder (shareholders, employees, community, customers) interests versus a rationale based on shareholder interests only.[9]

Participation   It's difficult for individuals to resist a change decision in which they participated. Prior to making a change, those opposed can be brought into the decision process. Assuming that the participants have the expertise to make a meaningful contribution, their involvement can reduce resistance, obtain commitment, and increase the quality of the change decision. However, against these advantages are the negatives: potential for a poor solution and great consumption of time.

Building Support and Commitment   Change agents can offer a range of supportive efforts to reduce resistance. When employees' fear and anxiety are high, employee counseling and therapy, new-skills training, or a short paid leave of absence may facilitate adjustment. Research on middle managers has shown that when managers or employees have low emotional commitment to change, they favor the status quo and resist it.[10] So firing up employees can also help them emotionally commit to the change rather than embrace the status quo.

Implementing Changes Fairly   Try as managers might to have employees see change positively, most workers tend to react negatively. Most people simply don't like change. But one way organizations can minimize the negative impact of change, even when employees frame it as a negative, is to makes sure the change is implemented fairly. As we learned in Chapter 6, procedural fairness becomes especially important when employees perceive an outcome as negative, so when implementing changes, it's crucial that organizations bend over backwards to make sure employees see the reason for the change, and perceive that the changes are being implemented consistently and fairly.[11]

Manipulation and Cooptation   *Manipulation* refers to covert influence attempts. Twisting and distorting facts to make them appear more attractive, withholding undesirable information, and creating false rumors to get employees to accept a change are all examples of manipulation. If corporate management threatens to close down a particular manufacturing plant if that plant's employees fail to accept an across-the-board pay cut, and if the threat is actually untrue, management is using manipulation. *Cooptation*, on the other hand, is a form of both manipulation and participation. It seeks to "buy off" the leaders of a resistance group by giving them a key role in the change decision. The leaders' advice is sought, not to seek a better decision, but to get their endorsement. Both manipulation and cooptation are relatively inexpensive and easy ways to gain the support of adversaries, but the tactics can backfire if the targets become aware that they are being tricked or used. Once discovered, the change agent's credibility may drop to zero.

Selecting People Who Accept Change   Research suggests that the ability to easily accept and adapt to change is related to personality—some people simply have more positive attitudes about change than others.[12] It appears that people who adjust best to change are those who are open to experience, take a positive attitude toward change, are willing to take risks, and are flexible in their behavior. One study of managers in the United States, Europe, and Asia found that those with a positive self-concept and high risk tolerance coped better with organizational change. The study authors suggested that organizations could facilitate the change process by selecting people who score high on these characteristics. Another study found that selecting people based on a resistance-to-change scale worked well in winnowing out those who tended to react emotionally to change or to be rigid.[13]

Coercion   Last on the list of tactics is coercion; that is, the application of direct threats or force on the resisters. If the corporate management mentioned in the previous discussion really is determined to close a manufacturing plant if employees don't acquiesce to a pay cut, then coercion would be the label attached to its change tactic. Other examples of coercion are threats of transfer, loss of promotions, negative performance evaluations, and a poor letter of recommendation. The advantages and drawbacks of coercion are approximately the same as those mentioned for manipulation and cooptation.

The Politics of Change

No discussion of resistance to change would be complete without a brief mention of the politics of change. Because change invariably threatens the status quo, it inherently implies political activity.[14]

Internal change agents typically are individuals high in the organization who have a lot to lose from change. They have, in fact, risen to their positions of authority by developing skills and behavioral patterns that are favored by the organization. Change is a threat to those skills and patterns. What if they are no longer the ones the organization values? Change creates the potential for others in the organization to gain power at their expense.

Politics suggests that the impetus for change is more likely to come from outside change agents, employees who are new to the organization (and have less invested in the status quo), or from managers slightly removed from the main power structure. Managers who have spent their entire careers with a single organization and eventually achieve a senior position in the hierarchy are often major impediments to change. Change, itself, is a very real threat to their status and position. Yet they may be expected to implement changes to demonstrate that they're not merely caretakers. By acting as change agents, they can symbolically convey to various constituencies—stockholders, suppliers, employees, customers—that they are on top of problems and adapting to a dynamic environment. Of course, as you might guess, when forced to introduce change, these long-time power holders tend to implement incremental changes. Radical change is too threatening.

Power struggles within the organization will determine, to a large degree, the speed and quantity of change. You should expect that long-time career executives will be sources of resistance. This, incidentally, explains why boards of directors that recognize the imperative for the rapid introduction of radical change in their organizations frequently turn to outside candidates for new leadership.[15]

Approaches to Managing Organizational Change

Now we turn to several approaches to managing change: Lewin's classic three-step model of the change process, Kotter's eight-step plan, action research, and organizational development.

Lewin's Three-Step Model

Kurt Lewin argued that successful change in organizations should follow three steps: **unfreezing** the status quo, **movement** to a desired end state, and **refreezing** the new change to make it permanent.[16] (See Exhibit 19-3.) The value of this model can be seen in the following example, when the management of a large oil company decided to reorganize its marketing function in the Western United States.

3 Compare the four main approaches to managing organizational change.

---

unfreezing *Changing to overcome the pressures of both individual resistance and group conformity.*

movement *A change process that transforms the organization from the status quo to a desired end state.*

refreezing *Stabilizing a change intervention by balancing driving and restraining forces.*

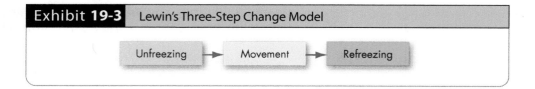

Exhibit **19-3** Lewin's Three-Step Change Model

The oil company had three divisional offices in the West, located in Seattle, San Francisco, and Los Angeles. The decision was made to consolidate the divisions into a single regional office to be located in San Francisco. The reorganization meant transferring more than 150 employees, eliminating some duplicate managerial positions, and instituting a new hierarchy of command. As you might guess, a move of this magnitude was difficult to keep secret. The rumor of its occurrence preceded the announcement by several months. The decision itself was made unilaterally. It came from the executive offices in New York. The people affected had no say whatsoever in the choice. For those in Seattle or Los Angeles, who may have disliked the decision and its consequences—the problems inherent in transferring to another city, pulling youngsters out of school, making new friends, having new coworkers, undergoing the reassignment of responsibilities—their only recourse was to quit. In actuality, fewer than 10 percent did.

The status quo can be considered to be an equilibrium state. To move from this equilibrium—to overcome the pressures of both individual resistance and group conformity—unfreezing is necessary. It can be achieved in one of three ways. (See Exhibit 19-4.) The **driving forces**, which direct behavior away from the status quo, can be increased. The **restraining forces**, which hinder movement from the existing equilibrium, can be decreased. A third alternative is to combine the first two approaches. Companies that have been successful in the past are likely to encounter restraining forces because people question the need for change.[17] Similarly, research shows that companies with strong cultures excel at incremental change but are overcome by restraining forces against radical change.[18]

The oil company's management could expect employee resistance to the consolidation. To deal with that resistance, management could use positive incentives to encourage employees to accept the change. For instance, increases in pay can be offered to those who accept the transfer. Very liberal moving expenses can be paid by the company. Management might offer low-cost mortgage funds to allow employees to buy new homes in San Francisco. Of course, management might also consider unfreezing acceptance of the status quo by removing restraining forces. Employees could be counseled individually. Each employee's concerns and apprehensions could be heard and specifically clarified. Assuming that most of the fears are unjustified, the counselor could assure the employees that there

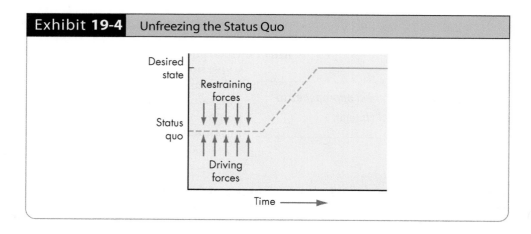

Exhibit **19-4** Unfreezing the Status Quo

Organizational development at Wal-Mart includes a new voluntary program called the Personal Sustainability Project that seeks to improve employee well-being and organizational effectiveness. Through workshops, retreats, and seminars, Wal-Mart informs employees about the benefits of issues ranging from physical fitness to energy conservation and then gives them the freedom to make positive changes in their personal lives and in their workplace. Wal-Mart employees in this photo sample healthy food as part of a seminar promoting the benefits of fitness and lifestyle improvements.

Source: Michael Stravato/ The New York Times

The OD paradigm values human and organizational growth, collaborative and participative processes, and a spirit of inquiry.[23] The change agent may be directive in OD; however, there is a strong emphasis on collaboration. The following briefly identifies the underlying values in most OD efforts:

1. *Respect for people.*   Individuals are perceived as being responsible, conscientious, and caring. They should be treated with dignity and respect.
2. *Trust and support.*   An effective and healthy organization is characterized by trust, authenticity, openness, and a supportive climate.
3. *Power equalization.*   Effective organizations deemphasize hierarchical authority and control.
4. *Confrontation.*   Problems shouldn't be swept under the rug. They should be openly confronted.
5. *Participation.*   The more that people who will be affected by a change are involved in the decisions surrounding that change, the more they will be committed to implementing those decisions.

What are some of the OD techniques or interventions for bringing about change? In the following pages, we present six interventions that change agents might consider using.

Sensitivity Training   It can go by a variety of names—**sensitivity training**, laboratory training, encounter groups, or T-groups (training groups)—but all refer to a method of changing behavior through unstructured group interaction.[24]

---

action research   *A change process based on systematic collection of data and then selection of a change action based on what the analyzed data indicate.*

organizational development (OD)   *A collection of planned change interventions, built on humanistic-democratic values, that seeks to improve organizational effectiveness and employee well-being.*

sensitivity training   *Training groups that seek to change behavior through unstructured group interaction.*

Members are brought together in a free and open environment in which participants discuss themselves and their interactive processes, loosely directed by a professional behavioral scientist. The group is process oriented, which means that individuals learn through observing and participating rather than being told. The professional creates the opportunity for participants to express their ideas, beliefs, and attitudes and does not accept—in fact, overtly rejects—any leadership role.

The objectives of the T-groups are to provide the subjects with increased awareness of their own behavior and how others perceive them, greater sensitivity to the behavior of others, and increased understanding of group processes. Specific results sought include increased ability to empathize with others, improved listening skills, greater openness, increased tolerance of individual differences, and improved conflict-resolution skills.

Survey Feedback   One tool for assessing attitudes held by organizational members, identifying discrepancies among member perceptions, and solving these differences is the **survey feedback** approach.[25]

Everyone in an organization can participate in survey feedback, but of key importance is the organizational family—the manager of any given unit and the employees who report directly to him or her. A questionnaire is usually completed by all members in the organization or unit. Organization members may be asked to suggest questions or may be interviewed to determine what issues are relevant. The questionnaire typically asks members for their perceptions and attitudes on a broad range of topics, including decision-making practices; communication effectiveness; coordination between units; and satisfaction with the organization, job, peers, and their immediate supervisor.

The data from this questionnaire are tabulated with data pertaining to an individual's specific "family" and to the entire organization and then distributed to employees. These data then become the springboard for identifying problems and clarifying issues that may be creating difficulties for people. Particular attention is given to the importance of encouraging discussion and ensuring that discussions focus on issues and ideas and not on attacking individuals.

Finally, group discussion in the survey feedback approach should result in members identifying possible implications of the questionnaire's findings. Are people listening? Are new ideas being generated? Can decision making, interpersonal relations, or job assignments be improved? Answers to questions like these, it is hoped, will result in the group agreeing on commitments to various actions that will remedy the problems that are identified.

Process Consultation   No organization operates perfectly. Managers often sense that their unit's performance can be improved, but they're unable to identify what can be improved and how it can be improved. The purpose of **process consultation (PC)** is for an outside consultant to assist a client, usually a manager, "to perceive, understand, and act upon process events" with which the manager must deal.[26] These might include work flow, informal relationships among unit members, and formal communication channels.

PC is similar to sensitivity training in its assumption that organizational effectiveness can be improved by dealing with interpersonal problems and in its emphasis on involvement. But PC is more task-directed than is sensitivity training. Consultants in PC are there to "give the client 'insight' into what is going on around him, within him, and between him and other people."[27] They do not solve the organization's problems. Rather, the consultant is a guide or coach who advises on the process to help the client solve his or her own problems. The consultant works with the client in *jointly* diagnosing what processes need

To improve dysfunctional relationships between management and union employees, American Airlines CEO Gerard Arpey (right in photo) formed problem-solving teams to find new ways to compete on efficiency and service. A joint leadership team of senior managers and union officials meets monthly to discuss strategy and finances, another team communicates with employees through American's and union Web sites, and other teams of flight attendants and airport workers are trying to improve customer service. To resolve the problem of funding pensions, Arpey is shown here joining pilots and flight attendants in lobbying Congress for support of pension reform legislation.

improvement. The emphasis is on "jointly" because the client develops a skill at analyzing processes within his or her unit that can be continually called on long after the consultant is gone. In addition, by having the client actively participate in both the diagnosis and the development of alternatives, there will be greater understanding of the process and the remedy and less resistance to the action plan chosen.

Team Building　As we've noted in numerous places throughout this book, organizations are increasingly relying on teams to accomplish work tasks. **Team building** uses high-interaction group activities to increase trust and openness among team members.[28] Team building can be applied within groups or at the intergroup level, at which activities are interdependent. For our discussion, we emphasize the intragroup level and leave intergroup development to the next section. As a result, our interest concerns applications to organizational families (command groups) as well as to committees, project teams, self-managed teams, and task groups. Team building is applicable where group activities are interdependent. The objective is to improve coordinative efforts of members, which will result in increasing the team's performance.

The activities considered in team building typically include goal setting, development of interpersonal relations among team members, role analysis to clarify each member's role and responsibilities, and team process analysis. Of course, team building may emphasize or exclude certain activities, depending on the purpose of the development effort and the specific problems with which

survey feedback　*The use of questionnaires to identify discrepancies among member perceptions; discussion follows, and remedies are suggested.*

process consultation (PC)　*A meeting in which a consultant assists a client in understanding process events with which he or she must deal and identifying processes that need improvement.*

team building　*High interaction among team members to increase trust and openness.*

the team is confronted. Basically, however, team building attempts to use high interaction among members to increase trust and openness.

It may be beneficial to begin by having members attempt to define the goals and priorities of the team. This will bring to the surface different perceptions of what the team's purpose may be. Following this, members can evaluate the team's performance—how effective is the team in structuring priorities and achieving its goals? This should identify potential problem areas. This self-critique discussion of means and ends can be done with members of the total team present or, when large size impinges on a free interchange of views, may initially take place in smaller groups followed by the sharing of their findings with the total team.

Team building can also address itself to clarifying each member's role on the team. Each role can be identified and clarified. Previous ambiguities can be brought to the surface. For some individuals, it may offer one of the few opportunities they have had to think through thoroughly what their job is all about and what specific tasks they are expected to carry out if the team is to optimize its effectiveness.

Intergroup Development

Intergroup Development   A major area of concern in OD is the dysfunctional conflict that exists between groups. As a result, this has been a subject to which change efforts have been directed.

Intergroup development seeks to change the attitudes, stereotypes, and perceptions that groups have of each other. For example, in one company, the engineers saw the accounting department as composed of shy and conservative types, and the human resources department as having a bunch of "ultra-liberals who are more concerned that some protected group of employees might get their feelings hurt than with the company making a profit." Such stereotypes can have an obvious negative impact on the coordination efforts between the departments.

Although there are several approaches for improving intergroup relations,[29] a popular method emphasizes problem solving.[30] In this method, each group meets independently to develop lists of its perception of itself, the other group, and how it believes the other group perceives it. The groups then share their lists, after which similarities and differences are discussed. Differences are clearly articulated, and the groups look for the causes of the disparities.

Are the groups' goals at odds? Were perceptions distorted? On what basis were stereotypes formulated? Have some differences been caused by misunderstandings of intentions? Have words and concepts been defined differently by each group? Answers to questions like these clarify the exact nature of the conflict. Once the causes of the difficulty have been identified, the groups can move to the integration phase—working to develop solutions that will improve relations between the groups. Subgroups, with members from each of the conflicting groups, can now be created for further diagnosis and to begin to formulate possible alternative actions that will improve relations.

Appreciative Inquiry

Appreciative Inquiry   Most OD approaches are problem-centered. They identify a problem or set of problems, then look for a solution. **Appreciative inquiry (AI)** accentuates the positive.[31] Rather than looking for problems to fix, this approach seeks to identify the unique qualities and special strengths of an organization, which can then be built on to improve performance. That is, it focuses on an organization's successes rather than on its problems.

Advocates of AI argue that problem-solving approaches always ask people to look backward at yesterday's failures, to focus on shortcomings, and rarely result in new visions. Instead of creating a climate for positive change, action research and OD techniques such as survey feedback and process consultation end up placing blame and generating defensiveness. AI proponents claim it makes more sense to refine and enhance what the organization is already doing well. This allows the organization to change by playing to its strengths and competitive advantages.

The AI process essentially consists of four steps, often played out in a large-group meeting over a 2- or 3-day time period and overseen by a trained change agent. The first step is *discovery*. The idea is to find out what people think are the strengths of the organization. For instance, employees are asked to recount times they felt the organization worked best or when they specifically felt most satisfied with their jobs. The second step is *dreaming*. The information from the discovery phase is used to speculate on possible futures for the organization. For instance, people are asked to envision the organization in 5 years and to describe what's different. The third step is *design*. Based on the dream articulation, participants focus on finding a common vision of how the organization will look and agree on its unique qualities. The fourth stage seeks to define the organization's *destiny*. In this final step, participants discuss how the organization is going to fulfill its dream. This typically includes the writing of action plans and development of implementation strategies.

AI has proven to be an effective change strategy in organizations such as GTE, Roadway Express, and the U.S. Navy. For instance, during a recent 3-day AI seminar with Roadway employees in North Carolina, workers were asked to recall ideal work experiences—when they were treated with respect, when trucks were loaded to capacity or arrived on time. Assembled into nine groups, the workers were then encouraged to devise money-saving ideas. A team of short-haul drivers came up with 12 cost-cutting and revenue-generating ideas, one of which could alone generate $1 million in additional profits.[32]

Creating a Culture for Change

4 *Demonstrate two ways of creating a culture for change.*

We've considered how organizations can adapt to change. Recently, some OB scholars have focused on a more proactive approach to change—how organizations can embrace change by transforming their cultures. In this section we review two such approaches: stimulating an innovative culture and creating a learning organization.

Stimulating a Culture of Innovation

How can an organization become more innovative? An excellent model is W. L. Gore, the $1.4-billion-per-year company best known as the maker of Gore-Tex fabric.[33] Gore has developed a reputation as one of America's most innovative companies by developing a stream of diverse products—including guitar strings, dental floss, medical devices, and fuel cells.

What's the secret of Gore's success? What can other organizations do to duplicate its track record for innovation? Although there is no guaranteed formula, certain characteristics surface again and again when researchers study

intergroup development *OD efforts to change the attitudes, stereotypes, and perceptions that groups have of each other.*

appreciative inquiry (AI) *An approach that seeks to identify the unique qualities and special strengths of an organization, which can then be built on to improve performance.*

Respected as one of the world's most innovative companies, Starbucks turned a commodity product that was declining in sales and invented specialty coffees as a major new product category. Starbucks relies on its employees to share customer insights with managers and takes product development teams on inspirational field trips to view customer behavior, local cultures, and fashion trends. Starbucks has extended its coffee shops from American college campuses and urban sites to locations throughout the world, including the shop shown here at a shopping center in Ramadan, Dubai.

innovative organizations. We've grouped them into structural, cultural, and human resource categories. Our message to change agents is that they should consider introducing these characteristics into their organization if they want to create an innovative climate. Before we look at these characteristics, however, let's clarify what we mean by innovation.

Definition of *Innovation* We said change refers to making things different. **Innovation** is a more specialized kind of change. Innovation is a new idea applied to initiating or improving a product, process, or service.[34] So all innovations involve change, but not all changes necessarily involve new ideas or lead to significant improvements. Innovations in organizations can range from small incremental improvements, such as Nabisco's extension of the Oreo product line to include double-stuffed cookies and chocolate-covered Oreos, up to radical breakthroughs, such as Toyota's battery-powered Prius.

Sources of Innovation *Structural variables* have been the most studied potential source of innovation.[35] A comprehensive review of the structure–innovation relationship leads to the following conclusions.[36] First, organic structures positively influence innovation. Because they're lower in vertical differentiation, formalization, and centralization, organic organizations facilitate the flexibility, adaptation, and cross-fertilization that make the adoption of innovations easier. Second, long tenure in management is associated with innovation. Managerial tenure apparently provides legitimacy and knowledge of how to accomplish tasks and obtain desired outcomes. Third, innovation is nurtured when there are slack resources. Having an abundance of resources allows an organization to afford to purchase innovations, bear the cost of instituting innovations, and absorb failures. Finally, interunit communication is high in innovative organizations.[37] These organizations are high users of committees, task forces, cross-functional teams, and other mechanisms that facilitate interaction across departmental lines.

Innovative organizations tend to have similar *cultures*. They encourage experimentation. They reward both successes and failures. They celebrate mistakes. Unfortunately, in too many organizations, people are rewarded for the absence of failures rather than for the presence of successes. Such cultures extinguish risk taking and innovation. People will suggest and try new ideas only when they feel such behaviors exact no penalties. Managers in innovative organizations recognize that failures are a natural byproduct of venturing into the unknown. When Barry Bonds set the Major League Baseball record for home runs (73), he also had more strikeouts (93). And he is remembered (and paid $20 million per year) for the former, not the latter.

Within the *human resources* category, we find that innovative organizations actively promote the training and development of their members so that they keep current, offer high job security so employees don't fear getting fired for making mistakes, and encourage individuals to become champions of change. Once a new idea is developed, **idea champions** actively and enthusiastically promote the idea, build support, overcome resistance, and ensure that the innovation is implemented.[38] The evidence indicates that champions have common personality characteristics: extremely high self-confidence, persistence, energy, and a tendency to take risks. Idea champions also display characteristics associated with transformational leadership. They inspire and energize others with their vision of the potential of an innovation and through their strong personal conviction in their mission. They are also good at gaining the commitment of others to support their mission. In addition, idea champions have jobs that provide considerable decision-making discretion. This autonomy helps them introduce and implement innovations in organizations.[39]

Creating a Learning Organization

Another way organizations can proactively manage change is to make continuous growth part of its culture—to become a learning organization.[40] In this section, we describe what a learning organization looks like and methods for managing learning.

What's a Learning Organization? A **learning organization** is an organization that has developed the continuous capacity to adapt and change. Just as individuals learn, so too do organizations. "All organizations learn, whether they consciously choose to or not—it is a fundamental requirement for their sustained existence."[41] However, some organizations just do it better than others.

Most organizations engage in what has been called **single-loop learning**.[42] When errors are detected, the correction process relies on past routines and present policies. In contrast, learning organizations use **double-loop learning**. When an error is detected, it's corrected in ways that involve the modification of the organization's objectives, policies, and standard routines. Double-loop learning challenges deeply rooted assumptions and norms within an organization. In this way, it provides opportunities for radically different solutions to problems and dramatic jumps in improvement.

---

innovation *A new idea applied to initiating or improving a product, process, or service.*

idea champions *Individuals who take an innovation and actively and enthusiastically promote the idea, build support, overcome resistance, and ensure that the idea is implemented.*

learning organization *An organization that has developed the continuous capacity to adapt and change.*

single-loop learning *A process of correcting errors using past routines and present policies.*

double-loop learning *A process of correcting errors by modifying the organization's objectives, policies, and standard routines.*

Exhibit **19-6**	Characteristics of a Learning Organization

1. There exists a shared vision that everyone agrees on.

2. People discard their old ways of thinking and the standard routines they use for solving problems or doing their jobs.

3. Members think of all organizational processes, activities, functions, and interactions with the environment as part of a system of interrelationships.

4. People openly communicate with each other (across vertical and horizontal boundaries) without fear of criticism or punishment.

5. People sublimate their personal self-interest and fragmented departmental interests to work together to achieve the organization's shared vision.

Source: Based on P. M. Senge, *The Fifth Discipline* (New York: Doubleday, 1990).

Exhibit 19-6 summarizes the five basic characteristics of a learning organization. It's an organization in which people put aside their old ways of thinking, learn to be open with each other, understand how their organization really works, form a plan or vision that everyone can agree on, and then work together to achieve that vision.[43]

Proponents of the learning organization envision it as a remedy for three fundamental problems inherent in traditional organizations: fragmentation, competition, and reactiveness.[44] First, *fragmentation* based on specialization creates "walls" and "chimneys" that separate different functions into independent and often warring fiefdoms. Second, an overemphasis on *competition* often undermines collaboration. Members of the management team compete with one another to show who is right, who knows more, or who is more persuasive. Divisions compete with one another when they ought to cooperate and share knowledge. Team project leaders compete to show who the best manager is. And third, *reactiveness* misdirects management's attention to problem solving rather than creation. The problem solver tries to make something go away, while a creator tries to bring something new into being. An emphasis on reactiveness pushes out innovation and continuous improvement and, in its place, encourages people to run around "putting out fires."

Managing Learning How do you change an organization to make it into a continual learner? What can managers do to make their firms learning organizations? The following are some suggestions:

- *Establish a strategy.* Management needs to make explicit its commitment to change, innovation, and continuous improvement.
- *Redesign the organization's structure.* The formal structure can be a serious impediment to learning. By flattening the structure, eliminating or combining departments, and increasing the use of cross-functional teams, interdependence is reinforced and boundaries between people are reduced.
- *Reshape the organization's culture.* To become a learning organization, managers need to demonstrate by their actions that taking risks and admitting failures are desirable traits. That means rewarding people who take chances and make mistakes. And management needs to encourage functional conflict. "The key to unlocking real openness at work," says one expert on learning organizations, "is to teach people to give up having to be in agreement. We think agreement is so important. Who cares? You have to bring paradoxes, conflicts, and dilemmas out in the open, so collectively we can be more intelligent than we can be individually."[45]

An excellent illustration of a learning organization is what Richard Clark is trying to do at Merck. In addition to changing Merck's structure so that innovation can come from customers (patients and doctors), Merck is also trying to reward researchers for taking risks, even if their risky ideas end in failure. Merck's transformed strategy, structure, and culture may or may not succeed, but that's part of the risk of stimulating change through creating a learning organization.

Work Stress and Its Management

Most of us are aware that employee stress is an increasing problem in organizations. Friends tell us they're stressed out from greater work loads and having to work longer hours because of downsizing at their companies (see Exhibit 19-7). Parents talk about the lack of job stability in today's world and reminisce about a time when a job with a large company implied lifetime security. We read surveys in which employees complain about the stress created in trying to balance work and family responsibilities.[46] In this section we'll look at the causes and consequences of stress, and then consider what individuals and organizations can do to reduce it.

5 *Define* stress *and identify its potential sources.*

What Is Stress?

Stress is a dynamic condition in which an individual is confronted with an opportunity, demand, or resource related to what the individual desires and for which the outcome is perceived to be both uncertain and important.[47] This is a complicated definition. Let's look at its components more closely.

Stress is not necessarily bad in and of itself. Although stress is typically discussed in a negative context, it also has a positive value.[48] It's an opportunity when it offers potential gain. Consider, for example, the superior performance that an athlete or stage performer gives in "clutch" situations. Such individuals often use stress positively to rise to the occasion and perform at or near their maximum. Similarly, many professionals see the pressures of heavy work loads and deadlines as positive challenges that enhance the quality of their work and the satisfaction they get from their job.

Exhibit **19-7**	Too Much Work, Too Little Time

With companies downsizing workers, those who remain find their jobs are demanding increasing amounts of time and energy. A national sample of U.S. employees finds that they:

Feel overworked	54%
Are overwhelmed by workload	55%
Lack time for reflection	59%
Don't have time to complete tasks	56%
Must multitask too much	45%

Source: BusinessWeek, July 16, 2001, p. 12.

stress *A dynamic condition in which an individual is confronted with an opportunity, a demand, or a resource related to what the individual desires and for which the outcome is perceived to be both uncertain and important.*

In short, some stress can be good, and some can be bad. Recently, researchers have argued that **challenge stressors**—or stressors associated with work load, pressure to complete tasks, and time urgency—operate quite differently from **hindrance stressors**—or stressors that keep you from reaching your goals (red tape, office politics, confusion over job responsibilities). Although research on challenge and hindrance stress is just starting to accumulate, early evidence suggests that challenge stressors are less harmful (produce less strain) than hindrance stressors.[49]

More typically, stress is associated with **demands** and **resources**. Demands are responsibilities, pressures, obligations, and even uncertainties that individuals face in the workplace. Resources are things within an individual's control that can be used to resolve the demands. This demands–resources model has received increasing support in the literature.[50] Let's discuss what it means.

When you take a test at school or you undergo your annual performance review at work, you feel stress because you confront opportunities and performance pressures. A good performance review may lead to a promotion, greater responsibilities, and a higher salary. A poor review may prevent you from getting a promotion. An extremely poor review might even result in your being fired. In such a situation, to the extent that you can apply resources to the demands—such as being prepared, placing the exam or review in perspective, or obtaining social support—you will feel less stress.

Research suggests that adequate resources help reduce the stressful nature of demands when demands and resources match. For example, if emotional demands are stressing you, then having emotional resources in the form of social support is especially important. Conversely, if the demands are cognitive—say, information overload—then job resources in the form of computer support or information are more important. Thus, under the demands and resources perspective on stress, having resources to cope with stress is just as important in offsetting stress as demands are in increasing it.[51]

Potential Sources of Stress

What causes stress? As the model in Exhibit 19-8 shows, there are three categories of potential stressors: environmental, organizational, and personal. Let's take a look at each.[52]

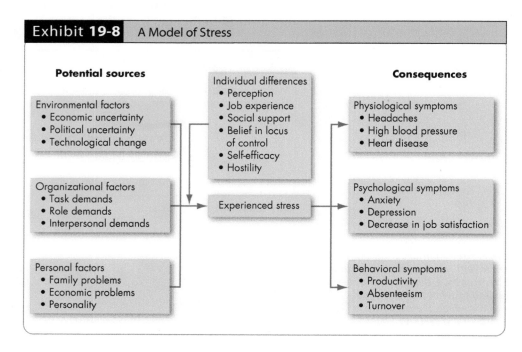

Exhibit 19-8 A Model of Stress

MYTH OR SCIENCE?

"Meetings Stress People Out"

*a*s a general rule, this statement is false. A recent investigation revealed that whether you love or hate meetings depends on your work environment, your personality, and your attitude about meetings.[53]

In one study of 676 employees, the researchers found that time spent in meetings led to positive reactions (higher job satisfaction, lower depression and intentions to quit) for people whose work was interdependent, but negative reactions for those whose work was independent. This result makes sense in that if you rely on other people to get your work done, meetings are a productive way to exchange information and coordinate efforts. If you do your work independently, however, meetings are likely to simply be interruptions to getting your work done.

Even more interesting were the results of the second study, of 304 employees in the United States and United Kingdom. The researchers found that for accomplishment-oriented people—those who were goal oriented and hard driving—meetings led to negative reactions. However, for people who scored low on this measure, time spent in meetings was positive.

Finally, the researchers also found in the second study that people's attitudes toward meetings mattered. If people had positive attitudes about meetings, then meetings were more enjoyable and less stressful. For people with negative attitudes, the opposite was true. So your attitude toward meetings is a bit of a self-fulfilling prophecy: If you think they're a waste of time, they will be. ∎

Environmental Factors   Just as environmental uncertainty influences the design of an organization's structure, it also influences stress levels among employees in that organization. Indeed, evidence indicates that uncertainty is the biggest reason people have trouble coping with organizational changes.[54] There are three main types of environmental uncertainty: economic, political, and technological.

Changes in the business cycle create *economic uncertainties*. When the economy is contracting, for example, people become increasingly anxious about their job security. *Political uncertainties* don't tend to create stress among North Americans as they do for employees in countries like Haiti or Venezuela. The obvious reason is that the United States and Canada have stable political systems, in which change is typically implemented in an orderly manner. Yet political threats and changes, even in countries like the United States and Canada, can induce stress. For instance, the threats by Quebec to separate from Canada, or the difficulties of East Germany integrating with West Germany, lead to political uncertainty that becomes stressful to people in these countries.[55] *Technological change* is a third type of environmental factor that can cause stress. Because new innovations can make an employee's skills and experience obsolete in a very short time, computers, robotics, automation, and similar forms of technological innovation are a threat to many people and cause them stress.

---

challenge stressors *Stressors associated with work load, pressure to complete tasks, and time urgency.*

hindrance stressors *Stressors that keep you from reaching your goals (red tape, office politics, confusion over job responsibilities).*

demands *Responsibilities, pressures, obligations, and even uncertainties that individuals face in the workplace.*

resources *Things within an individual's control that can be used to resolve demands.*

Organizational Factors   There is no shortage of factors within an organization that can cause stress. Pressures to avoid errors or complete tasks in a limited time, work overload, a demanding and insensitive boss, and unpleasant coworkers are a few examples. We've categorized these factors around task, role, and interpersonal demands.[56]

Task demands are factors related to a person's job. They include the design of the individual's job (autonomy, task variety, degree of automation), working conditions, and the physical work layout. Assembly lines, for instance, can put pressure on people when the line's speed is perceived as excessive. Similarly, working in an overcrowded room or in a visible location where noise and interruptions are constant can increase anxiety and stress.[57] Increasingly, as customer service becomes ever more important, emotional labor is a source of stress.[58] Imagine being a flight attendant for Southwest Airlines or a cashier at Starbucks. Do you think you could put on a happy face when you're having a bad day?

Role demands relate to pressures placed on a person as a function of the particular role she plays in the organization. Role conflicts create expectations that may be hard to reconcile or satisfy. Role overload is experienced when the employee is expected to do more than time permits. Role ambiguity is created when role expectations are not clearly understood and the employee is not sure what he or she is to do.

Interpersonal demands are pressures created by other employees. Lack of social support from colleagues and poor interpersonal relationships can cause stress, especially among employees with a high social need.

Personal Factors   The typical individual works about 40 to 50 hours a week. But the experiences and problems that people encounter in the other 120-plus nonwork hours each week can spill over to the job. Our final category, then, encompasses factors in the employee's personal life. Primarily, these factors are family issues, personal economic problems, and inherent personality characteristics.

National surveys consistently show that people hold *family* and personal relationships dear. Marital difficulties, the breaking off of a relationship, and discipline troubles with children are examples of relationship problems that create stress for employees that aren't left at the front door when they arrive at work.[59]

Economic problems created by individuals overextending their financial resources is another set of personal troubles that can create stress for employees and distract their attention from their work. Regardless of income level—people who make $80,000 per year seem to have as much trouble handling their finances as those who earn $18,000—some people are poor money managers or have wants that always seem to exceed their earning capacity.

Studies in three diverse organizations found that stress symptoms reported prior to beginning a job accounted for most of the variance in stress symptoms reported 9 months later.[60] This led the researchers to conclude that some people may have an inherent tendency to accentuate negative aspects of the world in general. If this is true, then a significant individual factor that influences stress is a person's basic disposition. That is, stress symptoms expressed on the job may actually originate in the person's *personality*.

Stressors Are Additive   A fact that tends to be overlooked when stressors are reviewed individually is that stress is an additive phenomenon.[61] Stress builds up. Each new and persistent stressor adds to an individual's stress level. So a single stressor may be relatively unimportant in and of itself, but if it's added to an already high level of stress, it can be "the straw that breaks the camel's back." If we want to appraise the total amount of stress an individual is under, we have to sum up his or her opportunity stresses, constraint stresses, and demand stresses.

Individual Differences

Some people thrive on stressful situations, while others are overwhelmed by them. What is it that differentiates people in terms of their ability to handle stress? What individual difference variables moderate the relationship between *potential* stressors and *experienced* stress? At least four variables—perception, job experience, social support, and personality—have been found to be relevant moderators.

In Chapter 5, we demonstrated that employees react in response to their perception of reality rather than to reality itself. *Perception*, therefore, will moderate the relationship between a potential stress condition and an employee's reaction to it. For example, one person's fear that he'll lose his job because his company is laying off personnel may be perceived by another as an opportunity to get a large severance allowance and start his own business. So stress potential doesn't lie in objective conditions; it lies in an employee's interpretation of those conditions.

The evidence indicates that *experience* on the job tends to be negatively related to work stress. Why? Two explanations have been offered.[62] First is the idea of selective withdrawal. Voluntary turnover is more probable among people who experience more stress. Therefore, people who remain with an organization longer are those with more stress-resistant traits or those who are more resistant to the stress characteristics of their organization. Second, people eventually develop coping mechanisms to deal with stress. Because this takes time, senior members of the organization are more likely to be fully adapted and should experience less stress.

There is increasing evidence that *social support*—that is, collegial relationships with coworkers or supervisors—can buffer the impact of stress.[63] The logic underlying this moderating variable is that social support acts as a palliative, mitigating the negative effects of even high-strain jobs.

Personality also affects the degree to which people experience stress and how they cope with it. Perhaps the most widely studied personality trait in stress is *Type A personality*, which we discussed in Chapter 4. Type A—particularly that aspect of

The Wieden & Kennedy advertising agency creates a socially supportive atmosphere that reduces the negative effects of employees' high-stress jobs. Open workspaces emphasize teamwork and neighborliness as employees collaborate on creating ad campaigns for clients such as Nike, Target, Nokia, and Starbucks. The employees in this photo cheer on coworkers during a company basketball game.

Source: Leah Nash/ The New York Times

Type A that manifests itself in hostility and anger—is associated with increased levels of stress and risk for heart disease.[64] More specifically, people who are quick to anger, maintain a persistently hostile outlook, and project a cynical mistrust of others are at increased risk of experiencing stress in situations.

HOW STRESSFUL IS MY LIFE?

In the Self-Assessment Library (available on CD and online), take assessment III.C.2 (How Stressful Is My Life?).

Consequences of Stress

Stress shows itself in a number of ways. For instance, an individual who is experiencing a high level of stress may develop high blood pressure, ulcers, irritability, difficulty making routine decisions, loss of appetite, accident-proneness, and the like. These symptoms can be subsumed under three general categories: physiological, psychological, and behavioral symptoms.[65]

6 Identify the consequences of stress.

Physiological Symptoms Most of the early concern with stress was directed at physiological symptoms. This was predominantly due to the fact that the topic was researched by specialists in the health and medical sciences. This research led to the conclusion that stress could create changes in metabolism, increase heart and breathing rates, increase blood pressure, bring on headaches, and induce heart attacks.

The link between stress and particular physiological symptoms is not clear. Traditionally, researchers concluded that there were few, if any, consistent relationships.[66] This is attributed to the complexity of the symptoms and the difficulty of objectively measuring them. More recently, some evidence suggests that stress may have harmful physiological effects. For example, one recent study linked stressful job demands to increase susceptibility to upper respiratory illnesses and poor immune system functioning, especially for individuals who had low self-efficacy.[67]

Psychological Symptoms Stress can cause dissatisfaction. Job-related stress can cause job-related dissatisfaction. Job dissatisfaction, in fact, is "the simplest and most obvious psychological effect" of stress.[68] But stress shows itself in other psychological states—for instance, tension, anxiety, irritability, boredom, and procrastination.

The evidence indicates that when people are placed in jobs that make multiple and conflicting demands or in which there is a lack of clarity about the incumbent's duties, authority, and responsibilities, both stress and dissatisfaction are increased.[69] Similarly, the less control people have over the pace of their work, the greater the stress and dissatisfaction. Although more research is needed to clarify the relationship, the evidence suggests that jobs that provide a low level of variety, significance, autonomy, feedback, and identity to incumbents create stress and reduce satisfaction and involvement in the job.[70]

Behavioral Symptoms Behavior-related stress symptoms include changes in productivity, absence, and turnover, as well as changes in eating habits, increased smoking or consumption of alcohol, rapid speech, fidgeting, and sleep disorders.[71]

OB In the News

The Ten Most Stressful Jobs—And One More That Didn't Make the List

According to the U.S. Centers for Disease Control and Prevention (CDC) and *Health* magazine, the top 10 most and least stressful jobs are:

10 Most Stressful Jobs	10 Least Stressful Jobs
1. Inner-city high school teacher	1. Forester
2. Police officer	2. Bookbinder
3. Miner	3. Telephone line worker
4. Air traffic controller	4. Toolmaker

10 Most Stressful Jobs	10 Least Stressful Jobs
5. Medical intern	5. Millwright
6. Stockbroker	6. Repairperson
7. Journalist	7. Civil engineer
8. Customer service/ complaint worker	8. Therapist
9. Secretary	9. Natural scientist
10. Waiter	10. Sales representative

One job that certainly seems like it should be on the list is flight attendant. Planes are more full than ever, passengers are grumpier than ever (due to full planes, smaller seats, fewer perks, and more delays), and the pay and job security seems to decline with every passing year.

Of these factors, perhaps none is more stressful than the increasingly tense relationship between passengers

and flight attendant. Lori Sheridan—a Northwest flight attendant since 1968—said her job description used to be all about providing "whatever the passenger wanted." Now, she said, "It's all about telling them what they can and can't do."

"It's one more level of stress on top of several years of pretty severe stress," said Patricia Friend, president of the largest flight attendant's union.

Sources: Based on *Helicobacter pylori and Peptic Ulcer Disease*, Centers for Disease Control and Prevention, U.S. Department of Health and Human Services; and M. Maynard, "Maybe the Toughest Job Aloft," *New York Times*, August 15, 2006, pp. C1, C6.

There has been a significant amount of research investigating the stress–performance relationship. The most widely studied pattern in the stress–performance literature is the inverted-U relationship.[72] This is shown in Exhibit 19-9.

The logic underlying the inverted U is that low to moderate levels of stress stimulate the body and increase its ability to react. Individuals then often perform their tasks better, more intensely, or more rapidly. But too much stress places unattainable demands on a person, which result in lower performance. This inverted-U pattern may also describe the reaction to stress over time as well as to changes in stress intensity. That is, even moderate levels of stress can have a negative influence on performance over the long term as the continued intensity of the stress wears down the individual and saps energy resources. An athlete may be able to use the positive effects of stress to obtain higher performance during every Saturday's game in the fall season, or a sales executive may be able to psych herself up for her presentation at the annual national meeting. But moderate levels of stress experienced continually over long periods, as

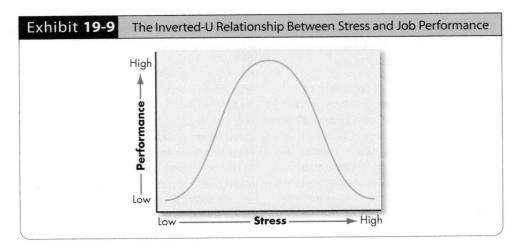

Exhibit 19-9   The Inverted-U Relationship Between Stress and Job Performance

typified by the emergency room staff in a large urban hospital, can result in lower performance. This may explain why emergency room staffs at such hospitals are frequently rotated and why it is unusual to find individuals who have spent the bulk of their career in such an environment. In effect, to do so would expose the individual to the risk of "career burnout."

In spite of the popularity and intuitive appeal of the inverted-U model, it doesn't get a lot of empirical support.[73] At this time, managers should be careful in assuming that this model accurately depicts the stress–performance relationship.

Managing Stress

From the organization's standpoint, management may not be concerned when employees experience low to moderate levels of stress. The reason, as we showed earlier, is that such levels of stress may be functional and lead to higher employee performance. But high levels of stress, or even low levels sustained over long periods, can lead to reduced employee performance and, thus, require action by management.

7 Contrast the individual and organizational approaches to managing stress.

Although a limited amount of stress may benefit an employee's performance, don't expect employees to see it that way. From the individual's standpoint, even low levels of stress are likely to be perceived as undesirable. It's not unlikely, therefore, for employees and management to have different notions of what constitutes an acceptable level of stress on the job. What management may consider to be "a positive stimulus that keeps the adrenalin running" is very likely to be seen as "excessive pressure" by the employee. Keep this in mind as we discuss individual and organizational approaches toward managing stress.[74]

Individual Approaches An employee can take personal responsibility for reducing stress levels. Individual strategies that have proven effective include implementing time-management techniques, increasing physical exercise, relaxation training, and expanding the social support network.

Many people manage their time poorly. The well-organized employee, like the well-organized student, can often accomplish twice as much as the person

International OB

Coping with Stress: Cultural Differences

Stress is a common complaint of workers worldwide. But how workers manage that stress, and whether they seek social support for relief, varies from one culture to another. A recent study examined this issue.

The study compared the tendency to seek social support to relieve stress among some Asian groups (Koreans and Asian Americans) to that of European Americans. Given that Asians tend to be more collectivist than European Americans (who tend to be more individualist), two possibilities arise. First, a collectivist orientation might increase the likelihood that one would want to talk about stressful problems, in essence seeking social support. Second, because collectivists strive for group harmony, they may keep problems to themselves and fail to use social support as a means of coping with stress.

The study found support for the latter suggestion: Koreans, Asians, and Asian Americans reported using social support less often than European Americans because they were concerned about maintaining group harmony. What's the upshot? Collectivists experiencing stress may be limiting themselves in terms of coping mechanisms and may need to find other means of coping with work-related stress.

Source: Based on S. Taylor, D. K. Sherman, H. S. Kim, J. Jarcho, K. Takagi, and M. Dunagan, "Culture and Social Support: Who Seeks It and Why?" *Journal of Personality and Social Psychology,* September 2004, pp. 354–362.

Cross-functional support for innovation efforts appeals to people in collectivist cultures like Finland. Hannu Nieminen, head of Insight and Innovation of Nokia Design, leads a global team of more than 300 people representing 34 different nationalities in developing cellular phones for the Finland-based company. The team includes designers, psychologists, researchers, anthropologists, engineers, and technology specialists who are based in major cities around the world. They collaborate by blending macro trends with insights from local cultures in designing products that appeal to country-specific customer needs and tastes.

who is poorly organized. So an understanding and utilization of basic *time-management* principles can help individuals better cope with tensions created by job demands.[75] A few of the most well-known time-management principles are (1) making daily lists of activities to be accomplished, (2) prioritizing activities by importance and urgency, (3) scheduling activities according to the priorities set, and (4) knowing your daily cycle and handling the most demanding parts of your job during the high part of your cycle, when you are most alert and productive.[76]

Physicians have recommended noncompetitive physical exercise, such as aerobics, walking, jogging, swimming, and riding a bicycle, as a way to deal with excessive stress levels. These forms of *physical exercise* increase heart capacity, lower the at-rest heart rate, provide a mental diversion from work pressures, and offer a means to "let off steam."[77]

Individuals can teach themselves to reduce tension through *relaxation techniques* such as meditation, hypnosis, and biofeedback. The objective is to reach a state of deep relaxation, in which one feels physically relaxed, somewhat detached from the immediate environment, and detached from body sensations.[78] Deep relaxation for 15 or 20 minutes a day releases tension and provides a person with a pronounced sense of peacefulness. Importantly, significant changes in heart rate, blood pressure, and other physiological factors result from achieving the condition of deep relaxation.

As we noted earlier in this chapter, having friends, family, or work colleagues to talk to provides an outlet when stress levels become excessive. Expanding your *social support network*, therefore, can be a means for tension reduction. It provides you with someone to hear your problems and to offer a more objective perspective on the situation.

Organizational Approaches   Several of the factors that cause stress—particularly task and role demands—are controlled by management. As such, they can be modified or changed. Strategies that management might want to consider include improved personnel selection and job placement, training, use of realistic goal setting, redesigning of jobs, increased employee involvement, improved organizational communication, offering employee sabbaticals, and establishment of corporate wellness programs.

Certain jobs are more stressful than others but, as we learned earlier in this chapter, individuals differ in their response to stressful situations. We know, for example, that individuals with little experience or an external locus of control tend to be more prone to stress. *Selection and placement* decisions should take these facts into consideration. Obviously, management shouldn't restrict hiring to only experienced individuals with an internal locus, but such individuals may adapt better to high-stress jobs and perform those jobs more effectively. Similarly, *training* can increase an individual's self-efficacy and thus lessen job strain.

We discussed *goal setting* in Chapter 6. Based on an extensive amount of research, we concluded that individuals perform better when they have specific and challenging goals and receive feedback on how well they are progressing toward these goals. The use of goals can reduce stress as well as provide motivation. Specific goals that are perceived as attainable clarify performance expectations. In addition, goal feedback reduces uncertainties about actual job performance. The result is less employee frustration, role ambiguity, and stress.

Redesigning jobs to give employees more responsibility, more meaningful work, more autonomy, and increased feedback can reduce stress because these factors give the employee greater control over work activities and lessen dependence on others. But as we noted in our discussion of work design, not all

Xerox Corporation employee Joanne Belknap took a four-month sabbatical to work as a volunteer for the American Cancer Society, where she visited businesses and informed managers and employees about the society's programs. Xerox grants employees fully paid sabbaticals to work on community service projects. Sabbaticals are one way that organizations can rejuvenate employees by allowing them to work on meaningful projects in the community.

employees want enriched jobs. The right redesign, then, for employees with a low need for growth might be less responsibility and increased specialization. If individuals prefer structure and routine, reducing skill variety should also reduce uncertainties and stress levels.

Role stress is detrimental to a large extent because employees feel uncertain about goals, expectations, how they'll be evaluated, and the like. By giving these employees a voice in the decisions that directly affect their job performance, management can increase employee control and reduce this role stress. So managers should consider *increasing employee involvement* in decision making.[79]

Increasing formal *organizational communication* with employees reduces uncertainty by lessening role ambiguity and role conflict. Given the importance that perceptions play in moderating the stress–response relationship, management can also use effective communications as a means to shape employee perceptions. Remember that what employees categorize as demands, threats, or opportunities are merely an interpretation, and that interpretation can be affected by the symbols and actions communicated by management.

What some employees need is an occasional escape from the frenetic pace of their work. In recent years, companies such as Charles Schwab, DuPont, L.L.Bean, Nike, and 3Com have begun to provide extended voluntary leaves.[80] These *sabbaticals*—ranging in length from a few weeks to several months—allow employees to travel, relax, or pursue personal projects that consume time beyond normal vacation weeks. Proponents argue that these sabbaticals can revive and rejuvenate workers who might be headed for burnout.

Our final suggestion is to offer organizationally supported **wellness programs**. These programs focus on the employee's total physical and mental condition.[81] For example, they typically provide workshops to help people quit smoking, control alcohol use, lose weight, eat better, and develop a regular exercise program. The assumption underlying most wellness programs is that employees need to take personal responsibility for their physical and mental health. The organization is merely a vehicle to facilitate this end.

Organizations can expect a payoff from their investment in wellness programs. And most of those firms that have introduced wellness programs have found significant benefits. For instance, a study of eight Canadian organizations found that every dollar spent on their comprehensive wellness programs generated a return of $1.64, and for high-risk employees, such as smokers, the return was nearly $4.00.[82]

Global Implications

Organizational Change   A number of change issues we've discussed in this chapter are culture bound. To illustrate, let's briefly look at five questions: (1) Do people believe change is possible? (2) If it's possible, how long will it take to bring it about? (3) Is resistance to change greater in some cultures than in others? (4) Does culture influence how change efforts will be implemented? (5) Do successful idea champions do things differently in different cultures?

> **8** *Explain global differences in organizational change and work stress.*

Do people believe change is possible? Remember that cultures vary in terms of beliefs about their ability to control their environment. In cultures in which people believe that they can dominate their environment, individuals will take a proactive view of change. This, for example, would describe the United States and Canada. In many other countries, such as Iran and Saudi Arabia, people see themselves as subjugated to their environment and thus will tend to take a passive approach toward change.

If change is possible, how long will it take to bring it about? A culture's time orientation can help us answer this question. Societies that focus on the long term, such as Japan, will demonstrate considerable patience while waiting for positive outcomes from change efforts. In societies with a short-term focus, such as the United States and Canada, people expect quick improvements and will seek change programs that promise fast results.

Is resistance to change greater in some cultures than in others? Resistance to change will be influenced by a society's reliance on tradition. Italians, as an example, focus on the past, whereas U.S. adults emphasize the present. Italians, therefore, should generally be more resistant to change efforts than their U.S. counterparts.

Does culture influence how change efforts will be implemented? Power distance can help with this issue. In high–power distance cultures, such as Spain or Thailand, change efforts will tend to be autocratically implemented by top management. In contrast, low–power distance cultures value democratic methods. We'd predict, therefore, a greater use of participation in countries such as Denmark and the Netherlands.

Finally, do successful idea champions do things differently in different cultures? Yes.[83] People in collectivist cultures prefer appeals for cross-functional support for innovation efforts; people in high-power-distance cultures prefer champions to work closely with those in authority to approve innovative activities before work is begun; and the higher the uncertainty avoidance of a society, the more champions should work within the organization's rules and procedures to develop the innovation. These findings suggest that effective managers will alter their organization's championing strategies to reflect cultural values.

wellness programs   *Organizationally supported programs that focus on the employee's total physical and mental condition.*

So, for instance, although idea champions in Russia might succeed by ignoring budgetary limitations and working around confining procedures, champions in Austria, Denmark, Germany, or other cultures high in uncertainty avoidance will be more effective by closely following budgets and procedures.

Stress   In considering global differences in stress, there are three questions to answer: (1) Do the causes of stress vary across countries? (2) Do the outcomes of stress vary across cultures? and (3) Do the factors that lessen the effects of stress vary by culture? Let's deal with each of these questions in turn.

First, research suggests that the job conditions that cause stress show some differences across cultures. One study of U.S. and Chinese employees revealed that whereas U.S. employees were stressed by a lack of control, Chinese employees were stressed by job evaluations and lack of training. While the job conditions that lead to stress may differ across countries, it doesn't appear that personality effects on stress are different across cultures. One study of employees in Hungary, Italy, the United Kingdom, Israel, and the United States found that Type A personality traits (see Chapter 4) predicted stress equally well across countries.[84]

Second, evidence tends to suggest that stressors are associated with perceived stress and strains among employees in different countries. In other words, stress is equally bad for employees of all cultures.[85]

Third, although not all factors that reduce stress have been compared across cultures, research does suggest that, whereas the demand to work long hours leads to stress, this stress can be reduced by the resource of social support such as having friends or family to talk to. A recent study found this to be true of workers in a diverse set of countries (Australia, Canada, England, New Zealand, the United States, China, Taiwan, Argentina, Brazil, Colombia, Ecuador, Mexico, Peru, and Uruguay).[86]

Summary and Implications for Managers

The need for change has been implied throughout this text. "A casual reflection on change should indicate that it encompasses almost all of our concepts in the organizational behavior literature."[87] For instance, think about attitudes, motivation, work teams, communication, leadership, organizational structures, human resource practices, and organizational cultures. Change was an integral part in the discussion of each.

If environments were perfectly static, if employees' skills and abilities were always up-to-date and incapable of deteriorating, and if tomorrow were always exactly the same as today, organizational change would have little or no relevance to managers. But the real world is turbulent, requiring organizations and their members to undergo dynamic change if they are to perform at competitive levels.

Managers are the primary change agents in most organizations. By the decisions they make and their role-modeling behaviors, they shape the organization's change culture. For instance, management decisions related to structural design, cultural factors, and human resource policies largely determine the level of innovation within the organization. Similarly, management decisions, policies, and practices will determine the degree to which the organization learns and adapts to changing environmental factors.

We found that the existence of work stress, in and of itself, need not imply lower performance. The evidence indicates that stress can be either a positive or a negative influence on employee performance. For many people, low to moderate amounts of stress enable them to perform their jobs better by increasing their work intensity, alertness, and ability to react. However, a high level of stress, or even a moderate amount sustained over a long period, eventually takes its toll, and performance declines. The impact of stress on satisfaction is far more straightforward. Job-related tension tends to decrease general job satisfaction.[88] Even though low to moderate levels of stress may improve job performance, employees find stress dissatisfying.

Point >< Counterpoint

MANAGING CHANGE IS AN EPISODIC ACTIVITY

*O*rganizational change is an episodic activity. That is, it starts at some point, proceeds through a series of steps, and culminates in some outcome that those involved hope is an improvement over the starting point. It has a beginning, a middle, and an end.

Lewin's three-step model represents a classic illustration of this perspective. Change is seen as a break in the organization's equilibrium. The status quo has been disturbed, and change is necessary to establish a new equilibrium state. The objective of refreezing is to stabilize the new situation by balancing the driving and restraining forces.

Some experts have argued that organizational change should be thought of as balancing a system made up of five interacting variables within the organization—people, tasks, technology, structure, and strategy. A change in any one variable has repercussions on one or more of the others. This perspective is episodic in that it treats organizational change as essentially an effort to sustain equilibrium. A change in one variable begins a chain of events that, if properly managed, requires adjustments in the other variables to achieve a new state of equilibrium.

Another way to conceptualize the episodic view of looking at change is to think of managing change as analogous to captaining a ship. The organization is like a large ship traveling across the calm Mediterranean Sea to a specific port. The ship's captain has made this exact trip hundreds of times before with the same crew. Every once in a while, however, a storm will appear, and the crew has to respond. The captain will make the appropriate adjustments—that is, implement changes—and, having maneuvered through the storm, will return the ship to calm waters. Like this ship's voyage, managing an organization should be seen as a journey with a beginning and an end, and implementing change as a response to a break in the status quo and needed only occasionally.

*t*he episodic approach may be the dominant paradigm for handling organizational change, but it has become obsolete. It applies to a world of certainty and predictability. The episodic approach was developed in the 1950s and 1960s, and it reflects the environment of those times. It treats change as the occasional disturbance in an otherwise peaceful world. However, it bears little resemblance to today's environment of constant and chaotic change.[89]

If you want to understand what it's like to manage change in today's organizations, think of it as equivalent to permanent white-water rafting.[90] The organization is not a large ship, but more akin to a 40-foot raft. Rather than sailing a calm sea, this raft must traverse a raging river made up of an uninterrupted flow of permanent white-water rapids. To make things worse, the raft is manned by 10 people who have never worked together or traveled the river before, much of the trip is in the dark, the river is dotted by unexpected turns and obstacles, the exact destination is not clear, and at irregular intervals the raft needs to pull to shore, where some new crew members are added and others leave. Change is a natural state and managing change is a continual process. That is, managers never get the luxury of escaping the white-water rapids.

The stability and predictability characterized by the episodic perspective no longer captures the world we live in. Disruptions in the status quo are not occasional, temporary, and followed by a return to an equilibrium state. There is, in fact, no equilibrium state. Managers today face constant change, bordering on chaos. They're being forced to play a game they've never played before, governed by rules that are created as the game progresses.

Questions for Review

1 What forces act as stimulants to change, and what is the difference between planned and unplanned change?

2 What forces act as sources of resistance to change?

3 What are the four main approaches to managing organizational change?

4 How can managers create a culture for change?

5 What is stress and what are the possible sources of stress?

6 What are the consequences of stress?

7 What are the individual and organizational approaches to managing stress?

8 What does research tell us about global differences in organizational change and work stress?

Experiential Exercise

POWER AND THE CHANGING ENVIRONMENT

Objectives

1. To describe the forces for change influencing power differentials in organizational and interpersonal relationships.
2. To understand the effect of technological, legal/political, economic, and social changes on the power of individuals within an organization.

The Situation

Your organization manufactures golf carts and sells them to country clubs, golf courses, and consumers. Your team is faced with the task of assessing how environmental changes will affect individuals' organizational power. Read each of the five scenarios and then, for each, identify the five members in the organization whose power will increase most in light of the environmental condition(s).

(m) = male   (f) = female

Advertising expert (m)	Accountant-CPA (m)
Chief financial officer (f)	General manager (m)
Securities analyst (m)	Marketing manager (f)
Operations manager (f)	Computer programmer (f)
Industrial engineer (m)	Chemist (m)
Product designer (m)	In-house counsel (m)
Public relations expert (m)	Human resource manager (f)
Corporate trainer (m)	

1. New computer-aided manufacturing technologies are being introduced in the workplace during the upcoming 2 to 18 months.

2. New federal emission standards are being legislated by the government that will essentially make gas-powered golf carts (40 percent of your current business) obsolete.

3. Sales are way down for two reasons: (a) a decline in the number of individuals playing golf and (b) your competitor was faster to embrace lithium batteries, which allow golf carts to go longer with a charge.

4. Given the growth of golf courses in other countries (especially India, China, and Southeast Asia), the company is planning to go international in the next 12 to 18 months.

5. The U.S. Equal Employment Opportunity Commission is applying pressure to balance the male–female population in the organization's upper hierarchy by threatening to publicize the predominance of men in upper management.

The Procedure

1. Divide the class into teams of three to four students each.

2. Teams should read each scenario and identify the five members whose power will increase most in light of the external environmental condition described.

3. Teams should then address the question: Assuming that the five environmental changes are taking place at once, which five members of the organization will now have the most power?

4. After 20 to 30 minutes, representatives of each team will be selected to present and justify their conclusions to the entire class. Discussion will begin with scenario 1 and proceed through to scenario 5 and the "all at once" scenario.

Source: Adapted from J. E. Barbuto, Jr., "Power and the Changing Environment," *Journal of Management Education*, April 2000, pp. 288–296.

Ethical Dilemma

STRESSING OUT EMPLOYEES IS YOUR JOB

Some of the most admired business leaders argue that the only way to get the most out of people is to stretch them. This view would seem to be backed by both business anecdotes and research evidence. "If you do know how to get there, it's not a stretch target," former GE CEO Jack Welch has said. "We have found that by reaching for what appears to be the impossible, we often actually do the impossible; and even when we don't quite make it, we inevitably wind up doing much better than we would have done."[91]

As for the research evidence, we noted in Chapter 6 that goal-setting theory—whereby managers set the most difficult goals to which employees will commit—is perhaps the best-supported theory of motivation.

The implication is that to be the most effective manager you need to push, push, and push more.

But does this pose an ethical dilemma for managers? What if you learned that pushing employees to the brink came at the expense of their health or their family life? While it seems true that managers get the performance they expect, it also seems likely that some people push themselves too hard. When Kathie Nunley, who travels more than 100 days a year, had to miss her son winning an

art competition, the only person she could share her news with was the Delta ticket agent. "It hit me how sad it was that I was sharing this moment with an airline agent rather than my son," she said.

On the one hand, you may argue that employees should be responsible for their own welfare, and that it would be paternalistic, and encourage mediocrity, to "care for" employees. On the other hand, if your stretch goals mean that your best employees are those who give it all for the organization—even putting aside their own personal or family interests—is that what you wish to be as a manager?

Questions

1. Do you think there is a trade-off between the positive (higher performance) and negative (increased stress) effects of stretch goals?

2. Do you think a manager should consider stress when setting stretch goals for employees? If you answered no, then what should a manager do if a valued employee complains of too much stress? If you answered yes, then how might this be done?

3. How do you think you would respond to stretch goals? Would they increase your performance? Would they stress you?

Case Incident 1

INNOVATING INNOVATION

Executives at Procter & Gamble (P&G) are pretty happy these days. P&G's stock has nearly doubled over the past 5 years, and the company's performance has been unusually resistant to the myriad changes that affect all companies.

Many at P&G might point to chief technology officer Gil Cloyd as one of the sources of this success. Although short-term performance is obviously important, Cloyd has been more focused on long-term change, specifically how P&G approaches research and development (R&D). Given the enormous variety of products that P&G offers, including toilet paper, laundry detergents, personal care products, and pet food, the ability to sustain a competitive level of innovation is a tremendous challenge. Says Cloyd, "One of the challenges we have is serving the needs of a very diverse consumer population, but yet be able to do that quickly and very cost effectively. In the consumer products world we estimate that the required pace of innovation has doubled in the last three years. That means we have less time to benefit from any innovation that we bring into the marketplace." Cloyd's approach is simple yet complex: Innovate innovation.

What is innovating innovation? As Cloyd explains, "What we've done is refine our thinking on how we conduct and evaluate research and development. We've made some changes. For example, historically, we tended to put the evaluation emphasis on technical product performance, patents, and other indicators of internal R&D efforts. Now there is more emphasis on perceived customer value." Cloyd describes P&G's innovation process as holistic, meaning it touches every department of an organization. Holistic innovation includes first setting appropriate financial goals and then implementing an innovation program for all aspects of the product—from its manufacturing technology to those aspects that the customer experiences directly, such as the product's packaging and appearance.

One of Cloyd's major goals at P&G is to acquire most product ideas from sources external to the organization, which it is close to doing. As a result, P&G has doubled the number of new products with elements that originated outside the company.

Though P&G is enjoying enormous success due in part to its innovation program, Cloyd is not resting on his laurels. He emphasizes learning as a critical element to continued innovation success. One area he's exploring is computer modeling and simulation. Previously, manufacturing was the main user of computer modeling. Now, Cloyd is using it in the product design process. Explains Cloyd, "A computational model helps us more quickly to understand what's going on. The simulation capabilities are also allowing us to interact with consumers much more quickly on design options. For example, Internet panels can engage consumers in as little as 24 hours. Digital technology is very important in helping us learn faster. Not only will it accelerate innovation, but the approach will greatly enhance the creativity of our people." By continually looking for new ways to design, produce, and market products, Cloyd and P&G are indeed "innovating innovation."

Questions

1. This book covers the notion of "idea champions." What characteristics of Gil Cloyd make him an idea champion?

2. Would you consider P&G to be a "learning organization"? What aspects of P&G lead you to your answer?

3. Although Cloyd is a major reason for P&G's innovation success, what are some structural features of P&G that might contribute to its ability to innovate so well?

4. The benefits of technological innovations for companies are often short lived because other companies adopt the same technology soon after. What factors do you believe contribute to P&G's ability to continually innovate at such a competitive level?

Source: Based on A. Markels, "Turning the Tide at P&G," *U.S. News & World Report*, October 22, 2006, pp. 1–3; and J. Teresko, "P&G's Secret: Innovating Innovation," *IndustryWeek*, December 2004, pp. 26–34.

Case Incident 2

THE RISE OF EXTREME JOBS

Before Barbara Agoglia left her job at American Express, she was spending 13 hours a day working and commuting. She also had to be available via cell phone 24/7. The last straw came when she didn't have time to wait with her son at his bus stop. Carolyn Buck also has an extreme job. She usually works more than 60 hours a week for Ernst & Young and often has to travel to India and China.

Agoglia and Buck are not alone. Most U.S. adults are working more hours than ever, but one group in particular stands out: those with extreme jobs—people who spend more than half their time working and commuting to and from work. More than 1.7 million people consider their jobs *too* extreme, according to a recent study.

What accounts for the rise in extreme jobs? It's not entirely clear, but the usual suspects of globalization, technology, and competitiveness are high on everyone's lists.

As extreme as Agoglia and Buck's jobs may seem, U.S. workers may have it comparatively easy. Most surveys indicate that extreme jobs are worse in developing counties. A 2006 *Harvard Business Review* study of managers in 33 global companies indicated that, compared to U.S. managers, managers in developing countries were more than twice as likely to have extreme jobs.

For those who hold extreme jobs, a personal life often takes a back seat. Among extreme job holders, 44 percent take fewer than 10 vacation days per year. Many individuals with extreme jobs see society changing into a "winner takes all" mode, where those who are willing to go the extra mile will reap a disproportionate share of the intrinsic and extrinsic rewards.

Why do people take extreme jobs (or allow their jobs to become extreme)? A 2006 study suggested that, for both men and women, the number 1 reason they work long, stressful hours is not pay. Rather, it's that the stimulating or challenging work gives them a rush. As one Asian manager said, "Building this business in markets where no one has done anything like this before is enormously exciting. And important. We've built distribution centers that are vital to China's growth—they contribute to the overall prospects of our economy."

Although this sounds all good, the situation is more complicated when you ask holders of extreme jobs about what their jobs cost them. Among such job holders, 66 percent of men and 77 percent of women say their job interferes with their ability to maintain a home. For those with extreme jobs who have children, 65 percent of men and 33 percent of women say it keeps them from having a relationship with their children. And 46 percent of male and female extreme job holders say their jobs interfere with having a strong relationship with their spouse. About half of each group say it interferes with their sex life. "I can't even fathom having a boyfriend," says one extreme job holder. Another extreme job holder, Chris Cicchinelli, was so concerned about being out of touch with work during his honeymoon that he got a satellite phone. Even that didn't help. He ended up cutting his 10-day honeymoon to 5 days. "I had major anxiety," he said.

Questions

1. Do you think you will ever have an extreme job? Are you sure? Explain.

2. Why do you think the number of extreme jobs has risen?

3. Do you think organizations should encourage extreme jobs, discourage them, or completely leave them to an employee's discretion?

4. Why do you think people take extreme jobs in the first place?

Sources: T. Weiss, "How Extreme Is Your Job?" *Forbes*, February 1, 2007, p. 1; S. A. Hewlett and C. B. Luce, "Extreme Jobs," *Harvard Business Review*, December 2006, pp. 49–58; and S. Armour, "Hi, I'm Joan, and I'm a Workaholic," *USA Today*, May 23, 2007, pp. 1B, 2B.

Endnotes

1. Based on "Is Merck's Medicine Working?" *BusinessWeek*, June 30, 2007, pp. 1–3; K. McKay, "Merck CEO Sets Sights on Change," *USA Today*, February 27, 2006, pp. 1B, 2B.

2. See, for instance, K. H. Hammonds, "Practical Radicals," *Fast Company*, September 2000, pp. 162–174; and P. C. Judge, "Change Agents," *Fast Company*, November 2000, pp. 216–226.

3. J. Taub, "Harvard Radical," *New York Times Magazine*, August 24, 2003, pp. 28–45+.

4. A. Finder, P. D. Healy, and K. Zernike, "President of Harvard Resigns, Ending Stormy 5-Year Tenure," *New York Times*, February 22, 2006, pp. A1, A19.

5. P. G. Audia and S. Brion, "Reluctant to Change: Self-Enhancing Responses to Diverging Performance Measures," *Organizational Behavior and Human Decision Processes* 102 (2007), pp. 255–269.

6. M. T. Hannan, L. Pólos, and G. R. Carroll, "The Fog of Change: Opacity and Asperity in Organizations," *Administrative Science Quarterly*, September 2003. pp. 399–432.

7. J. P. Kotter and L. A. Schlesinger, "Choosing Strategies for Change," *Harvard Business Review*, March–April 1979, pp. 106–114.

8. J. E. Dutton, S. J. Ashford, R. M. O'Neill, and K. A. Lawrence, "Moves That Matter: Issue Selling and Organizational Change," *Academy of Management Journal*, August 2001, pp. 716–736.

9. P. C. Fiss and E. J. Zajac, "The Symbolic Management of Strategic Change: Sensegiving via Framing and Decoupling," *Academy of Management Journal* 49, no. 6 (2006), pp. 1173–1193.

10. Q. N. Huy, "Emotional Balancing of Organizational Continuity and Radical Change: The Contribution of Middle Managers," *Administrative Science Quarterly*, March 2002, pp. 31–69; D. M. Herold, D. B. Fedor, and S. D. Caldwell, "Beyond Change Management: A Multilevel Investigation of Contextual and Personal Influences on Employees' Commitment to Change," *Journal of Applied Psychology* 92, no. 4 (2007), pp. 942–951; and G. B. Cunningham, "The Relationships Among Commitment to Change, Coping with Change, and Turnover Intentions," *European Journal of Work and Organizational Psychology* 15, no. 1 (2006), pp. 29–45.

11. D. B. Fedor, S. Caldwell, and D. M. Herold, "The Effects of Organizational Changes on Employee Commitment: A Multilevel Investigation," *Personnel Psychology* 59 (2006), pp. 1–29.

12. S. Oreg, "Personality, Context, and Resistance to Organizational Change," *European Journal of Work and Organizational Psychology* 15, no. 1 (2006), pp. 73–101.

13. J. A. LePine, J. A. Colquitt, and A. Erez, "Adaptability to Changing Task Contexts: Effects of General Cognitive Ability, Conscientiousness, and Openness to Experience," *Personnel Psychology*, Fall, 2000, pp. 563–593; T. A. Judge, C. J. Thoresen, V. Pucik, and T. M. Welbourne, "Managerial Coping with Organizational Change: A Dispositional Perspective," *Journal of Applied Psychology*, February 1999, pp. 107–122; and S. Oreg, "Resistance to Change: Developing an Individual Differences Measure," *Journal of Applied Psychology*, August 2003, pp. 680–693.

14. See J. Pfeffer, *Managing with Power: Politics and Influence in Organizations* (Boston: Harvard Business School Press, 1992), pp. 7, and 318–320.

15. See, for instance, W. Ocasio, "Political Dynamics and the Circulation of Power: CEO Succession in U.S. Industrial Corporations, 1960–1990," *Administrative Science Quarterly*, June 1994, pp. 285–312.

16. K. Lewin, *Field Theory in Social Science* (New York: Harper & Row, 1951).

17. P. G. Audia, E. A. Locke, and K. G. Smith, "The Paradox of Success: An Archival and a Laboratory Study of Strategic Persistence Following Radical Environmental Change," *Academy of Management Journal*, October 2000, pp. 837–853.

18. J. B. Sorensen, "The Strength of Corporate Culture and the Reliability of Firm Performance," *Administrative Science Quarterly*, March 2002, pp. 70–91.

19. J. Amis, T. Slack, and C. R. Hinings, "The Pace, Sequence, and Linearity of Radical Change," *Academy of Management Journal*, February 2004, pp. 15–39; and E. Autio, H. J. Sapienza, and J. G. Almeida, "Effects of Age at Entry, Knowledge Intensity, and Imitability on International Growth," *Academy of Management Journal*, October 2000, pp. 909–924.

20. J. P. Kotter, "Leading Changes: Why Transformation Efforts Fail," *Harvard Business Review*, March–April 1995, pp. 59–67; and J. P. Kotter, *Leading Change* (Harvard Business School Press, 1996).

21. See, for example, C. Eden and C. Huxham, "Action Research for the Study of Organizations," in S. R. Clegg, C. Hardy, and W. R. Nord (eds.), *Handbook of Organization Studies* (London: Sage, 1996).

22. For a sampling of various OD definitions, see N. Nicholson (ed.), *Encyclopedic Dictionary of Organizational Behavior* (Malden, MA: Blackwell, 1998), pp. 359–361; H. K. Sinangil and F. Avallone, "Organizational Development and

Change," in N. Anderson, D. S. Ones, H. K. Sinangil, and C. Viswesvaran (eds.), *Handbook of Industrial, Work and Organizational Psychology*, vol. 2 (Thousand Oaks, CA: Sage, 2001), pp. 332–335.

23. See, for instance, R. Lines, "Influence of Participation in Strategic Change: Resistance, Organizational Commitment and Change Goal Achievement," *Journal of Change Management*, September 2004, pp. 193–215.

24. S. Highhouse, "A History of the T-Group and Its Early Application in Management Development," *Group Dynamics: Theory, Research, & Practice*, December 2002, pp. 277–290.

25. J. E. Edwards and M. D. Thomas, "The Organizational Survey Process: General Steps and Practical Considerations," in P. Rosenfeld, J. E. Edwards, and M. D. Thomas (eds.), *Improving Organizational Surveys: New Directions, Methods, and Applications* (Newbury Park, CA: Sage, 1993), pp. 3–28.

26. E. H. Schein, *Process Consultation: Its Role in Organizational Development*, 2nd ed. (Reading, MA: Addison-Wesley, 1988), p. 9. See also E. H. Schein, *Process Consultation Revisited: Building Helpful Relationships* (Reading, MA: Addison-Wesley, 1999).

27. Schein, *Process Consultation*.

28. W. Dyer, *Team Building: Issues and Alternatives* (Reading, MA: Addison-Wesley, 1994).

29. See, for example, E. H. Neilsen, "Understanding and Managing Intergroup Conflict," in J. W. Lorsch and P. R. Lawrence (eds.), *Managing Group and Intergroup Relations* (Homewood, IL: Irwin-Dorsey, 1972), pp. 329–343.

30. R. R. Blake, J. S. Mouton, and R. L. Sloma, "The Union–Management Intergroup Laboratory: Strategy for Resolving Intergroup Conflict," *Journal of Applied Behavioral Science*, no. 1 (1965), pp. 25–57.

31. See, for example, R. Fry, F. Barrett, J. Seiling, and D. Whitney (eds.), *Appreciative Inquiry & Organizational Transformation: Reports From the Field* (Westport, CT: Quorum, 2002); J. K. Barge and C. Oliver, "Working with Appreciation in Managerial Practice," *Academy of Management Review*, January 2003, pp. 124–142; and D. van der Haar and D. M. Hosking, "Evaluating Appreciative Inquiry: A Relational Constructionist Perspective," *Human Relations*, August 2004, pp. 1017–1036.

32. J. Gordon, "Meet the Freight Fairy," *Forbes*, January 20, 2003, p. 65.

33. D. Anfuso, "Core Values Shape W. L. Gore's Innovative Culture," *Workforce*, March 1999, pp. 48–51; and A. Harrington, "Who's Afraid of a New Product?" *Fortune*, November 10, 2003, pp. 189–192.

34. See, for instance, R. M. Kanter, "When a Thousand Flowers Bloom: Structural, Collective and Social Conditions for Innovation in Organizations," in B. M. Staw and L. L. Cummings (eds.), *Research in Organizational Behavior*, vol. 10 (Greenwich, CT: JAI Press, 1988), pp. 169–211.

35. F. Damanpour, "Organizational Innovation: A Meta-Analysis of Effects of Determinants and Moderators," *Academy of Management Journal*, September 1991, p. 557.

36. Ibid., pp. 555–590.

37. See P. R. Monge, M. D. Cozzens, and N. S. Contractor, "Communication and Motivational Predictors of the Dynamics of Organizational Innovation," *Organization Science*, May 1992, pp. 250–274.

38. J. M. Howell and C. A. Higgins, "Champions of Change," *Business Quarterly*, Spring 1990, pp. 31–32; and D. L. Day, "Raising Radicals: Different Processes for Championing Innovative Corporate Ventures," *Organization Science*, May 1994, pp. 148–172.

39. Howell and Higgins, "Champions of Change."

40. See, for example, T. B. Lawrence, M. K. Mauws, B. Dyck, and R. F. Kleysen, "The Politics of Organizational Learning: Integrating Power into the 4I Framework," *Academy of Management Review*, January 2005, pp. 180–191.

41. D. H. Kim, "The Link Between Individual and Organizational Learning," *Sloan Management Review*, Fall 1993, p. 37.

42. C. Argyris and D. A. Schon, *Organizational Learning* (Reading, MA: Addison-Wesley, 1978).

43. B. Dumaine, "Mr. Learning Organization," *Fortune*, October 17, 1994, p. 148.

44. F. Kofman and P. M. Senge, "Communities of Commitment: The Heart of Learning Organizations," *Organizational Dynamics*, Autumn 1993, pp. 5–23.

45. Dumaine, "Mr. Learning Organization," p. 154.

46. See, for instance, K. Slobogin, "Many U.S. Employees Feel Overworked, Stressed, Study Says," *CNN.com*, May 16, 2001, www.cnn.com; and S. Armour, "Rising Job Stress Could Affect Bottom Line," *USA Today*, July 29, 2003, p. 1B.

47. Adapted from R. S. Schuler, "Definition and Conceptualization of Stress in Organizations," *Organizational Behavior and Human Performance*, April 1980, p. 189. For an updated review of definitions, see C. L. Cooper, P. J. Dewe, and M. P. O'Driscoll, *Organizational Stress: A Review and Critique of Theory, Research, and Applications* (Thousand Oaks, CA: Sage, 2002).

48. See, for instance, M. A. Cavanaugh, W. R. Boswell, M. V. Roehling, and J. W. Boudreau, "An Empirical Examination of Self-Reported Work Stress Among U.S. Managers," *Journal of Applied Psychology*, February 2000, pp. 65–74.

49. N. P. Podsakoff, J. A. LePine, and M. A. LePine, "Differential Challenge-Hindrance Stressor Relationships with Job Attitudes, Turnover Intentions, Turnover, and Withdrawal Behavior: A Meta-analysis," *Journal of Applied Psychology* 92, no. 2 (2007), pp. 438–454; J. A. LePine, M. A. LePine, and C. L. Jackson, "Challenge and Hindrance Stress: Relationships with Exhaustion, Motivation to Learn, and Learning Performance," *Journal of Applied Psychology*, October 2004, pp. 883–891.

50. N. W. Van Yperen and O. Janssen, "Fatigued and Dissatisfied or Fatigued but Satisfied? Goal Orientations and Responses to High Job Demands," *Academy of Management Journal*, December 2002, pp. 1161–1171; and N. W. Van Yperen and M. Hagedoorn, "Do High Job Demands Increase Intrinsic Motivation or Fatigue or Both? The Role of Job Control and Job Social Support," *Academy of Management Journal*, June 2003, pp. 339–348.

51. J. de Jonge and C. Dormann, "Stressors, Resources, and Strain at Work: A Longitudinal Test of the Triple-Match Principle," *Journal of Applied Psychology* 91, no. 5 (2006), pp. 1359–1374.

52. This section is adapted from C. L. Cooper and R. Payne, *Stress at Work* (London: Wiley, 1978); S. Parasuraman and J. A. Alutto, "Sources and Outcomes of Stress in Organizational Settings: Toward the Development of a Structural Model," *Academy of Management Journal* 27, no. 2 (June 1984), pp. 330–350; and P. M. Hart and C. L. Cooper, "Occupational

Stress: Toward a More Integrated Framework," in N. Anderson, D. S. Ones, H. K. Sinangil, and C. Viswesvaran (eds.), *Handbook of Industrial, Work and Organizational Psychology*, vol. 2 (London: Sage, 2001), pp. 93–114.

53. S. G. Rogelberg, D. J. Leach, and P. B. Warr, and J. L. Burnfield, "'Not Another Meeting!' Are Meeting Time Demands Related to Employee Well-Being?" *Journal of Applied Psychology* 91, no. 1 (2006), pp. 86–96.

54. A. E. Rafferty and M. A. Griffin, "Perceptions of Organizational Change: A Stress and Coping Perspective," *Journal of Applied Psychology* 71, no. 5 (2007), pp. 1154–1162.

55. H. Garst, M. Frese, and P. C. M. Molenaar, "The Temporal Factor of Change in Stressor-Strain Relationships: A Growth Curve Model on a Longitudinal Study in East Germany," *Journal of Applied Psychology*, June 2000, pp. 417–438.

56. See, for example, M. L. Fox, D. J. Dwyer, and D. C. Ganster, "Effects of Stressful Job Demands and Control of Physiological and Attitudinal Outcomes in a Hospital Setting," *Academy of Management Journal*, April 1993, pp. 289–318.

57. G. W. Evans and D. Johnson, "Stress and Open-Office Noise," *Journal of Applied Psychology*, October 2000, pp. 779–783.

58. T. M. Glomb, J. D. Kammeyer-Mueller, and M. Rotundo, "Emotional Labor Demands and Compensating Wage Differentials," *Journal of Applied Psychology*, August 2004. pp. 700–714; A. A. Grandey, "When 'The Show Must Go On': Surface Acting and Deep Acting as Determinants of Emotional Exhaustion and Peer-Rated Service Delivery," *Academy of Management Journal*, February 2003, pp. 86–96.

59. V. S. Major, K. J. Klein, and M. G. Ehrhart, "Work Time, Work Interference with Family, and Psychological Distress," *Journal of Applied Psychology*, June 2002, pp. 427–436; see also P. E. Spector, C. L. Cooper, S. Poelmans, T. D. Allen, M. O'Driscoll, J. I. Sanchez, O. L. Siu, P. Dewe, P. Hart, L. Lu, L. F. R. De Moreas, G. M. Ostrognay, K. Sparks, P. Wong, and S. Yu, "A Cross-National Comparative Study of Work-Family Stressors, Working Hours, and Well-Being: China and Latin America Versus the Anglo World," *Personnel Psychology*, Spring 2004, pp. 119–142.

60. D. L. Nelson and C. Sutton, "Chronic Work Stress and Coping: A Longitudinal Study and Suggested New Directions," *Academy of Management Journal*, December 1990, pp. 859–869.

61. H. Selye, *The Stress of Life*, rev. ed. (New York: McGraw-Hill, 1956).

62. S. J. Motowidlo, J. S. Packard, and M. R. Manning, "Occupational Stress: Its Causes and Consequences for Job Performance," *Journal of Applied Psychology*, November 1987, pp. 619–620.

63. See, J. B. Halbesleben, "Sources of Social Support and Burnout: A Meta-Analytic Test of the Conservation of Resources Model," *Journal of Applied Psychology* 91, no. 5 (2006), pp. 1134–1145; N. Bolger and D. Amarel, "Effects of Social Support Visibility on Adjustment to Stress: Experimental Evidence," *Journal of Applied Psychology* 92, no. 3 (2007), pp. 458–475; and N. A. Bowling, T. A. Beehr, and W. M. Swader, "Giving and Receiving Social Support at Work: The Roles of Personality and Reciprocity," *Journal of Vocational Behavior* 67 (2005), pp. 476–489.

64. R. Williams, *The Trusting Heart: Great News About Type A Behavior* (New York: Times Books, 1989).

65. Schuler, "Definition and Conceptualization of Stress," pp. 200–205; and R. L. Kahn and M. Byosiere, "Stress in Organizations," in M. D. Dunnette and L. M. Hough (eds.), *Handbook of Industrial and Organizational Psychology*, 2nd ed., vol. 3 (Palo Alto, CA: Consulting Psychologists Press, 1992), pp. 604–610.

66. See T. A. Beehr and J. E. Newman, "Job Stress, Employee Health, and Organizational Effectiveness: A Facet Analysis, Model, and Literature Review," *Personnel Psychology*, Winter 1978, pp. 665–699; and B. D. Steffy and J. W. Jones, "Workplace Stress and Indicators of Coronary-Disease Risk," *Academy of Management Journal*, September 1988, pp. 686–698.

67. J. Schaubroeck, J. R. Jones, and J. L. Xie, "Individual Differences in Utilizing Control to Cope with Job Demands: Effects on Susceptibility to Infectious Disease," *Journal of Applied Psychology*, April 2001, pp. 265–278.

68. Steffy and Jones, "Workplace Stress and Indicators of Coronary-Disease Risk," p. 687.

69. C. L. Cooper and J. Marshall, "Occupational Sources of Stress: A Review of the Literature Relating to Coronary Heart Disease and Mental Ill Health," *Journal of Occupational Psychology* 49, no. 1 (1976), pp. 11–28.

70. J. R. Hackman and G. R. Oldham, "Development of the Job Diagnostic Survey," *Journal of Applied Psychology*, April 1975, pp. 159–170.

71. E. M. de Croon, J. K. Sluiter, R. W. B. Blonk, J. P. J. Broersen, and M. H. W. Frings-Dresen, "Stressful Work, Psychological Job Strain, and Turnover: A 2-Year Prospective Cohort Study of Truck Drivers," *Journal of Applied Psychology*, June 2004, pp. 442–454; and R. Cropanzano, D. E. Rupp, and Z. S. Byrne, "The Relationship of Emotional Exhaustion to Work Attitudes, Job Performance, and Organizational Citizenship Behaviors," *Journal of Applied Psychology*, February 2003. pp. 160–169.

72. See, for instance, S. Zivnuska, C. Kiewitz, W. A. Hochwarter, P. L. Perrewe, and K. L. Zellars, "What Is Too Much or Too Little? The Curvilinear Effects of Job Tension on Turnover Intent, Value Attainment, and Job Satisfaction," *Journal of Applied Social Psychology*, July 2002, pp. 1344–1360.

73. L. A. Muse, S. G. Harris, and H. S. Field, "Has the Inverted-U Theory of Stress and Job Performance Had a Fair Test?" *Human Performance* 16, no. 4 (2003), pp. 349–364.

74. The following discussion has been influenced by J. E. Newman and T. A. Beehr, "Personal and Organizational Strategies for Handling Job Stress," *Personnel Psychology*, Spring 1979, pp. 1–38; J. M. Ivancevich and M. T. Matteson, "Organizational Level Stress Management Interventions: A Review and Recommendations," *Journal of Organizational Behavior Management*, Fall–Winter 1986, pp. 229–248; M. T. Matteson and J. M. Ivancevich, "Individual Stress Management Interventions: Evaluation of Techniques," *Journal of Management Psychology*, January 1987, pp. 24–30; J. M. Ivancevich, M. T. Matteson, S. M. Freedman, and J. S. Phillips, "Worksite Stress Management Interventions," *American Psychologist*, February 1990, pp. 252–261; and R. Schwarzer, "Manage Stress at Work Through Preventive and Proactive Coping," in E. A. Locke (ed.), *Handbook of Principles of Organizational Behavior* (Malden, MA: Blackwell, 2004), pp. 342–355.

75. T. H. Macan, "Time Management: Test of a Process Model," *Journal of Applied Psychology*, June 1994, pp. 381–391; and B. J. C. Claessens, W. Van Eerde, C. G. Rutte, and R. A. Roe, "Planning Behavior and Perceived Control of Time at Work," *Journal of Organizational Behavior*, December 2004, pp. 937–950.

76. See, for example, G. Lawrence-Ell, *The Invisible Clock: A Practical Revolution in Finding Time for Everyone and Everything* (Seaside Park, NJ: Kingsland Hall, 2002); and B. Tracy, *Time Power* (New York: AMACOM, 2004).

77. J. Kiely and G. Hodgson, "Stress in the Prison Service: The Benefits of Exercise Programs," *Human Relations*, June 1990, pp. 551–572.

78. E. J. Forbes and R. J. Pekala, "Psychophysiological Effects of Several Stress Management Techniques," *Psychological Reports*, February 1993, pp. 19–27; and M. Der Hovanesian, "Zen and the Art of Corporate Productivity," *BusinessWeek*, July 28, 2003, p. 56.

79. S. E. Jackson, "Participation in Decision Making as a Strategy for Reducing Job-Related Strain," *Journal of Applied Psychology*, February 1983, pp. 3–19.

80. S. Greengard, "It's About Time," *Industry Week*, February 7, 2000, pp. 47–50; and S. Nayyar, "Gimme a Break," *American Demographics*, June 2002, p. 6.S. Greengard, "It's About Time," *Industry Week*, February 7, 2000, pp. 47–50; and S. Nayyar, "Gimme a Break," *American Demographics*, June 2002, p. 6.

81. See, for instance, B. Leonard, "Health Care Costs Increase Interest in Wellness Programs," *HRMagazine*, September 2001, pp. 35–36; and "Healthy, Happy and Productive," *Training*, February 2003, p. 16.

82. D. Brown, "Wellness Programs Bring Healthy Bottom Line," *Canadian HR Reporter*, December 17, 2001, pp. 1+.

83. See S. Shane, S. Venkataraman, and I. MacMillan, "Cultural Differences in Innovation Championing Strategies," *Journal of Management* 21, no. 5 (1995), pp. 931–952.

84. J. Chen, C. Silverthorne, and J. Hung, "Organization Communication, Job Stress, Organizational Commitment, and Job Performance of Accounting Professionals in Taiwan and America," *Leadership & Organization Development Journal* 27, no. 4 (2006), pp. 242–249; C. Liu, P. E. Spector, and L. Shi, "Cross-National Job Stress: A Quantitative and Qualitative Study," *Journal of Organizational Behavior*, February 2007, pp. 209–239.

85. H. M. Addae and X. Wang, "Stress at Work: Linear and Curvilinear Effects of Psychological-, Job-, and Organization-Related Factors: An Exploratory Study of Trinidad and Tobago," *International Journal of Stress Management*, November 2006, pp. 476–493.

86. P. E. Spector et al., "A Cross-National Comparative Study of Work-Family Stressors, Working Hours, and Well-Being: China and Latin America Versus the Anglo World," *Personnel Psychology*, Spring 2004, pp. 119–142.

87. P. S. Goodman and L. B. Kurke, "Studies of Change in Organizations: A Status Report," in P. S. Goodman (ed.), *Change in Organizations* (San Francisco: Jossey-Bass, 1982), p. 1.

88. Kahn and Byosiere, "Stress in Organizations," pp. 605–608.

89. For contrasting views on episodic and continuous change, see K. E. Weick and R. E. Quinn, "Organizational Change and Development," in J. T. Spence, J. M. Darley, and D. J. Foss (eds.), *Annual Review of Psychology*, vol. 50 (Palo Alto, CA: Annual Reviews, 1999), pp. 361–386.

90. This perspective is based on P. B. Vaill, *Managing as a Performing Art: New Ideas for a World of Chaotic Change* (San Francisco: Jossey-Bass, 1989).

91. J. D. Breul, "Setting Stretch Goals Helps Agencies Exceed Their Reach," *Government Leader 1*, no. 9 (September/ October 2006), www.governmentleader.com/issues/1_9/ commentary/205-1.html); G. Stoller, "Frequent Business Travelers Pack Guilt, *USA Today*, June 22, 2006, www. usatoday.com/money/biztravel/2006-06-21-road-warriors-usat_x. htm.

Research in Organizational Behavior

For every complex problem, there is a solution
that is simple, neat, and wrong.

—H.L. Mencken

A number of years ago, a friend of mine was excited because he had read about the findings from a research study that finally, once and for all, resolved the question of what it takes to make it to the top in a large corporation. I doubted there was any simple answer to this question but, not wanting to dampen his enthusiasm, I asked him to tell me of what he had read. The answer, according to my friend, was *participation in college athletics.* To say I was skeptical of his claim is a gross understatement, so I asked him to tell me more.

The study encompassed 1,700 successful senior executives at the 500 largest U.S. corporations. The researchers found that half of these executives had played varsity-level college sports.[1] My friend, who happens to be good with statistics, informed me that since fewer than 2 percent of all college students participate in intercollegiate athletics, the probability of this finding occurring by mere chance is less than 1 in 10 million! He concluded his analysis by telling me that, based on this research, I should encourage my management students to get into shape and to make one of the varsity teams.

My friend was somewhat perturbed when I suggested that his conclusions were likely to be flawed. These executives were all males who attended college in the 1940s and 1950s. Would his advice be meaningful to females in the twenty-first century? These executives also weren't your typical college students. For the most part, they had attended elite private colleges such as Princeton and Amherst, where a large proportion of the student body participates in intercollegiate sports. And these "jocks" hadn't necessarily played football or basketball; many had participated in golf, tennis, baseball, cross-country running, crew, rugby, and similar minor sports. Moreover, maybe the researchers had confused the direction of causality. That is, maybe individuals with the motivation and ability to make it to the top of a large corporation are drawn to competitive activities like college athletics.

My friend was guilty of misusing research data. Of course, he is not alone. We are all continually bombarded with reports of experiments that link certain substances to cancer in mice and surveys that show changing attitudes toward sex among college students, for example. Many of these studies are carefully designed, with great caution taken to note the implications and limitations of the findings. But some studies are poorly designed, making their conclusions at best suspect, and at worst meaningless.

Rather than attempting to make you a researcher, the purpose of this appendix is to increase your awareness as a consumer of behavioral research. A knowledge of research methods will allow you to appreciate more fully the care in data collection that underlies the information and conclusions presented in this text. Moreover, an understanding of research methods will make you a more skilled evaluator of the OB studies you will encounter in business and professional journals. So an appreciation of behavioral research is important because (1) it's the foundation on which the theories in this text are built, and (2) it will benefit you in future years when you read reports of research and attempt to assess their value.

Purposes of Research

Research is concerned with the systematic gathering of information. Its purpose is to help us in our search for the truth. Although we will never find ultimate truth—in our case, that would be to know precisely how any person or group would behave in any organizational context—ongoing research adds to our body of OB knowledge by supporting some theories, contradicting others, and suggesting new theories to replace those that fail to gain support.

Research Terminology

Researchers have their own vocabulary for communicating among themselves and with outsiders. The following briefly defines some of the more popular terms you're likely to encounter in behavioral science studies.[2]

Variable

A *variable* is any general characteristic that can be measured and that changes in amplitude, intensity, or both. Some examples of OB variables found in this textbook are job satisfaction, employee productivity, work stress, ability, personality, and group norms.

Hypothesis

A tentative explanation of the relationship between two or more variables is called a *hypothesis*. My friend's statement that participation in college athletics leads to a top executive position in a large corporation is an example of a hypothesis. Until confirmed by empirical research, a hypothesis remains only a tentative explanation.

Dependent Variable

A *dependent variable* is a response that is affected by an independent variable. In terms of the hypothesis, it is the variable that the researcher is interested in explaining. Referring back to our opening example, the dependent variable in my friend's hypothesis was executive succession. In organizational behavior research, the most popular dependent variables are productivity, absenteeism, turnover, job satisfaction, and organizational commitment.[3]

Independent Variable

An *independent variable* is the presumed cause of some change in the dependent variable. Participating in varsity athletics was the independent variable in my friend's hypothesis. Popular independent variables studied by OB researchers include intelligence, personality, job satisfaction, experience, motivation, reinforcement patterns, leadership style, reward allocations, selection methods, and organization design.

You may have noticed we said that job satisfaction is frequently used by OB researchers as both a dependent and an independent variable. This is not an error. It merely reflects that the label given to a variable depends on its place in the hypothesis. In the statement "Increases in job satisfaction lead to reduced turnover," job satisfaction is an independent variable. However, in the statement "Increases in money lead to higher job satisfaction," job satisfaction becomes a dependent variable.

Moderating Variable

A *moderating variable* abates the effect of the independent variable on the dependent variable. It might also be thought of as the contingency variable: If *X* (independent variable), then *Y* (dependent variable) will occur, but only under conditions *Z* (moderating variable). To translate this into a real-life example, we might say that if we increase the amount of direct supervision in the work area (*X*), then there will be a change in worker productivity (*Y*), but this effect will be moderated by the complexity of the tasks being performed (*Z*).

Causality

A hypothesis, by definition, implies a relationship. That is, it implies a presumed cause and effect. This direction of cause and effect is called *causality*. Changes in the independent variable are assumed to cause changes in the dependent variable. However, in behavioral research, it's possible to make an incorrect assumption of causality when relationships are found. For example, early behavioral scientists found a relationship between employee satisfaction and productivity. They concluded that a happy worker was a productive worker. Follow-up research has supported the relationship, but disconfirmed the direction of the arrow. The evidence more correctly suggests that high productivity leads to satisfaction rather than the other way around.

Correlation Coefficient

It's one thing to know that there is a relationship between two or more variables. It's another to know the *strength* of that relationship. The term *correlation coefficient* is used to indicate that strength, and is expressed as a number between −1.00 (a perfect negative relationship) and +1.00 (a perfect positive correlation).

When two variables vary directly with one another, the correlation will be expressed as a positive number. When they vary inversely—that is, one increases as the other decreases—the correlation will be expressed as a negative number. If the two variables vary independently of each other, we say that the correlation between them is zero.

For example, a researcher might survey a group of employees to determine the satisfaction of each with his or her job. Then, using company absenteeism reports, the researcher could correlate the job satisfaction scores against individual attendance records to determine whether employees who are more satisfied with their jobs have better attendance records than their counterparts who indicated lower job satisfaction. Let's suppose the researcher found a correlation coefficient of +0.50 between satisfaction and attendance. Would that be a strong association? There is, unfortunately, no precise numerical cutoff separating strong and weak relationships. A standard statistical test would need to be applied to determine whether the relationship was a significant one.

A final point needs to be made before we move on: A correlation coefficient measures only the strength of association between two variables. A high value does *not* imply causality. The length of women's skirts and stock market prices, for instance, have long been noted to be highly correlated, but one should be careful not to infer that a causal relationship between the two exists. In this instance, the high correlation is more happenstance than predictive.

Theory

The final term we introduce in this section is *theory*. Theory describes a set of systematically interrelated concepts or hypotheses that purports to explain and predict phenomena. In OB, theories are also frequently referred to as *models*. We use the two terms interchangeably.

There are no shortages of theories in OB. For instance, we have theories to describe what motivates people, the most effective leadership styles, the best way to resolve conflicts, and how people acquire power. In some cases, we have half a dozen or more separate theories that purport to explain and predict a given phenomenon. In such cases, is one right and the others wrong? No! They tend to reflect science at work—researchers testing previous theories, modifying them, and, when appropriate, proposing new models that may prove to have higher explanatory and predictive powers. Multiple theories attempting to explain common phenomena merely attest that OB is an active discipline, still growing and evolving.

Evaluating Research

As a potential consumer of behavioral research, you should follow the dictum of *caveat emptor*—let the buyer beware! In evaluating any research study, you need to ask three questions.[4]

Is it valid? Is the study actually measuring what it claims to be measuring? A number of psychological tests have been discarded by employers in recent years because they have not been found to be valid measures of the applicants' ability to do a given job successfully. But the validity issue is relevant to all research studies. So, if you find a study that links cohesive work teams with higher productivity, you want to know how each of these variables was measured and whether it is actually measuring what it is supposed to be measuring.

Is it reliable? Reliability refers to consistency of measurement. If you were to have your height measured every day with a wooden yardstick, you'd get highly

reliable results. On the other hand, if you were measured each day by an elastic tape measure, there would probably be considerable disparity between your height measurements from one day to the next. Your height, of course, doesn't change from day to day. The variability is due to the unreliability of the measuring device. So if a company asked a group of its employees to complete a reliable job satisfaction questionnaire, and then repeat the questionnaire six months later, we'd expect the results to be very similar—provided nothing changed in the interim that might significantly affect employee satisfaction.

Is it generalizable? Are the results of the research study generalizable to groups of individuals other than those who participated in the original study? Be aware, for example, of the limitations that might exist in research that uses college students as subjects. Are the findings in such studies generalizable to full-time employees in real jobs? Similarly, how generalizable to the overall work population are the results from a study that assesses job stress among 10 nuclear power plant engineers in the hamlet of Mahone Bay, Nova Scotia?

Research Design

Doing research is an exercise in trade-offs. Richness of information typically comes with reduced generalizability. The more a researcher seeks to control for confounding variables, the less realistic his or her results are likely to be. High precision, generalizability, and control almost always translate into higher costs. When researchers make choices about whom they'll study, where their research will be done, the methods they'll use to collect data, and so on, they must make some concessions. Good research designs are not perfect, but they do carefully reflect the questions being addressed. Keep these facts in mind as we review the strengths and weaknesses of five popular research designs: case studies, field surveys, laboratory experiments, field experiments, and aggregate quantitative reviews.

Case Study

You pick up a copy of Soichiro Honda's autobiography. In it he describes his impoverished childhood; his decisions to open a small garage, assemble motorcycles, and eventually build automobiles; and how this led to the creation of one of the largest and most successful corporations in the world. Or you're in a business class and the instructor distributes a 50-page handout covering two companies: Wal-Mart and Kmart. The handout details the two firms' histories; describes their corporate strategies, management philosophies, and merchandising plans; and includes copies of their recent balance sheets and income statements. The instructor asks the class members to read the handout, analyze the data, and determine why Wal-Mart has been so much more successful than Kmart in recent years.

Soichiro Honda's autobiography and the Wal-Mart and Kmart handouts are case studies. Drawn from real-life situations, case studies present an in-depth analysis of one setting. They are thorough descriptions, rich in details about an individual, a group, or an organization. The primary source of information in case studies is obtained through observation, occasionally backed up by interviews and a review of records and documents.

Case studies have their drawbacks. They're open to the perceptual bias and subjective interpretations of the observer. The reader of a case is captive to what the observer/case writer chooses to include and exclude. Cases also trade off generalizability for depth of information and richness of detail. Because it's always dangerous to generalize from a sample of one, case studies make it difficult to prove or reject a hypothesis. On the other hand, you can't ignore the in-depth analysis that cases often provide. They are an excellent device for initial exploratory research and for evaluating real-life problems in organizations.

Field Survey

A lengthy questionnaire was created to assess the use of ethics policies, formal ethics structures, formalized activities such as ethics training, and executive involvement in ethics programs among billion-dollar corporations. The public affairs or corporate communications office of all *Fortune* 500 industrial firms and 500 service corporations were contacted to get the name and address of the "officer most responsible for dealing with ethics and conduct issues" in each firm. The questionnaire, with a cover letter explaining the nature of the study, was mailed to these 1,000 officers. Of the total, 254 returned a completed questionnaire, for a response rate just above 25 percent. The results of the survey found, among other things, that 77 percent had formal codes of ethics and 54 percent had a single officer specifically assigned to deal with ethics and conduct issues.[5]

The preceding study illustrates a typical field survey. A sample of respondents (in this case, 1,000 corporate officers in the largest U.S. publicly held corporations) was selected to represent a larger group that was under examination (billion-dollar U.S. business firms). The respondents were then surveyed using a questionnaire or interviewed to collect data on particular characteristics (the content and structure of ethics programs and practices) of interest to the researchers. The standardization of response items allows for data to be easily quantified, analyzed, and summarized, and for the researchers to make inferences from the representative sample about the larger population.

The field survey provides economies for doing research. It's less costly to sample a population than to obtain data from every member of that population. (There are, for instance, more than 5,000 U.S. business firms with sales in excess of a billion dollars; and since some of these are privately held and don't release financial data to the public, they are excluded from the *Fortune* list). Moreover, as the ethics study illustrates, field surveys provide an efficient way to find out how people feel about issues or how they say they behave. These data can then be easily quantified.

But the field survey has a number of potential weaknesses. First, mailed questionnaires rarely obtain 100 percent returns. Low response rates call into question whether conclusions based on respondents' answers are generalizable to nonrespondents. Second, the format is better at tapping respondents' attitudes and perceptions than behaviors. Third, responses can suffer from social desirability; that is, people saying what they think the researcher wants to hear. Fourth, since field surveys are designed to focus on specific issues, they're a relatively poor means of acquiring depth of information. Finally, the quality of the generalizations is largely a factor of the population chosen. Responses from executives at *Fortune* 500 firms, for instance, tell us nothing about small- or medium-sized firms or not-for-profit organizations. In summary, even a well-designed field survey trades off depth of information for breadth, generalizability, and economic efficiencies.

Laboratory Experiment

The following study is a classic example of the laboratory experiment. A researcher, Stanley Milgram, wondered how far individuals would go in following commands. If subjects were placed in the role of a teacher in a learning experiment and told by an experimenter to administer a shock to a learner each time that learner made a mistake, would the subjects follow the commands of the experimenter? Would their willingness to comply decrease as the intensity of the shock was increased?

To test these hypotheses, Milgram hired a set of subjects. Each was led to believe that the experiment was to investigate the effect of punishment on memory. Their job was to act as teachers and administer punishment whenever the learner made a mistake on the learning test.

Punishment was administered by an electric shock. The subject sat in front of a shock generator with 30 levels of shock—beginning at zero and progressing in 15-volt increments to a high of 450 volts. The demarcations of these positions ranged from "Slight Shock" at 15 volts to "Danger: Severe Shock" at 450 volts. To increase the realism of the experiment, the subjects received a sample shock of 45 volts and saw the learner—a pleasant, mild-mannered man about 50 years old—strapped into an "electric chair" in an adjacent room. Of course, the learner was an actor, and the electric shocks were phony, but the subjects didn't know this.

Taking his seat in front of the shock generator, the subject was directed to begin at the lowest shock level and to increase the shock intensity to the next level each time the learner made a mistake or failed to respond.

When the test began, the shock intensity rose rapidly because the learner made many errors. The subject got verbal feedback from the learner: At 75 volts, the learner began to grunt and moan; at 150 volts, he demanded to be released from the experiment; at 180 volts, he cried out that he could no longer stand the pain; and at 300 volts, he insisted that he be let out, yelled about his heart condition, screamed, and then failed to respond to further questions.

Most subjects protested and, fearful they might kill the learner if the increased shocks were to bring on a heart attack, insisted they could not go on with their job. Hesitations or protests by the subject were met by the experimenter's statement, "You have no choice, you must go on! Your job is to punish the learner's mistakes." Of course, the subjects did have a choice. All they had to do was stand up and walk out.

The majority of the subjects dissented. But dissension isn't synonymous with disobedience. Sixty-two percent of the subjects increased the shock level to the maximum of 450 volts. The average level of shock administered by the remaining 38 percent was nearly 370 volts.[6]

In a laboratory experiment such as that conducted by Milgram, an artificial environment is created by the researcher. Then the researcher manipulates an independent variable under controlled conditions. Finally, since all other things are held equal, the researcher is able to conclude that any change in the dependent variable is due to the manipulation or change imposed on the independent variable. Note that, because of the controlled conditions, the researcher is able to imply causation between the independent and dependent variables.

The laboratory experiment trades off realism and generalizability for precision and control. It provides a high degree of control over variables and precise measurement of those variables. But findings from laboratory studies are often difficult to generalize to the real world of work. This is because the artificial laboratory rarely duplicates the intricacies and nuances of real organizations. In addition, many laboratory experiments deal with phenomena that cannot be reproduced or applied to real-life situations.

Field Experiment

The following is an example of a field experiment. The management of a large company is interested in determining the impact that a four-day workweek would have on employee absenteeism. To be more specific, management wants to know if employees working four

10-hour days have lower absence rates than similar employees working the traditional five-day week of 8 hours each day. Because the company is large, it has a number of manufacturing plants that employ essentially similar workforces. Two of these are chosen for the experiment, both located in the greater Cleveland area. Obviously, it would not be appropriate to compare two similar-sized plants if one is in rural Mississippi and the other is in urban Copenhagen because factors such as national culture, transportation, and weather might be more likely to explain any differences found than changes in the number of days worked per week.

In one plant, the experiment was put into place—workers began the four-day week. At the other plant, which became the control group, no changes were made in the employees' five-day week. Absence data were gathered from the company's records at both locations for a period of 18 months. This extended time period lessened the possibility that any results would be distorted by the mere novelty of changes being implemented in the experimental plant. After 18 months, management found that absenteeism had dropped by 40 percent at the experimental plant, and by only 6 percent in the control plant. Because of the design of this study, management believed that the larger drop in absences at the experimental plant was due to the introduction of the compressed workweek.

The field experiment is similar to the laboratory experiment, except it is conducted in a real organization. The natural setting is more realistic than the laboratory setting, and this enhances validity but hinders control. In addition, unless control groups are maintained, there can be a loss of control if extraneous forces intervene—for example, an employee strike, a major layoff, or a corporate restructuring. Maybe the greatest concern with field studies has to do with organizational selection bias. Not all organizations are going to allow outside researchers to come in and study their employees and operations. This is especially true of organizations that have serious problems. Therefore, since most published studies in OB are done by outside researchers, the selection bias might work toward the publication of studies conducted almost exclusively at successful and well-managed organizations.

Our general conclusion is that, of the four research designs we've discussed to this point, the field experiment typically provides the most valid and generalizable findings and, except for its high cost, trades off the least to get the most.[7]

Aggregate Quantitative Reviews

What's the overall effect of organizational behavior modification (OB Mod) on task performance? There have been a number of field experiments that have sought to throw light on this question. Unfortunately, the wide range of effects from these various studies makes it hard to generalize.

To try to reconcile these diverse findings, two researchers reviewed all the empirical studies they could find on the impact of OB Mod on task performance over a 20-year period.[8] After discarding reports that had inadequate information, had nonquantitative data, or didn't meet all conditions associated with principles of behavioral modification, the researchers narrowed their set to 19 studies that included data on 2,818 individuals. Using an aggregating technique called *meta-analysis,* the researchers were able to synthesize the studies quantitatively and to conclude that the average person's task performance will rise from the 50th percentile to the 67th percentile after an OB Mod intervention.

The OB Mod–task performance review done by these researchers illustrates the use of meta-analysis, a quantitative form of literature review that enables researchers to look at validity findings from a comprehensive set of individual studies, and then apply a formula to them to determine if they consistently produced similar results.[9] If results prove to be consistent, it allows researchers to conclude more confidently that validity is generalizable. Meta-analysis is a means for overcoming the potentially imprecise interpretations of qualitative reviews and to synthesize variations in quantitative studies. In addition, the technique enables researchers to identify potential moderating variables between an independent and a dependent variable.

In the past 25 years, there's been a surge in the popularity of this research method. Why? It appears to offer a more objective means for doing traditional literature reviews. Although the use of meta-analysis requires researchers to make a number of judgment calls, which can introduce a considerable amount of subjectivity into the process, there is no arguing that meta-analysis reviews have now become widespread in the OB literature.

Ethics in Research

Researchers are not always tactful or candid with subjects when they do their studies. For instance, questions in field surveys may be perceived as embarrassing by respondents or as an invasion of privacy. Also, researchers in laboratory studies have been known to deceive participants about the true purpose of their experiment "because they felt deception was necessary to get honest responses."[10]

The "learning experiments" conducted by Stanley Milgram, which were conducted more than 30 years ago, have been widely criticized by psychologists on ethical grounds. He lied to subjects, telling them his study was investigating learning, when, in fact, he was concerned with obedience. The shock machine he used was a fake. Even the "learner" was an accomplice of Milgram's who had been trained to act as if he were hurt and in pain. Yet ethical lapses continue. For instance, in 2001, a professor of organizational behavior at Columbia University sent out a common letter on university letterhead to 240 New York City restaurants in which he detailed how he had eaten at this restaurant with his wife in celebration of their wedding anniversary, how he had gotten food poisoning, and that he had spent the night in his bathroom throwing up.[11] The letter closed with: "Although it is not my intention to file any reports with the Better Business Bureau or the Department of Health, I want you to understand what I went through in anticipation that you will respond accordingly. I await your response." The fictitious letter was part of the professor's study to determine how restaurants responded to complaints. But it created culinary chaos among many of the restaurant owners, managers, and chefs as they reviewed menus and produce deliveries for possibly spoiled food, and questioned kitchen workers about possible lapses. A follow-up letter of apology from the university for "an egregious error in judgment by a junior faculty member" did little to offset the distress it created for those affected.

Professional associations like the American Psychological Association, the American Sociological Association, and the Academy of Management have published formal guidelines for the conduct of research. Yet the ethical debate continues. On one side are those who argue that strict ethical controls can damage the scientific validity of an experiment and cripple future research. Deception, for example, is often necessary to avoid contaminating results. Moreover, proponents of minimizing ethical controls note that few subjects have been appreciably harmed by deceptive experiments. Even in Milgram's highly manipulative experiment, only 1.3 percent of the subjects reported negative feelings about their experience. The other side of this debate focuses on the rights of participants. Those favoring strict ethical controls argue that no procedure should ever be emotionally or physically distressing to subjects, and that, as professionals, researchers are obliged to be completely honest with their subjects and to protect the subjects' privacy at all costs.

Summary

The subject of organizational behavior is composed of a large number of theories that are research based. Research studies, when cumulatively integrated, become theories, and theories are proposed and followed by research studies designed to validate them. The concepts that make up OB, therefore, are only as valid as the research that supports them.

The topics and issues in this book are for the most part research-derived. They represent the result of systematic information gathering rather than merely hunch, intuition, or opinion. This doesn't mean, of course, that we have all the answers to OB issues. Many require far more corroborating evidence. The generalizability of others is limited by the research methods used. But new information is being created and published at an accelerated rate. To keep up with the latest findings, we strongly encourage you to regularly review the latest research in organizational behavior. The more academic work can be found in journals such as the *Academy of Management Journal, Academy of Management Review, Administrative Science Quarterly, Human Relations, Journal of Applied Psychology, Journal of Management, Journal of Organizational Behavior,* and *Leadership Quarterly.* For more practical interpretations of OB research findings, you may want to read the *Academy of Management Executive, California Management Review, Harvard Business Review, Organizational Dynamics,* and the *Sloan Management Review.*

Endnotes

1. J. A. Byrne, "Executive Sweat," *Forbes,* May 20, 1985, pp. 198–200.

2. See D. P. Schwab, *Research Methods for Organizational Behavior* (Mahwah, NJ: Lawrence Erlbaum Associates, 1999); and S. G. Rogelberg (ed.), *Blackwell Handbook of Research Methods in Industrial and Organizational Psychology* (Malden, MA: Blackwell, 2002).

3. B. M. Staw and G. R. Oldham, "Reconsidering Our Dependent Variables: A Critique and Empirical Study," *Academy of Management Journal,* December 1978, pp. 539–559; and B. M. Staw, "Organizational Behavior: A Review and Reformulation of the Field's Outcome Variables," in M. R. Rosenzweig and L. W. Porter (eds.), *Annual Review of Psychology,* vol. 35 (Palo Alto, CA: Annual Reviews, 1984), pp. 627–666.

4. R. S. Blackburn, "Experimental Design in Organizational Settings," in J. W. Lorsch (ed.), *Handbook of Organizational Behavior* (Upper Saddle River, NJ: Prentice Hall, 1987), pp. 127–128; and F. L. Schmidt, C. Viswesvaran, D. S. Ones, "Reliability Is Not Validity and Validity Is Not Reliability," *Personnel Psychology,* Winter 2000, pp. 901–912.

5. G. R. Weaver, L. K. Trevino, and P. L. Cochran, "Corporate Ethics Practices in the Mid-1990's: An Empirical Study of the Fortune 1000," *Journal of Business Ethics,* February 1999, pp. 283–294.

6. S. Milgram, *Obedience to Authority* (New York: Harper & Row, 1974). For a critique of this research, see T. Blass, "Understanding Behavior in the Milgram Obedience Experiment: The Role of Personality, Situations, and Their Interactions," *Journal of Personality and Social Psychology,* March 1991, pp. 398–413.

7. See, for example, W. N. Kaghan, A. L. Strauss, S. R. Barley, M. Y. Brannen, and R. J. Thomas, "The Practice and Uses of Field Research in the 21st Century Organization," *Journal of Management Inquiry,* March 1999, pp. 67–81.

8. A. D. Stajkovic and F. Luthans, "A Meta-Analysis of the Effects of Organizational Behavior Modification on Task Performance, 1975–1995," *Academy of Management Journal,* October 1997, pp. 1122–1149.

9. See, for example, K. Zakzanis, "The Reliability of Meta Analytic Review," *Psychological Reports,* August 1998, pp. 215–222; C. Ostroff and D. A. Harrison, "Meta-Analysis, Level of Analysis, and Best Estimates of Population Correlations: Cautions for Interpreting Meta-Analytic Results in Organizational Behavior," *Journal of Applied Psychology,* April 1999, pp. 260–270; R. Rosenthal and M. R. DiMatteo, "Meta-Analysis: Recent Developments in Quantitative Methods for Literature Reviews," in S. T. Fiske, D. L. Schacter, and C. Zahn-Wacher (eds.), *Annual Review of Psychology,* vol. 52 (Palo Alto, CA: Annual Reviews, 2001), pp. 59–82; and F. L. Schmidt and J. E. Hunter, "Meta-Analysis," in N. Anderson, D. S. Ones, H. K. Sinangil, and C. Viswesvaran (eds.), *Handbook of Industrial, Work & Organizational Psychology,* vol. 1 (Thousand Oaks, CA: Sage, 2001), pp. 51–70.

10. For more on ethical issues in research, see T. L. Beauchamp, R. R. Faden, R. J. Wallace, Jr., and L. Walters (eds.), *Ethical Issues in Social Science Research* (Baltimore, MD: Johns Hopkins University Press, 1982); and J. G. Adair, "Ethics of Psychological Research: New Policies, Continuing Issues, New Concerns," *Canadian Psychology,* February 2001, pp. 25–37.

11. J. Kifner, "Scholar Sets Off Gastronomic False Alarm," *New York Times,* September 8, 2001, p. A1.

Comprehensive Cases

<table>
<tr><td>Case</td><td>1</td><td>Arnold Schwarzenegger:
Leader of California?</td></tr>
</table>

The governor of California, Arnold Schwarzenegger, or "Arnold" as the state's residents like to call him, is arguably playing the biggest role of his career. Elected in the October 2003 recall election that featured a hodgepodge of 135 candidates, including celebrities Gary Coleman, Larry Flint, and Mary "Mary Carey" Cook, Schwarzenegger replaced incumbent Gray Davis as the governor of the most populous state in the country by raking in 48.1 percent of the popular vote. Californians, weary of Gray Davis's lack of progress, decided to put their trust in a man best known for his roles in action movies such as the *The Terminator* and *Total Recall.*

Schwarzenegger's ascent to the governor's seat is impressive when one considers his background. Born in the small town of Thal, Austria, on July 30, 1947, Schwarzenegger was the product of a modest and harsh upbringing. His parents strictly disciplined him—treatment that he says "would be called child abuse" today. Schwarzenegger explains, "My hair was pulled. I was hit with belts. So was the kid next door, and so was the kid next door. It was just the way it was. Many of the children I've seen were broken by their parents, which was the German-Austrian mentality. Break the will. They didn't want to create an individual . . . It was all about conforming. I was the one who did not conform and whose will could not be broken. Therefore I became a rebel. Every time I got hit, and every time someone said, 'You can't do this,' I said, 'This is not going to be for much longer, because I'm going to move out of here. I want to be rich. I want to be somebody.' "

Determined to leave Austria, Schwarzenegger began to search for a way out, a way to become "somebody." He found that way out through bodybuilding. As a child, he idolized bodybuilder Reg Park, a former Mr. Universe. Though his parents objected, Schwarzenegger pursued bodybuilding so vehemently that at one point he was able to bench-press 520 pounds

(for comparison, physical fitness experts typically say that it is good to be able to bench press one's own body weight).

At age 19, Schwarzenegger was crowned Mr. Universe. He continued to win championships, and, in 1970, he even defeated his idol, Reg Park, for the Mr. Universe title. Schwarzenegger now says that bodybuilding was instrumental to his success as an actor and as a politician. "I know it from my bodybuilding—that I can see my goals very clearly . . . It takes the confidence to ignore critics and naysayers," he states.

Having accomplished his goal of becoming Mr. Universe, Schwarzenegger set his sights on America to pursue acting and moved to the United States at age 21. Although he attended acting school, his odd last name and thick accent at first kept him from acquiring roles. He eventually landed a small role in the film *Hercules in New York* and continued to appear in other films such as *Stay Hungry* and *Pumping Iron.* In 1982, however, Schwarzenegger made his mark in the film *Conan the Barbarian,* which grossed more than $100 million worldwide. His on-screen charisma, massive physique, and uniqueness compared to American actors made him a standout. Since moving to the United States, Schwarzenegger has made 33 movies and has become one of the most highly paid actors in the world. For *Terminator 3,* Schwarzenegger earned an astounding $33 million—a record sum at the time.

After succeeding as a bodybuilder and an actor, Schwarzenegger began eyeing a bigger prize: the California governor's seat. During his acting career, Schwarzenegger had formed a strong network of powerful friends and advisors, including investor Warren Buffet, economist Milton Friedman, and Israeli Prime Minister Benjamin Netanyahu. As the recall election neared, Schwarzenegger consulted with his network of allies. Buffet told Schwarzenegger that California needed strong leadership, and Friedman gave him advice on how to improve California's dismal economy. All of this advice gave Schwarzenegger the vision he needed to propel himself to the rank of governor. Running as a moderate Republican, he sought to unite Democrats and Republicans, pass a balanced budget, reduce government spending, and resuscitate the business community. Once he accomplished these goals, Schwarzenegger would confidently state to the rest of the world that California was *back*. Schwarzenegger's vision came at a perfect time: Governor Davis witnessed the rise and fall of the tech boom. When the tech bubble burst, revenue plummeted. In 2001 and 2002, state revenue from the income tax fell 27 percent, yet spending remained the same. Although Davis was not solely responsible for the resulting Californian debt, Californians were eager to place blame.

Hungry for someone to take the reins from Gray Davis and steer California away from its troubles, many Californians embraced Schwarzenegger as he campaigned across the state. His name recognition and charismatic personality made him a leading candidate. Schwarzenegger's style is vastly different from other politicians. His wit, honesty, and lack of concern for political correctness struck a chord with voters. (As he told one interviewer at *Fortune* magazine following the election, "I love smart women. I have no patience for bimbos.") It was perhaps this larger-than-life persona that led him to "terminate" Gray Davis in the recall election.

Following the election, Schwarzenegger immediately began making policy for California. Within only a few days of his swearing in, Schwarzenegger had a viable economic recovery plan. To the praise of the state's residents, he repealed the car-tax increase, which would have raised almost $4 billion in revenue but was hated by Californians. He continued his strong push for reform, passing propositions that made a $15 billion bond offering possible and that paved the way for a balanced budget. In April 2004, he persuaded the state's legislature to pass a bill overhauling workers' compensation, a victory for businesses trying to reduce costs but a defeat for workers.

A testament to his approachable personality was the fact that he broke tradition by actually going from his office on the first floor to the upstairs offices of the legislators to meet with them. Schwarzenegger's chief of staff, Pat Clarey, can't remember the previous four governors doing that. All in all, the newly elected "governator," using his charisma and network of powerful friends, inched closer each day to his vision.

Even the Republican party took notice. Though more moderate than the Republican Party would like, Schwarzenegger knew that his popularity and charisma were an asset to the Republican convention during President George W. Bush's 2004 reelection campaign.

While the Republican party convention organizers were debating whether to invite the moderate Schwarzenegger to speak, Schwarzenegger told the *New York Times*, "If they're smart, they'll have me obviously in prime time." Schwarzenegger got his wish. Two days after the interview, he was invited to speak during his requested time. Republican operatives weren't disappointed with quips such as "This is like winning an Oscar. As if I would know! Speaking of acting, one of my movies was called *True Lies*. And that's what the Democrats should have called their convention." Schwarzenegger's speech at the convention electrified the crowd, further solidifying his role as a charismatic leader.

Not everything has been rosy. One of his major goals was to pass a $103 billion budget plan that he believed would be a tremendous step toward economic recovery. He set an optimistic timeline of passing the budget by June 30, 2004. Schwarzenegger worked tirelessly, negotiating budget reductions with state-affiliated organizations such as universities, prisons, and the teacher's union. However, negotiations began to fall apart when he made conflicting promises to the opposing parties on state and local budget linkages. Instead of victoriously passing his budget on time, the state legislature recessed for the July 4th weekend, leaving Schwarzenegger and his budget on hold.

Not to be dissuaded, Schwarzenegger began campaigning to the public to garner support for his budget. He even went so far as to call opponents "girlie men" at a public rally—an incident that infuriated his critics. Though eventually he was able to pass a revised version of his original budget, Schwarzenegger continued to attempt to fix California's financial crisis through various cost-cutting initiatives. He took on the California teachers' union, trying to persuade it to revamp entirely the way it hires, pays, and fires teachers. During this time, his approval rating fell to 55 percent. Though still high, his approval rating was down from a staggering 65 percent. Many of his ideas are abhorrent to the teachers' union. For example, Schwarzenegger wants to tie teachers' pay to test scores. Many teachers feel that this undermines their ability to teach what they think are important topics and will result in a narrow curriculum.

Some believe Arnold Schwarzenegger is a powerful politician, but he says that he really doesn't like the word *power* because it tends to have a negative connotation. Schwarzenegger says, "Power is basically influence. That's the way I see it. It's being able to have the influence to make changes to improve things." Schwarzenegger has a clear vision of how he wants to improve things; the question is not only whether he can create beneficial policies but also whether he has the ability and support to implement those policies. Although he realizes that his charisma helped him to become governor, Schwarzenegger also knows the importance of vision to a leader. As he puts it, "There is no one, and when I say no one, I mean no one, who will back me off my vision. I will go over burning coals for that."

Questions for Discussion

1. What words would you use to describe Arnold Schwarzenegger's personality? Do any of these fit into the Big Five taxonomy of personality? How might these personality traits influence Schwarzenegger's leadership skills? How might these traits have helped Schwarzenegger get to where he is now?

2. Based on the case, as governor of California, what types of power is Schwarzenegger likely to have? What types of influence tactics does Schwarzenegger appear to use?

3. How would you describe Schwarzenegger's leadership style using the leadership theories covered in this textbook? What details of the case lead you to these conclusions? Is Schwarzenegger's leadership style likely to be effective? Why or why not?

4. Applying concepts from goal-setting theory, explain how goals have influenced Schwarzenegger's progression to the governor's seat. What aspects of the case suggest that Schwarzenegger is committed to the goals that he has set for himself?

5. Are there any "dark sides" to Schwarzenegger's charisma and leadership skills? What might these be, and how might they affect his relationships with others and his ability to govern?

6. How might Schwarzenegger's personality and leadership style help or hinder his ability to effectively negotiate with other parties such as the teachers' union?

Source: Based on B. Morris, A. Gil, P. Neering, and O. Ryan, "Arnold Power," *Fortune*, August 9, 2004, 77–87; and R. Grover and A. Bernstein, "Arnold Gets Strict with the Teachers," *Business Week*, May 2, 2005, 84–85.

Case 2 — What Customers Don't Know Won't Hurt Them, or Will It?

Sitting at her desk at the car rental shop where she worked, Elena couldn't believe what she was hearing. Gripping the phone tightly, Elena listened as the head manager of the company's legal department told her that a car that she had recently rented to a customer had blown a tire while the customer was driving on a nearby highway. Although the customer, Jim Reynolds, tried to maintain control of the vehicle, he crashed into another car, seriously injuring himself and the other driver. Apparently, the tire had noticeable structural damage that caused it to blow. Elena stared at her desk in shock as the legal department manager asked whether she was aware of the tire's condition before renting the car to Mr. Reynolds.

"I . . . I'm sorry, what did you say?" asked Elena.

"I asked whether you were aware that the tire was damaged before renting the car to Mr. Reynolds," repeated the manager.

Elena paused, thinking back to when she had rented the car to Mr. Reynolds. Unfortunately, she knew the answer to the manager's question, but she did not know whether she wanted to answer it. Her mind raced with worried thoughts about how she let herself get into this position, and then she remembered when her supervisor first told her to lie to a customer.

Elena had started working for the rental car company 2 years ago. Fresh out of college, she was intrigued by the possibilities of joining a company and moving up the ranks into management. She worked hard, sometimes putting in 50 or more hours a week. And she was good at her job, too. Customers would frequently tell her supervisor of Elena's great service and courtesy. Within no time, the supervisor began telling her that she was a strong candidate for management and would probably be running her own rental office within the next year.

Intrigued with becoming a manager, Elena began to work even harder. She was the first one at the office each morning and the last one to leave. Things were going well, until one particularly busy day, when the rental office had more business than it could handle. The office typically had a few vehicles left for walk-in customers, but on this day the lot was empty except for one SUV, which a couple had reserved for their vacation. The couple's reservation was for 1 P.M., and it was now 12 noon. Proactive as usual, Elena decided to go check the SUV to make sure it was ready for the couple. As she got up from her desk, the door to the rental office flew open, and a man rushed toward the counter.

"Do you have anything to rent?" he quickly asked. "I don't have a reservation, but I really need a car right now for the rest of the week."

Elena apologized and explained that the only vehicle they had at the moment was reserved, but that he could wait at the office until another car was returned. In fact, she said, they expected to have two vehicles returned around 3 P.M.

"That's not good enough," the man replied. "I need a car now."

"Again, I do apologize sir, but it wouldn't be fair to those with a reservation to rent the only car that is available," said Elena.

With a frown, the man turned to leave. As he did, Elena's supervisor, who had been listening to the conversation, chimed in. "So you really need a car, huh?" he asked the man.

The man whirled around. "Yes, I do."

"I'll rent it to you for $150 a day," said Elena's supervisor. One hundred and fifty dollars a day was much more than the rental company's usual fee.

The man paused for a moment and then said, "Fine, I'll take it."

As he left with the only vehicle left on the lot, a stunned Elena asked her supervisor why he had rented the SUV when he knew that it was reserved—and at such a high price.

"That guy would have paid anything, and he ended up paying twice as much as we would have gotten out of it," her supervisor said, laughing. "Look, if you're going to be a manager, you need to know how to make money. Always take the best deal you can get."

"Even if it means losing another customer?" Elena asked. "What are we going to tell the couple who had a reservation for that SUV?"

"*You're* going to tell them that it broke down unexpectedly and it's at the shop. If you want to be a manager, start acting like one."

Soon after, the couple with the reservation walked into the rental office. Elena didn't want to lie to them, but she also didn't want to jeopardize her chances of obtaining a management position. She also figured that the couple would be more understanding if she told them that the SUV had broken down than if she told them that she had rented it to another customer. So Elena followed her manager's advice and lied to the couple.

In the months that followed, Elena encountered several more instances where her supervisor asked her to lie to customers because her office had reserved too many vehicles. Pretty soon, it became second nature, as she found herself lying to customers without pressure from her supervisor. To date, however, her lies hadn't caused any serious harm to anyone, at least as far as she knew. That track record changed, however, the day Jim Reynolds rented a car from her.

The day was routine in that the rental office was very busy. There were only two vehicles on the lot—a compact car and a new luxury sedan. Mr. Reynolds had reserved the less expensive compact car. However, when checking the car over before Mr. Reynolds arrived, Elena noticed a large lump on the outside well of the passenger-side front tire. From her training, she knew that this lump could be dangerous. But Elena also knew that she would have to give Mr. Reynolds the luxury sedan for the same price as the compact car if she decided not to rent him the compact car. She thought about what her supervisor had told her and knew that he probably would be upset if she didn't get a high rate out of their new luxury sedan. Besides, she reasoned, the car will be fine and Mr. Reynolds would have it for only a day. So Elena went through the routine. With a smile and a handshake, she rented the compact car to Mr. Reynolds, who didn't notice the tire because it was on the passenger side, and Elena didn't walk Mr. Reynolds around the car—a routine practice at the rental company.

Fast-forward one day and Elena's world had completely changed. Now, Elena was on the phone with the manager of the company's legal department, wondering how she ever thought it would be safe to rent the car to Mr. Reynolds. She could admit that she knew about the tire and decided to rent the car anyway, or she could lie and say that the tire looked fine when she rented the car. If she told the truth, becoming a manager would probably be out of the question, at least for a long while. Anger welled up inside her. She had worked hard to get where she was. She regretted not having told her supervisor that she wasn't going to lie to customers, even if it meant getting a better rate. But that moment had passed. She could tell the legal department manager that her supervisor had told her to lie to customers, but she knew that her manager would deny it. Either way, the options weren't too appealing.

"Hello? . . . hello?" asked the legal department manager.

Elena returned to the conversation. "Sorry, I lost you for a moment," she said. "Yeah . . . about Mr. Reynolds . . ."

Questions for Discussion

1. Using concepts from reinforcement theory, explain why Elena might be motivated to lie to customers. With reinforcement theory in mind, do you think that Elena will confess to the legal representative? Why or why not?
2. How might the rental office's climate influence Elena's behavior? What factors contribute to the current climate? What steps could you take to improve the ethics at this office?
3. Do you blame Elena for her behavior or do you attribute her behavior to external factors? How do concepts from attribution theory fit in?

4. Consider Elena's personality. Would you predict that escalation of commitment will occur (and she will lie to the legal representative), or will she decide to come clean? Explain your answer.
5. Do you think Elena would make a good leader some day? Why or why not? What factors might this depend on?
6. What emotions might Elena be experiencing? How might Elena's emotions affect her decision to tell the legal department manager about the incident with Mr. Reynolds?

Are Five Heads Better Than One?

Evan, Conner, Alexis, Derek, and Judy had been team members for only one week, but they felt that they were already working well together. Upper management at their company, Advert, a medium-sized marketing firm, picked the five employees for a special project: the development of a commercial promoting the launch of a client's 60-inch plasma flat-screen television. The project was especially critical because the television company was one of Advert's most important clients, and the firm's revenues had been slipping lately due to a few poor ad campaigns. Needless to say, upper management at Advert wanted the team to hit a home run with the project.

Upper management didn't have any trouble picking the five employees. All were bright, talented individuals who came up with creative ideas. More important, reasoned the top managers, the employees were similar on a number of characteristics. Evan, Conner, Alexis, Derek, and Judy were around the same age, had worked for the company for about the same amount of time, and because they all tended to be sociable, friendly, and valued getting along with others, their personalities seemed to mesh as well.

To give the team creative room, management allowed them as much autonomy as possible. It gave the team the freedom to see the project through from start to finish—coming up with their own ideas, hiring someone to film the commercial once the idea was in place, creating and maintaining a budget, and presenting the final commercial to the client. Advert's top managers had already met with and assured the client that it was in good hands with this team.

Excited to begin working, the team decided to meet in person to discuss ideas for the commercial. Conner, who was used to leading others in his previous work groups, took the head seat at the group's table. Immediately, he told the group his idea for the commercial.

"I've been thinking about this a lot since I was first told about the project," he said. "I know our client well, and I think they want us to do something out of the box—something that will grab people's attention."

Conner proceeded to explain his idea for the commercial, which centered on a college student "loser" trying to get a date. After one particular attractive female turns him down, and she and her friends ridicule him, the student returns sullenly to his dorm, plunks down on an old sofa, and turns on his small, black-and-white "loser" television. But in the next shot, the student is setting up a 60-inch plasma television in his dorm room, door ajar. While he's doing this, the group of attractive females walks by. In the final shot, the student is in his dorm room watching his new television, with the group of attractive females around him.

Following his explanation, Conner leaned back in his seat and folded his arms across his chest. Grinning proudly, he asked, "Well, what do you think?"

Alexis was the first to speak up. "Um, I don't know." She paused. "I think it's a pretty good start." Hesitantly, she added, "The only thing that I worry about is that our client won't like it. They pride themselves on being more sophisticated than their competitors. To them, this television is both an electronics device and a work of art." But then Alexis quickly added, "But I don't know, maybe you're right that we need to do something different."

Conner, with a slight frown on his face, asked the other group members, "What do the rest of you think?"

Evan responded, "Yeah, I think it's a pretty good idea."

"Judy?" asked Conner.

"I agree. It has potential."

"Well, everyone else seems to agree with me. What do you think Derek?" Conner asked, with the other three members staring at Derek.

Derek paused for a moment. He had his own ideas as well, and because he had worked with the client, perhaps more than any of the other team members, he wasn't sure about Conner's idea. Derek had pictured a commercial that placed the television in a stylish, contemporary Manhattan apartment, with a couple in their 30s enjoying a classic movie, a bottle of red wine on the coffee table.

Feeling the heat from his teammates' gazes, reluctantly Derek said, "Yeah, that sounds good."

"Great, it's settled then," beamed Conner. "We'll have this commercial to them in no time if we stay at this pace."

So the team fleshed out the commercial over the next month. Everyone got along, and the feeling of camaraderie strengthened. Once on board with Conner's idea, the team members became more confident that they would be successful, so much so that they made the commercial even racier than the original idea. The attractive girls would be dressed provocatively, and instead of watching the television, the student and the girls would be laughing and drinking, with the television on in the background. There were a few hesitations here and there as members expressed other ideas, but each team member, enjoying the group's solidarity, decided that it would be better to keep the team in good spirits rather than risk losing the team's morale.

The team quickly decided on a company to shoot the commercial and approved the actors. In a short time, they had completed their commercial. The next step was to present the commercial to their client. Conner took it upon himself to alert management that the team was ready to present the commercial.

"Impressive. Your team is a month ahead of the deadline," said one of the top managers. "We have a lot riding on this, so I hope that it's good. I presume everything went well then?"

Conner nodded. "Yes, very well. No problems or disagreements at all. I think we worked really well together."

On the day of the presentation, the team waited anxiously in a meeting room for their client to arrive. Advert's top managers took their seats in the meeting room. Soon after, three of the client's managers, dressed in professional attire, walked into the meeting room and sat down quietly. After welcoming the clients to the presentation, Conner and his teammates began the presentation, with Conner leading the way. He explained that the idea had come to the team almost instantly, and that given that everyone thought it was a good idea, he was sure that their company would feel the same. Then he dimmed the lights, pressed play, and let the commercial run.

It did not take long for the team to realize that the commercial was not having the effect they had wanted on their clients or their managers. The clients exchanged several sideways glances with one another, and the managers shifted nervously in their seats. After what seemed like an eternity, the commercial ended and the lights came back on. An awkward silence filled the room. The clients began murmuring among themselves.

"That was, um, interesting," said one of the clients, finally.

Conner replied that he thought the idea was "out of the box," and that, therefore, audiences would easily remember it.

"Oh, they'll remember it all right," smirked one of the clients. She then turned to Advert's top managers and stated, "This is not at all what we were looking for. The commercial doesn't fit our needs and doesn't portray the image that we are trying to obtain. Given that you told us that we would be in good hands with this team, my colleagues and I fear that your company will not be able to meet our goals. We appreciate the time that this took, but we will likely employ another advertising firm to film our commercial." With that, she and her colleagues left the room.

After a thorough lecturing from Advert's top managers, the team was disbanded. One month later, Derek was at home watching television when a commercial came on. Classical music played in the background as the camera swept through a modern home. The camera slowly rose up behind a tan leather sofa seating a couple enjoying a bottle of wine and watching a new 60-inch plasma television. In the bottom corner of the screen, in small writing, was the name of one of Advert's competitors. Apparently, Advert's former clients got what they were looking for in the end, but from a competitor. Derek shook his head and vowed to speak up next time he had an idea.

Questions for Discussion

1. What factors contributed to the poor performance of the Advert team? As a manager, what could you have done to help the team perform better?
2. According to the case, the Advert team was given a relatively high degree of autonomy. How might this autonomy have contributed to the presence of groupthink?
3. Teams can be either homogeneous or heterogeneous. How would you characterize the Advert team, and how did this affect the team's creativity and performance?
4. What are some group decision-making techniques that could have helped reduce conformity pressures and groupthink among the Advert team?
5. What different forms of communication could have been employed to improve the sharing of ideas among the Advert team? How might this have affected its performance and satisfaction?
6. How would you describe Conner's leadership style? Why do you think his style wasn't effective? In what situations might Conner be an effective leader?

Case 4 *Wal-Mart's World*

Just how does Wal-Mart, the world's largest retailer, maintain its corporate culture across all of its 4,000 stores? How does this giant, with sales a staggering $288 billion in fiscal year 2004, promote and preserve its image as a small-town store where the customer is king? Part of the answer lies in Wal-Mart's legendary Saturday Morning Meeting.

The Saturday Meeting started with Wal-Mart founder Sam Walton, who thought it unfair that he could take off on the weekends while his employees worked. So, in 1962, Sam Walton began arriving at his store, Walton's Five & Dime, in Bentonville, Arkansas, each Saturday between two and three in the morning. There, he would scrutinize the previous week's records to determine which merchandise was selling and which was not, as well as how sales were faring. However, Mr. Walton didn't stop there. When his store's "associates" (Walton called all his workers associates to emphasize that they were his colleagues as well as his employees) arrived, he would hold a quick morning meeting to openly share the store's information with them. He would also ask for their opinions on matters such as what items he should put on sale and how he should display certain products. Such meetings served not only to use the store's employees in multiple ways but also to convey to his employees that he valued their input and wanted them to learn the business.

Even as Wal-Mart grew into a multibillion-dollar company, the Saturday Morning Meeting continued.

Ever since, Wal-Mart has held them at the home office in Bentonville. Each Saturday morning, some 600 managers, many of whom live in Bentonville and make weekly trips to their respective territories, pack the 400-seat auditorium, waiting for their fearless leader to arrive. First, it was Sam Walton. Then, it was CEO David Glass. Now, at 7:00 A.M. sharp, current CEO Lee Scott heads the meeting. As usual, Scott starts off the meeting by leading the crowd in a Wal-Mart cheer: "Give me a W! Give me an A! Give me an L! Give me a Squiggly! . . . "

Though Saturday Morning Meeting topics typically include the company's financial performance, merchandising, and areas of improvement, the meeting is, above all else, a means to keep the company and its employees as close-knit as possible. Such solidarity is imperative to Wal-Mart's strategy of quick market response. When new ideas or problems surface, managers are comfortable sharing them with others. Decisions are made quickly, and action is taken.

For example, while discussing merchandising mistakes during a meeting, Paul Busby, regional vice president for the Northeastern United States, was concerned about a particular item that Wal-Mart was not carrying. "I went into a Kmart near one of my stores to look around and found an item that made me wonder why we don't have it." With a Kmart bag next to him, Busby pulls out a poker table cover and chip set that Kmart is selling for $9.99. "We should really have this product because it's a much better value than ours."

In response to Busby's concern, Scott McCall, the divisional merchandise manager for toys, replied, "We've got a pretty nice poker set in our stores, but I'll check with our sources and get back to you."

A mere 10 minutes passed before McCall asked for the microphone again. With cheers from the crowd, McCall stated, "Paul, I just wanted you to know that I've arranged for those Kmart poker sets to be acquired and be on the trucks rolling out to all the stores next week." Examples such as this illustrate the trust that Sam Walton had in his staff to make decisions. Instead of going through layers of red tape, Wal-Mart's managers can have their ideas implemented quickly. Of course, not all decisions are beneficial; however, those that are can result in immediate gains.

Such quick responses are difficult, if not impossible, for other large companies to execute. As former CEO David Glass explains, "The Saturday Morning Meeting was always a decision-making meeting to take corrective action, and the rule of thumb was that by noon we wanted all the corrections made in the stores." Glass clarifies, "Noon on Saturday." Glass further explains that since no other companies could even come close to the speed at which Wal-Mart executes strategy and change, Wal-Mart developed and sustains a competitive advantage. Wal-Mart's vast distribution network and purchasing power allow it to move products efficiently and sell them at a low price. For example, following the devastation of hurricane Katrina, Wal-Mart, rather than FEMA (Federal Emergency Management Agency), was one of the first organizations to distribute food and other goods to hurricane victims.

The Saturday Morning Meeting serves other purposes as well. Perhaps due to Wal-Mart's culture of retail fanaticism and continuous improvement of efficiency, the culture of Wal-Mart has been described as "neurotic." According to one Wal-Mart insider, "Mechanisms like these meetings keep that neurotic tension alive even at this enormous scale."

In fact, the Saturday Morning Meeting is not the only meeting Wal-Mart uses to maintain company culture. On Friday there is a merchandising meeting, where regional vice presidents get together to discuss what products are selling well. And not all meetings are for managers. Consistent with Sam Walton's emphasis on employee involvement, every Wal-Mart store has a 15-minute shift-change meeting three times a day. During these meetings, managers go over the store's performance numbers as well as ask their associates whether they have specific ideas that might improve sales. Managers send what they think are good ideas up to the regional vice president, who then proposes the ideas at the Saturday-morning meeting. The Wal-Mart greeter was one such idea, which a rank-and-file employee suggested. The greeter helped to put a friendly face on what might be viewed as a large, impersonal organization. Such structure helps to ensure that Wal-Mart's upper managers, who oftentimes are responsible for 100 or more stores, keep in touch with the daily happenings of their business.

One other aspect of Wal-Mart's culture is its frugality, a characteristic of Sam Walton that has endured even through Wal-Mart's tremendous growth and financial success. Walton began his strict focus on keeping costs low early on to gain an advantage over competitors such as Sears and Kmart. Walton was known to make executives sleep eight to a room on company trips. He himself drove a modest old pick-up truck and flew coach whenever he traveled. Amazingly, these characteristics have remained ingrained in Wal-Mart's culture. The current CEO, Lee Scott, drives a Volkswagen Beetle and has also shared hotel rooms to reduce costs.

But maintaining Wal-Mart's culture has not always been easy. In the late 1980s and early 1990s, attendance at the Saturday Morning Meetings grew tremendously, which made it impossible for everyone to speak. David Glass, CEO during that time, recalls complaints of boredom. So some of Wal-Mart's suppliers (who often attend the Saturday Morning Meetings), eager to impress and ingratiate themselves with the top brass, began bringing in entertainers such as singer Garth Brooks and former football player Joe Montana. However, the meetings began to lose focus. As Glass recalls of the entertainment, "You had to be careful how you did that because it becomes more fun to do that than fix the problems." By the late 1990s, the company began inviting guests who had more educational value, such as Bill Clinton and CEOs Jack Welch and Warren Buffet. These speakers were able to share their success stories with Wal-Mart's managers, giving them new ideas on how to conduct business and run the organization.

Perhaps the biggest obstacle to Wal-Mart is the increased public scrutiny that comes with being the world's largest company. In the past, the company had more tolerance for employee mistakes. It would strongly reprimand an employee who made an offhand sexist remark, for example, but if the employee altered his or her behavior, then the company let the employee stay. Today, however, Wal-Mart adheres to a stricter policy. As Mr. Scott explains, Wal-Mart is "not mean but less kind. Today, when you find somebody doing something wrong, you not only have to let them go, you have to document it so it is covered and people understand. That is a bit of a culture change. It's a company that operates in a different context than when Sam Walton was alive and when David Glass ran the company. Management cannot allow extraneous issues to bleed over. My role has to be, besides focusing on driving sales, to eliminate the constant barrage of negatives that causes people to wonder if Wal-Mart will be allowed to grow."

Indeed, Wal-Mart frequently finds itself in the news, though lately in stories that paint the company in a negative light. Controversies over Wal-Mart's anti-union position, its hiring and promotion practices (such as outsourcing the cleaning of its stores to illegal immigrants and working them seven days a week), and its treatment of employees (including accusations of discrimination and underpayment of employees) all make it increasingly difficult for Wal-Mart to maintain the image of a friendly, affordable retailer that Sam Walton had in mind when he founded the company. On this topic, Scott says, "Over the last couple of years I've been spending much of the time talking about all the negative publicity we've been getting, not from the standpoint that we hate the press, but by asking our people what we are doing that allows people to perpetuate these kinds of negative discussions about Wal-Mart."

If Wal-Mart is to enjoy continued success, it will have to find solutions to the above problems and the negative publicity that results. Perhaps the company should go back to its Walton roots? Or maybe it should alter its culture and market position to match its growth. For a company that has over 4,000 stores operating in the United States, Mexico, Canada, South America, Korea, China, and Europe; 1.5 million employees; and over 100,000 different products for sale, sustaining or changing the company's culture is a tremendous challenge. Thus far, however, Wal-Mart appears to be handling the challenge well.

Questions for Discussion

1. According to the textbook, there are seven primary characteristics that capture the essence of an organization's culture. How would you describe Wal-Mart's culture using these seven characteristics?
2. Based on this case, would you characterize Wal-Mart's culture as strong or weak? Why? How might Wal-Mart's culture contribute to its long-term performance?
3. As an upper manager of Wal-Mart, what steps could you take to either maintain or enhance the culture of Wal-Mart?
4. What are some aspects of Wal-Mart's culture that have persevered, but yet may be disadvantageous in today's economy?
5. How might Wal-Mart's negative press affect employee morale, job satisfaction, and organizational commitment? As a manager, what steps would you take to improve employee attitudes?
6. Characterize Wal-Mart's organizational structure. Is it mechanistic or organic? Does it have a high degree of centralization or decentralization? How might Wal-Mart's structure affect its employees in terms of their productivity and job attitudes?

Source: Based on D. Garbato, "Wal-Mart's Scott Concedes Size Impacts Corporate Culture," *Retail Merchandiser*, October 2004, p. 12; B. Schlender, "Wal-Mart's $288 Billion Meeting," *Fortune*, April 18, 2005, 90–99; and "Wal Around the World," *The Economist*, December 8, 2001, pp. 55–57.

Case 5   *Apple's Beethoven*

Management guru Jim Collins calls him the "Beethoven of business," Wall Street loves him, and Bill Gates was once his nemesis. Who is this powerful man? It's Steve Jobs, cofounder and current chief executive officer of Apple Computer. But despite its trailblazing start, Apple has suffered in recent years, losing sales and market share to big companies such as IBM and Microsoft. The slide even caused many analysts to question whether Apple had anything innovative left to offer. But Jobs, in characteristic fashion, has once again cornered a market, thanks to a small device—with big musical power—called the iPod.

Although Apple competed with computer giant Microsoft during the early 1980s, it soon found itself on the fringes of the computer industry because its computer, the Mac, wasn't compatible with many software programs that businesses needed. Personal computers (PCs), along with Microsoft's Windows operating system, began to dominate, sending the Mac to niche markets. By 1986, Apple's board of directors forced Steve Jobs out of the company. By the late 1990s, even the most fanatic Apple users were turning to different products because of the Mac's compatibility issues and Microsoft's ever-increasing dominance. Apple's share in the computer industry continued to decline, bottoming out at a mere 2 percent in the mid-1990s.

Apple knew it had to improve its operating system, so it bought the computer company Next in 1997, which, as circumstances would have it, Jobs himself was running. Along with Next came Jobs, who eventually returned to the forefront of Apple. Jobs's plan was simple: Rather than focus on hardware, Apple should focus on software. Create the right software, he reasoned, and the hardware sales would follow.

So Jobs began making moves that at first seemed risky but in the end paid off. One of the first things he did was to partner with his former rival, Bill Gates. Gates agreed to supply Apple with its popular Office and Internet Explorer programs as well as buy $150 million of Apple stock. Though this deal was good for Microsoft, it was even better for Apple, whose future was now tied to the more successful Microsoft in that Microsoft now had an interest in maintaining Apple's survival. Apple was no longer a competitor in a strict sense.

Because developing software is a costly undertaking, Jobs tried to keep the company afloat by offering computer hardware, which was simply a means to get into the software business. He pushed the company's managers for innovative thinking, which led to the introduction of the iMac in 1998. The iMac immediately stood out from its competitors for its odd, colorful styling, but compatibility issues with some widely used programs still remained. Though the iMac was not the innovative success that Jobs had hoped for, it bought him time to continue developing software.

During this time, Apple developed a new operating system that Jobs thought would revolutionize the computer industry: Mac OS X. The system was based on the operating system Unix and was superior to Windows in several areas, including stability and security. Now that he had the operating system, Jobs needed exciting software to go along with it. Knowing that he already had a deal with Microsoft, Jobs headed to Adobe Systems to ask them to develop a video editing program for his new operating system. Jobs recalled, "They said flat-out no. We were shocked, because they had been a big supporter in the early days of the Mac. But we said, 'Okay, if nobody wants to help us, we're just going to have to do this ourselves.'"

Adobe's rejection may have been a blessing in disguise for Apple. Jobs quickened the pace on software development, and in less than a year released two video editing programs, one for professionals and one for consumers. The software helped keep the buzz alive for Apple's innovative reputation. Feeling confident, Jobs knew that Apple needed to develop more software applications if it were to thrive, but he still hadn't noticed a phenomenon taking place on the Internet: the birth of online music.

In 2000, music lovers the world over, particularly young adults and teenagers, were downloading MP3s (digital music files) by the thousands from what were then illegal online music services, Napster being the company most in the news at that time. Online music delivery was an exciting product for consumers in that they could easily pick and choose what songs to buy and create their own music libraries on their computers. It was also a controversial issue in that there was no way (yet) to compensate artists and their record companies for the sales.

But for Jobs, the opportunity to deliver music to online consumers in a legitimate, user-friendly way was right up his alley. "I felt like a dope," he said. "I thought we had missed it. We had to work hard to catch up." He set out to develop the best "customer experience" possible.

So Apple began to install CD-ROM burners as a standard feature on all of its computers, hoping that it hadn't missed an opportunity. The burners allowed users to save electronic files, such as digital music files, onto a CD. The addition of burners as a standard feature was a crucial first step in marketing digital music because it offered a way to play digital music on devices other than a computer.

But Apple still needed to offer software that allowed users to manage their digital music files. Microsoft already sold several computer programs of this sort. For Apple, developing software that could easily manage and navigate through thousands of songs and allow a user to call up a song on a whim was no easy task. Jobs didn't have the answer himself, but he found it in a company called SoundStep. Jeff Robbin, the founder of SoundStep, teamed with several engineers and developed the program iTunes in just over three months. Not only was iTunes Apple's answer to comparable Windows jukeboxes, but many consumers found it a superior program with great search and sorting capabilities.

Jobs then hit on his big, Apple-saving idea: Develop a small, portable device, like the Sony Walkman, that could hold a user's entire digital music library. Jobs turned to Robbin again. In November 2001—a mere nine months later—Robbin and his team had developed the iPod, which is basically a small, handheld computer the size of a deck of cards (now, some are even smaller) with a simple interface for navigating through one's digital library and a set of earphones for easy listening. Music could be taken from a user's existing CD collection and "ripped" to the iPod via the user's computer, or online music file-sharing services such as Napster could be used to download songs onto the iPod.

Though Jobs believed that the iPod would be a success, he kept at his goal of developing the best "customer experience" possible. Napster, as well as other online music file-sharing services, was in the midst of lawsuits, leaving the door open for more legitimate, licensed services to emerge. By April 2003, Apple debuted its online iTunes Music store, allowing customers to legitimately buy songs for 99 cents that they could then download and store on their Mac computers and iPods. Major recording companies, such as Sony and Universal, agreed to sell their songs on iTunes, and the result was a tremendous success. As Eddy Cue, vice president for applications at Apple recalled, "We had hoped to sell a million songs in the first six months, but we did that in the first six days." While the iTunes store was busy selling digital music, Robbin and his team developed a Windows version of the iTunes store, further broadening Apple's market.

To say that Apple has done well with the iPod is an understatement. By January 2005, the company had sold more than 10 million iPods and 250 million songs. As a result, its stock price hit a record high of almost $80 per share in February 2005, and analysts estimated that Apple would earn $13 billion in revenues in 2005.

Jobs credits Apple's success to maintaining its core values of innovation and a continuous focus on the consumer. "The great thing is that Apple's DNA hasn't changed. The place where Apple has been standing for the last two decades is exactly where computer technology and the consumer electronics markets are converging. So it's not like we're having to cross the river to go somewhere else; the other side of the river is coming to us." Jobs further stated, "At Apple we come at everything asking, 'How easy is this going to be for the user? How great is it going to be for the user?' "

Though it appears that Apple is on a roll, its competitors are beginning to catch up. Not only has Microsoft entered the online music market but companies such as Wal-Mart and Napster (Napster is now on legal footing) are trying to capture some of the market share. As of the latest look, Wal-Mart was offering songs at 88 cents each, undercutting Apple's iTunes. Indeed, Apple's first-mover advantage will erode as competitors mimic Apple's product. Because they can copy Apple's online music store instead of creating it from scratch, start-up costs are lower for new entrants. What, then, will be the next move for Steve Jobs and Apple?

Questions for Discussion

1. Using the three-component model of creativity, describe what makes Steve Jobs, and by extension, Apple Computer, successful. Based on the case, which components does Jobs seem to possess in the highest degree? What aspects of the case led you to this conclusion?

2. What leadership theories are most applicable to Steve Jobs and why? How can these theories explain Jobs's recent successes?

3. Based on the case's description of Jobs, what can you infer about his personality? In other words, how would you describe his personality using terms from the book?

4. Are situational factors solely responsible for Apple's success, or is it due to the traits and leadership skills of Steve Jobs? If both contribute, which do you believe is more important and why?

5. Using Lewin's Three-Step Model of organizational change, explain Apple's development of and success with the iPod.

6. Would you characterize Apple as a learning organization? Why or why not? As a manager, what could you do to ensure that Apple continues to be innovative?

Source: Based on B. Schendler, "How Big Can Apple Get?" *Fortune*, February 21, 2005, 66–73.

Case 6 — *GM and the UAW: A One-Sided Negotiation?*

From 1947 through 1977, General Motors (GM) dominated the automobile industry, capturing an average of 45 percent of the auto market. Of the "Big Three" U.S. automakers (GM, Ford, and Chrysler), GM ranked first in sales in every year during this time frame and ranked first in profits for 16 of the 20 years. Needless to say, GM sat comfortably atop the automobile industry.

Now, decades later, GM's share of the U.S. automobile market is down to 25.4 percent, its lowest level since it competed with Henry Ford's Model T. Rumors of bankruptcy abound. In March of 2005, GM lowered its earnings forecast, which sent its stock price to its worst one-day fall since October 19, 1987, when the stock market crashed. Following this, GM announced that it had lost a staggering 1 billion dollars during its first quarter alone. Finally, adding insult to injury, GM disclosed that its sales were plummeting, and for this its stock earned Standard & Poor's grade of junk-bond status. What once was the world's largest and most profitable auto manufacturer is now puttering along in the slow lane.

So who or what is responsible for GM's decline? Though there are numerous factors that are hurting the company, one major factor has been the United Auto Workers (UAW) union and its long relationship with GM over the years.

The relationship first took shape during the Depression, when demand for cars overall fell sharply and almost half of all autoworkers lost their jobs as a result. Those autoworkers that did keep their jobs received greatly reduced pay because the major auto companies could barely afford to stay in business. However, GM, through the leadership of Alfred Sloan, remained competitive and profitable. But working conditions paled in comparison to today's standards. It was not typical for companies, including GM, to provide benefits such as health insurance, and pension plans were unheard of.

All of this began to change for GM in 1936, when two major players in the UAW, Walter and Victor Reuther, staged a sit-down strike at one of GM's primary plants, Fisher Body Plant No. 1, in GM's hometown of Flint, Michigan. Though the governor at the time, Frank Murphy, instructed over 4,000 guardsmen to maintain peace at the strike, he did not give them the authority to evict the strikers, forcing Sloan to negotiate with the UAW (though Sloan later stated that "we would not negotiate with the union while its agents forcibly held possession of our properties . . . we finally felt obliged to do so"). As a result of the strike, GM formally recognized the UAW as a legal organization in 1937. Shortly after, in 1941, Ford formally recognized the UAW, giving the union even greater power.

What followed was a relationship that endured over the years, giving the UAW and its members some of the best benefits in the country. Indeed, the UAW was a powerful negotiator. Victor Reuther, believing strongly that all workers should have health insurance, tried first to bargain with the federal government. After several failed attempts, he turned to Sloan at GM. Although Sloan initially viewed Reuther's request for health insurance and pension plans as "extravagant beyond reason," one of Reuther's proposals eventually persuaded him. Previously, GM and the UAW engaged in contract renegotiations each year, which made it difficult for GM's managers and workers to plan ahead because they were unsure what the costs would be for the following year. Reuther, capitalizing on this problem, offered to agree to longer contracts. As Sloan later stated, "Longer intervals gave the corporation more assurance that it could meet its long-range production schedules." What was the catch to the UAW's concession? In return for longer contracts, the UAW insisted that each and every contract be better for the UAW than the one before it. Sloan agreed to the terms of the negotiation, setting the stage for health insurance, pension plans, and other employee benefits.

During the economic boom following World War II, demand soared, leaving the auto industry rich with profit. As Reuther stated to the auto industry during these times, "It's a growing market—we have nothing to fight over." So, at first, contract renegotiations went smoothly and costs of employee benefits stayed at a minimum. But little by little, the UAW negotiated better benefits for its members. In 1943, GM allowed workers to purchase health insurance; however, GM did not incur any of the cost because workers put their money into a pool. Five years later, the union successfully negotiated two powerful benefits. The first, an "escalator clause," stipulated that GM give raises based on the cost of living. The second, the "improvement factor," rewarded workers for increasing efficiency. As a plant increased in efficiency, and lowered costs as a result, workers at the plant received raises. Then, in 1950, GM agreed to pay 50 percent of all its workers' health care premiums, including workers' families, and it also agreed to develop and pay for a pension plan. Three years later, GM extended these benefits to its retired workers.

Business was still booming in 1959, when the UAW persuaded GM to guarantee workers' wages—even for those workers the company had laid off. Thus, workers could be assured that they would receive no less than what GM had promised to pay them, even during economic hardship. The UAW continued to push GM to further sweeten its benefits—per their original deal—and in 1961, GM agreed to pay 100 percent of all health care premiums, again for workers and their families. Three years later, GM extended this benefit to its retirees.

GM's market share around that time peaked at 50.7 percent, but in 1966, the same year that Alfred Sloan died, a little-known company called Datsun exported a car to the United States, marking the entry of Japanese automakers in the U.S. market. During this time, Japan's influence was minimal, and GM continued to agree to increase benefits to its workers. In 1970, for instance, the UAW persuaded GM to provide full retirement benefits after 30 years of service. In addition, GM agreed to extend health insurance benefits to cover mental and prenatal and postnatal conditions. As UAW negotiator Douglas Fraser recalls, "We had a lot of arguments over mental health. I don't believe we had any arguments over full premiums."

From GM's standpoint, the concessions it made over the years may be relatively minor when considered in isolation, but their cumulative impact is now taking its toll. As the company has lost market share to increased competition from both domestic and foreign producers, particularly Japanese producers, more and more workers have retired, leaving GM with huge expenses. GM anticipates health care costs to top $5.6 billion in 2005 alone, and it is estimated that GM's long-term health care liabilities are $77 billion. To fund its pension plans, GM has long-term liabilities of $89 billion—a tremendous amount when one considers that GM's revenues in 2004 were $193 billion.

And costs continue to soar as baby boomers retire in droves, leaving younger workers to support retirees and causing large discrepancies in the number of current and retired workers. GM now employs 150,000 people, yet it funds health care for 1.1 million people. And because of the ever-increasing benefits packages that the UAW negotiated with GM over the years, GM's health care plan is far better than what the average U.S. company provides. While average U.S. citizens pay 32 percent of their medical costs, GM workers and members of the UAW pay only 7 percent. In fact, GM now spends more than double on health care what it spends on steel to produce its automobiles. As one former GM investor quipped, "When you invest in GM, you are not investing in a car company. You are investing in a money-management firm and an HMO."

All of these rising costs have caused GM considerable financial problems. Although some analysts suggest that GM should streamline operations, Thomas Kowaleski, a spokesperson for GM, said, regarding the enormous cost of benefits, "We cannot be profitable at 20 percent market share because legacy costs won't go away." Even closing a plant is no longer under GM's discretion—the UAW must approve it. To make matters worse, even if GM halts production at a given plant, it still has to pay its workers 95 percent of their regular wages, even though GM's wages are 60 percent more than the industry average.

All in all, GM may have negotiated itself into a stranglehold with the UAW. But there are two sides to consider. On the one hand, offering great employee benefits is a goal that all organizations should have, as workers should receive the best treatment possible and companies want to attract the best workers possible. On the other hand, if the UAW continues to press GM for improvements, and GM concedes, the company may no longer exist to provide those benefits.

Questions for Discussion

1. How would you characterize the type of conflict that exits between GM and the UAW using the various conflict-handling interventions described in Chapter 15?
2. Based on the case, would you conclude that GM and the UAW have engaged in distributive or integrative bargaining? Which type would be better for the two parties in the long term, and why?
3. What types of power does the UAW hold over GM? How has this power influenced its ability to negotiate with GM?
4. Based on the case, what decision-making errors with the union might have led GM to its current financial position? What can GM do to eliminate these errors in the future?
5. Although benefits such as a "guaranteed wage" likely are appealing to workers, how might such benefits affect employee motivation? How might they affect job satisfaction and organizational commitment? Could this be a case where management engages in the "folly of rewarding A, while hoping for B?"
6. As a manager of a large company such as GM that operates in a highly competitive environment, how would you attempt to strike an appropriate balance between employee treatment and company profitability?

Source: Based on R. Lowenstein, "What Went Wrong at GM," *Smart Money,* July 2005, 78–82.

Case **7**   *A Question of Motivation*

Alex and Stephanie have a few things in common. Both are students at their state's university, and both work full-time at a local supermarket to make ends meet and help pay for college. Though the pay isn't great, it's a steady job that allows them some flexibility, which helps when scheduling classes. Both students joined the supermarket two years ago, and, given their similar situations, became friends quickly.

Although Stephanie seems to enjoy her job, arriving and leaving work each day with a smile on her face, Alex often grumbles and complains about his work. Much of the time, Alex complains about his boss, Dan, who oversees the produce department. Stephanie works for Jonathan, a 10-year veteran who everyone generally admires for his friendly demeanor and relaxed management style.

Most employees want to work for Jonathan, as he often assigns his employees different duties each week so workers don't get bored. Stephanie, for instance, can be working at the checkout counter one week, stocking shelves the next, and the store's culinary center the following week.

The culinary center is a new service that the store is test-marketing. Employees show customers how to create exciting recipes from start to finish. It is Stephanie's favorite place in the store to work. She is also responsible for taking customers around the store to locate ingredients for a culinary center recipe, many of the ingredients being some of the store's finest. And she enjoys allowing customers to sample what she cooks. So far, the culinary center is a success, and many of the store's more expensive ingredients are becoming difficult to keep in stock. To help with this issue, Jonathan encourages his employees to notify him immediately when an item is running low and even empowers employees to reorder items from vendors. By doing this, Stephanie has quickly grasped how the supermarket operates.

Alex's supervisor, in contrast, prefers most of his employees to work in the same area each day—Alex is one of those employees. Dan believes that the best way to master a job is to do it over and over again. This means that Alex has to stock the same produce areas each day. As boxes of produce are delivered to the store's supply room, Alex unloads their contents onto the shelves. Alex also must constantly reorganize the produce already on the shelves to make them look as orderly as possible. Most of the time, though, he doesn't feel inclined to do either task.

After a particularly boring morning of restocking apples (the store had apples on sale that day), Alex met Stephanie for lunch in the break room. After sitting down, Alex reached into his lunchbox and pulled out an apple, a look of disgust on his face. "Ugh . . . If I have to look at another apple, I'm going to be sick."

"Bad day again?" asked Stephanie as Alex stuffed the apple back into his lunchbox.

"I stocked apples all morning—what do you think?" Alex retorted.

"Why don't you tell Dan you want to do something else?" Stephanie inquired. "I see that he lets Denise work in other areas." Stephanie leaned closer. "I've even heard that she gets paid more than you. Is that true?" she whispered.

"Apparently, she gets paid $2.00 more an hour, but I do the same things that she does. Oh, that's right. One thing I don't do is tell Dan what a cool shirt he has on or how awesome his car is. They're both pathetic if you ask me," frowned Alex.

"Two dollars more an hour, but she's been here for only 3 months!" Stephanie exclaimed. "And I know that you work just as hard as she does. No wonder you're so irritated all the time."

"I don't even care any more. What's the point? If I stock more apples, or something meaningless like that, what does it get me—another sticker that says 'good job'? Oooh, that's really great. Thanks a bunch Dan!" replied Alex, punctuating his last sentence with a sarcastic thumbs-up. "Anyway, enough about my day. How's yours going?"

"Pretty good, actually. Jonathan and I met earlier today, and we both set a goal for me to sell 10 bottles of truffle oil next week."

"Wow. That stuff is pretty expensive, isn't it?" asked Alex.

"Thirty-five dollars for four ounces," replied Stephanie. "It'll be tough, but I found a pretty good recipe that I'll be making for customers who stop by the culinary center." She paused, then said, "I think I'll be able to do it. I've made quite a few similar recipes before, and even though this one is more difficult, it shouldn't be too bad. Besides, if I sell the oil Jonathan said that he'll give me a $75 bonus. So I'm definitely going to give it a shot. The nice thing is that I'll be able to do this on my own, without someone breathing down my neck."

"Well that's certainly more than I'll be making this week," said Alex. "This job is okay, but I'd probably leave if I could. It's too risky right now to just quit. If I can't find something, then I'll be in trouble when that next tuition bill comes around."

"Look on the bright side. At least you make more than Jean. She's been here for 7 years, still working in the deli," replied Stephanie.

"That's true," sighed Alex as he returned to his lunch. He looked up at the clock. They had been at lunch for a half hour already. Dan was quite the stickler about keeping lunch to a minimum. Although store policy allowed employees 45 minutes for lunch, Dan often pushed his employees to keep it to 30 minutes. As Alex quickened his chewing, Dan strolled into the break room and opened the refrigerator, his back to Alex and Stephanie.

Wheeling around with a soda in hand, Dan commented, "Bit of a long lunch, hey Alex?"

Alex could feel the blood rising to his face. "It's been exactly a half hour, and I'm almost finished," he said.

"Well, we're running low on apples again. So quit lying around and get back to work." Dan walked toward the door, stopped, and turned around. "I thought that college students were supposed to be smarter than this. At the very least I would hope that they could tell time." He added, "I guess the university must have glossed over your application." And with that, Dan left.

"What a jerk," said Stephanie after Dan was out of earshot.

"What else is new," said Alex. "I'd guess I'd better get back to work." Alex got up and returned what was left of his lunch to the refrigerator. When he opened the door, he noticed a sandwich labeled with a post-it note that read "Dan's." After glancing quickly to the door, he casually swept the sandwich onto the floor. Stephanie turned around at the sound.

"Oops," smirked Alex. He paused, staring down at the sandwich. "Five-second rule!" he said as he picked up the sandwich, being sure to smear the underside of it on the floor. After putting it neatly back on the shelf, Alex turned to Stephanie. "Well Steph, have a good one. I think maybe I'll take my time on those apples."

Questions for Discussion

1. How can expectancy theory be used to explain the differences in motivation between Alex and Stephanie? What specifics from the case apply to expectancy theory?
2. Alex states that he is underpaid for the work he does. What motivational theory does this apply to, and how would it explain Alex's behavior?
3. Using concepts from organizational justice, explain why Alex knocks his boss's lunch to the floor. What should Alex's boss do to improve the fairness of his treatment?
4. Using concepts from the emotions and moods chapter, explain why Alex retaliates toward his supervisor. Was his behavior driven purely by emotion, or did cognition also play a role? How so?
5. Compare and contrast Alex and Stephanie in terms of each person's level of work stress. How might stress affect their attitudes and behaviors within their work environment?
6. Discuss Alex and Stephanie in terms of each person's job attitudes (for example, job satisfaction, organizational commitment). What factors might be responsible for any differences?

Case 8 — *The Big Promotion*

Devon and Isabella arrived outside their boss's office at the same time and took a seat. Both exchanged a cordial "hello," but they didn't say much else as they waited outside. Fidgeting nervously in their seats, the two knew that only one of them was going to receive what would be the biggest promotion of their careers.

Devon and Isabella worked for a large software company and each was responsible for managing one of the company's largest divisions. Both had been in their current position for years, hoping that a spot at the company's corporate headquarters would open up. That time had arrived a month earlier when one of the company's senior executives retired. Such positions did not open frequently, so Devon and Isabella knew that this was a tremendous opportunity.

For the past month, they had prepared for their meeting with the company's CEO, Paul McAllister. Although Paul already knew Devon and Isabella well, he wanted to meet with them at the same time to see how they handled the pressure of being interviewed in front of each other.

After waiting for what seemed like an eternity, Devon and Isabella looked up simultaneously as Paul opened the door to his office.

"Isabella. Devon. Good to see you. Come on in," said Paul.

Devon and Isabella entered Paul's office and took the chairs ready for them at the front of his desk.

Paul broke the silence by saying, "Well, you both know why you are here, so there's no need to waste time. I already know your resumes backwards and forwards, and I've gathered as much information as possible from those who know you best, so now it comes down to hearing it, 'straight from the horses' mouths.' I'm going to ask you both one question only, and it's the same question for both of you. Let me flip a coin to see who will respond first." He flipped the coin. "Devon, you're up."

Devon sat up with confidence, eyeing Paul.

Paul began. "To function effectively in an executive position requires strong leadership skills. Both of you have gained valuable experience as managers of your respective divisions, making decisions that have resulted in strong performances from those divisions. But you have also, as managers, followed directives that this corporate office has handed down. As an executive, this will change. You will no longer take directives—you will give them. In short, you will be responsible for guiding the future of this company, and its success will depend greatly on you. So my question to you both is: How do you plan to succeed as a leader if you are offered this position?"

"Well Paul," responded Devon, "That is an excellent question. I believe that, to be a successful leader, one must be able to exert influence. When you get down to it, that is what leadership is all about—the ability to influence others. I have demonstrated that I have this ability since I joined the ranks of management." Devon paused, collecting his thoughts. "It is my opinion that leadership boils down to what actions you take with your employees. For me, leadership is all about rewarding and punishing appropriately. I try to make my employees' jobs less complicated by stating exactly what they need to do, assigning particular tasks, setting appropriate goals, and ensuring that my subordinates have the resources they need."

Paul listened carefully as Devon continued. "Basically, I am an organizer. When employees accomplish a given task or goal, I reward them appropriately for their work. When employees fail to accomplish an assignment, an appropriate response from me is needed. If it is clear that the employee did not try to accomplish the task, then punishment is necessary, and this punishment could range from a verbal reprimand to termination, depending, of course, on the circumstances. If the employee did not have the necessary skills or resources to complete a task, then my job is to provide those skills and resources. By rewarding and punishing employees based on their performance, I am able not only to influence employee behavior to match the goals of the organization but also to send a clear message as to what I expect."

Devon added, "I also want to note that a strong sense of fairness guides all of my decisions—I reward and punish justly. As a result, my employees are satisfied with their work and perform at high levels. So I will bring my ability to influence behavior with me if I am offered this position, and in doing so will be able to shape the future of our company."

"Thank you, Devon," responded Paul. "Isabella, how would you answer this question?"

"Well, Paul," said Isabella, "I think you'll find that my perspective on leadership is different from Devon's. Although I certainly agree with Devon that giving clear guidance to employees, setting appropriate goals, and rewarding employees for accomplishing tasks is a fundamental leadership quality, I believe that it takes more than that to be a successful leader. You see, I do not believe that just anyone can be a leader. To be a leader requires a certain 'something' that not all people possess."

"And you believe that you possess that certain something?" interrupted Paul.

Isabella grinned. "I think you'll find that my record suggests that I do, in fact. You see, successful leadership is about motivating people beyond the formal requirements of their jobs. It is not enough in today's global economy to simply ensure that employees are completing their tasks. To survive, and moreover, grow, leaders must challenge employees to look ahead, to contribute ideas, and to make sacrifices for the good of the company. My job as a leader of this company is to create a vision of where we will be 5, 10, and 15 years from now. I see us creating new technologies, as well as merging existing technologies, to give our company the competitive advantage it needs to sustain growth in the long term. By sharing this vision with my employees, we will all be able to pursue the same goals."

Isabella continued, "I inspire my subordinates to see the company as their own, rather than as a means to a paycheck. I consider employee input and the different needs of each worker, and I challenge each and every one of them to think outside the box and develop innovative solutions to the problems facing us. The end result is, in my opinion, a highly motivated workforce with a common goal—to make sure our company is the industry leader."

Paul nodded, thinking about both answers. He had scrutinized each person's record carefully, and both were qualified for the job. However, the two candidates differed in important ways. Devon had built a strong reputation for being a traditional, straightforward leader, motivating his employees well, setting appropriate goals, and ensuring that employees accomplished tasks on time—even ahead of schedule. However, Devon was not known for developing the most creative solutions, and he lacked the vision that Paul knew was an important competency to have as an executive.

Isabella, in contrast, had built a reputation as being a visionary leader. Though her ideas were a bit unconventional at times, in many cases they were directly responsible for getting the company out of a jam. In addition, her magnetic personality made her a favorite among employees. However, Isabella often revealed a somewhat egotistical personality, and Paul was unsure whether this egoism would be amplified if she were in a more authoritative position.

Paul had to make a tough decision. He thought about his company's future. Things were relatively stable now, and business was good, but he knew that stability was not always certain.

"I would like to thank you both for coming today. You're making this a tough decision for me," said Paul. "I need to think about this a bit more, but I'll be getting back to you soon." He paused, then added, "You'll have my answer tomorrow morning."

Questions for Discussion

1. Using terms from the text, how would you describe Devon's leadership style? How would you describe Isabella's leadership style?
2. Whose leadership style do you believe would be more effective, Isabella's or Devon's? Why? What, if any, situational factors might their effectiveness depend on?
3. If you were Paul, who would you hire and why?
4. What are some potential downsides to each candidate's leadership style?
5. Whose employees do you think are likely to be more motivated, Devon's or Isabella's? Whose employees are likely to have higher job satisfaction, trust in leadership, and organizational commitment? Why?
6. Based on their leadership styles, in what type of organizational structure would Devon be most effective? What about Isabella? Why?

ILLUSTRATION CREDITS

Chapter 1
3. Mark Crosse/AP Wide World Photos
5. Matt Rourke/AP Wide World Photos
10. Elaine Thompson/AP Wide World Photos
17. Getty Images, Inc.
20. Melanie Stetson Freeman/The Christian Science Monitor/Getty Images, Inc.
22. AP Wide World Photos
24. Jessica Kourkounis/The New York Times
28. Greg Ruffing/Redux Pictures

Chapter 2
43. Dave Yoder/The New York Times
48. Douglas Healey/The New York Times
50. © Ed Kashi/Corbis
54. Mario Villafuerte/Redux Pictures
57. Toru Yamanaka/Agence France Presse/Getty Images
62. Joe Raedle/Getty Images, Inc.

Chapter 3
73. Eros Hoagland/Redux Pictures
77. © Jodi Hilton/Corbis
78. Aynsley Floyd/AP Wide World Photos
82. Kim Kyung-Hoon/Corbis/Reuters America LLC
88. Katsumi Kasahara/AP Wide World Photos
89. STR/Agence France Presse/Getty Images

Chapter 4
103. Fred R. Conrad/The New York Times
106. AP Wide World Photos
108. Manish Swarup/AP Wide World Photos
112. Chris Pizzello/AP Wide World Photos
113. Charles Rex Arbogast/AP Wide World Photos
120. Ben Baker/Redux Pictures

Chapter 5
137. Joyce Dopkeen/The New York Times
144. Misha Erwitt/The New York Times
147. © Kim Kulish/Corbis
148. © Ferran Paredes/Reuters/Corbis
156. Toshifumi Kitamura/Agence France Presse/Getty Images

158. © Darryl Bush/San Francisco Chronicle/CORBIS All Rights Reserved

Chapter 6
173. Christopher Gardner Media
180. AP Wide World Photos
187. Ralph Orlowski/Corbis/Reuters America LLC
190. Julia Cumes/AP Wide World Photos
192. Justin Sullivan/Getty Images, Inc.
201. CLARO CORTES IV/Reuters/Corbis/Bettmann

Chapter 7
213. Thomas Strand Studio
218. Thomas Broening Photography
221. Tom Strattman/The New York Times
224. Lawrence Bartlett/Agence France Presse/Getty Images
226. Chris Mueller/Chris Mueller/Redux Pictures
229. Ben Garvin/The New York Times
232. Pat Sullivan/AP Wide World Photos
234. Paul Sakuma/AP Wide World Photos

Chapter 8
249. Aijaz Rahi/AP Wide World Photos
255. Doug Mindell Photography
259. Beaver County Times, Lucy Schaly/AP Wide World Photos
261. © James Leynse/CORBIS All Rights Reserved
265. © Kimberly White/Reuters/Corbis
267. Stephen Chernin/Getty Images, Inc.
269. STR/Agence France Presse/Getty Images

Chapter 9
283. Ryanstock/Taxi/Getty Images
287. © Bob Daemmrich/CORBIS All Rights Reserved
289. Chris Graythen/Getty Images, Inc.
293. Courtesy of AT&T Archives and History Center, Warren, NJ
298. Tom Wagner/Redux Pictures
300. © Redlink/CORBIS All Rights Reserved

Chapter 10
321. Optimus Solutions
325. Alexandra Boulat/VII/AP Wide World Photos
330. Ruth Fremson/The New York Times

333. Jim Wilson/The New York Times
335. AP Wide World Photos
338. Harry Cabluck/AP Wide World Photos

Chapter 11
349. Cheryl Senter/AP Wide World Photos
352. Shizuo Kambayashi/AP Wide World Photos
354. Erik S. Lesser/The New York Times
363. Noah Berger/The New York Times
366. Alyson Aliano/Alyson Aliano Photography
369. Alyssa Banta/Redux Pictures

Chapter 12
383. Charles Rex Arbogast/AP Wide World Photos
385. Jason Kempin/FilmMagic/Getty Images, Inc.
390. Scott Cohen/AP Wide World Photos
392. Carlos Osorio/AP Wide World Photos
396. Patrick Allard/REA/Redux Pictures

Chapter 13
411. Ben Baker/Redux Pictures
414. Paul Sakuma/AP Wide World Photos
416. Koji Sasahara/AP Wide World Photos
418. © Michele Asselin/Corbis Outline
422. Mel Evans/AP Wide World Photos
426. Thaddeus Harden/Corbis/Outline
428. STRDEL/Agence France Presse/Getty Images
436. Djamilla Rosa Cochran/WireImage for CHANEL/Getty Images, Inc.

Chapter 14
449. © Alan Schein Photography/CORBIS All Rights Reserved
452. John Bazemore/AP Wide World Photos
455. Christopher LaMarca/Redux Pictures
459. Charles Bennett/AP Wide World Photos
462. AP Wide World Photos
465. George Frey/AP Wide World Photos

Chapter 15
483. Gene J. Puskar/AP Wide World Photos
488. Michele McDonald/The Boston Globe/Redux Pictures

Name Index

A

Aamodt, M. G., 356n
Abbas, Syed, 330
Abdala, Dianna, 378–379
Abele, A. E., 178n
Abramson, L. Y., 268n
Adair, W. L., 505n
Adams, J. S., 192n
Adams, J. Stacy, 192
Adams, R., 111n
Adams, S., 307n
Adams, Tom, 182
Addae, H. M., 648n
Aditya, R. N., 385n, 400n
Adler, N., 374n
Adler, N. J., 161n, 201n
Agoglia, Barbara, 653n
Aherarn, Liz, 276
Ainslie, Elizabeth, 167
Akst, D., 389n
Albarracín, D., 77n
Alderfer, C. P., 177n
Alderfer, Clayton, 177
Allen, Chap, 213
Allen, N. J., 79n, 81n, 270n
Allen, T. D., 429n, 430n
Allen, Woody, 212
Alliger, G. M., 433n
Alloy, L. B., 268n
Allport, G. W., 105n, 107n
Allport, Gordon, 105
Alsop, R., 5n, 158n
Amabile, T. M., 158n
Ambady, N., 260n, 265n, 268n, 272n
Ambrose, M. L., 193n
Amelinckx, A., 327n
Ames, D. R., 386n
Amis, J., 627n
Amusa, Gbola, 511
Anderson, C., 489n
Anderson, N., 46n, 587n
Anderson, P., 538n
Andersson, L. M., 296n
Anfuso, D., 633n
Ansberry, C., 218n, 591n
Anthony, W. P., 473n
Antonakis, J., 388n
Argyris, C., 635n
Arita, E., 230n
Armeli, S., 81n
Armenakis, A. A., 311n, 330n
Armour, S., 25n, 476–477n
Armstrong, Michael, 476
Arnold, J. A., 269n
Arpey, Gerard, 631

Arthur, M. B., 415n
Arthur, W. J., Jr., 594n
Arvey, R. D., 106n
Aryee, S., 81n, 467n
Asch, Solomon, 295–296
Ash, Mary Kay, 413, 416
Asher, J. J., 588n
Ashford, S. J., 9n, 375n, 623n
Ashforth, B. E., 250n, 269n, 272n, 468n
Ashkanasy, N. M., 264n
Ashmos, D. P., 570n
Atkins, Howard, 344, 598n
Atwater, L. E., 193n, 435n
Audia, P. G., 622n, 626n
Avolio, B. J., 79n, 421n, 423n
Axtell, R. E., 373n
Aycan, Z., 91n, 161n

B

Babcock, L., 497n, 502n
Babcock, P., 139n
Babkoff, H., 258n
Bacharach, S. B., 461n
Bachrach, D. G., 31n
Badal, J., 457n
Bader, P., 432n
Bahney, A., 364n
Bailey, D. E., 223n
Baker, Avery, 67
Bakker, A. B., 588n
Bakker, P., 588n
Balestreri-Spero, J. C., 588n
Balkundi, P., 329n
Ballmer, Steve, 269
Ball-Rokeach, S. J., 117n
Baltes, B. B., 308n
Balzac, Honoré de, 448
Banaji, M. R., 52n, 267n
Bandura, Albert, 57n, 188n, 189–191, 189n
Banks, W. C., 291n–292n
Barbarian, J., 591n
Barber, N., 64n
Barbuto, J. E., Jr., 651n
Bardack, N. R., 589n
Barker, B., 25n
Barnes-Farrell, J. L., 224n
Baron, A. S., 52n
Baron, H., 605n
Bar-On, R., 265n
Baron, R. A., 469n
Barrick, M. R., 105n, 109n, 331n, 587n
Barron, F. X., 158n
Barry, B., 111n, 501n
Barsade, S. G., 241n
Basch, J., 263n
Basilli, Seppy, 611

Bass, B. M., 416n, 419n, 421n, 436n, 451n
Bateman, T. S., 88n
Bates, J., 531n
Bauer, C. C., 308n
Baum, D., 420n
Baum, J. R., 421n
Bavetta, A. G., 502n
Bazerman, M., 148n
Bazerman, M. H., 165n
Beal, D. J., 273n
Beard, D. W., 537n
Beccalli, N., 437n
Bechara, A., 265n, 269n
Becker, Maggie, 315
Becker, T. E., 185n
Bedeian, A. G., 270n, 311n
Beehr, T. A., 123n
Begley, S., 54n
Belknap, Joanne, 646
Bell, Alexander Graham, 160
Bell, S. T., 331n, 594n
Bell, W. D., 233n
Belohlav, J. A., 52n
Benedict, C., 207, 207n
Benham, Bob, 350
Benjamin, Maria, 226
Bennett, R. J., 30n, 296n
Bennett, W., Jr., 594n
Bennis, W., 398n
Benson, Chuck, 487
Benz, M., 92n
Ben-Ze'ev, A., 253n
Berlo, D. K., 352n
Bernardin, H. J., 601n
Bernstein, A., 591n
Bershok, Joel, 442
Bertua, C., 46n, 587n
Bettman, Gary, 511
Bhatia, P., 79n, 421n
Bilefsky, D., 373n
Bilotta, J. G., 286n
Binney, E., 361n
Bishop, John, 96
Bitner, M. J., 89n
Black, M. M., 50n
Blackburn, R. S., 660n
Blair, C. A., 88n
Blake, R. R., 390n, 632n
Blanchard, Ken, 395–396
Blank, Steve, 316
Blau, G. J., 79n
Blomberg, M., 167n
Blombert, M., 132n
Blonk, R. W. B., 642n
Bloom, Jonathan, 476
Blum, M. W., 501n, 503n

Boal, K. R., 79n
Bobko, P., 51n
Bodinson, G., 324n, 326n
Bodnar, Andrew, 510–511
Bogg, T., 111n
Boje, D. M., 564n
Bolman, L., 475n
Bommer, W., 22n
Bonaparte, Napoleon, 386
Bond, M. H., 125n, 473n
Bond, R., 296n
Bonds, Barry, 69, 635
Bonett, D. G., 80n
Bono, J. E., 31n, 86n, 88n, 112n, 273n, 386n, 420n
Bonsteel, Michelle, 350
Booms, B. H., 89n
Boon, S. D., 424n
Bosson, J. K., 360n
Bouchard, T. J., Jr., 106n
Bowditch, J. L., 557n
Bowen, D. E., 89n
Bowerman, Bill, 564
Bowles, H. R., 497n, 502n
Bradlow, E. T., 427n
Brady, D., 131n, 361n
Brady, Kathryn, 271
Brady, Tom, 453, 584
Branch, B. J., 350
Branson, Richard, 385, 386, 559
Brass, D. J., 115n
Bravo, Rose Marie, 148
Brazil, D. M., 399n
Breaugh, J. A., 52n
Brechu, Brehm, 340n
Breckler, S. J., 75n
Brees, Drew, 584
Brennan, Jack, 418
Brett, J., 489n
Brett, J. M., 505n
Bridwell, L. G., 177n
Briles, Judith, 477
Brion, S., 622n
Britt, J., 28n
Broadwater, Gene, 185
Brockway, J. H., 153n
Brody, L. R., 259n
Broersen, J. P. J., 642n
Brokaw, Tom, 120
Brooke, P. P., Jr., 79n
Brooks, S. M., 21n
Brotheridge, C. M., 262n
Brouer, R. L., 458n
Brown, D., 647n
Brown, D. J., 79n
Brown, G. R., 256n
Brown, Kelvin, 224, 238n
Brown, M. E., 423n
Brunelli, M., 326n

Bryant, F. B., 153n
Brynaert, Didier, 568–569
Buchko, A. A., 232n
Buck, Carolyn, 653n
Buddha, 386
Budhwar, P. S., 467n
Buffet, Warren, 665
Buffett, Jimmy, 136
Bulger, Marc, 584
Bulkeley, W. M., 526n
Bunch, R., 324n, 326n
Buono, A. F., 557n
Burgin, Danny, 166
Burke, L. A., 12n
Burke, M., 96n
Burke, R. J., 602n
Burke, Sheila P., 152
Burnett, D. D., 128n
Burnfield, J. L., 639n
Burnham, D. H., 181n
Burns, J. M., 423n
Burns, T., 534n
Burris, Jeff, 578
Burrows, P., 143n
Burton, T. M., 366n
Busby, Paul, 671
Bush, George W., 441, 666
Buss, A. H., 107n
Buss, D. M., 255n
Butler, E. A., 226n
Butterfield, D. A., 51n
Byosiere, 649n
Byrne, J. A., 567, 658n

C

Cacioppo, J. T., 254n
Cadsby, C. B., 233n
Calabrese, Erin, 276
Caldwell, D. F., 217n
Caldwell, S., 624n
Caminiti, S., 223n
Campbell, Ann Marie, 305
Campbell, E. M., 220n
Campbell, Jason, 584
Campbell, W. K., 113n, 155n
Campion, M. A., 222n, 334n, 588n
Carbonara, P., 588n
Carl, D. E., 437n
Carlile, P. R., 364n
Carlson, K. A., 148n
Carlson, R. E., 589n
Carnahan, Kristin, 611
Carnevale, P. J. D., 489n
Carretta, T. R., 51n
Carreyrou, J., 511n
Carroll, G. R., 623n
Carroll, S. J., 601n
Carsten, J. M., 90n
Carstensen, L. L., 259n

Carstons, Rob, 406
Carswell, J. J., 81n
Carter, A., 264, 422n
Caruso, D. R., 264n
Cascio, W. F., 49n, 543n
Case, J., 556n
Castañeda, M. B., 80n
Castro, S. L., 467n
Cattell, R. B., 107n
Cavanagh, G. F., 157n
Cavanaugh, Kyle, 68
Cawley, B. D., 602n
Cervone, D., 189n
Chambers, John, 405
Champy, J., 387n
Chan, Donna, 611
Chandler, C., 144n
Charles, Lyria, 566
Chatman, J. A., 574n
Chemers, M. M., 393n
Chen, G., 220n, 562n
Chen, P. Y., 196n
Chen, Y., 503n
Chen, Z., 467n
Chen, Z. X., 81n
Chenault, Ken, 386
Cheng, Y., 80n
Cheraskin, L., 425n
Chereches, R., 121n
Cherniss, C., 265n
Child, J., 524n
Chiquet, Maureen, 436
Chouinard, Yvon, 411–412
Chow, C., 420n
Chow Hou, W., 161n
Christian, S., 459n
Christie, R., 112n
Chuang, A., 273n
Chuang, W., 15
Church, A. T., 124n
Churchill, Winston, 386
Cicchinelli, Chris, 653n
Cidambi, R., 79n
Clarey, Pat, 666
Clark, Carrie, 206
Clark, David, 97
Clark, Jim, 504
Clark, L. A., 253n
Clark, R. D., III, 306n
Clark, Richard, 617–618, 637
Clarke, L. D., 202n
Clinton, Bill, 264, 413, 441
Cloyd, Gil, 652–653
Coady, Tony, 474
Cochran, P. L., 25n, 592n
Coffman, Curt, 243
Cohen, F., 417n
Cohen, J. D., 259n
Cohen, Jennifer, 476
Cohen, R., 510n

Colbert, A. E., 217n, 395n
Collins, J., 418n
Collins, Jim, 673
Colquitt, J. A., 54n, 111n, 195n, 196n, 595n, 624n
Colvin, G., 131n
Conant, Douglas R., 422
Conchie, Barry, 568
Conger, J. A., 413n
Conlin, M., 214n, 436n, 572n, 610n–611n
Conlon, D. E., 196n
Connery, H., 155n
Consalvi, C., 298n
Conte, J. M., 266n
Coombs, T., 191n
Coons, A. E., 389n
Cooper, C., 301n
Cooper, C. L., 567, 642n
Cooper, Jarrod, 69
Copeland, J., 469n
Cosmides, L., 255n
Côté, S., 270n
Cottone, K., 220n
Coyle, Laurie, 330
Crant, J. M., 116n
Crawford, D., 525n
Cretul, Larry, 67
Cronin, Kevin, 240
Cropanzano, 253n
Cropanzano, R., 196n, 241n, 262n, 264n
Cruz, M. G., 303n
Culbert, S. A., 461n
Cullum, Leo, 454n
Curhan, J. R., 499n
Custer, H., 356n
Cutler, Jay, 584
Cyert, R. M., 455n

D
Daft, R. L., 367n, 368n
Dahle, C., 344n
Dalgaard, Lars, 130
Dalton, D. R., 222n
Daly, J. A., 370n
Damanpour, F., 634n
Damasio, A. R., 254n, 255n, 269n
Damasio, H., 269n
Dane, E., 149n
Darwin, Charles, 255, 616
Daus, C. S., 264n
Davidson, Diane, 546
Davidson, K. M., 155n
Davies, D. R., 49n
Davies, P. G., 145n
Davis, Gray, 665, 666
Davis, H. J., 202n
Davis, J. H., 304n, 424n
Davis, K., 359n, 360n
Davis, Vernon, 271

Dawson, C., 223n
Day, D. V., 113n, 114n, 436n, 587n
Deal, T. E., 475n, 556n
Dearborn, D. C., 142–143, 142n
Deaux, K., 259n
DeCenzo, D. A., 234n
de Charms, R., 182n
Deci, E. L., 182n, 184n
Decker, T., 266n
de Croon, E. M., 642n
De Dreu, C. K. W., 269n, 499n
Deeney, J. M., 286n
de Fruyt, F., 587n
de Hoogh, A. H. B., 416n
Deisenhammer, E. A., 50n
de Jonge, J., 638n
Delazer, M., 50n
Dell, Michael, 22
Deltas, G., 154n
DeMatteo, J. S., 338n
Denburg, N. L., 265n
den Dulk, L., 238n
den Hartog, D. N., 416n
Denison, D. R., 555n
Denny, Morgan, 611
DePaulo, B. M., 261n
Descartes, R., 252n
DeShon, R. D., 186n
DeShon, R. P., 469n
Dess, G. G., 537n
Deutschman, A., 546n
DeVader, C. L., 433n
DeVoe, S. E., 184n
Dickson, M. W., 308n
Diefendorff, J. M., 79n
Diener, E., 85n, 256n, 268n, 271n
Diener, M., 85n
Dienesch, R. M., 398n
Digh, P., 161n
Dill, F., 298n
DiMicco, Dan, 545
Dionne, S. D., 435n
Dipboye, R. L., 21n, 589n
Dirks, K. T., 329n
Dobbs, K., 593n
Doctoroff, Dan, 204
Dolan, Peter, 439, 510–511
Dolan, S. L., 554n
Dominguez, A., 505n
Donald, Jim, 365
Dorfman, P., 437n
Dorfman, P. W., 398n
Dormann, C., 638n
Dossett, D. L., 52n
Douglas, C., 458n
Downer, Alexander, 111
Drake, A. R., 15
Drasgow, F., 459n
Drasgow, R., 238n
Drewniak, Joann, 350

Drexler, A. B., 339n
Drickhamer, D., 235n
Dror, 462n
Drucker, Peter, 567n–568n
Duchon, D., 399n, 570n
Duffy, Michelle, 207
Dukerich, J. M., 433n
Dulye, L., 355n
Dumaine, B., 636n
Dumas, T. L., 605n
Dunagan, M., 644n
Dunham, R. B., 80n
Dunn, Patricia, 376
Dunnette, M. D., 6n, 45n, 114n
Dunning, D., 150n
Dunning, Kitty, 457
Durand, Douglas, 167–168
Durlach, P., 270n, 489n
Dutton, J., 25n
Dutton, J. E., 623n
Dvorak, P., 354n, 504n, 541n, 573n
Dyer, W., 630n, 631n

E
Eagly, A. H., 430n
Earl, Donna, 276
Earley, P. C., 185n, 186n, 607n
Early, P. C., 127n
Eaton, J., 304n
Eberhardt, J. L., 145n
Eby, E. T., 429n
Eby, L. T., 338n, 430n, 557n
Ecklund, Erik, 550
Eden, D., 146n, 399n, 437n
Edens, P. S., 594n
Edwards, J. E., 630n
Edwards, John, 388
Ehrhart, M. G., 24n, 640n
Ehrlich, S. B., 433n
Eid, M., 271n
Eisenberger, R., 81n, 82n
Eisenhower, Dwight, 441
Eisinger, J., 242n
Eisner, Michael, 417
Ekman, P., 252n, 260n
Elfenbein, H. A., 260n, 265n, 272n, 499n
Elias, M., 53n, 155n
Elliot, A. J., 184n
Elliott, E. K., 268n
Ellis, A. P. J., 331n, 469n
Ellison, Larry, 113, 388
Ellison, S., 459n
Elman, N. S., 429n
Elms, H., 297n
Elshafi, Motaz, 53
Emerson, R. E., 454n
Engelbrecht-Wiggans, R., 154n
Engemann, K. M., 589n
Ensari, N., 433n
Ensher, E. A., 594n

Erez, A., 88n, 111n, 112n, 268n, 297n, 624n
Erez, M., 91n, 161n, 186n
Erickson, P. B., 350n
Esterl, M., 525n
Evans, G. W., 640n
Evans, Todd, 233–234

F

Face, Andrew, 242–243
Fahr, J., 89n
Falbe, C. M., 457n
Falk, S., 64n
Fanelli, A., 417n
Farrell, D., 87n, 461n, 464n
Fast, J., 357n
Fastow, Andrew, 142, 305
Faure, C., 308n
Faust, Drew Gilpin, 622
Favre, Brett, 584
Fayol, Henri, 6, 6n
Fedor, D. B., 624n
Feild, H. S., 330n
Fein, M., 219n, 230n
Feist, G. J., 111n, 158n
Feldman, D. C., 561n
Felsenthal, E., 494n
Ference, R., 304n
Ferris, G. R., 49n, 458n, 467n, 469n, 471n, 473n
Festinger, Leon, 76–77
Fiedler, F. E., 390n, 393n, 395n
Fiedler, Fred, 392–395
Field, H. S., 644n
Finder, A., 622n
Fine, G. A., 360n
Fineman, S., 570n
Fink, C. F., 299n
Finkelstein, S., 538n
Fiorina, Carly, 143, 417, 439
Fischhoff, B., 150n
Fisher, A. K., 39n
Fisher, C. D., 263n
Fisher, G. G., 258n
Fisher, Martyn, 230
Fiss, P. C., 623n
Flanders, Scott, 430
Fleischhacker, W. W., 50n
Fleishman, E. A., 47n
Flint, J., 587n
Florida, R., 158n
Flynn, F. J., 386n
Flynn, James, 68
Foley, Jeremy, 436
Folger, R., 196n
Fong, E., 297n
Fong, S. C. L., 238n
Foote, N., 302n
Ford, Bill, 498, 517–518
Ford, Henry, 404

Ford, Henry, II, 564
Ford, J. K., 51n
Foreman, Ed, 96
Forrester, R., 339n
Forstmann, Teddy, 112
Foss, S., 611n
Fost, D., 387n
Foster, C. A., 113n
Foti, R. J., 110n
Foulkes, N., 456n
Frankel, L. P., 254n
Fraser, Douglas, 676
Frederick, W. C., 119n
Freeman, David, 379
Freeman, Howard, 131
Freeman, R. B., 87n
French, J. R. P., Jr., 452n
Frey, B. S., 92n
Friedman, A., 194n
Friedman, Milton, 665–666
Friedman, R., 489n
Friedman, R. A., 111n, 501n
Friedman, S. D., 605n
Friesen, W. V., 260n
Frieswick, K., 232n
Frijda, N. H., 241n, 272n
Frings-Dresen, M. H. W., 642n
Frink, D. D., 467n
Frost, P. J., 414n, 437n
Frye, Charlie, 584
Frye, N., 259n
Fryer, B., 365n
Fu, P. P., 458n, 472n, 473n
Fuller, J. A., 258n
Fulmer, I. S., 5n
Fumarelli, Thomas, 504

G

Gaertner, S., 50n, 52n, 194n
Gage, Phineas, 254–255
Galang, M. C., 467n
Gale, S. F., 558n
Galinsky, A. D., 463n, 497n, 498n, 502n
Gan, R., 415n
Ganzach, Y., 47n
Garbato, D., 673n
Garcia, Anne, 228
Garcia, J. E., 395n
Garcia, S., 554n
Gardner, Chris, 173–174
Gardner, Rich, 174
Gardner, W. L., 254n, 469n
Garnett, Terry, 249–250
Gates, Bill, 256, 360, 360n, 559, 602, 602n, 673–675
Gatewood, R. D., 52n
Gavin, J. H., 337n
Geber, B., 338n
Geenwald, J., 274–275n
Geier, J. G., 386n

Geis, F. L., 112n
Gelfand, M. J., 91n, 161n, 505n
Gellatly, I. R., 52n
George, J. F., 286n
George, J. M., 268n
Gerberding, Julie, 452
Gerhart, B., 5n
Gersick, C. J. G., 288n
Gerstner, Lou, 543
Gettelfinger, Ron, 498
Geyelin, M., 494n
Ghiselli, E. E., 587n
Giacobbe-Miller, J. K., 202n
Giacobbi, P. R., 259n
Gibson, D. E., 241n
Gigone, D., 303n
Gil, A., 667n
Gilbert, D., 151n
Gilbert, D. T., 258n
Giles, W. F., 330n
Gilmartin, Raymond, 439
Gilmore, D. C., 469n, 473n
Gilson, R. L., 81n
Ginnett, R. C., 287n
Ginsburg, David, 138
Gist, M. E., 502n
Glader, P., 545n
Gladwell, Malcolm, 153
Glasman, L. R., 77n
Glass, David, 671, 672
Glenn, E. S., 505n
Glomb, T. M., 262n, 640n
Goates, N., 489n
Goelzer, P., 555n
Goggins, Sara, 578
Gogoi, P., 384n
Gold, Jack, 526
Goldman, B. M., 197n
Goleman, D., 361n
Goleman, Daniel, 264n
Gomez-Mejia, L. R., 233n
Gonzalez, David, 155–156
Goodenow, Bob, 511
Goodman, P. S., 193n, 194n, 228n
Gordon, J., 365n, 633n
Gordon, W. J. J., 160n
Gore, Wilbert L., 545–546
Górska-Kołodziejczyk, Elżbieta, 568
Gosling, S. D., 107n
Gottfredson, L. S., 45n
Graen, G., 399n
Grandey, A., 260n
Grandey, A. A., 262n, 269n
Granovetter, M., 424n
Grant, A. M., 220n
Grant-Vallone, E., 594n
Grassley, Charles, 168
Grawitch, M. J., 268n
Gray, H. M., 268n
Gray, S., 484n

Grayson, C., 155n
Green, Bill, 362
Green, S. G., 273n, 399n
Greenberg, Hank, 417
Greenberg, J., 195n, 299n, 417n
Greene, C. N., 86n
Greene, K., 48n
Greengard, S., 646n
Greenhaus, J. H., 605n
Greenstein, F. I., 264n
Greer, Frank, 217–218
Gregersen, H., 116n
Grensing-Pophal, L., 560n
Griffeth, R. W., 50n, 52n, 90n
Griffin, R. W., 158n
Grossman, Rex, 584
Grow, B., 131n, 434n
Grube, J. A., 80n
Grubman, Jack, 476
Gruenfeld, D. H., 463n, 497n
Gruhl, Dan, 476
Guilbault, R. L., 153n
Guion, R. M., 89n
Gumbel, P., 557n
Gunj, Ljubica, 44
Gunnthorsdottir, A., 301n
Gurchiek, K., 83n, 354n, 362n, 471n
Gurtner, A., 336n
Guynn, J., 131n

H

Haaland, S., 555n
Hachiya, D., 90n
Hackett, R. D., 49n, 89n
Hackman, J. R., 216n, 219n, 241n, 642n
Hackman, J. Richard, 215
Hagemark, Bent, 74
Hai, Alexandra, 43–44
Hall, D. T., 79n
Hall, J., 494n
Hall, J. A., 259n
Hall, Kevin, 566
Hambley, L. A., 431n
Hambrick, D. C., 560n
Hamby, Sherry, 207
Hamm, S., 187n, 554n
Hammond, J. S., 150n
Hammond, Larry, 568
Hampson, E., 116n
Hance, Steve, 213
Haney, C., 291n–292n
Hanges, P., 437n
Hanisch, K. A., 91n
Hannan, M. T., 623n
Hanson, C. G., 233n
Hanson, T. J., 588n
Harkins, S. G., 300n

Harpaz, I., 202n
Harris, P. R., 309n
Harris, S. G., 644n
Harrison, D. A., 78n, 92n, 116n, 329n, 337n
Harrison, J. K., 601n
Hartel, C. E. J., 264n
Harter, J. K., 81n, 568n, 569n
Harter, L. M., 81n
Hartke, D. D., 395n
Harvey, O. J., 298n
Hasselbeck, Matt, 584
Hastie, R., 151n, 303n
Hastings, R., 130n
Hastings, R. R., 38n, 53n
Hauenstein, M. A., 110n
Hausenblas, H. A., 259n
Hauserman, N., 459n
Hausknecht, J. P., 587n
Hawn, C., 316, 316n
Hayes, T. L., 81n
Hays, K., 305n
Healy, P. D., 622n
Heaphy, E., 25n
Heath, C., 11n
Heidmets, L., 121n
Heine, S. J., 472n
Helfrich, David, 250
Helft, M., 74n
Heller, D., 217n
Heller, F., 226n
Hempel, J., 401n
Henderson, N. B., 603n
Heneman, H. G., III, 169n
Henley, N. M., 357n
Henningsen, D. D., 303n
Herbert, T. T., 202n
Herold, D. M., 624n
Herrnstein, R. J., 587n
Hersey, Paul, 395–396
Hershey, J. C., 427n
Hertel, G., 337n
Herzberg, Frederick, 178–180
Hess, K., 335n
Hetland, H., 421n
Higgins, C. A., 105n, 471n, 635n
Higgins, M., 505n
Highhouse, S., 629n
Hill, T. E., 375n
Hiller, N. J., 113n
Hilton, J. L., 144n
Hilton, Paris, 388
Hinings, C. R., 627n
Hira, N. A., 121n
Hirneise, Linda, 167
Hirschfeld, R. R., 330n
Hirschhorn, L., 360n
Ho, S. S., 195n
Hoch, S. J., 510n
Hochschild, A. R., 261n

Hochwarter, W. A., 467n, 473n
Hodgson, G., 645n
Hoffman, B. J., 88n
Hoffman, L. R., 501n
Hoffman, R. L., 494n
Hofstede, Geert, 124–126, 124n, 201n
Hogan, R., 128n
Hoge, W., 28n
Holden, E. W., 50n
Holladay, C. L., 190n
Holland, Christopher, 284
Holland, Dick, 517
Holland, J. L., 122n
Holland, John, 122–123
Holland, K., 91n, 600n
Hollenbeck, J. R., 154n, 186n, 331n
Hollon, J., 407n
Holman, D., 254n
Holmes, J. G., 424n
Holz, M., 273n
Hom, P. W., 50n, 52n
Hom, W., 80n, 90n
Honda, Soichiro, 660–661
Hornstein, Harvey, 206
Hosmer, L. T., 424n
House, R. J., 127n, 180n, 199n, 385n, 396n, 400n, 414n, 415n, 416n, 421n, 437n
House, Robert, 385, 396–397, 413, 421
Howard, J. L., 467n
Howard, Kevin, 305
Howell, J. M., 414n, 423n, 437n, 635n
Howell, J. P., 398n
Hsu, Ancle, 531–532
Hu, L., 311n
Huang, X., 236n
Huang, Y.-M., 269n
Huard, Damon, 584
Hudy, M. J., 84n
Hulin, C., 459n
Hulin, C. L., 80n, 90n, 91n, 186n
Humphrey, R. H., 250n, 269n, 272n
Humphrey, S. E., 154n, 331n, 334n
Hundley, Debra, 296
Hundley, K., 255n
Hunt, C. S., 261n
Hunter, J. E., 49n, 109n
Hurst, C., 86n
Huws, U., 223n
Huy, Q. N., 624n
Hyatt, D. E., 326n, 328n, 334n
Hymowitz, C., 362n, 430n, 522n, 528n

I

Iacocca, Lee, 416–417
Iaffaldano, M. T., 86n
Icahn, Carl, 484
Ilgen, D. R., 331n, 334n
Ilies, R., 217n, 268n, 270n, 386n, 395n, 422n, 459n

Immelt, Jeffrey, 5, 25, 130, 406
Imus, Don, 370–371
Inesi, M. E., 463n
Isen, A. M., 159n, 258n, 268n, 270n, 489n
Ivancevich, J. M., 186n, 601n
Iyengar, S. S., 184n

J

Jackson, Andrew, 441
Jackson, C. L., 191n
Jackson, S. E., 646n
Jackson, T., 161n
Jackson, Tarvaris, 584
Jaffe, D., 291n–292n
Jago, A. G., 400n
James, L. R., 107n, 435n
James, LeBron, 453
James, N., 259n
Jang, K. L., 106n
Janis, I. L., 114n, 304n
Janssen, O., 638n
Jarcho, J., 644n
Jauman, Scott, 213
Javidan, M., 127n, 437n
Jayne, M. E. A., 21n
Jay-Z, 453
Jefferson, Thomas, 423, 441
Jehn, K. A., 337n
Jermier, J. M., 434n, 435n
Jesperson, Daryl, 344
Jessup, L. M., 286n
Jewell, Sally, 390
Ji, David, 531–532
Jin, 144
Joan of Arc, 404
Jobs, Steve, 386, 404–405, 413–415, 417
Jodoin, David, 349
John, O. P., 107n
Johnsen, T. B., 421n
Johnson, A. B., 360n
Johnson, D., 640n
Johnson, D. E., 88n
Johnson, M. D., 222n, 264, 334n
Johnson, S. I., 145n
Johnson, Samuel C., 384
Johnson, Tamra, 366
Johnson, William R., 484
Johnson-George, C., 424n
Johnston, Larry, 95–96
Johst, Hanns, 548
Jones, J. R., 642n
Jordan, M. H., 330n
Jorm, A. F., 50n
Judge, T. A., 31n, 86n, 88n, 105n, 112n,
    113n, 169n, 191n, 217n, 259n,
    268n, 270n, 386n, 388n, 395n,
    420n, 421n, 471n, 587n
Judt, T., 121n
Jundt, D., 334n
Jung, D. I., 420n

K

Kacmar, K. M., 49n, 467n
Kafka, Franz, 516
Kahn, Cheryl, 406, 649n
Kahn, R., 390n
Kahneman, D., 149n
Kamin, A. M., 79n
Kammeyer-Mueller, J. D., 262n, 640n
Kamprad, Ingvar, 559
Kanazawa, Michael, 566
Kanhold, K., 373n
Kanter, Rosabeth Moss, 204, 450n, 473n
Kanungo, R. N., 413n
Kark, B., 415n
Karnitschnig, M., 373n
Karp, J., 436n
Katerberg, R., 80n
Katigbak, M. S., 124n
Katz, D., 390n
Katz, N., 341n
Katz, R. L., 8n
Katz, Robert, 8
Katzenbach, J. R., 323n
Kay, Ira, 242
Keeney, R. L., 150n
Keeping, L. M., 602n
Keirlin, Robert A., 560
Kekorian, Kirk, 484, 493n
Kelleher, Herb, 417, 552, 559
Keller, R. T., 79n, 421n
Kelley, H. H., 141n
Kelly, J., 431n
Kelner, S., 267n
Kemmler, G., 50n
Kennedy, A. A., 556n
Kennedy, D. A., 107n, 264
Kennedy, J. C., 458n
Kennedy, John F., 413, 423, 482
Kennedy, R. B., 107n
Kerr, N. L., 307n
Kerr, S., 434n, 435n
Kesmodel, D., 441
Kidd, Jason, 320
Kiefer, P., 44n
Kiely, J., 645n
Kiely, M., 357n
Kiesler, C. A., 294n
Kiesler, S. B., 294n
Kiewitz, C., 467n
Kifner, J., 663n
Kilduff, M., 114n, 115n
Kiley, D., 518n
Kim, D. H., 635n
Kim, H. S., 644n
King, L., 268n
King, Martin Luther, Jr., 413, 415, 423
Kirkpatrick, S. A., 386n, 421n, 440n
Kirn, S. P., 27–28n
Kitchen, P., 271n
Klein, Calvin, 113

Klein, H. J., 111n, 186n
Klein, K. J., 24n, 640n
Kleinfeld, Klaus, 525
Klimoski, R. J., 562n
Kline, T. J. B., 431n
Klineberg, S. L., 51n
Knight, Bobby, 256
Knight, Philip, 383–384
Knowles, Beyoncé, 453
Koeppel, D., 406
Kofman, F., 636n
Kogan, N., 114n
Koh, W., 79n, 421n
Kolb, D. A., 594n
Kolodinsky, R. W., 473n
Komaki, J. L., 191n
Konovsky, M. A., 89n
Konradt, U., 337n
Koogle, Tim, 493n
Koopman, P. L., 416n
Kopelman, S., 501n
Korman, William A., 378–379
Korsgaard, A. M., 237n
Kotter, J. P., 385n, 623n, 627n
Kotter, John, 385, 627–628
Kouzes, J. M., 425n
Kouzes, James, 410
Kowaleski, Thomas, 677
Kowalski, R. M., 469n
Kozlowski, Dennis, 417, 422
Kraatz, M. S., 297n
Kraimer, M. L., 116n
Kraut, A. I., 6n
Kravitz, D. A., 51n
Kray, L. J., 197n, 502n
Kreitner, R., 54n
Krell, T. C., 463n
Krensavage, Michael, 449–450
Kreth, Kelly, 364
Kristof, 470n
Kruger, J., 150n
Ku, G., 498n
Kumar, K., 340n
Kunreuther, H. C., 510n
Kurtz, Tony, 97
Kwon, S., 499n
Kwong, J. Y. Y., 152n

L

Labedo, O. J., 472n
Labich, K., 49n, 557n
Labroo, A. A., 270n, 489n
Lachnit, C., 587n
Laffey, A. G., 187, 240, 418
LaGanke, J., 308n
Lagarde, Christine, 502
Laland, K. N., 256n
Lam, S. S. K., 302n
Lambert, T. A., 557n
Lamborghini, Ferruccio, 456

Landrum, G. N., 108n
Landy, F. J., 49n, 266n
Langan-Fox, J., 353n
Lange, Eric, 243
Langford, P. H., 9n
Lanza, Frank, 436
Lapedis, D., 220n
Lapointe, J., 512n
Larsen, R. J., 256n
Larson, Gary, 371n
Larson, J., 155n
Latham, G. P., 185n, 299n, 440n
Laursen, B., 111n
Lavidor, M., 258n
Law, K. S., 265n
Lawler, E. J., 461n
Lawler, J. J., 238n
Lawrence, K. A., 623n
Lay, Ken, 142, 305
Lazarus, Shelly, 426
Lazear, Ed, 233
Leach, D. J., 639n
Leary, M. R., 469n
Leavitt, H. J., 31–32n
Ledford, G. E., Jr., 231n
Lee, B., 15
Lee, C., 81n
Lee, Kate, 81n, 220n, 270n, 283, 460n
Lee, R., 49n
Lee, R. T., 262n, 468n
Lee, S., 111n
Leftwich, Byron, 584
Lei, L., 497n, 502n
Leinart, Matt, 584
Lengel, R. H., 367n, 368n
Lentz, E., 429n, 430n
Leo, J., 371n
Leonard, B., 53n
Leong, J. L. T., 473n
LePine, J. A., 54n, 88n, 111n, 113n, 388n, 595n, 624n, 638n
LePine, M. A., 638n
Lescornez, Philippe, 568–569
Leung, K., 195n
Lev, Marty, 74
Leventhal, G. S., 195n
Levitz, J., 242n
Levy, P. E., 602n
Levy, R. I., 272n
Lewin, Kurt, 625–627
Lewis, J. D., 424n
Lewis, K. M., 268n
Lewis, M., 69n
Liao, H., 273n
Lichtenstein, S., 150n
Liden, R., 399n
Liden, R. C., 398n
Lidsky, D., 364n
Lieberman, Rhonda, 296
Lieberman, S., 290n

Lincoln, Abraham, 404, 441
Lisco, C. C., 489n
Liska, L. Z., 398n
Littman, M., 235n
Livesley, W. J., 106n
Lizzette, L., 430n
Locke, E. A., 64n, 89n, 185n, 186n, 191n, 386n, 421n, 440n, 626n
Locke, Edwin, 185
Lockwood, N. R., 81n
Loehlin, J. C., 106n
Loewenstein, G., 269n
Long, Jerry, 406
Longfellow, George, 350
Lopez, George, 343
Lord, R. G., 79n, 433n
Löscher, Peter, 525
Losman, J. P., 584
Lowenstein, R., 677n
Loyd, D. L., 310n
Lublin, J. S., 242n, 459n, 511n, 560n
Lucas, H. C., Jr., 533n
Luke, Jacob, 232
Lunsford, J. L., 423n
Luthans, F., 8n, 25n, 54n, 62n, 63n, 188n, 237n, 663n
Luthans, Fred, 8
Lux, S., 458n
Lyubomirsky, S., 268n

M
Maccoby, M., 113n
Machiavelli, Niccolo, 112
MacKenzie, S. B., 31n
Mackey, John, 441
Madjar, N., 268n
Maeriac, J. P., 88n
Magee, J. C., 463n, 497n
Mahar, L., 393n
Mainous, A. G., III, 87n
Majchrzak, A., 326n
Major, V. S., 24n, 640n
Makary, Martin, 329
Malhotra, A., 326n
Malmendier, U., 112n
Malone, John, 416
Man, D., 302n
Mandela, Nelson, 386
Manix, Sue, 222–223
Mann, L., 114n
Manning, Dennis, 102
Manning, Eli, 584
Manning, M. R., 641n
Manning, Peyton, 584
Mannix, E., 310n, 332n
Mannix, E. A., 503n
Manstead, A. S. R., 269n
Mao Zedong, 386
March, J. G., 148n, 455n
Marchionne, Sergio, 621

Margerison, C., 331n
Mark, Reuben, 232, 406
Markels, A., 653n
Markham, S. E., 235n
Marriott, Bill, 77
Marsalis, Wynton, 289
Marshall, J., 642n
Martin, L. L., 268n
Martin, Yiesha, 38
Martocchio, J. J., 238n
Maslow, Abraham, 176–177
Mason, P. A., 560n
Mathieu, J. E., 336n
Matson, E., 302n
Matsumoto, D., 272n
Matthews, G., 49n
Matthews, V., 564n
Maue, B., 154n
Maurer, T., 58n
Maurer, T. J., 54n
Mausner, B., 178n
Maxfield, M., 417n
May, D. R., 81n
Mayer, J. D., 264n
Mayer, R. C., 424n
Maynard, M., 643n
Mayo, Elton, 292–293
Mayo, Mike, 198
Mazerolle, M. D., 107n
McAlister, A., 121n
McAllister, Paul, 679–680
McAndrew, F. T., 589n
McCall, Scott, 672
McCann, D., 331n
McCarthy, S., 12n
McClellan, E. L., 50n
McClelland, D. C., 180n, 181n, 267n
McClelland, David, 180–181
McCormick, D. W., 572n
Mccown, Josh, 584
McCrae, R. R., 107n
McCroskey, J. C., 370n
McDevitt, Kelly, 213
McDivitt, Kristine, 418
McDonald, Andrew, 364
McDonald, Bob, 477
McDonough, J. J., 461n
McEvoy, G. M., 49n
McFarland, L., 605n
McGee, Linda, 406
McGehee, W., 54n
McGrath, R. G., 524n
McGregor, Douglas, 177, 177n, 424n
McGregor, J., 250n, 322n
McGrew, J. F., 286n
McGuire, Martha, 283
McGuire, Tim, 487
McGuire, Will, 439
McInally, Pat, 584
McIntyre, Joyce, 113

McKee, G. H., 235n
McKenna, D. D., 6n
McKersie, R. B., 496n
McKinnell, Henry, 439
McLaughlin, Edward, 578
McMahon, J. T., 186n
McNabb, Donovan, 584
McNair, Steve, 584
McNerney, James, 25, 130, 423, 439
Medlen, Paul, 38, 39
Medsker, G. J., 222n, 334n
Meglino, B. M., 117n, 237n
Mehra, A., 115n
Mehrabian, A., 357n
Meindl, J. R., 433n
Mellon, Jerry, 182
Meloy, M. G., 148n
Mencken, H. L., 658
Mendenhall, M. E., 463n
Merianne Liteman, 344
Merkle, George, 271
Mero, N. P., 194n
Merritt, J., 25n
Mesch, D. J., 222n
Mesquita, B., 272n
Metz, Mark, 321
Meyer, C. J., 334n
Meyer, J. P., 79n, 185n
Meyer, L. L., 501n
Meyer, Urban, 436
Meyers, Myles, 38
Michaelsen, L. K., 340n
Michaelson, Larry, 67
Milgram, Stanley, 661–663
Miller, D. J., 202n
Miller, E. K., 259n
Miller, J. D., 154n
Miller, M. D., 370n
Miller, M. L., 303n
Milliman, J., 608n
Milliman, J. F., 572n
Mills, J. A., 56n
Miner, J. B., 181n
Mintzberg, H., 6–8, 7n, 455n, 461n, 526n
Mirabile, M., 584n
Misangyi, V., 417n
Mitchell, T. R., 351n
Moberg, D. J., 157n
Moede, W., 300n
Mohr, L. A., 89n
Mohrman, A. M., Jr., 608n
Monroe, Marcel, 232
Moon, H., 154n, 331n
Moore, D. A., 497n
Moore, J. E., 12n
Moorhead, G., 304n
Moorman, R. H., 89n
Moran, R. T., 309n
Moregeson, F. P., 588n
Morgan, H. J., 252n

Morgan, John, 546
Morgan, P. M., 499n
Morgenson, G., 450n
Morgeson, F. P., 222n, 422n
Morris, B., 667n
Morris, David, 602–603
Morris, Saul, 602–603
Morrison, E. W., 562n
Moscoso, S., 46n, 587n, 589n
Motowidlo, S. J., 641n
Mount, M. K., 109n, 331n, 587n
Mouton, J. S., 390n, 632n
Mowday, R. T., 194n, 554n
Muchinsky, M., 86n
Muchinsky, P. M., 199n
Mueller, S. L., 202n
Mulally, Alan, 37–38, 242, 517–18
Mulcahy, Anne, 354, 526
Mullen, B., 301n, 311n
Mumford, T. V., 222n
Munson, J. M., 118n
Munson, L. J., 459n
Munz, D. C., 268n
Muoio, A., 594n
Murakami, F., 505n
Murdoch, Rupert, 404, 416
Murnighan, J. K., 498n
Murphy, Allison, 233–234
Murphy, Frank, 676
Murphy, S. E., 433n
Murray, A., 439n
Murray, C., 587n
Murtha, Narayana, 429
Musch, J., 154n
Muse, L. A., 644n

N

Nader, Fred, 477
Nadler, S., 431n
Nagele, C., 336n
Nagourney, E., 329n
Nahrgang, J. D., 422n
Nam, S., 160n
Namie, Gary, 206
Nanus, B., 424n
Naquin, C. E., 339n, 432n, 499n
Nardelli, Robert, 130, 391–392, 434
Nathan, B. R., 608n
Neale, M. A., 310n, 332n
Neck, C. P., 304n, 572n
Neeleman, David, 167
Neering, P., 667n
Nelson, D. L., 567, 640n
Nelton, S., 272n
Nesselroade, J. R., 259n
Neubert, M. J., 331n
Newby-Clark, I. R., 76n
Newman, D. A., 78n, 92n
Ng, K. Y., 196n
Nguyen, D., 459n

Nichols, E., 340n, 355n
Nicholsen, G., 587n
Nicholson, N., 66n
Nielson, T. R., 594n
Nieminen, Hannu, 645n
Nietzsche, Friedrich, 282
Nilekani, Nandan, 429
Nisbett, R. E., 51n
Nishii, L. H., 505n
Nixon, Richard, 264
Noah, Joakim, 258
Nocera, J., 76n, 198n
Noe, R. A., 54n, 595n
Nolen-Hoeksema, S., 155n
Nooyi, Indra, 108

O

Obama, Barack, 406–407
O'Connor, E. J., 225n
O'Connor, K. M., 269n
Odbert, H. S., 107n
O'Donnell, Trish, 466
Ohanian, L., 206n
Oishi, S., 271n
Okumura, T., 503n, 505n
Oldham, G. R., 220n, 241n, 268n, 642n, 659n
Oldham, Greg, 215–217
O'Leary, George, 474
O'Leary-Kelly, 296n
Olekalns, M., 489n
O'Neill, R. M., 623n
O'Neill, T. A., 431n
Ones, D. S., 587n
Oreg, S., 624n
O'Reilly, C. A., III, 175n, 333n
O'Reilly, C. A., 217n
Organ, D. W., 30n, 88n, 89n
Orlando, Janet, 3–4
Ornstein, S., 195n
Ortega, J., 219n
Osborn, A. F., 306n
Ostroff, C., 88n, 193n
O'Sullivan, M., 260n
Owyang, M. T., 589n

P

Packard, J. S., 641n
Page, R., 605n
Palmeiro, Rafael, 69
Palmer, Carson, 584
Pan, P. P., 228n
Pandya, M., 404n
Papper, 334n
Park, J., 267n
Park, Reg, 665
Parker, G., 373n
Parker, S. K., 217n
Parrish, Russell, 129
Parsons, Emma, 276

Pasupathi, M., 259n
Patterson, Bill, 289–291
Patterson, Neal L., 366–368
Patton, G. K., 86n, 88n
Patton, G. R., 31n
Patton, George, 404
Paulson, G. D., 432n
Pavlov, Ivan P., 55, 55n
Payne, J. W., 151n
Pearson, C. M., 296n
Pearson, Jane, 192
Pedigo, P. R., 6n
Peltz, Nelson, 483–484
Peng, T. K., 458n
Penner, L. A., 462n
Pennington, Chad, 584
Penttila, C., 5n
Perez, William, 383
Perot, Ross, 551
Perrewé, P. L., 458n, 467n, 468n, 473n
Perrone, J., 276n
Perrow, C., 455n
Perry-Smith, J. E., 160n
Persaud, R., 110n
Peters, L. H., 225n, 395n
Peters, P., 238n
Peters, Tom, 21
Petersen, J. C., 461n, 464n
Peterson, M. F., 237n
Pfeffer, J., 450n, 462n, 473n
Phillips, K. W., 310n, 605n
Picascia, S., 254n
Piccolo, R. F., 86n, 421n
Piekstra, J., 105n
Pierce, B. D., 66n, 232n
Piper, Sandra, 350
Plattner, Hasso, 187
Plous, S., 150n
Podsakoff, N. P., 86n, 638n
Podsakoff, P. M., 31n, 89n, 421n, 453n
Pohlmann, J. T., 395n
Polidoro, Joe, 283
Polk, James, 441
Pólos, L., 623n
Pondy, L. R., 489n
Poole, M. S., 485n
Pope, Charles, 344
Popp, G. E., 202n
Popp, P. O., 52n
Porath, C. L., 296n
Porges, S., 401n
Porter, C. O. L. H., 196n
Porter, L. W., 554n
Posavac, E. J., 153n
Posner, B. Z., 118n, 425n
Posner, Barry, 410
Post, Albert, 330
Posthuma, R. A., 588n
Poteet, M. L., 430n
Potosky, D., 51n

Poverny, L. M., 254n
Powell, G. N., 51n
Pratkanis, A. R., 305n
Pratt, M. G., 149n, 268n, 565n
Prehar, C. A., 196n
Preontaine, Steve, 564
Press, Jim, 406
Prest, W., 185n
Price, K. H., 337n
Probst, T. M., 238n
Proust, Marcel, 2
Provico, Auglaize, 568
Pugh, S. D., 21n
Pulkkinen, L., 111n
Pusic, E., 226n
Puska, P., 121n
Putnam, L. L., 485n
Pyszczynski, T., 417n

Q

Quinn, Brady, 584
Quinn, J. B., 538n
Quinn, R., 25n
Quinn, R. T., 27–28n
Quiñones, M. A., 51n, 190n

R

Rabinowitz, S., 79n
Rafaeli, A., 259n, 565n
Raffo, A., 206n
Rai, S., 592n
Raiffa, H., 150n
Raines, Franklin, 439
Randolph, Kim, 141
Ransdell, E., 564n
Rapoport, A., 301n
Rashotte, L. S., 357n
Rau, R., 270n
Raven, B., 452n
Raver, J. L., 505n
Ravlin, E. C., 117n
Reade, Q., 508n
Reagan, Ronald, 264, 413, 441
Reb, J., 197n
Ree, M. J., 51n
Reed, John, 476
Reeves, M. P., 557n
Reichers, A. E., 84n
Rempel, J. K., 424n
Renard, M. K., 601n
Ressler, Cali, 214
Reuther, Victor, 676
Reynolds, Jim, 667, 668
Reynolds, N., 269n
Rhoades, L., 81n, 82n
Rhodes, K., 561n
Rice, Condoleeza, 111
Rich, B. L., 86n, 113n, 191n, 388n
Richard, O. C., 20n
Richardson, R. J., 414n

Ricketts, C., 550n
Rigby, Darrell, 578
Riketta, M., 80n
Ringelmann, Max, 300
Rioux, S. M., 462n
Rist, R. C., 191n
Rivers, Philip, 584
Robbin, Jeff, 674
Robbins, S. P., 150n, 163n, 234n, 491n, 492n
Robert, C., 238n
Roberts, B. W., 111n
Roberts, J. L., 416n, 453n
Roberts, L. M., 25n
Robinson, M. D., 110n
Robinson, S. L., 30n, 296n, 297n
Robison, J., 568n
Rodriguez, Oscar, 131–132
Roehm, Julie, 274, 361–362
Roethlisberger, Ben, 584
Rogelberg, S. G., 639n
Rogers, G., 87n
Rogerson, R., 206n
Rokeach, Milton, 117n, 118
Rolland, Filip, 587n
Rolland, J. P., 587n
Rommel, Jeff, 166
Romo, Tony, 584
Roosevelt, Franklin, 264, 386, 404, 416, 441
Roper-Batker, John, 229
Rosen, B., 326n
Rosen, Scott, 477
Rosette, A. S., 501n
Rosnow, R. L., 360n
Ross, Susan, 221–222
Roth, L., 92n, 114n
Roth, P. L., 51n, 78n
Rothbard, N. P., 605n
Rotter, J. B., 424n
Rotundo, M., 262n, 459n, 640n
Rousseau, D. M., 12n, 81n
Roznowski, M., 90n, 91n
Rubenstein, David, 103
Rucci, A. J., 27–28n
Ruddy, T. M., 326n, 328n, 334n
Rudolf, C. J., 225n
Ruiz-Quintanilla, S. A., 237n
Rupp, D. E., 270n
Rusbult, C. E., 87n
Ruskin, John, 103
Russell, D. W., 79n
Russell, JaMarcus, 584
Russell, S. S., 258n
Russo, J. E., 148n
Ryan, A. M., 51n, 469n, 605n
Ryan, K., 88n
Ryan, O., 67n
Ryan, R. M., 184n

S

Saavedra, R., 270n
Sacco, J. M., 51n
Sackett, P. R., 459n
Sagan, Carl, 254
Sage, Alan, 611n
Salancik, G. R., 184n
Salas, E., 311n
Salavich, Brad, 53
Salgado, J. F., 46n, 124n, 587n, 589n
Salovey, P., 264n
Salter, C., 167n
Salter, S. B., 15
Salzberg, Barry, 78
Sandal, G. M., 421n
Sandberg, J., 244n, 284n, 316n, 369n, 477–478
Sanders, R., 146n
Sanders, Zachery, 342
Sandomir, R., 112n
Sandström, P., 121n
Sandvik, E., 85n
Sarkozy, Nicholas, 502
Sartre, Jean Paul, 273
Sashkin, M., 436n
Saunders, Maddie, 342
Saunders, Mark, 259
Sawyer, J. E., 158n
Sayles, L. R., 284n
Schafer, Lu Ellen, 592
Schaub, Matt, 584
Schaubroeck, J., 642n
Schein, E. H., 558n, 559n, 561n, 562n, 630n
Schelhardt, T. D., 338n, 602n
Schendell, Laura, 234–235
Schendler, B., 675n
Schepman, S., 191n
Schettler, J., 561n
Scheu, C. R., 51n
Schiller, Michael, 369
Schindler, P. L., 424n
Schkade, D. A., 151n
Schlenker, B. R., 470n
Schlesinger, L. A., 623n
Schmidt, F. L., 49n, 81n, 109n, 587n
Schmitt, N., 51n
Schneider, B., 89n, 559n
Schneider, C. P., 177n
Schneider, Gary, 131
Schon, D. A., 635n
Schoorman, F. D., 424n
Schor, Juliet, 95
Schriesheim, C. A., 453n
Schultz, P. W., 121n
Schulze, W., 336n
Schutzman, Charlotte, 222–223
Schwartz, Jonathan, 363–364
Schwartz, N. D., 104n
Schwartz, R. D., 298n

Schwarzenegger, Arnold, 665–667
Schwarzman, Stephen, 103–104, 130
Schweitzer, M. E., 427n, 510n
Schwochau, S., 459n
Sciarrino, J. A., 588n
Sclavos, Stratton, 420–421
Scollon, C. Napa, 271n
Scott, B., 191n
Scott, B. A., 259n
Scott, K. D., 50n, 89n, 235n
Scott, K. S., 5n
Scott, Lee, 671–673
Scott, Sir Walter, 474
Scott, W. E., 184n
Scott, W. G., 351n
Seers, A., 288n
Segal, Nancy, 106
Seibert, S. E., 116n
Seidenberg, Ivan G., 152
Seidlitz, L., 85n
Seijts, G. H., 299n, 336n
Selig, Bud, 69
Seligman, M. E. P., 85n
Seligson, Hannah, 271
Selye, H., 640n
Selznick, P., 551n
Semmer, N. K., 336n
Sendry, J., 463n
Senge, P. M., 636n
Shabbir, Mahnaz, 139
Shaffer, M. A., 116n, 238n
Shakespeare, William, 289
Shamir, B., 415n, 432n
Shani, A. B., 146n
Shapiro, D., 425n
Shapiro, H. J., 199n
Shaver, P. R., 252n
Shaw, George Barnard, 121
Shaw, J. C., 86n, 191n, 195n, 299n, 311n
Sheldon, K. M., 184n
Shellenbarger, S., 25n, 50n, 223n, 276–277n
Sheppard, B. H., 425n
Sheridan, J. E., 574n
Sherman, Barry, 510–511
Sherman, D. K., 644n
Sherman, M. P., 308n
Shiflett, S., 392
Shiv, B., 269n
Shleicher, D. J., 113n
Shonk, J. H., 324n
Siebel, Tom, 388
Silverman, E., 116n
Silverman, R. E., 366n
Silverstein, S., 459n
Simon, H. A., 142–143, 142n
Simpson, R. L., 353n
Sipe, Michael, 379
Sitkin, S. B., 11n
Skarlicki, D. P., 196n

Skelton, Clifford, 577
Skilling, Jeff, 305, 422
Skinner, B. F., 56–57, 56n, 66
Skorupski, Jessica, 350
Slack, T., 627n
Slater, William, 442
Sloan, Alfred, 676
Sloma, R. L., 632n
Slovic, P., 150n
Sluiter, J. K., 642n
Small, Lawrence M., 152
Smisek, Jeff, 232
Smith, Alex, 584
Smith, C. A., 79n
Smith, C. S., 95n
Smith, D. K., 323n
Smith, F. J., 89n, 90n
Smith, Fred, 559
Smith, J. J., 206n
Smith, K. G., 626n
Smith, Orin, 418
Smith, P. B., 296n
Smith, P. C., 258n
Smola, K. W., 119n
Smolinsky, Steve, 240
Snyder, M., 469n
Snyderman, B., 178n
Solomon, R. C., 252n, 253n, 261n
Solomon, S., 417n
Sommerfield, F., 494n
Song, F., 233n
Song, L. J., 265n
Sorensen, J. B., 557n, 626n
Sorenson, G., 370n
Spector, E., 84n
Spector, P. E., 90n
Spencer, D. G., 90n
Spencer, L. M. J., 267n
Spencer, S., 270n
Spirling, L. I., 110n
Spreitzer, G, 25n
Srivastava, S., 107n
St. Clair, L., 9n
Stajkovic, A. D., 54n, 62n, 63n, 188n, 237n, 663n
Stalker, G. M., 534n
Stanton, J. M., 224n, 258n
Staples, D. S., 309n
Staw, B. M., 152n, 659n
Steel, P., 460n
Steensma, H., 52n
Steers, R. M., 90n, 554n
Stefani, Gwen, 453
Stein, M. B., 106n
Steindl, J. R., 51n
Steiner, I. D., 335n
Stetler, David, 168
Stevens, C. K., 470n, 502n
Stevenson, K. A., 505n
Stewart, Julia, 235, 331n

Stewart, Martha, 271
Stewart, W. H., Jr., 114n
Stibal, J., 459n
Stockdale, M. S., 80n
Stogdill, R. M., 389n
Stonecipher, Harry, 439
Stoute, Steve, 453
Stover, Elaine, 129
Strauss, G., 226n
Strauss, J. P., 109n
Stringer, Howard, 416
Stuhlmacher, A. F., 501n, 502n
Sturman, M. C., 29n
Sullivan, Michael, 167
Summers, Lawrence, 621–622
Sundstrom, E., 338n
Surowiecki, J., 13n
Sutton, C., 640n
Sutton, C. D., 119n
Swann, W. B., Jr., 360n
Swap, W., 424n
Sweeney, Anne, 180
Sy, T., 270n
Symons, C., 311n
Szymanski, K., 300n

T

Taber, T. D., 399n
Taggar, S., 336n
Tait, Richard, 559
Takagi, K., 644n
Take Ko, 243
Talleyrand, 382
Tamir, M., 110n
Tan, C. S. F., 424n
Tan, H. H., 424n
Tang, T. L., 226n
Tanikawa, M., 606n
Tannen, D., 370n
Tapon, F., 233n
Tarantino, Quentin, 159
Tasa, K., 336n
Tate, G., 112n
Taub, J., 621n
Taylor, G. S., 89n
Taylor, M. S., 601n
Taylor, R. N., 114n
Taylor, S., 644n
Teachout, M. S., 51n
Tellegen, A., 253n
Tepper, Bennett, 207
Tett, R. P., 128n
Thacker, Roy, 38
Thatcher, Margaret, 386
Thayer, S. K., 414n
Thierry, H., 416n
Thomas, C. C., 424n
Thomas, David A., 442
Thomas, E. J., 299n, 490, 491n, 499n
Thomas, K., 490n

Thomas, K. W., 79n, 485n, 506n
Thomas, M. D., 630n
Thomas, S. C., 587n
Thompson, C. A., 604n
Thompson, Jody, 214
Thompson, John, 147, 214
Thompson, L., 501n, 502n
Thoresen, C. J., 31n, 86n, 88n, 105n
Thornburg, L., 243n
Thornhill, S., 116n
Thornton, Nigel, 550
Timberlake, Justin, 453
Timmerman, T. A., 553n
Tindale, R. S., 307n, 499n
Tischler, L., 97n
Todorov, A., 146n
Toney, Mike, 38
Tong, K., 195n
Tooby, J., 255n
Toosi, M., 20n
Tosi, H. L., 417n
Totterdell, P., 270n
Toyama, M., 505n
Tracy, K. B., 601n
Tranel, D., 265n
Trang, Mark, 571
Treadway, D. C., 458n
Trevino, L. K., 25n, 368n, 423n, 592n
Trevor, C. O., 29n
Tribe, Laurence, 406–407
Trottman, M., 167n
Trougakos, J. P., 273n
Truch, E., 365n
Truman, Harry, 441
Trump, Donald, 114
Tsai, W.-C., 269n
Tschan, F., 336n
Tse, Irene, 96
Tsui, A. S., 9n
Tuckman, B. W., 286n
Turezyn, Virginia, 316
Turner, M. E., 305n
Turner, Ted, 414
Twain, Mark, 248
Twenge, Jean, 240
Tynan, R. O., 339n
Tyson, Lynn, 442

U

Ulrich, M., 259n
Unckless, A. L., 113n
Unsworth, E., 238n
Useem, Michael, 316

V

Valasquez, M., 157n
Valle, M., 468n
van Breukelen, W., 52n
Vance, R. J., 81n
Vandebroek, Sophie, 455n

van den Berg, P. T., 416n
Vandenberghe, C., 185n
VandenHeuvel, A., 50n
van der Vlist, R., 52n
van der Weide, J. G., 416n
van der Zee, K. I., 105n, 588n
Van De Vlert, E., 236n
Van Kleef, G. A., 269n
Van Maanen, J., 561n, 562n
Van Rooy, D. L., 265n
Van Valen, Ellen, 48
Van Yperen, N. W., 638n
Vecchio, R., 399n
Vedantam, S., 52n
Veijo, A., 121n
Verney, T. P., 310n, 311n
Verquer, M. L., 123n
Vey, M. A., 273n
Vick, Michael, 584
Vickers, M. H., 276n
Victorov, V. I., 202n
Vigoda, E., 468n
Villa, J. R., 398n
Viswesvaran, C., 265n, 587n
Vleeming, R. G., 112n
von Hippel, W., 144n
Voss, K., 337n
Vowinkel, Ted, 296
Vroom, Victor H., 197n, 400, 400n

W

Wachner, Linda, 113, 391–392
Wageman, R., 334n
Wagner, R., 568n, 569n
Wagner, S. E., 123n
Wahba, M. A., 177n, 199n
Waldman, D. A., 416n, 417n
Wall, J. A., Jr., 495n, 501n, 503n
Wallach, M. A., 114n
Walsh, J. P., 375n
Walters, A. E., 501n, 502n
Walton, R. E., 496n
Walton, Sam, 564, 671
Wang, X., 648n
Wanous, J., 84n
Wanous, J. P., 219n
Ward, E. A., 452n
Warr, P. B., 639n
Washington, George, 441
Watson, C., 501n
Watson, D., 253n, 256n, 257n, 258n
Watson, W. E., 340n
Weaver, G. R., 25n, 592n
Weber, J., 119n, 384n, 436n
Weber, Max, 413
Week, Rena, 255
Wegman, Danny, 578
Wegman, John, 578
Wegman, Robert, 578
Wegman, Walter, 578

Weigert, A., 424n
Weill, Sanford, 476
Weingart, L. R., 336n, 499n
Weinstein, Elaine, 231
Weiss, E., 58n
Weiss, E. M., 50n
Weiss, H. M., 54n, 241n, 262n, 264n, 273n
Weiss, K., 604n
Weiss, L., 253n, 302n
Weiss, T., 654n
Welbourne, T. M., 233n
Welch, David, 462
Welch, Jack, 12, 25, 130, 240, 404–406, 417, 525, 532, 582, 652
Weldon, E., 336n
Weller, A., 258n
Wells, Mark, 213
Wells, S. J., 593n
Wenger, E., 302n
Werner, M., 386n
Werner, S., 194n
Wesson, M. J., 186n, 196n
West, B. J., 469n
Westhead, R., 512n
Wheeler, Janet, 442
Whitacre, Ed, 354
White, E., 227n, 231n, 233n, 343n, 566n
White, R., 66n
White, R. E., 116n
Whitehead, John, 418
Wicker, A. W., 76n
Wiener, L., 229n
Wiener, Y., 554n
Wigdor, L. A., 180n
Wiggins, J. A., 298n
Wilbur, E. R., 49n
Wild, E., 195n
Wildavsky, A., 155n
Wilde, Oscar, 42
Wilder, Colleen, 343
Wilemon, D., 327n
Wiley, J. W., 21n
Wilke, J. R., 441
Williams, C. R., 186n
Williams, Doug, 38
Williams, K. Y., 333n
Williams, M. S., 494n
Williams, R., 642n
Willis, J., 146n
Willness, C. R., 460n
Wilpert, B., 226n
Wilson, Gary, 129
Wilson, J. A., 429n
Wilson, T. D., 258n
Winter, D. G., 181n
Witmeyer, D., 505n
Witt, L. A., 127n
Wofford, J. C., 398n
Woggerman, Carrie, 38
Wojnaroski, P., 185n

Womack, Clint, 130
Womack, Sean, 274
Wong, C., 265n
Wong, C. S. K., 49n
Wong, J., 15
Wong, K. F. E., 152n
Wood, M. B., 592n, 598n
Wooden, M., 50n
Woodman, R. W., 158n
Woodruff, S., 288n
Woods, Tiger, 51, 152, 458
Woodyard, Chris, 19n
Workman, M., 22n
Wrenn, K., 58n
Wrenn, K. A., 54n
Wright, Bill, Jr., 383
Wright, P. M., 186n
Wright, T. A., 80n
Wright, W., 106n
Wrigley, William, Jr., 383
Wu, A., 420n
Wu, S. J., 252n
Wysocki, B., Jr., 229n

X

Xie, J. L., 642n
Xin, K. R., 9n
Xu, H., 499n

Y

Yamaguchi, S., 505n
Yammarino, F. J., 416n, 417n, 435n
Yang, J. L., 174n
Yetton, Phillip, 400
Young, Vince, 584
Youssef, C. M., 25n
Yukl, G., 457n, 458n, 472n
Yung, Chung Ju, 559
Yuriko, Otsuka, 298n

Z

Zaal, J. N., 105n
Zaccaro, S. J., 432n
Zajac, E. J., 623n
Zakaria, N., 327n
Zand, D. E., 424n, 427n
Zanna, M. P., 76n, 424n
Zapf, D., 273n
Zaslow, J., 442n
Zeidner, R., 362n
Zelezny, L., 121n
Zellner, W., 229n
Zernike, K., 622n
Zhao, H., 116n
Zhao, L., 309n
Zhou, J., 159n, 268n, 467n
Zhu, W., 79n, 421n
Zimbardo, P. G., 291n–292n
Zimbardo, Philip, 291
Zuckerberg, Mark, 363

Organization Index

A

AACSB International, 64
AAIPharmia, 450
Academy of Management, 663
Accenture, 362, 591
ADM, 53
Admiral, 569
Adobe Systems, 5
Advert, 669–671
AFLAC, 604
AFL-CIO, 544–545
AIG, 417
AirAsia, 573
AJet, 342
Alarm One, Inc., 3–4, 344
Albertsons, 95–96
Alcoa, 23, 564–565, 597
Alenia Aeronautica, 531
Allstate, 129
Alltel, 53
Amazon.com, 23
American Airlines, 166, 192, 226, 573, 631
American Cancer Society, 646
American Council on Education, 85
American Express, 21, 53, 89, 223, 386, 436, 653
American Psychological Association (APA), 663
American Society of Safety Engineers, 39
American Sociological Association, 663
American Steel & Wire, 231
America Online (AOL), 557–558
Amgen, 5, 549, 550
Amherst College, 658
Anheuser-Busch, 495
AOL (America Online), 557–558
AOL Technologies, 333
APA (American Psychological Association), 663
Apex Digital, 531
Apotex, 510–511
Applebee's International, 235, 242–243
Apple Computer, 108, 261, 364, 386, 405, 414, 415, 417, 541, 549, 673–675
Arizona State University, 129
A.T. Kearney, 557
AT&T, 108, 223, 354, 476, 533, 597
Auglaize Provico, 568
Aurora Café, 44
Autoliv, 218
Avon, 418, 603

B

Bain & Co., 364, 578
Baker & McKenzie, 502

Balliet's, 350
Bank of America (BOA), 129, 240, 577–578, 589
Bank of Floyd, 462
Bank One, 220
Baring Brothers Bank, 623
Bear Stearns & Co., 174
BellSouth, 354
Bentley Pharmaceutical, 449–450
Bertelsmann, 373
Best Buy, 213, 214, 609
Bethlehem Steel, 22
Blackstone Group, 103–104, 130, 525
BMW, 17, 326, 588
BOA (Bank of America), 129, 240, 577–578, 589
Boeing Company, 22, 130, 325–326, 418, 423, 439, 531, 541, 557, 565, 569
Bristol-Myers Squibb, 439, 487, 510–511
British Airways, 304
Broad Air Conditioning, 560
Broad's Furniture, 342
Burger King, 16, 344

C

Cabela's, 587
Cadbury Schweppes PLC, 483
Campbell Soup, 422
Canon, 298
Capital Alliance Partners, 97
Cara Program, 174
Carlyle Group, 103
Caterpillar, 23, 81, 535
Centers for Disease Control and Prevention (CDC), 452, 643
Cerner Corp., 366, 367–368
Cessna, 520
Champion Spark Plug, 232
Chanel, 436
Charles Schwab, 436, 646
Chicago Bulls, 258
CH2MHILL, 406
Chrysler Corp., 326, 391, 416. *See also* DaimlerChrysler
Cigna Corp., 228–229
Cingular, 354, 531
Cisco Systems, 5, 53, 405, 549, 593–594
Citigroup, 96, 108, 233–234, 476
CNN, 371, 414
Coast Guard, 190
Coca-Cola, 18, 430, 541, 603
Colgate-Palmolive, 232, 406
College Board, 611
Columbia University, 599, 663
Comedy Central, 364
Configuresoft Inc., 611
Container Store, 240
Continental Airlines, 232

Cranium, 559
Cytos Biotechnology, 396

D

DaimlerChrysler, 21, 38–39, 373
Dean Witter, 173–174
Dell Computer Company, 22, 23, 116, 416, 442, 500, 531
Deloitte & Touche, USA, 78
Delphi Delco Electronics, 287
Delta Airlines, 465, 652
Department of Defense, 334, 577
Descartes, René, 252
Deutsche Bank, 564
Diageo PLC, 373
Dial Corporation, 459
Dissero Partners, 566
Domino's, 23
Don Jagoda Associates, 457
Duff and Phelps, 37
Duke University, 599
Dunkin' Donuts, 138
DuPont, 440, 597, 646
DVS Shoe Co., 50

E

EA (Electronic Arts), 158
Eastman Kodak, 557
eBay, 265, 436
Eddie Bauer, 604
Edward Jones, 429
EEOC (Equal Employment Opportunity Commission), 138
Electronic Arts (EA), 158
Electronic Data Systems (EDS), 531, 551
Eli Lilly and Company, 221
Emerson Electric, 338
Emery Air Freight, 61–63
EMM Industries, 289, 290–291
Enron, 142, 167, 305, 417, 422
Equal Employment Opportunity Commission (EEOC), 138
Ericsson, 564
Ernst & Young, 30, 604, 609, 653
ExxonMobil, 16–17, 53, 573

F

Facebook, 312, 362–363
Factory Card & Party Outlet, 47
Fannie Mae, 439, 603
Fastenal Co., 560
Federal Bureau of Investigation (FBI), 557
FedEx, 89, 108, 559
Fiat Group Automobiles, 621
Firoian Café, 44
FleetBoston Financial, 577
Florida State University, 387
Ford Motor Co., 17, 23, 37–38, 182, 242, 326, 476, 498, 517–519, 536, 564, 570, 600

Four Seasons Hotels, 89
Freedom Communications, 430
Freescale Semiconductor, 38
Frito-Lay Corporation, 231

G

Gallup, 243
Garden of Eden, 144
Garnett & Helfrich Capital, 250
GEICO, 129
Gemological Institute of America, 131
Genentech, 569, 604
General Electric (GE), 5, 24–25, 95, 108, 130, 226, 240, 283, 405–406, 417, 437, 532–533, 569, 573, 596, 600, 652
General Foods, 322
General Motors (GM), 144, 155, 182, 201, 326, 364, 476, 493, 550, 675–677
GlaxoSmithKline, 259
Glazier Group, 406
Global Savvy, 592
Goldman Sachs, 96, 418
Good People Company, Ltd., 82
Google, 73–74, 130, 154, 364, 549–550
GTE, 633
Guardian Life Insurance Co., 102

H

H. J. Heinz Co., 53, 483–484
Habitat for Humanity, 344
Habitat International, 602–603
Hackensack University Medical Center, 533
Hallmark Cards, Inc., 338, 600
Hamilton High School, 185
Harley-Davidson, 326
Harrah's Entertainment, 589
The Hartford Financial Services Group, 221
Harvard Business School, 385, 627
Harvard University, 52, 599, 621–622
HealthSouth, 417
Herman Miller Inc., 495
Hewitt Associates, 230
Hewlett-Packard, 143, 223, 226, 376, 417, 439, 453, 495, 533, 570, 577
Hitachi, 532
Home Depot, 48, 130, 242, 391–392, 434, 544–545
Honda Motors, 17, 108, 326, 538
Honeywell, 597
H&R Block, 600
Hyundai, 559

I

IBM, 53, 124–125, 129, 214, 223, 226, 228–229, 230, 250, 326, 363–364, 406, 476, 495, 531, 543, 564, 591

ICU Medical Inc., 343
IDS Financial Services, 231
IKEA, 559
ImageNet Company, 606
IMG, 112
Imperial Chemical, 230
Indiana University's Kelley School of
     Business, 474
Infinity Capital, 316
Infosys Technologies, 429
Ingres, 249
Intel, 53, 591
Internal Revenue Service (IRS),
     30, 527
International Paper, 568
Ito Yokado, 593

J

J. D. Power, 167
J. M. Smuckers, 604
Jazz at Lincoln Center Orchestra, 289
JCPenney, 524
Jeep, 217–218
JetBlue, 166–167
John Deere, 228–229
Johns Hopkins, 329
Johnson & Johnson, 566–567, 604
JPMorgan Chase, 50

K

Kaiser Permanente, 361
Kaplan Inc., 611
Kavu, 315
KeySpan Corp., 231
Kinko's, 593
Kmart, 660–661
Koei, 573
Kohl's Department Stores, 213–214
KPMG, 224
Kraft, 483

L

Lands' End, 240
Lehman Brothers, 609
Leonardo's Pizza, 129
Levi Strauss, 597
Liberty Media, 416
Limited Brands, 561
Lincoln Electric, 218
LinkedIn, 363
Little People of America (LPA), 371
Liz Claiborne, 620n
L. L. Bean, 646
Lockheed Martin, 38, 591
L'Oreal, 267
Los Angeles Times, 371
Louis Vuitton, 325
Lowe's, 573
LSG Sky Chefs, 138
Lucent Technologies, 22, 604

M

Macy's, 620
Major League Baseball, 69
Manor Park Nursing Home, 587
March of Dimes, 551
Marks & Spencer, 304, 535
Marriott Corporation, 5, 77, 604
Mary Kay Cosmetics, 413
Masterfoods, 569
Matsushita, 455
MBNA, 577–578
McDonald's, 16, 18, 156, 453, 520–521,
     603
McGrath/Power, 476
Mead Paper, 232
Medex Insurance Services, 406
Medicare, 167
The Men's Wearhouse, 570
Mentor Graphics, 604
Menttium Corporation, 442
Merck, 439, 604, 617–618, 637
Merrill Lynch, 24, 223, 224, 242,
     366, 541
MGM, 530
Michigan State University, 334
Microsoft, 10, 108, 269, 522, 559, 573,
     589, 602, 673–674
Miller Brewing Co., 591
MIT Sloan School of Management, 4–5
Mitsubishi Motors Corporation, 531, 557
Molson Coors, 81, 344
Montgomery Ward, 22, 53
Morgan Stanley, 53
Motorola, 53, 226, 533
MTV, 97
MySpace, 312, 362–363

N

Nabisco, 634
Napster, 675
National Cooperative Bank, 233
National Football League (NFL),
     583–584
National Hockey League (NHL),
     511–512
National Institute of Learning, 591
Nationwide Insurance, 166
NBA, 258, 298
NEC Corp., 541
Nestle, 53
Neumann Homes, 561
New Balance, 335
News Corporation, 416
The New Yorker, 13
New York University, 463
New Zealand Air, 556
NFL, 47, 69, 583
Nichols Foods Ltd., 235
Nike, 364, 383, 509, 564, 646
Nissan Motor Company, 53, 88, 326, 440

Nokia, 17, 645
Northrop Grumman, 366
Northwest Airlines, 197
Northwestern University, 463
Novell, 564, 573
Nucor, 231, 440, 545

O

Office Depot, 89
Ogilvy & Mather Worldwide, 426
Ohio State University, 389–390
Optimus Solutions, 321
Oracle Corporation, 113, 234, 249–250,
     388
Osco, 95
Oticon A/S, 533

P

Pacific Coast Baptist College, 610–611
Patagonia, 21–22, 120, 411–412, 418
Peoples Flowers, 47
PepsiCo, 108, 603
Perot Systems, 551
Pew Research Center, 130
Pfizer, 5, 436, 439, 604
Philip Morris, 459, 460
Phoenix Inn, 235–236
Pizza Hut, 17, 228–229
Poker Channel, 269
Pomona College, 599
Portland Furniture Mart, 487–488
PricewaterhouseCoopers (PwC), 401,
     564
Princeton University, 599, 600, 658
Private Equities, 379
Procter & Gamble, 226, 240, 418, 455,
     476, 589, 652–653
Prudential, 604
Publix Supermarkets, 232, 589–590
Putnam Investments, 224

Q

QualityAgent, 243

R

R. W. Armstrong & Associates, 379
Radclyffe Group, 276
Radio Shack, 361
Raymond James & Associates, 449
Raytheon, 53
Recreational Equipment, Inc., 390
Reebok, 453
RE/MAX International, 344
RenaWeek, 255
Roadway Express, 633
Rubbermaid, 53

S

Safeway, 603
Salesforce.com, 571

Salomon Smith Barney, 476
Sanford C. Bernstein & Company, 511
SAP, 187
Saturn Corporation, 521
Savon, 95
S. C. Johnson, 384, 604
Scooter Store, 20
Seagate, 344
Sears, 22, 28, 90, 524
Sea World, 129
Security Alarm, 47
7-Eleven, 62
Seward Montessori School, 229
Shabbir Advisors, 139
Sharp Electronics, 532
Shea & Gould, 494
Siebel Systems, 388
Siemens, 373, 525, 593
Sierra Atlantic, 592
Singapore Airlines, 89, 218
Smith Corona, 22
Smithsonian Institution., 152
Smith & Wesson, 591
Society for Human Resource Management
    (SHRM), 94, 138, 476
Sony Corporation, 108, 416, 532, 675
SoundStep, 674
Southwest Airlines, 89, 417, 552, 559,
    570, 572, 589
Sprint, 597
Stanford University, 463
Starbucks, 5, 273, 365, 418, 585, 634
Stratus Technologies, 604
Subway, 47
SuccessFactors, 130
Sun Microsystems, 214, 363–364,
    549, 600
Symantec, 147

T

Taco Bell, 155
Takeda Chemical Industries, 230
TAP Pharmaceutical Products, 167–168
Texaco, 557
20th Century Fox, 530
3Com, 646
3M Co., 108, 533, 535, 569
Tiffany & Co., 483

Time Warner, 531, 557–558
Tommy Hilfiger, 453
Tom's of Maine, 570
Toshiba, 440
Toyota Motor Corporation, 57, 326, 352,
    406, 538, 587, 634
Trader Joe's, 441
Translation, 453
Trian Fund Management, 483–484
Trigon Blue Cross/Blue Shield, 338
TRW, 525
TSI Telecommunications Service, 591
TWA, 22
Tyco, 417, 422

U

UCLA, 85
Unilever, 330, 373, 436
United Auto Workers (UAW), 493, 498,
    675–677
UnitedHealth, 439
United Parcel Service (UPS), 20, 459,
    597
Universal, 675
University of Florida, 67–68, 436
University of Michigan, 390
University of Minnesota, 106
University of Northern Iowa, 440
U.S. Air Force, 267, 316
U.S. Army, 420
U.S. Coast Guard, 190
U.S. Department of Defense,
    334, 577
U.S. Federal Bureau of Investigation
    (FBI), 557
U.S. Internal Revenue Service, 30
U.S. Marine Corps., 561
U.S. Navy, 633
U.S. Postal Service, 129
U.S. Steel, 545
USAirways, 573

V

VeriSign, 420–421
Verizon, 152, 223, 538
Virgin Group, 385, 386, 418, 559
Volkswagen, 144
Volvo, 322

W

Wachovia, 550
Wackenhut Corp., 39
Wagner College, 611
Wallstrip.com, 536
Wal-Mart, 53, 95–96, 129, 228–229, 272,
    274, 361, 564–565, 629, 660–661,
    671–673
Walt Disney Co., 18, 180, 240, 556, 589
Walt Disney World, 129, 138
Warnaco, 113, 391–392
Warner Brothers, 530
Watermark, 504
Wegman's, 578–579
Wells Fargo, 344
Wendy's International, 483
Western Electric, 86, 292–294
Wetherill Associates, 570
Wharton School, 240, 385
Wheaton College, 599
Wheeler Landscaping, 590
Whirlpool, 233
Whole Foods Markets, 5, 338, 441
Wieden & Kennedy advertising agency, 641
Wild Oats, 441
Wipro Spectramind, 369
W. L. Gore & Associates, 232, 322,
    545–546, 560, 597
Wonderlic, 583–584
Woolworth, 22
Workforce Employment Solutions, 47
Workplace Bullying and Trauma
    Institute, 206
Worldcom, 417
Worthington Industries, 28
Wrigley, 383

X

Xerox Corporation, 226, 354, 455, 526,
    533, 569, 603–604, 646

Y

Yahoo!, 333, 493
YouTube, 312

Z

Ziggs, 363
ZoomInfo, 363

References followed by b indicate boxes; e, exhibits

A

Abilities *An individual's capacity to perform the various tasks in a job*, 44–48, 65
  intellectual, 45–47, 45e
  leader–follower relationship, 396
  motivation and, 224–225
  physical, 47–48, 47e
Absenteeism *The failure to report to work*, 28–29, 162
  job satisfaction and, 90
Abusive customers, emotions and, 276–277
Accommodating *The willingness of one party in a conflict to place the opponent's interests above his or her own*, 490, 506
  conflict and, 490
Accountability, 37–38
Achievement needs, 201
Achievement-oriented leader, 397
Acquisitions, barriers to, 557–558
Action research *A change process based on systematic collection of data and then selection of a change action based on what the analyzed data indicate*, 628
ACT test, 45
Adjourning stage *The final stage in group development for temporary groups, characterized by concern with wrapping up activities rather than task performance*, 286, 286e
Administrators, 6
Affect *A broad range of feelings that people experience*, 251, 251e
  relationship between emotions, moods, and, 251e
Affect intensity *Individual differences in the strength with which individuals experience their emotions*, 256
Affective commitment *An emotional attachment to the organization and a belief in its values*, 79–80, 82
Affective component of an attitude *The emotional or feeling segment of an attitude*, 75
Affective events theory (AFT), 262–264, 263e
African-Americans, job performance of, 51
Age
  job performance and, 48–49
  job satisfaction and, 49
  as source of emotions and moods, 259
  workforce and, 19e

Age discrimination, forced ranking programs and, 600
Aggregate quantitative reviews, 662–663
Agreeableness *A personality dimension that describes someone who is good natured, cooperative, and trusting*, 109
All-channel network, 358e, 359
Alternative work arrangements, 221–224
Ambiguity, conflict and, 488
Ambiguous responsibility, 303
Americans, values of, 126b
Analogies, effective use of, 160
Anchoring bias *A tendency to fixate on initial information, from which we then fail to adequately adjust for subsequent information*, 150–151
Anchors, 150–151
Anger, 252, 275
Anthropology *The study of societies to learn about human beings and their activities*, 15
Anticapitalism backlash, coping with, 17–18
Antisocial behavior, 29, 296
Apologies, impression management and, 470e
Application forms, 585–586
Appreciative inquiry *Seeking to identify the unique qualities and special strengths of an organization, which can then be built on to improve performance*, 632–633
Apprenticeships, 593
Arab discrimination, 145
Arbitrator *A third party to a negotiation who has the authority to dictate an agreement*, 503–504
Arousal, 190
Asia, teamwork in, 339
Assessment centers *A set of performance simulation tests designed to evaluate a candidate's managerial potential*, 588
Association, impression management and, 470e
Attentional processes, 57
Attitudes *Evaluative statements or judgments concerning objects, people, or events*, 75–83
  behavior and, 76–78
  components of, 75, 76e
  consistency of, 76–77
  identifying major job, 79–83
Attribution theory *An attempt when individuals observe behavior to determine whether it is internally or externally caused*, 141–142, 142e
  cultural differences in, 160

Attribution theory of leadership *The idea that leadership is merely an attribution that people make about other individuals*, 432–433, 434b
Auction sales, high bids and, 498b
Authentic leaders *Leaders who know who they are, know what they believe in and value, and act on those values and beliefs openly and candidly. Their followers would consider them to be ethical people*, 422–427
Authority *The rights inherent in a managerial position to give orders and to expect the orders to be obeyed*, 522
Autonomy *The degree to which the job provides substantial freedom and discretion to the individual in scheduling the work and in determining the procedures to be used in carrying it out*, 216, 216e
Availability bias *The tendency for people to base their judgments on information that is readily available to them*, 151
Avoiding *Desire to withdraw from or suppress a conflict*, 490, 507
  conflict and, 490

B

Baby boomers, 119e, 120
Background checks, 586–587
Bargaining
  distributive, 496–497, 496e, 497e
  integrative, 496, 496e, 498–499
  in negotiations, 500
  strategies in, 496–499
Barriers
  to acquisitions, 557–558
  to change, 557
  to diversity, 557
  to mergers, 557–558
Basic literacy skills, 591
Behavioral component of an attitude *An intention to behave in a certain way toward someone or something*, 75
Behaviorally anchored rating scales (BARS) *Scales that combine major elements from the critical incident and graphic rating scale approaches: The appraiser rates the employees based on items along a continuum, but the points are examples of actual behavior on the given job rather than general descriptions or traits*, 598
Behavioral symptoms of stress, 642–644
Behavioral theories of leadership *Theories proposing that specific behaviors differentiate leaders from nonleaders*, 389–390

Behaviorism *A theory that argues that behavior follows stimuli in a relatively unthinking manner*, 56
Behavior(s), 596
    attitudes and, 76–78
    conflict and, 491–492
    defensive, 468, 468e
    ethical, 26
    exit, 87
    externally caused, 141
    modification of, 61–63
    political, 461–462, 463–471, 464e, 471–472
Bias
    anchoring, 150–151
    availability, 151
    confirmation, 151
    in decision making, 162
    hindsight, 153
    overconfidence, 150
    reducing, 163e
    self-awareness, 152b
    self-serving, 142
Bids, auction sales and, 498b
Big Five personality framework, 109–111, 116b, 127, 386, 501, 587
Biofeedback, 645
Biographical characteristics *Personal characteristics—such as age, gender, race, and marital status—that are objective and easily obtained from personnel records*, 48–53, 65
    age, 48–49
    gender, 50
    race, 51
    tenure, 51–52
Blogs, 363–364
Board of directors' activities, 544–545
Board representatives, 226
Body art, hiring based on, 129–130
Body language, 357–358
Body movement, 357
Bonus *Pay program that rewards employees for recent performance rather than historical performance*, 230–231
Boomers, 119e, 120
Boundaryless organization *An organization that seeks to eliminate the chain of command, have limitless spans of control, and replace departments with empowered teams*, 532–533, 541
Bounded rationality *Making decisions by constructing simplified models that extract the essential features from problems without capturing all their complexity*, 149
Brainstorming *An idea-generation process that specifically encourages withholding any criticism of those alternatives*, 306–307

superiority of individuals over group, 307b
Brazil, cultural issues for leaders in, 401–402
Buck passing, 468e
Buffing, 468e
Bullying, impact of, on employee motivation, 206–207
Bureaucracy *A structure with highly routine operating tasks achieved through specialization, very formalized rules and regulations, tasks that are grouped into functional departments, centralized authority, narrow spans of control, and decision making that follows the chain of command*, 527–528, 530
Bureaupathologies, 530
Business, lying in, 37

C

Canada
    performance evaluations, 606
    stress, causes of, 648
    teamwork in, 339
Capitalism, 17–18
Cardinal traits, 128
Career burnout, 644
Case-analysis method, 536
Case study, 660–661
Causality, 659
Centralization *The degree to which decision making is concentrated at a single point in the organization*, 524
    job satisfaction and, 540
    in organizational structure, 524
Chain, 359, 359e
Chain of command *The unbroken line of authority that extends from the top of the organization to the lowest echelon and clarifies who reports to whom*, 522–523
Challenge stressors, 638
Change agents *Persons who act as catalysts and assume the responsibility for managing change activities*, 621–622, 625
Change *Making things different*, 620
    creating culture for, 633–637
    forces for, 619–620, 619e
    Kotter's eight-step plan for implementing, 627–628, 627e
    managing, 639, 650
    managing planned, 620–622
    politics of, 625
    resistance to, 622–625
    selecting people who accept, 624
    stimulating, 22–23
Channel, 353

Channel richness *The amount of information that can be transmitted during a communication episode*, 367, 367e
Character traits, 107
Charismatic attributions, characteristics of, 413–415, 413e
Charismatic leadership, 413–418
    influence on followers, 415–416
    key characteristics of, 413e
    situation and, 416–417
Charismatic leadership theory *Attributions of heroic or extraordinary leadership abilities when followers observe certain behaviors*, 413
Chief executive officers (CEOs)
    leadership style, 406–407
    level of pay for, 241–242
    managing, 439
    niceness, 130–131
China
    cultural issues for leaders in, 402
    emotion in, 271
    employees, organizational commitment of, 80b
    ethics in, 161
    influence tactics in, 458b
    stress, causes of, 648
Clarification in negotiations, 500
Classical conditioning *A type of conditioning in which an individual responds to some stimulus that would not ordinarily produce such a response*, 55–56
Climate of trust in creating effective teams, 329
Closure in negotiations, 500
Coalition *An informal group bound together by the active pursuit of a single issue*, 457
Coercion in overcoming resistance to change, 624–625
Coercive power, 452
Cognition, conflict and, 489
Cognitive component of an attitude *The opinion or belief segment of an attitude*, 75, 76e
Cognitive demands, relationship with pay, 262e
Cognitive dissonance *Any incompatibility between two or more attitudes or between behavior and attitudes*, 76–77
Cognitive evaluation theory *A theory stating that allocating extrinsic rewards for behavior that had been previously intrinsically rewarding tends to decrease the overall level of motivation*, 182–185
Cognitive resource theory *A theory of leadership that states that stress unfavorably affects a situation and that intelligence and experience can lessen the influence of stress on the leader*, 395

Cohesiveness *Degree to which group members are attracted to each other and are motivated to stay in the group,* 301, 302e
group, across cultures, 302b
Cohorts *Individuals who, as part of a group, hold a common attribute,* 333
Collaborating *A situation in which the parties to a conflict each desire to satisfy fully the concerns of all parties,* 490, 506
conflict and, 490
Collectivism *A national culture attribute that describes a tight social framework in which people expect others in groups of which they are a part to look after them and protect them,* 124, 126e
Command group *A group composed of the individuals who report directly to a given manager,* 284–285
Commitment
escalation of, 151–152
in overcoming resistance to change, 624
Common purpose in creating effective teams, 335–336
Communication apprehension *Undue tension and anxiety about oral communication, written communication, or both,* 370
Communication channel
choice of, 366–368
information richness of, 367e
Communication process *The steps between a source and a receiver that result in the transference and understanding of meaning,* 352–353, 353e
Communication *The transference and understanding of meaning,* 9, 351
barriers to effective, 368–372
computer-aided, 360–364
conflict and, 487
cross-cultural, 373–374
direction of, 353–355
face-to-face, 431
functions of, 351–352
gender and, 370
interpersonal, 355–358
lateral, 355
networked, 432
nonverbal, 357–358
oral, 355–356
organizational, 358–366
in overcoming resistance to change, 623
politically correct, 370–372
written, 356–357
Competence, 424
Competing *A desire to satisfy one's interests, regardless of the impact on the other party to the conflict,* 490
conflict and, 490
Competition, 506, 636
as force for change, 619e, 620

Composition in creating effective teams, 330–334
Compromising *A situation in which each party to a conflict is willing to give up something,* 490–491, 507
conflict and, 490–491
Computer-aided communication, 360–364
Computer-based training, 593–594
Conceptual skills *The mental ability to analyze and diagnose complex situations,* 8
Conciliator *A trusted third party who provides an informal communication link between the negotiator and the opponent,* 504
Conditioned response, 55
Conditioned stimulus, 55
Confirmation bias *The tendency to seek out information that reaffirms past choices and to discount information that contradicts past judgments,* 151
Conflict *A process that begins when one party perceives that another party has negatively affected, or is about to negatively affect, something that the first party cares about,* 484–495
benefits to organizations, 505–506
cultural differences in, 504–505
defined, 485
dimensions of, 491e
dysfunctional, 486
felt, 489
functional, 486, 493–494
human relations view of, 486
interactionist view of, 486
joint counseling sessions, 504b
levels of, in creating effective teams, 336–337
perceived, 489
process, 486
relationship, 486
task, 486
techniques in, 492e
unit performance and, 506e
Conflict-intensity continuum, 491e
Conflict process *Process with five stages; potential opposition or incompatibility, cognition and personalization intentions, behavior, and outcomes,* 487e
stage I: Potential opposition or incompatibility, 486–489
stage II: Cognition and personalization, 489
stage III: Intentions, 489–491
stage IV: Behavior, 491–492
stage V: Outcomes, 492–495
Conformity *Adjusting one's behavior to align with the norms of the group,* 294–296
impression management and, 470e

Congruence, 310
Connotations, 373
Conscientiousness *A personality dimension that describes someone who is responsible, dependable, persistent, and organized,* 109
Consensus, 141
Consideration *The extent to which a leader is likely to have job relationships characterized by mutual trust, respect for subordinates' ideas, and regard for their feelings,* 389–390
Consistency, 424
of attitudes, 76–77
in judging others, 141
Consultant *An impartial third party, skilled in conflict management, who attempts to facilitate creative problem solving through communication and analysis,* 504
Consultation, 457
Contagion effect, 270
Contemporary leadership, 428–432
Contemporary theories of motivation, integrating, 199–200, 200e
Contemporary work cohorts, 119–121, 119e
Context in creating effective teams, 328–329
Contingency organizational behavior (OB) model, 32–34, 33e
Contingency theories, 391–398
Contingency variables *Situational factors; variables that moderate the relationship between two or more other variables,* 16
predictions and, 397–398
Contingent reward leadership, 419e
Contingent selection, 589–590
Continuance commitment *The perceived economic value of remaining with an organization compared with leaving it,* 80, 80b, 82
Continuous reinforcement *Reinforcing a desired behavior each time it is demonstrated,* 59–60
Contract, psychological, 290
Contrast effects *Evaluation of a person's characteristics that are affected by comparisons with other people recently encountered who rank higher or lower on the same characteristics,* 143
Controlling *Monitoring activities to ensure they are being accomplished as planned and correcting any significant deviations,* 6
Cooptation in overcoming resistance to change, 624
Core-plus plans, 234
Core self-evaluations *Degree to which individuals like or dislike themselves,*

whether they see themselves as capable and effective, and whether they feel they are in control of their environment or powerless over their environment, 112

Core values *The primary or dominant values that are accepted throughout the organization,* 554

Correlation coefficient, 659–660

Cost-minimization strategy *A strategy that emphasizes tight cost controls, avoidance of unnecessary innovation or marketing expenses, and price cutting,* 535, 535e

Creative-thinking skills, 160

Creativity *The ability to produce novel and useful ideas,* 158
  emotions, moods, and, 268
  improving, in decision making, 162
  three-component model of, 159–160

Critical incidents *Evaluating the behaviors that are key in making the difference between executing a job effectively and executing it ineffectively,* 598

Cross-cultural communication, 372–374, 374e

Cross-functional teams *Employees from about the same hierarchical level, but from different work areas, who come together to accomplish a task,* 325–326

Cross-hierarchical teams, 532–533

Crying at work, 271b

Cultural barriers, 373–374

Cultural context, 374

Cultural differences, 160–161
  in attributions, 160–161
  in conflict, 504–505
  in group behavior, 309–310
  in negotiations, 505
  organizational change, 647–648
  organizational culture, 573
  performance evaluation, 606–607
  selection processes, 605–606
  stress, 648
  teamwork, implications for, 340

Cultural intelligence, 46b

Cultural training, 592b

Culture(s)
  for change, creating, 633–637
  in coping with stress, 648
  emotions and, 271
  formalization versus, 554
  group cohesiveness across, 302b
  Hofstede's framework for assessing, 124–125, 126e
  innovative organizations, 634–635, 636
  managerial evaluation of employees and, 197b
  negotiating across, 503b, 505
  organizational structure and, 540–541, 671–673

politics and power, 472–473
  status and, 299
  values across, 124–127
  working with people from different, 17

Customer-responsive culture, creating, 567–570

Customers
  departmentalization by, 522
  emotions and abusive, 276–277
  ethical handling of, 667–669
  job satisfaction and, 89–90

Customer service
  emotions, moods and, 269–270
  improving, 21–22

D

Data, 37–38

Day of week as source of emotions and moods, 256

Deadlines, temporary groups with, 287–288

Decentralization in organizational structure, 524

Decisional roles, 7e, 8

Decision making
  biases in, 162
  cultural differences in, 161
  emotions, moods, and, 267–270
  ethics in, 156–160
  gender differences in, 155
  group, 302–308
  individual, 162
  intuitive, 149–150
  organizational constraints on, 155–156
  personality and, 154–155
  skills in, 330

Decision(s) *The choices made from among two or more alternatives,* 146
  defined, 146
  link between perception and individual, 146–147
  making of, in organizations, 147–156
  rational model for making, 148–150

Decoding, 353

Deductive reasoning, 45

Deep acting *Trying to modify one's inner feelings based on display rules,* 262

Defensive behaviors *Reactive and protective behaviors to avoid action, blame, or change,* 468, 470e

Demands, stress and, 638

Demands *Responsibilities, pressures, obligations, and even uncertainties that individuals face in the workplace,* 638

Demographics
  changing United States, 20
  group, 333

Departmentalization *The basis by which jobs are grouped together,* 521–522
  functional, 529
  product, 529–530

Dependency *B's relationship to A when A possesses something that B requires,* 451
  factors creating, 455–456
  as key to power, 454–456

Dependent variable *A response that is affected by an independent variable,* 27–31, 659

Design
  change and, 633
  OB research, 660–663

Destiny, change and, 633

Destructive forms of conflict, 486

Deterrence-based trust *Trust based on fear of reprisal if the trust is violated,* 425

Development programs, 607

Deviant workplace behavior *Voluntary behavior that violates significant organizational norms and, in doing so, threatens the well-being of the organization or its members,* 29–30, 270, 296–297, 296e
  groups and, 297e

Directive leadership, 397

Disability, workforce and, 19e

Discovery, change and, 633

Discrimination, forced ranking programs and, 600

Disgust, 252

Displayed emotions *Emotions that are organizationally required and considered appropriate in a given job,* 261–262

Dissatisfaction with working conditions, 162

Disseminator role, 8

Distinctiveness, 141

Distributive bargaining *Negotiation that seeks to divide up a fixed amount of resources; a win/lose situation,* 496–497, 496e, 497e

Distributive justice *Perceived fairness of the amount and allocation of rewards among individuals,* 195, 196e

Disturbance handlers, 8

Diversity
  in creating effective teams, 332–333
  group, cultural issues and, 309–310
  managing, in organizations, 602–605

Diversity training, 605

Division of labor, 519

Domestic partners, workforce and, 19e

Dominant culture *A culture that expresses the core values that are shared by a majority of the organization's members,* 553

Double-loop learning *Correcting errors by modifying the organization's objectives, policies, and standard routines,* 635

Downward communication, 353–354

Dreaming, change and, 633

Dress codes, 476–477
Driving forces *Forces that direct behavior away from the status quo*, 626
Due process, providing employees with, 601
Dysfunctional conflict *Conflict that hinders group performance*, 486, 487
Dysfunctional outcomes, 494

E

Economic problems, 640
Economic shocks as force for change, 619e, 620
Economic uncertainties, 639
Education
    importance of, 65
    in overcoming resistance to change, 623
Effectiveness *Achievement of goals*, 27, 303
Efficiency *The ratio of effective output to the input required to achieve it*, 27, 303
Effort–performance relationship, 197
Egypt, cultural issues for leaders in, 402
Electronic mail, 360–362, 365b, 378–379
Electronic meeting *A meeting in which members interact on computers, allowing for anonymity of comments and aggregation of votes*, 308
E-mail, 360–362, 365b, 378–379
Emotional contagion *The process by which people's emotions are caused by the emotions of others*, 270
Emotional demands, relationship with pay, 262e
Emotional dissonance *Inconsistencies between the emotions we feel and the emotions we project*, 260–261
Emotional intelligence (EI) *The ability to detect and to manage emotional cures and information*, 264–266, 387–388
    case against, 266
    case for, 264–266
Emotional labor *A situation in which an employee expresses organizationally desired emotions during interpersonal transactions*, 260–262
Emotional recognition, 260b
Emotional stability *A personality dimension that characterizes someone as calm, self-confident, secure (positive) versus nervous, depressed, and insecure (negative)*, 109, 110
Emotion(s)
    organizational behavior applications of, 267–270
    relationship between affect, moods, and, 251e
    sources of, 256, 258–259
Emotion(s) *Intense feelings that are directed at someone or something*, 66, 251, 369
    abusive customers and, 276–277

basic set of, 252–253
conflict and, 489
defined, 250–259
displayed, 261–262
felt, 261
forecasting, 258b
functions served by, 254–256
global issues, 271–272
Empathy, 374
    as dimension of emotional intelligence, 264
Employee attitudes, 95–96
    organizational culture and, 568–569, 574e
Employee behavior, organizational designs and, 539–540
Employee engagement *An individual's involvement with, satisfaction with, and enthusiasm for the work he or she does*, 81–82
Employee involvement, 225–227
    global implications, 238
    as motivator, 323
Employee involvement program *A participative process that uses the input of employees and is intended to increase employee commitment to the organization's success*, 225
    as motivation, 239
Employee-oriented leader *Emphasizing interpersonal relations; taking a personal interest in the needs of employees, and accepting individual differences among members*, 390
Employee-oriented leadership, 390
Employee performance, 539–540
    downsizing and, 543
    socialization influence on, 574
Employee recognition programs, 234–235, 236b, 236e
Employee(s), 398
    culture in evaluation of, 197b
    expression, toleration of, 571–572
    forced ranking programs, 600b
    helping balance work–life conflicts, 24–25
    impact of bullying on motivation of, 206–207
    importance of, 538b
    learning of organizational culture, 564–566
    participation in decision making, 239
    paying not to work, 182b
    providing, with due process, 601
    providing performance feedback to, 601–602
    rewarding, 227–237
    saying thanks to, 243–244
    self-efficacy of, 607
    structure preferences, 541

Employee stock ownership plan (ESOP) *Company-established benefit plans in which employees acquire stock, often at below-market prices, as part of their benefits*, 232–233
Employee turnover, culture and, 554
Employment interview, 145–146
Empowerment in creating customer-responsive culture, 567–570
Enactive mastery, 189–190
Encoding, 353
Encounter stage *The stage in the socialization process in which a new employee sees what the organization is really like and confronts the possibility that expectations and reality may diverge*, 562
Entrepreneur role, 8
Entrepreneurs, personalities of, 116b, 131–132
Entry socialization, 562, 563e
Environment *Institutions or forces outside the organization that potentially affect the organization's performance*, 537–539
    in determining personality, 106
    organization structure and, 537–539, 538e
    as source of stress, 639
    worker satisfaction, 93
Envy, 270
Equity theory *A theory that individuals compare their job inputs and outcomes with those of others and then respond to eliminate any inequities*, 192–197, 193e, 202–203, 239, 608
ERG theory *A theory that posits three groups of core needs; existence, relatedness, and growth*, 177
Error(s)
    fundamental attribution, 142
    leniency, 600, 601
    randomness, 152–153
    rater, 601
    reducing, 163e
Escalation of commitment *An increased commitment to a previous decision in spite of negative information*, 151–152
Esteem needs, 176, 201
Ethical behavior, improving, 26
Ethical dilemmas
    social loafing, 314–315
    spying on organizational members, 577
Ethical dilemmas *Situations in which individuals are required to define right and wrong conduct*, 26
    board of directors' activities, 544–545
    résumés, shaping, 610–611

Ethical standards, 161, 166
Ethics
    of behaving politically, 471–472
    customer relations, 667–669
    in decision making, 156–160
    executive pay, 241–242
    goal-setting, 205
    health benefits for cohabiting partners, 67–68
    impression management, 474
    leadership and, 405, 423
    national culture and, 161
    negotiations and, 510
    OB research, 663
    in organizational cultures, 566–567
    résumé and, 610–611
    stress, employees and, 652
Ethics training, 592
Ethnic profiling, 145
E-training, 593–594
European Union cooperative trade arrangement, 19
Evolutionary psychology *An area of inquiry that argues that we must experience the emotions that we do because they serve a purpose,* 66, 255
Exchange, 457
Excuses, impression management and, 470e, 471b
Exercise as source of emotions and moods, 259
Exit behavior, 87
Exit *Dissatisfaction expressed through behavior directed toward leaving the organization,* 87
Expectancy theory *The strength of a tendency to act in a certain way depends on the strength of an expectation that the act will be followed by a given outcome and on the attractiveness of that outcome to the individual,* 197–199, 197e, 203
Experience, 641
Experiential exercise method, 536
Expertise, 159
Expert power *Influence based on special skills or knowledge,* 453
External equity, 228
Externally caused behavior, 141
Extinction, 59
Extraversion *A personality dimension describing someone who is sociable, gregarious, and assertive,* 107–110, 110e
Extreme jobs, 653–654

F

Face-to-face communications, 431
Failure as motivation, 204

Favors, impression management and, 470e
Fear, 252
Feedback *The degree to which carrying out the work activities required by the job results in the individual obtaining direct and clear information about the effectiveness of his or her performance,* 216, 216e, 353
    survey, 630
Feeling individuals, 108
Felt conflict *Emotional involvement in a conflict creating anxiety, tenseness, frustration, or hostility,* 489
Felt emotions *An individual's actual emotions,* 261
Femininity *A national culture attribute that has little differentiation between male and female roles, where women are treated as the equals of men in all aspects of the society,* 124, 126e
Fiedler contingency model *The theory that effective groups depend on a proper match between a leader's style of interacting with subordinates and the degree to which the situation gives control and influence to the leader,* 392–395, 394e
Field experiment, 662
Field study, 661
Figurehead role, 7
Filtering *A sender's manipulation of information so that it will be seen more favorably by the receiver,* 368
First impressions, 589b
Five-stage group-development model *The five distinct stages groups go through: forming, storming, norming, performing, and adjourning,* 286–287
Fixed-interval schedule *Spacing rewards at uniform time intervals,* 60
Fixed pie *The belief that there is only a set amount of goods or services to be divvied up between the parties,* 496
Fixed-ratio schedule *Initiating rewards after a fixed or constant number of responses,* 60
Flattery, impression management and, 470e
Flexible benefits *A benefits plan that allows each employee to put together a benefit package individually tailored to his or her own needs and situation,* 234
    global implications, 238
Flexible spending plans, 234
Flexible work hours, 222
Flextime, 221–222, 222e
Flynn effect, 68

Forced comparisons, 598–599, 600b
Foreign assignments, 17
Formal channels *Communication channels established by an organization to transmit messages related to the professional activities of members,* 353
Formal group *A designated work group defined by the organization's structure,* 284
Formalization *The degree to which jobs within the organization are standardized,* 524–525
    culture versus, 554
    in organizational structure, 524–525
Formal lecture method, 536
Formal power, 452
Formal regulations, 155–156
Formal small-group networks, 358–359
Formal training, 593
Forming stage *The first stage in group development, characterized by much uncertainty,* 286, 286e
For-profit organizations, decision making in, 157
Fragmentation, 636
Framing *A way to use language to manage meaning,* 412–413
    leadership and, 412–413
France, cultural issues for leaders in, 402
Friendship group *Those brought together because they share one or more common characteristics,* 285
Full range of leadership model, 419–420, 420e
Functional conflict *Conflict that supports the goals of the group and improves its performance,* 486, 487
    creating, 494–495
Functional departmentalization, 529
Functional outcomes, 492–495
Fundamental attribution error *The tendency to underestimate the influence of external factors and overestimate the influence of internal factors when making judgments about the behavior of others,* 142

G

Gainsharing *A formula-based group incentive plan,* 232
Galatea effect, 190–191
Gender
    in decision making, 155
    job performance and, 50
    motivation and, 178b
    in negotiations, 501–502
    as source of emotions and moods, 259
    workforce and, 19e
Gender identity, job performance and, 53

...ency postulate,
...–455

...eralizable, OB research, 660

Generation gap, 442

Generation Next, 121

Generation Y, 121

Geography, departmentalization by, 521–522

Globalization
impact on labor markets, 19b
job satisfaction, 91
personality traits, 116
responding to, 16–18
teamwork, 339–340

Global Leadership and Organizational Behavior Effectiveness (GLOBE)
framework for assessing cultures, 127, 401
leadership theories, 437

Global virtual teams, 327b

GMAT tests, 45

Goals, 420–421
in creating effective teams, 335–336
reducing biases and errors, 163e
in selection process, 559–560
setting, 645

Goal-setting theory *The theory that specific and difficult goals, with feedback, lead to higher performance,* 185–188, 199, 202

Grade inflation, 599e

Grapevine *The organization's informal communication network,* 359–360

Graphic rating scales *An evaluation method in which the evaluator rates performance factors on an incremental scale,* 598

Grief, workplace, 271b

Ground rules in negotiations, 500

Group decision making, 302–308
strengths of, 302
techniques in, 306–308
weaknesses of, 302–303

Group demography *The degree to which members of a group share a common demographic attribute, such as age sex, race, educational level, or length of service in an organization, and the impact of this attribute on turnover,* 333

Group interaction, status and, 298–299

Group-level variables, 32

Group order ranking *An evaluation method that places employees into a particular classification, such as quartiles,* 598–599

Group processes, effects of, 335–337, 335e

Groupshift *A change in decision risk between the group's decision and the individual decision that members within the group would make; can be either toward conservatism or greater risk,* 304, 306

Group(s) *Two or more individuals, interacting and interdependent, who have come together to achieve particular objectives,* 284, 285e
defining and classifying, 284–285
differences between teams and, 323, 324e
evaluating effectiveness of, 308e
formal, 284
friendship, 285
informal, 284
interacting, 306
interest, 285
job design and, 312
properties of, 288–301
reasons for joining, 285e
reference, 294–295
stages of development, 286–288, 286e
task, 285

Groupthink *Phenomenon in which the norm for consensus overrides the realistic appraisal of alternative courses of action,* 304–306, 305b
dangers of, 315–316

Growth, emphasizing, 568–569

H

Halo effect *Drawing a general impression about an individual on the basis of a single characteristic,* 143, 601

Hand gestures, 372e

Happiness, 252
job satisfaction and, 86b

Hawthorne studies, 86b, 292–294

Heredity in determining personality, 105–106

Heuristics, 267

Hierarchy of needs theory *A hierarchy of five needs—physiological, safety, social, esteem, and self-actualization—exists such that as each need is substantially satisfied the next need becomes dominant,* 176–177

High-context cultures *Cultures that rely heavily on nonverbal and subtle situational cues in communication,* 374, 374e

Higher-order needs *Needs that are satisfied internally; social-esteem and self-actualization needs,* 176

Hindrance stressors, 638

Hindsight bias *The tendency for us to believe falsely that we'd have accurately predicted the outcome of an event after that outcome is actually known,* 153

Historical precedents, 156

Human behavior, learning, 66

Humanistic work practices, 571

Human relations view of conflict *The belief that conflict is a natural and inevitable outcome in any group,* 486

Human resource management, 9
innovative organizations, 635

Human skills *The ability to work with, understand, and motivate other people, both individually and in groups,* 8

Hygiene factors *Factors—such as company policy and administration, supervision, and salary—that, when adequate in a job, placate workers. When these factors are adequate, people will not be dissatisfied,* 180

Hypnosis, 645

Hypothesis, 659

I

Idea champions *Individuals who take an innovation and actively and enthusiastically promote the idea, build support, overcome resistance, and ensure that the idea is implemented,* 635

Identification-based trust *Trust based on a mutual understanding of each other's intentions and appreciation of the other's wants and desires,* 425–426, 426–427, 432

Identity, role, 290

Illegitimate political behavior *Extreme political behavior that violates the implied rules of the game,* 461–462, 464, 477–478

Imitation strategy *A strategy that seeks to move into new products or new markets only after their viability has already been proven,* 535, 535e

Implementation in negotiations, 500

Implicit models of organizational structure *Perceptions that people hold regarding structural variables formed by observing things around them in an unscientific fashion,* 541–542

Impression management *The process by which individuals attempt to control the impression others form of them,* 469–471, 470e, 474

Incompatibility, conflict and, 486–489

Independent variable *The presumed cause of some change in the dependent variable,* 31–32, 659

Individual approaches to stress management, 640

Individual decision making, 162–163
link between perception and, 146–147

Individual differences recognizing, 236e
  motivation and, 238
  stress and, 641–642
  variables in, 219b
Individualism *A national culture attribute describing the degree to which people prefer to act as individuals rather than as members of groups*, 124, 126e
Individualizing formal training, 594
Individual-level variables, 31–32
Individual ranking *An evaluation method that rank-orders employees from the best to worst*, 599
Individuals, turning into team players, 337–339
Individual task outcomes, 595
Inductive reasoning, 45
Influence tactics in China, 458b
Informal channels *Communication channels that are created spontaneously and that emerge as responses to individual choices*, 353
Informal group *A group that is neither formally structured nor organizationally determined; appears in response to the need for social contact*, 284
Informal training, 593
Informational roles, 7–8, 7e
Information overload *A condition in which information inflow exceeds an individual's processing capacity*, 368–369
Ingratiation, 457, 470
Initial Public Offering (IPO) pricing schemes, 154b
Initial selection, 585–587
Initiating structure *The extent to which a leader is likely to define and structure his or her role and those of subordinates in the search for goal attainment*, 389
Innovation *A new idea applied to initiating or improving a product, process, or service*, 634
  comprehensive case study, 673–675
  defined, 634
  innovating, 652–653
  sources of, 634–635
  stimulating, 22–23, 633–634
  structural options, 535e
Innovation strategy *A strategy that emphasizes the introduction of major new products and services*, 535
Inspirational appeals, 457
Inspirational approaches, to leadership, 413–418
Instant messaging, 362
Institutionalization *A condition that occurs when an organization takes on a life of its own, apart from any of its members,*

and acquires immortality, 542, 550–551
Instrumental values *Preferable modes of behavior or means of achieving one's terminal values*, 118
Integrative bargaining *Negotiation that seeks one or more settlements that can create a win/win solution*, 496, 496e, 498–499
Integrity, 424
Integrity tests, 587–588
Intellectual abilities *The capacity to do mental activities—thinking, reasoning, and problem solving*, 45–47, 45e
Intelligence, 45
  benefits of cultural, 46b
  cognitive ability tests or, 587
  emotional, 264–266
  Flynn effect, 68
Intelligence quotient (IQ), 45–46
Intentions *Decisions to act in a given way*, 491
  conflict and, 489–491
Interacting groups *Typical groups, in which members interact with each other face-to-face*, 306
Interactional justice *Perceived degree to which an individual is treated with dignity, concern, and respect*, 196, 196e
Interactionist view of conflict *The belief that conflict is not only a positive force in a group but that it is also an absolute necessity for a group to perform effectively*, 486
Interest group *Those working together to attain a specific objective with which each is concerned*, 285
Interest inventories, 587
Intergroup development *Organizational development efforts to change the attitudes, stereotypes, and perceptions that groups have of each other*, 632
Intermittent reinforcement *Reinforcing a desired behavior often enough to make the behavior worth repeating but not every time it is demonstrated*, 59
Intermittent schedule, 59–60
Internal equity, 228
Internally caused behaviors, 141
International business, impact of negative perceptions on, 144b
International corporate deviance, 30b
International human resource practices
  performance evaluation, 606–607
  selection, 605–606
Interpersonal communication, 355–358
Interpersonal conflict, emotions, moods and, 270

Interpersonal demands, 640
Interpersonal roles, 6–7, 7e
Interpersonal skills, 330, 592
  importance of, to managerial effectiveness, 4–5
Interval schedules, 60
Interviews, 588–589
  employment, 145–146
  role of anchoring in, 150–151
  in selecting leaders, 435–436
Intonations, 357e, 358
Intrinsic motivation, 197b
Intrinsic rewards, 234–235
Intrinsic task motivation, 160
Introverts, 108
Intuition *A gut feeling not necessarily supported by research*, 12
  complementing, with systematic study, 11–13
  decision making by, 149
Intuitive appeal, 265
Intuitive decision making *An unconscious process created out of distilled experience*, 149–150
Intuitives, 108
Islam, job performance and, 53
Israel, performance evaluations in, 607

J
Japan
  decision-making differences in, 161
  performance evaluations, 607
Job attitudes
  as distinct, 82–83
  emotions, moods and, 270
  identifying major, 79–83
Job characteristics, cultural differences in, 236e, 237
Job characteristics model (JCM) *A model that proposes that any job can be described in terms of five core job dimensions; skill variety, task identity, task significance, autonomy, and feedback*, 215–217, 216e
Job design *The way the elements in a job are organized*, 215
  groups and, 312
  motivating by changing nature of, 215–225
Job enlargement *Increasing the number and variety of tasks that an individual performs results in jobs with more diversity*, 219–220
Job enrichment *The vertical expansion of jobs, increasing the degree to which the worker controls the planning, execution, and evaluation of the work*, 220–221, 220e
  global implications, 237
Job evaluation, 228

_, _he degree to which a ._son identifies with a job, actively participates in it, and considers performance important to self-worth,* 79

Job performance, 48
  job satisfaction and, 88
Job redesign, 217–221
Job-related stress, 641–642
Job rotation *The periodic shifting of an employee from one task to another,* 218–219, 593
Job(s)
  desire for challenging, 219b
  rewarding emotionally demanding, with better pay, 262e
Job satisfaction *A positive feeling about one's job resulting from an evaluation of its characteristics,* 31, 79, 83–91, 162, 178, 180
  absenteeism and, 90
  causes of, 84–86, 86e, 87e
  centralization and, 540
  core self-evaluations and, 112
  cultural differences in, 236e
  customer satisfaction and, 89–90
  happiness and, 86e
  heredity and, 106b
  job performance and, 88
  length of work week and, 96–97
  level of, 83b, 84, 85e
  measuring, 83–84
  organizational citizenship behavior and, 88–89
  productivity and, 86b
  role of managers in creating, 91
  turnover and, 90
  workplace deviance and, 90–91
Job sharing, 222–223
Job training, 66
Jordan v. Duff and Phelps, 37
Judgments
  about individuals, 108
  making, about others, 141–145
Jury behavior, 310
Justice
  distributive, 195
  as ethical criterion, 157
  interactional, 196
  organization, 195
  procedural, 195
Justification, 468e
  in negotiations, 500

K

Knowledge-based trust *Trust based on behavioral predictability that comes from a history of interaction,* 425–426
Knowledge management *The process of organizing and distributing an* organization's collective wisdom so the right information gets to the right people at the right time, 364–366
Knowledge worker, importance of, 538b

L

Laboratory experiment, 661–662
Labor markers, impact of globalization on, 19b
Laissez-faire, 419
Language, 369–370, 565–566
  translation and, 373b
Lateral communication, 355
Leader–member exchange (LMX) theory *The creation by leaders of in-groups and out-groups; subordinates with in-group status will have higher performance ratings, less turnover, and greater job satisfaction,* 398–399, 399e
Leader–member relations *The degree of confidence, trust, and respect subordinates have in their leader,* 393, 394
Leader-participation model *A leadership theory that provides a set of rules to determine the form and amount of participative decision making in different situations,* 400
  contingency variables in revised, 400e
Leaders
  authentic, 422–427
  charismatic, 413–418, 413e
  employee-oriented, 390
  finding and creating effective, 435–437
  importance of, 401
  managing, 439
  matching, 393–394
Leadership construct, challenges to, 432–435
Leadership role, 7
Leadership style, identifying, 392–393
Leadership *The ability to influence a group toward the achievement of a vision or set of goals,* 385–386
  attribution theory of, 432–433
  authentic, 422–427
  bad bosses, 387b
  behavioral theories, 388–391
  charismatic, 413–418, 413e
  comprehensive case, 665–667
  conflict and, 488
  contemporary, 428–432
  contingency theories, 391–398
  contingent reward, 419–420
  contrasting, 451
  in creating effective teams, 328–329
  emotions, moods, and, 268–269
  employee-oriented, 390
  ethics and, 423
  framing and, 412–413
  gender and, 430b
  online, 431–432
  substitutes and neutralizers to, 434–435, 435e
  trait theories, 386–388
  transactional, 420e
  transformational, 418–421, 420e
  trust and, 424–425
Leadership training, 404
Leading *A function that includes motivating employees, directing others, selecting the most effective communication channels, and resolving conflicts,* 6
Learning *Any relatively permanent change in behavior that occurs as a result of experience,* 54–55
  double-loop, 635
  managing, 636–637
  single-loop, 635
  theories of, 55–58
Learning organization *An organization that has developed the continuous capacity to adapt and change,* 635–637
  characteristics, 636e
  defined, 635
  managing learning, 636–637
Least preferred co-worker (LPC) questionnaire *An instrument that purports to measure whether a person is task- or relationship-oriented,* 392–393
Legitimacy, 456
Legitimate political behavior *Normal everyday politics,* 461
Legitimate power *The power a person receives as a result of his or her position in the formal hierarchy of an organization,* 452
Leniency error, 600, 601
Level-5 leaders *Leaders who are fiercely ambitious and driven, but whose ambition is directed toward their company rather than themselves,* 417–418
Lewin's three-step model, 625–627
Liaison role, 7
Long-term orientation *A national culture attribute that emphasizes the future, thrift, and persistence,* 125
Low-context cultures *Cultures that rely heavily on words to convey meaning in communication,* 374, 374e
Lower-order needs *Needs that are satisfied externally; physiological and safety needs,* 176
Loyalty *Dissatisfaction expressed by passively waiting for conditions to improve,* 87, 424
  values and, 121b
LSAT tests, 45

M

Machiavellianism *Degree to which an individual is pragmatic, maintains emotional distance, and believes that ends can justify means,* 112

Male advantage stereotype, 430b

Male competitiveness, 66

Management
functions of, 6
roles of, 6–8, 7e
skills in, 8

Management by objectives (MBO) *A program that encompasses specific goals, participatively set, for an explicit time period, with feedback on goal progress,* 187–188, 188e

Managerial action in creating customer responsive culture, 567–570

Managerial activities, effective versus successful, 8–10, 9e

Managerial effectiveness, importance of interpersonal skills to, 4–5

Managerial grid *A nine-by-nine matrix outlining 81 different leadership styles,* 390

Managers *Individuals who achieve goals through other people,* 6
comprehensive case study, 677–679
contemporary theories of, 181–200
in creating job satisfaction, 91, 92–93
influence of, on moods, 270
defining, 175
early theories of, 175–181
emotions, moods, and, 268
failure and, 204
functions of, 5–10
integrating contemporary theories of, 199–200, 200e
intrinsic, 197b
by job design, 215–225
by praise, 240

Manipulation, in overcoming resistance to change, 624

Masculinity *A national culture attribute describing the extent to which the culture favors traditional masculine work roles of achievement, power, and control. Societal values are characterized by assertiveness and materialism,* 124, 126e

Material symbols, 564–565

Matrix structure *A structure that creates dual lines of authority and combines functional and product departmentalization,* 529–530, 529e

MCAT tests, 45

McClelland's theory of needs *A theory stating that achievement, power, and affiliation are three important needs that help explain motivation,* 180–181

Mechanistic model *A structure characterized by extensive departmentalization, high formalization, a limited information network, and centralization,* 534, 534e, 535e

Mediator *A neutral third party who facilitates a negotiated solution by using reasoning, persuasion, and suggestions for alternatives,* 503

Meditation, 645

Meetings, stress and, 639b

Members
abilities of, in creating effective teams, 331–332
preferences in creating effective teams, 334

Memory, 45

Men, communication barriers between women and, 370

Mental models, team effectiveness and, 336

Mentor *A senior employee who sponsors and supports a less-experienced employee,* 428–430, 442

Mentoring, 428–430, 593

Mergers
barriers to, 557–558
organizational culture and, 577–578

Merit-based pay plan *A pay plan based on performance appraisal ratings,* 230

Message, 353

Metamorphosis stage *The stage in the socialization process in which a new employee changes and adjusts to the job, work group, and organization,* 562–563

Michigan, University of, studies on leadership, 390

Middle East, performance evaluations in, 606

Millennials, 121

Misrepresenting, 468e

Model *An abstraction of reality, a simplified representation of some real-world phenomenon,* 26–27
OB research, 660

Moderating variables, 77–78, 659

Modular plans, 234

Moods *Feelings that tend to be less intense than emotions and that lack a contextual stimulus,* 251
defined, 250–259
effect of time of day on, 257e
forecasting, 258b
impact of day of the week on, 257e
influence of managers on, 270
organizational behavior applications of, 267–270
as positive and negative affect, 254

relationship between affect, emotions, and, 251e
role of, in negotiation, 501
sources of, 256, 258–259
structure of, 253e

Motivating potential score (MPS) *A predictive index suggesting the motivating potential in a job,* 217

Motivation-hygiene theory, 178

Motivation theories
as culture-bound, 202
linking employee involvement programs and, 227
performance reviews and, 233b

Motivation *The processes that account for an individual's intensity, direction, and persistence of effort toward attaining a goal,* 175

Motor reproduction processes, 57

Movement *A change process that transforms the organization from the status quo to a desired end state,* 625–626

Multinationals, structural considerations in, 528b

Multiple evaluators, 601

Muslims
job performance and, 53
stereotyping and profiling of, 145

Myers-Briggs Type Indicator (MBTI) *A personality test that taps four characteristics and classifies people into 1 of 16 personality types,* 107–108, 127

Myth of rationality, 250

N

Narcissism *The tendency to be arrogant, have a grandiose sense of selfimportance, require excessive admiration, and have a sense of entitlement,* 113
leadership and, 388

National origin, workforce and, 19e

Natural disasters, decision-making and, 166–167

Need for achievement *The drive to excel, to achieve in relation to a set of standards, to strive to succeed,* 180

Need for affiliation *The desire for friendly and close interpersonal relationships,* 180

Need for power *The need to make others behave in a way that they would not have behaved otherwise,* 180

Need(s)
hierarchy of, 201
McClelland's theory of, 180–181
theories on, 202

Negative affect *A mood dimension consisting of nervousness, stress, and anxiety at the high end, and relaxation, tranquility, and poise at the low end,* 254

, deviant workplace
 ...iors and, 270
.autve leniency, 600, 601
Negative perceptions, impact of, on
    international business, 144b
Negative reinforcement, 58–59
Neglect *Dissatisfaction expressed through
    allowing conditions to worsen*, 87
Negotiation *A process in which two or more
    parties exchange goods or services and
    attempt to agree on the exchange rate
    for them*, 495–504, 500e
  bargaining strategies, 496–499
  comprehensive case study, 675–677
  cross-cultural, 503b
  cultural differences in, 503b, 505
  defined, 495
  effective, 503b
  emotions, moods, and, 269
  ethics and, 510
  hockey and, 511–512
  issues in, 501–502
  in overcoming resistance to change, 625
  role of anchoring in, 150–151
  third-party, 503–504
Negotiation role play, 509–510
Negotiator role, 8
Networked communication, 432
Networked organizations, working in,
    23–24
Networking, 9
Networking software, 362–363
Neutralizers to leadership, 434–435, 435e
Nexters, 121
Noise, 353
Nominal group technique *A group
    decision-making method in which
    individual members meet face-to-face
    to pool their judgments in a systematic
    but independent fashion*, 307–308
Non-Christian faiths, workforce and, 19e
Nonsubstitutability, 456
Nonverbal communication, 357–358
  value of, 377
Normative commitment *An obligation to
    remain with the organization for
    moral or ethical reasons*, 80, 80b, 82
Norming stage *The third stage in group devel-
    opment, characterized by close relation-
    ships and cohesiveness*, 286, 286e
Norms *Acceptable standards of behavior
    within a group that are shared by the
    group members*, 292–297, 310
  status and, 298
Number aptitude, 45

O

OB Mod (organizational behavior
    modification) *The application of
    reinforcement concepts to individuals
    in the work setting*, 62–63

problems with, 63–64
  task performance review, 662–663
Off-the-job training, 593
Ohio State University, studies on
    leadership, 389–390
Older workers, training for, 58b
Onboarding, 561
Online leadership, 431–432
On-the-job training, 593
Openness, 424
Openness to experience *A personality
    dimension that characterizes someone
    in terms of imagination, sensitivity,
    and curiosity*, 109, 110–111
Operant conditioning *A type of conditioning
    in which desired voluntary behavior
    leads to a reward or prevents a
    punishment*, 56
Opportunity to perform *High levels of
    performance are partially a function
    of an absence of obstacles that constrain
    the employee*, 225
Oral communication, 355–356
Organic model *A structure that is flat, uses
    cross-hierarchical and cross-functional
    teams, has low formalization, possesses
    a comprehensive information network,
    and relies on participative decision
    making*, 534, 534e, 535e
Organization *A consciously coordinated
    social unit, composed of two or more
    people, that functions on a relatively
    continuous basis to achieve a common
    goal or set of goals*, 6
  decision making in, 147–156
  managing diversity in, 602–605
  technology in reshaping, 542
Organizational approaches to stress
    management, 645–647
Organizational behavior modification
    (OB Mod) and task performance,
    662–663
Organizational behavior (OB) *A field of
    study that investigates the impact that
    individuals, groups, and structure
    have on behavior within organizations,
    for the purpose of applying such
    knowledge toward improving an
    organization's effectiveness*, 10–11
  absolutes in, 16
  challenges and opportunities for,
    16–26
  contributing disciplines to, 13–15, 14e
  dependent variables in, 27–31
  independent variables in, 31–32
  personality attributes influencing,
    111–117
  research, 658–664
  values and, 127
Organizational behavior (OB) model
    contingency, 32–34, 33e

Organizational change
  approaches to managing, 625–633
  as episodic activity, 647–648
Organizational citizenship behavior
    (OCB) *Discretionary behavior that is
    not part of an employee's formal job
    requirements, but that nevertheless
    promotes the effective functioning of
    the organization*, 30–31
  job satisfaction and, 88–89
Organizational communication,
    358–366, 645–647
Organizational constraints on decision
    making, 155–156
Organizational culture *A system of shared
    meaning held by members that
    distinguishes the organization from
    other organizations*, 551–574
  beginning of, 558–559
  boundaries of, 555b
  change and, 575
  comprehensive case study, 671–673
  contrasting, 553e
  creating ethical, 566–567
  employee learning of, 564–566
  formation of, 563, 564e
  functions of, 555–556
  keeping alive, 559–563
  as liability, 556–558
  spirituality and, 570–572
Organizational Culture Profile (OCP),
    129
Organizational designs
  boundaryless organization, 532–533
  bureaucracy, 527–528
  culture and, 541
  determinants and outcomes, 542e
  employee behavior and, 539–540
  flat structure, 545–546
  matrix structure, 529–530
  simple structure, 526, 526e
  stage in multinational companies, 528b
  team structure, 532–533
  virtual organization, 530–532, 532e
Organizational development (OD)
    *A collection of planned change
    interventions, built on humanistic
    democratic values, that seeks to
    improve organizational effectiveness
    and employee well-being*, 628–633
Organizational display rules, costs and
    benefits of, 273
Organizational factors as source of stress,
    640
Organizational justice *An overall percep-
    tion of what is fair in the workplace,
    composed of distributive, procedural,
    and interactional justice*, 195, 196e,
    202–203
Organizational politics, responses to,
    466–468, 468e

Organizational structure *How job tasks are formally divided, grouped, and coordinated*, 519, 519e
  centralization in, 524
  chain of command in, 522–523
  decentralization in, 524
  defined, 519
  departmentalization in, 521–522
  determinants and outcomes, 542e
  differences in, 534–539, 534e
  downsizing, performance and, 543
  employee participation, 525b
  environment in, 537–539, 538e
  formalization in, 524–525
  for learning, 636
  size in, 535–536
  span of control in, 523–524, 523e
  strategy in, 534–535
  technology in, 536–537
  work specialization in, 519–521, 521e
Organization size, structure and, 535–536
Organization systems level variables, 32
Organizing *Determining what tasks are to be done, who is to do them, how the tasks are to be grouped, who reports to whom, and where decisions are to be made*, 6
Others, shortcuts in judging, 142–145
Outcomes
  dysfunctional, 494
  functional, 492–495
Outsourcing, 242–243
Overconfidence bias, 150
Overconforming, 468e

P

Paper-and-pencil tests, 587–588
Parenting, 66
Participation in overcoming resistance to change, 625
Participative leader, 397
Participative management *A process in which subordinates share a significant degree of decision-making power with their immediate superiors*, 225–226, 226b
Path-goal theory *The theory that it is the leader's job to assist followers in attaining their goals and to provide the necessary direction and/or support to ensure that their goals are compatible with the overall objectives of the group or organization*, 396–398, 397e
Pay
  level of, for CEO, 241–242
  merit-based, 230
  skilled-based, 231
  variable, 228–233
Pay structure, establishing, 228

People
  managing, during war on terror, 18
  "reflected best-self," 25
People skills, improving, 22
Perceived conflict *Awareness by one or more parties of the existence of conditions that create opportunities for conflict to arise*, 489
Perceived organizational support (POS) *The degree to which employees believe the organization values their contribution and cares about their well-being*, 81
Perceiving individuals, 108
Perception *A process by which individuals organize and interpret their sensory impressions in order to give meaning to their environment*, 139–147, 162, 641
  cultural barriers, 373–374
  defined, 139
  factors influencing, 139–140, 140e
  impact of negative on international business, 144b
  link between individual decision making and, 146–147
  person, 141–145
  politics, 472
  role, 290
  selective, 142, 368
Perceptual speed, 45
Performance, 286, 310
  global teams, 340
  linking rewards to, 239
  organizational culture and, 574e
Performance evaluations, 146, 155, 465, 595–602, 607–608
  in creating effective teams, 330–331
  criteria for, 595–596
  international, 606–607
  methods of, 598–600, 599e
  purposes of, 595
  suggestions for improving, 601–602
Performance expectations, 146
Performance feedback, providing, 601–602
Performance reviews, motivation with, 233b
Performance–reward relationship, 197
Performance-simulation tests, 588
Performing stage *The fourth stage in group development, when the group is fully functional*, 286e
Personal appeals, 457
Personal factors as source of stress, 640
Personal favors, swapping, 476
Personality–job fit theory *Identifies six personality types and proposes that the fit between personality type and occupational environment determines satisfaction and turnover*, 122–123

Personality tests, 587–588
Personality *The sum total of ways in which an individual reacts and interacts with others*, 105–117, 127
  conflict and, 489
  in creating effective teams, 331
  decision making and, 154–155
  defined, 105
  determinants, 105–107
  global, 116b
  influence on organizational behavior, 111–117
  linking to workplace, 122–123
  proactive, 115–117
  as source of emotions and moods, 256
  type A, 115
  type B, 115
Personality traits *Enduring characteristics that describe an individual's behavior*, 107–108
  in predicting behavior, 128
  role of, in negotiation, 501
Personalization, conflict and, 489
Personal power, 452–453
Personal variables, conflict and, 489
Person–organization fit, 123
Person perception, 141–148
Peter Principle, 387
Physical ability *The capacity to do tasks demanding stamina, dexterity, strength, and similar characteristics*, 47–48, 47e
Physical distance, 358
Physical exercise, stress management and, 644–645
Physiological needs, 176, 201
Physiological symptoms of stress, 642
Piece-rate pay plan *A pay plan in which workers are paid a fixed sum for each unit of production completed*, 229–230
Planned change *Change activities that are intentional and goal-oriented*, 621
  managing, 620–622
Planning *A process that includes defining goals, establishing strategy, and developing plans to coordinate activities*, 6
  in negotiation, 499–500
Playing dumb, 468e
Playing safe, 468e
Political behavior *Activities that are not required as part of one's formal role in the organization but that influence, or attempt to influence, the distribution of advantages and disadvantages within the organization*, 461–462
  ethics of, 471–472
  factors contributing to, 463–466, 464e
  illegitimate, 461–462, 477–478
  legitimate, 461
  perception, global implications, 472

...ommunication, ...572

...cal skill, 458

Political uncertainties, 639

Politics, 461–473
of change, 625
culture and, 472
reality of, 462, 463e

Position power *Influence derived from one's formal structural position in the organization; includes power to hire, fire, discipline, promote, and give salary increases*, 393–395, 394e

Positive effect *A mood dimension consisting of specific positive emotions like excitement, self-assurance, and cheerfulness at the high end, and boredom, sluggishness, and tiredness at the low end*, 254

Positive emotions, 267

Positive organizational culture, creating *A culture that emphasizes building on employee strengths, rewards more than it punishes, and emphasizes individual vitality and growth*, 567–570

Positive organizational scholarship *An area of OB research that concerns how organizations develop human strength, foster vitality and resistance, and unlock potential*, 25

Positive reinforcement, 58–59

Positive work environment, creating, 25

Positivity offset *Tendency of most individuals to experience a mildly positive mood at zero input (when nothing in particular is going on)*, 256

Potential opposition, conflict and, 486–489

Power *Capacity that A has to influence the behavior of B so that B acts in accordance with A's wishes*, 451
bases of, 452–454
coercive, 452
contrasting, 451
cultural issues, 472–473
definition of, 451
dependency as key to, 454–456
expert, 453
formal, 452
legitimate, 452
personal, 452–453
politics and, 461–462
referent, 453
reward, 452

Power distance *A national culture attribute describing the extent to which a society accepts that power in institutions and organizations is distributed unequally*, 124, 126e

Power dynamics, 475

Power tactics, 456–458, 457e, 458
effectiveness, cultural differences and, 473

Prearrival stage *The period of learning in the socialization process that occurs before a new employee joins the organization*, 561–562

Preconceived notions, 12b

Preparation in negotiation, 499–500

Presidents, characteristics of great, 441

Pressure, 457

Prevention, 468e

Primary traits, 128

Proactive personality *People who identify opportunities, show initiative, take action, and persevere until meaningful change occurs*, 115–117

Problem *A discrepancy between some current state of affairs and some desired state*, 146–147

Problem solving
bounded rationality, 149
intergroup development, 632
in negotiations, 500
skills in, 592

Problem-solving teams *Groups of 5 to 12 employees from the same department who meet for a few hours each week to discuss ways of improving quality, efficiency, and the work environment*, 324

Procedural justice *The perceived fairness of the process used to determine the distribution of rewards*, 195, 196e

Process conflict *Conflict over how work gets done*, 486, 487

Process consultation *A consultant assisting a client to understand process events with which he or she must deal and to identify processes that need improvement*, 630–631

Process departmentalization, 522

Process in creating effective teams, 335–337

Product departmentalization, 529–530

Production blocking, 307

Production-oriented leader *One who emphasizes technical or task aspects of the job*, 390

Productivity *A performance measure that includes effectiveness and efficiency*, 27–28
effect of age on, 49
improving, 21
job satisfaction and, 86b
spirituality and, 572

Professional guidelines, 663

Professional sports, rewarding and punishing of behaviors in, 68

Profiling *A form of stereotyping in which a group of individuals is singled out—typically on the basis of race or ethnicity—for intensive inquiry, scrutinizing, or investigation*, 145
ethnic, 145

Profit-sharing plan *An organizationwide program that distributes compensation based on some established formula designed around a company's profitability*, 231–232

Programmed learning method, 536

Promotion decisions, 465, 679–681

Propensity for risk taking, 114

Protégés, 442

Psychological contract *An unwritten agreement that sets out what management expects from the employee, and vice versa*, 290

Psychological empowerment *Employees' belief in the degree to which they impact their work environment, their competence, and meaningfulness of their job, and the perceived autonomy in their work*, 79

Psychological map, 336

Psychological symptoms of stress, 642

Psychology *The science that seeks to measure, explain, and sometimes change the behavior of humans and other animals*, 12, 13–14
evolutionary, 66

Punctuated-equilibrium model *Transitions temporary groups go through between inertia and activity*, 287–288, 288e

Punishment
managerial use of, 67
rewarding versus, 568

Purpose, sense of, 571

Pygmalion effect, 146, 190

Q

Quality, improving, 21

Quality circle *A work group of employees who meet regularly to discuss their quality problems, investigate causes, recommend solutions, and take corrective actions*, 226–227

Quality-control manager, 7

Quality of life, work level and, 94

Quick fix, being wary of, 35

R

Race
job performance and, 51
workforce and, 19e

Randomness error *The tendency of individuals to believe that they can predict the outcome of random events*, 152–153, 163e

Rank and yank plans, 600b
Rater error, 601
Rational decision-making model *A decision-making model that describes how individuals should behave in order to maximize some outcome*, 148–150, 148e, 162
Rational *Making consistent, value-maximizing choices within specified constraints*, 148
Rational persuasion, 456
Ratio schedules, 60
Reactiveness, 636
Readiness, 396
Redesigning jobs, 645–646
Reference groups *Important groups to which individuals belong or hope to belong and with whose norms individuals are likely to conform*, 294–295
Referent power *Influence based on possession by an individual of desirable resources or personal traits*, 453
"Reflected best-self," 25
Refreezing *Stabilizing a change intervention by balancing driving and restraining forces*, 625
Reinforcement, 58–59
    processes of, 58
Reinforcement schedules, 60–61, 60e
    behavior and, 60–61
Reinforcement theory
    problems with, 63–64
Reinforcement theory *A theory that behavior is a function of its consequences*, 191, 200, 202
Relationship, causality and, 659
Relationship conflict *Conflict based on interpersonal relationships*, 486, 487
Relaxation techniques, 645
Religion, job performance and, 52–53
Representative participation *Workers participate in organizational decision making through a small group of representative employees*, 226
Research, in organizational behavior
    design, 660–663
    ethics, 663
    evaluating, 660
    purposes, 658
    terminology, 659–660
Resistance point, 496
Resistance to change, 622–625, 639
    overcoming, 623–625
Resource allocators, 8
Resources
    adequate, in creating effective teams, 328
    stress and, 638
Respect, in spiritual organization, 571
Restraining forces *Forces that hinder movement from the existing equilibrium*, 626–627

Résumé, ethics and, 610–611
Retention processes, 57
Reward power *Compliance achieved based on the ability to distribute rewards that others view as valuable*, 452
Rewards, 77
    for employees, 227–237
    linking, to performance, 239
    manipulating of, 66
    in shaping team players, 334, 338–339
    worker satisfaction, 93
Reward systems, 155
    conflict and, 488
    in creating customer-responsive culture, 568
    in creating effective teams, 334b
Rights as ethical criterion, 157
Risk avoidance, 66
Risk taking, 114–115
Rituals *Repetitive sequences of activities that express and reinforce the key values of the organization, which goals are most important, which people are important, and which are expendable*, 564–565
Rokeach Value Survey (RVS), 118e, 119
Role ambiguity, 465, 640
Role *A set of expected behavior patterns attributed to someone occupying a given position in social unit*, 7, 289–292
    allocating, in creating effective teams, 331–332
    decisional, 7e, 8
    figurehead, 7
    interpersonal, 6–7, 7e
    leadership, 7
    liaison, 7
    negotiator, 8
    spokesperson, 8
Role conflict *A situation in which an individual is confronted by divergent role expectations*, 290–291, 311, 640
Role demands, 640
Role expectations *How others believe a person should act in a given situation*, 290, 640
Role identity *Certain attitudes and behaviors consistent with a role*, 290
Role overload, 640
Role perception *An individual's view of how he or she is supported to act in a given situation*, 290, 311
Role stress, 646
Rumors, reducing negative consequences of, 360, 360e, 376

S

Sabbaticals, 646
Sadness, 252
Safety needs, 176, 201
Sales manager, 7

Satisfaction, 311
Satisfactory state of affairs, one person's problem as, 147
SAT tests, 45, 611
Scapegoating, 468e
Scarcity, 455–456
Secondary traits, 128
Secrecy, need for, 376
Selection, 435–437
    comprehensive case study, 679–681
    emotions, moods, and, 267
    international, 605–606
    organizational culture and, 574
    placement decisions and, 645
    in shaping team players, 337–338
Selection practices, 585–590, 607
    contingent, 589–590
    initial, 585–587
    substantive, 587–589
Selection process
    goal of, 559–560
    model of, 586e
Selective perception *Selectively interpreting what one sees on the basis of one's interests, background, experience, and attitudes*, 142–143, 151, 368
Self-actualization *The drive to become what one is capable of becoming*, 176, 201
Self-awareness as dimension of emotional intelligence, 264
Self-concordance *The degree to which a person's reasons for pursuing a goal are consistent with the person's developing interests and core values*, 184–185
Self-efficacy *The individual's belief that he or she is capable of performing a task*, 188–191, 190
    of employees, 607
Self-efficacy theory, 188–191
Self-esteem *Individuals' degree of liking or disliking themselves and the degree to which they think they are worthy or unworthy as a person*, 155
Self-fulfilling prophecy *A situation in which one person inaccurately perceives a second person and the resulting expectations cause the second person to behave in ways consistent with the original perception*, 146, 502
Self-leadership *A set of processes through which individuals control their own behavior*, 430–431
Self-managed work teams *Groups of 10 to 15 people who take on responsibilities of their former supervisors*, 324–325, 340
Self-management as dimension of emotional intelligence, 264

713

...sonality trait that ...s an individual's ability to adjust his or her behavior to external, situational factors, 113–114

Self-motivation as dimension of emotional intelligence, 264

Self-promotion, 470
impression management and, 470e

Self-protection, 468e

Self-report surveys in measuring personality, 112

Self-serving bias *The tendency for individuals to attribute their own successes to internal factors while putting the blame for failures on external factors,* 142

Sender, 353

Sensing, 108

Sensitivity training *Training groups that seek to change behavior through unstructured group interaction,* 629–630

September 11, 2001, terrorist attacks, 137
stereotyping and profiling after, 137, 145

Sexual harassment *Any unwanted activity of a sexual nature that affects an individual's employment and creates a hostile work environment,* 459–461

Sexual orientation, job performance and, 53

Shaping behavior *Systematically reinforcing each success step that moves an individual closer to the desired response,* 58–64
methods of, 58–59

Shortcuts
applications of, in organization, 145–146
in judging others, 142–145

Short-term orientation *A national culture attribute that emphasizes the past and present, respect for tradition, and fulfilling social obligations,* 125, 126e

Simple structure *A structure characterized by a low degree of departmentalization, wide spans of control, authority centralized in a single person, and little formalization,* 526, 526e

Single-loop learning *Correcting errors using past routines and present policies,* 635

Situations, matching, 393–394

Size, 299–301, 310

Skilled-based pay *A pay plan that sets pay levels on the basis of how many skills employees have or how many jobs they can do,* 231

Skill variety *The degree to which the job requires a variety of different activities,* 215, 216e

Sleep as source of emotions and moods, 258–259

Small-group networks, 358–359, 359e

Social activities as source of emotions and moods, 258

Socialization *The process that adapts employees to the organization's culture,* 561–563
encounter stage, 562
individuals doing themselves, 558b
influence on employee performance, 574
metamorphosis stage, 562–563, 562e
model of, 562e
prearrival stage, 561–562

Social-learning theory *The view that people can learn through observation and direct experience,* 57–58

Social loafing *The tendency for individuals to expend less effort when working collectively than when working individually,* 299–300, 309, 314–315, 337
in creating effective teams, 337

Social needs, 176, 201

Social psychology *An area within psychology that blends concepts from psychology and sociology and that focuses on the influence of people on one another,* 13–14

Social skills as dimension of emotional intelligence, 264

Social support, 641
network for, 645

Social trends as force for change, 619e, 620

Sociology *The study of people in relation to their social environment or culture,* 15

Span of control *The number of subordinates a manager can efficiently and effectively direct,* 523–524, 540
in organizational structure, 523–524, 523e

Spatial-visualization, 45

Speech coaching, 379

Spirituality
criticisms of, 572
organizational culture and, 570–572, 570e

Spiritual organization, characteristics of, 570–571

Spokesperson role, 8

Sports teams as models for workplace teams, 341

Status *A socially defined position or rank given to groups or group members by others,* 297–299
culture and, 299, 309
factors determining, 298
group interaction and, 298–299
norms and, 298

Status characteristics theory *Theory stating that differences in status characteristics create status hierarchies within groups,* 298

Status inequities, 299, 311

Stereotyping *Judging someone on the basis of one's perception of the group to which that person belongs,* 66, 137–139, 144–145

Stories, 564

Storming stage *The second stage in group development, characterized by intragroup conflict,* 286, 286e

Strategic alliances, 541

Strategy, organizational, 534–535

Stress *A dynamic condition in which an individual is confronted with an opportunity, demand, or resource related to what the individual desires and for which the outcome is perceived to be both uncertain and important,* 637
challenge, 638
consequences of, 642–644
coping with differences, 648
defined, 637–638
ethics, 652
extreme jobs, 653–654
hindrance, 638
managing, 644–647
meetings and, 639b
potential sources of, 638–640
as source of emotions and moods, 258
sources of, 638–640

Stressors, 639–640

Stretching, 468e

Strong culture *Culture in which the core values are intensely held and widely shared,* 554

Structural considerations in multinationals, 528b

Structural variables, innovation and, 634

Structure
conflict and, 487–488
in creating effective teams, 327

Structured interviews, 605

Subcultures *Minicultures within an organization, typically defined by department designations and geographical separation,* 553–554

Substantive evidence, 12b

Substantive selection, 587–589

Substitutes to leadership, 434–435, 435e

Supportive colleagues, worker satisfaction and, 93

Supportive leadership, 397, 398

Supports in overcoming resistance to change, 624

Surface acting *Hiding one's inner feelings and modifying one's facial expressions in response to display rules,* 261–262

Surprise, 252

Survey feedback *The use of questionnaires to identify discrepancies among member perceptions; discussion follows and remedies are suggested,* 630

Systematic study
  complementing intuition with, 11–13
  Looking at relationships, attempting to attribute causes and objects, and drawing conclusions based on scientific evidence, 11

System-imposed time constraints, 156

T

Tactics
  influence, 458b
  power, 456–458, 457e, 458
Target point, 496
Task conflict *Conflicts over content and goals of the work,* 336–337, 486, 487
Task demands, 640
Task group *Those working together to complete a job task,* 285
Task identity *The degree to which the job requires completion of a whole and identifiable piece of work,* 215, 216e
Task significance *The degree to which the job has a substantial impact on the lives or work of other people,* 215, 216e
Task structure *The degree to which the job assignments are procedurized,* 393–394, 394e
Team building *High interaction among team members to increase trust and openness,* 631–632
Team-building retreats, 344
Team efficacy in creating effective teams, 336
Team player, pressure to be, 342–343
Team(s)
  competitive reward conditions, 334b
  comprehensive case study, 669–671
  creating effective, 326–327, 328e
  differences between groups and, 323, 324e
  drawbacks of using, 339
  global extent of, 339–340
  global virtual, 327b
  popularity of, 322–323
  roles of, 331–332, 332e
  size of, in creating effective teams, 333–334
  spirituality and, 572
  surgical, 329b
  turning individuals into players, 337–339
  types of, 324–337, 324e
Team structure *The use of teams as the central device to coordinate work activities,* 532–533
Teamwork, 508

Technical expertise, 330
Technical skills *The ability to apply specialized knowledge or expertise,* 8, 591
Technological change, 639
Technology *How an organization transfers its inputs into outputs,* 536–537
  boundaries of, 378
  as force for change, 619e, 620
  in reshaping organizations, 542
Telecommuting *Refers to employees who do their work at home at least two days a week on a computer that is linked to their office,* 223–224, 224b, 242–243, 609
  global implications, 237
Temporariness, coping with, 23
Temporary groups, with deadlines, 287–288
Tenure, job performance and, 51–52
Terminal values *Desirable end-states of existence; the goals that a person would like to achieve during his or her lifetime,* 118
Testing in selecting leaders, 435e
T-form (technology-based) organization, 533
T-groups, 629–630
Thailand, cultural differences in, 161
Theory, OB research, 660
Theory X *The assumption that employees dislike work, are lazy, dislike responsibility, and must be coerced to perform,* 177
Theory Y *The assumption that employees like work, are creative, seek responsibility, and can exercise self-direction,* 177
Thinking individuals, 108
Third-party negotiations, 503–504
Three-component model of creativity *The proposition that individual creativity requires expertise, creative-thinking skills, and intrinsic task motivation,* 159–160, 159e
360-degree evaluation, 597, 597e, 601
Time management, 644–645
Time of day as source of emotions and moods, 256
Tone, language barriers caused by, 373
Top management, 560
Traditional management, 8
Traditional view of conflict *The belief that all conflict is harmful and must be avoided,* 485
Training, 436–437, 645
  computer-based, 593–594
  cultural, 592b
  diversity, 592b, 605
  employee evaluators, 601
  ethics, 592
  evaluating effectiveness of, 594–595

formal, 593–594
  individualizing formal, 594
  informal, 593
  job, 66
  methods of, 593–594
  for older workers, 58b
  on-the-job, 593
  programs for, 607
  sensitivity, 629–630
  in shaping team players, 338
  telecommuting, 609
  types of, 591–592
Training groups, 629–630
Traits, 596
Trait theories of leadership *Theories that consider personal qualities and characteristics that differentiate leaders from nonleaders,* 386–388
Transactional leaders *Leaders who guide or motivate their followers in the direction of established goals by clarifying role and task requirements,* 418, 420e
Transfer pricing, 30b
Transformational leadership, 418–421
  charismatic leadership versus, 421
  evaluation of, 421
Transformational leaders *Leaders who inspire followers to transcend their own self-interests and who are capable of having a profound and extraordinary effect on followers,* 418–421, 420e
Translation, 373b
Travel costs, reducing, 242–243
Trust *A positive expectation that another will not act opportunistically,* 465
  defined, 424
  deterrence-based, 425
  dimensions of, 424, 424e
  identification-based, 426–427, 432
  job satisfaction and, 90
  knowledge-based, 425–426
  leadership and, 424–425
  spiritual organization, 571
Turnover *The voluntary and involuntary permanent withdrawal from an organization,* 29, 162
  organizational structure, 575
Two-factor theory *A theory that relates intrinsic factors to job satisfaction, while associating extrinsic factors with dissatisfaction,* 178, 179e, 180
Type A personality *Aggressive involvement in a chronic, incessant struggle to achieve more and more in less and less time and, if necessary, against the opposing efforts of other things or other persons,* 115
Type B personality, 115

...oidance *A national culture attribute describing the extent to which a society feels threatened by uncertain and ambiguous situations and tries to avoid them*, 124–125, 126e

Unconditioned response, 55

Unconditioned stimulus, 55

Understudy assignments, 593

Unfreezing *Change efforts to overcome the pressures of both individual resistance and group conformity*, 625

United States
  decision making, 161
  executive pay, 241–242
  job satisfaction limited to, 91
  performance evaluations, 606–607
  stress, causes of, 648
  teamwork, extent of, 339
  value orientation, 125
  work hours in, 206

Unity of command *The idea that a subordinate should have only one superior to whom he or she is directly responsible*, 522, 529

Upward communication, 354–355

Utilitarianism *Decisions made to provide the greatest good for the greatest number*, 157

V

Validity, OB research, 660

Values *Basic convictions that a specific mode of conduct or end-state of existence is personally or socially preferable to an opposite or converse mode of conduct or end-state of existence*, 117–121, 127
  across cultures, 124–127
  conflict and, 489
  defined, 117
  importance of, 117–118
  linking to workplace, 122–123
  types of, 118–121

Values system *A hierarchy based on a ranking of an individual's values in terms of their intensity*, 117

Variable-interval schedule *Distributing rewards in time so that reinforcements are unpredictable*, 60

Variable-pay program *A pay plan that bases a portion of an employee's pay on some individual and/or organizational method of performance*, 228–233
  global implications, 238

Variable-ratio schedule *Varying the reward relative to the behavior of the individual*, 60

Variables
  defined, 659
  moderating, 77–78

Verbal comprehension, 45

Verbal persuasion, 190

Vicarious modeling, 190

Videoconferencing, 364

Virtual organization *A small, core organization that outsources major business functions*, 530–532, 532e, 542

Virtual teams *Teams that use computer technology to tie together physically dispersed members in order to achieve a common goal*, 326, 343
  global, 327b

Vision *A long-term strategy on how to attain a goal or goals*, 415–416

Vitality, emphasizing, 568–569

Vocational Preference Inventory, 122, 122e

Voice behavior, 87

Voice *Dissatisfaction expressed through active and constructive attempts to improve conditions*, 87

Voice mail, 365b

W

War on terror, managing people during, 18

Weak cultures, 554

Weather as source of moods and emotions, 256–257

Web logs, 363–364

Wellness programs *Organizationally supported programs that focus on the employees' total physical and mental condition*, 646–647

Western cultures, job satisfaction and, 91–92

Wheel, 359, 359e

Whistle-blowers *Individuals who report unethical practices by their employer to outsiders*, 157, 167–168

Wilderness survival, 309, 313–314

Willingness, leader–follower relationship, 396

Winner's curse *A decision-making dictum that argues that the winning participants in an auction typically pay too much for the winning item*, 153, 154b

Women, communication barriers between men and, 370

Wonderlic Personnel Test, 46–47

Work, level of, 95

Work design in creating effective teams, 334

Work-environment stimulants, 160

Workforce diversity *The concept that organizations are becoming more heterogeneous in terms of gender, race, ethnicity, sexual orientation, and inclusion of other diverse groups*, 18, 36–37

management implications, 20–21
  managing, 18–21, 19e

Workforce violence, 38–39

Work group *A group that interacts primarily to share information and to make decisions to help each group member perform within his or her area of responsibility*, 323, 508

Work–life conflicts, 603–605, 604e
  balancing, 24–25

Workplace
  impact of dissatisfied and satisfied employees on, 87–91, 87e
  linking individual's personality and values to, 122–123
  technology in, 639
  unequal power in, 459

Workplace deviance, 29–30
  job satisfaction and, 90–91

Workplace grief, 271b

Workplace inactivity, 29–30

Workplace incivility, 296

Workplace romances, ethics and, 274–275

Workplace spirituality *The recognition that people have an inner life that nourishes and is nourished by meaningful work that takes place in the context of community*, 570

Workplace teams, sports teams as good models for, 341

Work sample tests *Creating a miniature replica of a job to evaluate the performance abilities of job candidates*, 588

Works councils, 226

Work specialization *The degree to which tasks in the organization are subdivided into separate jobs*, 519, 540
  in organizational structure, 519–521, 521e

Work stress, management of, 637–647

Work team *A group whose individual efforts result in a performance that is greater than the sum of the individual inputs*, 323

Workweek, length of, and job satisfaction, 96–97

World politics as force for change, 619e, 620

Written communication, 356–357

Written tests in evaluation, 598

Written tests in selection, 587–588

X

Xers (Generation X), 120–121

Z

Zero-sum approach, 465

Zimbardo's prison experiment, 291–292